CONSUMER BEHAVIOR

HUMAN PURSUIT OF HAPPINESS IN THE WORLD OF GOODS

Jill Avery, Ph.D.   Simmons College

Robert V. Kozinets, Ph.D.   York University

Banwari Mittal, Ph.D.   Northern Kentucky University

Priya Raghubir, Ph.D.   New York University

Arch G. Woodside, Ph.D.   Boston College

OPEN MENTIS

CONSUMER BEHAVIOR

Human Pursuit of Happiness in the World of Goods

Jill Avery, Robert Kozinets, Banwari Mittal,
Priya Raghubir, and Arch G. Woodside

3rd Edition

Author credits and responsibilities for content are limited as follows:
Jill Avery: p. 509-513; Robert V. Kozinets: p. 501-508;
Banwari Mittal: p. 1-489, 514-570;
Priya Raghubir: 491-495; Arch Woodside: 496-500.

Editorial Consultants: Dr. Roxanne Kent-Drury, Maria Tenaglia-Webster,
            Julia Colterjohn, and Shirley T. Undicimo
Design Team: Andrew Curtis, Brad Dee, Md. Nazmul Haque, Mark Kruse,
            Manoj Prasanna Wimalasuriya, and Tania Yakimova

Library of Congress Control Number: 2012937546

ISBN-13: 978-0-979-1336-3-3
ISBN-10   0-979-1336-3-7

MY CB BOOK

CONSUMER BEHAVIOR

Jill Avery, Ph.D.
Simmons College

Robert V. Kozinets, Ph.D.
York University

Banwari Mittal, Ph.D.
Northern Kentucky University

Priya Raghubir, Ph.D.
New York University

Arch G. Woodside, Ph.D.
Boston College

**Human Pursuit of Happiness
in the World of Goods**

DEDICATION

To You, Dear Reader

For choosing to come along, as we explore and
illuminate the world of consumers.

Enjoy the journey!

OPEN MENTIS

P R E F A C E

Your Pet Topic Not Included

At first we were paranoid. What if we ended up not including someone's pet topic? Then the answer hit us: If we missed it, students would still get that topic—from you, and much better. Relieved, we focused instead on making sure we included as many key topics as possible.

Familiar Amalgam

Deeply conceptual. Utterly applied. Cognitive, information processing framework. Behavioral. Post-modernist. We couldn't choose. Aspiring to make this a comprehensive textbook to serve the needs of our discipline, we ended up with a little bit of everything.

Play with Theories

To make all topics accessible to the student, we named and renamed some concepts, redrew a few flowcharts, and "decoded" many theories for simplicity. And to fill gaps in current CB Theory, we built some anew. Not to worry: to the student, *all* theories are new anyway.

Teach Your Way

All content is made transparent to the student. So you won't have to spend all class time explaining the basics. It frees you instead to use the book as a launch pad for your own creative ways of teaching the subject.

Yes, Its a Textbook

Didactic. Conversational. Serious. Light. The book has the gravitas of the subject matter. But its prose and poetry is student-speak. We wrote it so even students who don't like textbooks may like it. Let's hope.

Lofty Goal Unmet

Actually, we wanted absolutely, positively to enchant the student. Alas, that lofty goal may have been met only partially. We offer this modest contribution for your consideration. And for a different kind of learning experience for your students.

You are the Gatekeeper

Your students have the opportunity to discover how enjoyable a book called a "textbook" can be. They will read it because they *want to*, not because they *have to*. You, dear professor, have the power to bring that opportunity to them. Or not.

Tell us, What, How?

If you do decide to, please do not hesitate to tell us how may we make your adoption a breeze. As a niche publisher, we will put out all our effort to meet your needs.

Read It, Anyway

Even if you are content with your present book, do turn the pages of this book and read a paragraph here and there. See for yourself that a "textbook" may reward even a topic scholar—at the very minimum by showing how to bridge the gap between the mind of an expert instructor and that of the 21-year-old student.

Thank you for, at our request, browsing the book.

FEATURES

Auto Customized

The book can be taught (and read) in any order. Part III (Consumers' Environment) before Part II (Inside the Consumer's Mind), for example. Or Part IV (Decision Making) before Part II. Most (80%) of the chapters can be re-sequenced. Yes, even Chapter 12 (Post-Choice) before Chapter 11 (Choice)! Each chapter is written to be understandable independently of the others.

Plenty To Do

Review+Rewind. Think+Apply. Practice+Experience. Fill in surveys. Score yourself on uniqueness, vanity, opinion leadership, and the like. And measure others a hundred ways (The book gives you that many measurement scales!). Analyze cases. Love stats? Survey data available. Satisfy your data craving!

Flags Are Free

Those Flags you see on the inside margins. And the globes. We placed them only where we say something substantive about a given country, rather than a mere mention of it. Rest assured, there is more global content than the flags and globes signal.

Facebook, Twitter, and Us

Yes, MyCBBook is on Facebook. And on Twitter. (Sorry, no Bebo.) Friend us. Follow us. Poke us. Share your discovery and joy from this book with other students and professors who may have missed this book. Tell them why it is important to browse this book even if they are content with another CB book.

Love Google

We explain all CB concepts but not all proper nouns. We know readers are Google-savvy. Hint, hint: Google, dear reader, Google. (Or Bing it.)

Pun Intended

Often you will come across some chuckle-producing tidbits. Like the one about the intriguing game of Chessboxing (Chapter 1). Or an example of … (shhhh..!) in the cognitive learning section of Chapter 4 on page …. (shhhh…!); Or (shhhh…!). Well, you get the idea. Please, please, let your fellow readers discover these by themselves.

World's Second Most Fascinating Book

And, these anecdotes and examples might make you forget that this is a *textbook*. That would be an illusion. It is a textbook alright. The world's second most fascinating book on CB, actually*. We count on you to help us keep it that way.

---

* Actually, one professor has called it the "most innovative CB book" and another has said, "This is the best CB book I have ever read!"

ACKNOWLEDGMENTS

1   To hundreds of CB scholars and researchers, whose labors and insights have produced the body of knowledge this book ventures to paraphrase and explain.

2   To the authors of all CB textbooks—Eric Arnould, Del Hawkins, Wayne Hoyer, Leslie Kanuk, Debbie MacInnis, Paul Miniard, David Mothersbaugh, Jerry Olsen, J. Paul Peter, Linda Price, Leon Schiffman, Jagdish Sheth, Michael Solomon, among others—who blazed the path this book now follows, albeit with a twist of its own.

3   To CB educators at various schools, whose professional reviews of the manuscript improved it exponentially, and whose enthusiasm for its distinctions sustained our resolve.

4   To CB professors and students who embraced our first and second editions—faults and all, and who, with their nurturing feedback and undiminished enthusiasm, helped us improve this book.

5   To the organizations (see photo and content credits) who have generously shared valuable images and information included in the book.

6   To our professional colleagues around the world, who, over the years, have supported our modest academic endeavor in knowledge dissemination. It is to their collective goodwill that we owe the desire and drive to offer this book.

TO YOU ALL, OUR SINCERE GRATITUDE.

FOR INTERNATIONAL READERS

HUMANS ARE HUMANS

Consumers are humans first. Their marketplace behavior gets its nourishment from the wellspring of human behavior. A majority of CB concepts (80%) are actually concepts and theories about universal human behavior. They are, at their core, country-neutral.

CONSUMERS ARE CONSUMERS

Consumers learn brand images through classically conditioned associations. In high involvement conditions, they elaborate the message. Rational consumer attitudes are based on brand beliefs. Consumers are "info-misers" and use heuristics (rules of thumb). Framing biases their judgments. Reference groups influence consumers in three separate ways. Consumers use products as identity markers. They use brand stories to enact their own life dramas. Consumers can't count their money correctly... On and on, the book reveals and explains these CB theories—with zeal unstoppable by context, country, culture.

This is because ALL consumers behave this way—whether they are shopping at a department store in New York, Toronto, or London, a boutique shop in Singapore, a floating market in Thailand, or medieval street markets in Morocco.

THE WORLD IS FLAT

Lenovo, LG, Samsung, Sony, Dove, Chanel, Diesel, Billabong, Yellow Tail, Oolong—these non-U.S. brands are today truly global. Among stores, Seven-Eleven, a U.S. headquartered company, has a store in every city block in Japan, and Hermès opened its first store in Sao Paolo in 2009. No good marketing book today can be anything but INTERNATIONAL.

GLOBAL REMIX SERVED

But country and culture do add alluring, vibrant colors on the canvas of universal consumer behavior. The book samples these from far and wide—not only in the examples (e.g., MOCCA's body paint campaign in Toronto, Beatlemania Tour in London, Lingerie Perdu in Saudi Arabia, and the Romancing Singapore Campaign) but also in concepts (e.g., *face saving* in China) and in research studies (e.g., brand communities in Spain, Austria, and Switzerland). Look for the globe icons.

TALES FROM THE WEST

About readers not from North America, one thing is certain. Either your marketplace is similar to the marketplace in the U.S. (many Western European countries and urban centers around the world are), or it is dissimilar. Either way, tales from the West can be fascinating—and which 20-something in the new century doesn't want to read about the New World consumers and marketplace? Admiration, curiosity, critiquing, differentiation—any reason is a good reason.

NOW TRANSLATE THIS, DEAR STUDENT!

When given a project to do, students often ask for a sample report as a guide. An ideal sample report is one that resembles, but is not a carbon copy of, the purported student report. So the book is an invitation to this general experiential project assigned to the student: "Here is how this specific CB concept works in the countries and world regions implied in the book. Now, go find out how it works in your country." Students learn if they find it to be similar. They learn even more if they find it to be dissimilar. True learning comes more from that which is different from the already-familiar.

WELCOME TO THE EXCURSION!

Where Is My Topic?

BEYOND THE CLASSROOM

The book offers a repertoire of CB knowledge. In a semester-long course, you will cover most of it and pave the way for the student to read the rest of it later, read all of it again, and re-read it selectively outside of the "read and test" framework. In the school of life, we are students forever, and the book is designed to serve as a resource beyond the classroom, for the life-long student in us, to keep and savor for years to come.

REQUEST TO REVIEWERS

Reviewers may excerpt up to 5 nonconsecutive pages* and copy the jacket and front and back end matter without seeking further permission.

They are requested, however, not to reveal the tidbits or their location in the book (except a small sample of them).

Thank you, and your professional courtesy is greatly appreciated.

INVITATION TO COPY

Whereas conscientious readers, aware of the U.S. copyright laws (which prohibit any copying and dissemination of this work in any form and for any audiences whatsoever, including for educational purposes) and maintaining respect for the intellectual labors of authors, would want to refrain from lifting material out of this book (unless the audience members have been required to obtain an individual copy), the publisher hereby grants permission to all individuals to copy and disseminate up to 10 pages (but not more than two consecutive pages), cumulatively over the work's lifetime.*

---

* Excludes Licensed Materials and third-party contributions. Excludes all contents not created by us. Excludes commercial uses. Excludes reprinting. Credit should appear on the same page, adjacent to the material.

 **R** EAD •  **A** PPLY •  **E** XPERIENCE

Augmented Reality

Authenticity

I see it, therefore it is.

Ambient Advertising

Social Media

Your Big Life Project

Bobos Lifestyle

With brands I build my Identity

Involvement as the Big Arbiter

Framing Effect

The Enchanted Consumer

Parody Consumption

You talk but I will listen to myself

Five Exchange Resources

Nostalgia

Brands to adore, brands to love

USER— The Code for Consumption-Value

Some of my decisions intrigue me

The idea that marketers create consumer needs is overrated

Collaborative Consumption

Status Crystallization

I like what marketers offer, but I have to be vigilant

Forming the Frame, not Targeting

SAVVY MARKETER

The Global Consumer

Consumption Tribes

Social Facilitation

5Ps of Marketing

BRIEF CONTENTS

MY CB

PERCEPTION **3**

Consumer Perception, Biases, and Sensory Marketing
The Only Reality That Matters **56**

4 LEARNING

Consumer Learning, Memory, and Nostalgia
From Classical to Cognitive **82**

DECISIONS **11**   **12** SATISFACTION

EPILOGUE

Marketing Meets the Consumer
480

Insight, Foresight, and
the Marketer Response

PART VIII   SPECIAL TOPICS   **ST**

PART IX   RESOURCES   **R**

CASES   PART IX
FROM Air Stocking to ZIPCARS

Classic*

Romantic*

* For definitions, see page 545

Resources   PART X

CONTENTS

SYLLABUS AT A GLANCE

(Master Sequence)

SEQUENCE OPTION 2
External Environment and Demographics before Internal Influences

SEQUENCE OPTION 3
Consumer Decision Making before Internal Influences and External Environment

FEATURES

» Each chapter is written so as to not require prior reading of the preceding chapters. This frees the reader to read the book in any sequence of one's choosing.

» SPECIAL TOPICS can be read anytime in the sequence. All of them pertain to the "Inside the Consumer's Mind" module. Special Topic 1 provides insights based on "positivist" research; Topics 2, 3, and 4 offer post-modernist perspectives; Topic 5 is a grand-tour of many overarching, enchanting, and trending consumer happenings.

» Cases connect with topics across chapters (more specifics within) and can be interspersed as needed.

» Resources R1 and R2 also require no knowledge of any prior chapters; however, re-reading them after reading a few chapters will add to your "take away."

CONSUMER BEHAVIOR

PART ▲

Welcome to the Future World of Consumption!!

Enter ❭

1 Welcome to the Fascinating World of Consumers

Where Offerings and Hopes Meet

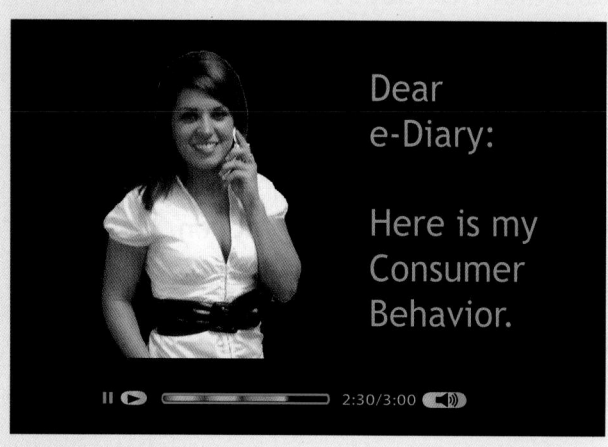

Dear
e-Diary:

Here is my
Consumer
Behavior.

2:30/3:00

LEARN . APPLY . EXPERIENCE

OBJECTIVES

1 How Consumer Behavior is Defined and What Its Elements are

2 Five Visions of the Consumer Marketers Should Recognize

3 Consumer Needs and Wants and How Marketing Shapes Them

4 Five Resources All Humans Possess and Exchange in the Marketplace

5 Four Consumption Values Humans Seek in the Marketplace

6 Four Reader Types to Benefit from This Consumer Behavior Book

I Love My *Keds!*

A Mere Ardent Consumer Till Yesterday, Now Suddenly, I Am A Marketer Too!

See my new Keds!

These are no ordinary shoes. They are uniquely mine. With some priceless elements of my autobiography built into them. They are my signal to the world as to who I am. I wear them with spirit, glee, and pride. I designed them, myself!

I had been dreaming of designing my own pair of shoes for some time. So, on the afternoon of November 22, 2011, I sat down at my laptop and launched Keds.com. The Keds design tab led me step-by-step through the process of creating the shoe I wanted. I had the option of choosing the basic style and then applying my own design and paint to the upper, lower, left and right quarters, tongue, sole, lining, laces, and even eyelets. I made these choices—giving shape to my needs and my tastes.

Buying the shoes I designed was a breeze. I made the online payment of $65

and then, ten days later, on December 3, the pair of shoes was delivered. And on the Keds.com Web site, I did one more thing: I put my design up for sale. Keds will make a shoe with my design for anyone who wants to buy it. Voila, I am now a co-creator, co-marketer!

—Arianna Osborn, Cincinnati, USA (March 5, 2012)

Designing my shoes; crafting my identity

Athletic shoes . Ice cream . Ketchup	Chocri . Coco Cola . eCreamery
Neckties . Skateboards . Soda	Heinz . M&M's . NIKEiD
Speakers . T-shirts	Threadless . Zazzle

Some of the other products you can custom-design and personalize, and the companies that are making it possible.
Welcome to the age of customized consumption!

WEB 2.0 AND THE EMPOWERED CONSUMER

Web 2.0 No, it is not our older brother's Web anymore. It is Web 2.0—the World Wide Web (www) with new capabilities that let us—the users—play a more active role in the Web experience. In the early life of the Web (i.e., Web 1.0), users were limited to viewing content passively. In contrast, Web 2.0 (building up progressively since about 2000) allows users to connect with other users (e.g., in discussion forums), create content (e.g., customer reviews on Amazon.com), and annotate others' content and messages (e.g., by posting comments on news and blogs). Interesting though this capability was, it was at first used by consumers mostly for hobby-like content creation (e.g., on YouTube) and for social networking (e.g., via Facebook). But lately, Web 2.0 has been deployed to give consumers new power: To let consumers become co-creators, even co-marketers! Keds is a prime example.

Keds: Shoes for Youthful Optimism You might have heard: Keds gave to the world, in 1916, the first shoe with a soft sole so quiet you could walk into a room without being heard. The company boasts that its shoes were once the choice of such icons as Marilyn Monroe and Jackie O. More recently, its Pro-Keds have been worn by numerous NBA stars. In 2007, the company collaborated with fashion designer Nanette Lapore and created *Nanette Lepore by Keds*—a fun, flirty summer style that delighted the stiletto-tortured feet of fashionistas around the world. In 2008, the company launched Keds Studio, allowing customers to design their own one-of-a-kind shoes. In 2010, it launched Keds Collective to collaborate with cutting edge designers and music and cultural icons. The goal was to transform its original sneakers into museum-worthy pieces of art and function. Now in 2012, the Keds site provides a much larger pallet of some 500-plus options (e.g., 10 to 15 colors and 8 to 10 prints for each of the 13 components of the shoe, such as upper, toe, insole, gore, stitching, etc.). You can also import your own images and write your own text in one of the 20-plus font styles. And you can do one more thing: You can post your creation for sale on the Keds Collective Web site itself.

Welcome to the age of Web 2.0! To the power of consumers-turned-marketers!

Welcome, in fact, to the fascinating world of consumers. In this book, we are going to describe, dissect, and discourse about consumer behavior—human behavior in the world of products. We will study how we think, feel, and act in the marketplace—how we come to see the products the way we see them, how we make our choices from the mind-boggling array of goods available, how we buy them and then weave them into the tapestry of our lives. How we consume them to sustain and energize our bodies, feed our minds, and construct our egos and our identities. This is the study of consumer behavior.

WE ARE CONSUMERS—24-7!

We are all consumers. This much must come as no surprise to you. But what you may not have realized is how much of your waking day you spend being a consumer—and we count not just when you are consuming or when you are buying something. Rather, as we will explain later, you are a consumer any time you are even thinking about acquiring and/or consuming anything. To be sure, we also live at least part of our lives not being consumers—such as when we are conversing with a friend (without using a phone or any other product), reflecting on our futures, or for that matter, on the future of mankind. But most of the rest of the day is filled with plotting and enacting consumption. Write a daily journal for a week, if you like, and see for yourself. A group of consumers did just that, at our request. We reproduce one of these journals (see box: Dear e-Diary). This journal was quite representative of all those we received in one respect; they all showed the same thing: We are consumers 24-7!

Dear e-Diary—Here is My Consumer Behavior
by Ellen Tibbs

MONDAY
- This morning on the way to work I bought a Sugar Free Red Bull and Special K blueberry breakfast bar.
- I was walking to my car earlier and saw a woman with a new Coach purse. I am getting sick of the one I am carrying now. Once I save up some money I might treat myself and buy one!
- My friend just called and said she had an extra ticket to go to the Journey concert in two weeks. I really want to go so I told her I would meet up with her later to pay for the ticket.

TUESDAY
- I got my hair colored at the salon, Madalyn San Tangelo this morning.
- My friend Lindsay and I wanted to eat sushi so I placed a carry out order at AOI, a Japanese cuisine restaurant at Newport on the Levee. We both ordered California Rolls, rice and we split an appetizer.
- I was online today and bought and downloaded music from iTunes. I bought some songs by James Blunt and Jack Johnson. .

WEDNESDAY
- I love my car, but I want a new one. I saw a new silver Scion today and want it badly. I called my mom and talked to her about trading my car in for a new car.
- I looked online for a desk for my room. I have a computer and printer, but no work station. I usually sit at my kitchen table or on the floor to do homework and it's getting really annoying. I looked at Pottery Barn, Bova and a couple of random sites, but didn't see anything I liked.

SATURDAY
- I bought an Icee Mango at Panera Bread...
- I went shopping today at Kenwood Mall for something to wear tonight. I went to a couple of stores, but didn't find anything. I went into Forever 21 and was excited when I found a white skirt and black camisole. I was even more excited when I found great accessories to match!

SUNDAY
- I had a headache this morning and was out of Advil so I went to Walgreen's. I bought water and a bottle of Advil gel caplets. In line I grabbed a new tube of Burt's Beeswax and bought that too.
- I had to buy gas again today. I feel like I filled up! I hate buying gas. It is so expensive and is a pain in the butt. The only thing worse than buying it is to know you will have to buy it again in three days!
- I work at J B Fin's on the Levee, so I went shopping on my break. I went to Hollister and PacSun. I didn't find anything I liked. However, I did buy a new belly button ring from the outside vendor.

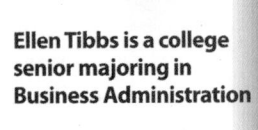

Ellen Tibbs is a college senior majoring in Business Administration

MY CB BOOK

CONSUMERS ARE FASCINATING

As consumers, we are fascinating. Consider a conversation we recently had with a consumer, Jackie, age 30 (see the box titled "A Consumer Interview: I Obey My Thirst"). We will let that interview speak for itself, and let you decide whether you agree that consumers are indeed fascinating.

When we think of consumers such as Jackie, several images come to mind. Consumers are the browsers in the department store, shoppers in the mall, patrons enjoying a meal in a restaurant, visitors standing in long lines at Disneyland, youngsters flocking to video arcades, and old ladies rushing to grab door-buster sale items. These and many other visions of the consumer can be aptly grouped into the following five categories:

1. **Consumer as Problem-Solver**
2. **Consumer as Economic Creature**
3. **Consumer as Computer**
4. **Consumer as Shopper**
5. **Consumer as Reveler**

FIVE VISIONS OF THE CONSUMER

Consumer as Problem Solver In this vision, consumers are searching for solutions to the needs of daily life, looking for a product or service that will meet those needs in the best possible way. Once they find the "solution product," they can relax and move on with their lives. The following self-report from a consumer illustrates this:

> After I purchased my new pants recently, I spent most of my free time thinking about the shoes I already have. Finally, I decided that I didn't have any shoes to go with my new pants. On Tuesday, I started my search at Payless Shoe Source, but didn't have any luck. I continued my search at Dillard's and JC Penny's but once again I just didn't see what I was looking for. I became very discouraged. I decided that later that evening, my final store to shop would be Shoe Carnival. As soon as I walked in, I saw them, the perfect pair of shoes. They were a little pricey at $38.99 but with a 10% sale, I bought them. I was very excited and relieved that I had found the shoes I was looking for. (Angie, 22)

Consumer as Economic Creature Consumers are also planners and managers of personal finances; they want to use their money wisely. As such they seek to buy products at the best prices available. This does not mean that they always go for the lowest price (although often they do), but always that they want to maximize their utility. As one consumer stated:

> My fiancée and I always cut coupons before we go grocery shopping. It always saves us at least $20 per trip. We both agree that Kroger and Thriftway are too expensive for our large bi-monthly shopping trips. We prefer to go to Meijer and likely save another $40 just by going there. Once at Meijer, we aren't too picky about the brands we buy. We can often be seen calculating the per unit price based on the Meijer brand versus the name brand with coupon. On almost everything, the lower per-unit cost always wins. Oddly enough ketchup is the one item that I purchase based on the brand name. (Christopher, 23)

Consumer as Computer We also see consumers reading package labels, checking-off items on a shopping list, pondering information in their heads, looking at ads, making sense of instructions on how to use a product—in other words, sorting out all the information about products and the marketplace. Indeed, our brains act like human computers. This vision can be seen in the following self-report from a couple:

> We were in the market for a house. We began by searching the MLS site on the Internet. We searched listings by price, by location, by school district, and by features. Then we found a realtor and let him do the searching. He showed us several houses on the computer within our price range. One house seemed to have all the features but was on a street with no sidewalks, and sidewalks were important to us because we have children. Another house had everything but the deck was small; a third house had a large deck but the kitchen was small. We tried to figure how much it would cost to make the deck bigger, and we thought that expanding the kitchen would be very cumbersome. We kept turning in our heads the three houses we liked and their various features, and finally, taking everything into account, we settled on the one with the small deck. (Jenny, 23, and Paul, 24)

Consumer as Shopper This is the familiar image of consumers, coming out of a store, loaded with shopping bags in both hands. Inside the store, they are totally taken in by the vast merchandise, enchanted by all that is on display, theirs to have if they like, but to enjoy the sight anyway. Stores and marketplaces are the proverbial Alice's Wonderland for the consumer as a shopper. As one of our research respondents put it:

> I shop all the time. Days, evenings, weekdays, weekends. Whenever I can get out. I shop at department stores and just as much at boutique shops. And I shop online—my favorite

Doing Yoga

Is this person, at this moment, being a _CONSUMER_?

"I Obey My Thirst!"

A Consumer Interview

We intercepted Jackie Cooper, a 30-year old male, walking with a shopping bag in hand, in the Downtown Mall, Cincinnati. Our interviewer was Pamela Ryckman, a junior marketing student, who conducted the interview as part of her class project.

Q. Excuse me sir, would you mind answering a few questions for my class project?

A. Sure, you can ask me anything.

Q. Great, thank you. (Pointing at the shopping bag) What did you buy today?

A. I just bought this new fly Fubu jersey. It is uh, blue and yellow, double zero on the back. It's phat.[1]

Q. How do you buy your clothing?

A. You know, whatever looks good. Stay away from stripes though.

Q. Why?

A. Oh, it could make you look bulky, you know.

Q. What kind of clothes do you buy?

A. Well, I have a lot of Nike. My favorite is Fubu, you know. I also got Sean-John. That is the only kind of stuff I buy.

Q. Why do you like these brands? What do you look for when you buy clothes?

A. Its gotta be comfortable. I have to be able to move in it, or play ball in it, and still go to the clubs … comfortable but still nice.

Q. Do you go on spending sprees?

A. Nah, I try to keep my platinum bill on the *D.L.*[2]

Q. Are you happy with the way you buy clothes?

A. Yeah, I got my own system. Hasn't failed me yet.

Q. Do you like shopping for clothes?

A. Clothes shopping? Yes, I like it. I love it. You know, I gotta keep my threads on top of the game.

Q. Is choosing clothes a problem for you?

A. Nah, I usually just try whatever catches my eye and I just buy it. I go in, do my business, and then I'm out. … I am like flash … you know flashin' in, flashin' out. Bling blingin'!

Q. What role does clothing play in your life?

A. See, I look at clothing like it's a part of me. It's like people be lookin' at my clothes. It is like they're seein' into my soul. You know what I mean? That's why I dress the way I dress.

---

1. Pretty hot and tempting; 2. Down-low

Makeup artist, Cincinnati, USA

Q. Do you pay attention to clothes advertising?

A. Nah, I just buy what I like; I will not bow to any sponsor. I buy what I want. I'm like Sprite—I obey my thirst. That is the way it is.

INTERVIEWER: Ok. Thank you for your time.

site is Alloy.com. I shop for sales and I shop for rare merchandise. If I am getting bored I will go to the mall. In fact if I don't go shopping for 2 or 3 days at a stretch, I begin to feel depressed. I buy very carefully, after full deliberation, but I browse a lot and I window-shop a lot. Mall is a place I couldn't live without. You could say I was born to shop. (Christy, 22)

Consumer as Reveler Finally, we all have visions of consumers just having a good time—at a restaurant, a rock concert, a beach resort on spring break—enjoying life with all the wonderful things the marketplace has to offer. Below are two excerpts from consumer interviews.

I am really big into smelling good. I spend hundreds of dollars on top name cologne. I feel that appearance and smell at first are what make the man what he is. I can be running to the grocery store and I put on cologne. (Chad, 22)

I love attending a live concert. Rap, country, rock, gospel, alternative—I love them all. My favorite band is Dave Matthews—I have got all 14 of their CDs and two live concert DVDs! (Joe , 23)

Here we have a snapshot of a group of consumers (see facing page). When it comes to consumers as revelers, a picture does speak a thousand words!

All of these visions are true. They exist not only in different consumers, but also sometimes in the same consumer. Thus, we are economic creatures at times, watching every penny; at other times, we just want to experience, just want to be revelers, with money as no object. Sometimes, we are assessing a product and soaking up all the information, with our internal computer drives whirring. A consumer is indeed multi-faceted. And our study will cover all these facets.

Now, we are ready to begin our formal study of consumer behavior.

WHAT IS CONSUMER BEHAVIOR?

We define **consumer behavior** as the set of mental and physical activities undertaken by consumers to acquire and to consume products so as to fulfill their needs and wants.

Our definition of consumer behavior has several elements worth noting. Let us discuss these one by one.

Mental and Physical Activities   First, consumer behavior includes both mental and physical activities. **Mental activities** are acts of the mind, and they relate to what we think, feel, and know about products. **Physical activities** are, in contrast, acts of the human body, and they relate to what we do physically to acquire and to consume products. When you are contemplating buying a product, even dreaming about it, you are engaging in a mental activity. You are also engaging in a mental activity when you are

> Just wondering if a three-button suit jacket will be proper is also *Consumer Behavior.*

mulling over a product's benefits and risks; making sense of an advertisement; trying to remember the price of a product in the store you previously visited; trying to recall what Dr. Oz said the other day, on his TV show, about the benefits of eating chia seeds; or just wondering if a three-buttoned suit jacket will be good to wear to a forthcoming job interview, or if, instead, you should stick to the more conservative two-buttoned jacket.

Physical activities include visiting stores, clipping coupons, talking to salespeople, test-driving a car, placing an item in the shopping cart, abandoning a shopping cart, and saving empty cartons for later recycling. Physical activities entailed in actual consumption are also included—such as preparation to consume (e.g., setting the table, blotting grease from pizzas and fries, etc.), consumption situations (e.g., choosing takeout or dining in, using a cell phone while driving), consumption rituals (e.g., a makeup regimen), or routine trivial behaviors (e.g., TV channel flipping). Indeed, it is by observing consumer inconveniences and improvisations during product use that marketers often conceive new products and tailor their communications. Some activities are hybrids— both physical and mental—such as reading *Consumer Reports* or product labels.

It should be noted that the mental and physical activities we study under consumer behavior are not limited to specific acts of buying and using products. Rather, they include activities that the consumer undertakes in preparation for and prior to the actual buying act, and they also include activities that continue long after a product is actually consumed or used. When a consumer hears a friend praising a product and makes a mental note to try it some time in the future, this preparatory activity is part of consumer behavior. Likewise, if a few months after using a product, the consumer suddenly recalls the experience of using that product and chuckles about it, enjoying the memory of past consumption, then that post-use mental activity is also consumer behavior.

Product   Second, we use the term *product* broadly, to refer to any physical or non-physical product or service that offers some benefit to the consumer, including a place, a person, or an idea offered for exchange. Thus, not only are physical products such as cars, shirts, and golf clubs included, but so too are services such as a fitness club, a college education, a TV program, and a "breakup letter service"—more on that later. Also included are places such as vacation destinations, outlet malls, or video arcades. And persons, such as political candidates seeking your votes are included. And, finally, ideas are included, such

as vegetarianism or promoting Occupy Wall Street. (The latter, a public protest, originally initiated by Canadian activist group *Adbusters*, was launched on September 17, 2011 in New York City. Since then, under a more generalized moniker, The Occupy Movement, it has spread worldwide: London, Ontario, Canada, November 9, 2011; Copenhagen, October 15, 2011; Paris, November 4, 2011; London, UK, October 15, 2011, repeated on February 27, 2012). The important point here is that casting your vote for a candidate is just as good an example of consumer behavior as is buying a brand of toothpaste; so is visiting a museum, choosing a college, reading Kim and Krickitt Carpenter's *New York Times* best seller, *The Vow*, displaying a "Save Our Environment" bumper sticker on your new, British-built Toyota Avensis, or deciding not to donate to the Octo-Mom (Nadya Suleman) fund.

Photos courtesy of Arden E. John, South Korea

Consumers as Revelers: Bo Ring Mud Festival South Korea

Consumers Third, our definition includes the concept of *consumer*. In general, a consumer is anyone engaged in the acquisition and use of products and services available in the marketplace. Although a few humans on our planet might well be living lives sustained entirely by self-produced products and services (rather than those acquired in the marketplace), most of us acquire the majority of the products and services we need and want through marketplace exchange. Each of us, therefore, is a consumer.

The use of the term *consumer* in this text is broader than in practice, where different marketers call them, instead, by different names. For example, retail stores generally refer to their patrons as *customers* (rather than as *consumers*); so do utility companies (e.g., electricity or phone service providers), financial companies (e.g., banks), and service providers (e.g., palm readers). Professional service providers (e.g., lawyers, real estate agents, tax advisors) refer to them as *clients,* or by their more context-specific roles (e.g., doctors call them *patients*, educators call them *students*, fund-raisers call them *donors*, etc.). Only manufacturers (e.g., Procter & Gamble, Unilever, Kraft, Cadbury, Molson, Britvic. etc.), who do not routinely deal with the end-users of a product directly, refer to these household end users as *consumers*. In this text, however, we refer to all of these kinds of acquirers and users of products and services as *consumers*.

Customers, clients, patients, tourists, donors, students— all are consumers.

Our use of the term *consumer* also goes beyond its literal meaning— persons who "consume." Of course, some products do get consumed, such as food items, but other products do not get "consumed" (i.e., depleted), such as household appliances or other durables. For these products, we are users rather than consumers. Again, we will use the term *consumers* to refer to the users of all products or services, whether these products are consumables or durables.

Correspondingly, we define **consumption** as any and all usage of products whether or not the products are actually "consumed" away; i.e., depleted. Thus, when we look at our digital pictures and we show them or e-mail them to others, we are consuming these pictures. And, of course, activities such as TV viewing, visiting art galleries, and tweeting and retweeting messages on Twitter also count as consumption.

Needs and Wants Finally, two important words in our definition are *needs* and *wants*. *Needs* and *wants* are perhaps the two words most freely used by consumers—"freely" in the sense that consumers seldom ponder before uttering these words. They utter these words merely, but unmistakably, to indicate their desire or intent to possess and/or consume something. Philosophers of diverse ilk have ruminated for centuries as to what *need* and *want* mean, and understandably there is no consensus. Consequently, consumer researchers who study consumer needs and wants also vary in their definitions of

Philosophers of diverse ilk have ruminated for centuries as to what *need* and *want* mean.

the terms. Indeed, it would be futile to search for a definition on which everyone would agree. So, below are the definitions we will use in this book.

A Need Is Not A Product. A Product Is Not A Need.

A **need** can be defined as a discomforting human condition. It can be discomforting in a physiological sense or in a psychological sense. Examples of physiologically discomforting conditions are sensations of hunger or cold; examples of discomforting *psychological* conditions are feeling bored, feeling insecure, or experiencing being looked down upon. As consumers, we seek products or services in the marketplace exchange so as to alleviate these conditions of discomfort. A **want** is a desire for a specific object or product. The consumer who wants a product judges that it would restore his or her condition to a satisfactory state. Thus, the felt discomfort of a hungry stomach is a need; desire for food and for a specific kind of food is a want. Feeling insecure is a need; desire for the latest model of Nike shoes, even when barely within one's means, is a want. Thus, a product is *not* a need; it is a *solution* to a need.[2]

The definitions we use here differ from common speech, where needs are equated with necessities, and wants with luxuries. There are good reasons for this, which we will explore in a later section. For now, just remember that *need* is your felt discomfort, period. And remember also that the discomfort has to be perceived by the person himself or herself. Thus, a need is not someone else's assessment of your condition. I cannot say that your hair looks long, so you need a haircut; Or, that you don't need an iPad, or the latest game for your Wii. Or that you don't need to have your Avatar reside in Second Life. It is for you to decide if not having these things is discomforting for you, psychologically speaking. Indeed, then, *need* is a very subjective word. It is a very personal feeling.

WANT? NEED? SAME DIFFERENCE

Need is a very subjective feeling—this important consumer sentiment is elegantly captured in this ad for Nissan 370Z.

Copyright, Nissan (2009). Nissan and the Nissan logo are registered trademarks of Nissan. Photo: Markus Wendler. (Used with permission.)

THE ALL-NEW NISSAN Z
Starting at $29,930. The attraction of the all-new Nissan 370Z™ is far more than physical. With its staggering 332 horsepower, the world's first SynchroRev Match Manual Transmission* and finely crafted interior, every detail only makes you want it more. Or is it need? For more information, visit us at NissanUSA.com.

SHIFT_the way you move

As shown $37,460. 370Z Touring with Sport Package. Prices are MSRP* excluding tax, title, license and destination charge. Dealer sets actual price. *Available feature. Always wear your seat belt, and please don't drink and drive. ©2009 Nissan North America, Inc.

EXCHANGE, RESOURCES, AND VALUE

Three Essentials of Consumer Behavior

There are three essential elements in all consumer behavior. Without these, no "consumer behavior" can occur. And they work in unison—inseparably, as three grand enablers of consumer behavior. These are exchange, resources, and value. Let us examine each.

EXCHANGE

Exchange refers to an interchange between two parties where each receives from the other something of more value and gives up something of less value. Within that specific exchange, what is given up is of less value to the giver than it is to the receiver, so that both parties gain more in value than they give up. Thus, when we buy a shirt, we part with our money (say, 20 dollars or 40 rubles or 25 Euros or 120 pesos or 80 yen) because, at that time, that particular shirt is more valuable to us than keeping that money in our pockets; conversely, when we sell that shirt in a garage sale for one dollar, at that time, that shirt's value to us is less than even one dollar.

Although an exchange can also occur between any two consumers, it is customary to call one of the parties the *marketer* and the other party the *consumer*. A **marketer** is an individual or an organization with an organizational goal that offers products and services in exchange for the consumer's money or (occasionally) other resources. When a marketer primarily seeks money and has the making of money as the principal organizational goal, then that marketer is referred to as a **commercial entity**. When a marketer offers products and services either free of cost or at a nominal charge insufficient to cover costs or make any profit, the marketer is typically a **non-profit** or social organization. Typically, non-profit or social organizations promote ideas (e.g., smoking cessation) or persons (e.g., a presidential candidate). An important point here is that the study of consumer behavior is just as useful for non-profit and social and community organizations.[3]

RESOURCES

A **resource** is something we own or possess that people value. Since people value those resources, more or less universally, we can, as consumers, use them to acquire a whole host of products and services. That is, as humans, we value resources ourselves, and, because other humans value them too, we can exchange some of them to satisfy our needs and wants.

Money

Time

Know-
ledge

Energy

Social
capital

Five Resources

There are five types of resources: money, time, skills and knowledge, body and physical energy, and social capital. Of these, money is the most often used resource for marketplace exchanges—when we acquire products and services, we typically pay for them with money. We also use money to acquire the other four resources. We buy time-saving devices to gain more time; we hire maids so we ourselves don't have to expend time in housekeeping chores. We buy books and take college courses to gain knowledge, we buy home-improvement books to learn to do handiwork, and we pay for lessons to acquire the skills needed to compete on *Dancing With The Stars*.

To build our bodies and enhance physical energy as a resource, we spend money and join a gym. We spend time doing yoga. And we buy vitamins and nutrition-supplements to get energy. Finally, we spend time and money to build **social capital**—the network of friends and professional connections that can be of help in our hours of need. We buy designer brand clothes that will help us gain acceptance among our peers. We spend time writing "thank you" notes and sending gifts to keep the friends we have. And we pay fees to join social clubs and associations to enlarge our social networks.[4]

Sometimes we use other resources so we can pay less in money. We pay, in part, with our time when we choose to take a cheaper airline flight with a stopover instead of a direct flight. Likewise when we buy a modular furniture system that we have to assemble ourselves, we exchange our time, physical energy, and skill set to save money. If we believe that we have the requisite skills, then we choose a low-fee discount broker rather than a full-service investment advisor, or we buy stocks online. We use our healthy bodies as resources when we donate blood or pledge to donate some organ. And good looks are themselves "exchanged" to attract a date, companion, or mate.

VALUE

The third essential element in all consumer behavior is value. **Value** is the sum total of net benefits we receive from an activity or an exchange. Indeed, value is the core goal of all exchanges that humans undertake.

> **Value, not money, is the basic currency of all human interaction. When we meet someone, we try to quickly assess how long it would be worth our while to be talking to that person. If an incoming phone call shows up on our caller ID, we promptly decide if we would gain anything by taking that call at that time…. It is even more true of marketplace exchanges. The only reason customers are even in the marketplace is that they are looking for something of value. (ValueSpace, 2001, p. 3-4.)[5]**

Value comes from all the benefits, all the desired outcomes that consumers obtain and experience from their use of products. When a cream eradicates our acne, that is a desired outcome to us and hence a value. When a musical play uplifts our moods, that is a desired outcome and hence it is a value. When wearing a particular suit or dress brings us compliments from others, we are receiving value. And when we feel good about ourselves having donated to a charity, we are experiencing value. In everything we buy, in everything we consume, in every advertisement to which we pay attention, from every salesperson to whom we lend our ears, in every store we enter, on every Web site we visit, we seek value.

Thus, value comes in multiple forms. Basically, value accrues when some need is satisfied. Because human needs are countless, so also are forms of value. However, they can be categorized into four major types, captured in the acronym USER: (a) utilitarian, (b) social, (c) ego/identity, and (d) recreational.[6]

Utilitarian value is the set of tangible outcomes of a product's usage (or of an activity). It comprises physical consequences of a product and its effects in the physical world around us and within us (i.e., in our bodies). Also called *functional value*, utilitarian value comes from objects when they enable us to manage our lives as biological and physical beings and to manage our external physical environments as well. Examples include filling our bellies with food, energizing our bodies with nutrients, moisturizing our skin with lotions, navigating physical distance by using a Segway™, etc. But don't mistake utilitarian value as referring only to basic physical necessities. A computer that allows us to write and save letters, a personal jet that enables us to reach places at will, and a digital camera phone that lets us shoot pictures anytime anywhere, and then e-mail them instantly to our friends—these products yield specific benefits that are also utilitarian.

Social value comes from our ability to manage our social worlds (as opposed to the physical world). This includes maintaining warm and harmonious relations with others, fitting in with peers, and generally projecting a good image to others. Thus, we get social value when we wear brand name clothing with a certain brand image, and we get social value when we buy someone a gift to affirm our relationship. We also receive social value when we donate blood as part of an office drive, as well as when we boycott French imported products just because all our coworkers do.

Ego/identity value comes from our need to construct and nurture our identities or self-concepts, our sense of ego, our ideas of who we are. Thus, we eat vegetarian food because we value the identity of being an animal saver. We gain ego/identity value by recycling because we believe in preserving the environment. We wear Polo and Donna Karen and drive a Jaguar because we think these brands are very urbane and sophisticated, and we also view ourselves as urbane and sophisticated. Or alternatively, we wear, say, American Eagle and drive a Blazer because we want to nurture our self-identities as being very rugged.

Finally, **recreation value** comes from objects and activities when they recreate our moods and regenerate our mental ability—removing our fatigue and boredom, stimulating the senses, and rejuvenating our minds. Also called **hedonic value**, recreation value is obtained from wide ranging forms of consumption: from mild mood-lifters like listening to one's favorite music to the extreme exhilaration of watching one's favorite sports team win the championship game; from a short coffee break to wallowing in pleasure at the Venetian in Las Vegas.

Of course, many products and activities could simultaneously produce multiple values, and two consumers could use the same product to derive two different values. Thus, a consumer could wear Polo or Donna Karen clothing purely to impress others, whereas another person could wear them, not because what others might think of them, but because he or she sees himself or herself that way. To us the clearest distinction between the two values (social and ego/identity) came from a consumer who said he buys name brand shirts and pants to make an impression, even though he thinks it is foolish to pay so much for them, and that when it comes to underwear, he buys a store brand; in contrast, another consumer bought only designer-brand underwear because he thought he "deserved it."

Make no mistake about it: we sometimes choose a product to impress others, but sometimes we choose it purely to play out our sense of identity. Tons of expensive designer brand undergarments and a dozen or more personal grooming gadgets from Sharper Image get chosen, not because of a desire to impress others (these products have low public visibility), but because we believe we are the kind of people who have the personalities suited for those brands.

Another point to note is that while a few products are entirely symbolic and have no physical utility (e.g., greeting cards), most products have utility as a minimal core. Many products have physical utility and not much more (e.g., hardware products such as duct tape), but most products have, surrounding a physical, utilitarian core, some social, ego/identity, or recreational value. Clothing, cars, colognes, and being seen in a Starbucks Café sipping a $4.50 Tazo® Vanilla Rooibos Tea Latte offer these multiple values, for example.

We will dwell on these more in subsequent chapters of the book, but for now remember the acronym USER as your code word to think of the four principal values consumers seek in the marketplace and in consumption.

Are These Two People *Consuming* at This Moment?

Yes, the clothes, for starters. Besides, whereas during yoga, we are expected to shut off our minds from all extraneous thoughts, few are able to. For all we know, these two persons might be thinking, individually, "I should, after all, buy a proper yoga mat." Or, he might be contemplating which movie they should see later that evening, *Hugo* or *Midnight in Paris*. And she, to buy TomTom GO 740 LIVE, as the ultimate answer to his aversion (arguably a typical male trait) not to ask for directions.

Remember, evaluating impending purchases or contemplating future consumption is also consumer behavior.

Whether in actions currently unfolding or in thoughts laced with objects of desire, we are, at any given moment, more likely than not, being consumers. Indeed, then, we are consumers 24/7!

Does Marketing Create Consumer Needs?

Some people blame marketing for creating consumer needs. They charge that marketing creates a desire for products we don't need. Does it? Let us examine this closely. Mainly, this charge is based on two prevalent views of what a *need* is. First, the charge comes from those who define true needs as only the basic things we require for survival. Consequently, they argue that we only need a basic car, not a fancy car, but marketers create in us a desire for a fancy car, and that we do not need $150 Nike shoes, but fancy advertising beguiles us into believing that we do.

The second definitional problem is that in common parlance, a need is confused with a product. This leads to the argument that no one needed an iPad until Apple introduced iPads, and no one needed Botox treatments until Botox treatments became available. A discourse on whether or not we needed something is impossible if we use the terms *need* and *product* interchangeably.

In contrast, we have defined *need* as a condition (an unsatisfactory one), not as a product that improves that condition. So the need to create, store, access, and watch digital content on-the-go always existed; iPads provided a solution—a better solution. And the need to impress peers and express ourselves has always existed; Nike offers, and Botox treatments offer, to some consumers, a way to do it. Consider digital camera cell phones. Before they became available, we did not need digital camera cell phones. In fact, we did not even need cell phones. But the need to be able to call our moms or friends from a place with no pay phone nearby had always existed. And every once in a while we were in a place looking at something, some product, some transient scene, and we wished we could capture it in a photo and show it to a friend far away in real time to get his or her opinion. We had always needed, too, the ability to see the caller's face in our tiny cell phone's screen. Since these possibilities were not available, we dreamed about them every once in a while and then pushed the thought away from our active attention. Until one day, science made the cell phone available, and then the cell phone with digital camera and e-mail capabili-

**Two consumers.
Two different self-identities.
Expressed through clothes.**

**Miguel Young, a "watch repair artist" (L), Sean Foley, an eco-design professor,
Fedora hat and tie-dye T-shirt—to each his own, courtesy of the marketplace.**

(Incidentally, no amount of clever marketing can make Miguel trade his fedora hat for the tie-dye T. And Sean will absolutely, positively not do the trade either. They might as well, but not because of marketing.)

ties, and we suddenly recognized these products as solutions to our long-dormant needs. But it was science that gave us those products, not marketing. Marketing brought the news and explained product functions and benefits. The same goes for every invention—from Post-it® Digital Notes to hair transplants, science made them available, and, *after* that, marketing brought us the information and offered the invention at a price (sometimes a hefty sum, mind you). And those who saw these products as solutions to their needs—the conditions that were bugging them—bought them immediately, without much persuasion, whereas others waited a while or never bought them at all (a high intensity marketing effort notwithstanding!).

Speaking of the products science has brought us, smart consumers would have discovered their benefits even in the absence of marketers, and from them, in turn, all consumers would have. Consumers who credit marketers with creating in them the need for all those new inventions are merely shifting responsibility from themselves to marketers.

What about products that are not scientific inventions, but mere packaging of image, you might ask. Like designer brands? Here, too, marketing receives more blame than it deserves. Imagine a world in which only one brand and one type of shoe (in all sizes, of course) was available, and only one brand and one style of clothes, and only one make and style of car. Would you then have been happier? There resides in us a need to differentiate ourselves, not to be stamped from a cookie cutter, to show something unique. What marketers do, to consumers' benefit, is simply to make those varieties, those differentiations in product offerings available. And in countries where these products are not freely available (and where, therefore, there is no marketing), many consumers would kill to get them from the gray market if they could!

Somehow, consumers have their ideas of what will make them happy, and they will do anything to get those things, marketing or no marketing. (Without any promotion, iPhone 4S, launched in Australia, Canada, France, Germany, Japan, the UK. and the US on October 14, 2011, was sold out on a pre-order basis on the first day of availability! And when Nike released its outer space-themed limited-edition shoe, Foamposite Galaxy, on February 24, 2012, people lined up at the stores on the previous evening, and in several cities armed police with riot gear had to be called in to manage the unruly crowd!!) The important question, therefore, is this: Where do consumers get their ideas? From diverse sources, actually. From the media for one. From seeing what the sports celebrities are driving, and what the rap artists are wearing. And they observe people around them. Who is wearing Seven7 ™ or True Religion jeans, who is driving the Scion, and who is walking with iPod ear buds as a fashion statement? Thus, it is the media, and it is the society as a whole, the culture, the world around us, and what we see on the streets we are roaming—these are the sources of our desires. Marketing is a part of this environment, no more, and no less.

The tattoo is already inside you!

Let us look at it another way. Consider how many products are introduced in a typical year, and how many of them become abysmal failures. With all the marketing prowess behind them, marketers just can't convince enough number of consumers to part with their money to buy those products. And then there is the battle of the brands. In clothing, there is Kenneth Cole, and there is Tommy Hilfiger. Open any issue of *GQ* or *Esquire* and you can find advertisements for both. Why, then, do you buy one brand and not the other? There is a very simple reason: Each brand makes a certain brand promise, each projects a certain image, each fits a certain consumer's inner self-image, and the consumer buys that which speaks to him or her. To other marketers, consumers vote "No"—with their wallets and purses. Yes, consumers respond to advertising, to marketing, but only to the brand and only to

The Tattoo is already inside you!
This consumer, Victor Strunk, used to sixth-sense extra-terrestrial characters protecting him from dangers both from outside and from within, got them etched on his skin.

the marketer that in fact responds first to what is within the consumer already. As one tattoo artist, describing how he helps his clients choose a design, put it: "The tattoo is already within the consumer; all I do is bring it out for the world to see!"[7]

Below, we summarize the arguments on the two sides of this debate.

REASONS FOR:

1. What consumers really need (for survival) are just the basics (e.g., food, clothing, shelter). As to all other products, consumers come to believe they need them because marketers tell them so.

2. Marketers create new products. Until then, consumers manage with whatever is available. By creating new products, marketers created consumer needs for those products.

3. Marketers package products and create messages that lure consumers. By themselves, many of the products would not have attracted consumers.

4. Marketers flood the media with commercials and deals; exposed to a barrage of commercial messages day-in and day-out, it is natural for consumers to succumb.

REASONS AGAINST:

1. To limit consumer needs to basic survival is to limit consumers to mere biological beings. As social and psychological beings, their social and psychological needs are just as important.

2. Products are not needs, so creating products cannot equal creating needs. Products are solutions to needs, which must already exist in consumers.

3. Many products fail despite heavy marketing. Thus, not marketing but the product's benefits (including social and psychological benefits) cause consumers to want them.

4. Consumers don't really trust marketers anyway. Rather, their product choices are based on advice from independent sources and influence from peers.

So now, dear reader, you must decide which side you are on.

SEEING THE FUTURE FIRST: MEETING CONSUMERS' LATENT NEEDS

Consider the telephone. It is a miracle. It was invented in 1876. Suddenly, two persons continents apart could talk to each other. Since then, the technology experts in phone companies have upgraded the device over the years, improving sound fidelity and adding new features such as pulse tone, and, later, speed dial, memory, and muting. But their gaze had for long remained focused on the telephone device itself. And while they kept in mind the consumer need the device served, that need seems to have been understood in its most obvious form: the need to talk to someone not within hearing range. They did not look deeper; it was assumed, inadvertently, that whenever someone wanted to talk to a distant person, that other person would be available at that location and at that time, and that he or she would want to talk to the caller, without knowledge of who was calling. Furthermore, it was assumed that the two would speak the same language! After all, it was not until 1971 that the answering machine was invented.[8] And it was not until 1987 that caller ID was first offered to consumers.[9] And finally, technology experts are only now building automatic, built-in translation software. It took more than a hundred years to address these telephone-related consumer needs. For nearly a century, scientists and marketers had failed to recognize these communication needs of consumers. No one had bothered to look deeper.

Marketing Is All About Satisfying a Consumer Need

Consider some other products to see if they *create* a new need, or, merely, albeit admirably, *satisfy* a latent need of consumers.[10]

Self-watering Flower Pot The pot has two chambers; the lower half is filled with water; a wick from the top half, which contains soil, reaches out to the bottom chamber. Would you want to buy it? If yes, that is because the moment you saw it, you recognized it as the perfect solution to a latent need—the challenge of taking care of plants while on vacation. If not, then no amount of marketing effort will make you buy it.

MyVu MyVu is a video eyewear system, equipped with a patented optical system (called SolidOptex®). It connects to your iPod and to other video source devices, and gives you a hands-free, full-screen, private viewing experience. Thus, you can watch your videos on the train, plane, or bus, in the mall, at the coffee shop, or even while standing in line to buy the tickets to the next Broadway show. And it looks high tech yet fashionably styled.

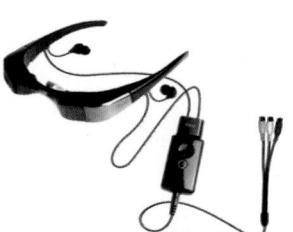

MyVu is a video eyewear

Hug Shirt It has *wearable electronics*. It enables a person to send you a hug from far away. Here is how it works: It has two high-tech components, embedded in the fabric: (1) *sensors* that can sense the strength of the touch, skin warmth, and the heart-beat of the sender at a distance; and (2) *actuators* that can reproduce the same sensations for the wearer. Yes, now you can hug your teacher everyday! (Check it out at the London-based design company, cutecircuit.com.)

Word Lens An app for iPhone 4S. Imagine that you are in a foreign country looking at a road sign in a language you can't read. Just activate this app and flash your phone camera, and, voilà, instantly the sign text is translated into English or Spanish.

Silent Dating This concept in social networking was invented a few years ago. You meet people in a group, but you are not allowed to talk at all. You are provided with a generous supply of index cards and a pen. Scribble a message on one and slide it over to the other person. Then wait for him/her to doodle back. Says one recent, happy, silent dater: "I haven't had this much fun since passing notes in school." Silent Dating parties are held in such cities as New York, San Francisco, Washington D.C., London, and even Beijing. Check out the schedule for the next party at www.quietparty.com.

Hug Shirt
from CuteCircuit

Will You Buy These Products?

Now, let us consider briefly what role marketing plays (or will play) for these products. Consider the Hug Shirt. Okay, "hugging your teacher" was the wrong pitch. How about hugging your significant others, when you are away from home? If the wearable vest doesn't cost too much, some of us just might buy it. But, and this is an important "but," only if the sensations are realistic and only if we can bring ourselves to believe that the hug we just experienced felt just as if the other person were in "touching proximity." If not, no amount of marketing prowess will get us to part with our money. The truth is, many of us can't wait to try it on. At least as a novelty experience, initially, and then, later, to use it as a real emo-interface with a loved one far away.

What is your response to MyVu—the private-viewing experience eyewear that lets you watch a video in the upper part of your visual field, while in the rest of your visual field you scan your surroundings? Consumers who are already into watching videos on their mobile screens, spend a lot of time away from home and office, and like the idea of being able to watch their favorite videos even when in public places while glancing at the surroundings (while keeping tack of the moving checkout line, for example) will embrace it readily; others will wait until they have determined if this ability is important to them.

What about the iPhone app, Word Lens? Introduced in December 2010 for Android phones and later for iPhone 4 and 4S, it has, at this writing (March 2012), become one of the most sought-after apps for travelers.

Silent dating—It was a "hot" idea once, but now it is limited to a niche segment. For this segment, that other dating scene, with loud music and the noise of a thousand conversations, has been utterly frustrating for any intelligent interaction. Silent Dating is also a breath of fresh air for the tongue-tied among that segment. And it is a low-risk venture. More than anything else, it is, for some, a new, alluring sport through which to play out their spontaneity. Those of us who have this mindset of constant exploration will find it a value; those who do not, will not, marketing or no marketing.

Will you buy any of these products? Yes or no, whatever your answer, it is *your* answer—the outcome of your determining if they will meet any of your needs. Would a million-dollar ad campaign make you buy it? No, a million-dollar ad campaign will make *you*, at most and if at all, reassess if it would satisfy your needs. That is all.

That's a loud shirt for a quiet party.

Yes, I am bilingual—English and Silence!

Notes from Silent Daters (www.quietparty.com)

| LA CAFETERÍA 10 MIDE ESTA MANERA → | + | Word Lens | = | COFFEE SHOP 10 METERS THIS WAY → |

As these examples show, rather than creating needs in consumers, what marketing does best is invent new solutions to meet consumers' needs (overt or latent), and communicate the new and enhanced value these new products bring to relevant segments of consumers.

CREATING CONSUMER VALUE: THE SUPREME PURPOSE OF BUSINESS

What is the purpose of marketing? For that matter, what is the basic purpose of business itself? To make money? "Wrong," says Harvard professor Theodore Leavitt, who explains this by an analogy: all humans have to breathe to survive, but breathing is not their *purpose*. Likewise, making money cannot be called the purpose of business.[11] The basic purpose has to relate to why society allows businesses to exist. It is, says Peter F. Drucker, one of the world's leading management gurus, "to create a satisfied customer."[12]

Marketing does not create a need. It creates a satisfied consumer. And in striving to do so, its practitioners—marketers—serve a very important role for consumers, and for society. They create products they hope will satisfy the latent needs of some segment of consumers; or they commercialize the inventions of inventors, adapting them to suit consumer needs and tastes. They bring, too, art, culture, aesthetics, design, and creativity to morph and sculpt a socio-cultural identity for a given product—the so-called *brand image*, the one they hope will resonate with the target consumer. However, creating that brand image in the marketer's own image will bring all that multi-million dollar effort and all that marketing prowess to naught (see the story of OK Soda in Chapter 7); creating it, instead, as they should, in the target consumer's image will bring the admiration (and economic votes; i.e., dollars or Euros or yen) of its target consumers.

MyVu Video Eyewear

To create a product in the consumer's image, marketers must labor to understand consumers' needs and wants, desires and motives, self-concepts and identities; they must then craft their products so that they solve consumers' relevant problems and fulfill their dreams. Marketers must labor, as well, to decide what price will make for a good value for the consumer and still bring the firm fair economic returns on its investment. Marketing brings the product to consumers' doorsteps, or to the Web portals on their cell phone screens. And it creates the physical, social, and cultural milieu that smooths the product acquisition process for consumers and that invites, enables, and enhances consumers' consumption experiences. The art of doing this right is the profession of marketing. This is, in effect, the supreme mission of marketing.

How do you fulfill this mission? How do you create a satisfied customer? How else but by studying consumers, by analyzing how a consumer thinks, feels, and acts in the marketplace and how he or she connects products and specific brands to his or her needs and aspirations. By seeing the "proverbial 'tattoo' that is already within the consumer," so to speak. That is why understanding consumer behavior is of paramount importance to the success of all organizations, commercial or social.

THE AGE OF THE EMPOWERED CONSUMER

Understanding consumer behavior has always been an essential prerequisite for business success. Throughout the 100-year-history of marketing in the 20th century, marketers were in control. John Wanamaker's Philadelphia store (now Macy's), opened in 1876, was the first store operated with what is now known as the *marketing concept*. The first marketing course was offered in 1905 by the University of Pennsylvania, and radio advertising (the first truly "mass" medium) began in 1922.[13] Consumers had the option of buying or not buying the products they were offered, but little else. But since the beginning of the 21st century, the introduction of Web 2.0 has changed all that. Individual consumers can now create brand messages on their own and broadcast them—see any number of "sucks.com" Web sites (e.g., Dell Sucks, Netflix Sucks, etc.). And with social media, consumers can now connect and band together by the millions. They now have access to media and they now have the strength of numbers. The 21st century is the Age of the Empowered Consumer. This (new) Age, in turn, has multiple facets; below is a list of four new developments in marketing and in the consumer mindset.

1. The age of co-creation and personalization
2. The age of the authentic and unique consumption experience
3. The age of collaborative consumption
4. The age of the consumer in the driver's seat

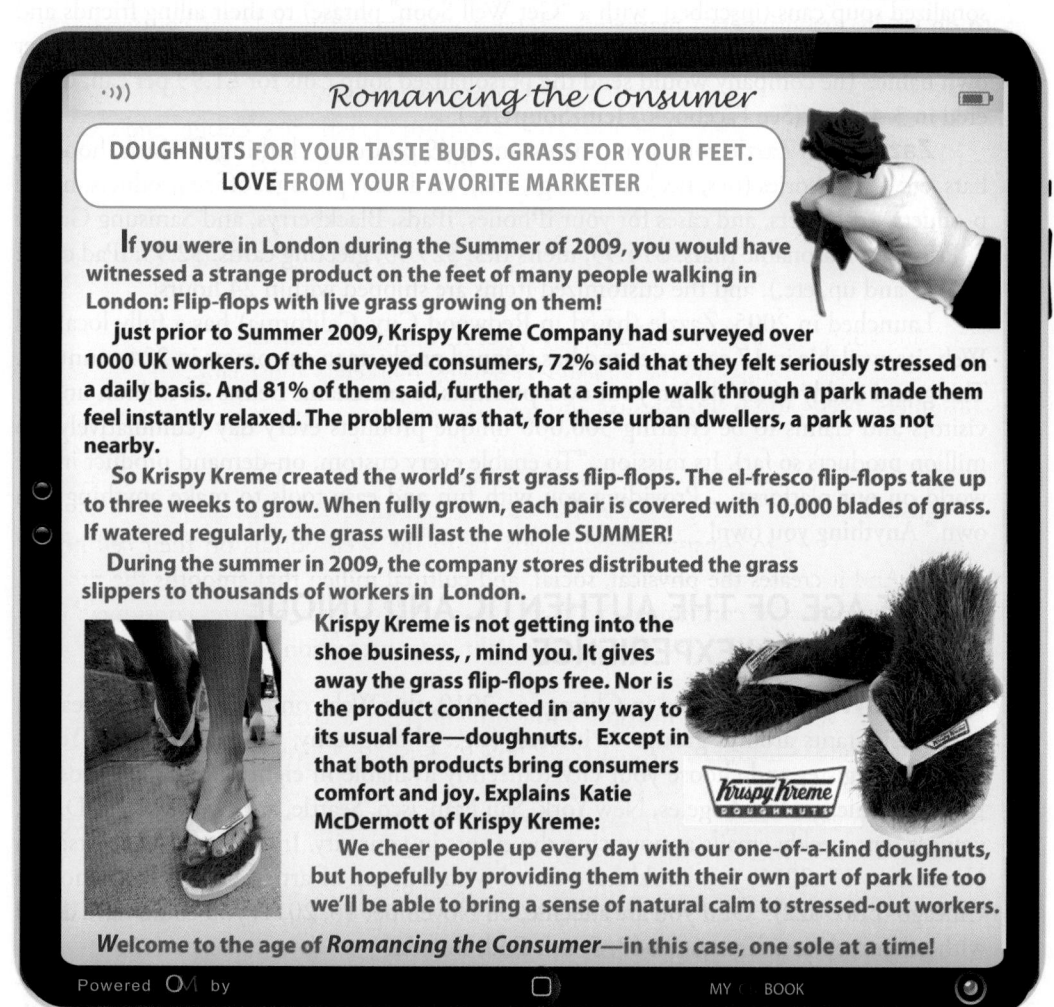

Romancing the Consumer

DOUGHNUTS FOR YOUR TASTE BUDS. GRASS FOR YOUR FEET. LOVE FROM YOUR FAVORITE MARKETER

If you were in London during the Summer of 2009, you would have witnessed a strange product on the feet of many people walking in London: Flip-flops with live grass growing on them!

just prior to Summer 2009, Krispy Kreme Company had surveyed over 1000 UK workers. Of the surveyed consumers, 72% said that they felt seriously stressed on a daily basis. And 81% of them said, further, that a simple walk through a park made them feel instantly relaxed. The problem was that, for these urban dwellers, a park was not nearby.

So Krispy Kreme created the world's first grass flip-flops. The el-fresco flip-flops take up to three weeks to grow. When fully grown, each pair is covered with 10,000 blades of grass. If watered regularly, the grass will last the whole SUMMER!

During the summer in 2009, the company stores distributed the grass slippers to thousands of workers in London.

Krispy Kreme is not getting into the shoe business, , mind you. It gives away the grass flip-flops free. Nor is the product connected in any way to its usual fare—doughnuts. Except in that both products bring consumers comfort and joy. Explains Katie McDermott of Krispy Kreme:

We cheer people up every day with our one-of-a-kind doughnuts, but hopefully by providing them with their own part of park life too we'll be able to bring a sense of natural calm to stressed-out workers.

Welcome to the age of *Romancing the Consumer*—in this case, one sole at a time!

Powered by ○ MY ○ BOOK

1. THE AGE OF CO-CREATION AND PERSONALIZATION

Arianna Osborne's experience with Keds is being replicated by millions of consumers around the world, all enabled by the new Internet technologies.[14]

NikeiD In a manner similar to that found on Keds, on NikeiD, you can design your own Nike shoes, both on its Web site, and now also in NikeiD Studios in select cities in Europe, China, and USA, where design consultants are also available. Design them from scratch, or you can customize classic models such as Nike Dunk, Nike SHOX, and Nike Air Max.

Threadless Threadless invites anyone to design a T-shirt and submit it for competition. The consumer entries are posted on the company's Web site for one week for the site visitors to vote. The highest scoring ideas are accepted for production. The original designers get a share of profits . The company has nurtured a community of a million creators.

Chocri On the Web site of Chocri, a German chocolate maker, you can create your own chocolate bar. You choose one of the bases (dark, milk, or white) and select one of over 100 toppings ranging from chili to candied rose petals. The company boasts over 27 billion combinations!

Jones Soda Jones Soda enables you to buy your Jones Soda with a customized label that you create, with any photo and text you want. Choose one of the eight flavors (e.g., Blue Bubblegum, Fufu Berry, etc.), and upload your photo and a message; For $29.99, a 12-pack of your personalized bottles of Jones Soda will be shipped to you.

Heinz In October 2011, Heinz in the U.K. invited its Facebook fans to send personalized soup cans (inscribed with a "Get Well Soon" phrase) to their ailing friends and family members. Each consumer had the option of adding the recipient's name and his/her own name. The company would send the personalized soup cans for £1.99 per can, delivered in 3-4 days. (See Facebook/HeinzSoupUK.)

Zazzle On Zazzle.com, you can customize 49 products: clothing (T-shirts, hoodies, hats, etc.), accessories (ties, necklaces, bags, etc.), cards and postage, office products, home products, art posters, and cases for your iPhones, iPads, Blackberrys, and Samsung Galaxy S. Prices are reasonable (hats: $14.95; men's ties: $29.95; greeting cards: $2.95; iPad cases: $49.95 and up, etc.), and the customized items are shipped within 24 hours!

Launched in 2005, Zazzle (based in Redwood City, California) has a fully localized Web site available in 17 countries and has shipped products to customers in 224 countries. This grand daddy of all "design your own products" e-merchants boasts 20 million unique visitors and claims to be creating 500,000 unique products every day (cumulatively, 86 million products so far). Its mission: "To enable every custom, on-demand product in the world on our platform… Providing you with fun and easy tools to make anything you own." Anything you own!

2. THE AGE OF THE AUTHENTIC AND UNIQUE CONSUMPTION EXPERIENCE

GrubWithUs Founded in Chicago in 2010, this Web company organizes meals in select restaurants around groups of interest (e.g., photography, Veggie Grubbers, Yoga). After you register and choose your city (currently available in eight U.S. cities—Boston, Boulder, Chicago, Los Angeles, New York, San Francisco, Seattle, and Washington, D.C.), you are sent weekly emails announcing the events in your city. Interested in the Arts? On November 17, 2011, you could have dined with a group of artists at The Parthenon in Chicago (price $22). Or if you are a techie, on November 16, 2011, you could have dined with other techies at Tremont 647, South End, Boston.

Lite Graffiti Elena C. of San Francisco offers what she calls a "light graffiti experience" at the UC Berkeley Campus. She explains "This involves capturing the light trails created by your flashlights; the camera captures what the eye cannot see so the results are amazing, even magical." She posts the offer on Vayable.com, a Web site that connects precisely this kind of unique-experience crafters with experience-seekers. For $25 a person for up to 8 persons in the group, Elena will bring the flashlights and a digital camera. And she will give you the digital pictures of the graffiti you create.

Java Trip On the same Vayable.com site, London resident Kardelen K. offers a coffee tasting tour of cafes in London. Her pitch: "I love coffee and I have been discovering the coffee shops in London for two years." You get to visit these cafes, and you get the inside skinny on the coffee beans, their origins, and the brewing processes involved. This three-hour experience will cost you $50 for a group of up to 6 people.

Piccadilly Circus, London

3. THE AGE OF COLLABORATIVE CONSUMPTION

Collaborative consumption refers to the practice of consumers coming together to consume a product without necessitating each consumer to own the product in its entirety. This practice is not new—roommates borrowing each other's clothes (or sports equipment, books, colognes, or leftover food!) have engaged in this practice for as long as shared rooming has existed. Only, now the practice has a new twist, thanks to the new means of consumer-to-consumer connectivity enabled by Web 2.0 and by social media. Consumers are connecting, these days, *with strangers* (sometimes via intermediary firms) to share the products they own—sometimes through barter or for a nominal price, but often at a good-value price. This trend is also known as peer-to-peer commerce.

Air BnB (Airbnb.com) This San Francisco-based start-up connects travelers who need a place to sleep with people who have a room to spare in their homes. The company calls its Web site, *the eBay for space*. Space owners are able to put their spare rooms to use, and travelers get access to distinctive spaces and the company of the hosts. The listed properties span some 20,000 cities in 192 countries. As of December 2011, the company boasts having booked 2 million nights!

Getaround This California-based company connects people who are willing to rent their cars to other consumers needing to rent one. On a recent visit (November 19, 2011), one member consumer in South Beach, California was offering his Mini Cooper for $7.50 an hour, and in Sunnyvale, CA, for $50 an hour, you could have rented a Tesla Roadster! Here is how the company describes its mission: "Car owners invest huge amounts of time and money into an asset they barely use. Cars are driven only about 8% of the time, while potential drivers walk past block after block of underutilized cars. We connect the dots…to help people get around… We want to empower people to travel more efficiently and cause a shift from personal to shared transport."

4. THE AGE OF THE CONSUMER IN THE DRIVER'S SEAT

Request anything

Zaarly

Zaarly This U.S. company, launched in May 2011, is eBay in reverse. Consumers post what they want, when, and how much they are willing to pay for it. Then other consumers (as well as conventional sellers) offer to fulfill the consumers' needs. The notable feature is the kinds and varieties of needs that you can post: baby-sitting services, a wedding singer, a chance to ride in a sports car, interior design advice, and the like. You can post your order on the Web and also on your mobile with an app; no need to tell it where you are—the "hyper-local" app already knows. Zaarly is a first, in that it is buyer-driven, and delivers in the "here and now" (e.g., want coffee delivered in an hour). The company boasts over 9.1 million posts in 200 U.S. cities (as of November 2011). And now its name is also a verb: its Web site offers a step-by-step guide, "How to Zaarly"!

David vs. Goliath On October 1, 2011, Molly Katchpole, a 22-year old Roger Williams University student, posted a petition on Change.org against Bank of America's proposed $5-a-month debit card fee. By the month's end, more than 300,000 people had signed the petition. And more than 20,000 people had pledged to close their Bank of America checking accounts. On November 1, the Big Bank aborted the plan!

ENLIGHTENED MARKETERS:
RESPONDING TO EMPOWERED CONSUMERS

Rather than feeling threatened by these trends, enlightened marketers are embracing the empowered consumer. In fact some firms are enabling, advancing, and celebrating the new consumer trends. Many of these trends have become possible due to the pioneering efforts of businesses. Many companies that enable these services are new ventures, and some were started by consumers who once faced the problem their businesses now solve. Keds and NikeID exemplify established companies that pioneered the co-creation processes. Zazzle is a new company conceived entirely to enable **mass-customization**—producing customized products for a "segment size of one" at close to the cost of mass production. Other companies are finding innovative ways of engaging consumers' hearts and minds in their products and in their marketing endeavors:

Maxwell House In July 2011, Maxwell House Canada opened its second Optimism Café in Toronto (the first was in Montreal), giving away a free cup of coffee throughout the month of July. As part of its Brew Some Good campaign, it launched its Is Your Cup Half Full or Half Empty Optimism campaign. It invited consumers to take an optimism break and post a video clip or a letter on its Web site. Among the posted videos were these two:

- Dave Tally, a homeless person, found $3,300, but returned it to the owner. Inspired by his honesty, the community offered help and now he is not homeless anymore.

> It is a beautiful day.
> But I can't see it!

- A blind person sat on a sidewalk with a cardboard sign that read "I'm blind. Please help." Passersby occasionally dropped a few small coins. Then a woman came by and wrote something on the other side of the cardboard. For the rest of the day, people came by and emptied their pockets of change. The woman had changed the sign to read: "It is a beautiful day. But I can't see it!"

Coke Australia Starting in September 2011, in time for Christmas 2011, Coca-Cola Australia introduced Coke bottles inscribed with the first names of people. These were not names of any specific persons, but rather merely common first names (e.g., Adrian, Kate, Matt, etc.). The company used 150 common names and printed them on millions of bottles. The expectation was that consumers would eagerly seek out not only their own names but also the names of their friends, and would then enjoy consuming the Coke out of these bottles together. The campaign was named Share a Coke.

It is only a matter of a few years (a single-digit number of years) before, to be successful, most marketers will have to remake themselves in the image of the newly empowered consumer. Like Keds and Nike and Zazzle, they will have to find ways of mass customizing their offerings; like Jones Soda and Heinz they will have to offer personalization; like GrubWithUS and Vayable, they will have to engineer authentic, unique, experiential consumption offerings. Like AirBnB and Getaround, they will have to enable product-sharing among consumers and offer their consumers access to the products without having to own the product. And like Canada's Maxwell House and Coke Australia, they will have to develop innovative marketing programs that connect their products to consumers' thoughts and feelings about their brand consumption experience. To prepare for that future, a future already upon us, it is imperative that we study how humans behave as consumers in their pursuit of happiness in the marketplace.

CONSUMER BEHAVIOR AS A FIELD OF STUDY

When we seek to understand consumer behavior, we seek to understand, basically, human behavior, albeit in connection with the world of goods. As an applied field of study, it draws on all four fields of basic social sciences dedicated to the study of human behavior; namely, anthropology, sociology, economics, and psychology. You already know what these fields are, but here is a quick refresher[15]:

Anthropology is the study of humankind in its habitat. It examines humankind's historic development—how people came to live the way they do. It is a study of the human in nature—how she/he survives and adapts and how a culture develops to help her/him live and adapt.

Sociology is the study of social systems—groups, organizations, and societies. It examines their structure and how individuals relate to one another in these social groups. It includes the study of social institutions, such as family, church, school, etc., and the part they play in society and in consumers' lives.

Economics is the study of goods—how they are produced, distributed, and consumed. As such it also deals with how societies and individuals allocate their resources on what to produce and what to buy. Economics helps us understand how we spend money, why we save it, and how to gain maximum utility from every transaction.

Psychology is the study of the human mind and the mental processes that influence a person's behavior. Here we study how we develop perceptions, how we learn, how we form attitudes, and what motivations drive our behavior.

As we cover various consumer behavior topics, we will constantly draw on related topics in these source disciplines, define the key concepts they use, and then go on to apply them to the behavior of humans as consumers.

Consider our shopper in the mall, Jackie, for example (see the Interview). We may find that Jackie has a world-view that is either perfectly normal or perfectly strange—depending on our own world-views. If our cultures and therefore our world-views are different from Jackie's, then we may find it a little strange that he thinks that people can look at his soul through his clothes. He also has a language (a dialect, actually) that is not standard English—in his culture, "brotha" does not mean one born of the same parents. An appreciation of these traits of his requires us to draw on anthropology, the study of man and his culture. Of course, his prime goal in buying clothes is to make himself attractive. Here

Anthro-pology

Sociology

Economics

Psychology

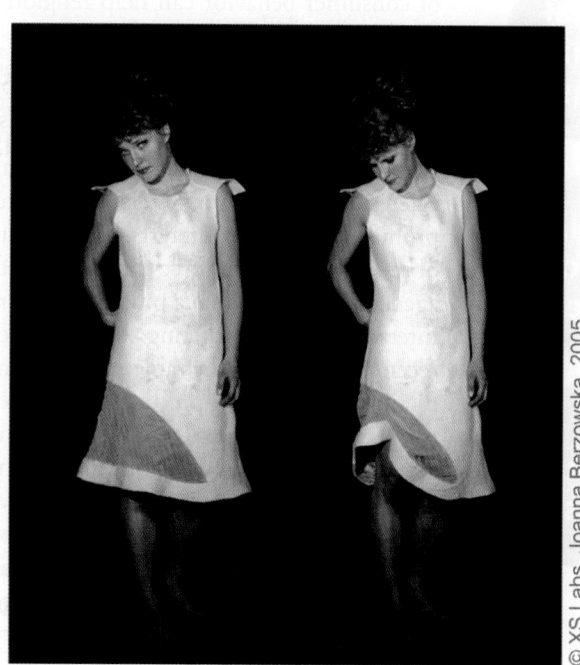

This is Vilkas, a kinetic dress. It has a mind of its own. The kinetic hemline rises (over a 30 second interval) about 2 inches to reveal the knee and upper thigh and then falls in a few minutes. And it does so autonomously—on its own. You cannot control it, except by manually pulling it down. States the company's official description: "This initiates a physical conversation between the wearer and the garment, as they fight over control of the body's real estate."
(Research Director: Joanna Berzowska)
If this has caught your fancy, then it brings you value; otherwise, it does not. Go ahead, make it a conversation starter. Play your playful self!
(Check it out at www.xslabs.net.)
If you think about it, life is about experiences. Products that enable, shape, embellish, and enrich those experiences become endearing to consumers, marketing or no marketing. Life as a human and as a consumer alike is an experiential journey. So is, as we will tell you at the end of this chapter, reading about consumer behavior, in this book. Enjoy the journey.

© XS Labs, Joanna Berzowska, 2005
(Used with permission.)

Model: Hanna Soder Photos: Shermine Sawalha

we see the mysterious but very real influence of significant others on his choice of clothes. Sociology helps us understand which other groups may have influenced his choices as a consumer. Also he is worried about not "maxing out" his credit card; so no matter how much he likes clothes (and other things), he is going to watch his money and make sure he gets good value for it. These are considerations that economics helps us understand.

There are other mental processes going on in Jackie's mind that we will need to understand: how did Jackie come to associate Fubu and Sean John with the kind of image he wants for himself? How is it that he equates his clothes with his soul? And why is it that he claims not to pay attention to advertising and not be influenced by it, even though he declares this accomplishment by using advertising's own slogan, I "obey my own thirst"? Psychology helps us understand these processes of the consumer's mind. Anthropology, sociology, economics, and psychology—all blended into one—that is the multidisciplinary study of consumer behavior.

WHO SHOULD STUDY CONSUMER BEHAVIOR?

There are four groups of people who should be interested in a study of consumer behavior and can benefit from understanding consumer behavior. They are (1) marketers, (2) social organizations, (3) public policy makers, and (4) consumers themselves.

Marketers Marketers are the people who connect a business (or organization) to consumers. They present the product and its message to consumers, hoping consumers will find it a source of satisfaction of their needs. And, equally important, marketers interpret consumer needs and preferences for the benefit of their own organizations so other departments in their firms can design and make products that will satisfy those consumer needs. To play this role effectively, all marketers need to understand consumer psychology and consumer behavior.

Social Organizations The study of consumer behavior is just as useful to organizations whose goals are not to make money but rather to promote public well-being. Indeed, everyone is a marketer. Political parties market candidates, and they should study voter preferences and views. The Red Cross and other agencies seeking volunteers and money are marketers offering "good feelings" in exchange, and they need to understand their donors' psychology. Arts organizations, educational institutions, social and human services agencies, and volunteer social campaign organizers such as Mothers Against Drunk Driving (MADD), all need to understand their consumers—donors, patrons, art aficionados, irresponsible consumers. Even religion is not beyond marketing; an understanding of consumer behavior can help religious organizations reach their goals and better serve their followers.

Public Policy Makers The third group with an interest in consumer behavior consists of public policy makers. They are concerned, as they should be, with protecting the consumer both from marketers' potentially deceptive practices and from consumers' own irrational consumption behaviors. While it always behooves marketers to act in the consumer's interest, sometimes marketers are tempted to engage in opportunistic practices that compromise consumers' interests. To prevent this, lawmakers make laws, and various agencies of the government enforce those laws, monitoring business practices. But in order for these agencies to know when a practice is harmful to consumers, it has to know how consumers interpret various marketing programs. For example, the Federal Trade Commission (FTC) recently sued QVC (a cable shopping network) for running infomercials promoting its dieting and slimming products for women. The FTC charged that the ads misled consumers.[16] For this charge to have legs, it would have to be based on an understanding of the psychology of perception and exactly what constitutes consumer deception.

Public policy makers are also concerned with protecting consumers from their own unhealthy behaviors. Thus, the government mandates warnings in all tobacco advertising, for example, but it must study whether anyone heeds such warnings, and whether increasing the size of lettering (as it recently required) would help. Thus, a study of consumer behavior is imperative also for public policy makers concerned with consumer protection.

Marketers

Social Organiza-tions

Public Policy makers

Consum-ers

Consumers Finally, a study of consumer behavior should be of interest (surprise!) to consumers themselves. We spend many of our waking hours and so much of our money contemplating and experiencing consumption that understanding what drives that behavior can be an interesting, even an eye-opening exercise. The good thing about this book and this subject as a field of study is that we can actually relate every topic to our own personal lives. By reading this book, you will understand your motives for buying or not buying something. You will learn the bases of your perceptions and misperceptions about products and brands. You will realize how our brains are imperfect computers, and yet how they process all product information reasonably well. You will understand, too, how you might be influenced by others and yet continue to believe that your marketplace choices are your own. And, you will recognize how, through consumption, you construct your own identity—connected with some groups but purposely distanced from others.

An Experiential Journey

Now the fun begins. We give you, so to speak, a universal template with a collage of mirrors of different shapes and sizes, and you can find for yourself which mirror reflects you the best. Here is where it becomes a learning experience. Or experiential learning. It is an expedition of discovery—about yourself and about the world of consumers. Welcome to the expedition!

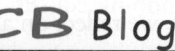 CB Blog

1

Mongolian Cow Sour Yogurt Super Girl's Voice
The Age of the Empowered Consumer

In 2005, Li Yu Chun became the winner of the Chinese version of American Idol-the show named Mongolian Cow Sour Yogurt Super Girl's Voice. This "Super Girl" was not, according to some judges of the show, the most outstanding talent on the show. And had it been left to judges, or any other music connoisseur, she would have been eliminated long before the final round. It was not her singing that saved her. Rather, it was her attitude that earned her millions of fans across the country—the same attitude that irked some of the establishment.

Throughout the show, Li wore jeans and a simple black top. Hair unkempt, no lipstick, no makeup. In most of the Western countries, this would pass as a mere "tom-boyish" persona. But in China, it was a major sociological and cultural experiment. Chinese girls are supposed to look and act like, well, girls. And Li, then 21, was defying an age-old gender role (for definition, see Chapter 14). While conservative elders balked, Li's defiant attitude touched a chord among the country's youth. At the show's climax, some 400 million Chinese stayed glued to their TV sets. And, exercising their rarely granted democratic privilege, they texted-in their votes for Li, in millions, crowning her the "Chinese Singing Idol."

This story demonstrates, at once, the capabilities of technology (the Internet and cell phones) to transfer power to consumers, and the power of market offerings that capture and reflect, even if accidently, consumers' inner moorings. Li Yu Chun did not try to persuade or to sway her audience. She wears the crown for singing, but she owes her claim to fame to an iconoclastic persona hitherto merely dreamed of, silently, by millions of Chinese youth. She gave voice to that silent dream, bringing out the consumers' inner tattoo, so to speak. That is why consumers voted for her, in millions. Just as they do in the marketplace, with their dollars.

Market offerings (products) are not the progenitors of consumer needs—unless we use the term "need" and "product" as synonyms, as in, "I need coffee, therefore coffee is my need." They are, rather, the solutions to consumer needs, latent or overt. Products succeed only when they come as response to consumer needs, desires, yearnings. Marketing's task is to cast its offerings in the consumers' image, not vice versa.
That truth requires that we understand Consumer Behavior.

SUMMARY

...hapter with a basic fact: ...ours as consumers. We ...se we defined consumer ...ying and consuming but ...ysical activities we under... experience products—an ...much before we actually ...duct, and continues, in our memories, ...

Taking the view... of consumers 24/7, we portrayed marketplace products as solutions to consumer needs and wants. We then defined *need* as a discomforting condition, whether physiological or psychological, and *want* as a desire for specific solutions to that condition. We next identified three essentials that frame all consumer behavior: exchange, resources, and value. Consumers' marketplace activities are basically an exchange with marketers, where consumers acquire products and part with their money. Money is one of the five resources consumers possess, the other four being time, knowledge and skills, body and physical energy, and social capital. In the exchange, what consumers seek first, foremost, and always is *value*.

We defined *value* as the set of net benefits consumers receive from an exchange. And we identified four broad categories of value: utilitarian, social, ego, and recreational (i.e., hedonic), captured in the acronym USER. We then raised a question, "Does marketing create consumer needs?" Marketing merely presents products and brings their benefits to consumers' attention, and consumers pick and choose what meets their needs. Satisfying a consumer need is the very purpose of business. And in order to do just that, marketers must, we argue, study consumer behavior. The study of consumer behavior is built upon the core disciplines of anthropology, sociology, psychology, and economics. And, besides marketers, social organizations and public policy agents too must study it. Lastly, consumers themselves should study it so they can understand their own consumer behavior. This book is directed at all "students" of consumer behavior—and who among us is not a student in the school of life? Our gain from reading the book is two-fold—first, we reflect on and understand our own behavior as consumers; and second, we become knowledgeable about how, as marketers, we must fashion our offerings so as to appeal to consumers.

KEY TERMS

Anthropology	Exchange	Need	Recreation value	Sociology
Consumer	Hedonic value	Physical activities	Resource	Utilitarian value
Consumer Behavior	Marketers	Product	Social capital	Value
Ego/Identity value	Mental activities	Psychology	Social value	Want

YOUR TURN

REVIEW+Rewind

1. What is consumer behavior? Isn't it basically people buying products? Why or why not?
2. How are *needs* and *wants* defined here? Are these definitions different from how we use the words *need* and *wants* in everyday language? Which approach to defining these is better and why?
3. What are the five resources all consumers have?
4. What is the USER model of consumer value?
5. Who should study Consumer Behavior and why?

THINK+Apply

1. Give an example from your own life in which you exchanged one resource for the other four.
2. Give an example of each exchange value you have sought in recent marketplace exchanges.
3. Some accuse marketing of creating consumer needs, making us buy things we did not need. Do you agree or disagree? Defend your answer.

A Must Do

1. Write a short memo to yourself, evangelizing how this book is going to benefit you personally in your role as (a) a consumer, and (b) a marketing professional (current or future).

PRACTICE+Experience

1. Write a journal of your own consumer behavior of the past one week. Record one episode each for when you were an economic creature, a problem solver, a computer, a shopper, and (here comes your favorite part) a reveler.
2. Find four advertisements that offer, individually, each of the four values of the USER model, and explain your selections.
3. Interview a consumer (similar to the interview of Jackie in the chapter), and then identify the four values of the USER model in his or her consumer behavior. (Direct your topics so that the interview reveals all four values.)

CASE 1

DON'T WEAR YOUR STOCKINGS! SPRAY THEM

Say goodbye to all those runs in your stockings. And in hot summer, no more need to suffer the confining fabric garment on your legs. Instead of wearing stockings made of fabric, now all you do is hold a can and spray the stockings directly on your legs. The can sprays silk powder and the powder coating makes it look like you are wearing a panty hose.

This innovative product is marketed in Japan by C.C. Medico CO. Ltd of Japan. Japanese women have bought it in droves. And they wear it with enthusiasm.

The sprayed-on stockings last a day. Don't worry, they won't wash away in rain—they are waterproof. Of course, you can wash them off with soap and a loofah.

You can buy it at beauty.com (search Air stocking). It comes in three colors: Terra-cotta, natural, and bronze. Alas, for the fish-net look, you will have to stay with the real thing. But in Air Stockings, you get to show your pedicured toes.

> A Southwest flight attendant who tried it on a flight had this to say,
> **" I haven't sweated it off. It hasn't rubbed off on my clothes or on the seat."**
>
> Said another:
> **"I would rather wear this than a hose; it makes my skin more smooth."***

Check it out at www.airstockings.com

DISCUSSION QUESTIONS

1. If women find this product appealing, does it not show that marketing creates new needs in consumers? Explain.

2. Why will women find this product appealing? Or, why not? Describe the mindset of the prospective consumer.

3. The product has yet to gain popularity in USA, Canada, UK, and other European and Asian countries. Why might its adoption by consumers be slower outside of Japan?

4. If this product were introduced in your own country, would women adopt it? Why or why not?
   (Perhaps you could interview some women to enrich your understanding.)

Note: We situated this case here as an end-of-chapter case, so as to alert the reader that cases are included in the book. Actually, this and all other cases raise multiple issues and apply to more than one chapter. Accordingly, rather than at the end of individual chapters, they are placed as a collective unit at the end of all 18 chapters.

A Case Study at the end of every chapter? No!

RESEARCHING THE CONSUMER

DEAR CONSUMER: MAY WE HANG OUT WITH YOU FOR A WHILE?

Laskerville—a code-named small town outside Chicago, with a population of 8,000, not counting the three or four visitors who slipped in and out of town. You could see them in the market square, in local bars, at car dealerships, even at the funerals. It was they who gave the town this code name, and the townspeople didn't even know it.

They were researchers from the Chicago-based Foote, Cone & Belding (FCB) advertising agency, whose founder's name was Albert Lasker. They would cast away their business suits and don jeans and boots. To mingle with the villagers. Trying to get a fix on what turns the wheels in small-town U.S.A. What better way to find out about consumer attitudes, lifestyles, concerns, and mores, than to observe those consumers firsthand in their natural habitat.

QUALITATIVE AND QUANTITATIVE

What the FCB researchers were doing is called *participant observation*, one of the many methods of researching the consumer. There are qualitative methods (*participant observation* is an example), and then there are quantitative research methods. Okay, answer the following question:

> **Q. Would you like to read up on consumer research methods now, or would you rather first read a few substantive chapters on CB?**
>
> ☐ **A.** I want to read them now as I am eager to do some CB research projects soon.
> ☐ **B.** I want to read the substantive CB concepts first so I may know which CB concepts to research.

If you answered A, please go to Research Appendix (at the end of the "topic chapters, p. 532)". If you answered B, turn the page to go to Chapter 2.

Incidentally, you have just participated in a quick quantitative survey research!

(To read full article, go to page 532)

MARKET SEGMENTATION

WHERE MARKETING STRATEGY MEETS CONSUMER RESEARCH

Perhaps no other concept in marketing is more potent than the concept of segmentation. The core idea is that all consumers are not alike, and that to satisfy individual consumers, we must bring them market offerings designed to meet their specific needs. **Market segmentation** is the process of identifying key differences among the population of consumers and clustering them into distinct groups corresponding with their different needs and characteristics. These resulting groups are called *market segments*.

In an absolute sense, seldom are any two consumers entirely identical. In this sense, then, every consumer is a segment unto himself/herself. But many of the differences are minor, and for practical reasons, it is wise to not pay heed to every little difference. We end up grouping consumers, therefore, into broad groups, using grouping criteria that imply significant differences. For example, we could simply group consumers by their sex, thus treating men and women as two distinct segments. Or we could cluster all people into brown-eyed and blue-eyed consumers, but this grouping is unlikely to be of any consequence (except perhaps for the marketers of eye makeup). Thus, the core purpose of segmentation is to identify consumer groups whose marketplace behaviors will be significantly different.

In this note, we describe various consumer characteristics—both demographic and psychographic—that serve as bases of segmentation

(To read full article, go to page 542)

The readers of this book can be divided into two broad segments, in terms of their preference for covering this topic:

SEGMENT A desires to read up on a significant application as prelude to reading various CB concepts and theories.

SEGMENT B believes that it is better to get a good grasp of the CB Concepts first to fully appreciate this application.

To meet the preferences of both these segments, we append this topic at the end of all of the "topic chapters." That way, readers may continue reading about the fascinating concepts of CB in the next and subsequent chapters, right away. They will also have the freedom to read this application after a few CB topic chapters, and re-read it later at the end of all of the CB topic chapters.

2 Consumer Motivation, Emotion, and Involvement

The Fire That Lights Within

Coffee...
Me ....
Life is a joy.

Visualize me and coffee together, and you will know what deep involvement is.

2:30/3:00

LEARN . APPLY . EXPERIENCE

1 Consumer Motivation as a Fundamental Inner Force

2 Maslow's Hierarchy of Needs and Its Fluidity

3 Unconscious Consumption Motives and Methods of Researching Them

4 Emotions and Moods: Definition, Types, and Measurement

5 Hedonic Consumption and Its Four Forms

6 Consumer Involvement and Its Role as a Yardstick for Consumer Actions

I Want Nicole Kidman's Nose and Halle Berry's Cheeks!

Beverly Hills, California. The cosmetic surgery capital of the world.

Consumers there, as elsewhere, are increasingly choosing to place their faces under the knife. They want their noses chiseled a bit (or a lot), eyebrows curved a little more, and twin-chins united. They come into the clinics with wish lists. And with photographs of their favorite celebrities. They point out a part of the face in the photograph—that is how they want it for themselves.

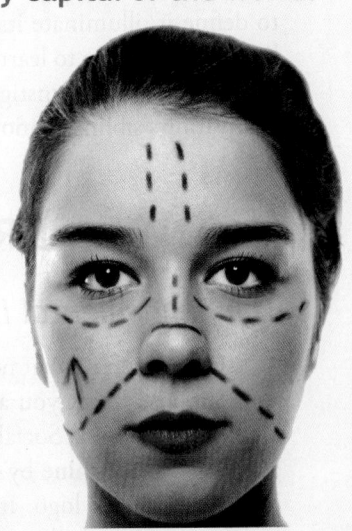

Which celebrities have the hottest facial features? According to a recent report, the hottest, most in demand features were these: the eyes of Brad Pitt and Heather Graham; the jaw lines of Cate Blanchett and Johnny Depp; the lips of Denise Richards and Benicio Del Toro; and the cheeks of Halle Berry and Dylan McDermott.[a]

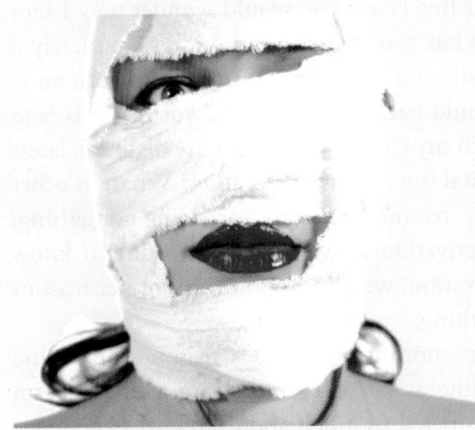

Julie L. is a 30-year old former NFL cheerleader who now works as a banking professional in North Hollywood. She got a nose job a few years ago; then another one. Still not satisfied, she is now planning a third one. "Especially in a town like Los Angeles, it's all about how you look," she explains.[b]

> I am driven to attain my goals.

INTRODUCTION

Meet the new consumer. The consumer with a new face—literally. Achieving it was no cakewalk. This altered face was under the knife for more than four hours. The costs were upward of 10,000 dollars. There was considerable post-surgery pain. The face had to stay in hiding for several weeks. And there was some risk that the face would suffer some permanent nerve damage. But appearance is very important to some consumers. It always has been. Only, until now, they couldn't do much about it. But now medical science has made it feasible. So those of us who can afford it can now have a better face. But more than money, we still need strong motivation.

---

a. Based in part on a report on ABCNews.com, "Looking like a Celebrity: Plastic Surgery at the Frontlines of Glamour," April 10, 2002; http://abcnews.go.com/Health/print?id=132633.
b. Ibid. Name (Julie L.) disguised in the present narrative.

Motivation is a powerful force in life. Without it, we would simply vegetate; with it, we can accomplish a lot. As consumers, too, we need motivation. It takes money and effort to acquire things—we must have the motivation to want something badly enough that we are willing to devote our time to it and part with our money. There are products we want, and, just as surely, there are products we don't want. It all depends on whether or not those products stir our motivations.

But just what is motivation? In this chapter, you are going to find out. We are going to define it, illuminate its true nature, and explain why it has such a strong grip on our lives. We are going to learn some theories of motivation and become familiar with a variety of motivations that instigate our consumption behavior. And, we will also meet two of motivation's siblings: emotions and involvement.

CONSUMER MOTIVATION

The Fundamental Inner Force

Motivation is what moves a person—it is the driving force for all human behavior.

Suppose I sent you a video message and a gift of a Pepsi that you could redeem at any nearby PepsiCo Social Vending System™. You would identify the new, sleek, blue and grey vending machine by its cool moniker, *Be Social*—with the "O" in "Social" replaced by the cool Pepsi logo. It is here that I would have recorded the video message, typed in your name and phone number, and paid for the beverage. My message would have

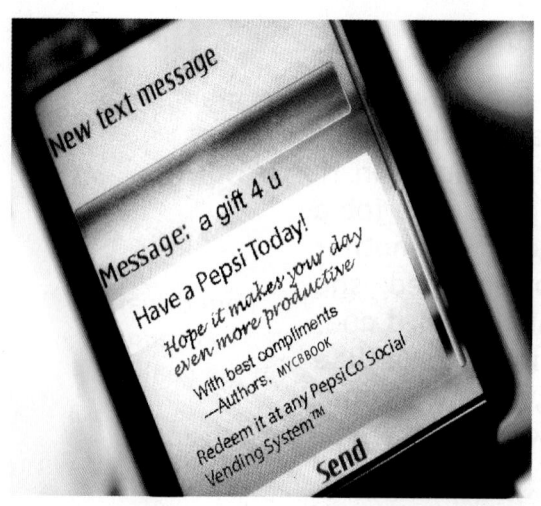

avoided revealing my intent (it would say, simply: "Hope this makes your day even more productive!"). Then, as you sipped your free Pepsi, you would wonder why I sent you this gift. What was my motivation? Was it merely a random act of sharing happiness? Or was it to earn an I-owe-you so I could later ask you for a favor? Or was it to impress you with my currency with the use of all the latest gizmos and digital fun stuff in the market? What, in other words, were my reasons? Reasons for doing something: this is what motivation is. Whenever we want to know someone's motivation, we want to know his or her reasons for doing something.

Describing motivation as a "reason for doing something" is fine as far as everyday usage of the term goes, but it doesn't tell us much about how we experience it. That experience is captured in the definition we will use here: **Motivation** is goal-directed drive. Let us consider each of the two components of motivation implied in this definition.

Drive Drive is energy. You might remember, for example, when you wanted to get a copy of *Gran Turismo 5 XL Edition* as soon as it was released (which was on January 17, 2012). You just felt driven to do it. "Felt driven"? That is right, motivation is actually a drive you feel; it is the surge of energy that impels you to do something. If you don't do it, or until you do it, you feel a state of discomfort. This energy, this drive, then, is a key ingredient in your motivation.

Goal Object That "something" you feel the drive for is not random, of course. Rather, it is something that you know will reduce your discomfort. You are driven to attain it. In other words, it is your goal. You judge it to be the thing that will reduce your discomfort. Goal object is, thus, the second ingredient of motivation.

We are now ready to formally define *motivation*. **Motivation** is the human drive to attain a goal object. A **drive** is a force or energy that impels us to act. And a **goal object** is something in the world the acquisition or attainment of which will bring us happiness—by reducing our current discomfort or tension.[1]

A Model of Motivation

Discomfort, drive, goal object, let us connect them in a model of motivation. Discomfort occurs when you lack something you desire; in other words, it occurs due to a gap between your desired state and your actual current state. This gap is felt as a discomfort and creates tension. Tension in turn produces the energy or drive to achieve the goal object. A drive is like a spring, compressed by felt discomfort and therefore under tension and ready to release with force. The greater the pressure (i.e., the discomfort), the greater the released force (i.e., drive). Drive provides the energy to act; goal object provides the direction in which to channel that energy. A person with goal objects but without the drive is just a daydreamer; one with energy but no goal object is akin to a hyperactive child. When energy is expended to attain some goal object, we call that use of energy motivated or **purposive behavior.**[2] (See Figure 2.1.) Remember, then, to be motivated, you should have both a drive and a goal object.

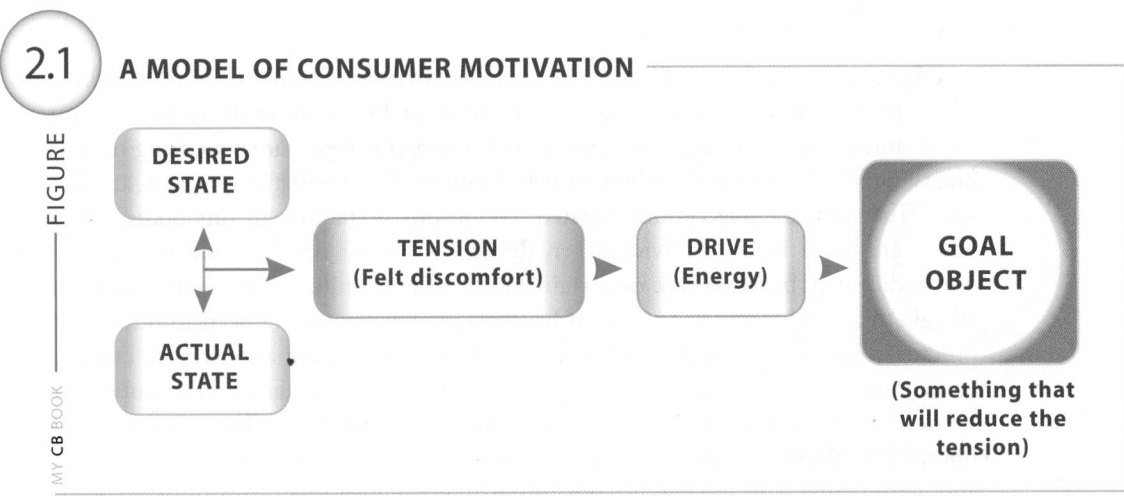

2.1 FIGURE — **A MODEL OF CONSUMER MOTIVATION**

DESIRED STATE → ACTUAL STATE → TENSION (Felt discomfort) → DRIVE (Energy) → GOAL OBJECT (Something that will reduce the tension)

MY CB BOOK

What about Needs and Wants?

Motivation is goal-directed energy. A motivated behavior (i.e., purposive behavior) is goal-driven behavior. Then, what about needs? Isn't it true that our needs drive all of our behaviors? We need food, for example, so we do whatever is required to get food. In the definition of motivation, where does need fit? How are motivation and need related?

In Figure 2.1, notice that the tension or discomfort produces the drive. Thus, tension or discomfort is NOT motivation itself, but rather a precursor to motivation. That tension or discomfort is what *need* is. That is how we defined *need* in Chapter 1 (review it if you'd like). And, as we explained in Chapter 1 and as shown in Figure 2.1, that need (i.e., felt discomfort) comes from a felt gap between the current state and the desired state. A need, then, is an instigator of the drive component of motivation. If you don't feel any need, then you will not have any drive.

Suppose you got a C in a course last semester. You are very concerned about its impact on your grade point average (GPA); you are now feeling discomfort and tension. Consequently, you now feel a strong urge to make up for it this semester, i.e., you are feeling the drive. The goal object is the grade A in your Consumer Behavior course this semester. Thus, given the drive and the goal object, you have the motivation to read this book closely. And to listen to your instructor with rapt attention!

Sometimes, there is only one goal object that can reduce a particular tension. But often the world offers us a range of solutions. To relieve hunger pangs, for example, we must get some food, but what kind of food? The kind of food we feel will satisfy us best becomes our goal object. The desire for a particular goal object is, as defined in Chapter 1, a consumer *want*. Thus, needs and wants are closely related to motivation. Needs provide the drive and the goal object provides the want. Our needs and wants are what make us different consumers.

Well, Then, From Where Do Needs Come?

Innate versus Learned Needs

Where do needs come from? Are we born with them, or do we acquire them? The answer is, both. Scholars classify needs into two types: innate and learned. **Innate needs** are needs with which we are born. They are common to all humans, rooted in our survival instincts. Thus, a hungry stomach creates an innate need, and so does a body shivering with cold or burning with heat, exposed to the harsh weather outside. In contrast are **learned needs**, which are acquired in the process of growing up and living. So when you say you feel lonely, dejected, ridiculed, bored, or burned out, you were not born with these needs, and your survival does not depend on overcoming these conditions. Not remedying loneliness or boredom or ridicule or peer rejection would not place our survival in peril, but not remedying them does cause us considerable mental anguish. Respectively, these two types of needs are also called *biogenic* and *psychogenic* needs.

What Our Bodies Need

Biogenic needs are conditions of discomfort stemming from our biology as humans. All bodily discomforts are included in this category, but such needs go beyond hunger, thirst, and exposure to rough weather. They include tiredness due to working or walking, illness, and loss of motor skills and sensory faculties due to aging (e.g., vision and hearing loss). They also include certain negative conditions pertaining to our bodies, many of which are based in our individual genes, such as oily or dry hair and bad breath. Or our bodies may be intolerant of certain foods, such as milk for the lacto-intolerant, or allergic to certain materials (e.g., bird feathers), which creates the need to find substitute products (e.g., hypoallergenic pillows). Finally, biogenic needs also include cravings for certain foods and substances (e.g., spicy food, caffeinated beverages, and narcotics), which we develop because of the conditioning of our bodies and tastes. Thus, strictly speaking, not all biogenic needs are innate needs. We learn some of them through repeated use, and, with strong wills, we can use our minds to extinguish them. But until we do so, the conditioned cravings of our bodies do qualify as biogenic needs.

And What Our Mind Needs

Psychogenic needs, in contrast, stem from our mental makeup, not from our bodies —the way we think about ourselves and about the world, how we define happiness and success, and what we consider to be good and bad. Lack of things we consider essential to our happiness produces a state of discomfort in our minds and thus creates psychogenic needs. We all want to look cool, and if we come to believe that a Billabong brand of shirt will make us cool, then the discomfort of not having that shirt is a psychogenic need. If we come to believe that adorning our bodies with tattoos will get us the admiration and popularity we seek, then that is a psychogenic need as well.

Then what about a facelift?

Now think back to the facial surgeries we mentioned at the beginning of this chapter. What kind of need do they exemplify? The correct answer is "psychogenic." Just because what we gain—the goal object—pertains to our bodies, it does not make it a bodily or biogenic need. Rather, this need stems from our psychological makeups, our ways of thinking—both that we are unhappy with our looks and that we covet certain facial features. Just because, to satisfy a need, we do something to our bodies, this does not make it a biogenic need. The need is produced by our views of ourselves as psychological beings, not biological beings; therefore, the perceived need for a facelift is a psychogenic need.

Why is a facelift a *psychogenic* need?

Some products and brands satisfy, of course, only a biogenic need (e.g., a generic brand of cotton swab); others satisfy a purely psychogenic need (e.g., a birthday greeting card). But most consumers seek most products to simultaneously satisfy both types of needs, and many brands strive to deliver that value to consumers, such as a designer brand of shoes or an eco-friendly skin care line of products.

APPROACH-AVOIDANCE MOTIVES
Things We Seek and Things We Avoid

We have defined *motivation* as a goal-directed drive. But this does not mean that goal objects are always desirable. Some goal objects are the ones we want to avoid. The drive we feel to avoid a goal object is also motivation. Consumer psychologists therefore recognize two types of motivations: approach and avoidance.

Approach motivation is the desire to attain a goal object. Approach goal objects (i.e., objects that attract us) are sought or even longed for, such as the latest game for Wii or Michael Jackson's left-handed glittery glove (sold at the "Music Icons" auction at the Hard Rock Cafe in New York City's Times Square, November 21, 2009). Being deprived of them creates discomfort and unhappiness.

Avoidance motivation is the desire to protect oneself from an object, such as a bee sting or a stale or unhygienic burger. Technically, approach and avoidance motives are called, respectively, *appetitive* and *aversive*. Of course, one consumer's poison may be another's nectar. Vegetarians love tofu, but avoid meat; most non-vegetarians love meat, and they avoid tofu—some of them may not even know (happily) what it is.

We haven't *gone* green.
We started that way.

ANAKIRI
BioEnergetic Skin Care

Brand Anakiri seeks to fulfill both biogenic and psychogenic needs of ecology-conscious consumers.

We all want the "approach objects" and we all want to avoid the "avoid objects." Sometimes we are lucky and have to choose between two desirable options—say, out of two toys, we can only have one. That lucky situation is called **approach-approach conflict**. Of course, sometimes we also get totally unlucky and face two options equally undesirable. Got a speeding ticket? Well, you can pay a fine, or you can attend three hours of safe-driving classes (purposely designed, it seems, to bore you!). You are facing what is known as an **avoid-avoid conflict**.

The above two types of conflicts occur when we are faced with two separate options—two equally enjoyable TV shows at the same time, two equally charming dresses, two equally mouth-watering deserts. Or, if we are unlucky, two equally tasteless diet foods, two equally boring classes, or two equally moist-eye movies that our significant others have shortlisted for us to watch together. But there is a third type of conflict, called **approach-avoid conflict**—a conflict we experience when we find an object desirable as well as undesirable. This happens for products that have both desirable and undesirable features. Unfortunately, products often are a mixed blessing: a part of them is good, but a part of them is undesirable. For example, the taste and sensory pleasure in Hershey's candy bars is desirable, but their fat and calorie content is not.

As a marketer, your greatest challenge is to minimize the negative aspects of your product while maximizing its desirable properties. Avoidance motives of consumers provide opportunities for marketers just as approach motives do. Blending two hitherto mutually opposed attributes (e.g., healthy and good-tasting) in a product can bring an unusual value to consumers by banishing their approach-avoid conflict.

Designing new products to banish consumers' approach-avoid conflicts creates market winners.

A Universal Dictionary of Motivations

Go to the Sharper Image Web site and look at the pictures of various objects. Which ones would you like to buy? Would you be interested in a Saxxy Synthesizer, an electric scooter, wireless boxing robots? A desktop arcade game or a Laser Baseball? If you are, then you have a motivation for each. What motivation is that? You could answer that it is a motivation for a Saxxy Synthesizer, a motivation for an electric scooter, or for a Laser Baseball, and so on. So then how many motivations are there? As many as there are products? If you are a typical consumer, you probably own thousands of things—does it mean you have thousands of motivations? And what can a marketer do with a list of, say, a thousand motivations?[3]

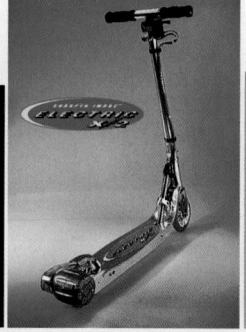

Goal Objects Galore
Photos courtesy Sharper Image

We therefore need to find a more sensible way of counting and specifying consumer motivations—a way that goes to the core of *why* we need these thousands of products to begin with. There must be, in humans, a core set of needs that make up a short list—short enough to remember and utilize in real-world marketing. The good news is that there is. Psychologists have studied human motives for years and have grouped all of the human motives into a few categories. One of them is psychologist Abraham Maslow, who gave us a short list of five core motives. There are, of course, other lists, but this one has stood the test of time and has become a classic in marketing and consumer behavior. No marketer can ever claim to understand why people buy things without understanding Maslow's theory of human motivation. It is, in other words, "a universal dictionary of motivations"—translating thousands of consumer purchases into five simple need categories.

MASLOW'S MODEL OF HIERARCHY OF NEEDS
Humans Live for Bread and Then More!

The five need categories in Maslow's theory are:

1. **Physiological needs**
2. **Safety and security needs**
3. **Belonging and love needs**
4. **Esteem and ego needs**
5. **Self-actualization needs**[4]

Actually, Maslow did more than simply propose this list; he also suggested a pecking order among them—that is, what humans must have first before they seek something else. His theory is called **Maslow's hierarchy of needs**—the order in which humans experience needs. The hierarchy is shown in Figure 2.2 as a pyramid. According to Maslow, the needs at the bottom of the pyramid must be satisfied first; until they are, the higher-level needs remain dormant. But the moment the lower level of needs becomes satisfied, then, almost inevitably, the next level of needs comes to life. Let us look inside this pyramid.

• **Physiological needs** At the bottom of the pyramid are **physiological needs**—i.e., our bodily needs (also called *biogenic needs*). These needs drive us all to seek food, clothing, and shelter. We must satisfy these needs before we worry about anything else. It is a no-brainer—if we are starving, then we must find food before we seek, say, *XBOX720*. And we must find clothes before we seek a facelift.

Furthermore, many of the differences in what consumers use and buy are due to physiological (that is, biological) differences; i.e., differences attributable to genetics, race, gender, or age. Examples include soy milk for lactose-intolerant persons (genetics), vision-correcting glasses for weak eyes (due to age or genetics), and custom-made shoes for people with feet of unequal size. For all humans, such needs are paramount. And these must be satisfied before consumers will feel other needs.

- **Safety and Security Needs**
Closely following physiological needs are **safety and security** needs—the need to be protected from danger. Personal safety is a motive as old as survival itself—early man developed arrows and spears to kill predatory animals that threatened his survival. In modern times, the new weapons are personal cell phones and community-supported police forces. In cars, marketers are now placing a renewed emphasis on advanced safety features—e.g., rear-view cameras and sensor-activated automatic steering correction for lane-straying drivers!

- **Belonging and Love** Next come social motives of **belonging and love**. We are all social creatures, and once our physiological and physical safety

FIGURE

2.2 **MASLOW'S MODEL OF HIERARCHY OF NEEDS**

A   A: Self-Actualization Needs

Esteem and Ego Needs

Belonging and Love Needs

Safety and Security Needs

Physiological Needs

MY CB BOOK

concerns are met, our social needs become active. We want to have friends and family, and we want to receive love and affection from others. Without love and affection, our lives will feel empty. To satisfy this kind of need, consumers buy products that are well-regarded by others and the use of which will bring them peer approval, affection, and a sense of belonging. The kind of car you choose to drive, the designer logos on the clothes you wear, and whether you get a tattoo or a piercing on your body—each of these is determined, at least in part, by how you think your peers and significant others will look upon your choice. Many products, such as greeting cards, flowers, and other kinds of gifts, are bought specifically to promote relationships with others.

- **Ego and Esteem** Next in the hierarchy are **ego needs**—the need to feel good about ourselves and to have self-esteem. We all work hard to gain success in our individual spheres of activity and to acquire the qualities others consider desirable and virtuous so that we can win our own and others' esteem. We also buy products and services we believe support our self-image. We drive cars, for example, that, beyond impressing others, in our judgment, reflect who we are; we visit stores in which we are treated with respect; and we even buy and give gifts to ourselves because we feel we "deserve them."

- **Self-actualization** Finally, once these physiological, security, social, and esteem needs are satisfied, people begin to explore and extend the bounds of their potential—to become what they are capable of being. This is the need for **self-actualization**—the need to realize one's true potential. To quote Maslow, "musicians must make music, artists must paint, poets must write if they are to be ultimately at peace with themselves. What humans *can* be, they *must* be."[5]

Indeed, the self-actualization motive is what drives many adults to go back to school and acquire a new set of skills. And many marketers appeal to consumers' ambitions. (A recent ad from Monster.com poked fun at people who were content with their current mediocre jobs.) Many not-for-profit agencies appeal to the consumer's sense of being a good citizen. The U.S. Army's long-running slogan "Be All You Can Be" and, later, "The Army of One" are calls to a person's need for self-actualization.

In Eastern philosophy, many see their self-actualization as meeting their Creator, becoming what they are supposed to be in a cosmic sense. They spend endless hours meditating and reflecting on the nature of life and its purpose. And in Eastern and Western societies alike, religious messages such as "God is within you" are designed to appeal to a believer's need for self-actualization.[6]

SAVVY
MARKETER

How the Hierarchy Works
The Storm Inside the Pyramid

If this pyramid were a five-story building, there would have to be an elevator that only went upwards and only one floor at a time—or at least that is how the foregoing description of Maslow's hierarchy reads. But that description was for starters, designed to explain the basic pattern. We can now move beyond and look more closely at the hierarchy. Rather than being a five-story building served by an upward-only elevator stopping at each floor, perhaps a more apt analogy is an ocean with five "layers" of water, being navigated by a submarine. The submarine moves relatively effortlessly between top and bottom layers of water, causing many cross currents. These cross currents occur because our needs at any one level of hierarchy recur. They occur, also, because we don't have to satisfy the needs at one level fully before moving on to the next level. Rather, we need to satisfy them only to a good degree. Thus, if we need a place to live, we can rent an apartment in whatever condition it is in and move in. Then we can attend to the task of studying for our classes. After the first test is done, we can attend to making the apartment more livable and buying the essential furniture we need.

The point of the hierarchy is that consumers have to feel at least some modicum of comfort at one level of their needs before they can become concerned about the next "higher" level of needs. You can't sell someone a necktie if his throat is desert-dry with thirst.

Product Journey up the Pyramid
Or Why a Chair Comes in So Many Shapes

There is another fascinating fact about our motivation to acquire things as it relates to Maslow's hierarchy of needs. Consider the three chairs shown here.

What motivates a particular consumer to buy one rather than the other of these three chairs? Their basic function is the same: to satisfy our physiological need to be seated. And that need is well-satisfied by the Hand Chair, for example, which costs only $90. The other two chairs also satisfy that need; but, in addition, they might meet higher-level needs as well. The Lips Chair would probably appeal to a consumer who thinks that it might be an icebreaker and that friends might hang out at his or her place more often. It will meet, in other words, his or her need for belonging and love. What about the Broadway Chair: Who is going to buy it—at $1460? Besides being rich, what else would motivate a person to buy something like this? Most likely, this person is an art connoisseur, or one who believes that others will hold him or her in high esteem, awed by his or her appreciation of the art and beauty of the chair. It will satisfy, in other words, his or her need for esteem.

Recall that we began this quest for coming up with a short list of motivations because counting them as "motives to acquire specific things" would have resulted in a long and unwieldy list of thousands. The short list in Maslow's hierarchy solves that problem. But there is also a bonus benefit. A product is no longer *tied* to a specific need; it can now meet more than one need. A chair must satisfy a physiological need, of course, but, in addition, it can satisfy the need for belonging or esteem as well. And this is where the real fun begins, for consumers and marketers alike. Consumers must decide how many and which needs they want a product to satisfy. And marketers must invent new versions of product classes so as to satisfy new combinations of consumers' needs.

Beyond Maslow—Murray's List of Needs
The Psychology of Flashmobs

A few years ago, *Flashmobs* suddenly became the latest craze among some cyber-consumers. (If you haven't heard about them yet, read all about them on Flashmob.com.) Would you ever join the mob? Why or why not? Why do hundreds of consumers join? Can you explain this behavior by using Maslow's scheme of needs?

Lips Chair
www.Sexyfurnishings.com

Hand Chair
www.Brightthrift.com

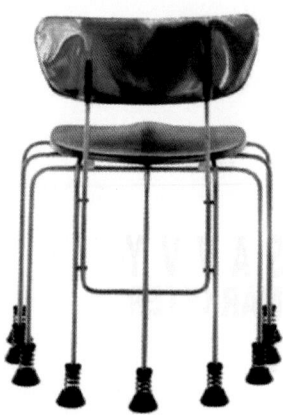

Broadway Chair
(Courtesy: Bernini SPA)

Chances are, you could not. We could say, of course, that it is to satisfy their need for belonging. That is at best a partial explanation, for the crowds disburse after a mere ten minutes. The Flashmob.com site describes its purpose: *Breathing life and vibrancy into the dull corners of modern life.* Perhaps there is something more, like a need for excitement, or a need to shock and surprise bystanders. The problem with Maslow's needs list is that it paints everything with a broad brush, and, as such, it does not pinpoint consumer motivation at this level of detail

Breathing life and vibrancy into the dull corners of modern life

There are a number of such consumer behaviors for which Maslow's list does not have an adequate answer. Why, for example, do customers walk away when salespersons try hard to sell them something? Why do some people enjoy telling stories to others? And why do some consumers happily pay upward of one thousand dollars for a celebrity-worn pair of jeans? Maslow's list gives us answers in broad terms but not precisely. And, it is not designed to—after all how could as few as five motivations cover all the thousands of reasons for human behavior?

Fortunately, other psychologists have proposed more detailed lists. One list popular in marketing is from psychologist Henry Murray. Murray proposed a list of 12 biogenic and 28 psychogenic needs. See a sampling of those needs in Table 2.1. Review that list and you will realize that Murray helps us define consumer needs at a more detailed level than does Maslow. With a list like this, you now can explain almost any consumer behavior. Looking at that list, what would you say is the motive behind flashmobs? Or behind such consumer behaviors as impulse buying, being a demanding customer, or playing an opinion leader?

UNCONSCIOUS CONSUMPTION MOTIVES

The Bliss of Not Knowing What Makes Us Buy Things

Suppose we told you that Jane Infosino, one of our neighbors, buys a lot of kitchen appliances; that Mark O'Connor, one of our friends in Denver, Colorado, always wears shoes that are rather heavy; and that Angelica Yoshida, one of our coworkers, always wears white cotton dresses. Why? What do we mean by "why"? Aren't their motivations obvious, you wonder? Jane most likely loves to cook; Mark perhaps does a lot of walking and likes to keep his feet warm in the cold weather of Denver; and Angelica feels that white cotton looks good on her.

TABLE 2.1 MURRAY'S LIST OF PSYCHOLOGICAL NEEDS (A SAMPLE WITH CONSUMER EXAMPLES)

NEED	DEFINITION	EXAMPLES
Autonomy	To be independent and free to act on impulse; To be unattached; To be irresponsible; To defy convention	Impulse buying; wearing unconventional clothes, etc.
Dominance	To direct the behavior of others	Aggressively demanding attention in service establishments
Nurturance	To give sympathy; to feed, help, and protect the needy;	Giving to humanitarian causes
Exhibition	To make an impression; To excite, amaze, fascinate, entertain, shock, intrigue, amuse or entice others	Wearing high-fashion clothing
Cognizance	The need to explore, ask questions, to seek knowledge	Visiting museums; learning about new technology
Exposition	The need to give information and explain, interpret, lecture	Playing opinion leaders

Note. Our descriptions are intuitive, intentded to explain Consumer Behavior. For original descriptions, see H.A. Murray. Explorations in Personality (New York: Oxford, 1998).

MY CB BOOK

These are all good reasons. And, most likely, these are actually the reasons these consumers, Jane, Mark, and Angelica, will give you. But Ernest Dichter disagrees. He believes that Jane Infosino's love of kitchen appliances arises from her desire to gain mastery over her environment; that Mark wears heavy boots to show off his masculinity; and that Angelica's penchant for white cotton is due to a sense of the moral purity she feels in the deep layers of her mind. "Who is Ernest Dichter," you ask, "and could there be anything weirder than these explanations?"

Ernest Dichter was a psychoanalyst who trained in Vienna in the early part of the 20th century. A strong believer in Sigmund Freud's ideas about the subconscious in human psyche, he believed that unconscious motives play a significant role in people's consumption decisions. He believed that we suppress a lot of our motives because they are not appreciated by society or that some of these motives seem unwholesome even to ourselves, the motive holders. So, we suppress them from our consciousness. But, buried inside the deep layers of our minds, they still influence our behaviors, both in life and in the marketplace. We remain unaware of them, of course—that is why they are called "unconscious motives"—and being unaware serves us just fine. Ignorance here really *is* bliss.

Dichter conducted in-depth interviews with consumers for some 200-plus products. Based on these interviews, he identified a set of subconscious motives/needs that explain why individuals consume certain products. (See Table 2.2.)

Marketers have always looked at Dichter-like claims of unconscious motives with less-than-total belief. But peeping into consumers' unconscious motives has not been entirely fruitless. Consider the following story:

> Back in the Sixties, the Pillsbury Company came out with a new product: quick-baking cake mix. No more need to diligently measure and mix various ingredients; no more need to skillfully monitor the baking process; hours of labor in the kitchen simplified. Homemakers should rush to buy it, right? For some unknown reasons, they were not buying it. When the company researchers asked them why, their typical answer was, "The cake wouldn't taste good." Yet, in blind taste tests, they couldn't tell the difference. Obviously, they had

TABLE 2.2 DICHTER'S LIST OF SUBCONSCIOUS CONSUMPTION MOTIVES (A Sample)

Motive	Examples of Consumption Decisions
Mastery over environment	Kitchen appliances, power tools
Status	Drinking scotch; owning a car in a third-world country
Rewards	Candies, gifts to oneself
Individuality	Gourmet foods; foreign cars; tattoos
Social acceptance	Companionship: sharing tea-drinking
Love and affection	Giving children toys
Security	Full drawer of neatly ironed shirts
Masculinity	Toy guns; heavy shoes
Femininity	Decorating (products with heavy tactile component)
Eroticism	Sweets (to lick); gloves (to be removed by women as a form of undressing)
Disalienation (a desire to feel connected)	Listening to and calling in talk shows
Moral purity/cleanliness	White bread; bathing; cotton fabrics
Magic-mystery	Belief in UFOs, religious rituals, crystals (having healing power), etc.; visiting Elvis Presley museum and buying related products

Note: Constructed by the author, based on information in Jeffrey F. Durgee, "Interpreting Dichter's Interpretations: An Analysis of Consumption Symbolism in the Handbook of Consumer Motivations," in H. Hartvig-Larsen, D. Mick, and C. Alstead, eds., Marketing and Semiotics: Selected Papers from the Copenhagen Symposium (Copenhagen, 1991). The original work by Dichter is documented in Ernest Dichter, *Handbook of Consumer Motivations* (New York: McGraw-Hill, 1964).

MY **CB** BOOK

some deep-seated motive against buying quick-baking cake mix, and they wouldn't tell it to us if we asked them directly. In-depth research revealed that the real reason was that this innovative product took away from women their opportunity to practice what they then considered the "art of cake baking."

If you are a total disbeliever in the existence of subconscious motives, ask any grandparents why they buy toys for their grandchildren. They will tell you, invariably, that it is because they love their grandchildren. They are not wrong, but often that is not the whole truth. Few, if any, will tell you that it is to also satisfy their own need to receive the love and affection of their grandchildren. Or ask people who call in to a radio talk show why they do it. "To express my opinion," will be the answer. Isn't it obvious? Yes, but the obvious answers can be deceptive. Probe deeper and you might discover that it is, at least for some of them, to mitigate their feelings of being alienated from society. The reasons people give may not be wrong. But sometimes they are only half-truths. The other half resides in their unconscious motives. It behooves marketers to uncover both conscious as well as unconscious motives. Since unconscious motives influence consumption decisions unconsciously, the Dichter's list of motives is most useful for incorporating symbolism into product advertising.

> The reasons people give us are sometimes only half-truths.

RESEARCHING CONSUMER MOTIVES

Raising Peek-a-boo to an Art Form

You must now be wondering how, if many of consumers' motivations are unconscious, marketers would ever find out about them. Actually, the same question also applies to conscious motives. For example, if you ask consumers why they bought a Lips Chair or a Broadway Chair, they would not admit, even if aware of it, that they bought it to win friends or to gain esteem. We like to keep some of our motives private. It is simply not cool to reveal that we are seeking status or affection or love, for example. Thus, there are two reasons why we would not learn, by direct questioning, what consumers' real motives for a given purchase might be. First, these motives might be unconscious, and second, consumers might want to keep them private. The question, then, is how to get consumers to reveal them. Fortunately, psychologists have devised a set of procedures to, in a sense, "trick" the consumers' minds into revealing them, unwittingly. We call this "Playing Dr. Motivation."

Playing Dr. Motivation

UNCOVERING HIDDEN MOTIVES

Motivation Research (MR)

Motivation Research is research directed at discovering the motives for a person's behavior—reasons of which the consumer is either unaware or is unwilling to admit to in direct questioning. It uses techniques that are disguised and non-structured. The techniques are disguised in that consumers are not able to figure out that you are trying to find out their deep motives. They are non-structured in that the answers are not pre-structured; rather, the consumer is encouraged to say whatever comes to mind.

The general characteristic of these techniques is that the respondent is given a fairly vague and open-ended stimulus and is then asked to interpret that stimulus. Since the stimulus is vague, interpreting it requires that the consumer "project" himself or herself into the stimulus situation. These techniques are therefore called *projection techniques*. From such self-projections from consumers, the researcher is able to infer each consumer's motives for a particular marketplace behavior. These techniques, described below, are all very simple, but they are amazingly effective. Read on.

Third-Person Question Phrasing

Instead of asking "Why don't you buy —— (say, quick-baking cake mix)," the question can be phrased as "In your opinion, why do people not buy ——?" Consumers would not be hesitant to answer this, and, of course, they are basically projecting their own motives onto other consumers. Their answers, on behalf of others, would reveal to us *their* own motives.

Word Association

Quick, say the word that comes to mind when we say the following words: Blue —— (write your answers in this and the following blanks); Angel ——; surfer ——; Europe ——. Your answers might reveal that *blue* is cool, *Angel* is good-hearted, *surfer* is sexy, and *Europe* is exotic. This is word association. For example, the words "instant-baking cake mix" might bring out such associations as "tasteless," "ordinary," "cheap," "lazy," and so on, revealing the reasons consumers might not buy it. Another group of respondents might respond with such words as "convenient," "quick," and "instant gratification," revealing why this group of consumers includes heavy users of instant cake mix.

Sentence Completion

Sentence completion techniques are similar to word association. Here, the consumer is presented with an incomplete sentence and asked to fill in the blank. E.g., an incomplete sentence like, "I drink instant coffee only when I am ——" might elicit such responses as "in a hurry," "in the office," and so on; or, alternatively, such responses as "entertaining at home," or "relaxing." These two sets of responses will reveal two different sets of motives for consuming instant coffee, and, correspondingly, two vastly divergent perceptions about it.

Story Completion

The most common form of story completion is the **Thematic Apperception Test** (TAT), which consists of a series of ambiguous pictures shown to the consumer. The consumer is asked to describe the story of which the picture is a part. To continue with the coffee example, a consumer might be shown someone preparing a cup of instant coffee and asked

---

EXHIBIT 2.1

MASON HAIRE'S PROJECTIVE TECHNIQUE

MEET CLEVER DR. HAIRE

Since you liked our description of projective techniques, we can't help giving you yet another version—this one by a clever MIT psychologist. His method was so innovative that it has come to be known by his name, Mason Haire. Back in the Sixties, when Maxwell House Coffee introduced instant coffee, homemakers chose not to buy it. When asked why, they gave the obvious reason: They did not like its taste. This perfectly innocent answer was not so innocent, for in product development research, consumers had indeed found the test product's taste comparable or better. Obviously, homemakers now had some other reason for not buying the new coffee, a reason they would rather not give. So to uncover that deeper motive, the company hired our clever Dr. Haire. Here is what he did it.[7]

He made two shopping lists with usual supermarket items, including coffee. The lists were identical except that one included Maxwell House Regular Coffee and the other included Maxwell House Instant Coffee. His research team then intercepted shoppers at random in supermarkets and showed them one or the other of the lists. Consumers were told that the list had been found in a shopping cart, and were asked to imagine and describe the kind of person the owner of the shopping list was.

The findings were revealing. The study respondents who had been shown the list containing regular coffee described the list owner as a very conscientious homemaker and a

good housewife. Those shown the other list thought the list owner was a lazy homemaker and a bad wife!

What is remarkable in the findings of this study is that consumers had no hesitation in saying that the shoppers who used instant coffee were lazy, whereas they never would have admitted that the reason they themselves never bought instant coffee was because of their fear of being perceived as lazy. How did they know what kind of a person the list owner who used instant coffee was? Obviously, by projecting their own motives onto those other consumers!

Although the technique is some fifty years old, it is eminently usable for a variety of products in modern times. For example, suppose that you want to find out whether consumers think that the type of person who reads Time magazine is different from the one who reads Newsweek. Put together two identical collections of magazines except that one includes Time and the other includes Newsweek. Then, show one set to some consumers and the other set to others, and ask each consumer to "guess" the type of person the subscriber is. Or, investigate the image of the users of Visa versus MasterCard credit cards by a "lost wallet" procedure: Show consumers a wallet supposedly found on the street. Thus, whenever the purpose is to identify the personality associations people make for the user of a product, these associations can be unearthed by using the Mason Haire technique. ■

to describe "the story" surrounding this situation. Someone might say, "The consumer shown in the picture is an office secretary preparing coffee for a high-level executive meeting"; another's story might be that the person in the picture is a bored housewife, getting ready to watch daytime TV. These two stories illustrate two very different sets of perceptions, attitudes, and motives for or against the consumption of instant coffee. It is in this story-writing procedure that the "projection," as this set of techniques is called, plays out fully (since the stimulus is quite vague).

A variation of this technique involves asking consumers to fill in a blurb in a cartoon, such as the one shown here, designed to find out the "real" reasons why some consumers build their own Web pages.

EXHIBIT 2.2

TWO SHOPPING LISTS

List A	List B
- apples	- apples
- oranges	- oranges
- milk	- milk
- peanut butter	- peanut butter
- cookies	- cookies
- cereal	- cereal
- Maxwell House regular coffee	- Maxwell House instant coffee
- bread	- bread
- eggs	- eggs
- cheese	- cheese
- muffins	- muffins
- soup	- soup

DO OUR SHOPPING LISTS REVEAL WHO WE ARE?
(Consumers themselves believe they do.)

MY CB BOOK

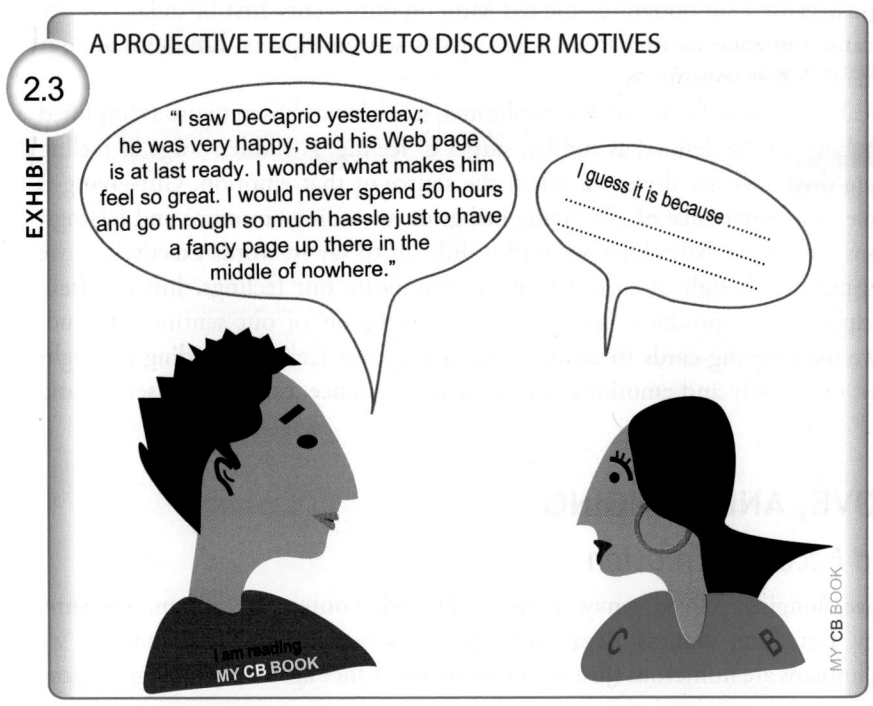

EXHIBIT 2.3

A PROJECTIVE TECHNIQUE TO DISCOVER MOTIVES

"I saw DeCaprio yesterday; he was very happy, said his Web page is at last ready. I wonder what makes him feel so great. I would never spend 50 hours and go through so much hassle just to have a fancy page up there in the middle of nowhere."

I guess it is because ....

I am reading MY CB BOOK

MY CB BOOK

CONSUMER EMOTIONS

The inset copy reads:

"Tenderness is a cup of friendship soup made from fun, dreams and laughter. Enjoy these tender moments. Because tomorrow you could wake up with food poisoning."

(Source: www.Diesel.com)

As every teen and twenty-something knows (or at least as the trendy or fashionable among them do), Diesel is the name on jeanswear from Europe that is "Oh, so cool." They like its denim, of course, but what they love even more is how the company whispers sweet nothings into their ears. Its advertising captures their world-view, echoes their sentiments, makes them chuckle, and, above all, tugs at their heartstrings. This is the art of emotional selling.

Motivation and emotion are closely related. Similar to needs, emotions are also capable of propelling the person toward relevant goal objects. As consumers, we desire certain goal objects (i.e. products), and, if we are deprived of them, we feel negative emotions. If we attain them, we feel positive emotions. Current negative emotions act as drive, and so do the expectations of positive emotions. Thus, positive emotions serve as approach motivations and negative emotions, as avoidance motivations. Much of the consumption or use of products and services is driven by and immersed in emotions. No wonder, then, that a wide range of products are sold through emotional campaigns, from "Diamonds Are Forever" (in a recent commercial, a young man screams at the top of his lungs, "I love this woman," in a public square, before presenting her with an engagement ring) to McDonald's Happy Meals (with a campaign showing cute babies with ear-to-ear smiles).[9]

What Is Emotion?

As humans, we are creatures of emotion. Emotions lace our lives and guide our everyday actions. We cuddle a baby because we feel affection and love for the little creature. We swear at a rude driver who cuts in front of us because we feel anger and frustration. We feel anxious because we are not prepared for the exam. We are delighted when we ace it. We are ecstatic because Dad bought us the red Mini on our twenty-first birthday. We are overjoyed because someone we met at last night's party sent us flowers. Emotions are our lives—as humans and as consumers.

The technical definition of emotion is complicated, so we have chosen to use a simplified version. **Emotions** can be defined as sudden surges of feeling. A sudden surge of feeling acts as a strong drive. We are driven to attain the source of that emotion. Gift-giving is an apt example. The experience of gift-giving brings us rewarding emotions and feelings. Most emotions are non-verbalizable—we find it difficult to say in words exactly how we feel toward someone, though often our faces communicate our feelings. Just as often, we find it helpful to use products (given as gifts) as symbols of our sentiments. And, sometimes, we use greeting cards to capture and convey our feelings. Finding the right card can be an immensely and emotionally gratifying experience, both for the sender and the recipient.[10]

LUST, LOVE, AND LONGING

A Hundred Faces of Emotion

Lust, love, longing. Greed, envy, jealousy. Hatred, contempt, disdain. Pleasure, happiness, joy. Boredom, sadness, depression. Pain, agony, torment. The emotions we experience as humans are numerous (just as our needs are). Once again, psychologists come to the rescue and offer us a manageable list. Psychologist Robert Plutchik has proposed that all human emotions can be summarized into eight types.[11] Each can vary in intensity as follows.

1. **Fear**—ranging from timidity to terror. A consumer might experience this if, when driving on the expressway, he or she discovers that the car's brakes are not working.
2. **Anger**—ranging from annoyance to rage. A consumer might become angry when a car rental agent says that the car the consumer reserved is not available.
3. **Joy**—ranging from serenity to ecstasy. A consumer might experience joy at an auto dealership when he or she spots a rare model he or she had been looking for.
4. **Sadness**—ranging from pensiveness to grief. A consumer may experience sadness when, calling an airline for a last-minute reservation, he or she is informed that the last seat was just sold.
5. **Acceptance**—ranging from tolerance to adoration. When a consumer goes to a hair salon and the stylist happens to be friendly and highly skilled, the consumer would experience acceptance.
6. **Disgust**—ranging from boredom to loathing. A consumer might feel disgust at finding an insect in his or her soup.
7. **Anticipation**—ranging from mindfulness to vigilance. This is the emotion a consumer experiences while awaiting the announcement of the winning lottery number.
8. **Surprise**—ranging from uncertainty to amazement. A consumer might feel surprise when his or her waiter announces that dessert will be on the house.

This is a list of human emotions we experience in everyday consumption situations. But products and brands also become sources of emotion.

WHEN BRANDS BRING EMOTIONS

Can you pack your brand with emotions? Yes, an increasing number of brands are doing just that. Here is how:

1. **Romantic Love** In 2009, Coke released the "Open Happiness" ad showing two teenagers in a library, flirting by drawing some images on their hands—the boy draws a Coke bottle on his hand and the girl draws on her hand a glass filled with ice cubes. As they bring their hands closer to touch, coke flows out of his hand into hers. The commercial ends with the superimposed tagline, "Open Happiness."
2. **Family Love** In 2011, Google created a video for its Chrome browser, in which a father catalogs his daughter's life story—from birth to her loss of her baby teeth—all using Google tools, from Gmail to YouTube (YouTube is now a part of Google).
3. **Human Connection** In a 1973 ad, a large number of people assembled on a hilltop in London and holding Coke bottles in hand, sang the song "I'd like to buy the world a Coke." In a 1979 ad, aired during the Super Bowl game, NFL star player "Mean Joe Green" is offered a Coke by a kid; the grateful Green rewards the kid by giving him his jersey.
4. **Joys of Everyday Life** In 2010, BMW ran a campaign which featured happy people enjoying their BMWs, feeling the breeze on their faces. Its tag line: "What you make people feel is just as important as what you make. We make joy." Joy is made by BMW.

The quintessential common element of these emotion-laden brand communications is that the brands are given a human face.

MEASURING EMOTIONS

Suppose you are a fragrance marketer and you are creating an advertisement for your brand of cologne. You want to evoke an emotional theme of romance. You create the ad and run the advertising campaign. How would you know the advertisement was successful in evoking the emotion of romance? It would be nice if you could measure the emotions your viewers feel when they see your advertisement, wouldn't it? Once again, consumer

SHADES

Romantic Love

of

Family Love

EMOTIONS

Human Connec-tion

in

Joys of Everyday Life

BRANDS

researchers can help.[12] There are two ways, they suggest, of measuring emotions: verbal rating and picture matching. In the verbal rating method, you simply present the names of the eight emotions to consumers and then ask them to circle the emotions they think they experienced when they were watching the ad. Likewise, as a marketer, you can also measure the emotions consumers experience when using your product—say, a videogame, a movie, or a brand of cologne.

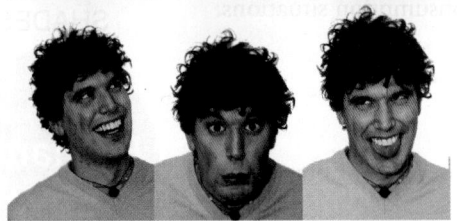

This method is simple, and that is good. But it does have one problem: it assumes that consumers recognize their emotions under these labels or that they can verbalize their emotions. Can you verbalize all your emotions? For example, how would you feel if you sat in that Lips Chair we showed you before (flip back to the page if you like)?

You are finding it difficult to name those emotions precisely, are you not? This is normal. The fact is that most of our emotional communication is nonverbal, i.e., we can't put our feelings in words; instead, we show and communicate our emotions through gestures and facial expressions. So why shouldn't we use a technique that capitalizes on this to measure emotions? Our second method does just that; it is called (what else?) the **picture matching method**. Ad agencies Foote, Cone, and Belding (FCB) and BBDO use it to test their ads. (They call it *visual image profiling*.) In this method, consumers who have just been shown a test advertisement are shown a set of faces with differing expressions, and are asked to mark the face that comes closest to how they themselves felt when they viewed the ad.

This method is very useful for testing commercials. If an advertisement does not produce the desired emotion, you, as a marketer, must modify it until it delivers the desired emotional effect.

CONSUMER MOODS

Almost Emotional

"Moods subtly insinuate themselves in everyday life, influencing what we remember of the past, perceive in the present, and expect from the future."

—-Morris Holbrook (2000)[13]

Emotions are quite an experience. But we can't be on an emotional high all the time. In fact, to feel emotions, we must have been in a state of "no emotion." Only then can we notice the change in our feelings. "But what," you might ask, "do we feel when we are in states of 'no emotion'?" The answer is that we are in such states as being relaxed, bored, curious, happy, etc. Now, if these are not emotions, what are they? You know them first hand. You even know their name. You call them *moods*.

Moods are simply emotions felt less intensely. They are "almost emotions," if you will. They are also short-lived. They are easy to induce, and they appear and disappear in our consciousness frequently and readily. They are pervasive, in that we are always in some kind of mood—a happy mood or a sad mood, an irritated or pleased, amused or bored, a pensive or a "brain-dead" mood. Moods affect our responses to marketing communications.[14]

When You Don't Know You Are in the Mood

We are not always conscious of our moods. For quite some time now, you have been busy reading this chapter. You have been in a relaxed and pleasant and absorbed mood, but you were not saying to yourself, mentally, "I am in a relaxed, pleasant, and absorbed mood." Yet, this mood kept you reading. If you grew tired of reading, you may have perhaps stopped for a while, still without consciously recognizing that you were tired. If you were always aware of your mood, then your mind would not be able to focus on the work you were doing. Thus, moods are not only milder forms of emotions, but sometimes they can be so mild as to not even register on our consciousness (in contrast, we are always aware of our emotions).

In this case, our moods act like a *backdrop* in our consciousness. They work in the background, almost autonomously. This helps us keep on doing whatever we are doing. Thus, if we are in a store and the ambiance and the piped-in music put us in a pleasant mood, we just linger on a bit longer. And buy more—which is very good for the marketer.

And When You Know You Are in the Mood

Then there are times when we do become conscious of our moods. And we also become aware of the source of our moods. When the music in the store just puts us in a pleasant mood without our awareness, for example, we may not even be conscious of the music being played; in contrast, if suddenly some tune or lyrics registered on our consciousness, then we would become aware of the mood and the source, and we, in fact, would focus on that source. We would pause to listen to the song or the tune. Thus, when we are aware of our moods, we want to approach or stay with its source if the mood is a positive one, and we want to distance ourselves from the source if the mood is negative. This type of mood acts as an active driver; in other words, it acts as a motivational force. We received good grades, so we want to buy a cappuccino. We got an e-mail from an old friend, so we want to grab a beer. You get bored reading your textbook, so you switch on your I-Pod. (Please, not right now!)

How Moods Make You...

Moods make us act in the marketplace, and basically these mood-based acts can be grouped into two categories:

Response to Market Stimuli Consumer researchers have found that consumers linger longer in positive-mood environments—as when good music is playing in a store, or when a salesperson is not shadowing them as they browse the merchandise. Consumers also tend to better recall those ads that create a positive mood. And they feel more positive toward brands whose advertisements create feelings of warmth.[15] Overall, good moods make us respond positively to market stimuli; bad moods make us respond negatively.[16]

Situational Consumption Choices Our moods also affect our consumption experiences. One of the findings of research on this topic is that consumers in negative moods engage in "immediate self-gratification," such as rewarding themselves (eating desserts, drinking, self-gifting, etc.); of course, consumers also engage in these activities when in positive moods ("Dessert? Forget dieting, I deserve it!"). Thus, both negative and positive moods (compared to neutral moods) produce self-gratification-oriented consumption. Another mood effect is that the consumption experience itself is more positive when we are in a good mood, and more negative when we are in a bad mood. Have you ever wondered why food in a restaurant tastes better when we are with nice company? Nice company produces a nice mood—that is why!

Good Mood—Marketers Owe It to You

If moods affect consumer responses to market stimuli, it behooves marketers to create the circumstances that create a positive mood in you. Moods are induced in two ways: (a) internal autistic thinking—this happens when you recall some past incident or fantasize about some future event; and (b) exposure to external stimuli—you see candy and you instantly feel in the mood to eat some candy. As a marketer, you can tap into both of these

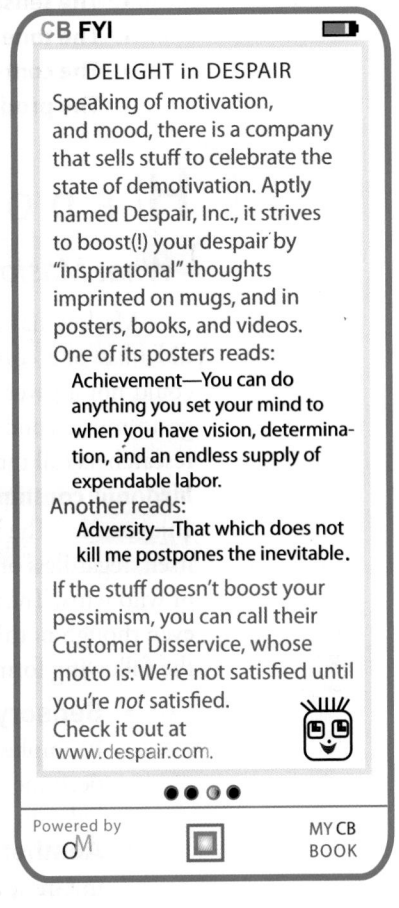

CB FYI

DELIGHT in DESPAIR
Speaking of motivation, and mood, there is a company that sells stuff to celebrate the state of demotivation. Aptly named Despair, Inc., it strives to boost(!) your despair by "inspirational" thoughts imprinted on mugs, and in posters, books, and videos.
One of its posters reads:
   Achievement—You can do anything you set your mind to when you have vision, determination, and an endless supply of expendable labor.
Another reads:
   Adversity—That which does not kill me postpones the inevitable.

If the stuff doesn't boost your pessimism, you can call their Customer Disservice, whose motto is: We're not satisfied until you're *not* satisfied.
Check it out at www.despair.com.

● ● ● ○

Powered by
oM

MY CB
BOOK

S A V V Y
MARKETER

sources; you can arrange marketing stimuli to induce the right mood in the consumer. Here are some marketing stimuli at your command:

- **The ambiance of the store**
- **The demeanor of the salesperson**
- **The sensory features of the product**
- **The tone and manner of the advertisement**
- **The content of the message**
- **The product packaging or the display of the product itself**

HEDONIC CONSUMPTION

What Maslow Missed

Maslow has done us a great service—by capturing all of our core motives. But he did miss one core type—pleasure, enjoyment, recreation, hedonism. Maslow's scheme could not answer such questions as "Why do consumers play solitaire?" or "Why do we go to music concerts?" Pleasure and recreation are also natural human needs. Consumer researchers call them **hedonic motives**—the consumer need and desire to obtain pleasure. **Hedonic consumption** refers to the use of products/services for the sake of intrinsic enjoyment.[17] The idea of "intrinsic" means that the activity or consumption is enjoyable in itself, regardless of the outcome of the activity. Thus, the game itself is enjoyable regardless of who wins. Theater, music, vacations, etc., are enjoyable while we are consuming them, even though nothing concrete may come from them. Intrinsic enjoyment comes in one of the following forms.[18]

- **Sensory pleasure**—pleasant sensations of sight, sound, taste, touch, or smell. Examples include: taking a bubble bath; luxuriating in a Jacuzzi or sauna; using perfume and colognes; looking at exciting colors in clothing; glancing at strobe lights in a discotheque; choosing home décor; listening to music.
- **Aesthetic pleasure**—reading poetry; visiting an art gallery; taking a course in Greek history.
- **Emotional experience**—watching movies or TV shows; sending gifts; receiving gifts; visiting relatives; long-distance social calling; dating; class reunions.
- **Fun and Play**—playing Angry Birds Space (released March 22, 2012); playing sports; dancing; vacationing.

Some activities may be a source of more than one kind of hedonic pleasures.[18]

SATISFYING YOUR HEDONIC MOTIVES:
BRINGING THE WORLD RIGHT INTO YOUR ROOM

Lie in Bed in Fantasy Land

There is an inn that offers you hedonic gratification like no other. Its themed rooms put you instantly in the midst of New York City's Central Park or in front of the Statue of Liberty, while you are watching TV or lying on   bed.

Other choices include a pirate hideout, Tennessee caves, race car room (the bed frame is a model race car), a rain forest, a Champaign room (with a Champaign bath on an open-view Mezzanine floor within the room) and, yes, Venice.

You can check out this *Romancing the Consumer* Inn at www.wildwood-inn.com.

The Venetian Room at Wild Wood Inn, Florence, Kentucky, USA.

MY CB BOOK

CONSUMER DESIRES

Do you remember your high school sweetheart? Do you remember the day you first approached her (or he approached you)? Or, do you remember how badly you wanted to go to Ibiza on your last spring break? Do you remember that you would have given up almost anything to get a ticket to a U2 concert? Is there anything you yearn for now? The things that you may have yearned for in your life and the things you yearn for now—these are called "objects of desire." Desire, you see, is more than a "want," and it is certainly more than a "need." Likewise, it is more than an emotion, and it is certainly more than a mood. It is a motivation, but it is a motivation of the most intense kind. It is an emotion involving a passion attached to an object—a product, a person, a cause, a life goal. A passion that entails fervent longing or yearning. It is a motivation so intense that it can become all-consuming.[19]

Desire works on the pleasure principle. We have desires because we seek pleasure. That is why some think of desire as sinful—as indulgence. Sometimes, we even feel guilty, giving in to our desires. And, desires can, in excess, lead to unhealthy compulsive consumption and obsession. That is the "dark side" of desire. Likewise, if we yearn for something out of our reach, then that, too, can lead to intense frustrations. Often, though, consumers satisfy their desires for unreachable objects by fantasizing about them. **Fantasy consumption** is vicarious consumption; thus, consumers who desire the lifestyle of the "rich and famous" live that lifestyle vicariously by watching TV shows about those lifestyles. A dose of realism often mellows unreachable desires for most people, most of the time. If desires for unreachable goals persist, they can lead to psychotic behavior.

Desire plays a significant role in every human's life. When we desire something, it becomes our life's goal to acquire it, to reach it. Our desires give us goals to live for, to strive toward. Fulfillment of desires is also a source of positive emotion, of satisfaction. Desire is just another name for living; when a person desires nothing, then he or she stops looking forward to anything in life. Absence of desire is lack of hope. Materialistic cultures promote desires; ascetic values curb desires—actually, they curb the number of objects to desire. For desire to serve as a life-force, the number of objects is not relevant; only that we desire something. And that something needs to be reachable and it does not have to be material goods or material success. "To desire is to hope; and to hope is to live."[20]

Some desires remain mere yearnings; some desires are fulfilled again and again. Some objects pique our interest continually. For these, we feel deep involvement. About "deep involvement" in a minute, but first let us learn about involvement itself.

www.anything4jetta.com

**The all-new Jetta.
You'll do anything to drive it.**

Toll-free Helpline: 18001020909, 18002090909

Terms and conditions apply.

Volkswagen. Das Auto.

Image courtesy of Mudra Communications, India.

The motivational power of desire for products

CONSUMER INVOLVEMENT

A Yardstick for All of Our Actions

Now we want to introduce you to a concept that is so powerful that it colors all our actions as consumers. And it will absolutely, positively leave its mark on every other concept we will cover in this book. The concept is *involvement*, and it describes our relationship with all of the products we consume or do not consume and all of the activities in which we do or do not want to engage.

How do you want your tea? Onkar Singh Kular, a London artist, has designed 128-Pantone colored mugs for you to choose *precisely*. Mark one and the hostess will know how much milk to add to satisfy your "high-involvement taste" for tea.
(Image: courtesy Onkar Singh Kular)

Involvement is a general term that can be defined as the degree of interest a consumer finds in a product, service, object, or activity. At the most basic level, involvement stems from the *personal relevance* of an object, product, or service to a consumer. Paul is not a hunter, so guns are not relevant to him, but he has a cat, so cat foods are relevant. Accordingly, Paul is not involved in guns but is involved in cat foods. Perceived relevance, then, identifies a consumer's involvement as a 'yes' or 'no'—involved or not involved—category.

Once we cross the relevance threshold, involvement becomes a matter of degree—high or low, corresponding to the *degree* of interest a consumer feels in a product or object. Thus, both table salt and golf clubs are relevant to Paul, but he takes less interest in table salt than in golf clubs.

Of the hundreds of products and services we consume in our lifetimes, we cannot be equally excited about each one. There are some products we consume casually and take for granted. In these, our involvement is low. There are other products we consume with some interest, pausing to savor their tastes, smell their aromas, feel their textures, or hear their sounds. Still others—a few in number—we consume with extreme interest. We like them; we enjoy them; we love them. Everyone has a favorite activity, a favorite product, a favorite brand. Some of us are fashion experts; others, car buffs; still others, computer jocks. We are eager to get to know these products—fashions, cars, and videogames—to find out everything there is to know. We get excited whenever the topic comes up. And, of course, we want to be shopping for or using them whenever possible. In these, we have high involvement; and, moreover, in these, we have *enduring* involvement. **Enduring involvement** is the degree of interest a consumer feels in a product or service on *an ongoing basis*.[21] The extreme form of enduring involvement is deep involvement.

There are some products or activities in which we become interested only in specific situations, as when buying a product or when consuming something in the presence of an important client or friend. This form of involvement is called **situational involvement**—defined as the degree of interest in an object in a specific situation or on a specific occasion. For example, you are unlikely to take much interest in dishwashers—you use them in your kitchen in a taken-for-granted manner. But the last time you were buying one, you became extremely interested (i.e., involved) in dishwashers—attempting to learn about them, deliberating over various options, and weighing them vis-à-vis your own needs. The involvement that arises at the time of purchase (as different from the consumption situation) has a specific name—**purchase decision involvement**—the degree of concern consumers experience in making the right choice. The other sub-form of situational involvement is *consumption-situation involvement*, the interest we experience in the usage situation. For example, consuming wine at home, unconcerned about the public image of the wine brand, versus consuming wine in company, concerned about the impressions you might make consuming a particular brand of wine.

Want to know whether you have enduring involvement in something? Or whether the next time you buy, say, a frozen entree, you will have high purchase decision involvement?

Take the surveys in Table 2.3 and find out.

The linkage between involvement and motivation should be self-evident. Involvement acts as a "master switch" that turns our motivation on or off. No involvement, no motivation. Low involvement, low motivation. High involvement, high motivation. Enduring involvement, perpetual motivation. Situational involvement: we are motivated when the right situation arises. As black and white as that! This concept, *involvement*, will keep us company throughout this book.

DEEP INVOLVEMENT

Extreme Interest in Things

One special case of enduring involvement is **deep involvement**—defined as a consumer's *extreme interest* in a product or activity on an ongoing basis. Often it borders on product fanaticism. One consumer in Sydney had the brand name 'Apple' tattooed on his forehead. We will have occasion to discuss this particular example further in a later chapter.

The phenomenon of deep involvement is important to study because it is a window on a consumer's key motivations and emotions. People are fanatical about things they care deeply about. They use them for enjoyment, to derive life satisfactions, and even to define their identities for themselves. What are you deeply involved in? Cars? Sports? Art? Gizmos? Cooking? Shoes? If you are, then you know how a significant part of your consumer behavior—contemplating, searching, browsing, buying, collecting, caring, nurturing, and relishing—is dedicated to the object of your deep involvement. You also know, firsthand, how your deep involvement is, for you, a constant source of motivation—perhaps even a reason to live!

Kimberly Rose of San Diego, caught in a moment of *deep involvement* with coffee

CB Blog

2

Self-Actualization—A Personal Journey for You

Have you reached your self-actualization? You won't think so if you believe that one must first "be done" with the lower level needs in Maslow's Hierarchy. That view, termed here the stage view, is true but limited. Later, Maslow articulated an additional view, termed here "stream of episodes." In this view, we experience self-actualization as an episode, an event, a creative moment in which we feel a sense of personal accomplishment, self-worth, extreme joy. Writes Maslow[22]:

> We may define it as an episode, or a spurt in which the powers of the person come together in a particularly efficient and intensely enjoyable way... He becomes in these episodes more truly himself, more perfectly actualizing his potentialities, closer to the core of his Being, more fully human.

Note that the events of extreme enjoyment are not by themselves episodes of self-actualization. Thus, joys of videogame playing and watching a thriller movie are not self-actualization. Rather, self-actualization is a performance (not consumption) episode, in which we perform and create something; and, in creating that thing, we see our true worth, our true self, our individual talent and fulfillment.

Among creative acts, all work counts: e.g., cooking, repairing cars, writing a research paper or a book, teaching, studying for a course. Not when we do these acts as mere chores, of course. They count only if we perform them to the best of our abilities. Thus, if cooking is your passion, then you are experiencing a self-actualizing episode every time you cook the best dish you wanted to cook. Likewise, every course you take with full conscience and dedicate to it the time and energy it warrants. The episodic view is, thus, an invitation to experience self-actualization every day.

Will you choose to avail yourself of this opportunity?

CONSUMER BEHAVIOR

MY CB BOOK .COM

Table 2.3   # MEASURING CONSUMER INVOLVEMENT
Baseline, Enduring, Deep, and Maven

A ENDURING/DEEP INVOLVEMENT

Strongly Disagree 1 2 3 4 5 Strongly Agree
1. Cars offer me relaxation and fun.   ___
2. Driving my car is one of the most enjoyable and satisfying things I do.   ___
3. I enjoy discussing cars with friends.   ___
4. I get bored when other people talk about cars.*   ___
5. Sometimes I get too wrapped up in my car. ___
6. I don't pay much attention to car advertisements.*   ___
7. Cars are nothing more than appliances.* ___
8. I generally feel sentimental attachment to the cars I own.   ___
9. I use this product to define and express the "I" and "Me" in myself.   ___
10. When I am with friends, I often end up talking about cars.   ___

* Item to be reverse-coded.

Add item scores. Scores below the mid-point, 30, indicate low or absent *Enduring Involvement*. Scores above 30 mean High *Enduring Involvement*.

(Adapted from: Peter Bloch, "Involvement with a Product Class," *Advances in Consumer Research* 8, 61-65.)

B DEEP INVOLVEMENT IN A SPECIFIC BRAND/PRODUCT

Strongly Disagree 1 2 3 4 5 Strongly Agree

1. I feel emotionally attached to my ___.   ___
2. My ___ holds a special place in my life.
3. My ___ is central to my identity—my sense of who I am.   ___
4. If I lose my ___, I would feel as if a part of me was missing.   ___
5. I take good care of my ___.   ___
6. I trust my ___.

Add item scores. Scores below the mid-point, 18, indicate low or absent *Brand Involvement*. Scores above 18 show presence of *Brand Involvement*.

(Adapted, in part, from Kimberly J. Dodson, "Peak Experiences and Mountain Biking: Incorporating the Bikes in the Extended Self," *Advances in Consumer Research*, 1996.)

C INVOLVEMENT OF THE MAVEN

Name of the product _____
Strongly Disagree 1 2 3 4 5 Strongly Agree

1. I would be interested in reading about this product.
2. I would read a Consumer Reports article about this product.
3. I have compared product characteristics among brands of this product.
4. I usually pay attention to ads for this product.
5. I usually talk about this product with other people.
6. I usually seek advice from other people prior to purchasing this product.
7. I usually take many factors into account before purchasing this product.
8. I usually spend a lot of time choosing what kind to buy.

Add all items. Scores below the mid-point, 24, indicate low or absent *Enduring Product Involvement*. Scores above 24 show presence of *Enduring Product Involvement*.

(Based on Edward F. McQuarrie and J. Michael Munson, "A Revised Product Involvement Inventory: Improved Usability and Validity," *Advances in Consumer Research*, Vol. 19 (Provo, UT: Association for Consumer Research, 1992), pp. 108-15. (Reprinted by permission.)

D BASELINE INVOLVEMENT IN A PRODUCT

To me, this product (_____) is:

Unimportant	1 2 3 4 5	Important
Insignificant	1 2 3 4 5	Significant
Not relevant	1 2 3 4 5	Relevant
Unexciting	1 2 3 4 5	Exciting
Uninteresting	1 2 3 4 5	Fascinating
Means nothing	1 2 3 4 5	Means a lot

Add item scores. Scores below the mid-point, 18, indicate low or absent *Involvement as Product Importance*. Scores above 18 show its presence.

(Adapted from: Judith L. Zaichkowsky, "The Personal Involvement Inventory: Reduction, Revision, and Application to Advertising," *J. of Advertising* 23, No. 4, December 1994, 59-70.)

SHADES of INVOLVEMENT

Involvement is a multifaceted concept. Different measurement scales capture different facets.

 Measures involvement in a product category as a whole, beyond a specific brand.

 Involvement in and attachment to the particular unit (or brand) the consumer possesses.

 Involvement in a product category as an object of knowledge in the marketplace. The consumer is constantly engaged with the marketplace information on the product. Product experts and market mavens display this sort of involvement.

 This measure captures the full range of involvement—particularly the total *irrelevance* of the product; it captures as well the high interest in a product, without necessarily implying total immersion or personal attachment.

Romancing the Consumer

C. H. E. S. S. B. O. X. I. N. G.

Welcome to a new sport called *Chessboxing*. Here, you play chess for four minutes and then box for 2 minutes. And then you repeat the same cycle for 11 rounds (six for chess and five for boxing). You can win by knocking down your opponent in the ring or by checkmating him/her.

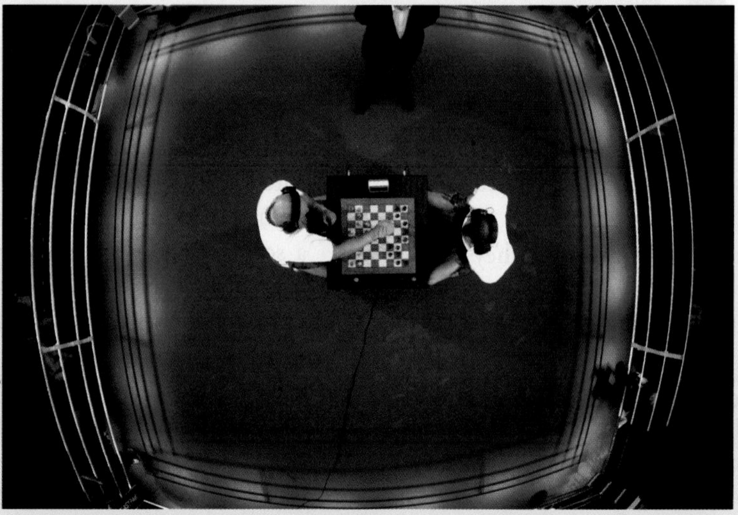

The sport was created by Iepe Rubingha, a Dutch artist, in 2003. Now it is run by the World Chess Boxing Organization (WCBO), based in Berlin. Through its affiliate clubs, WCBO organizes the games in various European countries.

Its London affiliate, the Great Britain Chess Boxing Organization (GBCBO), opened its first club in April 2008. If you happen to be in London, you can take in a training session for £7 at the Islington Boxing Club in North London.

There is logic to the sport, as WCBO puts it: It is a combination of the number one thinking sport and the number one fighting sport! So now you, dear reader, can exercise your mind and your body together, thanks to this innovative marketer!

Powered by Owl • MY BOOK

SUMMARY

In this chapter, we explored the three related topics of *motivation, emotion,* and *involvement*. *Motivation* is goal-directed drive or energy; this energy is provided by *felt needs*. Various scholars have classified human needs, and we discussed some of the prominent classifications. Maslow's Hierarchy-of-Needs classification is perhaps the most well-known of these, but we also outlined Murray's social needs system and Dichter's list of subconscious motives.

Human emotions play a significant role in motivating human behavior. We explained Plutchik's emotional classification system, and illustrated it with consumer behavior examples. We discussed moods as a milder and short-lived form of emotion and outlined some influences of mood on consumer behavior. One specific topic in our discussion of emotions and moods was *hedonic consumption*.

Finally, we discussed consumer involvement as a factor that separates the important from the trivial. It comes in two forms: situational and enduring—the extreme form of the latter is deep involvement. We learned how to measure these, and we came to understand that, as a "master switch" of motivation, involvement will color every topic in the rest of the book. How? We look forward to finding out in the chapters that follow.

KEY TERMS

Enduring involvement	Involvement	Purposive behavior
Emotion	Maslow's hierarchy of needs	Primary emotions
Goal object	Moods	Situational involvement
Hedonic consumption	Motivation	

YOUR TURN

1. Define and explain the concept of *motivation* and how it is related to the concept of *need*.

2. Explain each need in Maslow's Hierarchy of Needs. Explain any five needs suggested in the Murray's list of needs.

3. List any five of Dichter's motives. How do they differ from Maslow's needs?

4. What is the difference between conscious and unconscious motives?

5. List all methods of researching consumer motives, and explain each briefly.

6. What are emotions, and how are they related to motivation?

7. What are moods and how do they differ from emotions? Give examples of two uses of moods that a marketer can employ.

8. What is involvement? What is the difference between situational and enduring involvement?

9. What is meant by hedonic consumption? List your own hedonic consumptions.

10. Briefly explain the needs for cognition, arousal, and attribution. Give one example of each.

11. Write down scales to measure consumers' (a) enduring and (b) purchase decision involvement.

THINK**+Apply**

1. Do Maslow's needs always arise in the order of the hierarchy? Explain.

2. Think of one example for each of the motives in Dichter's list, where a consumer's action could be motivated, at least in theory and at least in part, by that particular motive.

3. With which of these products are you enduringly involved: (a) your car, (b) your MP3 player; (c) your cell phone; (d) any student or professional club; (e) your gym; (e) your brand of cologne; (f) your dishwasher and microwave oven. Explain your answer.

4. Describe a recent consumption (buying or using) activity that caused you to make attributions. List all the attributions that came to mind and then explain the one on which you settled. For this particular set of attributions, what could marketers do to avoid an attribution unfavorable to themselves?

PRACTICE**+Experience**

1. Find an ad on TV or in magazines that captures each of the needs in Maslow's Hierarchy.

2. Interview five consumers on their reasons for (choose one): (a) joining a health club or gym; (b) joining a sorority or a fraternity or another social club; (c) keeping a Web page (e.g., Facebook) or participating in discussion forums. Include a discussion of the sort of activities in which they participate and what sort of activities they enjoy (for a Web page, it would relate to what sort of content they maintain on the Web page). List and comment on the possible motives different consumers may have for these activities.

3. Design and conduct a study using the Mason Haire techniques to understand why consumers might (a) download music even when they know it is illegal, and (b) regularly participate in Flashmob events (see Flashmob.com).

4. Interview two consumers who might have enduring involvement in some consumption. Document the kinds of activities they engage in to manifest their deep involvement, and understand what kinds of needs it satisfies for them.

5. Interview two consumers on their net surfing behavior —when, why, how often, which sites, and with what feelings, pleasures, and frustrations do they surf the net? Also what role does the Internet occupy in their leisure life (i.e., exclude Internet surfing for work and employment related purposes)? Then, identify and compare these two consumers' (a) motives, where possible, relating them to any of the motives covered in the chapter, and (b) emotions experienced during Web surfing.

In the Marketing Manager's Shoes

Put yourself in a marketing manager's shoes. Most concepts in the chapter have some lessons for the marketing manager; i.e., they suggest what to do differently in practice. Indeed, often these applications are implicit in our explanations of the concepts and models in the chapter. Identify at least five specific applications of the chapter's concepts, all of which should be entirely new, different from the examples cited here.

AROUSAL, COGNITION, ATTRIBUTION

Essential Tonics for Your Mind

If you want to explore further, there are three special motives worth learning about. These are: to be engaged, to be informed, and to be a psychic. Their technical names: "need for arousal," "need for cognition," and "need for attribution." Our minds are hardwired for them, in a manner of speaking.

Eager to learn what these are? Well, you are already experiencing the "need for cognition." Cognition simply means thought, information, knowledge. **Need for cognition**—our discomfort with ignorance, our need for information, for understanding the world around us—this is instinctual. Driven by this need, we read newspapers, watch CNN, and eavesdrop on gossip; and, of course, we want to know the regular price of an item that is now on sale.

Our minds also have a need to be stimulated. Without stimulation, we experience the discomfort we call "boredom." The **arousal seeking motive** is the drive to maintain our stimulation at an optimal level. This need drives our many consumer behaviors: Hanging out at the mall, refurbishing our wardrobe, changing the paint in our living rooms, traveling to new places, etc.

Finally**, attribution** is the process of assigning causes—i.e., figuring out why something happened. If your best friend brought you no gift on your birthday, your mind would not rest easy until you figured out why. In the store, the salesperson steers you away from your favorite brand. Keep your mind wondering, or put it to rest by attributing some reason to the salesperson. Attribution, cognition, and arousal keep the mind, respectively, out of wondering, out of ignorance, and into something engaging.

NEED FOR ATTRIBUTION

Why Ask Why?

As humans we have the inherent motivation to assign causes to all events that we witness and all events that affect our lives. The process of assigning causes is called "making attributions." **Attributions** are "inferences that people draw about the causes of events, others' behaviors, and their own behavior."[23] The motivation to assign causes is called **attribution motivation**.

How do we assign causes? Basically, we think of all the possibilities, and then we accept the one that makes the most sense. If our listener did not laugh at our joke, perhaps she missed the punch line; or, perhaps, she thought the joke had a streak of racism. Our coworker did not compliment us on our hairdo, perhaps because she was just too preoccupied. Or maybe she did not like the hairdo and didn't want to say so. On and on we go—digging deeper and deeper, like a scientist trying one experiment after another, until we find an explanation that we feel comfortable with.[24]

Attribution Affects Future Behavior That explanation, the specific *cause* we choose for attribution, influences our subsequent action. If the listener perceived our joke to be racist, perhaps we should apologize. If indeed our coworker did not like our hairdo, maybe we should revisit the hair stylist and ask her to restore our previous, usual hairdo.

Consumer Attribution Behavior This human motivation also shapes our behavior as consumers and our responses to what marketers offer us. There are three specific situations where consumer attributions play a significant role: (a) a salesperson's recommendation for purchase; (b) an unsatisfactory product experience; and (c) a product offering that seems "too good to be true." Consider each in turn.

a. Salesperson Recommendation What happens when a salesperson recommends a particular product? We wonder why. We might assume that the salesperson makes more commission on that model, and we may then not follow his or her advice. Alternatively, we might think that perhaps the salesperson genuinely believes the model to be superior. In that case, we would heed his or her advice.

b. Unsatisfactory Product Experience You have bought a used car from a dealer and in six months the transmission failed (the 90-day warranty expired three months after the purchase). Would you buy a used car from that dealer again? That depends on the attribution you make. If you believe that the dealer knew about the defective transmission and did not tell you, then you would never buy from that dealer again. On the other hand, if you make the attribution that the dealer did not know, then, of course, you would consider buying from that dealer again.

c. An Incredible Product Offering When we find a product at a throwaway price, or if the marketer gives away something free, we wonder why. Suppose we find a silk shirt that usually retails for $40 now marked down to $10 in an upscale department store; we would ask why. Perhaps the store just got excess inventory; or perhaps, alternatively, savvy marketers of silk shirts have discovered that silk is going out of fashion. If we make the former attribution, we would buy that silk shirt; otherwise, we might not.

A MODEL OF CONSUMER ATTRIBUTIONS ———————— MY **CB** BOOK

PRODUCT TRIAL EXPERIENCE ▶ ATTRIBUTIONS ▶ FUTURE BEHAVIOR

Perceptions

CONSUMER PERCEPTIONS AND SENSORY MARKETING

3

The Only Brand Reality That Matters

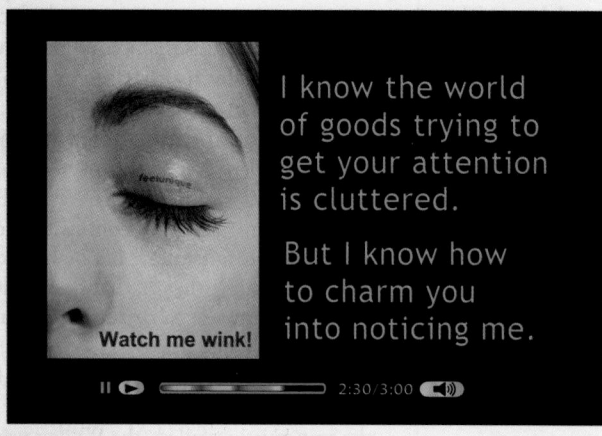

I know the world of goods trying to get your attention is cluttered.

But I know how to charm you into noticing me.

Watch me wink!

2:30/3:00

LEARN . APPLY . EXPERIENCE

Do You See What You See?

Photographer: Markus Wendler

Look at this picture. What do you see? We showed it to 10 MBA students and 10 Undergraduate students who had been reading the inaugural edition of *this book* (www.mycbbook.com). Their answers varied.

Three of them wrote that they had no idea what was going on in the picture. Six of them thought that it was an ad for a suitcase—that it was lightweight and/or strong (it was about to fall but, were it to fall, it wouldn't break). Many got the idea of balance but the specificity varied. Some thought it was conveying balance—in life in general. Only six respondents saw the tire as the main object being promoted, as a source of balance. Here too, three thought that it was conveying the physical quality of the tire (balance, traction, etc). Only three saw "balance" being used in a metaphorical sense—that the tire helps you run your life in *balance* (e.g., between work and home life).

No one saw that the tire had a Mercedes logo on the wheel. Only when it was brought to their attention did the students attribute the ad to the brand Mercedes, but in a variety of ways. Six of them thought that the ad was for Mercedes tires! Nine of them saw it as an ad for Mercedes cars. Of the latter, three thought Mercedes was promoting balance as the car's physical attribute. One respondent felt that the ad meant "Mercedes can transport everything!"

Three respondents thought that the ad was promoting the ability of the brand to bring balance to our lives and across our interests.

I see it, therefore it is.

INTRODUCTION

The story of this picture vividly shows a revealing truth about the workings of the human mind: It has a way of seeing things that may or may not reflect reality. Perception is about how our minds see things. It does not matter what a marketer says a product is or will do. It doesn't even matter in reality what a product is. What matters is how consumers perceive it.

One of the most famous stories about the monumental power of consumer perception in the annals of marketing is this. The year was 1985. In April of that year, the Coca-Cola Company launched "New Coke"—a sweeter concoction than its old product, which the company chose to withdraw from the market completely. The change was intended to take market share away from rival Pepsi. In blind taste tests, consumers had always rated Pepsi higher than Coke, and it was based on these research findings that the company's product development scientists had concocted a new formula. The result was New Coke. Just to be sure, prior to the launch of New Coke, the company had again conducted consumer taste tests, and, in these tests, consumers had consistently rated the new formula not only as better than the old Coke but also better than Pepsi.

So it was with great fanfare that the company launched the new product. Within days, however, there was a groundswell of consumer protest. Whereas a lot of consumers were just angry with the company for taking away something they had been used to drinking for decades, many of them found that the New Coke just did not taste as good. When the blind taste tests were repeated, the results were the same as before, but with a twist: consumers pointed to the drink that tasted better, but they thought they had selected the old Coke. When told that the drink they had picked was actually New Coke, they argued that they were probably confused or that the plastic cups must have made the drinks taste different. The fact was, they insisted, that the old Coke definitely tasted better. And that is why they said they would not buy New Coke.

Red wine? White wine? In the bottle and in the glass. Perceptual distortion aplenty!

Six weeks later, the company had to bring back the old Coke, under the name Coke Classic. And even two years later, the old Coke continued to outdo New Coke in sales—about 8 to 1. Such is the power of perception. Of things big and small. In our lives as humans and as consumers.

Perception is fundamental to us as humans. It is also the first and inevitable response consumers experience every time they face the marketplace, a marketplace filled with an amazing array of alluring products, all shouting out to be noticed, admired, and chosen. That fundamental response, perception, is the topic of this chapter.

We begin this chapter by defining perception, shaping your perception of the word *perception* itself, if you will. If someone were to ask why you perceive something the way you do, you would likely answer, "Because that is the way that thing is." We will explain how this is only half true, and we will tell you about the factors that make up the other half and influence your perceptions. We will then unravel the mystery of perceptual distortion, accounting for biases that distort your perception of reality, every day.

Since perception influences our way of looking at the world, it affects virtually every instance of consumer behavior in the marketplace. We bring this point home by highlighting the role of perception in five domains of consumer behavior: (i) the psychophysics of consumer price perceptions, (ii) country-of-origin effects, (iii) brand image and brand extensions, (iv) perceptual maps and positioning, and (v) sensory marketing.

THE PERCEPTION PROCESS

Perception is a basic, fundamental, and inescapable process of the human mind. "Basic" in that any time we encounter anything—absolutely anything whatsoever—our minds must first perceive it before they can do anything else with it. "Fundamental" in that the perception we form of a thing plays a central role in whatever we do with that thing subsequently. "Inescapable" or inevitable in that we can't stop it and we can't control it. Just how do our minds do that?[1] Let us define our terms first.

Perception is the process by which the human mind becomes aware of and interprets a stimulus. The process has three steps: *exposure, attention*, and *interpretation*. (See Figure 3.1.)

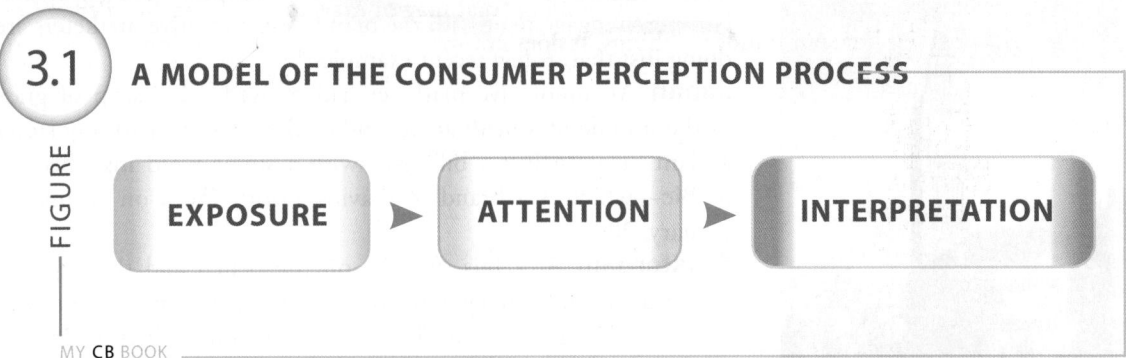

3.1 **FIGURE** **A MODEL OF THE CONSUMER PERCEPTION PROCESS**

EXPOSURE ▶ ATTENTION ▶ INTERPRETATION

MY **CB** BOOK

EXPOSURE

The Face-off with the Consumer

Exposure means that a stimulus comes within the reach of one or more of our five senses: seeing, hearing, smelling, touching, and tasting. A **stimulus** is any object or event in the external environment. Exposure determines whether a stimulus even has the opportunity to be sensed by the consumer. If you advertised Pocket God on a country music station, and if your target consumers—mostly teenagers—didn't listen to country music stations, then the commercial would gain exposure with your target audience. If you advertised *NDMX* golf balls in *Vogue* or *Vanity Fair*, for example, then again you would most likely miss your target audience. Thus, proper choice of message delivery media is the most crucial and first step. A wrong choice can cause the first step itself to fail. No face-off with the consumer occurs, and, consequently, no perception is created.

S A V V Y
MARKETER

Zipping and Zapping

Consumers often avoid commercials, sometimes by attending to other tasks and sometimes by switching channels, a process called **zapping**. And when consumers watch prerecorded programs (such as via Tivo), they fast-forward through the commercials, a process called **zipping**. To get past these commercial-avoidance habits of consumers, marketers must make their ads vivid (more on vividness later). And in terms of media choice, two (relatively) new options can do wonders in getting exposure: product placement and ambient advertising.

Product Placement

Product placement is the tactic of embedding the product in media content, such as featuring a product being used naturally by actors in a TV movie.

Product placement, if done adroitly, works wonders. In the James Bond films, Jaguar XKR is featured, and in the American film that spoofs James Bond, *Austin Powers*, actor Mike Myers endorses Shaguar (Jaguar). In the year 2002, when Austin Powers was playing in theaters, sales of Jaguar rose sharply in America.[2]

Ambient Advertising

Ambient advertising refers to the placement of advertisements or other product-related stimuli right in the midst of the consumer's natural environment.[3] Outdoor billboards technically qualify as ambient media, but they are a traditional medium that the consumer has learned to ignore. So these days, ambient advertising appears in such varied places as airport lounges, public restrooms, even sidewalks; and on a variety of other objects, e.g., shopping bags, coffee cups, and theater tickets. But merely taking over these new sites to broadcast the brand messages only clutters and contaminates the consumer's natural

environment. The real power of ambient media is to use them in a manner that (a) integrates the brand into the environment, (b) adds to the consumer experience of that environment, and (c) creates consumer engagement with the brand. Some creative marketers are doing just that. A few recent examples:[4]

Japan An innovative marketer had mowed a big strip of grass in the middle of a field; at the end of the "shaven" pathway stood a giant razor against a billboard with a single word inscribed on it: Bic—which is a brand of shaving razors. (Seen on ground in January, 2008.)

Amsterdam At a bus stop, sit on the bench and the adjacent screen panel will display your weight. At the bottom of the screen is the brand logo, Fitness First (an International Chain of Health Clubs). (Released in March, 2009.)

London, U.K. In the middle of a sidewalk, an inverted oversized bottle is suspended in mid-air, with thick pink liquid pouring out, making a big splash on the ground. All dried up. Apparently, it is the dried-up liquid column that is supporting the bottle in mid-air. That bottle contained Rimmel Quick Dry Nail Polish! (Bringing home the "quick dry" feature par excellence, this outdoor prop was seen on the streets of London in January, 2009.)

ATTENTION
Breaking through the Noise

Choosing the right advertising medium can give your product exposure to the consumer. But getting exposure does not mean that you will also get the consumer's attention. Or even awareness. For example, if you are in a classroom, all the other students have exposure to you, and you have exposure to them; but this doesn't imply you will have noticed each one of them. At the end of the class period, you will walk out without even being aware of some of them. Exposure, yes; awareness, no; and attention, definitely not.

Now let us take a marketing example. Suppose you are selling Lucozade Energy Drink, and you placed an ad in the Christmas 2012 issue of, say, *Hello*. Lisa, your typical target consumer for this product, is flipping through this magazine. She comes to the page that features your ad, but she flips past it too. Your ad has failed to get Lisa's attention. Again, exposure, yes; attention, definitely not.

Attention can be defined as allocation of mental processing capacity. When attention is given, the mind focuses on a stimulus, ready and willing to process further information from that stimulus. Getting attention is a major concern for marketers, because most consumers face a flood of stimuli. For a stimulus even to be noticed, it has to make its presence felt to one of our five senses. Thus, it should somehow "catch" our eyes, ears, or nose, or leave a taste on our tongue, or feel different on our skin (touch). On one or more of these five sensory characteristics, it should stand apart from the surrounding environment. That is, it should be vivid. **Vividness** refers to a stimulus' intensity and distinctness. Vivid sensory characteristics include bright colors, loud noises, strong aromas, strong tastes, or very rough or very silky textures. The key element required for producing the vividness effect is **contrast**—a stimulus' distinct difference from its environment or background. For an example, see inset (MOCCA: Get Doused in Art).

Although Lisa missed the Lucozade ad, she did stop to notice when she came to a page featuring Fleuvog shoes. Do you know why? Vividness. The colors (a black body frame behind a red shoe) and the image are so stunning that they can't be missed, even through the peripheral vision of a reader cursorily browsing the magazine. Lisa made a mental note to check it out later at Fluevog.com.

Voluntary and Involuntary Attention

Actually, attention comes in two forms: *voluntary* and *involuntary*. **Voluntary attention** is attention given by choice—the consumer chooses to pay attention. **Involuntary attention** is forced on the consumer.[5] It is an intrusion. Now, it is the case that, initially, all advertising must catch involuntary attention; i.e., the attention the advertising catches is of the involuntary sort, at least initially. This is because the consumer seldom proactively seeks an advertisement. Lisa was just turning the pages of *Hello*; she was not looking for shoes. The Fluevog ad had to intrude upon her attention. It did so by being vivid.

If consumers find an ad to be relevant, then they will pay voluntary attention. That initially involuntary attention turns into voluntary attention. Lisa, of course, decided to pay voluntary attention to the Fluevog ad. Consequently, she noticed, to her delight, that inscribed within the body frame is the phrase "Listen to Me!"

MOCCA: GET DOUSED IN ART

Toronto, Canada. The Museum of Contemporary Canadian Art (MOCCA), in October 2011, ran ads on bus shelters showing a man walking his dog, a woman pushing a shopping cart in a parking lot, and a man mowing his lawn (three different ads)—ordinary everyday situations except that these persons were drenched in pink paint! The headline read: *Get Contemporary*. The big idea was this: "The paint is like the art experience that sticks with you" (statement by Josh Day, the art director behind the campaign).** 🇨🇦

(Source: MOCCA press release, October 5, 2011)

Marketing Implications

All advertising (all marketing stimuli, for that matter) must necessarily first get involuntary attention. But with our lives so over-cluttered with things to do and with so many stimuli from so many directions vying for our attention, consumer attention these days has become a scarce commodity. Some have called the present times *the attention economy*.[3]

To survive in this attention-scarce economy, marketers must constantly reinvent new ways to gain exposure and attention. Commercial speech now shows up in strange places—on floor mats in fitness gyms, on TV screens in Wal-Mart, on mini-video screens mounted on shopping carts, and as place-based ads on cell phone screens—called **contextual advertising**. Beyond the ever-expanding media presence, clever message execution also influences consumer attention. Perhaps one of the cleverest recent examples of a "no fail attention getter" advertising is from Zelnorm®—yes, those exposed tummies used as billboards for marker pen-inscribed words like "Abdominal Pain," "Bloating," and whatever else those tummies might be suffering from.

This particular execution for Zelnorm® has a rare quality worth emulating that all students and practitioners of advertising must note: Anyone can get attention (by doing totally outrageous things, for example—remember the Paris Hilton Car Wash for the Carl's Jr. burger chain?). The creative challenge is to get attention in a manner such that the attention "prop" is also the message.

SAVVY MARKETER

INTERPRETATION
The Curse of Extreme Creativity

The third and final step in the perception process, **interpretation** is the process and outcome of understanding the meaning of a stimulus. When you see an abstract painting and you understand it to be a cubist style of art by Picasso, depicting three musicians, you have interpreted the painting.

When you first saw a can of 911 Smart Energy Drink on a store shelf, you wondered if 911 had anything to do with the September 11 World Trade Center tragedy. Then you read the label, which says that it is a drink made by a nutritional scientist in Switzerland. So you made a mental note to try it sometime. You interpreted this new stimulus properly.

A recent ad from Budweiser depicted some idle young men who phoned each other simply to ask and reply with a one-word slang contraction, "Wasssup?" In a later version, one of these young men is sitting at a bar when a more mature customer walks in. The young man habitually asks, "Wasssup?" and the older gentleman unloads his full story. (YouTube it.) Now, the older man did understand the meaning of the slang, but he didn't know that it was not meant to be taken literally. Among the viewers too, many older consumers might miss the point of the "Wasssup?" ad series. And certainly, consumers in foreign cultures would be at a loss. This exemplifies, simply, a consumer's inability to interpret the ad. In order to make the ad interpretable, an ad creator must understand both the vernacular (slang language) of the target audience as well as its culture.

FACTORS THAT SHAPE PERCEPTION

Or, Are Things the Way We See Them?

If we asked you why you see something the way you say it is, you would most likely answer, "Because that is the way it is." But is it? Sometimes, you will be right, but sometimes not. Look at this necktie. Do you perceive it to be "cool"? Your perception will depend on three factors, responsible for all our perceptions (see Figure 3.2).

1. **Stimulus characteristics—the properties of the stimulus itself**
2. **Context—the setting in which the stimulus is encountered**
3. **Consumer characteristics—consumers' own knowledge, interests, and experiences**

1. STIMULUS CHARACTERISTICS

A Thing Is What It Is

Some of the blame for our misperceptions and credit for correct perceptions should go to the object or stimulus itself. After all, the mind's goal is to capture the "reality" of the stimulus. So, when we perceive something, we can't perceive it to be considerably different from what it is. If we see a car, then that is because the stimulus really happens to be a car. If we perceive a brand of cereal to be healthy, it is because we see that it has whole-wheat flakes and nuts, and we do not taste much sugar in it. The reality of the stimulus, i.e., the stimulus characteristics, inevitably determines our perception. Stimulus characteristics themselves can be grouped into two types: *sensory characteristics* and *information content*.

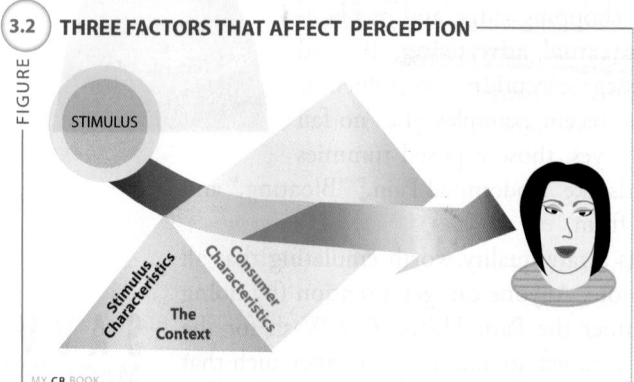

FIGURE 3.2 THREE FACTORS THAT AFFECT PERCEPTION

STIMULUS

Stimulus Characteristics

Consumer Characteristics

The Context

MY **CB** BOOK

Sensory Characteristics

A characteristic is **sensory** if it stimulates any of the five senses. Sensory characteristics influence perceptions and consumer responses in two ways: through sensory-experience and through cultural symbolism. **Sensory experience** refers to how we feel when a stimulus makes contact with our senses. We are biologically wired to find some sensory characteristics pleasant and, likewise, to find some unpleasant. Thus, we find loud, harsh sounds unpleasant and melodic sounds pleasant. We find sweet tastes pleasant and bitter tastes unpleasant. And so on. Some of these responses develop with conditioning (e.g., we may dislike Indian classical music by such artists as Ravi Shankar or country music by such artists as Garth Brooks simply because we have had no prior exposure to these styles). But eventually they all come to reside in our automated, biological sense responses.

Cultural symbolism refers to the meaning any characteristic or entity comes to have in a particular culture. Although the term applies to all entities, the focus here is on sensory characteristics of visual stimuli. All visual stimuli have three features: color, shape, and texture.[6] And each comes to acquire cultural symbolism.

Color The meaning of some colors differs across cultures; for example, black is the color of mourning in Britain, but white is the color of mourning in Japan. This meaning applies only to clothing, however, and not to cars—in both countries (and in most other countries in the world) black in cars is considered to signify affluence and gravity.

Marketers attempt to influence consumers' perceptions by packaging their products and messages in appropriate colors. Mouthwashes are colored green or blue to connote a clean, fresh feeling. One brand, Plax, makes its mouthwash red to distinguish itself from competing brands and also to create the perception that it is medicinal and therefore more effective. Consumers find blue to be the coolest color for display in electronic devices. Most cell phones have adopted this color as a popular option. And American Express introduced a blue card targeted at college students and even called it Blue Cash.

Shape Shapes, too, come to connote qualities that sometimes are culture-specific, and, with changing culture, their meanings may change for the same consumer group. This is most visible in clothing styles and in car designs. The boxy shapes of the cars of the sixties were replaced in the eighties by egg-shell bodies resembling a spaceships and connoting advanced aerodynamics; but at the beginning of the current century, the boxy look was back, with Scion and Element for the Gen Y set, and with the Mini for nostalgic boomers. In men's neckties, the fashion swings from broad to narrow. In jeans, from bell-bottoms to tapered to flared, changing shapes catch the fancy of the fashionable and trendy. In skirts, mini to midi to maxi define the wearer's identity.

Texture Textures, too, come to acquire culturally symbolic meanings. Silky textures in clothing, for example, are deemed luxurious in a gender-neutral way in Eastern cultures, but somewhat feminine in Western cultures (where rustic textures are considered masculine). The "distressed" look in clothing conveyed poverty in most cultures until recently; now, it is "engineered" at great expense in such Jeanswear brands as Seven7™, Rock & Republic, and True Religion and then celebrated by millions of young consumers as the coolest looking fabric on our planet!

Information Content

The second characteristic of a stimulus that influences perception is its information content. Information content moves the perceptual process beyond sensation or stimulus selection toward interpretation. For example, information about an automobile's engine horsepower, acceleration, and style enables one to categorize (i.e., interpret) it as a performance car or, alternatively, a family sedan.

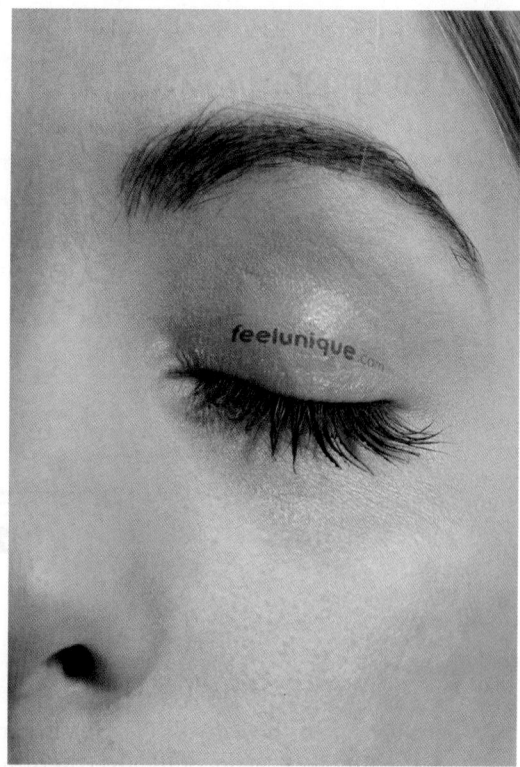

Watch me wink. Brand feelunique.com gets your attention, in a charming way.
Feelunique.com is a U.K. based online beauty boutique. Models/consumers sporting the temporary tattoo on their eyelids earned 10 pence per wink. (Creative agency: Mischief PR, U.K.)

CB FYI

EXPOSURE EVERYWHERE

In January 2012, Nick Symmonds, a 2008 Olympian, auctioned off his left shoulder space, offering to tattoo the Twitter handle of the bidder and to sport it during the 2012 London Olympic Games. The winning bid was placed by a Wisconsin-based active lifestyle marketing firm, Hanson Dodge Creative, at $11,100. Ironically, he would have to cover the temporary tattoo during the IAAF events. Not to worry: the bandage would be prominent enough to draw attention anyway, perhaps even more so!

Source: CNN TV Report, personal viewing, January 18, 2012.

Powered by
oᴹ   MY CB BOOK

Perception.

Reality.

To a new generation of Rolling Stone readers, pigs live on farms. You'll find the cops living in Beverly Hills or on Hill Street, now heralded instead of hated. If you're looking for an 18 to 34 year old market that is taking active part instead of active protest, you'll have a riot in the pages of Rolling Stone.

Rolling Stone

Marketing Practice

In the early 1980s, for instance, *Rolling Stone* magazine faced a serious perception problem: Many of its advertisers thought its readers were from the hippie generation of the Woodstock era. Starting with a campaign in 1984 with the theme *Perception versus Reality*, the management met this challenge head-on, educating potential advertisers about the changing profile of the magazine's readers and their attitudes. Note that this perception was modified by the information content in the ad (and, eventually, in the magazine).

2. THE CONTEXT AS A FACTOR

The Company the Stimulus Keeps

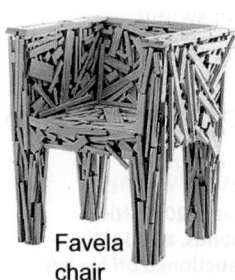

Favela chair

Context refers to the setting or surrounding in which a stimulus is situated. In interpreting a stimulus, we are always influenced by the context. Suppose that a restaurant waiter keeps a polite but impersonal demeanor. This waiter will most likely be deemed unfriendly in a low-to-mid-price, mass-market restaurant such as an Applebee's or a T.G.I. Friday's restaurant. The same demeanor in an upscale restaurant such as a Nobu or a Jean-Georges may be perceived, on the other hand, as respectful (i.e., not getting too personal).

Look at the Favela chair in the picture. What do you think of it? Is it cool? Or, alternatively, ugly? And how much do you think it costs? Write down your answers. Now, what if we were to tell you that we found it in an antique store in a rundown area amidst cheap furniture? Next, what if we were to tell you, instead, that we saw it at the home of MoMA director Glenn Lowry? Would your perceptions of the chair be different? If yes, that shows the power of the context.

Now read the actual description of the Favela chair a couple of pages later. If your perception has changed now, that, too, shows the power of the context, in this case the context being the price, the designer name, and that it is made in Italy.

3. CONSUMER CHARACTERISTICS

The Consumer Still Rules

Finally, consumers' own characteristics influence their perceptions. That is why two consumers may not perceive the same stimulus in a similar fashion. Most Americans love the game of football and find it perfectly normal, but many foreigners who watch the game for the first time are amused that players carry their "foot"-ball in their hands! An 8'x10' room in a European Hotel might look adequate to a Japanese tourist but look awfully small to an American tourist. And a dress that might look too risqué to 2012 Grammy winner jazz musician Terri Lyne Carrington might not look exciting enough to Lady Gaga. The consumer characteristics that influence perceptions include: (a) consumer needs and involvement, (b) consumers' sensory and cognitive skills, and (c) consumer familiarity and expertise. (See Figure 3.3.)

3.3 THREE CONSUMER CHARACTERISTICS THAT INFLUENCE CONSUMER PERCEPTIONS

FIGURE

NEEDS & INVOLVEMENT

SENSORY & COGNITIVE SKILLS

FAMILIARITY & EXPERTISE

CONSUMER PERCEPTION

MY **CB** BOOK

Consumer Needs and Involvement

Consumer needs give relevance to stimuli. If you are not hungry, you might ignore or not even notice a roadside restaurant. If you are not into body-piercing, then an ad for body-piercing might not even register on your senses, or if it did, you might not pay attention to it. Involvement is, as we discussed in the previous chapter, a state of mind in which a need is felt more intensely or when we are deeply interested in something on an enduring basis. Involvement, too, affects consumer perceptions. For example, if a consumer is involved in videogames, he/she will pay attention to the impending launch of Nintendo's Wii U game console (at press time, scheduled for sometime in 2012). Thus, after we have sensed a stimulus, whether or not we select it for further attention depends on our need and involvement in the topic of the stimulus.

Our needs and involvement affect not only our attention but also our interpretations. If we were very hungry, for example, then even insipid food would taste good. If we were bothered because our hair was very flat, and if a new brand of shampoo gave our hair even a little bit of body, then we would rate that shampoo highly. But if our hair had no "flatness" problem, then we might not even notice that brand's quality.

Consumers' Sensory and Cognitive Skills

As humans, we differ in the sensitivity of our senses: some of us have a more developed, keener sense of smell than others. This allows us to smell mild aromas that others cannot and to distinguish between two closely related aromas. Similarly, some of us have more sensitive faculties of hearing, vision, taste, and touch. Correspondingly, our perceptual skills differ. Some of us can perceive depth accurately; some can visualize linear distances or spatial dimensions better (e.g., "Would this table fit into our kitchen?"); and some can remember, while in a store, the exact visual image of the colors in their bedroom's wall paper design and judge, while in the store, whether a particular drapery color will match.

> As humans, we differ in the sensitivity of our senses.

Even more importantly, people differ in their **cognitive skills**—the mental abilities to hold and process information. Some of us can manipulate numbers more easily than others (e.g., "Per unit of the product, do these two brands have the same amount of fat?"); and some can hold more information in active memory while others need to write things down as they listen to a product demonstration or a food recipe. Some have a tendency to avoid technical information while others avidly seek it. These cognitive skills obviously influence how consumers interpret and encode a stimulus. A 21-year-old college student might find a textbook's prose and examples engaging, whereas a topic scholar (with highly developed cognitive skills) might dismiss it as lacking gravitas.

Consumer Familiarity and Expertise

Finally, consumer familiarity with the stimulus category or expertise on the topic influences consumer interpretation. We are able to recognize and quickly categorize something with which we are familiar. When we see a new product under a familiar brand name (i.e., a brand extension), we quickly know what it is—e.g., that Listerine mint strips are breath fresheners. Expertise goes beyond familiarity and entails some specialist knowledge. Because of this, expertise helps consumers to more accurately categorize and evaluate stimuli. Thus, wine connoisseurs are able to judge wines more accurately than can novice wine consumers, for example.

Expectations Influence Perception

Designer: Fernando and
Humberto Campana, 2002
Manufacturer: Edra, Italy
Materials: Brazilian Pinus wood
Dimensions: 29"x26.33"x24"
Price: $2,630.00
www.edra.com

Favela Chair

Familiarity produces expectations, and our expectations in turn influence our perceptions. We drink a soft drink, thinking it is Coke, our favorite brand, and we find that the drink tastes good, just as Coke should. We see a shirt with a Kenneth Cole label, and we think it is a high quality, fashionable shirt. We notice that the DVD player is made in China and we quickly conclude that it is a "cheap" import. Again and again, in everyday life, we form these perceptions and make quick judgments (sometimes false) because we *expect* things to be like that. And speaking of expectations, look again at the Favela Chair and see the power of context and how contexts shape our expectations and, in turn, our perceptions.

PERCEPTUAL BIASES

Or, Why We Don't See How Things Are

Since consumer characteristics influence consumer perceptions, these perceptions are seldom objective; rather, they are biased or distorted. Some of these distortions occur unintentionally; others occur because we actively control what we want to see or not to see. In either case, to cope with the mass of stimuli coming at us all the time, our minds employ three selective processes: selective exposure, selective attention, and selective interpretation (see Figure 3.4). These selective processes bias our perceptions.

SELECTIVE EXPOSURE

Avoiding Seeing Things

As a typical consumer, we face something like 3000 stimuli on an average day. If our minds were to attend to each one of these, we would go insane. Therefore, our minds cope with the barrage of marketing communications and products (and other information in everyday life), by becoming "selective." Consumers look at only a few advertisements, ignoring the rest of them. Want proof? Well, did you notice everyone in class today? Did you notice every billboard on your drive home today? The fact is that we choose what to expose ourselves to. In fact, we even go out of our way to seek exposure to certain things. We buy a newspaper to save the Super Bowl victory news report; we Google the pre-release reviews of forthcoming movies; we visit the mall to see new merchandise; and we play and replay YouTube videos to savor such posts as the JK Wedding Entrance Dance video (posted on July 24, 2009, watched over 73.970 million times as of March 31, 2012, 9:30 am). In these and other ways, we choose to expose ourselves selectively to market communications.

SELECTIVE ATTENTION

Avoiding Taking a Note of Things

You didn't notice all the students in your class and their T-shirts; but you did notice that one particular student with the T-shirt that said: "Procrastinate Now!" And when you were reading Bossypants and listening to CNN on your TV in the background, you let whiz past your ears the news stories about Israeli Prime Minister Benjamin Netanyahu's statement on Iran during his visit to the White House, Air Canada's strike during March Break (which was averted), and British MPs alarmed at the soaring costs of the forthcoming London Olympics (shooting past the budgeted £9.3bn); but you did pause reading the

3.4 BIASES IN THE PERCEPTUAL PROCESS

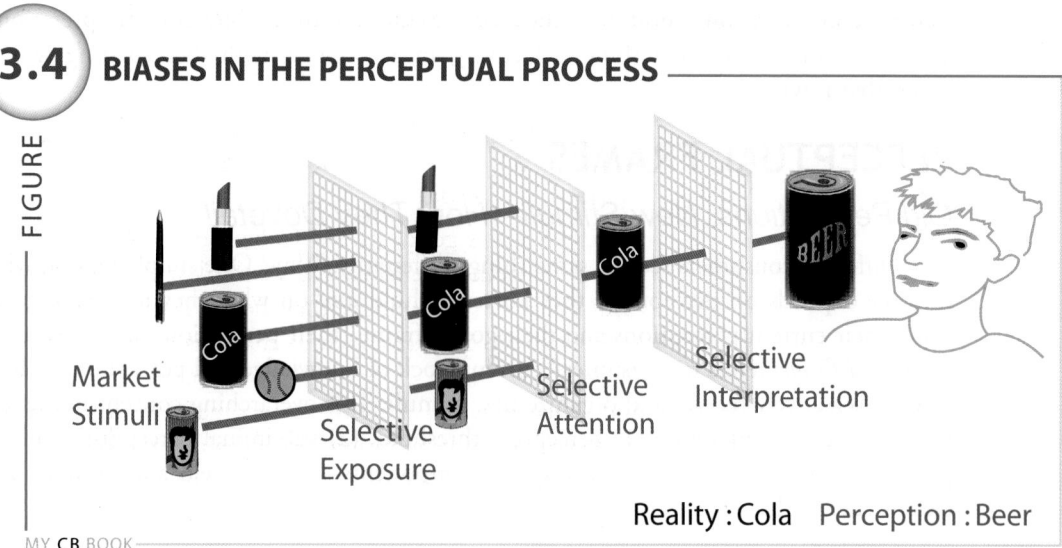

Reality : Cola   Perception : Beer

MY **CB** BOOK

book and turned fully to the TV as soon as you heard the words "Apple launches iPad-3" (on March 8, 2012). Why? Because you are interested in all new gizmos! Selective attention at work here.

SELECTIVE INTERPRETATION
Avoiding Knowing the Inconvenient Truth

Even if a marketer succeeds in getting the consumer's full attention, it still does not mean the marketer got the consumer to believe in the message. Consumers interpret the content and messages of marketing communications selectively. A call by the umpire was unfair if it penalized our favorite team; it was fair if it penalized the opposite team. This sort of selective interpretation is called *perceptual distortion*.

Perceptual distortion refers to information being encoded non-objectively. That is, the consumer sees it as different from reality. This distortion occurs because, as consumers, we see things in a manner that makes those things congruent with our prior beliefs.

Perceptions of Dan Brown's *The Da Vinci Code* are sharply divided among people with prior prejudice for or against the identity of Mary Magdalene and the Holy Grail, as a sampling of reviews on Amazon.com so vividly reveals. Same story with Dr. Seuss' classic tale The Lorax (released on March 2, 2012); check out, for example, critics' and

---

HALFTIME AT SUPER BOWL XLVI: WHOSE HALFTIME?

One commercial during Super Bowl XLVI was from American car maker Chrysler. Run at halftime and delivered by famed actor/director Clint Eastwood, the ad depicted Detroit's (car industry's) comeback. "Its halftime in America," says Eastwood, "... and our second half is about to begin!"

Yes, the game's halftime was about to begin. But in America, it was also going to be, possibly, the halftime for another event—Barack Obama's presidency. Was this a message, then, in disguise, for the Democratic Party? (After all, Detroit's auto industry was rescued by Obama's stimulus package!) Both Eastwood and Chrysler denied any such intent. But, according to the news chatter that followed, such was exactly the interpretation many viewers were making—at least the politically savvy ones.

Indeed, we interpret all stimuli the only way we can: according to our individual world-views! **Selective interpretation** at work here.

readers' comments on Rottentomatoes.com. Same stimulus, different interpretations! Why? Consumers interpret things selectively, in accordance with their existing world-views, that is why.

PERCEPTUAL FRAMES
Old Perceptions, New Stimuli—How They Dovetail

Different consumers see the same things differently. Why? One simple reason: what they see depends on perceptions they currently hold *and* on what they are looking for. Thus, their current perceptions and their goals "frame" their perceptions of new stimuli. *Perceptual frames* refers to consumers' current stock of knowledge and perceptions, which serve to selectively receive and organize new stimuli. This overarching concept influences three perception outcomes: (1) perceptual threshold, (2) subliminal perception, and (3) perceptual organization, with its three subcomponents—gestalt, field and ground, and closure. Let us discuss each.

1. PERCEPTUAL THRESHOLD
Or, How Can We Show up on the Consumer's Radar

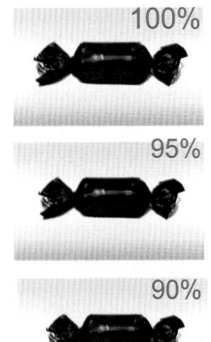

100%

95%

90%

Some stimuli are not registered by our senses because they fall below our **perceptual threshold** (sometimes also called **differential threshold**)—the minimum level or magnitude at which a stimulus begins to draw involuntary attention, begins to be sensed. A related concept is the **just noticeable difference (j.n.d.)**. This refers to the magnitude of change necessary for a change to be noticed. Marketers use this principle to reduce product quantity or size marginally in order to keep the prices constant in the wake of rising costs. Some years ago, a famous candy maker successfully reduced the size of its candy bars by keeping the size change small.

The magnitude of change needed for it to be noticed depends on the base quantity. The larger the base quantity, the larger the magnitude of change needed for the change to be noticed. This is known as **Weber's Law**, named after the German scientist Ernst Weber.[7] For example, a one-half inch reduction in the size of a five-inch candy bar will perhaps not be noticed, but the same reduction in a two-inch long stick of chewing gum is likely to be noticed.

Sometimes, marketers must draw consumer attention to certain features for consumers to notice them. The Canadian beer brand Molson, in an ad in early 2006, pioneered this concept—it portrayed its beer as a fragrance! The copy read:

> **"Embrace the fragrance of Molson. Saskatchewen barley, pure Canadian water, aromatic hops. The scent that brings people together. In bars since 1776."**

Now, when you consume your beer, at least if it is Molson beer, you won't only be drinking it but you will be partaking of its aroma as well!

No matter how vivid a stimulus, after a while our senses get used to it and we stop perceiving it. What makes a stimulus rise above the perceptual threshold is *change*. Savvy marketers can put this principle to good use and bring consumers enhanced consumption experiences. Case in point: Febreze® NOTICEables™ by Proctor & Gamble. The wall-plug-in air fresheners come in twin fragrance pouches that switch every 45 minutes. When the fragrances alternate, you are sure to notice them and enjoy the fragrant air in the room. You can have the choice of Calypso Breeze & Hawaiian Paradise™, Morning Walk & Cleansing Rain™, Pink Magnolia & Jasmine Breeze™, Vanilla Refresh & Vanilla Bean,™ and Clothesline Breeze & Meadow Songs™. (Learn more at www.febreze.com).

SAVVY MARKETER

Some stimuli fail to achieve registration on consumers' senses, but failing to achieve attention can sometimes be a good thing. Actually, some stimuli are deliberately kept "sneaky" so that, it is hoped, they fail to attract attention. It is like flying a fighter plane below an enemy's radar sensors. That brand of candy bar reducing its size just a tad is a case in point. In such situations, escaping notice is a good thing for marketers.

And it is also the basis of one of marketing's oldest folktales—*subliminal perception*.

2. SUBLIMINAL PERCEPTION

The Folklore of Sneaky Marketing

Perhaps no other story has been told in marketing more often than this one. In the 1950s, marketing researcher James Vicary conducted a test. In a theater, on the movie screen, the words "Drink Coca Cola" and "Eat popcorn" were flashed for 1/3000 second (below the perceptual threshold level) at five-second intervals. The sales of Coca Cola and popcorn reportedly increased during the test period.[8]

As a result of stories like this, people at large sometimes suspect marketers and advertisers of being mysterious con artists, trying to manipulate their minds without their knowledge. And since then, consumer advocacy groups and consumer activists have been trying to find hidden symbols in product package designs or in pictures in advertising. This quest for hidden images in commercial communications, however, has turned up no concrete evidence that such tricks exist or that they work. Marketing researchers who have tried to repeat the Vicary experiment have not been able to replicate his findings. And, indeed, in a 1962 interview with *Advertising Age*, Vicary himself confessed to having fabricated the whole thing.

A gift for you!:
Now you see it.
Now you don't.

On trial here is a phenomenon called **subliminal perception**—the perception of a stimulus without our being aware of it. **Subliminal stimuli** are defined as stimuli of which one is not conscious. Thus, the stimulus registers on our senses but without our being aware of the registration. For example, if music is playing in a store where we are busy finding what we want, we might not become conscious of it even though it might put us in a happy mood. Thus, without focusing our attention on it, we have perceived it below the threshold of awareness. This is subliminal perception.

Psychologists have done several experiments to test whether subliminal stimuli work. Typically, the subliminal stimulus is masked by or submerged in a more vivid stimulus on which people are focusing attention. Let us describe one such experiment.[9] A psychology researcher told a group of subjects (that is, people who participate in psychological experiments) that their task was to solve some problems on the computer. Each of them sat at a PC and went through the tasks presented on the computer screen, such as solving puzzles or building figures. While the steps to these tasks were being presented, some pictures of faces would briefly appear in a corner, where they would not interfere with the main task; they would flash so briefly that they would be below the threshold level of being seen by the human eye. The pictures flashed for half of the subjects were of pleasant faces; the other half were of unpleasant faces.

Sometimes, mere exposure can create a liking.

After some time, a message suddenly appeared: "F 11 Error: failure saving data. You must begin again from the beginning." Secretly, a camera recorded the facial reaction of all subjects. The finding? The subjects whose screens had flashed unpleasant faces were angrier than the other group of subjects!

While psychologists still debate if subliminal perception is real, experiments like this one show that it is possible for humans not to be aware of something but to be influenced by it anyway. What then is to be believed about subliminal perception?[10] Here is our summary of this issue:

1. **First, research has demonstrated that mere exposure to stimuli can create a liking for those stimuli and that this can happen even without consumers being aware of having seen the stimuli before. This is called *mere exposure effect*.[11]**

2. **Second, certain stimuli create an instant and automated response in humans. For example, if a commercial contains a soft melody, we might like the advertised brand a little bit more without even being aware of the melody. Making a package more pleasant to look at can have a similar subliminal effect.**

3. Whether consumers perceive a stimulus subliminally or consciously, it pays to make all elements of marketing stimuli pleasant. It is not necessary for marketers to cunningly embed unwholesome images in advertisements. Pleasant presentations of all elements of product offerings are all that are needed to create favorable impressions whether or not the phenomenon of subliminal perception actually existed.

3. PERCEPTUAL ORGANIZATION

Bringing Order to the Chaos of Life

Not only is our world full of stimuli but each stimulus also generates a multitude of sensations. If our minds took note of all these sensations, we would continuously experience a state of chaos. And our minds would be perennially overloaded with the work of "seeing" the stimuli. To cope with such an enormous task and to bring order to its sensing of stimuli, the mind quickly "organizes" the sensations in some sensible order. Three principles guide how consumers accomplish this perceptual organization: gestalt, figure and ground, and closure.

Gestalt   Look at the zebras in the picture. Done? Ok, now, without looking at it again, answer these questions: How many stripes does the standing zebra have? And which of its front legs is positioned forward of the other—the left or the right? Are the stripes on the side of its belly slanted upward from left to right, or from right to left? And is the seated zebra's head pointed toward or away from the standing zebra? You didn't notice? But you saw the picture and recognized it as a zebra, right? All of us register and encode stimuli this way—as an overall configuration, without sensing the details. This is called *gestalt*

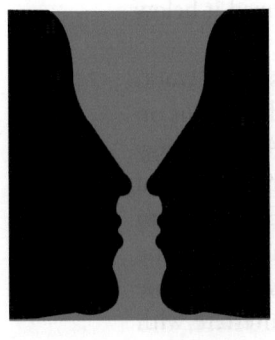

perception, derived from the German word **gestalt,** which means a general, overall image formed in the mind. Humans (and therefore consumers) seldom attend to all the details of a stimulus. Rather they form an overall impression based on a pattern within the stimulus (for a zebra, this pattern is a horse-like animal with stripes). It is efficient for consumers to do it this way.[12]

Marketers need to take note: sometimes consumers are paying only fleeting attention, so they form an overall impression of the brand based on some surface features or on the overall image in an ad. But even when they pay attention, consumers don't notice each feature, and often what they notice and retain in memory is merely an overall impression of the advertised product, i.e., a gestalt.

Figure and Ground   Now look at the Zebra picture again. Is it really a picture about zebras? Or is it about the outdoor terrain and vegetation in spring? That depends on how you stumbled onto this picture. Were you searching for pictures of animals? Or, alternatively, were you searching for pictures of seasons or landscapes? This is the concept of figure and ground: In any visual, something is the background (ground), and something is the focal object (figure).

Look at the picture of a vase. Is it really a vase, or is it, instead, a picture of two human faces? That depends on what you see as ground and what you see as figure. As an advertiser, you will want to make sure that your product and your message remains the figure rather than becoming the ground. Your message risks becoming part of the ground if you make the ad so humorous, for example, that people remember the joke or the humor but not your product story or even its brand name.

Courtesy: whozoo.org

Closure The closure principle suggests that consumers have a natural tendency to complete a partial stimulus, supplying the missing information from memory (assuming of course that they are already familiar with the complete stimulus).[13] If you hear the tune of a song, you automatically begin to hum it; if you read or hear a partial sentence of a familiar jingle, you fill in the rest. Partial information bothers us like an unsolved puzzle, and we make the effort to find the missing information and achieve closure. Utilizing this principle, if marketers omit a letter or two from a familiar brand name or jingle, then consumers will fill in the blank. In this way, consumers actively participate (rather than seeing the information passively), and this active participation makes the brand name or tagline more memorable. Not too long ago, an ad by a famous brand of Scotch whiskey did just that in its Christmas Holiday advertising. It wrote the headline phrase as _ingle _ells. Can you fill in the blanks to achieve closure (and notice the curious discomfort until you do)?

Actually, consumers need not be familiar with the brand name or slogan; they need only to be familiar with the words used. If you are preparing a poster, for example, for your campus club, say, the Young Entrepreneur's Club, try to leave out a letter here and there (for example: You g E trepne r's Cl b). The chances are that more viewers will register the poster and your club's name in their minds than if you had spelled it out. That is because achieving closure on an unfinished stimulus is an inherent human need.

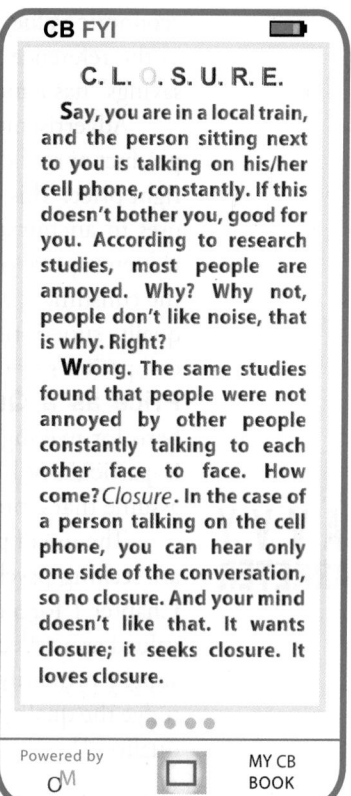

CB FYI

C. L. O. S. U. R. E.

Say, you are in a local train, and the person sitting next to you is talking on his/her cell phone, constantly. If this doesn't bother you, good for you. According to research studies, most people are annoyed. Why? Why not, people don't like noise, that is why. Right?

Wrong. The same studies found that people were not annoyed by other people constantly talking to each other face to face. How come? *Closure*. In the case of a person talking on the cell phone, you can hear only one side of the conversation, so no closure. And your mind doesn't like that. It wants closure; it seeks closure. It loves closure.

Powered by
oM

MY CB BOOK

MARKETING APPLICATIONS OF PERCEPTION PROCESSES

Marking out a section on "Marketing Applications" is akin to writing a whole chapter on the environment of fish and then marking out a section called "Water." The marketing applications of the perception process have been described throughout the chapter, enmeshed inseparably with the very description of these processes. What we do need to do here, however, is to present some special areas of application—entire topic areas that have developed in marketing simply as outgrowths of systematic research and practice development by marketers and consumer researchers, anchored in the concepts of perception. These are as follows:

1. **The psychology of consumer price perceptions**
2. **Country-of-origin effects**
3. **Brand image and brand extensions**
4. **Consumer perceptual maps and positioning**
5. **Sensory marketing**

PSYCHOLOGY OF PRICE PERCEPTION

$9.99 is Good, $10.01 is Too Much!

APPLICATION
#1

The psychology of price perception refers to the way in which consumers psychologically perceive prices. Noteworthy aspects of this phenomenon are reference price and price as a quality cue.

Reference Price A consumer who accidentally walks into a store and discovers a "20 percent-off" sale may be delighted, but if the same consumer came in after viewing an advertisement hyping a huge sale, he or she is likely to feel disappointed or even anguished. Why? The concept of reference price explains it. **Reference price** is the price consumers expect to pay.[14] If the actual price is lower than the reference price, it is perceived as a good economic value. The consumer who accidentally walks into the store has the full price as the reference price; in contrast, the consumer who has seen advertisements of "huge savings" has a much lower reference price and is therefore disappointed.

Advertisement or no advertisement, we all have some reference price in mind for a product or service; this is termed the **internal reference price**, the price we believe to be the right price. This differs from the **external reference price**, which is the price the marketer uses to anchor a price advantage (e.g., "compare at___"). Often, a consumer's internal reference price comes from knowing the competitors' prices. When a price is higher than the consumer's reference price, the marketer may have to "educate" the consumer on the quality superiority that makes the price a good value. One recent advertisement read: "Our competitor's price is lower. That is because it should be!"

Price as a Quality Cue Consumers often use price as a quality cue—that is, as a basis for making inferences about the quality of the product or service. Such use of price is particularly likely where quality cannot be independently judged. Consumers often assume that a product with a higher price is superior in quality to one with a lower price.

SAVVY MARKETER

The use of price as a quality cue can occur for products and services when consumers are seeking psychosocial satisfaction, that is, nonfunctional or non-utilitarian values (see Chapter 1 for a description of these values). For example, for pens, a higher price may be valued as a reflection of exclusivity and status. It also may occur for products and services sought primarily for their functional or utilitarian value, especially if consumers cannot judge the quality independently (e.g., judging a higher priced pen to be superior in writing quality).[15]

COUNTRY-OF-ORIGIN EFFECTS

High Fashion Suits from Timbaktoo?

APPLICATION #2

Would you buy a DVD player from Pakistan or Iran? High-fashion suits from Russia, Nigeria, or Timbaktoo? A fine wine made in Mauritius or China? Most probably, your answers are "no." What about a DVD player from Japan, a fashion suit from Italy, or a fine wine from France? Perhaps, your answers to these questions are "yes." If so, your answers may be driven by "country-of-origin" image.[16]

Country-of-origin effects refer to the bias in consumer perceptions of products and services due to the country in which these products and services are made (or are claimed to be made). Overcoming this bias requires well-conceived informational and educational campaigns, and tenacious attention to product quality. In 2005, Lenovo, a Chinese computer company, acquired IBM's ThinkPad and personal computer business, and by pursuing product innovation, established an image for itself, unaffected by the historical image of China for electronic products. (The Thinkpad was actually already manufactured for IBM by Lenovo, so actual quality was never in question; the challenge was simply to manage public perception of a China-made computer.)

While a country with a poor overall image suffers from this bias, a country with a good image benefits from it. A British marketer of electronic products, in fact, exploits the positive image of another country. It assembles its products all over the world, but not in Japan; yet it markets them under the brand name Matsui to imply (misleadingly) a Japanese origin.

BRAND IMAGE AND BRAND EXTENSIONS

Listerine Lipstick? You Must Be Kidding!

APPLICATION #3

Brand names influence the perception of products. For new products, brand names act as contexts. They are like pedigrees. Adidas started as a shoe company; now it also sells apparel. Good for Adidas—as the company's good name is going to bring good consumer perceptions to its apparel. But if you are a marketer, be careful before you rush to stick your famous brand name on anything. Brand names come to be known, you see, for certain product categories, and brand extensions must remain within the bounds of that category.

Listerine is perceived to be in an oral hygiene product. If the company (most known for mouthwashes) brought out a product extension into, say toothpaste, that would be easily assimilated and accepted by consumers. But if the company wanted to start marketing, say, sunglasses under the brand name Listerine, that would create an anomaly in consumer perceptions of the brand. Consumers would not be able to "organize" this new stimulus, and it would unsettle the brand image even for the company's oral hygiene products.

How Brand Names Affect Consumer Perceptions

Brand names clearly affect consumer perceptions of products. In one recent study in the UK, 800 consumers were surveyed about what they thought of the pair of jeans depicted in an advertisement they were shown. The ads (in print) were both for the

FIGURE **3.5** **PERCEPTIONS OF BRANDED AND UNBRANDED JEANS**

Attribute	Unbranded	Branded
Expensive	3.9	5.3
Well-known	3.4	6.4
High Quality	4.1	5.5
Original	3.5	4.7
Classy	4.3	5.4
Stylish	4.1	5.2
Makes a Statement	3.2	4.3

Legend: Unbranded Jeans / Branded Jeans

Adapted from: Susan Auty and Richard Elliot, "Social Identity & the Meaning of Fashion Brands," European Advances in Consumer Research 3, p. 1-10, 1998. Used with permission of the Association for Consumer Research.

MY CB BOOK

Levi's brand of jeans, but two versions were created: one showing the brand name on the product and the other without the brand name. In all other aspects, the two versions of the ad were identical. Half the consumers were shown one version and the other half the other version. Each group was asked to rate the pair of jeans on a number of adjective pairs (e.g., stylish/not stylish, expensive/inexpensive). The finding was unmistakable: On an average, consumers who saw the branded jeans ad rated the jeans higher than did the consumers who saw the unbranded jeans version. Even more important, they rated it higher not simply in overall terms but also on most of the attributes. See Figure 3.5. This amply illustrates what consumer psychologists have known all along; namely, that brand names, and the image and reputation those brand names have built, bias consumers' product perceptions.

PERCEPTUAL MAPS AND POSITIONING

APPLICATION **#4**

How Marketers Play the Photographer

Which pizza is tastier, Tombstone or DiGiorno®? Which is healthier? And which is the best value for the money? The answers are all a matter of perceptions—how you perceive these pizza brands. And these perceptions are in your mind. There is a map, if you will, in your mind of all these brands of pizza. And likewise, for other products. What marketers do is capture your mental map on paper, playing *the photographer of the mind*, so to speak. These maps on paper are called *perceptual maps*. **Perceptual maps** are visual depictions of consumer perceptions of alternative brands in a product category, in multi-dimensional grids. Dimensions are attributes of the product category—in the pizza example, these are taste, healthiness, price value, etc. Thus, the number of dimensions can be as many as the number of attributes. On paper, we can at best draw three-dimensional pictures, but for convenience we usually draw these maps in two dimensions at a time (along an X axis and a Y axis), covering all attributes with two attributes at a time. As an in-class exercise, two student groups drew their maps as shown in the figure. Notice how the perceptions of the two groups differ. Note that consumers may never have even tried some of these pizzas— their perceptions are merely impressions. As we know, not all perceptions are based on experience. Indeed, consumers never even try some products because of their unfavorable preconceptions about them. Also note that since the two consumers' perceptions are different, surely both of them cannot be correct, and therefore at least one of them differs from objective reality. It confirms one of our axioms: When it comes to how we see the world, there is no objective reality, only perception. And perceptions, not reality, are what matter. That is why marketers need to study such perceptual maps.

Four Uses of Perceptual Maps

SAVVY MARKETER

1. **Know who your competitors are** Your competitor is not the company whose brand has the highest market share, nor the company with the brand share closest to yours (in either direction). Rather, your competitor is the company closest to your brand in the consumer's perceptual space; i.e., on the perceptual maps your consumers draw for you. Thus, perceptual maps enable you to see the marketplace and various competitors in it from your customer's point-of-view.
2. **Know who your potential new target customers should be** Your potential target market should be the consumers of brands plotted closest to your brand on the map. They are the ones who are likely to have considered your brand and found it acceptable. If in a survey of consumers, along with the perceptual maps, you also elicit demographic and media information, then you can target this group of consumers.
3. **Modify the product** Consumers perceive your product as lacking certain features or qualities. This tells you what features you need to improve in your products so that you may advance your brand on the perceptual map.
4. **Correct the misperceptions** Finally, consider the case of the consumers who have judged your product to be inferior to the products of certain competitors, but who view your product as on par with (if not superior to) these competitors' products when the product is tested and/or analyzed objectively. Obviously, consumers have come to hold misperceptions about your brand. You need to correct these perceptions by communicating the true attributes of your product and by encouraging sampling of your product by these consumers.

Positioning and Repositioning

SAVVY MARKETER

The spot your brand occupies in the consumer's mental map is known as its *positioning*. More formally, **positioning** is defined as a consumer's perception of a brand relative to that of other brands and relative to consumers' goals relevant to the product category. Positioning encompasses the salient features consumers associate with the brand and the images the brand name evokes in consumers' minds. The images can relate to the product's benefits, the situations for which the brand is suited, the characteristics of people who consumers believe would typically use the brand, the emotive and symbolic experiences evoked by the brand, or the product's relationship with any other facets of consumers' lives.

If you don't like the positioning of your brand, you would want to change consumer perceptions about it. The practice of changing consumer perceptions about a brand is called **repositioning**. As a marketer, you can position and reposition your brand in one or more of the following ways.

By Functional Benefits When you think of Volvo, what comes to mind? Safety. Thus, Volvo is positioned as a safe car; Honda as a reliable car; Cadillac as a luxury car; and BMW as a performance car.

By Symbolic Image Some brands position themselves by an intangible attribute that goes beyond a product's utilitarian benefits. Notice how the Movado brand positions itself as an "artistic" watch whereas Tag Heuer positions itself as an endurance watch. (Google these brands if you have not already seen their print ads.)

By User Image Brands can also be positioned by a distinct personality. For example, Quicksilver projects a casual, playful image; in contrast, Just Cavalli embodies an ultra-glam, pulp-fiction-esque image. (You can find ads for these brands by Googling.)

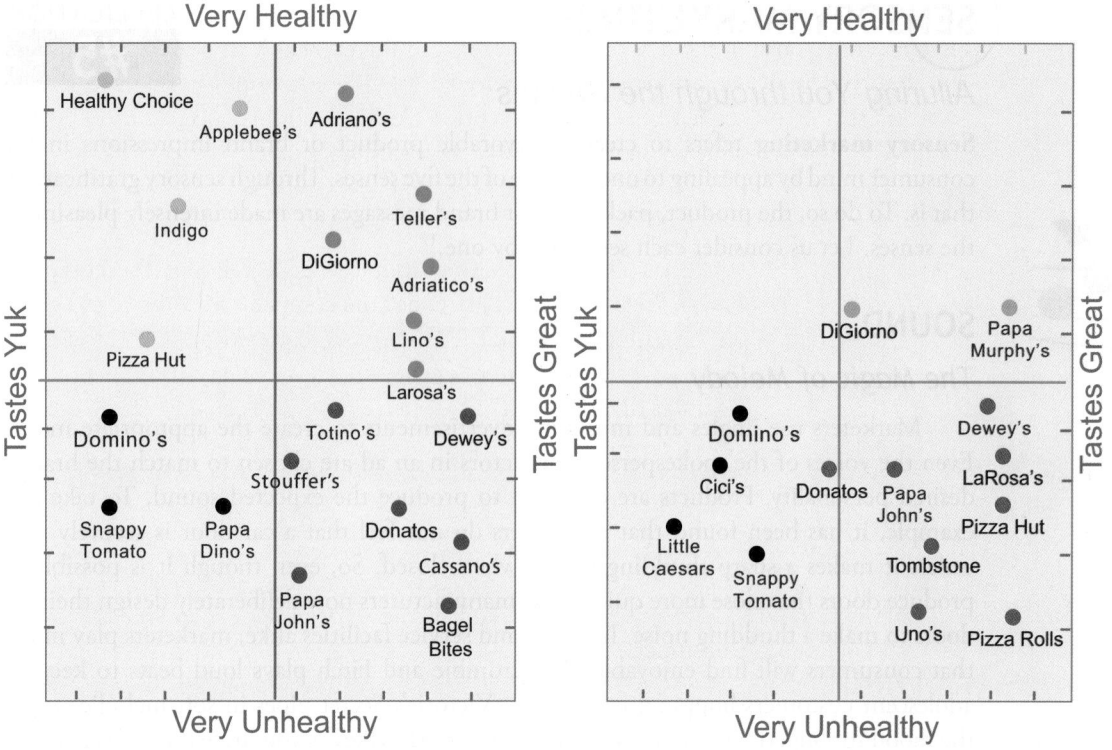

By Usage Situation When a beer advertises itself as "the one beer to have when you are having more than one," it is positioning itself according to a consumption situation.

By Competition Sometimes, brands position themselves by competitive advantage. A classic positioning battle was fought between Hertz and Avis—Hertz had been touting its "largest car fleet, and number 1" position. In response, Avis countered with the "Avis is only Number 2, so we try harder" campaign.

By Values A brand can also position itself according to the larger societal values it stands for. If you know anything about The Body Shop, then you know what stands out the most about it in the consumer mind: no animal testing. Likewise, Ben and Jerry's is positioned as an environmentally friendly company.

By Category Yet another way to position a brand is by carving out a new category. A classic example is Dial soap, which, in a campaign several years ago, wrapped itself in a prescription Rx label, thus positioning itself as a germ killer rather than merely as a cleanser. And, of course, you remember (perhaps from your "principles of marketing" text) that 7 Up staked out a new category: an Uncola drink.

Repositioning

Any of the above approaches can also be used for repositioning a brand. Sometimes, the goal of repositioning a product is to move consumers' attitudes toward it to a *different* position. Exemplifying this is an old campaign from Certs (which showed a bunch of cherries and proclaimed that the product contained less sugar than all those cherries). At other times, the goal of repositioning is to broaden the product's current position. An example is Izod's color campaign; Izod did not abandon its 20-something athletic casual clothing appeal; instead, the company just broadened the product's positioning to include a color extravaganza.

cookies

Well, oranges are round.

And moist.

And certainly sweet.

Okay, maybe you can't call one a cookie,

but don't let an orange hear you say

that it isn't a snack.

Better snacking.

Sunkist

sunkist.com

"Well, oranges are round and moist. ..."
Positioning against (and above) cookies

SENSORY MARKETING

Alluring You through the Senses

Sensory marketing refers to creating favorable product or brand impressions in the consumer mind by appealing to one or more of the five senses. Through sensory gratification, that is. To do so, the product, packaging, or brand messages are made intensely pleasing to the senses. Let us consider each sense one by one.[17]

SOUND

The Magic of Melody

Marketers use jingles and music in advertisements to create the appropriate mood. Even the voices of the spokesperson and actors in an ad are chosen to match the brand's desired personality. Products are designed to produce the expected sound. To take one example, it has been found that consumers do not feel that a car door is securely shut unless it makes a sharp thudding sound when closed. So, even though it is possible to produce doors that close more quietly, car manufacturers now deliberately design their car doors to make a thudding noise. In stores and service facilities alike, marketers play music that consumers will find enjoyable. Abercrombie and Fitch plays loud beats to keep its adolescent customers hopping; in contrast, Victoria's Secret pipes in soft melodies to set the mood for lingerie shopping. The sounds your car makes as you drive through changing surrounds—from city streets to highways to tunnels, and from wind to rain to snow—have you ever taken the time to enjoy them? Honda "celebrates" them in a 2-minute TV commercial that has a full orchestra play a medley of those sounds, introduced by the only spoken words in the commercial, "This is what a Honda feels like"! YouTube it and enjoy this outstanding example of sensory marketing.

TASTE

Thank Your Taste Buds for It

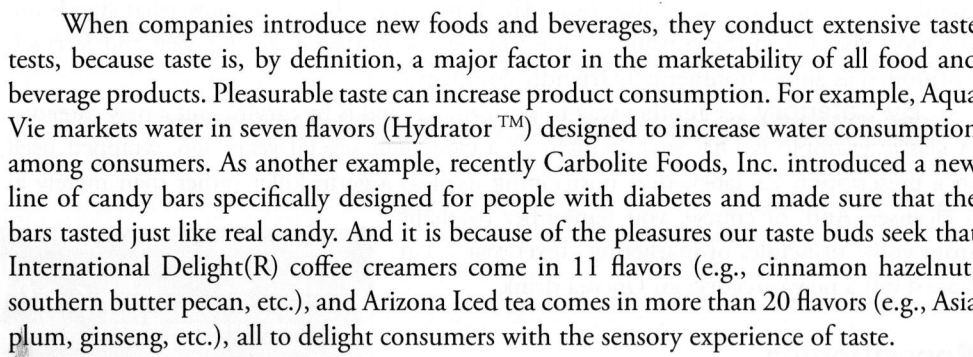

When companies introduce new foods and beverages, they conduct extensive taste tests, because taste is, by definition, a major factor in the marketability of all food and beverage products. Pleasurable taste can increase product consumption. For example, Aqua Vie markets water in seven flavors (Hydrator ™) designed to increase water consumption among consumers. As another example, recently Carbolite Foods, Inc. introduced a new line of candy bars specifically designed for people with diabetes and made sure that the bars tasted just like real candy. And it is because of the pleasures our taste buds seek that International Delight(R) coffee creamers come in 11 flavors (e.g., cinnamon hazelnut, southern butter pecan, etc.), and Arizona Iced tea comes in more than 20 flavors (e.g., Asia plum, ginseng, etc.), all to delight consumers with the sensory experience of taste.

THE SENSE OF SMELL

Oh, the Spell of that Hypnotic Fragrance

Who among us, while strolling through the mall, has not been tempted to buy a Cinnabon, or Aunt Annie's pretzel, or a cup of Starbucks cup of Caffe O'Lait? Smell plays a big role in attracting consumers to stores and products. At the very least, stores should have pleasing aromas.[18] A Phoenix-based company, Digital Tech Frontier, is now marketing a machine called Visual Scentsations. The machine electronically blends and emits aromas that don't stick to clothing or hair. Suppose a store sells bakery products but does not bake on the premises. Using the machine, it can create an authentic baking aroma. The machine can control how far the smell goes and when and where it is released. The company is also selling the machine to airports, public theaters, hospitals, theme parks, and hotels. Who knows, next time you go to a Rainforest restaurant, you might even enjoy the aroma of a rainforest!

THE SENSE OF TOUCH

Touch Me, Touch Me Not

We all know the feeling: we are in a store, we read a sign that says "please do not touch," and we feel as if someone has clipped our wings. We feel that we have been denied one of our basic pleasures while shopping—tactile sensation. Tactile sensation is a significant consumption experience for a number of products. The texture of clothes, bed sheets, and towels; the temperature of food and beverages (which affects not only taste but also touch sensation); the consistency of skin ointments (moisturizing creams, after shave lotions, bath oils, etc.)—these and many other product qualities bring consumers pleasure because they evoke tactile sensation.

Touch is so important to our experience of most of these products that, when not allowed to touch, as consumers we feel almost disabled—rendered helpless in judging and evaluating them. Fortunately, though, tactile surfaces have a rough visual code; that is, through a history of personal experiences of touching and viewing the same surface simultaneously, we learn to recognize the tactile feel of a material by its appearance. That is why we are sometimes content merely to look at the material or look at the picture of the product and evaluate its tactile properties. But often, there is nothing like the real thing and the opportunity to touch it. Recent research has found that the mere act of touching a pleasant product makes consumers want it more (the effect is opposite for inherently unpleasant products)![19]

This tactile sensory experience (along with the visual treat) is what makes shopping pleasurable. That is why retail stores display products in places where consumers can touch and feel them. And that is why many e-tailers who started out purely with Internet presences are now opening showcase brick and mortar stores. For example, bluemercury. com, a marketer of makeup, skincare, and spa products, started out as an "Internet only" company; but starting with five physical locations in 2006 (Georgetown and Dupont Circle in Washington D.C., Philadelphia, Ardmore, Pennsylvania; and Princeton, New

Romancing the Consumer

AN UNFORGETTABLE SENSORY CONSUMPTION EXPERIENCE!

There is a restaurant in Beverly Hills, California that really "stinks." Its name:

The Stinking Rose: A Garlic Restaurant.

You see garlic the moment you enter the narrow doorway. Rows of bottles of garlic pickles and sauces, garlic-shaped artifacts for décor, and a miniature garlic factory that is fun to watch.

One of its dining areas is named the Michaelangelo Room, and is remarkable for its 8' by 65' canvas mural with the Sistine Chapel painted on it, with one change—God hands Adam a garlic bulb!

But you go there not as much for the visual atmosphere as for food; or rather, for the garlic in it. It serves Californian-Italian cuisine generously seasoned with garlic: Garlic-Steamed Clams, Roasted Garlic Potato Onion Soup, Garlic Spinach Fontina Fondue, Forty Clove Garlic Chicken, and the like. And yes, there is garlic ice cream: Gilroy Famous Garlic Ice Cream with Caramel Molé Sauce! And the martini comes not with an olive but with a garlic clove in it. Its slogan promises: "We season our garlic with food."®

For vampires, they do serve some garlic-free dishes. (Vampires are, you might have heard, repelled by garlic.) But for the rest of us, it's garlic feast for our eyes, tongues, and noses. And for our skins. For hours after you eat there, your skin will smell of garlic. Perhaps you should take your friends along for an evening of garlic feasting.

Garlic is, incidentally, good for your body and for your heart. But more than anything else, eating at The Stinking Rose is an unforgettable sensory consumption experience!

Powered by · MY BOOK

Jersey, by February 2012, it had expanded to 38 locations. (Curious about whether your town has one? Well, Google it.)

SIGHT

The Eyes Never Had It So Good!

Finally, there is the sensory experience of sight. This experience works on two levels: visual identity and experiential pleasure. (Actually, all five senses can and do receive stimuli both as identity and as sensory pleasure, but it is easier to illustrate this dual experience for the sense of sight.)

Visual Identity When we think of any object, brand, product, etc., we visualize it. If we can see it, in our mind's eye, as distinct from other objects, brands, or products, then its visual identity has made an impression on us. Forming this impression means both that we are able to tell it apart from other similar things and that we have certain impressions about it. Brands do it by using brand logos, brand marks, or brand symbols. Thus, most consumers recognize McDonald's by its golden arches, Delta airlines by its the stylized Greek letter delta, and Target by the red bull's eye.

From a shield to a vibrant sunburst (named Helios, after the sungod of ancient Greece).

Companies sometimes change their logos to keep the brand or company's image contemporary. In 2003, petroleum company BP Amoco changed its brand mark from a shield to a multi-layered sunflower. Note that the company still kept the core colors (green ground with yellow figure), but changed the icon. The old shield stood for protection and stability, but that image was not considered relevant anymore. The new figure looks more contemporary, so it certainly creates the perception of a modern company. But beyond that, the company intended the interlocking pattern of sunflower petals (technically called Helio's mark) to symbolize the sun, energy, and BP's commitment to environmental leadership.

Visual identity also comes from all other visual aspects of the brand, such as the color and design on the package (e.g., Arizona Iced Tea), or colors of vehicles and employee uniforms in a service company (e.g., UPS's brown).

Experiential pleasure Beyond the identity, the visual stimuli related to a brand also offer a pleasurable sensory experience (just as stimuli do through other senses). The packaging of Arizona Iced Tea is a treat for the eye (both in the physical brand and in its presence on the company's Web site. And the visual cacophony of colors, shapes, and textures in stores and on merchandise beckon millions of consumers to malls and stores, whether or not they intend to buy anything. Some brands have showcase stores like Niketown and Apple to provide unusual sensory experiences. Some stores even commission renowned architects to design stores and merchandise displays that offer truly unique sensory experiences. Ed Tsuwaki, a well-known Japanese graphic designer, designed unusual swan-necked mannequins that now display clothing in *nakEd bunch* stores in Tokyo. And fashion retailer

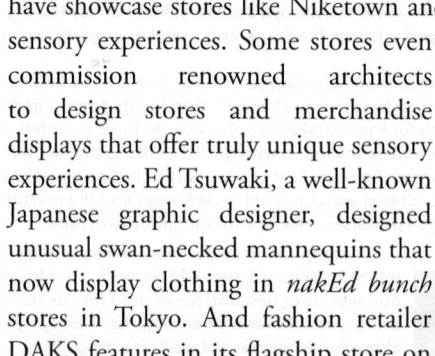

Attractive cans of Arizona Iced Tea

DAKS features in its flagship store on Old Bond Street in London a dramatic sculpture group designed by renowned Swedish artist Lars Nilsson.

No account of sensory marketing would be complete without the mention of a company that has turned it into an art form—Apple Computers. In 1998, the company introduced iMacs—housed in an egg-shaped translucent shell and five fruit colors that instantly changed the product category from pure hardware into designer decor eye candy! Then in 1998, the company introduced the iPod, a portable media player that instantly made it fashionable to walk around with white ear buds. iPod's main consumer utility is music (pleasure for our ears), but it's lure resided in its appeal to two of our other senses: lovely to look at and inviting to the touch, with our fingers addictively spinning the click-wheel!

Such is the power of sensory marketing!

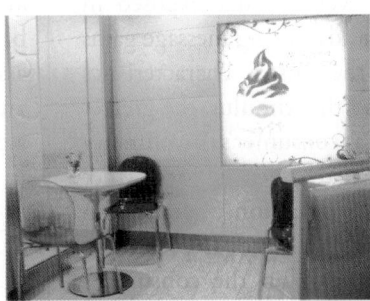

Yagööt, a Cincinnati-based eatery, dishes out delicious, innovative concoctions built around its brand of yogurt. But it is its decor that irresistibly lures the eyes.

Delight to the palate. Enchantment to the eye.

CB Blog

3

⌐ TRUISMS ABOUT CONSUMER PERCEPTIONS

This we have said before, but it bears repeating. More than the product's reality, consumer perceptions of it matter. Making your product with desirable qualities is good, even a necessity, but it is not enough. Beyond that, you have to get the consumer to perceive it correctly. And appreciate it. If consumer perceptions fall short of the product's reality, don't blame consumers for it. It is how our minds function. With efficient stimulus coding as our goal, our minds form a perception that sits well with our prior expectations—with our map of the world, so to speak. If we believe, as marketers, that consumer perceptions are currently distorted, then we have the onus, and some "power of product reality" on our side, to mold those perceptions. Savvy marketers have shouldered this responsibility with understanding and grace.

And they have grasped as well the following truisms about human perception:
- There are no facts in life, only statements of facts.
- There is no objective reality, only perceptions.
- Sometimes perceptions come close to reality, sometimes they are far off.
- All our perceptions are true; others' perceptions may be false.
- Perceptions, not reality, form the basis of our actions.
- Consumer perceptions, not reality, determine the fates of brands.

P o n d e r that!

CONSUMER BEHAVIOR

SUMMARY

In this chapter, we described consumer perception as a three-step process—exposure, attention, and interpretation. In this perceptual process, we identified the influence of the characteristics of the stimulus or incoming information, the influence of the context, and the role of the consumers' own characteristics. We described how marketers attempt to gain exposure by carefully targeting media audiences and lately through product placement in media events. Once exposed in the right media, the product or advertising message gains consumer attention based on the sensory characteristics of the stimulus—the more vivid the stimulus, the greater the likelihood of it gaining a consumer's involuntary attention. Consumers subsequently select it for further attention—termed *voluntary* attention, depending on the interest or involvement in the topic presented. And finally, interpretation depends on the consumer's prior expectations and the context of the stimulus. For a product, everything serves as context—brand name, package design, price, and the store in which the product is carried. Marketers, therefore, need to fashion these elements of their offerings so that the core products get perceived in the desired fashion.

Next, we described three biases in the perception process: selective exposure, selective attention, and selective interpretation. These processes allow us to escape from (selective exposure) and cope with (selective attention) the barrage of stimuli that constantly face us; they allow us also to complete the task of interpretation efficiently. Marketers should be aware of these biases and, where necessary, design their stimuli to harness these biases in their favor.

In the second half of the chapter, we put these concepts to practical application. Here, we examined five areas of marketing where perceptions influence consumer behavior: (i) the psychophysics of consumer price perceptions, (ii) country-of-origin effects, (iii) brand image and brand extensions, (iv) perceptual maps and positioning, and (v) sensory marketing. Any given price is perceived as good or bad depending on what is known as *reference price*. The country of a product's origin affects consumer perception of a product's quality. Some brand extensions are perceived as natural and are therefore assimilated by consumers; others are perceived as misfits and rejected. Perceptual maps place competing brands in a common space, and these maps then guide the marketer to reposition a brand. Discussion of these practical issues in marketing highlighted the role of perceptual processes in consumer response to marketing programs.

The last application, sensory marketing, concerns how marketers are structuring the entire marketplace environment to appeal to consumers' various senses. In this section, we highlighted the sensory experience of stimuli through each of the five senses: sight, hearing, smell, touch, and taste. Whatever the ultimate benefits and appeal of products, these must first pass through our sensory screens. It behooves marketers, therefore, to design all stimuli with noteworthy sensory experiences, with attention to each of the five senses. With the increasing deployment of multi-media technology, both in physical and digital worlds, the potential for sensory marketing is vast. As marketers and students of consumer behavior, becoming aware of consumer perception processes will help you fashion your marketing mix for maximum perceptual advantage.

KEY TERMS

Ambient advertising
Assimilation and contrast
Attention
Brand image
Closure
Context effect
Contextual advertising
Country-of-origin effects
Expectations
Figure and ground
Gestalt

Interpretation
Just Noticeable Difference (j.n.d.)
Mere exposure effect
Odd pricing
Organization
Perception
Perceptual distortion
Perceptual frames
Perceptual threshold
Perceptual maps

Positioning
Quality cue
Reference price
Repositioning
Stimulus
Subliminal perception
Sensory marketing
Visual identity
Weber's law

YOUR TURN

REVIEW+Rewind

1. Describe the three steps in the perception process and illustrate them with an example drawn from your own experience.

2. Define attention and its two forms: voluntary and involuntary. Give an example of each.

3. Perception is affected by three groups of factors—what are these? Illustrate each with an example from your personal experience.

4. Explain perceptual distortion.

5. Explain the concepts of just noticeable difference (j.n.d.) and Weber's law. How can marketers utilize these concepts?

6. What is "mere exposure effect" and its relevance to marketers?

7. Explain the concepts of (a) gestalt, (b) figure and ground, and (c) closure.

8. Explain the concepts of positioning and repositioning. The chapter describes several approaches to repositioning a brand in the consumer mind. Briefly explain each with a current example.

9. What is meant by internal and external reference price? What is its relevance to a company's pricing decisions?

THINK+Apply

1. As a consumer, have you experienced perceptual distortion? Why did these occur in your case?

2. Assess all ads in the book so far in terms of their effectiveness in creating distinct positioning for the advertised brand. Next, find an ad for each method of positioning and repositioning, and comment on their likely effectiveness in creating a distinct "brand perception" in the consumer mind.

3. What advice would you give a company considering a product line extension—should it use a family name or new, individual brand names?

4. Assume that you own a clothing company in, say, Malaysia. You wonder whether country-of-origin effects will work in your favor or against you in the U.S. and Canada. How will you research this issue? Write a memo "educating the rest of your marketing team," on exactly what effect country-of-origin has on consumers.

PRACTICE+Experience

1. Set up a blind taste test for two brands of cola or power drinks. Have consumers choose between the two brands with their brand names: (a) not revealed, (b) revealed correctly, and (c) revealed falsely (i.e., call each drink by the other's name). Tally, for each condition, the proportion of those who chos[e] and knowingly prefer, versus their brands. Summarize your [...]

2. Get three consumers to draw [...] (choose one):
   a. Five brands of jeans.
   b. Five brands of athletic shoes.
   c. Five brands of credit cards.

   Then adopt one of the brands as your company's brand, and suggest marketing action to improve its perceptual position, separately, for each of the three consumers.

3. Visit your local supermarket, and browse through the product displays of three categories: beverages, candies and cookies, and men's grooming products. Identify brands that do a good job of (a) establishing a distinct visual identity, and (b) creating pleasurable sensory experience.

4. Visit your local mall and make a list of all stores that utilize one or more of the five sensory stimuli to appeal to consumers. For each selected store, list and describe examples of each of the five sense appeals. Next, choose two stores that might be utilizing some but not all feasible types of the five sense appeals, and suggest how they could bridge this gap.

5. Take along a consumer on a cyber tour of www.evian.com. Then interview the consumer about his/her perceptions about this brand. Next, take him/her on a cyber tour of www.dasani.com and interview him/her to understand his/her perceptions of this brand. Repeat this for several other consumers (depending on time allocated to this assignment). Summarize how the two brand perceptions differ, and then exercise your brains (and analyze the two Web sites) to figure out what elements of these Web sites end up causing these differing perceptions. After a few interviews, you may want to structure consumers' responses somewhat. For this purpose, prepare a list of dimensions on which you might want to assess perceptions. And if you really want to add some more fun to the exercise, add www.vitaminwater.com to the mix, thus assessing and comparing consumer perceptions of the three brands.

In the Marketing Manager's Shoes

Most concepts in the chapter have some lessons for the marketing manager, i.e., they suggest to the marketing manager what to do differently in practice; indeed, often these applications are implicit in our explanations of the concepts and models in the chapter. Identify at least five specific applications of the chapter's concepts—all of which should be entirely new, different from the examples cited here.

Learning

4 Consumer Learning, Memory, and Nostalgia

From Classical to Cognitive

LEARN . APPLY . EXPERIENCE

OBJECTIVES

1 Four Models of Consumer Learning

2 Roles of Intrinsic Vs. Extrinsic Rewards in Winning Consumer Loyalty

3 Consumer Memories: Short-Term, Long-Term, Episodic, and Semantic

4 Three Methods of Transferring Information from STM to LTM for Brands

5 Six Innovation Characteristics That Aid Consumer Adoption

6 Two Motives for Nostalgia and Marketer Response to Satisfy Them

Look, Touch, Relish, Learn—
How a Cool Marketing Campaign Teaches You

If you were in New York City during a recent NYC Fashion Week, you could have witnessed some interesting people: Live fashion mannequins. They were decked out in haute couture designer outfits and toting a new electronic gadget the size of a clutch handbag—Sony's latest sleek 1.4 pound VAIO Lifestyle PC.

Coinciding with the NYC Fashion Week, the event was part of a marketing campaign by Sony Electronics to create a buzz for the Vaio. The models could be seen walking the streets on Fifth Avenue, in Chelsea and SoHo, at Grand Central Station and in trendy bars and cafes.

The mannequin women were updating their Facebook status using their Vaios, and they would often invite onlookers to look and feel the Vaio up close. In fact, they would lend you an extra Vaio, and, using your Vaio, you could IM them. You could find their schedules and whereabouts at www.sony.com/golightly. And you could later watch them on YouTube, and savor their activities on Flickr and Facebook.

And, incidentally, you would have "learned" of a cool new product—learned that it was sleek and light and, more importantly, that it was fashionable and hip!

©CHANCE YEH/PatrickMcMullan.com

> Engage me. And I will learn.

INTRODUCTION

Every marketer wants consumers to learn—learn the brand name, the product's benefits, its image, its story. The world of goods is filled with thousands of brands, and consumers learn about them over a lifetime. Some of these are things consumers are motivated to learn; others they learn inadvertently—without motivation, without trying, sometimes even without being specifically aware. Whether garnered with motivation or assimilated effortlessly, learning is critical to our growth as a person. And learning about the marketplace is absolutely essential for us to navigate the world of goods and pluck from it what will meet our needs and make our lives easier. And happier.

Since marketers are busy teaching consumers all sorts of things about their products, it would help to understand how consumers learn. We are going to explain consumer learning in this chapter, for marketers' benefit and for your benefit as well.

We begin this chapter by defining what it means for consumers to be learners, and we describe four different ways consumers learn. While you are constantly learning, in life and in this book, you should be intrigued by the idea of learning about learning itself. We will tell you about three modes of learning that humans share with other species. Then we will tell you about the fourth mode, unique to humans, and here we will take you deep inside the consumer mind, showing you how it works as a super-efficient computer, serving as a storehouse for a lifetime of information. Of all the things you learn, perhaps the most important to you, at least in your role as a consumer, is learning about new products and deciding what to do about them—adopt them, reject them, or wait a while. Your adoption of new products is especially important to marketers, since millions of dollars or Euros or yen are made or lost in their efforts to get you to learn a new consumption or shopping behavior (such as using the self-checkout registers), to learn a new trick, so to speak. We conclude this chapter, therefore, with advice to marketers about fashioning their products (innovations or otherwise) and their communications so as to mesh with the four modes of consumer learning. Let us begin at the beginning: by defining *learning*.

Consumer Learning Defined

Learning is acquiring a response to a stimulus. Suppose you are in a fruit and vegetable store in an Asian country (or an ethnic store in your own country) and you see persimmons—a fruit you have never seen before. What would you do? And if you saw, say, mangoes—a fruit you tried recently at a friend's home and liked—what would you do? Most likely, you would put the mangoes in your shopping basket and ignore the persimmons. Thus, you would have learned a response to mangoes but not to persimmons. And once you had acquired a response, you would use it automatically in similar future situations.

A learned response can be mental, or it can be behavioral. When we see a shirt with the Kenneth Cole name on it, we conjure up an image of well-made, prestigious clothing (a mental response); when we hear Adele Live is coming to town, we quickly buy a ticket for her concert (a behavioral response). As humans, we learn because it helps us to respond better to our environment. For instance, a child who accidentally puts his hand on a hot light bulb learns never again to touch a hot light bulb. Or, a consumer who gets trapped into buying a substandard product from a mail-order company learns never again to buy anything from that company, or perhaps from any mail order firm. Conversely, when consumers, wary of the authenticity of sellers on eBay, receive the product just as they expected, they learn to trust eBay sellers. Along the way, as they bid for items a few more times, they even learn the best strategies for bidding, avoiding the mistakes made the first time. With each experience, they learn to adapt their responses better. Thus, the purpose of all human learning is to acquire a potential for future adaptive behavior.

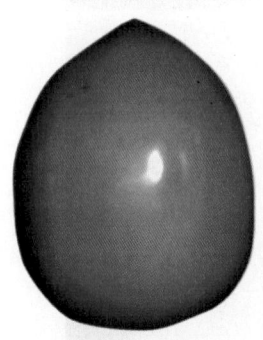

Persimmon

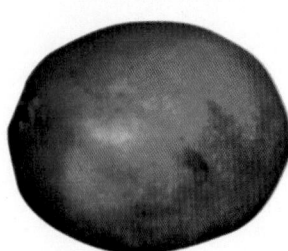

Mango

> The purpose of all human learning is to acquire a potential for future adaptive behavior.

FOUR MODELS OF CONSUMER LEARNING

Or How the Dog, Pigeon, Monkey, and Computer Get It

There are four mechanisms, or models, of consumer learning. Although you may not know about them, you use all four of them in your everyday life. Consider the following consumer scenarios:

Four Consumer Scenarios

- **You give an expensive cologne, Polo, to your friend Miguel on his birthday. But he is not thrilled. He tells you he only uses Curve. "Polo is a little too loud and stuffy... kind of like flaunting your riches," he tells you. "Curve is more subtle and sexy—if you know what I mean," he adds. How can he say that? You are actually wearing Polo yourself, but he has never been able to tell! Where did he learn this notion about Polo, anyway?**

- **Your friend Christèle always flies with JetBlue Airlines. Once, she opted to take a 6 a.m. flight even though another airline had a more convenient 7 a.m. flight. How does JetBlue get her to show such loyalty?**

- **Your neighbor's son, David, is in high school; he wears oversized shirts, baggy pants, baseball hats turned backwards, beads, headbands, and earrings. So do his friends. Where did they learn to dress this way?**

- **You run into your friend Christina at Coconut Grove (Miami), and she is all excited about a new keyboard she just saw at the Best Buy store a few minutes' drive away (19191 S Dixie Hwy, Point Royale Plaza). It was a keyboard that has a docking station for your iPhone, so you can type your text messages using the full-size keyboard. With one click you can switch back and forth between the iPhone and the PC/Mac. The keytops are sculpted, curved to fit your finger tips so that your fingers won't slide and mistype; and it comes with Anti-Ghosting Circuitry (*ghosts* are the missing or extra letters that result from fast-typing on ordinary keyboards). Christina is excited about buying this Tactile One Keyboard (from Matias, Canada, launched January 12, 2012, priced at $199.0) on her way back home.**

Each of these scenarios represents a distinct model of consumer learning: classical conditioning, instrumental learning, modeling, and cognitive learning. Let us learn more about each. See Figure 4.1.

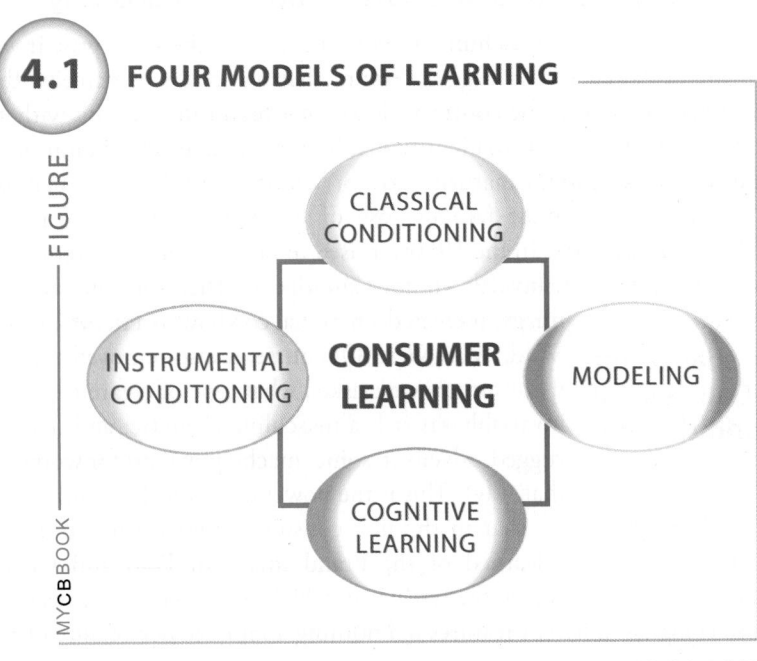

4.1 FOUR MODELS OF LEARNING

FIGURE

CLASSICAL CONDITIONING

INSTRUMENTAL CONDITIONING

CONSUMER LEARNING

MODELING

COGNITIVE LEARNING

MYCBBOOK

CLASSICAL CONDITIONING

The Most Famous Dog in Psychology

We will talk about consumers in a minute, but first a story about the most famous dog in psychology—known simply as Pavlov's Dog. Ivan Petrovich Pavlov was a Russian psychologist interested in understanding the learning processes of humans and animals. A giant in the field in his time (1849-1936), with a Nobel Prize in Physiology, Pavlov studied the human learning process by experimenting on animals. In his experiments, Pavlov harnessed a dog, gave him some meat powder, and observed that the dog salivated. This salivation is an inherited reflex. Next, Pavlov rang a bell just before giving the dog meat powder, and repeated this sequence several times; the dog salivated every time. Then, he merely rang the bell without giving the dog any meat powder. Now, you wouldn't expect the dog to salivate just with the ringing of the bell, would you? Yet in this experiment, the dog did!

This finding was groundbreaking in the study of human learning, but to appreciate it fully, you must first learn a few technical terms. In this experiment, the meat powder is called an unconditioned stimulus, and the bell is called a conditioned stimulus. An **unconditioned stimulus** (UCS) refers to a stimulus to which the consumer already has a pre-existing response. A **conditioned stimulus** (CS) is a stimulus to which the consumer either does not have a response or has a pre-existing response that needs modification, so a new response needs to be conditioned.[1]

In summarizing his findings, Pavlov said he had conditioned the dog to salivate to the bell. In other words, the dog had "learned" the salivating response to the bell. Note that the salivation response to the meat powder itself did not have to be learned, since it already existed as an instinctual response. Rather, the transfer (i.e., conditioning) of this response to the bell, a previously neutral stimulus, is what constitutes "learning."

Because you may have heard this story many times, nothing may seem unusual about it on the surface. But think deeper. The sound of the bell was not inherently appealing to the dog, and the dog had never before salivated on hearing it. However, now the bell successfully elicits that response.

This is **classical conditioning** at work—a process of learning by an extension of a pre-existing response from one stimulus onto another stimulus, through exposure to the two stimuli simultaneously.

What Does Pavlov's Dog Have to Do with Marketing?

Believe it or not, as humans, consumers learn the same way. If we see a new product or brand paired with a rugged terrain, then we come to perceive that brand as rugged and masculine. On the contrary, if we see a brand in a setting with soft colors and silky textures, then we come to identify that brand with a delicate, feminine image. Want proof? Just check out current magazine ads for Wrangler and Dolce & Gabbana clothing.

Perhaps the most famous case of classical conditioning is the repositioning of Marlboro cigarettes. In the 1960s, it used to be a woman's cigarette, complete with a filter and pink tip (so the lipstick wouldn't smudge it)! Then the company decided to change its image. It created a fictional cowboy, in a fictional countryside, out in the Wild, Wild West. Of course, it also removed the pink-tip filter. Today, if consumers were asked what type of cigarette Marlboro is, they would invariably say it is a masculine cigarette: and one for the independent, rugged, adventuresome, macho guy (and for women who see themselves that way). This is the power of classical conditioning!

Gender change for Marlboro—Courtesy of Classical Conditioning!

Now you know that in the first consumer scenario mentioned above, your friend Miguel must have learned of the brand image of Polo and Curve through classical conditioning—by seeing the settings in which these two brands were advertised, since the two colognes' inherent features tell nothing about the personality of the two brands.

Classical Conditioning is Everywhere

For classical conditioning to work, what is absolutely essential is constant pairing—your brand should be constantly paired with a desirable setting or with another desirable stimulus. The setting can include any number of things in the ad: color, look and feel of the ad, scenery, music in the jingle or commercial, or even the event being depicted (e.g., two people fighting versus showing affection). Other stimuli in the ad can include other objects or products (e.g., pair your brand of water, say, with a luxury car), sound bites (e.g., lyrics from an Elvis song or the voice of Glee star Dianna Agron), and, of course, specific persons (e.g., pair your brand of toupee with a tycoon or, alternatively, a hard-working athlete).

The magic of such pairings is constantly at work in ads everywhere. Thus, CK perfume is "youthful" because of the teenage models used in the brand's advertising, and Giorgio is "mature" and "richer" because of its Beverly Hills heritage. Coca-Cola uses real-life vignettes (with the tag line "Open Happiness") to convey its "real-thing" image, while Pepsi uses Kylie Minogue and Pink to promote its "New Generation" image.[2]

(Courtesy: Stacy Adams)

How do consumers learn which brand of shoes (and clothing) is for whom? Stacy Adams shows its shoes and clothing with fashionable, urban, trendy, young men; the brand and the wearer add to each other's allure. (*Allure*? See the admiring woman behind.) Here Classical Conditioning is at work, superbly, alluringly!

INSTRUMENTAL LEARNING

Or, How a Pigeon Learns to Peck

The second learning mechanism takes us to other animals. Psychologist B.F. Skinner experimented with pigeons. He built two doors in a pigeon feed box, one fake and one real. If a pigeon pecked on the fake one, nothing happened; if it pecked on the real one, food grains fell out. After a few trials, the pigeons learned to peck on the right door. This is **instrumental learning** (also called *instrumental conditioning* or *operant conditioning*)—a process where one learns behavior because it is rewarding. That is, we learn a response because it is instrumental to obtaining a reward. This is the familiar way we get children to learn good behaviors—"Eat your vegetables, and you'll get dessert," we tell them.

Can marketers use this method to help consumers learn? Absolutely. By rewarding the consumer if he or she buys the marketer's brand. Buy my product, and you get a chance to win a prize. Shop at my store, and you get a "double your coupon" deal. Use my credit card, and you get some cash back. Fly my airline, and you earn loyalty points good for a free trip—perhaps for this reason, your friend Christèle learned to always fly with JetBlue.

This reward comes in two forms: extrinsic and intrinsic. An **extrinsic reward** is external to the product; e.g., coupons, sweepstakes, rebates, and loyalty programs such as frequent flyer or frequent hotel stay rewards. Cigna, an insurance company, offers incentives to get its members to engage in pro-health behaviors. In contrast, an **intrinsic** reward is the reward built into the product itself—consumers learn to buy and use a product because they find the product itself rewarding. For example, we learn to use Bed Head shampoo

because it renders our hair just the way we want it, and we learn to drink Fruitopia because we savor its taste. We learn to visit the video game arcade Gameworks because we have a good time there, and we learn to buy Twelve Girls Band's new CD Romantic Energy because we found their previous releases—Eastern Energy, Journey to Silk Road, and Shining Energy—enchanting. (Check it out at www.twelvegirlsband.com.)

This distinction between intrinsic and extrinsic rewards is important to marketers. If the product is not, in itself, rewarding to the consumer (or not any more rewarding than competitors' products), then, to get the consumer to buy their product, marketers have to resort to extrinsic rewards, such as coupons, rebates, and frequent buyer rewards. However, consumer patronage won through such giveaways is rarely lasting. Rather than luring consumers through constant rebates and promotions, as marketers we should instead make our product itself intrinsically rewarding to the consumer. That way, the consumer buys our product not merely because of a coupon or sale (an extrinsic reward), but because he or she likes our product itself more. That is, as marketers, we have to get the consumer to learn to respond primarily to our product, not to extrinsic rewards. Frequency award programs, and indeed all extrinsic rewards, should serve, at best, as proverbial icing on the cake, but the real lure should be the cake itself.

Please, *instrumentally condition* me....

Journey to Silk Road	Eastern Energy	Red Hot Classic	Shining Energy	Romantic Energy
Enjoyed →	Bought Enjoyed →	Bought Enjoyed →	Bought Enjoyed →	Bought

i am a consumer. instrumentally condition me. and i will learn to buy your products. instrinsic or extrinsic—which reward is twelvegirlsband offering me? dare to figure that... or else i will take my money to another marketer who does!

MODELING

Monkey See, Monkey Do

Let's continue with animals. This time, a monkey—actually, a bunch of them. Watch them sometime. One monkey will start scratching his head, or making faces, or swinging from a tree branch, and then all the other monkeys will do the same. This is the third mechanism of learning, called **modeling**—a process whereby learning occurs by observing others.[3]

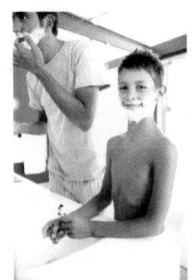

This "monkey see, monkey do" phenomenon is very much present in humans as well. Children learn much of their social behavior by observing and imitating their elders. We also learn from teachers, celebrities, coworkers, and other role models we admire. Many teenagers adopted the grunge looks of teen music artist Avril Lavigne or rapper Nelly. You now realize that in the third consumer scenario described above, this is how our neighbor's son, David, must have learned to dress the way he does.

In our day-to-day lives, we observe people we like or aspire to be like, and we learn what they consider good to wear, eat, and do. Thus, clothing with specific designer names becomes popular because influential people wear it. Hairstyles become popular on college campuses based on peer observations. And we choose careers because someone inspires us as a role model. Marketers harness this learning mechanism, for example, when they send product samples to influential and well-respected people, hoping that their followers will adopt the product when they see their leaders and role models using it.

COGNITIVE LEARNING

What an Amazing Supercomputer Our Mind Is!

For this fourth and last method of learning, we move from animals to machines. When people talk about learning, they are often thinking of cognitive learning (rather than the other three forms). **Cognitive learning** refers to learning by acquiring new information from written or oral communication. When we acquire information about something, whether incidentally and passively or deliberately and actively, we learn *cognitively*. It is through cognitive learning that we come to know who Ruari Mahon is (she is a fashion designer for Swedish denim brand Nudie Jeans—*Nudie* is intended to connote the firm's completely-organic production of its denim) or what Wexley School for Girls is (it is not really a school, much less for girls only; rather, it is the name of a quirky, Seattle-based ad agency). And in reading this book (and in listening to your instructor), you are actually learning cognitively.

Much of our learning about products also happens this way. Before we purchase technical products, we read product brochures, ask salespeople questions, and examine product features. In the fourth consumer scenario, this is how Christina, the friend you met at Coconut Grove, must have learned about the various features of Tactile One Keyboard. And of course, much of our learning about life or things that are useful to us every day also comes from cognitive learning—by reading informative articles in newspapers, magazines, or on Web sites, and by listening to words of wisdom from sages, consultants, soothsayers, and personal advisors. Read Exhibit 4.1, for example, courtesy of Solis Belt University (yes, that is really its name!). If you learn anything about belts, then, well, you will have just experienced cognitive learning.

Cognitive learning occurs on two levels: rote memorization and problem solving. With **rote memorization**, we rehearse the information until it gets firmly lodged in our long-term memory. Rote memorization can result from active rehearsal (as in trying to memorize the directions to that sushi place in Dallas, *Deep Sushi*), or from passive, repeated exposure to the information (seeing Deep Sushi ads often). A great deal of advertising aims simply to create a rote memory of the brand name or slogan by repeated presentation. Thus, most consumers around the world have learned by heart such slogans as "Coca-Cola: The Real Thing," and "Pepsi: The Choice of a New Generation."

In **problem solving**, we actively process information to reach certain judgments. Suppose you are wondering if you need to buy Spotify, a new music streaming service. You read about it, weigh it in your mind, and then say, "Now I understand what Spotify is and what it will do for me." This is cognitive learning about Spotify. This form of information utilization to form judgments is pervasive in our lives as consumers as we make brand choice decisions.

The problem solving type of learning obviously requires some mental effort, especially compared to rote memorization. The amount of mental effort depends on how much we want to learn about the product or brand. That depends, in turn, on the level of involvement we feel with the product.

EXHIBIT

4.1 SEVEN TIPS FOR WEARING BELTS

The belt you wear, and how you wear it, matters. Make your belt an afterthought at your own risk. Here are seven tips that will keep you looking good in your belt no matter the situation:

1 Match your belt to your shoes. As with any fashion advice, there are exceptions to this rule, but belts in general should be the same color as your shoes.

2 Wear a belt that fits your waist. If you're a 36 men's, a 32 inch belt will only emphasize your denial about it.

3 If you're going to own one belt, make it a black leather one with a silver buckle. (Go with a regular buckle.) It's the classic look. Canvas, suede, and studded belts work best if you're aiming for more of a casual or street look. A black leather belt is the right choice for dress pants and suits and it works in most casual situations as well.

4 Don't wear a belt with suspenders, unless you're trying to look goofy.

5 If you're going formal, get a dress belt that's an inch and a quarter wide without braids or special designs. Special designs and braids are for a more casual look.

6 If you're wearing gold jewelry, wear a belt with a gold buckle; if you're wearing silver jewelry, go with a silver buckle. Belts look best when they match your accessories.

7 If you've got an elastic waist, cover it with a belt.

Q. Now, you learned something from the above guide. Which model of learning did you just experience?

Source: http://store.soliscompany.com/belts.html
Courtesy: Solis Company.

MY CB BOOK

Involvement, you will recall, was defined in Chapter 2 as the degree of interest in an object or product. Thus, cognitive learning can be of two types: low involvement learning and high involvement learning.

In **low-involvement learning**, the product is relevant, but not much is at stake, such as a low priced item for routine use. We want to learn the brand name and possibly learn about its single, most relevant feature, if the information is readily available. So, with a quick glance at a print advertisement, we may learn the brand name Altoids (a mint), and we may also learn about its key feature, namely, that it is a strongly flavored mint. Consumers are unwilling to work hard to read an ad for a low involvement product; that is why these ads should be simple, featuring a visual, and merely a line or two of text if at all.[4]

In **high-involvement learning,** the product is very important to us as consumers, and a lot is at stake—such as an expensive purchase of an iPad 3, or even a cereal if we are very health conscious. Here, we want to choose the right product and the right brand, and therefore, we want to learn about several of the brand's features and capabilities. So, we read package labels, seek knowledgeable salespersons, search the Web for information, and read or watch the entire advertisement to understand as much information as possible. Let us summarize the four models in terms of what and how we learn (see Table 4.1).

We shall fight shoes in the street.
We shall fight shoes in the office.
We shall fight them in the park, the museum and the supermarket. We shall fight shoes because shoes are in league with hard surfaces to destroy our backs. And we shall fight them with something far superior to a shoe. Something that protects your spine. Something that tones your muscles. Something that helps you stand up straight and walk the way you were meant to. And if we have to step on a few toes to gain that victory, then with all our might, we will.

theantishoe.com
©2008 Masai USA Corp

The anti-shoe.

Helping consumers learn a "high involvement" product story: Most shoes are not designed to provide support against the pounding that your feet and your body receive from hard surfaces. The MBT shoe claims to be built to fight these other shoes (that are in league with hard surfaces). MBT shoe positions itself as an anti-shoe.

(Image used with permission)

TABLE

4.1 **FOUR MODELS OF LEARNING WITH MARKETING EXAMPLES**

MODEL	WHAT IS LEARNED	HOW	EXAMPLES
CLASSICAL CONDITIONING	Brand Image, in terms of associations NOT necessarily related to inherent features of the brand.	By exposure to the brand along with another stimulus, consumers associate & extend the image of this other stimulus to the brand.	Forming an impression that cologne Navigator is for an independent, rugged, determined athletic man (simply because of the mood of the person in the ad).
	Emotional response	If marketers pair an emotional stimulus with the brand, then the consumer begins to feel the same emotion toward the brand.	Tommy Cologne ads show an American flag; the consumer then feels patriotic toward the cologne brand as well.
	Behavioral response	Certain stimuli bring out certain behaviors in humans. Expose consumers to those stimuli along with your brand or place, and consumers will automatically begin to act that way.	Play a slow musical melody in the store, and consumers linger longer and buy more.
INSTRUMENTAL CONDITIONING	Brand purchase & use behavior	Because of some incentive we get every time we buy a product (extrinsic reward). Because we find the use of the product itself gratifying (intrinsic reward).	Renting movies from Hollywood (instead of another outlet) because of a free bonus movie. Can't wait to visit Gameworks whenever possible because we enjoy it very much.
MODELING	Product or brand use behavior	By observing people we like.	Buy a four-button jacket suit because you saw your favorite athlete wearing it.
COGNITIVE LEARNING	The intrinsic feature of the product or brand.	By paying attention to product information.	While searching the Internet for hotels in Seattle, you read about W Hotel & learn that it features contemporary urban chic decor, and is wired for Wi-Fi & i-Tunes.
(a) Low Involvement Learning	Brand name, jingles, etc.; at most one or two brand features for a simple and no-risk product.	By repeatedly being exposed to the advertisetment; By effortlessly looking at or listening to a simple ad or by simply seeing a a brand package on display.	Most consumers have learned "Can you hear me now" tagline for Verizon and know it means that the signal reception is good in all locations.
(b) High Involvement Learning	Consumers learn as much information about a product as there is to learn to solve a problem or make a product choice decision.	By reading the ad carefully or by paying attention to the commercial, or seeking advice from a salesperson or a professional.	A consumer considering the Botox procedure to erase facial wrinkles, reads its ad entirely, consults a professional and also checks out some information on the Internet.

MY CB BOOK

STIMULUS GENERALIZATION AND DISCRIMINATION

The Art of Not Having to Learn All the Time

Consider the child who burned his hand by touching a yellow light bulb. He will never touch a yellow light bulb again, for he has learned that a glowing, yellow, ball-shaped object is painful to touch. In fact, he has most likely also learned that he shouldn't touch a white, red, or blue light bulb either—or, for that matter, anything that glows, even if it is not hot. This is a good thing; otherwise, the poor child would have to learn a new response to each new object, and would never have any time to play. Likewise, as consumers, we don't have to learn to respond anew every time we encounter a new stimulus. We quickly and instinctively repeat the response we have made in the past to other *similar stimuli*.

Suppose we are new immigrants from a country where there are no big self-browsing and self-service stores. Suppose that, in fact, there are no stores in our home country where you can walk inside the store—instead all the stores are storage rooms with a service window or a storefront. (Indeed, most stores in many developing countries are set up this way!) Now in our new country, we find superstores where we can wander and browse. We go to one food store and learn that we are not supposed to run around, talk loud, or eat food inside the store; next, we would employ the same behavior in other stores even if these other stores sell different merchandise and have a different ambience, such as a department or jewelry store. This happens because humans learn to see the similarities even when two things are not exactly identical. Psychologists call this process **stimulus generalization**—a process wherein a consumer extends a learned response for one stimulus to other similar but unidentical stimuli.

However, the child who burned his hand by touching a hot light bulb will not have learned not to touch a hot pan or put his finger in a cup of coffee because he sees these objects as being different enough from the glowing bulb. Likewise, the immigrant consumer who has learned the behavioral protocol for a store might be at a loss when visiting a bar for the first time. This is just as well, for otherwise the consumer would have ended up making the wrong response (to his or her social embarrassment). This ability to see two stimuli as different helps consumers to respond to each

It is a good thing that our minds also know when not to use such shortcuts.

in an appropriate way. Psychologists call this ability **stimulus discrimination**—a process wherein a consumer perceives two stimuli as different so that the response learned for one stimulus is not repeated for the other. Stimulus generalization is a useful shortcut, but it is a good thing that our minds also know when not to use such shortcuts.

A Shortcut for Every Season

Do consumers use this shortcut in all four modes of learning? Yes, they do. In classical conditioning, Pavlov's dog still salivates if the bell is replaced by a device that makes a similar but non-identical sound. Analogously, consumers come to see a brand of chewing gum featured with outdoor winter scenery as refreshing, but also when it is featured with outdoor autumn or spring scenery. Consumers see Peyton Manning with Gatorade and learn to associate Gatorade as a thirst quencher for athletes; if the brand were to later feature Albert Pujols in a new ad campaign, consumers would still make the same association. Consumers who learn to buy clothing at the season's end to get a better price (an example of instrumental conditioning) also learn to buy snow-plowing equipment at the end of the season and visit tourist spots off season. And in the cognitive learning mode, suppose you happened to read Dr. Oz's advice for getting a good night's sleep: Sixty minutes before bed, turn off all electronics and dim all lights (see doctoroz.com); you would now assume that turning off all electronics is also a good idea while trying to get a nap, or to feel inner calm in your mind in the midst of a hectic day. Thus, stimulus generalization means we get extra mileage out of what we have learned.

SAVVY MARKETER

Savvy marketers utilize the concepts of stimulus generalization and discrimination to obtain favorable consumer responses. When a product is new, but marketers want it to be seen as being of the same high quality and prestige as the company's other brands, they give the new product the appearance of the familiar brand, by package similarity and the brand name. Thus, new flavors of soup, new varieties of pasta, and new versions of video games are given a brand family name and are packaged identically to the existing package. Store brands make their products resemble manufacturers' brands, hoping consumers will engage in stimulus generalization. In contrast, when marketers want to attract a new set of consumers, they name the new brand by a different and unique name—for example, Eternity and Obsession colognes (both from Calvin Klein).

CONSUMER INFORMATION PROCESSING

Memory and Remembering

Inside the Supercomputer

Whereas the other three models of learning are applicable to non-human creatures as well, only humans have the capacity for cognitive learning, because only humans have the capability to process information. Here is the phone number for University of Cambridge: 44 (0) 1223 337733; and for the Office of the Prime Minster of Canada: 613 992 4211; and, finally, for the White House: 202 456 1414. Can you memorize these? At least one of them? You are able to memorize the last one, or maybe even the middle number, right? This is because these are shorter, but also because they are only seven digits long (not counting the area code). Seven is also the number of digits (more exactly speaking, 'seven plus or minus two') a human can memorize at a time. Seven digits, seven letters, seven names, and so on. Psychologist George Miller has established through research that we are able to memorize seven bits of information, plus or minus two, at a time.[5] When we combine bits of information and treat the combined entity itself as a unit, with a meaning of its own, then that becomes a new single bit of information. This combination of bits into a new unit is called *chunking*. Thus, 911 is a single bit or chunk that stands for the emergency phone number in the US and Canada (and in a few other countries such as El Salvador, Fiji, and Uruguay) and 999 in the U.K. We can memorize seven bits of information, make it into a unit, and then move on to memorizing a new set of seven bits of information. Our minds also are able to quickly form into chunks some simple multi-digit numbers such as 3000, 6666, etc. (London Business School has cleverly chosen its number to be 44 0 (20) 7000 7000!) Furthermore, words we are already familiar with form a unit, no matter how many letters they may have. Thus, President's Delight as a brand name can be memorized quickly because both the words are already familiar.

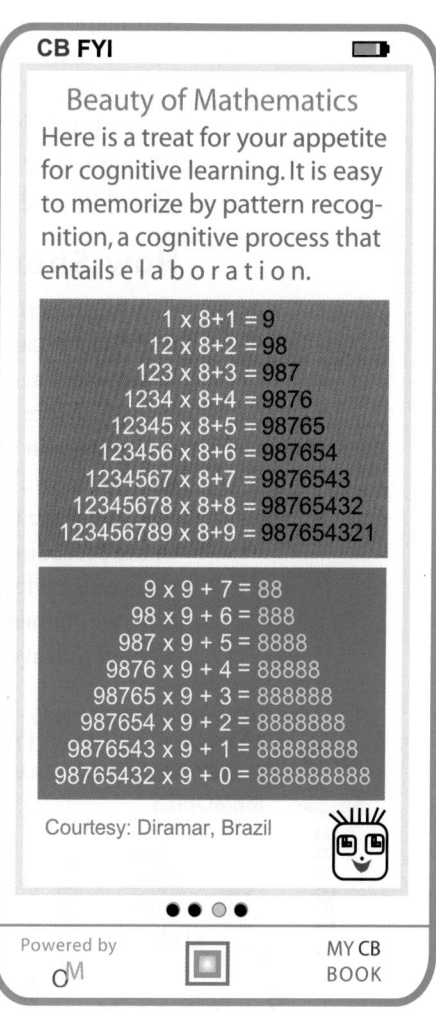

CB FYI

Beauty of Mathematics

Here is a treat for your appetite for cognitive learning. It is easy to memorize by pattern recognition, a cognitive process that entails e l a b o r a t i o n.

$$1 \times 8 + 1 = 9$$
$$12 \times 8 + 2 = 98$$
$$123 \times 8 + 3 = 987$$
$$1234 \times 8 + 4 = 9876$$
$$12345 \times 8 + 5 = 98765$$
$$123456 \times 8 + 6 = 987654$$
$$1234567 \times 8 + 7 = 9876543$$
$$12345678 \times 8 + 8 = 98765432$$
$$123456789 \times 8 + 9 = 987654321$$

$$9 \times 9 + 7 = 88$$
$$98 \times 9 + 6 = 888$$
$$987 \times 9 + 5 = 8888$$
$$9876 \times 9 + 4 = 88888$$
$$98765 \times 9 + 3 = 888888$$
$$987654 \times 9 + 2 = 8888888$$
$$9876543 \times 9 + 1 = 88888888$$
$$98765432 \times 9 + 0 = 888888888$$

Courtesy: Diramar, Brazil

Powered by o^M MY CB BOOK

HOW CONSUMER MEMORY WORKS

Pulp Fiction Bookpurses, Will You Remember Them?

Pulp Fiction Bookpurses—the fun purses from Maddie Powers, made with vintage pulp-fiction book jackets with titles like *Don't Push Me Around* and *Boy Chaser*. Will you remember this title, say, by tomorrow? Or, instead, will your memory fail you?

Memory is a place in the human brain where information is processed and stored. It is like a warehouse that holds all we know and all we will ever know over our entire lifetimes. Memory refers to both this storage area and its stored contents. It is divided into three parts: sensory, short term, and long term.

Sensory Memory **Sensory memory** is the ability of our senses to keep information alive briefly. While watching TV ads, for example, only the sounds (voice and music, if any) will register on our auditory senses, and only the visuals will register on our vision senses—only these sensory features of the entire ad, not any meaning or message. These features remain there for less than a second, long enough for us to decide whether we should pay any attention. If we decided not to pay any attention, then they would vanish. That is why you do not remember some commercials at all.

Short-term Memory If we decide to pay attention to the sensations, then the information enters our short-term memory. **Short-term memory (STM)** is the part of the brain where information is being held and processed currently. Thus, STM is working memory; that is, we are currently working with it and on it. All new information enters from our senses first into STM. Here, we decide what to do with it: we can decide to memorize it, file it, use it for some imminent decision or action, or discard it altogether.

Long-term Memory **Long-term memory (LTM)** is the part of the brain where information we do not currently need is stored away. It is stored there in some organized way, so that, when needed in the future, it can be accessed. We place it there so that our minds are not constantly occupied with the huge amounts of information and knowledge we acquire. It is because of this passive storage that we are not constantly burdened with the consciousness of everything that has happened in our lives and, instead, are free to focus on the matter at hand. In sum, STM is active memory, and LTM is passive memory.

How Short is Short?

Short-term memory has two characteristics: (a) limited capacity, and (b) limited duration. It can only hold very small amounts of information—seven plus or minus two bits, as we mentioned earlier. And it can hold it only for a very short time—just a few seconds. More exactly, STM is basically what we are currently, at this very minute, aware of; it is what is in our consciousness and what our attention is directed toward. For example, right now, you are thinking of Cold Stone Creamery ice cream—we made you think of it. No, you were not thinking of it even a millisecond before you read the word "ice cream" in the preceding sentence, and you will not be thinking of it the second you finish reading the words coffee, Coke, Pepsi, Snapple, Gatorade, Dr Pepper, and Mountain Dew. (Notice how we named seven beverages just to fill your entire STM capacity; of course, if we wanted to leave no chance at all for any of you, we should have named two more.)

Hundreds of Faces and Thousands of Words—All Stored in the Mind

Long-term memory also has two characteristics: (a) unlimited capacity, and (b) efficient organization. LTM is like a huge warehouse, with virtually unlimited capacity. In it, we hold names and faces of hundreds of friends, associates, and public figures; hundreds of events we have experienced in life and just as many more that we read about; words to hundreds of songs, poems, or stories; musical tunes, food tastes, and a spectrum of aromas and colors; and facts about and experiences with literally the thousands of products we consume.

Second, this massive pile of data and information is not just thrown into the storage area. Rather, it is organized systematically, for efficient access when needed. So if a waiter asks you what you would like to drink, you don't think of cereal, pasta, or salad; instead, you think of coffee, Coke, Pepsi, Snapple, Gatorade, Dr Pepper, or the Dew. Or to make it even more efficient, the fact that you only like to drink Dew with your dinner and Snapple with your lunch is also stored in your LTM. So you think only of Snapple if it is lunchtime and only of Dew if it is dinnertime. Without such efficient accessing of information in LTM, everyday living would be an uphill struggle.

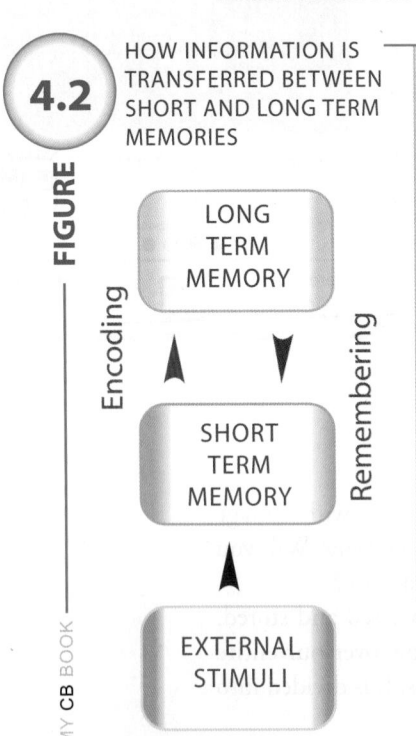

FIGURE 4.2 HOW INFORMATION IS TRANSFERRED BETWEEN SHORT AND LONG TERM MEMORIES

MY CB BOOK

Let us see how STM and LTM communicate with each other.

How STM and LTM Talk to Each Other

Information flows constantly between our two memories. (see Figure 4.2) All external information entering LTM must go through STM. And all the information stored in LTM must be brought back into STM to utilize it for a current task. An apt analogy is that of the theater: LTM is the backstage where all the actors and props assemble and wait to be called; STM is the front-stage where actors are currently playing their roles. The process of moving the information from STM to LTM is called *encoding*, and the process of withdrawing information from LTM to STM is called *remembering* or *retrieval*. Let us see how these processes work.

Keeping Information Alive in STM

When we are exposed to new products and services or new information, it is received in STM (via the sensory memory, of course). If we judge the information to be useless, we discard it. If we need it for some immediate task, we keep it alive in our STM. Keeping it alive simply means keeping it in our consciousness, currently. There are two ways to do this: (a) rote rehearsal, and (b) quick coding. (See Figure 4.3.) Rote rehearsal is repeating the information in our heads, mechanically, that is, without thinking about it. Thus, if the Spotify ad gave you a number to call (say, 1-800-579-5210), and you were trying to find a piece of paper on which to write it, you might repeat the number in your head.

The second method, *quick coding*, entails identifying some surface features in the information to help us remember it for the time being. Thus, in the phone number 579-5210, you might notice that there is a '5' at the beginning of both the exchange and individual number codes. So you memorize that. Then, you notice that in the first set, the digits jump by two—5, then 7, then 9—so you memorize that. Finally, in the second set, you notice that the remaining three digits are 0, 1, 2, backwards. So you make a mental note of that, thus concluding your task of memorizing. This is not very helpful but doing it a couple of times might just do, for some consumers. Non-numerical information lends itself to easier "quick coding." You remember the Maddie Powers pulp-fictionesque Bookpurse, don't you? You quickly remembered a classmate last semester who was into vintage accessories. Of course, none of these ideas might work for you; individual consumers have to find their own "tricks" to do the requisite "quick coding."

Transferring Information from STM to LTM

More often, the case is that we expect to use the information at some time in the future (rather than immediately), so we choose to store it in our LTMs. We do this by **encoding**—a process in which we assign it a meaning and then file it in a category of similar things. There are three ways of placing the information in the long-term memory: (1) repetition, (2) mnemonics, and (3) elaboration. See Figure 4.4.

MY CB BOOK

4.3 TWO WAYS TO KEEP INFORMATION ALIVE IN SHORT TERM MEMORY

FIGURE

QUICK CODING — SHORT TERM MEMORY — ROTE REHEARSAL

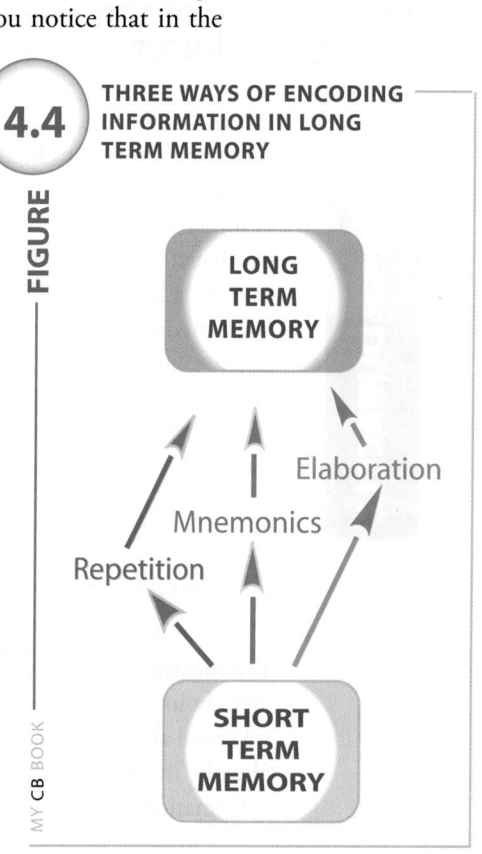

4.4 THREE WAYS OF ENCODING INFORMATION IN LONG TERM MEMORY

FIGURE

LONG TERM MEMORY

Elaboration

Mnemonics

Repetition

SHORT TERM MEMORY

Repetition

We all know numbers, and we all know the alphabet; we know them by heart. We can always recite them without fail at the spur of the moment. They reside in our LTMs, etched there permanently. We all learned them the same way—by repeating them many times. Thus, **repetition**—defined as the incidence of an occurrence more than once. Saying something again and again, hearing it often, observing a stimulus, touching it, smelling it—and doing so with the intent to memorize—indeed results in the information being placed into our LTM. This is similar to the rehearsal needed to keep something alive in STM, with two exceptions: First, the rehearsal itself needs to be repeated several times at various intervals (e.g., a day apart, every two to three days, a week later, and so on); and second, because our goal is to place it in LTM, we would be doing the repetition with more focused attention.

Rehearsal is the process of repetition, when the consumer is the one actively doing the repeating. Of course, repetition (but not rehearsal) can also occur without the consumer's intent and effort. Consumers can simply be exposed repeatedly to a stimulus. Such repeated exposure also lodges the stimulus information in LTM even with minimal attention, although some attention is still needed, and the more attention we pay, the quicker the information gets lodged in LTM.[6] This is how so many brand names (e.g., Adidas, PlayStation, MINI Cooper, etc.) got put into our LTMs even though we never tried! Marketers are interested in getting their brand names and messages into our LTM, and that is why they repeat their commercials so often.

Mnemonics

Mnemonics are memory devices that help us remember information through some nonsensical associations. Let us illustrate.

Assume you have a second date with someone you met a few days ago. During your first date, you learned that this person prefers Snapple for lunch and Mountain Dew for dinner. It is important for you to remember this information. How would you remember it? Here, mnemonics can help. You see, Dew and dinner both start with the letter "d"; and only Snapple has the letter "l", the first letter of the word "lunch." Got it? There is now a good chance that you would remember it for a while. That is the power of mnemonics!

You remember to order Snapple for lunch because of the common letter *l*.

As a marketer, can you utilize the power of mnemonics to help your consumers remember your product or message? To stimulate your thinking, we will give three examples. A few years ago, Halls Cough Drops hired comedian Richard Hall, who, in a TV commercial, walked into a room built with the packaged strips of Halls, called the Halls of Medicine. Richard Hall and Halls of Medicine—get it? Recently, Duracell's Coppertop Battery ads showed the product with the copper portion of the battery snapping into position on top of the remaining portion, as the voiceover mentioned the word "coppertop" in the tagline, "Nothing tops the Coppertop." "Coppertop"—get it? Our third example is about J&B—the brand that utilized the "closure principle" in the "–ingle –ells" Christmas print ad (mentioned in Chapter 3). In another print campaign, the company placed the letters J&B at strategic places in consumers' lives; one of these ads showed Hall of Fame baseball player Johnny Bench, and in the background were letters J&B placed on the home plate, and the headline read: "J&B at home." "J&B at home,"—get it?

Elaboration

The third and last method of placing information in LTM is called *elaboration*. **Elaboration** is the active processing of information in conjunction with other information already in the memory so as to identify meaning in the new information. Thus, whereas rehearsal also involves active processing, only elaboration entails utilization of information already in our memories. And while mnemonics may also include the use of some information already in long-term memory, only in elaboration do we try to link the information in terms of meaning (as opposed to surface or nonsensical features).

Suppose you wanted to commit to LTM the phone number, 1-800-592-5216. Given the motivation, you would suddenly realize that '92' is the year you were born and also that in that year the U.S. Declaration of Independence was 216 years old. Now this phone number will be lodged in your LTM (provided you were indeed born in 1992, and provided, of course, that it was your goal to lodge it into your LTM).

In elaborating on it, we try to find any connections the new information may have with our existing knowledge, judge its relevance to ourselves, and assess its future use. Thus, we are not merely accepting information as given but rather scrutinizing it for meaning, and, by active contribution of our own, adding to it. For example, suppose you hear an ad for the Segway Human Transporter—advertised as a revolutionary, high-tech, battery-powered, self-balancing transporter with a top speed of 12.5 mph and a range of up to 15 miles per charge. You chuckle about it and begin thinking:

4.5 AN ASSOCIATED NETWORK OF MEMORY

FIGURE

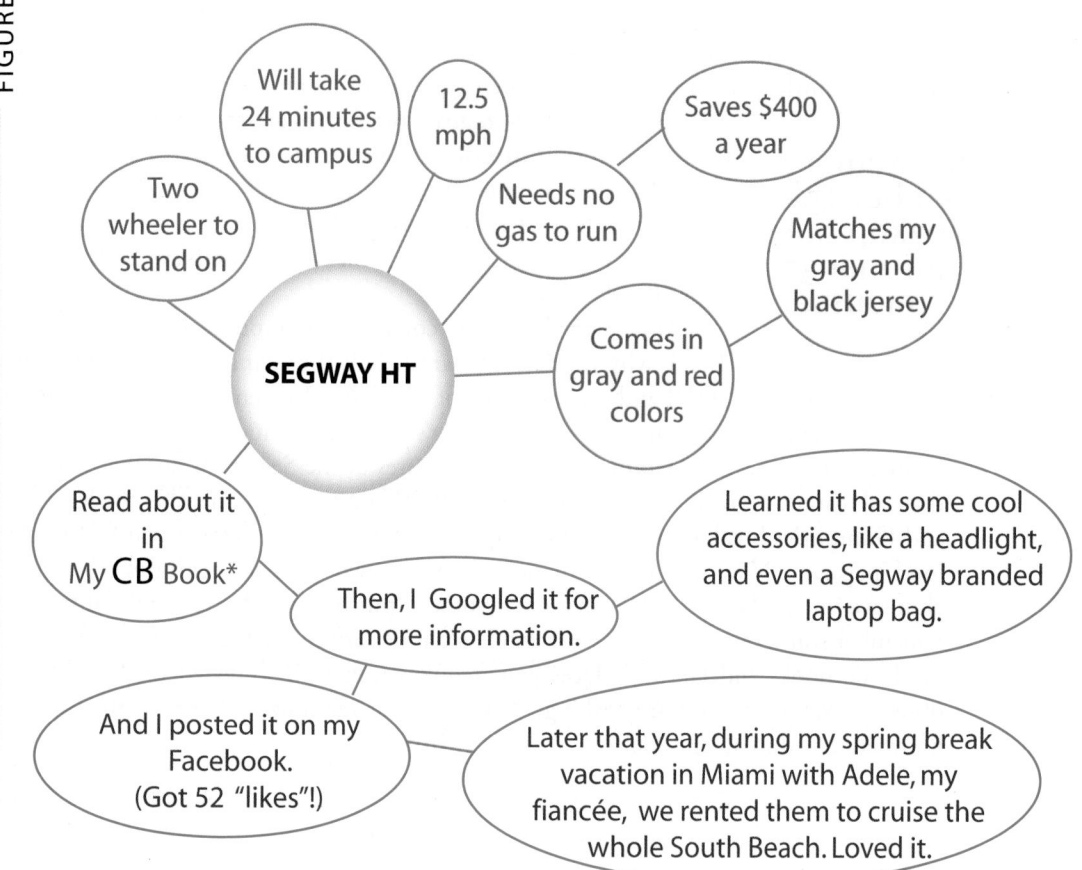

Note how, rather than being limited to the product itself, associated networks of memory spread into our lives at large. Ultimately, then, everything in a person's memory is interconnected, thus connecting even mundane consumption to memories of significant other events in our life histories. Activating one node (i.e., becoming conscious of one node) "spreads the activation" to other nodes, quickly to nodes connected only by a few links, but slowly and with focused effort to nodes farther away. Failure of remembering is then basically a failure of "spreading activation." "Spreading activation," aided by appropriate cues along the way, helps us remember things even from the distant past.

*see www.mycbbook.com

MY CB BOOK

Campus parking is a good 10-minute walk to the classroom, and the morning traffic is a nightmare, taking a good 20 minutes to drive the 4 miles from home. In that much time, with the Segway, I could be in class. I've got 500 bucks in my savings, and if I can get dad to fork over four grand, I can buy this machine. I will save about $400 a year on gas and $200 on parking, so that is a cool $600-a-year savings. Come to think of it, I will be the first one to use it on campus. Why, I can even imagine myself wearing my favorite gray/black jersey, to match the dual colors of my Segway. Did I say "my Segway" already?!

With elaboration like this, you are likely to have placed the advertised brand information in your LTM, along with images of yourself cruising around campus in your gray/black Segway.

Information Structure This elaboration actually results in knowledge being developed and stored as an **associated network**—a network of various concepts organized and stored in memory. (See Figure 4.5.) A **concept** is a name or label given to any object or quality of an object, person, situation, or an idea. Examples include mouse, jock, love, hot, cool, clean, culture jam, mojo, etc. These concepts are depicted as nodes interconnected by lines, which represent connections among those objects or qualities.[7]

Episodic and Semantic Memories

All knowledge is of two types: *episodic* and *semantic*. **Episodic knowledge** consists of descriptions of events; **semantic knowledge** consists of information about objects and their properties. If we show you a mouse, and tell you, "this is a mouse," that is semantic knowledge. So is your learning that it needs no food and dutifully conveys your wish to your PC. That you received it as a free gift from Microsoft just for being a buzzer on an online Web site that Microsoft sponsors (more on being a buzzer, later, in Chapter 10) is episodic knowledge. Correspondingly, the two types of memories are called *semantic* and *episodic* memories. **Semantic memories** are memories of objects and their properties. **Episodic memories** are memories of events—both those that have happened to you personally (e.g., when you tried a Segway for the first time at South Beach during a spring break) and those you only witnessed (e.g., the victory of New York Giants in Super Bowl XLVI).

Your episodic memory helps you remember the Kardashian breakup but not the recipe for mango mousse.

Now, which memory comes to you more easily? Right, episodic. That is why you can still narrate how the Giants sacked Tom Brady five times in Super Bowl XLVI and every episode of *The Office*. Remembering the definition of *involvement*, or subconscious motives in Dichter's list, or the names of all the nations in the United Nations Security Council, or all the features of the Segway is another matter, for that calls for the more difficult semantic memory. That's why you remember the Kardashian and Humphries breakup but not the recipe for mango mousse, which you had read in a food magazine. Now all this information about the two types of memories is not an idle chore we imposed on you. As a marketer, you can put it to good use. Want consumers to remember some key features of your wireless phone service, such as the fact that it works in all the nooks and faraway places you frequent (semantic knowledge)? Show it as an obsessive wanderer constantly asking, "Can you hear me now?" That is, embed semantic knowledge within an episode!

Over the river [] Through the woods. [] Past the broken elevator. [] Up six flights of stairs. [] Out the window. [] Up the fire escape. [] Back in the window. [] Down the hallway. [] In the office. [] To the client's desk we go.
Customer service is back in shipping.

Notice how this DHL ad transforms a semantic message into an episodic format!

Text of a recent ad by DHL.

To help consumers remember the brand name is a coveted goal of brand marketers (or should be). With a name like Yellow Tail (a wine from Australia), *Creatives* have a field day. When it comes to devising mnemonics for their brand name, this ad takes the prize.
(Image, courtesy of Deutsch and Sons, Ltd.)

Remembering the Information: Retrieving from LTM into STM

Okay, you have placed this information into LTM; now, how do you retrieve it? Basically, there are two mechanisms: (a) recognition and (b) recall.

Recognition and Recall

Recognition refers to identifying a stimulus as having been encountered before. Thus, it entails being able to access and retrieve the information from LTM based on an exposure to a relevant external stimulus object. In contrast, *recall* involves becoming conscious of some information residing in LTM without the stimulus being present. It is being able to access and retrieve information from LTM without an external stimulus object. Thus, when the consumer standing in front of a vending machine sees the cold drink Fruitopia and remembers having seen the same brand in an ad or at a friend's home, he or she is remembering through recognition. On the other hand, if the consumer enters the store and feels an urge to buy a soft drink and thinks, "Let me buy a Fruitopia," he/she is "recalling" the brand name.

Recall has two forms: unaided and aided. **Unaided recall** involves accessing information without any clues; **aided recall** is accessing information with some clues. So, if we were to ask you which advertisements you saw yesterday while watching *the 84th Oscar Academy Awards Show* (aired on February 26, 2012) and if you could recall any of the advertisements, then you would have recalled those ads unaided. If we then asked whether you saw an ad from Taco Bell, and you said yes, then this would be a case of aided recall. If you still didn't recall, and we then asked whether you remembered an ad that showed a bunch of animated pigs, and then you remembered and said that, yes, you saw that ad featuring animated pigs, it would still be an aided recall. Thus, recall can require cues of varying degrees. This depends on how strong the memory trace is—i.e., how strong was the impression made when the information was placed in LTM the first time. Strong traces enable unaided recall, and when aid is needed, memories may be activated with merely a hint; weak traces need strong cues.[8]

In the associated network shown here, a recall cue can basically pertain to any one of the nodes or links. When one of these links or nodes is activated, the activation then spreads to other nodes and linkages, bringing them into our consciousness—our STM. Psychologists call this process **spreading activation**—the phenomenon where consciousness of one of the nodes suddenly activates our consciousness of all the other nodes.[9] Thinking of Segway reminds you of My CB Book. It is like an electric current that quickly flows through the entire circuit.

CONSUMER ADOPTION OF PRODUCT INNOVATIONS

The Ultimate Learning Experience

One of the most challenging problems for marketers is getting consumers to buy new products. Okay, smartphones and iPads and Adele's and Bon Iver's new releases are actually awaited, but such innovations as Lasik eye surgery, TiVo, and hybrid cars take years to catch on. In marketers' minds, product innovations bring new value to consumers. Consumers should be excited about buying them. But about ten new products fail for each one that succeeds. That is a lot of money and effort wasted. And marketers wonder why. From the consumers' points of view, of course, buying new products means learning whether the new products are really better for their needs. Even more importantly, they have to learn new tastes as well as new habits.

Let us first define *innovation*. An **innovation** is a product or an idea that is new to the consumer. *Newness* has two dimensions: (1) uniqueness or how different it is from existing products, and (2) age or how long it has existed in the marketplace.[10]

Of course, uniqueness is a matter of degree. Some new products and services are only marginally dissimilar from their existing forms, whereas others are substantially dissimilar. Based on the degree to which they are unique, scholars classify innovations as *continuous*, *dynamically continuous*, or *discontinuous*. Consider innovations in vision correction products, and imagine some 50 years ago when eyeglasses were all that existed. With that anchor, the featherweight lenses of the 1990s would be called a *continuous innovation*, contact lenses (first made commercially available in 1973) *dynamically continuous*, and radio keratotomy (or the newer photo keratotomy)—a vision corrective laser-surgery procedure—a *discontinuous* innovation.

DESIRABLE CHARACTERISTICS OF INNOVATIONS

Or, What Makes an Innovation Hot

Now then, the million-dollar question is: How do consumers learn whether or not an innovation is worthy of their adoption? The answer to this question comes from sociologists who, during the 1960s, studied why some farmers would not adopt new hybrid seed and farming innovations. Sociologists actually turned the question on its head. Instead of asking why people would not adopt innovations, they asked: What is it in innovations that encourages their widespread adoption, or, alternatively, blocks their adoption. That question is more interesting to us as marketers anyway, because the answer permits us to try to build those qualities into our innovations. According to sociologists, good innovations have six desirable characteristics or attributes that help their adoption by consumers? They are:[11]

Performance men's compression undershirt from Equmen, Australia (*Equmen* was coined to mean equality for men).

- **Relative advantage** What consumers consider, first and foremost, is the innovation's **relative advantage**—how much better the innovation is compared to the current product for which it would substitute. For example, the relative advantage of laser eye surgery is that consumers don't have to use eyeglasses or contact lenses anymore.

- **Perceived risk Perceived risk** of innovations refers to uncertainty about whether a relative advantage will accrue and whether any unanticipated harm will occur. For example, some consumers might perceive risk in laser surgery or in irradiation of foods. Consumers are less likely to adopt innovations with a high perceived risk.

- **Complexity Complexity** refers to the difficulty involved in understanding an innovation. Consumers prefer an innovation that is easy to comprehend. The easier it is to figure out, the less complexity it has. For example, many consumers may find the Internet too complex to understand, so they may decide not to adopt it.

- **Communicability** Communicability refers to the extent to which an innovation is socially visible or is otherwise easy to communicate about in social groups. For example, taboo topics (such as personal hygiene products) have low communicability. Hairstyles are more visible and are therefore naturally more communicable. The greater the ease with which consumers can communicate about an innovation, the more rapidly and likely they are to adopt it.

- **Compatibility** Consumers want products that are compatible with their behavior and values. **Behavioral compatibility** means consumers won't need to alter their behavioral routines. **Value compatibility** means consistency with consumers' deeply held values. Examples of behavioral incompatibility would be vans that do not fit in the garage, electric cars that may require frequent battery charging, or a medication that adversely interacts with a person's favorite beverage, such as coffee (as do most homeopathic medicines). Examples of value incompatibility are contraceptives for consumers whose religion may prohibit contraception, or, for vegetarian consumers, new food products that use animal derivatives.

- **Trialability** Trialability refers to the extent to which it is possible to try out the innovation on a smaller scale. Trialable innovations are adopted more readily than those not trialable. Contact lenses are trialable, whereas keratotomy is not.

This innovation evaluation template can help marketers appraise their proposed new product innovations in respect of the readiness with which consumers will or will not adopt their products. For your learning experience, we bring you news about two innovations: one is a body shape firming *compression undershirt* from Eqimen, Australia. The other is a high-tech eyewear that enables private viewing of video content and looks cool, to boot. (See photos here). Read more about these at www.eqimen.com and www.myvu.com, respectively, and apply the evaluation template.

Which Model Do Innovation Adopters Use?

Adopting an innovation entails all four models of learning. First and foremost, the consumer has to learn the benefits and relative advantage of the innovation. If they do it by reading about it, then this is *cognitive learning*. Consumers who are not very skilled in evaluating new product information are not likely to complete the required *cognitive learning*. Consequently, they are unlikely to adopt the innovation, at least early on. With trialability, consumers basically want to see if the expected utility will materialize. If the trial proves the claimed product benefits, then consumers adopt it with the expectation of getting the reward—the relative advantage. Expectation of the reward is *instrumental learning*. So also is behavioral or value compatibility—if the innovation is compatible, then it serves *instrumental* utility.

Myvu personal media viewer from Myvu.com

If you are not a pioneer in adopting the innovation, you look to others for guidance. If others you trust are using the innovation, you assume it must be safe or effective, or sometimes you simply want to be like these others. You are learning the idea of adopting the innovation through *modeling*—becoming like these others. Finally, marketers often have a choice of how to "position" the new product. By placing the innovation in a proper setting, they create a proper image for the product. The image the consumer develops as a result of these positioning props or settings is, as you realize, *classical conditioning*. Thus, in adopting any innovation, most consumers have to use all four modes of learning.

Consumer Nostalgia

Down the Memory Lane: Nostalgia and the Pleasures of Consuming the Past

Life is a curious mixture of things. On one hand, we admire all of these innovations—products with space-age technology and futuristic designs, but on the other hand, we long for things from eras gone by. This is our way of staying connected to the past. Happy experiences leave memory traces—some of them so strong that we often find ourselves reminiscing about them. Like our 21st birthday. The childhood home in which we grew up. The high school football field on which we played. Our first cars. We reminisce, and we long for those past experiences and for those products from the past. Well, marketers have heard our prayers—they are bringing back those products. Let us understand just what sort of consumption pleasures such products from the past deliver to consumers.

One cute car you see on road these days is the Volkswagen Beetle, fondly called the Bug. The first convertible Bug was released in 2003, but its regular (non-convertible) version first showed up on the road a few years ago, in red, blue, white, black, and of course, its signature "mellow yellow," and it turned heads everywhere. Heads were turning, not because they were seeing something unfamiliar, but rather because they were seeing something old, something they had seen some 30 to 40 years before (or had seen them in pictures). And they were enchanted by this revival of the old. The car was actually first made in 1946 and was in vogue until the 1960s or so. Now, Volkswagen had decided to bring it back.

Welcome to the age of retro, or what marketers call the *retro-trend*. **Retro** products are products that are designed to capture significant stylistic aspects of some old, once popular, but since retired product. What Volkswagen did with the new Beetle, Chrysler did with its PTCruiser and BMW did with the Mini Cooper.

Just why are consumers so enchanted with retro products? There is a one-word answer—**Nostalgia**—defined simply as a longing for the things and lifestyles of the past.[12] This nostalgia stems from two motives whose satisfaction provides the enjoyment the consumer is seeking[13]:

1. **Reminiscing about the personal past**
2. **Re-experiencing the lure of a historical era**

The first motive, and its related source of satisfaction, is that we have fond memories of our pasts—where we lived, what we did, with whom we were friends, what we wore, and what we ate. Products are an integral part of most of these memories. A chance to re-consume these products simply gives us the pleasure of familiar experiences. And the familiar is often warm, cozy, and comfortable. Thus, we all like to revisit our alma mater and rejoice at school reunions. By the way, reunions today are a huge business and on the rise. Along the same lines, we enjoy looking through old albums and seeing movies from the times in which we grew up. Participation in these activities takes us back to our personal pasts and allows us to relive these moments from our once-cherished lives.[14]

> On Pioneer Court in Chicago stands a 26-foot tall statue of Marilyn Monroe, bringing onlookers the joy of nostalgic consumption.

The second reason is just a fascination with the past—even if one has not personally known that past. That is why one likes to go and see a medieval village, for example. Why so? Usually, we are so caught up in the complex life of the current times that when we hear the lore about how idyllic and simple life once was, we develop a fascination with the life of yesteryear. We see an escape, a psychological distancing from the demanding times of the present. This sense of nostalgia is captured by scholars in this observation, "Nostalgia is associated with melancholy and is the alienation of human beings in society as a consequence of their own limitations and finitude."[15] To escape the alienating realities of present times, we want to go back, even if only in a small slice of our lives, and in bits and pieces, to that simpler lifestyle of yesteryear.

MARKETING WITH NOSTALGIA

Marketers respond to consumer hunger for nostalgia in three ways:

1. **Retro fashions and products**
2. **Memorabilia from the past**
3. **Nostalgic Lifestyle Islands**

Retro Fashions and Products Retro clothing, retro cars, retro music—we hear these terms every day. What does *retro* really mean for these products? It means, simply, borrowing the product styles from a particular period of history. The late 1996 Beetle shares with its 1946 original only the exterior, egg-shaped signature body style. Everything else is different, not the least of which is that the original had the engine in the back. (Yes, it's true!) The new Beetle has it in the front. Yet the body style alone is enough to make the car a retro product, and it is enough to impart to consumers a nostalgic experience.[16]

Hot Topic has brought back characters and toys from the past; it sells both the actual merchandise and their imprints on T-shirts. Thus, it sells Care Bears and My Little Pony as eye jewelry. Fashion designers scout the globe for historic costume styles, and Target sells retro furniture. And in movies, *Good Morning, Vietnam* (made in 1987) appealed to baby boomers' need for nostalgia; *Dirty Dancing* (also made in 1987) captured a general fascination with the 1960s, using songs from that era, such as "My Girl" and "I Heard It Through the Grapevine." In May 2009, the movie *Star Trek* opened worldwide, to arouse and feed the nostalgia of its fans, grossing some 375+ million dollars within the first 9 weeks.[17]

Andy Warhol Retro Watch developed by Seiko Instruments Inc., under license from the Andy Warhol Foundation. (Courtesy: Seiko Instruments USA, Inc.)

Memorabilia The marketplace also satisfies consumer need for nostalgic gratification through **memorabilia**—products designed to capture the authenticity of a person, place, or event from a historic period. Thus, Elvis memorabilia is a vast collection of merchandise and images of Elvis and is popular worldwide—one Web site in the German language is doing a brisk business, for example. Likewise, memorabilia abounds for other film celebrities (e.g., Marilyn Monroe, James Dean, and Groucho Marx), for politicians (e.g., Ronald Reagan and Abraham Lincoln), and for movies (e.g., *E.T.* and *Star Wars*), among others. Many consumers devote considerable time and money to building collections of memorabilia on their pet subjects. Michael Jackson's left-handed glove was auctioned off amidst much fanfare on Nov. 21, 2009, at the "Music Icons" auction at the Hard Rock Cafe in New York City's Times Square. And since July 17, 2011, tourists in Chicago have been enjoying a nostalgic eye-full, staring at the 26-foot-tall statue of Marylin Monroe on Pioneer Court.

Nostalgic Lifestyle Islands The third market response is to create "islands" of particular historic lifestyles. An example is Colonial Williamsburg in Virginia—a showcase town of the colonial past. Another example is Club Med, the organized-vacation company, where resort properties are devoid of all modern-day amenities (no TVs or phones, for example). The Chinese Gardens in Sydney will rent you Chinese period costumes to wear while you roam the gardens and take pictures as keepsakes. What these market offerings do for the consumer is to create nostalgic "experiences." If you want to try one such experience while visiting Tel Aviv, for example, plan to stay in a place called *the Cinema Hotel.*

The Joy of Nostalgia: Rolls-Royce Silver Cloud III 1964

Courtesy: Schworer Beverly Hills Limousine Service, LLC (www.classicrollslimo.biz)

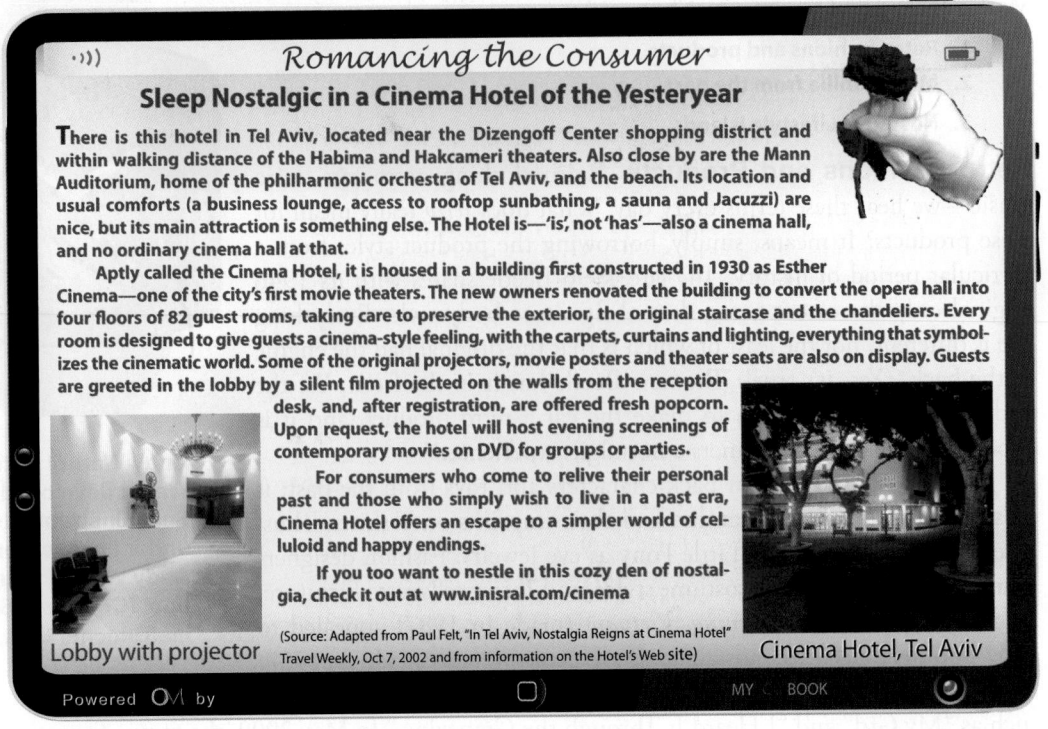

Romancing the Consumer

Sleep Nostalgic in a Cinema Hotel of the Yesteryear

There is this hotel in Tel Aviv, located near the Dizengoff Center shopping district and within walking distance of the Habima and Hakcameri theaters. Also close by are the Mann Auditorium, home of the philharmonic orchestra of Tel Aviv, and the beach. Its location and usual comforts (a business lounge, access to rooftop sunbathing, a sauna and Jacuzzi) are nice, but its main attraction is something else. The Hotel is—'is', not 'has'—also a cinema hall, and no ordinary cinema hall at that.

Aptly called the Cinema Hotel, it is housed in a building first constructed in 1930 as Esther Cinema—one of the city's first movie theaters. The new owners renovated the building to convert the opera hall into four floors of 82 guest rooms, taking care to preserve the exterior, the original staircase and the chandeliers. Every room is designed to give guests a cinema-style feeling, with the carpets, curtains and lighting, everything that symbolizes the cinematic world. Some of the original projectors, movie posters and theater seats are also on display. Guests are greeted in the lobby by a silent film projected on the walls from the reception desk, and, after registration, are offered fresh popcorn. Upon request, the hotel will host evening screenings of contemporary movies on DVD for groups or parties.

For consumers who come to relive their personal past and those who simply wish to live in a past era, Cinema Hotel offers an escape to a simpler world of celluloid and happy endings.

If you too want to nestle in this cozy den of nostalgia, check it out at www.inisral.com/cinema

(Source: Adapted from Paul Felt, "In Tel Aviv, Nostalgia Reigns at Cinema Hotel" *Travel Weekly*, Oct 7, 2002 and from information on the Hotel's Web site)

Lobby with projector

Cinema Hotel, Tel Aviv

Powered OM by   MY BOOK

SUMMARY

In this chapter, we discussed the consumer as a learner, describing four models of learning: classical conditioning, instrumental conditioning, modeling, and cognitive learning. Classical conditioning occurs when a preexisting consumer response to a stimulus (product, service, or person) is transferred to another stimulus, due to their occurrence together. Instrumental conditioning occurs when consumers learn to engage in a behavior repeatedly because the behavior is rewarding. Modeling occurs by observing other consumers whose behavior we find worth imitating. Finally, cognitive learning occurs when consumers obtain new information.

Marketers take advantage of these learning models by structuring their product communications in a fashion conducive to the learning of desired consumer responses. For example, they use classical conditioning by constantly pairing attractive celebrities or likeable non-celebrities with hitherto neutral brands. Through this pairing, the image of the celebrity rubs off on the product. Marketers also offer frequent buyer rewards as instrumental to consumers learning to patronize those marketers. The modeling method of learning is promoted by giving free product samples to people likely to serve as role models for other consumers. And cognitive learning is utilized by the appropriate design of messages for low-involvement versus high-involvement products.

Next, we discussed how consumers acquire and process product information and how they remember it. Here we described three types of memories—sensory, short-term and long-term—and examined how information travels between and among them. Understanding the workings of memory and remembering helps marketers create more effective product messages.

Next we discussed how and why consumers learn to adopt or not to adopt a new product innovation. Consumers desire certain characteristics in innovations, namely, relative advantage, low perceived risk, low complexity, easy communicability, behavioral and value compatibility, and trialability. Finally, we discussed the consumer desire for nostalgic consumption, and how marketers are satisfying this consumer need by bringing back retro products, such as the Volkswagen Beetle and the Andy Warhol watch.

CB Blog

WHAT THE CONSUMER WILL NOT LEARN

Learners—that is us. We are constantly learning something. Without learning, our progress as people would stop. Can you visualize your life if today you knew only as much as you had known, say, 10 years ago? Learning empowers you, in life and in the marketplace.

Fortunately, much of that learning comes naturally—without any effort, just by being exposed to stimuli in our world as we go about living everyday life.

All learning is, in essence, the learning of associations. Association between two stimuli (classical conditioning), between an act and a reward (instrumental conditioning), between an act and what that act will make you (role modeling), and between an object and its name (e.g., simple brand name awareness—cognitive learning) or between an object and a property or consequence (e.g., a brand claim —also cognitive learning).

These associations occur in our physical and social worlds, some created by nature, some by society at large, and not an insignificant number of them by marketers.

As a marketer, you pair your brand with a celebrity; pair it with certain lifestyle depictions; pair it with an upscale, trendy store; pair it with product benefits; with certain emotions; with certain consumer values and aspirations.

But you can't "manufacture" these associations in your image, in isolation from the pairings (i.e., associations) consumers have learned in their world-at-large. You can't put together a pairing of just any two entities you desire to be associated in the consumer mind, and say "Viola! The consumer will have learned (i.e., accepted) that association."

Consumers will accept only those pairings (associations) they find intuitively sensible. As a marketer, LEARN THAT!

MY CB BOOK .COM

CONSUMER BEHAVIOR

(K)EY TERMS

Associative network
Behavioral compatibility
Chunking
Classical conditioning
Cognitive learning
Communicability
Complexity
Conditioned stimulus

Elaboration
Episodic memory
Innovation
Innovation adoption
Innovators
Instrumental conditioning
Learning
Modeling
Nostalgia

Problem solving
Rote memorization
Semantic memory
Stimulus discrimination
Stimulus generalization
Relative advantage
Perceived risk
Value compatibility
Trialability
Unconditioned stimulus

A PHOTO QUIZ

Stacy Adams Shoes and Clothing

Yellow Tail, a wine from Australia

[yellow tail]

tails, you win.

MyVu personal media viewer

Equmen men's compression clothing

1. That Stacy Adams Ad you saw before—look at it again. In addition to the Classical Conditioning method of learning, which other method is at work? Perhaps all three, but at least one more. Can you name it? And explain how.

Note: Neither advertisers nor consumers need be aware of the specific method. Advertisers strive, simply but importantly, only to create and communicate an image association, and consumers learn it "naturally" by one of the four methods. Naming those methods, as this chapter does, is consumer researchers' (not consumers') tool of analysis.

2. Consider the three products pictured here. MyVu (personal media viewer) and Equmen (men's compression undershirt) are new products, i.e., innovations. Yellow Tail (wine from Australia) has been around for a few years but not every wine consumer may be familiar with it yet.

Assume you wanted to launch these products to target markets hitherto unfamiliar with each. As a marketer, what kinds of "ideas" would you like your target consumers to *learn* about your product over, say, the next three years? List these ideas, and then for each idea to be learned by consumers, identify (a) which learning model would be most relevant and useful, and (b) how would you harness that model—which marketing mix element, and (c) and in what manner (for example, if you suggest an ad campaign, spell out the message and creative elements).

Product _____ (Repeat this exercise for each product)

Ideas you want consumers to learn	a. Model that would be relevant	b. Marketing mix element to deploy	c. Implementation details
1. _____	_____	_____	_____
2. _____	_____	_____	_____
3. _____	_____	_____	_____
4. _____	_____	_____	_____
5. _____	_____	_____	_____
6. _____	_____	_____	_____
and so on ...	and so on ...	and so on ...	and so on ...

YOUR TURN

REVIEW+Rewind

1. Define conditioned and unconditioned stimuli, giving examples of each.

2. Explain extrinsic versus intrinsic rewards, citing examples. What are their relative merits and demerits?

3. In your own words, explain each of the four models of learning. Cite two consumer examples of each from personal experience.

4. Compare and contrast high-involvement and low involvement learning.

5. Describe what is meant by stimulus generalization and stimulus discrimination. Explain how marketers use these concepts.

6. How short is short-term memory? How long is long-term memory? Explain your answer.

7. Name and briefly describe the three processes by which information is placed into long-term memory.

8. Explain the difference between semantic and episodic memories.

9. List any six criteria that an innovation should meet in order to attain consumer acceptance.

10. Explain what is nostalgic marketing. What value do retro products bring to consumers?

THINK+Apply

1. Should marketers try to transform consumers from low involvement to high involvement mode of learning? Why or why not?

2. Given your understanding of how consumers' short and long term memories work, write down three things you would do to make the consumer memory work for your product, assuming your product is (a) a car and (b) yogurt.

3. Evaluate the following products/services in terms of the desirable characteristics of innovation that facilitate their adoption:
   a. Roomba automatic vacuum cleaner (go to www.sharperimage.com and search for Roomba)
   b. Teeth whitening strip (go to www. crestwhitestrips.com)

4. How can you use the concept of modeling in promoting a social cause, say an anti-drug program?

5. Visit two Web sites: Limited Express (http://www.limited.com/about/exp/index.jsp) and Dolce & Gabbana Website (http://eng. dolcegabbana.it/main.asp). You will notice that each uses a combination of methods to convey its message and brand story. Can you describe which of the four models of learning each Web site is utilizing? Be specific about what is it you learned and through which method. Also try to memorize a few items you see; comment on how you memorized them.

PRACTICE+Experience

1. Collect advertisements that illustrate, separately, how advertisers base their messages on one or the other model of consumer learning.

2. Interview 2 or 3 consumers who may have adopted a new product recently. Ask questions to understand how they viewed the new product on innovation characteristics described in this chapter.

3. Assume you have recently accepted a position as marketing director of a local museum. You recall the concepts of instrumental conditioning, and wonder if it can help you develop ideas for getting your member patrons to visit the museum more often. Write a memo for your director, outlining various approaches (utilizing both intrinsic and extrinsic rewards, specifying which is which) to get consumers to visit the museum more often.

4. Interview two consumers and ask them if they remember any commercials they saw the last time they watched TV. Ask them which ones (let them describe the storyline so you may assess how much they remembered). Next, ask them questions that would help you understand what factors help consumers remember or not remember commercials. Write a brief report on what you learned.

In the Marketing Manager's Shoes

Put yourself in a marketing manager's shoes. Most concepts in the chapter have some lessons for the marketing manager, i.e., they suggest what to do differently in practice; indeed, often these applications are implicit in our explanations of the concepts and models in the chapter. Identify at least five specific applications of the chapter's concepts, all of which should be entirely new, different from the examples cited here.

Values

5

Consumer Values, Personality, and Self-Concept

The Reality of Our Multiple Selves

LEARN . APPLY . EXPERIENCE

She Drives at 200 MPH and Adopts A Rainforest!

Leilani Münter—You are probably familiar with her name. She is a race car driver, finishing fourth at the 2004 Race at the Texas Motor Speedway, the highest finish for a female driver in the history of the racetrack. In 2007, she became the fourth woman in history to race in the Indy Pro Series, and Sports Illustrated named her as one of the top ten female race car drivers in the world.

Photo by Marc Roy

Leilani Münter

She is passionate about racing. But it is her other name that may surprise, and delight, you: *Carbon Free Girl*. Yes, she is also an environmentalist!

With a bachelor's degree in Biology, specializing in Ecology, Behavior and Evolution from the University of California, San Diego, she understands up close the ecological crisis our planet faces, and she is taking one giant step toward mitigating it: Getting car racing to find eco-religion. At the races, she is promoting the use of bio-fuels, eco-friendly materials, and recycling programs. And for every race she drives in, she is adopting one acre of rainforest.

She drives 200 mph race cars, which causes a waste of a lot of fuel, tires, and carbon fiber. "I know it is not the most eco-friendly sport in the world," says Ms. Münter, "but I am on a mission to change that."[1] ESPN magazine calls her an oxymoron: A race car driver and an ecologist! She is forming an Eco Dream Team—a group of sponsors for her eco-message-carrying cars. "If a sponsor didn't want to work with me because I promote recycling and caring for the environment, then... thanks, but no thanks, I don't want you on my race car anyway."[2]

> My consumption must honor my values.

Photo by:
Craig Davidson

Photo by Marc Roy
All photos are courtesy of
Leilani Münter

To this 36-year old and (according to some) "weird, greenie, vegetarian hippie chick,"[3] environment is a deeply held value!

Check out her site at carbonfreegirl.com.

1, 2, 3 Leilani Münter, "My Race to Save the World," August 11, 2008, *Huffington Post* (huffingtonpost.com); Also see: carbonfreegirl.com and leilanimunter.com.

INTRODUCTION

Leilani Münter. Preserving our planet is a deeply held value to her. And using the racing events as a platform, she is delivering her eco-action messages to more than a 100 million fans.

Core beliefs and actions such as these form our value system. Values are the foundation of all our thoughts and actions. Both as humans and as consumers. They also form the core topic of this chapter. We begin by defining the concept of value, and then present some important values humans possess, demonstrating their role in our consumption choices. Because our values constantly guide, covertly and overtly, our preferences and actions, we develop into a type of person, psychologically speaking, different from other persons. This "psychological person" is called *personality*. We describe selected personality traits, those that are considered significant in psychology, and likewise those considered important for consumer behavior.

An important facet of the psychological person that we are is our self-concept. This concept is not, we will learn, a singular entity; rather, it too is multi-faceted. We discuss our various selves, and account for their various components—from our bodies to our characters, for example. We end the chapter with an enumeration of how our material possessions, the goods we buy in the marketplace, become enmeshed with our identities, thus forming our so called *extended selves*.

CONSUMER VALUES

Definition

Should we really care for our environment? Should universities have minority quotas for student admissions? Should governments ban all violent videogames targeted at children? Or irreverent lyrics by Eminem? Should a fast food burger chain be held responsible if a consumer can show he got heart disease from eating its fattening burgers? And, should motorists be fined for using their cell phones while driving? All these questions call for "value judgments." Your answers will depend on what your values are.

Values are desired end-states of life and preferred paths to achieving them. As such, they constitute the purposes and goals for which we believe human life should be lived—ours and others'. They also serve as fundamental rules by which life should be lived. Thus, if we value not depleting the resources of our planet, then we will not consume without consideration of its ecological impact. Values are our beliefs about big things. *Beliefs* are our conceptions of what is or should be. This table is solid; Tylenol will cure a headache; it will rain soon—these are our *beliefs* about small things in life. Honesty is more important than profit; money is the source of happiness; it is our duty to help the poor and needy—these are our beliefs about big things in life, and are therefore our *values*. If we believe in helping the needy, then we will donate to social causes (e.g., relief for Haiti). If we believe in free individual choice, then we would not favor government regulation of music, videogames, movies, and the like. And, if we believe in individual responsibility, then we would hold ourselves, not fast food burger chains, responsible for our own eating behaviors.

Values require us to "take a position" on basic choices we make in the conduct of our lives. As such they undergird and inevitably influence our opinions and choices on all matters, big and small. And, of course, they intimately affect the choices we make as consumers.

How many end-states do we value? In other words, how many values are there? Psychologist Milton Rokeach identified 36 values, 18 in each of the two groups, called *terminal* and *instrumental*. **Terminal values** are the goals we seek in life (e.g., freedom, wealth, salvation, etc.), whereas **instrumental values** are the means, paths, or behavioral standards by which we pursue those goals (e.g., honesty, altruism, etc.). Rokeach developed these lists of values for understanding human psychology.[1] In recent times, marketing

> **One Chinese traditional value is "Man-nature orientation"—that man and nature must exist in symbiosis (as opposed to the pursuit of material progress at the cost of preserving nature). In a study of Chinese consumers, those who scored high on this value were found to be more ecologically conscious.**
>
> Source: R. Chan and L. Lau, "Antecedents of Green Purchases: A Survey in China," *J. of Consumer Marketing*, 2000, 17 (4), 338-357.

scholars have developed value lists more directly related to humans' consumption behavior.

What is Your LOV Profile?

Consumer researchers felt a need for identifying values that might be more directly relevant to everyday consumer behavior. For this purpose, consumer researcher Lynn Kahle (along with colleagues Sharon Beatty, Pamela Homer, and Shekhar Misra) developed a List of Values (LOV), consisting of nine terminal values:[2]

1. **Self-respect**
2. **Self-fulfillment**
3. **Security**
4. **Sense of belonging**
5. **Excitement**
6. **Sense of accomplishment**
7. **Fun and enjoyment**
8. **Being well respected**
9. **Warm relationships with others**

LOV 6

LOV 7

LOV 9

This list of values corresponds well to the needs in Maslow's Hierarchy of Needs, except that Maslow includes physiological needs, and LOV adds values of fun and excitement. Does LOV explain our consumption behaviors? The answer is a definite yes. In a number of studies, LOV has been found related to consumer activities: for example, people who valued a sense of belonging especially liked group activities. Those who valued fun and enjoyment especially liked skiing, dancing, backpacking, hiking, camping, and drinking. And people who valued a "warm relationship" with others tended to give gifts to others, often for no reason at all.[3]

Beyond these research findings, it makes sense to expect LOV to influence a wide range of consumer behaviors. For example, would you expect shoplifters to value "self-respect" more or less than an average consumer? Who would you expect to enroll in a master's program—someone with a low importance rating on self-fulfillment value or someone with a high rating on it? (And remember, enrolling in a master's program is also a consumer behavior.) Finally, who would you expect to forgo a visit with family for a chance for adventure travel: one who values sense of belonging or one who values excitement? We list several such expected behaviors in Table 5.1, with the caveat that these are based not on research but on our intuitive reading of the conceptual meaning of these values. In practice, as a marketer, you should always go beyond available research and build many more intuitive inferences for consumption topics of interest to you, and then verify them through pragmatic research.

Since consumers differ in their values, LOV can be used to segment consumers. Although any number of segments can be identified in a population, three most sharply distinct values-based segments would be Achievement, Hedonism, and Relationships (it is easy to see which of the nine LOV values would score high for each group).[4]

To the Achievement segment,

	TABLE 5.1 SELECTED BEHAVIORS PRODUCED BY *LOV*
LIST OF VALUES (LOV)	**SELECTED CONSUMER BEHAVIORS**
1. SELF RESPECT	Shoplifting, changing retail tags. (Lack of Self-esteem)
2. SELF FULFILLMENT	Enrolling in a part time master's degree course; donating to charities.
3. SECURITY	Not running up credit card high
4. SENSE OF BELONGING	Taking family vacations; visiting with friends & relatives rather than going to new places.
5. EXCITEMENT	Adventure travel.
6. SENSE OF ACCOMPLISHMENT	Saving for home ownership; self improvement courses; learning professional skills.
7. FUN AND ENJOYMENT	Watching sports; vacationing at resorts; etc.
8. BEING WELL RESPECTED	Avoid edgy and funky clothing; not drink much; shun all deviant consumption.
9. WARM RELATIONSHIPS WITH OTHERS*	Personal hospitality and participating in social get-togethers. Gift giving. Heavy use of communication products.

Source: LOV items (but not examples) are from Kahle, Beatty, and Homer, 1986, (See Lynn R. Kahle, Sharon E. Beatty, and Pamela Homer, "Alternative Measurement Approaches to Consumer Values: The List of Values (LOV) and Values and Life Style (VALS)," Journal of Consumer Research 13 (December 1986), pp. 405–409). LOV items are copyright © 1986 by Journal of Consumer Research, Inc. Published by The University of Chicago Press.

MY CB BOOK

accomplishment and self-fulfillment would be of high value; to the Hedonism segment, enjoying life would be most important; and finally, to the Relationships segment, a sense of belonging and warm social relationships would be of utmost value. Research has found that consumers who value relationships with others are more susceptible to interpersonal influence; consequently, when purchasing products, particularly socially visible products, such as clothing, these consumers place much more emphasis on style and brand image (as opposed to the product's functional features like durability, reliability, or fit).[6]

Beyond LOV: More Consumer Values

We don't want to leave you with the impression that LOV exhausts all consumer values. In fact, there are a number of other values—both general as well as consumption specific—that influence consumer behavior. Many of our personal values come from the culture in which we live, so we will cover them more comprehensively in Chapter 9. One such value is collectivism (versus individualism). In collectivist cultures, people are concerned about the wellbeing of their group and society in general. In individualist cultures, people are focused on their own personal wellbeing even at the expense of their group. Now, these cultural values are not equally assimilated by all members of a society. Thus, in collectivist cultures, some individuals will turn out to be individualists, and vice versa.

Will consumers who value individualism behave differently than those who value collectivism? Yes. A collectivism-valuing consumer will consume in a way that is good for the society as a whole, such as buying an eco-friendly car. In contrast, an individualist consumer will buy the car that pleases him or her regardless of its environmental impact. One study in Greece found that consumers who were collectivists were more prone to practice recycling than those who were individualistic.[7]

Another personal value is **materialism**—the extent to which one considers possessing and consuming more and more products as a sign of success. In the above-mentioned recycling study in Greece, materialistic consumers were found to recycle less than an average consumer. As should be self-evident, some consumers' never-ending possession sprees are driven and explained by their high materialism value.

LINKING PRODUCT ATTRIBUTES TO CONSUMER VALUES

As the foregoing examples show, values can affect the choices consumers make at three levels:

- **Marketplace Activity:** Shoplifting, shopping honesty, shopping constantly, the never-ending quest for possessions, patronizing minority sellers, etc.
- **Choice of Product Category:** Enrolling in personal development courses, purchasing gifts, joining social networking associations, consuming hedonistic products, etc.
- **Preference for Product Attributes:** Seeking travel with adventure versus connecting and socializing attributes, buying cosmetics that do not use animal testing, valuing symbolic and social prestige attributes of a product, etc.

Note the last point again: values cause consumers to seek different attributes in products. Put another way, consumers prefer different product attributes because of the values consumers possess. Wouldn't it make sense, then, to find out these underlying values behind consumer choice of product attributes? It does, and to accomplish this, consumer researchers build what they call **means-end-chains**—pathways connecting product attributes to ultimate consumer goals or values. (See Figure 5.1.) These are simply links between a product's physical features and the consumer's fundamental needs and values. Attributes lead to consequences or benefits, which in turn lead to still other, higher-level benefits. And these higher-level benefits ultimately lead to the fulfillment of values.

Marketers draw these links to understand the ultimate purpose for which consumers buy even seemingly mundane products.

To draw these links, consumer researchers use a technique called **laddering**—a procedure to map a consumer's view of how a product's use ultimately fulfills his or her higher level values. To implement the procedure, consumers are asked repeatedly in an iterative sequence: "Why is that feature important to you?" For example: "Why is quick acceleration important to you?" If the answer is, "to maneuver out of traffic situations," we next ask, "And why is that important to you?" And so on.[8]

FIGURE 5.1

A MEANS-END CHAIN FOR A HYPOTHETICAL CONSUMER

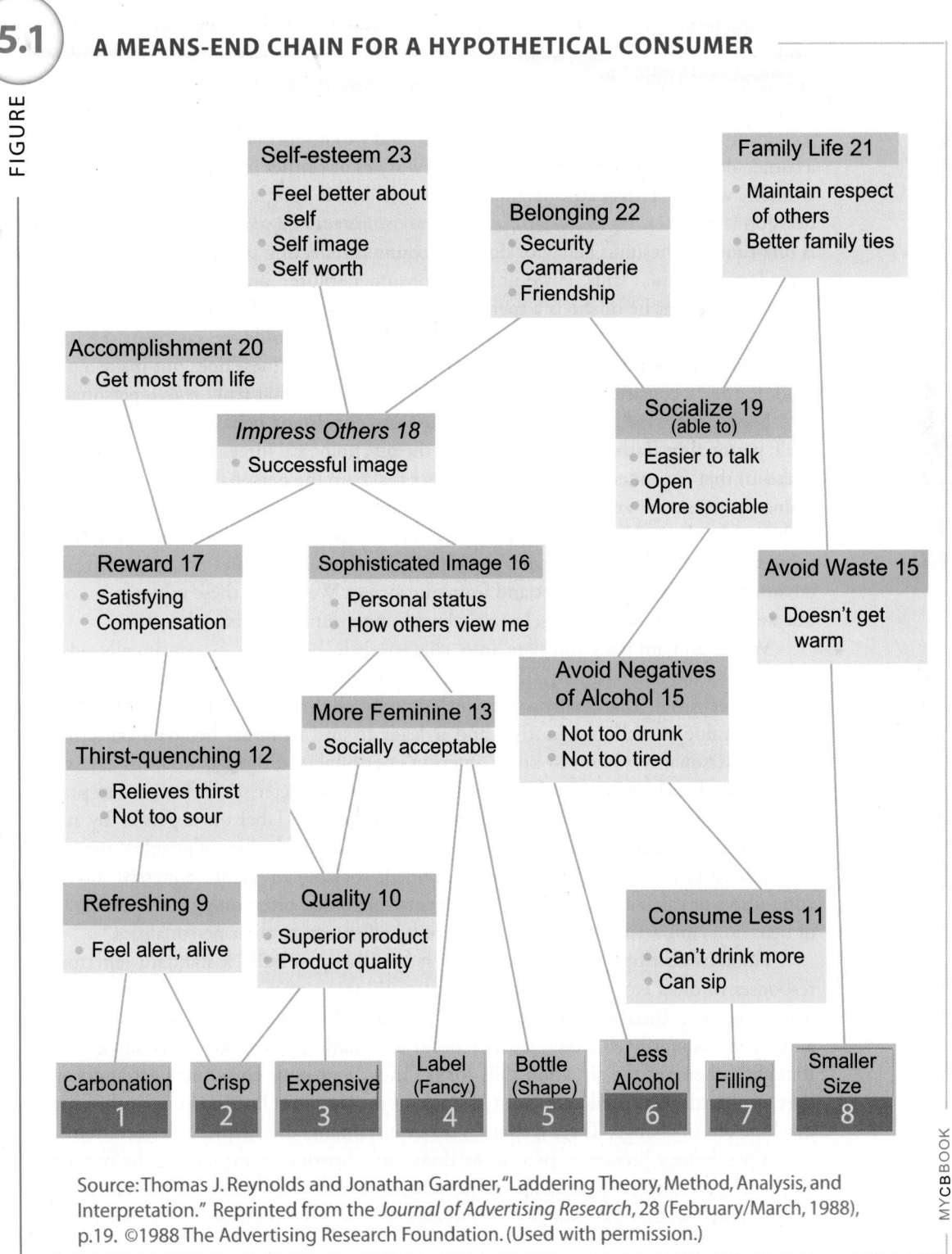

Source: Thomas J. Reynolds and Jonathan Gardner, "Laddering Theory, Method, Analysis, and Interpretation." Reprinted from the *Journal of Advertising Research*, 28 (February/March, 1988), p.19. ©1988 The Advertising Research Foundation. (Used with permission.)

MYCBBOOK

CONSUMER PERSONALITY

Our values make us the persons we are. A person's personality is one way of summing up that person. A part of personality is genetically given to us, and a part is formed by our social environment. But our personalities are also influenced considerably by our values. If we valued hedonism, for example, then we would develop a happy-go-lucky, pleasure-seeking personality. And if we valued human relationships over self-interest, we would develop a warm, affable personality.

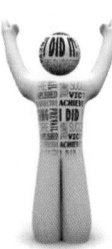

Personality refers to a person's psychological makeup that engenders characteristic responses to the environment in which he or she lives. By *environment*, we mean *social or physical situations*. By *response*, we mean *an action or behavior*. All of our actions or behaviors are our responses to environmental stimuli. At a cocktail party, for instance, we see a group of people (environmental stimuli), and we either try talking to them or stand in a corner aloof (response). If we see a lot of new styles of clothes in the store (environmental stimuli), we either rush to buy them, or we deliberate long and hard before making a decision (response). By *characteristic*, we mean *consistent or typical, natural or spontaneous*. A one-time and hesitant behavior does not count as reflecting personality; rather it is just a random response. Thus, if we notice a consumer splurge on an isolated occasion, we could not say that he or she is a spendthrift. If splurging were his or her typical behavior, and it seemed to come to him or her naturally, only then could we say he or she has the personality of a spendthrift. Likewise, a one-time act of kindness does not make a person kind. Rather, a consistent, repeated pattern of behavior is what truly *reflects* personality.

Notice the word *reflects*. This is because the consistent behavior pattern is not, by itself, personality. Rather, that behavior and the psychological forces (i.e., our psychological makeup) that engender or produce it together make up the personality. Those forces come primarily from our genetics and our values and motives. Some motives are biological or biogenic, that with which we are born; others—psychogenic motives—we learn and acquire based on the rewards and punishments we receive. Values are learned from the environment—from our culture and from our society. We receive these values from society, but we adopt (or reject) them selectively based upon our own personal motives.

Values and motives translate into characteristic behaviors as continually adapted responses to the environment. Thus, values, motives, and characteristic behaviors are all closely interwoven. That is why some words describe all three elements: e.g., "achievement" can be a value as well as a motive, and it leads to an "achiever" behavior pattern (i.e., achiever personality). Now, to know a person's personality, although we must assess both psychological makeup (i.e., values and motives) *and* characteristic behaviors, in practice and in everyday life, we conveniently stick a personality label on a person by merely observing that person's characteristic behavior. Everyday descriptions of people—innovative or tradition-bound, dogmatic or open-minded, sociable or aloof, aggressive or meek, compulsive or calculative, thrifty or indulgent—are based often only on our observations of behaviors, but actually we intend these to be references to their personalities.[9]

Humans develop personality because it is efficient to build a standard repertoire of responses to one's environment, as opposed to thinking up a new response every time a situation arises. These standard responses, by repeated occurrence, get etched in memory and are involuntarily elicited (i.e., they occur automatically without effort and conscious thought) whenever the situation calls for it. Thus, aggressive consumers get angry when they see that an advertised item is out of stock, or the checkout line too long, or the vending machine out of change. These responses occur instantaneously without deliberation.

In psychology literature, two of the dominant theories for explaining the concept of personality are the Freudian theory of personality and the personality trait theory.[10] Every consumer researcher is at least part psychologist. Now it is our chance to know what every psychologist knows.

FREUDIAN THEORY

Is Your Id Misbehavin'?

Recall that, in Chapter 2, we talked about some of our motives being unconscious. Sigmund Freud, the founder of psychoanalysis, was a leading psychologist who suggested the concept of the unconscious. He argued that human personality is driven by both conscious and unconscious motives. He proposed three divisions of the human psyche: id, superego, and ego. The **id** is the basic source of inner energy, directed at avoiding pain and obtaining pleasure; it represents unconscious drives and urges. The **superego** is the moral side of the psyche, reflecting the ideals of society. It is a person's conscience, trying to keep the id from misbehaving, so to speak. The **ego** is the conscious mediator between the id and the superego, that is, between the unconscious and impulsive desires of the id and the societal ideals internalized by the superego. The ego helps a person respond to the world in socially acceptable ways. According to Freud, a person's personality is crafted by the interplay of these three forces.[11]

The precise role of these three forces in shaping personality is complex. Suffice it to say, a broad way to classify people into personality types using Freudian theory is to look at the relative dominance of the id, superego, and ego forces. Persons with a dominant id would be mostly pleasure seeking and self-centered. Persons with a dominant superego would be mostly moralistic and altruistic. Finally, persons with a dominant ego would be mostly practical—and would, in fact, guard their sense of self. In consumer behavior, id-dominated persons would seek more hedonistic consumption and be unrestrained in their desire for buying and consuming. Superego-dominated persons would shun anti-social consumption and advocate pro-social consumption (e.g., shun environment-polluting products). Persons with a well-developed ego would show a consumption pattern balanced between the other two types; they would also more likely engage in self-growth oriented consumption (e.g., enrolling in skill-development courses).

Because many of the id's urges are socially unacceptable, they are suppressed. Subsequently, they find their expression in alternative ways that are more acceptable to society. Behaviors that express themselves in this manner are called *defense mechanisms*.

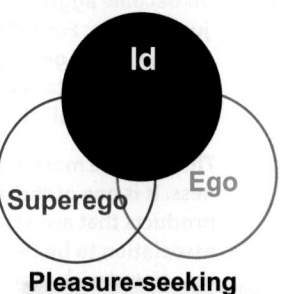

Pleasure-seeking & self-centered

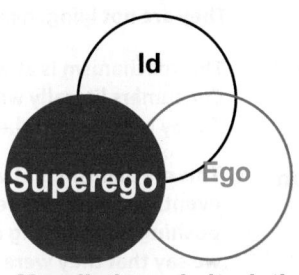

Moralistic and altruistic

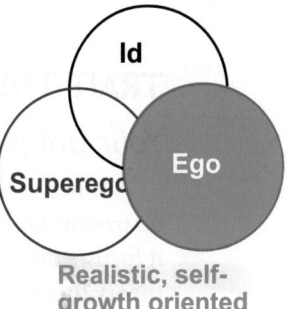

Realistic, self-growth oriented

DEFENSE MECHANISMS

Defense mechanisms are psychological processes we employ to protect our egos. These defense mechanisms make a behavior acceptable to our own sense of right and help us overcome guilt and frustration. When we use them, we either mentally redefine the stimulus (e.g., "That car is not really a luxury car") or redefine our motive for engaging in a particular behavior (e.g., "I didn't buy it because of its luxury features").

You know some of them already. *Rationalization*, for example. When someone tries to give a rational reason for a seemingly irrational behavior (like why he or she drove 5 miles to save 50 cents on gas), we say they are rationalizing. Other defense mechanisms include projection, aggression, repression, withdrawal, and regression. Read more about them in Table 5.2. We should have an understanding of the defense mechanisms consumers are employing. And we should thank Freud for this consumer insight!

TABLE 5.2 SELECTED DEFENSE MECHANISMS

Rationalization	This defense mechanism involves explaining an embarrassing action by a false motive, for which the real motive is suppressed from consciousness. For example, a consumer who bought a luxury car to impress others but does not want to admit this motive would rationalize the decision by citing a superior performance feature, even though that feature may have played no role in his or her decision.
Projection	This defense mechanism is at work when we project our own feelings onto others, or blame others for our own shortcomings or attribute personal feelings to others. For example, suppose we break an appliance by wrongful use, we would blame the manufacturer for poor workmanship. Or if we enjoy buying name brand clothes from off-price stores, we would assume that all our co-workers who wear nice clothes must have also been buying them from some off-price stores. Thus, by assuring ourselves that our own motive to buy nice clothes from off-price and irregular merchandise stores is a "normal" behavior in others, we protect our ego from anxiety.
Aggression	To become aggressive is to display or inflict pain on someone out of frustration and without justification. For example, a consumer who suspects a certain retailer of price gouging during a market shortage might spoil the merchandise in the store. Or a poor person who is deprived of basic transportation may slash tires of a luxury car. Now you know why some consumers do these sorts of "uncool" things!
Repression	This defense mechanism involves pushing unacceptable thoughts and feelings into unconsciousness. It is one of the most primitive mechanisms. Repression is at work when consumers avoid products that are associated with unattractive situations, and at the same time they deny that association to be the reason for their avoidance. For example, a consumer may avoid products associated with his ex-spouse (or products he consumed in a previous marriage). Or children of immigrants, eager to fit into their new environment, may avoid their own parental preferences; moreover, they would deny that they are trying to distance themselves from their ethnic origins. They are not lying, mind you, for their motive to distance themselves works subconsciously.
Withdrawal	This mechanism is at work when we withdraw from a situation in which we are not successful. Consumers literally withdraw from associations, PTA meetings, health clubs, book clubs, and so on, if they believe that they are not performing well in those settings.
Regression	This mechanism is at work when we revert to childhood behaviors. Attend a very special sales event, and you may very well witness regression. Sometimes adults resort to immature behaviors, pushing and shoving each other, or fighting over limited merchandise. Referring to adults, when we say that they were fighting like children, they in fact were. Freud would have said the same thing!

MY CB BOOK

TRAIT THEORY

Your Uniqueness Is What Your Personality Is

Whereas Freud's theory seeks to *explain* personality, "trait theory" merely seeks to *describe* it. Unlike the former, it does not deal with the inner, psychological forces; rather, it focuses directly on the "characteristic behavior" portion of the definition. That is, Freud's theory focuses on the "why" of personality; trait theory focuses on the "what."

The trait theory of personality is an approach used to describe a person's personality by means of a multitude of characteristics or traits. Each trait marks similarities and differences among people. A **personality trait** is defined as a person's stable and consistent way of responding to the environment in a specific domain.[12] Notice that the definition of a personality trait is virtually identical to the definition of personality. However, a given personality trait works in a specific domain, whereas personality is the sum total of all of the personality traits. For example, in the domain of group situations, how a person consistently behaves across group situations will be one of his or her personality traits (e.g., aggressive or friendly). Another domain centers on work and career, and how a person consistently behaves in the workplace will be another trait (e.g., striving or lazy). A third domain is product acquisition, and, again, how a person consistently behaves in this domain is another trait (e.g., materialistic or frugal). Consistency of response is a hallmark of a trait: persons with a compulsiveness trait consistently and characteristically act compulsively; persons with the personality trait of dogmatism consistently hold on to their beliefs; and variety-seeking persons are constantly changing their preferences.[13]

If personality is the sum total of all the traits, how many traits are there? The answer is, *thousands*—actually, 4500, to be exact. This magic number is the number of different words people use to describe other people (in the English language), a list painstakingly compiled by psychologist Gordon Allport in the 1930s. Of course, no single human being has that large a vocabulary, and the list would be too unwieldy to be of any practical use. Therefore, psychologist Raymond Cattell took Allport's list and (using a statistical technique called *factor analysis*) reduced it to 16 fundamental traits, phrased as pairs of opposite adjectives: e.g., reserved/outgoing, apprehensive/self-assured, etc.[14]

Consumer researchers have been interested, naturally, in predicting consumers' brand choices by their personalities. They did not succeed: for example, in the 1970s, researchers failed to find any personality differences between the buyers of Ford versus Chevy brands of cars. For a reason we will explain later, personalities should not be expected to predict brand choices, not directly anyway. What personalities can be expected to explain are, rather, consumers' natural behaviors, including marketplace behaviors. Take Cattell's two traits we listed earlier: reserved/outgoing and apprehensive/self-assured. If we are outgoing (instead of reserved), for example, then we are going to participate much more in group based consumption activities, and we are more likely to buy products with their public image in mind. In contrast, as reserved consumers, we are probably going to prefer that salespersons keep their distance, leaving us to browse by ourselves. If we are apprehensive, we might feel intimidated in a sophisticated, exclusive restaurant; as self-assured consumers on the other hand, we are likely to be more certain of our rights in the marketplace and seek to exercise them.

To show further that personality influences consumer actions, let us consider another set of personality traits, called the Edwards Personality Preference Schedule (EPPS), which consists of 15 traits. For illustration, we have chosen five of them (see Table 5.3).

TABLE 5.3	FIVE SELECTED PERSONALITY TRAITS FROM EDWARD'S PERSONAL PREFERENCE SCHEDULE (EPPS)
TRAIT	**BEHAVIOR**
1. Achievement	To do one's best, accomplish tasks of great significance, do things better than others, be successful, be a recognized authority.
2. Order	To have work neat and organized, make plans before starting, keep files, things arranged to run smoothly, have things organized.
3. Exhibition	To say clever things, tell amusing jokes and stories, talk about personal achievements, have others notice and comment on one's appearance, be the center of attention.
4. Autonomy	To be able to come and go as one pleases, say what one thinks, be independent in making decisions, feel free to do what one wants, avoid conformity, avoid responsibilities and obligations.
5. Affiliation	To be loyal to friends, do things for friends, form new friendships, make many friends, form strong attachments, participate in friendly groups.

MY CB BOOK

THE BIG FIVE OF PERSONALITY

Although the above two lists are quite useful to characterize human personality, psychologists were still not satisfied with the length of these trait lists. Over the 45-year period from 1945 to 1990, psychologists continued to seek a smaller set that would account for most of Cattell's traits, and other traits as well. The current view has now settled on five factors. This view argues that all of the adjectives people use to describe other people can be encompassed by five broad factors, called **the Big Five** of personality.[15] These are captured by the acronym OCEAN[16], which stands for:

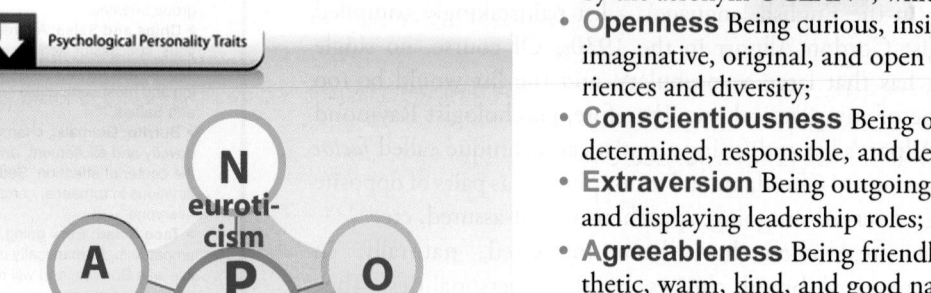

Psychological Personality Traits

- **O**penness Being curious, insightful, imaginative, original, and open to new experiences and diversity;
- **C**onscientiousness Being organized, determined, responsible, and dependable;
- **E**xtraversion Being outgoing, persuasive, and displaying leadership roles;
- **A**greeableness Being friendly, sympathetic, warm, kind, and good natured;
- **N**euroticism Being emotionally unstable, nervous, and anxious;[17]

Each of these is actually a *supertrait*, because each contains a number of more specific traits, as described above.

The Big Five theory is relatively new and has not yet been utilized for published research in consumer behavior. But if you solved the Personality Puzzle above, you can easily think of the marketing applications of OCEAN. For starters, Openness can make you adopt new products more readily. Conscientiousness can make you use shopping lists, evaluate product choices more thoroughly, and not take advantage of retailer errors. Agreeableness can make you naturally act like a nice customer in service establishments. Extraversion, perhaps a trait all too familiar, can lead you to engage more in social leisure activities. Finally, neuroticism would likely lead you to engage in escape or compensatory consumption behaviors, such as binge eating or gambling.

TABLE

5.4 MEASURING CONSUMER INNOVATIVENESS

	Strongly disagree				Strongly agree
	1	2	3	4	5
1. When new products (relevant to me) come out in the market, I am one of the first ones to buy them.					
2. I am interested in finding out about the latest innovations in products I use.					
3. Often I use products in unusual ways to get more out of them.					
4. It is too risky to buy products as soon as they come out.*					
5. Clothing, music, electronics, food products, or whatever, I usually wait for other people to try out new trends.*					

Note: To score yourself, reverse score the items marked *, and then add all item ratings. The higher the score, the more innovative you are, with 15 being the middle point. (Your score)

MY CB BOOK MEA SUR E

Source: Fashioned, in part, after Ronald E. Goldsmith and Charles F. Hofacker, "Measuring Consumer Innovativeness," *Journal of the Academy of Marketing Science,*" 19, 1991, p. 212, which is focused on consumer innovativeness in a product category. More specifically, only the first item in the present scale resembles (but is unidentical with) an item in the cited source. The present scale (which is intuitive and empirically untested) is easy to adapt for specific product categories (e.g., electronics, clothing, appliances, cosmetics, cooking, etc.) by simply inserting the name of the product category instead of the word *product* or *products*.

MY CB BOOK

MARKETERS' FIVE

To match the Big Five that psychologists have given us, we have culled five personality traits of more direct use to marketers. This is not a standard list, mind you, but we consider these important and worthy of study.

Innovativeness

Have you ever noticed how some people rush out to buy new products as soon as they are introduced? These consumers have the personality trait of **innovativeness**, defined as being predisposed to embrace *new* products, ideas, and behaviors. They are not necessarily seeking instant gratification, mind you, nor are they reckless, impulsive buyers. Rather, these consumers strive to push the boundaries of benefits current products offer, and they are quick to see the merits of innovative products. Want to know if you are innovative? Score yourself on the scale given in Table 5.4.

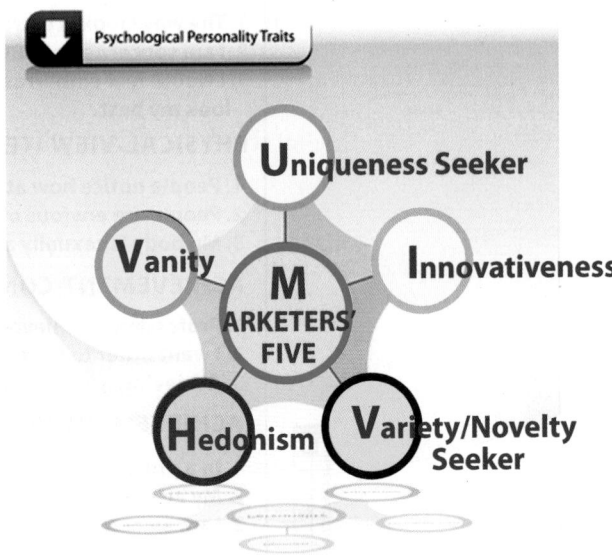

Variety/Novelty Seeker

Do you get easily bored with going to the same restaurant, pub, or park? Are you always excited whenever you meet new people? Do you change your wardrobe frequently? Do you have more than one (or two) wristwatches, more than one (or two) pairs of eyeglasses, more than one (or two) cell phones, and/or more than one (or two) stress balls (!)? If your answer to these questions is a yes, then you have the personality trait of *variety seeking*, defined as desiring new and diverse experiences. Variety-seeking consumers embrace change and, innovation or no innovation, they want a different "toy" every week, so to speak. Novelty/variety seeking has also been termed sensation seeking, and recent research has found it to be, at least in part, genetically produced.[18]

Hedonism

Would you listen to your favorite music 24/7 if you could? Would you go surfing often? Are you much more into sports, television, travel, or bungee jumping than most other people? If you answered "yes," then you have the personality trait of **hedonism**, defined as seeking maximal pleasure out of life. Underlying this personality trait is the belief that the most important thing in life is to enjoy yourself.[19] Hedonists make pleasure the central theme of life. A whole bunch of industries cater to hedonistic consumers. There is even a business called Club Hedonism and another called Hedonism II, where some consumers take their dream vacations. There is, of course, a little bit of hedonism in most of us, but it should not overtake our pursuit of more meaningful goals in life, like acquiring useful skills, mastering an art or profession, and making a name for ourselves. Yes, you can watch MTV, but not incessantly, and not at the expense of reading this book!

Vanity

The trait *vanity* refers to excessive pride in one's appearance and accomplishments.[20] Consumer researchers who have studied this topic have recognized these two aspects, appearance and accomplishment. Additionally, they argue that a consumer's view of vanity could take two forms: a concern or anxiety and a "positive (generally inflated) view." In effect, then, a consumer could either be dissatisfied with and anxious about his or her appearance; or, when satisfied, he or she could be proud of it and hold an inflated perception. Likewise, with respect to accomplishments, a consumer could be overly anxious, or, alternatively, conceited. Want to know how much "trait vanity" you have? You can score yourself on the scale shown in Table 5.5.

Although research on this topic is scanty, this trait has been found to correlate with materialism, consciousness of one's body in public, consumption of cosmetics, money spent on clothing, and consideration of cosmetic surgery.[21] In popular literature, sheer extravagance is considered vanity.[22] At any rate, vanity does result in consumption—consumers high in vanity will spend more on higher priced items and on conspicuous consumption.

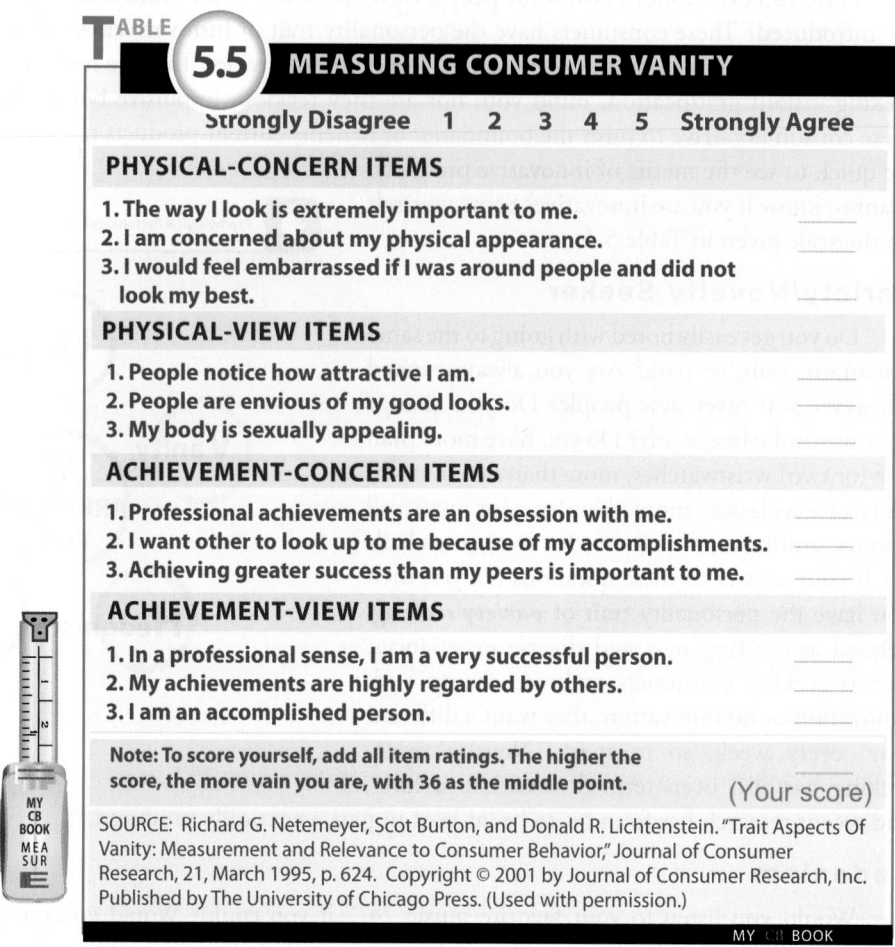

TABLE 5.5 MEASURING CONSUMER VANITY

Strongly Disagree 1 2 3 4 5 Strongly Agree

PHYSICAL-CONCERN ITEMS

1. The way I look is extremely important to me.
2. I am concerned about my physical appearance.
3. I would feel embarrassed if I was around people and did not look my best.

PHYSICAL-VIEW ITEMS

1. People notice how attractive I am.
2. People are envious of my good looks.
3. My body is sexually appealing.

ACHIEVEMENT-CONCERN ITEMS

1. Professional achievements are an obsession with me.
2. I want other to look up to me because of my accomplishments.
3. Achieving greater success than my peers is important to me.

ACHIEVEMENT-VIEW ITEMS

1. In a professional sense, I am a very successful person.
2. My achievements are highly regarded by others.
3. I am an accomplished person.

(Your score)

Note: To score yourself, add all item ratings. The higher the score, the more vain you are, with 36 as the middle point.

SOURCE: Richard G. Netemeyer, Scot Burton, and Donald R. Lichtenstein. "Trait Aspects Of Vanity: Measurement and Relevance to Consumer Behavior," Journal of Consumer Research, 21, March 1995, p. 624. Copyright © 2001 by Journal of Consumer Research, Inc. Published by The University of Chicago Press. (Used with permission.)

MY CB BOOK

TABLE 5.6 MEASURING NEED FOR UNIQUENESS

Strongly Disagree 1 2 3 4 5 Strongly Agree

1. I like to look different from an average person.
2. I believe my tastes and preferences are exclusive.
3. I like to stand out in a crowd.
4. Most customs and rules are made to be broken.
5. Clothing, music, electronics, food products, whatever, I usually wait for other people to try out new trends.*
6. I often look for one-of-a-kind products to create my own style.
7. I am an accomplished person.

*Reverse score this item.

Note: To score yourself, add all item ratings. The higher your score, the more uniqueness seeker you are, with 21 being the middle point.

(Your score)

Source: Items are excerpted from a much longer list in Kelly Tepper Tian, William O. Bearden, and Gary L. Hunter, "Consumer Need for Uniqueness: Scale Development and Validation," Journal of Consumer Research, 28, June 2001, 50-66. Copyright © 2001 by J. of Consumer Research, Inc. Published by The University of Chicago Press. (Used with permission.)

MY CB BOOK

Uniqueness Seeker

Another important trait, and the last one in our list of the *Marketers' Five*, is *uniqueness seeking*. As the name implies, **uniqueness seeking** is a personality trait wherein a person seeks to be unique, different from others. This trait is fueled by one's desire for differentiating oneself from the pack, so to speak. A few satisfy this desire through personal accomplishments—e.g., being a Pulitzer journalist, an Oscar-winning actor, a Nobel scientist, a Hall of Fame ball player, a celebrated artist, a mesmerizing orator, or a revered teacher, for example. For most of us, however, *need for uniqueness* takes the form of visible consumption. If a person looks different in products or objects he or she is donning—clothing, hairstyle, makeup, or body adornments—then he or she is seen by others to be unique, and, in turn, he or she sees him- or herself as unique.

Want to know if you have this trait? Take the survey in Table 5.6 and see for yourself.

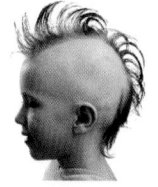

Pursuit of uniqueness

THE INFLUENCE OF PERSONALITY ON CONSUMER BEHAVIOR

The role of personality, just like the role of values, is overarching—affecting all domains of consumer behavior. In a sense, personality is the conduit through which the influences of all other psychological or even biogenic characteristics flow. For example, a person genetically prone to headaches or allergies could bear the discomfort stoically, shunning early medication, or, alternatively, he or she could show hypochondriac tendencies and seek intense medication at the earliest onset of symptoms. (Stoicism and hypochondria are indeed personality traits.) A young person could be staid and be content with "consuming" TV all the time, while a 70-year-old with an active personality could be hiking and skiing. A woman could wear unisex clothes and smoke cigars with a macho image, and a man could be a heavier user of cosmetics (men's fragrances, of course) than the average woman!

Marketers use the concept of personality in brand communications, presenting their brands along with some desired symbolic personality meanings. To accomplish this, they use three related approaches. First, they give a brand the desired personality by showing certain symbolic images in conjunction with the brand—e.g., placing the brand in an outdoor, rugged setting to give it a rugged personality. Second, they carefully choose spokespersons and human models whose known professions, skills, styles, and moods depict the desired personality. And third, they depict the brand in use by typical "target" users whose style, mood, and the "activity of the moment" capture and convey the intended personality image.

SELF-CONCEPT

Our Multiple and Extended Selves

Self-concept is the mirror image of personality. Your personality is who you *are*; self-concept is how you see yourself in your "mind's eye." **Self-concept** can be defined as a person's conception of himself or herself. It is "the sum total of all the thoughts and ideas the person conjures up when he/she thinks of him/herself."

Everyone has a self-concept—an image of who he or she is. This self-concept includes both an idea of who a person currently is and who he or she would like to become. These two concepts are respectively called **actual self** and **ideal self**.[23] Often, we also recognize that others don't see us the same way as we see ourselves. The way others see us is called **social self-concept**. Here too, there can be an *actual* social self-concept, and there can be an *ideal* social self-concept—the latter meaning how you would like others to see you.

How do we measure self-concept? For starters, we could simply ask people to describe themselves. For instance, "Tell me how would you describe yourself as a person?" We could then probe further with follow-up questions such as, "Is this how you see yourself

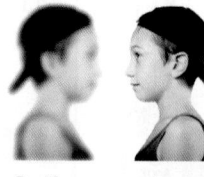

Self-concept: our looking-glass self

now?" or "How do others see you, that is, to them, what kind of a person are you?" and, "What kind of a person would you like to become, in your own eyes? And in the eyes of others?" See Exhibit 5.1 for a selection of some self-essays.

Of course, this approach would require that (a) consumers trust us enough to share their self-concepts (after all a self-concept can be a very private thought), and (b) consumers are articulate enough to put their self-concepts in words. Moreover, this in-depth interview method would be time-consuming and costly to implement on a large sample of consumers. So, to measure it more efficiently, we can give consumers a list of words that describe a person—any person—and ask them to check off words that apply to them individually. To implement this approach, marketing researchers have designed a scale of self-concept, shown in Table 5.7. Using this scale, we can ask consumers to rate themselves; furthermore, we can ask them to rate themselves separately in terms of their actual and ideal self-concepts, if we like.

SAVVY MARKETER

One marketing use of the scale is based on the theory of *image congruity*. **Image congruity** theory states that we like to associate ourselves with objects (things, activities, and people) whose image is congruent with our own image of ourselves. Thus, if we believe that we are contemporary, trendy, innovative, and vain, then we would likely keep friends who are also contemporary, trendy, innovative, and vain. We would avoid activities we see as traditional, old-fashioned, and modest, and we would want to consume only those products and brands (especially if they are conspicuous) that are contemporary and trendy. Being vain, we would want to show off a little, and we would be even more conscious of

TABLE

5.7 A SCALE TO MEASURE SELF IMAGE & PRODUCT IMAGE CONGRUENCE

Instruction: Please rate yourself, as you see yourself, on the following descriptive word pairs, by circling a number in each row closer to the word that describes you. Then connect all self-ratings with a solid line. Next, rate a specific brand, and connect your brand ratings with a dotted line. You can rate, likewise, more brands, connecting each brand's ratings with a visually different line.

1.	Rugged	1	2	3	4	5	6	7 Delicate
2.	Exciting	1	2	3	4	5	6	7 Calm
3.	Uncomfortable	1	2	3	4	5	6	7 Comfortable
4.	Dominating	1	2	3	4	5	6	7 Submissive
5.	Thrifty	1	2	3	4	5	6	7 Indulgent
6.	Pleasant	1	2	3	4	5	6	7 Unpleasant
7.	Contemporary	1	2	3	4	5	6	7 Uncontemporary
8.	Organized	1	2	3	4	5	6	7 Unorganized
9.	Rational	1	2	3	4	5	6	7 Emotional
10.	Youthful	1	2	3	4	5	6	7 Mature
11.	Formal	1	2	3	4	5	6	7 Informal
12.	Orthodox	1	2	3	4	5	6	7 Liberal
13.	Complex	1	2	3	4	5	6	7 Simple
14.	Colorless	1	2	3	4	5	6	7 Colorful
15.	Modest	1	2	3	4	5	6	7 Vain

Interpretation: Visually examine your self-rating profile vis-a-vis each brand's profile; you would prefer the brand with a profile most similar to your profile. Alternatively, you can also calculate an "image incongruence" score for each brand by taking the absolute difference between your self- and brand ratings on each scale item and then summing up the differences across all 15 items. The brand with the smallest incongruence score is the one you should prefer the most. A brand with an image incongruence score of zero matches your personality perfectly!

Source: Adapted from Naresh K. Malhotra "A Scale to Measure Self-concepts, Person Concepts, & Product Concepts," Journal of Marketing Research, Vol. 18 (November 1981), pp. 456-464, scale items on p. 462. Reprinted with permission from the Journal of Marketing Research, published by the American Marketing Association.

MY CB BOOK

the right image of things that are conspicuous. In short, our consumption is driven by self-concept-brand image congruence.

This congruence can be assessed by using the self-concept scale. In addition to asking consumers to rate themselves using this scale, we can then ask them also to rate their impressions of a brand, say, Tommy Hilfiger, Rock & Republic, or Stacy Adams. A comparison between self- and brand ratings would reveal which dimensions of a brand's image would need to be modified to bring the brand image closer to our target consumer's own self-image.[25]

Personality or Self-Concept—Which Do Consumers Consume?

At this point, you might wonder, which one explains consumer behavior better—personality or self-concept? Recall again that personality is who you are, whereas self-concept is who you think you are. Now, the latter does incorporate a part of the former—we are aware and accepting of some of our personality traits. If we are optimistic, outgoing, or introverted, for example, then our self-concepts will probably include these. On the other hand, if we are dogmatic, arrogant, selfish, etc., we are probably either unaware or in denial of those traits, and accordingly, our self-concepts would not include these traits. To the extent that selected personality traits are included in our self-concepts, their influence on consumer behavior is shared and overlapping. But what happens when the two don't overlap?

Personality leads to characteristic behaviors, which are, by definition, largely automated. Occasionally we can control them by consciously reining them in, but mostly they flow naturally (and to us, those ways of acting are perfectly normal anyway). Therefore, those of our marketplace behaviors that are our characteristic responses will be better explained by our personalities—marketplace behaviors such as getting angry at salespersons, rejecting high pressure persuasion, complaining at the slightest dissatisfaction, or, alternatively, feeling timid and avoiding confrontation even in the face of gross inconvenience caused by a marketer, compulsive shopping, compulsive eating, frequent gift giving, being stingy in sharing consumption with others, frequent grooming, and so forth.

S A V V Y
MARKETER

EXHIBIT 5.1

To Each, His or Her Own Self-concept

I am a 22-year old male who likes the outdoor activities such as freewheeling and boating. I like to enjoy life while at the same time being frugal. I am independent and hate to borrow or rent things. I would rather not finance vehicles and things and wait till I have the money. I have a strong drive for success and am proud of the fact that I have worked for everything I have got. ————O————

I am a fun loving lady who likes to go out with her friends. I am ready to graduate. I am creative—like to do my own things. I love animals, especially kitties. I am hungry all the time. I love food. ————O————

I am a male, 21 years old and am one of those who have no clue what they want in life. I work constantly and make a lot of money and spend that money on things I don't need. For example, I flat out purchased a '04 Mustang only to turn around and buy a second car—a 2003 Ford Mustang Cobra. So basically I have no direction in my life. When I should be thinking of the future, I can only think about what I want to do five minutes from now. My parents say I am stupid, but I'm enjoying life. Is there anything more to life? ————O————

[Excerpted from the author's research files, partially paraphrased and edited from written or verbal protocols.]

I take love very seriously

I am a strong woman and a woman of color. I have a big heart and I take love very seriously. I am honest and loyal. I believe in God. I am forgiving. I am confident. I am driven. I feel guilty about things others won't think about. I am sensitive and deep thinking. I analyze everything that happens to me. I am passionate. I love to laugh and I love to flirt. I love to make people feel good. I am open-minded. I am not concerned about following the crowd. I care about people's feelings and their rights as individuals. Finally, I am strong and I can't be broken.

Nicole Smith, a college senior majoring in Business Administration

In contrast are product and brand choices we make as consumers. Since these are acts of choice (not automated acts), our conscious thoughts about who we are, i.e., our self-concepts, rather than our personalities, should guide our choices. Accordingly, the kinds of cars we choose to drive, the clothes we choose to wear, the leisure activities we prefer, the food we buy and eat, the beverages we imbibe—for each of these product choices, and as long as we are able to afford them and buy them for reasons beyond pure survival, our choices are based on our self-concepts. Through products, we live our self-concepts. We buy clothing that is rugged or suave, we buy a house that is Victorian or contemporary, we buy a car that is sporty and muscular, or alternatively, luxurious and well-appointed, because we believe that we ourselves are suave or rugged, classic or contemporary, athletic or refined. That is why the self-congruency model described above can be a powerful tool for marketers.[26]

COMPONENTS OF SELF-CONCEPT

Let us ask, what is included in a person's self concept? Although it can include virtually everything that consumers ever come to own and live with, a systematic list would include the following[27]: See Figure 5.2.

Body For most consumers, their bodies are an integral part of their self images. Of course, the connection they feel between their sense of self and their bodies varies. If you ask a Hindu or a Buddhist monk, for example, and millions of their followers, they would tell you that their bodies have *nothing* to do with who they are. The soul within, not the body, is the real self. In fact, the very goal of life in Eastern philosophy is to get out of this temporary shell that the body is and meet one's creator. At the other extreme, many consumers (in Eastern and Western cultures alike) are obsessed with their bodies to the extent that the body is the end-all and the be-all of their being. To them, the body—its appearance and shape—defines identity, and sense of self. Consumers around the world spend billions of dollars, Euros, and yen on cosmetics and on beauty-enhancing services (e.g., hair salons, nail boutiques, tanning booths, fitness clubs, etc.). For many consumers, permanent body adornment with tattoos and piercings is becoming a new source of enjoyment and enhanced living. For those who find their bodies lacking in beauty and shape and who just can't shake their self-concepts off their view of their bodies, new medical techniques such as Botox injections and liposuction are becoming new beacons of hope.

Values and Character The second component of the self is the set of values a person holds. Earlier in the chapter, we defined *values* as "desired end-states in life and ways of achieving them." **Character** is the behavior of a person, being tested particularly in the face of tempting opportunities for opposite behaviors (e.g., not pointing out a cashier's mistake when given too much in change). Since we make deliberate choices in adopting certain values and discarding others, and we make sacrifices in living by those values, these choices define us. "I live by those values, because that is the kind of person I am," we tell ourselves. For many consumers, religion is a key source of their values and character, and consequently, it becomes a defining component of their identities.

Competence and Success The third component of self is one's perception of one's competence and success. If we view ourselves as competent and successful, then we build positive self-esteem. If we judge ourselves as failures, then we risk suffering from low self-esteem, anxiety, and even depression. How we define success, and likewise competence, varies, of course. To some of us, success is acquiring more money and living a materially comfortable life; to others it might be achieving the ability to put their children through college and raising them to be good citizens. For still others, it might be defined as gaining fame and reputation. This component of the self influences consumption of many competence-enhancing products and services, as consumers strive to upgrade their competence and skills, including educational and training programs, and skills classes in such wide-ranging areas as painting, dancing, music, etc.

Social Roles *Social Roles* are a set of behaviors society assigns to individuals based on

Consumers choose clothing that reflects their self-image. For consumers who see themselves as "colorful," and "contemporary," Stacy Adams brings just the clothing they can't resist.

their positions in social institutions. These institutions include family, workplace, public-service organizations, etc. Thus, society assigns roles to individuals, like a father's role, a mother's role, a supervisor's role, a minister's role, a judge's role, etc. And individuals not only accept these roles, but they take pride in playing them so much that they incorporate these roles into their self-concepts.

Personality Traits   Finally, we also view ourselves in terms of our stable and characteristic behavioral responses. These, you will recall, are personality traits—the enduring states of our action patterns in everyday life. Thus, we are (and view ourselves as being) patient or temperamental, macho or delicate, stoic or tender,

5.2 SELF-CONCEPTS OF TWO CONSUMERS

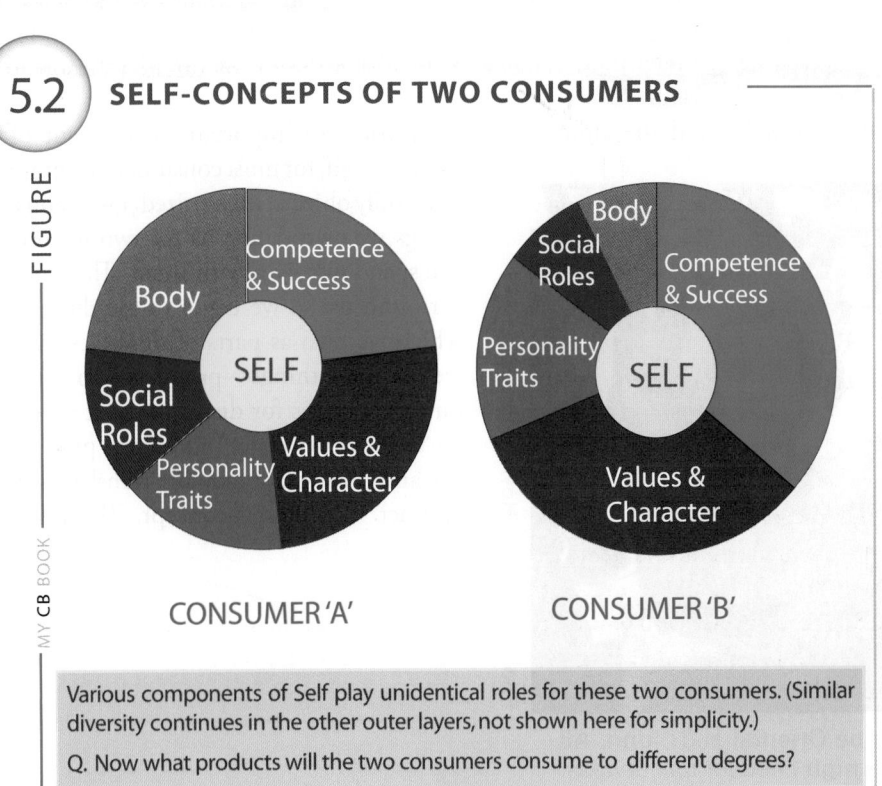

CONSUMER 'A'   CONSUMER 'B'

Various components of Self play unidentical roles for these two consumers. (Similar diversity continues in the other outer layers, not shown here for simplicity.)

Q. Now what products will the two consumers consume to different degrees?

dogmatic or open-minded, outgoing or shy, and so on. Of course, as already mentioned, we do not have to be aware of or acknowledge all of our personality traits. The self-concept includes only those personality traits that the person acknowledges.

THE EXTENDED SELF AND POSSESSIONS

We have all heard the expression, "you can take a boy out of a village, but you can't take the village out of the boy." That is, the village you live in becomes a part of your personality. Indeed, when we try to make sense of people, we don't merely look at the person and their personal characteristics (age, body shape, or temperament) and accomplishments (e.g., education, career, fame); we also want to know what family they come from, what school they attended, what company they work for, what kind of friends they have, what kind of car they drive, and what kind of clothes they wear. We look at others that way and we judge them that way, but what happens when others too look at us that way? We want them to judge us by some of these things but not by others. If we graduated from a big-name

school, for example, then, of course, we frequently name-drop our alma mater. If we have a famous dad, we may brandish our pedigree every chance we get. If we are on a typical student's budget and drive an old, dilapidated car, we don't think of that car as reflecting who we are. If we have a genuine Rolex watch, or an authentic Louis Vuitton handbag, then, of course, we want people to take notice.

Thus, it is a fact of life that people judge us by things that are not, strictly speaking, integral parts of ourselves. And we too define ourselves by these things that are outside of our skins, and our minds, and our personalities. This notion of viewing ourselves by things beyond and outside of ourselves is called the extended self. **Extended self** comprises all the external entities and objects that we consider, with pride, as parts of ourselves. By entities, we mean family, school, neighborhood, professional associations, and other institutions; by objects, we mean things we own. Not all the entities with which we have had associations, and not all objects we possess, form parts of our extended selves; only those in which we feel pride. Important entities that become, for most consumers, parts of their extended selves include (a) Ethnic & Cultural Identities, (b) Work Organizations, (c) Family Identities, and (d) Social Networks. See Figure 5.3.

Possessions Beyond the aforementioned entities, an important component of the

Photo Courtesy: Howard French

extended self, for most consumers, is comprised of worldly objects, their prized possessions. The things we own define us for two reasons: (1) We spend our lives with them. They virtually surround us, so we begin to see those things which we own as parts of ourselves. And (2) we use these things—products—to bring out our inner selves for display so that others can see us for who we are. Indeed, the products we use and possess are tangible translators of the abstract idea of self-concept. The following

Yes, you can be Oriental *and* **blond. All you need is a high** *need for uniqueness.*

three quotes from scholars put it well:

> **Our fragile sense of self needs support, and this we get by having and possessing things because, to a large degree, we are what we have.**[28]

> **A man's self is the sum total of all that he can call his, not only his body and his psychic powers, but his clothes and his house, his wife and children, his ancestors and friends, his reputation and works, his lands, and yacht and bank-account. All these things give him the same emotions. If they wax and prosper, he feels triumphant; if they dwindle and die away, he feels cast down—not necessarily in the same degree for each thing, but in much the same way for all.**[29]

> **Clothing, automobile, house are all acquired as "second skin" in which others may see us.**[30]

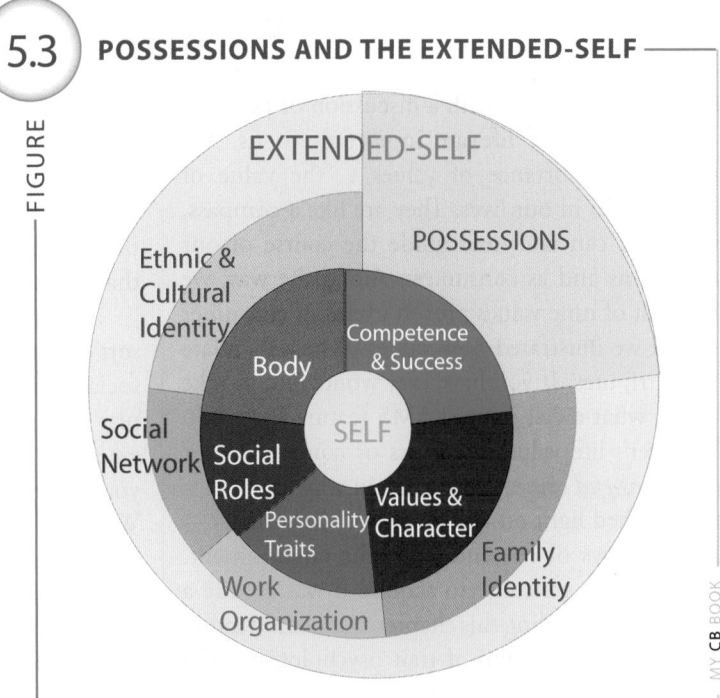

FIGURE 5.3 POSSESSIONS AND THE EXTENDED-SELF

If our clothing, automobiles, and houses serve us as our "second skin," does the hotel we stay in do the same? Embassy Suites employed this concept in a recent ad. An overnight stay in a small hotel the night before a big interview might make a candidate feel small and less important, the ad reminded the reader. A stay in a big comfortable hotel room, on the other hand, just might boost a candidate's self-confidence noticeably before the interview, as any number of business travelers would verify. Yes, good things in life are not merely pleasurable to consume; they are also, at least for some consumers, a source of their enhanced self-concept, an ingredient of their extended selves.

If you are a marketer, then you would like to know whether or not the product you are selling is part of your target consumer's extended self. You can find this out by using a short questionnaire, shown in Table 5.8.

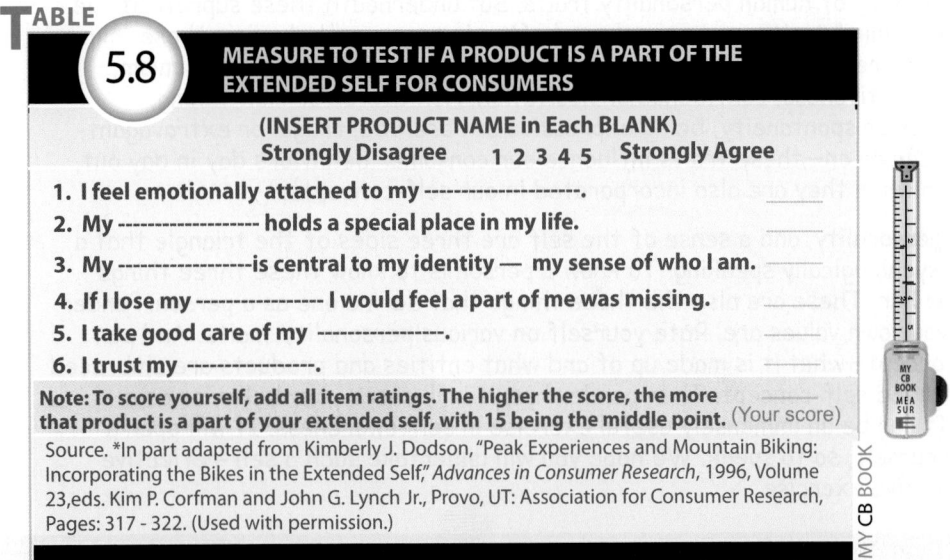

TABLE 5.8 MEASURE TO TEST IF A PRODUCT IS A PART OF THE EXTENDED SELF FOR CONSUMERS

(INSERT PRODUCT NAME in Each BLANK)
Strongly Disagree   1 2 3 4 5   Strongly Agree

1. I feel emotionally attached to my ----------------------.
2. My ------------------- holds a special place in my life.
3. My -------------------is central to my identity — my sense of who I am.
4. If I lose my ----------------- I would feel a part of me was missing.
5. I take good care of my ------------------.
6. I trust my -----------------.

Note: To score yourself, add all item ratings. The higher the score, the more that product is a part of your extended self, with 15 being the middle point. (Your score)

Source. *In part adapted from Kimberly J. Dodson, "Peak Experiences and Mountain Biking: Incorporating the Bikes in the Extended Self," *Advances in Consumer Research*, 1996, Volume 23,eds. Kim P. Corfman and John G. Lynch Jr., Provo, UT: Association for Consumer Research, Pages: 317 - 322. (Used with permission.)

SUMMARY

We began this chapter with a discussion of personal values—what aspects of life are important to us. We understood the importance of values ("the value of values," if you will) in our lives. They are like a compass, we learned, that can and does guide the course of our lives—as humans and as consumers. Along the way, we met LOV, a list of nine values proven useful in consumer research. And we illustrated how values ultimately relate to product attributes. If you have ever wondered, to take one example, what a cell phone's SMS feature has to do with a teenager's life value of success or competence or efficiency, *means-end chains* could explain why.

Next, we shed light on the concept of personality—our consistent ways of responding to the environment. What it is and how we come to acquire it was mostly a mystery to us before reading this chapter, but not anymore, thanks to Freud and a group of trait psychologists. The Freudian Theory illuminates the nature of personality as a set of conscious and sub-conscious motives and urges. Trait theory views personality as a set of patterned and consistent behaviors. Defense mechanisms were described as the ego's attempt to manage anxiety and protect the self from being slighted. Many defense mechanisms account for significant occurrences of product use or nonuse. We then described the *Big Five* theory of personality and its role in consumer behavior. We also presented what we call the "Marketers' Five"—our list of five personality traits that affect consumer behavior immensely.

Next, we discussed self-concept (our ideas about the sort of person we are), and we described actual, ideal, and social variations of it. We also discussed how possessions play a role in defining our identities as consumers—our extended selves. Are you obsessed with your body? Then your body plays an important role in your self-concept. What about your character, your friends, and your accomplishments—are these a part of your self-concept as well? They are if you choose to make them. And your possessions? Would you feel a void in your life if one of your possessions were taken away from you? If yes, then that possession is a part of your extended self-concept. Self-concept directs our purchases toward products that are congruent with our self-concepts; that is why it is important to marketers to understand the concept of self-concept.

CB Blog

5

VALUES, PERSONALITY, AND SELF-CONCEPT FOUNDATION FOR OUR BEING

Values, Personality, and our sense of self—these three concepts are so deep, and psychological literature on them so vast, that no single chapter can cover them comprehensively. Necessarily then, we have barely been able to sample a part of the subject matter. There are many important values, not covered here, that consumers around the world have embraced. And human personality traits, related to life in general and in the consumption domain in particular, can add up to thousands in number. The Big Five is personality psychologists' bold and innovative tool to reign in this vast inventory of human personality traits. But underneath these supratraits lie more specific, "mini" traits, so to speak, and often in consumer behavior, these "mini traits" play a more clearly discernible role. Traits such as optimism or pessimism, shyness or assertiveness, confidence or hesitation, risk-averse or risk-taking, thoughtfulness or spontaneity, being expressive or reserved, frugal or extravagant- and the list can go on—these traits influence our consumer behaviors day in day out, even more so when they are also incorporated in our self-concepts.

Values, personality, and a sense of the self are three sides of the triangle that a person is, psychologically speaking. To know a person is to know these three things about him or her. These are also the three things that define one as a person. Ponder over what your own values are. Rate yourself on various personality traits. And pen your self-concept—what it is made up of and what entities and products are embraced in your extended self-concept. Then ponder how it influences your behavior as a consumer. It can be an immensely useful exercise in self-awareness. It will open a window to yourself, so to speak. We hope you will undertake such a self-reflective and introspective exercise.

CONSUMER BEHAVIOR

KEY TERMS

Actual self	Image congruity	Personality	Terminal values
Aggression	Innovativeness	Projection	Trait theory
Character	Instrumental values	Rationalization	Uniqueness seek
Defense mechanism	Laddering	Regression	Values
Extended self-concept	List of values (LOV)	Repression	Vanity
Hedonism	Materialism	Social Roles	Variety seeking
Ideal self	Means-end chain	Social self-concept	Withdrawal

YOUR TURN

REVIEW+Rewind

1. What are values and what role do they play in consumer behavior?

2. How do values relate to product attributes?

3. How would you define personality and self-concept? How are the two concepts related?

4. Briefly explain the six defense mechanisms described in the chapter, and illustrate each with an example from your experience.

5. What are the *Big Five of Personality*? Explain each briefly, and cite one marketing application of each.

6. Explain the concept of self-concept brand image congruence. How does it explain a consumer's brand choice?

7. What components make a consumer's self-concept? Explain each concept briefly. What is meant by *extended self*, and what role does consumption play in this concept?

8. Briefly describe in your own words each of these traits: vanity, sensation-seeking, hedonism, materialism, and uniqueness seeker. What importance do these traits have in predicting consumer behavior?

THINK+Apply

1. Identify the relative importance of LOV components in your own LOV profile. How does your LOV profile affect your own consumer behavior?

2. Based on List of Values (LOV), consumers can be placed into one of the three segments. Find three advertisements, one for each segment, that would appeal to only that segment but not others.

3. In your own case, what relative roles do various component of self-concept play, individually, in your self-concept? How does the particular combination of these components affect your consumer behavior?

4. The chapter asks a question: "self-concept or personality: which do consumers consume?" In your own case, name five marketplace behaviors that are influenced more by your personality, and, likewise, name five behaviors that are influenced by self-concept.

5. Assume you are a brand manager for (a) a line of clothing; (b) organized tours abroad, and (c) one-of-a-kind items of home décor. Which of the personality traits mentioned in the chapter would be most relevant to your identification of your target market? Why?

PRACTICE+Experience

1. Interview two consumers and draw means-end chains for their clothing styles—the styles that make their wardrobe. Identify implications of the means-end-chain for clothing behavior of these consumers.

2. Get a sample of consumers to rate themselves on the self-concept scale; then have them rate two brands of jeans (or cars or colognes); also ask them which of the two brands they would prefer more. Calculate the congruence scores and see whether these congruence scores predict their relative preferences. Why do you think they might not have?

3. Find two consumers who you know differ on vanity. Verify that by using the vanity measurement scale. Then interview them to identify how their consumer behaviors are different. Repeat this for the uniqueness trait.

4. Interview several consumers to find out which possessions, if any, they consider a part of their extended self-concepts. Explore how. Then outline how a marketing manager can apply this kind o research.

In the Marketing Manager's Shoes

Put yourself in a marketing manager's shoes. Most concepts in the chapter have some lessons for the marketing manager; i.e., they suggest what to do differently in practice. Indeed, often these applications are implicit in our explanations of the concepts and models in the chapter. Identify at least five specific applications of the chapter's concepts, all of which should be entirely new—different from the examples cited here.

estyles

6 Consumer Lifestyles and Psychographics

The Art of Writing Consumer Biographies

The interesting
life you live!
We capture it.
We reflect it.

We are your
lifestyle brand.

LIVE THE INTERESTING LIFE MensJournal

‖ ▶ ▬▬▬▬▬▬▬▬ 2:30/3:00 ◀))

LEARN . APPLY . EXPERIENCE

OBJECTIVES

1 The Concepts of Lifestyle and Psychographics

2 Methods of Measuring Lifestyles and Psychographics

3 Psychographic Segmentation: VALS™ and Other Lifestyle Portraits of Consumers

4 Marketing Applications of Psychographics

5 The Concepts of Materialism and Voluntary Simplicity

6 The Concept of Your *Big Life Project*— A Profound Truth about Your Own Identity Project

Ripped Jeans. T-shirts, Polos, and Pearls—Please Give Me My Identity!

Hello, I am Bianca Hutton, the surfer, golfer, fashionista girl from Finland, now "living it up" in the American marketplace.

I am an upbeat, positive girl who likes to smile. I never really get angry or annoyed but feel that people sometimes act in a very disappointing way. I like attention but do not put myself in the spotlight. I aspire to be something great, but I cannot plan my life to the last detail. I live by the motto that everything happens for a reason. I also believe that people need to educate themselves constantly and I try to look for cues in books, in TV series, and from work and school experiences. I am compassionate and, in addition to my hobbies (golf, tennis, piano, horse riding, choir, skiing), I volunteer my time for many different causes.

Back home I am strictly the pearls-and-Polo girl. Here in the U.S., on any given day you can find me in as many as five different outfits: a casual, student look for the classroom; athletic sweats for the gym; a golfer ensemble in the afternoon; sorority girlwear in the evening; and a preppy business-suit look somewhere in between. My wardrobe betrays my inner dilemma—I have not yet determined exactly who I am inside.

My surfer girl outfit unlocks my passion for a carefree lifestyle, and the Bohemian side of me comes through more in conversation. My grown-up look makes me feel determined and motivated, ready to succeed in life and tackle any problem with a level-headed, intelligent approach. I have come to the conclusion that although I can put up a front of being mature and well-rounded, my desire to wear ripped jeans and a T-shirt with a surfer brand logo on it means that I am still a child at heart and that I am still discovering who I am and who I want to be.

Bianca Hutton, a not-so-ordinary consumer, still discovering her identity

With brands I build my identity.

INTRODUCTION

Bianca, the star of our story above, is in some ways a typical, recently graduated 20-something woman. And yet, in some ways she is unique as well. Like many Americans and Europeans, she juggles school, work, sports, and family and friends. But she juggles as well among her many identities. Her brief autobiography is a window into her personality and her sense of self. It is also a window into her consumption habits (although her present write up is limited to consumption of clothing). Marketers wish they could get every consumer to write such autobiographies. So they do the next best thing—they write them for their consumers. And call them *psychographics*.

PSYCHOGRAPHICS

Psychographics are characteristics of individuals that describe them in terms of their psychological and behavioral makeup. The word itself means *graphing* (or measuring) a person in terms of his or her psychological makeup. It describes a person in terms of his or her *mental* makeup and the *behaviors* it produces. It comprises the sorts of things people do in everyday life and what they think about those things and about matters that fill their world. All these clusters of thoughts and actions make up psychographics.

LIFESTYLE
Bohemians, Soccer Moms, and Other Consumer Types

Values, personality, and *self-concept* are abstract ideas. It is in our lifestyles that they materialize and take concrete shape. They form both the engine and the navigator of our lifestyles, driving and guiding their flow. **Lifestyle** is simply the way we live—our pattern of living. That pattern of living comprises the activities we undertake, the way we spend our money, and the way we use our time. Consider these two portraits:

Thelma Thelma stays at home, taking care of her two children. She spends her days productively, immersed in running a household. She enjoys cooking and baking, especially baking cakes. She sews her own clothes and dresses modestly. She wears very little makeup. And she spends most of her time at home even on the weekends, entertaining relatives and friends, rather than go out.

Candice Candice is a working mom. She likes to go out rather than stay at home and dislikes household chores. She attends parties where there are a lot of people and a lot of music and dancing. She also frequents art galleries, theaters, and museums. And she likes to dress in high fashion and loves to shop in boutiques.[1]

Different lifestyles warrant different products

Thelma and Candice live their everyday lives differently. That is, they have different lifestyles.

How do consumers live their lifestyles? How else, but by engaging in activities that entail, inevitably, the use of products and services? Thelma obviously eats out less, but she buys more food items from the supermarket than Candice does. Candice, on the other hand, uses baby-sitting services more than Thelma does. Candice also uses dry cleaner services more, whereas Thelma buys more laundry detergents. Candice is a frequent visitor to fashion boutiques, whereas Thelma sews most of her own and her family's clothing and buys the rest at a department store. Candice's ideal vacation would be a trip to Europe, whereas Thelma's would be a camping trip with family. When it comes to building a lifestyle, consumers are like artists, producing a piece of art, and they use products to build the beautiful mosaics of their lifestyles. Products are the building blocks of lifestyles. Because commercial products play a major role in consumers' enactment of their lifestyles, lifestyles can explain consumer behavior significantly.

Every consumer has a unique lifestyle. Consider, for example, two lifestyle types—both urban, identified through research—called *Bohemian Mix* and *Kids & Cul-de-sacs*.[2]

Bohemian Mix The Bohemian Mix are young residents of urban hodge-podge neighborhoods. The majority (3 out of 4) are never-married or divorced singles, and they are predominantly students, artists, writers, actors, and the like. They live somewhat adventuresome, funky lives, exercising both their bodies and minds, hanging out at sidewalk cafes, public libraries, bookstores, and health food stores. They participate heavily in social and voluntary organizations, benefit programs, and protest campaigns on social issues.

Kids & Cul-de-sacs This group defines the typical suburban family. With young children at home, they are predominantly upper-middle-class professionals, soccer moms, and barbecue dads. Their leisure activities are centered around their children: school games, class projects, video rentals, visits to the zoo or local theme park, and fast food or pizzeria restaurants. Their favorite vacation spot is Disneyland.

Sean Foley, an eco-conscious professional, happy with his bohemian, artistic persona

Notice how dramatically different these two lifestyles are. Do these lifestyles require different products? Of course, they do. How else would consumers live their lifestyles differently?

Products Consumed by the Bohemian Mix Bohemians shun domestic cars and disproportionately buy foreign cars. Since they live on apartment-lined city streets, their cars are compact—a MINI Cooper or a Volkswagen Beetle, or, if they can afford it, a used BMW. They consume healthy foods, and they shun fast food restaurants like McDonald's or Jack in the Box, both because they perceive the food to be unhealthy and because they dislike cookie cutter restaurants. You also won't find them hanging out in bars; instead, their hangouts are art galleries, coffee shops, and leftist bookstores.

Kids and Cul-de-sac consumers

Products Consumed by the Kids & Cul-de-sacs These consumers own multiple vehicles, at least one of which is usually a minivan or an SUV, perfect for carting around their kids. Their preferences are spread equally between domestic (e.g., Mercury Villager) and import cars (e.g., Toyota Previa). They read such magazines as *Golf Digest* and *Travel & Leisure*. On TV, they watch *Wall Street Week* and news and talk shows. They are not excessively health-conscious. They often barbecue, and they seek out family-style mainstream restaurants.

PSYCHOGRAPHICS—LIFESTYLES BY NUMBERS

Putting Humpty Dumpty Back Together

Values, personality, self-concept, and lifestyle—these all describe consumers' psychological makeup. Each one looks at it with a different lens, but together they provide a more comprehensive view. This view is woven together by psychographics. *Psychographics* are, as mentioned previously, characteristic profiles of consumers that describe them in terms of their psychological and behavioral makeup. By *makeup,* we mean a relatively enduring arrangement. Thus, psychographics include permanent mental (psychological) entities; e.g., values, self-concepts, even opinions. **Opinions** are our beliefs about things, and they derive from our values. Self-concepts are a specific type of opinion—they are our opinions about ourselves. Psychographics also include one's behavioral makeup, that is, relatively enduring behaviors; these are, you would realize, personality traits. And lifestyles are the manifestations of all these mental and behavioral entities in everyday living.

Psychographics accomplish one more thing—they measure these entities *quantitatively,* by a measure called the **AIO inventory**. *AIO* stands for "activities, interests, and opinions," and the inventory comprises a set of statements to which respondents indicate their agreement or disagreement on a numerical scale. For a sample, see Table 6.1.

To analyze and interpret the data from these AIO measures, researchers group together consumers with similar responses. These groups, thought to have relatively similar values, self-concepts, and lifestyles, can then be described in terms of their AIO profiles, called *psychographic profiles,* which are in turn used to identify psychographic segments. These are exemplified by the profiles of Thelma and Candice and of Bohemians and Kids and Cul-de-sacs, which you have just read.

PSYCHOGRAPHIC SEGMENTATION
Adventures in Dissecting the Consumer

VALS™: A PSYCHOGRAPHIC PROFILE OF U.S. CONSUMERS

A noteworthy lifestyle segmentation scheme is called VALS™ (formerly an acronym for Values and Lifestyles). Originally developed by SRI International, VALS is now owned by a spin-off, Strategic Business Insight (SBI). VALS divides consumers into eight groups, based on two dimensions: primary motivation and resources.

Primary Motivation According to SBI, in all behaviors, consumers are driven by three primary motivations: ideals, achievement, and self-expression. Consumers motivated primarily by ideals are driven by their principles and guided by knowledge. Achievement-motivated consumers seek products that reflect and communicate their success. Finally, consumers motivated by self-expression desire to engage in activities that give expression to their inner senses of self, engaging in a variety of social and physical activities.

Resources Resources refer to the full range of psychological, physical, demographic, and material means and capacities people have available to them. Resources encompass

TABLE

6.1 AIO STATEMENTS

SAMPLE ACTIVITIES, INTERESTS, AND OPINIONS DEFINING LIFESTYLE CATEGORIES

CHILD-ORIENTED

When my children are ill in bed I drop almost everything else in order to see to their comfort.
My children are the most important things in my life.
I try to arrange my home for my children's convenience.
I take a lot of time and effort to teach my children good habits.

COMPULSIVE HOUSEKEEPER

I don't like to see children's toys lying about.
I usually keep my house very neat and clean.
I am uncomfortable when my house is not completely clean.
Our days seem to follow a definite routine such as eating meals at a regular time, etc.

SELF-CONFIDENT

I think I have more self-confidence than most people.
I am more independent than most people.
I think I have a lot of personal ability.
I like to be considered a leader.

INFORMATION SEEKER

I often seek out the advice of my friends regarding which brand to buy.
I spend a lot of time talking with my friends about products and brands.

FINANCIAL OPTIMIST

I will probably have more money to spend next year than I have now.
Five years from now the family income will probably be a lot higher than it is now.

PRICE-CONSCIOUS

I shop a lot for specials.
I find myself checking the prices in the grocery store even for small items.
I usually watch the advertisements for announcements of sales.
A person can save a lot of money by shopping around for bargains.

FASHION-CONSCIOUS

I usually have one or more outfits that are of the very latest style.
When I must choose between the two, I usually dress for fashion, not for comfort.
An important part of my life and activities is dressing smartly.
I often try the latest hairstyles when they change.

HOMEBODY

I would rather spend a quiet evening at home than go out to a party.
I like parties where there is lots of music and talk. (Reverse scored)
I would rather go to a sporting event than a dance.
I am a homebody.

COMMUNITY-MINDED

I am an active member of more than one service organization.
I do volunteer work for a hospital or service organization on a fairly regular basis.
I like to work on community projects.
I have personally worked in a political campaign or for a candidate or an issue.

Source: Adapted from William D. Wells and Douglas J. Tigert, "Activities, Interests, & Opinions," *Journal of Advertising Research* 11 (August 1971), p. 35. "© Copyright The Advertising Research Foundation. (Reprinted with permission.)

education, income, self-confidence, health, physical energy, innovativeness, and leadership. It is a continuum, on the vertical axis, from minimal to abundant. Resources generally increase from adolescence through middle age, but decrease as age advances, as do depression, financial reversal (e.g., layoff), and physical or psychological impairment.

Using the *primary motivation* and *resources* dimensions, the VALS scheme defines eight segments of adult consumers who have different attitudes and exhibit distinct consumption tastes and practices. These segments are *Innovators, Thinkers, Believers, Achievers, Strivers, Experiencers, Makers,* and *Survivors.* See Figure 6.1 for the conceptual scheme and Exhibit 6.1 for a brief profile of these segments.

Want to know what group you belong to? The VALS classification survey enables marketers to identify a consumer's VALS type and is shown in Table 6.2, but to score yourself on it, you must go to the Internet at www.strategicbusinessinsights.com/vals/surveynew.shtml.

This classification survey is integrated into larger custom and syndicated surveys such as GFK's MRI Survey of American Consumers, which asks hundreds of questions about product ownership and media usage. GeoVALS™ estimates the percentage of each VALS type by US zip code.

FIGURE 6.1   VALS™ CONSUMER SEGMENTS

INNOVATORS   High Resources High Innovation

Primary Motivation
Ideals   Achievement   Self-Expression

THINKERS   ACHIEVERS   EXPERIENCERS

BELIEVERS   STRIVERS   MAKERS

SURVIVORS   Low Resources Low Innovation

Source: Strategic Business Insights (SBI) www.strategicbusinessinsights.com/vals (Used with permission)

MY CB BOOK

BEYOND VALS

Today, in every world region, there is a research enterprise, commercial or non-commercial, that has measured that region's (or for a country in that region) consumer psychographics.

SBI itself runs a similar research program in Japan (See Figure 6.2). The company also has a U.K. VALS, Venezuela VALS, Dominican Republic VALS, Nigeria VALS and a VALS Global Framework. (SBI is currently developing China VALS™.) Likewise, to understand European consumers as a unit, the ad agency Backer Spielvogel Bates Worldwide runs Global Scan, a program to survey consumers in 17 countries. It measures 250 attitudes (130 specific to one country, and 120 cross-culturally pertinent), and, based on the results, it has identified five global psychographic types: Strivers, Achievers, Pressureds, Adapters, and Traditionals. In a similar vein, the advertising agency DMB&B recently did a 15-country survey and found four European consumer groups: Successful Idealists, Affluent Materialists, Comfortable Belongers, and Disaffected Survivors.[7]

Notice anything different between the Japanese and the American VALS™ systems? Or between the Global Scan and the European system mentioned above? The names of many groups are different, as are their descriptions. At first, you might think this is so because these are from different countries, and you would be right, but only partially. In fact, the names (and descriptions) differ even among

EXHIBIT   LIFEMATRIX LIFESTYLE SEGMENTS

1. **Tribe Wired:** Digital, free-spirited, creative young singles
2. **Fun/Actives:** Aspirational, fun-seeking, active young people
3. **Dynamic Duos:** Hard-driving, high-involvement couples
4. **Priority Parents:** Family values, activities, media strongly dominate
5. **Home Soldiers:** Home-centric, family-oriented, materially ambitious
6. **Renaissance Women:** Active, caring, affluent, influential moms
7. **Rugged Traditionalists:** Traditional male values, love of outdoors
8. **Struggling Singles:** High aspirations, low economic status
9. **Settled Elders:** Devout, older, sedentary lifestyles
10. **Free Birds:** Vital, active altruistic seniors

MY CB BOOK

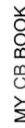

Japan-VALS™: Change Regions and Life Orientations

- Japan-VALS™ was designed to explain and model social change in Japan—not only change in institutions or ideas, but change in consumer markets and media as well.

Japan-VALS divides society into segments on the basis of two key consumer attributes: life orientation and attitudes to social change. Life orientation is simply what interests or animates a person the most—life, occupational duties, recreational interests. Japan-VALS identifies four primary life orientations: Traditional Ways, Occupations, Innovation, and Self-Expression. Each orientation provides a life theme around which activities, interests, and personal goals are woven.

Crosscutting the variety of life orientations, change attitudes stratify society into distinct layers, like overturned bowls nested one inside another. The change-leading segments are in the outermost layers of society; the change-resisting segments are at the center. Change diffuses from one layer to the next, primarily along the channels around different life orientations.

FIGURE 6.2 JAPAN-VALS™ FRAMEWORK

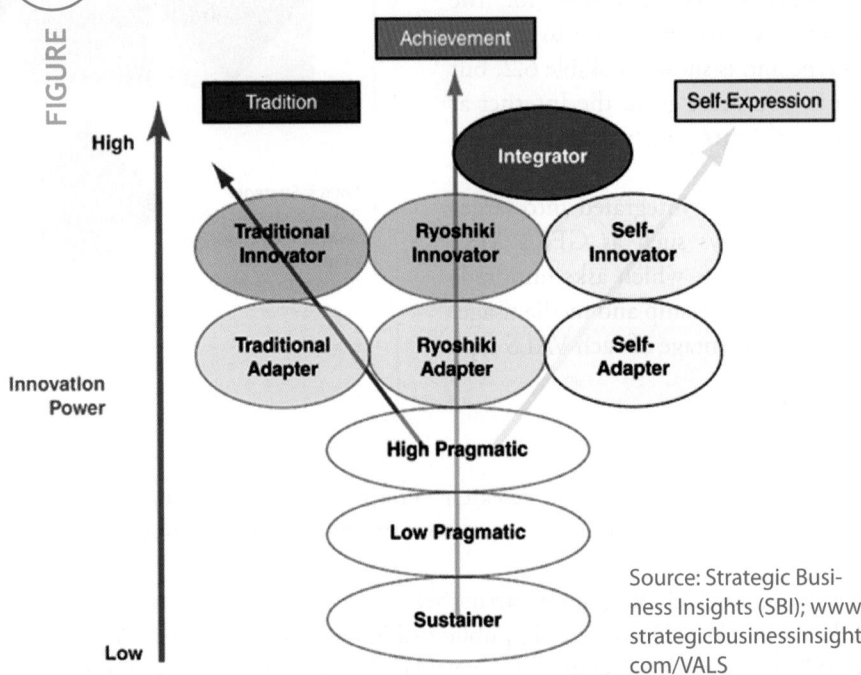

Source: Strategic Business Insights (SBI); www.strategicbusinessinsights.com/VALS

This design permits Japan-VALS to clarify the processes of social change and innovation diffusion in Japanese society. It also identifies the consumer segments at the core of most consumer markets:

- **Integrators** (4% of population) are highest on the Japan-VALS measure of Innovation. These consumers are active, inquisitive, trend-leading, informed, and affluent. They travel frequently and consume a wide range of media-print and broadcast, niche, and foreign.
- **Self-Innovators** and **Self-Adapters** (7% and 11% of population) score high on Self-Expression. These consumers desire personal experience, fashionable display, social activities, daring ideas, and exciting, graphic entertainment.
- **Ryoshiki Innovators** and **Ryoshiki Adapters** (6% and 10% of population) score highest on occupations. education, career achievement, and professional knowledge are their personal focus, but home, family, and social status are their guiding concerns.
- **Traditional Innovators** and **Traditional Adapters** (6% and 10% of population) score highest on the measure of Traditional Ways. These consumers adhere to traditional religions and customs, prefer long-familiar home furnishings and dress, and hold conservative social opinions.
- **High Pragmatics** and **Low Pragmatics** (14% and 17% of population) do not score high on any life-orientation dimension. They are not very active and not well informed; they have few interests and seem flexible or even uncommitted in their lifestyle choices.
- **Sustainers** (15% of population) score lowest on the Innovation and Self-Expression dimensions. Lacking money, youth, and high education, these consumers dislike innovation and are typically oriented to sustaining the past.

the psychographic profiles prepared by different research companies within the same country. Why?

The answer is multi-fold. First, note that these segment names are creative labels given by researchers. That is, they are nicknames their creators came up with to capture each segment's characteristics, and as nicknames they are inevitably subjective. Despite differing nicknames, however, some consumer segments are broadly the same type of consumers—they have to be, for, after all, humans are humans, no matter who researches and nicknames them. Just as surely, many lifestyle segments are different, unique to a country and culture—they have to be, for after all cultures across some countries differ greatly, and cultures necessarily and strongly influence and define the lifestyles of their people.

6.1

EXHIBIT

VALS™ PROFILE

Look What CB Researchers Found

- **Innovators (Formerly Actualizers):** are successful, sophisticated, take-charge people with high self-esteem. Because they have such abundant resources, they exhibit all three primary motivations in varying degrees. They are change leaders and are the most receptive to new ideas and technologies. Innovators are very active consumers, and their purchases reflect cultivated tastes for upscale, niche products and services.

  Image is important to Innovators, not as evidence of status or power but as an expression of their taste, independence, and personality. Innovators are among the established and emerging leaders in business and government, yet they continue to seek challenges. Their lives are characterized by variety. Their possessions and recreation reflect a cultivated taste for the finer things in life

- **Thinkers (Formerly Fulfilled):** are motivated by ideals. They are mature, satisfied, comfortable , and reflective people who value order, knowledge, and responsibility. They tend to be well educated and actively seek out information in the decision-making process. They are well-informed about world and national events and are alert to opportunities to broaden their knowledge.

  Thinkers have a moderate respect for the status quo institutions of authority and social decorum, but are open to consider new ideas. Although their incomes allow them many choices, Thinkers are conservative, practical consumers; they look for durability, functionality, and value in the products they buy.

- **Believers:** Like Thinkers, are motivated by ideals. They are conservative, conventional people with concrete beliefs based on traditional, established codes: family, religion, community, and the nation. Many Believers express moral codes that are deeply rooted and literally interpreted. They follow established routines, organized in large part around home, family, community, and social or religious organizations to which they belong.

  As consumers, Believers are predictable; they choose familiar products and established brands. They favor American products and are generally loyal customers.

- **Achievers:** Motivated by the desire for achievement, they have goal-oriented lifestyles and a deep commitment to career and family. Their social lives reflect this focus and are structured around family, their place of worship, and work. Achievers live conventional lives, are politically conservative, and respect authority and the status quo. They value consensus, predictability, and stability over risk, intimacy, and self-discovery.

  With many wants and needs, Achievers are active in the consumer marketplace. Image is important to Achievers; they favor established, prestige products and services that demonstrate success to their peers. Because of their busy lives, they are often interested in a variety of time-saving devices.

- **Strivers:** are trendy and fun loving. Because they are motivated by achievement, Strivers are concerned about the opinions and approval of others. Money defines success for Strivers, who don't have enough of it to meet their desires. They favor stylish products that emulate the purchases of people with greater material wealth. Many see themselves as having a job rather than a career, and a lack of skills and focus often prevents them from moving ahead.

  Strivers are active consumers because shopping is both a social activity and an opportunity to demonstrate to peers their ability to buy. As consumers, they are as impulsive as their financial circumstance will allow.

- **Experiencers:** are motivated by self-expression. As young, enthusiastic, and impulsive consumers, Experiencers quickly become enthusiastic about new possibilities but are equally quick to cool. They seek variety and excitement, savoring the new, the offbeat, and the risky. Their energy finds an outlet in exercise, sports, outdoor recreation, and social activities. Experiencers are avid consumers and spend a comparatively high proportion of their income on fashion, entertainment, and socializing. Their purchases reflect the emphasis they place on looking good and having "cool" stuff.

- **Makers:** Like Experiencers, Makers are motivated by self-expression. They express themselves and experience the world by working on it-building a house, raising children, fixing a car, or canning vegetables-and have enough skill and energy to carry out their projects successfully. Makers are practical people who have constructive skills and value self-sufficiency. They live within a traditional context of family, practical work, and physical recreation and have little interest in what lies outside that context.

  Makers are suspicious of new ideas and large institutions such as big business. They are respectful of government authority and organized labor, but resentful of government intrusion on individual rights. They are unimpressed by material possessions other than those with a practical or functional purpose. Because they prefer value to luxury, they buy basic products.

- **Survivors (Formerly Strugglers):** live narrowly focused lives. With few resources with which to cope, they often believe that the world is changing too quickly. They are comfortable with the familiar and are primarily concerned with safety and security. Because they must focus on meeting needs rather than fulfilling desires, Survivors do not show a strong primary motivation.

  Survivors are cautious consumers. They represent a very modest market for most products and services. They are loyal to favorite brands, especially if they can purchase them at a discount.

Source: Strategic Business Insights (SBI); www.strategicbusinessinsights.com/vals

MY CB BOOK

Another reason is that the questions asked in various surveys are not always the same; different researchers ask different questions that try to measure different aspects of consumers' personalities and lifestyles. Some measure only leisure activities, others measure people's beliefs and all activities or lifestyles, and still others measure lifestyles *and* values *and* self-concepts. Thus, different psychographic studies differ because they are different slices of the same (or similar) pie. But they are all real as views from different angles of the same prism.

TABLE 6.2   VALS CLASSIFICATION QUESTIONNAIRE

VALS™ Survey

Mostly disagree   Somewhat disagree   Somewhat agree   Mostly agree

1. I am often interested in theories.
2. I like outrageous people and things.
3. I like a lot of variety in my life.
4. I love to make things I can use everyday.
5. I follow the latest trends and fashions.

6. Just as the Bible says, the world literally was created in six days.
7. I like being in charge of a group.
8. I like to learn about art, culture, and history.
9. I often crave excitement.
10. I am really interested only in a few things.

11. I would rather make something than buy it.
12. I dress more fashionably than most people.
13. The federal government should encourage prayers in public schools.
14. I have more ability than most people.
15. I consider myself an intellectual.

16. I must admit that I like to show off.
17. I like trying new things.
18. I am very interested in how mechanical things, such as engines, work.
19. I like to dress in the latest fashions.
20. There is too much sex on television today.

21. I like to lead others.
22. I would like to spend a year or more in a foreign country.
23. I like a lot of excitement in my life.
24. I must admit that my interests are somewhat narrow and limited.
25. I like making things of wood, metal, or other such material.

26. I want to be considered fashionable.
27. A woman's life is fulfilled only if she can provide a happy home for her family.
28. I like the challenge of doing something I have never done before.
29. I like to learn about things even if they may never be of any use to me.
30. I like to make things with my hands.

31. I am always looking for a thrill.
32. I like doing things that are new and different.
33. I like to look through hardware or automotive stores.
34. I would like to understand more about how the universe works.
35. I like my life to be pretty much the same from week to week.

Source: Strategic Business Insights (SBI) www.strategicbusinessinsights.com/vals (Used with permission)

PSYCHOGRAPHICS + DEMOGRAPHICS
Double the Power

Marketers have always recognized that not all consumers are the same. Very early on, they recognized consumer differences in terms of demographics. Accordingly, consumers were differentiated by age, sex, income, family size, etc. Soon marketers realized that demographics told them "who" bought their product, but not "why" they bought it.

To bridge this gap, Motivational Research (MR) was invented. MR is, as we learned in Chapter 2, the practice of identifying some deep-seated consumer motives behind a purchase (or, alternatively, resistance to a purchase). This line of psychoanalytic research gave marketers some comfort, as researchers trained in the Freudian psychology of the unconscious mind solved the mysteries of consumer whims and/or deep, unexplainable consumer resistance to buying specific products.

Marketers' love affair with MR was short-lived, however, as MR findings sometimes stretched credulity. More sophisticated analyses applied to demographics could now yield multidimensional profiles. Yet demographics are demographics, and even a multidimensional profile, such as a consumer being "35 years old, married, with 2.5 children, and 1.2 dogs" could not satisfy marketers' thirst for real explanations for consumer behavior. To the rescue came the idea of applying the same quantitative analytical techniques to the measurement of consumer motives. From motives to other aspects of consumers' psychological makeup was then a short leap, and the craft of psychographics, as we know it today, was born.

Today, most psychographic surveys routinely include demographics as well. That is why many psychographic segment names and descriptions incorporate and are informed by demographics as well (e.g., "Renaissance Women," or "Accepting Mid-lifers").

PRODUCTS AS BUILDING BLOCKS OF LIFESTYLES

Lifestyles and Psychographics are very useful marketing tools today. Except some entirely utilitarian products such as detergents, lawn mowers, hamburgers, etc., most products such as clothing, cars, electronics, home furnishings, and even grocery shopping bags come adorned with content and/or stylistic features that serve to express consumers' self-concepts and identities. Consumers use them to build their lifestyles.

Multiple Applications

We are now ready to put some order to the vast array of lifestyle research options available to marketers eager to use them. (Remember, *lifestyles* is a term marketers use interchangeably with the term *psychographics*.)

Same product, different psychographics

- **General Population Lifestyles** A psychographic research project can take a random sample of an entire population (say, of a nation) and identify lifestyle segments of consumers. Many market research companies (e.g., SBI) have already done this for individual countries. Marketing companies can simply buy these standard databases. Most of these research surveys also include questions on consumer use of a wide range of products, and, based on product-use indexes, you can choose which psychographic segment to target for your product.

- **Subpopulation Lifestyles** Instead of looking at the general population, we could, of course, sample a specific subpopulation and repeat the same research process. Thus, we could prepare a psychographic profile of, say, only women, or only college students. If we were selling women's cosmetics, for instance, then we had better limit our sample to women only. The same research companies that offer general population lifestyle profiles will be happy to slice the data by demographics for you (sometimes for a fee, of course).

SAVVY MARKETER

- **Domain/Product Specific Lifestyles** Suppose your business is a travel agency; then you wouldn't want to target non-travelers. And you know also that all travelers are not alike. Therefore, you would want to identify psychographic segments among travelers only. Or if you were a sports marketer, then you would want to identify consumers interested in sports. For these purposes, you would limit your sample to domain-

Different consumers, different lifestyles

specific consumers. You can accomplish it by asking a screening question at the start of the survey. Even more importantly, in your AIO inventory, you would ask fewer questions about general psychographics and a lot more questions focused on traveling, or sports, or museum-visiting, or about whatever be your domain of interest. Instead of an activity domain, your focus could instead be a product: e.g., lifestyles of organic food consumers, or heavy users of energy drink.s

• **Customers' Psychographics** Having been immersed in psychographics for so long in this chapter, you cannot but wonder about the psychographics of your own customers, i.e., the target consumers for the specific products or services or brands you are marketing. You can certainly do a psychographic survey of your customers. Of course, you will have to build your AIO inventory carefully so that it covers, for the most part, only those psychographics that you would intuitively consider relevant to your product domain.

You Got Psychographics; Now What?

Alright, you have completed your research and have collected the psychographic profiles of various consumer groups—for the entire population in a country, for an age or gender group, for a specific domain area, or for your current consumers—whichever seemed relevant to you. Now what? How do you harness this information in your marketing strategy? Here are the steps:

1. **Choose your target market(s)**
2. **Create different programs for different segments**
3. **Court a segment of current consumers**
4. **Appeal to lifestyles**

MARKETING BY LIFESTYLE

Since consumers buy products to build the mosaic of their lifestyles, wouldn't it make sense that products be marketed by the lifestyles to which they belong? A lot of marketers are doing just that. These marketing applications can be divided into four broad categories: (a) products by lifestyles; (b) selling product constellations, (c) brand alliances, and (d) positioning by lifestyles.[3]

A. Products by Lifestyles Products are the building blocks of lifestyles. Therefore, many products are conceived and crafted to suit specific lifestyles. For example, American Eagle Outfitters makes its clothing for a casual and rugged persona; in sharp contrast, Stacy Adams clothing caters to urbane trendy suave men.

B. Selling Product Constellations Often, consumers don't choose their products haphazardly; rather, for each lifestyle, a certain set of products seems to fit together. For example, a surfer's lifestyle requires a surfboard, surfing gear, skin-protection products, surfing magazines and videos, an MP3 player, a utility vehicle, and perhaps even picnic-ware. These products form, for the surfer, a **consumption constellation**—defined as a group of products that are consumed together in a typical consumption lifestyle. Rather than having to buy these from different sellers or different areas of a store, it would be nice if the consumer could buy them in a one-stop shopping place. Several marketers are helping consumers do just that (e.g., Benchmark Outdoor Outfitters; Party City).

C. Brand Alliances A special case of product constellation is co-branding and brand alliances. You are no doubt familiar with how airlines and hotels award loyalty points that can be redeemed wih vendors of either service. Often other companies run joint promotions that make sense, such as a Broadway Theater ticket plan with an upscale restaurant offering, or a credit card offer from a fraternity with special discounts at stores near college campuses.

D. Positioning by Lifestyle Often marketers try to "position" their brands by lifestyle. To accomplish this, various elements of the marketing mix can be utilized. Products can be designed to appeal to consumers of specific lifestyles, and distribution outlets can be selected based on the lifestyle of consumers they attract. Moreover, product communication campaigns can depict the purported lifestyle. Consider these options:

Lifestyle Specific Media Products Visit any magazine store, and see how many magazines there are on very specific interests and leisure activities. There are magazines for women (e.g., *Woman's Day, Cosmopolitan, Perth Woman*); for golf fans (e.g., *Golf Digest*), for music lovers (*Spin*), for lovers of the outdoors (e.g., *Outdoors, Field & Stream*), for the techno-literati (e.g., *Wired*), and for transvestites (e.g., U.K. based *Repartee).* Likewise, Web sites such as iVillage.com, Oxygen.com, and DailyCandy.com are devoted to women's interests and feature wide-ranging interest areas (e.g., parenting, romance, cooking, etc.).

Clothing brands are often positioned by lifestyles. In this ad from Stacy Adams, color, fabric, style, and the model, all come together to depict the mosaic of a fashionable, out-on-the-town lifestyle.

Physical Presence in Lifestyle Events Here, a brand's connection to a consumer lifestyle is established by placing the brand in the contexts of consumers' lifestyle interests or events. For example, coffee itself has nothing to do with musical events or listening; however, Nescafé's Australian web site allows you to download selected music freely. And it shows vignettes of "slice of life" situations in which, as part of your lifestyle, the company hopes you will consume Nescafé. The company thus hopes to place its brand in the midst of your life-at-large.[4]

Lifestyle Niche Echoing In the foregoing two sub-strategies, the product is aimed at the general user of the product category; the marketer just looks for common ground, from a lifestyle point-of-view (e.g., love of music for the music concert event), In contrast is a strategy where the entire marketing program (from product design to distribution to advertising) is conceived, from inception, to echo a particular lifestyle niche.

In its immediate, utilitarian function, this cup is identical with almost all other cups. It distinguishes itself, however, in its visual style, which consumers of a certain psychographics will find more appealing than will others.

To illustrate this strategy, let us visit the store Hot Topic. If you want to meet some teenagers who are into punk or Goth (think Avril Lavigne), there is perhaps no better place, at least as far as a mall goes. This retail store sells clothing to the "definitely not mainstream" youth. A "welcome" sign here reads: "Come in or you suck." The background music is excruciatingly loud. Of course, it also sells CDs of the same music. On display are such brand names as Morbid Threads and Vamp, and T-shirts display such insulting sentiments as "Wow, you're ugly" and "I know how you feel, I just don't care." Its racks are filled with tons of body jewelry, and it sells licensed gift cards featuring images such as SpongeBob SquarePants and the rock group Korn. Many of its customers buy the cards not to send to someone, but to keep for themselves![6]

To reinforce your understanding of this last strategy, where the whole business concept is created around a particular psychographic, we take you to a consumer group diametrically opposite to the funky, gothic teenager of Hot Topic: the mature, aesthetic experience-seeking consumers of home furnishings and clothing. They are the Bobos. And the store that captured the hearts and minds of this segment: Anthropologie. Read about the Bobos in the inset and in the chapter feature *Romancing the Consumer.*

SAVVY MARKETER

If we were to buy tires, our principal concern would be performance—what the tire does for the car and for our driving. But its performance on the road (solid grip, for example) gives us ability, control, and confidence. "Precision control" and "groomed for grip" could very well be metaphors for our living itself. **Why, those tires that give our life a style even leave t-r-a-c-k m-a-r-k-s that are fashionable enough to adorn our clothing.** Such brand connections are subtle but real, and for reasons of subtlety even more gratifying for us—at least for those of us who see having control on the road as being part of our self-concepts. We are style-setters; why shouldn't our tires be? (Image used with permission.)

BOBOs—A New Consumer Segment

BOBOs are a new class of consumers who combine the traits of two other types: bohemians and bourgeoisie. The term was coined by New York Times reporter David Brooks in his book *Bobos in Paradise* (Simon and Schuster, 2001).

You have read about bohemians in this chapter earlier. Bourgeoisie were almost the opposite—the old aristocracy, the elite class in the pre-1960s and 70s. Born and raised in educated and affluent families, youngsters went to Ivy League schools, and later held positions of influence. For bourgeoisie, everything, from dress to table manners to social interactions had to be prim and proper.

Then, in the sixties, came the bohemian class—the hippies, the gypsy, the artsy people who spawned the sexual revolution and the pursuit of a care-free rather than materialism-burdened lifestyle.

In the post-1970 period, the old aristocracy gave way to meritocracy. Anyone who had the requisite aptitude and abilities could get into the Ivy Leagues. To advance in life, old family ties were no longer required. This new, elite class lacked the appetite for formal mannerism of the aristocrat class. Instead, they adopted the "more casual than thou" attitude of the bohemian class. And lo, Bobos were born!

Bobos are affluent (like bourgeoisie) but not materialistic (a trait they share with bohemians). They spend well but not conspicuously. Recall that bohemians shun mass-merchandised goods; in their time, the bourgeoisie did the same. However, the two groups pursued uniqueness in different ways: Bohemians by searching for quirky inexpensive goods (e.g., tie and dye); bourgeoisie by shopping at upscale, exclusive stores. Bobos shun both mass merchandise and glitzy, pretentious luxury brands. Instead they seek artisan products with unique style and aesthetics, in boutique stores. To cater to this new class, a new category of merchandisers has sprung up: Starbucks, Panera Bread, Pottery Barn, Restoration Hardware, to name a few. Although the term *Bobos* has not become popular, the Bobos phenomenon is real and Bobos are kicking and thriving. A store called Anthropologie is living proof.

(See Romancing the Consumer)

Bobos = Bohemians + Bourgeoisie

MY CB BOOK

Positioning by Lifestyles/ Psychographics

《   〉

Now notice how the same tire company, Bridgestone, fashions its offering to a younger consumer lifestyle. Even the tire name, Fuzion, is conceived to resonate with the youth mindset. (Image used with permission.)

Romancing the Consumer

Anthropologie--Welcome to Bobo Lifestyles

It is an academic discipline with a French spelling. But we are not speaking here of some college course you take for 3 credits. We speak, instead, of a store-chain that is part museum, part a modern day shopping enclave. Headquartered in Philadelphia and with some 85-plus stores in North America, the chain sells women's clothing and home furnishings. But that is just the store demographics. What is fascinating is the store chain's "psychographics."

Enter the store and you are inside a large warehouse-like high-ceilinged structure with exposed wooden beams. Happily, its largeness is broken down into small islands alongside a meandering pathway, a collection of some 30 or so borderless merchandise display areas, each with an intimacy of its own.

Quirky and artistic decorations abound—on the walls (mixed material curios) and on tabletops (e.g., pebbles, lentils, beads, oversized books). The tables, on which the merchandise is displayed, themselves are rustic, distressed wood you would expect to find in a peasant farmhouse a couple of centuries ago. In fact, most likely, that is where they came from. Hanging on a sparsely populated rack are jeans—one variety is an inconspicuously branded Level 99 (price $168). Other collections offer eclectic styles and fabrics—from Indian sari material to Moroccan embroidered motifs to vintage Italian. From long classy dresses to flirty midi skirts.

Stylistic home goods abound: folk-artsy ceramic tableware; artisan-made picture frames; contemporary linen. But what attracts a second (and third) look are vintage furniture pieces—being one of a kind, they vary, naturally, across stores and from season to season. Some recent sightings (priced from $1500 to $6000 and upward): a dining table with irregular, rough, broken edges, and with 6" diameter tree trunks as its legs; two gorgeous glass chandeliers hanging with jute/hemp ropes; a bench with a mini tiled-look sitting surface and thick tree branches in a crisscrossing pattern as back and arm support. (The table was priced $3800.) Such functional but quirky and definitely unique merchandise define the store's personality.

True to its name, the store merchandise looks like a collection of some cultural anthropologist. For chic Bobos—part bohemian, part high-culture consumers—Anthropologie is indeed an oasis for discovering material goods with nonmaterial stories that resonate with one's own identity and psychographics. Anthropologie was one of the first stores in Bobo land, and a visit there will, just like a college course, earn you some credit hours in Bobo lifestyles.

Powered OM by   MY C. BOOK

MATERIALISM VERSUS VOLUNTARY SIMPLICITY

The Yin and Yang of Consumption

In this section, we cover an overarching psychographic that captures our consumption style in its entirety (i.e., it covers everything we do as consumers). It is called *materialism*, and its exact opposite is *voluntary simplicity*. Of immense gratification to millions of consumers, the former (i.e., materialism) can become a never-fulfilled pursuit for some; the latter (i.e., voluntary simplicity), an exact antidote, can bring Nirvana to the same consumers. Read on.

MATERIALISM

Materialism is an overarching marker of consumer lifestyles. No matter which VALS group a person belongs to, and no matter what cluster of activities, opinions, and interests define a person, all individuals in their roles as consumers can be scored on a single psychographic factor—*materialism*.

Do you want to own a lot of things, indulge in luxuries, live a very rich and comfortable life, and have lots of money? Do you consider your possessions an important aspect of your self-identity? If so, then you are what social scientists and consumer researchers call *materialistic*. The Oxford English Dictionary defines **materialism** as "a devotion to material needs and desires, to the neglect of spiritual matters; a way of life, opinion, or tendency based entirely upon material interests." Consumer researcher Russ Belk defines **materialism** as "the importance a consumer attaches to material possessions."[8]

Materialism has three dimensions: materialists define success by material things one owns; their lives revolve around acquisitions; and they seek happiness in material possessions. Want to know your materialism score? Table 6.3 presents a scale to measure materialism.

Consumer researchers have identified several traits of materialists. First, materialists value acquisition of possessions more than they value other life goals. They value them more than they value relationships with others, for example. Second, materialistic people are self-centered. Accordingly, they are less likely to be sharing and giving—less likely to donate money to church organizations or charity and less likely to lend money to friends. Materialists also lead a life of material complexity—they rely on technology, they have positive attitudes toward growth, and they lack concern for things in nature. Finally, despite many possessions, materialists tend to be less satisfied with life than others. The lust for goods is insatiable; it always leaves materialists wanting more.[9]

VOLUNTARY SIMPLICITY

The opposite of materialism is simplicity and frugality. Some consumers live a simple and frugal life, of course, because of limited means and resources. But many consumers who are well-off realize that chasing material goods is a never-ending race, that acquiring more actually leaves us less contented, wanting more. Some realize it after a period of chasing after goods, and some develop that mode of thinking as they grow up as adolescents. When consumers live a simple life, not chasing material goods (and when they do so not because they can't afford but because they don't want to), they are living a life of voluntary simplicity. **Voluntary simplicity** refers to acquiring a belief system that too much consumption is undesirable, and, accordingly, choosing to live a life with fewer products and services.[10]

Voluntary simplicity entails both a belief system and a practice. It is based on the belief that true happiness comes not from materialism but from focusing on and reflecting on life itself—on the nonmaterial aspects of life. And it is practiced through reduced consumption,

CB FYI

Lifestyles of Billionaire Brides

Which bride had the most extravagant wedding in history? That honor, according to Forbes magazine's "Billionaire Weddings List," goes to Vanisha Mittal, daughter of India-born, London-based steel industrialist Lakshmi Mittal.

A graduate of the European Business School and the London Business School, and a board member in her father's business, Mittal took her wedding vows in June 2004, at the Château de Versailles, France. Pop singer Kylie Minogue sang, while wine from five thousand bottles of Mouton Rothschild flowed. Total tab: $60 million!

Read a fascinating account of this fairytale nuptial lifestyle in Verve magazine at www.verveonline.com/29/spotlight/pomp/excerpt1.shtml

Powered by oM   MY CB BOOK

TABLE 6.3 — A SCALE TO MEASURE CONSUMER MATERIALISM

Rate the following statements on this scale:

Strongly Disagree   1   2   3   4   5   Strongly Agree

SUCCESS SUBSCALE

I admire people who own expensive homes, cars, and clothes. _____
The things I own say a lot about how well I'm doing in life. _____
I like to own things that impress people. _____
I don't pay much attention to the material objects other people own.* _____

CENTRALITY SUBSCALE

I usually buy only the things I need.* _____
I try to keep my life simple as far as possessions are concerned.* _____
Buying things gives me a lot of pleasure. _____
I like a lot of luxury in my life. _____

HAPPINESS SUBSCALE

I have all the things I really need to enjoy life.* _____
I wouldn't be any happier if I owned nicer things.* _____
I'd be happier if I could afford to buy more things. _____
It sometimes bothers me quite a bit that I can't afford to buy all the things I'd like. _____

How to score. Reverse score the items marked *, and then add up all items. The higher the score, the more materialistic you are, with a score of 36 being the midpoint. _____ (Your score)

Source: Adapted and abbreviated from Marsha L. Richins and Scott Dawson, "A Consumer Values Orientation and Its Measurement: Scale Development and Validation," *Journal of Consumer Research*, 19, 3 (December 1992) pp. 303-17. © Journal of Consumer Research. Publisher: The University of Chicago Press (Used with permission.)

MY CB BOOK MEASURE

freeing one's mind of wealth and commercial products, and turning one's attention to inner growth. It also entails cleaning up one's calendar from the clutter of too many appointments and a rushed schedule, and taking the time to "smell the roses," so to speak.

For many, consuming is a process of identity construction. A product confers an identity, prestige, and blissful happiness. However, some who see consumption as a means of overcoming the stress of life actually find that, through consumption, stress is not reduced. In fact, they find that the race to acquire more (and for acquiring the resources to acquire more) creates its own stress. And if their purpose in consumption were to create a self, consumption creates, they realize, a self that is always incomplete and still dissatisfied with its new state or definition. One reaches a point in this self-creation enterprise, looks in the mirror, and wonders, "Is this what I wanted to become?" Then comes a U-turn—dispossession of goods and uncluttering of day-to-day calendars.

Psychologist V. Gecas describes the self as comprising three components: self-esteem, self-efficacy, and authentication. **Self-esteem** refers to holding oneself as valued. **Self-efficacy** refers to viewing oneself as effective, in control. Finally, **authentication** refers to realizing that one is what one truly is. One consumer notes his realization of how a consumption-based self is not authentic:

> " ...I had all the stuff that was supposed to make me successful—my car and my clothes, the house in the right neighborhood and belonging to the right health club. All the external framework was excellent, and inside I kind of had this pit eating away at me."

Another consumer said:

> "We had a big house and a housekeeper... and I was driving up and down the freeway to work all the time when I realized, 'This is not me, this is not who I am'"

(Respondents in a research study by Professor Stephen Zavestoski, Providence College).[11]

The importance of voluntary simplicity is brought home by a practice among some consumers around the world: they celebrate one day in a year as *Buy Nothing* day (see www.buynothingday.com).

STATUS CONSUMPTION

One key element of the psyche of consumer lifestyles is the need to keep up with the Joneses, so to speak. That means, consuming according to one's status, or status consumption. **Status consumption** can be defined as acquiring and consuming products that signify a status in society. Products acquire a status image through acceptance and appreciation among the social classes. Thus, Mercedes-Benz, for example, acquires a status image that is appreciated by upper social classes and the old wealth; a BMW (which is in the same price range), in contrast, connotes not as much social class status as a sporty, trendy, professional person's car.

The consumption of the upper classes is marked, naturally, by expensive lifestyles, encompassing big mansions, luxury cars, richly tailored clothes, and glittering gold. However, some of this consumption is driven by a desire to "show off," flaunting one's wealth. Sociologist Thorstein Veblen has termed this **conspicuous consumption**, defined as lifestyles that flaunt the wealth of the rich.[12] Note that not all upscale consumption need be conspicuous. The key is the desire to impress others with one's wealth.

The majority of the consumers in both upper classes and middle classes constantly remain very conscious of the product and brand status when making their selections. Of course, within the same class, not every consumer is equally status-conscious.[13] To measure how status conscious you are, take the short survey in Table 6.4.

CONTRARIAN STATUS CONSUMPTION

Three trends counter the mindset of conspicuous consumption: voluntary simplicity, quiet aesthetics, and parody display.

- Voluntary Simplicity As already discussed, this lifestyle entails a mindset wherein the consumer voluntarily simplifies his/her lifestyles and avoids the trappings of materialism. Accumulation of goods is reversed, and the chase after material wealth abandoned. Home, car, entertainment electronics, travel, etc., are downsized. Everyday consumption is oriented toward products of high quality and taste without being glittery or showy.
- Quiet Aesthetics **Quiet Aesthetics** (a term coined anew for this book) is a mindset where an affluent consumer seeks well-made and unique products of understated glory—high class in composition and aesthetics, and not mass-produced. Whereas

TABLE

6.4 A STATUS CONSUMPTION SCALE

Express your opinion on the following statements:

Strongly disagree	Mostly disagree	Disagree	Neutral	Agree	Mostly agree	Strongly agree
1	2	3	4	5	6	7

1. I would buy a product just because it has status.	1 2 3 4 5 6 7
2. The only products that I find appealing are the ones with status.	1 2 3 4 5 6 7
3. No matter what I buy I am always conscious of its status.	1 2 3 4 5 6 7
4. Paying more for a product just because of its prestige and status is unwise.*	1 2 3 4 5 6 7
5. Maintaining my status in everything I buy is important to me.	1 2 3 4 5 6 7

* Reverse score this statement, so that 1 is recoded as 7, 2 as 6, 3 as 5, 5 as 3, 6 as 2, and 7 as 1.

If you score more than 20, you are most likely status-conscious in your consumption and purchases. Let's hope you have the money to live out your status consumption desires.

Note: Composed by the author. For an alternative version, see Jacqueline K. Eastman, Ronald E. Goldsmith, & Leisa Reinecke Flynn, "Status Consumption in Consumer Behavior: Scale Development & Validation," Journal of Marketing Theory & Practice, Summer 1999, 41-51. Our item # 1 is borrowed as is, & other items are informed by but non-identical with their other items. Their other items are: I am interested in new products with status; I would pay more for a product if I had status; The status of a product is irrelevant to me; and, A product is more valuable to me if it has some snob appeal.

voluntary simplicity also shuns being extravagant, the seekers of "quiet aesthetics" are happy to spend for uniqueness, authenticity, and the quiet quality of a product. An ace example is the consumption of Bobos (described earlier) and the store they love: Anthropologie. Other favorites: Pottery Barn, Restoration Hardware, William Sonoma, Whole Foods Markets, etc. A considerable part of wealth is devoted to private collection of arts and support of public projects.

- Parody Display We owe this term to sociologist John Brooks, who coined it to capture a consumption trend among the upper social classes. He noticed that conspicuous consumption did not sit well with all affluent consumers. There was a segment of affluent consumers who disliked the flaunting lifestyles. This radical, breakaway group is not satisfied with the two foregoing lifestyle choices either. Their disdain for the flaunting lifestyle is so intense that they resort, instead, to mocking it, by consuming the products of exactly opposite kinds—"rags," so to speak. Torn, faded jeans were a prime example when the practice first started. Now, of course, designer jeans, distressed and holed, are ultra-expensive and have in themselves become a new status symbol. In every age, there will always be a radical, breakaway group, conjuring up new avenues of mocking the pretentious lifestyles of the affluent. Be on the lookout for the next product prop for parody display.[14]

A particular parody display is essentially a short-lived trend, not because it fades, but because its props become the new means of "keeping up with the Joneses"!

YOUR BIG LIFE PROJECT
A Profound Truth About Your Own Identity Project

We all have projects in life. Some are small—like doing the weekly laundry this coming Sunday; others are big—like finally getting rid of that tattoo. Or, if you are an appearance-anxious boomer, getting that twin-chin united by facial surgery. *Life projects* are significant goals and major events that we strive to bring to fruition. Thus, not all projects in life are life projects; only those that will have a major impact on our lives, with which we remain obsessed for considerable time, which currently occupy our minds constantly, whose completion we look forward to, and which entail considerable investment of time, money, and physical energy. Accordingly, updating your Facebook profile does not qualify, but enrolling in Mandarin classes certainly will. (Panama has made the teaching of Mandarin mandatory in all schools; the US Government has allocated more than $1billion to fund Chinese classes in schools. And in the U.K., the number of college students taking Chinese as their main subject has more than doubled during the past five years!)

Here are some others that would qualify. To graduate; to find a job; to remodel your home; to travel to Asia; to learn how to play guitar; to learn to tango; to learn to speak the French language fluently; to lose 15 pounds of body weight; to read all the books mentioned in this book; to get an eternal date (sign up on e-harmony.com); to get a spouse; to adopt a child from a Third World poor family; to start your own blog; to digitize all your photos; to re-read this book later, post-graduation, liberated from the hassled read-and-test framework.

Each of these projects reflects your lifestyle and entails significant consumption. Each also brings, when completed, immense satisfaction to the person striving toward that goal. These projects have a finite duration: one month, one year, five years. (Their accomplishment might take as little as a week, but, to qualify as a "life project," the total time of our obsession with them has to be much longer, say, at least a month). Life projects are important to give meaning to life. Without them, life remains dreary and purposeless. Most people have three or four life projects at any stage in their lives.

Now consider this. Over and above these life projects, which have a finite duration and which differ from person to person, there is one overarching and perpetual life project we all have. It begins very early in life and it never ends. It is, and here comes our big proposition, to build and implement our lifestyles.

We spend considerable amounts of time, money, and energy to choose and constantly build and bolster our self-identities, and flesh out our corresponding lifestyles. We go to the marketplace to collect the ingredients that will help us assemble a lifestyle. Then we constantly, day in day out, keep embellishing and adapting it. Every consumer, every one of us, has this BIG LIFE PROJECT. With no exceptions. Yes, even monks have it!

Marketers need to study their target consumers' BIG LIFE PROJECTS—their consumers' constant endeavor sto live their lifestyles. They need to map, in other words, their target consumers' identity projects, their lifestyles, their psychographics.

GEODEMOGRAPHICS

Where You Live Says a Lot About You

What is your ZIP Code? 01742? Then, you are a college graduate, earn about $75,000 a year, and are eager to learn Italian. 30132? In that case, you never finished college, have a blue collar job, make about $33,000 a year, love to read Civil War history, rarely lock your front door, and probably have a set of deer antlers hanging on your bedroom wall. Or did you say, 94598? Okay then, you are a Generation Xer, constantly socializing on your cell phone, obsessed with recycling, and can often be found at Starbucks, sipping a latte.

How did we know? We know because of geodemographics—the art of portraying people and markets by their geographic location.

Geodemographics is the study of relationships between demographics on one hand and geographic location on the other. The underlying premise is that people of similar demographic characteristics (age, income, occupation) tend to live in similar geographic locations. Moreover, since the natural and economic resources of a geographic location enable and constrain our activities, geographic location helps shape our lifestyles and activities. For example, if we don't live near a river, or ocean, or lake, then we won't be engaging in water sports—not frequently, anyway. If you live in a big city, your lifestyle is going to be that of a big city person; your friend, who lives in an industrial town, is going to have a different lifestyle. Thus, in a very real sense, our lifestyles and consumption are determined by where we live—i.e., by our geodemographics.

PRIZM

The Psychology of 90210 and Other ZIP Codes

The company that has given us a neighborhood clustering scheme for U.S.A. is Claritas, Inc. Claritas has grouped various neighborhoods in America based on their Zip Codes into the so called PRIZM clusters.

The company grouped some 250,000 neighborhoods, based on their ZIP Codes, ZIP+4 postal codes[15], and census tracts (about 500-1000 households). All geographic units whose inhabitants have the same demographics and lifestyles are grouped together, producing a total of 66 clusters. Thus, ZIP Codes 10021 (Upper East Side, New York), 60614 (Lincoln Park, Illinois), and 90292 (Marina Del Rey, California) are placed, along with other Zip Codes, into a single ZIP Code Cluster, called *Urban Gold Coast*.

People sharing a cluster also share a lifestyle. Why? For two reasons: first, as already mentioned, because the geography and resources and activities available in a place determine what consumers can and will do. And, second, we choose to live in the neighborhoods that fit our lifestyles. **"Birds of a feather flock together,"** as they say. Since our lifestyles influence what we buy and consume, the clustering scheme also tells the marketer what people in a given ZIP Code are likely to buy. Hence, the clustering scheme is given the name PRIZM (Potential Rating Index by ZIP Code Markets).

In fact, one of the two lifestyle segments we described earlier—Bohemian Mix—was taken from this list. Let us now view a fuller profile of that consumer segment, and, for contrast, one more, *Urban Achievers*. See where they live in Exhibits 6.2A and 6.3A.

Bohemian Mix You have met this group earlier in this chapter as an example of lifestyle profiles. Now we've got more information for you, so read on. Bohemian Mixers are young residents of urban hodge podge neighborhoods; the majority (3 out of every 4) are neve-married or are divorced singles. They are predominantly students, artists, writers, actors, and the like. They live somewhat adventuresome, funky lives, exercising both their bodies and minds, hanging out at sidewalk cafes, public libraries, bookstores, health food stores, social and voluntary organizations, benefit programs, and protest campaigns on social issues. "Day and Night," writes Michael Weiss, the author of an influential book on the Prizm Clusters (titled Clustered World)[16], "residents drift along the sidewalks, cruising, holding hands, and window shopping ... Many exposed limbs bear at least one tattoo." They enjoy aerobic activities like biking and rollerblading, and buy healthy foods. They stay hip by reading such magazines as GQ, Harper's Bazaar, Rolling Stone, etc. Their open-mindedness makes them early-adopters of new products like organic pet foods and computer online services. What Bohemians value most is their uniqueness, and their rejection of the mainstream. National chains and fast food restaurants will not survive in these areas because residents resist cookie-cutter businesses so as to preserve their uniqueness. What do well, instead, are sidewalk cafés, art galleries, and leftist bookshops. See Exhibit 6.2B.

Bohemian

Urban Achievers Urban Achievers are a mix of the young and the old, single students and older couples, with a disproportionate number of foreigners. They live in city centers, in upper-middle class apartment buildings in multi-ethnic group neighborhoods. They seek to avoid mono-ethnic suburban communities, and they enjoy multicultural city festivities and shows. Imported food, newspapers, alternative medicine, libraries, adult classes, and listening to public radio (PBS) are popular among this group. "As consumers, Urban Achievers behave," writes Weiss, "like many upper-middle-class metropolitan sophisticates. They surf the Internet, go to movies, eat out and travel abroad at high rates." They are similar to the Bohemian Mix in their liberal progressive views and in their support of such causes as gay rights and racial issues. But unlike Bohemian Mix, they do not have

Urban Achiever

Brief Profiles of Two Selected PRIZM Clusters

BOHEMIANS

bohemian mix

1.7% of U.S. households

Primary age groups: **under 24, 25–34**

Median household income: **$33,700**

Median home value: **$135,452**

Thumbnail Demographics

inner-city singles neighborhoods

multi-unit rental housing

ethnically mixed households

college graduates

white-collar professionals

Politics

Predominant ideology: liberal Democrat

1996 presidential vote: Bill Clinton

Key issues: gay rights, legalizing marijuana, defusing racial tensions

Sample Neighborhoods

Dupont Circle, Washington, D.C. 20036

Greenwich Village, New York, New York 10014

West Los Angeles, California 90025

Forest Park, Illinois 60130

Broadway, Seattle, Washington 98102

URBAN ACHIEVERS

urban achievers

1.6% of U.S. households

Primary age groups: **25–34, 65+**

Median household income: **$35,600**

Median home value: **$109,900**

Thumbnail Demographics

midlevel urban couples and singles

multi-unit rental housing

ethnically mixed households

college graduates

professionals and managers

Politics

Predominant ideology: liberal Independent

1996 presidential vote: Ross Perot

Key issues: gay rights, defusing racial tensions, increasing military spending

Sample Neighborhoods

Outer Richmond, San Francisco, California 94121

Hoboken, New Jersey 07030

Reseda, California 91335

Clearwater, Florida 34619

Bitter Lake, Seattle, Washington 98133

Source: Michael J. Weiss, The Clustered World, Little Brown and Company 2000, p. 212, 292 (Used with permission.)

any desire to distinguish themselves from the mainstream (in some ways, they think they *are* the mainstream). Full of optimism, they wish to achieve and hold on to the American Dream—a prosperous, happy, fulfilled life. See Exhibit 6.3B.

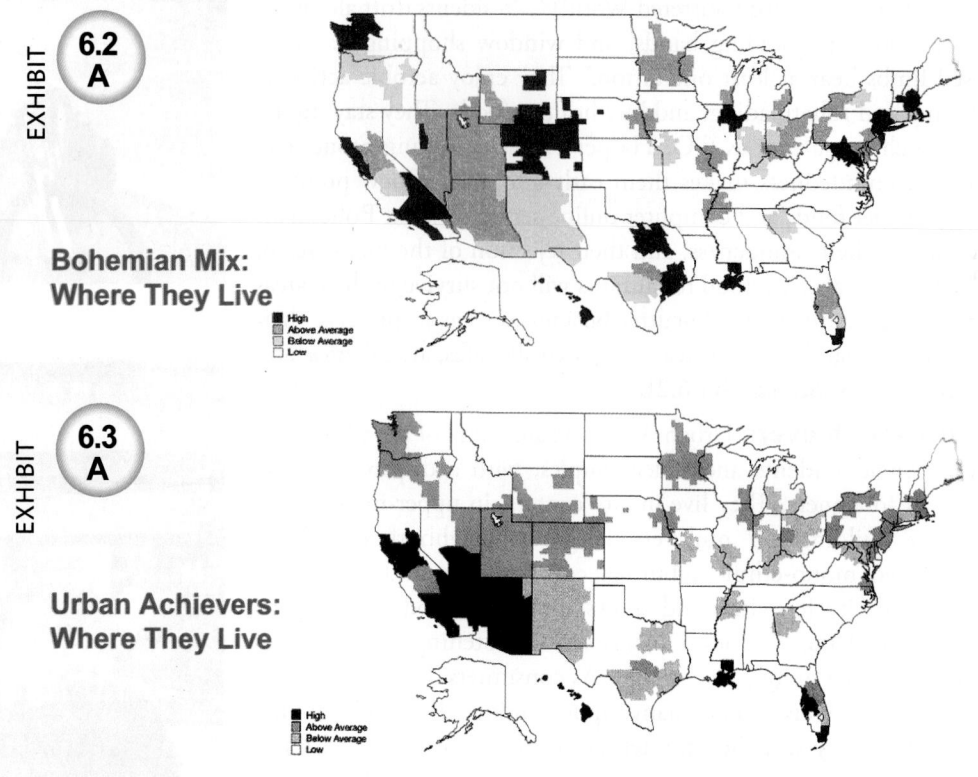

EXHIBIT 6.2 A

**Bohemian Mix:
Where They Live**

High
Above Average
Below Average
Low

EXHIBIT 6.3 A

**Urban Achievers:
Where They Live**

High
Above Average
Below Average
Low

Product Usage Variations Across Prism Clusters

If the lifestyles of PRIZM clusters are different, as we saw above, then it follows that the consumption of products must also vary across these clusters. And the fact is, it does. *The Clustered World* contains information linking product purchase rates for hundreds of products to the PRIZM cluster profiles. Figure 6.3 shows what clusters shop at Victoria's Secret, for example. As that figure shows, Bohemian Mix, God's Country, American Dream, and Norma Rayville are the top four clusters, while Middleburg Managers, Urban Achievers, Gray Power, and New Beginnings are the bottom four.

What other products are consumed more by some PRIZM clusters and less by others? In Figure 6.4, we show selected products and stores and name the top two and the bottom two clusters for each. Read on and marvel at this fascinating information about product use variations. These illustrations show how useful geodemographics can be to marketing managers for segmenting and targeting their consumers for different products.

FIGURE 6.3 **WHO SHOPS AT VICTORIA'S SECRET**

Cluster	Index
Bohemian Mix	217
God's Country	175
Military Quarters	162
Norma Rae-ville	133
Middleburg Managers	65
Urban Achievers	64
Gray Power	62
New Beginnings	7

Note: Average consumption is indexed at 100.
Source: Compiled by Author from: Michael J. Weiss, *The Clustered World,* 2000.

MY CB BOOK

6.2 B — BOHEMIAN MIXERS —PRODUCT PREFERENCES

LIFESTYLE PRODUCTS

WHAT IS HOT		WHAT'S NOT	
Foreign videos	246	Golfing	49
Jogging	236	Country music	46
Victoria's Secret	217	Woodwork	30
Espresso makers	189	Gas grills	21
European travel	188	College football	13

OTHER PRODUCTS WITH ABOVE AVERAGE CONSUMPTION

FOOD/DRINK		MAGAZINES/NEWSPAPERS	
Imported beer	201	New Yorker	440
Gourmet coffee beans	191	GQ	340
Imported wine	180	Mademoiselle	292
Brown rice	174	Rolling Stone	167
Bottled water	146		
Pita bread	145		

CARS/TRUCKS		TELEVISION/RADIO	
Alfa Romeos	277	Nightline	270
Saab 900s	212	Contemporary rock radio	184
Land Rovers	192	America's Most Wanted	162
Honda CRXs	172	Simpsons	136

SOURCE: Michael J. Weiss, The Clustered World, Little Brown, 2000, p. 212-213. (Used with Permission.)

MY CB BOOK

Bohemians eat brown rice nearly twice as much as an average American but watch college football only one eighth as much.

6.3 B — URBAN ACHIEVERS —PRODUCT PREFERENCES

LIFESTYLE PRODUCTS

WHAT IS HOT		WHAT'S NOT	
Theater	170	Golf Vacations	80
Passports	166	Victoria's Secret	64
Condoms	164	Pro Football Games	62
Exercise Clubs	163	Cellular Phones	38
Gambling Casinos	142		

OTHER PRODUCTS WITH ABOVE AVERAGE CONSUMPTION

FOOD/DRINK		MAGAZINES/NEWSPAPERS	
Brie Cheese	233	Esquire	217
Malt Liquor	207	Popular Photography	204
Taco Bell	137	Cosmopolitan	180
Bagels	120		
Kool Aid	118		

CARS/TRUCKS		TELEVISION/RADIO	
Kias	217	News Radio	248
Nissan NX1s	172	BET	240
Toyota Corollas	150	Beverly Hills 90210	222
		NYPD Blues	157

SOURCE: Michael J. Weiss, The Clustered World, Little Brown, 2000, p. 222-223. (Used with Permission.)

MY CB BOOK

Urban Achievers' favorite car is Kia. And they are not into golf vacations or into Victoria's Secret. Their favorite TV shows: Beverly Hills 90210 and NYPD Blue!*

*90210 ran during 1990-2000 and NYPD during 1993-2005. The present-day favorites of this group need to be studied.

6.4 FIGURE — TOP TWO AND BOTTOM TWO CLUSTERS FOR SELECTED PRODUCTS/SERVICES

BOTTOM TWO			TOP TWO	
Norma Ray-ville	40	Gap	196	Hispanic Mix
Sunset City Blues	43		183	Young Literati
Blue Blood Estates	80	Burger King	152	Old Yankee Rows
Young Literati	70		126	Red, White & Blues
New Empty Nests	82	Taco Bell	187	Boomtown Singles
Inner Cities	79		159	Young Influentials
Boomtown Singles/Inner Cities	20	Price Club	280	Blue Blood Estates
Gray Collars/Short-guns & Pick-ups	14		247	Young Literati
Rural Industrial	62	Builder's Square	191	Gray Collars
Grain Belt	60		187	Boomers & Babies
Mines & Mills	47	Diet Pills	154	South Side City
Starter Families	41		140	Rural Industrial

Note: Average consumption is indexed at 100.
Source: Compiled from: Michael J. Weiss, The Clustered World, 2000. Used with permission.

SUMMARY

Using Bianca's brief autobiographical narrative as a launch pad, we began with an introduction to psychographics. Psychographics include personal values, personality traits, and self-concepts, all culminating in lifestyles—the way we live. Here, we understood a crucial fact of consumers' marketplace behaviors: consumers choose products to build the mosaics that comprise their lifestyles.

Psychographics are ways of "graphing the psychological makeup of the consumer." This is done, we learned, through AIO ("activities, interests, and opinions") statements, in response to which the consumers' numerical ratings enable us to identify psychographics-based segments. As an example, we reviewed VALS, a values and lifestyle segmentation scheme for North American consumers.

One particular application of psychographics is *geodemographics*—the art of profiling a person based on his or her place of residence. In this scheme, consumers of similar neighborhoods (counted as ZIP+4) are grouped together, resulting in 66 clusters for the entire USA, called the PRIZM segments. We showcased the marketing utility of this scheme.

Finally, we discussed two overarching consumer psychographics: materialism and voluntary simplicity. Without these, no chapter on psychographics would be complete. They hover over our entire lives, both in our roles as humans and as consumers, serving us as servants, or, alternatively, controlling us as masters. Read about them and decide for yourself what they do for you!

KEY TERMS

AIO inventory
Authentication
BOBOs
Consumption constellation
Geodemographics

Lifestyles
Materialism
Parody consumption
PRIZM
Psychographics
Quiet Aesthetics

Self-esteem
Self-efficacy
Status consumption
VALS
Voluntary simplicity

YOUR TURN

REVIEW+Rewind

1. Explain in your own words the concepts of *lifestyles* and *psychographics*.
2. How are psychographics measured? What is an AIO inventory and how is it useful for psychographics?
3. What is the VALS scheme of psychographic segmentation? Name each of its consumer types and explain each briefly.
4. Why do different psychographic segmentation studies for the same population come out with segment names that differ across studies?
5. Explain the concepts of (a) parody consumption, (b) status consumption, (c) materialism, and (d) voluntary simplicity
6. What is meant by "positioning by lifestyles"? Explain various options of implementing this.
7. Is PRIZM a good scheme to segment the market? Why or why not?

THINK+Apply

1. Why should psychographics explain consumer behaviors?

2. Explain the relationship among the following concepts: values, personality traits, self-concepts, lifestyles, and psychographics. Should all psychographic studies measure all these concepts? Why or why not?

3. From the AIO statements (given in the chapter), select only five factors you consider most relevant to differentiating heavy users versus light or nonusers of (choose one) (a) hair styling mousse, (b) wines, (c) video games. Alternatively, identify AIO factors that would distinguish between consumers whose favorite store for clothes is: (a) Limited Express versus Gap, (b) Pacific Sun versus Hollister.

4. Should a marketer construct a separate AIO inventory for each product category? Why or why not? Why can't you use the same AIO inventory for all products?

5. As a manager, what would you do differently if you were located in a Zip Code with a predominantly Bohemian Mix presence versus in a Zip Code with a predominantly Urban Achievers presence, assuming you were (a) a supermarket; (b) a clothing store, and (c) a multi-brand car dealership?

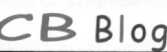
TO EACH BY HER OWN PSYCHOGRAPHICS

Lifestyles are the way people live—how they spend their resources (time, money) and what products they consume. No two lifestyles are the same, but by grouping consumers with more or less similar lifestyles, marketers have created hundreds of research-based lifestyle segmentation schemes. The inventory and examples given here will serve you well. Yet the creativity and challenge—and fun—is in identifying and defining the psychological makeup—values, personality/self-concept, and lifestyles—unique to your target consumers.

Self-concept is a powerful thing. It determines our course of life—what we become and what we accomplish. And it determines, even more immediately and in real time, what we consume and the lifestyle we live. The power of that self-concept is visible in the short narratives from Bianca, our chapter opener,
Like Bianca, all consumers live their lifestyles and consume the products they do because of who they think they are and want to become. Violate their self-concepts, and they will avoid your products and your marketing messages like poison ivy. To each consumer (or segment), according to his/her psychographics!

Geodemographics is in a class by itself. What can we say about it? We want to say that it is perhaps the most holistic, most insightful segmentation scheme for marking similarities and differences among consumers, but even that would be an understatement. The scheme's prowess comes from the fact that it incorporates, simultaneously, both consumers' psychographics and demographics. Its building block is ZIP+4, and within it, believe it or not, it implicitly contains age, income, social class and other demographics (such as family lifecycle, even ethnic identity) as well as lifestyle and values and self-concepts and other ingredients of our psychological makeup. After all, our choice of the place we live in is based on all these factors.

Of course, any single identifier of segment membership (ZIP+4 is the identifier for geodemographics) that is supposed to capture a whole host of consumer characteristics is bound to have internal fission in it. The basic assumption of PRIZM is that people in a neighborhood are alike, and for some consumers, this assumption is bound to be false. The lack of fit for some consumers not withstanding, PRIZM clusters are as good a description of neighborhoods as possible.

Indeed, we believe that if you want to know America and read a flesh-and-blood portrait of its people, you can do no better than read Michael Weiss's timeless classic, The Clustered World. If you want to truly understand the vibrant diversity among people—you will find that book immensely enlightening as well as deeply fascinating. We hope someday you will take the time to read it.

CONSUMER BEHAVIOR

PRACTICE+Experience

1. Consider two of your friends who are ostensibly different in their psychographics. Make a prediction in terms of the VALS segments to which each would belong (both primary and secondary segment). Then ask them to take the online survey. Review the survey results. Then interview them to understand why their computer-scored VALS profiles are different from your predictions.

2. Using the AIO inventory constructed in the earlier section, survey a sample of consumers, say 10, in each group (e.g., Limited Express vs. Gap Shoppers). Calculate the mean scores (manually or through a computer) on each AIO statement, and then for each factor, and compare and contrast the psychographic profiles of consumers who shop at the Limited Express and Gap. Likewise compare and contrast the psychographic profiles of other groups.

3. In your city, select two neighborhoods far apart. Identify the PRIZM Clusters you are likely to find in each. Drive or walk through those neighborhoods and observe people's lifestyles and activities. Do these activities match with the PRIZM Clusters these neighborhoods belong to according to their individual ZIP Codes?

In the Marketing Manager's Shoes

Put yourself in a marketing manager's shoes. Most concepts in the chapter have some lessons for the marketing manager; i.e., they suggest what to do differently in practice. Indeed, often these applications are implicit in our explanations of the concepts and models in the chapter. Identify at least five specific applications of the chapter's concepts, all of which should be entirely new, different from the examples cited here.

...ttitudes:
...el-Do Models

...ng What to Want and What to Shun

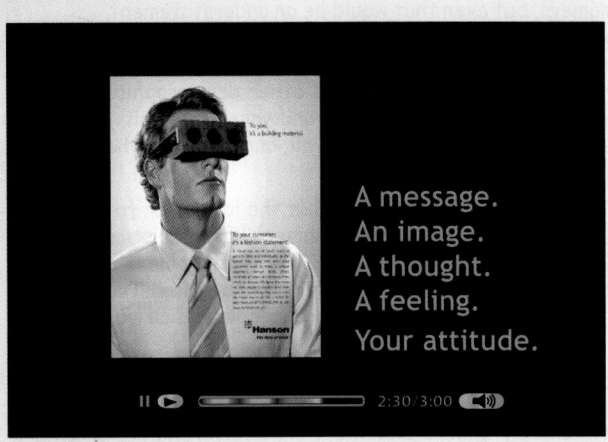

A message.
An image.
A thought.
A feeling.
Your attitude.

II ▶ ━━━━━━━━━━━━━ 2:30 / 3:00 ◀))

LEARN . APPLY . EXPERIENCE

OBJECTIVES

1 The Definition of Attitude and Its Properties

2 The ABC Model of Attitude and Its Measurement

3 Know-Feel-Do Hierarchies and How Involvement Affects Them

4 Four Functions That Attitudes Serve for Consumers

5 A Theory of Reasoned Action and Its Application in Consumer Brand Attitudes

6 Three Routes to Molding Attitudes— Convincing, Charming, and Inducing the Consumer

What is the Point of OK?

OK—it was the name Coca-Cola Company gave its new citrus-flavored soda concoction, back in Summer 1994, targeted at young adults.

The taste was a cross between Dr. Pepper, Lemonade, and Coca-Cola, and in pre-launch taste tests, young consumers had liked it—saying it was different and it had, well, oomph!

The can was decorated with facial images of apparently young people with no particular expression. A message around the lip of the can read: "OK soda says 'Don't be fooled into thinking there has to be a reason for everything.'" According to one comment, the company wanted to appeal to teenagers and Gen Y consumers—who had a "sense of themselves as sardonic and unsurprisable ('Yeah—it's OK, I s'pose')." It tried to soothe teen angst and anxiety. One brand slogan read: OK-ness is the belief that, no matter what, things are going to be OK.

By Summer 1995, a year after its introduction, the company decided to pull the brand. The teens and youth it targeted just did not see the brand as echoing their emotions. In one of the brand slogans, the company used a rhetorical question: "What is the point of OK? What is the point of anything?" The consumer seemed to have replied. "Nothing. Nothing is the point of 'OK,'" they seemed to say—and they didn't want *nothing!*

My attitude tells me what not to buy.

INTRODUCTION

The story of OK soda carries an important lesson for all students of marketing. It does not matter what a marketer says a product is or will do. What matters is what consumers come to think of it. The teen and youth of that time period did not think well of OK soda. And based on this opinion, they acted—tossing the brand into the dustbin of history. This fate is meted out to thousands of brands every year.

Before we rush to gloat over our insight as to how the OK Soda idea was doomed to fail, let us remember it is hindsight, not foresight. Indeed, OK soda briefly enjoyed a cult following, active even years after it was officially withdrawn. Fans reminisced in newsgroups at alt.fan.ok-soda and held onto unopened and opened soda cans as keepsakes. You can find some unopened cans on eBay even today. There is no telling if the campaign wouldn't have succeeded if continued longer, or in another place and time. A product's success or failure alike depend on consumer attitudes, and this is our point.

---

*Based on various sources including "OK Marketing— A retrospective of the OK marketing campaign by suck.com (February 14, 1996), www.suck.com/daily/96/02/14/daily.htm; en.wikipedia.org/wiki/OK_Soda; www.geocities.com/the_dolce/ok.html.

At this very moment, thousands of marketers are pitching their products and services to millions of consumers around the world. Standing at consumers' doorsteps, on the telephone, at business expos, at the mall, on eBay's auction Web site, through TV and radio ads, at upscale boutiques in Florence and Madrid, and from thousands of trailer trucks at flea markets around the world. Are consumers listening to them? How are they reacting to this cacophony of slogans and promises, and to that visual parade of product images? Aside from these marketers of material goods, also soliciting the favorable opinion of consumers are charities, schools, tourist spots, casinos and nightclubs, films, TV shows, sports teams, and even presidential candidates. How do consumers come to form an opinion about these entities? What persuades them to embrace some of these marketplace offerings, while spurning others? And how can marketers win favorable consumer reactions to their offerings?

This chapter is our answer to these questions. In this chapter, we explain the concept of attitude—the supreme precursor to all of our actions in the marketplace. We take you deep inside the mind of the consumer and witness the dynamic interplay of our thoughts, feelings, and intentions. Here you will also meet TOVA, TORA, and TOTA—no, these are not the names of some new renditions of Depeche Mode's 1981 album or of some mountains in Afghanistan; these are, instead, the nicknames of three models of attitude.

We also take a look at the motivational basis of attitudes, explaining the four functions that attitudes serve for us, and, through examples, we invite you to examine the motivations for some of your own deeply held attitudes—attitudes toward people (stereotypes) and attitudes toward products. Understanding attitudes can help you fashion your market offerings—advertising and all—to be consumer-friendly. This chapter is a key, in other words, to getting consumers to develop a good attitude toward your product offerings, and, consequently, to throw some dough your way. It is also a key to avoiding the fate of OK Soda. Read on.

(A)TTITUDE: DEFINITION

Do You Have it?

Do you have an attitude? Toward Lady Antebellum and their album *Own the Night*? Toward Lady Gaga and the lyrics of her song *Bad Romance*? Do you like or dislike them? And were you repulsed by Charlie Sheen's charades? And charmed by Tim Tibow's signature expression of gratitude? And which college courses did you like the most? The least? What is your attitude toward this book? What do you think of GoDaddy.com's Superbowl commercials featuring Danica Patrick? Which is your favorite drink—Coke, Pepsi, or the Dew? And if OK Cola were introduced today, would you have a more favorable reaction? All of these questions are designed to elicit your attitudes. So, just what is an attitude?

In common parlance, when we refer to your attitude, we simply refer to your "like" or "dislike" of something, your opinion about something. If you like something, then your attitude toward it is positive; if you dislike it, then your attitude is negative. However, to fully understand the nature of attitudes, we need to examine a classic definition of attitudes, offered by psychologist Gordon Allport: **Attitudes** are learned predispositions to respond to an object in a consistently favorable or unfavorable way.[1]
This definition has several elements:

- **Attitudes are learned.** That is, no one is born with them. You were not born with an attitude toward Stefani Joanne Angelina Germanotta (Lady Gaga), Charlie Sheen, Tim Tibow, Coke, or Pepsi, for example, were you? Instead, you have acquired (i.e., "learned") your attitudes during your time here on this earth. And how did you learn them? On the basis of some experience with or information about these things or persons.

- **They are targeted toward an object or a class of objects.** If we ask you what your attitude is or what your opinion is, you would ask, "Opinion about what?" or "Attitude toward what?" That "what" is the "object" in our definition—attitude toward an object. And that object can be anything—a brand, a product, a company, a class, a movie, a presidential candidate, and even an idea (e.g., the idea of 'freedom of speech'). Thus, we hold different attitudes toward different objects.

- **Attitudes cause responses.** That is, they are the reason we respond, or act, in a certain way toward these objects. Thus, we drink Coke and avoid Pepsi (or the other way around) because of our attitudes toward Coke and Pepsi. And our attitude toward Lady Gaga and her music makes us buy or not buy her albums.

- **The response that an attitude causes is consistent.** Thus, we don't buy Eminem's music today and avoid it tomorrow. And we don't choose Coke today and Pepsi tomorrow (unless our attitudes toward each are equally favorable). Instead, we act toward a given object the same way over a period of time; i.e., consistently.

- **Attitude is a predisposition.** By predisposition, we mean it is our "inclination." Thus, it resides in our minds. We are predisposed to doing something or not doing something. For example, we are predisposed (or inclined) to buy Lady Antebellum's music for our iPods, and we are predisposed to drink Coke and not drink Pepsi.

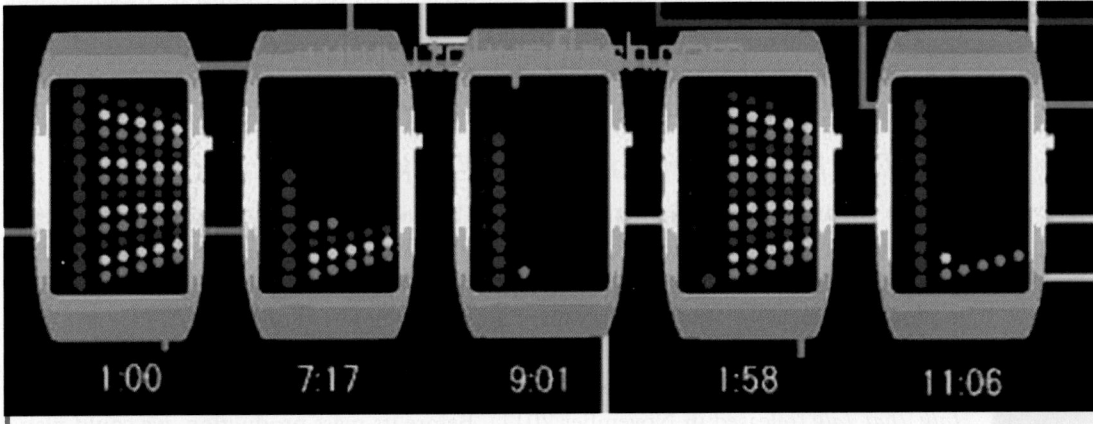

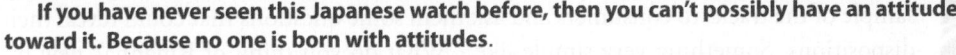

If you have never seen this Japanese watch before, then you can't possibly have an attitude toward it. Because no one is born with attitudes.

Now look at it, grasp how time is read on this watch, and then decide if you like or dislike it.

You now have an attitude, and we mean attitude toward the watch. You just learned it. And now you want to get one—that is your response. You want it today, and you would want it tomorrow (consistency), unless, of course, you change your attitude itself (toward the watch). You will buy it as soon as the opportunity arises (predisposition). You can buy it from www.tokyoflash.com.

YOUR ATTITUDE IS WAITING FOR ACTION!!!

PREDISPOSITION

Pregnant with Meaning

This word, *predisposition*, is a wonderful word, pregnant with rich meaning. It is the key to the concept of attitude and to understanding the true nature of this concept. No other term can cut it as well. We could say, for example, that an attitude is your opinion about something, and broadly speaking we would be right, but opinion is what you think of something. That is all. It is not quite the same thing as predisposition. We could say attitude is your general evaluation of something—whether you view it as a good thing or a bad thing—and we would be approximately right. But the word *evaluation* does not quite capture it either. *Predisposition*—it means you have something in your mind—a thought, an opinion, an evaluation, a view, even a feeling—and that you are going to do something about it. You are going to act toward the object of your attitude. Predisposition makes you inclined to act. Thus, an attitude is our mental code to release some action toward something. It is an *action in waiting*.

Action in Waiting

This idea of attitude as predisposition and predisposition as *action in waiting* is very useful to marketers. Marketers are interested, you see, in predicting consumers' future actions or future behaviors. A behavior is something we *do*; an attitude (predisposition) is something we have in our minds. So marketers use consumer attitudes to predict consumer behaviors. Thus, for example, if marketers knew that you had a positive attitude toward say, Adele's music, but a negative attitude toward Coldplay, then they could predict that you would be likely to buy Adele's music but not buy Coldplay albums. Marketers want to predict consumers' behavior—specifically whether consumers will or will not buy a product, *before* marketers invest the money to make and market that product.

Remember, then, the key elements in the definition of attitude:

(1) learned (2) predisposition, (3) toward an object (or a class of objects), (4) to respond or act (toward that object and in a favorable or unfavorable way); (5) consistently.

Review this definition a few times, so you don't think of it as difficult. We want you to have a favorable attitude toward this definition. So that you will be predisposed to do more with it—which is the focus of this chapter. Are you ready— oops, we mean, are you *PREDISPOSED*?

MEASURING CONSUMER ATTITUDES

How Do I Know What Consumers Think of My Product?

As a marketer, you might argue that all this conceptual understanding is fine, even great, but what I am interested in is finding out my consumers' attitudes toward my product. You convinced me, you might say, that attitude is a great concept, so I want to utilize it. How do I measure what my customers' attitudes are? Good question.

Because a disposition resides in the consumer's mind, we cannot, of course, directly observe it. Suppose we wanted to find out consumers' attitudes toward Rihanna's album *Talk That Talk* (released in November 2011). Before its mass production, we could play a sample of the tracks to consumers and ask them some questions that could reveal their predispositions. Something very simple like, "What do you think of Rihanna's new music?" And consumers would reveal in their own words, as we all do when asked questions like this, all that was in their minds about Rihanna. This 'view of something in their minds' revealed by consumers in their own words is the closest we can come to measuring their predispositions. If we want to do it on a large scale, i.e., for a large number of consumers, and in a way that allows us to compare the answers from different consumers, then we should do it using a paper-and-pencil set of questions with numerical rating scales. Such scales are designed to elicit consumers' overall mindsets (i.e., predispositions) toward something. Every researcher has his or her own favorite way of phrasing these rating statements. Below, we provide what a majority of consumer researchers would consider an efficient set of measures.

We can average the three items to arrive at the attitude score. Suppose this score comes to −1.67 for consumer Ross, -1.33 for consumer Joey, and +1.33 for consumer Chandler; then, Chandler's attitude toward Rihanna' music would be favorable, Joey's attitude unfavorable, and Ross's attitude even more unfavorable. We can use this measurement method for any product, new or old.

Next, a marketer would want to know what underlies an attitude. For this, we need to learn the ABC model of attitude.

ABOUT RIHANNA'S NEW MUSIC ALBUM, *TALK THAT TALK*:						
MY OPINION IS:	NEGATIVE	-1	-2	0	+1	+2	POSITIVE
I FEEL:	UNFAVORABLY	-1	-2	0	+1	+2	FAVORABLY
I DISLIKE IT VERY MUCH		-1	-2	0	+1	+2	I LIKE IT VERY MUCH

THE ABC MODEL OF ATTITUDE

ABC—this acronym stands for Affect, Beliefs, and Conation.

Psychologists now believe that attitudes are composed of three underlying dimensions: feelings, knowledge, and action intent. That is, when we hold an attitude about an object, typically it is based on some knowledge and beliefs about the object; we feel some positive or negative emotion toward it; and we want to act in a certain way toward it; for example, either embracing it or spurning it. Thus, an attitude is like a three-legged stool, the three legs being thoughts or beliefs (also called *cognitions*), feelings or emotions (technically called *affect*), and action intent (technically called *conation*). These three components comprise the ABC Model of Attitude (see Figure 7.1). Let us look at each component closely.

BELIEFS

What Do You Know About Me?

Although, sometimes we mindlessly form an attitude toward someone or something, often we base that evaluation on a more detailed appraisal of the person's qualities or of a brand's features. Remember, we are not born with attitudes, but rather we learn them based on some knowledge or information about the product. This knowledge about a person or product, these appraisals of a person's qualities or a brand's features, are called *beliefs*. More specifically, **beliefs** are expectations about what something is or is not, or what something will or will not do. Statements of belief connect an object (person, brand, store, etc.) to an attribute or benefit. Accordingly, a **brand belief** is a thought about a specific property or quality of the brand. (See Figure 7.2.)

Note that just because a marketer claims a particular quality or feature, it does not mean that consumers will make it part of their brand beliefs. Sometimes, because of distrust of the marketer, personal trial experience, or misperceptions, a consumer's brand beliefs could be exactly the opposite of the marketer's claims. Thus, for example, consumer Monica could come to believe that

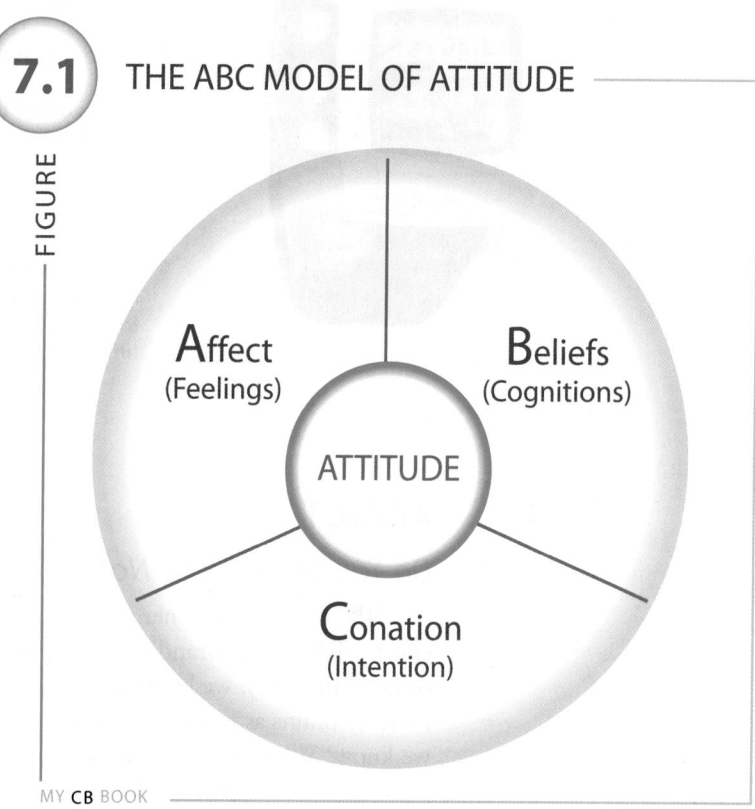

7.1 THE ABC MODEL OF ATTITUDE

FIGURE

Affect (Feelings) — Beliefs (Cognitions) — ATTITUDE — Conation (Intention)

MY **CB** BOOK

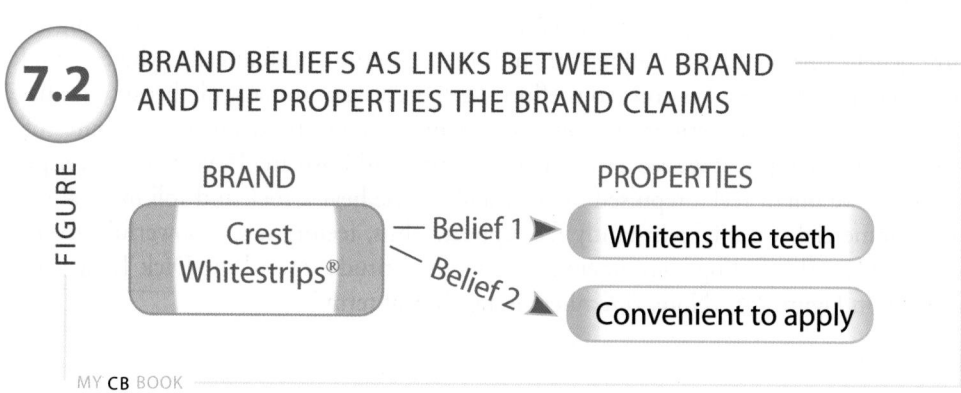

7.2 BRAND BELIEFS AS LINKS BETWEEN A BRAND AND THE PROPERTIES THE BRAND CLAIMS

FIGURE

BRAND — PROPERTIES

Crest Whitestrips® — Belief 1 ▶ Whitens the teeth — Belief 2 ▲ Convenient to apply

MY **CB** BOOK

Whitestrips® do in fact whiten the teeth, whereas consumer Rachel could come to believe that the whitening effect would be barely noticeable, if at all. Figure 7.3 shows how beliefs are the basis of consumer attitudes about Wrist Net Dick Tracy FX3200 (you can read more about it on www.Fossil.com).

Now, to the question: what underlies a particular attitude (i.e., an overall predisposition) toward something? The answer is simple: *Our beliefs about that something.* That is, beliefs are the foundations for our attitudes. Beliefs are detailed thoughts; attitude is an overall inclination of the mind.

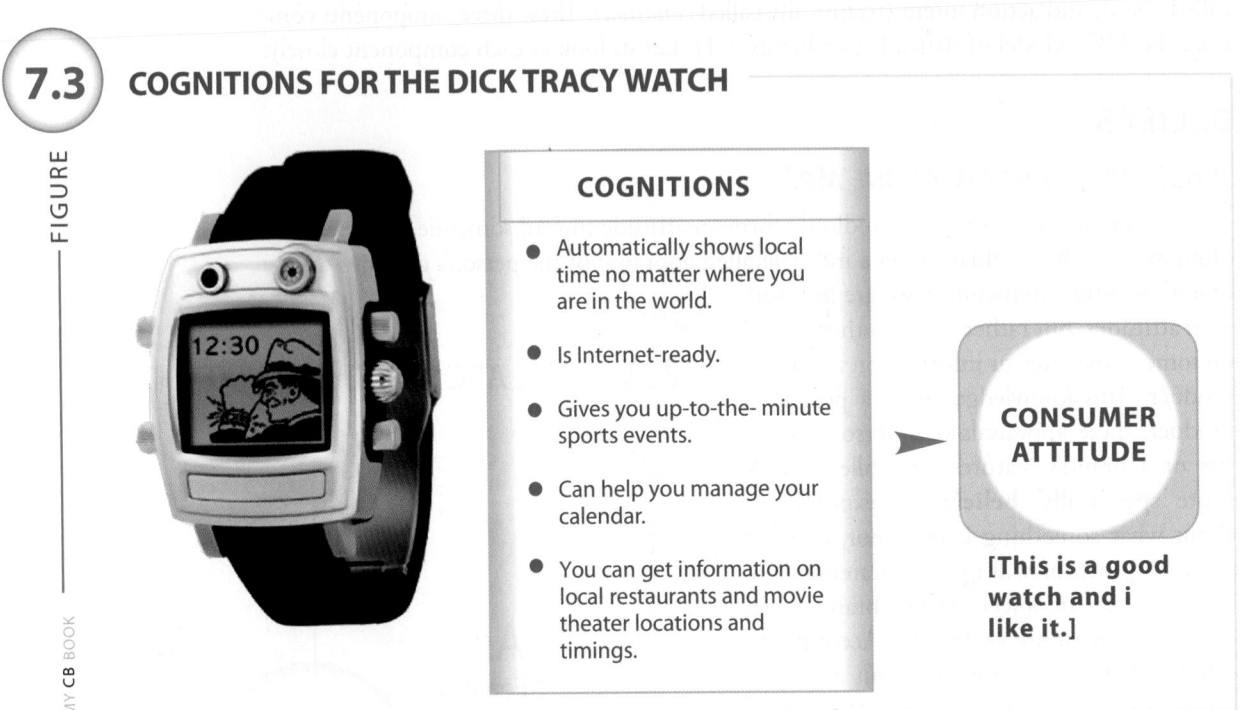

7.3 **COGNITIONS FOR THE DICK TRACY WATCH**

FIGURE

COGNITIONS

- Automatically shows local time no matter where you are in the world.

- Is Internet-ready.

- Gives you up-to-the- minute sports events.

- Can help you manage your calendar.

- You can get information on local restaurants and movie theater locations and timings.

CONSUMER ATTITUDE

[This is a good watch and i like it.]

MY CB BOOK

AFFECT

Do You Love Me or Not?

The second component of attitude is *affect* (or feelings). The belief component says in effect, "Tell me the brand's features, and its qualities, and I will tell you if I like the brand or not." In reality, we know this is not always the case. We know that a dislike for frog or monkey brains as food, for example, has nothing to do with its taste feature. How would we know? We have never eaten these things, but we dislike them anyway. Just the vision of these as food gives us the creeps. Thus, thinking (i.e., forming beliefs) is not always necessary for attitudes. Rather, feelings or emotions can also account for attitudes in some situations.

In fact, for many objects, our feelings occur even before we initiate thinking and form beliefs; this is because feelings can and often do arise automatically, whereas thinking (belief formation) takes conscious effort. Feelings arise automatically because we have been conditioned to experience various feelings upon exposure to various attributes of a product. For example, if we see a neon-colored shirt, and if we are 35-year-old career professionals, we might feel a repulsed by it, whereas if we hear a rock and roll musical tune in a commercial, we might instantly feel upbeat. Thus, feelings are a powerful driver of our attitudes. This feeling component as a basis for attitude toward the Dick Tracy watch is shown in Figure 7.4. (Note: *Affect* here is a technical term.)

7.4 **AFFECT FOR THE DICK TRACY WATCH**

FIGURE

AFFECT

● This watch is so cool.

● I feel thrilled to see it.

● What a joy this product is!

CONSUMER ATTITUDE

[This is a good watch and i like it.]

CONATION
So Do You Have Any Intentions of Buying Me?

So we hold certain beliefs about an object—person, product, or brand—and we experience certain feelings about it. What else? Action. We also act toward that object. We see ice cream, and we want to eat it. We see tofu, and we won't put it in our cart. Action often (if not inevitably) follows our thoughts and our feelings.

But there is more. Sometimes, actions come as an immediate responses to some objects—even before we have had time to think or feel. We see a dollar bill on the street, and we pick it up. We see a cute child, and we kiss or hug him/her. We see a bull running wild, and we run away from it. Quite often then, our attitudes take the form of immediate action rather than an expressed opinion (a belief) or even some focused feelings. Indeed, if we observe someone taking some action or engaging in some behavior, we can infer that person's attitude. This conation component as a basis for attitude toward the Dick Tracy watch is shown in Figure 7.5.

Now note that behavior itself is not the *conation* component of attitude. Rather, *conation* means intention; i.e., intention to act in a certain way. Thus, **conation** is our instruction to the mind that next time the occasion arises, we are going to buy this thing. This conation is what makes attitude an action in waiting. That said, in practical applications, consumer researchers may treat conation as if it were behavior itself.

Now you know what the three components of attitude are. Our attitudes about any product come from what we know about it, how we feel about it (what emotions and feelings it evokes in us), and whether we have intentions to buy that product. **Think-Feel-and-Do** thus sums up our attitudes.

7.5 **CONATION FOR THE DICK TRACY WATCH**

FIGURE

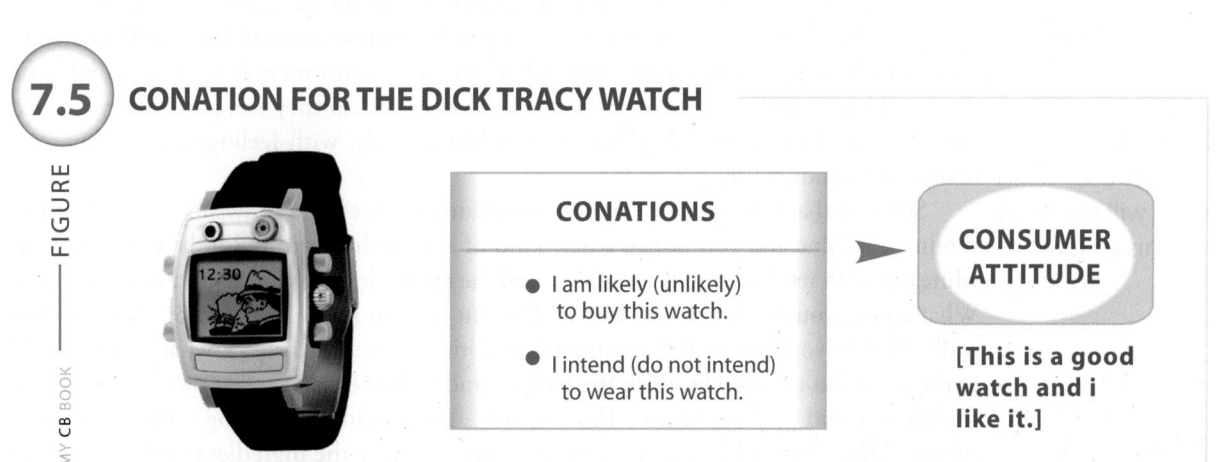

CONATIONS

● I am likely (unlikely) to buy this watch.

● I intend (do not intend) to wear this watch.

CONSUMER ATTITUDE

[This is a good watch and i like it.]

HIERARCHIES IN ATTITUDE

What Comes First? And What Comes Last?

If you have read this far, you can't help asking, how are the three components—think, feel, and act—interrelated? Do we think first and then act, or do we act first and think afterwards? This issue is addressed through the concept of *attitude hierarchy*. **Attitude hierarchy** refers to the sequence in which the three components occur. Scholars have identified three different hierarchies: (a) Learning Hierarchy, (b) Emotional Hierarchy, and (c) Low-Involvement Hierarchy. See Figure 7.6.

Learning Hierarchy In the **learning hierarchy,** cognitions come first, affect next, and action last (see Figure 7.6, Panel A). That is, we think first, feel next, and act last. We learn about the brand and form brand beliefs first; these brand beliefs then lead to brand feelings, which in turn lead to brand purchase intent, purchase and use.[4]

Consider an example. Let us say that you need to decide where to go for spring break: Florida (say, Miami Beach) or Cancun. You find out how far these places are in terms of the travel time, the cost of travel, and the cost of a hotel room. What activities does each site offer? Can you do snorkeling there, or white water rafting, for example? Then, after thinking over all this information, you begin to have pleasant, good feelings toward one of these destinations, and a bad feeling toward the other. Or you feel so-so toward the one (say, Florida), and much more excited about the other (say, Cancun). Based on these feelings, you then choose Cancun. We call this learning hierarchy a *rational hierarchy*. Your attitude towards a product or brand is based on a rational way of looking at it.

Emotional Hierarchy "Wait a minute," you might say. "The last time I decided on my spring break plan, well, what happened was that we—a bunch of friends—were watching this show on cable TV, *MTV Spring Break*. It was basically a live scene from Cancun, where lots and lots of college students were having one big party on the beach. And we said, "That is it. That is where we are going." This exemplifies an **emotional hierarchy** of attitude. Here you *feel* first, then act, and think last (see Figure 7.6, Panel B). Based on your emotions—attraction or repulsion toward certain brands or persons or things—you embrace or avoid them, buy them, use them. Finally, through experience, you learn more about them.

Low-Involvement Hierarchy Now, you might say, "Well some of my friends do choose their vacation spot this way. Me? I just go along wherever my friends are going. I don't even care if I go." One universal truth about consumers is that they differ in their degrees of involvement in various activities and likewise in their product choices. Recall that we defined *involvement* (in Chapter 2) as the degree of interest a consumer takes in a product or activity. When consumers have a stake in a product choice, it is a case of *high involvement*. With low stakes in the choice, involvement is low. Your involvement in the vacation destination choice is low.

The learning and emotional hierarchies described above are high-involvement hierarchies, as both occur when consumers have high stakes in the decisions, such as the choice of a spring break destination for most consumers. In contrast are decisions with low stakes, such as picking up a new variety of bread. With these, consumers don't want to take the time to think or acquire a lot of product knowledge, nor do they feel particularly thrilled about the product. Rather they buy the product casually, with feelings and thoughts to follow with product use.

Suppose that you are in a neighborhood convenience store browsing the cold drinks vending machine and you notice a new kind of energy drink from South Africa, *911*. Its white can with red lettering is attractive, and the energy logo is vibrant and looks inviting. What would you do before you buy it? Do you have to know a whole lot about it? Not really. Nor do you have to feel any notable emotions about it. Instead, what you are likely to do is just put the coin in, push the button, and grab the can. Out of the store, you take the first sip, and you say "Umm! This is good." And you like it (Feeling). Then you pause to note what flavor it has, and then maybe you even read the ingredients information on

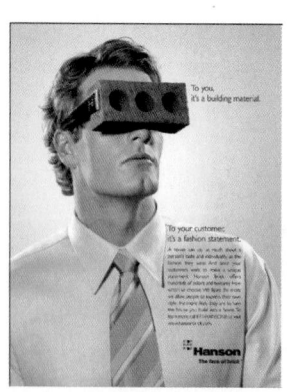

Here is an ad from Hanson Bricks. Which hierarchy does it use? Read on and we will return to consider this ad later.

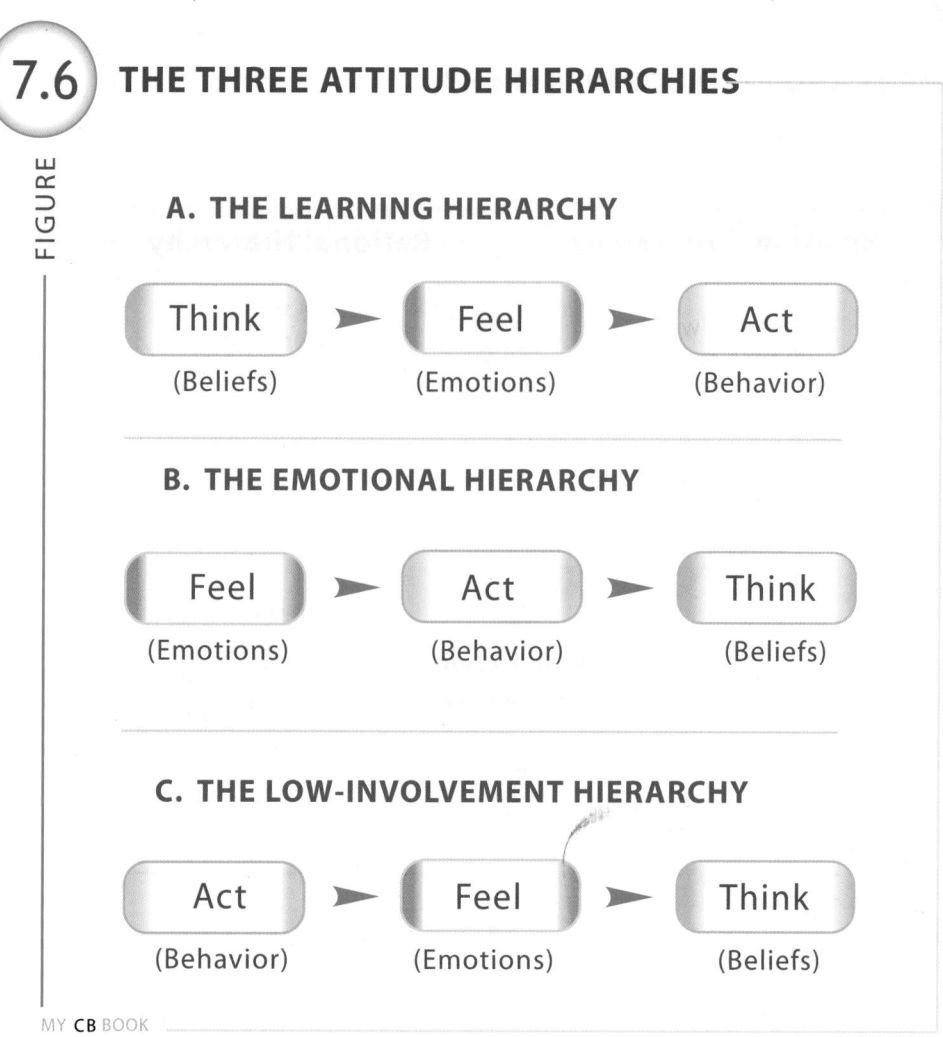

7.6 THE THREE ATTITUDE HIERARCHIES

A. THE LEARNING HIERARCHY

Think (Beliefs) ➤ Feel (Emotions) ➤ Act (Behavior)

B. THE EMOTIONAL HIERARCHY

Feel (Emotions) ➤ Act (Behavior) ➤ Think (Beliefs)

C. THE LOW-INVOLVEMENT HIERARCHY

Act (Behavior) ➤ Feel (Emotions) ➤ Think (Beliefs)

MY **CB** BOOK

the label (Cognition). Thus, in this case of a low-involvement product selection and consumption, action comes first. Feelings come next, and cognitions or thoughts last. This low-involvement hierarchy is shown in Figure 7.6, Panel C.

HOW INVOLVEMENT SHAPES THE HIERARCHY

Involvement and Attitude Formation

One clarification about involvement is in order. Involvement is not dichotomous (i.e., just high or low). Rather, it is a matter of degree. The low-involvement hierarchy described above occurs at the very low-end of involvement when something is of utterly no consequence to the consumer. In the middle range, the high-involvement hierarchies occur, but with less intensity of thought or feeling. The emotional hierarchy still begins with affect (or feeling), but at the middle range it is likely to begin with a mood rather than deep emotion. And the rational hierarchy is still relevant, except that instead of the extensive thoughts of the high-involvement condition, just a few thoughts will drive feelings. This situation is depicted in Figure 7.7.

MARKETING IMPLICATION OF ATTITUDE HIERARCHY

These hierarchies have marketing implications. We all know that consumers look at some products as primarily rational purchases and at others as primarily emotional purchases. We want consumers to have a positive attitude toward our products. So how do we go about building it? Here the hierarchies come to our aid. For primarily rational products

SAVVY
MARKETER

FIGURE

7.7 INVOLVEMENT AND ATTITUDE HIERARCHY

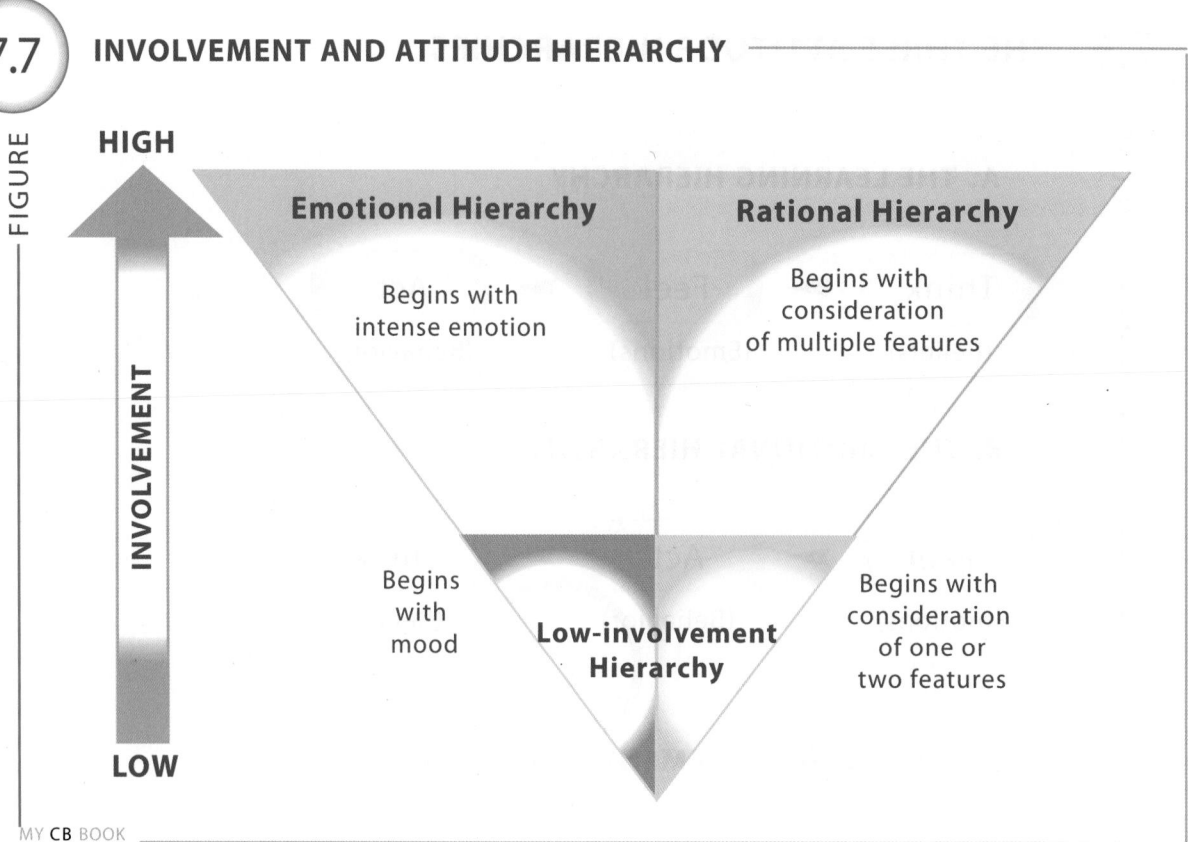

HIGH

INVOLVEMENT

Emotional Hierarchy

Begins with intense emotion

Rational Hierarchy

Begins with consideration of multiple features

Begins with mood

Low-involvement Hierarchy

Begins with consideration of one or two features

LOW

MY **CB** BOOK

(like home appliances), we must provide to consumers a lot of product knowledge, so that they may then base their decisions on rational grounds. We would fail if instead we began to appeal to their emotions. But once they have formed beliefs, then some emotional appeals will help to move them to action.

For emotional products, in contrast, we should first hook consumers emotionally. Talk about product features would only fall on deaf ears. Consider what would happen if we tried to sell someone a product like a diamond as a romantic gift by enumerating its physical and performance features. In this case, though, once consumers are hooked emotionally, our next step should be to make it very convenient to buy (remember, in the emotional hierarchy, feelings are followed immediately by action).

For extremely low-involvement products, on the other hand, we don't need to tell consumers much about the brand—as long as we have made the brand name familiar. Our first priority should be to make it very convenient for them to buy it. Marketers stimulate low-involvement purchases by using attractive product displays. Consumers see them, and they just reach out for them. In the middle range of involvement, if the product has some performance features that consumers usually worry about, then we should advertise those features—but we should limit our advertisement or sales-story to one or two features and not beat them over their heads with details (remember, consumers are not much motivated to devote mental effort). Or if the product is of an emotional nature but elicits only moderate involvement, then we should try to evoke some mood (not deep emotions). In either case, convenient display and availability is the next most important thing, as consumers will take action soon after giving it a little bit of thought or experiencing a little bit of feeling, as the case may be.[5]

For this low- involvement product, 911 drink, this "Nurse Your Thirst" ad seeks to create, via its imagery, a mood in the consumer.

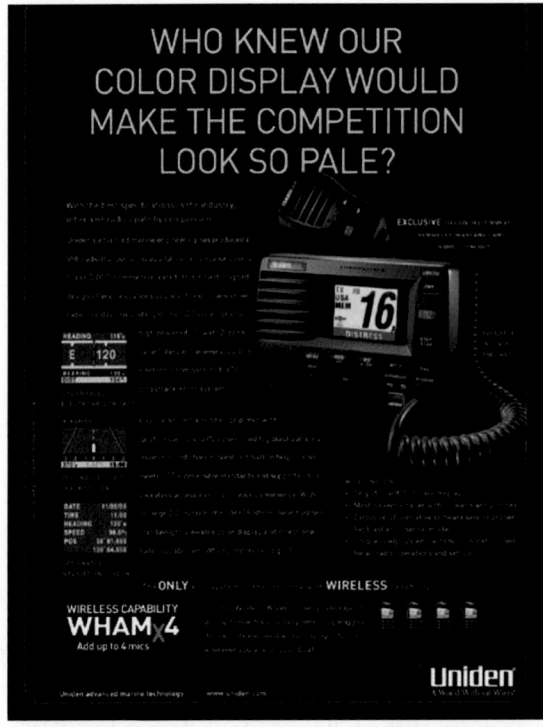

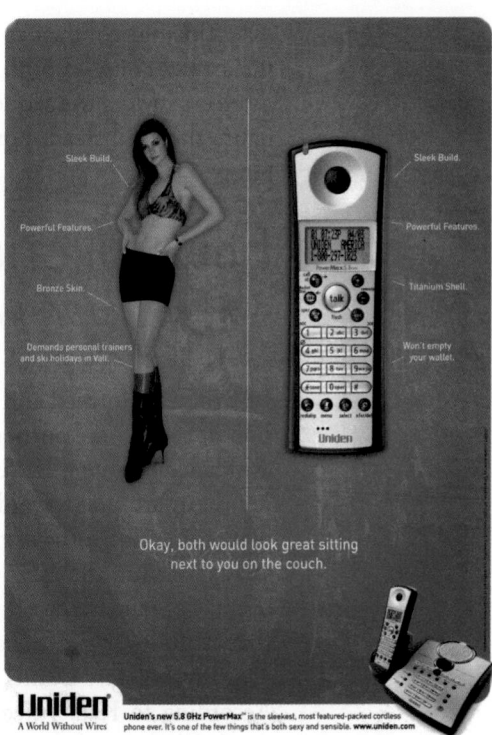

These two ads from Uniden serve your attitude formation through, separately, the rational and emotional hierarchies. Can you figure which does which?

Note. Although the small text in the ads is not readable (without a magnifying glass), their overall visual images are adequate to enable a comparison of their implied attitude formation hierarchies.

Consistency among Think, Feel, and Do

If you could just look inside the consumer's mind where these three components of attitude reside, what kind of relationship would you expect to find? Would they be fighting among themselves, or alternatively, living in harmony? The answer, according to psychologists, is that they wouldn't be fighting, although each would be trying to mold the other in its own image. That is, if there is a favorable thought about a product and an unfavorable feeling, then the thought would be trying to bring the feeling into line with itself; on the other hand, the feeling would be attempting to tell the thought to think of some negative belief about that product. This shouldn't seem farfetched to you, as we all know how sometimes our hearts are trying to persuade our thinking minds, and vice versa.

The fact is that although the three components develop in a hierarchical fashion, they always imply one another. That is, no matter which formed first in the consumer's head, after they have stabilized, they exist together. And they exist in harmony. That is, consumers cannot harbor a set of thoughts and beliefs about a brand without bringing into line their feelings about it. Nor can they harbor some feeling about the brand without also bringing brand beliefs into line. Likewise, a consumer cannot have thoughts or feelings and not have a corresponding intention to act. The consumer cannot continue to believe, for example, that Honda is a more reliable car than Ford, but continue to buy a Ford time after time. And a consumer cannot feel repulsed and angry every time he or she hears Eminem but still continue to buy his music. Consumers' thoughts, feelings, and actions have to exist in harmony.

FIGURE 7.8 THREE ATTITUDE COMPONENTS IN HARMONY

Do — Think — Feel

MY CB BOOK

Thus, in contrast to the previously described hierarchical models, Figure 7.8 shows the arrows going in both directions among all three of the components. The hierarchical models show us the sequence in which the components initially got formed. The present figure shows, instead, how the three components shape one another and co-exist in harmony.

FOUR FUNCTIONS OF ATTITUDE
Why Should We Hold Attitudes at all?

So far we have described what attitudes consist of and how they are formed, but not why they are formed and why we hold them. The answer is that they perform some function or serve some purpose for us. Their overall function is that they guide our approach/avoidance behavior. If we see an acquaintance across the hallway, we walk toward him or her if our attitude toward him or her is positive; if our attitude is negative, we turn away, pretending not to have noticed. If we see a five-cheese pizza on the menu and a Greek salad, we shun the pizza and order the salad or the other way around. But beyond this overall, proximate/direct function of approach-avoidance, are there any deeper functions that attitudes serve? The answer is yes.

Psychologist Daniel Katz called this perspective the **functional theory of attitude**.[6] According to Katz's theory, people hold certain attitudes (or come to acquire those attitudes) because these attitudes serve one or more of the following four deeper functions: utilitarian, value-expressive, ego-defensive, and knowledge. To illustrate these functions, we take you to the U.S. Primaries of 2012. See Table 7.1

Four Functions in Voter Attitude

In the U.S. Presidential primaries of 2012, the leading Republican candidates were Mitt Romney, Newt Gingrich, Rick Santorum, and Ron Paul. Suppose you watched their fiery debate on February 22 in Mesa, Arizona. During the debate, Senator Santorum attacked Governor Romney for his healthcare bill that had mandated Massachusetts citizens to purchase healthcare coverage. Now, as is inevitable, some voters had a favorable attitude toward Romney and others toward Santorum. Why?

Here is how functional theory would explain it. Some voters expected to benefit personally from Governor Romney's expected Massachusetts-like healthcare reform (they believed that it will bring their health insurance costs down) and also from his promised tax cuts. In effect, then, their favorable attitude toward Romney served a **utilitarian function**—offering them a personal benefit.

Other voters may not have cared for the tax relief or reduced insurance costs; rather, what was important to them was the idea that government mandating of insurance coverage violated the individual's rights, and individual rights of citizens were a very important "value" to them. This **value-expressive** attribute made them like Santorum more than Romney.

Still other voters might have liked governor Romney more because he had been more visible on the national political stage. Governor Romney had in fact visited their town and they had seen him face-to-face. Accordingly, some felt as if they knew governor Romney personally, that he was a familiar person. Santorum was, at least to them, an unknown quantity. All other things being equal, we feel more comfortable with familiar people. This is the **knowledge** function. As humans, we like familiar things; we dislike uncertainty.

Finally, suppose a candidate had inadvertently slighted a group of voters or even an individual voter. That group or individual voter might then feel his/her ego hurt; in return, the voter would have to dismiss that candidate as being unworthy of his/her vote. That is, the voter would defend his/her ego tit-for-tat, by discrediting that candidate, or by developing a dislike for him or her. This is the **ego-defense** function of attitude.

(P.S. Senator Sentorum suspended his campaign on April 10, 2012, in part due to his 3-year-old daughter's illness and hospitalization.)

Four Functions in Market Exchanges

Now to the commercial products scene. Consumer attitudes toward most everyday products are based, actually, on the utilitarian function. We like the Vidal Sassoon brand of shampoo, for example, because it leaves our hair looking full. We like Honda cars because they will last a long time. And we may like fur coats because they keep us very warm.

Many consumers like recyclable products because they have pro-environmental values. Many like Body Shop shampoos because the company does not use animal testing. And many do not like fur coats because they abhor the killing of animals. These are examples of value-expressive reasons for consumer attitudes. (Note that, contrary to some early consumer research, *value-expressive* does not mean expressive of our images or symbolic associations, but expressive of our deeply held values about life. The ability of a product to help us express our identities or self-images is also, in truth, a utilitarian function.)

Next, many consumers like to read *People* magazine, for example, because it keeps them informed about their favorite stars. If we are taking a date to dinner—we had better go to a restaurant we know well so there will be no mishaps. Try a Tofu burger? We had better not—we do not know what it will taste like. Such attitudes are attributable to the knowledge function. Some good examples of knowledge function are provided by "knowledge products," such as the Discovery Channel, or an encyclopedia like Encarta (a Microsoft software product), or a Web site full of information. The knowledge (i.e., familiarity) function is the reason we like to go to our familiar supermarkets, familiar restaurants, familiar clubs, and opt for familiar servers and sellers.

And now to the ego-defensive function. A consumer might dress nicely and drive a nice car (perhaps beyond his means) so that his neighbors will think he is successful in his career. He will take his date to a steak place rather than to the famous French restaurant in town because he can't pronounce the names of the exotic menu items there. Thus, this consumer's positive attitude toward dressing up nicely and his negative attitude toward French restaurants are both based on the ego-defense function. Table 7.1 summarizes these four functions with marketing examples.[7]

Why is it important to know the function of an attitude? Because if we want to change a consumer's attitude toward something, we need to address the deeper function it serves for that consumer. Telling a consumer how good the product's ingredients are (i.e., explaining the product's utilitarian function) would not help if the basic reason the

TABLE

7.1 FOUR FUNCTIONS OF ATTITUDE

FUNCTION	DEFINITION	EXAMPLES	
		Political	Products
Utilitarian	The attitude object serves some utility.	I like Mitt Romney because he will reduce my taxes and health insurance costs.	I like Vidal Sassoon because it does wonders for my hair.
Value-expressive	The attitude object expresses one's values.	I dislike Mitt Romney because he will violate individual rights with his healthcare bill.	I like Body Shop shampoo because the company does not use animal testing, a cause I value.
Knowledge	The attitude object reduces uncertainty; gives us the comfort of knowing.	Mitt Romney is more familiar to me than Rick Santorum; I feel more comfortable with Romney.	I love People magazine because it keeps me informed about all the stars.
Ego-defense	The attitude object helps us protect our ego (self-esteem).	I dislike that other candidate because he has slighted my ethnic group.	I don't like French restaurants, period. [Real reason: Not being able to pronounce menu items threatens this consumer's self-esteem.]

MY CB BOOK

After taking in this ad from Europe's Bisley Office Furniture Company:

You will like the brand for its utilitarian function ("organizes clutter"). And like the ad for its knowledge function ("Bisley does that").

SAVE LOTS OF SPACE
Introducing BISLEY InnerSpace

(Courtesy: Bisley Kolle Rebbe)

consumer dislikes the product is because of the company's exploitation of child labor or because of its adverse effects on the environment (both relate to the value-expressive function), for example.[8]

MULTI-ATTRIBUTE MODELS OF ATTITUDE AND BEHAVIOR: TOVA, TORA, TOTA

One of the ideas we described earlier in the chapter is that beliefs are the basis of attitudes, particularly in the learning or rational hierarchy. Consumers learn about product features and form brand beliefs; these brand beliefs then lead to attitudes. But not all of our brand beliefs are equally important to us. How would you combine these diverse beliefs to form an attitude?

The answer lies in multi-attribute models. **Multi-attribute models of attitude** suggest that overall attitude is based on the component beliefs about the object, weighted by the evaluation of those beliefs. There are three such models: (1) Theory of Value Assessment (TOVA), (2) Theory of Reasoned Action (TORA), and (3) Theory of Trying to Achieve (TOTA).[9] Of these, TORA is the one most commonly used by marketers, and you will find it useful too. Let us explore it.

THEORY OF REASONED ACTION (TORA)

Martin Fishbein, a well-known scholar and a professor of psychology at the University of Illinois at Urbana-Champaign, proposed this theory. According to the **Theory of Reasoned Action** (TORA),[10] our attitude toward an object is based on the consequences the object has, weighted by the desirability or undesirability of these consequences. (See Figure 7.9.)

Attitude = [the extent to which the object will lead to a consequence (or the product will yield a certain benefit or cause certain harm] X [the desirability or undesirability of that consequence]—calculating this for each consequence and then summing across all relevant consequences.

FIGURE 7.9

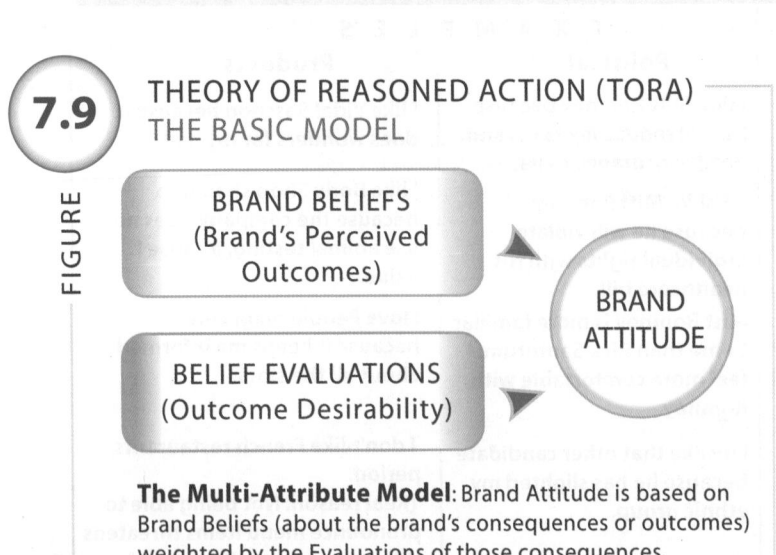

THEORY OF REASONED ACTION (TORA)
THE BASIC MODEL

BRAND BELIEFS (Brand's Perceived Outcomes)

BELIEF EVALUATIONS (Outcome Desirability)

BRAND ATTITUDE

The Multi-Attribute Model: Brand Attitude is based on Brand Beliefs (about the brand's consequences or outcomes) weighted by the Evaluations of those consequences.

MY CB BOOK

TABLE 7.2 — EXAMPLES OF CONSUMER ATTITUDES: TWO INTERNET SERVICE PROVIDERS

ATTRIBUTES	EXPECTATIONS about ATTRIBUTES (Unlikely 1 2 3 4 5 Likely)		EVALUATION OF CONSEQUENCES Very Bad -3 -2 -1 0 +1 +2 +3 Very Good
	Earthlink	NetZero	
1. The connection will be established successfully every time.	3	5	+3
2. The connection will be established speedily.	4	4	+2
3. The connection will be dropped in the middle of the session.	3	3	-3
4. The price (fee) will be high.	2	5	-1

Note: All attribute ratings are hypothetical and are used here merely for illustration. At any rate, even these hypothetical attribute ratings are examples not of any objective ratings but of consumer perceptions of one hypothetical consumer.

As an example, assume that consumer Nicole rates two Internet service providers, Earthlink and Netzero, as shown in Table 7.2. Using the data from the table, we can compute her attitude toward each service provider by using Fishbein's formula, as follows:

$$A_{EARTHLINK} = 3(3) + 4(2) + 3(-3) + 2(-1) = 6$$
$$A_{NETZERO} = 5(3) + 4(2) + 3(-3) + 5(-1) = 9$$

In this example, Nicole's attitude toward both services is positive, but it is more positive toward NetZero. Other consumers might well have different perceptions about the four attributes, as well as different evaluations (desirability or undesirability) for the attributes; consequently, they will have different attitudes.

Just so you don't think this math work was unnecessary busywork, look at Table 7.2 again. If we told you only what Nicole's brand beliefs about the two Internet services were, you wouldn't know how to figure out Nicole's attitude toward each brand. The multi-attribute model, TORA, helps you figure that out.

And TORA helps you figure out something else. Suppose we know that two of our friends, Colin and Bridget, have the same brand beliefs about tofu. Both believe that tofu is good for health but doesn't taste all that great and is rather cumbersome to cook. Yet, their attitude toward tofu is not the same—Colin's attitude is unfavorable, whereas Bridget's is favorable. Why? Look at Table 7.3. The reason is that Colin and Bridget differ in how desirable or undesirable they consider taste versus healthfulness of food. Now use the multiattribute model and calculate the attitude score to see for yourself how TORA explains why Colin dislikes tofu whereas Bridget likes it. In fact, if we hadn't told you that they did, you would have predicted it. And most marketers want to predict consumer attitudes toward their brands; TORA enables them to do just that. (Further reading: Exhibit 7.1.)

SAVVY MARKETER

TABLE 7.3 — MEASURING CONSUMER ATTITUDES WITH TORA
(Example: Two Consumers and Tofu)

	Colin	Bridget
Beliefs about Attributes*		
• Eating tofu will be good for your health.	4	4
• Tofu will not taste good.	5	5
Evaluations of Attributes**		
• Being good for health is...	+2	+3
• Not tasting good is...	-3	-1

* Measured as Unlikely 1 2 3 4 5 Likely
** Measured as Very Undesirable -3 -2 -1 0 +1 +2 +3 Very Desirable

Calculating Attitude Scores:
Colin = 4(+2) + 5(-3) = -7
Bridget = 4(+3) + 5(-1) = +7
Accordingly, Colin's attitude toward tofu is unfavorable whereas Bridget's attitude is favorable.

EXHIBIT 7.1

FISHBEIN's EXTENDED MODEL of BEHAVIOR

TORA actually covers more than attitude; it goes on to explain how attitudes then lead to behavior. Fishbein argued that an attitude captures our personal beliefs but that sometimes we are forced to act not entirely in accord with our wishes and our own brand beliefs; rather, and often, the expectations of others also influence our behavior. For example, someone may personally have an unfavorable attitude toward giving donations to an abortion clinic but may end up doing so due to the expectations of his or her co-workers or neighbors. These wishes of others are captured in the concept of **subjective norm**—what others expect us to do (i.e., normative expectations). These normative expectations are formed because of other people's desires and our own motivations to comply with them. These are computed by the same multiattribute weighting; i.e., the expectation of a specific person multiplied by our motivation to comply with that person's wishes (and then totaling this across all such persons who have expectations of us).

The personal attitude and subjective norm are then adjusted according to their relative weights (i.e., how important it is for a consumer to follow his or her own attitude versus the perceived need to comply with the expectations of others) and then summed. This weighted sum then leads to behavioral intention, which in turn, and finally, drives actual behavior. See Figure 7.10.

The distinctive advantage of Fishbein's extended model is that it accounts for social normative pressures as well as one's own internal beliefs about the consequences of a particular behavior—such as buying a specific brand of car. Explain to a teenager all you want about how utterly injurious to health smoking is, or how wearing a seatbelt can save his or her life in an automobile accident; yet if the teenager's peers consider smoking cool or wearing a seat belt "uncool," then your fact-laden pleas are probably going to fall on deaf ears. In many situations, the consumer's own assessments and personal attitudes are in favor of one alternative, but subjective norms temper them in favor of another.[11]

FIGURE 7.10 THEORY OF REASONED ACTION (TORA)
THE FULL MODEL

Fishbein's Extended Model of Behavioral Intention: In an Extension of the Basic Model, the Full Model considers both personal attitudes and expectations of people we consider our referents (here called Subjective Norm).

MOLDING CONSUMER ATTITUDES

How May I Persuade Thee?

As marketers, we are interested not only in understanding and measuring consumers' current attitudes but also in molding and shaping them. If our brand is new, then we want to form, in the consumer's mind, a favorable attitude toward our new brand. If our brand has been in existence for some time, and consumers already hold an attitude toward it, and if that attitude is negative or less positive than their attitudes toward competing brands, then as marketers, we would surely want to modify that attitude. How can we accomplish that?

Here, the three-component model comes to our aid. The three-component model says, you remember, that beliefs (or cognitions), feelings, and action all influence one another; furthermore, a consumer tries to maintain them in harmony. Therefore, if we changed one component, the other two components would follow suit, and the attitude (which consists of all three components) would be changed. (See Figure 7.11.)

SAVVY MARKETER

COGNITIVE ROUTE TO ATTITUDE MOLDING

I Am Going To Convince You

To follow the cognitive route, as a marketer, we provide an association (i.e., Brand A has property X) with the product or service; if the consumer accepts that association, then a brand belief is formed. For example, suppose you knew nothing about soya, a Chinese food crop; then you read somewhere that soya is a good source of protein. Thus, you acquired a new belief about soya (cognition formation). Or suppose you had a belief, say, that potatoes are fattening. And then the potato company gave you the facts: potatoes are fattening only if consumed as fries; by themselves, they have only about a hundred calories a piece. Then, your belief about baked potatoes might change. Consequently, you would look more favorably at the potato as a food item. Notice here that we succeeded in changing your attitude about potatoes by first changing your belief about its fattening property (or lack of it). In this case, the marketer has taken the cognitive route.

AFFECTIVE ROUTE TO ATTITUDE MOLDING

I Am Going To Charm You

As marketers, we may also mold consumer attitudes by first changing their feelings directly and by creating an

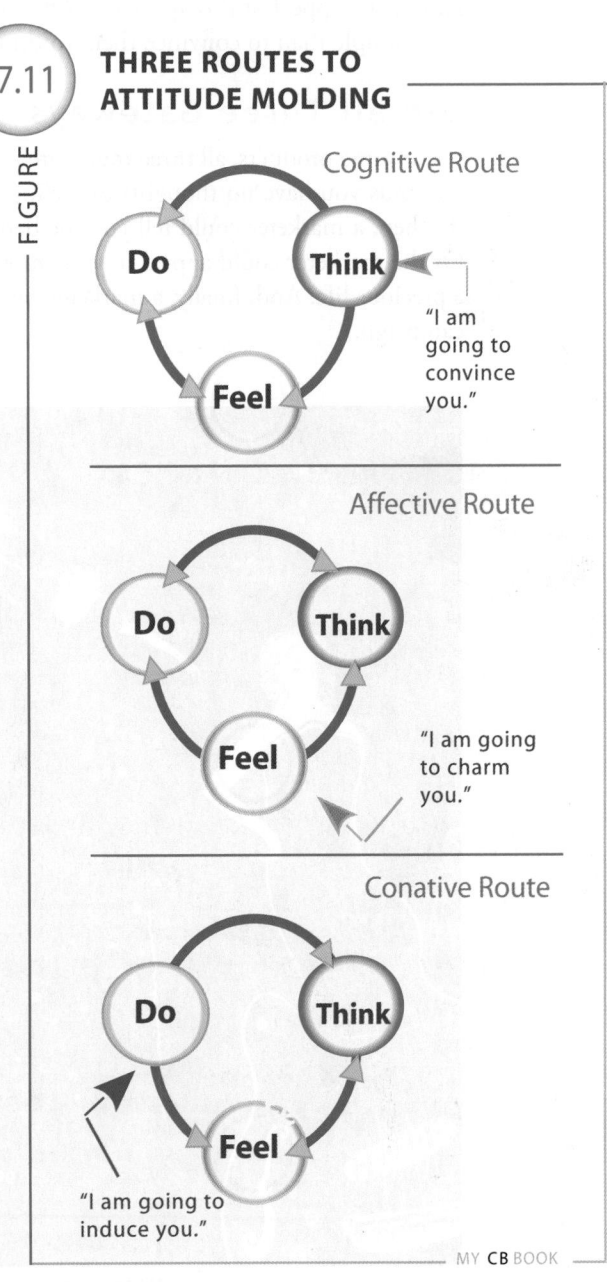

7.11 FIGURE

THREE ROUTES TO ATTITUDE MOLDING

Cognitive Route

Do — Think — Feel

"I am going to convince you."

Affective Route

Do — Think — Feel

"I am going to charm you."

Conative Route

Do — Think — Feel

"I am going to induce you."

MY CB BOOK

emotional connection between the brand and the consumer. Domestic marketers could appeal to a sense of patriotism, for example. Marketers often promote products such as soft drinks, colognes, and food with mood-inducing upbeat music. Just presenting appealing images of a product creates good feelings—as does a mere photo of iPod or a recent Fuse TV print ad. These feelings then create more favorable thoughts and create an intent to buy the product.[12]

CONATIVE ROUTE TO ATTITUDE MOLDING

I Am Going to Induce You

SAVVY MARKETER

Finally, in this third approach, we can change your attitudes by first changing your behavior. For example, suppose you are unaware of a new shampoo (and therefore have no existing attitude toward it), and you receive a free sample and try it. In getting consumers to try it, marketers induce their behavior directly. Upon trial, a consumer may come to like the product—thus developing a favorable attitude.[13] Marketers also induce a consumer to buy a product with special deals and coupons. Once the behavior is induced (e.g., the consumer buys a brand because of coupons), the cognitions and feelings fall into place. Part of the appeal of this approach is that it may sometimes be easier to get consumers to try a sample than to convince them to think or feel in a new way.

Use all Three Gateways

For some products, all three routes are possible. Suppose you have never donated blood, and thus you have no thoughts or feelings about it—that is, you have no attitude about it. Then, a marketer could tell you the benefits (to you and to others) of donating blood. Or the marketer could appeal to you emotionally by explaining how you could be saving a precious life. And, finally, a marketer can just get you to donate blood as part of a group campaign.

Molding your attitude through *Affecive* Route.

(Image courtesy of Fuse TV)

Romancing the Consumer

Visualize this. A man in his fifties decked up in tux is proposing a wedding toast. You hear him speak: "Good evening, Ladies and Gentlemen. ... I have dreamed ... that the day we sent her off to start her own family is every bit as memorable as the day she first joined ours." And then he concludes: "But I am just her financial advisor. Now let's hear a few words from her dad."

The commercial is from Morgan Stanley, in a product category (investment advice) historically considered serious business, where consumers supposedly make rational decisions based on considerations of pure economics rather than social relations.

Then there is the heart-warming story of an HSBC taxi seen a few years ago in New York City. HSBC is an Asian bank, which, in an act rare in the industry, decided to run a cab service for its customers. If you have an HSBC bank card, you simply hail this red-and-white checkered cab and ride to your destination—FREE!

An HSBC Courtesy Cab

Image by Tasha Walters
(Reprinted with permission from brandchannel.com)

The driver is dressed in khaki pants, a white button-down shirt, and a bright red bow tie. And he is one of the most knowledgeable cabbies, familiar with every street in New York City and also able to talk about a wide range of subjects. He is a happy-faced person, proud that he is an ambassador of the bank. **And the cab itself? It is a vintage 1981 model with a red and white checkered design and totally cool looks.**

These are all well-established, solid brands, and they have sought, and attained, a respectable consumer brand attitude. Only, now, they are pursuing an emotional basis for that attitude.

SOURCE: The HSBC story based on "Branded Life, Johnnie Morello drives customers to the brand," brandchannel.com, November 3, 2003. (http://www.brandchannel.com)

Powered OM by ☐ MY C BOOK ◎

UTILITARIAN PRODUCT • EMOTIONAL POSITIONING

Now let us consider these Hanson Brick ads.

Bricks are bricks. What do you look for when you are buying bricks? That they should be strong, and evenly shaped; their color should not fade; their material should not decay; and they should come in a choice of colors. It is a pretty drab and dull thing to choose. Its basically, and entirely, a utilitarian product. Right?

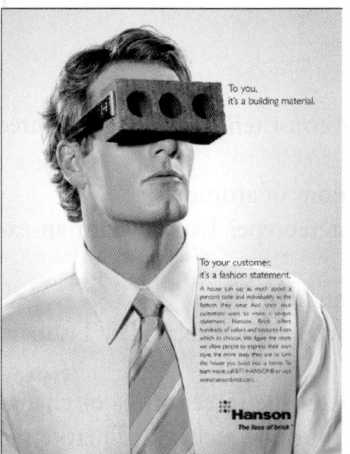

Think again. At least, a company named Hanson Bricks sees bricks otherwise. In these print ad, the company shows us how bricks are a "fashion statement." Or should be.

Can all utilitarian brands successfully switch consumers from a learning hierarchy and a cognitive/learning route to an emotional hierarchy of attitude formation? This assumes a certain degree of prior consumer knowledge of the brand and a skillful creative communication of the brand's personality.

SUMMARY

Like OK Cola, countless products fail in the marketplace every day, and for only one reason: They have failed to win a favorable consumer attitude. Must we, as marketers, not know, therefore, what an attitude is and how it is formed? We must. Therefore, we embarked upon an in-depth exploration of the classical definition of attitude—a learned predisposition. Next, we opened up its internal structure, and we found, lying underneath, three components: beliefs or cognitions (thoughts), affect (feelings), and conation (action tendency or intent to act). We learned also that as consumers we acquire these three components in a specific sequence, depending on how rational or emotional we are. And we learned also that the three components exist in harmony.

Next, we discussed a functional theory of attitude. Advanced by psychologist Daniel Katz, this theory expounds on the motivational reasons why consumers hold attitudes at all. They hold attitudes, according to Katz, because these attitudes serve one or more of four functions: utilitarian, value-expressive, ego-defense, and knowledge. Often marketers, particularly of more important causes, don't take cognizance of these functions, and, consequently, they fail to address the root causes of attitudes.

Next, we introduced you to TORA—a multi-attribute model of attitude structure. While somewhat complex to describe, understanding it is proportionately rewarding. We learned that TORA—theory of reasoned action—proposes that our attitude toward something is based on our component beliefs about the outcomes weighed by our evaluation (i.e., relative desirability) of these outcomes. That sounds sensible and logical, and TORA allows us to analyze consumer attitudes numerically and for a large number of consumers.

Having understood what attitudes are, we turned attention, naturally, to how to mold them. Here, we immediately recalled an inside secret we learned earlier: no matter where you begin, all three components eventually come into sync and come to live in harmony. If they live in harmony, then we could, as marketers, set the process in motion by introducing any of the three components. It is true, we learned, that there is a cognitive or belief formation route to attitude formation—tell consumers about product attributes; an emotional or feelings route—appeal to their emotions about the product; and a direct action route—induce the consumer to try our product. In time, all three components will converge.

We are now ready to deal with attitudes, ours and those of our consumers. If we apply the lessons of this chapter correctly, we will ensure that our product does not meet the fate of OK Cola!

KEY TERMS

Affect	Ego-defense function	Multi-attribute model of attitude
Attitude	Emotional hierarchy	Predisposition
Attitude hierarchy	Fishbein's extended model of behavior	Stereotypes
Belief	Functional theory of attitude	Theory of reasoned action
Brand belief	Knowledge function	Utilitarian function
Conation	Learning hierarchy	Value-expressive function

YOUR TURN

REVIEW+Rewind

1. Define the concept of consumer attitude. Explain each of its elements.
2. How are attitudes measured?
3. Name and explain the three components of the ABC model of attitude.
4. Define belief and illustrate it with one belief statement about any brand.
5. Describe the statements by which each of the three components is measured.
6. What is meant by the word *hierarchy* in attitudes? How do learning and emotional hierarchies differ, and how do these in turn differ from the low-involvement hierarchy of attitudes? Illustrate each with a consumer example.
7. What is meant by the consistency between the three components?
8. Explain the four functions of attitude?
9. What is a consumer stereotype? Explain with an example.
10. Describe the TORA model.
11. Describe the extensions in the "Extended Fishbein Model."
12. Name and briefly explain the three modes of changing people's attitudes. Illustrate each with a marketing example.

CB Blog

CONSUMER ATTITUDES—JUDGMENTS FOR BRANDS ON TRIAL

Consumer attitudes are not about the consumer per se; rather they are about his or her reactions to products and brands. They at once enmesh both the consumer and the product or brand. They are a projection by the consumer, of his or her will, his or her desires, onto the products. They are the final judgment for brands in the consumer's court.

In a free marketplace, marketers live or die by consumer attitudes. That is why it is important for us to understand how consumer attitudes are formed—attitudes that range from simple description such as "like/dislike" to complex characterizations such as "predispositions"; and from rational and emotional to complex multi-dimensional structures.

In the game of life, we are all marketers, trying to persuade others to adopt our points of view. Next time you find yourself persuading someone, consider what you have learned about how people form attitudes. Then consider what you can do to shape that attitude in your favor.

Most of all, as marketers, we should never forget that the way to a consumer's wallet is through his/her mind. Whether through rational or emotional appeals, you have to win favorable consumer attitudes. Winning consumer attitudes is not a matter of clever advertising or some gimmicky promotion, mind you. And you can't shoot from the hip and hope that your market offerings and your messages will find believers.

Rather, to build positive and enduring consumer attitudes, you will need every bit of knowledge about how attitudes are formed and shaped. For that knowledge, read and reread this chapter, and do it with involvement.

CONSUMER BEHAVIOR

MY CB BOOK .COM

THINK+Apply

1. What significance does the concept of attitude have for marketers? Why would you, as a marketer, want to measure consumer attitudes?

2. For each of the three attitude components, give two examples, drawing on your own attitudes toward any products or services.

3. Think of your current attitude toward any product, brand, organization, celebrity, musician, TV show, course, book, or whatever. Now identify one of these attitudes that serves, say, the utilitarian function; likewise identify one attitude for each of the other three functions.

4. Write down a complete survey to measure your attitude (all three components of it) toward (a) your wireless service, and (b) your hair salon.

PRACTICE+Experience

1. Construct a questionnaire to measure consumers' attitudes toward body-piercing. Then administer this survey to two consumers, one with body-piercing and the other without. Compare all attitude components. Do their attitudes differ along all components, and if not, how do you explain it?

2. Interview two consumers with significant body-piercing and/or tattoos to understand their atti-

tudes toward consumption of tattoos and body-piercing. Identify which of the four functions these consumer attitudes serve for each of these two consumers.

3. Survey three consumers using a questionnaire that measures (a) the three components of attitude, (b) the Theory of Reasoned Action, and (c) the Extended Fishbein Model. Measure these for two competing brands of a high-involvement product well-known to the consumer. Then compute the models for each consumer and see if the models work—the brand that is rated higher on components of the model is also the brand the consumer prefers more. Explain your results.

In the Marketing Manager's Shoes

Put yourself in a marketing manager's shoes. Most concepts in the chapter have some lessons for the marketing manager; i.e., they suggest what to do differently in practice. Indeed, often these applications are implicit in our explanations of the concepts and models in the chapter. Identify at least five specific applications of the chapter's concepts, all of which should be entirely new, different from the examples cited here.

TOVA AND TOTA

Two Models to Explain Complex Attitudes

THEORY OF VALUE ASSESSMENT (TOVA)

You have already read about TORA; now meet its cousin TOVA. Well-known psychologist Milton Rosenberg proposed this theory, actually called the *value-instrumentality model* (TOVA being our name for it). According to the **theory of value assessment** (TOVA), our attitude toward an object is based on how well it promotes the values in which we believe, weighted by the relative importance to us of those values:

Attitude = the extent to which the object will promote a value X the importance of that value to the consumer—calculating this for each value and then summing across all relevant values.

Take a consumer who is considering patronizing a store owned by a minority person. His response depends on his attitude, and to find his attitude, we need to add together each of the values this behavior satisfies (e.g., patriotism, encouraging the disadvantaged, rewarding the spirit of enterprise, and so on), weighted by the importance of these values to the consumer.

How does TOVA differ from TORA? In TOVA, the beliefs are about our deeply held values—thus, it applies to attitudes that serve a value-expressive function. The objects of attitude here are such that they evoke our deeply held values. These objects include fur, animal tested products, products made with inhuman labor, artificial foods, products proscribed by religion, etc. In contrast, in TORA, the consequences are all "value neutral" product benefits or harms. This model applies, therefore, to products where attitudes are based on the utilitarian function—cars, appliances, food products, etc. And one more thing. TOVA works well with value-based consumer segments (e.g., pro-choice versus pro-life voters; pro-environmental voters and their counterparts; and so on). In contrast, TORA works best with benefit segmentation (e.g., health-conscious versus taste craving consumers of food; economy versus status image for a car; etc.).

THEORY OF TRYING TO ACHIEVE. (TOTA)

TORA and TOVA have one more cousin, one with a bit more muscle, if you will. Accordingly, it can handle a bit more complicated situations, and it is called TOTA.[14] The problem is that TORA and TOVA work well when the "reasoned behavior" in question is a one-time action—like buying an SUV instead of a gas-economizing small car, or undergoing laser eye vision surgery, or getting a tattoo. How about dieting, trying to quit smoking, becoming a vegetarian, taking up an exercise program, etc.? These require repeated concerted actions, and there is no guarantee you will succeed. Theory of Trying to Achieve (TOTA) models how a consumer would decide whether or not to try to achieve some goal, such as weight reduction or adopting a healthy eating pattern. This model is shown in simplified form in Figure 7.12, and is illustrated for a consumer trying to lose weight.

As this figure shows, attitude toward trying (ATT) is based on three sub-attitudes: attitude toward success, attitude toward failure, and attitude toward the process itself. We may love the idea of becoming slim or, instead, be merely pleased; e.g., "It will be kind of nice; that is all" (attitude toward success). On the flip side, if we fail, we may feel miserable, or instead we may see the failure as no big deal (attitude toward failure). And finally, we may feel good or bad about the very regimen of exercise and eating (attitude toward process).

Of course, each of these three sub-attitudes are in turn based on their own multi-attribute models—i.e., perceived consequences of succeeding, of failing, and the process, weighted by the desirability of these consequences (not shown in figure). This is illustrated by two consequences of each attitude, shown below the main figure. These can be measured by asking the consumer to indicate how likely he or she thinks it is that each consequence

7.12 A THEORY OF TRYING TO ACHIEVE (TOTA)

FIGURE

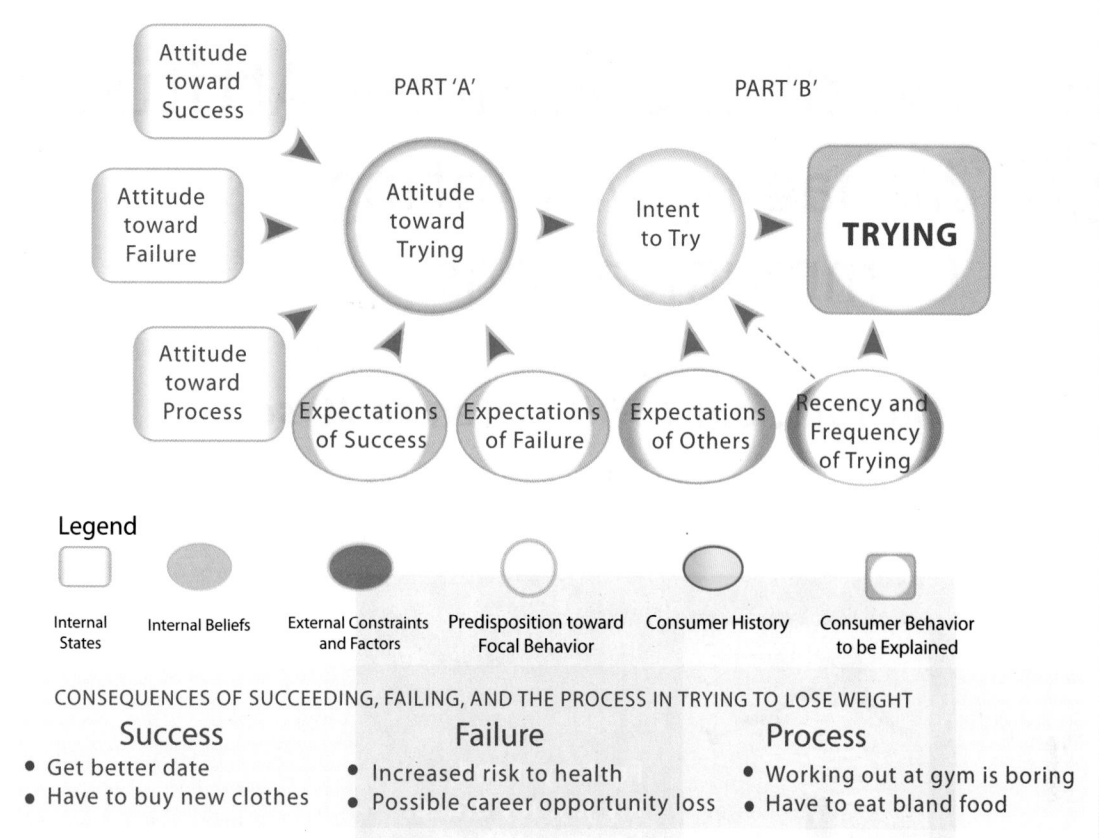

Legend

Internal States | Internal Beliefs | External Constraints and Factors | Predisposition toward Focal Behavior | Consumer History | Consumer Behavior to be Explained

CONSEQUENCES OF SUCCEEDING, FAILING, AND THE PROCESS IN TRYING TO LOSE WEIGHT

Success
- Get better date
- Have to buy new clothes

Failure
- Increased risk to health
- Possible career opportunity loss

Process
- Working out at gym is boring
- Have to eat bland food

MY CB BOOK

will occur and then also how desirable/undesirable each consequence is. Multiplying the two and adding up across all consequences would give us the three attitudes.

Next, the Attitude toward Trying is also affected by two expectations: expectations of success and expectations of failure. If a consumer expected to succeed, then he or she would likely keep at it; instead, if he/she expected to fail, then he/she may not even begin. (Success and failure are not always exactly opposites; a consumer may define success only when he or she loses say 10 lbs but may define failure only if no weight were lost at all.) This completes part 'A' of the model (see Figure 7.12).

Part 'B' extends the model from "attitude toward trying" to "intent to try and actual trying." Here, two new factors enter the picture. The first is "social norms toward trying"—i.e., the expectations of our significant others. As we all know, when it comes to trying lifestyle changes, expectations of significant others can sometimes play a big role, even more than our own attitudes. And the second factor is

"the recency and frequency of past behavior." The more recently you tried and the more frequently you have tried some difficult change, the more likely are you to try again.

This, then, is the theory of trying. See for yourself how it works for some of your endeavors. For starters, you may want to complete the list of the consequences of trying for weight loss in the above list, and then complete all other components of the model. And then reflect on each component—what can you change so as to help yourself get better at trying?[15]

Molding Consumer Attitudes— Managing Marketing Communications

You Talk, but I Will Listen to Myself

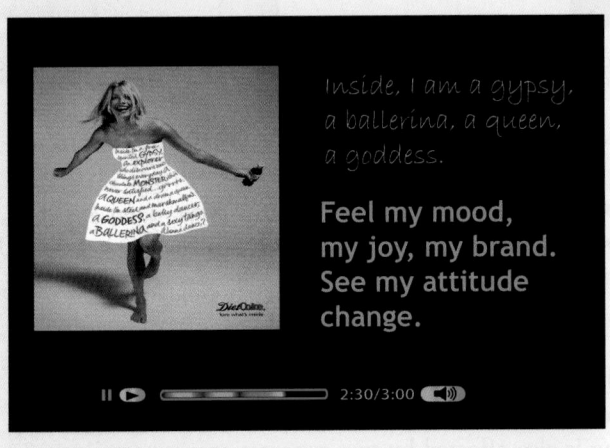

Inside, I am a gypsy,
a ballerina, a queen,
a goddess.

Feel my mood,
my joy, my brand.
See my attitude
change.

2:30/3:00

LEARN . APPLY . EXPERIENCE

OBJECTIVES

1 Seven Theories of Attitude Change

2 How Low Involvement Advertising Works

3 The Roles of Emotion, Humor, Fear, and Sex in Ad Appeals

4 Source Credibility and Match-Up Hypothesis

5 Five Factors of Persuasion in Interpersonal Selling

6 The Proposition That Consumers, Not Marketers, Control Attitude Change

Bull-Running versus Nude Running in Spain

Every year from July 7th to 14th, Pamplona, Spain is busy with activities surrounding Encierro, the famous bull-running festival of San Fermin.

On the morning of July 7, hundreds of young men gather at Santo Domingo. Then a herd of bulls is released from their corral, and the young men start running, with the bulls behind them. At first the bulls are far behind, and the runners are running slowly. Then, as the bulls get closer, the runners start running faster, making their way through city streets filled with cheering spectators. In the mile-long run, some drop out, some get trampled and a few, fueled by a fresh adrenaline rush, make it safely to the finish line. Later that day, there is a bullfight in a big arena where the bulls fight until they get killed.[1]

The Naked Truth: Bullfighting is Cruel

Photo by Andy Simms. Courtesy: PETA, UK

Of immense thrill to thousands of spectators, this event displeases one particular group—People for the Ethical Treatment of Animals (PETA). To protest against the event, PETA organize a different kind of run: "Encierro Human," humans only—clothes optional. Started in 2002, members and activists run just two days before the event, many unclad, with only a poster in hand, much to the delight of an amused crowd of spectators, chanting "Stop the bloody bullfights!"

"These runners are telling the world," says PETA's campaign coordinator, William Rivas-Rivas, "that the torture of bulls will not be tolerated and that caring, daring, and baring individuals will be back every year until the bulls are left out of the annual festivities."[2]

Protesting on issues; changing attitudes.

INTRODUCTION

Will PETA and its "Running of the Nudes" campaign succeed in stopping the bullfight? It is difficult to predict—for three reasons. First, the bull run is a sacred ritual, honoring patron saint, San Fermin. Second, it is a big tourist attraction that pulls in a good deal of money for local businesses. And third, it is, well, a time-honored tradition, and a source of thrill to millions of Spaniards all across Spain. So, only time will tell.

The NHS (National Health Services) of the Department of Health, U.K., offers a "support program" to pregnant mothers.

Stopping the bull run and bullfighting in Spain will require a change of attitude. Enough Spaniards have to stop patronizing the event, and, furthermore, petition their government to ban this bull-unfriendly sport. This requires a group action, propelled by an attitude shift among a large proportion of the population. Actually, protests such as these are bearing fruit: As of January 1, 2012, the government of Barcelona banned bullfighting (but the practice continues in other regions of Spain).

Other consumer actions are individual in scope and require a change of attitudes within the person himself or herself, such as switching brands, carpooling, or favoring hybrid cars over SUVs. What does it take to change people's attitudes? Look at the "smoke-free pregnancy" campaign image from the British Department of Health. Would the campaign succeed in making consumers think less favorably of smoking? Why or why not? This question is of great interest to marketers. In this chapter, we are going to describe various theories about and methods of changing consumer attitudes.[4] If you suspect that these theories, being *theories*, are, well, dull, then, along the way, we are also going to change your attitude toward these theories themselves. Attitude change, you'll find, is a fascinating topic, and it is also one of the most practical ones—a tool marketers deploy every day. So read on.

ATTITUDE CHANGE: SEVEN THEORIES

When You Care Versus When You Don't

1. INVOLVEMENT AND THINK-FEEL GRID FOR ATTITUDE CHANGE

If you think of all the issues in your life that require decisions (e.g., which hairstyle to get for the upcoming college reunion) and all the product and brand choices you have to make (e.g., which cola to drink, which movie to see this weekend, which ear to pierce, etc.), your attitudes toward these issues and objects can be divided into four quadrants on a grid. This grid is formed by two axes (or dimensions): the "involvement axis" and the "think-feel axis."

Is your involvement in the issue high (e.g., should you sign up for the U.S. Army, should you paint your car pink or green, etc.)? Or is it low (e.g., should you cut through the lawn or take the pathway, should you save the can for later recycling or just toss it in the nearest trash can, etc.)? And, is the issue or the choice of the brand or product a rational (THINK) matter for you (e.g., Which cereal is good for my health?)? Or do you get pretty emotional (FEEL) about it (e.g., "Is there a less permanent way to show her my love than to tattoo her name on my arm?")? Cross these two dimensions or axes, and we can locate your attitude-change problem in one of the four quadrants. This grid was invented by the ad agency Foote, Cone, and Belding (FCB), so it is aptly called the FCB Grid.[5] See Figure 8.1.

Now, our message will have to be designed differently depending on the quadrant. First, in the two THINK quadrants, our message will have to be rational—this means that we will have to tell you what the product does and what concrete benefits it will deliver to you. In the HIGH INVOLVEMENT THINK quadrant, we will present you with as many features and benefits as our product has, giving you the strongest argument we can muster (e.g., "You should join the Army because it will train you in rare and useful skills, and you will learn discipline, stay fit, earn a good salary, and build a career."). In contrast, in the LOW INVOLVEMENT THINK quadrant, you want to hear a rational argument, but you don't want to exert too much effort in thinking about it. You will want to quickly learn one or two good things about that brand. Accordingly, in this quadrant, we will focus only on one or two simple rational brand benefits.

For the *feel* issues or product choices, with high involvement (HIGH INVOLVEMENT

FEEL) we will have to make the message emotional. Rather than tout the product's physical or rational benefits, we will have to move you emotionally—whether that emotion is fear, hope, love, guilt, pride, or whatever. "You should join the Army," we might say, "because it will make your nation proud, you will protect innocent civilians against barbarian oppression, and you'll serve an honorable cause."

Lastly, in the fourth quadrant (LOW INVOLVEMENT FEEL), we will present the brand visually to create a positive impression, and/or we will set it up in a good mood setting. Essentially and foremost, the purpose of our ad here is to create a positive mood in the consumer—provide the consumer with a pleasant or humorous thought or image and cause him or her to smile or chuckle about our brand, thereby creating an *affectively* charged cloud in the consumer's mind. (Note: *Affective* is a technical term, meaning *emotional*.)

2. ELABORATION LIKELIHOOD MODEL

Central and Peripheral Routes

A "low involvement ad" should present a brand visually and present only a single *simple* product benefit. But what happens if we present an ad with long copy and many brand details even for a low involvement product? Well, for starters, consumers are not going to read a long ad for a brand of salt or mouthwash, for example. But suppose a mouthwash company did advertise its brand using a long copy. How would different consumers read it?

Questions such as these have always intrigued consumer researchers. Recently, researchers have found a pretty good answer, summed up as the "Central and Peripheral Route to Persuasion."[6]

Through the **central route**, as consumers, we process the message with attention. We center our attention on the message, read the entire text or listen to all the words, think them over, and then choose to accept the message or, alternatively, to dismiss it. If we find the message believable, then we accept it and are persuaded; if not, then we dismiss the message and are not persuaded.

Through the **peripheral route**, we process the message superficially. We don't pay attention to the exact words, nor do we bother to read or listen to the entire message text. Instead, we are impressed (or unimpressed) by some superficial elements of the ad. For example, if the ad is visually pleasing, or if there is a character in a TV commercial who is funny or annoying, or if a spokesperson has, say, a French accent, then, based on these merely peripheral elements, we form a quick impression about the brand. This is attitude change occurring through the peripheral route, a route we choose when we are not involved with the product being advertised.[7]

Back to the mouthwash ad: The high involvement consumers are very likely to read

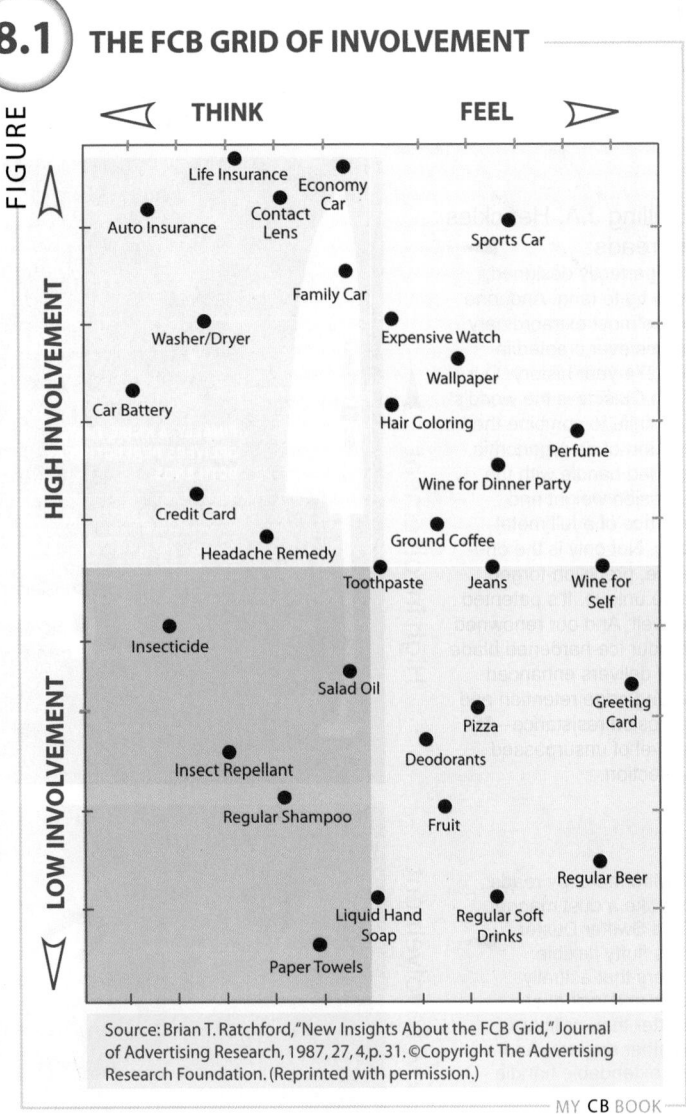

8.1 THE FCB GRID OF INVOLVEMENT

FIGURE

THINK ◁   FEEL ▷

HIGH INVOLVEMENT

Life Insurance
Economy Car
Auto Insurance
Contact Lens
Sports Car
Family Car
Washer/Dryer
Expensive Watch
Wallpaper
Car Battery
Hair Coloring
Perfume
Wine for Dinner Party
Credit Card
Headache Remedy
Ground Coffee

LOW INVOLVEMENT

Toothpaste   Jeans   Wine for Self
Insecticide
Salad Oil
Greeting Card
Pizza
Deodorants
Insect Repellant
Regular Shampoo   Fruit
Regular Beer
Liquid Hand Soap   Regular Soft Drinks
Paper Towels

Source: Brian T. Ratchford, "New Insights About the FCB Grid," Journal of Advertising Research, 1987, 27, 4, p. 31. ©Copyright The Advertising Research Foundation. (Reprinted with permission.)

MY CB BOOK

The FCB Grid in Action

◀ Think   Feel ▶

Zwilling J.A. Henckles ad reads: ▶
It is perfectly designed, from tip to tang. And, one of the most extraordinary knives ever created in our 274-year history. Our Twin Cuisine is the world's first knife to combine the comfort of an ergonomic, molded handle with the precision weight and balance of a full metal tang. Not only is the one-piece, precision-forged knife unique. It's patented as well. And our renowned Friodur ice-hardened blade now delivers enhanced cutting edge retention and corrosion resistance—for a level of unsurpassed perfection.

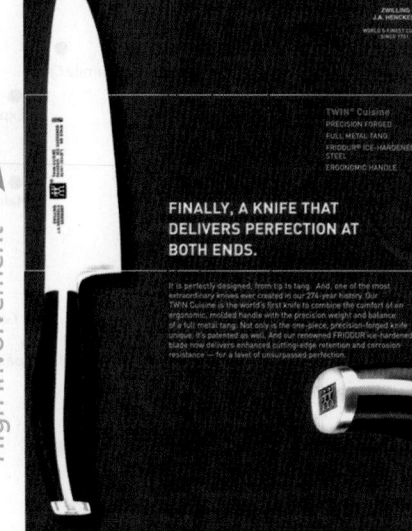

High Involvement

Courtesy: J.A. Henckles

Courtesy: NHS, Dept. of Health, U.K..

Swiffer ad copy reads:
It's like a dust magnet. The Swiffer Duster has fluffy flexible fibers that actually trap and lock dust better than ordinary feather dusters. And its extendable handle reaches virtually everywhere. ▶

Low Involvement

Photo courtesy of Proctor & Gamble

Courtesy: VCD, Paddington, NSW, Australia.

It might shock you to see the Swiffer and Diet Coke ads in the low involvement quadrants. Let us clarify. The ads themselves are NOT low involvement ads. Rather, the point is that dusting is not a highly involving topic, not at the time they are seeing the ad anyway; and the Diet Coke consumer may be involved in the brand, even highly involved, but there is not much more he/she cares to know about a soda. The task then is to say something simple and quick (THINK—the Swiffer ad), or show a quick-impression visual (FEEL—diet coke). To get attention and catch the fancy of such "low involvement," "I am not concerned about it now," consumers is precisely the challenge low involvement ads typically face. The vibrant colors in the Swiffer ad serve to capture attention, and the simple "ordinary duster+magnet=Swiffer" message, presented both visually and in the text, drives home the brand benefit to the otherwise low-involvement consumer.

In the Diet Coke ad, it is the admirable creativity that will in fact engage the reader, transforming him/her into a more involved consumer. As to the **J.A. Henckels knife** ad, it communicates the "high tech" features of this precision-perfect knife. The ad will attract mostly "high-involvement consumers," but it has to hope also, rightly, that those not currently involved will, should they take the time to read the ad, feel educated that not all knives are the same. As to the NHS anti-smoking ad, its intended audience is one that values appearances highly, a state of high FEEL INVOLVEMENT.

the entire ad, and, based on their acceptance of the argument, they will most likely be persuaded. Low involvement consumers, on the other hand, may only notice the colorful bottle, and will perhaps infer, without reading the copy, that the ad contains a scientific explanation of how the product works. And because there is a scientific explanation, they would figure, then the brand must be good. That is their peripheral processing at work!

Massaging the Message

Actually, through the central route, consumers do more than merely pay attention to the entire ad content. They elaborate on it. They construct a vision of the product or of themselves using the product. An ad for a new mountain bike makes them visualize how the new drive chain in the bike would give them more thrust for the same amount of legwork, or how they would enjoy the bike itself at the next summer camp. This happens, of course, only when consumers have high involvement in the product. Just as the **Elaboration Likelihood Model (ELM)** states: the higher the consumer's involvement, the higher the likelihood that the consumer will elaborate on the message.[8]

What is the advantage if consumers "elaborate"? First, the message will get processed fully, so consumers will have noted all the points made in the ad. And, second, since they will have personally and consciously interacted with the message, they will be more likely to remember the message later. Of course, processing with elaboration is a double-edged sword: The message goes through intense scrutiny, and, therefore, if the message is hype (flimsy, hollow, and not credible), then the attitude change will happen in the wrong direction; i.e., against the brand.[9]

Ponder This

Of course, "wrong" means "wrong from the marketer's perspective"; from the consumer's perspective, an elaborated message always leads to more realistic brand perceptions. In peripheral processing, consumers trade efficiency for accuracy. Some brand perceptions are formed quickly and may be inaccurate, but because the product or brand choice is not very consequential (that is why the consumer used low involvement processing), the slight inaccuracy is not harmful.

Want to see more elaboration in the ELM itself? Follow this description with Figure 8.2. It begins when the consumer is exposed to the message. He or she judges the message topic as either high or low involvement, and based on that judgment he or she decides to pay high (focused) or low (cursory) attention. High attention stimulates central processing and, correspondingly, high elaboration; in contrast, low attention results in peripheral processing and low elaboration, or, in fact, no elaboration at all.

With elaboration, the message is either judged relevant and truthful, and, consequently, positive brand beliefs are formed. Or, alternatively, the message is evaluated as hyped and untruthful, and negative brand beliefs are consequently formed. These beliefs (e.g., "This wine is well made.") and associations (e.g., "It is for really cool people.") are strong (i.e., the consumer is confident about them), well-considered as they are. These beliefs and associations are also multiple in number, based either on a multi-claim message or on internal elaboration, and, in turn, produce attitudes that are well founded in the consumer's mind, attitudes that are more certain, strong, and marked by conviction. In turn, they lead to a strong intent to buy (if the formed attitude is positive), or an equally strong intent not to buy (if the formed attitude is negative).

In the low elaboration, peripheral processing mode, quick impressions are formed pertaining to the brand as a whole (e.g., "Here is this new soda.") or its single attribute (e.g., "Okay, so this soda has fewer calories."); based on a single, quickly-formed belief or impression, the resulting attitude is weak (e.g., "I am not sure, but then it doesn't really matter—I mean I don't have to be absolutely sure.") and ephemeral (not enduring), with a "take it or leave it" intent (e.g., "Okay, maybe I'll try it sometime.").

8.2 ELABORATION LIKELIHOOD MODEL

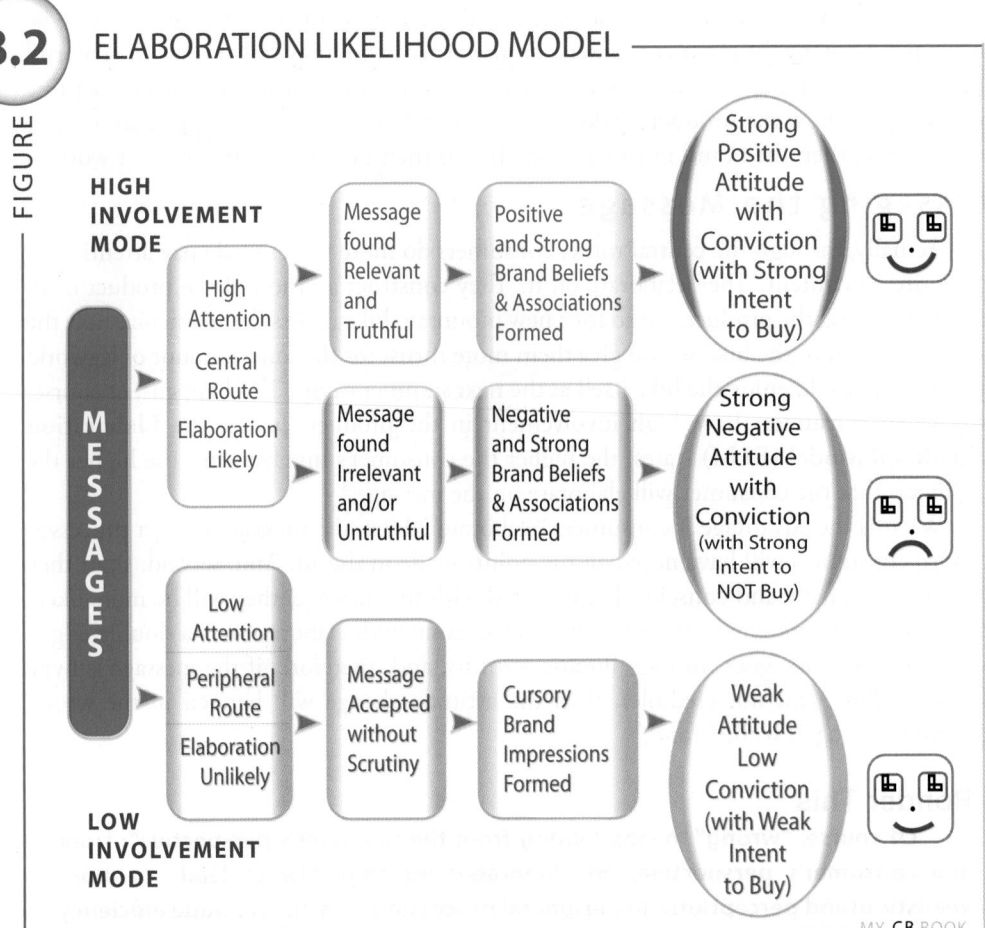

MY **CB** BOOK

3. MOLDING ATTITUDES VIA MULTI-ATTRIBUTE MODELS

The essence of the multi-attribute model (TORA) is the multi-attribute format of the attitude structure (i.e., beliefs weighted by evaluation of belief content). (See Chapter 7.) Given this structure, we can change consumer attitudes in three ways[11]:

- **By changing a specific component belief, which can be accomplished by changing the perception of the corresponding attribute level or associated consequence.**
- **By changing the importance that the consumer assigns to an attribute or to the evaluation of that consequence.**
- **By introducing a new attribute (i.e., evaluation criteria) into the consumer's evaluation process.**

Let us consider the example of EarthLink versus NetZero, discussed in the previous chapter. To improve consumer attitude toward its brand, EarthLink has the following options:

- **The company can improve its connection success rate and communicate this improvement to the consumer.**
- **Since it already has a superior rating on speed, it can try to emphasize the desirability of high speed, thus raising the speed's evaluation from the current rating of +2 to, say, +3.**
- **EarthLink can offer some new feature like a spam filter or privacy protection, and then communicate the importance of this new feature to the consumer.**

For technological products, this last option is particularly appealing. Since technological products are always evolving (e.g., portals like EarthLink, browsers, cell phones, PDAs, etc.), consumers are always looking for new features, and companies that can bring new features to the market sooner are more likely to win the consumer attitude battle.

Consider the new features EarthLink has introduced within only the last five years:

the user now has the ability to check email by phone; to check PC performance and fix errors; to protect against email viruses; to block unwanted email; to sort emails by date, sender name, and subject; to have sent customized reminders, alerts, sports scores and other information to mobile phones; to automatically forward IMs (Instant Messages) to a mobile phone; to get notification when a buddy is online; to send and receive emails via a PDA; and so on. These are new attributes for many consumers; these are also the new frontiers of the attitude battle over all sorts of gizmos.

4. HEIDER'S BALANCE THEORY

You love and adore pop princess Hilary Duff. And it is good that she loves animals and, being an animal lover yourself, you are thrilled that she has just come out with a cosmetics line of her own which is kept animal-cruelty free. Made by Townley Cosmetics, it is called "Stuff by Hilary Duff." Now, suppose that one day Ms. Duff decides to start promoting fur coats by Donna Karan? This is going to cause you some mental anguish,

In this ad, from India, Levi's flashes its Button Fly feature, hoping the new attribute will further bolster consumer attitudes toward the brand.
Copy reads: Made from the same steel that goes into your car's chassis. Button Flies.
Courtesy: J. Walter Thompson, Bangalore, India.

Ponder This
While we call them "tools of attitude molding," marketers should not assume that they give them a "manipulative" ability to sway consumer attitudes any which way they desire. And when we say "you can change an attribute perception," we don't mean that it is possible to change it in thin air. Rather, we mean that IF your product indeed has some attributes to a degree consumers have somehow underestimated, THEN you may hope to bring their perceptions in line with the product's reality (but not beyond).

for sure, but the question is, how are you going to make peace with it? Heider's Balance Theory can help us answer that question.

Fritz Heider, a social psychologist, proposed a theory in 1946 that explains how we deal with conflict in our attitudes toward any given two entities.[12] In the above example, the two entities are Ms. Duff and fur. **Heider's Balance Theory** maintains that, in any relationship between three entities, a state of imbalance cannot be sustained, and it will be resolved by altering one of the relationships. The third entity here is "you." The relationships among these three entities are imbalanced, which is why you are experiencing a conflict or dissonance. There are three options available to you: a) you start liking fur, b) you start disliking Ms. Duff, or c) you get Ms. Duff to stop liking and promoting fur. Each option represents an attitude change. Either your attitude toward fur will have to change, or your attitude toward Ms. Duff will have to change, or you will have to change Ms. Duff's attitude toward fur.

Achieving any of these options is easier said than done. Which way the change will occur depends upon which current attitude is stronger. If you really like Ms. Duff a lot, then you will have to modify your attitude toward fur. You don't have to start liking it, but you do have to stop disliking it, so that seeing Ms. Duff wear and promote fur doesn't keep you from enjoying her music. But if you cannot stand fur at all, then you must give up watching Ms. Duff on MTV.

Seen any application of this theory lately? Firms always use likable celebrities to endorse their brands. At press time, pro-basketball player Jeremy Lin had suddenly become a much sought-after brand ambassador. Weeks before, his winning streak for the New York Knicks had charmed sports lovers everywhere; but it remains to be seen if his personal glory will rub off on the brands he chooses to endorse.

5. ATTRIBUTION THEORY

You have encountered this theory before—remember the motive for attribution. As humans, we are hardwired to assign causes to events. To whom or to what we assign causes is something we learn, but the basic instinct to assign causes is an innate motive.[13] Marketers need to make sure that consumers don't misattribute a product's failure to the company, if in fact the consumers themselves are at fault.[14]

Marketers can and do also use attribution theory to mold attitudes. Suppose there is a brand of cereal you have never tried and have felt no desire to try. Now, suppose there is a $1 coupon (for a $2 box!); would you buy it? Many consumers would. And then what? They use it and don't think much of it; their attitude toward that cereal then remains unimproved. Why? Because, they attribute the reason for their buying and consuming that cereal to the hefty deal they got. Instead, give them a smaller incentive, say a coupon worth only 25 cents; in this case, they will attribute the cause for choosing and using it to their own preferences. And if the brand of cereal is any good, they will begin to think of it in a positive light.

Although there is the possibility that many consumers will not be attracted by a small deal (such as only 25 cents off), is it really worth getting people to buy your product with a huge bribe (i.e., a big coupon)? Do you really want them to attribute the purchase to

FIGURE 8.3 **HEIDER'S BALANCE THEORY**

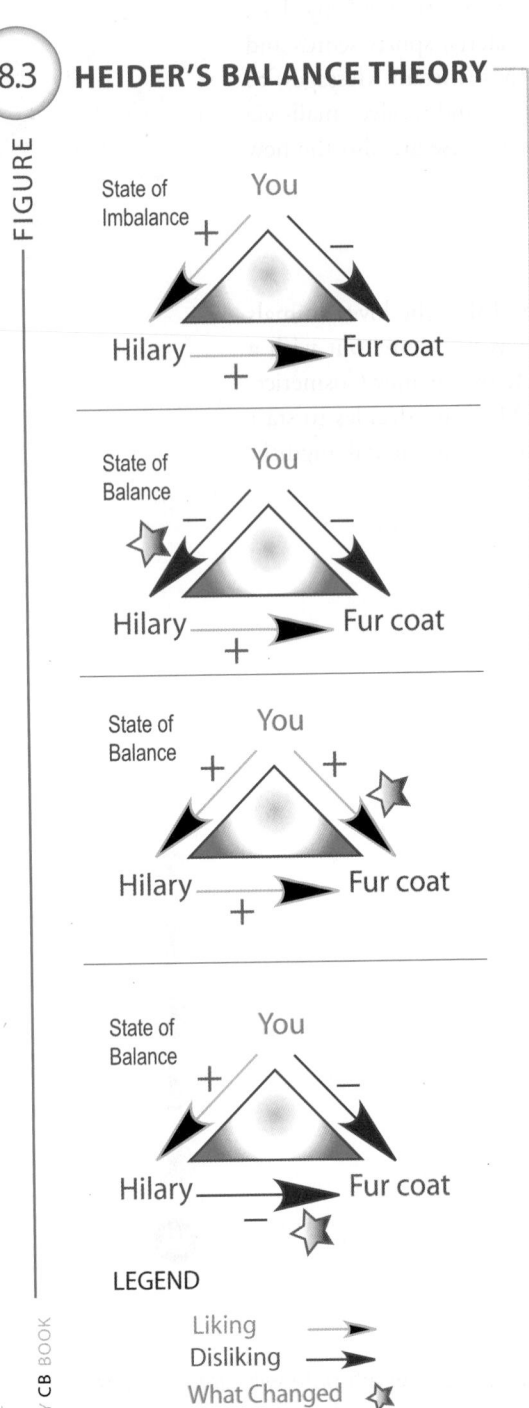

State of Imbalance

You

Hilary   Fur coat

State of Balance

You

Hilary   Fur coat

State of Balance

You

Hilary   Fur coat

State of Balance

You

Hilary   Fur coat

LEGEND

Liking

Disliking

What Changed

the external (coupon) rather than an internal (themselves) factor? Remember, blame or credit, it is best when consumers direct it internally, i.e., toward themselves.

6. SELF-PERCEPTION THEORY

A related theory is **self-perception,** advanced by psychologist Daryl Bem.[15] Bem proposed that we infer our attitudes from our own behavior. If we are screaming (behavior), then we must be angry and annoyed (attitude). In case the "new idea" in this theory has not hit you, recall that the classical theory we covered in the previous chapter was that our attitudes cause our behavior. But Bem's theory says, instead, that sometimes we don't have attitudes of which we are conscious; put differently, we are sometimes not conscious of our attitudes just *prior* to our behavior. If so, our attitudes don't cause our behavior—the

behavior erupts as a direct response to some stimulus, or perhaps the attitude operates at a subconscious level. In these cases, says Bem, if we go looking for our attitudes, we end up inferring them by observing our behavior and assigning a logical attitude to it. "If I am using this product," we tell ourselves, "then I must like it. So, yes, I do like it." Our attitude toward that product? "Well, of course, it is favorable!" Got it?

There are two pragmatic versions of the theory that marketers can use; these are called *foot in the door* and *door in the face*. With the **foot in the door** technique, a marketer makes a small request that the consumer cannot (or usually won't) refuse; subsequently, the marketer makes a larger request. A political campaign organization will ask you, for example, to display a small sign in your front yard, or to show up at a short meeting in the neighborhood. If you comply, then, later, you may be asked to put a larger banner in your front yard or to become an active volunteer in the campaign. How is this "foot in the door" technique explained by self-perception theory? Well, consumers figure that because they have put up the small signs in their front yards, then they must actually like the political candidate. This inferred attitude then acts as a precursor to subsequent behavior (and here we fall back on the classical attitude-causes-behavior theory).

With the **door in the face** technique, the marketer makes a large request that is sure to be refused; subsequently, after the consumer declines the first request, the marketer then makes a much smaller request, which is what the marketers wanted of the consumer in the first place. Having refused the larger request, the consumer happily accedes to the smaller request. Ask a resident voter to put a big sign in the front yard, and, when refused, ask if he/she won't at least agree to place a small sign. This is actually a combination of self-perception and another theory called the **law of reciprocal concession**.

From the self-perception point of view, the consumer looks at his behavior of having refused, and finds it at odds with his usual "nice person" behavior. It brings to salience the consumer's attitude of being a "nice, helpful" person. This attitude then leads the consumer to comply with the more reasonable request. From the "reciprocal concession" perspective, the consumer notices that the requester has made a concession, and the consumer feels that it is now his or her turn to reciprocate.

If you are now wondering how to choose between these two exactly opposite techniques (foot in the door versus door in the face), there is no easy answer. Savvy persuaders develop a knack for knowing which one will work in a particular circumstance.

Sure, political campaigners are marketers too, but if you are looking for

CB FYI

To Each, His Own Poison

In 2001, Police in West Palm Beach, Florida, broadcasted classical music (Bach, Mozart, etc.) in the evenings in Rosemary Village near downtown, a neighborhood plagued by loiterers and criminals. In a few weeks, the loiterers disappeared, and crime had been reduced noticeably.

Similar success was obtained in London, England, where, in 2004, the British Transport Police piped classical music in some crime-ridden London Underground stations, resulting in a one-third decline in robberies and vandalism.

Good thing, even bad behavior follows rules of attitude.

Source: "How Classical Music Can Reduce Crime, Benefit Your Mood and Increase Your Spending," www.SixWise.com, Oct 5, 2006.

Powered by oM   MY CB BOOK

an example from conventional business firms, then consider the following. A business gets a consumer to sign up for a basic service plan with an initial low payment (foot in the door), and then convinces the consumer to add on extra services. "I must have bought the service," the consumer would figure, "because I wanted and liked the service." Alternatively, you could quote a customer the full price and then offer a reduced price (door in the face).

The next time you find a salesperson playing this persuasion game, try to infer which technique he or she is deploying.[16]

7. ACTIVE VERSUS PASSIVE AUDIENCE THEORY

Seen any silly commercials lately? Or any that assume that consumers—that's us—are totally stupid, clueless, and gullible? How come such ads even get made? Do their creators believe that they can get away with anything, say whatever they wish to, and that we will believe it? The answer is, *yes*. These advertisers literally believe that they have total control over the consumer's mind; they truly think that consumers will accept whatever they are told. This is called the *passive audience theory*.

According to the **passive audience theory**, consumers' minds sit there, passively, and absorb whatever is thrown at them. Does it really work that way? Only infrequently, and in a very limited way. We might get irritated a bit, or pay no mind, and whatever little does happen to stick in our minds might stay there for some time. Perhaps we will remember the brand name; and if there is a fairly simple message (e.g., "It now comes in three colors."), we might absorb that message without thinking it over.

Diametrically opposite is the *active audience theory*. The **active audience theory** holds that consumers are actively processing the information in the ad, and that it is they who are persuading themselves. Here is how to prove it. After showing consumers an ad, ask them what they think of the advertised brand. Their answers will contain ideas that were not there in the ad to begin with! Let us repeat, they will give you totally new "arguments" about the brand—arguments the advertiser didn't even make in the ad. This is proof that, rather than passively absorbing the information, consumers are actively debating an ad's message and generating their own arguments—what are known as, *cognitive responses*.[17] **Cognitive responses** are simply the thoughts generated in the mind upon exposure to a message.

Indeed, to understand why consumers were or were not persuaded by an ad, marketers conduct ad processing research. Consumers are shown an ad and are then asked to write down everything that came to mind while viewing the ad. Each unit of thought (usually each sentence), called a *cognitive response*, is then coded into one of these three categories: (a) support arguments (e.g., "Yes, if it is made with no preservatives, then it is healthier."), (b) counter arguments (e.g., "How could such a big car be fuel-efficient?"), and (c) source derogation (e.g., "What does this spokesperson know about gizmos!?"). If you also measure consumers' overall attitudes toward the advertised brand, you will find that:

Attitude toward the advertised brand = f((support arguments – counter arguments) – source derogation), where f is some "function" or coefficient.

Across consumers, then, those for whom "support minus counter minus source derogation arguments" are fewer will be less persuaded than those who generated more positive than negative arguments. This method helps advertisers diagnose and then change those elements of the ad that might be causing the negative cognitive argument.[18]

You must already be suspecting that such active processing—generating cognitive arguments—must be occurring only for high involvement topics/consumers. You are right. Low involvement advertising works in a different way.

HOW LOW INVOLVEMENT ADVERTISING WORKS

Recall the *passive audience theory*; yes, we do look at commercials this way, acting like couch potatoes—lazy and passive, mentally speaking, of course, but only when we are not involved in the advertised brand, which is most of the time. In what kinds of products are we uninvolved? Well trivial products like super market items. What about cars, cell phones, refrigerators, or home security? Yes, these are important, but we are not really involved in processing any information about these products either, unless, of course, one of them breaks down and we need to buy it again. It doesn't matter, then, whether the product is a high or low involvement product by itself (meaning, whether it is expensive or low in cost, among other things); instead, most of the advertising hits us in our low involvement mode—when we are not paying attention. So, what good is this advertising if consumers are not paying attention? Actually, a lot, and precisely *because* consumers are not paying attention. This is an intriguing paradox. Here is how it works:[19]

When we are in a low involvement mode, our minds are on strike, so to speak; we do not want to exert our faculty of arguing. We are not paying attention, but a little bit of information gets through and becomes lodged in our minds. When the ad is repeated several times, a lot of information in the ad eventually succeeds in lodging itself in our minds—minds that were passive, and absorbing information unwillingly but also unknowingly, like sponges. When we are highly involved, in contrast, we are alert, and we actively counter-argue; but when we are not involved, we are uninterested. At the same time, and by virtue of our lack of interest, all of our defenses are down! What an opportunity for a commercial message! Now you have it: Most advertising doesn't do much on any single occasion, because we are not paying attention; but by repeated exposure, that advertising succeeds in making an impression on our minds, sometimes an even better impression than if we had been paying attention and scrutinizing the message.

Attitude Toward the Ad

Have you sometimes noticed that an ad is cute, but you still don't think much of the product? Or alternatively, that you find the ad annoying, but you buy the product anyway? Does your opinion of the ad itself affect what you think of the product? The answer is that sometimes it does, and sometimes it does not.

Here is what happens. In the high involvement mode, we pay close attention to the message, and, based on that close attention, we form brand beliefs. Based on these brand beliefs, we will buy the product, despite an annoying or unlikable ad. Or, alternatively, based on brand beliefs, we will not like the brand and will not buy it, despite a likable ad. Now then, it is not that the likability or unlikability of the ad has not played a role. It has, but it is only one of the factors, and, for high involvement products, it is a relatively less important factor. The more important factor is the message content and resulting brand beliefs. And where brands are otherwise comparable and the consumer loyalty or preference is divided between two brands, the one with a likable ad might well win.

For the low involvement consumer, on the other hand, brand beliefs are hardly there, and whatever few brand beliefs are there, they may not play a major role. Instead, the ad itself acts as a peripheral element, which can then play a major role in creating brand

1-800-CALL DHL   www.dhl.com

WE EAT, DRINK AND SLEEP YOUR BUSINESS.
THEN WE COME BACK FOR SECONDS.

Customer service is back in shipping.   *DHL*

Low Involvement advertising* works by repeated exposure to simple messages. But involvement or no involvement, all ads have to be interesting, perhaps low-involvement ads even more so. DHL here delivers a significant message—that it serves its customers with zeal, dedication, even enjoyment ("We come back for more."). Its challenge, and accomplishment, in these ads is to say it simply, with strong visual brand identification.

*Recall that low involvement is a characteristic of the target consumer, not of the ad itself; thus by "low involvement advertising," a convenient phrase in use by consumer researchers, we mean advertising directed at consumers who are not much involved in the product at the time. (Images Courtesy of DHL and its ad agency, Ogilvy Mather.)

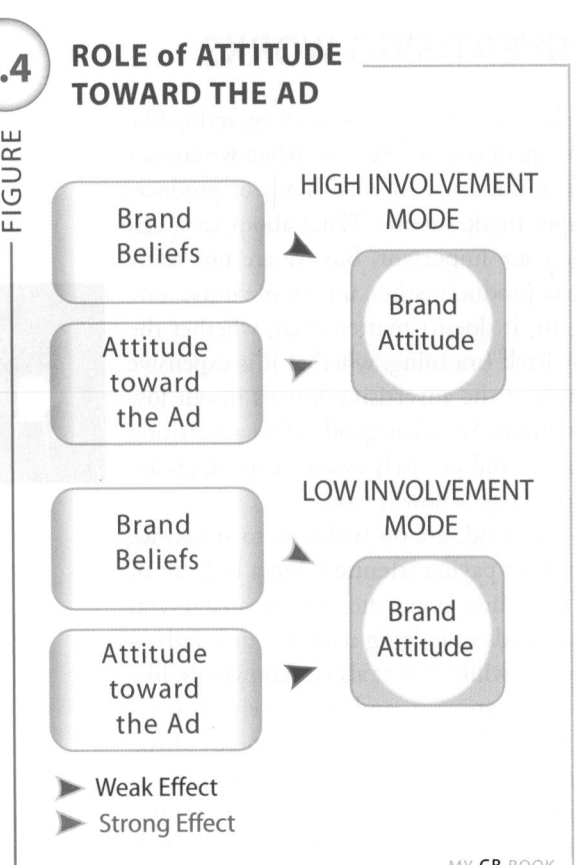

FIGURE 8.4   ROLE of ATTITUDE TOWARD THE AD

HIGH INVOLVEMENT MODE

Brand Beliefs → Brand Attitude

Attitude toward the Ad → Brand Attitude

LOW INVOLVEMENT MODE

Brand Beliefs → Brand Attitude

Attitude toward the Ad → Brand Attitude

▶ Weak Effect
▶ Strong Effect

— MY **CB** BOOK

attitude. And that's why *attitude-toward-the-ad* itself matters a lot for low involvement products; indeed, that's why low involvement product ads should be likable, interesting, and entertaining.[20] See Figure 8.4.

This does not mean that high involvement ads can afford to be dull and boring; rather, given a strong message, they might work *despite* the ad being boring. Involvement or not, it still behooves ad creators to try to make every ad *engaging*.

APPEAL TYPES

The Anatomy of an Ad

If an ad itself can contribute to the resulting brand attitude, it behooves us to look at the ad messages themselves. Are some message appeals more effective than others, and under what conditions? How do various appeals work or not work on the consumer mind? The main types of appeals are: (a) emotional versus rational, (b) humor, (c) fear, (c) sexual, (d) two-sided versus one-sided, and (e) comparative versus non-comparative.

Emotional versus Rational Appeals

Whereas rational appeals are made to mold our thoughts, emotional appeals are made to mold our feelings. Because, as humans, we experience many emotions, emotional

Beverages are a "low involvement" category. The attitude-toward-the-ad plays a big role in consumer attitude toward the brand, or at least toward the idea of trying out the brand. In low involvement conditions, consumers tend to process ads visually, and this ad with its vivid, eye-catching imagery, seems a winner.
(Image courtesy Brawndo Co.)

appeals can use one or more of the following emotions:

- **Romance—"Buy some chocolate and feel the romance."**
- **Sympathy—"Please donate to feed the hungry."**
- **Altruism—An appeal to deeper goodness in us (e.g., "Donate your time to church activities.").**
- **Ego-massaging—"You deserve it; you have earned it."**
- **Relationships and nostalgia—An appeal to evoke memories of deep connections (e.g., "This anniversary, make her a bride again; buy her a second diamond.")**
- **Fantasy and excitement—"Dream on. Buy this car and imagine _____ hitching a ride with you."**

Obviously, emotional appeals primarily work best for expressive products, whereas rational appeals are required (and work better) for functional products.[21]

Humor Appeals

Humor works by:

- **Aiding exposure—Preventing zapping and zipping, i.e., having consumers not want to avoid the commercial by switching channels (zapping) or by fast-forwarding while watching a prerecorded program (zipping).**
- **Holding attention—Getting people to listen to or watch the ad (rather than shift their attention to something else);**
- **Helping memory—Making people remember the ad because they remember the joke.**
- **Gratification: The enjoyment people derive from the use of media. It leaves a pleasant feeling by having amused the consumer, which then rubs off on the brand.[22]**
- **Multiplier effect—Repeated self-rehearsal. People like to tell jokes and talk about funny commercials; doing so further helps memorizing.**

Humor works best when:

- **Consumers already have a positive attitude toward the brand. (With initially negative consumer attitudes, humor might work only if it is self-deprecating.)**
- **The product is low in involvement.**
- **The product is not upscale, and gravitas is not the aspired positioning for the brand.**
- **The product pokes fun at itself (rather than at other brands or other people).**
- **The joke and brand message are integrated. For example, in an airline ad, a man comes home with flowers for his wife. He begins to undress (to bare briefs) as he walks toward the interior of the house, only to discover his in-laws waiting. The airline was promoting its cheap fares! (Had this ad been for a company selling flowers, the humor would have stood unconnected with the message.)**

Remember, humor can backfire when:

- **The ad makes fun of a specific group.**
- **The ad is in bad taste, relative to the sophistication or culture of the audience.**

Below, we leave you with a few examples of recent ads with humor. Judge for yourself whether and how humor would work in these ads.

- **Brand Energizer's Pink Bunny shows up in all the places (e.g., in the shower).**
- **Cheaptickets.com: A father and son are standing at the edge of a public swimming pool. The son points out a quarter on the pool deck, and the father lets go of the son (who falls into the pool) just to get the quarter. Tagline: We like cheap customers!**

This chuckle-inducing campaign from Chick-Fill-A has endured for years. One of the most outstanding illustrations of the use of humor in advertising, this ad manages both to amuse and to homes in on the brand message at the same time.
(Image courtesy of Chick-Fill-A Company)

Coke Sues Coke Zero:
How a Brand Uses Humor to Drive a Brand Benefit Home

In 2005, Coca-Cola Company launched a new brand extension: Coca-Cola Zero, a diet cola product with zero calories, intended for those consumers who might not have been attracted to Diet Coke, because of the word "diet" in the name, or because of its taste. The brand's principal benefit claim: whereas it has zero calories, it tastes exactly like its flagship brand Coca-Cola Classic. The challenge: How to communicate this to consumers.

The brand's marketing people and its advertising agency, Crispin Porter+Bogusky, came up with an idea. Two managers (supposedly from the Classic Coke division) would become upset that Coke Zero tasted exactly like Coke Classic did, and would want to sue Coke Zero (supposedly another division of the company). In the commercials that the ad agency produced, the two brand executives are seen consulting with their corporate lawyers about the possibility of suing Coke Zero, while the

lawyers, perplexed and even annoyed, inform them that one division of the company can't sue another division of the same company.

The grapevine has it that the corporate lawyers (who were indeed Coca-Cola Company legal counselors) were unaware that the two Coke Classic managers were two actors hired by Coke Zero: in other words, the counselors were part of a scene being enacted for a commercial to market Coke Zero! In effect, the lawyers were punked!

It is this "staged authenticity" that makes the commercial so believable, and so enjoyable. While its humor is delightful, and the scene induces enough of a chuckle to make the buzz (in the so-called viral marketing campaign), it executes its core message loud and clear: Coke Zero tastes exactly like Coke Classic. So, now take your pick.

MY **CB** BOOK

Fear Appeals

Fear Appeals bring home the severity of the impending consequences, but they can also alienate consumers if the ads do not offer immediate remedial steps that are feasible. The fear induced should not be very strong. And message arguments or sources should be strong enough to discourage counter arguing.[23] Fear works best when:

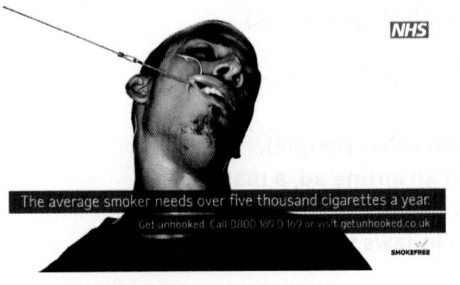

NHS

The average smoker needs over five thousand cigarettes a year.
Get unhooked. Call 0800 169 0 169 or visit getunhooked.co.uk

SMOKEFREE

Fear appeal at work.
(from NHS, U.K.)

- **Consumers are not sufficiently motivated. It raises the problem's salience; it can help to lift consumers out of apathy and inaction.**
- **The solution is clear and not too difficult to implement.**

Fear may backfire if consumers can't implement the solution or decide they do not want to. Then there is, for them, only one option—to dismiss the threat and disparage the fear-mongering ad.

Most consumers have self-selectivity bias—they dismiss a negative-consequence ad by rationalizing, "It won't happen to me." To counter this tendency, an ad should show not only the risk consequences but also the risk probability as well. A current TV commercial for Zocor (a cholesterol-control medication) shows two identical and perfectly normal looking persons going about their chores, when one of them falls down suddenly—due to high cholesterol. The message: "Anyone may be suffering from high cholesterol!"

Sexual Appeals

Sexual appeals come in two forms: (a) sexual suggestiveness and nudity, and (b) sexual themes or romance. They induce emotions through arousal, excitement, even lust. This type of appeal is implemented in one of the following forms:

- Skin is shown.
- The female and/or male body is shown in suggestive poses.
- Couples are shown in an intimate embrace, especially in states of partial undress.
- Sexual innuendo is presented in the text. Two examples from past ads: "Does she or doesn't she?" And "Nooner" (for Houlihan's Restaurants offering quick lunch service).

Sexual appeals work by[24]:
- **At the very least, attracting and holding attention.**
- **Raising the salience of the brand-name.**

This type of appeal can backfire when:
- **Sexual standards of a culture are violated.**
- **Sexual appeal is unrelated to the message.**

Even if it doesn't backfire, a suggestive ad may simply fail to accomplish anything at all, when it doesn't relate to the product's message. In a now-famous 2005 commercial for Carl's Jr./Hardee's, Paris Hilton is shown in a revealing bathing suit, striking sexy poses while washing a car and eating a burger. The ad received a lot of publicity, but it did very little for Carl's Jr./ Hardee's sales.

Sexual appeals work best when:
- **They are integral to some product benefit; e.g., for colognes, yes, but for hamburgers, no.**
- **The use of sex is tongue-in-cheek. In one of the now famous GoDaddy.com ads, female employees suggestively unbutton their tops to reveal their T-shirts with the GoDaddy logo, making a point to a (female) job applicant that, if hired, she will have to wear one of these T-shirts.[25]**

Note also that simply showing flesh—even a lot of it—does not automatically make an ad sexual—or at least it does not make the ad sexual in a bad sense. The human body is, after all, a beautiful thing, and it can be shown with class and celebrated, so to speak. Two campaigns come to mind. In a campaign released in 2004 (and still running), a Dove ad shows a lot of skin (with women in underwear). However, because its pretext is to show realistic consumers in many shapes and sizes, the ad is unlikely to produce any lewd thoughts. Instead, it is likely to enhance the perceived relevance of the ad. Another example is a 2005 print ad by Pirelli showing a totally naked, statuesque male body, ready to sprint off a tire. (See www.Pirelli.com.)

Two-Sided (Versus One-Sided) Appeals

One-sided or two-sided—that is the question. **Two-sided messages** present both the merits and demerits of a product, brand, or issue. Consequently, they help by raising the credibility of the advertising company itself. They also break the initial resistance consumers have toward any advertising in general ("Here comes another self-hyping commercial!"), especially for a consumer with an initially negative view of the brand.

Research has found that two-sided messages work better when the audience is initially opposed to an issue or has an unfavorable attitude toward the brand. For consumers already in favor of the brand, one-sided messages are more persuasive.[26]

There are two ways of making brand messages two-sided. In one version, you acknowledge the shortcomings of your brand while promoting its merits. In a milder version, you acknowledge "no superiority" of your brand on some less important features, and then claim superiority on the more important features.[27]

The negative side acknowledges the brand's past mistakes or inherent shortcomings and, consequently, makes the company look more honest. (The simplest example is, of course, "Yes, we are expensive, but we are worth it.") The negative side also *immunizes* against a competitor's potential negative advertising (i.e., by anticipating counter messages).

Use a two-sided message when the negative pertains to a minor attribute and when involvement is high. Don't use two-sided or comparative messages for low involvement consumers—the negative side may stick.

Two-sided messages work best when:
- **A negative attribute is already well-known and is acting as a blocker of consumer preference, and you can explain it away.**
- **The negative attribute is a minor irritant. You present it in the context of other benefits, thus trying to switch consumer evaluation from, say, a lexicographic to a compensatory mode. (These modes are described in Chapter 11.)**
- **You can refute a negative.**
- **The message shows humility: Acknowledging the brand's weakness can lower audience**

Broccoli and Tofu
To change your consumers' attitudes, would you use a one-sided or a two-sided appeal?

defenses, putting the audience in a more receptive mood. (This is especially effective when it shows a human weakness, when the weakness is "unavoidable," or when it is not under the marketer's control.)

- You can explain that the negative attribute was necessary to get the positive benefits.

Example: "When is a diet pill worth $153? When it works, really works." (TV Commercial for *Leptoprin* seen recently). Also, the same brand uses another two-sided message to this effect: "When you need to lose only 5 or 10 pounds, Leptoprin is not for you; use other products. But when you need to lose 20, 30, or even 50 pounds, consider Leptoprin." [Note: The author implies no endorsement of this product and claims no knowledge of it—beyond having watched the ad.]

Two-sided messages also work because of a phenomenon called *immunization* or *inoculation*. "My opponent will tell you that I have tried marijuana. Let me tell you under what circumstances." This is a hypothetical quote. By admitting it before hand, the speaker is prepping you, the voter, for an imminent accusation by the opposition party. This is called **inoculation theory**.[28]

"Our competitors can offer you a cheaper price, but ask them whether they use sweat shops" is the kind of inoculation that can save firms some lost customers when competitors come charging with their lower price messages.

Comparative (Versus Non-comparative) Advertising[29]

In **comparative advertising**, the advertised brand compares itself to competing products or brands. There are two versions of this approach: direct and indirect. In the direct version, the advertiser names a specific competitor; in the indirect version, the brand simply mentions competitors as a group, as in "compare with leading brands." The direct version is bolder, but it also must stand on truth—i.e., the claim of superiority being made must in fact have been proven. Direct-comparison advertising works best for utilitarian products with objectively measurable and demonstrable features.[30]

Sometimes a brand compares itself, not to other brands, but to another product category. For example, a Lifesavers ad once showed a page full of the mints against a single cherry, with the one-line copy: "There is more sugar in this cherry than in all these Lifesavers!" Comparative advertising works well for smaller brands; this is because people feel sympathy for an underdog brand. Avis' now famous "We try harder; we are only #2" illustrates this type of advertising.

An extreme form of indirect comparison is "implicit comparison" or comparison by implication only. Here, the competitor is not named at all; however, viewers who have suffered the competition can make the connection. A recent Discover Card print ad proclaims: "In less than a minute, you get a knowledgeable live person."

Remember, all such tricks are culture-specific. In the non-combative, cooperative cultures of the East, comparative ads may not go over well, especially if they are too brutal. Economic interests do rule supreme everywhere, so if your ad pointed out some real difference that consumers value, then consumers would like it because they will benefit from it. Yet it shouldn't be too harsh or cruel. Do it gently.[31]

SOURCE CREDIBILITY

Consumer persuasion depends not just on the message but also on the source's credibility. A **source** is any person or organization that is conveying a message or stands behind the message. At the most obvious level, the source is the person shown in the ad. Where no person is shown, the source is the company marketing the product. Actually, even when there is a spokesperson, the ultimate source is always the marketer, although some consumers may never consciously think of this ultimate source.

Types of Sources Sources are of the following types: (a) stars and celebrities, (b) experts, (c) company spokespersons, (d) actors and ad models, (e) real users, real people who are unidentified, and (f) real people identified by name. Have you ever wondered how advertisers decide what type of source to use? If you were an advertiser, what source would you use? To answer that question, you have to understand some things about source characteristics.

Source Characteristics There are three characteristics of sources that affect persuasion: credibility, attractiveness, and similarity. **Source credibility** refers to how credible (believable or trustworthy) the source is judged to be by the target audience. Credibility depends, in turn, on two sub-characteristics: source expertise and source independence. Judgments of **source expertise** are made based upon the profession, education, or personal experience of the source. Thus, a doctor promoting a drug, or a sportsperson promoting a sports shoe, or a computer professor promoting software, will all garner credibility, whereas a claim that "I am not a doctor but play one on TV" will not.[32]

Source independence refers to the separation of the source from the company that would benefit from the message. Independent sources such as *Consumer Reports*, product critics in the media (e.g., restaurant reviews published in newspapers and magazines), and unpaid spokespersons earn their credibility by virtue of their independence. Professionals shown in the ads are often paid by the advertiser, but the public either doesn't know or doesn't dwell on such payments. Some consumers assume, often correctly, that, fee or no fee,

Flies 21 feet into the air
Makes birds jealous

For Silk Soymilk, Kirsten Lawton, champion trampolinist, lends her support. Her profession requires good health, strength, agility, and energy for the "day's work." As an ace trampolinist, she soars high, and so does *source credibility* for this ad. (Image used with permission.)

the professionals have a code of not lying just for the money. It is assumed also that the professionals who claim that they benefit from a product do actually use that product.

The second source characteristic that determines a source's effectiveness is **source attractiveness**—the quality of making an emotional connection with the viewer. Often this quality comes, literally, from the source's physical appearance or talent. Stars and celebrities are, in their very physical persona, attractive, and they inspire a viewer's own pro-message attitude because viewers aspire to be like them. R&B superstar and nine-time Grammy winner Alicia Keys is featured in an infomercial for Proactiv Solution (an acne eradicating cream—a good commercial if you want to see the normally not seen acne-spotted face of the music diva). And on the company's Web site, www.proactiv.com, you can watch a video featuring Vanessa Williams! Incidentally, another recent product promotion Alicia Keys recently (2009) did was for Glacéau's Vitaminwater.

In these examples, these celebrities bring to the brand, by logical inference-making on consumers' part, mainly a utilitarian benefit (eradicating acne is important to these public faces, and therefore the brand must really be effective in eradicating acne), although some "social" and "ego/identity" benefits (by a classical conditioning-based association made by consumers) might also accrue.

Using celebrities, however, does have a few drawbacks (in addition to costing the advertiser a lot of money, that is). Consumers often dismiss, as unattainable, the product benefits that celebrities imply or proclaim (e.g., "Paris Hilton is beautiful to begin with, so of course this makeup product works on her. But it won't work on me."). Consumers may also, as a sort of a defense mechanism, reject the physical beauty or talent of these stars as unworthy of pursuit. In short, the stars are considered to be too different from the consumer.

The third and last characteristic that influences persuasion is **source similarity**, which refers to how similar to themselves consumers judge the spokesperson to be. This is the reason ordinary people used as spokespersons may sometimes have a more persuasive effect on the audience than would a celebrity. This is also why a lot of advertisers have always used models that look like most of us. Lately, even star-heavy brands such as Nike have

> **A Step Forward To Ensure Source Independence**
>
> Effective December 1, 2009, bloggers in the U.S. must declare, by law, any freebees they have received from companies about whose products they have blogged. Penalties include up to $11,000 in fines per violation and reimbursements to consumers of blogger-endorsed products.

resorted to depicting more realistic women in their ads.

Next question: How would you make the ad messages themselves credible? Answer: By one of these strategies:

1. **State the facts.** Support the message with statistics, objective numbers, etc.;
2. **Cite authorities** (e.g., JD Powers, government studies, etc.);
3. **Obtain testimonials from experts, and real users; and**
4. **Build corporate reputation.** Your company's reputation carries the strongest weight in message credibility;

One potent means of making a message more credible is by avoiding any hype. One recent advertiser went further: "Aleve helps me play, but it does not make me a better player." We will call it *preemptive anti-hype*. It takes guts, and it takes sincerity.

MATCH-UP HYPOTHESIS

You wouldn't use Gwen Stefani to pitch, say, the economic manifesto of the Republican Party's next presidential candidate, would you? Or ask U.S. Treasury Secretary Timothy Franz Geithner to pitch a new brand of grunge clothing, would you? No. This obvious or conventional wisdom is technically called **match-up hypothesis**—the celebrity chosen for promoting a brand should have an image similar to the brand's image (or desired image). Celebrity sources have, as you know, two different kinds of appeal: expertise and attractiveness. Decide which one you need for your brand and seek that kind of celebrity.[33] Moreover, within each kind, you should match the specific image you desire for the brand; e.g., Gwen Stefani for Hot Topic and Brittany Spears for Bebe, for example, but not the other way round; Robert Kiyosaki (Author of *Rich Dad Poor Dad*) for financial investments and CNN's Dr. Sanjay Gupta for stem cell research.

Now, you could, of course, pair Hollywood star Angelina Jolie and Columbia University economist Jeffery Sachs to film a documentary on the economy of Kenya—this innovative idea was implemented by MTV in late 2005. How and why this teaming idea satisfies a match-up hypothesis—and satisfy it certainly does—is a question we will leave you to ponder. Or *Bing* it. (*Bing*—a Microsoft Web search engine, launched in June 2009).

PERSUASION IN INTERPERSONAL SELLING
GETTING CUSTOMERS TO LIKE YOU

A special kind of source is a salesperson. A real human being communicates with consumers face-to-face or on the phone. How does persuasion work for the salesperson? No matter how deserving your message, if your audience does not like you, the messenger, they are not going to hear your message. Every salesperson first has to get the customer to like him or her as a person. And in the game of life, everyone is a salesperson. So, here is how to get others to like you.[34]

You could meet a total stranger, and, within five minutes, that person can decide whether or not he or she likes you. How does that happen? Basically there are five factors at work: (1) good looks, (2) common ground, (3) aspirational persona, (4) utility, and (5) being liked in return. Let us briefly discuss each.

Good Looks   Let's face it, other things being equal, looks matter. We are perhaps biologically wired to feel pleasant when we look at a person with good looks. This is unfair, but let us note that, to look good, one doesn't have to be a beauty queen or a handsome body builder. Personal grooming and a happy facial expression can make most of us look good. That is why most service establishments have personal grooming prescriptions, and many explicitly advertise "hiring happy faces."

Common Ground   The second factor that creates affinity between two persons is some "common ground," i.e., the sharing of some characteristic. This can be a common ethnic background, profession, technical background, alma mater ("Oh, you are a Hoosier too!"), common interest and hobbies, or a common favorite sports team. Sometimes even an indirect similarity of background or interest helps (e.g., "You are from Belgium? My brother lived there once!")

Aspirational Persona If we find out that a person has a quality we admire or to which we aspire, we immediately begin to look at that person in a favorable way. This is why we like sports personalities and other celebrities; this is also why we have role models in our lives. However, this is also the reason we can develop an instant liking for someone we have just met. If we come to know that the person we are meeting is an accomplished author (perhaps textbooks don't count!), or a champion chess player, or is heavily involved in community work, etc., then we might find that person inspiring; we might find his or her persona to be something we would aspire to. Consequently, he or she would earn our respect, and in turn, our liking.

Utility The fourth factor relates to whether the person can be of some use to us. If two persons move into the neighborhood, we like the one who has a pick-up truck and would be willing to loan it to us. We like a classmate who can teach us how to prepare a multi-media presentation. We like a salesperson who can give us free product samples. Whereas all other factors are psychological/emotional, the prospect of any utilitarian gains is, here, the only rational consideration. Too rational, actually—devoid of valuing a person as a person.

Being Liked Finally, the single most important factor is knowing that the other person likes us. We like people who like us. Period. It doesn't matter if they have nothing else to offer, we like them because they like us. Alternatively, no matter how much talent they have and how useful they might be, if we sense that they don't like us, then we won't like them, either. And of course, the more we think that they like us, the more we like them.[35]

CB Blog

8

The Grand Persuader: The Consumer Herself

We all want others to see the world our way. That is the crux of attitude change. How we form our attitudes, and once formed how we modify them, is not random or arbitrary.

Are you frustrated as marketers that sometimes it is just impossible to persuade consumers, knowledge of the underlying theories (covered in this chapter) notwithstanding? Why? Don't the same theories explain why persuasion will NOT occur?

It would be presumptuous to believe that as a marketer you have the power to mastermind consumer attitudes. Consumers, most of the time, persuade themselves (remember the "active audience" theory); your job is simply to provide the right information the right way. Yes, sometimes, or even often, consumers absorb information passively. Sure, sometimes, they let the ad and commercial communication do its trick on their unguarded minds. But that too is their choosing—certain matters are simply not important enough to them. It is consumers who choose, in life and in the marketplace, what messages they will soak in unguarded and what they will accept and with what sort of message-validity indicators (remember "source credibility"?). Once again, if you read these parameters of the consumer mind correctly, then you will be able to fashion your message so that it agrees with consumers' modes of persuading themselves.

Wouldn't you as a consumer want to keep personal autonomy and allow marketers to guide your attitudes in a manner that serves, merely but amicably, your own modes and goals of self-persuasion? Why should it be any different when the roles are reversed—i.e., when you become the marketer and assume a persuader's role?

And it is just as well that marketers can't mold consumer attitudes any which way they like. That way, both the fur merchant and PETA have an equal opportunity to lure the consumer mind, err, to serve consumers' agendas of self-persuasion.

CONSUMER BEHAVIOR

MY CB BOOK .COM

SUMMARY

This chapter gave us a repertoire of techniques to mold and change consumer attitudes, many of which are segregated according to low and high involvement. To begin with, the Involvement and Think-Feel Grid showed us how products and consumer concerns can be positioned by a low/high involvement level and by whether the consumer decision is a rational (thinking) or an emotional (feeling) decision. Persuasive messages then have to be crafted accordingly. Also related to involvement levels, two modes of processing—peripheral and central—were described, and movement from the peripheral to the central mode was captured in the model called the Elaboration Likelihood Model (ELM). The multi-attribute model of attitude of the previous chapter was also shown to offer us three different options for molding consumer attitudes.

Next, we made acquaintance with (a) Heider's Balance Theory, (b) attribution theory, (c) self-perception theory, and (d) active versus passive audience theory. Heider's Balance Theory helps us resolve the dilemma we face when a person we love or admire is friendly toward a product or issue we detest. Attribution theory explains attitude change as a process wherein we as consumers internally answer "why" something happened.

Self-perception theory works akin to the attribution theory's precepts: We infer our attitudes by attributing the cause of our behavior to our own attitudes! Finally, active versus passive audience theory portrays consumers as passive recipients versus active thinkers when they are exposed to a message. When in the active mode, consumers generate their own arguments, called *cognitive responses*, which, rather than the message's original content *per se*, then determine the resulting attitude.

Attitude toward the ad itself was identified as an influencer of brand attitude, albeit in a less or more intense fashion, depending on the level of involvement. Given the role of the ad in brand attitude molding, we looked at various appeal types. We reviewed (a) emotional, (b) humor, (c) fear, (d) sexual, (e) one- versus two-sided, and (f) comparative messages, describing their relative effectiveness. In this context, we also came to understand how source characteristics make ad spokespersons and celebrities effective or ineffective.

We ended the chapter with a short treatise on how attitude-molding works in interpersonal encounters—how you can, in other words, get others to like you!

KEY TERMS

Active audience
Central route
Comparative advertising
Cognitive response
Door-in-the-face
Elaboration Likelihood Model
Foot-in-the-door

Heider's Balance Theory
Law of reciprocal concessions
Match-up hypothesis
Passive audience
Peripheral route
Self-perception theory
Source attractiveness

Source credibility
Source independence
Source similarity
Two-sided messages
Zipping
Zapping

YOUR TURN

REVIEW+Rewind

1. Draw the Think-Feel and Involvement Grid, and show two products in each quadrant.
2. Explain the concept of Central and Peripheral Routes to Persuasion. Explain how these concepts relate to consumer involvement.
3. Explain the Elaboration Likelihood Model and its relationship with consumer involvement.
4. Does attitude toward the ad affect consumer brand attitude? How?
5. List the three options for changing consumer attitude, using the multi-attribute model of attitude.
6. Describe Heider's balance theory, and explain how it is related to consumer attitude change.
7. What is self-perception theory and how is it related to attitude change?
8. Give an example each of "foot-in-the-door" and "door-in-the-face" strategies of attitude change.
9. Describe active versus passive audience theory and its relevance to advertising message creation.
10. Describe the conditions under which each of the following types of ad appeals is likely to work: (a) humor, (b) fear, and (c) sexual appeals.
11. Give an example of a two-sided message, and explain why and when it is likely to be more effective than a one-sided message.
12. What makes a source credible? What is the principal advantage of using a celebrity?
13. Explain the concept of *match-up hypothesis*. How does it relate to the use of celebrity in ads?

THINK+Apply

1. Suppose you have developed expertise in (a) Web site design, (b) teaching the game of chess, (c) golf tutoring, or (d) being a DJ at ethnic weddings, and you want to advertise your services. Which of the various attitude change methods would you employ for each of these services and why?

2. As an advertiser, suppose you were using a celebrity endorsement. In the midst of the campaign, a news story develops that questions the celebrity's behavior: (a) the celebrity is not actually a user of the product, (b) the celebrity faked his/her talent (e.g., a singer is caught lip-syncing) or had unethically bolstered his/her performance (e.g., an athlete is caught using steroids, etc.). For each of these instances, how would Heider's Balance Theory play out in terms of consumer attitudes toward your brand if your brand is (a) closely related to the celebrity behavior in controversy, and (b) not related to it?

3. Think of two examples each of "foot-in-the-door" and "door-in-the-face" techniques that you yourself can utilize to receive a favor from someone who is (a) a friend, or (b) a stranger.

PRACTICE+Experience

1. Next time you see a commercial for a product new to you, soon after watching it, write down all the thoughts that occurred while you were watching the commercial. Now review these thoughts and flag them as support and counter arguments. How do these thoughts relate to your overall attitude toward the advertised product?

2. Ask a few friends to write down their thoughts for any two commercials they watch during the forthcoming week, and also to rate their overall attitude toward the advertised brands. Ask them to give you only their thoughts (and keep the overall attitude ratings with them). Then score the and predict their attitude friends. How good was your why not?

3. Find an ad that uses comparative comment on whether it employs di comparison, and whether the ad woul more effective without a comparison.

4. Ask (a) a friend and (b) a total stranger for th you thought of in an earlier question. Were successful? Comment on why or why not.

5. Survey a sample of consumers to assess all three components of attitude toward vegetarianism. In the survey, include at least two vegetarians and three heavy meat eaters with a negative view of vegetarianism. How would you change the latter group's attitude so that they would consider reducing meat consumption, if not eliminate it altogether? Describe alternative approaches.

6. Visit American Legacy Foundation's Website for TRUTH campaign (legacyforhealth.org) and review its current campaign. Using everything you know about attitudes and behavior from this chapter, evaluate the campaign in terms of its potential to accomplish its goals.

In the Marketing Manager's Shoes

Put yourself in a marketing manager's shoes. Most concepts in the chapter have some lessons for the marketing manager; i.e., they suggest what to do differently in practice. Indeed, often these applications are implicit in our explanations of the concepts and models in the chapter. Identify at least five specific applications of the chapter's concepts, all of which should be entirely new, different from the examples cited here.

(Courtesy: VCD, Australia)

A Photo Quiz

Was our tagging of this ad as a "low-involvement" feeling ad (in the FCB Grid) an oversimplification? Does it not also reflect a consumer's total immersion in the brand—the consumer is totally wrapped in the brand, enchanted, and experiencing the beverage as an elixir?
In fact, the mere sight of this ad is infectious—we almost feel the mood ourselves!
Do you agree?

...sumers' Culture and Meaning Transfer

Our Shared Code for Living

Through culture
I code myself.

Through culture
you decode me.

II ► ━━━━━━━━━━ 2:30/3:00 ◀))

LEARN . APPLY . EXPERIENCE

OBJECTIVES

1 The Definition and Six Characteristics of Culture

2 Six Universal Cultural Value Dimensions

3 Cultural Practices— Rituals, Customs, and Myths

4 How Meaning Is Created and Communicated Within a Culture

5 Cross-Cultural Marketing *Faux Pas* and the Wisdom of Acculturation

6 Profiles of Selected Cultures from Around the World

Welcome to Snake Alley, Taipei: The Home of the World's Most Bizarre Beverage

Taipei, Taiwan. From the moment we arrived in Taiwan, and even beforehand, there was a constant buzz among the students about DRINKING THE SNAKE BLOOD.

At the logistical pre-port meeting the night before we docked in Keelung, the ship's physician, "Dr. Milt," stood before the student body, and, as he always did before a port of call, rattled off a list of health warnings specific to the destination. Number One on his list that evening was "Whatever you do, please don't drink the blood of snakes." He cited hepatitis and salmonella as possible complications. Only an idiot would want to expose himself or herself to either one. So, naturally, at the first opportunity, several groups of students headed for Snake Alley in Taipei to drink the snake blood. We witnessed it firsthand. But I am getting ahead of myself.

The big attraction at Snake Alley has always been, and probably always will be, the cobras. If you happen to be a cobra in Snake Alley, you are out of luck. First, you are likely to be taunted by your captor in front of a group of squirming bystanders. Then you'll get hit on the head and strung up. The crowd

Rachel Barnett, a dance major at San Jose State University (left), and Jennifer Temple, then a junior at Colorado State University, at Snake Alley

will gasp as your underbelly is slit open with a sharp knife. Your skin will be peeled back and your heart exposed, still beating. Things only get worse. Your heart is ripped out and placed on a table, where it continues to beat. Then your main artery is cut. You bleed out into a glass.

New cultures: fascinating experiences!

The bile from your gall bladder is emptied into another glass. Meanwhile, your heart is still beating over on that table. By then you probably don't care anymore. But the audience does. They are anxious to drink your body fluids. Chinese folklore holds that your essence has curative properties and can act to "strengthen masculinity." Your blood or bile will be mixed with rice wine and served in shot glasses—for a price, of course. The buyer may or may not be Chinese. That night a large number of SAS students, male and female, were scrambling over each other for a chance to chug some snake blood. ... That night, lots of the kids drank snake blood.

During the long bus ride back, a student who was apparently having second thoughts, asked our faculty biologist, "Surely it's safe to drink the snake blood. Otherwise the government wouldn't allow it?"

Hey, Dorothy, I have news for you. You're not in Kansas anymore!

(Excerpted with permission from Ginnie Saunders (www.ginnie.com)

INTRODUCTION

Do you find this practice of drinking snake blood strange? Why do certain behaviors seem strange to some people and normal to others? It all depends on culture. We will more formally define culture shortly, but for now—so we can begin to talk about it—we can think of culture simply as a way of life. And by *way of life* we mean the different things we do in everyday living and the manner in which we do them. In Taiwan, eating snakes, critters, dog parts, etc., is considered normal, whereas in many other countries, this would be unthinkable. And, of course, such differences are not limited to food. Consider some other things people do differently around the world:

- **In Asia and the Far East, young boys and girls don't date; they just marry someone their parents select. (This time-honored practice is now changing, especially among educated, urban families.) In contrast, in much of the West, extensive dating often precedes marriage between two people.**

- **In the United States, Western Europe, and Australia, most teenagers begin to earn their own money and must make many of their purchases from their own earnings or do without those products. In many Eastern countries, the young are full-time students until graduation from college, with no part-time jobs, and their parents provide for all their needs.**

- **In Amsterdam and much of the Netherlands, when you visit a restaurant, you are basically assigned a seat, not a table. So, expect to share it with a stranger. In much of Western Europe and most of North America, this would be considered absurd.**

On and on it goes. Everywhere you look, people of different cultures do things differently. And that way of doing things comes naturally to them; it is deeply ingrained. As far as they are concerned, that is the only way it is, and should be, done. This manner of doing things, this "way of life," should influence our behavior as consumers. It does—immensely and pervasively.

This chapter is about culture—that all-pervasive force in our lives. First, we define culture and describe its essential properties. We also open the big treasure box that culture is and examine its diverse contents. It includes values and norms, customs and traditions, arts and crafts, and myths and material goods. We describe the roles these entities play in consumers' lives.

We then describe how cultural values differ across societies. Culture survives and, where necessary, adapts, because it serves certain useful functions in society; we learn about these functions. Culture is, we find out, the dictionary that translates the meaning of everything we do and everything we consume. Let us see how.

CULTURE: DEFINITION

The Blueprint for Everyday Living

What is culture? **Culture** can be defined as everything humans learn from and share with members of a society. That "everything" includes both what to do and how to do it. As such, it is an unwritten blueprint for how to conduct everyday living in a society so as to fit into that society. It is the implicit knowledge we acquire simply by living in a social group or community. That implicit knowledge tells us what is deemed edible and what is not, what to wear at home and what to wear in public, how to interact with people, and what the relationships should be between men and women, between adults and children, between the preacher and her disciples, and between strangers on the street. It is part of our collective mental conditioning that makes us act properly as if it were our second nature. And because it is collective conditioning, we share it with other members of our nation, region, or group.

Learning and *sharing* are two essential processes of culture. Our biological behavior and our genetically inherited instincts are not culture, since these are not learned. Likewise, our individual, idiosyncratic behaviors are not culture, since they are not shared. Thus,

Culture:
What we learn and share

our biological nature—to feel hunger pangs, to walk with our heads at the top and legs on the ground, to smile when happy—these are all matters of our biological nature, not culture. But eating with a spoon and fork or chopsticks is a matter of culture. So too are break-dancing, covering our mouths when yawning, and not double-dipping our piece of celery.

The opposite of culture is "nature," both human and physical. Our human nature is what we are born with. And outside our bodies, physical nature exists—distinct from man-made alterations. Thus, our human nature is to be utterly selfish, but culture reins in our personal desires. And in the physical world, rivers, oceans, and trees are nature, but bridges and shirts and genetically altered foods are culture (specifically, material culture; see below).

Nature vs. Culture

ELEMENTS OF CULTURE
The Rich Contents of the Treasure Box

Because culture is everything, literally everything, that humans learn and share, it is a vast and deep treasure box, with rich contents that include the following elements:

Values **Values** are a society's ideas as to what in life is worthy of pursuit and how those pursuits should be conducted. Thus, values include desirable ends as well as desirable means to those ends. Democratic and modern societies value liberty, equality, and individual rights, for example. In contrast, in many traditional societies, individual rights are deemed subservient to the rights of the group, tribe, or clan.

Norms **Norms** are unwritten rules of behavior. They are "do's and don'ts" guides. Norms are more specific than values and dictate acceptable and unacceptable behavior. For example, to be polite to strangers is a norm in much of the civilized world; so is to lower the window shades while undressing.

Rituals **Rituals** are sets of activities performed in a fixed sequence and repeated periodically. They can be either (a) utilitarian or (b) symbolic. Utilitarian rituals have demonstrable useful outcomes. Examples include daily baths or afternoon tea (a British ritual). Symbolic rituals have no practical utility, but are followed for the sake of tradition and have symbolic meanings in specific cultures. An example is wedding rituals, which differ markedly from one society to another. Table 9.1 lists various rituals.

Customs **Customs** are ways of doing things. For example, when to wear which clothes is dictated by customs. They differ from rituals, in that a ritual is an event or activity, whereas a custom can be a ritual, but it can also be an act that is not like an event. To wear a black tie to a formal dinner is a custom (i.e., a convention), not a ritual; but for the bride and groom to do the first dance at the wedding reception is a custom and a ritual. Customs also differ from norms, in that violation of norms is strongly sanctioned, whereas violation of custom is merely ridiculed.

Myths **Myths** are stories that express some key values of a society. For example, the story of Santa Claus is a myth in much of the Christian world. It expresses the value that if you live your life as a "good" person, then good things will come to you (e.g., Santa will bring you gifts).

Knowledge, Science, and Technology All knowledge is also culture. Knowledge is fundamentally the basis of beliefs on which we base our actions. Only a century ago, many people, especially in underdeveloped countries, believed that sickness and disease were curses from evil spirits. Based on this belief, they shunned all medication and would instead commission voodoo rites to exorcise the ghost of the evil spirits. The modern age of enlightenment and scientific advances sets us culturally far apart from the societies of yesteryear.

Science and technology are also culture, since they are learned and shared and reflect a society's belief and practice in attaining mastery over nature. The large-scale adoption of microwave cooking, wireless communications, and eyeglasses is as much a part of our culture as is the absence of these same things from such protected societies as the Amish.

Laws Laws are norms with legal sanctions. For example, smoking in a friend's house

VALUES

NORMS

RITUALS

CUSTOMS

MYTHS

KNOW-LEDGE

LAWS

ARTS

TABLE

9.1	VARIOUS RITUALS IN SOCIETY
RITUAL	**EXAMPLES**
Exchange rituals	Giving gifts; the practice of dowry in India (now illegal but still practiced covertly by many).
Possession rituals	House warming party; worship ceremony in many Asian countries before starting a business.
Grooming rituals	Bathing; using or not using scents and perfumes.
Divestment rituals	Redecorating a house; exorcising ghosts and spirits.
Religious rituals	Going to church on Sundays (Christians); praying five times a day (Muslims).
Rites of passage	Marriage, graduation , birthday, and so on.
Social rituals	Greeting, empathizing, mentoring, mating, and so on.
Family rituals	Mealtime, bedtime, story-time, and so on.

MY CB BOOK

may violate a norm but is not illegal. In contrast, smoking inside an airplane is now illegal and punishable. A society's laws reflect that society's values. For example, the anti-cloning law recently passed by the U.S. Congress reflects our values about the dignity of human life. Similarly, the anti-dowry law in India passed in 1971 reflects modern Indian society's values of equality of the sexes and the dignity of women.

Arts   The arts—music, painting, literature, etc.—are also culture. They represent a society's appreciation of the aesthetic experience; often the arts of an era and of a society also represents its values, obsessions, and life-conditions.

Material Culture   Finally, all man-made objects are also part of culture. They represent the degree of affluence and progress of a society in contrast to the life lived entirely in and with nature. It may at first appear jarring to you, but the fact is that all man-made materials and man-made objects are part of our culture—thus, the chairs, cell phones, wines and beers, and toupees—all represent culture, specifically **material** culture.

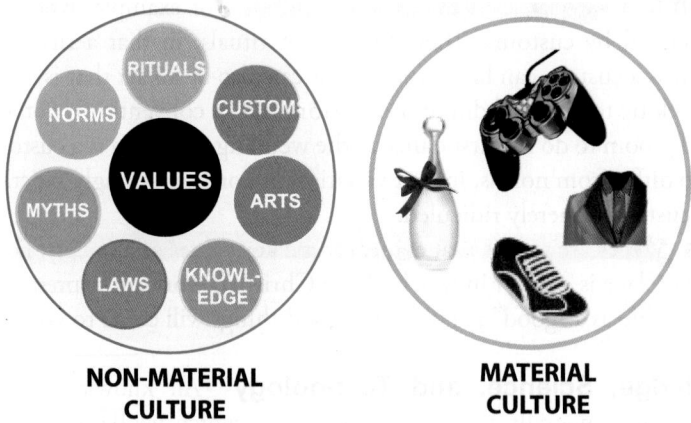

NON-MATERIAL CULTURE

MATERIAL CULTURE

Getting Culture—How Do We Learn It?

How do we learn our culture, as children and as adults? Learning one's own culture is called **enculturation**. Learning a new culture is called **acculturation**. Enculturation happens during childhood, mostly, as we are growing and learning the ways of the world. Acculturation happens when we migrate to a new society, or when we befriend persons from other cultures. Immigrants learn the host culture by acculturation, even as they retain the culture of their country of birth. As part of this culture, they also learn new consumer behaviors.

CHARACTERISTICS OF CULTURE

Every concept, every thing has certain characteristics—the essential, defining properties of that thing or concept. Culture also has characteristics—six of them (see Figure 9.1).

First, **culture is learned.** We are not born with it. Accordingly, instinctive behavior, which we possess from birth, is not culture. Thus, the act of crying or laughing is not culture; however, knowing when it is proper to cry or laugh in public is culture, since that is something we have to learn. Some cultures, such as the Chinese culture, "condition" people not to express emotions in public, whereas Italians learn to be very expressive of their emotions in public. If we lived in America, Canada, or Britain, for example, and if we moved to, say, Japan, South Africa, or Egypt, then we would have to learn the local culture—do's and don'ts of food, clothing, and social interaction.

Second, **culture regulates society**. Culture makes everyone behave. It does so by offering norms and standards of behavior and by sanctioning any deviations from those norms. Everyone in a culture knows what rules to live by. Life runs smoothly because, for example, we queue up in supermarkets and at bus stops, we don't toss garbage in our neighbors' yards, we show up on time for meetings, and we don't abuse, slight, or inconvenience strangers on the street or other shoppers in the mall.

Third, **culture makes living more efficient.** Because culture is shared (by definition), we don't have to learn things anew as we encounter new people and new situations within the same culture. Once you have learned the Egyptian culture, for example, you can use the same etiquette in interacting with all Egyptians. Living in your own culture, you know whether to take a gift and what gift to take when invited to someone's house, so you do it without having to think up a new "solution" for every host.

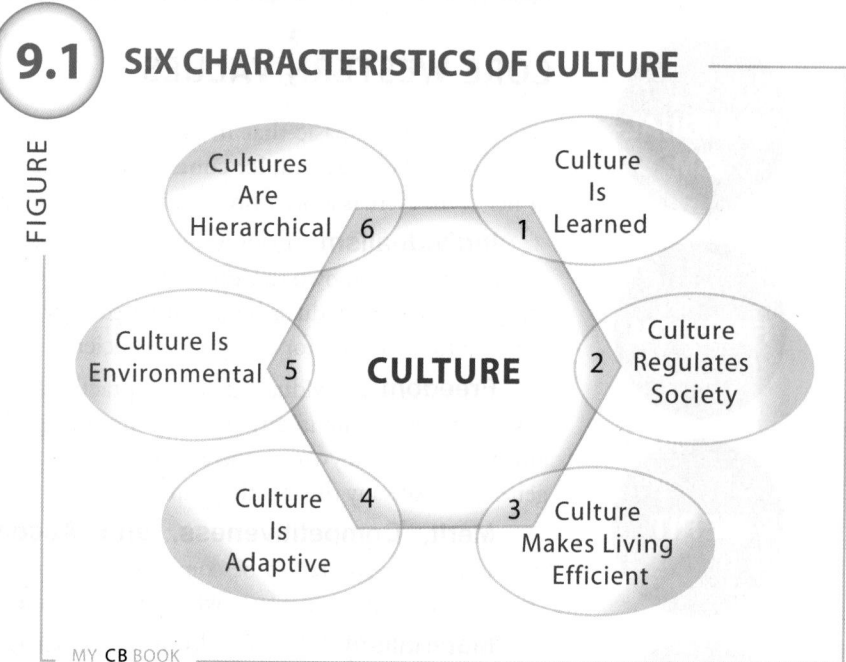

FIGURE

9.1 SIX CHARACTERISTICS OF CULTURE

- Cultures Are Hierarchical — 6
- Culture Is Learned — 1
- Culture Is Environmental — 5
- CULTURE
- Culture Regulates Society — 2
- Culture Is Adaptive — 4
- Culture Makes Living Efficient — 3

MY **CB** BOOK

Fourth, **culture is adaptive.** Culture is a human response to the environment, and as the environment changes, culture is likely to adapt itself to the new environmental demands. For example, when there were no telephones, people would visit their friends without an appointment; in the modern age of ubiquitous and instant connectivity, such "dropping by" is frowned upon.

Fifth, **culture is environmental.** It envelops everyone's life alike and always. As with environment, we take culture also for granted, acting in sync, without even being aware of its presence, until someone breaks a norm. Strangers in an elevator don't directly face each other and this is done without thinking, until someone actually deviates from this automatic behavior.

And, sixth, **cultures are hierarchical.** Multiple cultures are nested hierarchically. The culture of the larger group constrains and shapes the culture of the smaller groups within it. Imagine that you are a member of a middle-income Hispanic family in the United States. What is the culture in your family? It is actually the culture of the middle class, nested inside the culture of the Hispanics, in turn nested inside the U.S. culture.

CULTURAL VALUES
The Foundation of Culture

Values are our ideas about what is desirable in life, why life is worth living. As individuals, we have values—and in Chapter 5, we called them *personal values*. We might value freedom more than wealth, or a relaxed life more than fame, or environmental preservation more than technology. Now, we can ask, "Where did these personal values come from?" The answer is, from culture. Our society instills them in us, as part of socialization. Thus, whereas many values differ across individuals, many personal values are common. The values a society as a whole embraces are called **cultural values.**

Societies differ in many aspects of everyday life—dress, language, food habits, living arrangements, family formation, etc. These are substantial and very visible differences; but even more important are the differences in cultural values. Values are not tangible and therefore not visible, but they influence everything else in that culture. If you want to understand why people in a society act the way they do, you have to know what its values are. As such, values are the foundation of a culture. They are like the hidden, underwater radar system that silently keeps guiding the ship of a society's everyday life.

WEST

INDIVIDUAL-ISM

FREEDOM

MERIT

MATERIAL-ISM

CHANGE

EQUAL OPPOR-TUNITY

CORE WESTERN VALUES

Values are so basic that in fact every citizen must know the values of the society in which he or she lives, and, for contrast, the values of a few other societies different from his or her own. Here is a brief profile of six of the many Western core values:[1]

Individualism North American and Western European cultures consider individuals responsible for their own success, which is achieved through individual effort. It is considered acceptable that individuals be self-oriented, serving and guarding their personal interests (as opposed to sacrificing for the group or society).

Freedom Individuals are free to practice any religion, support any political party, play any sport, participate in any peaceful protest, speak their minds, pursue any career, choose any product, live anywhere, travel anywhere, adopt any line of work or employment, and, in general, pursue any dreams they fancy.

Merit, Competitiveness, and Accomplishment In Western cultures, individuals are expected to be competitive to gain success; it is a merit-based society where you get what you deserve (not what you need) and personal accomplishments are honored.

Materialism Western cultures value material success. As such, these cultures do not look down upon someone pursuing material wealth (in some cultures this might be deemed greed), and a wealthy person is considered successful with or without any nonmaterial accomplishments.

Change and Scientific and Industrial Progress Western cultures value change over tradition and believe in the power of science and technology to bring solutions to problems such as disease, aging, poverty, resource shortages, etc., and to produce new comforts and opportunities such as space travel, virtual experiences, and anti-aging miracles. they also value industrialization and the efficiency of mass production.

Belief in the Equality of Opportunity All persons living and breathing on American, Canadian, British, and many other Western soils (including those who are visiting there only temporarily) are deemed equal in the eyes of the law of the land. And such equality is not merely protected by law, but indeed valued as a natural human right. *Equality* means, of course, only equality of opportunity, not of status, position, or outcomes.

East Versus West

Many of the core cultural values of the East differ sharply from those of Western societies. Some Eastern values, in visible contrast to Western values, include the following:[2]

Collective Identity   Individuals are expected to show consideration for the well-being of their family, group, or organization. Individual identity is often known by the group's identity; individual personality is submerged in the group identity.

Inner Harmony   Rather than striving for mastery of the external environment, and achieving material success or individual triumph at the cost of bruised competitors, harmony with others, inner peace, and stability are valued. Happiness is sought in spiritual triumph over desires rather than in material acquisitions.

Respect for Tradition   While the West is oriented toward the future, sometimes even disparaging the past as backward looking, Eastern societies value the past as a source of wisdom and order, and they sustain and practice tradition for continuity and to counterbalance the supposed upheaval and chaos of modernity and radical change.

Respect for Hierarchy   In the West, interpersonal relationships are nurtured horizontally—among peers and equals. In the East, hierarchical relationships (e.g., parent-child, teacher-disciple, etc.) are valued just as much and relished as sources of emotional gratification.

Particularism   In Western societies, universal laws apply, and everyone is treated according to the same set of governing rules—a practice termed *universalism*. In contrast, in the East, matters are considered in a much more personal way, taking the individual's circumstances into consideration. Under this practice, called *particularism*, favors are expected and routinely granted due to personal relationships. Neutral rationalism is de-emphasized in favor of personal considerations.

Consensus   Eastern societies also value consensus rather than confrontation.

UNIVERSAL CULTURAL VALUE DIMENSIONS
What Tells Societies Apart

While reading through the lists of core Western and Eastern values, did you notice that some values are unique to each? This poses a problem: How do we prepare a coherent portrait of value differences for all the countries together? Wouldn't it be nice if there were a common template? Luckily for us, a Dutch social scientist named Geert Hofstede asked the same question. And with meticulous research that measured and compared cultural values across some 50 countries, he identified five dimensions on which societies differ.[3] Hofstede is a cultural anthropologist, mind you, not a market researcher, but the field of consumer behavior is rich precisely because it has borrowed from diverse, basic disciplines in the social sciences. If you ever had the opportunity to market to consumers around the globe, these five universal cultural value dimensions would prove immensely useful as a template to understand differences as well as similarities among these consumers. See Table 9.2. To understand these dimensions, answer the quiz question for each dimension below.

Individualism Versus Collectivism
The 'Me' Culture Rules

The Quiz Question: In my society, most people will:

   a. **Not usually sacrifice personal pleasure for the good of the society at large.**
   b. **Usually put the good of society above their personal interests.**

If you checked 'a,' your society is individualistic; otherwise, it is collectivistic. **Individualism** versus **collectivism**, one of the most significant cultural value dimensions, concerns whether, in a society, the wellbeing of an individual is considered more important than the wellbeing of the group as a whole. Cultures marked with individualism value self-interest over group interest, and they value unlimited personal freedom and survival of the fittest. In contrast, cultures of collectivism exhibit close ties between individuals, allow only

EAST

COLLECTIVE IDENTITY

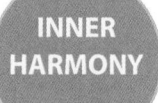

INNER HARMONY

RESPECT FOR TRADITION

RESPECT FOR HIERARCHY

PARTICULAR-ISM

CONSENSUS

a limited amount of personal freedom, and seek protection of the group. Simply put, this cultural value dimension classifies societies as "me" cultures versus "we" cultures.

The principal implication of this for marketers is that individualistic appeals (e.g., "stand out from others") so commonly found in Western advertising would be unsuitable for collectivist societies of Asia or for Asian and Hispanic consumer groups in the West.[4]

Power Distance

No Egalitarians Allowed

The Quiz Question: In my society, most people will:

a. **Always bow to people of higher status, and boss over people of lower status, even in off-work, social situations.**
b. **Expect to be treated with dignity and respect by all no matter what their station in life might be.**

If you checked 'a,' your society values large power distance; checking 'b' shows it values small power distance. **Power distance** refers to the extent to which the less powerful members of the society accept the authority of those with greater power. In societies with large power distance, superiors or persons of higher social strata are expected to maintain their distance from subordinates, and members of lower strata are expected to act in a subservient way. Follow the same practice in small power distance societies, and you would likely get in trouble.

The sources of power can be many: money, education, political position, etc. But don't confuse 'power distance' with power difference—it is not about absolute "power" differences among people that matter; rather it is the submissive role the less powerful willingly accept toward those more powerful. For example, there is a great divergence in power in the U.S. and Western Europe, just as much as say in Bangladesh or Russia (e.g., the business executive vs. the mailroom clerk, the affluent diner vs. the waiter; the movie star vs. the fan); but psychologically, everyone in North America and Western Europe feels equal, and those with fewer resources need not kowtow to those with more.

Does this value influence our consumer behavior? Yes, it does. In cultures of small

TABLE **9.2**	**COUNTRIES AT THE OPPOSITE ENDS OF *UNIVERSAL CULTURAL VALUES***
CULTURAL VALUE	**COUNTRIES**
INDIVIDUALISM/COLLECTIVISM	
Individualism	USA, Australia, the U.K. Netherlands, Canada, Italy, France.
Collectivism	Panama, Venezuela, Indonesia, China, South Korea, Mexico.
POWER DISTANCE (PD)	
Large PD	The Philippines, Mexico, China, Arab World, Brazil, France
Small PD	Austria, New Zealand, Great Britain, Canada, United States.
UNCERTAINTY AVOIDANCE (UA)	
High UA	Greece, Portugal, Guatemala, Belgium, Japan, Spain, France.
Low UA	Singapore, Jamaica, Denmark, Hong Kong, Sweden, UK, USA.
MASCULINITY/FEMININITY	
Masculinity	Japan, Austria, Venezuela, Switzerland, Italy, Mexico, UK, USA
Femininity	Sweden, Norway, Netherlands, Denmark, Thailand, South Korea
HIGH/LOW CONTEXT	
High Context	Most Asian countries (e.g., Japan, China, etc.)
Low Context	Most Western countries (e.g., USA, Canada, etc.)

Note: Countries are listed in descending order with the highest-scoring countries listed first.

Sources: Adapted from Geert Hofstede (2001), Culture's Consequences: Comparing Values, Behaviors, Institutions, and Organizations, Beverly Hills, CA, Sage Publications; Nitish Singh and Arun Pereira, The Culturally Customized Web Site, Burlington, MA: Elsevier, 2005.

power distance, decision-making is more participative. Thus, if you were selling a product in, say, Egypt or Malaysia (countries with large power distance), you would have to appeal to the head of the household (to whom all family members defer). In contrast, in western countries, you would have to appeal to the individual member of the family.

Uncertainty Avoidance
The Torture of Not Knowing

The Quiz Question: In my society, most people would:

   a.   **Feel uncomfortable going on a blind date**
   b.   **Consider blind dating a thrill**

   If you checked 'a,' your society values certainty; checking 'b' shows that uncertainty doesn't bother people much. **Uncertainty avoidance** refers to the extent to which people in a society feel threatened by ambiguous situations and want to avoid them. Some societies accept the "unknowability" of the future, while others deem and desire the future to be predictable. The former socialize their members into getting used to a certain degree of uncertainty and living each day as it comes. Other societies value knowing as much as possible and planning for all contingencies. Uncertainty avoidance leads people to not take risks and, consequently, to become less entrepreneurial and less innovative.

   Northern Europeans generally have lower tolerance for uncertainty than do people in Mediterranean nations. Therefore, consumers in Northern Europe, compared to those in the Mediterranean nations, would be less likely to buy products without first being certain about their benefits, and less likely to try unfamiliar service providers. And you can imagine where you would be able to sell more insurance!

Masculinity versus Femininity
Why Do Men Cry?

The Quiz Question: In my society, most people will:

   a.   **Desire money, success, and power over harmony and peace of mind**
   b.   **Embrace harmony and tranquility over money and success**

   If you checked 'a,' your society values masculinity; checking 'b' shows femininity is valued. Some societies value such things as money, success, power, and mastery of the environment, and such qualities as assertiveness, etc. (deemed to be *masculine* traits in humans). As such these are called **masculine cultures**; in contrast, those societies that value such concepts as harmony, peace of mind, caring for others, and quality of life (deemed to be 'feminine' traits in humans) are called **feminine** cultures.

   Accordingly, in feminine cultures, consumers tend to reject environmentally unfriendly products and products whose benefits are primarily materialistic in nature. Consumers in masculine cultures, in contrast, seek products that promise material success and adventure rather than tranquility. A new car, for example, may be positioned in masculine cultures as an outdoor adventure car with a high power engine—a 'macho' car, so to speak—whereas in feminine cultures, the more desirable appeal would be the aesthetics of the car and of the peaceful, harmonious experience of riding or driving it.

High Context versus Low Context
Why We Have To Ask What You Mean?

The Quiz Question: Which statement do you better understand?

   a.   **The professor said there would be no surprise quizzes in this course**
   b.   **The saleswoman said, "I am no Paris Hilton."**

   You don't have to answer this one. It is obvious that everyone would understand Statement 'a,' whereas only those familiar with Paris Hilton would understand Statement 'b.' Analogously, in some cultures, people communicate in a manner such that no special knowledge of that culture is required; in other cultures, everyday speech is full of idioms and clever phrasing so that, to understand it, you need to be familiar with that culture.

   This difference is captured by the universal cultural value of high versus low context.[5]

In **high context cultures**, to understand something, you need to know the context. Behind everything, there are layers of meaning not immediately apparent. People in high context cultures use symbols and nonverbal cues in communicating with others. They are much more polite to one another and very indirect in conveying their unpleasant reactions. In **low context cultures**, in contrast, to understand the meaning of something, you don't have to look at the context; the thing in itself is self-explanatory. And people are explicit in their communication. Asian societies are high-context and Western societies are low-context cultures.

If a Western consumer doesn't like a product, he or she will simply announce to the salesperson that he or she doesn't like it. A Japanese consumer would say, instead, that he "would think about it." This is because in the Japanese culture, rejecting someone's offer is considered impolite, even in commercial settings. The important point is that interpreting "would think about it" would require familiarity with the context, the Japanese culture. Also, in high context cultures there is greater use of soft-selling. Advertisements emphasize harmony and oneness with nature and use indirect, symbolic messages, avoiding direct comparisons with competitors. Low context cultures use simplicity, directness, and explicitness in communications.

CULTURAL PRACTICES, RITUALS, CUSTOMS, AND MYTHS

The Power of Protocol

If values form the bedrock of culture, cultural practices form its flora and fauna, making our journey through life more enchanting, and, as always, channeling our consumption. Cultural practices are behaviors that are rooted in the traditions and history of a cultural group. We discuss three of these practices: rituals, customs, and myths. Their one essential characteristic is that they are supra-logical—they cannot be explained by logic.

RITUALS

Rituals of a culture serve no ostensible function in the present time and make no sense to outsiders. However, historically, they did have a purpose, and they are all rooted in traditions. Consider two of the wedding rituals in Western culture: See Exhibit 9.1.

Today of course they serve no utilitarian purpose, but they do serve two non-utilitarian purposes: one is symbolic, giving the wedding a sacred status. The other is hedonic—we enjoy these rituals because they take us away from everyday drudgery. Seeing the bride in a bridal gown is an aesthetic pleasure, and seeing the bride throw her garter for some lucky person to catch is enchanting.

While the wedding ritual itself has a large number of consumption events, all of which can cost huge sums of money, there are umpteen other rituals in everyday consumption, as described in Table 9.1. Take the grooming ritual, for example. We simply need to examine our dressers and our makeup kits to realize how much of our money and time is happily expended everyday in personal grooming. From aftershave lotions to spray-on colognes to hair gels, from foundation creams to mascara to artificial eyelashes, and from bath oils to aromatic soaps to bottled perfumes, the extensive grooming accessories and even more extensive grooming techniques (gleaned from thousands of pages of advice and tips in glamour and lifestyle magazines) are as essential to our lives as modern consumers as are food and shelter.

9.1
EXHIBIT

ANCIENT WISDOM OF WEDDING RITUALS

Honeymoon. In the Anglo-Saxon days, grooms got their brides by kidnapping them, with the help of a friend--in modern times, we call him the Best Man). Then, the friend would hide the couple from the bride's family, until the bride got pregnant.
Tossing the Bridal Garter In France, several centuries ago, the groom's friends believed it to be good luck to tear off the bride's garter. To avoid the hassle, the brides took to giving away their garters voluntarily, by tossing them into the air. The lucky man to catch it is believed it be the next to find a bride for himself.

Read more on these rituals in Diane Ackerman, A Natural History of Love (Random House, 1995, p. 268-273).

CUSTOMS

Turning to customs, an example is the unique clothing that people of a given culture wear. Consider the Japanese kimono. Not only is wearing the kimono itself a custom, but custom also dictates what kind of kimono is appropriate, depending on the person's age and marital status, the season or event. Young unmarried women wear a kimono with long sleeves called *furisode*—a colorful kimono—very vibrant, colorful and rich with patterns and with flowing sleeves that hang almost to the ankles. Older women or those who have married, wear a kimono with short sleeves called *tomesode*—designs are smaller or solid and the colors are more subdued.[6]

Today, and for most Japanese women, kimonos are reserved for ceremonial occasions such as weddings. Most Japanese wear regular Western style clothing. Why then, you might ask, are we discussing kimonos? Kimono-making was once a thriving industry in Japan; today, it is an industry in decline. That is precisely our point—a clear illustration of the power of customs in dictating consumption behavior. A custom can start and sustain a whole industry; its decline and demise (often due to cultural adaptation to emerging circumstances) can banish it.

Bridal Showers and Bridal Registries

In modern times and in Western cultures today, bridal showers and registries are big business. Every department store and gift shop has a bridal registry set up: Go there and ask for it by the bride's name. You will get the bride's wish list, specifying exact size, color, and brand name. Violate this custom—by not contributing to the bride's gift chest, and see how much you endear yourself to the bride. If you really want to be remembered as a favorite contributor, thanks to an enterprising tour marketer, *TheBigDay.com*, you can now buy the couple their honeymoon trip to a resort island—or you can buy pieces of it. And let us remind you that this practice—of bridal registries—is not universal, and it is therefore a very cultural thing. Indeed, the practice of going on a honeymoon is itself a Western cultural concept—now, of course, well permeated into at least the urban population segments everywhere. But none of these socially learned concepts—dating, wedding, honeymooning—none of these would endure if they were not widely shared and accepted in a given society.

RITUALS

CUSTOMS

MYTHS

An African M Y T H
The Man with the Goat

Once upon a time, looking for employment, a barefoot villager left home with his only prized possession, a goat.

Along the road, hiding in the bushes, was a hungry thief wearing new shoes. Sighting the traveler with a goat, he instantly thought of a trick to steal the goat. He placed his shoes in the middle of the road, each a few hundred yards apart. When the villager arrived near the first shoe, he looked at it but left it untouched and moved on. A few minutes later, when he saw the second shoe, he got so excited that he forgot about the goat and ran back to get the first shoe. However, the thief had by now already retrieved back the first shoe. Feeling sad, when the villager came back to the spot where he had left his goat, he found neither the second shoe nor the goat.

Source: http://eev2.liu.edu/
e3/stargazer/africa.htm

Hindu Monkey God Hanumana

Prince Rama (actually, an incarnation of the Hindu God Vishnu) was roaming the forests (in a 13-year-long exile engineered by his jealous stepmother), with his wife and brother in tow. One day, something bit the brother, and to save his life, a sage prescribed an herb. The herb was grown on a distant mountain and it had to be brought in before daylight. Hanumana, who had enlisted himself as Rama's disciple and helper, and who was bestowed with the power to fly, was dispatched to fetch the medicinal herb. The herbal plant was to be recognized by the special glow it emitted.

When Hanumana arrived at the mountain, he found all of the bushes glowing. A demon, who would love nothing more than to see Rama's brother die, had, by his magical powers, created a glow in every bush on that mountain. Perplexed, Hanumana uprooted the entire mountain, put it on his palm and flew back the whole distance. The sage identified the medicinal herb and saved young prince Rama's brother's life.

MYTHS

The third cultural practice is the promulgation of myths. **Myths** are tales and stories handed down through history without known origins and with no tests of their truth. Nobody knows if they happened, but they ring true (albeit sometimes with some stretch of credulity). They amuse us, and they have a kernel of "feel good" after-taste to them—as when goodness triumphs over evil. There are two kinds of mythical stories: (1) superhuman, (2) human. Superhuman stories entail some mythical character performing superhuman feats, or some superpower bestowing an incredible, impossible blessing or curse on someone, based on his/her deeds. In contrast, human myths entail mythical stories of ordinary people doing ordinary things, with good things or bad things coming to them. Such human stories are myths because their historic truth cannot be proved. In myths, the star of the story can be a hero or an anti-hero. The mythical story of the Hindu monkey god Hanumana is of the former kind—superhero and hero; the African mythical story of the goat and the shoe is of the latter type—human but anti-hero. (Read them in insets.)

Now, these myths have a "moral" to teach. The Hindu monkey god's feat has two morals: (a) no evil power will succeed over good intentions, and (b) total loyalty and dedication means you should be willing even to "move mountains." The African myth of the man with a goat teaches that if you stray from a promise you have made to your family (or a goal you have set yourself) and are tempted by other distractions, you can lose everything.

MODERN DAY MYTHS AND URBAN LEGENDS

The mythical stories of Hanumana and the man with the goat illustrate the role of myths as value conveyors in popular culture. What do they have to do, you might ask, with consumer behavior? But myths are myths, and modern day consumption myths are no different. Perhaps the most famous of these is the myth of Santa Claus. Millions of consumers around the world believe in Santa Claus and embrace the moral 'value' lesson of that myth: "Good things will come to you if you do good deeds." And that myth now accompanies an elaborate ritual—the celebration of Christmas as a big holiday when everyone is supposed to give a gift to family and friends. Retail businesses do as much business during the week of Christmas as they do over several months during the rest of the year!

A special type of myth is one whose origins are located in our lifetimes. These are called **urban legends**.

As an example, consider the urban legend about Dr Pepper's new can, supposedly introduced in late 2001, in the wake of 911, to capitalize on the intense patriotic feelings the 911 event had aroused in Americans. Its substance as well as its *modus operandi* (i.e., how urban legends spread in a population) can best be gleaned from a news group entry on a Web site, as follows:

> **For those who have not heard, the bottlers/manufacturers of Dr Pepper and their other products have started a "new" can campaign. They are putting patriotic scenes on them. One is the Empire State Bldg. with the pledge of allegiance ...but ... they left off the words... "under God." They felt it might "offend" some. I don't know about you, but as a Christian, I am boycotting their products! They said they didn't "have room" for those words, but yet they had room for "indivisible" on the can!**
>
> **Please pass this along to others and see if we can get a message out to Dr Pepper ... if having "under God" on cans offends them, then they don't need our money with "in God we trust" on it!**

(Source: Courtesy Murray Wells, Urban Legend Blog, ulblog.org)

Does this urban legend serve any purpose? Yes, it does. In the U.S.,

there had been a move for some time, by some interest groups to delete the words "under God" from the Pledge of Allegiance because their use in government business violates, as some argued, the constitutionally guaranteed separation of Church and State. In fact, the San Francisco Ninth Circuit Court of Appeals ruled in favor of the argument in June 2002. Later that same month, the U.S. Senate unanimously voted to support the Pledge, rebutting the court's decision. While the urban legend arose and spread before these legal and political decisions, the genesis of the legend and the rash of email activity it generated in the wake of the constitutional debate proves the point—for the supporters of "under God," the legend was a handy tool to oppose the secular forces, and in this case, it was also closely tied to consumption.

The Deeper Functions of Ritualistic Cultural Practices

If you found this tour of wedding rituals, honeymoons, and monkey gods amusing, that is because most cultural practices do contain an element of amusement. But there is a deeper side to all this: all ritualistic practices (customs and myths included) serve deeper, fundamental functions. These functions are: (a) achieving sacredness, (b) value inculcation, and (c) meaning communication (see Figure 9.2).

a. Achieving Sacredness

Precisely because ritual practices cannot be explained logically, they acquire the status of sacredness. Thus, in a Hindu wedding, for example, the bride and groom 'walk' around the fire seven times; in one African wedding culture, the bride and groom sweep together with a broom. Why? Answer: This is how it is done; without it, the wedding has *not* occurred. As humans, we constructed a concept called *wedding*, and we wrote a script for it. That is the way it is, and it is not to be questioned. After all, so it may not be taken lightly, a wedding does need to be sacred.

But those rituals do have a meaning, you might argue. Those knowledgeable about these rituals will point out, correctly, that the seven circles in the Hindu wedding accompany the seven vows the groom takes, and that the broom-jumping signifies a public display of intended cooperation and sharing of responsibilities by the couple. But think again: Couldn't the Hindu groom say his vows another way? And why couldn't the African couple take a vow to cooperate and share, instead of doing the broom-sweeping? How about printing those vows in a document that is signed and notarized? You could do that, but that, you see, would make the whole thing totally "earthly," removing from it the aura of it being something "heavenly," something sacred. Of course, many Hindu couples are now getting married in civil courts, but those are not Hindu weddings. And many Christians are getting married in civil courts, but then those are not Christian weddings.

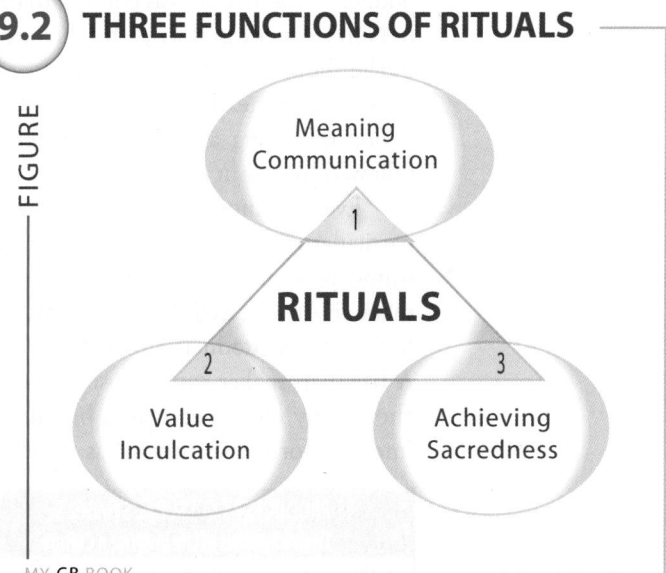

FIGURE 9.2 THREE FUNCTIONS OF RITUALS

Meaning Communication

1

RITUALS

2   3

Value Inculcation   Achieving Sacredness

MY CB BOOK

If this topic of sacredness has caught your fascination, and we hope it has, then you should read, in this chapter, the inset **CB BrainDish: The Sacred and the Profane.**

b. Value Inculcation

Rituals, customs, and myths also inculcate values—remember values are the bedrock of culture. Many values are inculcated through indoctrination by our elders—"Johnny, you can't steal your friend's toy." or "Lisa, nice girls don't lie." Every day, we receive value lessons, as direct exhortations and through rewards and sanctions. But there is another, less painful, way to receive values. In bedtime stories, folktales, and epics, values get passed from generation to generation. These tales and stories are called *myths*. And you have seen how mythical stories all have a moral, a life lesson.

c. Meaning Communication

Rituals as well as customs have symbolic meanings. In many countries, wearing black when in mourning is a custom that conveys that you feel sorrow. It could have been any other somber color, but we settled on black, and now the problem of how to communicate your sorrow and sympathy is solved. Chinese and Indians wear white to mourn, and that is fine too, for in their communities white has come to communicate sorrow. Likewise, if you wear a conservative suit, you communicate that you mean business. Companies that are now making it their custom for employees to wear "business casual" are communicating that they are innovative and are open to new ideas. Communication of meaning is an important function of culture; let us look at it more closely.

Cultural Practices and Marketing

We have been citing the marketing and consumer behavior implications of culture throughout this chapter, but this is a good place to pull together a more extensive account of how culture and its various elements impact consumer behavior and marketing practices.

Most rituals and customs entail consumption of products and services. Many holidays are customs, and they entail elaborate ritualistic activities. Christmas is perhaps the most celebrated ritual around the world. The fourteenth of February, celebrated as Valentine's Day in much of the Western world, generates the highest 24-hour floral sales of the year and is second only to Christmas in the number of greeting cards sent. Products such as candy, stuffed animals, wine, perfume, and restaurant meals receive a big boost on this day. Overnight on one February the 13th, Federal Express delivered more than three million pounds of roses! That was enough to fill seven 747 cargo jets—flying from South American to North American florists. By the next morning, there were $331 million worth of flowers in the shops of florists and retailers around the country.[7] Likewise, in Israel, Passover is celebrated in nearly every household. In much of the Muslim world, Ramadan is the period of fasting and prayers (when many businesses and stores actually close down), followed by a bout of festivities and consumption.

Even to know what products and services are needed, you have to know what the particular rituals or customs of a particular society are. Suppose you set up a business to supply products for African weddings. You would have to know what rituals and customs make an African wedding ceremony, and what products are used in these rituals as symbols. Secondly, for products and services used in rituals and customs, **fidelity of form** matters. A bar soap maker can choose any color and shape for the soap, and a soup maker can choose any container shape, but the form—the packaging and presentation—of goods intended for use in rituals has to be exactly as specified in the script (written or oral) of the ceremony.

PRODUCTS AS CULTURAL SYMBOLS
Twelve Symbols of Life in African Culture

In African wedding ceremonies, the officiant may administer the twelve symbols of life, each representing the love and strength that brings two families together:

Wine	The mixing of the blood of the two families
Wheat	Fertility and the giving of life and land
Pepper	Heated times the families will have
Salt	Healing and preservation of marriage
Bitter Herbs	Growing pains of married life
Water	Purity, dissolution of bitterness
Spoon, Pot	Healthy food that builds strong families
Broom	Cleanliness of health and wellbeing
Honey	Sweet love between a black man and woman
Spear	Protection of the sanctity of home and community
Shield	Honor and pride of the home
Bible or Koran	Symbol of God's truth and power

Source: Adapted from
http://www.africanweddingguide.com/history/symbolsoflife.html

CULTURE: A WEB OF MEANING

If we were to put our fingers on the single most significant purpose of culture, and, indeed, its very essence, we would say it is *meaning*. Meaning is what culture is all about; culture serves as the conduit of all meaning in life. Much of our everyday living depends on social communications—our communication of 'what we mean' to other humans. Culture is like the underground wiring that lights up the whole city; it is our underground cable that conveys meaning to all inhabitants of society. All these social communications can be grouped into four categories: (a) desires and expectations—what we want and expect from others; (b) values and tastes—what our values, tastes, and preferences are; (c) identity—what our self-concepts and our identities are; and (d) sentiments—perhaps the most important, what our feelings toward others are, and what sorts of relationships we desire with them.

We communicate through language, in which we use words to mean more than they literally do; but even more frequently, we communicate through gestures, actions, public displays of our possessions, and consumption of products that have symbolic meanings. We choose the products we believe carry the intended meanings. Put another way, we encode our intent in these products. At the receiving end, our listeners and audiences decode the message, inferring our intent. Two people of the same culture understand the figurative meaning of words and gestures they exchange, and they understand the silent language of our actions, our possessions, and our consumption choices. People from two different cultures either may not see the same meaning, or they may misread it. Culture is the grand interpreter; it is the dictionary of the silent language.[8] See Figure 9.3.

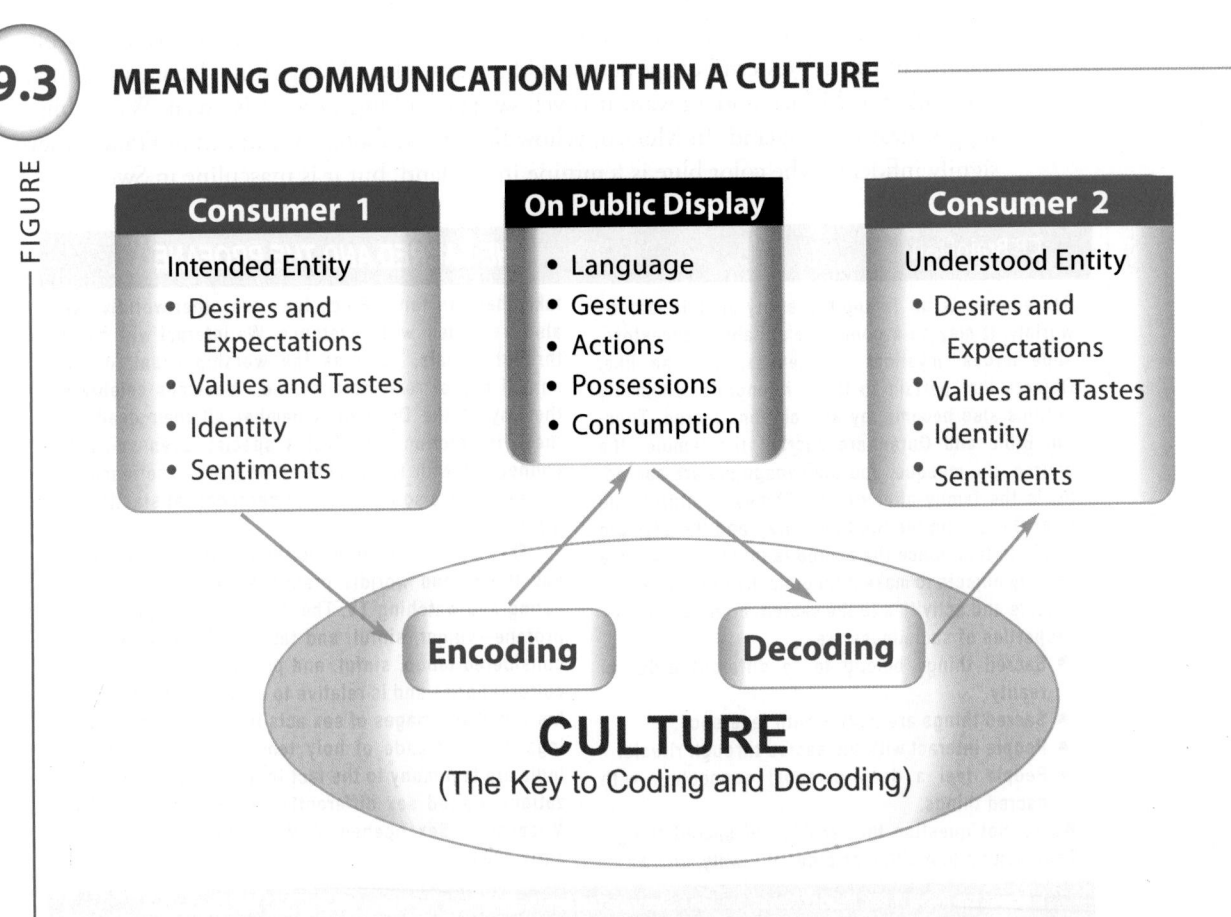

FIGURE 9.3 MEANING COMMUNICATION WITHIN A CULTURE

Consumer 1

Intended Entity
- Desires and Expectations
- Values and Tastes
- Identity
- Sentiments

On Public Display
- Language
- Gestures
- Actions
- Possessions
- Consumption

Consumer 2

Understood Entity
- Desires and Expectations
- Values and Tastes
- Identity
- Sentiments

Encoding   Decoding

CULTURE
(The Key to Coding and Decoding)

CROSSING CULTURES: MARKETING BLUNDERS

An understanding of cultures—all elements of culture—is required for all manner of marketing. The annals of marketing are filled with stories of cross-cultural marketing blunders committed by unsuspecting marketers. Blunders committed just because the marketers forgot to check the local culture. Below is a brief litany of actual blunders, potential traps, and some pointers for future reference.[9]

Lost in Translation Foremost among these blunders are the ones due to an obvious factor: differences in languages. These mistakes come in two forms: (a) the brand name acquires some undesired meaning in a foreign language, and (b) when translated, a message loses its original meaning.

When Colgate introduced its toothpaste in France, under the brand name Cue, it learned that in France, the word *cue* is sexual slang. And Coca-Cola's Fresca was Mexican slang for "lesbian." Likewise, taglines may be translated inaccurately. In Spanish, Hertz's tagline "puts you in the driving seat" became "Let Hertz make you a chauffeur."

Across cultures, product meanings get lost or distorted because everyday behaviors of people differ in meaning. An American underarm spray ad showed a woman applying the spray to a shaved underarm; the ad backfired in Italy because Italians do not consider a woman respectable if she shaves her armpits.

To avoid such blunders, as a marketer, you should use *back-translation*, a method in which a foreign translation is translated back into the original language by a different person. The back-translated version is then compared with the original version.[10]

Written Script Another aspect of language is how it is written and read. Arabic is read from right to left. So, before and after comparison ads, when translated into Arabic, would be totally absurd if the before and after placement of images were not reversed (e.g., comparison of clothing before and after a wash).

Colors Various colors mean different things in different cultures. In Brazil, purple signifies death; in Western Europe and the U.S., it is black; in Hong Kong, Japan, and India, it is white; in Mexico and Taiwan, it is yellow; and in Singapore, it is green. White lilies suggest death in England. In Mexico, yellow flowers symbolize death; but in France, they signify infidelity. The color blue is feminine in Holland, but it is masculine in Sweden.

CB BrainDish   *THE SACRED AND THE PROFANE*

Sacredness is an intangible entity that is other-worldly. It may be a god, angels, saints, ancestors, superheroes, mystical experiences, and the like. Objects that pertain to these intangible, unearthly entities also become, by association, sacred. Thus, the Bible and Quran are sacred; the temple, the church, the mosque, and the synagogue are sacred. So is the family alter (in the Chinese culture), the river Ganges (in the Hindu culture), and the Olympic torch. In fact, since the sacred is intangible, we use worldly objects to make it tangible, by linking certain objects and activities to the sacred. Four noteworthy properties of sacredness are:[1]

- Sacred things belong to "a different order of reality."
- Sacred things are treated with reverence.
- People interact with the sacred through rituals.
- People feel a deep personal connection with sacred things

We do not question the "reality" of sacred things. They belong to a different order of reality, and we take them on faith. Since they are other-worldly, we also treat them with reverence. We interact with them through rituals, such as the worship ritual, or an annual day of remembrance, i.e., Mexicans celebrate the Day of the Dead to remember all their dead. In these interactions, we feel a special, even spiritual connection with them. That is why the experience of the sacred is a source of great personal satisfaction to many consumers.

The absence of sacred is the mundane—the everyday things and worldly practices like grooming and eating and watching TV. The diametrically opposite is profane—vulgar, sinful, and taboo. Of course what is considered taboo, sinful, and prurient is itself part of cultural norms and is relative to a culture and a time in history. Vivid images of sex acts in ancient stone carvings on the façade of holy temples of Khajuraho in India are testimony to the fact that some ancient civilizations viewed sex differently. In modern times, The Museum of Sex opened in Manhattan, New York, in early 2003.[2]

1. Adapted form Russell W. Belk, Melanie Wallendorf, and John F. Sherry, Jr., "The Sacred and the Profane: The Theodicy of the Odyssey," *Journal of Consumer Research*, 16, June 1989, 1-38.
2. Joel Stein, "Having Sex, Museum Style," TIME, October 21, 2002, p. 92.

Furthermore, the meanings of colors changes with products and contexts. In the countries where black is used for mourning, the same color is considered trendy and classy in evening dresses, and majestic in cars. In India, white clothes are worn for mourning, but that is because death rituals are deemed to be sacred; indeed, in clothing, white is considered a color of "purity" and is accordingly used for all worship ceremonies and in everyday clothing. In China, wear a white carnation to a business meeting, and you might as well forget about doing any business—there and in other Pacific countries, the white carnation is a symbol of death. The moral of the story: It is a good idea to check with your local culture guide about what colors are appropriate for specific uses.

Numbers and Other Symbols Likewise, numbers have symbolic meanings that differ across cultures. In many countries (e.g., the U.S., Canada, UK, India), the number 13 is considered unlucky. In Japan, it is the number 4. So, in Japan, you don't want to package your products in fours. An owl is a symbol of bad luck in India, but owls signify wisdom in North America and Western Europe.

Standards of Nudity and Taboo Topics Standards in the acceptance of nudity vary across cultures. In Western Europe and Australia, nudity in public media is accepted much more than in the U.S., which in turn is more accepting than Eastern countries such as India, China, Thailand, etc., are. It is least accepted in Islamic countries such as Saudi Arabia. A perfume ad for Guerlain (Paris) showed a scantily clad woman strolling on the Champs-Élysées in Paris with the Arc de Triomph in the background. In the Arabic version, while the Arc de Triomph was retained in the background (the French association is valued for perfumes in Arabic countries as well), the model had to be fully clad.

Sex and personal hygiene products are discussed freely on American TV. In much of Asia, they are taboo. So, you couldn't advertise contraceptives, for example, on Chinese, Thai, or Filipino TV until after it was past bedtime for children, and magazine ads for Viagra and Levitra, so common in U.S. and Western magazines, could not be run in these countries.

Product Consumption Differences

Product consumption differs across cultures. Wine is a staple beverage in Europe, to be consumed with every meal; in the U.S., it is a leisure and celebration drink. Two-wheeler mopeds and horse-driven carriages are still used as the principal means of transportation in some countries, as are water-taxis. Miniskirts or even midis are not worn in Arab countries. Foods obviously differ not only across countries but also across different ethnic groups within the same nation.

For consumption with a cultural twist, consider alcohol consumption in Japan: Japanese culture sanctions it, even in excess! Male employees generally go out to drink after work with their coworkers and bosses. It is considered an insult to coworkers or to one's boss to refuse a drink. Often, people get drunk. But in Japan, getting drunk is not seen as a stigma. In fact, there is implicit support for it—it is seen as an emotional outlet for the Japanese who, under the norm of consensus-based decision-making, otherwise keep their personal feelings bottled up! To market your product to consumers of a foreign culture, your number one priority should be to adapt your product to suit the local culture.

As this litany shows, the nuances in each culture are so many and so subtle that your best bet is to have a

local culture

CROSS-CULTURAL *FAUX PAS*

Toyota Ads Bite the Dust in CHINA

In Late 2003, Toyota launched an advertising campaign in China for its new brand Prado. Within months, the company had to pull back the campaign and apologize. As the flood of scathing emails sent to the company revealed, the campaign had hit a nerve with many Chinese consumers. The reason: unbeknownst to the company, the campaign was insulting to the Chinese sense of patriotism in a way only someone familiar with Chinese culture and history would reckon.

The campaign showed stone lions saluting and bowing to a Prado Land Cruiser SUV. The ad copy said: "You cannot but respect the Prado." The ads were supposed to reflect the car's imposing presence on the road, according to an agency spokesperson. But to Chinese, it was a surrender of national pride.

For starters, Prado translated into Chinese as badao, which means "overbearing," or "rule by force." Next, the stone lions resembled those flanking the Marco Polo Bridge near Beijing, which is the site of the opening battle in Japan's invasion of China in 1937. Patriotism ranks high among Chinese values (as it does in most other nations), so one can imagine the wrath the campaign would engender. This cross-cultural marketing blunder is a vivid commentary on how an insider understanding of cultural symbolism—symbols in culture—is an absolute prerequisite for sensible marketing in any culture.

Note that on the car company's part, this is an innocent mistake. The company withdrew the ads immediately, and, in good conscience, apologized: "We want to express our sincere apology for the unpleasant feelings they have generated among Chinese readers."

Based on a report in "JAPAN: Toyota recalls 'offensive' sports vehicle ads in China," Asia Media, The Straits Times, Friday, December 5, 2003. People's Daily, Beijing, Friday, December 05, 2003.

local culture guide check all your marketing communications. And don't ever send abroad a salesperson who is highly *ethnocentric*. Here is why.

CULTURAL ETHNOCENTRISM

Most people are proud of their values and customs, as they should be. But this is no reason to be smug. Other nations have different values, and they too are proud of their values, as they should be. Rather than being smug, we need, as world citizens, to be aware and appreciative of other cultures and their values. Every cultural value has a rationale behind it; the need is to see a foreign culture through the eyes of the people of that culture.

Do you believe that your culture is superior to all other cultures? Many people do. This is called *ethnocentrism*—the belief in the superiority of one's own culture over all others. This helps ethnocentric people and nations maintain a degree of self-esteem, as individuals and as a nation. But taken to extremes, it can result in ill will toward other cultures and an unwelcoming attitude toward foreigners. People who travel around the world become more cosmopolitan in their outlooks and more appreciative of other cultures. While they retain a healthy respect for their own culture, they acquire an understanding and appreciation of foreign cultures and greater tolerance of foreign cultural practices.

Do you qualify to visit with your overseas customers? To find out, you need to take a test, shown in Table 9.3. Go ahead, take it. How did you do? If you scored high, then you would be too ethnocentric. You need some exposure to other cultures, and to learn to admire their uniqueness.

The consumer behavior most affected by ethnocentrism concerns buying products of foreign origin. Consumer researchers have called this particular behavior consumer **ethnocentrism**—consumers' proclivity to view the buying of foreign goods as unpatriotic. Consumer ethnocentrism is easy to measure by using a scale called CETSCALE, shown in Table 9.4. Rate yourself on it too, and see where you stand. Individuals with high "consumer ethnocentrism" are—(least or most, you decide) likely to buy foreign made goods.[11] But don't confuse this score with your *general* ethnocentrism. Your "consumer ethnocentrism" means only that you take pride in buying domestically and in helping your nation in that way. High *general* ethnocentrism means, on the other hand, that you consider all other cultures inferior to your own, and that, most likely, you are a chauvinist. Contrarily, if your general ethnocentrism score is low, it signifies that you have an enlightened mind that respects all cultures of the world and that you have a curiosity to learn about other cultures.

TABLE **9.3**	A SCALE TO MEASURE GENERAL ETHNOCENTRISM

Strongly Disagree			Strongly Agree	
1	2	3	4	5

1. My group's culture is the best. ____
2. I have no desire to learn about other cultures. ____
3. The world would be better off if all countries adopted the culture of my country or group. ____
4. I feel that most of the customs and rituals observed by people of other cultures are silly and absurd. ____
5. I believe that all cultures can learn from one another. ____

Note: Some items need to be reverse-scored; can you figure out which ones? After scoring each item in the correct direction (to align with the direction of item '1'), add the scores across all items.
If your overall score is 20 or higher, you are definitely ethnocentric.   ____ (Your score)

MY CB BOOK

THE SILENT LANGUAGE OF CULTURE

Acculturation: Key to Avoiding Putting Your Foot in Your Mouth

Even if you score well on the general ethnocentrism scale—scoring well means not being too ethnocentric—you are still not ready to meet your client in a foreign culture. You also need to become *acculturized* in diverse cultures—understand certain invisible and unwritten cultural nuances. Full acculturization will come from participating in these cultures up, close, and personal. But you can begin that journey by reading, below, a brief account of what cultural anthropologist Edward Hall calls, "the silent language of cultures,"[12] summarized here as six dimensions:

Formality and Protocol Westerners value and exhibit informality, addressing you by your first name even in the first encounter. Easterners, on the other hand, maintain a formal approach, reserving informality for close friends. To an Easterner, then, the informality of the Western salesperson can be off-putting.

There is a particular protocol that the Japanese follow when they meet a business counterpart. It is called *meshi*, an exchange of business cards. Each person presents the card to the other—*presents*, not *gives*, mind you; that means, the card is handed over with both hands and turned so it is ready to be read by the receiver. Each person then reads the card loudly, in turn, and acknowledges the other. This reading of the card also enables each person to understand the other in terms of hierarchy and status.

Friendships In Western cultures, friendships are formed easily, or rather the word *friend* is used quite casually. This is a mixed blessing: on the one hand, people are friendly and helpful even to strangers and even in first encounters. But, on the other hand, this dilutes the meaning of the word *friendship*. In Eastern cultures, the word is reserved for someone for whom you have true affection, and friendships are considered lifelong commitments.

Another protocol among Easterners is about "offering and sharing." If an Easterner goes out with friends, he or she never buys something to eat or drink for him/herself alone; if two

---

TABLE

9.4 CETSCALE: A SCALE TO MEASURE CONSUMER ETHNOCENTRISM

	Strongly Disagree				Strongly Agree	
	1	2	3	4	5	
1. We should always buy products made in our own country rather than imports.						____
2. Our country should import only those products that are unavailable here.						____
3. Buy products made in our own country; keep our country working.						____
4. Purchasing foreign-made products is unpatriotic.						____
5. All imports should be curbed, banned, or heavily taxed.						____
6. Foreign manufacturers should not be allowed to put their products on our markets.						____
7. It may cost me in the long run but I prefer to support and buy domestic products.						____
8. We should not buy foreign products because it hurts our nation's industry and puts our own people out of work.						____
9. It is always best to purchase products made in our own country.						____
10. For me, to buy domestic products rather than imports is a matter of national pride.						____

HOW TO SCORE. Add your ratings across the ten items. They should add up to a number between 0 and 100; scores above 50 indicate that, as a consumer, you tend to be ethnocentric. The higher the score, the more "consumer ethnocentric" you are. A perfect score of 100 shows you are devoted to always buying the products made in your own country.

____ (Your score)

Note. The original scale is 17-item long, phrased for American consumers. To make it shorter as well as country-neutral, we adopted nine items, paraphrased them for generality, and added a new tenth item. [The remaining 8 items in the original scale are these: (a) American products, first, last, and foremost. (b) it is not right to purchase foreign products. (c) A real American should always buy American-made products. (d) We should purchase products manufactured in America instead of letting other countries get rich off us. (e) There should be very little of trading or purchasing of goods from the countries unless out of necessity. (f) Foreign products should be taxed heavily to reduce their entry into the U.S. (g) We should buy from foreign countries only those products that we cannot obtain within our own country. (h) American consumers who purchase products made in other countries are responsible for putting their fellow Americans out of work. Note that to make it applicable to any country, the context "American" should be modified as we did in the items we adapted.]

Source: Adapted by the author from Terence A. Shimp and Subhash Sharma, "Consumer Ethnocentrism: Construction & Validation of the CETSCALE," J. of Marketing Research, 24, August 1987, p. 282. © American Marketing Association. (Used with permission.)

MY CB BOOK

friends go out, each will ask the other person for his/her choices, order for both, share the purchased item, and each will offer (sometimes insist) to pay for both no matter who ordered. "Going Dutch" is a Western norm that would make most Easterners uncomfortable.

Personal Space Cultures also differ in what is considered personal space. Latin Americans and Saudis stand much closer to each other than do Westerners. Standing far away, Westerners can seem aloof and cold to Latin American customers. Ads should show, therefore, proper distance between the people depicted in the ad.

Time The sense of time is different across cultures. First, cultures differ in whether life is fast-paced or slow-paced, and, correspondingly, in whether consumers in general are rushed and value time too much or are relaxed and less concerned about time. Westerners, for example, are generally time-conscious, and Netherlanders and Japanese are extremely so. In contrast, Mexicans and Latin Americans are more relaxed. Thus, Western sellers want to accomplish a business deal quickly and move on. Mexican customers, on the other hand, want to take their time, and may feel that the Westerner, always in a rush, is being rude.

This difference in sense of time implies that the North American concept of fast food restaurants would not receive the same enthusiasm in cultures with a relaxed pace, such as Mexico and Latin America. In these and many Eastern countries, McDonald's and other fast food outlets must position themselves, as they in fact do, as sources of "different" food and convenience (as opposed to speed).

Also, the importance placed on punctuality differs greatly. Much of the Western world and industrialized nations value punctuality; perhaps Japan takes the prize for running its commerce with precise punctuality. In contrast, in many Eastern countries, to be late is the norm rather than an exception. Perhaps India and Mexico would take the prize for lateness.

Explicitness Westerners are more true to their word, saying exactly what they mean. It is considered just good practice to be open and clear. In contrast, Easterners are hesitant to be candid because they think they would be hurting your feelings. In normal discussions, Westerners participate with visible energy, often eager to fill any silent moment. Easterners, on the other hand, seem more quiet and brooding, as if contemplating what is being said, and in fact letting several moments of silence pass before volunteering an opinion.

Relationships and Business Cultures also differ in terms of whether they keep business and social relationships apart. Latin Americans and Middle Easterners, for example, are unwilling to discuss business unless they come to know you and can trust you. Westerners, on the other hand, see business as a formal, impersonal transaction, where contractual obligations substitute for personal trust. To Americans, what matters is the reputation of the company with which they do business; to Latin Americans, the identity of the person with whom they are doing business matters. They are not buying from a company; rather, they are buying from a person.

CULTURES THAT SAVE *FACE!*

One particular cultural value in the Eastern societies is so unique that we "got to" tell you about it. This entails the concept of face found in the Asian cultures, most prominently in China and Japan. Face refers to self-respect, and everyone in these societies is expected to "maintain face." Now, keeping self-respect is important in all societies, but nowhere is "losing face" deemed so disgraceful as in China and Japan (along with a few other Asian nations). Keeping face is every human's right and losing it implies that you have even fallen below being a human. Because it is every human's right (unless he or she does something wrong), others are expected to honor it and not cause anyone to lose face. That means you must not criticize a person, and if you need to call attention to his or her poor performance, you must do so indirectly. Thus, if a waiter brought you a wrong order, for example, you would politely ask for a different order (not a "correction" but a "different" order). If you disagree with someone, you would not say so explicitly (this would mean you are causing him or her to lose face); rather, you would say that you are "not sure." One has to be intensely acculturated to understand both the nuances of behavior necessary to help others keep face and to realize its prowess on peoples' psyche in those cultures. **MYCBBOOK**

POSTMODERN GLOBAL CULTURE

A Myth or Reality?

In this concluding section of the chapter, we ponder a question that has, for some time now, occupied the minds of social scientists, guardians of public policy, and consumer activist groups. There is a fear, in some quarters, that Western-style consumption and the related consumption values of materialism and commercialism are corrupting otherwise sane consumer societies everywhere. Is this true? Scholars disagree. One camp argues:

Today's global culture has ties to no place or period. It is contextless, a true mélange of components drawn from everywhere and nowhere, realized through the network of global communication systems.[13]

Today, in almost any corner of the earth, you will be able to find your favorite brands of clothes, toiletries, watches, soft drinks, and even fast food. Coke is everywhere, and McDonald's and Kentucky Fried Chicken (KFC) are opening stores in the once forbidden economies of China and Russia. In every sense of the word today, Gucci and Banana Republic, Timex and Rolex, Apple and Zyinga are global brands. The TV series *Survivor*, *Friends*, and *The Apprentice*, or their reruns are being watched worldwide. *The Office*, originated in the U.K., is now a popular TV show in North America. The Volkswagen Beetle mania is back worldwide, and American-style rap music is being integrated with domestic music in India and other countries, and Western music bands are taking a fancy to Bollywood melodies (American pop group *Pussycat Dolls* created a remix number with Slumdog Millionaire's flagship musical number *Jai Ho,* in their single, entitled *You Are My Destiny!)*. In dress, cuisine, and media viewership, Western capitalism is evident everywhere. Such shared consumption is cited by some as cause for concern that cultural diversity is on its way to extinction, and that we are headed toward a culturally homogenized world!

Russell W. Belk, a creative consumer researcher and marketing professor at York University, disagrees, arguing that obliteration of distinct cultures is not a real threat. Belk cites three factors resisting such a threat.[14] First, consumers admit foreign cultural symbols and icons, but as they do, they keep the foreignness of these foreign things visible (as opposed to absorbing them seamlessly)—for example, Tokyo Disneyland has an American façade. Second, consumers view global culture as hyper-real (i.e., as a make-believe reality to be indulged in occasionally), distinct from the local culture, which is real. For example, Bollywood films are now watched on DVD by consumers of many nationalities around the world (check out *Bride and Prejudice*, for example, an Indian film maker's adaptation of Jane Austen's classic, available in movie rental stores such as Blockbuster). And third, consumers individualize foreign products and practices before adoption—for example, McDonald's offers non-beef burgers to Hindus in India.

BECOMING EDUCATED—CULTUREWISE

The significance of learning other cultures goes beyond being a savvy marketer. To lack curiosity about other cultures is to have a mindset that is, well, "so yesteryears." To be a cool person in the 21st century, one must be a "global person." Indeed, our college degrees in science, technology, and business are incomplete without considerable self-study of other cultures. Besides, this stuff is simply so fascinating! Read about the cultures of a few selected countries in the Appendix to this chapter.

global person

SUMMARY

We began this chapter with a definition of culture and a description of its elements—what is included in it. Defining it as the sum of all that we learn and share with others, we argued that it serves as a blueprint for everyday living. Values form its foundation, serving as a source of personal values for us, and serving also as the wellspring for all of its other elements: norms, cultural practices, science and technology, and material objects. Cultural practices include rituals, customs, and myths.

Why does culture exist? It exists because, we argued, it serves certain functions: it regulates society, and it makes living more efficient. Along with these two purposes, culture has other properties: it is learned (by definition), it is adaptive (otherwise it will lose its function), it is hierarchical (subcultures are nested within broader cultures), and it is environmental (we are immersed in it and, consequently, are seldom aware of it).

Cultures differ, and these differences can be captured in five universal value dimensions. All countries of the world can be differentiated with this template of five universal values.

Moving on, we described the role of rituals, customs, and myths, both in life, *per se*, and for consumption. Rituals, customs, and myths are all value carriers, and often they also serve a function. Ritualistic cultural practices often give sacredness to activities they surround (e.g., wedding rituals), thus making those activities and events of special value to us as consumers. In all cases, and at the very least, rituals have symbolic value, attaching and conveying meaning to otherwise ordinary consumption. In this context, we presented a model of how culture acts as a meaning communicator.

Following this theoretical treatise, albeit interspersed throughout with practical examples of

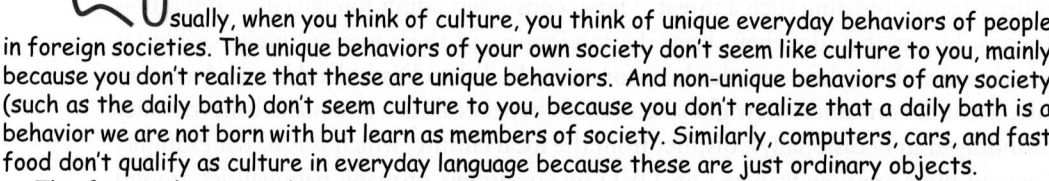

CB Blog

9

Be Noble: Understand Global Cultures

Usually, when you think of culture, you think of unique everyday behaviors of people in foreign societies. The unique behaviors of your own society don't seem like culture to you, mainly because you don't realize that these are unique behaviors. And non-unique behaviors of any society (such as the daily bath) don't seem culture to you, because you don't realize that a daily bath is a behavior we are not born with but learn as members of society. Similarly, computers, cars, and fast food don't qualify as culture in everyday language because these are just ordinary objects.

The fact is, however, that everything humans learn to make and everything humans learn to consume, and if that way of making things and that way of consuming things is shared across people in a society, then all of those things are, by definition, culture.

Culture takes many forms, depending on the people who inhabit it. Popular culture, trash culture, counter culture, heroin culture, rap culture, Hollywood culture, Washington D.C.'s political culture and Vancouver's bohemian culture, Amish culture, and Silicon Valley culture—all are cultures worthy of study and, for marketers, worthy of note. If you want to study any of these cultures, you can simply watch the consumption practices (that include customs, rituals, and everyday activities) of its people. From these overt practices, you can infer the cultural values that necessarily underlie and produce those behaviors.

One thing we cannot afford to do, however, is to bring an attitude of smugness about our own ways of living. That would make us extreme ethnocentrics—a trait that would turn us into modern day cave dwellers, blind to all the rich experiences our culturally diverse world has to offer.

The best way to experience and appreciate culture and its all-pervasive influence is to get exposure to people of foreign cultures. Travel abroad if you get a chance. But you can find plenty of it within your homeland. Diverse subcultures abound in most countries, the prime examples being ethnic subcultures.

In the present chapter, we chose to focus only on the universal concepts of culture. In this endeavor, we leave no stone unturned, and neither should you. We excerpt for you cultural profiles of selected countries (Appendix 'A', attached at the end of this chapter). We have tried to make these cultural profiles as fascinating as they come. Even if you decide to do nothing else in life, but especially if you decide to, at least read Appendix 'A,' and later the book from which that Appendix is excerpted—Understanding Global Cultures (Martin J. Gannon, Sage, 1994).

If you read that book in its entirety, you will never look at the world the same way again; and for that you will be a better person—a better consumer and a better marketing thinker.

CONSUMER BEHAVIOR

consumer behavior, we turned explicitly to an extended account of culture's impact on marketing practices. Here, we illustrated the sources of historical marketing blunders, ranging from naive translation to ill-fitting adaptation of product offerings and disastrous lack of awareness of cultural symbolism in advertising.

Finally, and to conclude the chapter, we dwelled on a burning issue that has been hotly debated by social scientists and public interest groups alike: Is the spread of Western materialistic culture corrupting us all; and is such diffusion of culture and consumption homogenizing us, with dilution of cultural heritage and diversity? Are we becoming global consumers, and is it a good thing or a bad thing? Don't think for a moment that this is merely an academic question; its answer will affect all marketers, immensely. If consumer resentment were to increase, for example, against the so-called *McDonaldization* of the world, there could be a backlash against marketers who seek to target consumers beyond their borders. The arguments on both sides are rich and thoughtful, and we believe you should read them yourself. On that note, we conclude this chapter.

KEY TERMS

Acculturation
Collectivism
Culture
Cultural values
Enculturation
High-context culture
Individualism

Low context culture
Materialism
Myths
National culture
Particularism
Popular culture
Power distance

Religion
Rituals
Sacred
Subculture
Universalism
Voluntary simplicity

YOUR TURN

REVIEW+Rewind

1. How is culture defined in the chapter? What are its characteristics? Discuss why it is important to study culture to understand consumer behavior.

2. Explain the six characteristics of culture.

3. Explain in your own words the terms *myth*, *custom*, *ritual*, *norm*, and *value*, and give a new (not used in the chapter) example of each.

4. What are the universal cultural value dimensions? Explain each and then name two countries that provide an illustration of each end of each of the cultural value dimension.

5. In face-to-face meetings with foreign customers, why is it important to understand the cultural differences that deal with friendships, time, and personal space?

6. Explain the concept of cultural ethnocentrism? What is its relevance and usefulness to marketers?

7. What functions are served by cultural ritual practices? Illustrate each with a cultural practice with which you are familiar (different from the ones described in the chapter).

8. Draw the model that depicts how culture transfers meaning.

THINK+Apply

1. Review, in your mind, the six universal cultural value dimensions. Suppose you were designing an advertisement for a brand of car for a Western country like Canada, America, or France, and separately for an Eastern country like Saudi Arabia, China, or Japan. How would you make that ad different so it is in harmony with each of the six cultural value dimensions? Now repeat this exercise for a brand of cologne.

PRACTICE+Experience

1. Select two consumers from different national cultures. Interview them to identify how their values and norms differ and how this influences their consumption.

2. Choose any *one* of these countries: (i) Qatar, (ii) Australia, (iii) Portugal, (iv) Malaysia, or (v) Nigeria. Do an Internet search to learn about some prominent cultural values in that country. Next, research any rituals surrounding (choose one): (a) the birth of a baby; (b) a wedding, (c) a religious festival, or (d) a non-religious festival. Then identify any cultural values that are reflected in these rituals. Next, identify any special products and services that are used in these rituals.

In the Marketing Manager's Shoes

Put yourself in a marketing manager's shoes. Most concepts in the chapter have some lessons for the marketing manager, i.e., they suggest what to do differently in practice; indeed, often these applications are implicit in our explanations of the concepts and models in the chapter. Identify at least five specific applications of the chapter's concepts, all of which should be entirely new, different from the examples cited here.

A MODEL OF MEANING PRODUCTION AND CONSUMPTION IN A CULTURE

When we consume products, it is their meaning we consume—this we have said already. Also we understood how two people in the same culture communicate meaning. Now we raise our understanding to a higher level. We ask an even more fundamental question: How do products come to acquire meaning in the first place? Who produces this meaning? And what role does culture play in the consumption of meaning? The answer to these questions is captured in the model of meaning production and consumption.

It all begins with culture. Using language, humans in all cultures give names to objects (e.g., we choose to call them pants, skirts, flowers, colognes, etc.), persons (e.g., man or woman, jocks or geeks), and qualities (e.g., masculine or feminine, slim or plump, sophisticated or simpleton). Note that the point is not that we choose to call a skirt a *skirt* or a geek a *geek* or a sophisticated quality *sophisticated*; rather, the point is that we choose to call some type of person a *geek*, a garment of a particular shape *pants*, and a certain quality and characteristic *sophisticated*. That is, the object, person, and quality exist already; culture and language just give them names. All objects have certain qualities, both physical (e.g., slim or plump, long or short) and conceptual; i.e., conceived only in our minds (e.g., ugly or beautiful, useless or effective). Physical qualities are integral to objects. As to conceptual qualities, we assign them, based on their (the objects') tangible sensory features (i.e., how they look, sound, taste, smell, and feel to the touch) and based on what they do for us; i.e., their outcomes, their consequences (e.g., fruits nourish, tattoos embellish, wines intoxicate). These qualities and outcomes are seen as desirable or undesirable, based on the values and norms of the culture. Thus the fundamental source of meaning is cultural values. The meanings to the properties/qualities come from cultural values—what a culture and society consider desirable. Sociologists call them *cultural categories*—the division of the world's objects and qualities into groups with given names; e.g., masculine or feminine, upper class or lower class, intellectual or peasant, nerd or jock, modern or traditional, sophisticated or simpleton. All of these are cultural categories, and culture assigns them meaning.[1]

Take jocks and geeks. Certain objective qualities go with them—by definition. Jocks are into sports, have strong bodies, and are not much into studying or intellectual pursuits; geeks are studious, high in academic achievement, not likely to be in sports and not likely to have muscular bodies. Are they desirable or undesirable? That depends on whom you ask. In western countries, high school students are in awe of jocks, and they ridicule geeks; in eastern cultures, while jocks are not necessarily ridiculed, they sometimes tend to be dismissed as dimwits, and it is, instead, the academically accomplished who are held in high esteem.

Take another example: If a woman wants to look attractive, should she be slim or plump? That again depends on what culture you are in. In Europe, for example, slimness was not always as valued as today; plumpish figures were. Just look at all the classical paintings by European artists, most notably by Peter Paul Rubens whose art even gave a name to women with figures of that genre—Rubenesque (as in the famous Greek bride Nia Vardalos).

One more example: In much of the Western world, men don't wear silk (except in ties); in contrast, in such Eastern countries as China, India, Thailand, Philippines, and Japan, men's silk shirts are considered more prestigious than shirts made of other materials. And, whoever decided that men shouldn't wear skirts (they don't—except in Scotland), and that women shouldn't wear pants (though now they do)? Again, culture. Now then, we know that objects, persons, and properties (both physical and conceptual) derive their names and associated meanings from culture at large. The next question is, how do *specific* products and brand names acquire these meanings?

MARKETER SYSTEM AND FASHION SYSTEM

Products are given meaning by (a) *the marketer system*, and (b) *the fashion system*. The *marketer system* consists of all the agents involved in bringing the product to the market. Principally, these are product makers, product sellers (salespersons and retail stores), and product advertisers. Product makers place the physical qualities in the product (and in its packaging) that have the desired meaning in the broader culture. Sellers (salespersons and retail stores) put in meaning by pricing (price has quality and class connotations in a culture) and by their own characteristics and qualities (e.g., the lifestyle of the salesperson, the atmosphere of the store), which in themselves have specific meanings in a culture.

Finally, advertising (or, more generally speaking, marketing communications) is the most powerful means of associating extraneous qualities with the product. Advertising uses symbols, language, and other objects and people (ordinary people as well as celebrities) chosen from desired cultural categories. A Piplin leather purse ad features a friendly, personable hometown American girl, so that is the meaning transferred to the Piplin brand of leather purses. A Dooney & Bourke ad, in contrast, features an avant garde, European girl with an attitude, so that is the image and cultural meaning that comes to be attached to the Dooney & Bourke brand. (Go ahead, Google these brands, or browse a current issue of Vanity Fair, Vogue, or Cosmopolitan, and see for yourself.)

Ideas adapted from "Culture and Consumption: A Theoretical Account of the Structure and Movement of the Cultural Meaning of Consumer Goods," Grant McCracken, *J. of Consumer Research*, 1986, 13 (June), 71-84.

The Fashion system refers to a society's collective ideas (or conventional wisdom) about what is in fashion and what is out. The agents in this system are what we will call cultural gatekeepers—people who, through their position and reputation, exercise influence and promote certain cultural meanings. There are three types of cultural gatekeepers: (a) designers, (b) the media, and (3) celebrities and other cultural icons. Designers are creative, innovative artists, collecting ideas from eclectic sources, and through their designs they communicate what is fashionable in a culture and for whom. Media include books, movies, TV programs, magazines, newspapers, etc., and all of them promote the cultural meanings of things. They do so, first, by depicting persons in conjunction with certain objects and qualities in their entertainment programs (e.g., show certain style of furniture in a show about upper class nobility), and, second, by editorializing certain opinions. Finally, celebrities serve for many as role models, and their images rub off onto the products they are seen using in real life.

Consumers as Meaning Producers

The next question is, what role do consumers themselves play in determining the final meaning of products. First, consumers acquire products with certain meaning (as produced by the marketer and fashion systems). Some of these products are adopted and consumed "as is." In so doing, consumers directly embrace the cultural meanings that come with these products. For example, Mercedes comes with the cultural meaning of material achievement, and Mercedes owners happily consume that meaning. Second, in some cases, following the acquisition, consumers modify product meanings by certain augmentation processes, called rituals— and rituals are activities that follow certain protocols (steps to carry them out) and have symbolic meaning (whether or not they have any tangible effect). Four rituals are relevant here: (a) possession rituals, (b) exchange rituals, (c) grooming rituals, and (d) divestment rituals.

Possession rituals are rituals, or sets of activities, that we perform to transform or modify products obtained from the marketplace. We may wash new clothes, install new software on PCs, wait to buy our cars in the right color, repaint and re-decorate a house we just bought, have a religious ceremony (in many Eastern cultures) when first entering a new home, or hold a house-warming party (in many Western cultures). In so doing, we add onto the objects certain qualities that have the cultural meaning we desire. Exchange rituals are bestowed on products we receive as gifts. Gift-giving is a highly symbolic ritual, and the gift item we receive acquires meaning from the sentiment of the gift-giver. Grooming rituals are two-fold: grooming ourselves and

grooming the product. In grooming ourselves, we use a variety of products, and although some of their meaning came with them when we bought them in the marketplace, the final and total meaning really comes from how we put together all the grooming products—using the same makeup products we could create for ourselves either a basic, well-groomed look, or alternatively, a look others in that culture would consider sexy. Second, we also groom the product—for example, we could wear a polo shirt casually, or we could have it starched and ironed. We can keep our cars clean and shiny or let them accumulate everyday dirt. We customize our PC desktops by getting them the skins we like. These product-grooming rituals give these products (and, by association, us) the meaning we desire. Finally, divestment rituals are activities we perform before discarding or parting with a product. Sometimes, we want to keep the meaning we have invested in a product intact, so, if we have to part with it, we try to identify and give it to someone who will keep that meaning intact (e.g., we transfer a family heirloom or a pet). If we don't want others to share that meaning, then we try to remove what we might have added to the product. All these factors are brought together in Figure 9.4.

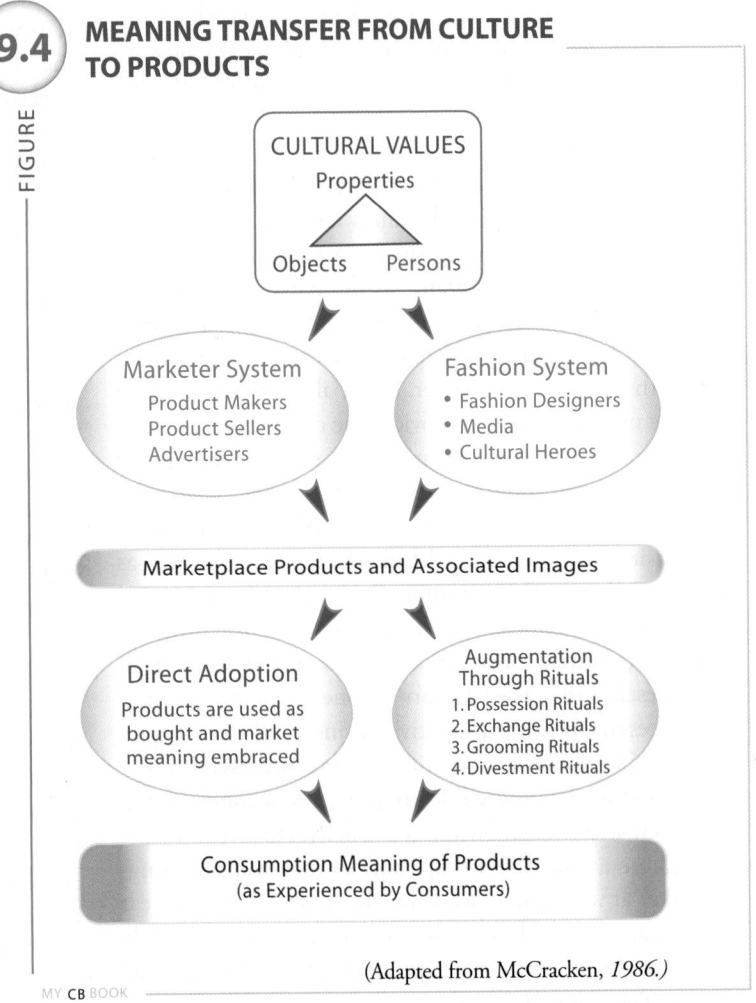

FIGURE 9.4 MEANING TRANSFER FROM CULTURE TO PRODUCTS

(Adapted from McCracken, *1986.*)

MY CB BOOK

SELECTED CULTURES FROM AROUND THE WORLD

A marketer aiming to communicate with consumers around the world needs to develop an awareness, nay appreciation, of the cultures of various countries. Here is a starter:

CHINA

Historically, the Chinese tend to be ethnocentric, considering their country to be the center of the universe, and their race to be superior. The Chinese character for the name *China* means the "central nation"!

Family is very important in China and its well-being comes before anything else. Senior family members are revered and obeyed. Aging brings dignity and status (unlike in Western cultures where youth is at a premium) and elders are sought for advice as well as for blessings.

An important Chinese value is faith in *feng shui*, meaning "wind and water," implying the principle of harmony between man and nature. Before constructing any building or business site, the Chinese will consult with a feng shui man, who will advise on how to design the structure and its furnishings to embody that harmony.

The Chinese pride themselves for not showing emotions in public, and, therefore, tend not to smile at strangers. In initial business contacts, connections and relationships help. The term *Guanxi* means both "connections" and "graft," as the party providing the connection expects to profit from the favor. Thus, using a connection or Guanxi helps you get the contact with the target consumer, but it also obligates you to the middle man who provides the connection.

Personal space is smaller so people stand closer together. In non-business settings, they greet one another with a slight bow or a nod of the head; in business settings, a handshake upon greeting as well as upon departure is common. Business cards are handed with both hands. Meetings begin with tea drinking and informal conversation, including introduction of oneself and a brief history of one's business. Trust is necessary before substantive business talks can begin. The Chinese tend to remain formal at business meetings. Negotiations proceed slowly and are best conducted in a low-key tone and without publicity. Furthermore, the Chinese don't like to say "no," so they will say things like "It will be inconvenient." In general, you will hear them say "yes," but this implies not agreement but only that "I am listening." It is important to them that all parties maintain "face."

FRANCE

French business organizations are highly centralized, with well-defined formal command and control lines of authority. On the surface, at least, there is rigid formality in how managers interact with each other and in adherence to written rules. Below the surface, however, there is an invigorating subculture of informal networking

and tacit flexibility. While rules are seldom flagrantly broken, they are constantly distorted or ignored.

The French seek novelty and elegance. This shows up in French consumers' quick adoption of gadgets and other innovations, and in their valuing aesthetics in product design and also in the use of language. They prefer wit to a belly-laugh and use humor that is more intelligent and satirical. However, in business presentations and meetings, humor is rarely used.

French people enjoy abstract thought and consider themselves philosophers. The pragmatic matters less than clarity of logic. They will tolerate the impractical but not the inconsistent. In business dealings, they may react negatively to your idea initially because they want to hear your arguments. Rational arguments supported by facts rather than sentimental pleadings are key to successful negotiations.

French managers are very competitive (as opposed to cooperating in teams). Indeed a manager would be dismayed if others did not compete with her or him. Group consensus takes the back seat to individual initiative. Most of the decision-making oriented communication is via written reports and proposals. Managers call meetings with a detailed agenda to inform and coordinate, rather than to discuss. Business colleagues use last names, at least in public, and they shakes hands no matter how well they know each other. Bosses do not socialize with subordinates after work; and a business lunch with the boss is rare and formal. Usually, lunch is regarded as "private time," and food is deemed to deserve the main attention.

Business begins with establishing a personal relationship. The French want to know you and expect you to show interest in their country. Personal relationships are valued for their own sake. The French believe that there is more to life than work; accordingly, they admire hard work but not workaholism. Work and family are considered separate. Being successful at the job is not considered adequate. Colleagues are expected to be lively and interesting, and well-informed and appreciative of the finer things in life.

When you meet people, as well as when you take

leave of them, you must shake hands with everyone, including children. The French are well-informed about other countries and cultures, so it pays to be informed about French history, politics, and culture.

GERMANY

The Germans are very ambitious, success-oriented, and competitive. The outward signals of success are the size of a person's office and the car he or she drives. Work and home are considered separate, and few Germans ever take their work home.

German organizations are hierarchical, with strict lines of authority. Everyone's role is well-defined, and everyone is supposed to work by the book. Decisions are taken by senior management rather than by consensus. Subordinates are expected to offer opinions only if they are well-informed. Compliance rather than consensus is expected.

Perfectionism both in business and private life is a hallmark of the Germans.

The Germans are very formal and private persons. German society is very normative, and eccentricity of even the mildest form is frowned upon. A German would not hesitate to point out if you do something out of line, even something as trivial as taking off your jacket. Policing each other's behavior is deemed a social duty.

German businessmen and managers always keep their jackets on unless alone. They address each other formally by their last names, especially in meetings. There is no place for humor in business meetings. Joking is common among close colleagues in private, but among strangers or in formal meetings, it makes people uncomfortable.

Punctuality is very important to the Germans. Everyone arrives on time and leaves on time. Working late is neither expected nor rewarded. During the working hours, you work hard, but that is the end of it.

INDIA

As the largest democracy in the world, India embodies the value of egalitarianism alongside the deeply rooted caste and class system. Labor or menial work, historically the exclusive occupation of lower castes, continues to be considered undignified. Most middle-class and upper-class families will hire household help for dishes, laundry, and cleaning, not necessarily because the homemaker is working but simply because it is the proper thing to do.

In businesses, rank and the respect that comes with

it are zealously guarded. Accordingly, subordinates display subservient behavior, and superiors treat their subordinates in a condescending manner. A Westerner who behaves in a more egalitarian manner toward the subordinates of his or her counterpart at the negotiating table may therefore discomfort both the subordinates and the superior alike.

Age is revered in India, as in most other parts of Asia (unlike in the West). Family members are respected.

Indians have a strong belief in destiny or fate and, for this reason, tend to work less hard or work fewer hours, and also tend to be contented with what they have.

Guests and visitors to homes are considered a godsend and are welcomed with a sense of duty and reverence ("A guest/visitor is a god" is a popular adage in India, followed in deeds as well as words). Even a stranger who knocks on the door will be welcomed, invited into the house, and offered at least a glass of water. Friends drop by without announcement, a carryover from the days when virtually no one had phones to make a prior appointment.

Indians are famous for being late, although in business, this is changing. In part, this habit is the consequence of Indians (as in Latin and Arab cultures) marking time not as much by clock as by events.

Indians generally greet one another with a *Namaste*—the word is audibly spoken along with a gesture in which both palms are placed together at the chest level with a slight bow of the head. However, when greeting customers, a handshake is accepted and appropriate, with these exceptions: when greeting female consumers, a "namaste" is appropriate, not the handshake (though younger women executives or younger businesswomen will gladly shake hands if offered); when greeting very senior or older executives or business customers; when greeting government officers; and, definitely, when greeting political cabinet members, even a junior minister in the foreign trade department.

In consumer markets, haggling over price is common. Even though fixed-price shops and one-price merchandise are becoming prevalent, especially in large cities, the practice of bargaining or seeking some concessions is alive and well.

ITALY

In sharp contrast to the German organizational culture, rules and formal procedures are almost always ignored, and flexibility is considered an Italian virtue. Getting things done is what counts.

Personal relationships are valued among colleagues. The delegation of responsibility is by trust in the individual rather than by position. Meetings are small and informal. Often they appear to be social

gatherings. Formal presentations are not common. People use meetings as an opportunity to exhibit their status, style, and elegance. Everyone is entitled to offer an opinion, and everyone is expected to be agreeable to the speaker. The worth of the idea depends more on the speaker's status than on its intrinsic validity.

For business, Italians dress formally. Looking sharp is considered a sign of good taste. Business managers consider it important to demonstrate intelligence and education. Even the most mundane conversations about business are filled with references to such notable figures as Aristotle, Adam Smith, and John K. Galbraith. Being well-educated and familiar with the classics is considered a social necessity.

Italians are not sticklers for punctuality, but it is considered rude to keep others waiting. While it is considered desirable not to be late for the next appointment, it is also considered rude to break off the current meeting or engagement. Thus, punctuality is considered a tool to organize activities rather than an end in itself.

JAPAN

To the Japanese, harmony is more important than honest opinion or truth. Saving face and maintaining dignity are critical in all situations. Individuality is

sanctioned, and blending in and being a team player are rewarded. People with higher rank, seniority, or age are respected and obeyed.

Japanese corporations are very hierarchical. Decisions are made by consensus. The consensus building process, called *ringi seido,* is very time consuming. Written proposals, called *ringi-sho,* are circulated throughout the departments, with prolonged discussion and analyses at each level. In business, the Japanese follow procedures and rules closely and disfavor any bending of rules.

The Japanese smile generously. They speak softly and dislike the aggressive mannerism of some Western businesspersons. They stand two to three feet apart, in part to allow body language such as the bow. They will escort you to the door or the elevator and expect you to do the same.

The Japanese place great importance on relationships and contacts. Accordingly, cold-calling is unwelcome, and a business person must obtain an introduction from third parties, and yet be careful not to ask too much of them, for this will obligate them to those whose favor they are seeking for you. A great deal of time is spent at first meetings just to get acquainted.

Socializing among business colleagues and with clients is important and considered part of a workday, so much so that many will leave the office in the early

evening hours to socialize (eat and drink) and then return to the office in the evening to conclude the workday. Many business deals are, in fact, made in social settings such as over dinner or on a golf course.

Japanese businesses are tied into a web of financial and non-financial relationships of cross-ownership and mutual obligation, called *Keiretsu.*

Presenting business cards is an elaborate protocol. The card is presented with both hands and facing the receiver, who then reads it slowly and carefully to show respect for the giver of the card. The receiver then places it on the table so he/she can refer to it from time to time; it is rude to put it in the pocket right away.

To the Japanese, bowing is an art form. Junior executives and younger persons bow first and at a steeper angle than do senior executives and older persons, although they do not expect this from foreigners. Handshakes, offered in deference to Western custom, are light.

Gift-giving is a conspicuously noticeable part of Japanese social life, and, by extension, of business life as well. The gift selection and its presentation (i.e., packaging) is made with great deliberation and care. Aesthetic presentation is as important as the appropriateness of the gift content. First-time business gifts should be low- or moderately-priced, lest they obligate the receiver more than is in order, and because room is needed for subsequent gifts that need to be more expensive. But more than the price, the reputation and quality of the gift is of paramount importance.

MEXICO

If you learn only one thing about the Mexican culture, it should be the *mañana* syndrome. *Mañana* is Spanish for  "tomorrow," but the cultural meaning of the term goes deeper than its literal meaning. It connotes priorities rather than procrastination.

To Mexicans, family and social obligations come first; business later. The *familia* (Spanish for "family") is a broad term extending to several generations, and horizontally to aunts and uncles, nephews and nieces, grandparents, cousins, and their families. Holidays are grand family reunion days, and the old and the young alike enjoy these gatherings. Teenagers do not view these as social obligations and they do not look bored. They enjoy their elders and respect them and, in turn, receive much-valued affection. If you are invited into a Mexican home, remember that your hosts are putting their family, their lifestyles, and their pride on display for you to admire and respect. Show interest in the family, treat all family members with respect, and never, never ask or expect a Mexican to postpone a family concern to deal with the business at hand.

Mexican businesspersons work at a relaxed pace and they like flexibility, refusing to be pushed by deadlines.

Lunch hours are long, lasting two to four hours, with a multi-course meal in a relaxed atmosphere of conversations about friends and family. A business lunch with a salesperson is the same, without any talk of business. But the Mexican customer is trying to assess you in this social set up as to your worthiness of his trust and dealings with you; this, therefore, from the Mexican's viewpoint, is a *business lunch*!

Along with *mañana* and *familia*, a third cultural element guides the Mexican cultural life, namely *fiesta*. Fiesta means fun, enjoyment, pleasure. If you see men drinking and dining with friends, with free-flowing tequilas, with Mariachi bands, colorfully dressed señoritas, and colorful piñatas for children, you are witnessing a fiesta in progress. This zeal for living, for fun and celebration, is what sustains a Mexican's morale and high productivity during work hours. Whatever else you may sell to Mexicans, you can't sell them "stress-release seminars"!

NETHERLANDS

The Dutch have a strong belief in the power of human aspirations and effort; at the same time, however, they believe that the forces of nature have to be respected. The Dutch like to innovate but also wish to minimize risks.

The Dutch are predominantly egalitarian; they tend to be frugal, using money wisely. Dutch organizations are generally egalitarian and open, and it is common for people to cut across reporting lines if needed. The hierarchical nature of organization and authority seen in other cultures is anathema to the Dutch. Authority is to be camouflaged rather than exhibited. The boss is deemed to be "one of us," a collaborator rather than an authority figure.

Communication in the Netherlands is open and sincere. Nobody attempts to hide things or manipulate information. There is a preference for oral communication rather than written. This practice is termed *buurten,* which means "visiting" (i.e., exchanging or communicating information orally).

Dutch businesses have frequent and regular meetings based on formal agenda. The Dutch are open to and welcoming of new ideas, but will adopt them only after thorough research and clarity. Decisions are made by consensus (not by majority vote), which may take a long time to reach. But since these are based on consensus, their implementation is fast.

Dutch businesses value frugality. Showing off is to be avoided. Offices, clothes, cars, even food—all are kept simple and subdued. Socializing takes place over coffee rather than over meals, so if you are invited to someone's home, it is more likely to be after dinner.

Punctuality is valued, and there is an obsession to use every minute productively. The Dutch look for solid personal relationships and consider it important to honor commitments.

UNITED KINGDOM

Meetings are considered very important in the United Kingdom. Most decisions are made in meetings. Issues are discussed, analyzed, ratified, and implemented in meetings. Meetings take up a good proportion of any given business day, but they are not considered an interruption of work. They are informal in style and participants are expected to make comments and express opinions. Decisions are made by consensus, and all meetings have to have a resolution and a decision; otherwise they are considered a failure.

The British are generally group-oriented. Collective initiatives are preferred over individual ones. Individuals always seek group support before implementing any idea or action plan.

The British tend to use first names among colleagues and also among all business contacts, often even before meeting face-to-face. Handshaking is limited to first meetings. The usual greeting is "How do you do?" with the expected response being the same interrogative. Rank and status distinctions are acknowledged and respected.

In sharp contrast to German and French business etiquette, humor is expected and desired. Business discussions are filled with levity and witty remarks. Both men and women participate equally in humor. In British businesses, it is quite natural for women to occupy managerial positions, particularly in service industries.

It is common for colleagues and business associates to lunch together. Conversations can be social or shop-talk. After-hours socializing at pubs is also common.

In social dealings, it is important to be "a nice person." One is supposed to be courteous and unassuming, rather than assertive and arrogant. Humility and self-deprecation are also valued. Being polite in conversation is a British trademark. Direct confrontation and argument are avoided, and vagueness and hints mark the British conversations.

Adapted from: *Understanding Global Cultures: Metaphorical Journeys Through 17 Countries,* Martin J Gannon and Associates, Sage, 1994.

Reference Groups, Opinion Leaders, and E-fluentials

Experts, Heroes, Minders, and Connectors

Running away.
Running toward.

But running always with my *reference groups*.

2:30/3:00

LEARN . APPLY . EXPERIENCE

OBJECTIVES

1 Various Types of Reference Groups

2 Three Forms of Referent Influences

3 Roles and Traits of Opinion Leaders

4 Innovation Adopter Categories and How Early Adopters Influence Late Adopters

5 The Role of the Media in Stimulating Market Conversations

6 Word of Mouth/Mouse Marketing and Igniting the Fire of Buzz

What Will You Not Do For a Dozen Free **Doughnuts?**

On a cold February morning recently, at about 9:45 a.m., if you happened to be in downtown Raleigh, North Carolina, you would have seen a hoard of people, some 5000 strong, racing toward you—if you happened to be standing between them and the Krispy Kreme Doughnuts (KKD) Shop, that is. They were all heading to get their free doughnuts, a dozen each, courtesy of the Krispy Kreme Challenge. The challenge required participants to assemble at the University's Bell Tower, run to the downtown KK store, eat a dozen KK doughnuts, and run back to the finishing line.

Although the throng of runners included people of all ages including children, a majority were students from the NC State University. Many wore doughnut tubes around their waists, and some even wore their Halloween costumes, thus adding to the excitement. KKD uses the event as a fund raiser, donating the money ($247,000 so far as of January 26, 2011) to the North Carolina Children's Hospital. The Krispy Kreme Challenge started in 2004 as a dare among a few friends, and had about 12 participants. It has now grown to include 5000-plus runners. Participants run 4 miles, burning 400 calories, and then gorge on 2400 fat-laced, sugar-coated calories, followed by, for many, upset stomachs. But that is, for students, a small price to pay for checking off an important milestone in their lives: Indeed, the run is listed by *Sports Illustrated* as one of the 100 things you must do before you graduate!

My referents— love 'em, follow 'em!

Sources: based on Maria Martinat, "NC State Students Compete in Krispy Kreme Challenge," MYNC.com, February 11, 2009; Krispy Kreme Challenge Web site (KrispyKremechallenge.com. (DoA: March 13, 2009).

INTRODUCTION

On any other Saturday, these students of NC State University would be sleeping till noon. Why did they get up so early, in such large numbers, on that chilly morning in February? Altruism—to help the fundraiser, maybe. The lure of the free doughnuts, perhaps. As a dare or a prank—students will do anything for fun. But most of all, because it is a group activity.

Consumers are social creatures. As such, they live, work, play, and consume with groups of other consumers. These groups influence consumer decisions immensely, as consumers buy and consume products and services that will please the groups to which they belong. The purpose of this three-part chapter is to describe these group influences and the intricate ways in which they both guide and constrain our behavior as consumers. In the first part, we define reference groups and identify three forms of influence they exercise. If you have been wondering why your coworker's wardrobe has come to resemble that of André 3000, and likewise why your neighbor dresses like Maya Jupiter, now you will now know why. We next discuss variations in consumer susceptibility to interpersonal influence (SIPI)—allowing you to understand why your best friend may not have followed your lead, as far as wardrobe goes.

In the second part, we describe opinion leaders—a group of people whose opinions matter—who are also known as *influentials*, along with its e-subtype, *e-fluentials*. Highly coveted by marketers, these individuals can make an innovation a market success. In the last and third part, we discuss how innovations spread—how members of this elite reference group carry and diffuse the pro-innovation (and occasionally, anti-innovation) virus. We also discuss word-of-mouth and word-of-mouse and their marketing applications: viral marketing and buzz marketing. You cannot be studying consumer behavior in the new millennium and not know what the 'buzz' on buzz marketing is about. After reading this chapter, you will.

REFERENCE GROUPS
Limiting Extreme Individuality

Castellers—Spanish sport team—forming human pyramids at a Spanish festival

Groups share goals and recognize interdependency

Photo courtesy of Brian Long, London

Reference groups are the persons, groups, and institutions that one uses as points of reference. These are people one looks to for guidance in establishing one's own values and behaviors.[1] Reference groups influence individual behavior by serving as points of reference, as sources of norms, values, and conduct.

Note that a reference group does not have to be a "group." It can be a person, such as one's parent, or a role model. And of course, it can be a group, like one's fraternity members. It can also be an organization or an institution. **Institutions** are more permanent groups or entities with a pervasive and universal presence in a society, such as schools, religions, and families. Any person, group, or institution that serves as a point of reference is called a **referent**.

Because no one lives in isolation, every consumer has at least one referent—even Bohemians and Goth girls. Most have several. No one lives totally by himself or herself, for him/herself, and of him/herself.

What is a Group Anyway?

Just what is a group? A **Group** can be defined as two or more persons sharing a common purpose. The essential and defining quality of a group is a common purpose. To pursue this common purpose, group members:

- **share some values**
- **recognize interdependency**

- assume specific roles
- communicate mutual expectations and evaluations
- are able to provide some reward or punishment, tangible or intangible

Not All Groups Are Alike

Family, coworkers, professional organizations, fraternity brothers and sorority sisters—these are all groups. Certainly, they are not alike and they do not influence you equally and in the same manner. To identify key differences, sociologists have classified them in many ways. See Tables 10.1 and 10.2

Primary versus Secondary Groups—**Primary groups** are groups with whom a person interacts frequently (not necessarily face-to-face) and considers their opinions or norms important to follow. Examples are family, work organization, church groups, etc. With **secondary groups**, the contact is infrequent, and the norms of the group are considered less binding. Examples are distant relatives, occupational groups like associations of doctors, professors, musicians, and so on.

TABLE 10.1 TYPES OF GROUPS

TYPE OF MEMBERSHIP	PRIMARY	SECONDARY
MEMBERSHIP	• Family • Coworkers • Church groups • Fraternities/Sororities	• Professional associations • Political campaign volunteers • YMCA/YWCA
SYMBOLIC	• Personal role models • Significant others • The person one secretly admires	• Celebrities • People successful in their professions

MY CB BOOK

TABLE 10.2 CLASSIFICATION OF GROUPS BY MEMBERSHIP TYPE

TYPE OF MEMBERSHIP	INFORMAL	FORMAL
BY CHOICE	• Volunteer groups • Community • Friendship groups • Cultural Heroes	• School • Workplace • Fraternities
ASCRIBED OR ASSIGNED	• Family	• Religion

MY CB BOOK

Formal Versus Informal Groups—In **formal groups**, membership is granted by a formal admission. There are written rules for admission into the group and for the conduct of members. **Informal groups**, in contrast, have few explicit rules about member behavior. A family is an informal group, whereas the American Marketing Association is a formal group.

Ascribed Versus Choice Groups—A **choice group**, as its name implies, is a group a person voluntarily decides to join. An **ascribed or assigned group** is one in which membership is automatic—you don't have a choice. Examples of ascribed groups (membership by birth) are family, relatives, and tribes. Examples of assigned groups are coworkers, sports team members, or fellow prisoners.

Associative Versus Dissociative Groups—**Associative groups** are those with which we want to associate or to which we want to belong. In contrast, **dissociative groups** are those from which we want to dissociate. Generally, consumers want to associate with peers who have similar values and lifestyles, and they want to dissociate from groups they find unappealing, as is evidenced by the mutual distaste among the so called *jocks* and *geeks*.

Membership Versus Symbolic Groups—**Membership groups** are those in which an individual claiming to be a member is so recognized by the head and key group members, even when the membership is informal. **Symbolic groups**, on the other hand, have no provision for granting membership. Symbolic group memberships operate on a psychological level; the consumer simply deems himself or herself to be

a member of that group (or desires to be a member) and voluntarily adopts the group's norms and values. Membership groups include the family, the YMCA or other community organizations, professional associations, and so on. When a person is not already a member of a group (real or symbolic) but desires and expects to become a member, it is called an **aspirational** group. Most people aspire to be members of some group, and they expect to move up into this group. Since they aspire to be like this group, they emulate and often adopt the behavior of its members.

CONDITIONS FOR REFERENCE GROUP INFLUENCE

Although the influence of reference groups on consumers' choices is pervasive, reference groups do not influence every consumer decision for every product or service. When we buy mulch for our lawns, or decide where to go for a quick lunch, we are not thinking of any reference groups we have. But if we were buying a tree to plant in the front yard, we might worry about our neighbors' opinion of it. Or if we were taking a date out for dinner, we had better think about the kind of wine we would order.

The important question, therefore, is this: when and under what conditions does reference group influence occur? Behavioral scientist Francis S. Bourne gives this answer: Reference group influence occurs the most for products that are conspicuous.[2]

Moreover, Bourne proposes that there are two dimensions of conspicuousness: exclusivity and public visibility. If everyone owns and uses a product or service, then the ownership and use of that product or service has no *exclusivity*. Accordingly, there will be no basis for being concerned about others' opinions of it. The second dimension, *visibility*, is critical because a product or service has to be visible and identifiable in order for reference group members to approve or disapprove of it.

Based on Bourne's ideas, consumer researchers have suggested that the reference group influence may occur for the ownership of the product *per se*, or for the choice of a specific brand, or both. This will depend on whether a product is a luxury or a necessity and whether the product is used in private or in public. Combining the two dimensions yields four combinations (see Table 10.3).[3]

1. **Publicly Consumed Luxuries** In this case, reference groups will influence both whether or not the product will be owned and which brand is purchased.

2. **Privately Consumed Luxuries** Here, reference group influence will be strong for the ownership of the product (because it is a luxury) but weak for the brand choice (since it will be used in private, out of public visibility).

3. **Publicly Consumed Necessities** In this case, product ownership influence will be absent or weak since everyone owns it anyway, but brand level influence will be strong due to public visibility.

4. **Privately Consumed Necessities** Finally, for products that are necessities and, in addition, are consumed privately, neither product ownership nor the choice of specific brands is likely to be influenced by reference groups.

Eating in a group

Eating alone

Private vs. public consumption—which one invites referent influence more?

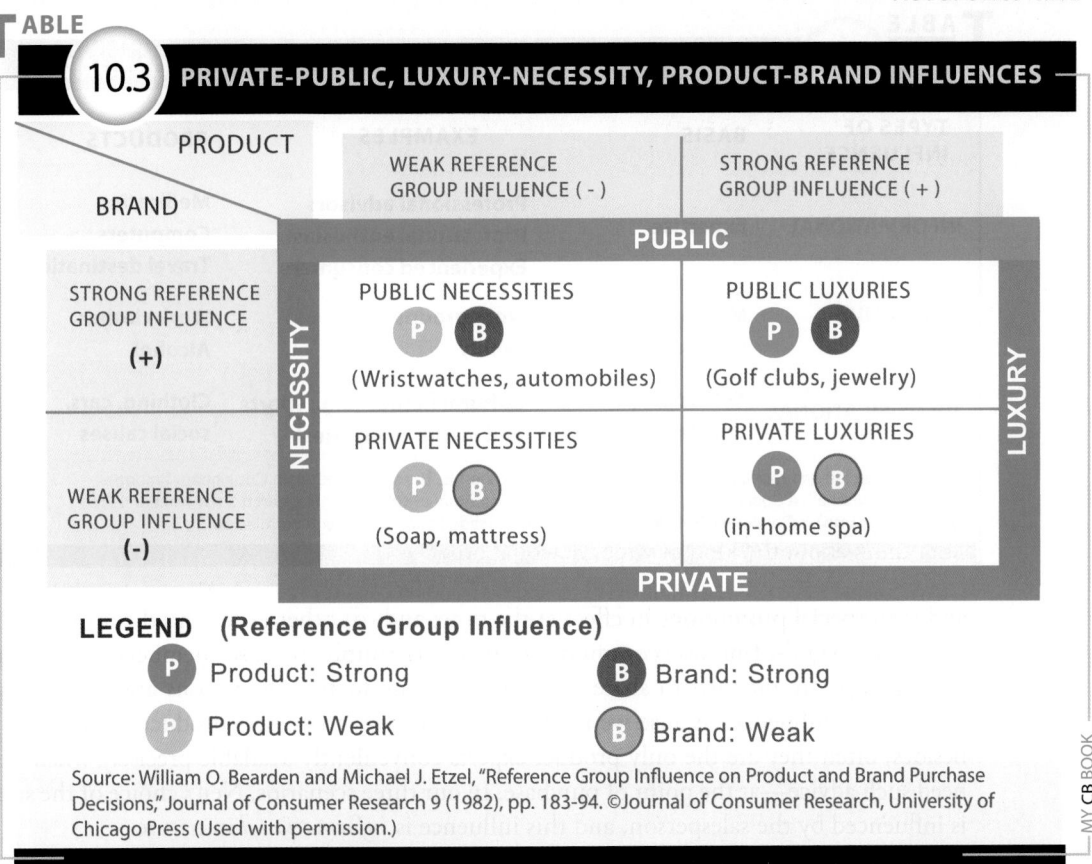

TABLE

10.3   PRIVATE-PUBLIC, LUXURY-NECESSITY, PRODUCT-BRAND INFLUENCES

PRODUCT

BRAND

	WEAK REFERENCE GROUP INFLUENCE (-)	STRONG REFERENCE GROUP INFLUENCE (+)
	PUBLIC	
STRONG REFERENCE GROUP INFLUENCE (+)	PUBLIC NECESSITIES P B (Wristwatches, automobiles)	PUBLIC LUXURIES P B (Golf clubs, jewelry)
WEAK REFERENCE GROUP INFLUENCE (-)	PRIVATE NECESSITIES P B (Soap, mattress)	PRIVATE LUXURIES P B (in-home spa)
	PRIVATE	

NECESSITY — LUXURY

LEGEND   (Reference Group Influence)

P   Product: Strong   B   Brand: Strong

P   Product: Weak   B   Brand: Weak

Source: William O. Bearden and Michael J. Etzel, "Reference Group Influence on Product and Brand Purchase Decisions," Journal of Consumer Research 9 (1982), pp. 183-94. ©Journal of Consumer Research, University of Chicago Press (Used with permission.)

MY CB BOOK

THREE FORMS OF REFERENCE GROUP INFLUENCE

Good to, Love to, Have to

The next question is, why do we as consumers accept influence from our reference groups or referents? What power do they possess over us to affect how we spend our money and what we consume? Consider the following three consumer purchases:

- **Neil, 26, wanted to buy a suit he could wear in winter as well as in summer. He went to a department store and tried on a few suits. He liked one that was dark gray, but the salesman recommended another one that was olive as being more appropriate for year-round use. So Neil bought the olive colored suit.**

- **Julia, 19, had been fancying the idea of wearing a low-cut pair of jeans, the kind she had seen Christina Aguilera wear. So this past weekend, she finally took out her savings and bought a pair. On Monday she would wear them to school.**

- **Hirosho, 35, got laid off from a dot-com company in the Bay Area, where he was a product developer. He then took a job as an industrial salesman in the Midwest. His job title was not the only thing that changed for him; now, he could no longer wear his cargo pants and tee-shirts to the office. Instead, he had to wear a white shirt and a tie—something he dreaded. Reluctantly, he bought a couple of each.**

All three consumers have been influenced by reference groups—however, those influences are not of the same kind. There are three kinds of reference group influences: informational, normative, and identificational.[4] (See Table 10.4.)

1. Informational   Informational influence occurs when a consumer is influenced by the product information someone provides. A person's power to exercise this influence on another person comes from his/her expertise. There are four types of "expert" referents: (a) professional advisors, such as doctors, tax accountants, and car mechanics; (b) product enthusiasts, such as computer buffs who get excited whenever new software is released; (c) **market mavens**—individuals who are generally knowledgeable about the marketplace happenings and possess information about a range of products, prices, distribution outlets,

MARKET MAVEN
In the know about all market happenings!

10.4	**TYPES OF REFERENCE GROUP INFLUENCES FOR CONSUMERS**		
TYPES OF INFLUENCE	**BASIS**	**EXAMPLES**	**PRODUCTS**
INFORMATIONAL	Expertise	Professional advisors Professional enthusiasts Experienced consumers	Medication Computers Travel destinations
NORMATIVE	Material rewards Sanctions	Work groups Family	Work clothes Alcohol
IDENTIFICATIONAL	Self-concept enactment	Cultural heroes (e.g., sports and media celebrities)	Clothing, cars, social causes

Source: Adapted and modified by the authors based on Robert E. Burnkrant and Alain Cousineau, "Informational and Normative Social Influence in Buyer Behavior," *Journal of Consumer Research* 2 (December 1975), 206-15. ©*Journal of Consumer Research*, University of Chicago Press (Used with permission.)

MY CB BOOK

and even special promotions in effect at the time; and (d) other experienced consumers.

Much word-of-mouth communication occurs simply because members of the last three groups are inclined to share their views on products. Salespersons also frequently exercise this influence because we naturally expect them to possess product information; besides, often they are the only product experts conveniently available precisely when we need such advice—at the point of purchase. In our three scenarios, Neil's choice of the suit is influenced by the salesperson, and this influence is *informational* in nature.

2. Normative **Normative influence** occurs when a consumer's decision or action is based on his or her desire to conform to the expectations of someone else. The force behind this influence comes from the referent's power to reward or punish the consumer's behavior. There are four types of normative referents:

Normative Influence: Work organizations dictate what you can wear

A. Parents and Family Members They influence youngsters because they have the power to reward or punish them. Children and adolescents may not watch, read, eat, wear, or drive what their parents do not approve of. For dependent children, especially, this reward/punishment often comes in the form of money—if parents are not willing to pay for a style of clothing, junior must simply compromise on his preference. Similarly, spouses influence each other's consumption choices simply by showing pleasure or displeasure (social reward/punishment).

B. Friends and Peers Identifying the power of reward and sanction that friends and peers possess is straightforward. If you want to keep your friends, then you must keep them happy. You must fit in, or you may become an outcast or a target of ridicule.

C. Regulatory Bodies and Other Public Institutions Governments and other regulatory bodies simply mandate, under threat of punishment, certain behaviors (which include consumption behaviors). Thus, you must wear a helmet if you want to ride a bicycle, and you must cover your body if you want to roam the streets! Schools mandate dress codes, and religious institutions mandate wide ranging consumption. For example, Sikh males in India must cover their heads with turbans; and Moslems may not eat pork.

Identificational Influence: Yo, Elvis, you are my hero.

D. Work Organizations Employers exercise referent power because they control a resource of great value to us—our wages! You have to follow the company code in personal behavior as well as in what you may choose to consume at work; e.g., the kind of clothing you wear, the kind of car you drive, and even what office decor you choose. In our scenarios, you would recognize Hirosho as the target of precisely this type of reference group influence.

3. Identificational **Identificational** influence occurs when a consumer emulates the behavior of another person. The force behind this influence is the referent's attractiveness as a role model or as an identity definer. We all have a role model, someone we look up to, someone we admire, someone we aspire to be like. We then emulate his or her tastes, his or her lifestyle, even his or her mannerisms. These referents define for us a self-concept, a personal identity, which we adopt and then enact with the accoutrements that go with that identity. There are three subtypes:

A. **Personal Acquaintances** For many of us, our role models come from among those we know intimately in our everyday lives. A parent, a senior in college, the president of our literary club, the coach of our basketball team—some aspect of their lives touches us, some accomplishment of theirs inspires us, some visible aspect of their lifestyles as consumers intrigues us. To identify with such persons, we acquire the same consumption accoutrements that we see them using.

B. **Cultural Heroes** Cultural heroes such as sports celebrities and film and music stars inspire millions of consumers around the world. Children and adolescents in their impressionable years are particularly mesmerized by these celebrities, whom they watch for several hours a day, often at some cost to their productive hours. But many celebrities inspire positive behaviors as well, supporting good causes such as Live Aid (U2's Bono), pro-environmentalism (Robert Redford), and human rights (Brad Pitt and Angelina Jolie).

C. **Social Archetype Groups** **Social archetype** groups are categories of persons sharing a lifestyle, such as bohemians, literati, jocks, cowboys, etc. Even some consumers outside of these groups find these groups fascinating—some of them anyway. They want to associate with these groups, assimilate their culture, and invariably emulate some consumption choices to gain at least a token identity of the group.

In our three scenarios, Julia's purchase of low cut-jeans is an example of identificational influence. Her referent for this choice is the cultural hero Christina Aguilera. Unlike normative referents, this cultural hero can neither punish nor reward Julia; to wit, Miss Aguilera is not going to write Julia a personal letter of commendation for her choice! Instead, what Miss Aguilera does for Julia, and for millions of other young women around the world, is to define a self-identity—one of a young, effervescent, fun-loving, trendy, accomplished diva.

To help you remember these, we nickname them as *good to, love to, and have to*. Go figure which is which.

Identity Adoption versus Identity Distancing

Identificational influence can work in either direction. When we find some group's image appealing, we want to adopt that identity, and, consequently, we want to emulate their behaviors, preferences and tastes, and consumption choices. On the flip side, if we find some group's image unappealing, then we want to distance ourselves from its identity, its image. In the former case, the group serves as an associative identification group; for the latter, it serves as a dissociative identification group. In the 1980s, in America, break dancing, rap music, and hip hop baggy clothing started out as features of the urban black teenagers' lifestyle, primarily as symbols of an anti-establishment stance; however, unexpectedly, suburban white teenagers found these style choices "cool," and adopted them en masse.

Identities to distance from and identities to adopt

In sharp contrast are motorcycle riders, in their leather jackets, chains, and tattoos. One particular group is known as the Hell's Angels, and most people do not want to be like them. Of course every "extreme" consumer inspires *identity adoption* among some consumers; just as likely, he or she also inspires *identity distancing* among others. But identity adoption and distancing occurs routinely even with normal consumers as referents. Many adolescents grow up in the image of their same-gender parent, but many also develop their tastes in styles that are diametrically opposed to those of their parents. Consequently, they wish to carve out their identities in ways that are sharply distanced from their images of their parents.

SOME OF NEW YORK'S MOST INFLUENTIAL ROLE MODELS
WILL NEVER WEAR THE YANKEE UNIFORM.

JOIN NEW YORK'S BRIGHTEST
TEACH NYC
WWW.TEACHNYC.NET

Ad
Council.org   NYC DEPARTMENT OF EDUCATION   Appleseed

In an age where most young people look to sports celebrities as role models, here the NYC Department of Education presents a more rewarding alternative—a role model that shows a career path rather than merely offering spectator entertainment, and the one that is both more personally fulfilling and societally more needed.

(Courtesy New York City Department of Education, The Appleseed Foundation, and the Advertising Council.)

Battle of Referents

It would be nice if we could choose our referents; sometimes we can, and sometimes we can't. For example, we can choose Andrè 3000 but not our parents. Many times diverse referents are in conflict—we can please one only by displeasing another. We want to dress up like Andrè 3000, but our parents would rather not see us decked out in that bright, checkered jacket. An expert (e.g., a movie critic) may advise us to go see *The Artist*, but our significant other might make us see *Magic Mike*. Many of our choices are conflicted precisely because different referents pull us in divergent directions. How we resolve such approach-avoidance dilemmas depends, in part, on how gullible we are—i.e., on our susceptibility to influence.

SUSCEPTIBLE TO INTERPERSONAL INFLUENCE (SIPI)

Although all of us are influenced by reference groups, we differ in our abilities to follow our own minds. Some of us are pretty independent-minded, not much concerned with pleasing others; but some of us are always anxious about other people's opinions. This individual characteristic is called **Susceptibility to Interpersonal Influence** (SIPI), defined as consumer motivation to follow other people's expectations and advice.[5] This characteristic is not simply a matter of habit or of casually following someone's advice for the sake of expediency. Rather, it is rooted in strong motivations to please and/or emulate others. High SIPI's (highly susceptibles) are very uncomfortable at the very idea of what others might think of their actions or market choices; as such they are driven by a desire to avoid disapproval and to win kudos. In contrast, "low SIPI's" are relatively less conscious of and anxious about others' views of their consumption practices.[6]

What makes consumers more or less susceptible? Three factors: autonomy, risk averseness, and consumption as identity marker (see Figure 10.1).[7]

• **Autonomy** refers to the desire to feel free to do whatever one wants. It comes from a level of confidence in one's own ability and tastes. Autonomy-exhibiting consumers have high self-esteem—i.e., they feel that they are competent. They are also high in self-efficacy—i.e., they are in fact able to control outcomes or achieve their goals. So they are less susceptible to others' influence.

• **Risk Averseness** refers to how much risk people are willing to accept. All consumer decisions, and life choices for that matter, entail certain risks, and risk-averse consumers want to tread cautiously. One way they minimize their perceived risk is by seeking and following others' advice. So they are more susceptible to others' influence.

• **Consumption as Identity Marker** refers to the extent to which a person defines his or her identity by consumption. At one extreme are consumers who believe that "you are what you consume"; at the other end are consumers who feel that a person is defined by his or her knowledge and character and goodness of the heart rather than by consumption.

Furthermore, corresponding with the three types of influences, consumers can differ in their susceptibility to the type of influence. Some consumers may be susceptible only on information, others on norms, and still others on identification. Information-based

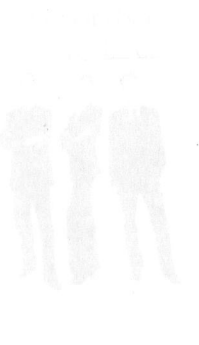

10.1 THREE-FACTOR MODEL OF SIPI

FIGURE

Autonomy

Risk Averseness

Consumption as Identity Marker

CONSUMER SUSCEPTIBILITY to INTERPERSONAL INFLUENCE (SIPI)

MY **CB** BOOK

TABLE 10.5   MEASURING CONSUMER SUSCEPTIBILITY TO INTERPERSONAL INFLUENCE (SIPI)

Please mark your opinion by writing a number in front of each question using the following scale:

Strongly Disagree	More Disagree than Agree	Feel Neutral	More Agree than Disagree	Strongly Agree
1	2	3	4	5

NORMATIVE

1. In making my selection of products and brands, my overriding concern is that my friends and significant others would like it.
2. When I am in the marketplace, I buy what I like without bothering about what others would think of my choice.*
3. I rarely purchase the latest fashion styles unless I am sure my friends approve of them.
4. If people would know the make or brand of a product I use, I would purchase only the brand they expect me to buy.
5. In life, for the most part, I do my own thing without worrying about what others might say.*

INFORMATIVE

1. I often depend on information from other people for making my product selections.
2. I can and do buy most of the products without a salesperson's advice or help.*
3. I am never sure of my selection without asking a few people if they think those products are good.
4. When people talk about their experiences with products, I listen.
5. Whatever decisions I make in life, I frequently look to information from others on the subject.

IDENTIFICATIONAL

1. I often identify with other people by purchasing the products and brands they use.
2. I like to look like people I like.
3. To make sure I buy the right product or brand, I often observe what people similar to me are buying and using.
4. Keeping up with Joneses—trying to have or do what the so-called 'successful people' have or do—is not my thing in life.*
5. I am happy with who I am, with no desire to imitate anyone else.*

Notes: (1) When giving the survey to consumers, remove the headings and jumble up the questions. Later, sort them back under the three headings. (2) Reverse score the questions marked*, and sum the scores within each heading and also compute a grand total. (3) No national norms exist, so mid-point scores (i.e., 15 for each heading and 45 for the grand total) may be considered as being middle-of-the-road. The overall score would range from 15 to 75, and dividing this into three equal intervals, we could say that a score of 35 or less would make you a low-SIPI, and a score of 55 or more, a high-SIPI.

Source: Composed by author, with adaptations and extensions of scales suggested in the literature--for example: William O. Bearden, Richard G, Netemeyer, and Jesse E. Teel, "Susceptibility to Interpersonal Influence," Journal of Consumer Research, 1989, March, 473-481; and William O. Bearden and Randall L. Rose, "Attention to Social Comparison Information: An Individual Difference Factor Affecting Consumer Conformity," Journal of Consumer Research, 1990, March, 461-471. © Journal of Consumer Research. Published by The University of Chicago Press. (Used with permission.)

MY CB BOOK

susceptibles are likely to be performance-risk averse, eager to avoid products that might turn out to be lemons. Norm-based susceptibles are paranoid about peer disapproval and about fitting in. They seldom deviate from a group's expressed wishes, and, in fact, they actively seek out advice to ensure that their choices will be approved. Finally, identification-based susceptibles are fascinated by certain others (be they remote celebrities or people they personally know in their lives); they are driven to imitate or emulate these others. Of course, some consumers are susceptible on all three counts, and some are susceptible on none.

How susceptible are you? Take the test (Table 10.5) to find out.

SOCIAL COMPARISON THEORY

One of the foundational theories of reference group influence is **Social Comparison Theory**.[8] The theory is a two-part statement: (1) As humans, we have an innate need to evaluate ourselves; and (2) because we do not have objective criteria, we look to others similar to ourselves for an evaluation template. In other words, we compare our own performance and our own traits against others whom we judge to be similar to ourselves. When we judge ourselves to be doing as well or better than our friends and persons of similar age, education, etc., we feel happy.

Such social comparison extends to consumption in two ways: (1) We use others as normative standards, with others' approval as an implicit goal in our marketplace choices. Thus, we wear clothing that we believe our bosses and coworkers will like (even if we ourselves may not like them as much). And (2) we adopt the styles and consumption patterns of those consumer groups to which we believe we should or do belong, so as to achieve at least outward similarity. Thus, if our graduate school class fellows were driving luxury European cars, then we too would try to buy one (even when beyond our means) just so the world at large would not think we were less successful in our careers than our cohort members.

Social Comparison Theory also explains why most consumers like to shop with a friend or shopping pal. Taking a friend along helps us make choices and ensures that the purchase will meet the social comparison test. In one study of teens[9] (teens are in their identity formative years and therefore engage in social comparisons more than do adults), it was found that teens who thought their teen friends were knowledgeable about clothing took their teen friends along when they shopped. They also enjoyed shopping more when with friends. And they spent more money in the store. The researchers point out that retailers wary of teen groups wandering in the store need to recognize that teens in groups are likely to end up buying more. Shopping with friends facilitates social comparison. And it also generates another referent influence, *social facilitation*.

S A V V Y
MARKETER

SOCIAL FACILITATION

Social facilitation refers to the effect that the mere presence of others has on our performance. This effect can be positive, eliciting improved performance, or negative, eliciting reduced performance. What does it depend on? Task ease and expertise. On easy tasks, in the presence of onlookers, we tend to push ourselves a bit more, seeking to accomplish more. This is because the ease of the task gives us confidence that we will reach the goal. But with a hard task, the presence of onlookers induces anxiety that we might fail the task. Task ease is, of course, a function of expertise. A given task will be easier for experts than for novices. Therefore, the presence of onlookers will make experts perform better, whereas it can turn a novice into a nervous wreck. Now you know why star players (sportsmen, musicians, theater actors) do better with a crowd of spectators than they do in practice sessions; in contrast, novices tend to botch their tasks. And in consumer behavior, shoppers unsure of what to buy will resent a salesperson shadowing them. But consumers with confidence in making product choices will welcome a salesperson's help and attention.[10]

Onlookers make novices nervous!

SOCIAL LOAFING

One of the most pervasive outcomes of normative influence (or rather of perceived liberation from it) is social loafing. **Social loafing** refers to the propensity of individuals in a group to put in less effort because their individual contribution (hence its absence) would not be visible. When individuals are not accountable, they will withhold effort. This is similar to free riding—partaking in the fruits of collective labor without contributing one's share of costs.[11]

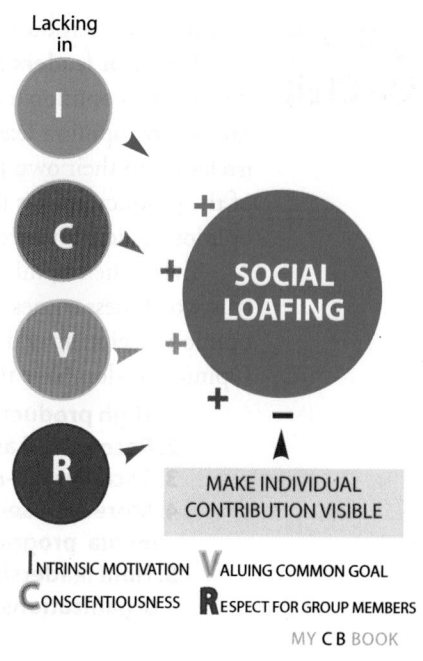

Thus, if you set up a coffee station for co-workers on a voluntary contribution basis, some of us will not make the contribution. In a group assignment, some will not work, or will not work as hard. But, just as surely, some will. What accounts for social loafing? A lack of certain personal qualities. Intrinsic motivation for the task, for one: Those intrinsically motivated (i.e., those who really like the task) will put in the effort. Conscientiousness (see Chapter 5 for a definition) is another factor: Those who are conscientious will drop their quarters in the common coffee pool. Valuing the achievement of the common goal is a third factor. Finally, respect for group members will also suppress social loafing. These four intrinsic personal qualities drive group members NOT to engage in social loafing. If you are the leader of a group with members lacking in these personal qualities, then you can curb social loafing by making the individual contribution *visible* (for example, by assigning the members individual parts of the task).[12]

In consumer behavior, all public consumption (that shares common resources) happens in an *implicit group*—so social loafing occurs when a person (consumer) ignores the implicit rules of public consumption (e.g., driving beyond the speed limit, smoking in a non-smoking place when no one is looking, shop-lifting, littering, not-flushing, etc., etc.)!

OPINION LEADERS

Basically, when we want to influence others' behavior, we can take three routes: First, we can simply go on living our normal lives, let them observe us, and hope that they find our behavior and tastes appealing and that they therefore emulate us. Second, we can explicitly tell them to "just do it," brandishing our power to reward or punish. Finally, we can tell them what we think of something and hope that they follow our advice. If they do, and if a lot of people like them also do, then we have become opinion leaders.

Opinion leadership is defined as the giving of information and advice, leading to the acceptance of the advocated position by the recipient of the opinion. This definition has two elements. First, the opinion leader must hold an opinion on a topic and recommend an action pertaining to it (e.g., recommend adoption of a new product); second, the opinion-recipient must follow the advice and adopt the recommended course of action.

Opinion leaders have two essential qualities, both necessary for their success: expertise and trustworthiness. **Expertise** is defined as possession of knowledge about a topic, or product—especially knowledge that is not yet common knowledge. Since a person cannot be an expert on everything, opinion leadership is by necessity topic-specific. Thus, no one is an opinion leader across the board. Rather, opinion leaders are experts on a single product or service. For example, John may be an expert on DVDs and Steve an expert on fashionable clothing.

Trustworthiness, the second requisite for opinion leadership, refers to the perceived benevolence and dependability of the opinion-giver. It is founded on the requirement that the opinion giver has no vested interest in promoting a position. That is why, despite expertise, the salesperson is often not an opinion leader. Some salespersons are exceptions:

S A V V Y
MARKETER

they make it their business to earn their customers' trust by giving impartial advice.

Opinion leaders are generally the first wave of adopters of new products. As such they serve as opinion leaders for those who have yet to adopt an innovation. Nonadopters can also be opinion leaders, but only if their nonadoption is due to the innovation being irrelevant to their own personal needs. In such cases, their expertise, not their personal use of the product, makes them opinion leaders. For example, physicians and pharmacists are opinion leaders for medicines, even if they have not used the medicine themselves.

Even when opinion leadership is based on personal adoption, another dimension of trustworthiness comes into play: Is the adopter similar to the opinion follower? If not, the opinion receiver may discount the opinion leader's experience as irrelevant or less relevant. Opinion leaders have the following personal characteristics:[10]

1. **High product-involvement**
2. **Recognized as leaders**
3. **Socially well-integrated**
4. **More exposed to a variety of media sources, especially news and information media programs (rather than merely entertainment-oriented media)**
5. **Hold leadership and formal office positions in social and community organizations**

IDENTIFYING OPINION LEADERS

Suppose you want to find out who in your community are opinion leaders, say, for new fashion clothing. You could use one of these four methods:

1. **Observation**
2. **Self-Designation**
3. **Sociometry**
4. **Key-Informant**

To use the **observation method**, we simply go to a community and observe people's patterns of interaction; from these observations, we identify persons who interact with many others and who seem to command respect from others. To identify opinion leaders among students, for example, we would just hang out in the college cafeteria, library, and hallways for a few days and observe who interacts with whom.

In the **self-designation method**, we ask members of a community themselves to answer a few questions that would reveal if they believe people seek their advice on a topic. The self-designation method, then, is simply a survey method we use to measure consumers' opinion sharing activities. One such survey, used by sociologists and consumer researchers, is shown in Table 10.6.

The above two methods are, of course, useful for measuring many aspects of consumer behavior—motivations, personality traits, perceptions, attitudes, lifestyles, and so on. The next two methods are especially useful for identifying opinion leaders.

In **sociometry**, a researcher asks the residents of a community or members of a group who they (each one individually) would consult with or look to for information about the given topic. Persons receiving the highest number of mentions are considered opinion leaders.

HASHERS—A REFERENCE GROUP WITH A RUNNING PROBLEM

Yes, indeed there is a group that runs, dressed just like this, in red. Typically, they run about 9-10 miles on impromptu trails. And then, at the finish line (which is often in a park), they stop, only to start a bout of frenzied merry-making—chugging beer, playing games, posing for pictures. They are members of their local chapter of a worldwide organization called the Hash House Harriers.

Today there are some 1000 local chapters in 137 countries—Australia, Mexico, Singapore, India, Russia, Great Britain, etc.

In the **key informant method**, instead of asking everyone, we ask prominent people in a community to name a few persons they consider able to influence others' opinions on a given topic. Of course, the key informants may themselves be opinion leaders, and, as such, may be named by other key informants.[11]

10.6 A SCALE TO MEASURE OPINION LEADERSHIP

In answering the following survey, please think of the conversations you generally have with others about consumer electronic products such as TVs, DVDs, computers, MP3, PDAs, cell phones, etc. (Note: The product used here, for illustrative purposes, is consumer electronics. The survey is adaptable for any product category.)

Q1. Compared to other people you know, are you more likely to be asked, less likely to be asked, or about as likely to be asked for your opinion about consumer electronic products?

Much more likely to be asked	Somewhat more likely to be asked	About equally likely to be asked	Somewhat less likely to be asked	Much less likely to be asked
1	2	3	4	5

Q2. During the past six months, to how many people have you given an opinion about one or more of these products?

To no one	To very few	To quite a few	To many	To a lot of persons
1	2	3	4	5

Q3. In your discussions with other people you know, if the topic turns to consumer electronic products, are you more likely to give or receive information and opinion?

Much more likely to give	Somewhat more likely to give	About equally likely to give and receive	Somewhat more likely to receive	Much more likely to receive
1	2	3	4	5

Q4. How likely are you to be used as a source of advice?

Not at all likely	Somewhat likely	Fairly likely	Quite likely	Very likely
1	2	3	4	5

Q5. Thinking back over the past year, would you say you have influenced others' decisions on consumer electronic products--about buying or not buying and about which brands and makes to buy or not buy?

Never	Rarely	Sometimes	Often	Frequently
1	2	3	4	5

Q6. When it comes to making buying decisions on consumer electronic products, do you depend a lot on other people's opinion, or are you able to determine on your own which product and brand and make to buy or not buy?

1. Depend almost entirely on other people's opinion
2. Depend a lot on other people's opinion
3. Balanced use of my own view and other people's advice
4. Largely able to decide on my own with some advice from others
5. Able to make up my own mind almost independently

Computing the score: Reverse code Q3 and then add up all questions. The score can range from 6 to 30. Since the middle point is 18, the following interpretation is suggested:

5-11	Not an opinion leader at all
12-15	More of an opinion follower than an opinion leader
16-20	Opinion exchanger rather than a leader or a follower
21-24	Opinion leader rather than a follower
25-30	Strong opinion leader

Note: The survey is composed by the author based on measures used by various researchers—principally, "Overlap of Opinion Leadership Across Consumer Product Categories," King, Charles W.; Summers, John O. *Journal of Marketing Research*, Feb70, 7(1), p43-50; Fred D. Reynolds and William R. Darden, "Mutually Adaptive Effects of Interpersonal Communication," Journal of Marketing Research, 8 (November 1971), pp. 449-454. See also Leisa Reinecke Flynn, Ronald E. Goldsmith, and Jacqueline K. Eastman, "Opinion Leaders and Opinion Seekers: Two New Measurement Scales," Journal of the Academy of Marketing Science 24, Spring 1996, 137-47; and Terry L. Childers, "Assessment of Psychometric Properties of an Opinion Leadership Scale," Journal of Marketing Research, 1986 (23), May, 184-88. No population distributional norms exist on the scale scores but you should expect a majority to be, by definition, opinion seeker/follower rather than opinion leaders. © Open Mentis Publishers, 2007, 2010.

INFLUENTIALS

Influentials They are the leading indicators of what Americans will be buying.

Two researchers, Ed Keller and Jon Berry, surveyed a national sample to identify opinion leaders and published their findings in a book entitled *Influentials*.[12] Their findings confirm what classical research has found to be the characteristics of opinion leaders (described above). Demographically, opinion leaders are slightly older, more educated, more likely to be dual-income couples, have a higher median income, and hold executive or professional jobs. In their psychological makeup, influentials are, compared to an average person, much more optimistic about their own future, believing in the prospects of achieving a "good life"; and they have an internal locus of control, believing in their own abilities to influence their life chances. Influentials read more newspapers, books and magazine, are much more active in their communities, volunteering in social and charity work, and are much more interested in current events and in civic issues.

E-FLUENTIALS

A New Breed of Influentials in the Cyber Age

Keller and Berry also researched (collaborating with the market research companies called Burson-Marsteller and RoperASW) **e-fluentials**—a subgroup of Influentials, consisting of the persons who are net-savvy and influence other people both offline and online. State Leller and Berry[13]:

E-fluentials make waves. They project their opinions far beyond the scope of their individual contacts. An e-fluential imparts an experience to 14 individuals on average. ... And, these electronic town criers are as likely to share information on products and services offline as they are to relay their experiences online.

E-fluentials comprise about 10% of the U.S. online population (i.e., about 11.1 million). By definition—since they are opinion leaders, they get asked about twice as often as others for advice on wide-ranging topics, from healthcare to new technologies. And, also by definition, they express more confidence in sharing their opinions with others. They visit both company Web sites and opinion sites (such as Planetfeedback.com) more than do other online consumers, and they double check the information found on these Web sites. They are online more often than others, and they participate in newsgroups, discussion forums, bulletin boards, and listservs (a type of online channel). Most importantly, they believe, much more than do others, in the power of the Internet as a channel for influencing opinion.[14]

DIFFUSION OF INNOVATIONS

How They Go Viral

First, look at *Coffee Joulies*. Coffee Joulies™ are shiny metal beans. The shells are stainless steel; inside is a plant based material—called phase change material (PCM)—that melts exactly at 140°F. So if your coffee is too hot, these Joulies eat up heat; if it is too cold, they emit heat. The result: Your coffee stays at 140°F—the ideal coffee temperature that will not burn your lips.

The set of five Joulies costs $49.00 (you need five of them to keep a 20 oz cup of coffee at the "just right" temperature). Launched in December 2011, at press time they were under limited scale production. Check it out at Joulies.com. Will you? And, even more importantly, will you be one of the first ones to buy them? Of interest to marketers is a study of how product innovations spread and what roles opinion leaders play in this process.

Sociologists and consumer researchers have studied this process, and they call it *diffusion*. The word *diffusion* means "spreading," and, therefore, the **diffusion process** refers to the spreading of an innovation's acceptance and use through a population. How does an innovation spread through a population? The answer: like an epidemic! A few

Coffee Joulies™

people get it at first—maybe only one person gets it, and then it spreads to two, then four, then eight, then sixteen, and so on. That is it spreads exponentially, at first, and then it slows down—only because there are few people left to catch it. The same thing with an innovation. A few people adopt it at first, say about 100; then they spread it to 400 (each one to four), who then spread it to 1600, then to 6400, then to 25, 600, to 102, 400, to 409, 600, then to 1.63 million, then to 6.55 million more, then to 26.21 million more, then to 105 million, and so on—you get the picture. The important point is that, when it comes to people adopting a new idea or innovation, they do it the same way they catch a contagious disease! See Figure 10.2.

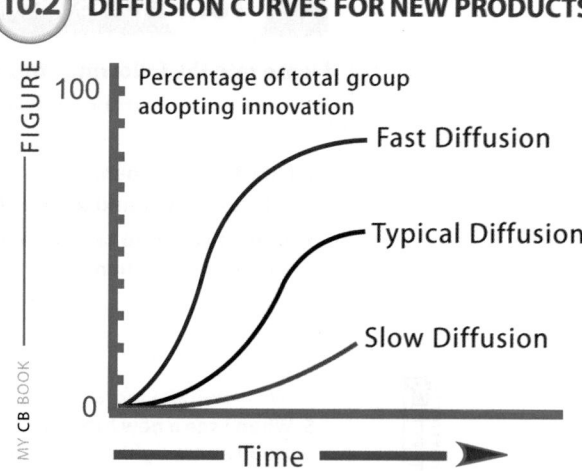

10.2 DIFFUSION CURVES FOR NEW PRODUCTS

What has this got to do with opinion leaders and followers? Well, it does, and in this respect the process differs from the spread of epidemics. Epidemics treat everyone equally, spreading to whoever is exposed. That is because people have no control over catching a disease (once they are exposed); in contrast, when it comes to adopting an innovation, they do it, for the most part, of their own free will. Accordingly, they decide whether to adopt it sooner or, alternatively, later. They choose, in other words, to take the plunge and show leadership, or alternatively, to be cautious and follow others' leads.

We can actually plot the adoption timing of these leaders and followers on a graph showing how quickly or how late various consumers in a society adopt innovations. What is the idea, you might ask? Because the products are so different, every graph would look different, wouldn't it? If so, then what could we possibly learn by plotting such graphs? Well, an interesting thing happens here: All the graphs look alike! And this common form is a bell-shaped curve, shown in Figure 10.3.

OPINION LEADERS AND FOLLOWERS
Innovators and Laggards, and All the Consumers in Between

Marketers have given these consumer groups names, depending on how early or late they adopt an innovation. On the bell curve, they are divided into five groups. The first groups of adopters are called *innovators*. The middle three groups that follow are called

10.3 INNOVATION ADOPTER CATEGORIES

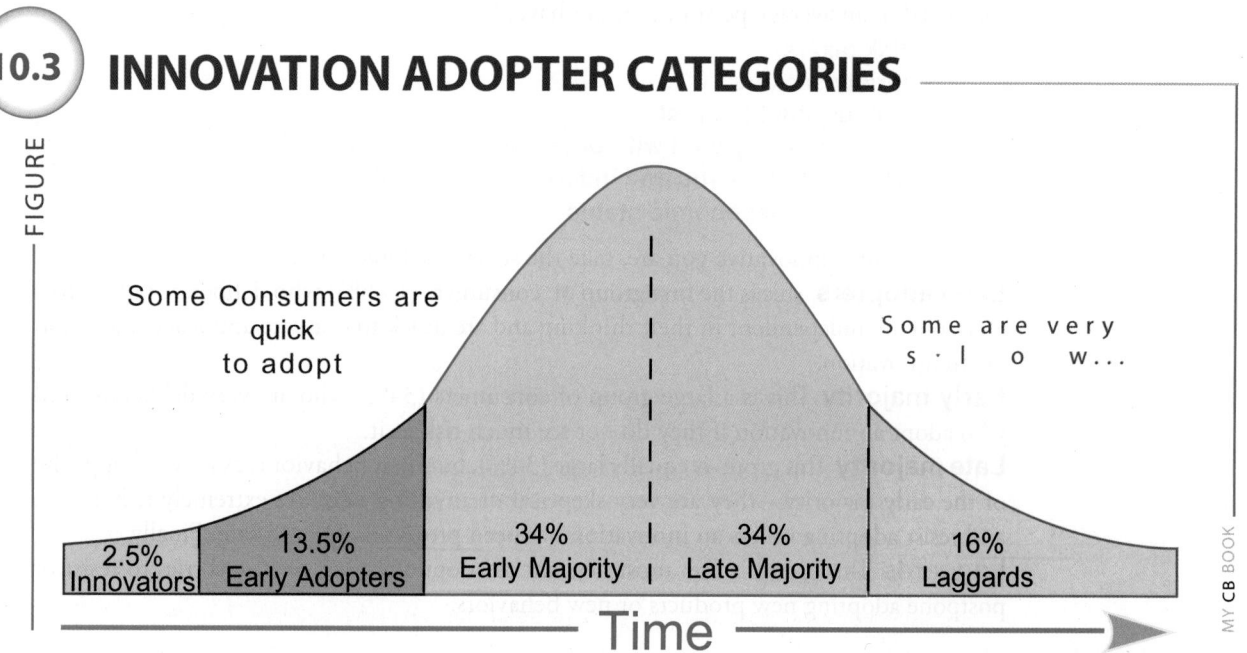

TABLE

10.7   **MEASUREMENT OF CONSUMER INNOVATIVENESS**

Please rate the following statements in terms of your agreement or disagreement.

	Strongly Disagree				Strongly Agree
	1	2	3	4	5

1. I like to take a chance.	1 2 3 4 5
2. I like to try new and different things.	1 2 3 4 5
3. When it comes to taking chances, I would rather be safe than sorry.*	1 2 3 4 5
4. I like to wait until something has been proven before I try it.*	1 2 3 4 5
5. If people quit wasting their time experimenting we would get more accomplished.*	1 2 3 4 5
6. When I see a new brand on the shelf, I usually pass right by.*	1 2 3 4 5
7. In general, I am the first (last) in my circle of friends to buy a new _____ when it appears.	1 2 3 4 5
8. I like to buy new _____ before others do.	1 2 3 4 5

* These items must be reverse-scored.

Note: 1. In the blank spaces, fill in broad product categories such as fashion clothing, tech gizmos, new products, etc. 2. While there is no normative score standard, a score above the middle point (after summing up all eight items) would indicate innovativeness; i.e., scores above 24 would indicate innovativeness.

Source: Items compiled from several sources, e.g., Clark Leavitt, John Walton (1975), DEVELOPMENT OF A SCALE FOR INNOVATIVENESS, in *Advances in Consumer Research*, Vol. 02, eds. Mary Jane Schlinger, : Association for Consumer Research, Pages: 545-554. Ronald E. Goldsmith and Charles F. Hofacker, "Measuring Consumer Innovativeness," *Journal of the Academy of Marketing Science*, 19 (1991), 209-221; Fred D. Reynolds and William R. Darden, "Mutually Adaptive Effects of Interpersonal Communication," *Journal of Marketing Research*, 8 (November 1971), pp. 449-454.

MY CB BOOK

early adopters, *early majority*, and *late majority*, in that order. The last to adopt are called *laggards*—an unfair label, actually, so take it sportingly if you are the last one to adopt. The dividing line between groups is drawn based simply on statistical distribution (i.e., one and two standard deviations in either direction from the mean). That is why the groups divide the bell curve so symmetrically.

Innovators The first 2.5% of the population to adopt an innovation are called *innovators*. Their defining characteristic is that they adopt *independently* of other people.

According to scholarly research in this field, innovators are a different type of people—compared to an average person, they are/have:[15]

1. **Risk takers**
2. **Variety seekers**
3. **High product interest**
4. **Less well-integrated with other members of the society**
5. **More individualistic and independent in thinking**
6. **Upper socioeconomic status**

To see how innovative you are, take the survey in Table 10.7.

Early adopters This is the first group of consumers (13.5%) who deliberate rather than rush, but are independent in their thinking and are quick to evaluate and reach a decision on an innovation.

Early majority This is a large group of consumers (34%) who are very deliberate, and who adopt an innovation if they do not see much risk in it.

Late majority This group is equally large (34%), but their behavior is exactly the opposite of the early majority—they are very skeptical of anything new, are extremely risk-averse, and resist adopting unless an innovation has been proven useful and safe. Finally,

Laggards This group is the most hesitant to adopt anything new, and tries to resist or postpone adopting new products or new behaviors.

THE ADOPTION PROCESS
Why Are Imitators Late to the Party?

The **adoption of an innovation** refers to the consumer acceptance of an innovation for continued use. Some innovations are adopted relatively quickly, whereas others take a long time before receiving widespread adoption. Two principal factors distinguish innovations from current products and cause most people to be cautious: (1) As new product categories, innovations lack evaluation criteria, so consumers don't know how to appraise them; and (2) their benefits and negative outcomes are unknown or not established by experience. Therefore, consumers engage in a long, deliberative process before adopting the innovation. This adoption process has been characterized by the acronym, AIDA (See Figure 10.4).

FIGURE 10.4 THE AIDA MODEL : STAGES IN CONSUMER ADOPTION OF INNOVATIONS

MY CB BOOK

- ACTION
- DESIRE
- INTEREST
- AWARENESS

The AIDA model suggests that when adopting an innovation, consumers pass through these four mental states in a hierarchical order. First they become aware of the innovation. Then they become interested in it and learn more. If what they learn tells them that the product would be of use to them, then they feel a desire for it. Finally, they take the necessary action to acquire it. Awareness, Interest, Desire, and Action–AIDA. Remember it; it applies to all of us, for all innovations.

Because innovators and early adopters are independent thinkers, they are able to progress through these four steps quickly. Those who adopt later can be called *imitators*. They are risk avoiders; they wait to see whether the risk takers' experience has been satisfactory.

SAVVY MARKETER

There you have it—later adopters (imitators) use early adopters as role models and opinion leaders for their adoption. That is why innovation adoption is, just like the spread of an epidemic, a process of group and social influence.

Contrary to the popular view, rejection does not make a person non-innovative. Putting off the trial adoption does. Or, even more strictly, a non-innovative consumer is someone who does not show curiosity to learn more (i.e., to gather more information) after exposure to a new stimulus, or avoids further information and puts off active evaluation of the innovation.

THE MEDIA AND MARKET CONVERSATIONS

TWO-STEP VERSUS MULTI-STEP FLOW COMMUNICATION THEORY
Whom Can Followers Trust—and Why Advertising Does Not Suffice

Since the advent of the mass media, it has become easy (though not inexpensive) to spread the word about your product to millions of consumers around the world. Just put it on TV or the radio, and the whole world will know who you are and what you are selling. The truth is that mass media doesn't really reach the masses; it may reach their ears and eyes alright, but it does not reach their minds. Only some people are persuaded by the mass media; you have met them before—opinion leaders. The rest of the masses look to opinion leaders for their news and for their tips on products.

When something is buzz-worthy, buzzers have a field day

This insight was first advanced by sociologist Paul Lazarsfeld, under the rubric of "the two-step flow of communication theory." **The two-step flow of communication theory** suggests that communication from mass media reaches the masses in two-steps—first, from mass media to opinion leaders, and then from opinion leaders to the masses.[13]

Is the theory valid today? Yes, in its overall insight, it is. But in details, it is much more complex, entailing many more flows. Accordingly, it is proper to call the modern version of the theory a "multi-step flow of communication theory." This theory captures the following multiple flows and processes (see Figures 10.5a and 10.5b):

1. **Mass media do reach the masses, but the masses pay attention mostly to entertainment media; in contrast, the news media reach opinion leaders who are much more tuned into news and new developments.**

2. **Even if the masses are exposed to product and event news through mass media, mass media, at best, only make them aware. In contrast, opinion leaders seek and receive detailed information about new products and events from media.**

3. **Opinion leaders are able to make up their minds based on the news and information they receive from mass media; in contrast, the masses do not make up their minds without seeking advice from opinion leaders. For the masses, then, mass media serve the crucial function of bringing awareness so they can seek further information and advice from opinion leaders.**

4. **Of course, as in the two-step flow, opinion leaders still spread some of the word proactively to the masses.**

S A V V Y MARKETER

Thus, this multi-step flow theory does not negate the two-step theory; rather it augments and extends it. And it further bolsters the role of opinion leaders in the persuasion process. As a marketer, you need to target both groups. Put general brand news in mass media, and put more detailed and technical information in special interest media—remember that opinion leaders are interested in specific interest topics!

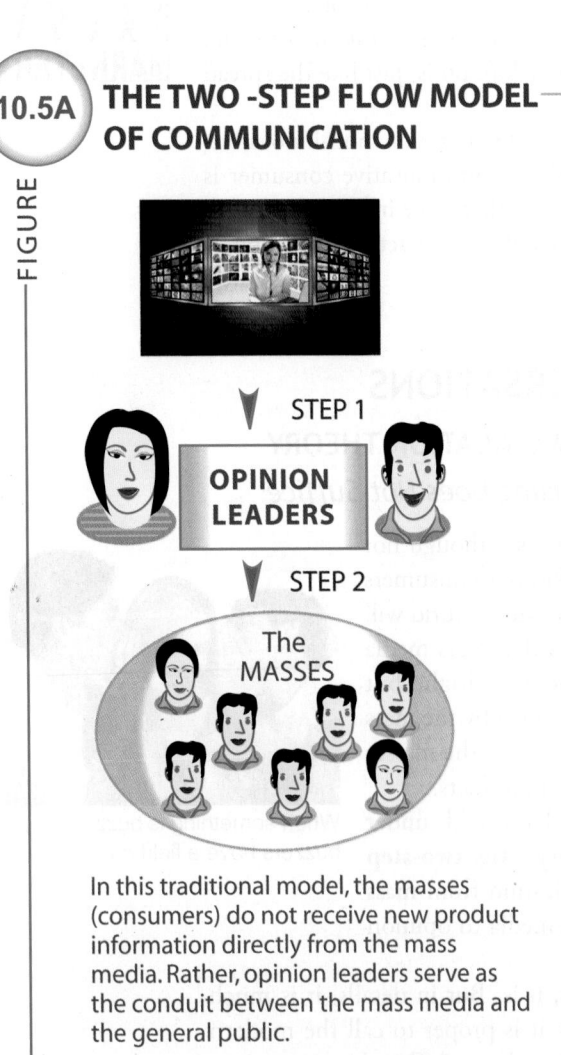

FIGURE 10.5A

THE TWO-STEP FLOW MODEL OF COMMUNICATION

In this traditional model, the masses (consumers) do not receive new product information directly from the mass media. Rather, opinion leaders serve as the conduit between the mass media and the general public.

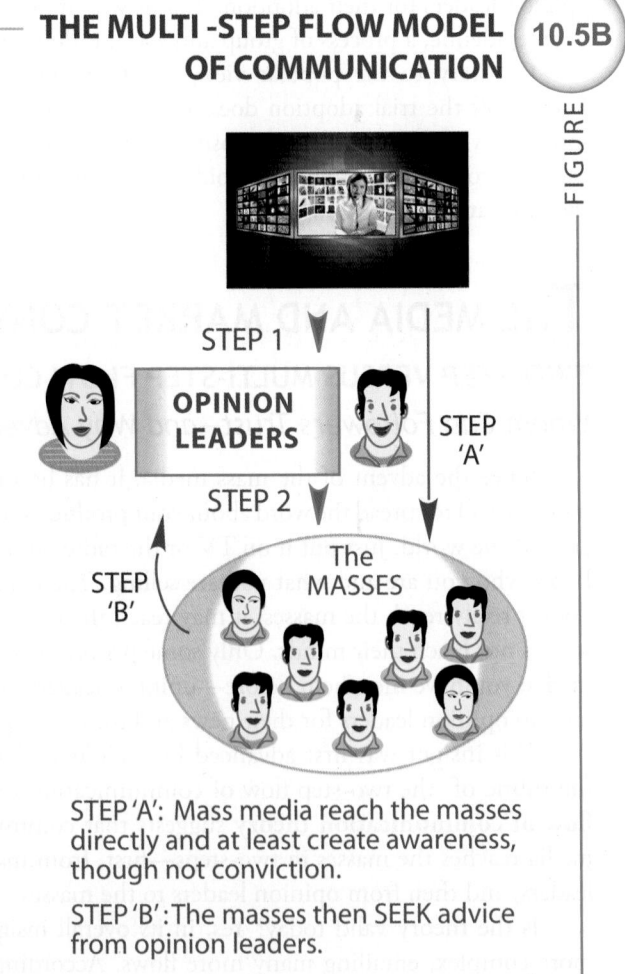

FIGURE 10.5B

THE MULTI-STEP FLOW MODEL OF COMMUNICATION

STEP 'A': Mass media reach the masses directly and at least create awareness, though not conviction.

STEP 'B': The masses then SEEK advice from opinion leaders.

MY **CB** BOOK

WORD OF MOUSE: SHARING OPINIONS IN CYBERSPACE

eMails, Web Forums, Social Networking Sites (*SoNets*), and Weblogs

The Internet is a powerful medium—a pervasive, omnipresent channel not only for marketer-initiated messages, but also for consumer-initiated messages. The chatter on the Net is a source both of enjoyment and opinion sharing for a substantial number of consumers. There are five platforms for expressing one's opinion in cyberspace: (a) e-mail, (b) feedback sites, (c) Web Groups and Forums, (d) social networking sites (*SoNets*), and (e) Weblogs.

Email Email is, of course, simply the cyber equivalent of old-fashioned letters. But there are several key differences, three of which are particularly relevant to spreading opinion by word-of-mouse. First, email is easier, faster, and free; second, it can reach many people at once; and third, it has *viralability*—with "forwarding" to each new layer of recipients, the email content can spread like a virus, one to many, quickly. Because of this spontaneity and immediacy, more consumers are likely to use e-mails (and now SMS text messages) to share their opinions on the experiences of the day (of marketplace objects as well as life activities) with their friends, family, and other contacts.

Feedback sites Many retailer Web sites provide consumers the opportunity to post their opinions about their products. Amazon.com, for example, posts reader reviews of the books and music it sells. Then, there are organizations that operate Web sites solely for the purpose of offering such opportunities to consumers. Two prominent sites are Epinions.com and Planetfeedback.com. On Epinions.com consumers post their reviews of products and retailers they have used. The Planetfeedback.com site similarly invites readers to post their views, although here the comments take the form of complaints, compliments, and suggestions. Both sites provide the opportunity for other readers to post their reactions to the original comments.

WORD OF MOUSE IN ACTION
One Recent Post

planetfeedback
The Voice of One, The Power of Many

↳ *LOVING your mascara that works for this red head!*
by Amie K. written to Max Factor
I just wanted to say "THANKS!" for having a mascara for redheaded women. I absolutely love your 2000 Calorie Deep Auburn Mascara, and use it whenever I can find it.
Reply

Web Groups and Forums Online chatrooms are Web sites with an instant messenger-enabled (IM) message-posting window where a consumer can post messages in real time and others can respond to the messages immediately. The format is conversational, with real-time interactivity. Other related formats are Newsgroups, Message boards, and Lists (technically called Listservs). A consumer registers on these sites and then posts messages; some sites allow unscreened postings, whereas others are screened by a moderator. The Yahoo! site (http://www.yahoo.com), for example, hosts thousands of groups, organized by interest area, where members and fans post messages about their favorite topics, including choice of music, artists, movies, colleges, UFOs , and other consumption objects.

Social Networking Sites (Sonets) The über communication media of the new millennium consumer are, of course, the social networking sites (*SoNets*) on the Web, such as Facebook, Myspace, Bebo, etc. Using them to stay in touch with friends and to gather new friends, members post their biographical information and their daily activities including the news about their favorite consumption. In "real time" information relay, Twitter takes the

---

BARBIE: BALD AND BEAUTIFUL

On December 20, 2011, two young women launched a campaign on their Facebook page, showing a bald Barbie. Their goal was to get Mattel, the iconic Barbie's toymaker, to make a bald Barbie. Their purpose: to help young girls who have lost their hair (say, due to cancer) to feel that bald girls can be beautiful.

Launched by Rebecca Sypin (of Lancaster, California) and Jane Bingham (New Jersey), by January 28, 2012 noon (EST, USA) it had reached 141,700 "likes."

Check it out at www.Facebook.com/BeautifulandBaldBarbie.

cake; using your mobile phone, you could quickly type in (140 characters maximum): "Dining at Prime One Twelve (South Beach, Florida); just tasted my first Rubyy Blood Orange Energy. Ooh, so yum yum!" With its *retweet* feature, Twitter also trumps on virability. (More on *SoNets* in Chapter 17.)

Weblogs The fourth medium for spreading the word in cyberspace, **Weblogs** are journals or logs people keep on their personal Web sites. Called *blogs* for short, they are personal accounts of users' own lives as well as opinions about things at large, including opinions on products and brands. Some of the bloggers are celebrities with a fan following, and their blog words reach and influence large audiences of readers.

Why Blog W-O-M Works

Are bloggers opinion leaders? Are they influentials? Why does their word-of-mouse matter? It matters because even if they do not carry any expert power or role model influence, bloggers are perceived to be independent commentators, sharing their opinions for no personal gain. This independence is what makes them trustworthy, in cyberspace and in the physical world alike. But in cyberspace, because we connect with strangers and never see their faces, trusting total strangers seems to have become second nature for cyber surfers. Actually, bloggers are not opinion leaders, but opinion sharers. And an opinion shared is an opinion influenced, particularly in cyberspace.

BUZZ MARKETING
W-O-M with a Twist

If you were sitting around in one of the cafes on Sunset Boulevard in Los Angeles on a summer evening in 2001, chances are that an attractive 20-something guy would have pulled up outside on his eye-catching Vespa and dropped in. (The story is some 12 years old but it is still a classic.) This handsome guy might even have bought you a latte, and if you admired his Vespa, a scooter you had never seen before, he would promptly have scribbled the address of the nearby dealer for you. And as a bonus, he would have whispered a secret in your ear—that is where rap artist Sisqo and Hollywood star Sandra Bullock bought their Vespas! This was classic buzz marketing at work. These seemingly enchanted Vespa riders were actually marketing messengers hired by the European motorbike company's US affiliate, Piaggio USA, to spread the word.

This is buzz marketing in action. **Buzz marketing** refers to the rapid-spread of product news through word-of-mouth. Perhaps the most colorful description of buzz marketing was penned by a business writer, Nancy K. Austin:

Buzz is busy talk. The CNN of the street. It's hugely influential. Buzz is not merely onomatopoeic; it is a big-time, no nonsense force. Once it is on the move, buzz is potent and widespread and lawless, which of course makes it irresistible. Brisk and a little unstable, buzz is a weather system that whirls into, and eventually out of, your life. Buzz is the Tornado Alley of communication.

—Nancy K. Austin, "Buzz: In Search of the Most Elusive Force in All of Marketing," Inc. Magazine, May 1998, 44-50.

The buzz-bees (the carriers of buzz) differ from celebrity influencers in one aspect: they are not celebrities at all. "We weren't looking for celebrities," says Julie Roehm, the then communications manager at Ford Motor Company who managed a buzz campaign for the company's Gen Y model *Focus*. "We were looking for assistants to celebrities, party planners, disk jockeys—people who seemed to influence what was cool." She gave them a *Focus* to drive around for six months and simply be seen driving it. (See also Recipe for Successful Buzz, Exhibit 10.1)

Peer-to-peer Marketing Peer-to-peer marketing is a special case of buzz marketing, where the goal is not just to spread the word but to get

CB FYI

From Sussex to the World
How a Cool PSA Went Viral

On January 20, 2010, Sussex Safer Road Partnership released a PSA on seat belt safety. In the 90-second advert, a man is shown driving a car, with wife and daughter in the back seat. Suddenly, he bumps into an apparent obstacle on the road, and, unable to swerve the car away from it, crashes the car, with glass shrapnel from the windshield flying out all over. The wife and daughter had seen this coming and had formed a "functional seat belt" around his body with their arms, thus saving him from injuries.

Okay, it was not a real car, and, sitting in his living room next to his wife and daughter, the man was merely pretending to be driving a car! But the "pretend feature, executed convincingly, added to the effect of the advert. It avoided the gory details of an actual car crash and conveyed the lesson with charming simplicity.

Although the PSA was broadcasted only in the Sussex area, it soon found its way into social media and on YouTube. From there, it quickly became an international phenomenon, garnering more than a million views in just two weeks.

Watch this charming video on YouTube. Also note the number of "views" and admire the power of viral diffusion!

Powered by
ᴓM

MY CB BOOK

the target audiences to act on the word which comes from their peers. If you are a college student, you might have seen some fellow students sitting in the hallway at a table loaded with T-shirts, pens, or cookies; you fill out an application for, say, a credit card, and you get one of these prizes. They are just collecting some money for their campus organization, they will tell you—and they are—but they are not unbiased communicators by any standard. Yet, you happily comply, for the sake of friendship, if not for the freebies. This is peer-to-peer marketing.

SAVVY MARKETER

EXHIBIT 10.1

RECIPE FOR SUCCESSFUL BUZZ

Not every marketable product or service lends itself to buzz marketing. Based on a reading of various writings and after pondering past case histories, we suggest the following ingredients of a successful buzz campaign:

1. Unique product or message First and foremost, the product has to be unique and interesting enough to become the topic of social conversations. When someone sees the product, it should arouse curiosity so the consumer looks at the product closely and finds and learns something about it worth telling others. And what he or she learns should be interesting enough so that he or she is eager to talk. Uniqueness of the product was a favorable factor both for the Vespa and the PT Cruiser, and, of course, recently for the Wii and Equmen.

2. Inherent human interest story Beyond uniqueness, what helps tremendously is that the product or topic be of inherent human interest (beyond its utilitarian value). Celebrity gossip spreads like a buzz because people find celebrities an interesting part of their world. It is doubtful that one could create a buzz around commodity products, which are used to do mere chores. Thus, Rumba, the new robotic vacuum cleaner, is less likely to get any buzz; but a product like bow-lingual (a gizmo, available from Sharper Image, that translates "woof" and a dog's emotions, into words) will, well, buzz!

It is the marketers' creative challenge to find ways of building human-interest stories in otherwise mundane products. Cigarettes themselves are a commodity product, at least for non-smokers. But makers of Lucky Strike undertook an innovative public relations campaign few years ago. It hired young people to roam the streets in major cities; they would offer you a beach chair to sit on and a cup of hot coffee to sip if you were forced out of "no smoking" buildings while you wanted to take a puff—and you could be smoking any brand. The gesture is, at least in appearance, so humane and touching that even anti-smoking crusaders would chuckle about it.

3. Scarcity and Mystery The product should not be in abundant supply. One that is easily available or easily seen will kill a buzz even before it begins. Of course, large-scale mass awareness is its ultimate goal, but in the initial stages of the buzz, the product should be rare, and the story about it should be known only to a select few. Thus, a mass advertising campaign and a buzz could never coexist. The topic information should look like "secret knowledge." Buzz makers want to feel and look like they have an inside scoop, that they are "in the know," and they are doing you a favor by letting you know. In turn, then, you feel privileged to become the new "in the know." And of course you can't wait to show off your being "in the know," so you carefully tell a "chosen few" others about it. This "mystery chatter" is the modus operandi of buzz.

4. Authenticity The buzz topic has to be authentic. A buzz maker can't sing rave praise about a product that turns out to lack any umph. In this respect at least, buzz is like all advertising: a false product performance claim kills a product; a false claim that is mass advertised kills it faster. The author of a book titled Purple Cow packaged the book in a milk carton and sent it to a select few (yours truly included), but this would have been all in vain if the book's contents had not vividly demonstrated the success stories of marketing programs that stood out by being truly different, just as the purple cow does from the herd of white and black and brown cows.

5. Free Agent The buzz-bees should be free agents, not hired hands. Before the movie Titanic was released, a glowing review of it appeared on a Web site called www.aint-it-cool-news.com; the Website was run by an Austin, Texas based geeky guy named Harry Jay Knowles, who published the site to disseminate the inside scoop on Hollywood happenings. The thing about Knowles was that he was no hired hand; instead he published stories the movie moguls tried hard to keep hush hush. That pre-release review is credited in part for the skyrocketing success of Titanic. Thus, buzz depends on the apparent impartiality of the talker.

6. Non-commercialism Finally, and related to the principle of Free Agent, the buzz should have the appearance of a social phenomenon rather than commercial advertising. When Lee Jeans Co. emailed its video clips, the recipients could play the video clips without knowing the sponsor's identity; only after a few months did the company reveal that to play the fuller version of the game, the consumer had to get a code from the label of the Lee Jeans in the stores—by which time the company had already created a following among teenagers who found the video clips rather fun (though silly).

These six ingredients are not absolute requirements, individually, but they are highly desirable. If a campaign lacks any one or more of these ingredients, it would be harder to sustain the buzz. And if one of these ingredients is missing or weak, other ingredients have to work that much harder. For example, the more transparent the commercial aspect, the stronger the other drivers of buzz, such as uniqueness, human-interest, scarcity, etc., would have to be. Vespa's commercialism was apparent, but the product and the 'visual personality' of the riders were attractive.

Further reading: Seth Godin and Malcolm Gladwell, Unleashing the Ideavirus (Hyperion 2001); Gerry Khermouch and Jeff Green, "Buzz Marketing," Business Week, July 30, 2001, p. 50-56; Nancy K. Austin, "Buzz: In Search of the Most Elusive Force in All of Marketing," Inc. Magazine, May 1998, 44-50; Emanuel Rosen, The Anatomy of Buzz : How to Create Word of Mouth Marketing (Currency 2002).

MY CB BOOK

During one recent school year, a small group of student "volunteers" at Brandeis University collected 200 names, complete with personal information—information fellow students would not easily give a business company. The Magma Group, the youth marketing company that sponsored the project, has some 6000 student volunteers in colleges across the nation who at its bidding will get their fellow classmates to fill out surveys for a freebee.[14]

Viral Marketing   We all know how a virus spreads—from one person, to two, four, eight, sixteen, thirty-two, and so on. Only ten iterations later, it would reach 65,000 people. With still 10 more, it would have reached 66 million people. **Viral marketing** refers to spreading product acceptance from one consumer to another in an exponential fashion. It has been practiced for quite some time, under such alternative names as *pyramid marketing* and *multi-level marketing*. An accomplished practitioner of this method is Amway. A company associate recruits three (or a number like that) of his or her friends to become associates and buy some of the company's product. Each in turn recruits three friends, who in turn do the same. And pretty soon, the number of associates (who are also the consumers of the products Amway sells) reaches thousands, or even millions. A similar program was used a few years ago by MCI under its *Friends and Family Campaign*, in which an MCI long distance phone service customer would qualify for some discount if he or she recruited friends and family members.

Viral marketing got a new life with the advent of the Internet. Here, the idea of viral marketing is simply to spread the message using the Internet channel. Viral marketing can occur in two ways: (1) voluntary or (2) incentivized. Voluntary viral marketing occurs when an email recipient finds the content interesting and voluntarily forwards it to friends. In incentivized viral marketing, the marketer offers an incentive for forwarding a message to a certain number of people.

SAVVY
MARKETER

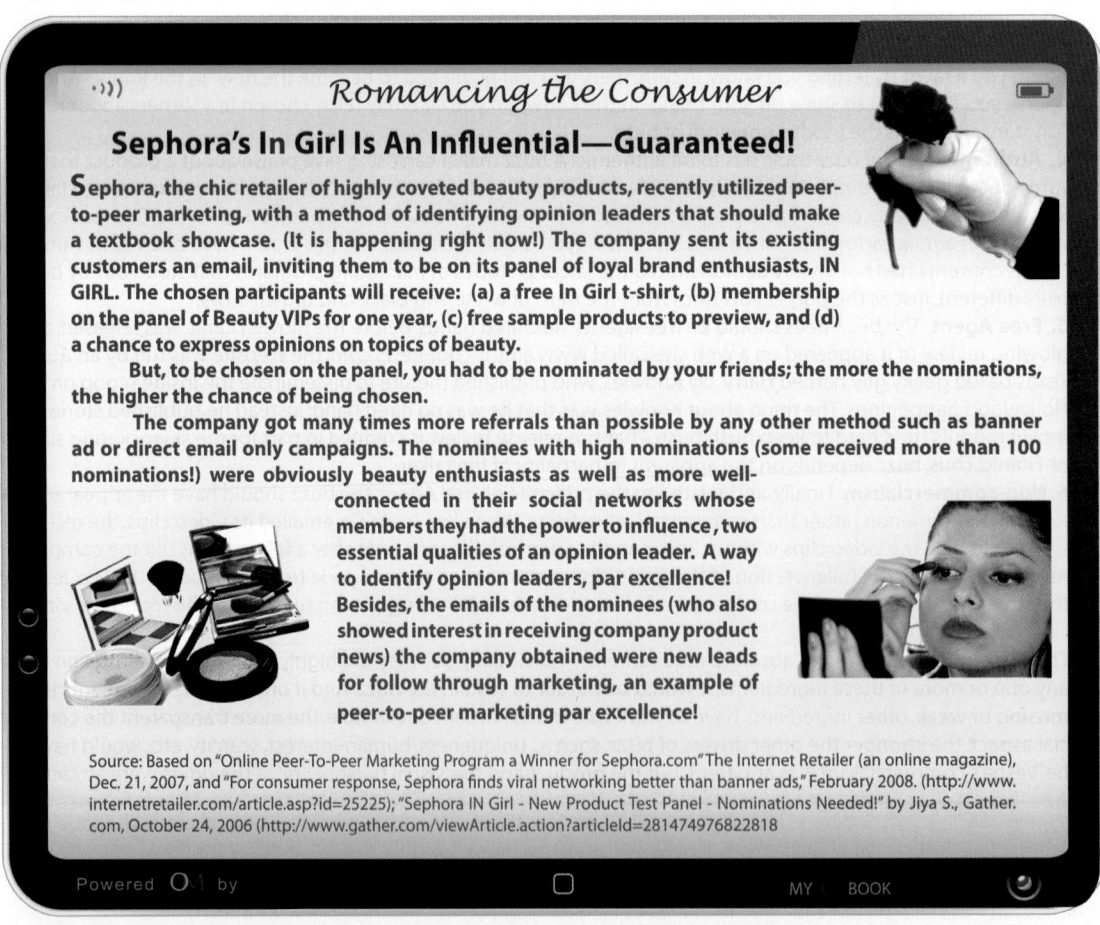

Romancing the Consumer

Sephora's In Girl Is An Influential—Guaranteed!

Sephora, the chic retailer of highly coveted beauty products, recently utilized peer-to-peer marketing, with a method of identifying opinion leaders that should make a textbook showcase. (It is happening right now!) The company sent its existing customers an email, inviting them to be on its panel of loyal brand enthusiasts, IN GIRL. The chosen participants will receive: (a) a free In Girl t-shirt, (b) membership on the panel of Beauty VIPs for one year, (c) free sample products to preview, and (d) a chance to express opinions on topics of beauty.

But, to be chosen on the panel, you had to be nominated by your friends; the more the nominations, the higher the chance of being chosen.

The company got many times more referrals than possible by any other method such as banner ad or direct email only campaigns. The nominees with high nominations (some received more than 100 nominations!) were obviously beauty enthusiasts as well as more well-connected in their social networks whose members they had the power to influence, two essential qualities of an opinion leader. A way to identify opinion leaders, par excellence! Besides, the emails of the nominees (who also showed interest in receiving company product news) the company obtained were new leads for follow through marketing, an example of peer-to-peer marketing par excellence!

Source: Based on "Online Peer-To-Peer Marketing Program a Winner for Sephora.com" The Internet Retailer (an online magazine), Dec. 21, 2007, and "For consumer response, Sephora finds viral networking better than banner ads," February 2008. (http://www.internetretailer.com/article.asp?id=25225); "Sephora IN Girl - New Product Test Panel - Nominations Needed!" by Jiya S., Gather.com, October 24, 2006 (http://www.gather.com/viewArticle.action?articleId=281474976822818

Powered by   MY BOOK

Cyber-buzz Cyber-buzz is buzz through the Internet channel. Although all Internet-based viral marketing is technically cyber-buzz, it is best to reserve the term to refer to the voluntary forwarding of emails, or to posting on social networking sites (*SoNets*) like Facebook, Twitter, etc. The voluntary forwarding of an email implies that the content is inherently interesting, a requirement for forwarding to an exponentially increasing number of recipients and to spreading at a super-fast speed, which is what buzz is, by definition. An example is the campaign by VF Corporation, the maker of Lee Dungarees. The company carefully identified 200,000 young Web surfers and emailed them a video, with a built-in click-through icon labeled "Send to a friend." The goal was to get the recipient to visit the company's Web site to watch a video game and, hopefully, along the way, to browse the new merchandise. Within four months of the initial e-mail, 436,000 consumers had visited the company's Web site.[17]

REFERENT INFLUENCE IN THE MARKETPLACE

Now You See It, Now You Don't

Reference groups, or referents, influence our consumer behaviors in three ways: (1) When we feel indecisive or inadequate to make product choice decisions, we ask referents whose opinions and judgment we trust. (2) Sometimes, people give us advice whether or not we want it. Sometimes this advice conveys factual material, such as which product would work better in a utilitarian or functional sense, and we take this advice if we trust their expertise. At other times, their advice is on matters of personal taste, such as what is in fashion or what purchases and consumption they consider undesirable. (3) Finally, referents influence us silently, just by being there, as we consider their implicit preferences and taste in making our own choices. This influence-from-a-distance, so to speak, occurs both for normative factors—we expect to be rebuked if we ignored referents' tastes—and for identification factors—we relish imitating our heroes' tastes and consumption choices.

SUMMARY

In this chapter, we reviewed the types of reference groups and explained the nature of their influence. Depending on the frequency of contact, groups can be primary or secondary; they can also be membership or symbolic, choice or ascribed. Their influence depends on conspicuousness in consumption, and as such it can occur at the product or brand-choice level. Such influence is of three types: informational, normative, and identificational. We then described a personality trait of consumers, their susceptibility to interpersonal influence (SIPI), and identified factors that make a consumer more or less SIPI.

Next, we described opinion leaders, people whose opinions consumers seek and respect. We described their characteristics and explained four methods of identifying them in a community. Next, we discussed influentials, a group of people who influence consumers by word-of-mouth (w-o-m). Among this latter group, we described a subgroup, e-fluentials, who affect opinion in cyberspace as well as outside of it, i.e., by word-of-mouth as well as by word-of-*mouse*. These opinion leaders play a crucial role in influencing consumers at large, especially in the adoption of innovations. Innovation spreads through consumer populations like an epidemic, and we described this diffusion process. Along this path, we identified five groups, from innovators who are the first to adopt an innovation, to early adopters, early majority, late majority, and laggards. The latter groups depend on the former groups for a favorable w-o-m. Finally, we discussed the relatively novel twin approaches to employing w-o-m—buzz marketing and viral marketing.

KEY TERMS

Ascribed groups
Buzz marketing
Consumption as identity marker
e-fluentials
Groups
Identificational influence
Informational influence
Influentials

Institutions
Key informant method
Membership groups
Normative influence
Opinion leaders
Primary groups
Reference groups
Secondary groups
Self-designation method

Social comparison theory
Social facilitation
Social loafing
Social networking sites
Susceptibility to interpersonal influence (SIPI)
Symbolic groups
Viral marketing
Weblogs

CB Blog

10

We And Our Referents— Obeying Our Own Thirst Is A Myth

Every consumer has reference groups. They are a fact of life. They influence us intensely, materially, constantly. Is it a good thing? Does a consumer need reference groups? The answer is Yes. Because alone we can't master all the information about all the products we need to buy. So we turn to other experts for advice, and we feel grateful, as we should, that they exist.

As to products of taste (rather than merely of function), there is no such thing as 100% "personal" taste. All our personal tastes come from people we admire; i.e., referents we choose.

Okay, we appreciate the informational and identificational influence, but what of the normative influence? We sometimes accept it gladly, but sometimes we resent it; e.g., a dress code. Either way, for the organizations and referents that impose various norms, they always serve some important function. Show up in faded distressed jeans at a wedding and you would spoil the look and feel of the event. If your yearning for extreme individuality is intense, you would no doubt find ways of excusing yourself from attending those events and indeed from the shackles of those normative referents. And you would find, instead, other referents whose norms you would gladly embrace.

For the rest of us—with no particular desire for extreme individuality, it is tempting to believe we make many choices of our own free will, uninfluenced by any referents, whether identificational or normative. Oh, really? Think again. What evaluation criteria did you use in choosing your products? Now, where did that evaluative template come from??

The fact is that other people who inhabit our personal world (family members, friends, coworkers, role models, and cultural heroes) influence our worldviews over our lifetimes. That influence occurs in small doses, overtly or subtly, but it is as certain as sunrise. Referents thus influence our consumer behavior in two ways: directly through brand advice or brand endorsement (overt or covert) and indirectly by molding our values and tastes. Thus:

Reference Groups have a pervasive influence on Consumer Behavior. They influence what we buy and what we consume, of course. But they influence more—our values, our beliefs, our preferences, our tastes. To understand reference groups is to understand how social forces shape our lives as humans and as consumers. No consumer behavior is untouched by reference groups. "Obeying your own thirst" is a myth. Now you know better!

CONSUMER BEHAVIOR

YOUR TURN

REVIEW+Rewind

1. How are groups defined? Name various classifications of groups and give an example of each.
2. Name and explain the three types of reference group influences with an example of each.
3. Explain what is meant by Susceptibility to Interpersonal Influence (SIPI); name and explain the three factors that make a person high or low on SIPI.
4. Define opinion leadership and name two "essential qualities" of opinion leaders. Also name some personal characteristics of opinion leaders.
5. Write down some questions to measure opinion leadership.
6. Name the five consumer groups based on the timing of their adoption of an innovation; briefly describe the characteristics of each group.
7. Explain the AIDA model and its significance in the adoption of a new product by consumers.
8. Explain the theory of two- and multi-step flow of communication and its purpose in marketing.
9. What is meant by (a) word-of-mouse, (b) buzz marketing, (c) peer-to-peer marketing, and (d) viral marketing? Give an example of each.
10. Explain Social Comparison Theory and how it affects consumer behavior.

THINK+Apply

1. Explain how normative and identificational types of reference group influences are different. Give two example of each from your own life as a consumer.
2. Name some people who serve as your opinion leaders, and describe to what extent these persons possess the characteristics of an opinion leader. Also identify what kind of influence each of these persons exercises on you as a consumer.
3. How does the concept of five adopter categories help a marketer of an innovative product? Think of two innovations, and then outline a long-term marketing program to appeal to each of the five innovation adopter groups.
4. What are the requisites of a successful buzz campaign? Assess whether a buzz campaign could be used by the following marketers: (a) a toothbrush that beeps after 2 minutes of use; (b) a shoe polish that would last for one year; and (c) a hair crème that would grow hair at a much slower rate so that the consumer would need a hair cut only once a year, and available only in selected salons on a limited basis; (d) this book (assuming there were an annual convention of all consumer behavior students). Explain your answer.

5. Think of two or three new products or services to be launched next year that would be suitable for creating buzz. Justify how these products are apt candidates for buzz. Next, prepare a plan for creating buzz for one of these products. Your plan should dwell on (a) which groups will be targeted and how you would identify and harness opinion leaders; and (b) which types of influence would be relevant to each buzz agent.

PRACTICE+Experience

1. Select one of the following "products": (a) clothing fashions; (b) electronic devices like computers, cell phones, DVDs, etc.; or (c) art shows. Now for the selected product category, administer a survey to 10 of your friends to measure their opinion leadership. Before surveying them, write down your perceptions about each friend in terms of whether or not they are opinion leaders. Also talk to them about the topic area and their topic-related conversations with others. Then compare their actual scores with your predictions, and explain possible reasons for a mismatch, if any.
2. Select a group (e.g., class, church group, ball league, etc.) of which you are a member and apply sociometric and key informant methods of identifying opinion leaders. Did the two methods lead to the same persons being identified as opinion leaders in those groups? Why or why not?
3. Locate a Hash Harry Harriers group in your city, and interview some of its members to understand what group norms exist and what kind of reference group influence the members of the group exercise on one another. Specifically identify what sorts of consumptions their membership in this group has influenced.
4. Search blogs on the Internet, and identify some that reflect consumption-related word-of-mouse.

In the Marketing Manager's Shoes

Put yourself in a marketing manager's shoes. Most concepts in the chapter have some lessons for the marketing manager, i.e., they suggest what to do differently in practice. Indeed, often these applications are implicit in our explanations of the concepts and models in the chapter. Identify at least five specific applications of the chapter's concepts, all of which should be entirely new—different from the examples cited here.

Decisions

11 Consumer Decision Making
Rational and Emotional

Choosing—It Is a Privilege. It Is a Hassle.

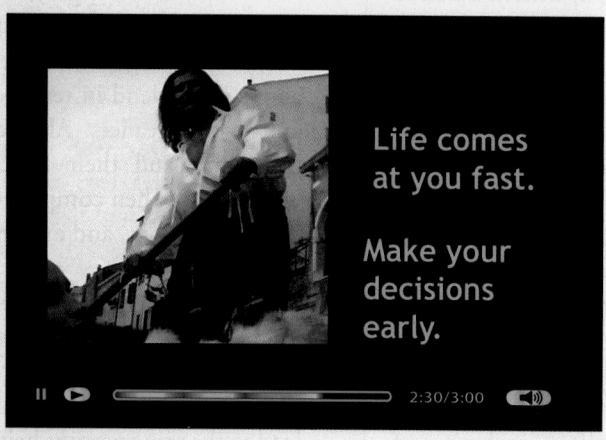

Life comes
at you fast.

Make your
decisions
early.

2:30/3:00

LEARN . APPLY . EXPERIENCE

OBJECTIVES

1 Five Steps in the Consumer Decision Process

2 Four Avenues of Problem Recognition by Consumers

3 Two Strategies and Five Determinants of Consumer Information Search

4 Compensatory and Noncompensatory Decision Models in Alternative Evaluation

5 ACM—The Model for the Consumer's Choice of Expressive Products

6 The Role of Involvement as a Pervasive Arbiter of Choice Processes

iPhone or Galaxy Nexus—That is the Question

Ever since the smartphones were introduced, I have been loyal to my Blackberry. But the lure of the iPhone has always been present, and now, with the launch of iPhone 4S, it has become irresistible. I hear that within one week of its launch in seven countries on October 14 2011, it sold out 4 million units. So today I had almost decided to buy the 4S, but then I saw this pop-up ad for Samsung's Galaxy Nexus, touting its killer differential advantage: a 4.65-inch display screen (versus iPhone's 3.5-inch). So I decided to compare the two closely.

First off, iPhone 4S upgraded its camera from 5 to 8 megapixels. Yes, I take a lot of phone-pictures and I had always wished for a more "empowered" camera in my phone. Unfortunately, Samsung's Galaxy models remain limited to 5 mpx.

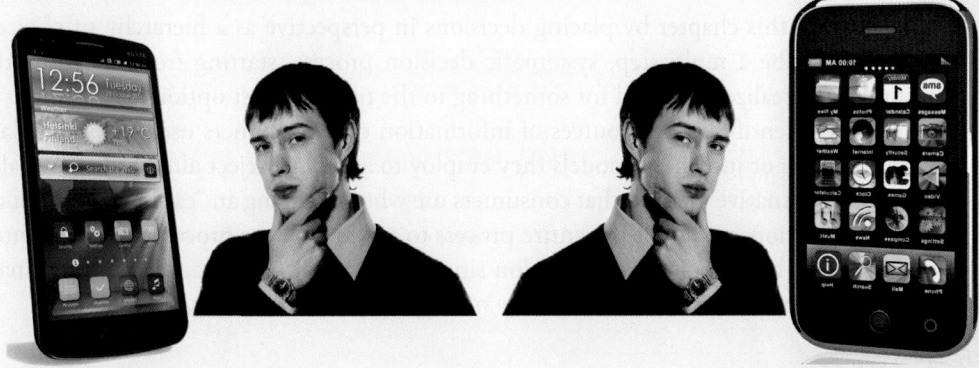

Some expert reviews quibbled about the display quality, praising the superior resolution in the iPhone versus the sharper contrast in the Nexus, but my eyes don't register such minutiae. What really impressed me about the Nexus was its 4G capability, especially since Apple disappointed fans on this dimension. With 4G, I read that you could download stuff 10 times faster—for me, a big PLUS!

Besides, Samsung's Nexus also has swap-up battery and swap-up SD storage options. With a spare battery and an extra SD card, my phone will never be out of juice or memory. Finally, it amazed me that with Nexus I have the freedom to download third-party keyboards, and I hear that some of those keyboards make typing a breeze.

So I am all excited about this new Samsung model. But then I hear Siri tell me things I want to know. What time is it now? Can you ping me in half an hour? How many calories in a regular Coke? When is my foot masseuse appointment? Will I need an umbrella? She—Siri—has answers to all. And if I try to double-book an appointment, she warns me!

So the 4G speed, the 8MPX camera and the swappable battery draw me to Nexus, but the charm of Siri is mesmerizing. And having to choose between the two is driving me nuts. If you have any suggestions, please sms me.*

> Some of my decisions intrigue me.

---

*I know, I know, by the time you read this, it will have become history (the way technology moves these days). iPhone will have introduced its much awaited iPhone 5, or, who knows, even 6; and the Android's Ice Cream Sandwich might empower the Samsung (and other Android- fueled phones like the Motorola's Razr, Hitachi's Sensation, etc.) to altogether new highs. But right now, at the time of writing, my decision dilemma is this: Siri or 4G, the 4S or the Nexus? Well, I will have to sleep on that.

INTRODUCTION

Decisions, decisions, decisions. Life is full of them. From choosing a smart phone to choosing a wedding ring, from choosing a college to choosing a fraternity to join, and from choosing a president for the nation to choosing the costume for the upcoming Halloween party, as consumers we face a marketplace of choices galore. Some decisions are easy to make, and we make them in a split second. Others are difficult, and we agonize for days and weeks. Our decisions have consequences. We have to live with our choices. And our choices determine the fates of businesses; some flourish because we choose their products, and others vanish because we reject their offerings. Businesses need to understand how consumers make these decisions

It is one thing to make decisions, but it is quite another to know how we make them. Although all consumers make decisions, not all understand the process. As students of consumer behavior, it is our opportunity—even our mandate—to understand this process.

We begin this chapter by placing decisions in perspective as a hierarchy of choices. We then describe a multi-step, systematic decision process, starting from the time the consumer first realizes the need for something to the time the best option is identified. In doing so, we identify various sources of information that consumers use, and we explain various decision or judgment models they employ to accept or reject alternatives. We also describe an alternative method that consumers use when choosing an "expressive" product. In the final section, we revisit the entire process to reveal how the process is implemented in high- versus low- involvement decision situations. In sum, the chapter will illuminate what goes on in consumers' minds as they make decisions in the marketplace.

THE CONSUMER DECISION PROCESS

Think about it: when you are in the marketplace, what decisions are you called upon to make about any product? Yesterday, you bought a *Some of us lamp*, an art nouveau creation of designer Gaetano Pesce.

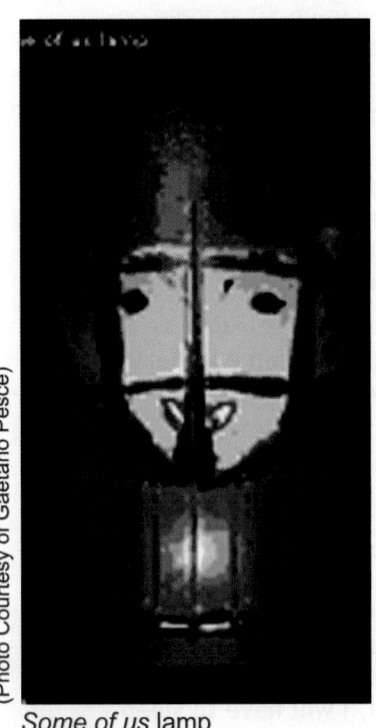

(Photo Courtesy of Gaetano Pesce)

Some of us lamp
by Gaetano Pesce

But it is not like you got up yesterday morning, and said, "Today, I am going to buy a Gaetano Pesce lamp." Instead, a few months ago, you started thinking about buying something spectacular for your living room in time for the New Year's Party at your new apartment. At first, you wondered if you should bother to spend that much money on one more home décor item at all. And then, even if you were so inclined, wouldn't you be better off, you asked yourself, to buy instead a big wall hanging from Morocco that you had seen at a Bal Harbor boutique? For several days thereafter, you debated these options.

All consumers typically face such dilemmas—deciding whether to purchase something entails weighing alternative uses of money and time resources. Consumers have finite money and time, and they must allocate them judiciously.

Once a consumer does make up his/her mind to buy a product, he/she must then decide which brand to buy, when to buy it, and where to buy it. These decisions at various levels of hierarchy can all be called *alternatives*, and the consumer's task is to choose from among the available alternatives. That decision-making process consists of the five steps shown in Figure 11.1.

Step 1:
PROBLEM RECOGNITION

You are combing your hair, looking in the mirror, as usual. You are about finished, when something about your eyes catches your attention. Under your eyes, some dark rings are beginning to form! In consumer behavior, we would say that you have just "recognized a problem."

The decision process begins when a consumer recognizes a problem to be solved or a need to be satisfied. As a consumer, you notice, for example, that you are hungry and need to get some food, or that your Nuvi is misdirecting you again and needs repairing, or that Sally has not called in a while, so you, Harry, had better send her a friendship card.

As this last example shows, a consumer "problem" is not necessarily a physical problem, such as a hungry stomach or dark circles under the eyes. Rather a **consumer problem** is any state of deprivation. It is a state wherein a consumer feels discomfort—physically or only mentally. In other words, it is a gap between the current state and the desired state, as felt by the consumer in his/her mind. You may recall from Chapter 2 that this gap is also called a "need"—problem recognition and need recognition are, then, one and the same thing. We will call this the Gap Concept of Consumer Need (see Figure 11.2).

Correspondingly, **problem recognition** is the consumer's realization of the gap between his/her current state and the desired state. It occurs as soon as the consumer becomes dissatisfied with his/her current state and wants to do something to achieve a desired state. (See Figure 11.3.)

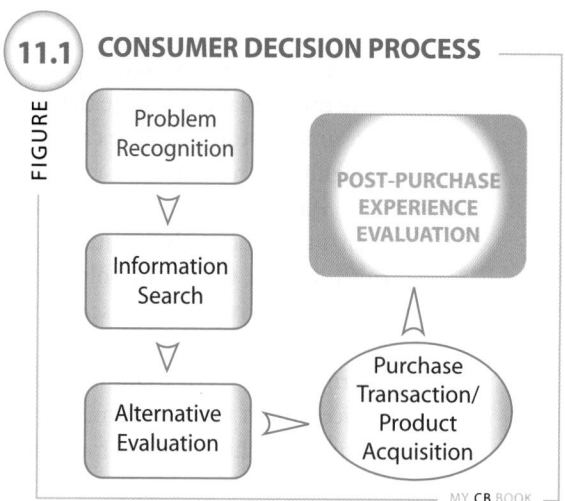
11.1 CONSUMER DECISION PROCESS

FIGURE

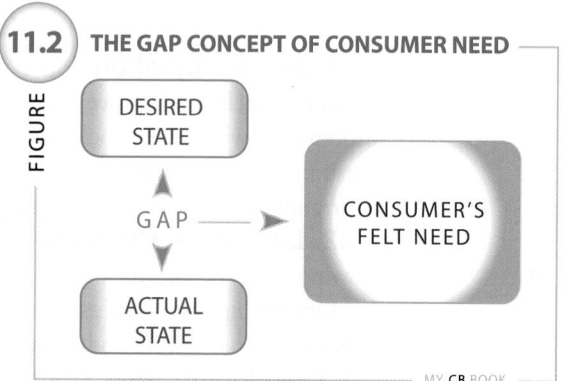
11.2 THE GAP CONCEPT OF CONSUMER NEED

FIGURE

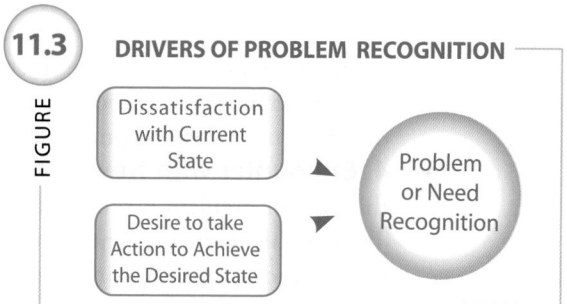
11.3 DRIVERS OF PROBLEM RECOGNITION

FIGURE

FOUR AVENUES OF PROBLEM RECOGNITION

Think of all the problems or needs you have recognized as a consumer within this past week. What causes us to recognize these problems? Basically, there are two causes: internal stimuli and external stimuli. **Internal stimuli** are perceived states of discomfort arising from something inside you. This can be a physical condition of your body (e.g., hunger or thinning hair), or it can be a psychological condition, originating in your mind (e.g. boredom, or anxiety about Sally). **External stimuli** are sources of information you see outside—in the marketplace and on the street. Seeing certain things makes you want those things. You smell coffee beans in a mall store, your body begins to crave coffee (a current state of discomfort), and your mind says it is time to have some coffee. You see a Camaro ZL1 on the road, and you begin to dream of driving it (desired state).

Opportunity Knocking—Ah, the Sweet Smell of Chocolate

External stimuli come in two forms: "problem stimuli" and "solution stimuli." A **problem-stimulus** is one in which the problem itself is the source of information, such as the sight of dirty laundry or a burnt-out light bulb. A **solution stimulus** is the information emanating from a solution itself. Here, exposure to a potential solution arouses the recognition of the need or the problem; for example, exposure to a new style of dress in a store might make us realize that the dress will come in handy for an upcoming party. Some consumer researchers have called this, appropriately, **opportunity recognition**[1]—problem recognition aroused by an external, solution stimulus.

Marketing communications, product or service samples, window shopping, etc., have their utility precisely because they serve as solution-stimuli for problem-recognition. In other words, they—the solution stimuli—entice us even when we are not feeling any internal deprivation or discomfort to begin with. Opportunity recognition occurs when a consumer is exposed to some external stimulus that promises to improve the current "normal" state. For example, your friend Lisa is at ease with her facial age lines; she has noticed them but has dismissed them as inevitable; and she is not currently bothered by them. Then she sees an ad for Botox, the wrinkle-removal medical treatment, and suddenly she becomes driven to do something about the wrinkles. Botox is the "solution-stimulus," and your friend Lisa was smart enough to have this "opportunity recognition."

For problem recognition, there are four avenues:

1. Stock Depletion Some "problems" occur simply, and repeatedly, due to stock depletion, such as when we empty a box of cereal. But sometimes consumers are caught unprepared when the stock depletion occurs. Some marketing communications help consumers by reminding them of imminent stock depletion (e.g., your pharmacy) or even by arranging an automatic replenishment (e.g., Chicago's Peapod for groceries).

2. Life Stage Changes New problems arise with new life conditions, such as a growing body, becoming a college student, leaving the parental home, becoming a parent, etc. Embarking on a professional career? Perhaps you will need to find a tattoo parlor to remove all those visible body tattoos!

3. Developing New Tastes Often, we develop new tastes, like tastes for fine arts and theater. We acquire new hobbies (e.g., digital designing); we get drawn to yoga, sushi, and organic food, etc. Developing a new taste doesn't necessarily mean acquiring a more mature taste or a taste for the finer things in life. We mean, rather, a desire for anything new, anything not tried before. It includes fantasy realization—suddenly seeing that we can make our fantasies come true; for instance, by buying a Mustang or a Ducati bike.

4. Encounter with New Technology/New Products Unlike the preceding three, this type of problem is subtle, lurking just behind (or below) our level of consciousness. These problems are brought to our consciousness when we see a solution stimulus—e.g., a new technology, or someone of our own type using a product we never thought of using, or someone telling us how cool some product would be for us. Sometimes, marketers make us realize how a product that we never paid attention to has relevance for us—like a a Spotify music library.

HELPING CONSUMER PROBLEM RECOGNITION

Marketers bring consumers value by bringing solutions to the problems consumers have recognized. For new life stage changes, while the consumer is aware of the need to prepare for the new stage, he/she needs "education" on the full spectrum of products needed to play on the new life stage. Wardrobe consultants (personal shopping advisors) fill this role for new career seekers; and college orientation information packets list the "essentials" that the new student must bring to campus.

But marketers can also bring value by helping consumers recognize the problems they otherwise may not. There is a category of problem recognition tasks that consumers don't see readily, or that they deny or resist being told about. We can call them **invisible problems**.

Marketers try to overcome this gap by educational communication; e.g., health education. Artful communications that bring the distant risk or future need into the consumers' visual field, so to speak, also help (see Nationwide's *Life Comes At You Fast*

campaign). Do consumers need to drink milk? Orange juice? Coffee? Red wine? More than the quantity they are currently consuming? If the scientific answer is yes, then marketers, by educating consumers on this need, can do society some good as well as earn themselves some dough.

This is a profound thought: Marketers usually are busy fighting battles for more market share for their brand, by getting product users to switch to their brand—a practice called **secondary demand creation**. In contrast, creating problem recognition converts nonusers into users (or infrequent users into more frequent users), thus expanding the total market size—a practice called **primary demand creation**.

Step 2:
INFORMATION SEARCH

Once you have recognized a need—like you need to do something about your thinning hair—you proceed to the next step, called *information search*. Here, you seek out information, first about what alternatives are available in the marketplace and then about various features of these alternatives. On the surface, the process looks simple and straightforward. But there is more to it. For starters, it takes two forms, depending on how novel the problem is for you, i.e., on how familiar you are with the available solutions.

When You are Unfamiliar with the Product

If you are totally unfamiliar with the solution product for your problem (e.g., thinning hair), then this is how you would most likely proceed: You find out about one alternative, learn a little about it, then come to know of a second alternative, learn a bit about it, then a third, and a fourth, and then you explore these a bit more, learning more about them, going back and forth from one alternative to another. Eventually, there comes a time when you feel that you have explored enough. For your thinning hair, for example, through a search for information, you might have discovered (one by one) some special shampoos, some herbal medicines, and the prescription medicine Propecia. You might closely explore two or three brands of shampoo, or a couple of herbal medicines, and so on.

LIFE COMES AT YOU FAST

Consumers often remain oblivious to their future needs. Nationwide helps consumers recognize this problem with its now famous Life Comes At You Fast campaign. Bringing that point home in this creative masterpiece execution is none other than Fabio Lanzoni, the Italian-born American actor and an international fashion icon.

And When You are Familiar

Suppose you want to buy a car. Here, the product category is familiar to you, so the information search focuses on the familiar alternatives. However, you would rarely perform an information search on all the brands with which you are familiar, much less all the brands in existence. Consumer researchers believe that brands are organized in our minds as sets and subsets as follows (see Figure 11.4):

Awareness set This comprises all the brands of which you are aware as a consumer.

Evoked set This is the subset of brands (in the awareness set) that you remember at the time of decision-making.

Inert set The brands you don't remember at the time of decision-making.

Inept Set The brands you do remember but consider unsuitable for your purpose.

11.4 AWARENESS, EVOKED, AND CONSIDERATION SETS

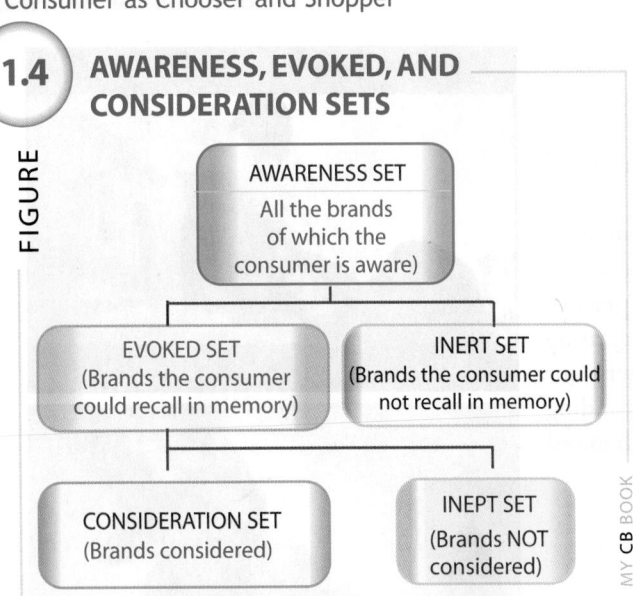

FIGURE

MY CB BOOK

Consideration set These are the brands you, as a consumer, will consider buying. This is the most important set. It is this set that you will evaluate further.

Try this for yourself. Quickly, what brands of low-fat candy come to your mind? Which ones would you consider buying? And what can marketers do to make you think of their candy brand when you think of candy bars?

Please Put My Brand into Your Consideration Set

Initially, consumers seek information about the consideration set of brands—which is a subset of evoked sets. New information can bring additional brands into the awareness, evoked, and consideration sets. It should be the minimum objective of all marketing communications to place the advertised brand in their target consumers' consideration set (rather than merely in the awareness or evoked set). This is accomplished by highlighting a feature of the brand that the target consumers will find desirable. For example, Shirts Taste Good is a brand of T-shirt that brings to life YouTube videos that went viral. By mentioning it, we have placed Shirts Taste Good into your awareness set. By mentioning that it features motifs of insanely popular YouTube videos (and that they sell at $14.95 for new releases and at $17.95 for oldies!), we may have succeeded in placing it into your consideration set as well. Or maybe not. It is for you to decide. If we did, then now you know what it takes for marketers to put their brand into the consumer's consideration set. In essence, marketers have to offer, in advertising and in fact, brand features that the consumer will find valuable.

For net-savvy consumers, the concepts of awareness and consideration sets work somewhat differently. If you are a net savvy consumer, and if you wanted to search cell phones, for example, you could go to RadioShack's Web site at www.RadioShack.com; and would find information on cell phones supported by five wireless service providers: Sprint, Verizon, Alltel, AT&T/Cingular, and US Cellular. Click on "Sprint" and you would see twelve cell phones; ditto if you clicked on "Verizon"; and you would see thirteen more if you clicked the combined link for the other three (some alternatives overlap, but many don't). Given that the list of alternatives is available on Web sites, as consumers we do not have to depend on our memories (called *internal memory*). Instead, we can depend on Web sites (which here serve as *external memory*) to store all the brand names.

In the Web information environment, therefore, the concept of awareness and evoked sets should give way to what we call the **recognition set**—the brand names the consumer recognizes as being familiar. The consideration set will be a subset of the recognition set.

Perhaps you realize, especially if you are net-savvy, that it is easy to find information about cell phones. But information on other products is not as easy to come by. Try finding information, for example, on low-carb foods, on remedies for thinning hair, or on tennis rackets with *liquidmetal* frames. And we mean try finding it in the *offline* world! Where would you begin? How much time and effort would you be willing to expend? And what would that depend on? Your interest in the product? Your mood? Or what?

Fortunately, consumer researchers have addressed these questions.

- What sources of information do consumers use?
- What search strategies do consumers utilize?
- What factors determine how extensive the search will be?

SAVVY MARKETER

SOURCES OF INFORMATION

The first place you would invariably look is your own memory. You would simply try to recall whatever you knew about that product category—the brand you last bought, or the ad you saw recently. This is termed **internal search**. Sometime that search is adequate to make your decision (e.g., buy the brand you bought last time), but sometimes you have to go beyond your existing knowledge and perform an **external search**—looking for information in market communications, media, and from other consumers.

In searching for solutions for your thinning hair, for example, you might ask a friend or a pharmacist. You might remember seeing an ad for Propecia in magazines, so now you might search through your stack of old magazines. And, of course, you could simply go to the Web and type the keyword "thinning hair" into a search engine. All these are "external sources of information." They can be organized as shown in Table 11.1.

First, they are grouped into two groups: marketer and nonmarketer. **Marketer sources** are those associated with the marketer of the product or service. Examples: advertising, salespersons, product/service literature and brochures, and in-store displays. And, of course, the Internet. There is one problem with the Internet, though. If you are looking to send an electronic greeting card, for example, you could go to the Apple's .Mac site at www.apple.com/dotmac/, but only if you knew, to begin with, that Apple offers iCards on its Web site!

Do You Trust Commercial Speech?

There is another problem with all these marketer sources: Can we trust them? That depends, to a degree, on the reputation of the company. In any case, one thing is certain: All marketer sources have a vested interest in providing biased information. That is why they are also referred to as **advocate sources**—sources that have a vested point-of-view to advocate or promote. As such, consumers view these sources as lacking credibility. That is why advertisers and salespersons should avoid hyping their product messages.

Corporate Web sites are a useful source of information for net-savvy consumers. If you knew, for example, that Propecia was made by Merck, then you could go to that company's Web site at www.merck.com to get information about the drug's efficacy and side effects. "The fact is," says the site, for example, "that 2 years of clinical testing showed that 2 of 3 men regrew some hair (vs. 7% with a sugar pill)."

Don't Forget Your Friends

Now let us look at the other half of the story— the nonmarketer sources. **Nonmarketer sources** are those that are independent of the marketer's control. Since these have no personal interest in providing biased information, they are viewed as **nonadvocate sources** and are considered more credible.

PUTTING THE BRAND IN CONSUMERS' AWARENESS SET

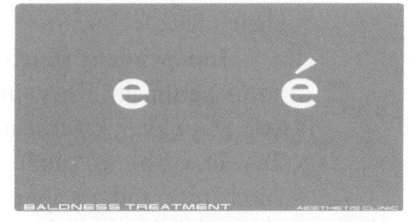
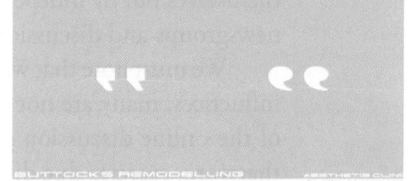

Baldness treatment and "buttocks remodeling" (as the clinic puts it), available at Aesthetic Clinic, Paris.

TABLE 11.1 SOURCES OF INFORMATION FOR CONSUMERS	
MARKETER SOURCES	**NON-MARKETER SOURCES**
ADVERTISING **Traditional:** Magazines, TV, radio, magazines, newspapers, bill boards **New:** Online banners, mobile phones, social networking sites, such as Facebook, QR codes, etc. **Sales Promotion** **Product brochures** **Store Displays** **Company Web Sites**	**PERSONAL SOURCES** Friends and acquaintances Past experiences **INDEPENDENT SOURCES** Public Information (e.g., Consumer Reports, Better Business Bureau, news reports in media, government publications; Product or service experts (e.g., Auto Critic, home appraisers, pharmacist, etc.) Internet (e.g., bulletin boards, forums, independent portals)

MY C3 BOOK

These, in turn, are of two types: personal and independent. **Personal sources** are individuals we know personally (e.g., friends). As consumers, we seek them out, and we surely value their advice.

Independent sources are those not controlled by marketers and also not known to us personally. They, in turn, fall into three subgroups: (a) independent publications (e.g., *Consumer Reports*) and organizations with relevant expertise (e.g., the Better Business Bureau, BBB); (b) product and service experts such as pharmacists, financial advisors, car mechanics, and art appraisers; and (c) various Web sites, run not by product marketers themselves but by independent organizations (e.g., ecolivingcenter.com) or by individuals, newsgroups and discussion forums.

We must note that while these sources are "independent" of specific product marketers' influences, many are not objective or unbiased by any means. Some sources (such as some of the online discussion groups) may even be based on ill-informed opinions; you must, therefore, exercise due diligence in paying heed to the information found there.

If You Are Not Knowledgeable

Do you have a tendency to use some of these sources more than others? If you do, one relevant factor is how knowledgeable you are about the product category. In an exploratory study, marketing professor Cheryl Burke Jarvis found that, when buying expensive products like electronics, computers, cars, vacations, etc., the inexperienced consumers' first source was friends-and-families, followed by a visit to retail stores and a strong reliance on salespersons. In contrast, the experienced and knowledgeable consumers' first source was non-marketer independent media like *Consumer Reports*, or expert ratings of computers in magazines, etc. They also consulted with friends, family members, and company Web sites; salespersons were seen as the last resort, and that too for the limited purpose of seeking price and other objective feature information—not recommendations.[2]

If you are a salesperson, here is an obvious lesson: To cater to experts, you should become highly knowledgeable about the product. Your product knowledge matters to novices as well, but to them your trustworthiness matters just as much. Finally, don't ever think that whatever you say goes. Consumers rely heavily on non-marketer sources, often to verify the information obtained from marketer sources. Thus, your product's reality (and, based on it, its reputation) speaks louder than does your commercial speech. So don't make your commercial speech dishonest. It is worth repeating: Consumers rely heavily on non-marketer sources!

NON-MARKETER SOURCES   *Blessings of the Information Age*

INFORMATION ON WOMEN'S HAIR LOSS ON THE WEB

QUESTION: By Anonymous on Sunday, June 16, 2002 - 05:58 pm:
I'm 40 years and I've loss hair problems since the 30 years. I began with Minoxidil 2%, after 5%, Propecia and now Propecia and Minoxidil 5%. ... my hair loss became worst and worst. ... I'm terryfied now! How could I work? How could I go to the street?

REPLY: By Tom Hagerty (Admin) on Monday, June 17, '02 - 09am:
Anonymous: Since you posted under Female Pattern Baldness, I gather that you are a woman. But why would a woman take Propecia or use 5% Minoxidil? Seeing a good dermatologist ..... The dermatologist should also give you some tests to rule out possible thyroid or low iron problems.

REPLY: By Rose on Tuesday, July 02, 2002 - 01:48 pm:
I don't think that women should use Propecia. It's a drug only for male pattern baldness. There are warnings on the drug that females should not use it.

REPLY: By mwoods on Sunday, July 14, 2002 - 06:18 pm:
I think I can help. Go to http://www.minoxidil.com - there is a solution called Xandrox.... Use the 5% Xandrox DAYTIME formula. [i USED IT]. After 3-4 wks hair falls out a lot, but my hair was already in the telogen stage, but after it stopped, growth began slowly but surely .... Try this, have faith in God...I!

Source http://www.hairloss-reversible.com/discus/messages/2/10.html?1035255600 (Reprinted by permission. from Tom Hagerty)

MY CB BOOK

SEARCH STRATEGIES AND DETERMINANTS

Are You a Simplifier or an Extender?

Okay, you have all these sources of information. What do you want to do next? Search all of them? Only a few of them? Which ones? If you want to save time and effort, you need a "search strategy." What is a search strategy? A **search strategy** is the pattern of information acquisition that consumers utilize to solve their decision problems. This pattern can be organized or *ad hoc*, "effortful" or convenience-based, quick or prolonged, and comprehensive or patchy. Correspondingly, we can group the search strategies as (a) systematic and (b) heuristic.

Systematic information search proceeds in an organized pattern, directed at answering specific questions. The questions pertain to problem solving: What features do various product alternatives have, and what are the relative merits and demerits of various brands or alternatives? Consumers carry these questions in their minds, and their searches conclude when those questions have been answered. In contrast, **heuristic search** refers to *ad hoc* acquisition of information to reach intuitive judgments. **Heuristics** are quick rules of thumb and shortcuts used to make decisions.[3]

SYSTEMATIC	HEURISTIC
Organized	Ad hoc
Effortful	Convenience-based
Prolonged	Quick
Comprehensive	Patchy

Rules of Thumb

Here are some examples of how consumers use heuristics (rules of thumb):

Quick inferences Consumers use partial information to draw broad inferences quickly. Do you think, for example, that because Smartwater is laced with electrolytes, it must be somehow "high-tech" and hence superior? Most consumers infer product superiority from technical sounding terms, even though they may not quite know what that feature meant (e.g., *Dolby sound, pH balanced, air-dried*, etc.).

Brand name Often consumers use brand names as a guide to making a choice; e.g., "If this new phone is from Nokia, then it must be good." (Incidentally, did the name SmartWater by itself make you think that this water must be really *smart*?)

Past experience Consumers also use past experience to make their choices; e.g., "Last time I flew by JetBlue, everything went well, so I will fly the same airline again."

Recommendation Consumers seek others' judgments and make their choices based on these recommendations; e.g., "My coworker says Honda INSiGHT is a cool car, so I will just buy an INSiGHT."

We might not see anything odd in the above examples of heuristics. They might seem to us perfectly normal and sensible ways to make decisions. Yet, the fact remains that they are easy ways out—if we really wanted to avoid missing out on the best option, we would really need to search the information fully and on our own, in addition to using these heuristics. But, instead, we often use these shortcuts, thus saving time and effort. That is the whole point of using heuristics after all—they save time and effort. Do note that although heuristics are not systematic, they are also not irrational. They are rational to their users in terms of the cost-benefit trade-offs.

cookies

Well, oranges are round.

And moist.

And certainly sweet.

Okay, maybe you can't call one a cookie,

but don't let an orange hear you say

that it isn't a snack.

Better snacking.

Sunkist

sunkist.com

Image: Courtesy of Sunkist Company

Round and moist and sweet. Just like a cookie. Helping consumers use their heuristic to choose an orange. **Better snacking**.

Simplifiers versus Extenders?

The next question is, "Which strategy would you employ as a consumer, and when?" This depends on two broad factors: (a) your own cognitive style, and (b) problem complexity. First, consumers differ in their proclivities or zones of comfort in dealing with information; i.e., they differ in their cognitive styles. **Cognitive style** refers to consumer mindset about the task of processing information. When it comes to processing information, we could be "extenders" versus "simplifiers," undertaking an extensive search task, or, alternatively, looking for simplified, quick answers.

Which type are you? You are an extender if, for most decisions, you conduct a systematic search, seeking information extensively, consulting a variety of sources, taking the requisite time, and deliberating a lot. Alternatively, you are a simplifier if you often adopt the heuristic strategy, drawing quick inferences and relying a lot more on other people's opinions than on your own consideration of information.

Do you sometimes feel overwhelmed with information? When that happens, you are experiencing what is called an **information overload**—a condition in which the information being presented is too much for you to process as a consumer. Although the sheer volume or complexity or the speed of information is the major cause, your own cognitive style too deserves some of the credit.

The second factor is **problem complexity**—how simple or seemingly difficult the apparent solutions appear at the beginning of the search. This, of course, depends on how new the problem is—if we ran out of cereal this morning, no problem, we have dealt with it before. But if we are losing hair, now that requires some serious searching.

Losing Your Hair is No Routine Matter

On this dimension of problem complexity, all problems can be divided into three types: routine, extended, and limited. **Routine problems** are those that you, as a consumer, have solved many times in the past. Hence, you will solve them again routinely; i.e., without any new information search effort. **Extended problems** are purchase tasks for purchases never made before, or made long ago, or where risks of wrong choice are high. Finally, **limited problems** are nontrivial, but risks are moderate, and the product or service is not overly complex or technical in terms of its features.

In **routine problem solving**, generally, no new information is considered, and consumers usually solve these problems simply by repeating their previous choices. At the other extreme lies **extended problem solving**, where the information search is extensive and deliberation prolonged. In the middle lies **limited problem solving**—here, the consumer invests some limited amount of time and energy in searching and evaluating alternative solutions.

Here we will mention three problems, one from each category, leaving you to figure out which is which. (1) On your way to class, you felt hungry; (2) You needed to buy an engagement ring; and (3) You needed to buy a tire for your Prius. Now you are on your own!

DETERMINANTS OF SEARCHING

Even for extensive problems, we do not always search for information exhaustively; on the other hand, even for routine problems, sometimes we end up searching for some information. For example, you may have bought greeting cards several times before, but on every one of your sweetheart's birthdays, you go to the store and spend several minutes, if not hours, making your selection. Why? Researchers have found that the extent of information search depends on five factors: perceived risk; involvement; familiarity and expertise; shopping style; and time pressure. (See Figure 11.5.)

Perceived Risk Perceived risk is the degree of loss (i.e., amount at stake) in the event that a wrong choice is made. It consists of two subfactors: (a) the degree of uncertainty that a choice may be wrong; and (b) the severity of the consequences of a wrong choice; i.e., what is at stake, should a wrong choice occur. Buying a new flavor of coffee with a

THREE TYPES

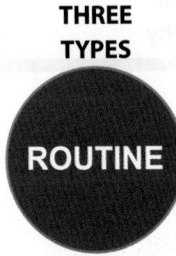

ROUTINE

OF

LIMITED

CONSUMER

EXTENDED

DECISION PROBLEMS

known brand name entails uncertainty about whether you will like the flavor, but the consequences are mild. Buying a suit without trying it on has the similar uncertainty about the suit's fit, but, in this case, and in addition, the consequences of an ill-fitting suit are considerable, especially if you are buying it for an important event. There are five types of risks:

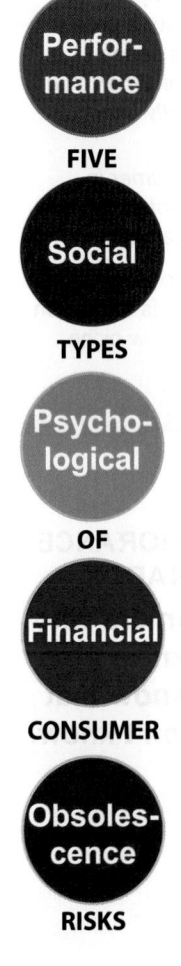

1. **Performance risk** The product or service may not perform well or not as well as some other alternatives. Also included here is the physical safety risk (such as the risk of your SUV rolling over).
2. **Social risk** Reference group members and significant others may not like it.
3. **Psychological risk** The product or service may not reflect oneself.
4. **Financial risk** The product may be overpriced; there may exist a lower price option.
5. **Obsolescence risk** The product may be replaced by newer substitutes.

If you buy a cell phone, for example, you will be concerned that the brand you buy might turn out to be unreliable, that the voice quality might be poor, or that when, dropped it might break. These are all performance risks. If you are considering buying a Scion iQ and are anxious over potential reactions from friends and coworkers, you are experiencing social risk. If you are unsure, yourself, that the Scion iQ would go well with your own self-concept of being, say, a successful executive, then you are experiencing psychological risk. We all know what a financial risk is—the product goes on sale the day after we have already bought it, for example. And obsolescence risk is high for fashion fads and technological products—the end of the season clearance item at the clothing store may seem like a great steal, but perhaps the style will be history by next year!

The higher you perceive the risk to be, the more extensive will be your information search. Marketers attempt, of course, to overcome these risks by using various strategies: performance risks by offering product warranties, financial risks by price guarantees, obsolescence risk by allowing trade-ins, and social and psychological risks by offering liberal return, exchange, or refund policies. If you judge that the product does not fit your style, or if significant others dislike your purchase, you may return it to the store without any liability, provided that it is unused. If you have used it, then of course you are on your own. In life, as well as in the store, it helps to know your mind and to have some confidence in yourself!

Involvement Involvement is defined in Chapter 2 as the interest a consumer takes in a product. In buying a greeting card, for example, you would take more interest if you were buying it for a special friend. This involvement means that you would be motivated to make as good a choice as possible. Consequently, you would search for more information before making your selection.

Familiarity and Expertise When it comes to buying a product, sometimes we are familiar with the product already. In that case, obviously, we would not engage in an elaborate information search. We would quickly know what to buy. Familiarity and prior experience also imply that the purchase problem is solved in the routine problem-solving mode.

The same is not true with expertise, though. *Expertise* is different from *familiarity*. We define **expertise** as the understanding of the attributes of a product or service class. It includes knowledge about an object or a product's composition, properties, and

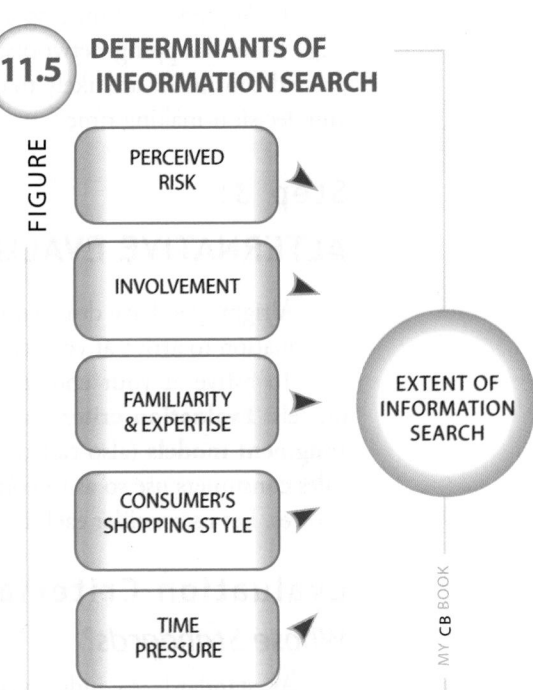

11.5 **DETERMINANTS OF INFORMATION SEARCH**

FIGURE

- PERCEIVED RISK
- INVOLVEMENT
- FAMILIARITY & EXPERTISE
- CONSUMER'S SHOPPING STYLE
- TIME PRESSURE

EXTENT OF INFORMATION SEARCH

MY CB BOOK

Speaking of involvement and greeting cards, a few years ago, a company brought out a greeting cards series called *For When You Are Slightly interested*!

It is *consumer involvement* that drives niche markets.

Indeed, consumer involvement is the raison d'être for new niche markets.

THE IGNORANCE PARADOX

Consumers who don't know also don't know that they don't know.

functioning—what it is made of, what capabilities or qualities that composition gives it, and how (and how well) it does whatever job it is supposed to do.

Interestingly, the role of prior expertise is counter-intuitive. At first, you would think that consumers with low prior expertise would seek more information to overcome their knowledge deficits—we call this the **deficit hypothesis**. However, it turns out that consumers with prior expertise seek even more information about the impending purchase than do those less knowledgeable.[4] For example, in one recent study of 1,400 car buyers, it was found that the amount of prior experience (i.e., familiarity) was, as expected, correlated negatively with the amount of consumer search effort. However, consumers' general interest in cars correlated positively with their product knowledge (i.e., expertise), and, in turn, both interest and expertise correlated positively with the amount of search effort.[5]

Ignorance Is Bliss

Although it seems counter-intuitive, the fact is that expert consumers seek more information than do novices—even though novices need it more. This occurs because naive consumers do not know what questions to ask; experts do. This explains why sports enthusiasts visit and buy from sports specialty stores, whereas non-enthusiasts buy their sports products from mass merchandisers. This is also why specialty stores have to employ more knowledgeable salespersons than do mass merchandisers. But novices are perfectly happy with their ignorance. You see, experts know what they know; they also know what they don't know. And they want to bridge that gap. In contrast, novices don't know that they don't know. To them, ignorance is bliss. This is called the **ignorance paradox**!

Consumer Shopping Style Consumers differ in their shopping styles. Some are avid comparison shoppers who search extensively to get the best value.[6] Others are brand loyal, sticking to known and tried brands, thus finding it unnecessary to search anew for information. Moreover, some find shopping interesting, whereas others find it a boring chore. Naturally, the latter type would search for information minimally.

Time Pressure One of the most conspicuous characteristics of the consumer in the new millennium is time pressure. Time has become scarce due to: (a) both spouses being employed, (b) people re-enrolling in school to acquire new skills necessary for a more complex employment market, and (c) new leisure activities, enabled by technology (e.g., cyber surfing). In a way, today's "always on the go" consumer is a "harassed decision maker."

Time pressure is making consumers look for more convenient outlets for shopping (e.g., home-shopping networks, catalog shopping, and the Internet). In addition, time-pressed consumers are likely to cut short their information search, comparison-shopping, and decision-making time.[7]

Step 3:
ALTERNATIVE EVALUATION

Alright, you have done enough information searching. Now, how do you use all that information to arrive at your choice?

To arrive at your choice, you need two things: evaluation criteria and judgment models. **Evaluation criteria** are standards against which consumers evaluate a product. **Judgment models** (also called "decision models" and "choice rules") are procedures and rules consumers use so as to consider various product attributes to arrive at their product choices. Let us consider each in turn.

Evaluation Criteria
Whose Standards?

As standards to judge various alternatives, **evaluation criteria** are simply what consumers want in a product. In a cell phone, for example, you would perhaps want long battery life, good sound fidelity, a large readable display, a 100-number memory, one-touch dialing, and Web readiness. If so, then all of these are your evaluation criteria. Do you want customizable ring tones, also? And voice activated dialing? A built-in speaker? If you do, then these, too, become your evaluation criteria.

Let us ponder a simple question: from where do these criteria come? How did you learn of them? At first, you might think, "The answer is simple: These are the features I want, so these became my criteria." You are right, but only partially. The full answer is this: they come from three sources: Motivation and need, solution feature availability, and perceived value vis-à-vis costs. (See Figure 11.6.)

In a sense, the features we want simply reflect our motivations and needs at a greater level of detail. Thus, we not only need food, but we also need hot, nutritious, and tasty food. We not only need a phone to meet the need to communicate anytime and anywhere, but we also need to be able to do it conveniently (hence, one-touch dialing), and we want to be able to communicate without using our hands (hence, a built-in speaker phone).

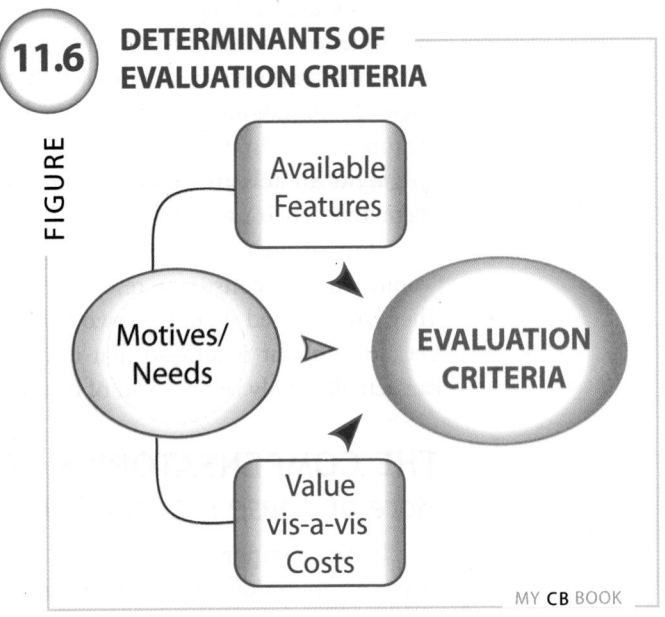

FIGURE 11.6 DETERMINANTS OF EVALUATION CRITERIA

MY **CB** BOOK

Next, if a solution feature is not available in the product (in any of the available alternatives), we would not even think of it as required. (We would still seek convenience, but it would not occur to us to translate convenience into hands-free dialing.) Note, however, that not all features of a product become evaluation criteria—only those that meet some need or address some motive. Thus, a motive and an available feature together make an evaluation criterion.

Finally, if a feature costs money, then we have to assess its value relative to its cost—*value* here being defined as the benefit to be derived from that feature. Voice-dial costs $50 extra? Well, we will do without it. Thus, when we enter the marketplace, so to speak (that means when we start the search process), we have an initial and tentative set of criteria in mind; later, we construct more (or drop some of the initial set) as we gather information.

Determinant Attributes

Thus, evaluation criteria comprise a subset of product attributes. We apply evaluation criteria to appraise alternatives. Often some of these evaluation criteria fail to distinguish among alternatives, because the alternatives under consideration are equal or on par. The evaluative criteria on which the alternatives differ from one another become determinant evaluative criteria, more formally known as **determinant attributes**. (See Figure 11.7.)

S A V V Y MARKETER

Marketers should constantly monitor competing brands and consumers' evaluative criteria so as to understand which brand features have become *determinant attributes* for their product categories.

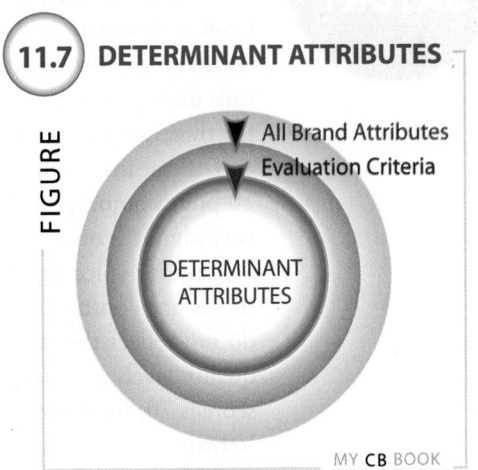

FIGURE 11.7 DETERMINANT ATTRIBUTES

All Brand Attributes
Evaluation Criteria
DETERMINANT ATTRIBUTES

MY **CB** BOOK

DECISION MODELS: COMPENSATORY AND NONCOMPENSATORY

Beauty Contests and Brand Battles

First, let's talk about models of a different kind. You might be familiar with beauty contests. Beauty contestants are first scored in different categories: talent, looks, outlook (attitude toward self and world view—remember, contestants are often asked a question or two about some big issue in life), etc. Then the judges add up all the scores. Sitting in the audience, you might wish that they gave more weight to talent; your friend, who is also watching the show, might wish that they based their final choice exclusively on looks. These are all judgment models; your judgment model is different from that of the event organizers, and, in turn, your friend's judgment model is different from yours. Very simply, **judgment models** are procedures and rules for taking into account various qualities of an alternative. Their utility? Very simply, again—they guide our choice decisions.

Just so we can talk about these various judgment models (or "decision rules" or "choice rules"), consumer researchers have given them more specific, technical names. They have divided them into two broad categories: compensatory and noncompensatory.[8] Let's learn about them—so that next time, as you watch the Miss Universe contest, you can actually apply them! And of course, you can apply them to the battle of brands.

THE COMPENSATORY MODEL
More of These if Less of Those

In the **compensatory model**, the consumer arrives at a choice by considering all of the attributes of a product or service (or benefits from a product or service) and by mentally trading off the alternative's perceived weakness on one or more attributes with its perceived strength on other attributes. A consumer may go about making this calculation in two ways. First, he or she might simply add the number of positive attributes, subtract the number of negative attributes each alternative has, and then choose the one that has the most positive and fewest negative attributes.

Whereas we sometimes do make decisions based on a simple numerical count of the pluses and the minuses, often we do not consider each plus or minus as equally significant. Some considerations are clearly more important than others, and every minus may not cancel a plus on some other feature. Therefore, we use a truer version of the compensatory model. This, the second, more systematic approach, is to weigh every product attribute in terms of its relative importance. Let us say that we want to make a choice between wireless service providers Verizon, AT&T, and Sprint. To keep the example simple, let us say there are just three evaluation criteria that we will use: reliability (calls not dropped, calls dialed correctly), voice quality, and customer service. Suppose we could rate each of the three services on these three criteria on a 0 to 10 rating scale (where 0 means very poor and 10 means excellent). Suppose we could also assign an importance rating by dividing 10 points among the three attributes: 5, 3, and 2—reliability is most important to us, so we assign it 5 out of 10 points; customer service is next most important, and we assign it a 3; and to voice quality we assign a 2 (the importance scores add up to 10). Table 11.3 shows one consumer's ratings (note that these are one consumer's hypothetical ratings and do not reflect the actual quality of these three services). Now, all you do is multiply the quality levels with importance weights and add them up for each company. The highest score is 70, for Verizon (see Table 11.2), so using this judgment model, you would choose Verizon.

This model is called *compensatory* because a shortfall on one attribute may be compensated by a good rating on another attribute. In the above hypothetical example, Verizon is actually not as good on customer service as is AT&T, and not as good on voice quality as is Sprint (all these being hypothetical statements, of course), but these shortcomings are more than compensated for by its superiority on reliability, which is of the highest importance to our hypothetical consumer.

NONCOMPENSATORY MODELS:

No Substitutions, Please

While sometimes we want it all (so we consider all the features or qualities and accordingly use the compensatory model), sometimes we just want one feature or maybe two. Or we want a few features to a certain degree, but we don't necessarily want them all. If there were one particular feature that we wanted, and if an alternative didn't have that feature, then it will be out, no matter what other features it had—those other features won't compensate. We call these judgment procedures *non-compensatory models*, and we will discuss four of them: conjunctive, disjunctive, lexicographic, and elimination by aspects.[9] To help us remember these, let's also give each of them a phrase:

Conjunctive model	**"Must have at least this much of these."**
Disjunctive model	**"Okay I am flexible; must have either this or that."**
Lexicographic model	**"I will take the best on the most."**
Elimination by aspects	**"At least this much on the most."**

TABLE

11.2 APPLYING COMPENSATORY MODEL TO THE CHOICE OF A WIRELESS SERVICE

Evaluation Criteria	Importance	Brand Ratings Verizon	Sprint	AT&T
Reliability	5	8	7	5
Customer-Service	3	6	4	8
Voice quality	2	6	7	4

Total weighted score for: Verizon = 8x5 + 6x3 + 6x2 = 70
Sprint = 7x5 + 4x3 + 7x2 = 61
AT&T= 5x5 + 8x3 + 4x2 = 57
Therefore, this specific consumer will choose Verizon.

MY   BOOK

The Conjunctive Model In the **conjunctive model**, the consumer uses certain minimum cutoffs on all salient attributes. Each alternative is then examined on each attribute, and any alternative that meets the minimum cut-offs on all attributes can potentially be chosen. If an alternative failed to reach the cut-off, even on one attribute, it would be dropped from further consideration. If all alternatives failed to reach the cut-off levels, then the consumer would revise his or her minimum cut-off levels or use another decision model. On the other hand, if more than one alternative met all the minimum cut-off levels, the consumer would likely resort to another decision model to eliminate further alternatives until only one survived the process. We will illustrate this for the three wireless companies shortly, but first let us define the other three models as well.

The Disjunctive Model The **disjunctive model** entails trade-offs between aspects of choice alternatives. Here, the consumer is willing to trade off one feature for another. For example, a home buyer might say that the house should have either five bedrooms or, if it has only four bedrooms, then it must have a finished basement. Although these trade-offs are also made in the compensatory model, there are important differences. First, the disjunctive model considers the sheer presence or absence of attributes, rather than the degree or amount in which these attributes are present. Second, in the compensatory model, the attributes traded off need not serve the same purpose, whereas in the disjunctive model, they tend to do so (e.g., a finished basement and an extra bedroom both imply more living space).

The Lexicographic Model In the **lexicographic model**, the consumer rank-orders product attributes in terms of importance. The consumer examines all alternatives first on the most important criterion and identifies the alternative that ranks the highest on that criterion. If more than one alternative remained in the choice set, the consumer would consider the second most important criterion, examine the remaining alternatives with respect to that criterion, and select the best. The process would continue until only one alternative remained.

Elimination by Aspect The **elimination by aspect** (EBA) model is similar to the lexicographic model, but with one important difference. The consumer rates the attributes

CONJUNC-TIVE

DISJUNC-TIVE

LEXICO-GRAPHIC

ELIMINA-TION by ASPECT

NONCOMPENSATORY

in order of importance and, in addition, defines the minimum required values. He or she then examines all alternatives first on the most important attribute, admitting for further consideration only those contenders that satisfy the minimum cut-off level on this most important attribute. If more than one alternative met this requirement, then the consumer would go to the next step, appraising the remaining alternatives on the second most important attribute, and retaining only those that met the minimum cut-off level on this attribute, and so on.[10]

Judgment Day—Models in Action

Now let's apply these models to a choice among the three wireless service companies.

For the conjunctive model, let us assume that you require all attributes to be at least average (a value of 5). Then, Sprint fails on customer service and AT&T is rejected on voice quality; only Verizon meets the cut-off minimum of 5 on all attributes. So Verizon is chosen ("Must have at least these"). To apply the disjunctive model, suppose you are willing to compromise and would accept a brand with either good voice quality or good customer service (good being defined as 7), and reliability doesn't matter to you. Now, then, Verizon is rejected, but both Sprint and AT&T are acceptable. (Your choice is not made, since you must now choose between the two, but you may do it now by looking at reliability, which is better for Sprint, or by some other criterion.)

Next, applying the lexicographic model, you will simply look at all three services, and, because reliability is most important to you (according to the table above), you will first judge them all on reliability and choose the one with the highest value on this—meaning that you would choose Verizon ("the best on the most"). Suppose that Sprint had also rated 8 on reliability; in that case, you will be left with both Sprint and Verizon, and in the second step you will use customer service as the next criterion, and you will ultimately choose Verizon (since it rates 6 on customer service versus Sprint's 4).

Finally, to apply EBA, let us keep the same importance ratings, and, in addition, suppose we wanted these attributes to be at least 6. Note that we don't want all the attributes to be 6, but, if we bother to look at an attribute at all, then it should be 6 or better. Now, AT&T is eliminated in the first step itself (it has less than 6 on reliability). In the second step, we evaluate the remaining two brands on customer service and select Verizon. (Incidentally, suppose Verizon had rated a 5 on voice quality; it wouldn't matter because our choice had already been made.)

Are These Models Sensible?

You are probably thinking to yourself, "This can't be real!" As far as you know, no consumer uses these models; perhaps they are a figment of the imagination of this textbook writer or of some other scatter-brained professor. Let us assure you, consumers do use these models all the time, and so do you. Before we show you how, two clarifications are in order. First, the models are not rules that the consumer "knows" he or she is applying. Rather, the consumer just goes about selecting and rejecting alternatives in some ways, but those ways represent the patterns of these models. Consumers don't have to know them by these names; we consumer researchers have to, so that, when we study consumers' decision processes, we can classify what proportion of our target market uses which models.

Second, consumers don't really assign numbers or do the calculations. Instead, they rate and rank and weigh and select and reject alternatives "qualitatively." They use qualitative labels such as "good," "poor," etc., rather than using numbers. We as researchers assign numbers so that we are able to analyze, using the computer, a large sample of consumers. Thus, in practice, consumers use these patterns in a qualitative and therefore somewhat imprecise manner.

Now let us show you how you use these models in your own choices. Remember the beauty contest mentioned earlier. If you wanted to value all three criteria— looks, talent, and outlook (not necessarily equally)—then you would be using a compensatory model. If all three criteria were important to you, and the beauty contestant should at least be, say, average on each, then you would be using a conjunctive model. If you thought that a contestant should be either very good on looks or very good on talent, then you would be using a disjunctive model. And if talent were all you cared about, and if you would declare the contestant with the most talent as the winner, then you would be using the lexicographic model. You'd have realized that if, out of all contestants, two contestants were equally outstanding on talent, then you might go for looks—whichever of the two had the better looks would take the prize (this is still the lexicographic model, remember!).

Finally, you would be using elimination by aspect (EBA) if you eliminated contestants based on whoever did not get a minimum score on talent (if talent was most important to you), and then the remaining contestants would be evaluated on the next test, outlook. Here, more would be eliminated for not making a minimum score on outlook, and so on. That is elimination by aspect. So, you see, believe it or not, you do use these models—as does every other consumer. All of the time!

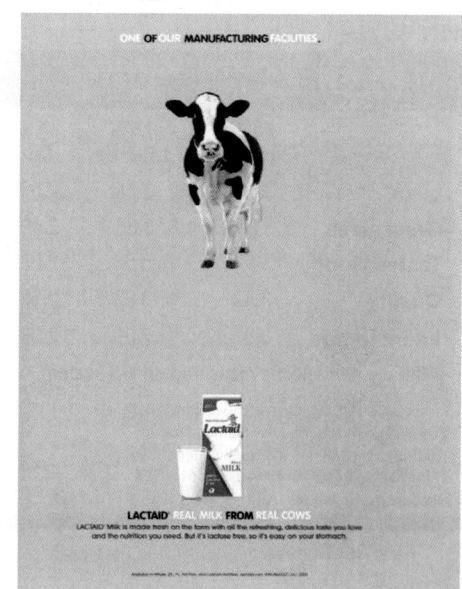

The headline reads: One of Our Manufacturing Facilities (shows the cow). Copy reads: Lactaid milk is made fresh on the farm with all the refreshing, delicious taste you love and the nutrition you need. But it is lactose free, so it is easy on your stomach. Lactaid® Real Milk from Real Cows.
For consumers whose most important criterion is that the milk be natural and real, this Soymilk ad communicates that it is. Helping consumers with their "lexicographic" strategy.

IMPERFECTIONS IN CONSUMER JUDGMENTS

While the foregoing decision models give the appearance of consumers making logical decisions, consumer judgments are seldom perfect. The human mind is not exactly like a computer. It does take in information, but then it does not analyze it precisely. Rather, to save time or mental effort, it interprets that information quickly and intuitively. Consequently, its judgments and interpretations are approximate and often not entirely logical or factual. Let us consider six notable imperfections: (1) framing effects; (2) heuristics as biases; (3) mental accounting; (4) top-down versus bottom-up customization; (5) inference making; and (6) *satisficing*.

Framing Effects on Judgment
The Case of Glass Half-full or Half-empty

For which would you pay more: a glass of wine that is 2/3 full, or a glass of the same wine that is 1/3 empty? You may think this question is silly because you believe that anyone can see that the two options are exactly equal. But think again: Do consumers perceive as equal two food items, one labeled 98% fat free and the other labeled 2% fat? The surprising answer, based on research, is "No." Consumer researchers have found that when consumers are presented with two equal options, one stated in positive terms and the other in negative terms, they invariably tend to prefer the option stated in positive terms. This result is called the *framing effect*. **Framing** refers to the context in which information is presented. **Framing-effect** refers to the bias in the interpretation of the

Half-full or half-empty? That depends on your FRAME!

TABLE 11.3	HOW FRAMING AFFECTS CONSUMER INFERENCES		
	75% lean	75% fat-free	25% fat
Lean	3.48	3.54	2.50
Greaseless	3.20	3.35	2.49
Tastes Good	3.42	3.53	2.58
Quality	3.42	3.33	2.58
Intent to buy	3.01	2.89	2.30
(Attribute perceptions measured on 1-5 scales)			

Source: Robert J. Donovan and Geoffrey Jalleh, "Positively versus Negatively Framed Product Attributes: The Influence of Involvement," *Psychology & Marketing*, 16 (7), October 1999, p. 613-630. (Used with permission)

MY CB BOOK

information resulting from its framing or context.

A recent research project illustrates this effect. In an experiment, consumers were randomly divided into three groups. One group was told that a specific meat product was 75% lean; another was told that it was 75% fat-free; and the third was told that it had 25% fat. Consumers were then asked to rate the meat product on leanness, greasiness, quality, and tastiness; they were also asked how likely they would be to buy that meat product. The findings are shown in Table 11.4. Consumers rated the meat labeled 25% fat much more negatively than did those who saw the other two labels. These results are a vivid commentary on how, as consumers, we do not always think rationally. Rather, we interpret the information based on its framing context. Illogical as it may seem, the fact is that as consumers we often think that a glass 3/4 full is better than a glass 1/4 empty!

Heuristics as Biases

We introduced this concept earlier, as shortcuts consumers use to simplify decision making. Two Nobel Prize-winning economists (Amos Tversky and Daniel Kahneman) have done some fascinating research and uncovered three general heuristics that produce significant biases in how humans make judgments.[11] All students of consumer behavior should learn and ponder these.

Availability Heuristics.

Quickly, what causes more people to die every year: car accidents or cancer? Most consumers in research studies have answered: Car accidents. Why? Because they hear of car accidents everyday; seldom of cancer deaths. (Fact: Cancer deaths exceed car accident deaths—in 2010, this ratio was 17 to 1, for the U.S.).

Consumer Behavior Implication: If ever in your life you have experienced a flood, you will now be more inclined to buy flood insurance; more likely than, say, have fire insurance, even if fires maybe more likely than floods.

Representative Heuristic

If you had a fellow student in your class from, say, Australia and he had the habit of volunteering frequently in class discussions, you would then assume that all Australians are outspoken and vociferous. Or at least, if you encountered another Australian, you would assume a high probability of him/her too being outspoken. This bias is called *representative heuristic*.

Consumer Behavior Implication: Consumers exposed to an immigrant merchant or service employee tend to then assume that all other immigrant salespersons of that nationality have the same attributes. This can, of course, be misleading. This consumer tendency to generalize or to stereotype based on a single instance is ever-present. That is why, as a marketer, you have to be careful to avoid flawed behavior or flawed performance, even on one occasion. Sell one stale donut, and consumers will quickly use representative heuristics to avoid all donuts that carry your brand name.

To overcome both these biases, you will need to (1) pay attention to **base rate information**—what is the proportion of Australians in Australia (not just among college students who come to USA) who are outspoken? and (2) avoid the tendency (perfectly natural) to give more weight to case histories or anecdotal evidence (e.g., that you know someone personally whose baggage was lost by, say, British Airways) over statistics (Does British Airways have an overall poor record of baggage misplacement?).

Anchoring and Adjustment

This is a heuristic where we use some pre-existing information as an anchor to evaluate

THREE

Availability

HEURISTIC

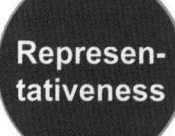

Representativeness

BIASES

Anchoring & Adjustment

subsequent information. Suppose you are negotiating with a car dealer for a car whose official retail price (MSRP) is $22,000; what price would you consider a good value? That depends on what the dealer is asking: If $21,000, then you might settle for, say, $20,000; if the asking price was $20,200, then you would most likely settle for $19,000 or $19,200 (not $19,800, even though it is $200 less than the $20,000 you were willing to settle for). Marketers often use this both to their own and to consumers' advantage: They suggest external reference prices ("regular price was —"; or "compare at —"); airlines now build slack into their scheduled arrival times; and fundraisers guide you with mention of "suggested donation amount." Anchoring bias dictates that our estimates of any property are biased by and toward the initial value information we have.

These have become habits of the adult human mind and, consequently, they influence every judgment we make in everyday living—large and small, in the marketplace and in life at large.

Mental Accounting

The Quirky Accountant Inside Our Minds

If you are a college student and earn money with a part time job as well as receiving occasional cash gifts from parents, do you treat these two types of income in like manner? Many consumers don't. They somehow deposit these, in their mind, in two separate accounts, so to speak. They will use one (say, the regular income account) for everyday expenses, and reserve the other (say, the cash gift income account) to draw on for personal indulgences. Salaried employees might treat regular income and bonus income as separate accounts, at least mentally, even if they deposit both in the same bank account. Likewise, many consumers also keep separate accounts in their minds for spending categories (e.g., food, clothing, entertainment). Thus, in effect, they will spend on food (eating out, etc.) until that month's food account is spent. If a dress caught their eye and it were not within the budget in their spending account for clothing, then a logical thing would have been to shift money from, say, the food account into the clothing account. But this would not happen, even if there were extra money in the food or entertainment account. In the same vein, consumers budget for an evening out. If the dinner ended up costing less than what they had budgeted, they would go ahead and spend it on extra food (e.g., dessert) rather than saving it for another occasion or making a purchase in another category, even during the same outing. This is called **mental accounting**[12]—the consumer habit of forming and keeping separate income accounts for different sources of income and, likewise, separate spending accounts for different spending categories. It is also called, particularly forming and managing the spending categories, *mental budgeting*. As consumers, of course, we don't call them as such, but most of us do keep mental accounts.

Top-Down versus Bottom-Up Customization

Imagine that you are out buying a car. You are considering a Ford Taurus, you are told the price of a basic Veloster Turbo (say, $18,000), and you are given a list of options with individual prices. You choose options one by one, until you believe you have included all the options you want. This is called **bottom-up customization**—a process wherein consumers build a product starting from the basic version.

Now suppose, instead, that you are given the price of a loaded car with all the options (say, 20,800), and you have the option of deleting the options (with individual prices specified). You delete the options one by one until you feel you have deleted the options you don't want. This is called **top-down customization**—a process wherein consumers build back a product starting from the loaded version.

Do you think you would end up with the same car in the two scenarios? The answer is "no"—most consumers will end up with a more loaded car (with a higher price ticket) in the top-down than in the bottom-up process. Why does this happen? Researchers have proposed several reasons, two of which are most likely:[12]

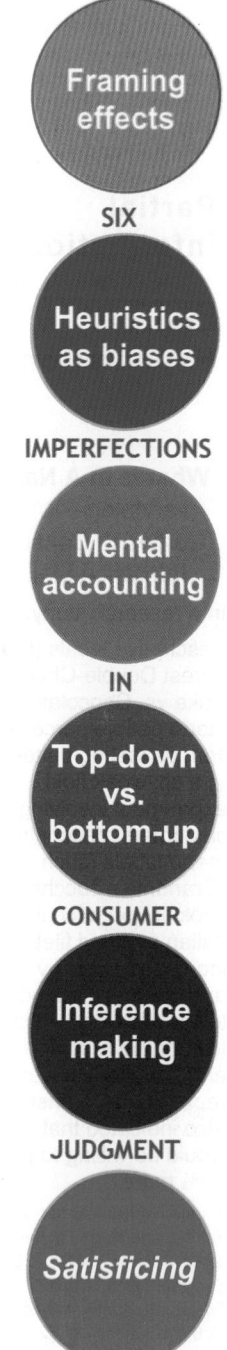

Framing effects

SIX

Heuristics as biases

IMPERFECTIONS

Mental accounting

IN

Top-down vs. bottom-up

CONSUMER

Inference making

JUDGMENT

Satisficing

a. Cognitive Effort Both adding options and deleting options take cognitive effort—i.e., the consumer has to think each option over and appraise its utility and cost. Suppose consumers want to undertake the effort to process only three options; then, starting from a ten-option loaded car, they will settle on a seven-option car. In contrast, starting with a basic car, they will end up with a three-option car.

b. Anchoring Effect The starting price acts as an anchor, as a comparison point, from which consumers judge how much they have moved. Suppose consumers want to move away by 5%; then from a starting price of $18,000, they end up at $18,900; but with $20,800 as the anchor, they will come down to $19,760, thus ending up with a customized item that is $860 more expensive in the top down than in the bottom-up version.

SAVVY MARKETER

This phenomenon is of great interest to marketers. If they offer a fully loaded model, consumers are likely to end up buying a "more-features" version, but a higher initial price might discourage some consumers at the outset. Thus, marketers must balance these two opposite effects.

Inference Making

It would be nice if we had all the information we wanted about a product. Often, we don't. So we try to guess at the missing information. That is, we try to make an inference about the missing attribute information. **Inference making** refers to the consumer act of assuming the missing information to make a judgment about a product. For example, a consumer may reason, "This pair of shoes is twice as expensive, so it must be more durable." In this manner, based on some partial information and some logical expectations, the consumer fills in the missing information.

Partial information + Logical Expectation = INFERENCE

Just how do consumers fill in missing information? Scholars have suggested three approaches; read them below and see which one is your favorite:

1. **Inter-attribute inference** The value of one attribute is inferred based on another attribute. For example, thickness of the fabric in an item of clothing might be used to infer crease-resistance (whether correctly or incorrectly).

2. **Evaluative consistency** The missing attribute is assumed to conform to the overall evaluation of the brand. Thus, if a brand were positively evaluated in overall terms, then the brand would be assumed to be good on the missing attribute as well, e.g., a VCR's repair record is assumed to be "good" just because consumers judge other attributes to be good.

3. **Negative cue** The consumer may simply treat the missing information as a negative cue and then use one of the two sub-strategies: avoid altogether the option with the missing information, or assume a low or poor value on this attribute.[13]

Chances are you have used all three of them, but do you favor one of them more than the other two?

SATISFICING

No matter what decision model they use, consumers as decision makers can never consider and appraise all of the alternatives exhaustively. Indeed, consumers *do not* typically make the most optimal choices. As already pointed out, the use of lexicographic, EBA, or other noncompensatory models might eliminate a brand from further consideration based on the first attribute, even though the brand's other features could have made the brand more attractive in overall terms. Yet consumers are perfectly happy making choices by using noncompensatory models. This is a concept that Nobel Prize winning economist Herbert Simon calls *satisficing*.[14] **Satisficing** refers to a consumer's (or a decision maker's) acceptance of an alternative that he or she finds satisfying, even though there might be a better alternative. Thus, even ardent comparison shoppers finally give up and buy the product or service they find most acceptable from among those they have considered so far, even though they recognize that there might well be a slightly or even substantially better product or service or deal at the next store. This is *satisficing*. If you are a satisficer (note it is *satisficer*, not *satisfier*), don't worry; most consumers are, most of the time!

CHOOSING EXPRESSIVE PRODUCTS
Or the Art of Buying Diamonds, Cologne, and Lingerie

The decision processes we have described, especially the decision models, seem to work well for appliances, cars, office products, tools, etc. But surely we wouldn't buy, you would argue, diamonds, cologne, dresses or lingerie this way. In fact, for many of these products, we just fall in love with them at first sight. How do consumers choose emotional products?

To address this issue, consumer researchers have divided products into two categories according to whether they serve, primarily, utilitarian (i.e., functional or performance) needs or, instead (and primarily), social-psychological needs or motives. We would call the former *functional* and the latter *expressive*—we use the latter to express ourselves and our personalities, moods, lifestyles, and tastes. We assess functional products (such as appliances and tools) by assessing their performance features; we process the information, and use the judgment models we described earlier. We call this the **information processing mode (IPM)**. In this mode, "the consumer is thought to acquire information about brand attributes, to form evaluative criteria, to judge the levels of these attributes in various brands, and to combine these attribute-levels for overall brand evaluation."[15]

Emotional Choices

In contrast, expressive products are chosen for their social-psychological values. They are assessed by what is known as the **affective choice mode (ACM)**. In this mode, affect or liking for the brand ensues based not on attribute information but on judgments that have three properties: holistic, self-implicative, and nonverbalizable. That is, individual attributes matter less than the overall style, appearance, and total impression (holistic); the

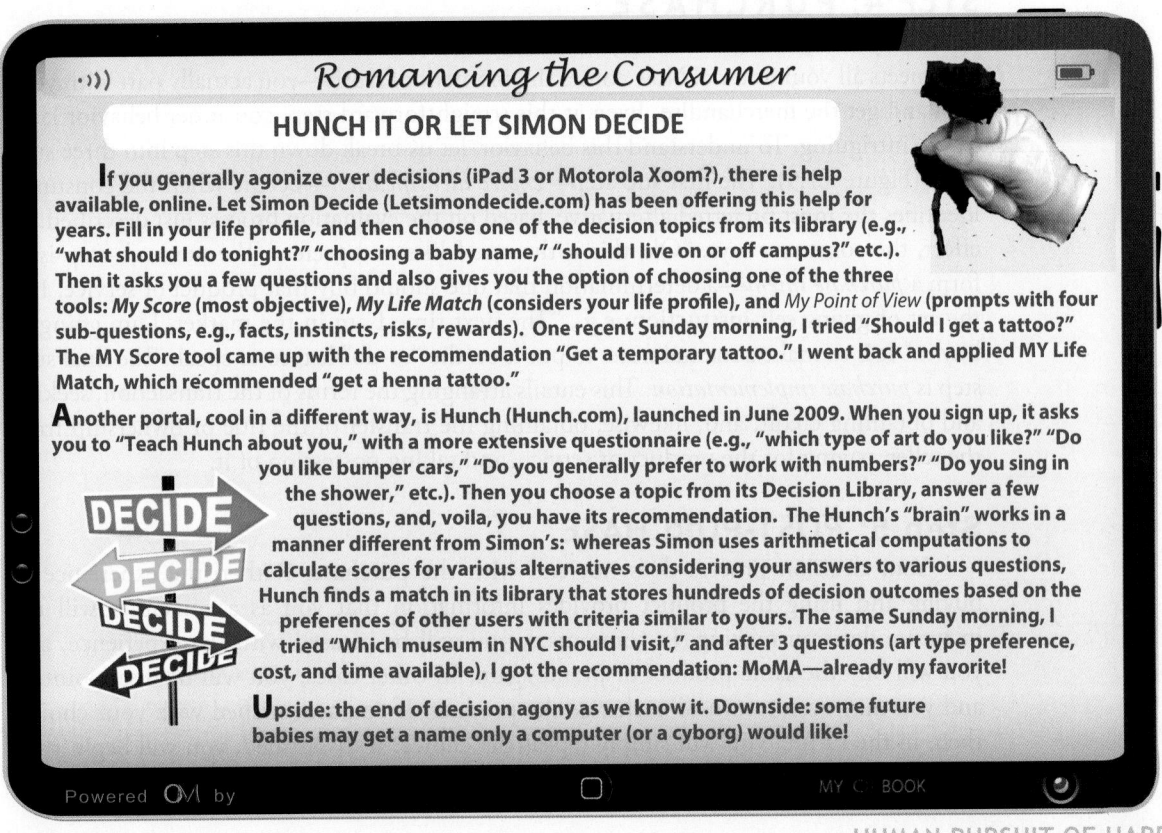

Romancing the Consumer

HUNCH IT OR LET SIMON DECIDE

If you generally agonize over decisions (iPad 3 or Motorola Xoom?), there is help available, online. Let Simon Decide (Letsimondecide.com) has been offering this help for years. Fill in your life profile, and then choose one of the decision topics from its library (e.g., "what should I do tonight?" "choosing a baby name," "should I live on or off campus?" etc.). Then it asks you a few questions and also gives you the option of choosing one of the three tools: *My Score* (most objective), *My Life Match* (considers your life profile), and *My Point of View* (prompts with four sub-questions, e.g., facts, instincts, risks, rewards). One recent Sunday morning, I tried "Should I get a tattoo?" The MY Score tool came up with the recommendation "Get a temporary tattoo." I went back and applied MY Life Match, which recommended "get a henna tattoo."

Another portal, cool in a different way, is Hunch (Hunch.com), launched in June 2009. When you sign up, it asks you to "Teach Hunch about you," with a more extensive questionnaire (e.g., "which type of art do you like?" "Do you like bumper cars," "Do you generally prefer to work with numbers?" "Do you sing in the shower," etc.). Then you choose a topic from its Decision Library, answer a few questions, and, voila, you have its recommendation. The Hunch's "brain" works in a manner different from Simon's: whereas Simon uses arithmetical computations to calculate scores for various alternatives considering your answers to various questions, Hunch finds a match in its library that stores hundreds of decision outcomes based on the preferences of other users with criteria similar to yours. The same Sunday morning, I tried "Which museum in NYC should I visit," and after 3 questions (art type preference, cost, and time available), I got the recommendation: MoMA—already my favorite!

Upside: the end of decision agony as we know it. Downside: some future babies may get a name only a computer (or a cyborg) would like!

Powered by MY C BOOK

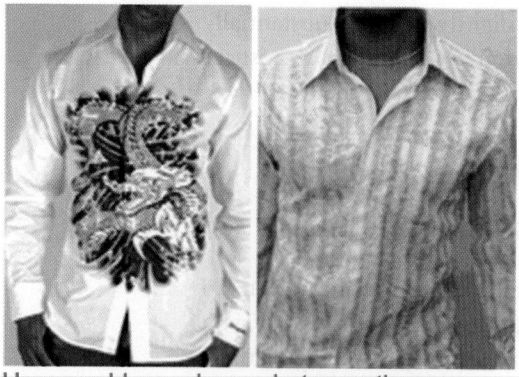

How would you choose between these two shirts? Most consumers use ACM for choosing between expressive products.
(Shirts available at www.soliscompany.com)
(Photos courtesy of the Solis Company)

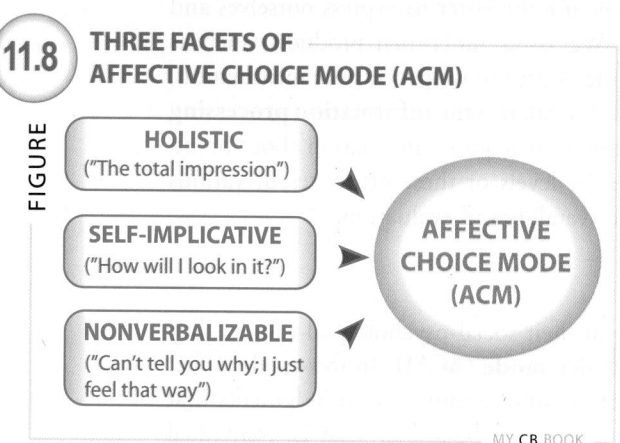

FIGURE **11.8** THREE FACETS OF AFFECTIVE CHOICE MODE (ACM)

HOLISTIC ("The total impression")

SELF-IMPLICATIVE ("How will I look in it?")

NONVERBALIZABLE ("Can't tell you why; I just feel that way")

AFFECTIVE CHOICE MODE (ACM)

MY **CB** BOOK

product or service is judged in relation to oneself, as in, "How will *I* look in this dress?" (self-implicative). Also the decision cannot be verbalized since it was based on nonverbal cues (i.e., picture, appearance) and vicarious emotional experience. See Figure 11.8.

The implication of this distinction is two-fold. First, for expressive products, you would not seek much feature information, but this would not mean that you don't care and that you are executing a routine problem-solving strategy. Actually, the deliberation time may be just as long. Second, marketers of these products should not burden the consumer with a lot of attribute information; instead, they should portray the product in its entirety (i.e., holistically) and create social/psychological symbolism via nonverbal communication and via association with positive role models or attractive personae.

Having described the ACM process, we must now balance the picture. It is not that, for expressive products, IPM is not used at all; rather, both of the processes are used. IPM is used initially to eliminate some choices using the noncompensatory models. Thus, the consumer may eliminate all dresses that are above a thousand dollars in price and all those that are not pastel in color. But then, when it comes to making the final selection, the ACM process is likely to be the one that determines the consumer's choice.

STEP 4: PURCHASE

Okay, so by now you have rejected many alternatives and have identified the one that best meets all your criteria. Now comes the moment of truth—you actually part with your cash and get the merchandise. Even at this straightforward step, consumer behavior is, at times, intriguing. To understand this behavior, let us break down this step into three sub-steps (Figure 11.9). The first sub-step—*choice identification*—occurs when the consumer identifies the most preferred alternative, based on the evaluation process just described. In effect, the consumer says, "Ok, this is the one I like and prefer." The next sub-step is to form a *purchase intent*—a determination that one should buy that product or service. It is the act of giving self-instruction; e.g., "The next time I am in the market, I am going to buy it." It is to make a mental note, to put it on the "to-do" list, so to speak. The final sub-step is *purchase implementation*. This entails arranging the terms of the transaction, seeking and obtaining credit, and, likewise, obtaining the transfer of the title or ownership from the seller, paying for the product or service, and taking possession of it.

Step 5: POST-PURCHASE

Your decision process does not end with the purchase. Rather, the experience of buying and using the product provides information that you as a consumer will use in future decision making. In some cases, you will be pleased with the experience, and you will buy the same product or brand again. In other cases, you will be disappointed, and you may even return or exchange the product. If you are satisfied with your choice, then, in the future, you will simply repeat the choice. If dissatisfied, you will begin your decision-making process again. Of course, you do not have to start at the very beginning

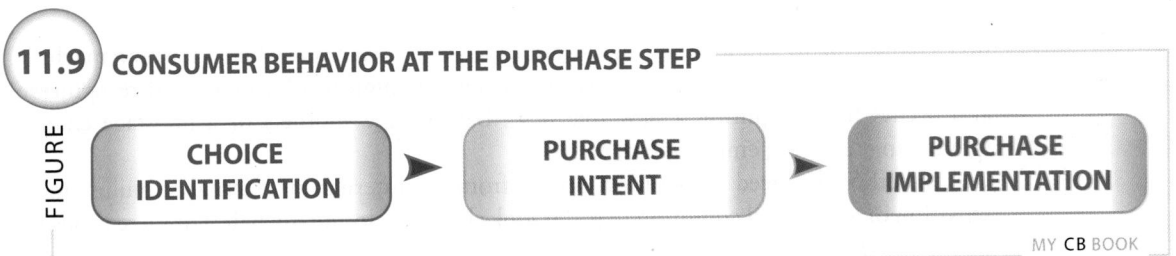

CHOICE IDENTIFICATION ▶ PURCHASE INTENT ▶ PURCHASE IMPLEMENTATION

MY **CB** BOOK

(i.e., at Step 1, Problem Recognition). Nor, in fact, do you have to search for information from scratch. Rather, you re-open the alternative evaluation process, and you pick up the threads from the previous occasion. Thus, you might remember which brand was your second choice, so you would go back to that brand, give it a last-minute check, and buy it. Or you might gather additional information about one or more of the alternatives you had eliminated or not considered in detail the last time, and then apply the relevant decision model again to identify a new choice.

To the marketer, nothing should be more important than to ensure that consumers' post-purchase experiences are good and that consumers are satisfied with their purchases. Only satisfied consumers will become loyal consumers. And loyal consumers are the backbone of a brand or business. We will study these fascinating topics of consumer satisfaction and loyalty further in the next chapter. For now, and before we conclude this chapter, we must address one final question. How do consumers choose from among various decision processes themselves? Our answer is summed up in one word—*involvement*.

SAVVY MARKETER

INVOLVEMENT— THE PERVASIVE ARBITER OF CHOICE PROCESSES

Involvement—you have encountered this concept before in this book and, indeed, in this chapter. Let us recap what it is. It is, very basically, *the importance of a product or issue to us as consumers*. We purchase and consume hundreds of products and services in our lives, but we are not equally involved in all of them. We take some for granted, not even noticing them unless something wrong happens. And we purchase them routinely, just repeating the last purchase, or just buying whatever is convenient, the cheapest, or the most available. For these low involvement products, we have neither the time nor the motivation to follow very deliberative processes. We reserve the more thorough and systematic processes for a few highly involving, substantive, significant purchases (such as buying a car or getting a facelift). Involvement helps us choose appropriate processes for each step of the decision model. See Table 11.4 for the first three steps.

Problem Recognition

Problem recognition differs for low- and high-involvement purchases. Low-involvement purchases consist of (a) frequently purchased items (e.g., cereal, milk, pencils, etc.); and (b) first-time purchases of small-ticket items (e.g., a new type of detergent or candy). Need recognition for such purchases occurs due to (a) stock-outs of frequently consumed products (e.g., being out of milk); (b) the incidence of repetitive body needs, such as feeling hungry; and (c) exposure to external stimuli, such as a low-ticket price or an ad. Need recognition for frequently consumed products is readily acknowledged. "We are out of milk? Okay, noted." Even for new items, low-involvement consumers are quickly able to visualize the value (or lack thereof) of consuming that product. They are unlikely to appraise that need thoroughly.

High-involvement need recognition occurs, in contrast, first, when a consumer experiences a first-time (not recurring) internal, discomforting condition; e.g., a first-time realization of weakening eyesight, thinning hair, etc. Second, it occurs due to exposure to a new external environment; e.g., making a trip to a foreign country or having to find a dentist in a new city. Third, it occurs when a durable product currently in use becomes defunct and needs replacement, and it entails significant expense; for example, when a washing machine breaks down or our dress shoes are worn out. Finally, high-involvement need recognition also occurs from acquiring a new role (e.g., becoming a mother) or a life-stage change (graduating, entering employment, etc.).

Whether the need recognition occurs from an internal or external stimulus, mere sensation of an internal condition (e.g., "It looks like I am losing my hair") or mere exposure to the external or solution stimulus (e.g., "That dress in the store window could come in handy at the next big office party") will not suffice when it is a high involvement decision. Rather, we engage in an in-depth needs assessment; we want to assess the seriousness of the condition and its consequences (e.g., "Am I really losing hair significantly, and should I really care about my appearance that much?").

Information Search

For most low-involvement choice decisions, the information search is minimal. The moment your mind labels a problem as "low involvement," it goes into sleep mode, so to speak. "Least effort" becomes its self-instruction and operating mode. Most of your low involvement decisions are repeat purchases, so the brand choice is already made—most likely you have a couple of brands you have used, or, alternatively, you have no brand loyalty at all and are quite open to buying whatever brand maybe available or on sale. In either case, the search will be short (confined mostly to *internal search*) and is likely to be limited in duration, often confined to one search episode (e.g., one visit to one store and a quick scan of items on adjacent shelves).

In contrast, for high-involvement decisions, the information search is prolonged and extensive and will definitely include *external search*. Our minds get into high-energy mode. Because the product entails risks, we compare multiple brands, and we use all the available sources—marketer-, independent-, and personal sources. We read advertisements and product brochures and on-pack product information in depth, and we also examine and compare the product alternatives thoroughly. If the product is enduringly involving, then the information search is ongoing already, but it intensifies when we are considering a purchase in that product category. The search continues for several days and over multiple search episodes. Learning a lot about alternative brands and stores, not effort minimization, becomes the objective of the information search.

Alternative Evaluation

For low involvement purchases, the minimal effort strategy adopted during the information search phase also continues during the alternative evaluation phase. First, since the search phase is short and the search is limited to a single stimulus exposure episode, the evaluative judgment is also concluded in the same episode. The goal is merely to judge whether the product will, in broad terms, fit the purported need.

Much of this evaluation occurs in a store where multiple alternatives are physically available for side-by-side inspection. Evaluative criteria are few (often one or two) and are used in a way that calls for the least cognitive effort. Accordingly, compensatory models of judgment are not used (as they require significant deliberation and effortful weighing of pros and cons). The non-compensatory model most likely to be used is lexicographic, employing one or two features and choosing the alternative that is best on these features.

For high-involvement products, the evaluation becomes effortful, prolonged, even agonizing. This is when your brain is operating full-steam—fully engaged. The consideration set is likely to be large, at least initially, and evaluation criteria are many. Therefore, evaluation typically proceeds in two stages. Consumer researchers Bettman and Park call it a **phased decision strategy**.[16] In the first stage, termed the **alternative elimination stage**, consumers narrow down the set of alternatives for closer comparisons. In the second stage, termed the **alternative selection stage**, the smaller set of alternatives is further examined. The objective of the first stage is thus to identify all *acceptable* alternatives, whereas the second stage is meant to identify the *best* alternative.

In the alternative elimination phase, the focus is to quickly eliminate the less desirable alternatives and arrive at a shorter list of brands or alternatives. This is done easily by using some non-compensatory model, such as the "elimination by aspect" model, and can be done even before going to the store or without having the alternatives physically available to examine (e.g., eliminate all foreign car brands).

Next, in the second stage (the alternative selection stage), the goal is to identify the final choice. The consumer uses the compensatory model, considering each alternative in its entirety, with simultaneous consideration of all the features, weighing them, pitting one feature's worth against another's, mentally compensating for the lack of one feature with the presence or superiority of another feature. If you think that this is a difficult and mind-boggling task, indeed it is; recall, if you will, how agonizing and difficult it was for you to make a very involving, very risky purchase decision the last time you had to make one, like which home you should buy.

How do you want your tea? Onkar Singh Kular, a London artist, has designed 128 Pantone colored mugs for you to choose *precisely*. Mark one and the hostess will know how much milk to add to satisfy your "high involvement taste" for tea. (Image: courtesy Onkar Singh Kular)

Choice and Post-Purchase

Once the choice has been delineated, you might think that the product purchase and post-purchase experience steps ought to be easily implemented, involvement or no involvement. Not so fast—the fact is that involvement influences these last two steps, as well. That influence is, however, so counter-intuitive and multi-layered that it would take a whole chapter to study it. We will do just that, in the next chapter. For now, we should be "satisfied" with how much ground we have covered in our understanding of consumer decision processes and of the greatly helpful arbiter's role that involvement plays in navigating

TABLE 11.4 DECISION PROCESSES FOR LOW VS. HIGH INVOLVEMENT SITUATIONS

DECISION STEP	LOW INVOLVEMENT	HIGH INVOLVEMENT
Need Recognition	. Mostly stock replenishment of frequently consumed products. . Seeing new but small ticket items . Mere exposure to product communications	. First time experienced condition of discomfort . A significant/expensive product breakdown . A new role (e.g., becoming a mother) . A life-stage change . New external environment
Information Search	. Limited . Focused on price and sale . Completed with a single episode of information exposure . Single source considered adequate	. Extensive . Focused on product features as well as price . Carried over several information acquisition episodes . Multiple sources consulted
Evaluation	. Single stage process . Use of non-compensatory model only . Mostly inside the store . Relatively quick communications	. Two stage process . Use of non-compensatory and compensatory models . Outside and inside the store . Long drawn and agonizing

MY CB BOOK

SUMMARY

In this chapter, we studied consumer decision making as a five-step process: problem recognition, information search, alternative evaluation, choice, and post-choice. The consumer decision process begins with problem recognition, which occurs due to an internal cue coming from one's unfulfilled needs, from external stimuli evoking these needs, or from related motivations. Once problem recognition occurs, the consumer (a) either relies on prior knowledge and previously learned solutions; or (b) searches for new solutions through new information acquisition and its evaluation and integration. In the information search stage, several determinants come into play, such as perceived risk, involvement, familiarity and expertise, shopping style, and time pressure.

Evaluation of alternatives entails the use of compensatory and noncompensatory decision models. The latter include conjunctive, disjunctive, lexicographic, and elimination-by-aspect models. The outcome of these evaluation processes is the identification of a preferred brand and the formation of purchase intent. Such purchase intent is then implemented by the actual act of purchasing. In the post-choice phase, the consumer is either satisfied or dissatisfied with the outcome of product use. If satisfied, he or she simply repeats the choice for future purchases; if dissatisfied, he or she revisits the decision process.

The consumer decision process is determined by the consumer's individual characteristics, such as demographics, personality, and motives (all discussed in previous chapters). This chapter focused on the decision process itself—how the individual consumer makes a selection out of an array of product alternatives facing him or her. It gave some further order to those processes by delineating the differences between how these processes unfold for low-involvement versus high-involvement decisions. Understanding this process should help you to be aware of your own future product choice decision making processes. And understanding these processes is helpful to marketing managers so that they may determine why some consumers choose their products and others choose competitors' products. Ultimately, it behooves marketers to structure their offerings and their communications in a fashion that responds to and resonates with consumers' decision-making processes.

CB Blog

11

Involvement—a Secret Code For Your Decider Mind

In this chapter, we have given you a grand, panoramic view of consumer decision-making processes. You must be amazed at the workings of your DECIDER mind—how, standing in the middle of the marketplace, so to speak, your mind sorts out a vast array of products and brands, puts some in memory to be recalled later, labels them as possible candidates for future use or not, considers their various features and expected outcomes, ignores some, contemplates some, weighs them, dismisses some, embraces others; and this cycle goes on, over and over, for choosing a product today, and another tomorrow, and yet another the day after, and so on.

Our mind is indeed an amazing machine, a super-efficient computer. It works hard, to help us choose and consume and experience. But it also works smart—it has a self-regulating mechanism, a meta-software program if you will, which tells it when not to work hard. "Simply skip working, it is no big deal," the meta-software sometimes tells it.

You know the feeling: for every task you face, every moment of the day, as a consumer and as a human, your mind is always asking, "How important is this?" That question, you may now realize, is designed to assess your involvement in the product choice at hand.

Involvement is indeed a powerful concept as it directs our minds' energies toward those decision tasks that are of great import to us as consumers. Involvement gives some order to what would have been, otherwise, a chaotic decision process. But that process is still very profound and complex. Our mind learns to execute some of the decision processes as second nature; but for others, called for in high-stakes choice decisions, it does agonize.

If you want to become more aware of these decision processes, keep a journal for a year, recording the decisions your mind agonized over for days, and the ones it made as second nature. Try also to map the specific processes using Table 11.5. If you are like most consumers, then these decision processes will map perfectly. If they don't, are you sure you are not involved even in trivial product choices—like you wanted to buy some M&Ms, but you wanted them all in the colors of your dress of the day!

CONSUMER BEHAVIOR

MY CB BOOK .COM

KEY TERMS

Advocate sources
Affective choice mode
  (ACM)
Awareness set
Compensatory model
Conjunctive model
Consideration set
Consumer problem
Disjunctive model
Elimination by aspects

Extended problem solving
External stimuli
Evoked set
Framing
Framing effect
Heuristics
Ignorance paradox
Independent sources
Information overload

Information processing mode
  (IPM)
Internal stimuli
Involvement
Lexicographic model
Limited problem solving
Marketer sources
Nonmarketer sources
Perceived risk

Personal sources
Primary demand
Problem recognition
Processing by attributes
Processing by brand
Secondary/Selective demand
Search strategy
Systematic search
Routine problem solving
Satisficing

YOUR TURN

REVIEW+Rewind

1. What is problem recognition in consumer behavior? Describe what causes it and when. Describe each type of problem recognition, with two examples. How can marketers utilize this classification?

2. What is meant by *search strategies*? Explain systematic versus heuristic search strategies.

3. What factors influence the extent of search in which a consumer would engage?

4. Explain the following concepts, with examples: (a) judgment models, (b) ignorance paradox; (c) affective choice mode (ACM), (d) *satisficing*, and (e) solution stimuli.

5. What would you say is the principal difference between compensatory and noncompensatory choice rules? Describe how the following choice rules work: conjunctive, disjunctive, lexicographic, and elimination by aspects.

THINK+Apply

1. Review in your mind the most recent important marketplace decision you made. What sources of information did you use in that decision? Please name each type, and comment on which ones were more useful and why you think so.

2. After a consumer has made a choice, would he or she buy immediately? Why or why not? What can a marketer do to reduce the barriers to consumer acquisition of products immediately after they have made the choice?

3. Reflect on how you might choose each of the following products or services:

   a. Graduate business schools
   b. A restaurant for dinner with your spouse or date on your anniversary
   c. Hotel for a business trip to Eastern Europe
   d. Toothpaste during a business trip to an Asian country where none of your usual brands is available and you don't know any brand names.

   For each, please indicate:

   i. How you will come to know what evaluation criteria to use
   ii. Which choice model you would use and how

4. In explaining the top-down versus bottom-up processing, we used the example of a consumer choosing a car. Can you think of other consumer choice situations where these concepts apply? Explain your answer. Next, what should a marketer do to benefit from this concept?

5. You are the marketing director of a hotel company. You discover through research that most guests during the week use a conjunctive model in choosing their hotels; in contrast, most weekend guests use a lexicographic model. First, visualize how these two models will work for choosing a hotel. Next, discuss whether your brand messages should be different across the two consumer groups and in what manner.

PRACTICE+Experience

1. Interview two consumers, each on his or her recent purchase of (a) a major appliance and (b) a grocery product never purchased before. The purpose of the interview is to find out how they went about making their brand selections and which decision model they used. Comment on whether the decision process differed for the two consumers, and likewise, for two products. How?

2. Collect two or three advertisements that address various problem-recognition situations; likewise, collect ads that respond to different choice rules.

3. Table 11.5 maps the processes for three decision steps across low and high involvement products. Choose two of your recent consumer decisions, one low and the other high involvement. Do the process and steps you took match those described in the table? Explain any discrepancies.

In the Marketing Manager's Shoes

Put yourself in a marketing manager's shoes. Most concepts in the chapter have some lessons for the marketing manager; i.e., they suggest what to do differently in practice. Indeed, often these applications are implicit in our explanations of the concepts and models in the chapter. Identify at least five specific applications of the chapter's concepts, all of which should be entirely new, different from the examples cited here.

APPENDIX 11A   FAMILY DECISION PROCESS

If you live with your family, invariably you buy some things as an individual and other things as a member of the family. You probably experience a different decision process when you buy something as a family member versus when you buy something as an individual. The steps remain the same as those described for individual-decision-making, namely, 1) problem recognition, 2) information search, 3) alternative evaluation, 4) choice, and 5) post purchase experience. However, each step unfolds with a somewhat more dynamic and complex process. This is because various members of your family have different tastes and preferences; moreover, not all members have the same stakes in the decision.

If you think back to a recent purchase decision made in your family, you might recall that various members undertook various activities, en route to the final decision. Suppose that it was a family vacation your family was considering over last Summer. Your parents wanted to go to South America (Akumal to Tumul) to see Mayan civilization. Your little sister and brother wanted to go to, naturally, Disney World. You are in college and are fascinated by rainforests (a fellow student, on exchange from Samoa, has been showing you a lot of wonderful pictures from his homeland), so you have been dying to make a family trip to Samoa. Your parents are open to your suggestion and since you are in college, you are the one assigned to gather all the information about rainforest sites as well as Mayan civilization sites in Mexico. You are planning to explore the Web this weekend.

But right now, you are studying this book on consumer behavior, and reading about how families make decisions. You cannot help but see a pattern in the present decision your family is making and the many others that you and your family have made in the past. This pattern consists of some steps your family goes through in making major purchase decisions, shown in Figure 11A1.[1]

Someone Proposes, and That Sets the Ball Rolling

The decision process begins when some member of the family recognizes a need. This much is similar to the first step in the "individual decision making" we studied in a previous chapter. What is different is that now the need recognizing member must make the proposal to other members of the family. This of course is not a formal or written proposal. Rather, it is a suggestion or request to consider a purchase. It does entail, however, that the person suggesting the purchase justify the need. In individual decision-making there is no one to justify one's need to. One may rationalize, but one is not called upon to justify to others.

Next, the proposal approval process begins. Typically, proposals for products that will serve some need of all members are readily accepted. Proposals for needs specific to the proposing member alone call for a more thorough justification. Thus, if Mom suggests replacing the washer, it is a shared need. If Junior wants a video game, or if Dad wants a treadmill, that would require more persuasion. When family members generally agree about the need, the proposal is deemed approved. Next, the tasks of information search are assigned to different members, depending on each member's area of familiarity. Alternative evaluation can be a prolonged process and different members may disagree because they differ on their evaluation criteria. Sometimes, conflict ensues, and resolving it may require certain negotiations.[2]

Following the decision and acquisition, post-purchase experience is likely to be explicit, for two reasons: One, if the product is consumed jointly, members tend to express their feelings (and having to express your feelings makes you more explicit); two, even if the product is used more by a specific member (rather than shared), other members who had participated in decision-making may want to know how their selection was working out. The

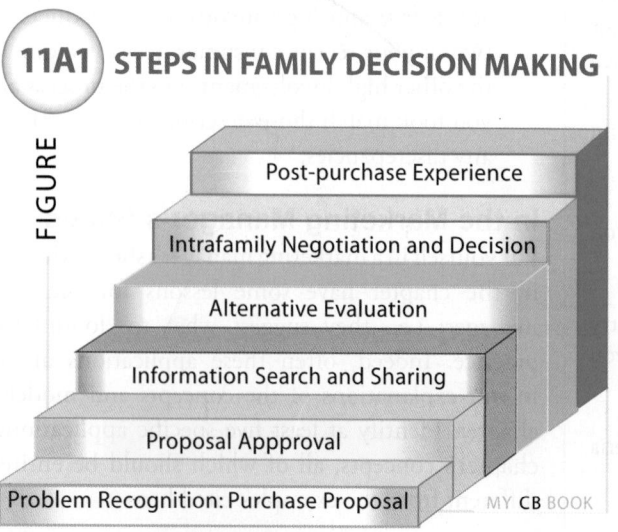

11A1 STEPS IN FAMILY DECISION MAKING

FIGURE

- Post-purchase Experience
- Intrafamily Negotiation and Decision
- Alternative Evaluation
- Information Search and Sharing
- Proposal Appproval
- Problem Recognition: Purchase Proposal

MY **CB** BOOK

important issues in the above process are joint decisions (say, between spouses) and conflict resolution.

HUSBAND-WIFE DECISION ROLES
A Muddling Through Process

Suppose you are a salesperson in an appliance store, and a couple walks in. Who would you direct your sales pitch at? That depends on what assumptions you make about how spouses make joint decisions. Who plays an active role, and who influences the decision more? To address this question, consumer researchers have identified five patterns of relative influence. These are: (1) autonomous decision by the husband only; (2) husband-dominated decision; (3) syncratic decisions (equal role by both); (4) wife-dominated decision, and (5) autonomous decision by the wife. **Autonomous decisions** are decisions made independently by the decision maker. **Syncratic decisions** are decisions in which all play an equal role in making the decision (see Figure 11A2).

A lot of consumption happens together in families
(Photo courtesy: Ian Shipley, second from right)

FIGURE 11A2 — PATTERNS OF JOINT DECISION MAKING

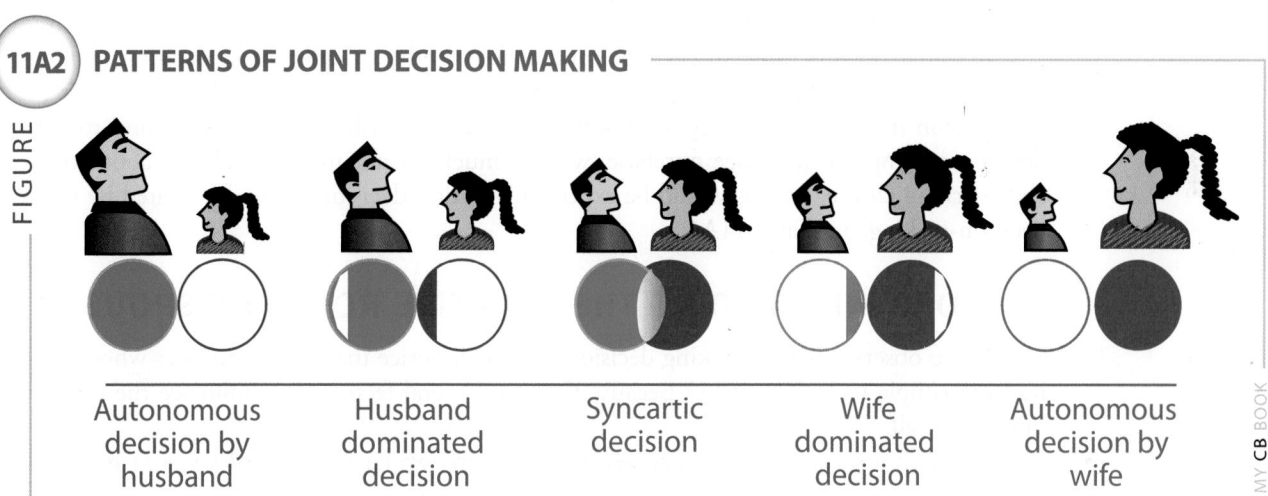

| Autonomous decision by husband | Husband dominated decision | Syncartic decision | Wife dominated decision | Autonomous decision by wife |

MY CB BOOK

Which of these patterns is followed will differ from one family to another, and also across product categories. Yet, it is reasonable to expect some common prevalent patterns in any given society. In an early study of 200 U. S. families, for the purchase of three products (washing machines, carpeting, television), the wife's influence was stronger for washers and carpeting, while the husband's influence was greater for televisions. The study was based on asking each spouse separately who had influenced the decision more. An interesting fact was that while mostly the spouses agreed on whose influence was more, for appliances, husbands tended to view themselves as the predominant or even solo decision makers, while wives reported more joint decision making.

Joint decisions are those in which more than one decision participant makes the decision. When couples report they made joint decisions for a specific purchase, it is not easy to visualize exactly how each member participated to make it a joint decision. If you ask the couple, each spouse is likely to say he or she influenced the decision more than did the other partner!

Consumer researchers consider such answers too simplistic and believe that the interpersonal dynamics of joint decision-making is more complex. In fact, noted consumer researcher C. W. Park has termed joint decisions as a "muddling through" process. His study of 45 couples, all recent buyers of a home, revealed very interesting patterns of interpersonal dynamics among the spouses.[3] Park's findings, summarized in Exhibit 11A1, reveal that joint decision-making is often a process of compromise as well as make-believe as to one's own role in the decision.

EXHIBIT

11A1

JOINT DECISIONS: A GAME OF COMPROMISE AND MAKE BELIEVE

A study of 45 couples, all recent home buyers, revealed the following:

■ Each person has some idea of what features the product alternative "must have." The spouses discuss these features and then agree on a common set of "must have" features.

■ Spouses grant each other the right to the "optional features" provided that these features do not interfere with the utility of the product or do not raise costs.

■ Spouses also grant each other certain role specialization with respect to the feature on which they consider the other person an expert. Thus, both spouses might agree that the husband is an expert on insulation, and the wife an expert on interior design.

■ On these role-specialized features, spouses acknowledge the partner's relative influence. On other features, each believes he or she influenced the decision more than did the other partner.

■ Spouses agree more with each other on salient objective dimensions (e.g., number of bedrooms, presence of a swimming pool, and so on) than on subjective dimensions (the interior design, the amount of insulation, and so on).

■ When spouses agree on features that the product must have, this agreement on "must have" features leads them to perceive that their decision plans are similar (even when they disagree on other optional features). Contrarily, when there is disagreement on these "must have" features, spouses perceive conflict.

■ Individual spouses are more satisfied with some features of the product purchased than with others, and the features with which the spouses are satisfied differ between the spouses. Each spouse feels greater satisfaction with the feature whose inclusion was influenced more by him or her.

Source: Adapted from C. Whan Park, "Joint Decisions in Home Purchasing: A Muddling-Through Process," *Journal of Consumer Research* 9 (September 1982), pp. 151-62. © *Journal of Consumer Research*. Published by The University of Chicago Press. (Used with permission.)

Research on this topic shows that spousal roles and participation in decision making varies across different product or service categories. And it also varies at different stages of the decision making process. A recent study showed that husbands played a greater role in decision making for insurance purchase, wives a much greater role in decisions about their child's school choice, and, as would be expected, vacation decisions were dominated by joint decision-making. See Table 11A1.

FACTORS INFLUENCING THE RELATIVE ROLES OF SPOUSES

If you observe spouses making decisions, you will notice that who influences whom varies from couple to couple. Why? Because there are several factors that influence the relative influence itself.

Based on a survey of consumer research literature, we have identified seven factors that affect the relative influence of spouses in joint decision making. These are: gender role orientation and role specialization, the wife's employment status, family life cycle stages, time pressure, purchase importance, consumer involvement, and socioeconomic development level of the population group (see Figure 11A3).

GENDER ROLE ORIENTATION **Gender roles orientation** refers to our concepts of the specific behaviors expected of a person by virtue of that person's gender. For example, in a family, the wife may be expected to take care of food preparation, and husband, of cleaning and laundry. These gender role orientations can be placed on a continuum of traditional-modern. In the traditional orientation, found in pre-industrialized societies and underdeveloped and developing countries, generally, wife is expected to be the homemaker and husband the breadwinner. In the modern orientation, there is more sharing of responsibilities between the two sexes.[4] Therefore, modern gender role families will in general exhibit more joint decision-making, and some wife-dominated or autonomous decisions made by the wife. In contrast, in traditional role families, more decisions will be husband-dominated.

In general, even in traditional families, purchase decisions are domain-specific. In many Asian, Middle Eastern, or other third-world countries, for example, buying cooking-related raw materials and kitchen supplies is the domain of women; likewise, certain aspects of engagement and marriage ceremonies are in women's domain. Accordingly, women decide what products need to be bought and in what quantities, although sometimes it is men who go to the market to do the actual buying. Since many staple products do not carry brand names, brand decisions are not always pertinent in these third-world countries. One of the most fascinating aspects of family decision making is the variation in gender role orientation you find across diverse countries and cultures, and how this gender role variation influences interspousal decision sharing in different population groups.

WIFE'S EMPLOYMENT STATUS The wife's employment status significantly influences gender-role orientation. In families where a wife is employed outside of the home, there is greater acceptance of her role in important family decisions. Not only does she make many decisions autonomously, but even in decisions historically the prerogative of the husband alone, the wife is often consulted. This occurs partly because the wife acquires greater recognition as a contributor to family finances. In addition, the greater exposure to the world outside of the home makes the wife more knowledgeable about a variety of products and services.

TABLE

11A1 RELATIVE ROLES OF SPOUSES

Decision Stage		Insurance	Child's school	Vacation
Purchase Proposal	H	42	4	25
	W	20	35	22
	H + W	34	50	30
Choice	H	42	3	23
	W	15	21	27
	H + W	42	57	48
Made the Actual Purchase	H	39	2	24
	W	17	50	29
	H + W	44	41	46

Note: Percentages do not add up to 100 due to omission of roles played by other family members.
Source: Adapted from M.R. Stafford, G.K. Ganesh, and B.C. Garland, "Marital Influence in the Decision-Making Process for Services," *Journal of Services Marketing*, 10, no. 1, (1996), p.15. (Used with permission.)

MY CB BOOK

STAGE IN FAMILY LIFE CYCLE Family life cycle has also been found to influence decision making in the families. Recently married couples tend to make more joint decisions; as the marriage ages, the chores become allocated along with the purchases that accompany those chores (e.g., grocery supplies for cooking, car wax for car washing, and so on) and get to be decided autonomously. However, the age of the marriage would tend not to affect important purchases. For important purchases, if the couple used joint decision making at the early stage of marriage, they would most likely continue to do so during the later years of marriage as well.

TIME PRESSURE Families with high time pressure tend to rely less on joint decision making, since autonomous or one-member dominated decision processes are generally perceived to be more time-efficient. However, such decisions may sacrifice effectiveness; the decision may not be optimal. Furthermore, the spouse with greater time pressure is likely to delegate the buying decisions to the spouse less busy.

IMPORTANCE OF PURCHASE Purchase importance refers to how important the family perceives the product to be. The importance of the purchase may stem from the financial outlay or from the centrality of the product to the individual—that is, whether the product is an important part of one's life. The more important the purchase, the more the decision making is going to be a joint one. This is for two reasons: One, multiple members have a stake in a large expense (as it would affect everyone by draining family resources). Second, the members will have to live with the decision for a long time.

CONSUMER INVOLVEMENT A related factor is that purchase importance may be different for different members of the family. That is, some members may be more involved (or interested) in a specific purchase. For example, the spouse who enjoys cooking may be more involved in kitchen

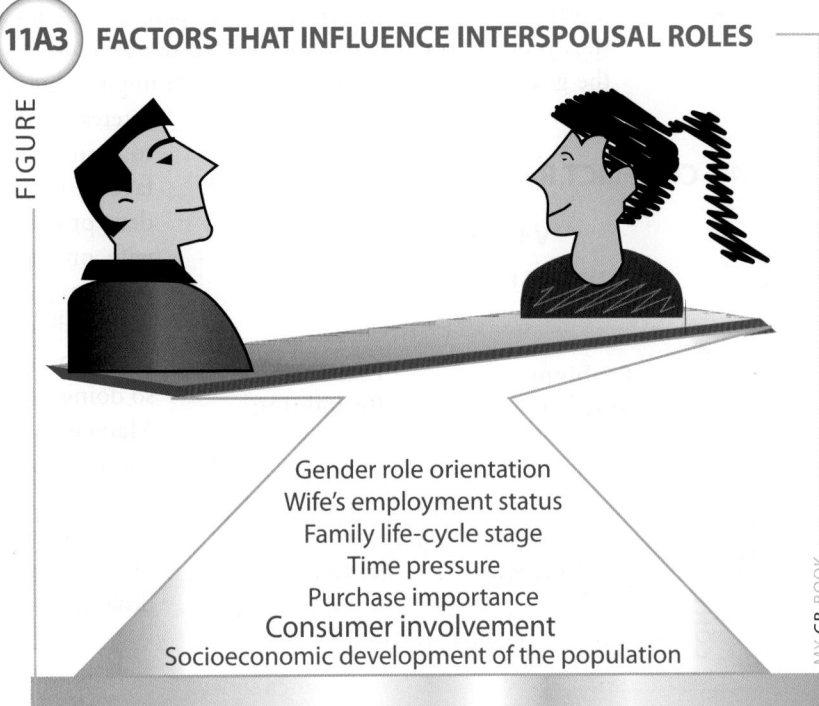

FIGURE

11A3 FACTORS THAT INFLUENCE INTERSPOUSAL ROLES

Gender role orientation
Wife's employment status
Family life-cycle stage
Time pressure
Purchase importance
Consumer involvement
Socioeconomic development of the population

MY CB BOOK

tools, whereas the spouse who enjoys "fixing" things, may be more involved in buying home repair tools.

SOCIOECONOMIC DEVELOPMENT OF THE POPULATION Gender role orientations and role specializations vary from one culture and country to another. Specifically, the culture of a country is related to the stage of socioeconomic development of the population. Underdeveloped countries have a more traditional gender role orientation than do more developed countries. With development and the resulting modernization, urbanization, and concomitant rising employment of women outside of the home, women's influence on marketplace decision-making increases.

At least three factors account for the increasing role of women in modernizing societies. First, with modernization and urbanization, families become increasingly nuclear, as young adults take up jobs in urban areas, leaving their parents and grandparents behind in their rural homes. Nuclear family forms necessitate more sharing of all household responsibilities, including procurement of goods. Second, in advanced countries, with increasing dependence by the husband on the wife's supplemental income, husbands feel obligated to consult with their working spouses on at least the major purchases. Finally, smaller family units generate a greater egalitarianism among the sexes, which leads to more participatory decision-making.

CONFLICT IN FAMILY DECISIONS

The family decision process is often marked by conflicts among various family members. The conflicts arise due to differences in the goals of various members. In a family vacation decision, for example, parents want to visit relatives, but the child wants to visit an amusement park. Or the husband wants a stylish, youthful car but the wife wants a large, safe car, for example. Or the other way around. Conflicts can also arise when perceptions of alternatives differ; for example, both parents and children agree it should be a fun vacation, not a family reunion; but children think that Disney World would be more fun and parents think that New York City would be more fun. The husband thinks a convertible is more youthful and stylish, while the wife thinks an SUV is more in style.[5]

Conflict Resolution

How do you and your families resolve such conflicts? Scholars have suggested four strategies: problem solving, persuasion, bargaining, and politicking (see Figure 11A4). Problem solving entails members trying to gather more information, or adding new alternatives. When motives/goals are congruent and only perceptions differ, obtaining and sharing information (i.e., problem solving) often suffices to resolve conflicts. Persuasion requires educating about the goal hierarchy; for instance, the wife might argue how a safe and large car is in the best interest of the whole family since the car is needed to transport children. Bargaining entails trading favors (the husband gets to buy a house with a den, provided that the car he buys is the one his wife prefers). When goals as well as evaluations (i.e., perceptions) are so divergent that bargaining is infeasible, try politicking. Here, members form coalitions and subgroups within the family and by so doing simply impose their will on the minority.[6] Marketers can help household members resolve a conflict by aiding the problem-solving mode— they can provide additional information about alternatives. Such interventions are most feasible in interpersonal selling situations such as at the car dealership or with a real estate agent

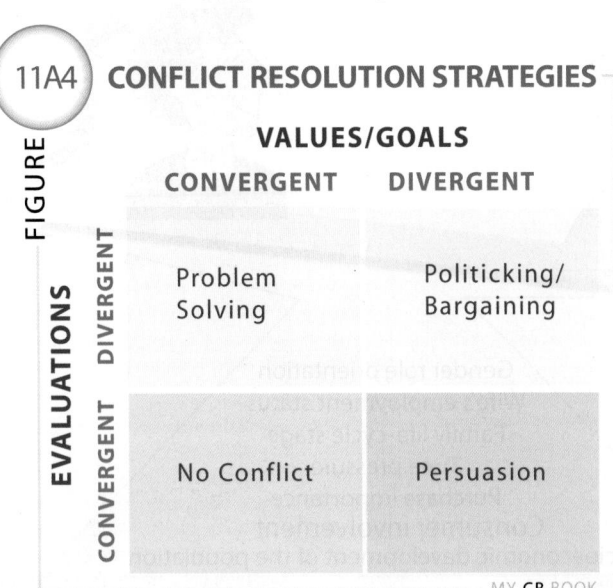

FIGURE 11A4   CONFLICT RESOLUTION STRATEGIES

EVALUATIONS	VALUES/GOALS	
	CONVERGENT	DIVERGENT
DIVERGENT	Problem Solving	Politicking/ Bargaining
CONVERGENT	No Conflict	Persuasion

MY **CB** BOOK

CB Level 2.0

A GENERAL FRAMEWORK FOR FAMILY DECISION MAKING

We have covered a lot of ground on family buying process. Wouldn't you like to see it all put together in a neat model and a neat diagram. Once again, several consumer researchers come to our rescue. And once again, we synthesize and adapt their models to give you an organizing framework that is comprehensive and yet easy-to-follow. See Figure 11A5. Since we have already discussed most of the variables contained in this figure, we describe the model only briefly here.

DECISION PROCESS

The linchpin of the model is the decision process, which can be either autonomous (i.e., decision made by a single family member), or joint decision making. Conflict occurrence is a significant component of the decision process. The conflict may arise either because the family members do not agree on purchase goals and criteria or because they disagree on their perceptions as to which alternatives would best meet these goals and criteria. The conflict can sometimes be intense, cloudingthe entire decision process. It may be manifested in angry arguments and agonizing frustration with the "irrationality of the other members." Its resolution would typically follow one of the four strategies discussed earlier: problem solving, persuasion, bargaining, or politicking.

INFLUENCES ON THE DECISION PROCESS

The extent to which a decision process will be autonomous or joint will depend on the nature of the purchase (e.g., degree of perceived risk), separation of the buyer/payer/user roles (who will be the principal user of the product, who is paying for it, and who actually will do the transaction)[7], individual member characteristics (e.g., wife's employment status), and family characteristics (e.g., authoritarian versus democratic families). And, of course, sources of information will influence the decision process. Different members may be exposed to different sources of information, and they will then view the alternatives differently.

11A5 ## A COMPREHENSIVE MODEL OF FAMILY DECISION MAKING

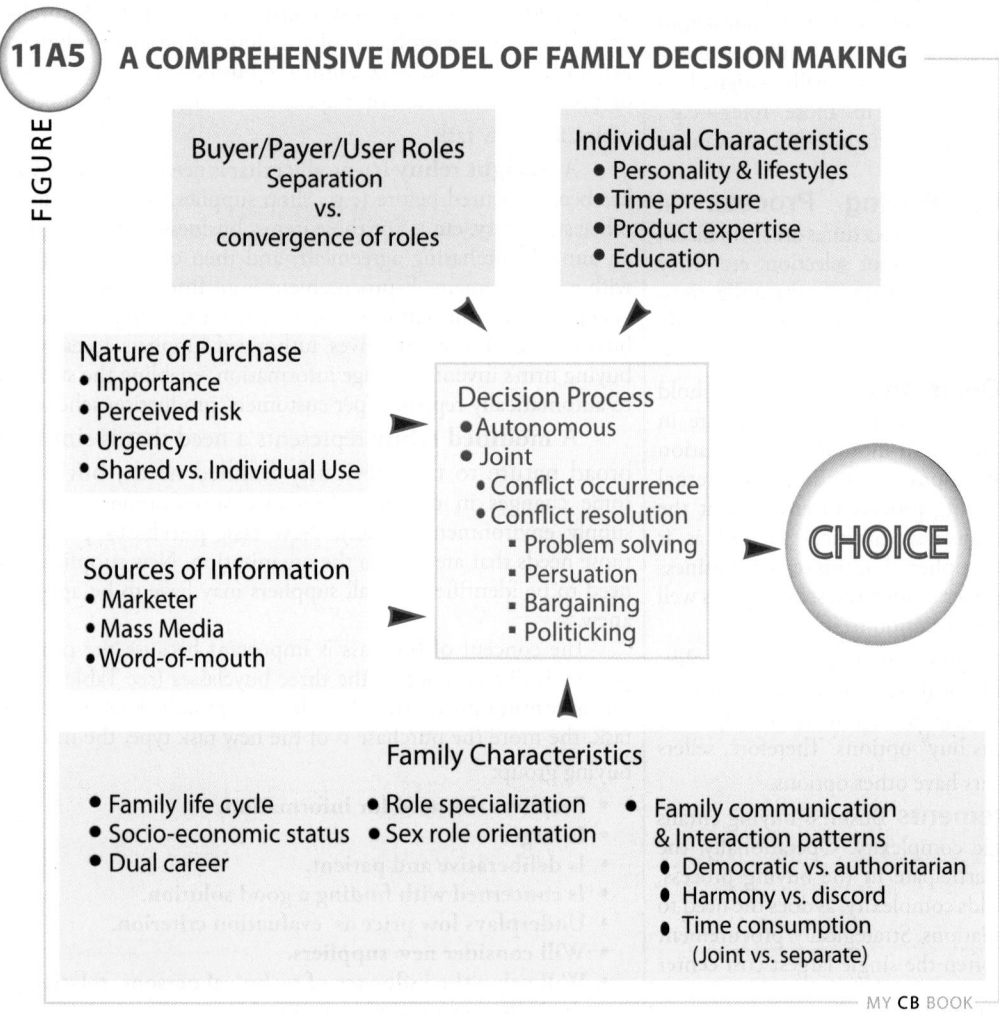

FIGURE

Buyer/Payer/User Roles
Separation
vs.
convergence of roles

Individual Characteristics
• Personality & lifestyles
• Time pressure
• Product expertise
• Education

Nature of Purchase
• Importance
• Perceived risk
• Urgency
• Shared vs. Individual Use

Sources of Information
• Marketer
• Mass Media
• Word-of-mouth

Decision Process
• Autonomous
• Joint
  • Conflict occurrence
  • Conflict resolution
    ▪ Problem solving
    ▪ Persuasion
    ▪ Bargaining
    ▪ Politicking

CHOICE

Family Characteristics
• Family life cycle
• Socio-economic status
• Dual career
• Role specialization
• Sex role orientation
• Family communication & Interaction patterns
  • Democratic vs. authoritarian
  • Harmony vs. discord
  • Time consumption (Joint vs. separate)

APPENDIX 11B | THE BUYING BEHAVIOR OF BUSINESS CUSTOMERS

Business customers have more demanding decision criteria.

11B1	COMPARISON OF HOUSEHOLD & BUSINESS BUYING	
Characteristic	**Household Buying**	**Business Buying**
Specilization of Customer Roles	Combined or slightly specialized	Moderate to very specialized
Formalization of the Buying Process	Informal	Slightly formal (small businesses) to formal (large businesses)
Accountability for Decision	Usually not formally measured	Strict measures
Internal Capabilities	Weak	Weak (small businesses) to very Strong (large businesses)
Complexity of Requirements	Little Complexity	Operational & strategic complexity

MY CB BOOK

BUSINESS VS. HOUSEHOLD BUYING BEHAVIOR

Business buying typically differs from individual or household buying in five key ways (see Table 11B1):

Greater Role Specialization In individual buying, the same person performs all the tasks needed to make a purchase—e.g., identifying a need, evaluating options, etc. In household buying, these tasks are sometimes shared among family members. For organizations, they are much more formally assigned to different functionaries who specialize in those roles—e.g., production department to requisition, engineering to evaluate the options, purchasing to negotiate, etc.

Formalization of the Buying Process In organizational buying, the policy and procedures are formalized, with written policies and rules for vendor selection, etc. They prepare and sign detailed contracts that specify the obligations of each party. This degree of formalization is rare in family buying behavior.[1]

Accountability for Decisions Unlike household buying, business buying holds accountable those who are in charge of procurement. This results in more formal evaluation and feedback on purchase decisions. There are also internal and external audits of the buying process to ensure that the procurement follows sound business practices as well as it obtains maximum value from suppliers. For this reason, business buying encourages formal supplier ratings and scorecards as well as constant feedback and communication to its suppliers.

Internal Capabilities More often than households, business customers are capable of producing certain items in-house. This capability requires business customers to analyze the economics of the "make versus buy" options. Therefore, sellers need to be aware that customers have other options.

Complexity of Requirements Business buying entails both operational and strategic complexity. Operationally, the number of employees who participate in the buying process, often from several locations, adds complexity, as does the need to comply with government regulations. Strategically, procurement is often a strategic function, often the single largest cost center to a business organization.

COMPONENTS OF THE BUSINESS BUYING PROCESS

With purchasing being such a significant and complex function, organizations typically have formal procurement systems, with several components, described below (see Figure 11B1). By determining the way the components fit together in a particular business, marketers can describe the business's buying behavior.

Nature of the Purchase Not all purchases are equal; some are more complex than others. This complexity is captured by two interrelated dimensions: buyclass and perceived risk.

Buy Class For an individual consumer, we classified purchase needs into routine problem solving, limited problem solving, or extended problem solving. Similarly, businesses have three types of procurement needs, or buyclasses: straight rebuy, modified rebuy, and new task.

A **straight rebuy** is a product that is needed repeatedly and has been procured before (e.g., shop supplies, worker uniforms, office stationery, etc.). For these items, businesses often negotiate an annual purchasing agreement, and then often implement it with e-procurement. E-procurement is an Internet based buying system, with information sharing between the supplier and the buying firm. The system gives authorized suppliers access to the buying firm's inventory usage information, enabling the suppliers to automatically replenish per customers' production schedules.

A **modified rebuy** represents a need that is similar in broad nature to the previously fulfilled needs, but entails some changes in design/performance specifications or in the supply environment. Finally, **New task purchases** pertain to those needs that are new to the organization. New suppliers may need to be identified and all suppliers may have to be appraised anew.

The concept of buyclass is important because the purchase process is different across the three buyclasses (see Table 11B2). On a continuum of straight rebuy to modified rebuy to new task, the more the purchase is of the new task type, the more the buying group:

- Perceives the need for information.
- Is large.
- Is deliberative and patient.
- Is concerned with finding a good solution.
- Underplays low price as evaluation criterion.
- Will consider new suppliers.
- Will value the influence of technical persons, relative to the influence of buying agents.[2]

Perceived Risk Each type of purchase involves a different level of perceived risk, importance, and complexity for the decision maker. Business customers use information such as the type of purchase to estimate risk, importance, and complexity. Then they adjust their decision-making strategy accordingly.

Perceived risk refers to the loss that would accrue were a wrong choice made. It has two components, namely (a) the degree of uncertainty that a choice may be wrong, and (b) the amount at stake should a wrong choice occur. Uncertainty stems from the absence of prior design/performance specifications and from lack of experience with potential suppliers. Thus, new tasks have the most uncertainty, and straight rebuys the least. Amount at stake is the financial loss or performance loss from a suboptimal choice. In part, perceived risk depends on (a) importance of purchase and (b) complexity.

Importance of purchase is a combination of the amount at stake and the product's strategic role in the organization. A large fleet of transportation vehicles might cost more than, say, a communication network; yet the latter might be viewed as a more important purchase due to its strategic role in equipping the firm for the information age.

Complexity refers to the extensiveness of effort it takes to comprehend and manage the product during its acquisition. Complexity has two dimensions: (1) the number of performance dimensions, and (2) the technical and specialist knowledge required to understand those dimensions. Thus, a single dimensional product like a chemical is simpler than a multidimensional item like a computer server system.

Together, the buyclass and perceived risk influence how extensive the purchase decision process will be. As perceived risk increases, more individuals will participate in the decision, who will deliberate more, consult a wide range of information sources, and experience greater conflict and role stress.[3]

Organizational Characteristics

Four organizational characteristics of the customer firm affect buying behavior: (1) size, (2) structure, (3) purchase resources, and (4) purchase orientation.

Size First, the size of the business determines not only the customer's potential dollar volume, but also the sophistication of its buying process. Small business organizations behave more like a family in their buying behavior; large organizations, in contrast, have larger buying groups and more formalized procedures.

Business Structure—comprising the number of departmental units, geographical locations, and its degree of centralization—influences the buyer behavior: The more departments or geographic locations a business has, the larger the buying group and more prolonged the buying process is likely to be.

Purchase Resources refer to the availability of professional buyers and product experts. Generally, large and professionally managed firms have better resourced purchasing departments, and consequently, a more rigorous and formal vendor evaluation.

Purchase Orientation Finally, The organization's **purchase**

TABLE 11B2 BUYING BEHAVIOR ASSOCIATED WITH BUY CLASSES

BUYCLASS	DESCRIPTION OF NEED	BUYING CENTER	INFORMATION SEARCH
STRAIGHT REBUY	Item is frequently needed & has been satisfactorily bought before	Very small; ordering may even be automated	Brief or nonexistent; new suppliers rarely considered; technical expertise rarely sought
MODIFIED REBUY	Need is broadly similar to one that has been fulfilled before but requires some change in specifications or the supply enviornment	Moderate	Some information is gathered; new suppliers may be considered; technical experts may have input into decision
NEW TASK	Need is completely new to the organization	Large	Extensive; new suppliers often considered experts usually have major input into decision

MY CB BOOK

orientation—its purchasing philosophy—can be placed along a continuum: At the one end purchasing may be viewed simply as an administrative function that finds the most economical sources of materials needed; at the other end, it may be viewed as a strategic, managerial function expected to bring value to the organization. As a strategic function, purchasing is engaged in several key activities:

- Scrutinizing 'make versus buy' decisions
- Continually finding better products, materials, and technology
- Developing long-term sources of supply and building relationships with the suppliers.

These two ends of the continuum may be referred to as reactive and proactive buying, respectively.

FIGURE 11B1 COMPONENTS OF BUSINESS BUYING PROCESS

NATURE OF PURCHASE
- Buy Class
- Perceived Risk

ORGANIZATIONAL CHARACTERISTICS
- Size
- Purchase orientation
- Buying center

BUYING CENTER

RULES & PROCEDURES
- Minority supplier policy
- Centralized buying

DECISION PROCESS
☐ ➜ ☐ ➜ ☐

MY CB BOOK

The Buying Center

In most organizations, purchase decisions are handled by a formal or informal buying center—a multifunction, multilevel internal organization that is responsible for the centralized purchasing function. It comprises various individuals who play the following roles:

- **User** This is the user department that would use the product.
- **Buyer** Alternatively called *purchasing manager*, purchasing executive, and so on, has the formal authority to execute the purchase contract.
- **Analyzer** One who performs technical analysis of suppliers by using such tools as cost analysis, value analysis, etc.
- **Influencer** By their expert advice, these role holders influence the evaluative criteria and supplier ratings and/or the final decision itself. Typically, these are design engineers and external consultants.
- **Gatekeepers** They regulate the flow of information from suppliers to the other members of the buying center. They permit or deny salespersons access to design and user departments or to other executives. Often purchase managers, receptionists, and secretaries play this role.
- **Decider** The deciders make the final decision. This role may be played by a formal buying committee, or by the CEO, CFO, or purchasing executive alone.

Note that buying center is a concept, not an actual group or committee name. Therefore, a salesperson selling to organizations must always try to identify all the individuals, spread throughout the organization, who might be playing the various roles in the buying center.

Rules and Procedures

Businesses generally set up elaborate policies (e.g., favor a minority supplier), rules (e.g., purchase needs must be consolidated for the entire organization), and procedures (e.g., minimum number of bids required). The degree of formalization and decision freedom varies from company to company.

Decision Process

Organizational buying decisions entail a multistage process, comprising the following stages:[4]

1. Need assessment Deciding the technical and performance specifications for the needed item.

2. Developing choice criteria Identifying supplier selection criteria.

3. Request for proposals (RFPs) Calling for proposals by publishing requests for quotes (RFQs) and inviting suppliers to submit bids.

4. Supplier evaluation Rank-ordering vendors. Some negotiations may occur toward reconciling differences both on technical aspects and on price variations among various bidders or suppliers.

5. Supplier selection Awarding the contract or placing an order.

6. Fulfillment and monitoring Monitoring for smooth fulfillment in a timely fashion and to the satisfaction of the buyers and users.

These steps are similar to individual decision-making except that there is a lot more formal analysis as well as use of more structured procedures.

Various roles in the buying center participate more in some stages than others (see Table 11B3). Generally, users exercise more influence at the need assessment and choice criteria stages; buyers shoulder the major responsibility at the RFP, supplier search, and fulfillment stages; analyzers help most at the supplier evaluation stage; influencers, at supplier evaluation and selection stages; and decision makers, at the vender selection stages. Gatekeepers, of course, would be active throughout, depending on the inflow of information, influence, and salesperson communications, all vying for the decision makers' attention. This pattern is not universal and business-to-business marketers should identify and map this pattern for each business client individually.

The decision-making process is primarily driven by two psychological processes: (1) expectations and (2) perceptual distortions.

. **Expectations** One factor that sets organizational decision making apart from individual and household decision making is that the various members of the buying center tend to have a set of different expectations, influenced by their background and their satisfaction or dissatisfaction with past purchases.[5]

. **Perceptual Distortions** Business customers, like individual consumers, encode incoming information selectively and in a biased manner. Expectations play a major role in selective perceptions. Thus, some buying center members might expect that only engineers are able to understand product specifications; they might then discount as unreliable any information that salespeople with non-engineering backgrounds provide. Such a premise might be entirely misguided, but the resulting perceptual distortion might cost a supplier an order.

THE CHANGING BUSINESS BUYING BEHAVIOR

Business buying behavior has undergone a sea change in recent years. Three forces have driven this change:

- Supplier partnering and relationship buying
- Information technology
- Global sourcing

More and more business customers are now entering into supplier partnering (signing long term contracts) and firms are engaging in relationship buying and relationship selling. Relationship buying and selling refers to doing business in a collaborative mindset to bring long-term gains to each party in a mutually satisfying exchange.6

Information technology has also changed procurement, basically by (a) better dissemination of information about procurement needs and supplier offerings, and (b) automating certain procurement processes. On the Web, business customers can explore the entire world just with the click of a mouse. This has made global sourcing—being able to conveniently find a supplier anywhere in the world—possible even for small businesses. Moreover, the Internet has now enabled new types of marketplaces—called online exchanges—such as auctions.

Technology continually changes business procurement practices, and students of business customer behavior must keep a keen eye on the changing environment of business buying and selling.

Customer Value

It is the be-all
And the end-all
Of all business activity.
The only purpose
Of organizations.

It is the only justifiable goal
Of all reengineering,
Organizational renewal,
Entrepreneurship,
And corporate
innovation.
And it is the only path
For sustained growth,
And for winning the battle
For market leadership.

www.myvaluespace.com

TABLE 11B3 — VARYING INFLUENCE OF BUYING CENTER MEMBER ROLES

BUYING CENTER ROLES	USER	BUYER	DECIDER	ANALYZER	INFLUENCER	GATE KEEPER
Need assessment	√√		√		√	
Vendor search		√√				√√
Choice criteria	√	√		√	√√	
RFP		√√				
Supplier evaluation				√√	√√	
Selection	√	√	√√	√	√	√√
Fulfillment/monitoring	√√	√√				

√ Influence   √√ Strong Influence

MY ⬜ BOOK

A COMPREHENSIVE MODEL OF BUSINESS BUYING BEHAVIOR

To bring together all of the ideas and concepts on business buying, we synthesize from various models available in the literature, and present a framework that is comprehensive as well as easy to follow. See Figure 11B2.

As Figure 11B2 shows, the nature of purchase and organizational characteristics (including rules and procedures) influence the structure of the buying center—whether a formal buying center exists, how many members it has, who its members are, what its charge may be, and so on. The buying center is constituted within the framework of buying policies, rules, and procedures (which are determined by the organizational characteristics), and the buying center in turn influences these by interpreting, implementing, and/or deviating from them. Decision process is influenced by the buying center as well as by the policies, rules, and procedures. Sources of information form an input at the supplier search stage of the decision process. This input is routed, of course, via the gatekeeper and is filtered through the perceptual distortion processes of the buying center members. Conflicts may occur at the supplier evaluation and selection stage, and if they do, they are resolved by one of the four methods described earlier for family buying, namely, problem solving, persuasion, bargaining, and politicking.

Macroenvironment

One factor not shown in the figure is the macroenvironment. It consists of the economic, political, legal, cultural, technological, and marketplace (i.e., suppliers and competitors). These envelop the entire buying system. For example, legal restrictions might exist against seeking foreign sources of supply. Economic uncertainty might engender shortage or surplus of certain products. The marketplace may offer no current suppliers so that a new supplier

may have to be commissioned expressly, making competitive bidding irrelevant. Technology that suppliers use to offer product information (e.g., Internet) or one that buyers require (e.g., electronic ordering) might render some suppliers or buyers unsuitable for each other. And certain suppliers or supplier cultures (especially involving cross-national dealings) might mandate certain styles of negotiations (e.g., misrepresenting information) unacceptable. Thus, the entire procurement system is facilitated and constrained within the framework of the macroenvironment surrounding it.

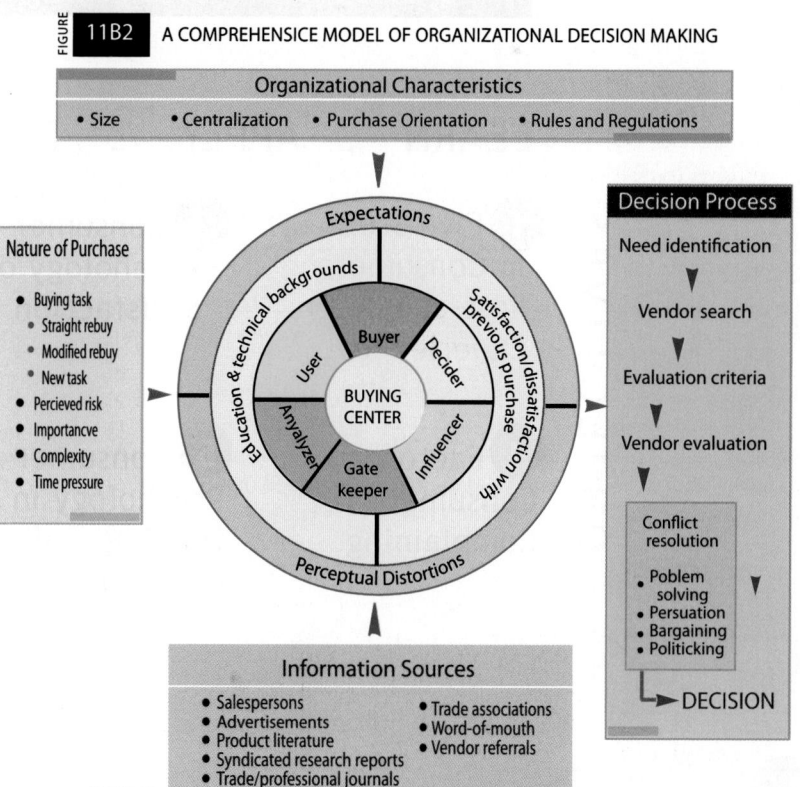

FIGURE 11B2 A COMPREHENSICE MODEL OF ORGANIZATIONAL DECISION MAKING

Organizational Characteristics
• Size   • Centralization   • Purchase Orientation   • Rules and Regulations

Nature of Purchase
• Buying task
  • Straight rebuy
  • Modified rebuy
  • New task
• Percieved risk
• Importancve
• Complexity
• Time pressure

Expectations
Education & technical backgrounds
Satisfaction/dissatisfaction with previous purchase
Perceptual Distortions

BUYING CENTER
User — Buyer — Decider — Influencer — Gate keeper — Analyzer

Decision Process
Need identification
Vendor search
Evaluation criteria
Vendor evaluation
Conflict resolution
• Poblem solving
• Persuasion
• Bargaining
• Politicking
DECISION

Information Sources
• Salespersons
• Advertisements
• Product literature
• Syndicated research reports
• Trade/professional journals
• Trade associations
• Word-of-mouth
• Vendor referrals

My CB Book

12 Consumer Post-Choice Experience

Doubt, Satisfaction, Voice, and Loyalty

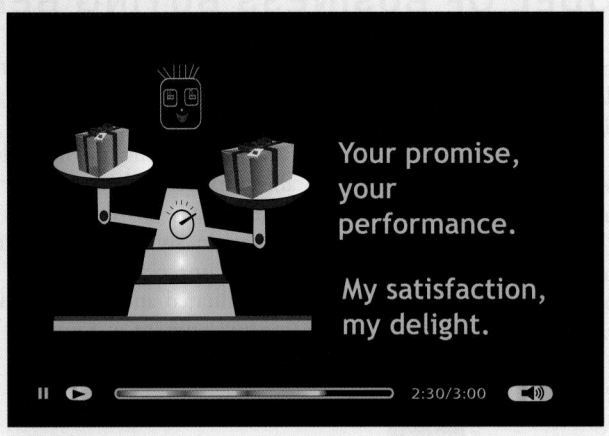

Your promise, your performance.

My satisfaction, my delight.

2:30/3:00

LEARN . APPLY . EXPERIENCE

OBJECTIVES

1 Five Steps in Consumers' Post-choice Experience

2 Consumer Psychology of Satisfaction

3 Five Faces of Satisfaction

4 Factors in Consumer Complaining

5 Consumer Psychology in the Disposal of Goods

6 How Involvement Affects Consumers' Post-choice Experience

Cold Feet in a Hot Dress

I haven't felt even a slight tinge of fear or doubt about marrying Ch

I am worried about being a good wife, yes. I am worried that I'm for
something important that I need to do to make the wedding and reception
go smoothly, yes. I am worried that I will forget my passport as we are t
hop the plane to Mexico, yes.

SECOND

THOUGHTS

But I'm lucky because I know that all of that stuff will work itself out. I will
do my best and enjoy the rest. And I'm lucky because I can tell that even in my
subconscious states, marrying Chris is one of the best things I can do in
my life. ... So while I've had jitters about the event,
I have fortunately not had jitters about the guy. This hasn't stopped me
from having cold feet about my dress, however.

I doubt
because I
care!

I bought it last fall. Before the flowers were chosen. Before the brides-
maid and flower girl dresses were selected. Before I was able to imagine
how everything would come together.

I fell for a big, foofy dress. Lots of beading. Fairly substantial train. Needs
a crinoline to lie properly. That kind of dress. The dress is gorgeous. There's a
reason I chose it.

But as everything comes together, I've realized: It doesn't work with the big
picture. I think I'm breaking up with my dress. Or I'm at least going to tell it I'm
thinking about seeing others.

So I took up with a second dress last night. It's sleeker, a slimmer silhouette,
more metropolitan. It is more appropriate to me, to us, our combined style and
the tone of the event itself.

I don't know why I feel guilt and a need to apologize to the first dress.
...There's still a chance that it will work with that dress. Something about that
just feels wrong, though. I will wake up on the morning of the wedding and
choose between the two. :)

Nicole M. Sikora, a consumer who wrote this entry (in May 2004) in her blog diary at
http://nicole.wiw.org/archives/2004_05.htm. (Reprinted with permission.)

INTRODUCTION

Everyone has heard at least one story like this. It would be nice if, after making an important decision, we could put the agonizing choice problem to rest and move on. Alas, the reality of life is different. Whether it is a wedding dress or a prom dress, a house, a car, a paint color for living room walls, or tattooing the name of your significant other on your body—every important choice decision unleashes a new train of thoughts and feelings. Ranging from doubt to gloating and from guilt to elation, these post-choice mental processes deeply influence the consumer's experience with a product and, indeed, the consumer's experience with life-as-a-consumer itself. In this chapter, we describe these processes.

We begin by describing a three-stage model of post-choice consumer experience. This experience culminates in a mental feeling consumers call *satisfaction* (or *dissatisfaction*). Simple on the surface, satisfaction is actually quite an intriguing process; here we examine its nature and uncover its five fascinating facets. We also discuss the drivers of satisfaction and the role product or service performance plays in it. We then discuss two post-consumption consumer actions—complaining and product disposal. Building a model of consumer complaining, we explain why consumers sometimes complain and sometimes don't. Finally, at the disposal stage, we describe consumer attachment to old possessions and motivations for recycling.

In the last section of the chapter, we revisit the entire post-choice process to identify how that process unfolds differently when the consumer is involved in the purchase decision and in product consumption itself versus when the consumer is not involved. As the present chapter will make clear, your experience of the consumption process is worlds apart when you as a consumer care versus when you don't care. Read on.

POST-CHOICE EXPERIENCE

After the Choice Has Been Made

Let us pick up the threads from the last chapter. In that chapter, the decision process was shown as a five-step process. Our goal at that point was to maintain the widely respected five-step process model, along with the standard nomenclature for the last two steps, namely *purchase* and *post-purchase*. Our goal in the present chapter is to unravel those last two steps in greater detail. We have redrawn these last two steps in Figure 12.1. Let us take a closer look.

Decision Confirmation

As mentioned in the previous chapter, the outcome of Step 3 of the five-step decision process, namely, *alternative evaluation*, is, actually, not purchase, but rather **choice identification**—acknowledging one of the alternatives as the one to choose. This is when the alternative evaluation step culminates and the consumer says, "Okay, this is the one I will buy." Choice identification sets in motion a whole spectrum of thoughts and feelings in the consumer's mind, comprising the next set of steps.

Immediately following the choice identification step comes **decision confirmation**—reaffirming the wisdom of one's decision. After a consumer makes an important decision, he or she experiences an intense need to reassure him/herself that it was the right decision. On the flip side, the consumer wants to avoid disconfirmation. This step occurs immediately after choice identification and continues through product purchase (acquisition) and consumption. Sometimes, following an important decision and after the purchase is made, consumers also experience post-purchase **cognitive dissonance**—also known as buyer's remorse—post-purchase doubt about the wisdom of one's choice.[1]

To reduce dissonance and to confirm the soundness of their decisions,

12.1 A MODEL OF CONSUMER POST-CHOICE PROCESSES

FIGURE

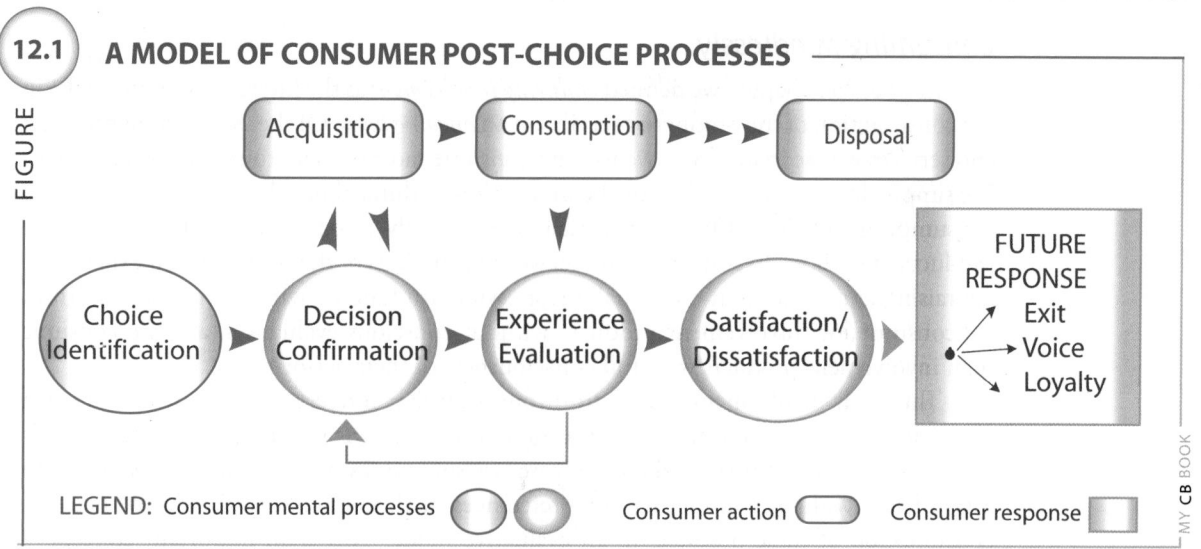

LEGEND: Consumer mental processes ◯ ◯   Consumer action ⬭   Consumer response ▢

MY CB BOOK

consumers seek further positive information about the chosen alternative and avoid any negative information about it. They reread product literature, review the brand's positive features, and avoid competitors' advertisements, for example. They also seek out friends to tell them about their purchases, hoping that their friends will validate their decisions by praising their choices.

Fighting Buyer's Remorse

Marketers can put this principle to use: After the purchase (say, during product or service delivery), the salesperson could review with the customer all the features of the product or service, some of which the consumer might not have noted before. This could help to improve the perceived attractiveness of the chosen product.

Marketers might also communicate directly with recent buyers, conveying a reassuring message. These communications might be targeted through in-pack brochures, personal letters, or emails following the sale. The message might include testimonials from other recent buyers, particularly from residents in the local area, and reiteration of or additional information about the post-sale customer support available from the company. For example, a car dealership might send a letter to recent buyers, assigning a specific customer service representative by name in the dealership's service department.

SAVVY MARKETER

Experience Evaluation

After the dissonance has been resolved and the wisdom of the decision is confirmed, the consumer acquires or purchases the product. Of course, there can be certain barriers that delay or derail the actual purchase. For our present purposes, we assume that the consumer has acquired the product. We assume also that the post-purchase dissonance, if it occurred, has also been put to rest. After the acquisition, the next action is, naturally, consumption. However, we sometimes acquire products we never end up using—such as when we acquire a product as a gift, when we make impulse purchases for which we later lose enthusiasm, or when we acquire products in anticipation of future events or conditions (e.g., travel to a specific destination, a wedding, or a slimmer body) that never materialize. That said, for the majority of products we acquire, consumption does occur. With this next action step comes the mental process of "experience evaluation." The experience of using the product and the realized benefits feedback into the "decision confirmation" process, further affirming the wisdom of the choice or, occasionally, disconfirming it.

How do you evaluate your consumption experience? Or, in fact, do you always evaluate your consumption experience? The answer is that sometimes you do, and sometimes you don't. This depends, you guessed right, on your involvement with the product, and on what we call **preference finality**—the certitude (versus tentativeness) of your judgment that had caused you to prefer and buy this product in the first place.

Consuming Mindlessly

In an earlier chapter, we defined *enduring involvement* as the interest consumers take in the consumption of the product or service on an *ongoing basis*. Of the hundreds of products and services we use in our lives, we use and consume most of them routinely or mindlessly. We simply do not have the time or the motivation to think about them at the time of each consumption incident. On the other hand, everybody is very enthusiastic about some products or services. In consuming these, we are conscious of the consumption experience, appraising and relishing it continually (e.g., wine drinking by wine connoisseurs). Thus, we consume low involvement products without conscious evaluation, and we consume high involvement products with full consciousness of their performance.

This high involvement comes from our enduring interest (e.g., in music CDs); it also comes from the continuing need to find good solutions to our still unsatisfied needs (e.g., persistent dandruff). In the latter case, we sometimes buy products and services on a trial basis, without considering our preferences final. Consequently, we undertake the consumption of these products in an evaluative mode. This is an important concept—consuming in an **evaluative mode**—consuming with the intention of evaluating the product's performance. Think of all the products you consumed yesterday; how many of them did you consume mindlessly, without being in an evaluative mode?

Evaluation occurs differently in the low versus high involvement mode. In the former mode, we notice the performance only if something does not work as expected. Or, alternatively, if it works exceptionally well. Thus, vivid performance difference (positive or negative) is required for low involvement consumers to notice the product performance. For high involvement consumers, in contrast, product performance must meet their requirements and expectations.

Smile, the credit card bill is here.

Discover Card understands the value of making product use experience a rewarding one. **(Used with permission.)**

Free Sampling—Does It Help?

This raises an important question for marketers: Should they distribute free product samples? If consumers don't always consume new products with an evaluative mindset, does free product sampling help? The answer is, it depends. Two things determine the productivity of free product sampling. First, if free samples were targeted only to consumers who were not fully satisfied with their current product, they would actively appraise the sampled product or service. Second, free sampling is more useful when the product or service's superiority is substantial and would be conspicuous in consumption—noticeable even when the consumer is not in an evaluative mode. Of course, "me too" products can also benefit from free sampling simply by creating awareness and use-familiarity, but the benefit would not be as substantial as it is for products of noticeable superiority.

SAVVY MARKETER

SATISFACTION/DISSATISFACTION

Whether or not we actively evaluate a product or service while using it, whether we use it mindlessly or mindfully, one thing is certain. In the end, when the product has been used or consumed, we are left with a feeling. That feeling is a feeling of satisfaction. Or dissatisfaction.

Satisfaction/dissatisfaction can be defined as the positive or negative feeling consumers get with the outcome of product or service consumption. It is this feeling of happiness or unhappiness that sets in motion the consumer's future actions toward the brand and the company, which is the next step in our model. Measuring overall satisfaction/dissatisfaction is easy. Consumer researchers can simply ask, "How satisfied or dissatisfied are you with— (the product or service name)?" In reality, though, satisfaction is quite a mysterious process. Let us unravel its mystery.[2]

THE PSYCHOLOGY OF CONSUMER SATISFACTION

Getting satisfaction is the ultimate purpose of all consumer behaviors. The choices consumers make in the marketplace must satisfy them, or else the whole choice decision process has been in vain, and the money has been wasted. And the problem of finding a solution to the recognized need has remained unsolved. So, just what is satisfaction? Why are consumers satisfied or dissatisfied with a product or service?

At first, the answer seems to be obvious and simple: When a product or service performs well, then the consumer feels satisfied; when the product or service performs poorly, then the consumer is dissatisfied. But this obvious and simple answer is deceptive. Consider a practical example: You bought a shirt at a flea market for $5, and after about five washes it began to fade. You also bought another shirt from a department store for about $40, and after five washes it too began to fade. However, you are still satisfied with the shirt from the flea market but you are dissatisfied with the shirt from the department store. This is because your expectations from the two shirts were different.

So satisfaction, or dissatisfaction, is caused by the product or service performance *relative* to our expectations. When performance meets or exceeds our expectations, *expectation confirmation* occurs, and the consumer feels satisfaction; when performance falls short of expectations, *expectation disconfirmation* occurs, and the consumer feels dissatisfaction. (Academic consumer researchers refer to these two conditions respectively as *positive disconfirmation* and *negative disconfirmation*—a technicality we will overlook.) This is called the expectations-confirmation-disconfirmation model of satisfaction. See Figures 12.2 and 12.3.

Please Stop that Advertising Hype!

Now, as a marketer, what can you learn from the model? If you want to satisfy your consumers, there are, the model tells you, only two ways to do it: (1) improve your product's performance, and (2) don't raise your customers' expectations so high that your product cannot meet them. As a marketer, stop all that advertising hype. It can be suicidal.

SAVVY
MARKETER

Moreover, when possible, as a marketer, you should actively shape consumer expectations.[3]—by realistic market communications, in advertising and personal selling,

FIGURE

(12.2) **THE ROLE OF EXPECTATIONS IN CONSUMER SATISFACTION**

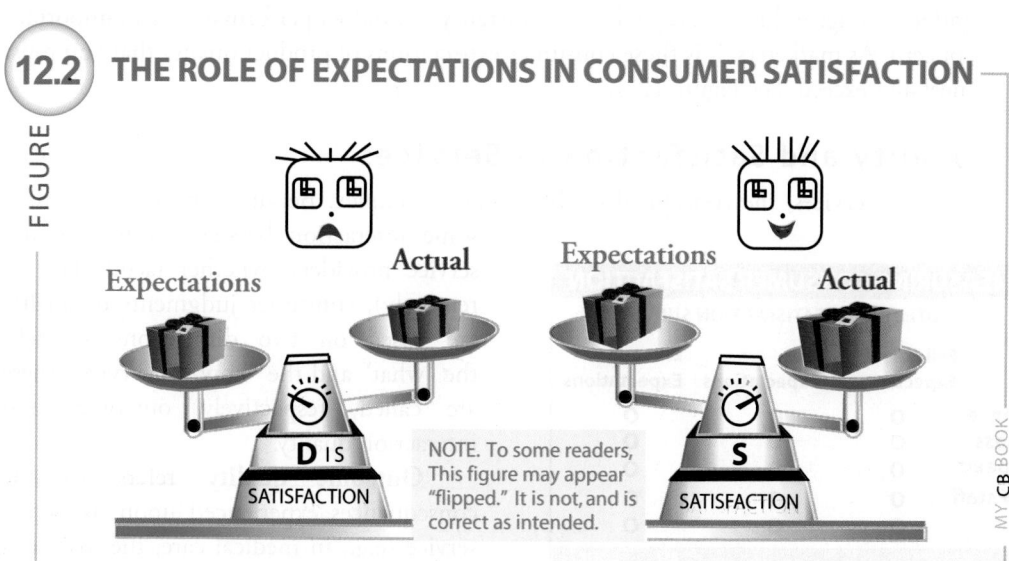

NOTE. To some readers, This figure may appear "flipped." It is not, and is correct as intended.

MY CB BOOK

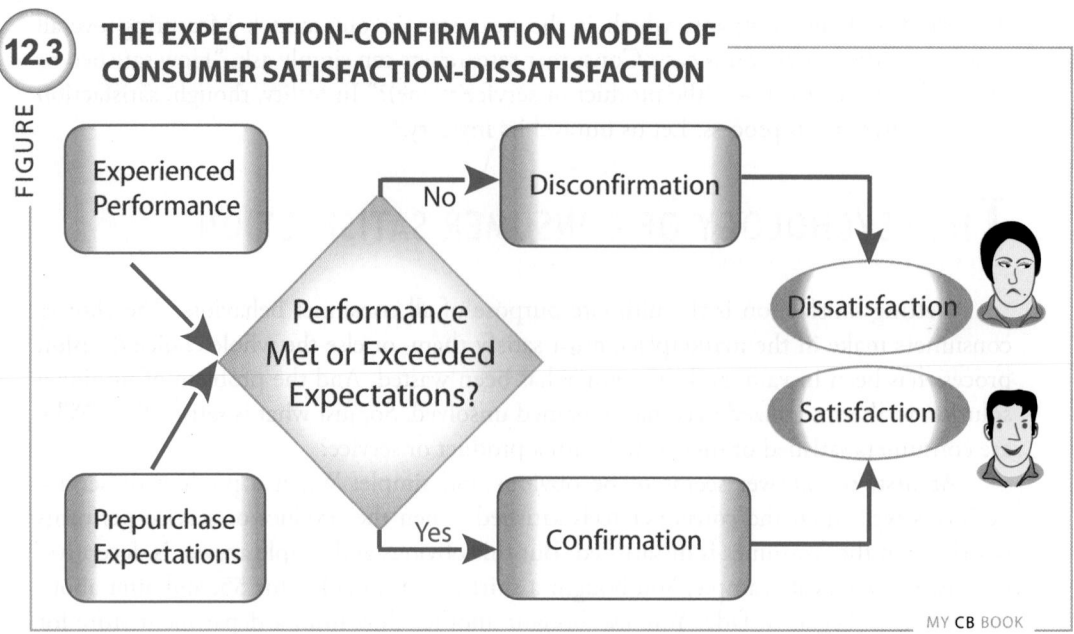

FIGURE 12.3 THE EXPECTATION-CONFIRMATION MODEL OF CONSUMER SATISFACTION-DISSATISFACTION

and even in order-taking. That is why savvy restaurant managers tell customers that the wait time will be 30 minutes when they expect it to be only 25 minutes.

To measure customer satisfaction, simply use the consumer survey card shown in Table 12.1.

Consumer Satisfaction and Quality

Achieving consumer satisfaction requires meeting consumer expectations. The next question is: expectations about what? What do consumers expect from a product? The answer: Product quality. Consumers are satisfied if they find the product's quality to be just what they expected or better.[4]

Product quality is judged by two criteria: performance level and consistency. **Performance** is the outcome of the product's use. When a shampoo cleanses your hair well, your cell phone does not drop calls, and your mascara does not drip onto your cheeks, these are all performances. And these performances must occur every time. For a brand of beverage like Coca Cola, good performance means that it tastes good, and it does not go flat quickly. Moreover, its performance should not differ from one can to another (consistency). With mass production and standardization, consistency is not a concern for consumers in most of the advanced economies; however, in underdeveloped economies, and for cottage industries everywhere, consistency of product performance is an important concern. As marketers, it is these consumer expectations of product quality that you must meet and exceed. See Figure 12.4.

Quality and Satisfaction in Services

For services, the concept of quality is more complex. Because services often entail some interaction between customers and service providers (whether face-to-face or remotely), consumer judgments of quality are based on two dimensions—namely, the "what" and the "how" of service. These are called, respectively, outcome- and interaction quality.[5]

Outcome quality refers to the consequences experienced upon using the service (e.g., in medical care, the disease is

TABLE 12.1 MEASURING CONSUMER SATISFACTION

HOTEL GUEST SATISFACTION SURVEY

How did we do? How was our:	Fell Below Expectations	Met Expectations	Exceeded Expectations
Room appearance	O	O	O
Room cleanliness	O	O	O
Registration speed	O	O	O
Friendliness of staff	O	O	O
Room service	O	O	O

MY CB BOOK

diagnosed correctly, and medication is prescribed correctly). **Interaction quality** refers to the pleasantness of the social interaction experience in the acquisition and use of the service—e.g., the doctor explains the diagnosis and treatment well. As a marketer of services, it is the consumer expectations of these two components of quality that you must meet and exceed. See Figure 12.5.

Some service marketing researchers have proposed a model of service quality called SERVQUAL. According to SERVQUAL, customers judge service quality along five dimensions as follows:[6]

Interaction quality in services

Reliability The service is performed right the first time.

Responsiveness The service company responds to customer problems and resolves them effectively.

Assurance The service company instills confidence in you.

Empathy Service employees empathize with, understand, and respect the consumers.

Tangibles All tangibles that go with the service (e.g., the physical facility itself, service vehicles, employee uniforms, and even the company stationary) are neat in appearance.

S A V V Y
MARKETER

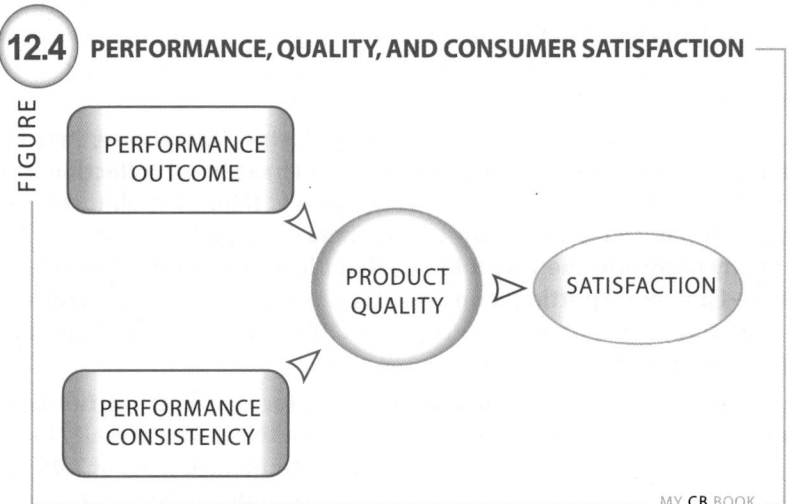

FIGURE **12.4** PERFORMANCE, QUALITY, AND CONSUMER SATISFACTION

PERFORMANCE OUTCOME → PRODUCT QUALITY → SATISFACTION

PERFORMANCE CONSISTENCY →

MY **CB** BOOK

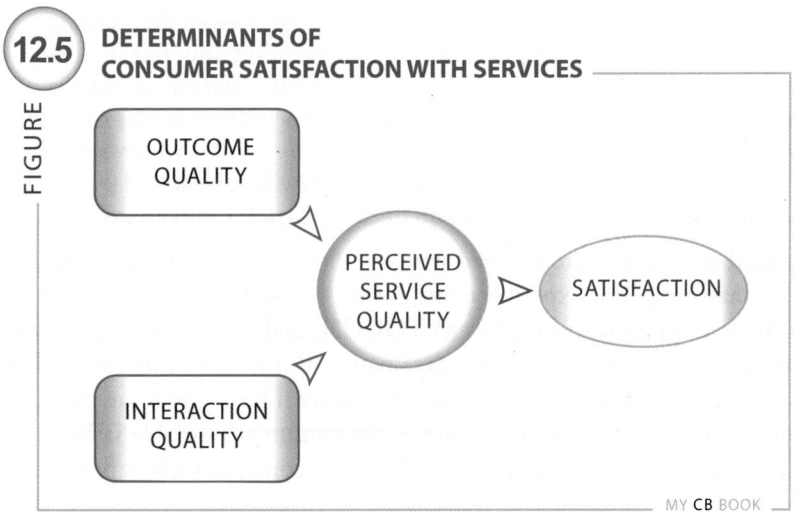

FIGURE **12.5** DETERMINANTS OF CONSUMER SATISFACTION WITH SERVICES

OUTCOME QUALITY → PERCEIVED SERVICE QUALITY → SATISFACTION

INTERACTION QUALITY →

MY **CB** BOOK

FIVE FACES OF SATISFACTION

From Mere Satisfaction to Extreme Delight

For customer patronage, satisfaction is the minimum requirement. It is necessary but not sufficient. Merely satisfying your customers will not win them over. Instead, you will need to *delight* them. From dissatisfaction to mere satisfaction to delight, satisfaction has five faces.[7] Let us view them closely.

Consider five recent consumption experiences of a consumer who calls himself Ross (the famous character, Ross, from *Friends*, is his favorite). Here, in his own words:

- **My tooth brush—I have used various brands; all name brands, of course. One day, while traveling, I bought one of those national brands (allow me to refrain from naming it). After a week of use, I felt the bristles in my mouth—on my tongue. When I examined the brush, sure enough the bristles had come loose. I found it incredulous. Vowed to never buy that brand again!**

- **I have a good collection of shirts. Name brands. Store brands. Whatever is on sale. They wash well, fit well. They please me when I wear them. But there are some that seldom "get chosen," because there is always some other shirt I would rather wear. But I still keep these "second-choice" shirts. For some "just in case" occasions. They "hang out" happily with my "first choice" shirts.**

- **My cell phone is LG enVTOUCH, serviced by Verizon. I got it two years ago. It has voice command, speaker phone, 3.2 megapixel camera and camcorder, a touch screen and a full Qwerty keypad, MP3, Bluetooth, and html Web browsing. It is sleek enough to hide comfortably in my pocket without making it bulge. It also offers me an organizer, a calendar preview, a notepad, a calculator, an alarm, a stop watch, and even a world clock. Yes, I know, since then a lot of even cooler smart phones have been launched. Maybe someday I will buy one. But for now I have no desire to reopen the "phone-shopping project," and I am "settled and happy" as far as my wireless communication needs are concerned.**

- **In the second example above, when I spoke of my shirts—"first choice," "second choice" alike, I was not thinking of one particular shirt I have in my collection. This one is a Mossimo, in dark blue. The fabric in this one is thin, so it almost sticks to my body, and it has a chic European collar. There is something about it, the way it feels on my body and the way it looks, that I just love. Never mind that it wrinkles easily—I postpone putting it on until it is time to go out, so it would look unwrinkled at least for some time at the 'big event.' When I wear it, I feel just a bit more self-confident, a bit more spirited.**

- **Recently, I visited Mitchell's Salon and Day Spa, for one hour of full body massage, turning in my $75 gift certificate. I had been told I would really like it (thus, my expectations were quite high). My masseuse, Nathan, met me at 7:05 and began to work on my body. First legs, then hands, then shoulders, back, face, head, and so on. I was really liking it. Soon, I lost track of time. And I had gotten enough of it—enough kneading, heavy pressing, big time muscle loosening—I really felt I had had enough (not in an "enough is enough" sense, mind you, but in a "boy, it feels great" sort of way). By now I no longer cared if Nathan gave me an entire hour. But if I thought I had had the best of it, and I did, I was in for a further surprise. The hot-towel wrap was still to come, and when it did, by itself it was worth every dollar my gift-giver had paid. Finally, it was 8:10 when he finished, and we warmly shook hands, and I made a mental note to go back and ask for him again.**

Now, if we asked Ross if he were satisfied with his tooth brush, shirt collection, his cell phone, and his massage parlor experience, his answer would be "Yes" for all but the tooth brush. Yes, he is satisfied with his LG enVTOUCH, and he is definitely satisfied with his blue Mossimo shirt, and with the massage parlor. But is he satisfied with them all in the same way? Certainly not. By just asking a consumer if he or she is satisfied with a product, we wouldn't really know the true depth of the consumer's variable satisfaction. As a marketer, it pays to recognize that consumer satisfaction comes in various flavors[7] (see Figure 12.6):

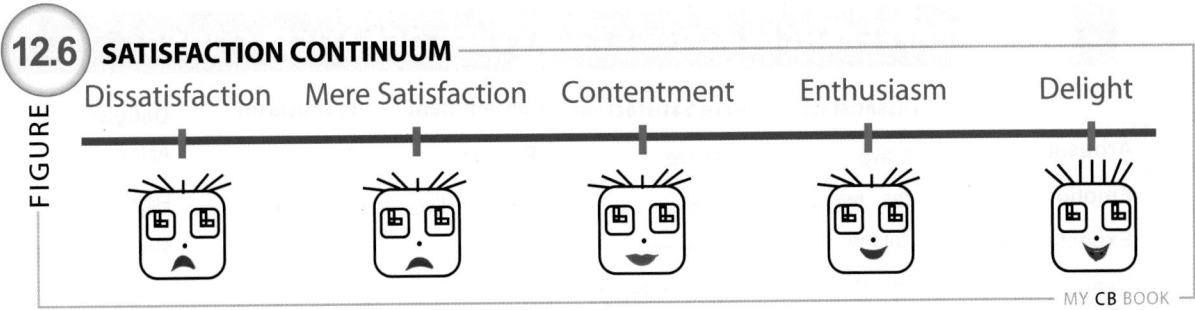

FIGURE 12.6 SATISFACTION CONTINUUM

Dissatisfaction　Mere Satisfaction　Contentment　Enthusiasm　Delight

MY CB BOOK

Dissatisfaction This is clearly a negative experience. Dissatisfaction is what Ross feels toward his tooth brush that he had once bought while traveling. Dissatisfaction is not mere absence of satisfaction. Rather, it is a decidedly negative state of unhappiness.

Mere Satisfaction At the lowest level is "mere satisfaction," defined more by an absence of any dissatisfaction, of anything negative, rather than by the presence of anything positive. Ross' "second choice" shirts present an example of "an absence of dissatisfaction." Ross is aware of his satisfaction with them merely by not experiencing any dissatisfaction. He wears them on non-important occasions, or not at all, still taking satisfaction in knowing that they are there if he needed them.

Satisfaction as Contentment With his cell phone, Ross is more than merely satisfied. Not only does he feel no dissatisfaction, but in fact he is quite content. It sits in his shirt pocket, and every once in a while, he chuckles about it: "What a nice thing it is to have in your pocket." It's not just a wireless phone *per se*, but this particular model has shape, size, and features that serve him well. He is so content, in fact, that he resists the idea of upgrading it with newer incarnations. More than mere absence of dissatisfaction, it is a positive feeling of having his need fulfilled and one of life's problems solved in an admirable way. This is satisfaction as contentment.

Satisfaction as Enthusiasm Recall that with his shirt collection in general, Ross feels simply fine. But his blue Mossimo shirt—now that is something special. When it comes to how Ross feels about it, he can't put it in the "they are just fine" group with his other shirts. Instead, the very thought of it and certainly its use makes him feel elated. He looks forward to the occasions to wear it. So his satisfaction with it is much more than mere satisfaction and, for that matter, more than contentment. He feels positive enthusiasm.

Satisfaction as Delight Finally, with respect to Ross' massage parlor experience, the word "satisfaction" would actually do injustice to it. Ross sees his experience with Mitchell's Salon and Day Spa as nothing short of pure delight. Delight as in what you feel when you see your old buddy after decades; delight as in when you get to buy your dream car. Delight as in when your name is called at the Oscars! **Delight** is an experience deluged with positive, pleasant emotions. It is the ultimate in satisfaction!

Delight is an experience deluged with positive, pleasant emotions. It is the ultimate in satisfaction!

Note that these five kinds of satisfaction differ not merely in degree but also in kind. We experience them differently. We feel activation or arousal for some (i.e., we feel energy and the desire to do something) and passivity for others. Also we feel emotional for some but not for others. Thus, our mental states differ for different kinds of satisfactions. Table 12.2 summarizes some important differences. To review them briefly, *dissatisfaction* activates us, whereas with mere *satisfaction* and *contentment* we feel passivity. With *enthusiasm* and *delight*, we feel activated again. In terms of emotion, with *dissatisfaction*, we feel negative emotion; with *mere satisfaction*, we feel no emotion. With *contentment*, *enthusiasm*, and *delight*, we feel positive emotion, in mild, moderate, and strong degrees, respectively. Thus, *mere satisfaction* is based entirely on cognitions—beliefs about how the product performed. All five states relate, of course, to expectations, but in diverse ways. *Dissatisfaction* results, clearly, when expectations are not met. *Mere satisfaction* is the outcome when product performance barely meets consumer expectations. *Contentment*

TABLE

(12.2) DIFFERENCES ACROSS FIVE TYPES OF SATISFACTIONS

	Dissatisfaction	Mere Satisfaction	Contentment	Enthusiasm	Delight
Arousal	Active	Passive	Passive	Active	Active
Emotion	Yes, negative	None	Mild, positive	Moderate	High
Expectations	Not met	Barely met	Well met	Exceeded	Positive Surprise
Usage	Discontinued	Matter-of-factly	Welcome	Looked forward to	Pursued
Search for new Solutions	Yes, definitely	Maybe	No, not really	Not at all	Definitely not
Open to Switch/ Change	Yes, pursue	Yes	No	Not at all	Definitely not
Repurchase	No	Maybe	Yes	Yes, definitely	Yes, at all costs
Loyalty/ Commitment	None	Weak	Moderate	Strong	Fanatical

MY CB BOOK

follows when prior expectations are well met. *Enthusiasm* requires that expectations be exceeded. Finally, *delight* occurs when there is some element of surprise.

Surprise! Here is Your Delight!

Surprise can take two forms. First, consumers experience surprise when product performance is markedly superior on one or more of the attributes, better, in fact, than what the consumer might have ever wished for. The product or service not only exceeds but in fact defies (in a positive sense) consumer expectations. When traveling by air, for example, we expect (and desire) the food to be reasonably tasty rather than bland. When we find that the food tastes great—so great in fact that we want to know the recipe and inquire if we can buy some additional food to take home—here, our expectations are exceeded and there is some degree of surprise. Or, when we notice that the coffee the airline serves is Starbucks, we are surprised. Thus, exceed expectation by a wide margin on an attribute, and you will delight the consumer.

The second source of surprise is when the product (or service) offers an attribute the consumer did not expect at all from that product category (e.g., if an airline offered a hot shower on the plane). It is surprises of this nature that produce delight.

Delighted Consumers Seek You Out

Do consumers who experience mere satisfaction behave differently than those who are delighted? Of course, they do. Indeed, consumers' future behaviors with respect to your product differ vastly across the five levels of satisfaction. With *dissatisfaction*, consumers simply discard and discontinue using the product, or they use it reluctantly if they are stuck with it. With *mere satisfaction*, we use the product matter-of-factly, without reservations but also without any fanfare, so to speak. With *contentment*, occasions to use the product are welcome. With *enthusiasm*, the consumer looks forward to using the product. Finally, with *delight*, consumers actively seek out or pursue the product-use occasions.

Still Looking?

Do consumers continue looking at alternative products, hoping to find better solutions, and are they open to competitors' sales pitches? That too depends on the kind of satisfaction the consumer experiences. With *dissatisfaction*, of course, they do, pursuing alternatives actively. With *mere satisfaction*, they might search for other solutions if it is convenient, and they would also be quite open to competitors' pitches. With *contentment*, consumers wouldn't want to bother searching for alternatives, as their problem is in a state of "closure." With *enthusiasm*, they would be totally closed off and unwelcoming of competitors' sales pitches. And with *delight*, they would, in fact, resist the alternatives. Thus, *mere satisfaction* does not insulate the consumer at all from the promotional trappings of competing brands. Only *enthusiasm* and *delight* do. In fact, with *mere satisfaction*, consumer repurchase of the brand is by no means guaranteed; they are completely open to change. This openness to change progressively diminishes and repurchase likelihood progressively solidifies as we move along the continuum toward *delight*.

Finally, consumer loyalty and commitment depends on the kind of satisfaction experienced. With *mere satisfaction*, it is weak at best; loyalty gathers strength first with *contentment* and then with *enthusiasm*. With *delight*, consumer loyalty becomes fanatical!

FUTURE RESPONSE: EXIT, VOICE, OR LOYALTY

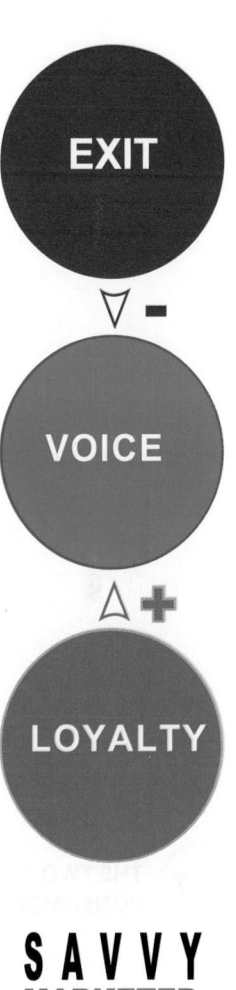

Following the experience of satisfaction or dissatisfaction comes the last step in our model, *future response,* which is comprised of exit, voice, or loyalty.

Exit As a consumer, if you are dissatisfied with your experience with a brand, then there is only one thing to do: Dump the brand, and never buy it again. In other words, you would exit from that brand. You would now consider other brands. Maybe you remember that when you were making your choice the last time, there was a brand you had judged "second best." So now you might buy that brand. Or alternatively, you might want to go back to the start of the decision process, engaging in the arduous process of information search, alternative evaluation, and so on, all over again. Yes, that is a price we sometimes pay to find a satisfying product.

Voice *Voice* refers to the act of expressing one's satisfaction or dissatisfaction. Voice is not an alternative to exit or loyalty but instead is an additional response. Voice can be further divided into three sub-categories: (a) the consumer complains (or occasionally expresses appreciation) to the company; (b) the consumer complains to a third party such as the Better Business Bureau or local and federal governmental agencies; and (c) the consumer complains (or praises) to friends. This last avenue is called **word-of-mouth** (WOM), defined as consumers' conversations with other consumers about a product or service. After complaining, and depending on how your complaint is resolved, you might decide to give the brand or marketer another chance. Or, you might decide simply to exit.

Loyalty The third response is loyalty. Consumer loyalty means the consumer buys the same brand repeatedly and feels a psychological commitment to it. The consumer returns to buy the product again. And he or she spreads positive word-of-mouth. Recent consumer research has shown that, although consumers are less likely to switch brands or companies when they are satisfied than when they are not, being satisfied does not guarantee loyalty. One study showed that despite satisfaction, as many as 30% of consumers were likely to switch suppliers.[8]

There are several reasons for this. First, consumers report being satisfied with a brand, but they may also be satisfied with some other brand. The implication of this is that you (*you* being the marketer) should measure consumer satisfaction with your brand *relative* to your competitors' brands. This can be done easily by asking consumers a question like, "Are you more satisfied, less satisfied, or just about as satisfied with Brand A than with Brand L?" The second reason is *perceived value*—consumers may expect to receive even greater value from some other brand.

The Public Chatter About Products

Voice as Word-of-Mouth Word-of-mouth by consumers is a significant factor in marketing. Positive word-of-mouth (i.e., product praise) can make a company; negative word-of-mouth (i.e., product criticism) can tarnish its reputation.

If there is only one thing that can be said about people, it is that they talk about their feelings and experiences. Both satisfied and dissatisfied consumers talk about their experiences with products and companies. The sad fact (sad for the marketer) is that

MY CB BOOK

EXHIBIT 12.1

PUBLIC COMPLAINING ON THE NET

I tried to exchange a tee shirt at the (name omitted) store at the Northshore Mall in Peabody, MA. When I gave the salesperson the receipt he told me this was the store copy. I told him obviously if I had the store copy the store had my copy, he then told me he could only give me the price it was now because i didn't hv the customer copy. Also, the store copy did hv the actual price. What kind of crap is that!!!!!!

I WILL NEVER SHOP IN THERE AGAIN AND I WILL ALSO TELL ANY PERSON WHO WILL LISTEN TO ME TO DO THE SAME

User (Name omitted). Posted on 23 Jan 2003 at 08:26.14 PM. USA

Source: Posted on http://www.thecomplaintstation.com

consumers spread more word-of-mouth when they are dissatisfied than when they are satisfied. Studies have shown that satisfied customers tell five other people; dissatisfied customers tell thirteen others![9]

The Internet offers a new avenue for consumers to vent their dissatisfaction publicly with a company. There are quite a few Web sites where you can post your complaint about any company. Exhibit 12.1 excerpts one such posting we found at thecomplaintstation.com. Eager to read some more peeves? Try complaintstation. tribe.net; there you will find postings with titles like UPS Sucks, Whole Foods Sucks, and Comcast Sucks Too. Under an entry entitled *T-Mobile Sucks*, a consumer named Lynda writes: "T-Mobile? T Mob more like it." With such public airing now made feasible by the Internet, no marketer can afford to leave dissatisfied consumers out in the cold.

CONSUMER COMPLAINING

Not for the Faint of Heart!

As a dissatisfied consumer, you might decide to complain to the company directly and give them an earful.

Imagine you are dining at Applebee's and your steak is not done well. What would you do—eat it quietly, eat the portion that looks good, or ask your waiter to take it back? Consumer researchers have studied just such consumer behavior situations and have built a model to explain why and when consumers do or do not complain. First, a general model —general in that it would apply to *all* behaviors. It is a two-factor, MAO model— motivation and ability/opportunity—shown in Figure 12.7.[10]

The motivation to complain itself depends on three factors (1) How much it hurts? (2) Who is to blame? and (3) Do you have the guts? Of course, scholars give these factors more technical names: *dissatisfaction intensity, attribution (who is to blame?)*, and *personality trait* (specifically, self-confidence and aggressiveness). See Figure 12.8.

Now let us apply this model to your Applebee's situation. If you feel that the steak was cooked really poorly (you feel dissatisfaction), and that serving the steak shows the cook's carelessness (attribution), then you would feel like telling your waiter. However, whether you would actually have the courage to tell depends on whether you have the self-confidence (personality trait). Have you sometimes noticed that when you complain, your friends squirm in their seats? Obviously, they lack self-confidence.

These three factors determine consumer motivation to complain. Whether or not that motivation materializes in the consumer act of complaining depends, as the two-factor model in Figure 12.7 shows, upon the opportunity being available to complain, i.e., how easy it is to complain. Of course, those who are strongly motivated will end up complaining even in the face of inconvenience, but more people who want to complain actually do so only if it is easy to complain. If, to complain, you have to jump through hoops, then you might just say, "Forget it."

FIGURE 12.7

THE TWO-FACTOR MODEL OF CONSUMER COMPLAINING BEHAVIOR

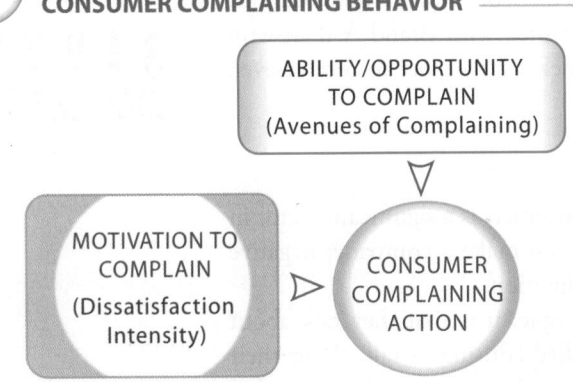

MY **CB** BOOK

The Art of Dodging the Whiners

Some companies love it when you say, "Forget it." Then they don't have to deal with you. So in order to keep you from complaining, they make you jump through hoops—fill out long tedious forms, no toll-free number, and no person designated to send complaints to. If you run a company, what other clever means of stopping dissatisfied consumers from complaining can you think of? The more ways you can think of, the more you push the consumer to take the exit option. The more consumers take the exit option, the fewer consumers you will have to worry about! However, if you don't want that to happen, then start thinking of all the ways you can encourage dissatisfied consumers to complain. And stop acting like you think (as many marketers do) that the consumer who complains is just a habitual whiner.

According to one research study, about 19% of dissatisfied consumers complain; of the complaining consumers, a significant majority continue to buy the product or service, compared to those who are dissatisfied but do not bother to complain.[11] Thus, complainers care enough to complain. Non-complainers simply walk out, taking their patronage to a competitor. Believe it or not, complaining is good for your business. Consumers leaving with dissatisfaction or in disgust is bad!

After the Complaint—Is There Justice?

What happens after the complaint? Do consumers stay with the company? That depends on how the company addresses the complaint. Turn a deaf ear, and your company will get even more bad word-of-mouth. Conversely, resolve the complaint, redress it to the consumer's satisfaction, and the consumer is likely to repatronize your company. Also, the consumer is unlikely to engage in negative word-of-mouth.[12]

At this point you might wonder what determines successful redress. To answer this question, you must learn a new concept called *perceived justice*. **Perceived justice** is the consumer's perception that he or she was treated fairly during the complaint resolution process.[13] This means that the offered remedy made up for the harm done by an unsatisfactory product or service.

When perceived justice seems not to have occurred—e.g., if the dry cleaner spoiled your shirt and merely refunded the dry cleaning charges, which is hardly a *just redress*—consumer hostility increases. Turn a deaf ear to consumer complaints, and you will increase consumer hostility and unleash a stronger wave of negative word-of-mouth. On the contrary, resolve a complaint to the customer's complete satisfaction, and he or she will become a stronger supporter of your company—stronger than if he or she had not even been dissatisfied in the first place! Why is that? The complaining experience gave the consumer the opportunity to learn how good your company really is. The lesson here is not that you should go about making consumers dissatisfied so they complain. Rather, the lesson is that if and when an occasional consumer becomes dissatisfied, go the extra mile to win him or her over. And, as a reward, reap a lifelong loyal supporter.[14]

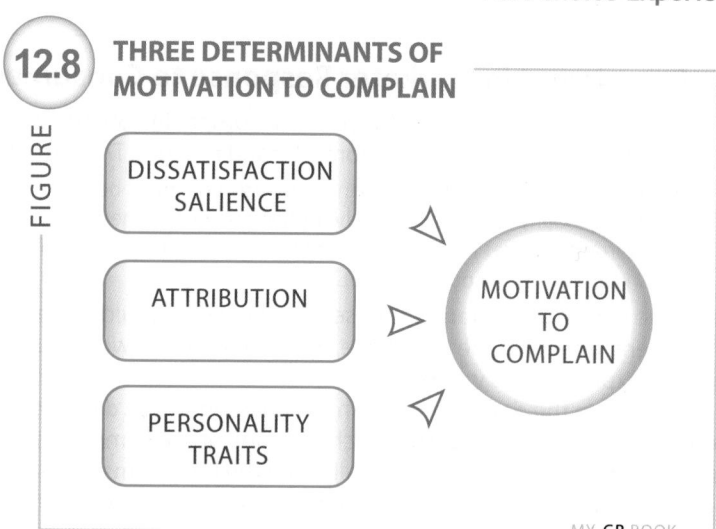

FIGURE 12.8   THREE DETERMINANTS OF MOTIVATION TO COMPLAIN

DISSATISFACTION SALIENCE
ATTRIBUTION
PERSONALITY TRAITS
→ MOTIVATION TO COMPLAIN

MY CB BOOK

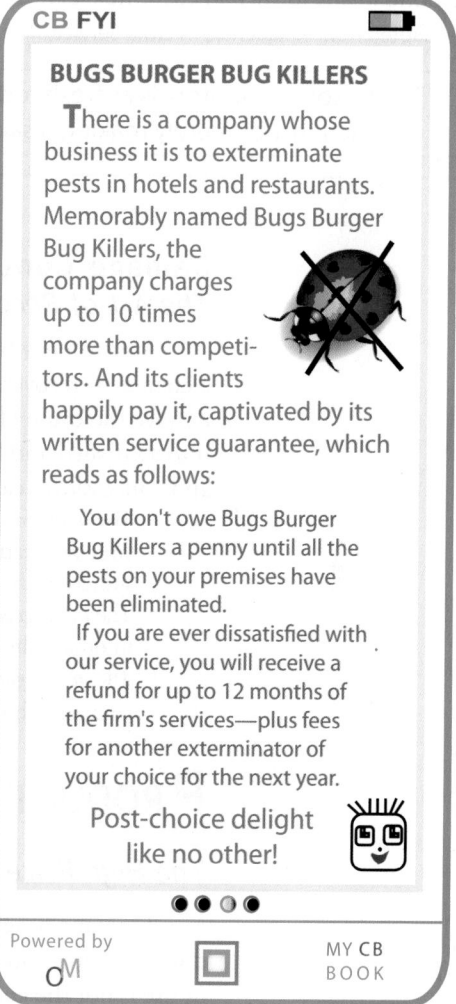

CB FYI

BUGS BURGER BUG KILLERS

There is a company whose business it is to exterminate pests in hotels and restaurants. Memorably named Bugs Burger Bug Killers, the company charges up to 10 times more than competitors. And its clients happily pay it, captivated by its written service guarantee, which reads as follows:

You don't owe Bugs Burger Bug Killers a penny until all the pests on your premises have been eliminated.

If you are ever dissatisfied with our service, you will receive a refund for up to 12 months of the firm's services—plus fees for another exterminator of your choice for the next year.

Post-choice delight like no other!

Powered by oM   MY CB BOOK

SAVVY MARKETER

An Experiment in Marketer Response to Consumer Complaints

Just to see the responsiveness of various car companies, an Advertising Age reporter wrote a complaint letter to the CEOs of 25 carmakers (both domestic and foreign). The letter read, in part:

> I was a big believer in your company's advertising when I bought my car late last year.... Now, a mysterious "clucking" sound is coming from the right-front wheel. The selling dealer hasn't been able to correct it. My warranty expires in two weeks, and I have a car I don't even know is safe to drive.... Can you suggest how I can get my car out of this rut?

Under the old model of transaction-selling, the letter would be sent to some clerk in the consumer service department, unread in the CEO office, where a salesman would just smirk when he or she reads "My warranty expires in two weeks."

But these are the days of relationship marketing. These days, enlightened companies go the extra mile to keep the customer satisfied. Mitsubishi was one of the companies that responded early; its reply letter claimed that the chairman had actually read the letter himself. Saab, Rolls-Royce, Volkswagen, BMW, and Volvo actually looked up the "presumed" consumer's phone number in the phone book and left several messages and sent mailgrams persistently.

The reporter notes: "In general, the imports were more prompt to respond than the domestics, and they used faster means (phone, mailgrams, rather than postal mail); and seven of the 25 companies failed to respond in any form! Bad customer service? Most assuredly. Bad consumer retention practice? Absolutely."

—Adapted from T. Kauchak, "A Little Service, Please!" Advertising Age (January 21, 1991), p. S-8. (Used with permission.)

MY CB BOOK

> The lesson of the story is as fresh today (in 2012+) as it was some 20 years ago. Total customer satisfaction, not merely making a sale, is and should be the goal of enlightened businesses.

Damage Control
The Art of Recovery

A customer who simply exits is lost forever. One who complains gives you, the marketer, a chance to recover. **Customer recovery** refers to the actions the company undertakes to remove the cause of dissatisfaction and to convert the dissatisfied and unhappy consumer into a satisfied and happy consumer. This is done usually by offering the customer refunds and concessions, called **make goods**. Some guidelines for effective *make goods* are these:

- The *make good* should be more than commensurate with consumer costs. If a hotel misplaces your reservation record and denies you a room, merely refunding the deposit would not suffice, as the alternative hotels at short notice might be much more expensive.
- The *make good* should be easy to obtain—the customer shouldn't have to go through hoops to obtain the *make good* award (e.g., fill out lengthy forms).
- The *make good* does not make an apology redundant—a mistake is a mistake, and the company should give the *make good* with sincere apology and cheerfully.[15]

PRODUCT DISPOSAL

The High Price of Consuming

Humans have another problem. All other species eat and drink and move on. They don't have to clean up after themselves. For humans, unfortunately, product consumption or use is not the end of consumer behavior. Following consumption, humans must decide how to dispose of whatever is left of the product. **Product disposal** refers to dispossession of product remnants after use. These remnants take two forms: for consumable products, the remnants are the containers in which the products were acquired from the market, like empty cereal boxes or empty milk bottles. For durable products, the remnants are the old products that have become unusable, like old computers, torn leather shoes, or used light bulbs.

Disposing of these remnants is no small problem. Every time you consume something, you must make the effort to dispose of the remnants properly. Or someone else must, on your behalf (as in a restaurant). And the problem is not over as soon as you dispose of it from your house. Somebody in the community or local government must find a way to permanently get rid of it. And it is not easy. That is because it is, in sheer volume, massive. And there is not enough space on our planet to "put it all to rest," so to speak.

So, What Can You Do About the Big Waste Problem?

Now the big question is: What are you going to do about it? There are three actions you can take—the "3Rs of waste action": reduce, reuse, and recycle. We discuss 'reduce' and 'reuse' in a later chapter and focus on recycle here. Recycling refers to submitting the used product to institutions that will place the whole or a part of the product or its constituents to reuse in the making of new products suitable for human (or animal) consumption.

12.9 FIGURE

THE TWO-FACTOR MODEL OF CONSUMER RECYCLING BEHAVIOR

ABILITY/OPPORTUNITY TO RECYCLE
(Recycling Facilities)

MOTIVATION TO RECYCLE
(Valuing the Environment)

CONSUMER RECYCLING ACTION

MY **CB** BOOK

Want to know what to recycle? Just Google "recycling guide." We did, and one entry on the very first page that caught our eye was (when accessed on February 10, 2012) titled "The World's Shortest Comprehensive Recycling Guide," available at www.obviously.com/recycle. Check it out.

Recycling can make a big difference. The question is, will enough consumers do it? Will you? This depends on two factors: your motivation and your ability or opportunity to recycle.[16] We call it the Two Factor Model of Recycling Action. See Figure 12.9.

The fundamental source of your motivation comes from whether or not you value the environment.[17] If you are deeply concerned about the environment (and our depleting resources on the planet), then you will be motivated. But motivation alone is not enough. It should be feasible to recycle—there should be facilities in your city that enable you to recycle.

Disposal of Personal Possessions
Saying Goodbye is Not Easy

It is one thing to recycle product packages and other items that have lost their utility to the consumer. They are simply garbage, and disposing of them entails no emotions. But consumers come to be deeply attached to many possessions. Memories of the past are tied to them. Many consumers come to see them as an inseparable part of their life histories. Accordingly, they save them as keepsakes. When circumstances force them to part with those possessions (such as moving into a smaller dwelling or to another city), they give them away to friends and relatives they can trust. And they continue to be concerned with the afterlife of these possessions; so to speak.

In 2000, an interesting project was undertaken by a Generation Xer, John D. Freyer, living in Iowa, who decided to sell everything he owned on the eBay auction site, but on one condition: the buyer of each item had to keep him informed of that possession's life in its new home! Freyer's experiences, now documented in a book, *All My Life for Sale*, are living proof that, to many consumers, disposing of personal possessions does not come easy.

CONSUMER INVOLVEMENT: THE SUPREME ARBITER OF POST-CHOICE EXPERIENCE

How It Colors Our Post-choice Experience

In the preceding chapter, we covered the role of involvement in the three pre-choice processes. Let us complete that story now.

Involvement and Product Purchase

For low-involvement products, once the evaluation is complete, and the alternative to be chosen is identified, the purchase is implemented immediately and in the same episode—e.g., at the online or offline store at which the alternative was identified. To acquire the product, typically, you don't want to drive far, and you don't want any hassle. If the item is out-of-stock at the store, you are more likely to buy another comparable brand (identified with a quick search or drawn from memory), rather than wait or go to another store. This is a purchase for which you can afford to be lazy, and convenience is your guiding criterion.

> **For low involvement purchases, you can afford to be lazy, and convenience is your guiding criterion.**

In contrast, after a high-involvement choice is identified, product purchase may have to wait. For high-ticket items, until we accumulate enough savings. Or to decide on other ancillary services or products—e.g., an extended warranty, or add-on options. Sometimes the entire decision process may have to be re-opened. For example, if the preferred brand is not available or not available with the desired options (e.g., a car in red), rather than casually choosing a substitute, we are likely to re-open the alternative evaluation process. Thus, for a high-involvement purchase, the product acquisition process itself can often become quite a project, with the need to coordinate several smaller decisions and multiple resources.

Involvement and Post-Purchase Consumption Experience

For low-involvement products, the product fits into the ongoing consumption pattern, especially when it is a frequently consumed product. Once the purchase is made, we put the decision and the product out of our minds, and we consume the product without conscious thought. We notice the performance only if it is substantially inferior or superior.

If dissatisfied, we are unlikely to complain, writing the experience off instead as a one-time mistake. We may initiate some word-of-mouth communication among friends, but we are not going to talk about it with passion, either favorably or unfavorably. Finally, at the product disposal stage, convenience is going to rule; we dispose of them in whatever fashion is convenient.

For high-involvement products, we continue to be actively involved beyond the actual acquisition of the product. If the final choice was not a clear winner (as is often the case), cognitive dissonance would likely afflict us. To resolve it, we would likely continue to pay attention to all product-related information (including watching the ads). And even if there were no dissonance, just to reassure ourselves, we would pay attention to all communications about the product. And we are going to be talking about it with friends, simply out of enthusiasm about the very acquisition of the product.

> **And we are going to be talking about it with friends, simply out of enthusiasm about the very acquisition of the product.**

During use, we are going to be attentive. If the experience is unsatisfactory, we are likely to complain and seek redress. And, we are likely to engage in word-of-mouth, perhaps passionately. If the product should meet all our expectations, we likely would develop strong brand loyalty and commitment to buying the same brand again. And, of course, post our "like" for the product on Facebook.

At the disposal stage, for high price items, we are likely to seek maximum salvage value. We are likely also to stretch the product's useful life (e.g., we might keep using our worn-out, favorite chair), and sometimes keep it forever as a keepsake. If we must give away the item, we often do so with concern for its afterlife (i.e., we give it to someone we know would take good care of it). In our own way, each of us writes a memorable obituary for the products we once loved but with which we must now part. These differences are summarized in Table 12.3.

TABLE 12.3 — POST-CHOICE DIFFERENCES BETWEEN LOW & HIGH INVOLVEMENT DECISIONS

DECISION STEP	LOW INVOLVEMENT	HIGH INVOLVEMENT
PURCHASE	• Convenience most important • Decision implemented immediately • Willing to substitute	• Requires further planning • Decisions on accessories • Willing to wait • Not willing to substitute
POST-PURCHASE	• Consumed inattentively • Consumed without any fanfare or rituals • Less likely to complain if dissatisfied • Disposal based on convenience	• Consumption is mindful • Often consumed with some possession rituals • More likely to complain if dissatisfied • Disposal with care and concern for after-life

MY CB BOOK

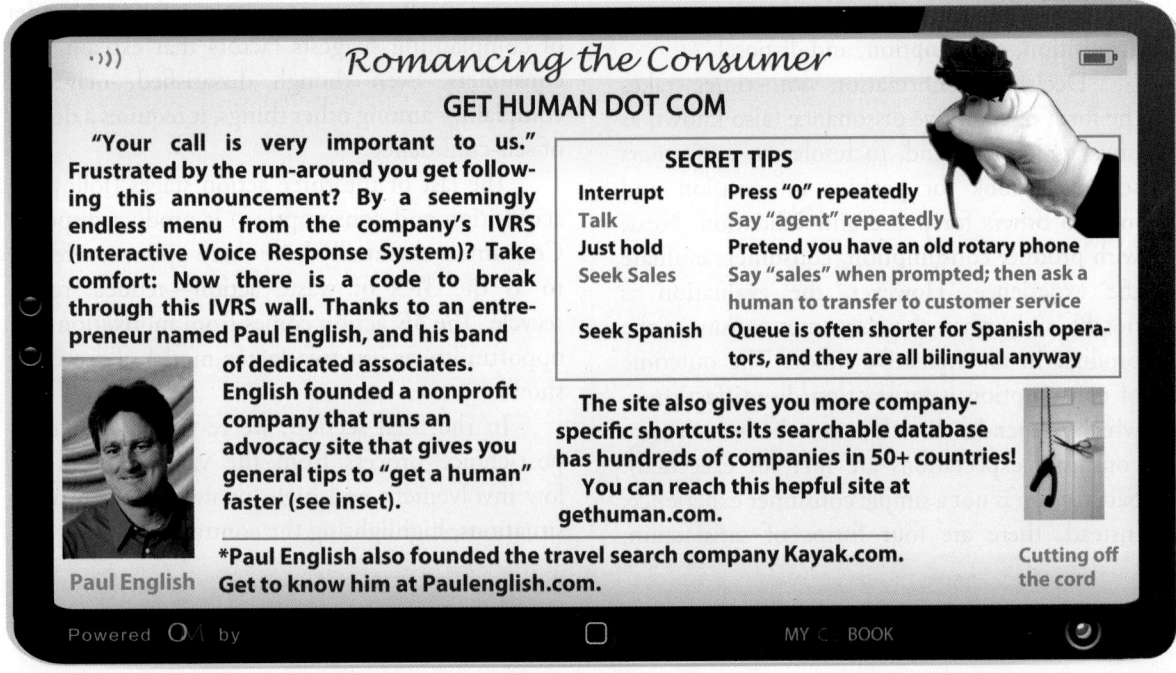

Romancing the Consumer

GET HUMAN DOT COM

"Your call is very important to us." Frustrated by the run-around you get following this announcement? By a seemingly endless menu from the company's IVRS (Interactive Voice Response System)? Take comfort: Now there is a code to break through this IVRS wall. Thanks to an entrepreneur named Paul English, and his band of dedicated associates.

English founded a nonprofit company that runs an advocacy site that gives you general tips to "get a human" faster (see inset).

Paul English

SECRET TIPS	
Interrupt	Press "0" repeatedly
Talk	Say "agent" repeatedly
Just hold	Pretend you have an old rotary phone
Seek Sales	Say "sales" when prompted; then ask a human to transfer to customer service
Seek Spanish	Queue is often shorter for Spanish operators, and they are all bilingual anyway

The site also gives you more company-specific shortcuts: Its searchable database has hundreds of companies in 50+ countries! You can reach this hepful site at gethuman.com.

*Paul English also founded the travel search company Kayak.com. Get to know him at Paulenglish.com.

Cutting off the cord

Powered O\ by   MY C. BOOK

CB Blog

Consumption: Multi-layered Product Experience

In the preceding chapter, we spoke of the amazing ways of the human mind. Like how it sorts out a vast array of products in the marketplace. Those amazing ways continue in the post-choice phases.

Following choice identification, the mind often rethinks over the chosen products, acquires some of them, uses them, gets rid of what cannot be used, finds a home for some it no longer needs or loves, evaluates some, experiences satisfaction (occasionally delight) or disappointment, gets angry, complains, chatters in praise or disparages, leaves in disgust or returns looking for more, and on and on it goes.

In these multi-layered experiences, the mind navigates, guided by involvement.

You can understand these processes by observing up close your own post-choice experiences. Just think back to any two low-involvement products you acquired, consumed and disposed of most recently, and likewise, two high-involvement products. How do the processes you experienced map against the entries in Table 12.3?

If they didn't map well for you, are you sure your involvement was low in the post-choice consumption experience of the trivial products? Like you had bought some M&M candies in various colors and then you wanted to eat them one by one to see if the candies tasted differently based on their color!

MY CB BOOK .COM

SUMMARY

In this chapter, we unraveled consumers' post-choice processes—processes set in motion following alternative evaluation and choice identification. These processes occur both as thoughts and as actions. The thought processes are captured in a series of three steps: decision confirmation, experience evaluation, satisfaction. In parallel occur three action processes: acquisition, consumption, and disposal.

Decision confirmation sometimes takes the form of cognitive dissonance (also known as buyer's remorse), and, to resolve it, consumers selectively look for positive information and look to others for praise and validation. Next, with product consumption, consumers evaluate the experience. However, the evaluation is notable only when the consumer consumes the product in an evaluative mode. The outcome of consumption is satisfaction/dissatisfaction— which depends directly on whether or not consumer expectations are met (or exceeded). Satisfaction is not a simple consumer experience; instead, there are four forms of satisfaction, ranging from mere satisfaction to delight. There is, of course, also the exact opposite of satisfaction— dissatisfaction.

The outcome of satisfaction/dissatisfaction is exit, voice, or loyalty, with dissatisfied consumers either abandoning the brand or complaining. Complaining—especially complaining to the company itself—does not come easily. Our model of complaining suggests factors that explain why consumers, even though dissatisfied, may not complain—among other things, it requires a degree of self-confidence.

The last of the three action stages (following acquisition and consumption) is product disposal. Consumers essentially have three options, referred to as the 3R's of waste action—reduce, reuse, recycle. The 3R action comes from motivation and opportunity, as our two-factor model of recycling shows.

In the final section, we re-visited the entire post-choice process from the vantage points of low involvement and high involvement consumer situations, highlighting the contrast.

KEY TERMS

3R's of waste action
Buyer's remorse
Cognitive dissonance
Customer loyalty
Customer recovery
Disconfirmation model

Evaluative mode
Exit
Perceived justice
Expectations
Interaction quality
Make goods

Outcome quality
Purchase-decision involvement
Product disposal
Reverse channel
Satisfaction/dissatisfaction
Voice

YOUR TURN

REVIEW+Rewind

1. Name the steps consumers experience soon after they have identified their product choice. Briefly explain each.

2. Name various forms of consumer satisfaction, and briefly explain each.

3. What is the expectation disconfirmation model of consumer satisfaction? What lesson does it teach marketing managers?

4. What are the factors that motivate consumers to complain? As a marketing manager, would you want to discourage or encourage consumer complaining? Why or why not?

5. What factors determine whether or not consumers will recycle? Explain each briefly.

6. Briefly explain how consumer activity differs in each of the following stages of decision making between low and high involvement conditions:
   a. Product purchase; and
   b. Post-acquisition evaluation

THINK+Apply

1. Review the description of *decision confirmation* in this chapter. Next, think back to two or three recent significant decisions you made as a consumer. Did you feel the need for decision confirmation, and if yes, what did you do to satisfy it?

2. For each type of satisfaction discussed in the chapter, give an example from your own consumption experiences over the last week (or month). Briefly outline each experience and then justify why you called it that type.

3. Are you generally a complainer or a non-complainer as a consumer? Why or why not? Are any of your friends different from you when it comes to complaining as a consumer? How are these persons different from you, as far as complaining goes? Answer these questions with the model of complaining in mind.

PRACTICE+Experience

1. Interview two or three consumers about their recent acts of complaining and ask them what caused them to complain and whether complaining by itself made them happy. Also, ask what response they got from the company and whether that response satisfied them or not. Also explore in the interviews the sense of the justice (or injustice) they received.

2. Interview two consumers and ask them to describe consumption experiences from their own lives that represent different forms of satisfaction. Then compare your findings for these two consumers, and whether the source of each type of satisfaction experience is similar.

3. As a marketing manager, describe how you will motivate consumers to recycle. How does the model presented in the chapter help you plan appropriate actions?

In the Marketing Manager's Shoes

Put yourself in a marketing manager's shoes. Most concepts in the chapter have some lessons for the marketing manager; i.e., they suggest what to do differently in practice. Indeed, often these applications are implicit in our explanations of the concepts and models in the chapter. Identify at least five specific applications of the chapter's concepts, all of which should be entirely new, different from the examples cited here.

13 Consumer As Shopper

Store Choice, Loyalty, and Impulsivity

It is a store.
It is eye candy.
It is social space.

It is my favorite
third place.

2:30/3:00

LEARN . APPLY . EXPERIENCE

OBJECTIVES

1 Eight Shopper Motives and Four Shopping Orientations

2 Three Factors That Induce Browsing and Unplanned Buying

3 Consumer Impulsivity and Three Properties of Impulse Buying

4 Store Choice Processes for Food and Non-Food Products

5 Factors in Store Loyalty and in Choosing Store Brands

6 Pop-up, Exhibition, and Play Stores: Hedonic and Social Roles of Fantasy Marketspaces

Brides, Brides-to-Be, and Bride-Wannabes

It is four o'clock on a cold winter morning. Women from all over Boston leave on a consumer pilgrimage to a destination a few miles away. Joining them are many out-of-towners, having arrived in Boston the previous evening. The destination: Filene's Basement, an off-price clothing store and Boston landmark so famous that it attracts 15,000 to 20,000 shoppers, including many tourists, every day.

Image courtesy Rocio B. Garza

On this particular day, the store is holding its bridal gown sale, a world-famous event held every year since 1947, to clear unsold inventory and samples. Bridal gowns that are regularly priced from $800 to $9,000 are marked down today to $249 and $499 (with a few upscale designer gowns for only $699).

The store will open at 8 a.m., but customers start lining up at 5 a.m. to get a good place in line. As soon as the doors open, the crowd instantly turns into a frenzied mob, rushing to the racks of gowns—thousands of them. Shoppers grab them by the dozen, without regard to size or style. A thousand gowns disappear in less than one minute. The shopping teams hold onto them, hoarding their inventory while the brides-to-be try them on one by one. Rather than wait for the fitting rooms to become available, the hopefuls don't mind undressing in the aisles, "public stripping" in plain view of bystanders. They try on one and then another. The gowns they discard are quickly grabbed by others waiting and hovering around the shopping teams. The media has described this event as "a magical event, a mystery tour, a lovable, thrilling hole in the ground, as transforming and madcap as Alice's entry into Wonderland."[1]

> I have the will to race to the goods I want.

By the end of the day, many lucky "Alices" will have walked away with the gown of their dreams. Many of them are soon-to-be-brides. But the lure of the merchandise is such that others—with no wedding plans in the near future—also come seeking and purchasing the dress of their dreams—just in case! Filene's Basement—an extraordinary shopping paradise for consumers; consumers—brides-to-be and bride-wannabes alike.

INTRODUCTION

A Planet Full of Shoppers

We are a planet of shoppers. Every day millions of consumers get out of their homes to hit the stores. Two of the most important questions every marketer, every store manager has to ask are: (1) How do consumers choose which stores to visit, and (2) Once in the store, what influences their buying behavior? In this chapter, we examine these questions.

We begin this chapter by defining shopping itself and identifying all the motives consumers have for shopping. No matter how much you have thought about shopping,  our list is bound to include some motives that will surprise you. Once in the store, consumers browse—many don't, but just as many do. And browsing is good for the marketer. As a marketer, how would you encourage consumers to browse in your store, and then how would you convert browsers into buyers?

Along the way, we also cover a special kind of shopper behavior that sometimes causes consumers some regret—impulsive buying. In fact, we will build an explanatory model so that you can understand your own impulsive buying behavior and try to control it if you will. We will also reveal the answer to the ultimate question every store manager asks: How to win their customers' loyalty?

In this chapter, we ask you to wear your usual consumer hat, but we also ask you, occasionally, to wear the hat of a store manager. For now you can keep your consumer hat on. Let us begin with an exciting new concept in retail stores, *pop up stores*.

POP UP STORES

Now You See It, Now You Don't!

Soho, New York British designer Katherine Hooker brought her spring/summer 2012 collection to a pop up store in Soho during the week of March 3rd to March 11th, 2012. In the collection were dresses never offered anywhere before!

Toronto, Canada You could have shopped Target at 362 King Street, Toronto, but only on February 23, 2012, never before, and not in the days following—not until Target comes to Canada in 2013. It opened this particular store just for one day, primarily to showcase its new limited-edition collection by designer Jason Wu, and within five hours it sold $60K of merchandise!

London, UK Stylistpick is a fashion footwear store with only an online presence. But for ten days from 24th February to 4th March, 2012, you could have shopped the store in physical space at Westfield Shepherds Bush. To celebrate the launch of the pop up shop, pop singer Cheryl Cole designed a premium shoe collection.

Welcome to a new concept in retailing—**Pop up Stores**. The concept, so named by creative folks at an online enterprise called Trendwatching.com, started some 10 years ago (Target was a pioneer) and has since been embraced by a handful of brands: Levy's, Gap, Meow Mix, Comme des Garcons (a German clothing company), Marc Jacobs, and even Hermès and Prada, among others.

In January 2009, Gap opened a Gap/Pantone store within its Fifth Avenue (NYC) concept retail space, for two weeks, featuring shirts in Mimosa hues (a color showcased by Mimosa as the color of the year 2009). Lux haute couture brand Hermès opened a store during the summer of 2009 (June to September), in Hampton East (NYC), featuring a more casual store ambience. Likewise, in July 2009, PRADA opened a temporary store at the Place Beauvau in Paris, with a remarkable storefront designed to simulate the look of the famous Mirabeau Bridge. The store merchandise (women's fashions) was displayed in settings that mirrored the outdoors life of Paris. The store remained open, as intended, only for five months.

The concept is now spreading to other types of goods—spas, magazines, artist shows, and even restaurants and bars. During the 2011 Christmas Season, Polar Bar opened at the Liverpool One Shopping Centre (UK), serving up comfort food to shoppers during the day and winter cocktails and live music at night (open until the first week of 2012). The French Laundry—a California-based internationally acclaimed restaurant—served its fusion of French and American cuisine at its temporary home at London's Harrods from 1st to 10th October, 2011. And on March 28, 2012, Food Network Canada host Bob Blumer brought to Vancouver's Waldorf Hotel a restaurant he dubbed one of the "World's Weirdest Restaurants"!

The pop up stores of this sort create heightened consumer excitement. This is due to their temporariness, rarity of merchandise, special prices, and an event-like experience. When consumers go shopping (anywhere), product purchase is not their only purpose. Often they have multiple motives, and they are able to satisfy a much broader range of these motives in the pop up event than in regular, permanent stores. Of course, permanent stores too cater to various consumer motives; and because of their permanency, they are the only assured sources of satisfying many of our shopper motives, in close proximity to the time we sense these motives arising. Let us look at what these shopper motives are. Keep your consumer hat on.

SHOPPER MOTIVES

I Am a Shopper, But I Don't Have to Buy Anything, Do I?

Shopping refers to all activities the consumer undertakes while in the store—permanent or pop up, physical or virtual. This set of activities includes "walking through stores at a relaxed pace (or navigating a Web site), examining merchandise, comparing products, interacting with sales staff, asking questions, trying things on, and ultimately, though not always, making purchases."[2]

Consumers don't always make a purchase when they go shopping. In fact, they often don't have plans to buy anything. Consumer researchers have identified a number of shopping motives.[3] As you read them below, check off the ones that apply to you.

Browsing Browsing refers to looking at merchandise without a specific purchase-intent. Browsers may end up buying something as a result of browsing, but they do not start out with the specific intent to acquire something. For some consumers, browsing is a habit, almost a personality trait. For them, browsing-motivated shopping trips often occur as independent, stand-alone activity. For others, it is an extension of a purchase event, extending the visit just to look around.

A consumer's browsing activity is usually product and store category specific, limited to a few store types and a few product types. Thus, bookstore browsers may not browse other stores, and sports-oriented consumers may browse only or mainly sports stores.

Bargain Hunting Some consumers go shopping mainly to look for bargains, often without an imminent need for the product and without a specific purchase intent. Bargain-hunting is a subcategory of browsing—the latter can be undertaken to discover a terrific bargain, but it may also be undertaken to discover new and interesting merchandise.

The mall at Center World, Bangkok

Socialization Shopping offers many an opportunity for social interaction with other people. Some hope to run into friends while at the mall. Some enjoy interacting with salespersons. Many stores hire employees who are similar in demographics and even psychographics and tastes to the intended target consumers. Indeed, some stores even become hangouts for consumers who want to meet other consumers with similar tastes, such as Barnes & Noble for those wanting to meet other people with literary interests.

Seeking Status Good store employees often attend to consumers with respect and courtesy, responding to their needs for information and assistance, especially at high-end stores. If you want to try on a suit, for example, they will carry the suit for you to the dressing room and wait for you outside while you try it on. Thus, store visits can give consumers a sense of social status.

Market Learning Many find that visiting stores can be a good way to acquire information about what is new in the marketplace. Some consumers have a strong interest (i.e., enduring involvement) in particular product categories, and they like to stay well-informed about these. Computer buffs want to learn about the latest software; music fans about new albums; and fashion experts about new styles in clothing. **Market Mavens**, described earlier in this book, often visit stores to satisfy this motive.

Mall visits are a good way of market learning (display at Center World, Bangkok)

Recreation Visiting the stores can also be fun. Many stores are set up to provide sensory experiences; the rock video blasting at Hot Topic, the mellow tunes at Victoria's Secret, the strong aromas in coffee bean stores, and the fragrant air of The Body Shop. Even the hustle and bustle of people walking, chatting, and browsing can be very stimulating. In fact, some writers have argued that, for many consumers, going shopping is therapeutic, a means of overcoming loneliness, boredom, or depression,[4] and satisfying their *hedonic* motive.[5]

Self-Gratification In contrast to all other motives, this one does require making a purchase. The act of purchasing, however, is not driven as much by the utility of the product or service, but rather by the sense of rewarding oneself through spending money. You might have felt such gratification if you have ever bought something to cheer yourself up when you felt depressed, or alternatively, when you felt that you deserved a reward.

Acquisition The most obvious reason to go shopping is, of course, to buy something. In this case, consumers engage in information search activity directed at a specific product category. The search can be extensive or quick, depending on the risk involved, but it begins with the intent of buying and ends when the decision to buy has been consummated; i.e., the product has been acquired.

SHOPPING ORIENTATIONS

Acquisition or Leisure?

Keep your consumer hat on. How many of these motives apply to you? Generally, it is also the case that, for each shopper, there are one or two motives that dominate his or her shopping pursuits. This determines a consumer's **shopping orientation**—his or her predominant motives for shopping activity. Being more or less permanent, it is like a personality trait.

Broadly, this orientation can be divided into two types: task oriented and leisure oriented. **Task-oriented** shoppers focus on finding what they seek, and they want to finish the shopping task efficiently. For **leisure-oriented** shoppers, in contrast, actual buying is secondary; enjoyment is primary.

If you are a task-oriented shopper, then shopping is a purely utilitarian chore for you. To finish it efficiently, you often wish to be left alone for self-paced information gathering, and you look to salespersons only as sources of product information, not for social chitchat. For task-oriented shoppers like you, a salesperson's product knowledge is what determines your liking for him or her.

If you are, instead, a leisure-oriented, socialization-seeking shopper, then your liking of the salesperson flows from the stylistic aspects of the salesperson's personality and the extent to which you feel you are valued by the salesperson. As a leisure-oriented shopper, you also enjoy mingling with other shoppers or simply enjoy being in the midst of other humans; you may even thrive on the hustle and bustle.

Orientations of Acquisition Shoppers

When acquisition itself is the principal goal, i.e., when the shopper is task-oriented, the consumer's shopping orientation can be further divided into four types according to the principal shopping attribute he or she seeks. These four types are:[8]

Product Quality Shopper This type of consumer seeks good product quality, buys name brands, and tends to be brand loyal. He or she usually limits his or her shopping to a few stores known to carry high quality merchandise.

Economic Shopper This consumer seeks the best price possible, is deal prone, uses coupons heavily, engages in comparison shopping, and tends not to be brand or store loyal.

Convenience Shopper To this consumer, convenience is most important. Accordingly, he or she buys products only when needed and from the stores most conveniently located.

Experience Shopper This type of shopper seeks personalized attention. He or she seeks stores reputed to be high on personal service. Store atmospherics are also important, as shopping to them must be an enjoyable activity.

Now then, what type of a shopper are you? What type is your friend? Your shopping pal should have a shopping orientation similar to yours. Otherwise, going shopping together may not be a good idea.

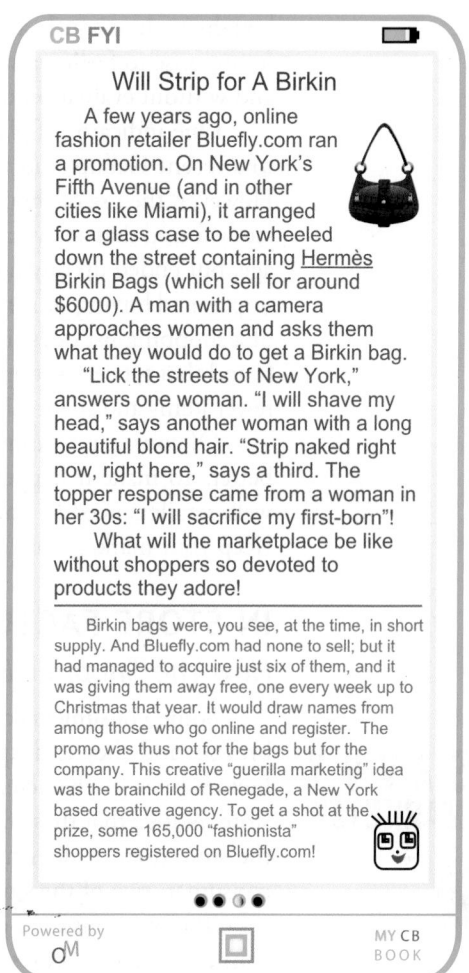

CB FYI

Will Strip for A Birkin

A few years ago, online fashion retailer Bluefly.com ran a promotion. On New York's Fifth Avenue (and in other cities like Miami), it arranged for a glass case to be wheeled down the street containing Hermès Birkin Bags (which sell for around $6000). A man with a camera approaches women and asks them what they would do to get a Birkin bag. "Lick the streets of New York," answers one woman. "I will shave my head," says another woman with a long beautiful blond hair. "Strip naked right now, right here," says a third. The topper response came from a woman in her 30s: "I will sacrifice my first-born"! What will the marketplace be like without shoppers so devoted to products they adore!

Birkin bags were, you see, at the time, in short supply. And Bluefly.com had none to sell; but it had managed to acquire just six of them, and it was giving them away free, one every week up to Christmas that year. It would draw names from among those who go online and register. The promo was thus not for the bags but for the company. This creative "guerilla marketing" idea was the brainchild of Renegade, a New York based creative agency. To get a shot at the prize, some 165,000 "fashionista" shoppers registered on Bluefly.com!

Powered by oᴹ   MY **CB** BOOK

PLANNED, UNPLANNED, AND IMPULSE BUYING

Often consumers make unplanned purchases. And marketers love it. How does a marketer convert a browser into a buyer? Put on your store manager hat and read on.

All purchases that consumers make in a store (whether in a physical store or an Internet store) can be classified as either planned or unplanned. **Planned purchases** are those that the consumer planned to make before entering the store. **Unplanned purchases** are those that the consumer did not intend to make before entering the store. The consumer doesn't necessarily decide *not* to buy those products beforehand; rather, the consumer simply doesn't think about those products before visiting the store.

Planned purchases are, of course, self-explanatory. The consumer came in with a plan to buy something and bought it. No mystery there. Unplanned purchases, on the other hand, are more interesting. They can be of three types:

1. Unplanned Restocking Purchases These are items the shopper had not thought about buying at the time but has been using regularly. He or she buys them in response to an in-store display or special deal, knowing that the item will be needed in the future.

2. Unplanned, Evaluated, New Purchases These are items the consumer needs, but the need for them was not recognized prior to this purchase occasion. These may either be products already in use but not yet in need of a replacement or products not already in use by the consumer (e.g., hair color). The need recognition occurs in the store when the consumer sees the merchandise; however, once the need recognition occurs (i.e., the thought to buy it comes to mind), the consumer evaluates the purchase carefully.

3. Impulse Purchases These are the extreme kind of unplanned purchases—items bought spontaneously and completely in an unpremeditated fashion. The consumer buys in response to feeling a sudden urge to buy something. These purchases are made quickly and without evaluation of need.[9]

One indicator of planned buying is the consumer's use of shopping lists. According to a recent Gallup study, about 55 percent of supermarket shoppers use a shopping list. However, the use of shopping lists does not rule out unplanned buying. The same Gallup study found that an average shopping list user had planned to buy 10.5 items, on the average, but ended up buying 16. Conversely, the absence of a list does not necessarily imply unplanned buying, as some consumers make mental rather than physical lists. Still, the use of a shopping list does signify greater use of planned purchases. A study in New Zealand found that grocery shoppers who had come to the store with a shopping list bought seven fewer items and spent $13.13 less than other shoppers who did not bring a list.[10]

Of course, unplanned buying by consumers is good for the marketer. The more, the better. To make it happen, stores try a few tricks. Some work, but some don't. To do it well, retailers need to understand what makes consumers do what they came to do: buy. Keep your marketer hat on. Here is a brief guide.

IN-STORE FACTORS
How the Shopper Becomes the Buyer

SAVVY MARKETER

Some consumers come with an intent to buy, but they don't. Others come just to browse, and they end up buying. Why? Some in-store factors are responsible. **In-store factors** refer to characteristics that surround the consumer's decision process inside the store. Notice that these factors are not limited to the characteristics of the store, i.e., what the store does or does not do. There are six factors in all: two are characteristics of the consumer; two of the situation; and two of the store. See Figure 13.1.

The two consumer characteristics are *familiarity* with the store and *mood*. Generally, consumers prefer stores wherein they are familiar with merchandise display and store procedures. Familiarity with the store gives them a feeling of control. This encourages **exploratory shopping**, just browsing around after collecting the planned items. In the unfamiliar stores, on the other hand, consumers tend to be disoriented, and they must focus on finding what they need, rather than exploring the store in general.

The second consumer factor is mood. When in a pleasant mood, the consumer tends to engage in exploratory shopping and liberal spending, and quite often, he or she purchases unplanned merchandise as a reward. An unpleasant mood, in contrast, leads the consumer to leave the store immediately. Consumers bring moods into the store, but moods are also created by some situational and store characteristics.

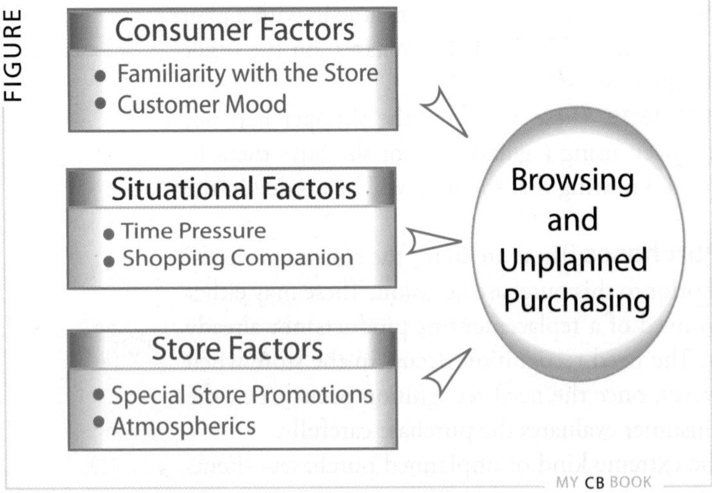

There are two situational factors—*situational* because they occur during some store visits but not during others: time pressure and the presence of a shopping companion.

First, consumers who are hassled with time pressure tend to limit their purchases only to preplanned purchase items.[11] Second, companions can also influence purchases. Do you shop with a friend or family member? More than half of consumers do.[12] Companions can promote add-on buying (e.g., family members suggesting or requesting new items); they can also hinder browsing, and consequently more buying (e.g., friends in

FIGURE 13.1 INSTORE FACTORS AFFECTING BROWSING AND UNPLANNED PURCHASING

Consumer Factors
• Familiarity with the Store
• Customer Mood

Situational Factors
• Time Pressure
• Shopping Companion

Store Factors
• Special Store Promotions
• Atmospherics

Browsing and Unplanned Purchasing

MY **CB** BOOK

Perdu, a Lingerie store in Saudi Arabia. Notice the two-story high ceiling, open spaces, and feminine hues. Can anyone resist this serene and romantic ambience? The *atmospherics* in this lingerie store invite lingering! (Courtesy: Chase Design Group; www.chasedesigngroup.com)

Perdu by night

a hurry).

Finally, there are two store factors. *Special store promotions*, for one, encourage unplanned purchases. Some consumers find special promotions and discounts simply irresistible. During grand sales events, browsers and bargain hunters visit stores in droves. The second store factor is called *atmospherics*. **Atmospherics** can be defined as the physical setting of the store. Atmospherics include lighting, colors, cleanliness and organization, scents, and of course, background music. Atmospherics can make consumers want to linger in a store or, alternatively, to get out quickly.[13] Incidentally, atmospherics is one factor under a store's control that can alter a consumer's mood.[14]

STORE DESIGNS FOR HEDONISM

Of all the above-mentioned consumer motives, the hedonic (or recreational) motive is a powerful motive to get consumers to visit your store even when they have no plans to buy. A major source of recreation is sensory excitement, which is produced by store environment—both physical and social. **Physical environment** comprises four elements: (a) design factors—the architecture, decor, furnishings, and the look and feel of the place; (b) ambient factors—the sights, sounds, and smells of the place, which are in turn created by lighting, colors, music, and aromas; (c) layout—the openness of the space, the ease of walking through the store, the comfort facilities, etc; and (d) the merchandise variety and

---

In the Store, Aroma Makes Consumers Buy More

The Power of Atmospherics

Recently, a group of students in a consumer behavior class taught by Professor Frank Wallace at the University of Louisiana conducted an experiment in a grocery store, to study the effect of aromas on consumer purchases. Here is their report.

Once a year, Albertson's Grocery Stores offer a week long Rose Sale. This year, the sale started on February 26, only 12 days after the Valentine's Day and ended March 4.

With permission of store managers, we introduced the artificial aroma of roses into the floral department at the Albertson's Grocery Store in Broussard, Louisiana. The aroma was released in the customer service area by a ScentCannon mounted on a shelf. (A ScentCannon looks much like a security camera, and uses a tiny fan to gently pull air over a small cardboard wafer soaked in an essential oil that produces the desired aroma.)

"Customer reactions were great. Everyone noticed the wonderful aroma," remarked the floral manager, Jana Babineaux. "It made us feel like a flower shop and not just part of a grocery store. Overall it was a slow week for the store. However, we did well. Sale prices this year were the same as last year and yet we had a 17% increase in our total sales, 65% of which were roses. That's the most roses we have ever sold. And yes, we came out NUMBER 1 nationally. Almost all of the customers reacted and commented about the aroma of the roses. Customers would purchase 2 dozen roses at a time."

The study was repeated in the bakery department with cinnamon bun (rolls) aroma. Similar effects were obtained. Of the 40 customers who were observed making a purchase and subsequently interviewed, 80% reported making a purchase due to smelling the aroma. Of these, 50% purchased a cinnamon bun; and the remaining 30% made the purchase of another bakery item. Some customers reported that they purchased another bakery item instead of the bun due to health and diet concerns. But the purchase occurred because of the aroma!

Source: Professor Frank Wallace, Marketing Professor, University of Louisiana at Lafayette, LA.

its order and arrangement.

Social environment refers to "the vibe" emanating from the store employees and the customers. Their appearance, personality, attitudes, and interactions make up the social setting. If you ever manage a store, make sure that your employees are dressed neatly, as well as are pleasant and courteous to customers. They should be "people persons" who truly enjoy interacting with customers. Some stores explicitly advertise "Hiring happy employees!"

Other customers also are part of the social environment in the store, but you can't do much about that, except to make sure that their shopping experience is as pleasant as possible. Don't despair: the quality of merchandise and the physical ambience of the store will attract like-minded customers. It will intimidate and dissuade the type of consumers who don't fit in with your major clientele.

S A V V Y
MARKETER

The design and ambience, especially, play a major role in producing sensory excitement.[13] No wonder, then, that many stores invest so heavily in design factors that contribute to the principal distinction of their brand. Indeed, store environment is a key theme of many shopping spaces, such as Abercrombie and Fitch, Victoria's Secret, and the Apple stores. These are what Mica Nova, a consumer sociologist, calls *fantasy palaces*.[14]

CONSUMER IMPULSIVITY

When You Gotta Have It!

Has this ever happened to you? You are in a store, you see a dress, and you suddenly feel, "I gotta have it!" Don't worry, it is quite normal, and most of us occasionally feel and act in this way. Acting in this way is called *impulse buying*. In a national survey of American consumers, as many as 38% of the survey respondents admitted to being impulse buyers. Many are impulse buyers only occasionally, but some do it frequently—buying on impulse every so often. They have what we call *impulsivity*—a personality trait.

Consumer impulsivity is defined as a consumer's tendency to buy and/or consume spontaneously, whenever exposed to the stimulus product. Correspondingly, **impulsive consumer behavior** refers to a specific purchase and/or consumption activity undertaken on the spur of the moment.[15] It is worth repeating that *consumer impulsivity* is a personality trait, whereas impulsive consumer behavior is a specific purchase episode.

Impulsive consumer behavior has three characteristics (see Figure 13.2):[15]

1. It is unreflective The consumer does not think it over, and does not seriously evaluate the need for the product or weigh costs versus benefits.

2. It occurs in proximity to the stimulus. If you see an advertisement for a wrist watch and make a mental note to buy it the next time you go to the store, then that desire and intent is not impulsive behavior because you are not exposed to the stimulus in a buying situation (and thus cannot implement spontaneous purchase or spontaneous consumption).

3. It is emotion-driven The spontaneous and unreflective acquisition or consumption behavior is driven by a strong emotional attraction for the product; the consumer just feels an irresistible "urge" to buy/consume it.

In other words, it is a fatal attraction. The moment you see a product, you just get sucked in. Your mind (or perhaps your heart) says, "I want it! I want it!"

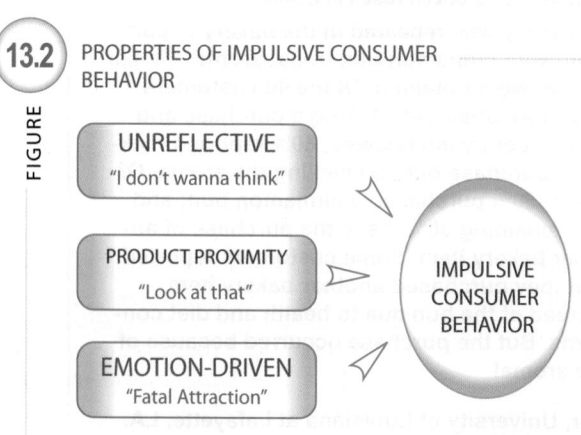

13.2 PROPERTIES OF IMPULSIVE CONSUMER BEHAVIOR

FIGURE

UNREFLECTIVE "I don't wanna think"

PRODUCT PROXIMITY "Look at that"

EMOTION-DRIVEN "Fatal Attraction"

IMPULSIVE CONSUMER BEHAVIOR

MY **CB** BOOK

HOW CONSUMERS CHOOSE THEIR STORES

It is Not Random At All

Now we turn to that 64 million dollar question: how do consumers decide at which store to shop? Here is how it usually happens.

If you live in a fairly typical city, you most likely have the option of at least three or four general merchandise stores at which to shop and just as many supermarkets. As every store manager will tell you, the number one factor in store choice is location. This, in fact, was also the conclusion of a survey conducted by *Consumer Reports* of about 10,000 supermarket shoppers.

But location is a relative criterion, not an absolute one. You know for yourself that you don't always go to the nearest store. Nor do most consumers, even though they want to minimize travel distance. Sometimes, they will go to a distant store if they can get better quality, selection, or price. Merchandise quality and price were the second and third criteria in the *Consumer Reports* study. In actuality, consumers do not choose a store on the basis of a single factor, or do not always value various factors in a specific priority order. Rather a dynamic interplay of factors influences their choice.[16]

THE INTERPLAY OF DECISION CRITERIA

Although no two consumers are exactly alike in their food shopping (and shopping for other products), the interplay of factors for a typical consumer's store choice can be described as follows (see Figure 13.3):

- **Distance is an important consideration, but it is not always measured from home or in kilometers/miles; rather, it is measured by convenience, such as whether it is on the way to work and on or off the main road or main commuting route. Moreover, small differences in distances are ignored, so that a slightly more distant store may be chosen on occasion even without any other advantage.**

- **If two or more stores are equally convenient from the standpoint of distance, then other factors (e.g., quality, assortment, and price) influence the store choice. Moreover, if these other factors are significantly inferior at the nearest store, then too a distant, less convenient store is likely to be chosen for regular shopping. The most convenient store may continue to be chosen, however, for filler trips.**

- **A typical consumer does not limit food shopping to just one store. Rather, consumers have a repertoire of stores, with one store shopped most frequently and regularly. For example, an average American household makes an average of 2.2 visits per week to a supermarket. However, for a majority of households (over 80 percent), only one visit (out of 2 or 3 total visits) is made to their most preferred supermarket; at least one visit every week is made to their less preferred store—albeit for less substantive shopping. Thus, a majority of American households rely on more than one food store to meet their food needs.[17]**

- **If there are stores that specialize in quality, assortment, or price deals, these stores are likely to be included in the repertoire of stores (i.e., into the consideration set), even if they are not conveniently located. They will be visited despite the locational disadvantage, but only on special occasions rather than on a regular basis.**

Spice Bazzar Istanbul

Consumers visit specialty shops like this despite distance disadvantage

The most important point is that consumers have a repertoire (i.e., assortment) of stores at which to shop. The choice of a specific store from the repertoire is based on the exigencies of the specific situation—for example, whether it is an emergency, a major shopping trip, or a filler trip, or whether one of the stores in the repertoire is running a price special, etc.[18]

As shown in the flow chart of the decision process in Figure 13.3, a store decision begins, but often does not end, with distance considerations.[19] This flow chart is most appli-

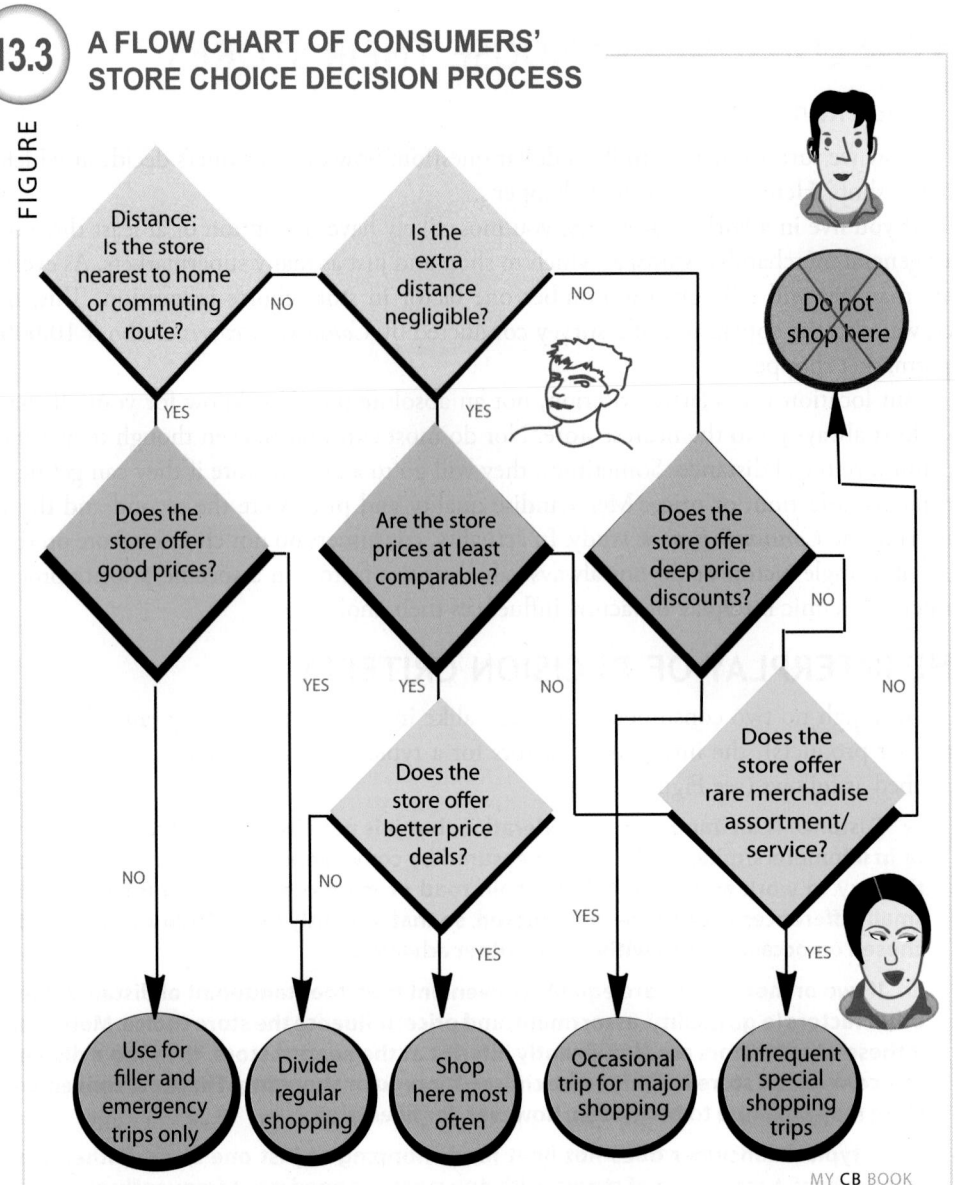

FIGURE 13.3 A FLOW CHART OF CONSUMERS' STORE CHOICE DECISION PROCESS

MY **CB** BOOK

cable to food shopping. Because shopping for groceries is repetitive, a sort of pattern emerges, dividing shopping chores over periodic "fixed schedule trips" and then "filler trips" and "special trips." Now, why don't you try drawing a flow chart for your own thought processes in choosing a supermarket choice?

Battle of the Stores—How They Differentiate Themselves

Since merchandise quality, assortment, and price all play important roles in helping consumers choose stores, retailers naturally try to distinguish themselves on one or more of these criteria. Supermarkets tend to offer a medium assortment of merchandise at moderate prices, levels considered acceptable by the mass market. Some supermarkets, such as Food Lion, and some supercenters, such as Meijer, feature lower prices. Warehouse stores offer a limited selection of merchandise, but at very attractive prices. Similarly, wholesale or membership clubs, such as Sam's and Costco, appeal principally to price-point sensitive consumers (to shop at these stores, you must be a member and pay an annual fee).

Specialty stores, such as Jungle Jim's in Fairfield, Ohio, or H-E-B Foods in San Antonio, Texas, focus on merchandise selection and assortment. Some supermarkets such as Harris-Teeter make fresh produce their special attraction. Such differentiation strategies work by focusing on a process of consumer self-selection—consumers self-select themselves to be the customers of the store that offers the advantage they seek.[20]

NONFOOD SHOPPING

Or When Man Does Not Live by Bread Alone

Of course, consumers buy more than food. They also buy apparel, jewelry, electronics, fragrances and cosmetics, to name a few products. This is when shopping gets interesting. For one thing, it is not repetitive, so it does not become a chore. Consumers are often excited about going shopping for these items. Besides, often these are high involvement purchases. Consequently, location takes a backseat. Merchandise quality, assortment, and price assume greater prominence. A few other factors also come into play:

Customer Service The courtesy and helpfulness of store personnel.

Wayfinding The ease of finding one's way around the store. Wayfinding depends on store layout, in-store displays, and signage.

Atmospherics The physical ambience of the store. Atmospherics entail the art of designing a physical space so as to create a pleasurable sensory experience for the customer. Ambience comprises such elements as lighting, colors, background music, scents, and, overall, the cheeriness or the gloominess of the store.

Often all of these factors work in unison. By that, we mean consumers form an impression about a store based on all these factors. This impression then, by and large, determines whether they visit the store or not. Even so, some factors are more important than others. Typically, the first set of factors—merchandise quality, assortment, and price (along with location)—form the first set of screening factors. The remaining three factors—service, wayfinding, and atmospherics—serve as the second tier of screening criteria. That is, when the first-tier factors are equalized, consumers are likely then to choose a store that offers one or more of the second-tier advantages. See Figure 13.4.

Are service, wayfinding, atmospherics, and the like not as important for food shopping, you might ask? They are, to some extent. However, these factors really play a determinant role for non-food shopping (which is not routinized).

Have we accounted for all the factors? Almost. You might notice that we did not mention advertised sale specials as a factor. This is because the advertised specials are just that—*special*. As such, they play a distinct role: they influence a particular *trip*. You see, the two-tier criteria depicted in Figure 13.4 determine the choice set. How do consumers select from this set of choices? They do so based on two criteria: locational convenience and advertised store specials. See Figure 13.5. Locational convenience here refers to situation-specific proximity; that is, wherever the consumer happens to be at the time he or she thinks about going shopping (e.g., home, office). Second, consumers often plan shopping trips specifically around advertised specials.

For nonfood, store atmospherics are a big draw.

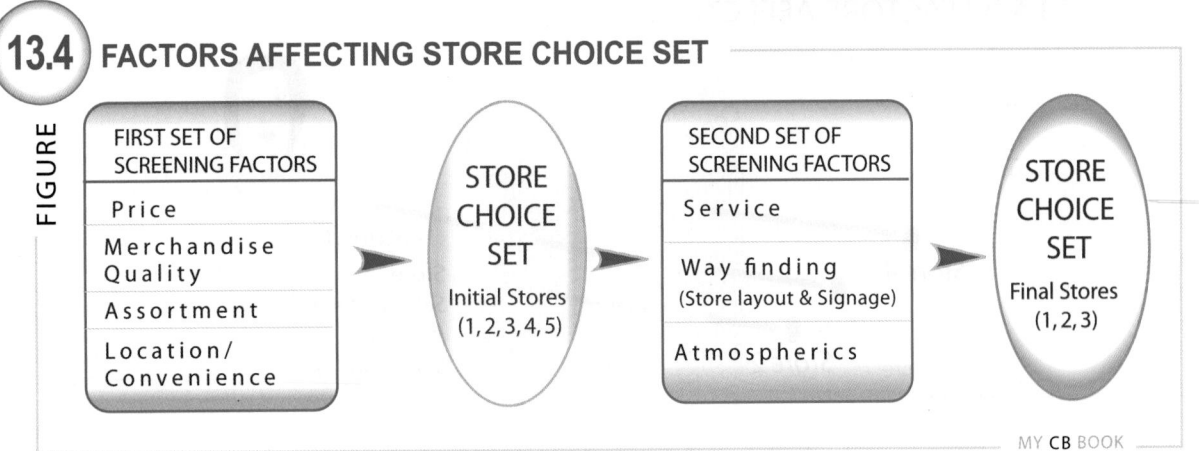

13.4 FACTORS AFFECTING STORE CHOICE SET

FIGURE

FIRST SET OF SCREENING FACTORS	STORE CHOICE SET	SECOND SET OF SCREENING FACTORS	STORE CHOICE SET
Price		Service	
Merchandise Quality	Initial Stores (1, 2, 3, 4, 5)	Way finding (Store layout & Signage)	Final Stores (1, 2, 3)
Assortment			
Location/ Convenience		Atmospherics	

Speaking of **advertised specials**, these days, this marketing tool is being given a few new twists. One such twist is contextual marketing. **Contextual marketing** is the program that offers to consumers price deals based on their physical location of the moment—their mobile phone identifies their location and is then sent coupons from nearby merchants, or, within a store, for nearby merchandise. The second twist is the use of social media to aggregate a large number of consumers into a membership group, and then, based on the group's massive buying power, wrench from merchants a huge price deal. Because being connected into social networks on these new social media is trendy, this practice has suddenly made couponing cool. See inset.

STORE IMAGE AND STORE PERSONALITY

As we said earlier, all of these factors work in unison. In the consumer's mind, they create an overall impression, called **store image**—the sum total of perceptions that consumers have about the store.

Store image is determined, first and foremost, by merchandise, service, and price factors; it is also determined by atmospherics, which drives the look and feel of the store. The clientele of a store is also an important determinant of store image, as consumers form impressions about the store from the type of customers who frequent it. Actually, the relationship between store image and clientele is mutual: store image determines the kind of clientele a store will attract, but the clientele also feeds back into store image. Finally, store image is also determined by the quality and appearance of store employees. The hip and youthful employees at Nike Town create a different image, for example, than do the more mature, warm, folksy greeters and cashiers at Wal-Mart stores.[21]

Closely related to store image is the concept of **store personality**, which refers to the characterization of a store on personality-like qualities. Many qualities that we apply to humans can also be applied to stores—such as sophisticated, modern, traditional, tacky, etc. Thus, store image is the sum total of consumer perceptions, and store personality is a subset—i.e., it refers to those perceptions that pertain to human-like qualities. That is,

> Store image = Store personality (human-like qualities) + other features of the store; i. e., non-personality-like attributes (e.g., price, merchandise variety, wayfinding, etc.

In a pioneering study on this topic, researchers have identified five store personality dimensions: *enthusiasm, sophistication, unpleasantness, genuineness,* and *solidity*. A scale to measure these personality dimensions is shown in Table 13.1.

Store image and store personality play an overarching role in how consumers choose stores. This is because, in selecting stores, consumers try to match stores with their own self-concepts. That is, they come to believe, for example, that Abercrombie & Fitch is their type of store whereas Chico's is not; or the other way around.

A survey of consumers in a major metropolitan area in Canada revealed the personality profile of selected stores in the city, presented in Table 13.2

FIGURE 13.5 FACTORS AFFECTING STORE CHOICE SET

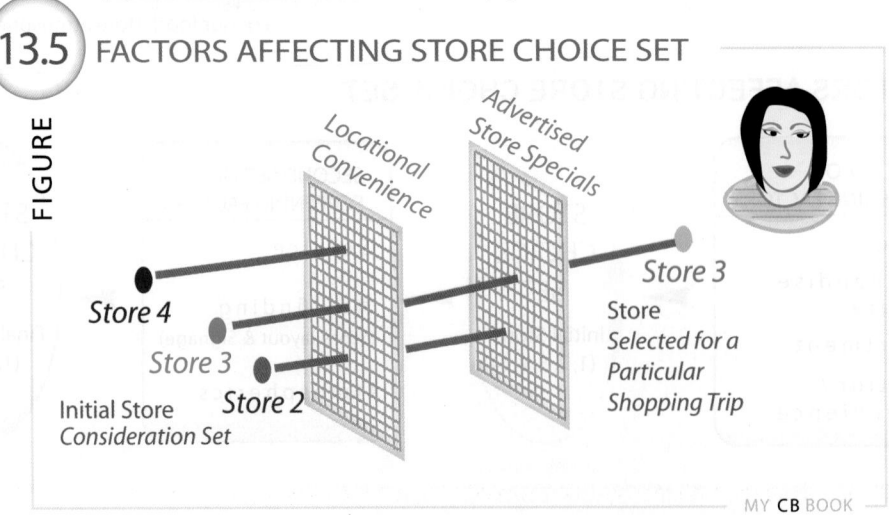

Locational Convenience

Advertised Store Specials

Store 4

Store 3

Store 3

Store 2

Initial Store Consideration Set

Store 3

Store Selected for a Particular Shopping Trip

MY **CB** BOOK

How Couponing Became Cool!

Historically, couponing was a game played by price sensitive consumers willing to put in the time and effort required to search for, clip, save, organize, and carry to the store, and then precisely match the coupon's redemption conditions to the merchandise in the store! Redeemers found value in the savings, and some even prided themselves on being prudent shoppers. Many consumers, however, wouldn't be bothered to make the effort. This process was eased considerably when stores started offering automatic deals to customers holding their membership or "loyalty" cards. Still, for some consumers, couponing was a stigma, or, at any rate, it was nothing to brag about. All that is now changing with the advent of new Web based coupon creators and distributors. Among them:

Groupon A Web based company called Groupon sends you a daily email with the "deal of the day"—discounted gift certificates for products from selected local merchants—from some 150 markets in North America and 100 markets in Europe, Asia, and South America. The site boasts more than 35 million registered users. You can receive the deal on, and redeem it from, your mobile phone.

LivingSocial Similar to the deals from Groupon, you can get daily deals from a company called LivingSocial, with one additional twist. Forward the deal to your friends, and if some of them buy the deal, you get your deal free of cost to you!

These new "deal makers" have changed couponing into a game. Consumers eagerly await their daily deals to arrive on their phones (thus there is an element of anticipation), make a project out of the consumption/purchase event ("We go for lunch at Johnny Rockets today!"), happily share the deal with their friends, and chat these up on Facebook. They pride themselves on being "in" on the deal, and on being the members of the community of this new breed of networked consumers. After all they are in it together with their friends! Ah, it feels so cool!

(Source: Information available at company Web sites and personal experience.)

TABLE **13.1** MEASUREMENT OF STORE PERSONALITY

Enthusiasm	Sophistication	Unpleasantness	Genuineness	Solidity
Enthusiastic ___	Chic ___	Annoying ___	Honest ___	Hardy ___
Welcoming ___	High-class ___	Irritating ___	Sincere ___	Solid ___
Lively ___	Elegant ___	Loud ___	Reliable ___	Reputable ___
Dynamic ___	Stylish ___	Superficial ___	True ___	Thriving ___

Source: Alain d'Astous and Melanie Levesque, "A Scale for Measuring Store Personality," Psychology and Marketing, Vol. 20/Number 6, May 2003, p. 455-469. © 2003 Wiley Periodicals, Inc. (Used with Permission.)

MY CB BOOK

TABLE **13.2** PERSONALITY PROFILE OF SELECTED STORES IN CANADA

Store Name	Enthusiasm	Sophistication	Genuineness	Solidity	Unpleasant
Wal-Mart	3.83	2.29	3.65	3.92	2.48
Sears	3.31	3.17	3.86	3.80	2.19
Zellers	3.00	2.14	3.35	3.16	2.42
La Baie	3.22	3.65	3.63	3.61	2.53
Canadian Tire	3.47	2.75	3.87	4.05	2.21
Future Shop	3.21	2.91	3.10	3.52	2.53

Note: Measured on 1-5 scales where a higher number meant more of the personality trait.
Source: Alain d'Astous (HEC, Montreal), personal communication

MY CB BOOK

CONSUMER LOYALTY TO STORES

Let us keep our store manager's hat on. We now know how consumers choose their stores. And we know how to get them into our store. But getting them once is only the beginning; our real goal is, and should be, to get them to visit our store again and again. In other words, how do we make a first time visitor a loyal customer?

For this purpose, we need to understand why consumers become store loyal. Obviously, many of the factors that influence a first time visit would also induce loyalty. But a few new factors also come into play. These factors are shown in Figure 13.6.

The determinant factors of store loyalty are of two kinds: the "what" factors and the "how" factors. The "what" factors refer to the products and services the consumer gets at the store. These are the factors for which the consumers go to the store in the first place, and these are what they walk out with when they leave the store. The "how" factors refer to the process entailed in a consumer's acquisition of those products and services.[22]

THE "WHAT" FACTORS

A consumer goes into a store to acquire some mix of merchandise quality, assortment, and price value—factors we have already considered—and also one more factor, namely, availability of store brands. Although self-evident, let us make brief comments on each. Discussing these factors again in the context of store loyalty gives us an opportunity to shed light on some important nuances. Understand these nuances, and you will be richly rewarded when and if someday you get to manage your own store.

Merchandise Quality Merchandise quality refers to the quality of the products the store carries and offers. Stores differ vastly on this element, with merchandise ranging from shoddy to premium quality (e.g., produce that is fresh or withered; clothing that is well tailored or hurriedly sewn). The merchandise quality is generally controlled by the brand names the store decides to carry. It is immensely important, therefore, to be very careful in selecting brands to carry in your store.

Assortment A store's **assortment** refers to the number of different items the store carries. This includes the number of diverse product categories (e.g., appliances versus food), product varieties (e.g., organic, flavors, styles, etc.), the number of brands of the same product category (e.g., for photo films, Kodak, Fuji, etc.), and the size and color varieties.

Although assortment will influence a consumer's patronage, the relationship is not straightforward. Consumers do not necessarily want an unlimited, vast assortment—indeed too large an assortment could create shopper confusion. Instead they want the store to carry their preferred brands as well as a few other related major brands. Why? Because consumers want to compare brands—both initially when their brand preference is still fluid, and later from time to time when they want to compare leading brands. Also, in many product categories, such as clothing, cosmetics, perfumes, jewelry, music CDs, and books, consumers intrinsically desire variety.

Assortment also appeals to consumers' desire for one-stop shopping—finding all of their requirements of related products in one place or from one source. The motivations for one-stop shopping are convenience and time savings. Stores like Meijer, Sam's, and Wal-Mart in the United States, and Food Giant and Asda's Dales in the United Kingdom attract consumers by offering an assortment of product categories far greater than a typical supermarket (such as Kroger in the United States or Tesco or Sainsbury's in the United Kingdom) and yet at comparable prices.

Price Value Consumers seek the best possible price for the merchandise they buy. This is the appeal of deep discounters such as Costco (United States), Matalan (United Kingdom), Aldo (Netherlands), Dia/Dirsa (Spain), or Netto (Denmark). However, consumers do not always, or even often, seek low-price merchandise; rather, for the quality of merchandise they desire, they seek the lowest or near lowest price. This point is important: Consumers

FIGURE 13.6 A MODEL OF CONSUMERS' STORE LOYALTY

"WHAT" FACTORS
Merchandise Quality
Assortment
Price Value
Store Brands

CONSUMER'S STORE LOYALTY

"HOW" FACTORS
Ease of Self-selection
In-store Information & Assistance
Convenience
Problem Resolution
Personalization
Atmospherics

MY **CB** BOOK

seek low prices for acceptable quality of merchandise, not low prices in the absolute. Of course, some consumers on some occasions find very low quality acceptable, so they seek very low-price merchandise. Still, merchandise acceptability comes first; low price comes later.

Store brands Yet another attraction for the consumer is **store brands**, the brands that carry a store label and are available exclusively at that store chain. As store brands are considerably lower in price, the availability of store brands becomes an attractive feature for the consumers, driving consumers' loyal patronage.[23]

THE "HOW" FACTORS

Store loyalty also depends on how positive the shopping experience is. This requires six "how" factors: (a) ease of merchandise selection, (b) in-store information and assistance, (c) convenience, (d) problem resolution, (e) personalization, and (f) atmospherics. If you are keeping track, these factors are just a more unbundled version of the three second-tier factors shown in Figure 13.4. We break them down in this way for ease of managing them as a store manager. Here is how.

Ease of Merchandise Selection This factor refers to how easily and effortlessly consumers are able to browse, inspect, and select products. This depends on several features: layout of aisles and shelf displays (wayfinding), shelf tags, product information cards, and signage. Merchandise should be arranged for easy access and for easy inter-brand comparisons. Also, correct price and brand shelf tags should allow easy evaluation, and comparable size and quality brands (including store brands) should be placed side-by-side for easy comparison. Finally, items should not be out of stock.

In-store Information and Assistance Merchandise selection ease provides efficiency in the self-selection of items, and most stores in the Western world are organized for self-selection. But beyond ease of self-selection, consumers sometimes need information and assistance from salespersons (for example, to see a product demonstration). They expect salespersons to be knowledgeable and fair and impartial in their advice. Assortment and knowledgeable salespersons are distinguishing features of some stores such as Modern Sound in Brazil.

Convenience Consumers also want convenience in getting to the store and getting out of it once they have selected their merchandise. Consumers are satisfied if the store location, parking availability, and checkouts (customer service) are convenient. Once a consumer has completed his or her product selection, nothing is more important to the consumer than to be able to checkout and go home as soon as possible.[24]

Have you noticed how some big supermarkets now have a separate entrance and independent checkout for the pharmaceutical, banking, and dairy departments? If you want to buy just a gallon of milk, you don't want to waddle your way through the labyrinthine aisles to go to the back of the store; you would rather just go to a convenience mart like Seven-Eleven or C-Space (South Korea).

PRICE VALUE
(As consumers see it)
- If there is a number in a store sign (Buy 6 for a dollar), shoppers buy more.
- Signs with suggestive selling (e.g., buy 12 for the weekend) increased consumer purchases.
- Signs with high purchase limits (e.g., limit 12 per family) doubled the number of purchases a shopper made.
- Multiple Unit pricing (3 for $3 vs. 1 for $1) increased sales by 35%.

As reported in: Wansink, Brian, Robert J. Kent, and Stephen J. Hoch (1998), "An Anchoring and Adjustment Model of Purchase Quantity Decisions," *Journal of Marketing Research*, 35:1 (February), 71-81.

Problem Resolution When consumers need problem resolution or a remedy for a store's mistakes or oversights, they want this service to be easy and hassle-free. Stores that have a liberal return policy, allowing consumers to return unused merchandise within a reasonable time, or stores that will repair or replace faulty merchandise within a reasonable time, even beyond the warranty period, are likely to earn consumers' repeat patronage.

Personalization By personalization, we mean positive employee behavior toward consumers. Stores that hire employees with poor interpersonal skills and low aptitude for socialization with consumers are likely to earn less loyalty from their consumers. For many consumers, personal attention from salespersons is very important, and it is expected from upscale stores like Lord & Taylor or Hermès. But personalization is a matter of attitude and culture, not of pricy sophistication.

Atmospherics Finally, a factor we have already defined before, atmospherics means the physical setting and ambience of the store. Atmospherics influence the whole shopping experience. And the shopping experience in itself, quite apart from the products one buys at the store, can be of inherent value, and a pull toward the store.

Perdu by Day

Another view of Perdu, a Lingerie store in Saudi Arabia. Worth visiting just for its *atmospherics*

A MODEL OF STORE BRAND CHOICE

Who Buys Store Brands?

Keep your store manager's hat on for just a little while more. There is one more model, learning which will pay off—the model of who buys store brands. Store brands are, you may recall, one of the factors in winning customer loyalty. There is money to be made in store brands. There is only one snag: not everyone is lured by store brands. If you knew who was and why, you would be able to milk your store brand program for better profits. Fortunately, consumer researchers have the answer.

Two studies, one from the U.S. and the other from the U.K., explored this issue. In the U.S. study, 582 shoppers were surveyed about their purchase of 28 product categories (e.g., bacon, soups, juices, frozen vegetables, paper towels, laundry detergents, etc.). The study found that consumers who bought store brands came from larger families and lower-income groups. But the buyers and non-buyers of store brands did not differ on age and education levels. Consumers who bought store brands (compared to those who did not) saw store brands as a better "perceived value for the money" and did not see any risk in buying store brands. They were also more tolerant of ambiguity.[25]

In the U.K. study, 1000 grocery shoppers were surveyed. All consumers perceived national brands to be superior to store brands in terms of quality, packaging, consistency, and image, but store brands were perceived to be a "better value for the money." Naturally, then, consumers to whom value-for-the-money was more important were the ones who bought store brands. These consumers were somewhat less educated, were younger, were of lower socio-economic status, and had at least one child living at home. There was one more interesting difference: store brand shoppers shopped more frequently and longer. Obviously, they were comparison shoppers who shopped often, looking for deals and taking advantage of sales. Figure 13.7 pulls together these factors.

FIGURE 13.7 A MODEL OF STORE BRAND BUYING

"WHO" FACTORS	STORE BRAND BUYING	"WHY" FACTORS
Lower socio-economic status		Motivation to save money
Larger families/Families with children		Better value for money
Price sensitive/Comparison shoppers		Quality gap not significant

MY CB BOOK

MARKETING IMPLICATIONS

Almost all of the concepts and factors we covered in this chapter have implications for marketing managers. Consumer motivations for shopping, factors in store choice, store image, store brands—each concept and each model suggests how to fashion your store so as to appeal to your target market. We choose three of them here to reiterate and to highlight managerial recommendations: Impulse buying, atmospherics, and store loyalty.

Milking Consumers' Impulsivity

The products that lend themselves to be purchased impulsively have four characteristics: (1) they are small ticket items—so that money does not become a major constraint; (2) they are sensory products, creating an immediate "fatal attraction" (i.e., candy, drinks, and magazines with sensational headlines on the cover); (3) they do not require detailed feature evaluation, so an impulse purchase is feasible; and (4) they are consumable immediately—perhaps as soon as we pay for them. Thus, impulse buying is immediately going to satisfy the motive that started the process to begin with—instant gratification. Accordingly, placement of such items for easy visibility in the store is a key factor.

Crafting Store Atmospherics

When consumers are just browsing for joy, the mood and the emotion of the moment play a crucial role. This mood is created by store atmospherics—so pay attention to the lights and sounds in the store you manage. The store ambience, the aesthetics, and the demeanor of salespersons can affect whether consumers make the unintended purchase or leave the store quickly.[26] It is within your power as a store manager to design and create an atmosphere that encourages browsing and impulse buying.

Winning Customer Loyalty

There are four "what" factors and six "how" factors that drive customer loyalty to stores. Among the four "what" factors, as a store manager you need to decide on which factor you will differentiate your store. With some merchandise savvy, you can combine all four—for example, Target store carries designer brands from celeb designers made exclusively for Target, such as the clothing styles by Alexander McQueen. These designer brands capture good quality, add to assortment, are offered, compared to high-fashion boutiques, at alluring price points, and give store-brand exclusivity. Other stores seek to differentiate themselves on "how" factors: best Buy on knowledgeable store employees, Amazon.com on convenience (one-click shopping cart), Nordstrom on personalization, etc. Now put your store manager's hat on. And decide which factor(s) you will harness to win your customers' loyalty.

SAVVY MARKETER

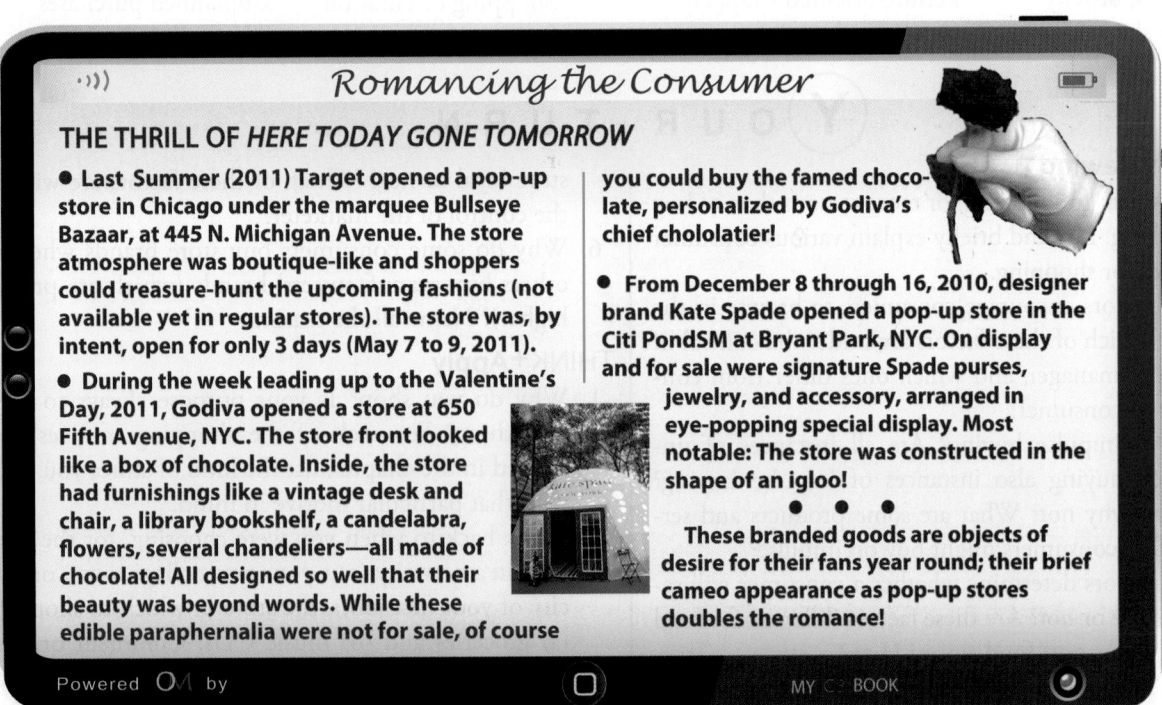

Romancing the Consumer

THE THRILL OF HERE TODAY GONE TOMORROW

● Last Summer (2011) Target opened a pop-up store in Chicago under the marquee Bullseye Bazaar, at 445 N. Michigan Avenue. The store atmosphere was boutique-like and shoppers could treasure-hunt the upcoming fashions (not available yet in regular stores). The store was, by intent, open for only 3 days (May 7 to 9, 2011).

● During the week leading up to the Valentine's Day, 2011, Godiva opened a store at 650 Fifth Avenue, NYC. The store front looked like a box of chocolate. Inside, the store had furnishings like a vintage desk and chair, a library bookshelf, a candelabra, flowers, several chandeliers—all made of chocolate! All designed so well that their beauty was beyond words. While these edible paraphernalia were not for sale, of course you could buy the famed chocolate, personalized by Godiva's chief chololatier!

● From December 8 through 16, 2010, designer brand Kate Spade opened a pop-up store in the Citi Pond℠ at Bryant Park, NYC. On display and for sale were signature Spade purses, jewelry, and accessory, arranged in eye-popping special display. Most notable: The store was constructed in the shape of an igloo!

● ● ●

These branded goods are objects of desire for their fans year round; their brief cameo appearance as pop-up stores doubles the romance!

Powered OM by   MY C BOOK

SUMMARY

We began this chapter with a discussion of consumer motives to go shopping. Consumers generally shop to make a purchase. Often, however, other motives also exist. These include recreation, socialization, status seeking, self-gratification (i.e., rewarding oneself by spending some money on oneself), and acquiring market information.

We next discussed three types of purchases: planned, unplanned, and impulse. Consumers do not always buy just what they planned to buy. Rather, unplanned and impulse purchases also occur. Several in-store factors play an important role in a consumer's shopping experience; they also account for whether or not unplanned and impulse purchases would occur. These factors include knowledge of the store, time pressure, special store promotions, store atmospherics, consumer mood, and whether there is a shopping companion. Impulse buying was defined as a spur of the moment decision, and we identified the kinds of products that are more likely to be bought as impulse purchases. We introduced browsing as a necessary activity that precedes unplanned and impulse buying, and we identified factors that promote browsing. Marketers can harness these factors to encourage browsing and, consequently, unplanned buying.

For every marketer, it is important to understand how consumers choose stores for shopping. Consumers choose stores based on location and distance as their first criterion, but this criterion is tempered by a consideration of other factors: quality, assortment, and price. These factors lead consumers to choose a repertoire of stores at which they usually shop. We presented a flow chart model of how consumers identify this repertoire and then utilize it.

We then presented a model of store loyalty, accounting for factors that induce consumers to become store loyal. These included "what" factors—what consumers get in the store—and "how" factors—how efficient and pleasing they find the experience of shopping. One of the "what" factors is *store brands*. So, next, we considered why consumers buy or do not buy store brands. Our model explains that store brand buying is more predominant among consumers who have large families, come from lower socio-economic strata, and are price sensitive. They buy store brands, motivated by a need to save money, and because they do not see product quality as significantly lower. They also see store brands as a better value for their money. Because store brands can be quite appealing in building store loyalty, store managers should understand these factors that influence consumer purchasing of store brands.

KEY TERMS

Assortment	Forward buy	Planned purchases	Store image
Atmospherics	Impulsive consumer behavior	Self-selection	Store personality
Browsing	In-store factors	Shopping	Task-oriented shoppers
Consumer impulsivity	Leisure-oriented shoppers	Shopping orientation	Unplanned purchases
Exploratory shopping	One-stop shopping	Store environment	Wayfinding

YOUR TURN

REVIEW+Rewind

1. Consumers go shopping for more reasons than to buy something. List and briefly explain various consumer motives for shopping.
2. What factors encourage consumers to browse in the store? Which of these factors are under the control of the store manager, and which ones differ from consumer to consumer?
3. What is impulse buying? Are all instances of unplanned buying also instances of impulse buying? Why or why not? What are some products and services that consumers might buy on impulse?
4. What factors determine whether a consumer will select a store or not? Are these factors different for food stores versus non-food stores? How?
5. What factors explain whether a consumer would be store loyal or not? Which of these factors are within the control of the marketer?
6. Why do some consumers buy store brands whereas others buy manufacturers' brands (which are priced higher)? Name all the reasons.

THINK+Apply

1. Why do you shop? Is your purpose always to buy something? For each of the shopping motives described in the chapter, list the kind of stores you visit with that particular motive in mind.
2. Think back to when you were choosing, for the first time in a new city (say, your new college town, or the city of your first job,), the store in which to shop for (a) groceries and (b) music CDs. Comment on the extent to which the store choice flow chart described in this chapter captures your own process.

CB Blog

Modern Day Malls: Fantastic Third Places For Consumers

In mankind's history of thousands of years, only a hundred or so years ago, if someone said "I am going shopping," it would have meant only one thing: That person was going to the market to buy something. (By some accounts, John Wanamaker's Philadelphia store, opened in 1877, is considered to be the origin of the modern day department store.) In some developing countries, this has been the case as recently as 20 or so years ago. But in a substantial part of the world and for a majority of consumers today, this phrase has now come to mean a multi-faceted event. Spending money and buying is a part of it, sometimes, not always. But the event full-blooms as a diversion: it is to meet friends, to hang out with them; to do some people-watching. It is also to discover new objects of desire—dresses, stilettos, colognes, books, music CDs, gadgets, body-pampering potions, and more. And it is, in general, just to soak up the atmosphere—listen to the sounds, take in the aromas, the colors, textures, and shapes of the merchandise and of the surrounding spaces we call *malls*.

For a modern day consumer, it may be difficult to imagine what life would be without the modern day shopping spaces. Ostensibly, the raison d'être of department stores, and now malls, is to enable one-stop shopping; in practice, however, their real worth springs from their ability to serve a larger societal purpose: because of their large physical space, on one hand, they allow for a degree of anonymity infeasible in a mom-and-pop store. On the other hand, they serve as "public spaces"—for people to meet, chat, mingle, watch, walk, sit, hang out, and yes, not infrequently, buy something. In fact, many consumers today "live" so much of their lives just hanging out at these malls, stores, and cafes that some have called these public spaces "third places" (after homes and offices).

Now there is no turning back. These days and going forward, consumers will do much of their nonessential buying only in these "fantasy marketspaces." And marketers—retail stores—had better offer them. The experience they offer customers in these marketspaces will help them sell their wares. But even more important, they will serve a larger societal purpose at the same time, namely, making enjoyable spaces available to the public. The modern mall, then, performs a great public service—bringing citizens the small delights of diversions in the world of goods, without necessarily having to buy them.

MY CB BOOK .COM

3. Apply the model of store loyalty to yourself and discuss which "what" and "how" factors apply to your own behavior in patronizing stores for the following products: (a) clothing, (b) music, (c) cereals, (d) books, (e) electronic equipment, and (f) haircuts.

4. As a store manager, you just read the model of store loyalty described in this chapter. You are excited because you believe you have found the key to making your customers loyal to your store. Briefly outline your action plan.

5. As a store manager, how would you improve the chances that consumers living in your area will choose your store rather than the one across the street?

6. As a store manager, what would you do to encourage consumers to browse while they visit your store?

PRACTICE+Experience

1. Interview five consumers to understand their store selection process for supermarkets. For each consumer, create a flow chart of his or her store selection process similar to the flow chart shown in the chapter.

2. Interview a few consumers on their recent impulse purchases. For each such purchase, probe the circumstances and thought processes that led to the purchase. Does the three-factor model of impulse buying hold for the consumers you interviewed? Comment briefly on why or why not.

In the Marketing Manager's Shoes

Put yourself in a marketing manager's shoes. Most concepts in the chapter have some lessons for the marketing manager; i.e., they suggest what to do differently in practice. Indeed, often these applications are implicit in our explanations of the concepts and models in the chapter. Identify at least five specific applications of the chapter's concepts, all of which should be entirely new, different from the examples cited here.

14 Gender and Age in Consumer Behavior

Two Permanent Markers of Our Identities

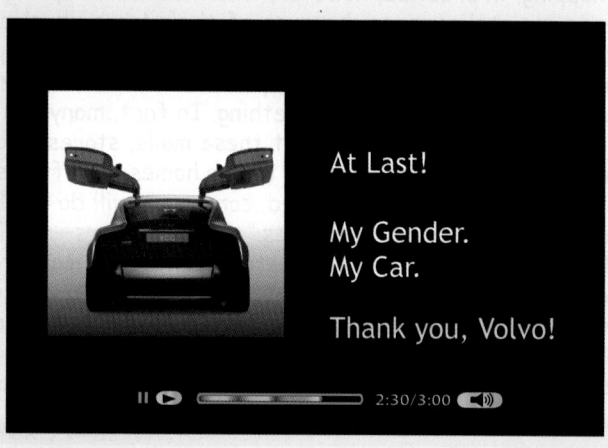

At Last!

My Gender.
My Car.

Thank you, Volvo!

2:30/3:00

LEARN . APPLY . EXPERIENCE

OBJECTIVES

1 The Concept of Gender Role Identity and Gender Identity Consumption

2 The Differences Between Men and Women in Shopping, Consuming, and Gift-Giving

3 Metrosexuals, Retrosexuals, Pomosexuals, and Übersexuals

4 Boomers to Teens— Age Segments in Consumer Populations

5 Family Life Cycle, the influence of children in Household Purchase Decisions and IGI

6 The Big Picture of Age and Sex, and How These Markers Affect Our Life as Humans and as Consumers

I Am A Normal Woman But Marketers Seem Not To Notice!

I am satisfied with most of my body. I have always liked my face, my hair, and my upper body. I am confident in a social environment and like when other people look at me while I am walking by. Clothes are something I really enjoy because I like to get dressed up. Also, I enjoy makeup and jewelry, anything that brings out my femininity.

It is my lower body that causes me some anguish. My mood changes drastically from good to miserable whenever I go shopping in search of a pair of pants. It seems that pants only look good in sizes 2 to 4, at least when they are on mannequins. When I pick up a size 8 and hold it up side-by-side a size 4, for some reason, size 8 just doesn't hold up to size 4. Size 8 looks big, saggy and out of shape, while size 4 looks elegant, long legged, and fashionable. When I try on the size 8, the pants would fit in width but are too long for me. What had looked so good on the mannequin in the display when I entered the store now appears so unfit on my body.

Isabell Haage battling fitting room blues in a store

"Do I have the wrong body?" I ask myself. I start questioning whether I am abnormal. And while I can escape being exposed to the ultra-thin models in advertising, I cannot escape the fact that most fashionable label clothes are designed for exactly those ultra-thin models. Why do fashion designers force average sized women into stretch jeans, which only look good when they are not "stretched" by the rather strong thighs of a normal woman? Shouldn't it be the objective of a clothing company to make its customers look good and feel happy? I don't feel happy when I want to buy pants. I feel frustrated and vulnerable. At that moment, I am nothing like the person who likes herself when looking into the mirror.

I think that most women for whom appearance is important become more depressed with their bodies after viewing very skinny models. I should perhaps not go shopping at certain stores anymore. Why do advertising and fashion magazines convey that those stores, which don't design their clothes to fit my normal body, are hip and trendy? Are the marketers supposed to cater only to skinny models? Do they not know that a majority of women are "normal" women, just like me? Or don't they know what normal women want?

Can you make clothes that fit my "normal" body?

INTRODUCTION

Isabell speaks for a lot of women. Her anguish is shared by "normal-sized" women everywhere. At least two marketers have heard their call, loud and clear—Nike and Unilever's Dove brand. More on them later. The point to note presently is that consumers' gender influences their product desires and preferences. Popular literature also suggests that men and women consume differently and they shop differently as well.

Men don't shop; they don't clean; they don't cry; they don't connect. Women shop; they find fulfillment in home-making; they build relationships. On and on, the stereotyped gender images persist. We will study these stereotypes as well as the new roles that modern-day men and women are assuming and how it is changing their consumption and shopping patterns. Gender (actually, *sex*—see below) is a fixed characteristic that deeply affects our consumption behaviors. Two other unalterable characteristics are our age and our ethnic identity. Together, these three characteristics influence our consumption behaviors and differentiate one consumer from another. We will discuss the first two of these individual differences (as well as a third demographic formed by the combination of these two, namely, *family*) in this chapter (leaving ethnicity for the next chapter). Let's begin with gender.

GENDER

Men Are from Mars, Women Are from Venus

First, a clarification. The terms "sex" and "gender" are sometimes used interchangeably but mean different things. Sex is defined as "either of the two major forms of species that differ biologically and are typically referred to as *male* or *female*; in contrast, "gender" refers to the roles and traits typically associated in a society with one or the other sex.[1] Thus, sex is biological; gender is sociological. We will use the word "gender" to refer to both.

Every society has men and women, but not in equal numbers. In the world as a whole, their numbers are about equal (male to female ratio, 1.018), but across nations, their ratio varies widely—from 2.2 to 0.84 (see Table 14.1).[2] We can observe vivid differences in their consumer behaviors, but these vary from one society to another. These differences emerge from three sources: (1) biology; (2) motivations and psychology; and (3) socialization and cultural norms.

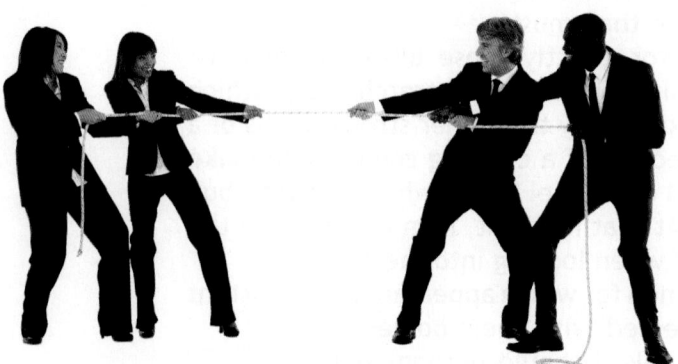

Biology creates different needs in men and women, and some of their consumption is determined by those needs. Popular literature (such as the book *Men Are from Mars, Women Are from Venus*) also suggests that men and women differ in their mental makeup—such as women are more emotional, are more nurturing, and are more motivated to seek long-term relationships. Finally, society socializes men and women into different roles and imposes different expectations for dressing, careers, and domestic responsibilities. Indeed, many of the consumption and behavioral differences attributed to biology and psychological makeup of the two genders are instead culturally induced differences. Cultures and societies have historically assigned women home-making and child-rearing roles; so, popular literature suggests that women have more of a nurturing instinct. Defying old stereotypes, women are now taking up careers historically assigned to men, and men are engaging in home-making and child-rearing tasks. One factor that shapes these changes is gender roles—the social roles assigned to a person based on sex. Let us see how.

GENDER ROLE IDENTITY CONSUMPTION

"Real men don't cry!"

"Real men don't cry." This popular adage is a window to our attitude toward the sexes—our ideas of what men and women are supposed to do. **Gender role identity** refers to how society thinks of a person simply by virtue of the sex of that person. In other words, society says, "you are a man (or woman), so this is how you are supposed to behave." Every person adopts some notion of gender role and molds his/her own behavior and his/her expectations of others based on gender. Gender role identity has two components: (1) work and career, and (2) personality and behavior.[3]

Work and Career

Some societies hold notions about what a man's job is and what a woman's job is. Because these notions are based entirely on gender, these are termed "traditional sex role attitudes." **Traditional sex role attitude** refers to a view that a woman's place is in the home and a man's place is out of home, working and earning a living. In contrast are **egalitarian sex role attitudes**—the view that men and women are both equal and must share equally in all tasks. In this view, women are as entitled to and capable of pursuing a career as men are.

In traditional sex role attitudes, if women work at all, their jobs are usually more subservient roles (e.g., office secretary). In contrast, with the egalitarian sex role attitude, women are viewed as entitled to all sorts of jobs—jobs in the Army, in science and technology, and in influential positions in politics and business. Indeed, recent surveys report just such a trend: many women are employed, while their male spouses are laid off and are assuming the role of male homemaker. In U.S., by 2008, 34.56% of the wives earned more than did their husbands (up from 26.6% in 1090). In Canada, about 31 percent of the wives made more than did their husbands in 2009, a jump from just 12 percent in 1976. And in the U.K., 19% of the wives or girl-friends out-earned their husbands or boy friends.[4]

We must clarify that while the homemaker role was historically assigned to women by traditional sex role attitudes, in modern times not all homemaking reflects traditional sex role attitudes. In many otherwise egalitarian families, women assume the homemaker role simply for practical reasons (e.g., the man in a higher paying job). Although she stays home and assumes the homemaking chores, in all other matters the couple functions as equals, making decisions jointly. If you are a marketer, and if a woman lists her occupation as homemaker, do not assume that she does not play a significant, if not a major, role in important family purchase decisions.

Personality by Gender

People also hold a notion about differences in personalities of women versus men. Men are supposed to exhibit masculine behavior, and women feminine behavior. **Femininity** refers to the personality traits of compassion, sensitivity, and politeness. Persons with these traits tend to value interpersonal relations over self-centered gains. **Masculinity** refers to the personality traits of independence, competitiveness, assertiveness, and instrumentality— valuing things and people merely for their utility.

The overall life orientation of persons with the masculinity traits is **instrumentality**— "how a particular object or person would be useful to me, what it will do for me personally." In contrast, the overall life-orientation of femininity is **expressiveness**—how an object or person facilitates or hinders expression and experience of emotion and interpersonal relations. (See Table 14.2.)

In general, men are more focused on impersonal or individualistic goals, whereas women are more focused on achieving the goals of the groups of which they are members (e.g., family, neighborhood, coworkers, or society). Personal victory is more important to men, whereas women are more concerned with how everybody involved feels in a situation. So, masculinity is focused on achieving goals without concern for the interaction process; in contrast, femininity is focused on goals related to the interaction process itself—that the people involved in the interaction feel good about the outcome.[5]

These traits are gender determinant. This is because, in large part, society channels our socialization according to our biological sex. Men are socialized to possess more masculinity,

TABLE 14.1	SEX RATIO	
(Selected Countries)		
	M/F	Rank
UAE	2.20	1
India	1.08	14
China	1.06	20
Australia	1.01	73
Canada	.98	121
U.K.	.98	12
USA	.97	146
Japan	.95	178
Russia	.85	226
Estonia	.84	228

Note: These are ratios in the total population. At birth they range from 1.133 (highest, China) to .837 (lowest, Nauru). Total population ratios are affected by male vs. female survival rates and net immigration.

CIA WORLD FACT BOOK as used in NationsMaster.com, 2011.

MY CB BOOK

while women are socialized into more feminine roles. Of course, this socialization is not polarized for all people. Some men possess more feminine than masculine traits, and some women possess more masculine than feminine traits.[6]

TABLE 14.2	MASCULINITY & FEMININITY TRAITS	
	MASCULINITY	FEMININITY
Life Orientation	Instrumentality	Expressiveness
Valuing people	For their utility	Just because they are persons
Attitude and behavior	Competitive	Cooperation and harmony
	Independence	Nurture and dependence
	Unemotional in relations	Derive emotional satisfaction in relations with others
	Selfish attitude	Helping attitude

MY CB BOOK

DIFFERENCES IN MEN AND WOMEN AS CONSUMERS

SAVVY MARKETER

One of the popular stereotypes about men as shoppers is that they focus on buying what they went to the store to buy, and they do not look around. Now, this stereotype has been confirmed by extensive observational studies. These studies confirm that men move faster through stores, and do less browsing. "And they also shop the way they drive—never ask for directions!"[7] They like to read the product information on their own. In contrast, women like to get information by asking a store employee. In one study at a wireless phone retailer, men were observed walking into the store, walking up to the product display, reading the product information, taking a brochure and a blank application and walking out to return later. Women, on the other hand, entered the store and walked directly up to the customer service counter, and had all their questions answered by a salesperson.[8] And as an example of focused shopping, men were found to take fewer items of clothing to the fitting or dressing room than did women. (See Table 14.3.)

We should note that many of the differences are relative to a time period and to particular societies. As gender roles change, marketers should be on the lookout for the changing patterns of male/female differences in consumer behavior.

Man or Woman: Who Decides?

In terms of decision-making in the household, for a long while, a stereotypical view has been that men are the principal decision makers for machine-like products—cars, kitchen and laundry appliances, lawn and garden tools, and home building and repair tools; and that women are the main decision makers for products that go into everyday living and homemaking, such as groceries, and kitchen supplies, and home furnishings. This conventional picture needs to be updated in two aspects: First, many products have both functional and aesthetic features, and for these products, women tend to be concerned with aesthetic features (color and style), influencing choices even for products where men take the lead. Second, more and more men as well as women are staying single longer (either never married or divorced). Consequently, product categories that were hitherto the predominant shopping domains of one sex are crossing over to encompass the other sex as well. Thus, men are spending more time in the kitchen and are shopping in the supermarket. Likewise, single women are becoming sole decision-makers—buying cars, appliances, and tools. Seeing this trend, the U.S. home improvement retailer, Home Depot, has positioned itself as a woman-friendly store, offering home improvement in-store classes for women.

TABLE

14.3 MEN VS. WOMEN DIFFERENCES IN SHOPPING

MEN	WOMEN
Finding Merchandise	
Men don't like to ask for directions in the store, but attempt to find it on their own.	Women would readily ask any available store employee, "where is -------------"?
Browsing	
Men move faster in the store and tend not to engage in much browsing. They focus on what they came to buy.	Women move at a relaxed pace and browse through merchandise even if they came to the store with a definite purchase in mind.
Seeking Product Information	
They like to get their product information by reading merchandise tags, pack-labels, brochures, etc.	Women like to get their information not by reading labels., etc., but by asking a salesperson.
Trying Things On	
Men try out what they must. In a clothes store, they will take only a few clothes to the dressing room, the clothes they have already decided to buy provided they will fit. Trying a product is the last stage in their purchase decision.	Whatever be the product—lipsticks, perfume, underwear—women will try a lot of styles or variations. Trying a product is just a part of the consideration process for them, not a final stage in the decision.

SOURCE: Compiled from *Why We Buy: The Science of Shopping*--Updated and Revised for the Internet, *The Global Consumer and Beyond* (Paperback), Paco Underhill, Simon & Schuster; Upd Rev edition, 2008. (Used with permission.)

MY CB BOOK

FOOD, CLOTHING, HOME, AND BEYOND: TASTES BY GENDER

Let us consider principal men-women differences in the three important product areas, food, clothing, and home-making, and then in consumption-at-large.

Food Concerning food, gender differences exist in health-oriented perceptions of foods and beverages. Women tend to buy fresh vegetables more because these are healthier than canned vegetables. Diet foods and diet drinks are also more popular among women than among men. In the 25-34 age group, single men spend more of their food budget (65 percent) away from home compared with women, who spend 55 percent.

Clothing In clothing, some men-women differences exist around the globe (e.g., skirts limited to women except in Scotland), but many differences are culture-based, such as preferences for color, fabric, and style. Bright, full-spectrum colors are usually used for women, whereas men are mostly clothed in white, blue, black, brown, and gray. And women's clothing entails a wider range of styles.

While fashion and public image consciousness may be present to the same degree among men and women alike (although this too varies across cultures), the range of fashion accessories and accoutrements suitable to reflect shades of moods and personality are much broader for women than for men in almost all cultures. Consequently, the drive to obtain a good "fit" (from a psychological standpoint) is generally much more intense among women than among men.

Furthermore, except in a few very liberated cultures, women are also more thoughtful and concerned about what they wear, lest they inadvertently send, by their clothing, a wrong message to men around them. Even though unjustified, the male interpretation of women's clothing as "signaling"—implicitly communicating one's attitudes and desires—is widespread in many cultures. Therefore, in office settings, there are some unwritten rules about what is correct office wear. The marketers of clothing understand these differences. Firms like Anne Klein have gone to the extent of setting up hot lines for women who may need advice about their choice in clothing for the office.

S A V V Y
MARKETER

Home Men-women differences can also be observed in their home style preferences. According to a survey done by Home Furnishings Council, in redecorating their homes, husbands focus mainly on dens (where men generally gather during parties or to watch

The Middle East

India

Oriental

Nigeria

Russia

Mexico

Gender role identities differ across cultures. For women, these gender role identities are reflected, in part, in their clothing styles. Of course, in many cultures, modernization of gender role identities has proceeded alongside the preservation of the norms of modesty in women's clothing.

sports), whereas wives focus on the living room and kitchen, where they spend a lot of time daily. Marketers should be watchful, however, for changes in gender-based preferences since many of the traditional gender roles around the world are changing.

Consumption-at-large Men-women differences permeate many other domains of consumption.[9] For example, one study of U.S. brides and grooms found that brides considered the wedding ceremony itself as the most important event, whereas grooms considered the reception as the key event. Thus, brides considered the wedding dress immensely significant and even sacred, requiring great planning and extensive deliberation. Also greatly significant to the bride was the choice of the church and the minister, the flowers, decorations, and the music. In contrast, grooms saw the success of the wedding more closely associated with a judicious selection of the reception hall, hearty food, and good socialization during the reception.[10]

Men and women also differ in how they look at sexual content in marketing messages differently. Men view sex as recreational and casual; women accept it only as part of romance and commitment.[11] Most sexual ads place sex in a context that is outside of commitment and relationship; therefore men are likely to like sexual ads whereas women tend to feel averse.

One noteworthy point is that men-women differences attenuate with education: the more educated the spouses, the more their preferences tend to converge.[12]

MARKETING IMPLICATIONS

Successful marketers use their knowledge about male-female preferences to meet the needs of both groups of consumers. Today, a large number of men are buying groceries, and women are buying cars. By the early 1990s, women had already become 49 percent of all new-car buyers! Today they exercise an influence on some 80 percent of all new-car sales. So carmakers are paying attention to women's needs. Chrysler Corporation has an advisory committee on the Women's Auto Market. And Volvo has now designed a car entirely for women, although the company would be happy if men like it too (see Case, in

SAVVY MARKETER

this book, titled, "A Car For Women By Women"). The woman-orientation continues in many car show rooms. Some car dealers have built play areas for children and diaper-changing stations in restrooms. And, salespersons are learning not to disregard women who accompany their husbands for car shopping.[13]

Since men's visits to a store are acquisition-focused whereas women's visits are browsing-oriented, men often make very impatient companions when they accompany a woman on shopping trips. While women are still browsing, men just hang around impatiently. It behooves retailers, therefore, especially of women's apparel, to find ways to occupy men. For example, retailers could provide a lounge area with a TV turned on to ESPN or some other sports program channel.

A Concept *Car for Women by Women* from Volvo (Photo courtesy Volvo Corporation)

One more point about men as shoppers is worth noting. Although men don't usually browse, they are not averse to buying what was not on their initial list, if it catches their attention. They are not impulsive but they are not very deliberative either. For instance, when a child accompanying his or her dad makes a request, the dad usually gives in. A well-known retail store researcher, Paco Underhill, describes it thus:

> It is here [in the supermarket], with thousands of products all within easy reach, that you can witness the carefree abandon and restless lack of discipline for which the (male) gender is known…. Giving him a vehicle to commandeer, even if it is just a shopping cart, only emphasizes the potential for guyness in the experience. Throw a couple of kids in with Dad and you have got a lethal combination; he is notoriously bad at saying no when there is grocery acquisitioning to be done. Part of being Daddy is being the provider, after all. It goes to the heart of a man's self-image." (p. 100).[14]

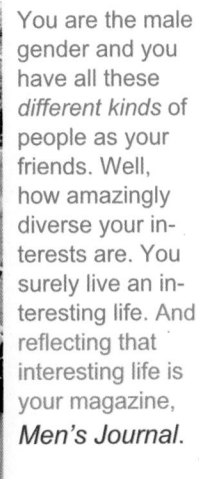

SAVVY MARKETER

As an aside, men make very attractive consumers on one particular shopping day: Valentine's Day. That day, men spend considerably more than do women. In a January 2009 survey by National Retail Federation (NRF), the average amount for an American male consumer was $128 (down from $163 in 2008), versus $78 (down from $84 in 2008) by female consumers.[15]

You are the male gender and you have all these *different kinds* of people as your friends. Well, how amazingly diverse your interests are. You surely live an interesting life. And reflecting that interesting life is your magazine, *Men's Journal*.

'Live the Interesting Life' Advertisement from Men's Journal
© Men's Journal LLC. All Rights Reserved. Reprinted by Permission.

METROSEXUALS, RETROSEXUALS, AND ÜBERSEXUALS

Trends in Male Branding

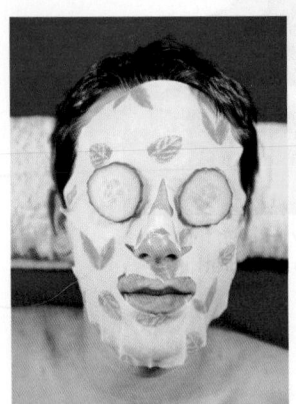

Metrosexuals **Metrosexuals** are urban males who have a strong aesthetic sense and spend a great deal of time and money on their appearances and lifestyles. The term was coined in 1994 by Mark Simpson, a British journalist, to refer to a type of male—a heterosexual man who is in touch with his feminine side. Popular media has illustrated the term by pointing to such celebrities as Brad Pitt, George Clooney, and David Beckham.

If you have browsed (even if only occasionally) men's style magazines such as GQ, Esquire, or The Face, you might have sometimes wondered, "Who wears those dapper, fashionable clothes and extensive accessories?" Wonder no more—it is the metrosexuals. Their excessive grooming also has a new term—**manscaping**. Introduced in 2004 by the American TV Show *Queer Eye for the Straight Guy*, it is shorthand for "landscaping" the male body by shaving, trimming, waxing, or brushing the body hair.[16] The idea of depilating the whole male body was yet unborn until the Queer Eye celebrated this grooming ritual.

Retrosexuals The **Retrosexual** is the anti-metro—a man with a generally poor sense of style. The retrosexual is not necessarily a boor; it is just that he abhors the idea of being finicky about physical appearance. While metrosexuals would chide any male who does not pluck his eyebrows (that would definitely include retrosexuals), retrosexuals would consider metrosexuals positively, scornfully dandies. The retrosexual lifestyle is most popular and socially accepted among men aged 18-24. However, the term is rarely used as a self-descriptor by such men, who tend to prefer, instead, such terms as "real man," or "masculine."

Übersexuals The word "über" has German roots and means above or superior. Thus, an übersexual is a variant of metrosexual, a more "refined" male, who is more confident and more focused on his mind than body. The term was coined by the authors of the book, *Future of Men*, who describe it thus: "The future of men is not to be found in the primped and waxed boy who wowed the world with his nuanced knowledge of tweezers and exfoliating creams. Men, at the end of the day, will have to rely on their intellect and their passion, their erudition and professional success, to be acknowledged and idealized in contemporary society. Called the übersexual—a degree of greatness and perfection, an acknowledgment that this is an evolved species of man—he is so perfect as to leave little margin for error and fallacy."[17]

All these are nifty labels for psychographic types, and for that reason they are immensely useful. Marketers who can decipher and dissect the consumption lifestyles of these types can sight opportunity. What marketing opportunities do you see?

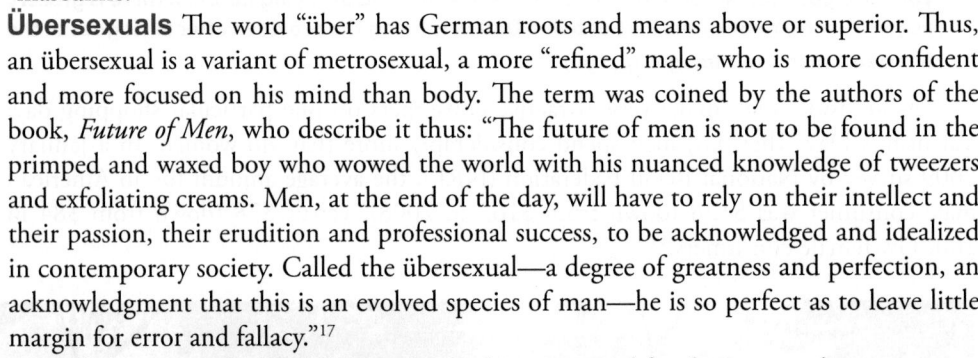

Romancing the Consumer

Woman Magic in Store Design

If you are selling clothing for women, shouldn't your store design revolve around them?

Levi's Jeans for Women's Shop at Macy's Harold Square, New York takes this idea to the apex.

Notice the furniture, the mannequins, the laminated glass panel behind the cashwrap. They all share an alluring feature with the target audience—womanly curves!

In this masterpiece store design by San Francisco's creative design firm Morla Designs, every visual detail is designed to charm its target customer—the woman. Even the script on the carpet has, well, womanly curves—in all shapes and sizes.

MY CB BOOK

Powered OM by

A G E

Why Marketers Want To Know How Old You Are

How old are you? Yes, we know it is impolite to ask. Still, we need to know. We are, you see, the marketer. And in a minute, you will appreciate why it is important for us to know your age.

Let us guess: Looks like you are twenty-one, right? Then you wouldn't be interested in a radio-monitored toy car, would you? Or a video of Frank Sinatra? And your dad, now in his early fifties, wouldn't be interested in a music video of Eminem, Justin Bieber, or Lady Gaga, would he? Your age, you see, has a monumental influence on your behavior as a person and as a consumer. You see it in everyday life—people older than you generally buy different things than what you buy. Likewise, people younger than you are just not interested in many products that interest you. But being or not being interested in a toy here and a music CD there is just the tip of the proverbial iceberg. These differences go deeper: persons of different age groups differ in their abilities, resources, needs, and desires; consequently, they differ in their views of themselves and of the marketplace.

It is important for marketers to understand age-related differences for two reasons. One, since consumer behavior differs sharply across different age groups, marketers often need to fashion their products and marketing programs by age groups. And two, age is the only factor which changes (i.e., increases) simply by the passage of time; so today's 25-year-olds will not stay that way tomorrow. This constant aging of consumers means that marketers must change their marketing programs as well. How?

First, we should adjust our products if we want to serve the same consumers as they age. For example, suppose we want to provide healthcare to Salma, in her 20s, and Alfred, in his 30s, for the rest of their lives. For this, we would need to adjust our healthcare resources and services as they age. To do this, we will need to know, ahead of time, what kind of healthcare will 30, 40, 50, and 60-year-olds need.

Second, suppose we don't want to serve Salma and Alfred as they age; rather, we just want to serve whoever is 20-30-years old. The problem with this is that our market size will fluctuate. For example, if today there are 20 million 20-30-year-olds, then 10 years from now, there could be 25 million of them or only 15 million of them—this depends largely on how many babies were born ten years ago. This will expand or shrink our market opportunity significantly. Are we ready to exploit that expansion, or cope with that shrinkage in the total number of consumers? That is why, as marketers, we need to keep track of age distribution in a population. Let us see how age distribution is changing around the world.

AGE DISTRIBUTION OF POPULATIONS

The Changing Landscape of the Market

If we want to market our products to consumers in any country, the first thing we will (or should) want to know is how many consumers are there. On October 31, 2011, the world population reached 7 billion. The U.N. recognized Danica May Camacho, born in Philippines 3 minutes before the midnight of October 31, 2011, as the 7-billionth baby. (Many other parents from around the world and the governments of their countries also claimed the landmark honor).

As of 2010, the largest population was in China (1.339 billion), with India the second largest (1.184 billion) and U.S.A. was a distant third (309.97 million). (See Table 14.4.)

Do these numbers matter to marketers? To savvy marketers, they do. Kentucky Fried Chicken (KFC), a U.S. based fast food franchise, operates more than 900 stores in China, and earns 15% of its total profits from feeding some 20 million Chinese every day. Guess which country is next on its list? India.

TABLE 14.4

POPULATION

THE TEN LARGEST COUNTRIES (2010)

	MILLION	%
China	1,339	19.22
India	1,184	17.36
USA	310	4.48
Indonesia	234	3.41
Brazil	193	2.74
Pakistan	170	2.55
Nigeria	158	2.27
Bangladesh	164	2.17
Russia	142	2.05
Japan	127	1.84

FIVE OTHER COUNTRIES		
Mexico	113	1.62
UK	62	8.90
S. Africa	50	7.17
Spain	46	6.60
Canada	34	4.88

United Nations Statistical Bureau. October 30, 2011.

MY CB BOOK

China and India are the most coveted consumer markets for many global brands today—Coca Cola and Pepsi, General Electric and Sony, Nestlé and Unilever, to cite just a few. In marketing, such is the magic of large numbers. Large numbers of consumers, that is.

Age Group Distribution Knowing the total number of consumers is, however, just the beginning. The next thing we would want to know as marketers is their age distribution: How many children, how many adults, and how many old people, etc. In U.S., consumers less than 14 years of age are 20.1% of the population. Do you suppose this ratio of young consumers to total population is the same for other countries? The answer is no. In fact, one of the most fascinating aspects of studying different countries' populations is the discovery of how the ratio of old to young people varies.

Table 14.5 gives the age distribution in selected countries for years 2010 and 2030 (projected), arranged here by the percentage of 65 years or older 2030 population. Japan will have the highest percentage of them (29.6%), UAE the lowest (2.32%). Conversely, Japan will have the smallest proportion of children in its population (11.3%), and Niger, the largest (46.9%). Guess where you would want to sell Disney cartoon movies!

Another interesting thing to note here is the projected change in these proportions over the next 20 years. In Brazil, China, and India, the proportion of 65-year-olds will nearly double (rising from 5-9% to 9 to 16%). Conversely, the proportion of other age groups will decline, most noticeably the youngest age group (0-14 years). In Brazil, for example, you start out with 26.2% children in 2010 and will be left with 20.9% in 2030. And in Japan, the young will be in the worlds' smallest minority (11.3%). Guess you will have to convert some of those Disney cartoon movies into artsy operas!

Since this is a wealth of knowledge, you must be eager to know why age distributions vary. Here is why: the total population as well as the age distribution is affected by three factors: birth rate, life expectancy, and migration. As these factors change, so does the age distribution. Most importantly, the aging of the population as seen in Table 14.5 is happening because, globally, the birth rate is declining and the life expectancy is increasing.

POPULATION PYRAMIDS

As Table 14.5 shows, the age composition of a population can change dramatically over time. This shift in population age distribution is captured in **population pyramids**—a layered depiction of males and females by age groups.

These are shown in Figure 14.1, for U.S.A., Canada, the U.K. and Japan, for 2010 and 2050. If you are a marketer in Japan, selling clothing, music, food, cell phones, or whatever, you would realize how dramatically your product offerings and marketing communications (e.g., advertising, personal selling, etc.) will have to change over time, because of changes in the age distribution of your target customers. And, of course, the pyramid is changing in all other countries as well. (See Figure 14.1.)

TABLE 14.5 — AGE DISTRIBUTION of POPULATION for SELECTED COUNTRIES

	2010			2030 (est.)		
	0-14	15-64	65+	0-14	15-64	65+
Japan	13.1	64.0	22.9	11.3	59.2	29.6
Italy	13.8	65.9	20.3	11.9	59.0	29.1
Germany	13.3	66.1	20.6	14.0	59.5	26.6
S. Korea	18.6	72.0	9.4	12.7	63.9	23.4
Canada	15.7	68.5	15.9	15.6	61.1	23.3
U.K.	17.3	66.2	16.5	17.3	61.3	21.4
Australia	18.3	67.7	14.0	17.4	62.0	20.6
U.S.A	20.1	66.8	13.1	18.1	62.6	19.2
China	17.6	73.6	8.9	16.9	66.8	16.3
Brazil	26.2	67.0	6.7	20.9	66.6	12.5
India	29.7	64.9	5.5	22.6	68.1	9.3

Source: CIA World Factbook, 2010

MY BOOK

1925

The year in which India overtakes China in population, crossing 1.394 billion

COUNTRIES of DISTINCTION FOR THEIR POPULATION AGE DISTRIBUTION

0-14

Highest	Uganda	50.1*
Lowest	Hong Kong	13.8

65+

Highest	Monaco	22.8
Lowest	UAE	0.9

* % of population, 2010
(Source: CIA World Factbook)

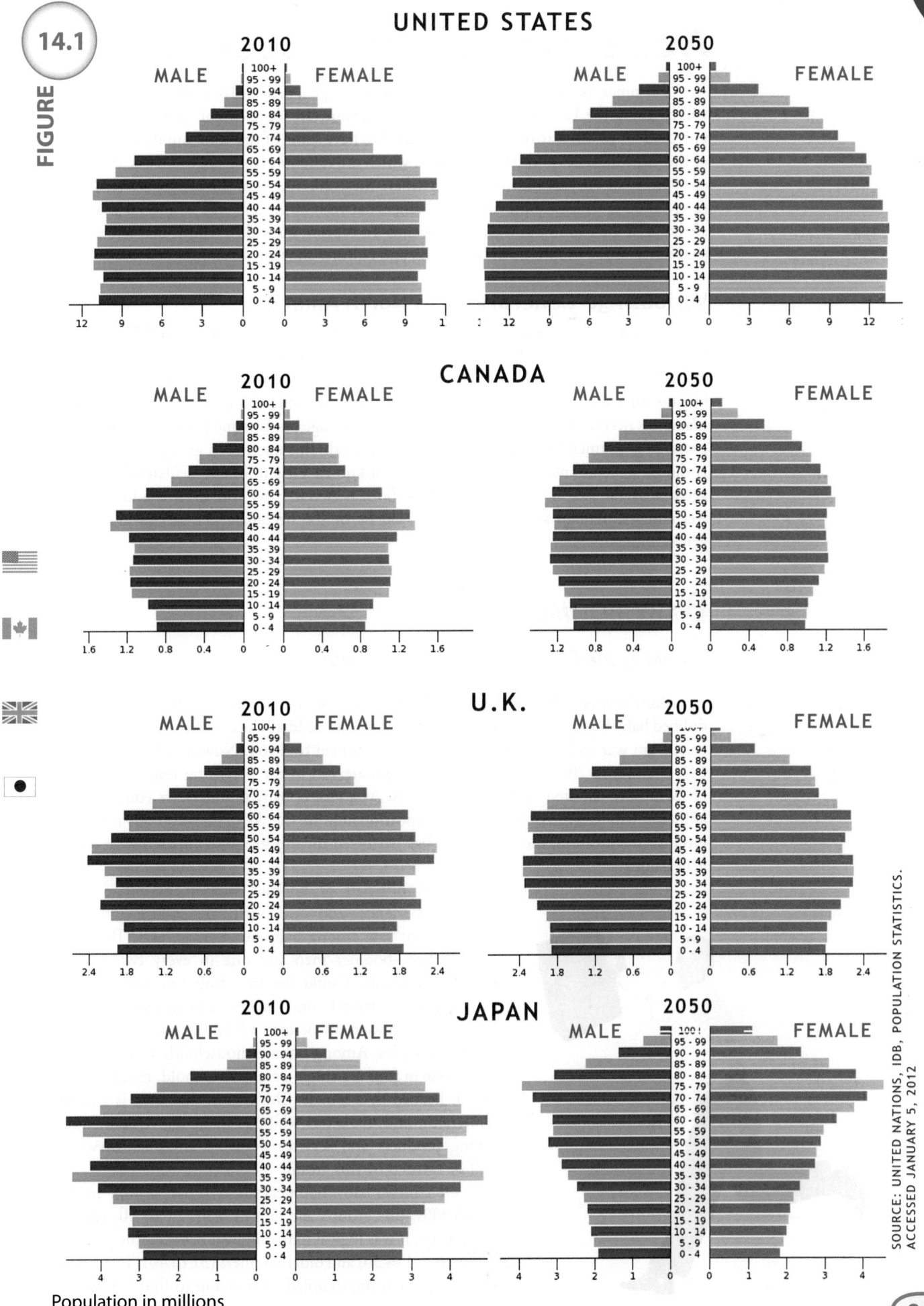

SOURCE: UNITED NATIONS, IDB, POPULATION STATISTICS. ACCESSED JANUARY 5, 2012

FIGURE 14.1

UNITED STATES

2010

MALE   100+   FEMALE
        95 - 99
        90 - 94
        85 - 89
        80 - 84
        75 - 79
        70 - 74
        65 - 69
        60 - 64
        55 - 59
        50 - 54
        45 - 49
        40 - 44
        35 - 39
        30 - 34
        25 - 29
        20 - 24
        15 - 19
        10 - 14
        5 - 9
        0 - 4

12 9 6 3 0   0 3 6 9 1

2050

MALE   100+   FEMALE
        95 - 99
        90 - 94
        85 - 89
        80 - 84
        75 - 79
        70 - 74
        65 - 69
        60 - 64
        55 - 59
        50 - 54
        45 - 49
        40 - 44
        35 - 39
        30 - 34
        25 - 29
        20 - 24
        15 - 19
        10 - 14
        5 - 9
        0 - 4

12 9 6 3 0   0 3 6 9 12

CANADA

2010

MALE   100+   FEMALE
        95 - 99
        90 - 94
        85 - 89
        80 - 84
        75 - 79
        70 - 74
        65 - 69
        60 - 64
        55 - 59
        50 - 54
        45 - 49
        40 - 44
        35 - 39
        30 - 34
        25 - 29
        20 - 24
        15 - 19
        10 - 14
        5 - 9
        0 - 4

1.6 1.2 0.8 0.4 0   0 0.4 0.8 1.2 1.6

2050

MALE   100+   FEMALE
        95 - 99
        90 - 94
        85 - 89
        80 - 84
        75 - 79
        70 - 74
        65 - 69
        60 - 64
        55 - 59
        50 - 54
        45 - 49
        40 - 44
        35 - 39
        30 - 34
        25 - 29
        20 - 24
        15 - 19
        10 - 14
        5 - 9
        0 - 4

1.2 0.8 0.4 0   0 0.4 0.8 1.2 1.6

U.K.

2010

MALE   100+   FEMALE
        95 - 99
        90 - 94
        85 - 89
        80 - 84
        75 - 79
        70 - 74
        65 - 69
        60 - 64
        55 - 59
        50 - 54
        45 - 49
        40 - 44
        35 - 39
        30 - 34
        25 - 29
        20 - 24
        15 - 19
        10 - 14
        5 - 9
        0 - 4

2.4 1.8 1.2 0.6 0   0 0.6 1.2 1.8 2.4

2050

MALE   100+   FEMALE
        95 - 99
        90 - 94
        85 - 89
        80 - 84
        75 - 79
        70 - 74
        65 - 69
        60 - 64
        55 - 59
        50 - 54
        45 - 49
        40 - 44
        35 - 39
        30 - 34
        25 - 29
        20 - 24
        15 - 19
        10 - 14
        5 - 9
        0 - 4

2.4 1.8 1.2 0.6 0   0 0.6 1.2 1.8 2.4

JAPAN

2010

MALE   100+   FEMALE
        95 - 99
        90 - 94
        85 - 89
        80 - 84
        75 - 79
        70 - 74
        65 - 69
        60 - 64
        55 - 59
        50 - 54
        45 - 49
        40 - 44
        35 - 39
        30 - 34
        25 - 29
        20 - 24
        15 - 19
        10 - 14
        5 - 9
        0 - 4

4 3 2 1 0   0 1 2 3 4

2050

MALE   100+   FEMALE
        95 - 99
        90 - 94
        85 - 89
        80 - 84
        75 - 79
        70 - 74
        65 - 69
        60 - 64
        55 - 59
        50 - 54
        45 - 49
        40 - 44
        35 - 39
        30 - 34
        25 - 29
        20 - 24
        15 - 19
        10 - 14
        5 - 9
        0 - 4

4 3 2 1 0   0 1 2 3 4

Population in millions

AGE BASED CONSUMER SEGMENTS

Consumer behaviors differ markedly across age groups. To understand how, we will be using the U.S. as an illustration throughout. To some extent, the differences are universal—i.e., 20-year-olds everywhere tend to have some of the same mindsets and some of the same lifestyles and product tastes, which are different from the mindsets and tastes of 30 or 50 or 70-year-olds, no matter where these 20, 30, 50 or 70-year-olds live. Just as surely, though, at least some of the differences between 20 and 30 and 50 and 70-year-olds are going to be country and culture specific. To capture these differences, marketers must study diverse age groups in the countries and cultures they are serving.

Various Age Generations in North America

In many ways, a young person (say, 25-year-old) fifty years ago behaved like a young person behaves today, and this young person in turn behaves today just like a 25-year-old will behave 50 years from now. At the same time, there are important differences simply because that was then and this is now. Therefore, to understand consumer psychology, marketers need to divide the population not only by age but by time period and examine a group of consumers born in a particular time period. This manner of grouping consumers is called "generations." For example, the well-known Generation X is identified not by age but by the year of its birth. Everyone born between 1964 and 1976 is a Generation Xer and will remain so no matter how old he or she becomes. Let us consider major generations.[18]

BABY BOOMERS

Seeking the Fountain of Eternal Youth

Born between 1946 and 1964, baby boomers number about 76 million.[19] They were dubbed baby boomers because in 1946 the birth rate suddenly sky-rocketed (soldiers came back from war and made, well, babies!) and subsided by 1964. Now middle-aged (46 to 64 years old, in 2010), the youngest of them are still in the parenting trap—about half of them have children under the age of 18. As a group, baby boomers are educated and affluent. This group contributes disproportionately to the $75,000-$200,000+ income groups. In education, the gender gap has narrowed for this group, compared with earlier generations.

About one-half of boomer women have had some college experience, and one-fourth are college graduates. Employment rate among baby boomers is high. Three out of four baby-boomer men and one in every two women have full-time jobs. Unlike the preceding generations, nearly four out of five baby-boomer women are employed outside the home.[20] About 60 percent of boomer households are married couples. Among boomer households with children, about one in four is a single-parent household, mostly (9 out of 10) headed by a female. This means that time is a major constraint, and marketers who can make convenient, time-saving products and services available anytime, anywhere will be favored by this group.

Of course, baby boomers are a broad group. In the mid-1980s, this group's age ranged from 21 to 40. During these years, it was logical to distinguish between the younger boomers (21 to 30) and older boomers (31 to 40). The former group was then preoccupied with trying to find a good job and a marriage partner. Their older cohorts were living a more settled life. In the 1990s, and even more so in the new millennium, the two groups became more similar, as most had the responsibilities of parenting and home ownership. The spending patterns for most baby boomers became similar, driven by the needs and wants of their children, including the need to save for college.

One phenomenon many of the baby boomers are experiencing in the new millennium has resulted in their being dubbed the "Sandwich Generation"[21]—a generation sandwiched between the twin burdens of caring for their own children as well as their aging parents. This latter burden is becoming heavier due to the fact that many of the seniors are living well into 90 years of age and beyond (due to improved life expectancy), and they are becoming the responsibility of their adult children, the baby boomers.

Now, in the second decade of the new century, the oldest of the baby boomers, say those born between 1946 and 1955, have entered their empty-nest years, freed from the burdens of child-rearing. This has freed them to spend both money and time more on themselves and also accelerate their investment in retirement plans. These older boomers will once again differ from their younger cohorts. Thus, baby boomers are a moving target, and marketers must learn to move along with them.[22]

The baby boomers are the most self-absorbed of all four generations. They have been preoccupied with career and material success. But now they have a new obsession, and it is one that cuts across both the groups (the younger and the older baby boomers)—it is to defy aging. Their number one concern these days is looks. Psychologically, they don't feel old, so physically, they don't want to look old. In a survey, boomers expressed the least satisfaction about their appearance. Only 39 percent of boomers felt happy about their appearance (compared to 53% among their seniors and 45% among their juniors).

BOOMERS

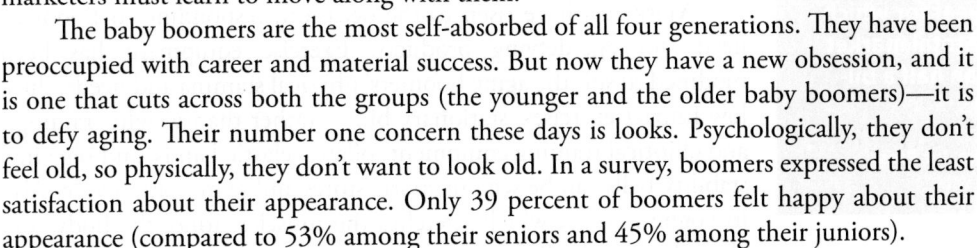

Sandwich Generation

Most self-absorbed

Age defiant

Financial Planning (At last)

The obsession with youthful looks has baby boomers searching for the proverbial fountain of youth. In a recent survey by the AARP (American Association of Retired Persons), half of the boomers admitted having depressive thoughts about aging, and one in every five reported that they were doing something to resist it. That something entails a three-pronged attack: (1) exercise and dieting, (2) nutrients and chemicals—pills, creams, and gulps, (3) surgical augmentations.

1. **Exercising and Dieting** Increasingly, Boomers are taking to exercise and diet, driven as much by a desire to look good as the desire to be healthy. About 33 million Americans go to the gym and more than half of them are over 40. Health clubs are now targeting the so-called "New Me's" and "Second Chancers,"—body conscious and divorced Boomers who want to look young again. Both gyms and spas and home exercise equipment companies are fast growing businesses.

2. **Nutrients, Cosmetics, and Chemicals** The second front in the Boomer's war against aging is the use of nutrients, cosmetics, and chemicals. Nutrients work on the body internally to keep cells healthy; cosmetics and chemicals work externally to mask the signs of aging. U.S. consumers spend about $30 billion on these anti-aging products every year. Boomers are increasingly consuming health pills ranging from ginko biloba for mental alertness, glucosamine for joints, and coEnzyme Q10, which some call the miracle vitamin of the 1990s. Anti-aging creams are also popular—35% of women have used some age-defying cream such as Nivea's Visage or Neutrogena's Visibly Firm. Then, there is hair color—designed to hide the unflattering gray. Fifty three percent of Boomer women use hair color to hide their graying hair (not counting women who use it to alter their color from non-gray to other shades); among men, 6% of them use hair color and their ranks are growing.

3. **Surgical and Medical Procedures** The last and most recent front in the anti-aging war is various medical and surgical procedures to actually alter the appearance

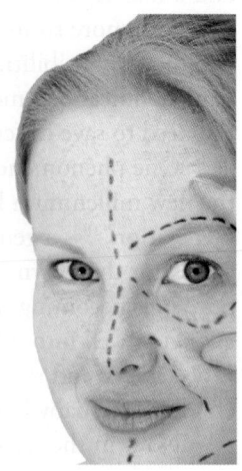

of the body and face. Americans spent nearly $10.7 billion on cosmetic procedures in 2010, of which $6.6 billion was spent on surgical procedures. Since 1997, there has been 71% increase in surgical and 228% increase in non-surgical cosmetic procedures. Although women accounted for 92% of all cosmetic procedures, even among men total cosmetic surgeries had an increase of 88% since 1997.

Marketers are paying close attention to this booming opportunity. Christie Brinkley was a model for Covergirl brand of cosmetics during the 1970s and 80s; the company recently brought back the 51-year-old superstar. Why? To appeal to Boomer women!

MARKETER RESPONSE

Marketers have risen to the occasion, responding to Boomers' needs for age-defying products. Exercise equipment has been modified to suit the aging boomers' physical stamina and needs; thus, low impact exercises, stationary bikes (rather than weight training), and elliptical training equipment, pilates, elastic bands, and big vinyl stability balls can be seen in sports stores and gyms nationwide. Also in vogue is yoga, which stretches the muscles, tones the body, and also relaxes and relieves stress.

Sports equipment itself is seeing a "facelift" and "liposuction" as well. For example, Wilson Sports has brought out a trimmed, lighter weight tennis racket and golf clubs. Solomon, a maker of skis, has come out with "lighter" skis, and even Nike has a line of shoes and clothing with "leaner mass" for the aging Boomer bodies.

Functional foods are now a $30 billion business. These include organic foods, soy milk, and new formulations of cereals (such as General Mills' Harmony that is enriched with antioxidants). There is even a new name for the product category: Nutraceuticals. These are new beverages fortified with nutrients: Aquafina Essential, Reebok Fitness Waters, and SoBe Beverages. With these cool sounding names, they are simultaneously healthy and trendy.

Gen X

- Avoid rat race
- Family Life
- Gender Equality
- Financial Planning (Already)

GENERATION X
X-ing Boomer Values

After the boomers came this next group, born between 1965 and 1975. Because they represent those born during the years of low birth rate, thus busting the sharp growth of the preceding baby-boomer era, they are sometimes also called "baby busters." And, due to their negation of most boomer values, they also have been dubbed *Generation X*. More than any other generation, Gen X are pragmatics, not ideologues. Their image of the boomers is that of Woodstock—that the boomers had a big party and didn't clean up.

The psychological makeup of Xers differs from that of boomers. Baby boomers, whether younger or older, came of age when the U.S. economy was sound. Therefore, boomers have been optimistic and have had confidence in their ability to succeed. The Xers feel, on the other hand, financially less secure. They also rejected the boomers' obsession with career and making money. Instead, they sought to work just enough to get by, and for this reason, and somewhat unfairly, they got dubbed as *slackers*.

Numbering some 45 million, the majority of them are in the workforce and also in the family formation and child rearing stage. And they want to raise their family differently than their parents did. A significant proportion of them experienced being "home alone," and many grew up in broken homes (due to divorced parents). They want to raise their children in two-parent families; therefore, dual-careers are less important to them. Many of them believe that one parent should stay home with the children. Gen X men are more involved than men from preceding generations in child rearing, and more of them are advocates of equal gender roles. With family-building, Gen Xers are realizing their financial responsibility and a majority of them (68% by a recent estimate) have already begun to save for their retirement (not far behind the 77% of Boomers today, although boomers didn't begin thinking about saving for retirement when they were as young as Gen Xers are today).

Of course, not all Gen Xers are slackers (and they never were). Many are shaking off that moniker with upward careers.

Xers' major purchases today comprise of setting up a home—house buying, appliances, furnishings, etc. The youngest of them are starting out or have recently started a career and are first time buyers of a new car. Their partaking of music, concerts, pubs, fast food and restaurants—which filled their consumer lives of the student days—is slowing as they settle down.

GENERATION Y
The Most Globally Homogeneous

Born between 1977 and 1984, Gen Y get their name simply because they followed Gen X. Actually, there is no consensus on whom to count as Generation Y. Some authors start counting from 1985, and some authors extend it to those born in 1995. Depending on how one counts, this group can range from 35 to 70 million. However, our profile below will focus on the group born between 1977 and 1984—this was the group that marked a departure from the previous two generations.

Gen Y—Ethnically the most open-minded

Like Gen X, Gen Y has disowned the Boomer values of self-absorption and materialism. But they do differ from Gen X on an important aspect. Gen X did not adopt any alternative ideology, staying uninvolved in any social issues. In contrast, Gen Y is ideological, embracing social issues such as environmentalism, animal treatment, vegetarianism, racial integration, etc. Growing up in the age of the computer (when home PCs are widespread), and coming of age in the era of the Internet, they are the most tech savvy of all generations. You can see them in constant chatter with their friends on their cell phones, on Myspace, Facebook, and Bebo, and via emails, sharing stories, music, and photos. They are the most ethnically inter-mingling, and more than any other generation, they exhibit global homogeneity. Today, youth everywhere dress alike, listen to the same music, and share the same chat rooms.

Gen Y

Globally alike

Tech savvy

Cynical of ad hype

Social Issues

Some 35 million in number, these 22 to 29-year-olds can be found mostly on college campuses, military bases, in their first jobs in corporations, in their parental homes, and, as shoppers, in stores like Express, Abercrombie & Fitch, and J. Crew. Their individual buying power is small, but collectively it is a large sum, totaling more than $200 billion. The older of them have joined the workforce and now make their own money to participate fully in the marketplace. The younger of them still get some allowance from home or make some money doing odd jobs. With it, they buy clothes (e.g., T-shirts, baseball caps), shoes, athletic wear, team sport memorabilia, fast food, books, movies, cell phones and personal items, and they patronize restaurants and bars.

According to a recent report, nearly half of the never married adults aged 20 to 25 live with their parents. Many return after a brief sojourn living out of the home. They find

Targeting Gen 'Y;

living at home attractive because food is generally free, and the rent is either waived or subsidized, and chores are also shared. Many who live at home are motivated to save and build their bank accounts so that they can buy a car, or when they get a job, they can afford the down payment on a house. All youth, whether they live at home, on college campuses, or at military bases, differ from their boomer parents (although they are in many respects, similar to Gen Xers.)

Their music is not rock 'n' roll or classic rock or retro; instead, it is rap, urban rhythm and blues, and industrial dance music. They will be known most for embracing hip hop as a mainstream music style—it is they who made white rapper Eminem's *8 Mile* a box office hit. They wear clothing that ranges from punk to preppie, from sloppy grunge to environment-friendly eco shirts. They are dead serious about getting a job and about getting an education so they may get a job—unlike their parents (Boomers) who were sometimes in college just for the experience, or to engage in political protest and reform. Social issues have a big appeal for today's youth. Issues like the environment, drug abuse, AIDS, and discrimination arouse young people, and young adults reward those businesses that support such social causes. Another important characteristic of this group is its dislike of hype in advertising. They dislike overstatement, hypocrisy, and false pretense of status image for the advertised products. To them, a product must be advertised and sold on its utility, rather than hype. This is not to imply that Gen Yers don't buy for image, but the image is the one they give a product, and the one they perceive from their social observations and from peer groups, not the one that the advertising hypes. And they reject conspicuous consumption.

TEENAGERS

The Early Consumer Socialization

TEENS

- Wanna look a bit older
- Addicted to small-screen
- Learn the buying skills early
- Internet market mavens

Also called *millennials*, because they came of age in the new millennium (i.e., those born after 1981) teens are a significant consumer segment for marketers, accounting for some 30 million in 2000. The older among them earn a small amount on their own, but nearly all get some allowance from their parents. Even more important, they influence a number of purchases of the family; indeed, the more significant the purchase, the more they influence it—the car and family vacation destinations, for example. Of all the people, teenagers have the most time available to spend in the checkout lines. Not surprisingly, a large number of them do family shopping. Many live their lives as latchkey children with parents working, and many parents leave a note for the older teenager (who can drive) to go to the supermarket and buy a few things. And they often accompany their parents on shopping trips. More than any other generation, then, this generation is becoming socialized into being a consumer at an early age—learning the art of buying. And this is happening more for teenagers today than it happened for the teenagers of yesteryear.

One of the important teen traits is that they like to look a couple of years older than they are (i.e., 14-year-olds like to look 16). An older teen will never seek advice from, or be influenced by, younger teens. As a group, teens like to go shopping and hang out in the mall. But the younger teenagers are constrained by not being of driving age yet; as such they depend on parents or older siblings to bring them to the mall.

One company recognized this "problem" as an opportunity, and started a catalog

TIGI Bed Head hair care products
Targeting teens with vibrant colors and images
(Used with permission.)

business for teen girls in high schools, and because of the trendy clothing style and casual presentation, it became popular among them. Using their parents' credit cards, they could order the clothes they liked from home, without having to find someone to drive them to the mall. A couple of years ago, the company began experimenting with mall stores (in addition to keeping the catalog). That company is Delia's, which was acquired in early 2003 by Europe's Alloy. Another retailer, Ulta, recognized the potential of the teenagers hanging out in the mall and made special efforts to respond to their needs.

Teenagers are the heaviest and constant consumers of new small-screen media devices and content—for communication and entertainment, of course, but also for information. Indeed, this has awakened them into becoming informed about all things—including marketplace happenings. As a result, they have become *Internet market mavens* (see definition in Chapter 10), so much so that many parents look to them for online product searches for family purchases. Marketers should take note!

SAVVY MARKETER

CHILDREN

Consumers in the Making

In the United States, children 5 to 12 years old numbered 33 million in 2000. Even more significant than their own purchases is the amount of influence they exercise on their parents' purchase decisions. Children influence such adult decisions as where to dine out, where to vacation, which entertainment and electronic gadgets to consider, and which brands of household groceries to purchase.

Growing up in the age of the Internet and the wireless and multimedia entertainment, kids of the new millennium are much more sophisticated than their predecessors, and in many aspects of life, more knowledgeable than their parents. Their influence stems both from personal preference (e.g., which brands of cereals they like and insist their parents buy) and from product expertise. Older kids can offer expert advice on such high-tech products as athletic shoes, video equipment, and even automobiles! One 10-year-old told in a Simmons Kids Study, "My little brother begged my dad to get a sports car. He got it."[23]

SENIORS

Anything but Sedated

Born before 1945, this group accounts for some 46 million Americans. Of course, it has now been some 20 years since the oldest of them entered the retirement age. In their 80's now, the older segment of this group is not very active. But don't dismiss them as sedate, depressed, indigent, or consuming only such elder care services as nursing homes and health care services. Many of them participate in regular shopping activity in national supermarkets and in the mall, and live life with good natured humor, typified by the TV Series *The Golden Girls'* 80-something Sophia Petrillo (played by actress Estelle Getty, 84, who passed away on July 22, 2008).

The youngest of the seniors are still in workforce, and only a few years away from being eligible to retire. More and more of them expect to continue to remain usefully employed (although not necessarily full-time), in part because they remain healthy and able-bodied and in part because a significant portion of their pension and retirement funds has been wiped out by the stock market nosedive first due to the bust of the so called Internet Bubble (1999-2002), and more recently of the housing bubble (2008-09), which led to bank failures and which in turn brought to the brink of bankruptcy an all time great corporation, General Motors! But even the oldest among this generation remain active, and able to provide for themselves. Their income is lowered after retirement, but they have the luxury of their house having been paid off, so their expenses are considerably less as well. Many are affluent, and indeed many support their grandchildren's education (thus lightening the burden on these grandchildren's struggling parents).

According to a recent survey done by the Georgia State University's Center for Mature Consumer Studies, 35.3 million Americans aged 65 or over had discretionary incomes of roughly twice that of debt-immersed baby boomers. These seniors were heavily into traveling and other leisure activities. Of course, at the other end, many were unable to provide for themselves, and are a financial burden on their adult children—the Boomers.

Seniors are also heavier consumers of leisure travel, both domestic and foreign. More than 47% own cell phones. And more than any other age groups, they are readers of the printed word, accounting for a disproportionately high readership of newspapers and magazines. They are not as attracted by fantasies or escapist appeals; rather, products must be shown to help them attain their values. With aging, consumers process information more slowly, but they have a richer store of information to supplement the slowly acquired new information. Therefore, older consumers don't fall for advertising hyperbole. And they have more time to do comparison shopping and product research.[24]

CONSUMING BY AGE

Food for the Young, Food for the Old

Yes, there really is such a thing as "food for the young" and "food for the old." You would know if you ever took a youngster to lunch or to a supermarket. For children and teenagers the main food feature has to be "fun." Supermarket aisles are filled with fun foods—foods with fun shapes, colors, flavors, and package pictures. There is Cheeto's Mystery Color Snacks (in cheesy neon orange color), green ketchup by Heinz, Magic Nestle's Wonderball, Hi-C, string cheese, spaghetti-shaped liquorices, and animal shaped candies.

For Gen X and Gen Y, convenience is most important in food buying. They want to eat on the go, so there are now supermarket foods to go, such as Go-GURT® by Yoplait® and Yoplait Express. Convenience is also important to dual career boomers, but to them, especially with advancing age, nutrition is also becoming important. The popularity of

SENIORS

Still vibrant

Have time for leisure

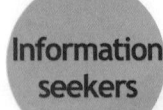

Information seekers

Shun ad hyperbole

bagels owes itself to this on-the-go convenience feature. Boomers, who don't have time to sit down to eat breakfast, cannot eat cereal in their cars; but bagels they can. And supermarkets also sell pre-mixed salad bags and ready-to-go meal solutions (either to cook at home or pre-cooked and ready-to-eat). Concern about nutrition grows as consumers age, and for the aged, some medical conditions, such as diabetes, introduce dietary restrictions. For aging seniors, foods also need to be less spicy, thus compatible with their less tolerant gastrointestinal systems.

S A V V Y
MARKETER

Clothes for the Young, and for the Old

The intergenerational differences are even more acute for clothing. Seniors are much more concerned with performance aspects of clothing like durability and quality, and also with price. Middle-aged Boomers wear high quality brand names, valuing the classic over the trendy.

The youngsters are, in contrast, exclusively focused on the trend of the day. Popular brands of clothing and shoes such as Skechers and Silver Tab certainly appeal to the younger consumer's desire for social image. Among teenagers and Gen Y, grunge clothing is popular, and more than to any other generation, price is most important to them, so much so that only they consider recycled clothing entirely prestigious—even the stores that buy and sell these have "cool" names—e.g., Snooty Fox and Plato's Closet.

For Whom The Zesty Life Begins at 50

Meet the women of the Red Hat Society. All decked in purple dresses and red hats. All 50+ in age.

The idea of what would later become a worldwide organization began with a whimsical purchase of a red hat by Sue Ellen Cooper (now the society's Queen Mother) a few years ago. About a year later, she read a poem by Jenny Joseph, "Warning," which depicts an older woman in a purple dress and a red hat. Moved by the poem, she decided to give to her best friend as a birthday gift a copy of the poem and a red hat. Later, she expanded the gesture to her other friends, who were all so moved by the poem that they decided to acquire purple dresses to complete the ensemble. All dressed up in the regalia, one day they went out to tea, and the idea of the society was born.

Today with chapters all around the world, the society holds national and regional conventions, and local chapters organize events like lunch meetings, train hoots, cruise trips, parades, and games.

On the society's Web site, a text banner reads, in part:

"The Red Hat Society began as a result of a few women deciding to greet middle age with verve, humor and elan. ... Underneath the frivolity, we share a bond of affection, forged by common life experiences and a genuine enthusiasm for wherever life takes us next." —Sue Ellen Cooper, Queen Mother (www.redhatsociety.com)

CROOKED FASHION AMONG JAPANESE TEENS

In Japan, there is a new fashion trend: Young women want to *disarrange* their teeth and pay the dentist to do just that. Dentists affix fake teeth to their real teeth to create the yaeba (double teeth in Japanese) look. And men find it more attractive—with imperfect teeth, women appear younger (children and adolescents have such teeth) and also more approachable.*

Before

After

F. A. M. I. L. I. E. S.

Households and Families

We all have a family. But your family is not the same as your friend's. And we all live in a household. But all households are not the same either. What is the difference between a household and a family? If you live with your parents, are you a member of a household? The answer is, "Yes." If you live with your fellow students, are you a member of a family? The answer is, "No." Here is another clue: All family members living together make a household, but not all households are families. Now for the definitions: **Families** are two or more persons related by blood, marriage, or adoption. **Households** are one or more persons living in the same dwelling unit. Thus, there can be single person household but a family requires at least two persons.

As Figure 14.2 shows, there are two types of households: family and nonfamily. Family households can further be classified into four types: (1) married couples, (2) married couples with children, (3) single parents, and (4) extended families. This last category includes grandchildren, uncles and aunts, brothers and sisters, and even cousins. Note that "extended" does not necessarily imply a larger family—two brothers living together become an extended family, as is a family of, say 20, comprising three generations related by blood or marriage. Also, family members who live apart are still a family; yet they are not a "family household."

Non-family households are of two types: (1) single person, and (2) roommates or housemates. Note that all students living in a dormitory are not a household since they do not make their purchasing decisions as a unit. Roommates and housemates, likewise, too may not make all of their purchasing decisions as a unit (e.g., clothing), but at least they make some decisions as a unit, or with consideration of the needs of all members of the unit (e.g., cleaning products or even appliances for the household as a whole).

According to the U.S. Census 2010, there are now 114.82 million households; of these, 78.8 million (68.62 %) are family households and 39.02 million (31.38%) are non-family households. In the last decade, since 1990, non-family households grew faster than family households (23% versus 11% growth). Among the family households, 59.3 million (74%) are married coupled households. Among the non-family households, unmarried couple households were 5.47 million (with 4.88 million of them being opposite sex partners, and 594,391 being same sex partners). Thus, 57% of all households are couples households (married and unmarried). Among the married couples households, 46% had at least one son or daughter living with them.[25]

14.2 TYPES of HOUSEHOLDS

FIGURE

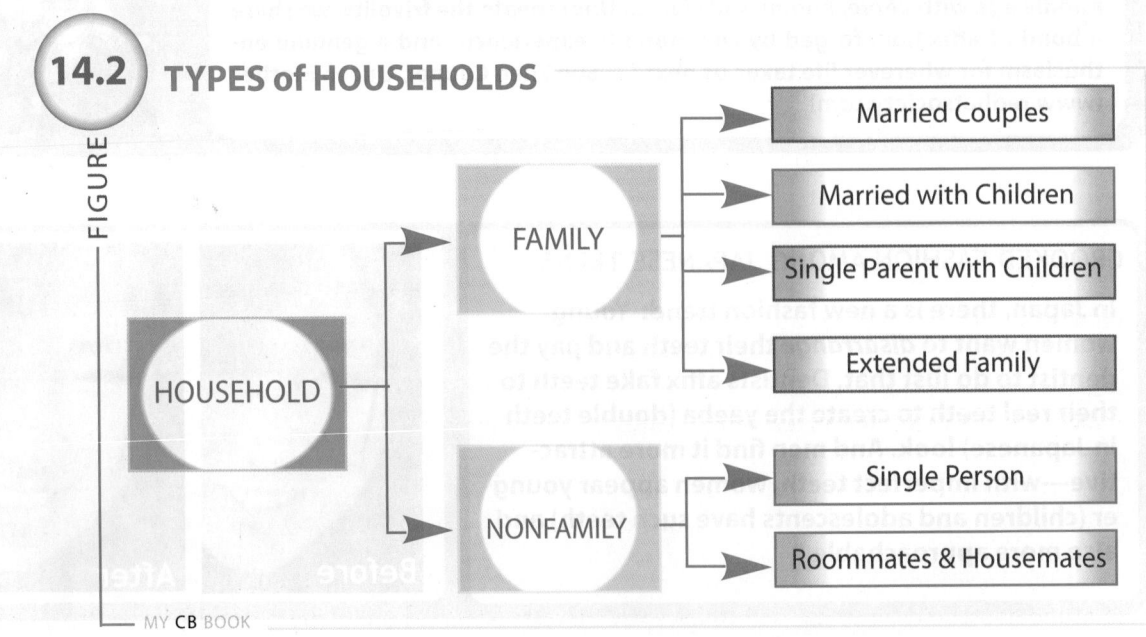

Married Versus Single

A person's marital status is an important parameter. It determines our lifestyles and consumption. The marriage rate has been falling in the Western nations. In USA, never-married rose from 34.9% in 2000 to 46.3% in 2009. In Canada, married couples declined from 83.1% in 1981 to 68.6% in 2006. In the UK, per 1000 unmarried males, 66 males got married in 1950, 27 in 2001, and 21.3 in 2009, with corresponding number for females being 51.7, 23.7 and 19.2. Currently, in each of the three major countries we showcase in this book (USA, Canada, and the UK), singles outnumber the married people! (See inset.)

MARITAL STATUS OF POPULATION			
	USA	CANADA	UK
MARRIED	49.3	48.8	42.8
SINGLE	51.7	51.2	57.2

Sources: US Census 2010, Census of Canada 2006; Office of National Statistics, 2010.

FAMILY LIFE CYCLE

Empty Nesters and Other Kinds of Families

How a person advances from one stage of family formation to another is called **family life cycle**. Historically, marketing researchers have broken this cycle into five stages: bachelor, couple, full nest, empty nest, and survivor. Marketing researchers have further divided full nesters into three substages: I, II, and III. Full nest I are families with young children under the age of six, full nest II are families with children between the ages of six and 18, and full nest III are families with grown-up children still staying at home. Similarly, empty nesters are further divided into two substages: I and II. Empty nest I refers to an early period when children have just left home, the parent is still fully employed, and, for many, children are out of college, thus eliminating a big drain on money; empty nest II refers to the later years (usually several years after children have left home) when the parent is retired and consequently has a much reduced income.

With aging, a person advances through these stages and lives as a different type of family—starting with being a single, to becoming a young married couple without children, moving on to becoming a middle-aged married person with children, to older married couple with children who have left home, and finally to becoming an older widower. Historically, a person typically advanced through these stages in this sequence. These days, of course, a person can live his or her entire life as an unmarried person, can become a parent without being married, can divorce at any age and thus become single again, and so on. To capture these trends, marketers recognize two types of family life cycles: Traditional and Modern. The Traditional Family Life Cycle (TFLC) refers to the five-stage model where a person advances, always, in a standard sequence and unidirectionally. In the Modern Family Life Cycle (MFLC), a person can move back and forth from one stage to the other, and these movements can occur in a number of patterns, e.g., sometimes jumping two sequential stages.[26] These two family life cycle patterns are shown in Figure 14.3.

The Modern Life Cycle is Not Universal

Don't abandon the traditional life cycle yet. In marketing, it is still useful, for two reasons. First, in many countries around the world, especially in the Eastern cultures, it is still the prominent form. Second, even for more westernized cultures, the TFLC serves as a basic platform on which the diverse departures of the MFLC can be overlaid. Of course, neither TFLC nor MFLC can account for all the diverse paths different families may take. Yet the scheme is useful for marketers to identify the changing needs of a family.

Married with Children

Now, Fewer of Them

In the U.S., "married with children" families are on the decline. In 1960, nearly half of the households were married couples with at least one child under the age of 18.

In the UK, the number of marriages has fallen by one-third every year since 1981!

—Office of National Statistics, UK

CANADA

MORE SINGLES

2006 51.5%

2001 49.9%

USA

MARRIED WITH CHILDREN

1960   50%

2010   20%

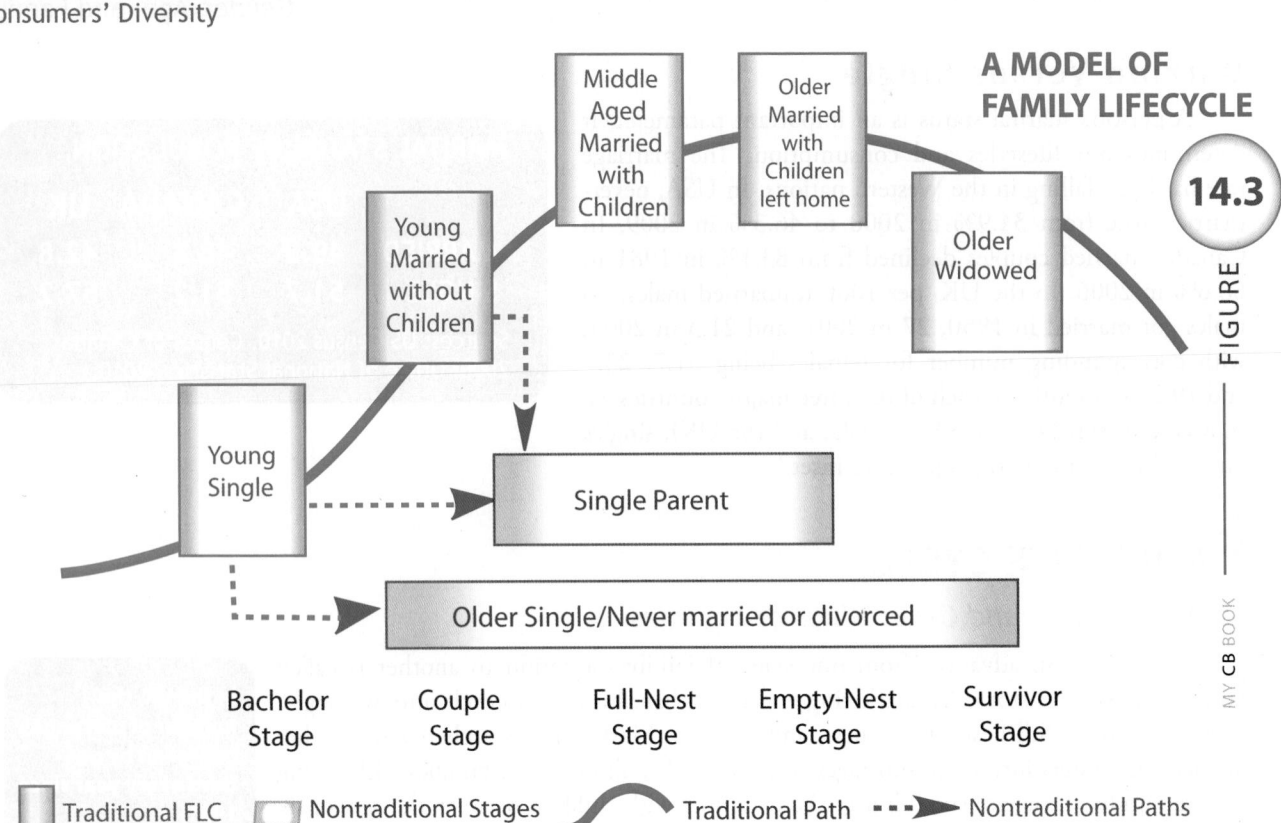

A MODEL OF FAMILY LIFECYCLE

FIGURE 14.3

MY CB BOOK

Bachelor Stage | Couple Stage | Full-Nest Stage | Empty-Nest Stage | Survivor Stage

☐ Traditional FLC   ☐ Nontraditional Stages   〰 Traditional Path   ┄► Nontraditional Paths

In the Census 2010, only one in five (20.1%) households fit this mold. That means, as a proportion of all households, in fifty years since 1960, America's "married with children" households have been reduced to less than half!

This trend of decline peaked during the 1970s. Why? Because baby boomers delayed getting married and/or having children. Also because older singles and empty nesters lived longer so the proportion of married couples with children became a smaller number. Now that declining trend is bottoming out. Why? For two reasons: first, because the baby boomers are no longer of the "postpone marriage and delay having a child" age. Second, the Asian and Hispanic immigrant families are on the rise and they are young and they value the traditional family pattern.[27]

Marketing Implications

Is Your Brand Tuned To Family Life Cycle Changes?

Suppose you want to market your product, say, cars, to families. What kind of family would you show in your advertising? Try selling cars, or any other product of household use, without understanding family life cycle, and the chances are your marketing efforts would prove unproductive. Indeed, it would pay to recognize the following FLC based consumer segments.

Young Married Couples Their principal "life project" is building a starter home. Thus, young married couples are a prime target market for all sorts of products needed for setting up a home—furniture, furnishings, small appliances, kitchen and cleaning tools and supplies. As they are generally starting out on their careers, they are likely not to have saved a lot of money. Therefore, when buying durable goods, they will be seeking the "bottom of the line," least expensive alternatives.

Full Nesters These are families with children living at home. In the early years (i.e., younger families with young children), this group is a prime prospect for child products (e.g., children's furniture, children's clothing, toys, etc.). They are usually strapped for time and seek time-saving products and services (e.g., easy-to-cook meal solutions, etc.)

As full nesters' children grow older, consumption gets structured around the needs of adolescent children. Many of these families move up from the starter home to a larger home with individual rooms for every member of the family. Once again, they become a

SAVVY MARKETER

USA

SINGLES
Men   45.2 M
Women 51.4 M
(USA, 2010)

prospect for furniture, furnishings, and appliances for the new house. Families that can afford buy additional TVs and entertainment centers for adult children, additional cars, computers, etc. Dining out at fast food and affordable restaurants, visits to amusement parks, family outings to ballgames, and vacations to destinations like Disneyland become frequent purchases. Later, with children in college, many full nesters are strapped for resources; as such, these families often buy bulk-sized packages of everyday household products, shop at warehouse stores, and take advantage of special sales and coupons.

Empty Nesters With children gone to live on their own, these consumers experience a sudden new-found resource: Time. Consequently, they seek more leisure activities—vacations, theater, eating out, or whatever suits their tastes. By now the children are out of college and the mortgage has been paid off; therefore, older empty nesters also become financially more secure. Many buy recreational vehicles (RVs) to travel in, and many sell off their big suburban houses and move into urban condos.

Single Parents An important departure from the traditional family life cycle comes in the form of single parents, shouldering the burden of child rearing without a spouse to share and receive support from. By the 2010 Census count, there were a total of 1.8 million single fathers and 7.2 million single mothers in the USA. Perhaps the most significant factor in this group's consumer behavior is time pressure. A single parent is always time starved and hassled. What this segment looks for most are time-saving product alternatives and services. Increasingly for this segment, home-based shopping and buying is useful. For this reason, Internet shopping (including home delivery of groceries ordered on the Internet) would appeal to this segment.

Singles The other important departure from the traditional family life cycle comes in the form of singles—men and women staying single well into their mature years, or divorced and not yet remarried. According to the 2010 U.S. Census, there were 45.2 million single men and 51.4 million single women.

There are two areas of consumption that are markedly different for singles. One, all of their visible public consumption has to look "cool" to a potential date. Thus, clothes, jewelry, car—whatever they are buying that would be seen in public—has to impress the opposite sex (or a potential date). Second, they end up eating out a lot, rather than fix a meal at home, and when they do go grocery shopping, the foremost need is for "single-serving" size. During the decade 2000-2010, single person households increased by 15%; food marketers need to address the "single-serving" size need of this segment of the population.[28]

Christian and Martina Haag, in Hamburg, Germany—*Empty Nesters* "Free" again!

CONSUMER BEHAVIOR IN FAMILIES

CHILDREN'S INFLUENCE IN FAMILY DECISION MAKING

Children—they are everywhere. And when they are not plotting pranks, they are cute. For marketers, they are also a goldmine. From fast food, to designer clothes, to video games and toys, they keep retailers' cash registers ringing. To the tune of some $30 billion a year, in U.S.A. alone. And this is only for children 12 years and under, and that too, counting only their direct purchases. They also influence the market spending by mom and dad—to the tune of over $300 billion.[29] And this influence increases with age. In one study it was found that 21 percent of mothers of five to seven-year-olds yielded to their children's requests, while 57 percent of mothers of 11 to 12-year-olds yielded to children's requests.[30] Today, the influence of children, especially the teen children, is likely to be even greater.

Children influence household buying in three ways. First, by having individualistic preferences for products paid for and bought by parents (e.g., toys). Second, children in

UK

SINGLES
Men   39.1%
Women 32.2%
(Office of National Statistics, UK, 2010)

their teen years begin to have their own money and become their own buyers of items of self-use, opening up a very valuable market to corporations selling a broad range of products and services. Third, they influence their parents' choice of products that are meant for shared consumption (e.g., family vacation or home entertainment system).[33] Exhibit 14.1 describes summary findings of a research study on children's influence.

George P. Moschis, a marketing professor at Georgia State University, is one of the leading scholars who has studied the role children play in family decision making. One of his insights is that children's influence in the family decisions depends on whether the family has a "social" or a "concept" orientation. Social-orientation families are the ones more concerned with maintaining discipline among children, whereas concept-oriented families are those that are concerned with the growth of independent thinking and individuality in children. Children from families with social orientation are less likely to make independent decisions and less likely to be involved in family decisions. Those with concept orientation are likely to have greater product knowledge, and their parents are more likely to involve them in family decision-making.[31]

Another way of classifying families is by how authority is exercised in the family. On this basis, worldwide, families can be classified into four types:[32]

1. Authoritarian families The head of the household (mother in matriarchal and father in patriarchal societies) exercises strict authority on children, and children learn to obey their elders in all matters. Such families are found mostly in Asian societies. Although a culture of obedience to elders is considered to be a virtue, especially in Asian cultures, it does curb individuality among children and consequently their influence on family buying decisions.

2. Neglectful families Parents are distant from their children, who are neglected in these families because the parent(s) place more priority on their individual affairs. Single-parent families risk this behavior most, some due to time pressure, others due to undisciplined lifestyle of the single parent, which engenders being irresponsible toward one's children. Of course, and hopefully, only a few single parents neglect their children.

3. Democratic families Every member is given equal voice. Most family matters are discussed among family members, especially those who would be affected by the decisions. Self-expression, autonomy, and mature behavior are encouraged among children. While opinions are sought from all affected members, the decision could be a joint one, or it could be exercised (or arbitrated) by the family head(s).

4. Permissive families Children are given relative independence in conducting their own affairs, especially in their adolescent years. Unlike parents in the neglectful families, however, permissive parents closely watch children's interests and exercise of freedom.

The relative prevalence of these types differs across different countries, and their proportions would change in the same country over time. Also, families could have partial tendencies of more than one type.

Children's influence would obviously differ across these four types. It would be lowest among authoritarian families. In neglectful families, children would exercise no influence on parents' purchases. For products needed for their own use, however, they are likely to exercise relative autonomy, provided they have an independent source of income. If not, their resources would be rather limited, since the neglectful parent is unlikely to support most of their requests. In democratic families, children would share influence with other members. Finally, in permissive families, children would exercise relative autonomy for products of which they are the principal or sole user.

Democratic Justice

A related concept is Democratic justice. **Democratic justice** refers to a family norm in which each family member is given a voice in family decisions. Often parents accept the norm that family members should be allowed to develop their individual identities and be treated as individual citizens of the household, with an equal voice in family matters. In the purchase of products for shared use (e.g., car, furniture, and so on), many families

CHILDREN'S INFLUENCE ON FAMILY DECISIONS

EXHIBIT 14.1

Consumer researchers Ellen Foxman, Patria Tanshuhaj, and Karin Ekstrom studied the role of adolescent children and found the following:

〉 Children (adolescents) had more influence for products for their own use.
〉 The greater the teenager's financial resources, the greater the influence he or she exercised.
〉 The greater the perceived knowledge, the greater the perceived influence.
〉 The greater the importance to the teenager of the product category, the higher the teenager influence.
〉 Teenager influence was higher in dual income families.
〉 Teenagers exercised more influence at the initiation stage than at the search and decision stage.

Mothers attributed less influence to their children than did children themselves. This discrepancy was lesser between mothers and their daughters than between mothers and their sons.

In an extension of this research, consumer researchers Sharon E. Beatty and Salil Talpade collected new data and analyzed purchases of durables (TV, stereo, phone, and furniture) made for family use versus made primarily for the use by the teenager. Some of their findings were as follows:

〉 Financial resources of teenagers influenced only those durable purchases that were for the teenager's own use (as opposed to family use) and only in the purchase initiation stage, not in the search and decision stages.
〉 Children's product knowledge was influential only in the initiation of purchase consideration and only for products intended for teenager use. For family purchases, teenager influence was significantly enhanced with product knowledge but only in the search/decision stage and only for stereos (not for the other products investigated).
〉 Importance of purchase to teenagers affected their influence for both for-family and for-teenager purchases, and in both initiation and search/decision stages.
〉 When teenagers were the major users of for-family durables, they exercised more influence (than if they were not going to be the major user) in both initiation and search/decision stages.
〉 Children had greater influence in dual-income families than in single-income families; however, this influence was significant only for purchases made for shared family consumption. For purchases for their own use, children had influence alike in both single and dual-income families.

Source: Adapted from Ellen R. Foxman, Patria S. Tanshuhaj, and Karin M. Ekstrom, "Family Members' Perceptions of Adolescents' Influence in Family Decision Making," *Journal of Consumer Research* 15 (March, 1989) pp. 482-91; and "Adolescents' Influence in Family Purchase Decisions: A Socialization Perspective," *Journal of Business Research* 18 (March 1989), pp. 159-72; Sharon E Beatty and Salil Talpade, "Adolescent Influence in Family Decision Making: A Replication with Extension," *Journal of Consumer Research*, 1994, vol. 21, #2, pages 332-41; © *Journal of Consumer Research*. Published by The University of Chicago Press. (Used with permission.) **a**lso see George E. Belch, M. A. Belch, and G. Ceresino, "Parental and Teenage Child Influences in Family Decision Making," *Journal of Business Research* 13 (1985), pp. 163-76.

MY CB BOOK

may consider it legitimate to give youngsters a voice. For products consumed by children exclusively (e.g., their own clothes or food) or primarily (e.g., a CD player and sound system), children are allowed to exercise their preference simply because parents grant children their democratic right to individuality.

Democratic justice can sometimes cause tensions in a family. When the offspring's preferences become incongruent with their parents' values (e.g., getting a punk style haircut), the value incongruence can become a source of conflict. As long as the offspring are living under the same roof, parents may resent, and, consequently, may attempt to change their sons' and daughters' counter-value purchases.

CONSUMER SOCIALIZATION OF CHILDREN

Consider these episodes:

- A single parent is clipping coupons on a Sunday afternoon. His 10-year-old daughter is nearby, helping her dad organize them—by product categories and by date of expiration. She makes a mental note: next time she sees a coupon in the newspaper, she would clip it and place it in these sorted envelopes.

- A mother is window shopping in a department store with her eight-year-old son. Suddenly, she begins to examine gym bags. She looks at one, puts it aside noticing its high

price, loudly speaking her thought (as people generally do when they are with a "shopping pal"). The son points to another. "No, I am looking for one in black only," she says. Then she looks at another. The son "scoops out" yet another black bag. The mother looks at it briefly and rejects it, saying, "It doesn't have the pocket." "It does," says the son, pointing at the zippered pocket. "No, I mean a meshed pocket (i.e., the one made of net fabric)—like this other one does," says the mother. Then the dialogue proceeds as follows:

Son:	**Why is it made of a net?**
Mother:	**To put your wet swimming suit in it.**
Son:	**You can put it in the other kinds of pockets too.**
Mother:	**Then it won't dry off.**
Son:	**Why can't we dry it off at home?**
Mother:	**We can. But if it is left in the bag for long, the bag will smell musty.**
Son:	**It will?**
Mother:	**Yes.**

Children's socialization begins early in life

How do children learn to become consumers? By this we do not mean merely how they learn to consume. Rather, we mean how they learn to shop, to value things, and to save money. How do they, in other words, become socialized to engage in marketplace exchanges? Socialized they do become, to an amazing degree. In one study, children 7 to 12 years old were found to possess strong brand preferences. And children who cannot yet read have been found to be able to recognize brand symbols, such as McDonald's arches and the Tony the Tiger mascot for Kellogg's Frosted Flakes.[33] Some observers believe that school and kindergarten children have had more experience with the marketplace than with arithmetic or writing!

Consumer socialization refers to the "acquisition of knowledge, preferences, and skills to function in the marketplace."[34] That is, consumer socialization occurs when one or more of the following are learned or acquired by children:

- **Awareness of various products and of their role in solving their personal needs and problems;**
- **Knowledge about the marketplace (e.g., what is available where) and about various product features;**
- **Skills in judging the utility of various product features;**
- **Preferences among alternative brands and products;**
- **Skills in making "smart decisions," such as making price and product comparisons, discounting advertising and salesperson claims, and evaluating trade-offs across options (including the option "to buy or not to buy");**

That is, children learn about desirable product features, alternative products, brands, stores, and other market options, and make this information a part of their stock of marketplace knowledge. They can learn, for example, that a particular toy is available at a particular store at a particular price, or that Sony Walkman comes in an attractive, neon-colored sports model, or that "Swatch" watches are cool, since they are worn by the coolest girls seen on TV and in the mall. And, finally, children can learn the knowledge and skills to make "smart choices." They can learn to clip coupons, do comparison-shopping, and select items from mail catalogs. Delia's catalog is very popular among young teen girls, and high school kids dig catalogs from Gap and J. Crew, for example.

Learning and socialization are lifelong processes, continuing through a person's mature years. We focus here on childhood socialization, since that is when the first wave of socialization occurs and that is when the family has the greatest opportunity to influence the socialization process. Two factors play a role in consumer socialization of children: (a) cognitive, and (b) environmental.

Cognitive factors refer to a person's mental abilities. Very young children, for example, are unable to discriminate between a TV program and a commercial and do not understand the persuasive intent of advertisers.[35] They are also driven by immediate perceptual features of the stimuli rather than by its substantive meaning. For example, a smaller glass filled to the top is judged to contain more juice than a larger but half-full glass.[36] Cognitive development proceeds with age, and so does children's consumer socialization.

Environmental factors refer to sources of information and influence surrounding the growing child. These sources include mass media, peers, and family. Family exercises the first and strongest influence on children's socialization.[37] As the child becomes older, peer influence grows, and the influence of family likely declines. In our experience, weakening of family influence with advancing years is less in Asian and third-world countries than in the more industrialized Western countries.

LEARNING MECHANISMS

How Children Learn to be Consumers

The socialization influence from parents to children occurs basically through the learning mechanisms described in Chapter 4: instrumental conditioning, modeling, and cognitive learning. These three mechanisms correspond to the three bases of reference-group influence (a topic covered in Chapter 10): normative, value-expressive, and informational, respectively.

1. Instrumental conditioning This refers to learning to do those things that are rewarded. In the early years of a child, parents control most resources and inculcate values through rewarding what they consider "good" behavior. Children learn those behaviors and the underlying values that receive rewards from their parents.

2. Modeling Here children look up to their parents as role models and try to internalize and adopt their values, roles, aptitudes, and so on. Thus, for example, a child who watches a father dressing up in the morning in "office clothes" is quietly making plans to wear similar clothes one day.

Modeling at work

3. Cognitive learning This third mechanism is at work when parents become the source of information about the product. In low involvement cognitive learning, children notice the products parents are using and in later life adopt them without much thought (e.g., Crisco oil or Morton salt). This is not modeling because the product choice is not driven by a desire to be "like them." High involvement cognitive learning occurs when parents communicate and educate about various brands or buying strategies. A mother might "educate" a daughter, for example, about what hygienic products are good, or when to use which of the several cough medicines she has in the family medicine chest.

Learning from the media can occur through cognitive and/or modeling processes. Learning from peers is predominantly via modeling. Occasionally it can be cognitive—i.e., peers can provide information. At times, peers even use instrumental conditioning, rewarding by offering approval.

INTERGENERATIONAL INFLUENCE

Learning from Your Cool Mom and Dad

Some of your consumer behavior is inherited from your parents. By this we do not mean that you inherited the genes for consuming certain products. Rather, we mean that you "learned" certain consumptions from your parents. We have already illustrated this behavior above. But there is a new name for some of this manner of acquiring consumption behavior, *Intergenerational Influence* (*IGI*).

IGI: Learning to dress like Mom (Jamie Schworer with daughter Katey)

Intergenerational Influence (IGI) of family members refers to the transmission of values, attitudes, and behaviors from one generation to the other.[38] In the context of consumer behavior, IGI refers to the transfer of consumption-related values, brand perceptions, and brand choices themselves (i.e., simply adopting the brands parents had been using). In a number of studies spanning last 3 decades, adult children were found to have adopted a broad range of product choices from their parents.[39] In a 2000 study of mothers and their grown-up daughters (who lived on their own), soup brand choice was the same for 76% of the mother-daughter pairs; for toothpaste it was common for 43%, and for facial tissue, 55%. The sharing was much less for such products as coffee (20%), vegetables (11%), and household cleaners (3%). (Also see Exhibit 14.2.)

That mothers and daughters share their brand preferences is merely the visible tip of the proverbial iceberg. Parents and their offspring share much more—the IG influence extends into three general areas:

a. Consumption preferences of products, brands, and stores;
b. Consumer skills (how to choose, compare, evaluate, etc.); and
c. Marketplace beliefs and attitudes (views on prices, advertisements, salespersons, etc.; e.g., the belief that "private brands and sale merchandise are good value").[40,]

Product Differences. According to recent research, IG influence occurs more for products that are merely utilitarian (e.g., cleaning products, food, etc.); in contrast, it occurs less for stylist products, which the offspring might use to express their individuality (e.g., clothing).[41]

Forward and Reverse Influence

IGI can take place in both directions: forward (from parents to children) and reverse (from children to parents). Forward influence occurs because as children are growing up, they observe parents using certain products. And they "adopt" those products for use in later, independent living. The reverse influence begins to occur as children grow up. In school and on the street, children are exposed to new knowledge and to new role models. Consequently, they begin to depend less on parents as role models or for guidance and begin to carve out their individual identity. In exercising their individual identity, they begin to influence what gets bought for family consumption, such as the type of home furnishings. Also, often parents begin to look to their grown-up children for advice on new developments in the marketplace and on new products.

IGI is a good reflector of the vitality of families. As the authors of a recent study have noted:

> Countervailing the lamentations of disintegrating families in popular literature, and of dilution in family sharing, our research shows that in consumer socialization of off-spring, and, even more importantly, in the inculcation of life values, family life is "alive and well."[42]

Marketing Implication IGI contributes to brand equity by perpetuating a brand's adoption through successive generations of offspring. This applies, however, only to utilitarian products, not individual/identity-expressing products. Marketers of utilitarian products must, therefore, extend their effort to milk the positive role of parental influence on offspring's product and brand adoptions.

For stylistic products that youth choose based on peer group popularity or other external influences, marketers might run parallel communications campaigns for intended users and their parents—the former with a lifestyle and "cool and trendy" theme, and the latter presenting the brand's more intrinsic and tangible benefits.

Marketers can measure IGI by using a scale shown in Table 14.6.

SAVVY MARKETER

TABLE 14.6 A SCALE TO MEASURE IGI

To what extent have you been influenced by your parents in acquiring or not acquiring the following personal skills:

Not at all   1   2   3   4   5   To a great extent

1. Planning, budgeting, saving money, etc. _____
2. How to choose between products and brands _____
3. How to assess product information _____
4. How to judge a brand in comparison to others _____

To what extent have the following tastes and preferences of your parents influenced your own tastes and preferences as consumers:

Not at all   1   2   3   4   5   Greatly

5. Their preferences of brands and products _____
6. Their preferences of stores _____
7. Their views of advertising, sales, and other marketing practices _____
8. Their personal involvement or lack of it in shopping, possessing things, conspicuous consumption, simplicity, etc. _____

Your Total Score _____

Scoring: The scores (when summed across the eight questions) could range from 8 to 40. Although national standards based on any representative study are unavailable, it is reasonable to deem consumers scoring above the mid-point ($3\times8=24$) to have been influenced more by IGI than those scoring below 24.

Source: "Consuming As A Family: Modes of Intergenerational Influence On Young Adults," Banwari Mittal and Marla Royne, *Journal of Consumer Behaviour* 2010, 9 (4, July-Aug) 239-257; also see "The Measurement of Intergenerational Communication and Influence on Consumption: Development, Validation, and Cross-Cultural Comparison of the IGEN Scale," Viswanathan, Madhubalan; Childers, Terry L.; Moore, Elizabeth S., *Journal of the Academy of Marketing Science*, Summer2000, 28(3), p406-424.

MY CB BOOK

SUMMARY

In this chapter, we discussed two important consumer characteristics: sex and age.

We began with a discussion of the consumer behavior differences between the two sexes. These differences relate to the consumption of clothing, personal items, and emotional or mood-related products. Historically concerned with homemaking, the roles of modern day women are changing to encompass decision-making for all sorts of product categories; so are men increasingly participating in home-making chores and shopping for domestic staples. A related concept we discussed was gender roles—the social roles assigned to a person based on sex. We noted that sex roles are changing in contemporary societies, and accordingly, marketers must keep an eye on changes in redistribution of decision making between the sexes.

Age plays a significant role in defining the market size for any product and shifts in markets over time. We explored age groups as different consumer segments. Here, we enumerated the diverse categories of age groups in America: GI Generation, Silent Generation, Boomers, Generation X, Generation Y, teenagers, and children. Consumers in these age groups differ vastly in their needs and wants, desiring different products and services, both because their physical characteristics are different and because their tastes differ according to the subculture of their age groups.

Many of the age-based consumer behaviors are related not to the number of years passed since birth, but to how old a person sees him- or herself to be. This notion is captured in the concept of "cognitive age." We described the consumer behavior influences of cognitive age. In particular, we noted how this explains why consumers often don't act their age.

CB Blog

(14)

GENDER AND AGE—OUR SUPERGLUED IDENTITY MARKERS

Gender and Age—the two markers of our identity, stuck to us as if "superglued."

Is there any moment in our waking life when we are not conscious of them? We are conscious of them in buying our clothes, in partaking of our foods, in choosing our recreation. We visit only those stores that sell the merchandise that suits our particular gender and age, buy music CDs that echo our generation's psyche, and flock to places —public as well as commercial—where people similar to our age and of interest to our gender congregate.

Males and females do make different consumers. Tons of observational studies tell us that. To get a full skinny on that, a reading of these three books will be worth every minute of your time:

1. Why We Buy: The Science of Shopping by Paco Underhill (Simon & Schuster, 2000);
2. Marketing to Women: How to Understand, Reach, and Increase Your Share of the World's Largest Market Segment by Martha Barletta (Kaplan Business, 2006); and
3. The Future of Men: The Rise of the Ubersexual and What He Means for Marketing Today, by Marian Salzman, Ira Matathia, and Ann O'Reilly (Palgrave MacMillan, 2006).

But keep in mind, these consumption differences are a moving target. The phrase "homemaker" has long stopped being tied to a specific gender, and the ritual of obsessive personal grooming has invaded the male specie. Bold consumers everywhere are defying the stereotype of their gender. Take comfort, however, in the knowledge that "putting more heart into gifts" is one thing on which men will never match up with women—except on Valentine's Day, that is.

Age, our second unalterable characteristic, marks the progression of our lives. It affects what we consume, both when we are celebrating it and when we are defying it.

Celebration and defiance consumptions offer distinct opportunities to marketers. To harness these, keep a close watch on the psychology of the generations. Seniors, Boomers, Gen Xers, Gen Yers, teens—they all represent unique and individually alluring islands of opportunity. Commune with them, grasp their mojo, and then fashion your offerings for each age group separately.

And, for the population as a whole, keep a watch on the changing numbers. The fortunes of whole industries can swing as today's Boomers reach their golden years and the Millennials become tomorrow's 30-somethings. Marketers: Ignore population pyramids at grave consequences!

CONSUMER BEHAVIOR

KEY TERMS

Baby boomers
Baby busters
Cognitive age
Consumer socialization of children
Democratic justice
Egalitarian sex role attitude
Family
Family life cycle

Femininity
Gender role identity
Generation X
Generation Y
Households
Intergenerational Influence
Manscaping
Masculinity

Metrosexual
Millennials
Population pyramids
Retrosexual
Signaling
Traditional sex role attitude
Übersexual

YOUR TURN

REVIEW+Rewind

1. List some notable differences between men and women in terms of their consumer behaviors.
2. How are gender roles changing lately in the Western Societies and elsewhere? What should marketers do to respond to these changes?
3. Explain why a marketer should study age as a consumer characteristic.
4. What is meant by the term "population pyramids"? Why should a marketer study them?
5. Explain the differences in the psychological makeup of consumers who are:
   a. Gen X and Gen Y
   b. Seniors and Baby Boomers
6. Who are metrosexuals? How do retrosexuals, and übersexuals differ from metrosexuals?
7. Explain the concept of Family Life Cycle and its utility to marketers.
8. Explain the concepts and sources of consumer socialization of children and IGI.

THINK+Apply

1. Which age group do you belong to? Does the description of consumer behavior for that age group hold true for you? To what extent? Why or why not?
2. Collect five ads targeted at seniors. Scrutinize them for any elements that might betray any stereotypes of seniors that are likely to displease seniors themselves?
3. Would a store targeting metrosexuals have good market opportunity? Why or why not?

PRACTICE+Experience

1. Interview two couples similar in demographics but differing on their gender role attitudes (traditional and egalitarian). Understand and describe how their consumption roles are affected by their gender role attitudes.
2. Interview two Baby Boomers and then two Generation Xers, if possible from the same family. Focus your interview on (a) their clothes buying habits, (b) use of credit cards and the importance of budgeting and savings, and (c) the importance of money in life. Summarize the differences and similarities you find.
3. Survey all of the marketing activities of companies marketing (a) soft drinks, (b) clothing, and (c) electronic music and communication devices, directed at Generation Y. Describe how well these marketing programs fit with the attitudes and tastes of Gen Y described in the chapter.
4. Interview two adolescents (one male and one female) to identify the IGI they have received, and compare your findings.

In the Marketing Manager's Shoes

Put yourself in a marketing manager's shoes. Most concepts in the chapter have some lessons for the marketing manager, i.e., they suggest what to do differently in practice; indeed, often these applications are implicit in our explanations of the concepts and models in the chapter. Identify at least five specific applications of the chapter's concepts, all of which should be entirely new, different from the examples cited here.

ETHNICITY

15 Ethnic, Religious, and Class Identity in Consumer Behavior

The Three Indelible Markers of Our Identities

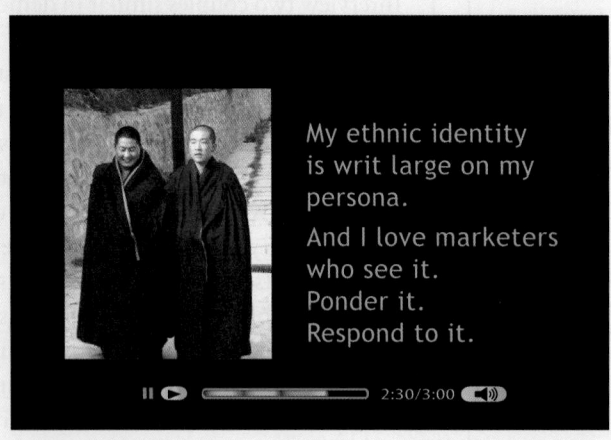

My ethnic identity is writ large on my persona.

And I love marketers who see it.
Ponder it.
Respond to it.

2:30/3:00

LEARN . APPLY . EXPERIENCE

OBJECTIVES

1 The Difference Between Race and Ethnic Identity

2 Various Ethnic Segments in Consumer Populations

3 Religious Identity as a Consumer Demographic

4 The Differences Among Income, Wealth, and Social Class

5 The Psychology of Poverty and Consumer Behaviors of Various Social Classes

6 The Concepts of Social Mobility, Status Discord, and Masstige Consumption

Let's Talk **Hair!**

I am mixed w/black and white and I have really coarse hair... I keep it short cause it's hard to keep clean and good looking. I've tried a lot of different products, but I need some advice on what products I should use that will give me those small sexy curls...

* * *

I decided to grow out of my relaxer and wear my hair natural... overcoming my psychological struggle in accepting my naturally curly hair... The book has great tips on options for growing out of a relaxer... [It] is a must-read for the black woman who has even slightly considered wearing her natural hair.

* * *

I want to keep my afro puffy and big , but I don't think it looks good , it looks dry and the color isn't dark black like when my hair is short.

* * *

My ethnicity.
My needs.
My identity.

I have relaxed hair and I am about to go to the Caribbean on vacation for 1 week. I am thinking of having my hair braided so that I would not have to style it every morning. However, I also plan to spend a lot of time swimming. Is braiding recommended? If so, how should I take care of my hair after swimming? If you don't recommend braiding, how should I take care of my relaxed hair after swimming?

* * *

Note: The four comments are from, respectively, Lightskinguy posted on Afrohair.com forum; a post on forum.afrohair.biz1; Lady De Q and A thread on Afro Hair.com; and a reader review of the book *Let's Talk Hair*

INTRODUCTION

Hair. Short, long, silky, thin, thick, blonde, dark, graying, brittle, oily, kinky. No matter what shape it comes in, it is on our heads and we love it. We spend anywhere from 50 to 300 hours a year on it.[1] How much time we spend depends in part on the type of hair we have and/or keep. That in turn depends in part on our ethnicity. And on our religious affiliations as well. And how much money we spend on our hair depends on our incomes, and on our tastes, which in turn depends on our social class.

Many other consumption behaviors also depend on these four characteristics—ethnicity, religion, income, and social class. All are also very sensitive issues—calling for a discourse with an open mind. In the marketplace, marketers ignore them at their own peril. Or harness them to serve diverse consumers. Let us learn more about them.

ETHNICITY VS. RACE

Your Bio-Cultural ID

Hello, what race are you? Yes, we know, it is impolite to ask. And politically incorrect. But you want some Sulfur8 for your braids, some apHOGEE shampoo, Afrikan Beauty Shea Butter Skin Care System, tamales, tortillas, Pan de Muerto, silk sarees, naan, basmati rice, bowls of pho and skeins of soba, hand-pulled mein and hand-pulled udon, don't you? We are marketers, and we can't offer you these products if we don't know your race. At any rate, you can't really hide your race and ethnic identity—it is writ large on your face and on your persona. Most of the time. Besides, ethnicity is a matter of pride with you, as it should be, and as it is with us. So let us talk about it.

Race or Ethnicity: Which Do We Mean?

Political incorrectness is not the only problem when discussing race and ethnic issues. There is no consensus among scholars as to the definition of these terms, or the criteria on which race and ethnic distinctions should be made. Skirting this controversy, we would define these two terms as follows:

- **Race** refers to the distinction among humans based on their genes, from which stem basic differences in the subspecies of humans.
- **Ethnicity** refers to distinctions among people based on their national or cultural heritage.

Thus, race is a biological concept. It is rooted in the differences in the biological makeup of humans, and represents one of the three such distinctions that *physically* separate people as a group—the other two biological distinctions being age and sex. In contrast, ethnicity is a sociological concept.

There are four original race groups among humans: Caucasians, Africans, Mongolians, and Aboriginals (or Australoids). These subspecies are said to have originated in, respectively, Northern and Western Europe, Africa, Mongolia (the Chinese region), and Australia. (Some scholars believe that this last group originated in South-East Asia and later migrated to Australia. If you are contemplating the feasibility of such migration—on foot, that is—remember, the sub-continental plates have drifted apart since.) Note that race itself can be a major criterion for ethnicity, so that, for example, Caucasian can be both a race and ethnicity. At the same time, an ethnic identity can cross more than one race, and within any one race multiple ethnic identities can exist. To illustrate, most Italians and French are Caucasians, but they are two distinct ethnic groups. In our view then, race is your bio-genetic identity; in contrast, ethnicity is your bio-cultural ID.[2]

In the United States, the Census Bureau specifies the following five race categories: 1. White; 2. Black or African American; 3. American Indian or Alaska Native; 4. Asian; and 5. Native Hawaiian, Pacific-Islander. The U.S. Census also asks a separate question about whether a person is Spanish/Hispanic/Latino. It is interesting to note that Hispanics are

Aboriginals at Sydney Harbor

not identified as a separate race category (correctly so, since *Hispanic* is not a race but an ethnic identity). Yet, on the race question, many Hispanics mark themselves in the "other" category.

Another point to note is that not all Asians have the same genetic roots, and, therefore, are not the same race. Chinese, for example, are of Mongolian race, whereas Indians have either Aryan (another name for Caucasian) or Dravidian (another name for Aboriginal/Australoids) roots[3]. Thus, *Asian* is a regional identity, not a race; as such the use of this term in U.S. Census as a race category is merely an administrative designation rather than a scientific or cultural classification. Asians tend to mark the race category because they interpret it as a geographic identity group rather than race.

MULTI-ETHNIC WORLD CITIES

- **Los Angeles, USA** A quintessential multi-ethnic city. People (9.83 million in 2010) here speak 80 plus languages and come from 100 plus cultural and ethnic backgrounds. Perhaps only in the offices of the United Nations in New York City will you find a more diverse population. In Los Angeles, at every turn of the road, you will see people who look different from you, no matter what your own race is. You will meet Filipinos, Koreans, Mexicans, Salvadorans, as well as Chinese, Ethiopians, Indians, Indonesians, Iranians, Pacific Islanders, Druze, Tamils, and Vietnamese, and, of course, less frequently, white Americans. As Marlene S. Rossman, the author of *Multicultural Marketing* observes, you can eat every night in a different ethnic restaurant without repeating the food for a year![4]

- **Toronto, Canada** A very vibrant city with 2.48 million people (5.5 million in The Greater Toronto Area). People of diverse ethnicities have made it their home (see chart); 30% of Canada's immigrants live here, and they speak some 150 languages. There are six Chinatowns here offering a rich cornucopia of Chinese, Korean, Vietnamese and other East Asian food. And on Gerrard Street, you are, for all practical purposes, on a market street in South Asia (India, Pakistan, Bangladesh).

- **London, UK** is the ethnically and culturally most diverse city in the world. Fully one-third (31%) of its residents (7.82 million in 2010) are non-white. South Asians (e.g., Indians, Pakistanis, etc.) make up the largest minority (13.3%), with blacks (10.6%), and East Asians—e.g., the Chinese—(3.5%) adding to the mix.[2] (See chart.) London is considered to be a world food capital. With over 100 Indian/Asian restaurants, the most popular cuisine here is of non-British origin: *curry*!

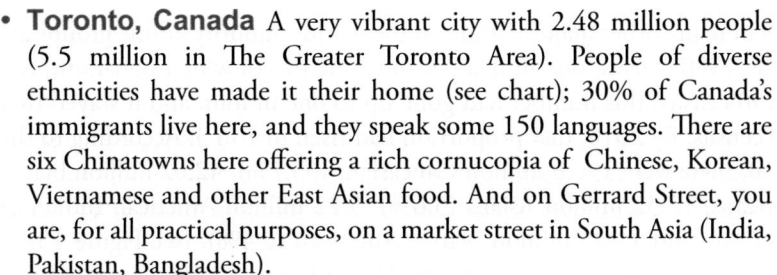

LOS ANGELES
The Land of the Ethnics

	(%)
WHITE	27.79
Hispanics	22.48
Black	8.30
Asian	13.72
Other	21.80

U.S. Census 2010

TORONTO
A Vibrant Multicultural City

(%)	
CANADIAN	53.0
South Asian	12.0
Chinese	11.4
Black	8.4
Filipino	4.1
Latin American	2.6

Census of Canada 2006

LONDON
The Europe's Most Ethnic City

(%)	
BRITISH WHITE	57.71
White (other)	11.10
South Asian	13.30
Black	10.61
East Asian	3.50

2007 estimate (UK Census)

ETHNIC DIVERSITY AROUND THE WORLD

Although the ethnic potpourri is not as dramatic elsewhere, its presence is unmistakable almost anywhere in the United States. And likewise elsewhere in the world. We will examine the ethnic diversity in the US fully below, but first a brief look at two other major Western countries, Canada and the UK, as cases in point.

- **Canada** Of the total population of 33.476 million in 2011, 18.4% (6.16 m) listed themselves as Canadian; an additional 13.8 % listed as "Canadian and other," thus making up one-third (32.2%) of the population as being native Canadian. In effect then, fully 2/3rd of the population is of non-Canadian origin. Among the latter, the largest minorities were English and French—4.38 and 3.94% by single response but 21.03 and 15.82% by multiple response categories. Among the non-Europeans, the largest ethnic groups were Chinese (3.63 by single- and 4.3% by multiple response categories) and East Indians (2.5% by single- and 4.63% by multiple response categories).[5] (See chart.)

- UK In the U.K., Whites comprise the largest segment of the population (83.35%) but the ethnic minorities are significant—Asian 5.87%, Black 2.81%, and Chinese 0.82%. In recent years, ethnic minorities have grown rapidly: Since 2001, the non-white British population grew from 6.6 million to 9.1 million in 2009, equivalent to 4.1% growth per year. The largest growth among minorities was in the Chinese segment: 8.6% annually; blacks were next, with 6.2% annual growth, and Indians third, with about 5% annual increase. Of the estimated 62.3 million people in UK (2010), 9.1 million are non-white British.[6] (See chart.)

- **USA** In USA, as in many other major nations in the world, minority ethnic groups are on the rise. In the 1980 census, one in five persons were of nonwhite, non-European origin; in the 1990 census, this number had gone up to one in four, and it stayed that way in the 2000 census. By 2010, that proportion had risen to 1 in 3. According to the U.S. Census 2010, there were 196.8 million Caucasians (63.7%), 42.02 million blacks or African Americans, 17.32 million Asians (5.6%), 5.22 million American Indian or Alaska Native (1.7%), and 1.225 million Native American (0.4%). (see Figure 15.1).

2003
The year Hispanics became the largest minority ethnic group in USA

Of the total population, 16.3% was Hispanic and 83.7% non-Hispanic. With 50.48 million strong, the Hispanics are now the largest minority (next largest, blacks, 42.02 million). This reversal occurred in 2003, when for the first time in history, Hispanics surpassed blacks (38.8 million versus 38.3 million in that year).[7]

ETHNIC DIVERSITY IN CANADA

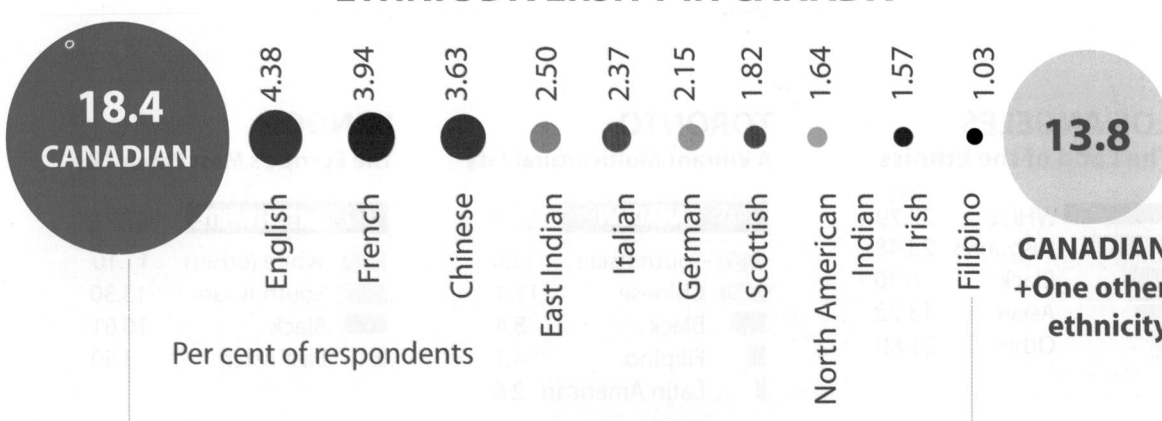

| 18.4 CANADIAN | English 4.38 | French 3.94 | Chinese 3.63 | East Indian 2.50 | Italian 2.37 | German 2.15 | Scottish 1.82 | North American Indian 1.64 | Irish 1.57 | Filipino 1.03 | 13.8 CANADIAN +One other ethnicity |

Per cent of respondents

SINGLE RESPONSE

Census of Canada 2006

ETHNIC DIVERSITY IN THE UK

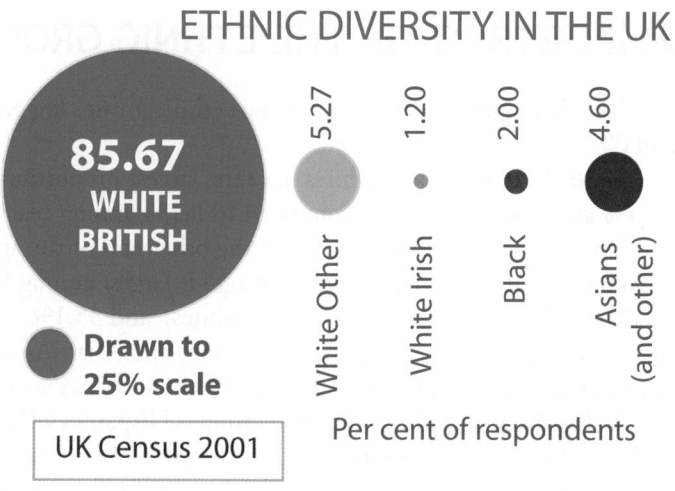

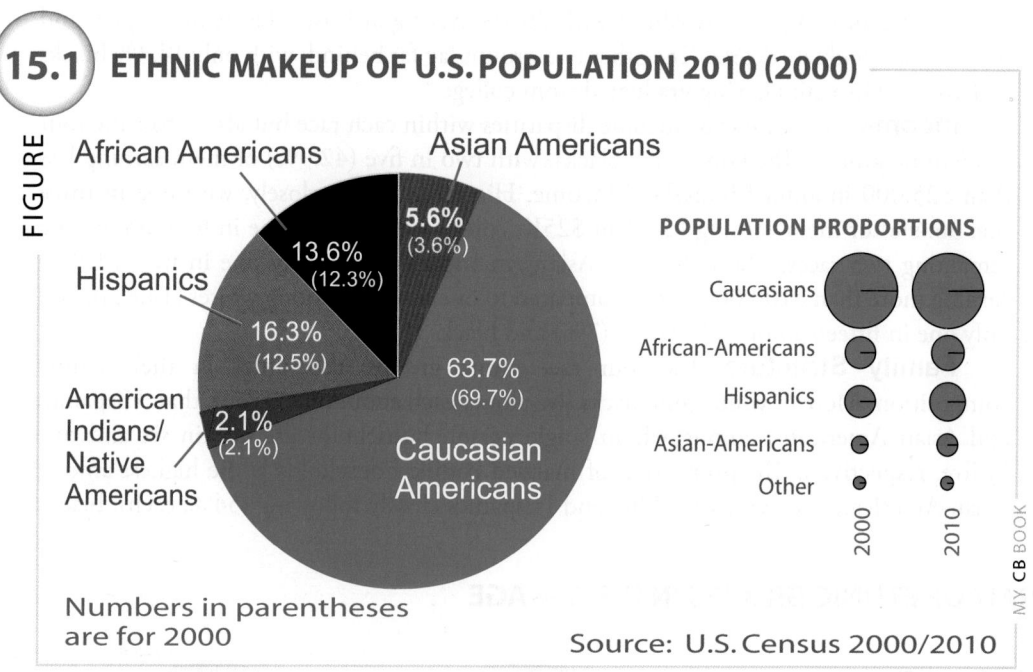

15.1 ETHNIC MAKEUP OF U.S. POPULATION 2010 (2000)

Numbers in parentheses are for 2000

Source: U.S. Census 2000/2010

The ever-increasing presence of immigrants and their U.S.-born offspring is altering mainstream culture and customs. Consider some popular foods in America: bagels, pizza, hamburgers, sushi, Szechwan chicken, burritos—all are ardently consumed by Americans of all ethnic backgrounds. Today, tortilla chips are consumed in 62% of U.S. households, and salsa outsells ketchup! Given such diversity, marketers need to understand the ethnic makeup of U.S. consumers.

The marketing literature identifies four race/ethnic groups in the United States: European Americans, African-Americans, Hispanics, and Asian-Americans. The culture, values, norms, and behaviors of these four race/ethnic groups differ markedly. As noted earlier, *Hispanic* is not a race but an ethnic group. Hispanics can be black or white, but they tend to identify themselves as just Hispanics rather than blacks or whites. And when people speak of blacks or whites, they mean, usually, non-Hispanic blacks and non-Hispanic whites.

A PORTRAIT OF THE ETHNIC GROUPS IN U.S.

The demographic profiles of various ethnic groups are graphed in Figure 15.2 (A, B, and C).

Age In terms of age, whites have the largest proportion of the oldest population—14.4% are 65 years or older, compared to 8.1% among blacks, 4.9% among Hispanics, and 6.5% among Asian-Americans; at the other end of the age spectrum, the proportion of young persons (less than 25 years of age) is largest among Hispanics–48.4% compared to 42.4% among blacks, 32.3% among whites, and 35.1% among Asian-Americans. The boomer age group is the largest among whites and Asian-Americans—30.4% and 30.6%, respectively, compared to 27.7% among blacks and 23.4% among Hispanics.[8]

Education The least educated group is Hispanics with nearly half of them (47.6%) with less than high school education. In comparison, among blacks, less-than-high-school educated are 1 in four (27.7%), and they are one in five among Asian Americans (19.6%) and one in six among whites (16.4%). The most educated group is Asian-Americans—44% of them have at least a bachelor's degree and 17.4% have a post-graduate degree. The next most educated group is whites with 26.1% having at least a bachelor's degree and 9.5% a post-graduate degree. The other two groups lag far behind, with only 14.3% blacks and 10.5% Hispanics having graduated from college.[9]

Income There are wide income disparities within each race but also across the four race/ethnic groups. The poorest are blacks, with two in five (42.9%) of them earning less than $25,000 in annual household income. Hispanics follow closely, with one in three (i.e. 36.4%) of them earning less than $25K, compared to about one in four among the remaining two races. The richest are Asian Americans with nearly one in five (21.9%) earning more than $100,000 a year, compared to one in seven among whites (14.8%), and only one in fifteen among Hispanics (7%) and blacks (5.6%).[10]

Family Structure The four race/ethnic groups also differ in their family composition. More of whites and blacks live alone, each about one in four, than Hispanics and Asian Americans, among whom single person households are one in six and one in five, respectively. The proportion of married couple households is the highest among Asian-Americans (61%), with whites and Hispanics closely following (54%, each); blacks

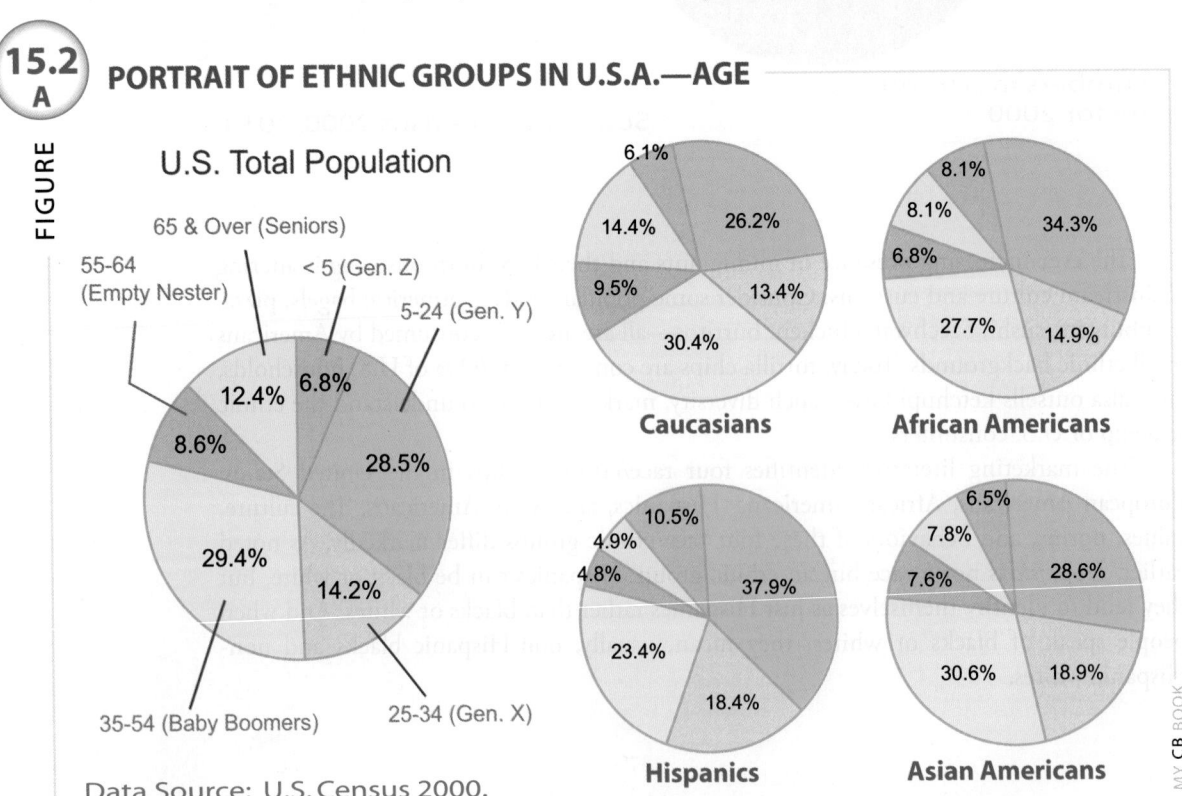

15.2 A **PORTRAIT OF ETHNIC GROUPS IN U.S.A.—AGE**

FIGURE

U.S. Total Population

65 & Over (Seniors)
55-64 (Empty Nester)
< 5 (Gen. Z)
5-24 (Gen. Y)
6.8%
12.4%
8.6%
28.5%
29.4%
14.2%
35-54 (Baby Boomers)
25-34 (Gen. X)

Data Source: U.S. Census 2000.

Caucasians: 6.1%, 14.4%, 9.5%, 30.4%, 26.2%, 13.4%

African Americans: 8.1%, 8.1%, 6.8%, 27.7%, 34.3%, 14.9%

Hispanics: 10.5%, 4.9%, 4.8%, 23.4%, 18.4%, 37.9%

Asian Americans: 6.5%, 7.8%, 7.6%, 30.6%, 28.6%, 18.9%

MY CB BOOK

have only one in three (31%) households that are married couples. The nuclear family (i.e., married couples with children) is found most among Hispanics and Asian-Americans, with about one in three (36% and 34%, respectively) such families in each group. Conversely, the number of single mothers (with children <18 years old) is the highest among blacks, with nearly one in five such households; the next highest number is Hispanics, with about

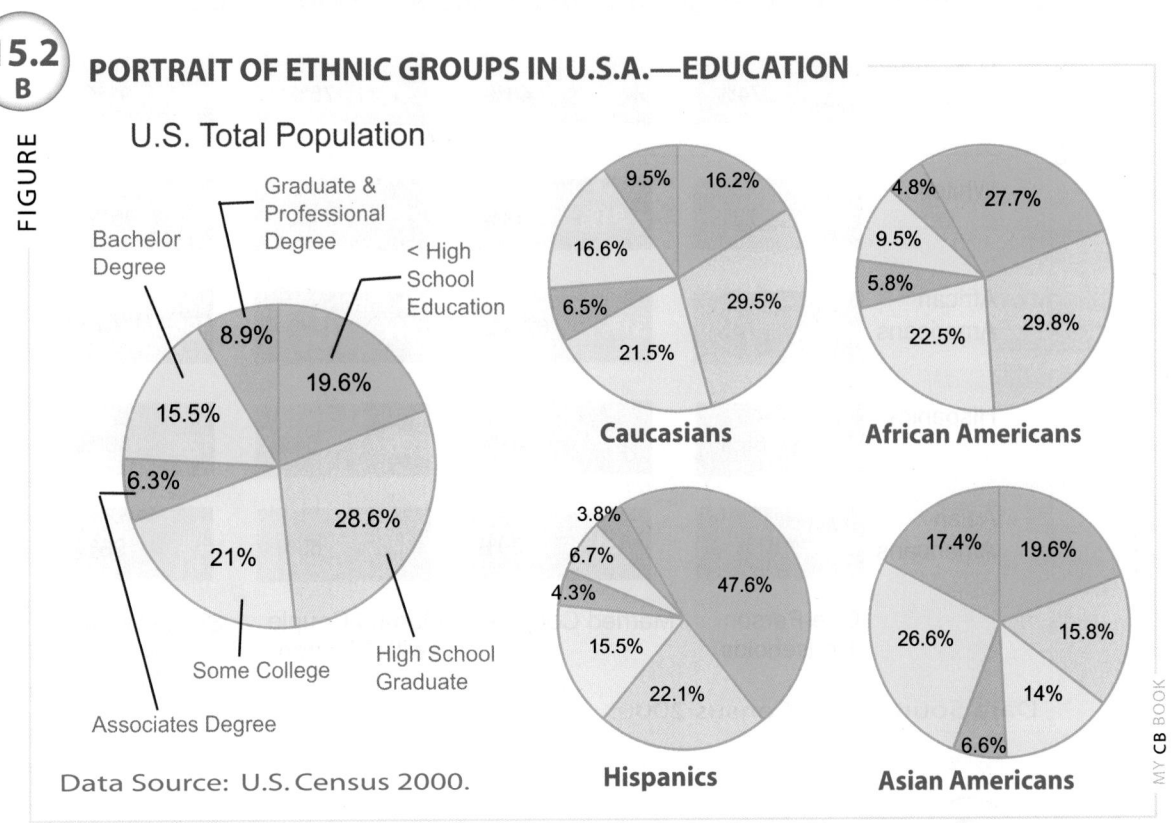

15.2 B
FIGURE

PORTRAIT OF ETHNIC GROUPS IN U.S.A.—EDUCATION

U.S. Total Population

Data Source: U.S. Census 2000.

Note. U.S. 2010 Census data for population subgroups were unavailable at press time.

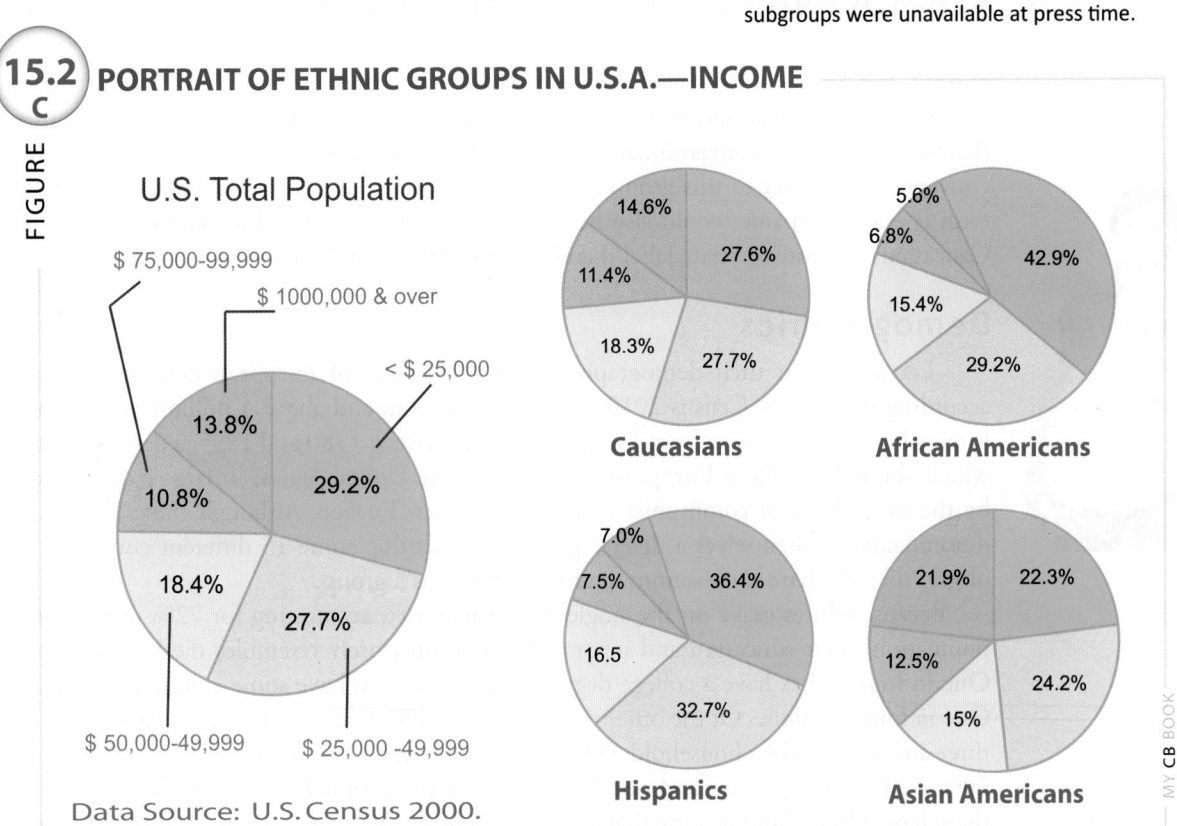

15.2 C
FIGURE

PORTRAIT OF ETHNIC GROUPS IN U.S.A.—INCOME

U.S. Total Population

Data Source: U.S. Census 2000.

one in ten (12%) single mother households. Among Asian-Americans and whites, this proportion is much lower—only one in twenty households is a single mother household.[11] (See Figure 15.3.)

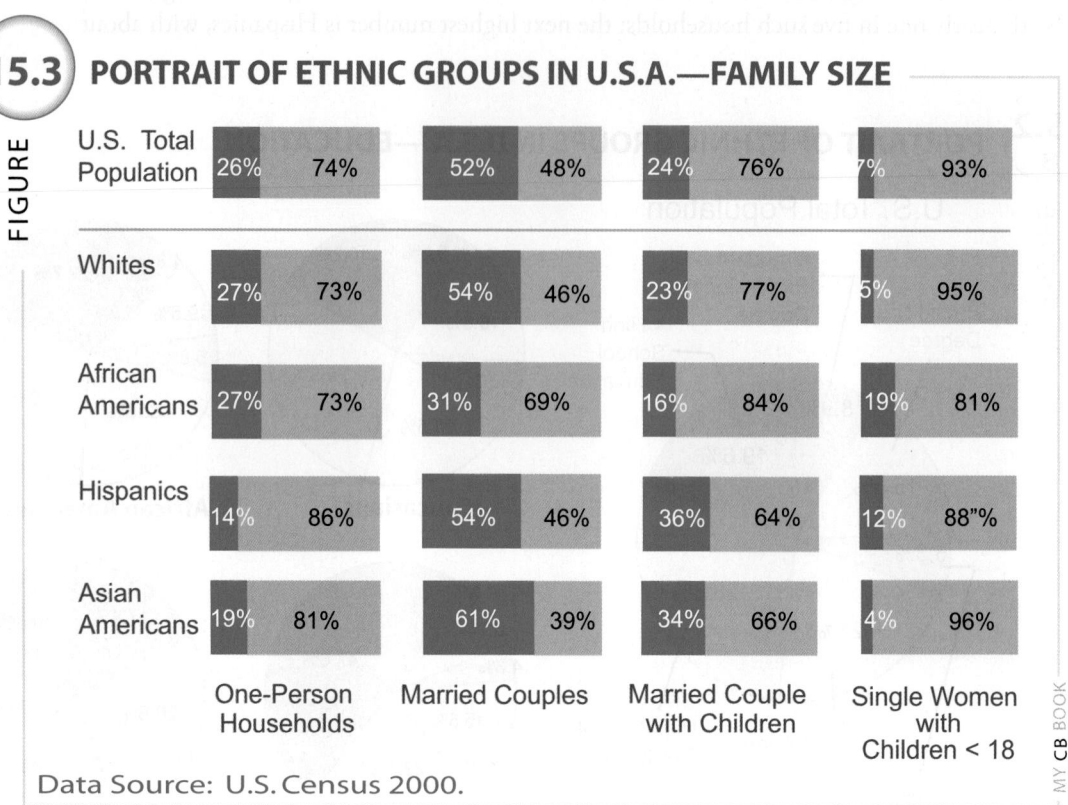

15.3 PORTRAIT OF ETHNIC GROUPS IN U.S.A.—FAMILY SIZE

	One-Person Households		Married Couples		Married Couple with Children		Single Women with Children < 18	
U.S. Total Population	26%	74%	52%	48%	24%	76%	7%	93%
Whites	27%	73%	54%	46%	23%	77%	5%	95%
African Americans	27%	73%	31%	69%	16%	84%	19%	81%
Hispanics	14%	86%	54%	46%	36%	64%	12%	88"%
Asian Americans	19%	81%	61%	39%	34%	66%	4%	96%

Data Source: U.S. Census 2000.

CAUCASIANS (NON-HISPANIC WHITES)

Who They Are

Even though European Americans are the descendants of European immigrants themselves, it is now conventional to deem them as the mainstream population. It is also conventional to refer to this group simply as "whites" or "Caucasians," although neither term is exact. Hispanics could also be white, and they are counted in the U.S. census as Caucasians. A more accurate label therefore would be "non-Hispanic Caucasians."

Demographics

Let us look at their demographics first. Americans of European descent number, according to the U.S. Census 2010, about 223 million, and about 4 million of them are foreign born. Immigration from Europe boomed between 1980 and 1995, a period during which about 1.2 million Europeans migrated to the United States, in large part spurred by the breakdown of communist regimes in Eastern Europe. Although these European descendants are themselves a diverse group, representing some 15 different countries of origin, they do share some common characteristics as a group.

Because whites make up the single largest majority, accounting for 72% of the total population, their education and income distribution closely resembles the U.S. average. One in four whites have a college degree, and one in two have some college experience. One in four live alone. Of the other three fourths, 64% are married couples. About one in three are members of a household with two or more persons working full-time. More than 10% are business owners, and one in four have a professional job. Forty-five percent of them have a household income that exceeds $50,000 a year, and for one in four, it exceeds

$75,000 a year, indicating the relative prosperity of this population. Of course, the prosperity of different ethnic consumers within this population varies: in general, the more recent the immigration, the poorer or less prosperous the group. Thus, the median household income is highest among European Americans of French origin ($75,000 for 40% of them), the majority of whom have been in the U.S. for more than ten years. The lowest income is among those of Polish origin ($25,000 for about 40% of them), the majority of whom have had a U.S. residence of less than ten years.[9]

Edmond and Teuta Cata, Caucasians and European Americans (recent immigrants from Albania)

Inside their minds

Next, let us look at their psychology. What is on their minds? What are their motivations and values, and what do they seek from life? From the marketplace? Among all the ethnic groups, Caucasians represent the Western cultural values the most: Individualism, competitiveness, merit, accomplishment, etc. (see Chapter 9). They desire change and progress and consider time as "money." They value youth and seek material success. These cultural values and norms influence their marketplace behaviors. Market transactions tend to be impersonal, apparently rational, and efficiency-driven. Products and services are purchased with personal benefits in mind.

Not all European Americans think of themselves as ethnic, but many do. Members of this latter group maintain strong ties with their homelands. These "ethnic Europeans" exhibit different marketplace behaviors from (non-Hispanic) whites in general, and from other ethnic minorities in particular.

These ethnic European Americans work longer hours than other (non-Hispanic) whites, and they spend the fruits of their labor liberally on material goods and on recreation. For example, they take cruises substantially more than does an average American: Compared with a 3% rate among the general population, the cruise travel rate among Americans of Swiss origin is 6%, and among those of Russian or Norwegian origin is 17%.

Conspicuous consumption is especially conspicuous among the "ethnic whites." Home electronics (VCRs, stereos, etc.) are owned by more than 90% of ethnic whites, compared to about 50 to 60% among all non-Hispanic whites. Indeed, among the recent immigrants from Eastern Europe, buying American consumer goods is a symbol of having become an American. One European immigrant explained it thus: "It takes a long time to become a citizen or to be able to vote or to perfect one's English. But as soon as a person has a steady job and an income, he or she can start buying the symbols of what it is to be an American, whether it be the TV and the VCR or the designer sneakers."[10]

Caucasians—How Marketers Should Respond

To reach ethnic Europeans, that is, those Americans of European descent who still maintain ties with their homeland and its language and culture, marketers must adapt their mainstream strategies. Cruise marketers catering to ethnic Europeans, for example, target different cruises to ethnic segments— Greeks, Italians, Eastern Europeans—and they customize food and

> ⚠ **CAUTION**   **Enter with an Open Mind**
>
> Profiling ethnic (and religious) groups by demographics is an easy task. This relates to objective data. But psychographic and consumption profiles are subjective and tentative. This is because research is thin on these topics, and many descriptions drawn here are based on occasional and sometimes dated studies. Some tend to confirm popular views, whereas some are revelations.
>
> Any profile that paints an entire category of people (whether based on age, income, profession, religion, or ethnicity) has, by definition, some elements of stereotype—not necessarily false, but not applicable to every consumer by any stretch. Furthermore, some traits can be understood only by in-group members; and some only by out-group members. Not all readers may therefore interpret them in the same way. What is of interest here is to learn what the current body of knowledge—comprising systematic studies, anecdotal evidence, and conventional wisdom—says about various ethnic groups. Read these with an open mind and enjoy the colorful cultural consumption portraits various ethnic groups offer.

entertainment to each group. Another strong marketing tool is the use of ethnic languages in advertisements—German, Italian, French, Russian, and so on. Ethnic whites still find their mother tongue very appealing.

SAVVY MARKETER

Often, the product benefit or appeal needs adaptation. For instance, AT&T found that its "True Voice" campaign with Whitney Houston had no appeal for recent ethnic European immigrants. The quality of the sound (true voice) was not a value to them because they were used to having to scream into the phone in their homeland. Actually, to an immigrant from Eastern European countries, true voice often meant "the voice of Pravda," and Whitney Houston had no relevance to them either. So on Russian-language TV, AT&T instead used a Russian comic promoting its service.

Such customization is not needed for the larger group of European Americans (i.e., those other than recent immigrants). Those having lived longer in America constitute, as already mentioned, what has come to be known as the "mainstream culture."[12]

AFRICAN-AMERICANS

DEMOGRAPHICS
Bridging the Economic Divide

African Americans number some 38.9 million (13% of the total U.S. population, per 2010 U.S. Census). (Worldwide, consumers of African origin number one billion.) They are concentrated in the South, mostly in major metropolitan areas such as Atlanta, Chicago, Los Angeles, Detroit, Washington, D.C., and New Orleans. Their median age is 25.6 years (compared with 43 years for whites), and the average household size is 3.1 (compared to 3.5 for whites). Many children live in single parent families (19% of all households are single women with children compared to 7% in the population as a whole). A large proportion is poor: the annual household income is less than $25,000 for 42.9% of them, compared to only 29% of whites. In education, they lag the average population somewhat: 27.7% of them have less than a high school degree, compared to 19.6% among the average population.[13] At the same time, many have middle and upper level incomes and are well-educated. The most notable thing about this ethnic group is that its members are entrepreneurial and determined to bridge the economic divide.

Values and Psychographics
Successful and Celebrating

Family and religious values are very important to African-Americans. Taking care of their loved ones comes first. Middle-class African-Americans display a high degree of achievement motivation, attempting to succeed financially, and they are keen to make a mark. They are self-image conscious and like to display style. They are trendsetters and tend to define their own style. In his book, *African Americans: A Celebration of Life*, author Ronald L. Freeman writes: "Style—whether captured in an elegant hat, an eloquent phrase, a sophisticated step, or a smooth move—lies at the very heart of African-American culture."

Among the distinguished icons of this ethnic group are such names as Oscar winner Halle Berry, basketball superhero Michael Jordan, TV show host Oprah Winfrey, and ace filmmaker Spike Lee. Two notable celebrations for this community are Black History Month (celebrated in February) and Kwanzaa (celebrated annually between December 26 and January 1).

African-Americans have a strong racial awareness and ethnic pride and support marketers and stores that show respect for their ethnic pride. In a recent study, more than any other ethnic group, they reported that their preference of stores depended on how the stores treated them based on their race.[14]

Ethnic, Religious, and Class Identity **15**

And How They Love Shopping!

African-Americans enjoy shopping, many using it as a social occasion. Compared to the general population, African-Americans spend disproportionately more on clothing, shoes, and home electronics. Although all kids are fashion and brand conscious, African- American kids are substantially more so. African-Americans show loyalty to well-known brands, but they are also willing to try new brands. African-Americans tend to drink regular colas (rather than diet versions) and flavored drinks such as Mountain Dew. In many product categories, African-Americans tend to buy premium brands. Many middle- and upper-class African-Americans spend a good deal on clothing, cars, audio equipment. They also buy other luxury products simply because doing so signifies their lifestyle, tradition, and relative affluence.

James Hughes and Ruth Champion-Hughes (entering a restaurant)

How Marketers Should Respond

Until recently, marketers had not directed much of their resources toward African Americans. Until the 1980s, cosmetic companies marketed the same make-up products for whites and African Americans; then Flori Roberts introduced a new line of foundations and make-up products specially formulated for the dark skin. Likewise, for years, African American children had to make do with white dolls, white cartoons, and even white fairy tales (Goldilocks). Today, Huggy bean dolls, and Kulture Kids, smaller dolls wearing kente cloth (a fabric motif style popular in Africa), and black hero comic books are in the offing. In another exemplary case of custom-targeting African Americans, *Essence* magazine created a designer line of eyeglasses that would fit the African American consumer's style better.

There are, of course, special media for African Americans that offer opportunity for marketers to target this group. Black Entertainment Television (BET) network reaches more than half of African-American households. Magazines such as *Ebony*, *Essence*, *Black Enterprise*, *Emerge,* and *YSB* are very popular among African Americans. Some marketers and advertisers have begun to adapt their efforts for this segment. For example, the Allstate logo is a pair of hands along with the slogan, "You are in good hands with Allstate." In some advertisements, those hands are black.

SAVVY MARKETER

HISPANICS

DEMOGRAPHICS

Now the Largest Minority

With over 35.30 million in number, Hispanics overtook as the single largest minority in the U.S. Census 2000, edging out African Americans by a small margin (the latter, 34.65 million). By 2010, their number grew to 50.5 million. As a group, Hispanics are the youngest of all groups in the U.S., with a median age of 24 years. Their median income, counted in U.S. Census 2000, was $33,565 (compared to the U.S. average of $42,228). This largest minority will represent a huge spending power, accounting for an estimated $900 billion in the U.S. marketplace, up 300% since 1990. To target them, U.S. advertisers spent $3 billion in 2004.[15]

Presently, they are concentrated in Miami—accounting for a little more than half of the total local population (57%). In Los Angeles County, they account for a little more than 40% of the population, and in New York, about 25%. There are four major subgroups:

1. Mexicans Sixty-seven percent of Hispanics are of Mexican origin, and two-thirds of them are U.S. born. Most of them live in the West and

HUMAN PURSUIT OF HAPPINESS **377**

Southwest. They are the youngest of all the Hispanic groups, and some have entered the country illegally, crossing the border and taking any job in the border states. Low-income Mexican Americans tend to stay in these border towns and states such as in Arizona, Texas, and California.

2. Puerto Ricans About 12% of U.S. Hispanics are of Puerto Rican origin. However just as many are of Puerto Rican ancestry but born in the United States. Puerto Ricans have been entitled to U.S. citizenship since 1917, when Puerto Rico became a U.S. commonwealth. Half of all immigrants from Puerto Rico have settled in New York. Many college-educated Puerto Ricans have settled in the Sunbelt States. They can move freely between the US and Puerto Rico; however, many feel that their home is Puerto Rico. This reduces their interest in assimilation. Puerto Ricans, like other Hispanics, are warm and sociable people.

3. Cuban Americans Only 4 to 5% of U.S. Hispanics are of Cuban origin, and 72% of them were born in Cuba. A vast majority of them live in South Florida (e.g., Miami, Tampa), although a large concentration can also be found in the New Jersey area. Cuban Americans are the most affluent Hispanics, and they are also the most educated: Of all Cubans above 25 years of age, 20% have completed four years of college; this compares with 6% for Mexican Americans and 10% for Puerto Rican Americans.

4. Dominicans Immigrants from Dominican Republic are new in the United States and were half a million in the 1990 census. Black and brown in skin color, most tend to settle near the Puerto Rican communities in the North (although a few do live in Miami and New Jersey), and yet they don't really assimilate with Puerto Ricans. They make up 40% of New York's Hispanics, and own 70% of Hispanic small businesses (predominantly supermarkets).

While these four groups broadly share a common language, cultural values, and customs, there are many important differences in tastes and activities. The style of music is different. They have different holidays and like different sports—Mexicans play soccer, whereas Cubans and Puerto Ricans play baseball. Their family size is different. Cubans tend to have smaller families than Mexicans (3.2 versus 4.4, on average).

Hispanics as a group also differ by their region of U.S. residence. In San Francisco, about half of them are churchgoers, whereas in Phoenix and Tucson, only about one in four is. Hispanics also differ by income groups, as do all customer groups. Affluent Hispanics are more assimilated than are low-income Hispanics. Finally, they differ by the length of their residence in the United States. Recent immigrants exhibit more of their native culture and customs.

What they Value

Family and children are very important to Hispanics and take precedence over work. Religion and tradition are also respected. Hispanics are more religious than Caucasians, and a greater proportion of them are churchgoers. Play and work are interwoven; during a normal workday, they entertain social visitors or engage in extensive social conversation with business visitors. On the flip side, they tend to work late hours (especially if they have had a prolonged, fun-filled lunch hour) and make substantial business deals over food and beverage fiestas. Hispanics—both men and women—have a strong interest in appearance. Finally, Hispanics are fascinated by technology.

Building Identity in the Marketplace

Good looks and appearance being important to Hispanics, they are heavy buyers and users of cosmetics and toiletries, much more than mainstream America. Hispanics love to shop. On a typical weekend, either the whole family will go to the mall, or the women will pick up their children and go shopping with a group of friends. They prefer shopping in person rather than through catalogs or online. Hispanics also have a tendency to buy from those

Maria Clay, born a Mexican, MBA from USA, now enjoying her Hispanic American ethnic consumer identity.

companies that are involved in community activities.

Hispanics tend to be more brand loyal; about half of them buy their usual brands. Many U.S. brands have made inroads in their native countries, so Hispanics continue to show loyalty to those brands. One reason is that since family is very important to them, they want to do the best for the family by buying prestige goods. Many Hispanics, of Mexican origin, in particular, don't trust putting checks in the mail because back in their homeland of Mexico, they trust neither the bank nor the post office. So they tend to pay by cash. Nationally, only one in three Hispanics has a checking account or owns a credit card (compared to more than two-thirds of all Americans).

How Marketers Should Respond

In a 2004 study, child-friendliness in restaurants was much more important to Hispanics than to an average American (24% versus 8%).[14] Since Hispanics are family oriented, marketplaces (e.g., restaurants, stores, public vehicles, travel programs, etc.) would need to be much more child-friendly.

Since Hispanics are close knit and community oriented, word-of-mouth is very effective for them; hence, event marketing (sweepstakes, music festivals, sporting events, religious holidays) is a good tool. In media communications, it helps to use Hispanic spokespersons; one study found that members of Hispanic minority ethnic groups viewed the "same-ethnicity" spokespersons as more trustworthy.[15] In mass media, Spanish TV, and among magazines, Hispanic and Hispanic Business are important. Some marketers have adapted their products to Hispanic tastes; an example is the introduction by Dannon yogurt of guava, papaya, mango, and pineapple flavors.

One vexing question facing marketers is whether the Hispanic customers of different origins can be treated as a single market. The most significant common factor is their common language, Spanish.[16] To account for differences among Hispanic groups, Donnelley Marketing Information Services (DMIS) of Stamford, Connecticut, has identified as many as 18 segments. For example, two of those segments are "Puerto Rican high-income, younger, established homes," and "Mexican, lowest income, younger, low-mobility Hispanic neighborhoods."[17] Such microsegmentation helps local, regional, and national marketers temper national campaigns with local variations. These local adaptations can supplement a national effort, which should be based on an understanding of common Hispanic cultural values: family and relationship orientation, respect for tradition and elders, religiosity, equal importance of play and work, and desire to acquire "Americanness," without losing pride in their own language and culture.

SAVVY
MARKETER

ASIAN-AMERICANS

DEMOGRAPHICS

Oh, What a Potpourri!

By the U.S. Census 2010, Asian-Americans—people of Asian origin—numbered 14.7 million, representing about 5% of US population. This group grew by 43% since 2000 census. Asian-Americans' median age is 27 years, and they have the highest median household income, $56,200 in 2010 (compared with $42,200 for the U.S. population as a whole). They also have a high rate of completing college, 44%, compared to the 24% U.S. average. About half of all Asians live in California, greater New York, or Honolulu. Their share of population ranges from 65% in Honolulu to 18.8% in San Francisco, 11.4% in Los Angeles, 6.7% in New York, 5.1% in Baltimore-Washington D.C. and 4.2% in

Chicago metropolitan area.[18]

Many live in acculturated neighborhoods and pricey suburbs. *Asian American* is merely a convenient label, since, in fact, it comprises immigrants from several countries:[19]

- Chinese Americans (23.75%)
- Filipinos (18.06%)
- Asian Indians (16.4%)
- Korean Americans (10.5%)
- Vietnamese Americans (10.95%)
- Japanese Americans (7.7%)
- Others (12.5%)

Chinese Americans Chinese Americans are about 2.43 million in number and account for over 23% of all Asian Americans. They sometimes identify themselves as either American-born Chinese (ABC), who are more educated and well-to-do and live in upscale communities and are more assimilated into the mainstream culture; or as fresh off boats Chinese (FOB), who live in downtowns and Chinatown and tend to be patriarchical, blue-collar, and conservative. They may speak one of the two major Chinese languages: Cantonese (spoken in Hong Kong) and Mandarin (spoken in Taiwan).

Sanghoon Chang and Ju Won Suh, strolling on Michigan Avenue, Chicago

Filipino Americans There are about 1.85 million Filipinos in America, constituting the second largest and probably the best assimilated of all Asian Americans. Because of the 400-year-long colonization by Spain, the Philippines is a Christian nation; hence, 85% of Filipino Americans are Roman Catholic. They are concentrated in San Francisco and Los Angeles, and, in lesser numbers, in Chicago, New York, New Jersey, and Connecticut.

Asian Indians About 1.67 million in number, immigrants from India, Pakistan, and Bangladesh are, as a group, the most educated of the entire U.S. population. A large number are professionals, and many are owners of small businesses (e.g., motels, gas stations, and convenience stores). Among recent immigrants, most came to study in polytechnic schools and in Ivy League colleges. Indian students are the most significant presence of all foreign students on college campuses, especially in doctoral programs, and lately in the Silicon Valley high-tech companies.

Korean Americans There are a little over one million Koreans in the United States, and 90% of them are foreign-born. They tend to cluster in large metro areas, mostly in New York, Los Angeles, Chicago, and Honolulu. They have the highest self-employment rate and the highest business ownership rate of any group in America. Many of them own small supermarkets and convenience stores.

Japanese Americans There are about 796,000 Japanese Americans in the United States, and more than 80% of them live on the West Coast. Close to 50,000 Japanese describe themselves as "salarymen," people who are sent by corporations to the United States on temporary assignment and have extended visas. Due to loyalty to their employers, they return to their country. Accordingly, they attempt to "stay Japanese" and believe that others have turned their backs on their homeland. However, a majority (close to 90%) are born in the United States, most have attended college, and this group's median family income is 32% above the U.S. average. Many are well assimilated, breaking the stereotype and doing things the mainstream population does. Overjoyed at Kristi Yamaguchi's success in figure skating, one young Japanese-American fan commented, "We are not all math or science wizards or laundry operators or restaurant owners, but skaters, architects, writers. And more. And less. Without hyphens."[20]

Yukari (Japanese-American) and Charles Infosino (Italian-American) (with son Nino)

Vietnamese Americans Vietnamese comprise the largest number of the rest of the Asian Americans, numbering more than a million. About half of them live on the West Coast (about one-third in California). Their median income is lower than that of all other Asian Americans.

VALUES
Not Mainstream at all

Confucianism has had a big influence on many Chinese. This system of beliefs (propagated by the Chinese philosopher Confucius) values hard work, long-term reciprocal relationships, respect for authority (especially, teachers and parents), harmony in all things, and discipline or delaying gratification. Accordingly, the cultural values of Chinese Americans emphasize familial relationships and obligations. Many Chinese Americans do not trust banks, preferring to borrow within their own community, and to put cash in a safe rather than in the bank.

Core Japanese-American values are hard work, loyalty to the group (work group, employer, family, community, or other groups they may join), an obligation to return favors, and respect for age and tradition. Education is also valued highly, so much so that doing well in school is considered an honor to the family or community.

An Asian Indian Family: Rajiv (second from right) and Shelley Chopra with daughters Aarti (extreme left) and Vini. U.S.A.

Filipinos share many cultural traits with Hispanics: family values, courtship rituals, allowing enough "play" time, and so on. They are outgoing and sociable; they love having a good time and enjoy a good laugh.

Like other Asians, Korean Americans value family loyalty, education, and frugality, and show respect for elders. They value self-reliance and are very hardworking.

Among Asian Indians, one of the most remarkable traits (but not easily visible to outsiders) is a faith in the Hindu philosophy of *Karma*. **Karma**, a gospel from Hindu Lord Krishna, emphasizes two seemingly contradictory dictums: (1) a person is predestined to get and achieve whatever is his or her due, based upon his or her deeds in a previous life, or, otherwise, whatever the God has willed for him or her; and (2) at the same time, it is a person's duty to do his or her work diligently since that work too is willed by God. Many outsiders confuse Karma with fatalism (belief in fate), implying a lack of desire to make the effort. Traditional Indians are fatalists, but this does not imply that they shirk the effort; rather, it implies that they must make peace with whatever is the outcome of their effort (i.e., whatever is their *Karma*). Likewise, Asian Moslems often use the expression, "Insha Allah," which means "whatever be Allah's (God's) wish."

Asian Indians value their families and many live in extended families, where adults and children care for the elderly. Many are deeply religious and like to maintain their tradition and customs. Many Asian Indian families, especially those with U.S.-born children, who act as acculturation agents for their parents, adopt modern lifestyles but at the same time preserve their customs in their activities at home and within the community, such as in dress, language, food habits, and religious rituals. They, like other Asians, are hard working; like Japanese, they are very ambitious. But unlike most other Asians, they are also content with what they manage to achieve, a trait acquired by their faith in Karma.

MARKETPLACE BEHAVIOR
Most Utilitarian of Them All

The marketplace behavior of Asian Americans differs from the mainstream population as well as from other racial/ethnic minorities. Notable among these differences are these:
- Japanese Americans, both permanent immigrants and salarymen, are very sophisticated consumers, have a good deal of money to spend, and buy high-quality

mainstream brands;

- Many Asian Indians are vegetarians. But even among those who are not, certain kinds of meats are prohibited; for example, Hindus will not eat beef, and Muslims will not eat pork or drink alcohol. To avoid meat, many Indians prefer Pizza Hut to McDonald's, for example;
- Saving face is very important to Asians. Therefore, they do not take kindly to advertisements that disparage a competitor's product. It is considered bad to make someone (e.g., a competitor) lose face;
- Koreans prefer a soft sell and face-to-face shopping.
- In Hawaii, Chinese tend to pay cash for a car, whereas Japanese finance it;
- Looking the customer in the eye is expected in the United States, but Asian customers would view that behavior as impolite. Similarly, in the United States, it is a practice to smile generously at customers, but for many Asian-American customers this would be out of place, since smiling is done selectively in Asia, reserved for good acquaintances and friends only. In some Asian-American cultures, smiling at strangers is considered artificial or "false."

If you observe any Asian-Americans in the marketplace, there is one thing that will stand out: They are not swayed by the fad of the day, and what they seek most is utilitarian value. Every purchase is highly deliberated, and while they do comparison-shopping, big time, they are willing to spend money—since they have the money—for quality.

SAVVY MARKETER

How Marketers Should Respond?

Language obviously is a key factor in targeting ethnic consumers. Marketing communications need to be in the language that minorities are comfortable with. Most businesses in Miami offer Spanish as a menu option on their voice mail. Chemical Bank teller machines offer a Russian language option in its Brighton Beach-Brooklyn branch to cater to the significant number of Russian immigrants living there. The New York Downtown Hospital, near Manhattan's Chinatown, serves Chinese food. And Dreyfus Corporation offers, at its San Francisco investment center, a money market prospectus in Chinese. But targeting ethnic groups goes beyond a simple language translation.

Many ethnic minority consumers can't identify with the American models most advertisers predominantly use. In a recent analysis, Cover Girl was found to have shown only one minority model out of 236 ads! Beyond the use of different models, the communications should reflect the particular minorities' cultural values and marketplace norms. Since Filipinos enjoy a good laugh, humor works very well for them. Also, because of their strong community orientation, sponsorship of community events is a very effective marketing tool for all Asians. For example, the Moon Festival banquet is a very special festival in the Chinese culture. And Deepawali is the Christmas-like festival for Asian Indians of Hindu origin. Many local marketers take advantage of these ethnic events and sponsor contests, prizes, and so on.

Marketing communication appeals need to be adapted to specific cultures of specific minorities. To Japanese Americans, don't advertise "You will stand out with this car," because Japanese Americans do not value standing out; they desire to blend in. All Asians value tradition, so the "new and improved" appeal is likely to be unattractive to them; instead, marketers should emphasize how long the company has been in business, how well established the brand is, and how long-standing its reputation is.

Food, Clothing, and Beyond—
Consumption Differences Across Ethnic Groups

Some consumption effects of race stem from genetics, which can cause differences in biological needs—such as differences in skin color and texture and hair type. Therefore, consumers from different races need personal care items with specific performance characteristics. Beyond physiology, other differences stem from cultural differences, which in turn affect values, lifestyles, and tastes. Customs and tastes differ among different ethnic groups, for example, in food, clothing, home decoration, and leisure preferences. Food is vastly different from the main-stream population for Asian-Americans and Hispanics, and to some extent also for African-Americans. Ethnic restaurants in America come mostly from Asia, catering to Asian-American minorities, but increasingly also to the mainstream population of whites and blacks. Asian-Americans and Hispanics also cook a lot more of their meals at home, so ethnic grocery stores can be found in most major cities. According to a recent report, U.S. Hispanics spend $117 per week on groceries compared to the U.S. national average of $87.[21]

Similarly, clothing also differs for minorities, most notably for Asian-Americans. Although most have adopted Western clothing in offices and on the street, at home they continue to feel more comfortable in their native clothing, and they prefer lounging in loose-flowing clothing from their homeland. On festive occasions and at in-group large social gatherings, they can be seen donning festive clothing of their native origin. Many of them buy these clothes from their homeland, but there are also full-scale stores in some major cities (e.g., Chicago, New York, and Toronto) catering to their needs.

SAVVY MARKETER

In terms of clothing, Hispanics are most assimilated into the mainstream, but they are also much more fashionable than (and not nearly as casual as) the mainstream population. Likewise, African Americans sport mainstream western clothing for the most part, particularly in the workplace, but in casual clothing they seek—much more than do most other groups—athletic clothes with images of sports teams and name brand clothing.

In clothing and beyond, minorities differ in conspicuous consumption. Asian Americans tend to be frugal, and they are interested in value and quality (rather than in showing off) even when they buy luxury. Hispanics are quite conspicuous, particularly in appearance related consumption. So are many (though not all) African Americans. Some minority ethnic groups tend to seek socially prestigious consumption to bolster their public image.

15.1 ETHNIC SKINCARE MARKET

EXHIBIT

How Marketers Respond

What is the most conspicuous difference between the three major ethnic consumer groups? Skin complexion. Ethnic skins differ in their pigment cells, and in their sensitivity to melanin and other ingredients in cosmetics. Likewise, hair care needs differ across ethnic consumers in pronounced ways. One recent estimate by Packaged Facts places the total ethnic spending in U.S.A. on hair care, cosmetic, and skincare products to be $1.5 billion. And marketers are waking up to this reality. Here is a sampler:

- Colomer USA launched African Pride Multi-Length Texturizer—a product that helps African Americans to maintain defined curls and waves.
- Universal Colors Cosmetics bills itself as a dermatologist recommended line for ethnic women. It has adopted a four-step skin care method (in contrast to the usual and traditional "3-step, cleanse, tone, moisturize, method") comprising deep cleansing exfoliation, toning, and moisturizing.
- Carol's Daughter offers a long line of hand-made products for African American women; recently, it launched its new Mango Collection—mango body butter, cherry mango cocoa butter body soufflé, mango lip balms, etc., enhanced with vanilla, coconut, lime, blended with cocoa and shea butter.
- Makari's skin lightening cream claims to gradually lighten the skin.

Apart from these niche marketers, mass market brands such as Cover Girl and Revlon also market ethnic-targeted cosmetics. Among these big players, L'Oreal has launched a major initiative in ethnic beauty care products. In the year 2000, it established L'Oreal Institute for Ethnic Hair and Skin Research in Chicago. The Institute researches the problems peculiar to African hair as well as all types of ethnic skins, In recent years, it acquired two black-centered companies, SoftSheen and Carson. But its efforts go beyond U.S. ethnic groups. It has a foothold in markets worldwide and caters to consumers of all race and ethnic origins. In China, for example, Maybelline (a L'Oreal line) is the preferred cosmetic brand for 44% of Chinese women.

Source: Based on: Hair Care Needs Are Different, Diverse.(Merchandising), MMR, June, 2005. Jennie James, "Because They're Worth It," Time.com, January 18, 2004; Ethnic Skin Care As Consumers Demand More Ethnic-specific Products, The Market Continues To Expand. By Susan A. Eliya, Happi, October 2005 http://www.happi.com/articles/2005/10/ethnic-skin-care.php).

MY CB BOOK

Money Talks

SAVVY MARKETER

Financial resources affect consumption differently across the races. Races differ in economic conditions. This is due to historical differences in accessing opportunities, as well as race-based cultural differences in individual achievement, motivation, and belief in upward mobility. There has also been a systematic bias against certain ethnic minorities in credit approval. Both of these factors limit the buying power of some ethnic minorities. Other ethnic minorities, such as Japanese Asians or Asian Indians, are affluent, but at the same time they shun credit, thus limiting their purchases to what they can afford.

Seeking Love from Merchants

Ethnic groups also differ from the mainstream whites in their choice of merchants and salespersons. They prefer to do business with stores and firms owned or operated by persons of their own ethnic origin. This is especially the case with financial, insurance, real estate, and health care services because these services and products entail a considerable risk (and they feel greater trust with salespersons of their own ethnic background). That is why a lot of insurance, financial services, and real estate companies hire ethnic salespersons. Having said this, we must also note that many ethnic consumers are totally assimilated in the mainstream and are indifferent or even prefer mainstream salespersons. This is in part because they wish to maintain the confidentiality of their financial and medical matters, and they may suspect ethnics to gossip in their close-knit ethnic communities. Therefore, a company seeking to target minorities should employ salespersons both of ethnic and mainstream origins. (By the way, and at least for this context, Asian Americans and Hispanics consider both blacks and whites as mainstream.)

Finally, ethnic groups differ also in the kind of interaction they seek from marketers—retailers, salespersons, agents, customer service persons. In some races and ethnic cultures, friendship is limited to personal friends, and consequently, in commercial transactions, there is politeness but not personal warmth, so none is offered and none is expected. However, expectations may be different between the customer and the salesperson, if they come from different ethnic backgrounds. This causes a problem when blacks or whites visit Asian-American stores and restaurants, for example, where the level of casual warmth and personalized social interaction is often absent. Of course, many of these service providers of ethnic origin are becoming acculturated enough now to diminish this glaring gap as time goes on.

ETHNIC IDENTITY

So far we have looked at ethnicity as an objective, an "all or none" descriptor of the consumer—a consumer is or is not Hispanic (or African American or Asian or whatever). In truth, it is not a matter of degree. But many of you might know some consumers who don't act like their ethnic type, or who don't see themselves in ethnic terms. This phenomenon is captured in the concept of ethnic identity. **Ethnic identity** refers to a person's knowledge of his or her membership in a social group and the value and emotional significance attached to that membership.[22]

Thus, it is a person's view of himself or herself as more or less ethnic, how closely he or she sees a sense of self in ethnic terms. Consumers with low ethnic identity view themselves

CB FYI

UAE—WHERE NATIVES ARE A MINORITY

United Arab Emirates is a young country with vibrant ethnic diversity. It was created in the early 1970s, following the withdrawal of British forces and the end of imperial treaties. Comprising a loose federation of seven independent states–Abu Dhabi, Ajman, Dubai, Al Fujayrah, Ra's al Khaymah, Ash Shariqah, and Umm al Qaywayn, its population was only 248,000 in 1970.

The population grew to 3 million in 2000 (up from 1.77 million in 1990). By Year 2007, the UAE population had surged to 4.488 million, and by mid 2010 to 7.56 million. (est.)

Its ethnic makeup: Emirati 19%, other Arabs and Iranians 23%, South Asians 50%, other expatriates (includes Westerners and East Asians) 8%. Thus, less than 20% are UAE citizens. Its major religion is Islam (96%, with Shi'a 16%), with Christians, Hindus, and others accounting for a mere 4%. While its official language is Arabic, other languages are in widespread use: Persian, English, Hindi, and Urdu.*

It is a modern country with growing economy. Its per capita GDP for 2010 (est.) was, in international dollars, 40,875, compared to 47,000 for USA, but well ahead of such modern nations as U.K. (36,600) and Japan (34,200).** And among the students at the UAE university, 75% are women!

Proof positive that ethnic diversity is good for a nation!

* UAE Interact, Ministry of Information and Culture, UAE. **Source: CIA Factbook.

Powered by
ℳ

MY CB BOOK

as simply "a human person," period, rather than as "Hispanic" or "Asian." They get more assimilated in the mainstream culture. They may not necessarily abandon the consumption rituals of their ethnic groups, but they feel equally at home in the marketplace marked by mainstream culture. One characteristic of Hispanics, for example, as we learned earlier, is that Hispanics shun coupons. But what about those Hispanics who do not feel strong ethnic identity? One study found that Hispanics with weak ethnic identity tended to use coupons just as the mainstream consumers did.[23] Marketers should not assume, therefore, that all ethnics would find various marketing tools equally attractive, or that non-ethnic media would not appeal to any persons of ethnic minorities, or that they can reach all ethnic affiliation persons relying exclusively on ethnic media or ethnic salespersons.[24]

SAVVY MARKETER

EXHIBIT

15.2 THE CHARMS OF ETHNIC DIVERSITY

Because race-based distinctions are easily visible (due to physiological features) and non-race-based ethnic distinctions are not, we tend to overlook that ethnic diversity exists in every country and in ample measure. We have compiled for you a sample of ethnic group composition of selected nations of the world. Peruse and be amazed.

And the next time you get to travel to any of these countries, look for the rich cultural experience these ethnically diverse marketplaces provide.

Australia Caucasian 92%, Asian 7%, aboriginal and other 1%

The Bahamas Black 85%, white 12%, Asian and Hispanic 3%

Belgium Fleming 58%, Walloon 31%, mixed or other 11%

Brazil White 53.7%, mulatto (mixed white and black) 38.5%, black 6.2%, other (includes Japanese, Arab, Amerindian) 0.9%, unspecified 0.7% (2000 census)

Burma Burman 68%, Shan 9%, Karen 7%, Rakhine 4%, Chinese 3%, Indian 2%, Mon 2%, other 5%

Canada British Isles origin 28%, French origin 23%, other European 15%, Amerindian 2%, other, mostly Asian, African, Arab 6%, mixed background 26%

China Han Chinese 91.9%, Zhuang, Uygur, Hui, Yi, Tibetan, Miao, Manchu, Mongol, Buyi, Korean, and other nationalities 8.1%

Cuba Mulatto 51%, white 37%, black 11%, Chinese 1%

Cyprus Greek 77%, Turkish 18%, other 5% (2001)

Ethiopia Oromo 40%, Amhara and Tigre 32%, Sidamo 9%, Shankella 6%, Somali 6%, Afar 4%, Gurage 2%, other 1%

India Indo-Aryan 72%, Dravidian 25%, Mongoloid and other 3% (2000)

Indonesia Javanese 45%, Sundanese 14%, Madurese 7.5%, coastal Malays 7.5%, other 26%

Iran Persian 51%, Azeri 24%, Gilaki and Mazandarani 8%, Kurd 7%, Arab 3%, Lur 2%, Baloch 2%, Turkmen 2%, other 1%

Israel Jewish 80.1% (Europe/America-born 32.1%, Israel-born 20.8%, Africa-born 14.6%, Asia-born 12.6%), non-Jewish 19.9% (mostly Arab) (1996 est.)

Latvia Latvian 57.7%, Russian 29.6%, Belarusian

4.1%, Ukrainian 2.7%, Polish 2.5%, Lithuanian 1.4%, other 2% (2002)

Malaysia Malay 50.4%, Chinese 23.7%, Indigenous 11%, Indian 7.1%, others 7.8% (2004 est.)

Mexico Mestizo (Amerindian-Spanish) 60%, Amerindian or predominantly Amerindian 30%, white 9%, other 1%

Netherlands Dutch 83%, other 17% (of which 9% are non-Western origin mainly Turks, Moroccans, Antilleans, Surinamese, and Indonesians) (1999 est.)

New Zealand European 69.8%, Maori 7.9%, Asian 5.7%, Pacific islander 4.4%, other 0.5%, mixed 7.8%, unspecified 3.8% (2001 census)

Nigeria Nigeria, Africa's most populous country, is composed of more than 250 ethnic groups; the following are the most populous and politically influential: Hausa and Fulani 29%, Yoruba 21%, Igbo (Ibo) 18%, Ijaw 10%, Kanuri 4%, Ibibio 3.5%, Tiv 2.5%

Philippines Tagalog 28.1%, Cebuano 13.1%, Llocano 9%, Bisaya/Binisaya 7.6%, Hiligaynon Ilonggo 7.5%, Bikol 6%, Waray 3.4%, other 25.3% (2000 census)

Russia Russian 79.8%, Tatar 3.8%, Ukrainian 2%, Bashkir 1.2%, Chuvash 1.1%, other or unspecified 12.1% (2002 census)

Singapore Chinese 76.8%, Malay 13.9%, Indian 7.9%, other 1.4% (2000 census)

Switzerland German 65%, French 18%, Italian 10%, Romansch 1%, other 6%

United Arab Emirates Emirati 19%, other Arab and Iranian 23%, South Asian 50%, other expatriates 8%, (1982)

United Kingdom White (English 83.6%, Scottish 8.6%, Welsh 4.9%, Northern Irish 2.9%) 92.1%, black 2%, Indian 1.8%, Pakistani 1.3%, mixed 1.2%, other 1.6% (2001 census)

Source: World Factbook, 2010

MY CB BOOK

RELIGIOUS AFFILIATION

Consumers' religious identity exercises substantial influence on consumers—on their values, customs, and habits. **Religion** refers to a system of beliefs about the supernatural, spiritual world, about God, and about how humans, as God's creatures, are supposed to behave on this earth. Religious institutions indoctrinate and offer tenets by which their followers ought to live. As such, these institutions influence consumer values, both in respect to the importance and value of material possessions and the goals or benefits desired of products. As a historical example, sociologist Max Weber attributed the industrialization and rise of capitalism in Western Europe to the Protestant ethic.[25]

Major denominations (i.e., religious affiliations) in the United States are Catholics, Protestants, and Jews. Major religions of the world include Christianity, Islam, Judaism, Hinduism, Buddhism, and Confucianism. The major ideas and tenets of each are summarized in Exhibit 15.4.[26]

In thinking about the role of religion in consumer behavior, it is useful to distinguish between religious affiliation and religious identity. **Religious affiliation** refers to a consumer's membership, in objective terms, in a religion. In contrast, **religious identity** (or identification) is the degree of involvement and commitment in that religion as a system of belief and practice. For most consumer behaviors in the domain of religious practice and rituals, a consumer's religious identification would be more influential than mere religious affiliation.[27]

Religious affiliation affects consumer behavior principally by influencing the consumer's personality structure, that is, his or her beliefs, values, and behavioral tendencies. These personality structures, in turn, affect consumers' marketplace behaviors. For example, if you contrast the personality structures of, say, Protestants and Catholics, you would find that compared with Catholics, Protestants are more stoic, nationalistic, and ascetic individualists who believe they have control of their fate and accept delayed gratification. In contrast, Catholics are more traditional, trusting in faith that God controls their life. They believe in collectivism, and family and home are priorities. On the other hand, Jews differ from both of these groups. They tend to be more innovative and more achievement- oriented. These personality differences in turn affect consumer preferences for products or services.

Oh, we almost forgot about hair (the topic of our chapter opening vignette) and religion. One particular religion prohibits hair cutting altogether—the Sikh religion; so Sikh men grow

---

EXHIBIT 15.3

Islamic Food: A Big Market Opportunity

How Marketers Respond

At the American Muslim Consumer Conference 2010, chocolates placed on the tables were special: They were made according to Islamic dietary laws. Islamically permitted goods are called halal. To qualify, meat should come from animals not already dead prior to slaughtering, and that are slaughtered by prescribed ritualistic procedures that are humane and that minimize pain to animals; the meat is to be devoid of blood, and ingredients in foods must exclude pork and alcohol. Moreover, the funds obtained from banks or other commercial lenders to run these businesses must be without interest (called usury-free). With 25% of the world's population being Muslim (1.6 billion people), worldwide, the market for halal products is estimated to be $632 billion annually. The largest markets for halal foods are in Indonesia, India, Pakistan, Egypt, and the gulf countries like UAE, Saudi Arabia, Oman, and Kuwait.

Businesses have been courting Muslim consumers for long; Nestle, for example, has about 20 factories in Europe with halal-certified production lines. In U.S., McDonald's, Wal-Mart, and Whole Foods sell halal food items. In the U.K., National Halal Food Group is a major supplier. Canada is a big exporter: In 2010, Canadian agri-food exports to halal markets exceeded $3.2 billion. With a market opportunity like that, marketers would need to understand the culture and values of religion-based ethnic communities like Muslims and, in a similar vein, other religious minorities as well.

Further reading: "US Muslims: A New Consumer Niche," Rachel Zoll, December 12, 2010. Copyright 2010 The Associated Press. Accessed from Forbes.com on January 15, 2012; "Halal Food," by Saad Fayed, About.com, accessed January 17, 2012. World Halal Forum 2009. "Global Halal Food Market," Agri-Food Trade Service, Canada, Report, May 2011.

   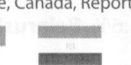

MY CB BOOK

their hair waist long, and to cover their long hair, they wear headgear (turbans), just as do many Saudi Muslims. In the Hindu religion, a child receives his or her first haircut amidst religious ceremonial pomp and show. Buddhist monks shave their heads, thus eliminating one more trap of the material world—*tress love*. For most consumers, however, *tress love* is their significant consumer behavior.

EXHIBIT 15.4

MAJOR RELIGIONS OF THE WORLD

BUDDHISM The Buddhist religion branched out of Hinduism in the sixth century B.C. and is found in such countries as China, Tibet, Sri Lanka, Japan, and Korea. Buddha, the Enlightened One, preached, "Blessed is he who overcomes sin and is free from passion ... and the highest blessedness comes to him who conquers vanity and selfishness." The tenet of Buddhism most relevant to customer behavior is the one about asceticism— rigorous self-denial and active self-restraint in consumption. Buddhism teaches that material things cannot bring happiness.

CHRISTIANITY Christianity comprises two main groups--Catholics and Protestants. Roman Catholicism centers around the church and its religious order. The church is supposed to mediate between God and humans. In the Catholic religion, the proper source for rules on the way to live is considered to be the Vatican. Therefore, outside knowledge not originating from the clergy is considered invalid. Consequently, Catholics are likely to be more fatalistic, traditional, and less innovative. In the United States, Catholics identify themselves with the Democratic Party.

Protestants believe that everyone has direct access to God (without the mediation of the church) and that God has intended for every person to do His work. Thus, work becomes important as a means of carrying out God's will. This work ethic, referred to as Protestant ethic, leads its followers to produce more material wealth. Protestantism does not seek to provide to its followers knowledge of the external world. It encourages them, instead, to seek scientific knowledge for that purpose. Compared to Catholics, Protestants are less authoritarian, more open to change, and have a work ethic; they consider leisure nonproductive and hence a waste of time. Politically, they may be conservative and align themselves, in the United States, with the Republican Party. Protestants believe in getting ahead by personal effort rather than by government handouts, and they strive for upward mobility.

CONFUCIANISM There are about 350 million adherents of Confucianism, mostly in China, Japan, Burma, and Thailand. Confucianism is a philosophy rather than a religion. It guides almost every aspect of Chinese life. Confucians urge people to strive for righteousness and improvement of one's character. Prominent Confucian values are harmony in the family, order in the state, and peace in the empire. Human duty is emphasized, and the ideal of the "superior man" rather than the divine is stressed. Man is supposed to cultivate the qualities of benevolence, propriety, wisdom, and sincerity.

HINDUISM Perhaps the oldest of all religions, Hinduism holds a strong belief in "Karma"—the idea that a person's activities determine his or her destiny in the next life and liberation of the spirit from the human body and its union with God. An important element of its belief system is the caste system, the group each person is born into; caste defines one's status. In India, the home of Hinduism, class mobility would be an inappropriate appeal for promoting products. Family is highly valued in this religion, and most Hindus live in extended families and even operate businesses as a family unit.

ISLAM Islam is the religion of the followers of the Prophet Mohammed. These followers, called Muslims, are concentrated in India, Pakistan, and the Arab nations of the Middle East. Muslims follow a detailed way of life and daily routine prescribed in the Koran, their sacred book. This routine includes prayer five times a day, a practice marketers visiting their Muslim customers should be aware of. Another noteworthy practice is fasting, especially during the lunar month of Ramadan, when Muslims must eat or drink nothing during the day. This religion holds rather traditional views on women, which may entail their seclusion and permits polygamy. Finally, Islam is a missionary religion--the faithful are supposed to uphold their religion and oppose the unbelievers.

The number of Moslems in America is estimated to be three to four million. About one in four Moslems in America is black. Moslems favor close-knit families, support religious education, and have conservative social values. Use of alcohol, dating, and sexual freedom are prohibited among traditional Moslems, although the younger generation growing up in America tends not to adhere to such strict norms of their religion.

JUDAISM In Judaism, God is viewed as an abstract and omniscient presence; however, God is presumed to be inclined to communicate with the individual directly (as opposed to through the clergy as in the Catholic system). Judaism believes that man can only comprehend God through self-education. It also believes, similar to Protestants, that man is responsible for his own actions and for his destiny or position in life.

The Jewish personality has been described as follows: Compared to Protestants and Catholics, Jews are more liberal and democratic, more flexible and rationalistic, higher in achievement motivation, more enthusiastic, gregarious, and emotional, more impatient and hurried, more inclined to postpone gratification, and politically most liberal.

Sources: Based on multiple sources: Benson Y. Landis *World Religions*, New York: E.P. Dutton & Co. 1965); "Understanding Islam in America," *American Demographics*, January 1994, pp 10-11. dictionary.com.

MONEY AS A CONSUMER DIFFERENTIATOR

Money is another factor that (after age, gender, race, and ethnicity) visibly distinguishes us in society. It's writ large on our persona—in the clothes we wear, the houses we live in, the cars we drive, and the restaurants we frequent.

It also determines, at least in part, our attitude toward the world and our market choices. Money affects them all. Money and a few other things, actually—like our education, occupation, and pedigree, for example. These characteristics are captured in the twin concepts of (a) income and wealth, and (b) social class. Let us consider each in turn.

INCOME AND WEALTH

First things first. Let us define income and wealth. A person's **income** is the amount of monetary earnings that person receives periodically on a more or less regular basis. This can comprise of wages and salaries, or income from one's business if self-employed. Income is of course only one component of a person's financial resources. Other components are inherited wealth, savings, and lottery winnings. A consumer's total financial resources are collectively known as "**wealth**." Your wealth is what determines whether you are poor or rich, or somewhere in between. For most consumers, though, their income is the principal or even the only determinant of their wealth. Therefore, our discussion of consumers' financial resources centers on income.

INCOME AND CONSUMER SPENDING

One universal fact of life in all societies is that income is not equally distributed across population, and also that a vast majority of population earns a low income, whereas a very small percentage of people earn a very high income. This can be seen in the distribution of income in the U.S.A. See Figure 15.4.

GINI INDEX Economists use a yardstick called *Gini Index* to measure inequality in a country. **Gini Index** is computed by subtracting from 1.0 the ratio of the proportion of income earned by a specific proportion of the population, counting from the bottom. Thus, if 20% of the population at the bottom earns 20% of total national income (and likewise 30, 40, 60% earn 30, 40, and 60% of the total income), then that ratio for this perfect-equality nation will be 1.0, and the Gini Index value will be zero (=1.0-1.0). Table 15.1 shows the Gini Index (converted to 100 basis) for selected countries. As that table shows, Finland has among the most equal and South Africa among the most unequal income distributions.

> On income equality, Finland ranks among the highest and South Africa among the lowest nations.

FIGURE 15.4 INCOME DISTRIBUTION OF POPULATION

Number of Families (%)		Annual Income ($)
5.2%		$200,000 and more
20.5%		$100,000 to 199,999
13.5%		$75,000 to 99,999
33.2%		$35,000 to 74,999
27.8%		< $35,000

Data Source: U.S. Census 2010

MY CB BOOK

TABLE 15.1 GINI INDEX

Australia	30.5
Brazil	53.9
Canada	32.1
USA	45.0
UK	34.0
Singapore	47.8
Russia	42.9
China	41.5
India	36.8
Japan	37.6
S. Africa	65.0
Germany	27.0
Norway	25.0

Gini index of 1 implies perfect equality and of 100 perfect inequality.

Source: CIA World Factbook Accessed Jan. 30, 2011.

MY CB BOOK

Food, Clothing, Or Video Games—What Do You Want To Buy With Your Money?

How do consumers allocate their money over different product categories, such as food, clothing, transportation, etc.? Although no two families will spend their money in exactly the same way, there is, on the average, quite a consistent pattern of how income is allocated over expense categories.

Poor families spend their incomes largely on food, housing, and some basic clothing. As income increases from low to moderate levels, people tend to eat more food, and also more of the foods that are not considered staples (which are therefore more expensive). Thus, with rising income, the amount spent on food increases; however, as a proportion of income, it remains the same. Subsequently, as income increases even further, the proportion spent on food declines—after all one can eat only so much!

The proportion of income spent on housing rises with income in the very low-income range, but then it remains fairly constant. As regards clothing, automobiles, and luxury goods, expenditures on these items rise sharply with income, until a very high upper limit is reached. These spending patterns are described by Engel's law—after the 19th century Prussian statistician Ernst Engel. According to **Engel's law,** the lower the per capita income of a nation or people, the more they tend to spend on basic necessities such as food, housing, and clothing. Consumption items other than these necessities are called discretionary products. Consumers buy these with **discretionary income**—personal income left after taxes and after the purchase of necessities. As discretionary income rises, consumers spend more on discretionary items, such as video games, vacations, art collections, or plastic surgery. (See Table 15.2.)

TABLE 15.2 HOW CONSUMERS SPEND THEIR MONEY

	PERCENTAGE OF TOTAL SPENDING		
	All Households	Households in Income Groups	
		$20-30 K	$70+K
Housing	34.4	37.6	32.0
Transportation	15.6	16.0	17.9
Food*	13.0	14.8	11.2
Health Care	6.4	8.6	4.8
Apparel	3.5	3.8	3.8
Entertainment	5.5	3.7	5.5
Other	21.6	15.3	24.7

*Comprises 7.65% spent for food consumed at home and 5.35% away from home.
Source: Consumer Expenditure Survey, 2010, U.S. Bureau of Labor Statistics.

MY CB BOOK

CONSUMER SENTIMENT

How much money will consumers spend (versus save)? That depends on, obviously, how much they have. But it also depends on their mental outlook on how good the economy is. Researchers call it *consumer sentiment.*

Consumer sentiment refers to a consumer's expectation about his or her financial well-being in the near future. This expectation or outlook can be optimistic or pessimistic, which will either spur or curb consumer spending.

The economic optimism/pessimism of consumers has been tracked since 1946 by the University of Michigan Survey Research Center. Termed **"The Index of Consumer Sentiment,"** the measure is based on monthly surveys in which a national probability sample of 500 households are asked the following questions:

1. **We are interested in how people are getting along financially these days. Would you say that you are better off or worse off financially than you were a year ago?**
2. **Now looking ahead, do you think that a year from now you will be better off financially, or worse off, or just about the same as now?**
3. **Now turning to business conditions in the country, do you think that during the next 12 months we'll have good times financially or bad times?**
4. **Looking ahead, will we have continuous good times during the next five years, or that we'll have periods of widespread unemployment, depression, or what?**
5. **About the big things people buy for their homes—such as furniture, a refrigerator, television, etc., generally speaking, do you think now is a good or a bad time for people to buy major household items? Why do you say so?[4]**

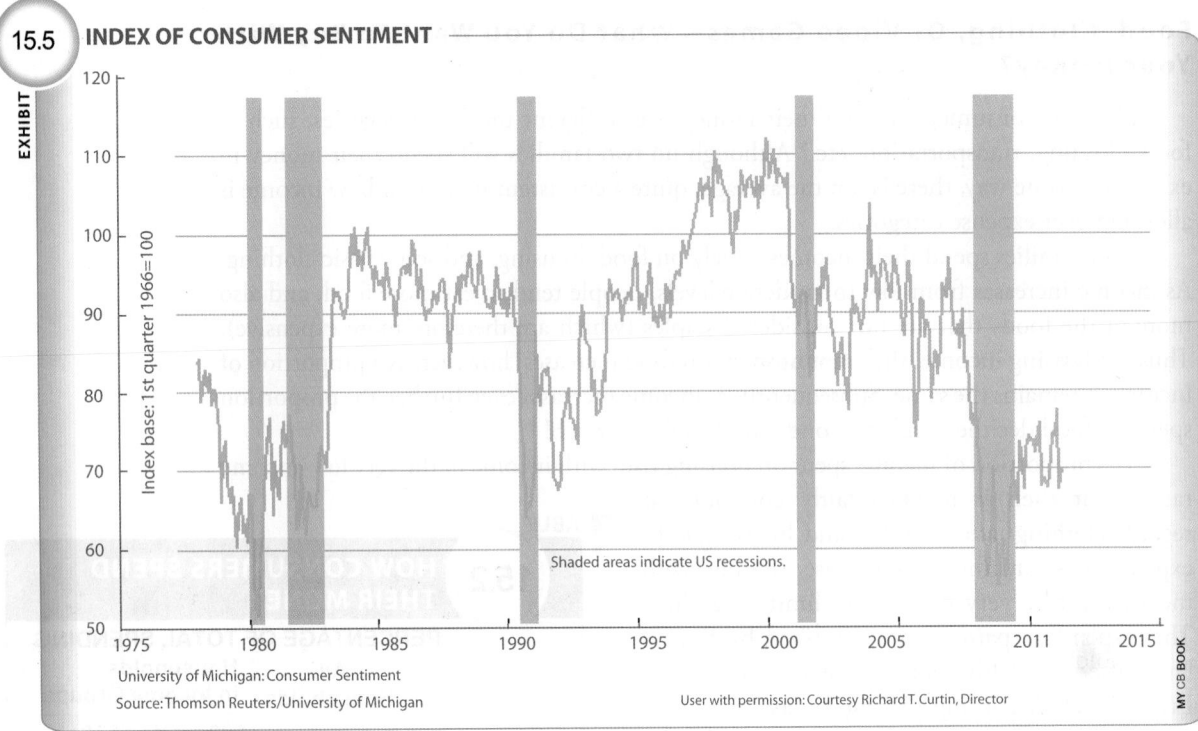

INDEX OF CONSUMER SENTIMENT

Index base: 1st quarter 1966=100

Shaded areas indicate US recessions.

University of Michigan: Consumer Sentiment

Source: Thomson Reuters/University of Michigan

User with permission: Courtesy Richard T. Curtin, Director

MY CB BOOK

The index is computed with 1964 value used as basis (100) and has fluctuated widely with a low of 52 in 1980 to a peak of 109 in 2000 (see chart) at the height of the so called "irrational exuberance" period of the stock market boom. The index has fallen since, reaching a low of 56.4 in June 2008, 57.6 in October 2008, and 56.3 in February 2009—the lowest in the last 3 years. In recovery since then, the index rose to 75.0 in January 2012.

MONEY AND THE MIND—MONEY ATTITUDES

No, we don't mean that money itself has an attitude. But the money holder certainly does. Some money holders flaunt it; others keep it under their skin. Some see only one purpose for having money—to spend, spend, spend. Others want to see it accumulate. These diverse views show your "money attitude." **Money attitude** refers to a consumer's view of and orientation toward money—what it means to him/her and how he/she wants to utilize it.[28]

For the same amount of income, consumers' money attitudes determine their spending and consumption habits, yielding four consumer types:

Flaunters These are consumers who have money and want to show it. They derive pleasure in displaying their wealth, hoping to impress or arouse envy in others. They buy conspicuous items (expensive cars, luxurious clothes, diamonds, etc.) and enjoy their possessions and acquisitions more for their exhibition value than their utilitarian value.

Big-spenders These consumers are not necessarily rich; they just like to spend. Often they live beyond their means and accumulate large debt. They buy and acquire stuff not as much to impress others, but for personal enjoyment. Thus, their purchases comprise a lot of personal, inconspicuous consumption such as eating out, travel, vacationing, cosmetics, entertainment systems, and household items. They also tend to be impulse buyers.

Planners & Savers To these people, money is a means of providing for a reasonable living and assuring a secure future. They like to save and accumulate wealth for the future. They assess their purchase needs carefully, and search for value in all they buy. Unlike Big-spenders, they are avid comparison shoppers and coupon clippers, and they invest their savings for long-term wealth accumulation.

FLAUNT-ERS

BIG SPEND-ERS

PLAN-NERS & SAVERS

TIGHT-WADS

Tightwads At the other end are *tightwads*, people who are obsessive about saving as much money as possible. They avoid buying a thing, unless it was absolutely needed; and they seek no-frills, barebone versions of products at the lowest price possible. Most notably, they learn the ways of putting the things they already own to new uses or extend their useful life. There is even a journal just for this type of consumers. Check it out for some tips for tightwad living at www.tightwad.com.

THE POOR, THE RICH, AND THE MIDDLE INCOME CONSUMERS

Every society is divided into these three broad groups, and people in every society refer to themselves and to others as "poor," "rich," or "middle income." There are other finer subdivisions, of course, but these three are the broad divisions most commonly used in everyday conversations. Let us look at each income group briefly.

THE POOR

Definition of Poverty If we are going to talk about poor people, then we should first define poverty. In general, **poverty** is a level of personal wealth at which a household cannot even pay for all of its basic needs, such as food, clothing, and shelter. For the U.S. population, the federal Department of Health and Human Services defines the poverty level relative to the cost of food. To do this, the department first specifies a daily market basket of foods needed to provide an adequate, nutritious diet on an "emergency" basis (i.e., when income is very low) for families of various sizes and composition. This food basket is then priced according to prevailing prices, and in turn multiplied by three because at low-income levels food represents about one-third of all expenditures. This figure defines the poverty-threshold income level. This figure for 2010 was ($11,139 for a single person household, $14,218 for two persons, $17,374 for three persons, and $22,314 for a family of four. The number of people in U.S.A. below the poverty level in 2010 was 46.2 million, representing 15.1% of the U.S. population.[29]

See Table 15.3 for poverty levels for selected countries of the world.

> **Poverty Line**
> 1-person family $11,139
> 2-person family $14,218
> 3-person family $17,374
> 4-person family $22,314
> (U.S. 2010)

> **46.2 million (15%)**
> The number of people below the poverty line in 2010 (US)

The Psychology of Poverty

What does poverty do to the poor? Fundamentally, it changes their outlook—their view of themselves and of others. Just as affluence does for the rich.[5] The poor see themselves as relatively deprived, powerless, cut-off from the rest of the society, and manipulated. If you peek deeper into their psyche, you are likely to find:[30]

Insecurity—The poor feel that their jobs are unstable, that their resources are inadequate to take care of sickness or other emergencies, and that police and courts exercise excessive and unfriendly vigilance against them.

Helplessness—The poor feel they lack political muscle, and because of their low education and limited life experiences, they are subject to the whims of others.

Fatalism—The poor feel that their own destinies are not in their hands and that chance, luck, or others control their future.

Present orientation—Since they perceive a lack of personal control of future events, the poor feel they might as well enjoy life now and let the future take care of itself.

TABLE 15.3

POPULATION BELOW POVERTY
(Selected Countries)

Chad	80	1
Nigeria	70	7
S Africa	50	26
Brazil	26	64
India	25	86
Spain	20	102
Mexico	18	108
U.K.	14	124
Russia	13	127
USA	12	131
Canada	9.4	138
China	2.8	152

Note: The poverty line is defined differently by each country. China, for example, defines it as per capita annual income of $90; international poverty line standard is $2 a day. The available CIA estimates are for various years (2000-2010).
Source: CIA WORLD FACT BOOK, accessed November 30, 2011.

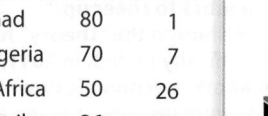

THE MIDDLE-INCOME GROUP

Again, we should first define what middle income is. There is no single definition, of course. One conventional grouping deems household income levels of less than $35,000 as low income, from $35K to $100K as middle income, and greater than $100K as upper income. The 2010 Census places the percentages of U.S. households in these three groups at 27.8, 46.7, and 25.6 percent respectively. Note that this approach defines the low-income group (income <$35,000) more broadly than the "poverty group" identified earlier.

In Europe, average income has gone up in most European Union (EU) nations. In Belgium, France, Italy, the Netherlands, and the United Kingdom, however, the trend is toward a two-tier income distribution, where both upper- and lower-income groups are expanding but the middle-income group is shrinking. What does this mean for marketers? This two-tier pattern has resulted into a simultaneous demand for luxury products and for inexpensive products.

THE AFFLUENT

There is, of course, no universal definition of affluence either. The group with $100,000 to 149,999 can be called "near affluent," those between 150,000 to 200,000 *affluent*, and those with incomes above $200,000 *super affluents*. According to the 2010 U. S. Census, these three subgroups were 15.1, 5.4, and 5.2% of the total population, respectively.

The affluent (which amount to 25.6 percent of US households) account for some 35 percent of all wine consumption in the United States, more than 60 percent of all airline travel, and 50 percent of all new-car sales. Obviously, the exquisite products advertised in such magazines as *Town and Country, Smithsonian, Architectural Digest, Southern Accent,* and *Worth* are consumed almost exclusively by the affluent. In third world countries, domestic servants—chauffeurs, butlers, valets—and imported cars are the status symbols for the affluent.

Why the Poor Pay More?

Would you believe it if we were to tell you that the poor actually pay more for their purchases—more than, say, the middle income groups? The fact is they do.[31] Why? This occurs for two reasons: (1) Lack of resources: poor consumers do not have transportation, storage space (refrigerator and pantry), and access to coupons; and (2) lack of skills and aptitude. They lack the skills to shop for bargains and wherewithal to avoid being exploited by merchants. Also to blame is their psyche: Their attitudes are responsible, according to some researchers, for why they accumulate debt, do not save, and buy unwisely (without putting in the required effort to obtain a good price).[32]

Some studies have found that the poor do not follow wise purchasing strategies. That is, the poor are less likely to read newspapers (and therefore sale advertisements in newspapers), less likely to do comparison shopping, less likely to patronize low-price discount and warehouse stores and buy private or generic brands, and are more likely to accept high-interest credit. Whereas some may view these as *ir*rational behaviors, the poor might actually be quite rational, given their goals and constraints.[33]

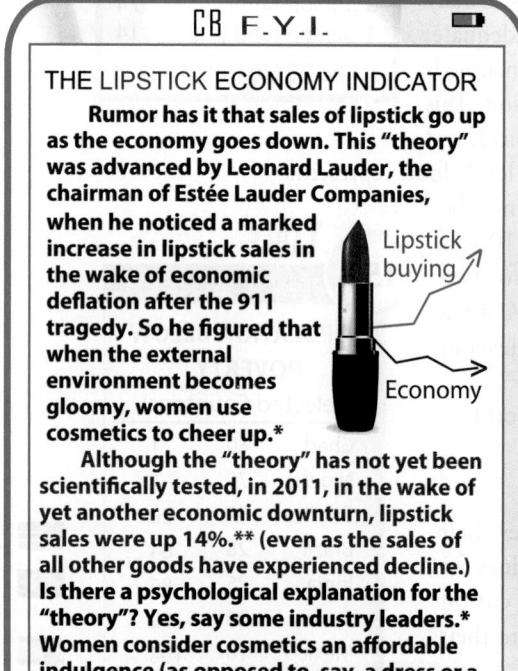

CB F.Y.I.

THE LIPSTICK ECONOMY INDICATOR

Rumor has it that sales of lipstick go up as the economy goes down. This "theory" was advanced by Leonard Lauder, the chairman of Estée Lauder Companies, when he noticed a marked increase in lipstick sales in the wake of economic deflation after the 911 tragedy. So he figured that when the external environment becomes gloomy, women use cosmetics to cheer up.*

Although the "theory" has not yet been scientifically tested, in 2011, in the wake of yet another economic downturn, lipstick sales were up 14%.** (even as the sales of all other goods have experienced decline.) Is there a psychological explanation for the "theory"? Yes, say some industry leaders.* Women consider cosmetics an affordable indulgence (as opposed to, say, a dress or a pair of shoes). So, they tend to buy them as compensatory purchases—using them to take comfort in looking good and to boost their confidence to face the situation. And, among cosmetics, lipstick has a special place as compensatory consumption: It can be applied often, instantly, and almost anywhere. So, women view it is as a quick mood-lifter and a means to instantly feeling good about themselves.

* Industry leaders quoted in "Hard Times, But Your Lips Look Great" Kayleen Schafefer, New York Times, 2008, May 1, 2008. **2011 sales growth reported in Time, Oct 10, 2011.

Powered by ⓜ MY CB BOOK

MARKETER RESPONSE TO CONSUMERS OF DIFFERENT ECONOMIC MEANS

Marketers respond to consumers of different income groups by different offerings. Some companies have broadened their consumer base by targeting consumers at multiple points along the economic spectrum. For example, clothing retailer Gap sells apparel under the brands Gap, Banana Republic, and Old Navy to appeal to consumers of different economic means. Since middle class consumption can be deemed to lie in the middle, marketer responses can be best understood by profiling it for the other two extreme groups.

Marketing to the Low-income Consumer

The marketer response to poor consumers has not always been admirable. A recent book, *The Low-Income Consumer: Adjusting the Balance of Exchange,* explains how low-income consumers get the short shrift at the hands of marketers.[10] One reason may be that when it comes to low-income consumers, marketers do not trust poor consumers to have enough resources to pay for the goods they want to buy, and to shop with honesty. As a result, retail stores in low-income areas tend to keep low quality merchandise and maintain extra vigilance. Sellers may also not value as much what poor consumers have to offer in exchange (e.g., food stamps, low revenue per transaction, etc.), so they may offer even less variety and charge higher prices. Marketers may also act less responsibly in dealing with poor consumers, such as not caring about crowding at checkout registers meant for food-stamp-paying consumers only, keeping poor patients waiting longer, and so on.[11]

Although individually their buying power is low, as a group, lower-income consumers constitute a substantial market. Business strategy guru CK Prahalad has drawn attention to the mass of poor consumers (especially in the third world countries) who collectively constitute an attractive market. Prahalad calls this untapped market a "fortune at the bottom of the pyramid." Some marketers recognize this market potential and are increasingly targeting this group with newer value-oriented strategies, or as *Business Week* states, by providing "affordable simulations of good life."[12] This is epitomized by a store called *Children's Orchard,* which sells used clothing in a non-thrift atmosphere, packaging many of the clothing items in shrink-wrap to make it look new!

SAVVY MARKETER

Marketing to the Affluent

In contrast to the widespread ambivalence about serving the poor, most marketers are eager to target affluent consumers. Everywhere, from free market to command economies, and in industrialized as well as non-industrialized nations, there is at least a small group of affluent consumers, for whom marketers make available the finest, ferreting goods from all corners of the world. You can thus find the most exclusive designer brands in Western Europe as well as in the newly liberated Eastern European countries, in Japan as well as in Africa, and in Australia, Canada, the UK and the United States as well as in China, India, and Mexico.[13, 14]

Marketers offer a wide variety of products to the affluents, such as Bugatti Veyron 16.4 Super Sport (at $2.3 million, the World's most expensive car), a Scott Henshall dress (worn by Samantha Mumba at the premier of Spider-Man II, the dress consists of transparent web laced with about 3000 diamonds estimated at 5 million British pounds), Stuart Hughes iPhone4 Diamond Rose Edition at $8 million, and the world's most expensive bagel sold at the Westin Hotel in New York City (the bagel, priced at $1000, comes with rare, white truffle cream cheese and Reisling jelly that is infused with goji berries and golden leaves and, rumor has it, a smell that is aphrodisiac). These define the limits of boundless occasional indulgence, an exception rather than the rule. For everyday consumption, marketers realize that affluents too, while buying upscale products, are value seekers. Costco is a warehouse store, selling packaged goods in bulk, appliances, furniture, and electronics to the upper middle and well healed. And it lures the affluents with diamond jewelry sold at super value prices.

A portrait from the lifestyles of the Russia's new rich (Millionaire Fair, Moscow, 2009)

SOCIAL CLASS

Life Beyond Income

Many sociologists, economists, and consumer researchers consider social class, rather than income or financial resources, a more meaningful characteristic of consumers to understand and predict consumer behavior. But isn't social class the same as income? Not quite. Consider this: how much money does a priest make? And a politician—say, a member of parliament or a congressman? We don't have to know their exact income, but we do know that many small business owners, like your local car dealers, most likely make more money. Are the priest and the member-of-parliament or congressman in a lower social class than the car dealer? No, and here is why.

Social class is the relative standing of a person in society in terms of status. A person in higher social class is deemed to have a higher social status than those in the lower social class. Thus social class is a prestige hierarchy in a society.[34]

Social Class—How to Get It?

What determines a person's social class? There are four factors: money, education and occupation, talent and accomplishment, and social capital. See Figure 15.5. These four things provide a person major resources that can get him or her prestige. (Health, beauty, race, age, and gender will not, not directly anyway.) Money is usually valued and given prestige everywhere, but not always above other three factors, and prestige given to education and occupation differs across societies.

Education is valued highly for its own sake in Eastern societies; a learned man is revered just because he is learned, no matter what his income. In Western societies, however, education is valued mostly for its instrumental outcome—that is, if it helps you earn more money or a better occupation. Likewise, certain occupations are more valued in some societies than in others. For example, teachers and professors and priests are highly respected in Eastern societies. So are engineers and doctors, and most government officials, including even a police constable. In Western societies, professions such as doctors,

judges, sportsmen, and college presidents are respected, as are managers and executives, and big businessmen. A recent poll conducted by Harris Interactive revealed that the five most prestigious occupations in the USA were firefighters (57%), scientists (56%), doctors (53%), nurses (52%), and teachers (52%); and the five lowest prestige occupations were entertainers (15%), bankers (15%), accountants (15%), stockbrokers (10%), and real estate agents (6%). Commenting on these results, Harris Interactive makes two interesting observations: (1) Income and prestige do not always go hand-in-hand across occupations; and (2) people are fascinated by actors and celebrities but do not necessarily deem them prestigious.[35]

Next, the third factor is your talent and accomplishments. If you are an accomplished artist, singer, poet, author, athlete, or scientist, for example, then you get social recognition, status, and prestige. Perhaps, of the four sources of social prestige, this one goes farthest in getting you status. Maya Angelou, J.K. Rowling, Luciano Pavarotti, Ravi Shankar, Al Gore, Santiago Calatrava, Elon Musk, Alex Rodriguez, Adele Laurie Blue Adkins, Landau Eugene Murphy, Jr., Brian Joseph Burton (Danger Mouse)—accomplished people like these have just as much status as the world's top billionaires, like Bill Gates and Prince Alwaleed Bin Talal Alsaud.

The fourth and final force is your **social capital**—your connections, the network of people you know.[19] People who get close to influential and powerful people also come to exercise influence of their own, and acquire status. Thus, personal advisors (even astrologers) of presidents and CEO's, personal trainers of models and star athletes, stylists, butlers, valets, and chauffeurs of kings and queens, and co-workers, subordinates, and even neighbors of politicians and other movers and shakers acquire and exercise influence among those without access to such resourceful people.

In part, of course, all four of these resources are interrelated. To get close to resourceful people, for example, one needs to have (often, though not inevitably) some talent and accomplishments of one's own. Education and occupation are channels to wealth, accomplishments, and personal connections. In turn, connections feed one's career and success, and, accomplishments often produce wealth. Yet, these four resources can and do exist independently and are garnered individually. Acting in sync, they bring to the person possessing them social status, and consequently, place him or her in a social class.

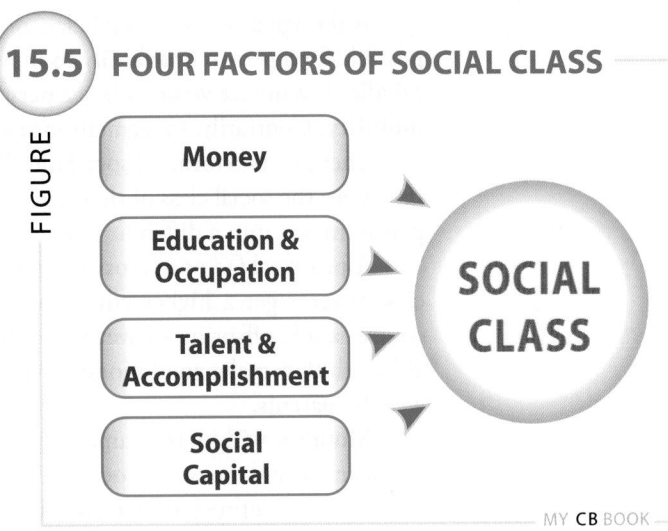

15.5 FOUR FACTORS OF SOCIAL CLASS

FIGURE

Money

Education & Occupation

Talent & Accomplishment

Social Capital

SOCIAL CLASS

MY **CB** BOOK

A Pervasive Phenomenon

Social classes exist everywhere. In the centrally controlled economies and polities (such as the former Soviet Union and China), social classes are based on political power, comprising the ruling classes, those close to the ruling class, and the masses. In once-traditional societies such as India, social class is based on the caste a person is born in, although these caste barriers are weakening (even breaking down) in modern India.[20] In feudal systems, classes are the landlords and the peasants; in pre-Civil War America, classes consisted of the slaves and other servants and the white European gentry. In industrializing nations, the bourgeois and the proletariat form the social classes. Democratic societies boast egalitarianism, but the class system is alive and well. Everywhere, class distinctions are almost a sociological need: People need, it would seem, a class system with hierarchical categories to distance from, belong to, and aspire to. Persons belonging to the same class share certain values, follow certain common customs and activities, and tend to acquire similar products and possessions.

Consumers need a class system with hierarchical categories to distance from, belong to, and aspire to.

The Psyche of Social Classes

One of the interesting ideas about social classes is that they also influence a person's "modes of thought." People of different social classes come to acquire differing ways of looking at the world and themselves, and consequently, different psychological attributes. Paul Henry, a consumer researcher, has identified the following psychological attributes on which members of different social classes are thought to differ.[36]

- **Future versus Present Orientation** Higher social classes have a future orientation versus lower social classes; the latter are more preoccupied with the present.
- **Drive to Stand Out** The higher the social class of a person, the higher the drive to stand out.
- **Preference for Stability** Higher social classes also prefer stability over change and they like to avoid challenges, preferring the comfort of the easy life.
- **Socially Engaged** Finally, higher social classes are more socially engaged.

SOCIAL MOBILITY AND STATUS DISCORD

Are You Going Up or Down?

The TV show *The Apprentice*, "starring" Donald Trump, begins with several participants, all seeking only one thing: upward mobility—both in Donald Trump's screening process, and in their life.

Although a person's social class does not change year-to-year (or even less often), it is possible for a person or a family to move in and out of a social class, such as from lower to middle class or vice versa. When a person moves to a higher social class, it is called **upward mobility**. Contrarily, movement into a lower class is called **downward mobility**.

There are two forms of social mobility: (a) across generations, when grown-up children rise above the social class of their parents or fall below it, and (b) over time, the same adult person moves into a different class.

A principal factor of cross-generational mobility is education; children of lower social class parents get a higher education and move into better paying jobs. Sometimes, of course, adult offspring of wealthy parents may experience downward mobility because, although they make good money, living on their own they can't afford the lifestyle of their wealthy parents.

Mobility within the same generation comes mainly from shifts in one's career or in business outcomes. In societies that believe in meritocracy, like Western Europe, a competent, hardworking, and motivated person can often rise in his or her career to jump more than one class. But this does not usually happen in tribal societies and underdeveloped countries. There, one's social class is determined by birth, period. These societies have what is called an **ascribed social class** system. In contrast, in much of the developed world, one can change one's social class through effort and accomplishments. These societies have an **achieved social class** system. Here, you can move up by your achievements, whether material (e.g., wealth) or otherwise (e.g., education, work success, political position, etc.), and of course, you can move down as well, by running high credit card debt, for example, or by wasting away your life.

> **SOCIAL MOBILITY**
> Some consumers achieve it *downward* by running high credit card debt.

STATUS DISCORD

When the four factors of social class are not congruent, a state of what we term *status discord* occurs. It takes two forms: a lack of status crystallization and being underprivileged.

STATUS CRYSTALLIZATION
Have You Got It?

Are you "status crystallized"? No, it won't make you cool, rich, or high status; but it sure will give you less cause for worry. Because social class is made up of multiple characteristics, two persons could be placed in the same class and yet have considerably different incomes, occupations, or education. When all components are in sync, the consumer is likely to experience more harmony. Sociologists refer to this phenomenon as **status crystallization**—a condition when all components of social class become consistent. When the components are out of sync, status crystallization will be missing and the consumer would experience psychological unease.

> **STATUS CRYSTALLIZATION**
> won't make you cool, rich, or high status; but it sure will give you less cause for worry.

For example, John, a chemist with a Ph. D., has a much higher education but relatively lower income than an average person with a Ph.D. degree; Larry, a self-made small business owner, has only a high school diploma but makes much more money than an average American. Each is experiencing a discrepancy between income and education. Because of higher education, John may want to live in "high culture" residential areas and consume "high culture" activities, such as the arts and theater; but, due to a restricted income, he may be unable to do so. And Larry, with high income, may want to join an exclusive country club, but because of his lack of social connections, he may not be able to. Or once a member, he may feel intimidated with the "high culture" attitudes of the more educated members. Such out-of-sync status, so to speak, can cause consumers considerable frustration in terms of their unfulfilled consumption wants.

UNDERPRIVILEGED AND OVERPRIVILEGED

One reason for a lack of status crystallization can be the income diversity within the same occupation and education groups. A recent M.B.A. graduate could earn, for example, anywhere from $50,000 to $150,000, depending upon his or her alma mater and employer. The median income of a recent MBA in America is about $75,000.[37] Those earning substantially below the median income feel **underprivileged**; those earning substantially above the median are **overprivileged**. Both groups have to strive to keep up the appearance of the social class defined by their education and occupation—namely, "a young executive with an MBA." The underprivileged struggle to keep up with the Joneses—buying homes, home furnishings, cars, and leisure activities that show the tastes of their fellow executives. At the other end, the overprivileged curb their desires to indulge in super-luxury for fear that they would be envied by their peers and be perceived as flaunting their disproportionate wealth. This is true for people of all occupations: engineers, doctors, businesspersons, entrepreneurs, professors, blue-collar workers, white-collar workers, etc.

What the overprivileged do is buy better things that would not be vividly conspicuous. For example, home furnishings, home appliances, better quality and prestigious brand clothing that does not look super-luxurious, higher level models of the same car (e.g., a loaded Toyota Camry or Nissan *Altima* rather than say a more basic Toyota Corolla or Nissan Maxima), or cars that are expensive but do not have the reputation of affluence (e.g., a Lexus or Acura rather than a Mercedes or Jaguar). And they would trade in their cars more often for a newer model. They would also be the first to buy new gadgets for the home that would not be conspicuous (e.g., Roomba, plasma TV, etc.).

SAVVY
MARKETER

The underprivileged, on the other hand, seek the same quality and prestige products as most people of their class, but they seek them at sale prices. Income hard-pressed professionals, for example, do not divert their clothes shopping trips to K-Mart or Wal-Mart; rather they still seek brand name clothing, but at discount stores like T.J. Maxx. They patronize department stores like Macy's or Bloomingdale's, but prefer to buy their clothing when on sale or at end-of-season clearance.

From Class to Mass—Pushing the Class Boundaries

There is a new market these days. Consider Starbucks. It sells plain coffee for $1.25 to $1.50. (You can get plain—though not identical—coffee for 75 cents at a convenience store). And then, there is a mouthful delicious menu of such coffee-latte drinks as White Chocolate Mocha, Tazo® Chai Latte, and Iced Caramel Macchiato that sell for 3 to 5 dollars. Why would consumers spend this kind of money? Simply because, these days, a considerable segment of middle-class consumers want some prestige. So they are buying an 8oz. bottle of Bath & Body Works lotion for $9, roughly three times more expensive than a run-of-the-mill brand; an $8 lunch at Panera Bread instead of a $4 lunch at one of the burger chains; and a $35,000 BMW instead of a $24,000 Honda.[38] This class of products—a sweet spot between the conventional middle market and the conventional luxury market—is known as the *masstige* (also called 'new luxury') products.

MASSTIGE

They buy $8 lunch at Panera Bread instead of a $4 lunch at one of the burger chains

Until recently, the conventional middle class consumers patronized such stores as Sears and J. C. Penney. The luxury stores like Neimen Marcus and Lord & Taylor were largely out of reach. The new masstige stores for trendy middle class are Pottery Barn and William Sonoma. Discount retailer Target caters to, it is said, two different clientele: traditional middle and lower middle class consumers who buy its "regular" wares; and the distinction and aesthetics seeking middle class consumers, for whom Target offers home furnishings by such designers as Philippe Starck, clothing by designers Mossimo Giannulli and Marc Ecko, and cosmetics by Sonia Kashuk. In September 2011, it launched fashion diva Missoni's signature "zigzag design" clothing collection. In 2011, H&M stores introduced Karl Lagerfeld designed affordable street wear, And in February 2012, this high couture designer brought his masstige "Fashion Kollection" to online-only store Net-a-Porter.

Consumption Differences Across Social Classes

As already mentioned, people identify with and associate themselves with other people in their own social class. To be accepted in and belong to that class, consumers adopt the visible consumption of their class. It is an inevitable fact of life that almost every visible consumption—the clothes we wear, the house we live in, and the leisure we partake in—shows our class.

Correspondingly, our possession, tastes, and product choices differ markedly across social classes. In leisure, for example, lower classes prefer and engage in such sports as bowling, and such pastimes as boxing, fishing, watching wrestling, hunting, visiting casinos, and watching TV. Upper-class groups play golf and polo, go on cruises, attend symphonies, operas, and plays. People of middle class play team sports (e.g., volleyball), play cards, and spend a lot of time shopping and visiting friends.[39]

Romancing the Consumer

Haute Couture for Your Ethnic Pride

Ask consumers of any ethnic affiliation what products from their ethnic culture are so near and dear to them that they almost could not live without them, and they will invariably name two products: foods and clothing from their native lands.

Bringing it to them, in every country and every city, are ethnic merchants. For African-Americans, a company called TeeKay Designs showcases festive clothing of African origin—from evening dresses and suits to wedding gowns.

Among Hispanics, one popular item in their native land is Zoot Suit, a festive suit many Hispanics wear on special occasions such as a wedding. Bringing it to Hispanics in America, is an online store named El Pachuco.

The company also offers, of course, other items of Hispanic clothing, such as shirts, pants, and hats.

For Chinese consumers living in America, an online store called *Britablue.com* offers such native clothing as dresses, qipaos, and mandarin jacket, etc.

For Asian-Indians living in America, Chicago based store Sahil offers colorful women's and men's clothing—saris, salwaar kameez, kurtas, and sherwanis.

These and other merchants bring extreme delight to these ethnic consumers. Thanks to these merchants, no matter where you live, ethnic products are now within reach, bringing you delight as you live out your ethnic pride.

Powered OM by

Income or Social Class? Who Done It?

At this point, you might wonder, are all these consumption differences across social classes really differences across income groups? The answer is, "Yes" but also "No." *Yes*, in as much as affordability does constrain what we can acquire. *No*, in as much as given the same prices, which style of products—furniture, home, clothing, leisure—we consume depends more on our tastes rather than available money. Our tastes are molded much more by social class than by income per se. Income affects our tastes, indirectly—by first affecting, in part, our social class.[40] Upper *income* consumers could afford to watch as much TV as they like, for example, but upper *social class* consumers actually watch less of it.

And you realize, of course, that the whole masstige phenomenon is energized by social class, not income. Proof positive that the concept of social class has teeth. And it offers marketers mighty avenues of rising out of parity branding for the middle classes. With that thought we rest this chapter!

S A V V Y
MARKETER

CB Blog

15

SOCIAL CLASS—THE GPS FOR YOUR PLACE IN SOCIETY

Age, race, and gender are given to you by birth and you cannot alter them. They define "who you are." Income and social class are, in contrast, your creation, the outcomes of the path you take in life and the choices you make. As such, they define and serve as markers of "what you are."

Income is our key resource. You know its immense utility to you as a consumer, and with enough of it, you can pick and choose from the marketplace what you dream of. Marketers fashion their offerings—products, prices, distribution outlets—according to income segmentation of consumers, and it is a good thing; it lets you know where you can shop without burning a hole in your wallet.

As you now know, income and social class are not the same thing. Income is a part of it, but it is social class that is truly an index of your social standing. Your education could be a means to your income as well, but it brings you social prestige in its own right. So does your occupation, albeit dissimilarly across cultures. Lastly, your social network determines your influence and prestige. Building social networks requires opportunity of access (often enabled by your education, money, and occupation), we agree, but it also takes initiative and a certain wherewithal. Pay attention to this factor, cultivate it, and watch how it "upgrades" your social standing.

Social class is more consequential than you might have realized. While we all chase money because it is a tangible target, it is the intangible social class that channels our experience both as social creatures and as consumers. Implicitly, we identify ourselves with our social class and use members of that class for social comparison. Perhaps no other variable has a greater effect on our tastes and on our views of how 'noble' and 'becoming' our tastes are, or should be. This "should be" issue arises when we are being pulled in different directions by the different components of the social class (i.e., when we are not status-crystallized!). The 'masstige' trend is good news, satisfying our yearnings for more aesthetic and/or upscale tastes hitherto restrained by our out-of-sync incomes.

Unfortunately, social class is out of vogue with practicing marketers. They are content with using income as their targeting variable. The nuances of social class do pepper the brand positioning deliberations of the more informed marketers; they know that, almost always, it is not the consumers of a particular income who find a product/brand appealing; rather, it is the consumers of a certain income with certain tastes! The next time you finish defining your target segment by income, fine-tune your focus with considerations of social class. Enjoy your contemplations!!

CONSUMER BEHAVIOR

S U M M A R Y

In this chapter, we discussed four important consumer characteristics: race/ethnic identity, religious affiliation, income, and social class. We began the chapter by clarifying the difference between race and ethnic identity, and profiled the four major ethnic/race groups in the United States, namely, Caucasians, Hispanics, African Americans, and Asian Americans. In the U.S., although Caucasians are a majority (comprising some 70%), minorities are growing rapidly. In the 2000 Census, Hispanics became the single largest minority ethnic group, surpassing African Americans by a small margin. Among Asian Americans, Chinese are the largest subgroup, and Japanese are the smallest. Each ethnic group differs from others in demographic as well as psychographic characteristics. Correspondingly, they differ in their consumption preferences as well. Some of these differences are based on biological needs being different; others are produced by cultural practices and habits. Specifically, race and ethnic backgrounds influence a consumer's needs for hair and skin-specific personal care items, taste differences in food and clothing, and in preferred interaction styles with marketers. We outlined how marketers need to respond to these ethnic differences.

Among religious affiliations, we covered major religions of the world: Christianity, Judaism, Hinduism, Islam, Buddhism, and Confucianism. A person's religious affiliation influences his or her consumer behavior by shaping values, beliefs and preferences. Some products are prohibited by some religions, and many consumption rituals are tied to religious practices and customs.

Next, turning to income and wealth, we defined income as a person's monetary earnings received periodically. It can comprise wages, salaries, and earnings from self-employment. It determines consumers' spending power and influences what they buy and when. As income increases, expenditures on clothing, automobiles, and luxury goods rise sharply. These patterns of spending are captured in Engel's law. Consumers also have what we call "money attitude," defined as their orientation toward money, which gives us four consumers types: Big-Spenders, Flaunters, Planners & Savers, and Tightwads. Along with money attitudes, consumers' expectations about their financial well-being in the near future—called consumer sentiments—influence how much they will spend currently. Marketers usually target the three income segments—the poor, the rich, and the middle classes—with different offerings.

We next discussed social class—defined as the relative standing of a consumer in society. The more prestige you have, the higher your social class, which comes from four factors: money, education & occupation, talent & accomplishments, and social capital. When these four elements are in sync, status crystallization occurs. Within each class, consumers who are on the fringe (far away from the average) are overprivileged or underprivileged—a condition that influences consumers' purchases. Social classes determine, of course, consumers' lifestyles and therefore their marketplace behaviors. We described the marketplace behaviors of each social class, and we noted how marketers are bringing prestigious products within the reach of the not-so-rich consumers, a phenomenon called masstige.

K E Y   T E R M S

Achieved social class
Ascribed social class
Asceticism
Buddhism
Christianity
Confucianism
Consumer sentiment
Discretionary income

Downward mobility
Engel's law
Ethnicity
Ethnic Identity
Hinduism
Income
Index of Consumer Sentiment
Islam

Karma
Money attitude
Overprivileged
Poverty
Poverty level
Race
Religious affiliation
Religious identity

Social class
Status crystallization
Underprivileged
Upward mobility
Wealth

YOUR TURN

REVIEW+Rewind

1. Explain the difference between race and ethnic identity.
2. Briefly outline the comparative demographic profiles of four major ethnic groups in U.S.A.
3. Briefly outline psychographic profiles of four major ethnic groups in U.S.A.
4. Briefly summarize the core theme the four major religions and suggest how each religion might affect consumer behavior of its followers.
5. Cite some examples of what marketers do differently (or should) when targeting different ethnic groups.
6. What is the difference between income and wealth? And between income/wealth and social class?
7. Why is wealth a better predictor of consumer behavior than income? And why is social class a better predictor of consumer behavior than wealth alone?
8. What is meant by "money attitude" and how does it affect consumer behavior?
9. Name and briefly describe the four segments of consumers based on their money attitudes.
10. How is poverty defined? What is the current threshold for poverty in USA?
11. What is The Index of Consumer Sentiment? What is its utility? What questions are asked to measure this index?
12. What is meant by the term "Social Class"? Name and explain important characteristics of the concept of social class.
13. Briefly describe three social classes in America in terms of their motivations and outlook on life. Also, name some important differences among the three social classes in America in terms of their food, clothing and leisure consumption.
14. What is meant by (a) status crystallization, and (b) underprivileged and overprivileged? Explain briefly.

THINK+Apply

1. Assume your firm was located in a college town that attracts students from all ethnic minorities in USA in large numbers. Outline some marketing ideas you would pursue if you were (a) a supermarket, (b) a movie theater, and (c) a food mall.
2. "Poor generally pay more." Do you agree or disagree with this statement? Why?
3. Is status crystallization a good thing or a bad thing for consumers? What problems does it (or lack of it) cause consumers?
4. If the "masstige" trend continues, what opportunities does it offer to marketers? What product categories (food items, clothing, cars, electronics, home improvement, service businesses such as banks and hospitals, and personal services such as hair salons, dry cleaning, lawn maintenance, etc.) will or will not be influenced by it? Explain your answer.

PRACTICE+Experience

1. Interview eight adult females, two each of Hispanic, African-American, Caucasian, and Asian-American identity, about their use of cosmetics and how their ethnic identity influences it.
2. Interview a couple of mixed ethnic identity about how the spouses shoulder and share responsibility for homemaking. Probe how they found their ethnic culture to affect the home-making expectations each had from the other? Summarize your findings.
3. Visit two online Hispanic supermarket stores, and survey the merchandise. For comparison, also visit the Web sites of two national chains like Kroger and Safeway. Summarize the differences you notice between these two categories of stores.
4. At your university or college or organization, find one person who belongs to and represents each of the five major religious institutions presented in the chapter (you may include yourself if appropriate). First, ask them to think about the various routines in their daily life (e.g., food preparation, dressing, grooming, etc.). Next, ask them to describe two rituals that are based on their religion. Based on your reading of the chapter, discuss if the ritual served any function when they started and if they serve any function now.
5. Review the consumption patterns of the three social classes described in the chapter. Which consumption pattern under each head best matches with your own consumption? Is there a discrepancy between your own consumption and consumptions of most other consumers in your social class? Explain why.
6. Visit the homes of three consumers, one from each social class, and make a note of the kind of things in the home. Summarize your observations.
7. Try to identify a consumer in each of the four segments based on "money attitudes" and interview them to understand how their consumption behavior differs for (a) food, (b) clothing, and (c) leisure activities.

In the Marketing Manager's Shoes

Put yourself in a marketing manager's shoes. Most concepts in the chapter have some lessons for the marketing manager, i.e., they suggest what to do differently in practice; indeed, often these applications are implicit in our explanations of the concepts and models in the chapter. Identify at least five specific applications of the chapter's concepts, all of which should be entirely new—different from the examples cited here.

Fandom

16 Consumer Relationship With Brands

Loyalty, Romance, and Brand Tribes

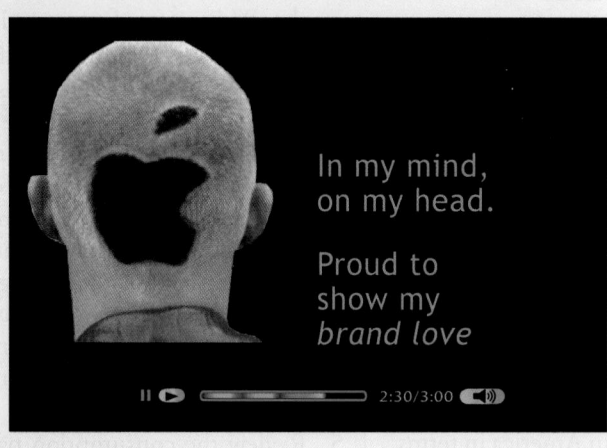

In my mind,
on my head.

Proud to
show my
brand love

▶ ━━━━━━━━━━ 2:30/3:00 ◀))

LEARN . APPLY . EXPERIENCE

OBJECTIVES

1 The Concept of Brand Loyalty and Ways of Measuring It

2 Four Types and Three Drivers of Consumer Brand Loyalty

3 The Concept of Brand Personality, How It Is Measured, and How Brands Acquire It

4 Six Drivers of Consumer-Brand Relationships

5 Concepts of Brand Communities, Brand Tribes, and Brandfests, and Their Roles in Building the Brand

6 Four Methods of Researching Brand Communities and Three Marketing Applications

Dear iCar, Will You Marry Me?

Extreme Brand Romance

A few years ago, this really happened. In relation to Miata. A sunny afternoon in a small town in Pennsylvania's Pocono Mountains. An outdoor wedding ceremony. A mass wedding, actually. 250 people gathered.

Each one a bride or a groom. All love-struck. All eager, all ecstatic. And then the voice of Reverend James A. Massie, Jr., an Episcopal priest, came through the microphone. He read a few vows, and then, with a deep breath, he uttered the sentence all had gathered to hear: "By the power vested in me, I pronounce that you are... car and driver." Suddenly, 250 happy people, all married that day to their Mazda Miatas!

Reverend Massie himself is an ardent fan. Besides praying, his only other passion is driving around in his white 1996 Miata, with religious songs playing on its CD player. It is a "spiritual endeavor," says Massie of his leisurely ride. Then there is Peter Warrick, a 53-year-old advertising executive in Fort Lauderdale; he owns 28 Miatas. He survived a heart attack recently, and what does he credit it to? His passion for the Miata![1]

Brands to adore. Brands to love.

INTRODUCTION

The fanatical devotion some consumers show toward their Miatas is exceptional but not unique. Many consumers feel similar passion for Puma sneakers, Krispy Kreme Doughnuts, Harley-Davidsons, and of course, their iPods and iPads. Apple computer fans, for example, make an annual pilgrimage to the Macworld Expo. There, they—graphic designers, artists, musicians, techies—browse through a galaxy of Apple products and devices, and, with great enchantment, they listen to Steve Jobs, cheering his every word. And whenever a new Krispy Kreme Doughnut store opens up, people form long queues all night long, just to taste their first bite of the legendary doughnut.

Other stories of fierce consumer loyalty show up in the media from time to time. The groundswell of protest at the brief withdrawal of Coca-Cola Classic was legendary. For Harley-Davidson motorcycle owners, now banded together in a group called HOG (Harley Owners Group), their attachment goes beyond the vehicle; in donning Harley paraphernalia, they have a lifestyle that is almost defined by the brand. Less visible but no less commanding of their owners' and consumers' strong loyalty are such products and services as Wii, Nike, and Virgin Airlines, and retail stores like the upscale Saks, European haute couture Louis Vuitton, the ace purveyor of pampering potions Body Shop, and surfer haven Pacific Sun.

On the flip side of the coin, not all consumers are loyal to any one product or brand, nor is any one consumer loyal to everything he or she buys and uses. And some products and brands command almost no loyalty from their consumers—for a few cents off, consumers would just as easily buy another brand. For packaged goods, for example, U.S. consumers' loyalty to manufacturers' brands ranges from only 10 to 40 percent. The picture is no better for services. For a broad range of services, as many as half of all consumers are willing to switch their current service providers. In Europe, consumer purchases of private labels or store brands (which is an indicator of lack of loyalty to manufacturers' brands) is remarkably high, as much as 50 to 60 percent for such supermarkets as Sanisbury's.[2]

Why such variation in consumer loyalty? Why are consumers loyal to some brands and not to others? What can marketers do to win consumers' loyalty? These questions are the subject matter of this chapter.

We begin this chapter by defining brand loyalty and describing ways to measure it. Next, we describe a model of brand loyalty that demystifies the three factors that drive it. In the final section, we take you to a higher plane—giving you glimpses of fanatic consumption and a peek inside consumption communities and brand tribes.

BRAND LOYALTY: THE CONCEPT

I Have Always CHOSEN You, Haven't I?

At first, brand loyalty seems like a simple idea. Ask consumers if they are loyal to any of the brands they use—shampoos, soft drinks, colognes, whatever. They are likely to say, yes, they have bought the same brand of shampoo, drunk the same soda, and used the same cologne for many years. Therefore, they would say, they are brand loyal. Or, conversely, because they don't stick to the same brands, they are not brand loyal, they would tell us.

Pretty good, at least for starters. Indeed, early marketing scholars viewed brand loyalty just this way—as the consistent purchase of the same brand. Every time a consumer repurchased a product (shampoo, cologne, wine, jeans, shoes, frozen pizza, motor oil, hospital for delivering one's babies, or whatever), if the consumer bought the same brand of a product or service repeatedly, then that consumer could be considered a brand-loyal consumer for that product category.

Totally consistent repurchase of the same brand would show **perfect** brand loyalty. However, in practice, even brand-loyal consumers occasionally deviate from their regular brand and instead buy an alternative brand. Therefore, practical estimates of brand loyalty allow for imperfect consistency. Such imperfect but still consistent repurchase can be estimated in three ways: proportion of purchase, sequence of purchase, and probability of purchase. See Table 16.1 for details.

THE POWER OF BEHAVIOR SCANS

Measuring consistent purchase is easy. Actually, marketing science has mastered this task. Here is how it works. When you buy a branded product, it gets scanned at the checkout register. This scan automatically records the brands you are buying. So if you are

TABLE
16.1 MEASURING BRAND LOYALTY BY PURCHASE HISTORY

Three Methods: Proportion, Sequence, Probability	
Proportion of purchases	The number of times the most frequently purchased brand is purchased divided by the total purchases. Thus, if you buy a brand, say, eight out of ten times, then your brand loyalty is 80 percent.
Sequence of purchases	Consider two consumers, Sarah and Kristin. On the last ten purchase occasions, Sarah bought the brands in the sequence AAABAAABBB, and Kristin bought them in the sequence ABABABABAB. Both patterns reflect divided loyalty, with 60% loyalty toward Brand A; however, Sarah's pattern shows a more consistent sequence than does Kristin's pattern. Accordingly, we would consider Sarah a more brand loyal consumer than Kristin.
Probability of purchase	A third way to combine the proportion and sequence is to compute the probability of the next purchase as follows: First, we would compute the proportion of the brand purchase (as described above). Let us say, this is 60%. Then, at any point in time, this proportion is adjusted to reflect the most recent purchase. Every time the consumer purchases a specific brand, the statistical probability of repurchasing that brand on the next occasion rises. If the consumer's most recent purchase was for our brand, we would "up the probability" to, say, 63%; if our brand has been bought twice most recently, we would raise it further to, say, 66%, and so on. This figure is merely illustrative; the exact upward or downward revision is based on statistical probability estimation.

MY CB BOOK

buying the same brand again and again, then the marketer knows, even without asking you, that you are a brand loyal consumer. Because the scanner is recording your behavior (i.e., which brand you bought), it is called a *behavior scan*. Of course, the marketer would have to know it is you at the cash register buying that item. How does the scanner machine know that? There are a few tricks to it. First, the store might give you a loyalty card that you scan every time you shop. Second, some marketing research companies such as A.C. Nielsen recruit a research panel from a national sample of consumers. These research panel members scan their membership cards every time they shop. Today, the company also runs a program called Homescan, wherein panel members are given a small hand-held scanner and asked to scan the UPC of everything they buy—groceries, medicine, clothes, shoes, electronics—when they return home from shopping.[3] Of course, when you signed up for the loyalty card or the A. C. Nielsen consumer panel membership, you gave them information about yourself. That is how, from behavior scan data, marketers can tell not only which brands command loyalty, but also what demographic groups of consumers are loyal to specific brands.

SAVVY
MARKETER

From Behavior Scan to Mind Scan

This way of defining brand loyalty—consistent repurchase of the same brand—is based on behavior, i.e., what consumers actually do, and is therefore called *behavioral brand loyalty*. And the ease of measuring it (by behavior scans) is wonderful. There is only one problem: It is based on what consumers DO, not what consumers THINK. For marketers, this is not good enough. Here is why.

Suppose your coworker always hangs out with you. Hangs out, that is all. You have no idea what your coworker THINKS of you. Would you feel certain your coworker is a loyal friend? Would you feel confident that if a new coworker joined your company, your current, constant buddy would not desert you? No? Why then should merely consistent repurchase assure marketers that a consumer is brand loyal?

The problem with behavioral brand loyalty is that it only shows that consumers repurchase the same brand, not whether they actually like the brand more than other brands. A consumer could buy the same brand merely out of habit or convenience, without thinking much about it. This kind of loyalty cannot be stable; if a competing brand offers a price deal, the consumer would perhaps readily buy the cheaper brand.

Thus, just counting the actual purchase consistency may not show true brand loyalty. Therefore, marketing scholars have argued that in measuring brand loyalty, we should also assess consumers' attitudes toward the brand. That is, we need to move beyond behavior-scans to mind-scans. We said, *mind-scan*, mind you, not brain-scan (the latter being an electro-magnetic imaging process). *Mind-scan* means probing what is in your mind, and this we can do by asking questions, as we did in Chapter 7 to measure consumer attitudes.

Only if the consumer attitude toward a brand is more favorable than it is for competing brands should the marketer consider that consumer loyal to that brand. This way of looking at brand loyalty—that is, a greater liking for the brand—is called **attitudinal brand loyalty**. This can be measured by asking consumers to rate various brands in terms of how much they like each brand or which brand they prefer the most.

Brand Loyalty as Attitude-Based Behavior

Marketing scholars who had initially proposed behavioral measures of loyalty began to later view loyalty in both behavioral and attitudinal terms. A leading consumer researcher Jacob Jacoby proposed a new definition of brand loyalty: "Brand loyalty is the biased (i.e., nonrandom) behavioral response (i.e., purchase), expressed over time, with respect to one or more alternative brands out of a set of such brands, and is a function of psychological (decision-making, evaluative) processes."[4] Another leading marketing scholar, George S. Day, currently a professor at the Wharton School, has defined brand loyalty as "consisting of repeated purchases prompted by a strong internal disposition." The phrase "internal disposition" refers to a favorable attitude. Thus, true loyalty incorporates both a behavior and an attitude.[5]

If these scholarly definitions are, well, a bit too technical for you, let us synthesize and simplify them for you. We define **brand loyalty** as *consumer commitment to a brand based on favorable attitude and preference, manifested by the consistent repurchase of the brand.* Remember four key elements: *consistent repurchase, favorable attitude, preference, and commitment.* That is, not only does the consumer buy the brand repeatedly, but he or she also likes the brand (holds a favorable attitude), prefers it over other brands (shows preference), and has commitment to it. Commitment means the consumer would stick around, not be lured by competing offers. In personal relations and brand relations alike, this is what commitment means, and commitment is what is required to claim loyalty.

Thus, to measure true brand loyalty, we must assess all four elements. And these can be measured through paper and pencil questions. See Table 16.2. In that table, the first three statements are meant to assess whether the consumer is loyal to any brand in a product category at all. The next six statements measure the extent to which a consumer is loyal to a specific brand. Note that these six statements capture all four elements of brand loyalty: attitude, preference, actual behavior, and commitment to repeated future behavior. Of course, you can use the same statements to measure consumer loyalty toward your competitors' brands as well.

So Should You Abandon Behavior Scans?

No, let's not go overboard. To begin with, recall what we learned about *attitudes* in an earlier chapter. Attitudes underlie and produce behavior. And, normally, attitudes and behaviors are correlated. Why would you act contrary to how you think and feel toward something? Why would you buy a brand if you did not also like and prefer it? Thus, measuring behavior implies tapping into attitudes as well—most of the time.

Yes, "most of the time," but not always. Sometimes, your consistent brand purchasing behavior may not reflect your true attitude. First, you may be buying a brand simply

MY CB BOOK

TABLE 16.2 ILLUSTRATIVE MEASURES OF BRAND LOYALTY

Rate the following statements using this scale:

Strongly Disagree   1   2   3   4   5   Strongly Agree

Existence of Loyalty (Name the product category _____)

1. In this product category, I have a favorite brand. _____
2. When buying——, I always buy my favorite brand no matter what. _____
3. If my favorite brand of——- is not available in the store, I would go to another store rather than buy a substitute brand. _____

Loyalty toward a Specific Brand (Name the brand _____)

4. I like this brand very much. _____
5. This brand is my favorite brand. _____
6. I prefer this brand to all others. _____
7. In the past, almost all of my purchases of this product have been this brand. _____
8. In the past, I have gone out of my way to buy this brand. _____
9. I am committed to buying this brand in the future. _____

Note 1. Specify the product category, such as yogurt, detergent, soft drink, jeans, athletic shoes, etc. Do not write the section headings on the survey form itself.
Note 2. Compute the average across these statements (the first three and the last six, separately). The closer the score is to '5' (meaning "strongly agree"), the stronger the brand loyalty.

---

because it is always on sale. You like it all right, but not as much as some competing brands. In fact, one of the competing brands may even be slightly higher on your attitude and preference meter, but the lure of the deal might be making you buy our brand, instead. This means if the price of the competing brand were to be reduced by a few cents, you might easily switch over. That hardly makes you brand loyal, your current consistent behavior notwithstanding.

Second, you simply might not care which brand you buy—your involvement in the brand choice in that product category could be low. You might buy our brand simply because it happened to be convenient. Tomorrow if this brand were temporarily out of stock, you would just as happily buy a competing brand. This, too, hardly makes you brand loyal.

That is why we ask for preference and commitment. But behavior does reflect attitude, often enough. Often is not bad. So we should not abandon behavior scans. Behavior scans give us, after all, automated measures of behavior—who is buying which brands. We should continue, therefore, to use behavior scans, and then periodically supplement them with measures of attitude (including preference and commitment, of course) by surveying consumers. Indeed, this is what marketing research companies that maintain behavior scan consumer panels do (such as A.C. Nielsen Research). In effect, they have the best of both worlds. Now, you have the complete picture.

SAVVY MARKETER

CONSUMER LOYALTY

Brands and More

The concept of loyalty that marketing scholars have developed for brands applies equally well to use of stores, service suppliers, and other vendors. To refer to all of these targets of loyalty, we can use the general term *consumer loyalty*. Thus, **consumer loyalty** *is a consumer's commitment to a brand or a store or a supplier, based on a strongly favorable attitude and preference, and manifested in consistent repatronage.*

Accordingly, **store loyalty** can be defined *as a consumer's predominant patronage of a store, based on a favorable attitude and preference.* That is, the consumer shops at that store (more than at any other store for that type of merchandise) and has a more favorable attitude toward that store. Just as we measured brand loyalty, we can measure a consumer's store loyalty by using a set of questions, as shown in Table 16.3.

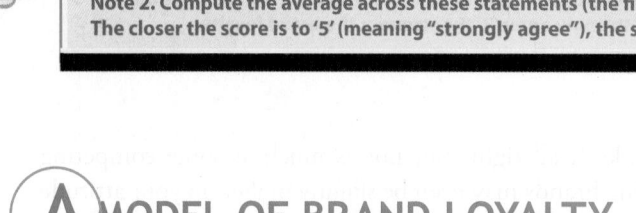

TABLE **16.3**	**ILLUSTRATIVE MEASURES OF STORE LOYALTY**

Rate the following statements using this scale:

Strongly Disagree   1   2   3   4   5   Strongly Agree

Existence of Loyalty (Name the product category _____)

1. For this group of products, I have my favorite store. _____
2. When buying this group pf products, I usually divide my shopping between 2 or 3 stores, to get the best deal.* _____
3. When buying this group of products, I would always go shopping at my usual store, no matter what. _____

Loyalty Toward a Specific Store (Name the store _____)

4. I like this store very much. _____
5. This store is my favorite store. _____
6. I prefer this store to all others. _____
7. When buying this group of products, I always shop this store first. _____
8. In the past 3 months, a majority of my shopping trips have been to this store. _____
9. I prefer to shop at this store even if another store advertises some deal. _____

Note 1. Specify the product category, such as yogurt, detergent, soft drink, jeans, athletic shoes, etc. Do not write the section headings on the survey form itself.

Note 2. Compute the average across these statements (the first three and the last six, separately). The closer the score is to '5' (meaning "strongly agree"), the stronger the brand loyalty.

MY **CB** BOOK

A MODEL OF BRAND LOYALTY

Or How to Make Julia a Believer

Measuring and knowing who is brand loyal and who is not is well and good, but now what? What do you do with that information? Let us say, you are a marketer of Swiss Mocha Chocolate Coffee Drink, and your measurements have told you that 20 percent of all consumers are loyal to Swiss Mocha Chocolate. Twenty-three year old college student Britney is loyal to your brand—she has a favorable attitude toward it, prefers it, drinks it often, and is committed to it. Thirty two year old stockbroker Julia is not—no favorable attitude, no preference, no consistent use, and no commitment.

The question is, how would you make Julia, and some of the other 80 percent of consumers like her, loyal to your brand? You would like to convert Julia into a believer, wouldn't you? You can. But to do so, you must first understand what makes consumers brand loyal. Consumer research literature has proposed many diverse factors, but here we synthesize them for you into a short list. (See Figure 16.1):

1. Performance Excellence The product (or service) must do what it is supposed to do and do it remarkably well. Thus, the shampoo must cleanse the hair well, the cell phone must not drop calls, and a pair of jeans must not fade or shrink. Honda and Toyota cars, Sony and Toshiba consumer electronics, Lands' End and Ralph Lauren clothing, and Jif peanut butter and Cold Stone Creamery ice creams in edibles command consumer respect because of their unfailing performance quality.

2. Self-Connection Beyond physical performance, the brand should somehow rise to make a personal connection with the consumer. The consumer must feel that the brand is cool and that it reflects him or her. This personal connection occurs because of the public persona of the brand—the brand's personality, carefully nurtured by the firm's entire marketing mix. Some brands acquire such consumer self-connection because of their adoption by other people whom the consumer considers cool and admirable. BMW and Saab cars, Diesel, Kenneth Cole, and Boca Wear clothing, Oakley and Chanel No. 5 eyewear, and, of course iPods, iPhones, and iPads, all owe consumer loyalty to this "cool" factor.[6]

3. High Involvement Finally, consumer involvement should be high in a given product category. Not all consumers are involved in a product. For some consumers, cars are simply transportation, while others take keen interest in their cars. No matter how flawless the performance, and how cool the other product users, if I am not much involved in, say, listening to music, then I am not going to be loyal to iPod, or to any other MP3 player for that matter. Only when the activity for which I need the product occupies a significant place in my life, would I bother to notice a brand's superior performance or care about how cool it is.

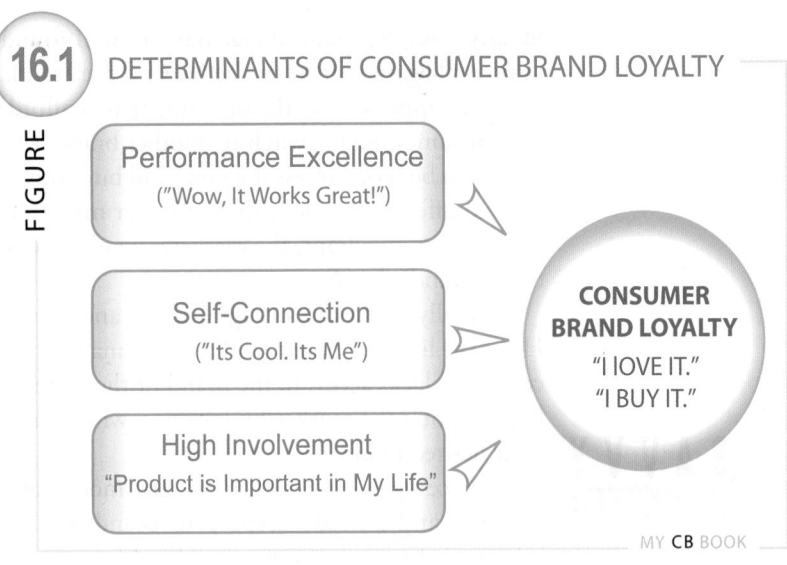

16.1 FIGURE DETERMINANTS OF CONSUMER BRAND LOYALTY

Performance Excellence ("Wow, It Works Great!")

Self-Connection ("Its Cool. Its Me")

High Involvement "Product is Important in My Life"

CONSUMER BRAND LOYALTY "I lOVE IT." "I BUY IT."

MY **CB** BOOK

All three of the above factors are necessary for developing consumer brand loyalty. What does this mean to you as a marketer? First, that if you want to develop consumer loyalty toward your brand, you should target consumers for whom the product category is of deep personal interest. To attract and keep the high involvement consumer, you will have to adopt the high ground of superior quality. And also carefully nurture its symbolic image. On the other hand, if you choose to target low involvement consumers, then price and promotion (or frequent buyer loyalty cards) would have to carry the major burden of keeping consumers coming back to you. But remember, "coming back," yes, true brand loyalty, no. "They choose it," yes; "They love it," no.

Study Figure 16.1 now and commit to memory these three factors of consumer brand loyalty. And let these always guide all of your marketing plans.

SAVVY MARKETER

FOUR FACES OF BRAND LOYALTY

Why did we say that keeping consumers coming back by using promotions is not an indicator of true brand loyalty? Because the definition of loyalty includes, you will recall, both behavior and attitude. Cross these two components, and you get four possible situations—four faces of brand loyalty, only one of which is true brand loyalty. See Figure 16.2.

When both attitudes and behaviors are weak, no loyalty exists. Weak attitude means the consumer does not have any liking or preference for the brand. Weak behavior means purchase of the brand is sporadic (i.e., the same brand is not purchased consistently). When both are strong (i.e., attitude is very favorable, and the same brand is purchased consistently), strong loyalty exists. These two cases reflect consistency between attitude and behavior, just as the chapter on attitudes told us.

Loyalty Needs Both Attitude and Behavior

The remaining two cases are more interesting. They show that attitude and behavior are out of sync. One of these cases describes what happens when behavior is high but attitude is low—here, the consumer has **spurious**

16.2 FIGURE FOUR TYPES OF BRAND LOYALTY

		BEHAVIOR	
		WEAK	STRONG
ATTITUDE	STRONG	Latent Loyalty	True Loyalty
	WEAK	No Loyalty	Spurious Loyalty

Source: Adapted from Alan S. Dick and Kunal Basu, "Customer Loyalty: Toward an Integrated Conceptual Framework," Journal of the Academy of Marketing Science, 22(2), 1994, 101. Used by permission..

MY **CB** BOOK

loyalty—loyalty that is incidental, not well-founded. The consumer buys the same brand again and again, but he or she feels no preferential attitude toward it. Perhaps this brand or store happens to be the only one that is affordable or convenient; given more choices, the consumer might switch to another brand. Or, perhaps the consumer perceives all the brands to be more or less the same and buys this one merely by inertia. If the other brands were to offer a price deal, the consumer might easily switch. To move this consumer into the "loyalty" quadrant, the marketer would have to strengthen the consumer's perception of the brand's *benefits*.

Finally, in the case of high attitude and low behavior, the consumer has **latent loyalty**. He or she likes the brand but has been unable to buy it. Perhaps the price is too high or the consumer lacks access to the brand or the store. Here, the marketer needs to tap into this hidden potential market by lowering whatever barriers prevent consumers from buying their desired brand.

SAVVY MARKETER

Once again you realize, as this model in Figure 16.2 shows, that tracking both behavior and attitude keeps your brand loyalty meter ticking—keeping you correctly informed about your consumers' loyalties.

CONSUMER BRAND LOYALTY: A COMPREHENSIVE MODEL

The three-factor model of brand loyalty (Figure 16.1) tells us three qualities consumers must feel in a product. An important question for marketers is, what market and competitor factors lead consumers to experience those three qualities and consequently become loyal to a brand. To answer that question, we build a comprehensive model, showing all market and competitor factors that together drive consumers' brand loyalties. In this model, we represent these factors as positive and negative forces. See Figure 16.3.

POSITIVE FORCES

These are divided into (a) product factors, and (b) consumer factors.

Product Factors

Product factors are two: performance fit, and psychological bonding.
Performance Fit How well a product's performance fits the consumer's need is the first and most important factor. Brands targeted to specific consumer segments are more likely to fit particular needs better than those mass-marketed to the public at large. That is why consumer loyalty is generally higher in niche markets than in mass markets.
Psychological Bonding Psychological bonding can be defined as the connection consumers feel toward the brand. Psychological bonding comes from the symbolic and emotional value of the brand. Brands that reflect social self-concept—the kind of person you like to be—become a part of your identity, your "extended self." This extended self-connection also results from other aspects of a brand's persona—the things the brand stands for in larger society; i.e., the societal values the brand espouses. Companies that espouse desirable societal values are referred to as **socially conscious businesses**. One avenue of showing social consciousness is **cause marketing**. In cause marketing, companies sponsor and support some social causes such as an AIDS awareness program or a "feed the hungry" program. Cause marketing programs create psychological bonding by connecting with consumers at the level of life's important values—the big causes and societal goals that are important to consumers.

Consumer Factors

Consumer factors also are two: enduring involvement and familiarity.
Enduring Involvement Consumers with enduring involvement take a keen interest in the product and therefore begin to feel an attachment to the brand.
Familiarity Familiarity creates fondness, as consumers want to repeat what they already know and like.[24]

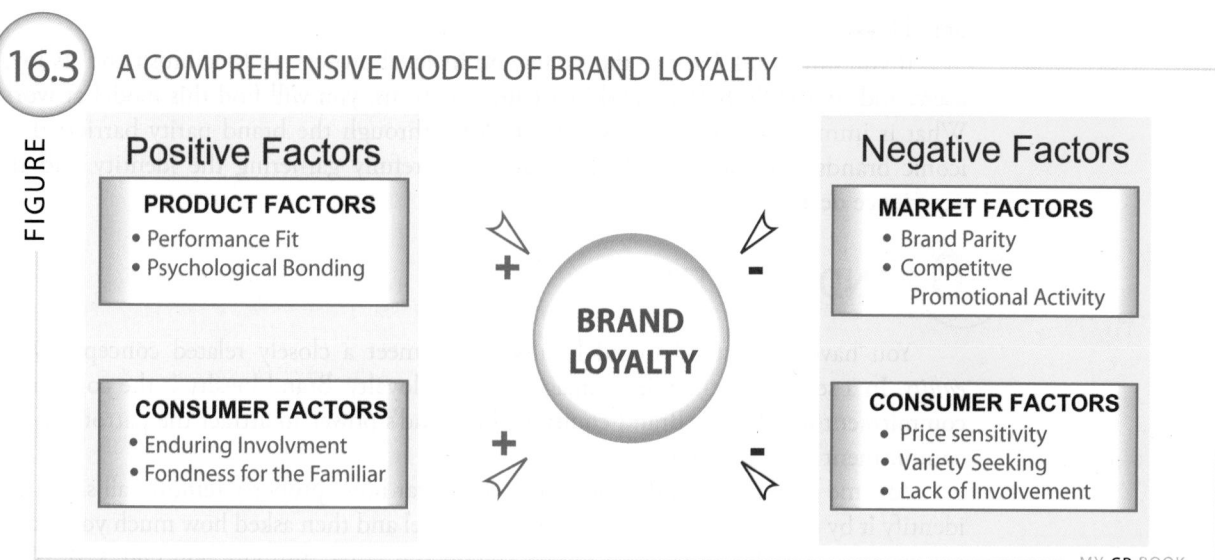

16.3 A COMPREHENSIVE MODEL OF BRAND LOYALTY

FIGURE

Positive Factors

PRODUCT FACTORS
• Performance Fit
• Psychological Bonding

CONSUMER FACTORS
• Enduring Involvment
• Fondness for the Familiar

BRAND LOYALTY

Negative Factors

MARKET FACTORS
• Brand Parity
• Competitve Promotional Activity

CONSUMER FACTORS
• Price sensitivity
• Variety Seeking
• Lack of Involvement

MY CB BOOK

NEGATIVE FORCES

While performance fit, psychological bonding, enduring involvement, and familiarity contribute to brand loyalty, some factors work against it. These relate to the market environment and consumer characteristics.

Market Factors

Two market factors that work against brand loyalty are brand parity and competitive promotions.

Brand Parity **Brand parity** refers to how similar and mutually substitutable the brands are. The more alike the brands in a product category are, the less motivation there is for a consumer to stick with a particular brand.

Competitive Promotions **Competitive promotions** refers to the special price deals available on competing brands. These price deals provide the motivation to switch from a favorite brand to a featured brand. Of course consumer response to promotional activity depends on the consumers' price sensitivity.

Consumer Factors

Three consumer factors work against brand loyalty: price sensitivity, variety seeking, and low purchase-decision involvement.

Price Sensitivity Price sensitivity is one consumer characteristic that discourages consumer loyalty. Consumers differ in their price sensitivity. Some consumers check the prices even on small items and notice even small price differences. Others are generally unaware of price variations across brands and, if aware, do not value small savings enough to switch brands. A number of marketing studies have found that consumers' price sensitivity is negatively related to brand loyalty and positively to coupon use.[25]

Variety Seeking Some consumers like to seek variety in their experience; they get bored with the same product or life experience. These consumers switch from one brand to another, not because they are dissatisfied with a brand, but rather simply for the sake of change and variety. The more variety seeking a consumer is, the less brand loyal he or she is likely to be.

Low Purchase Decision Involvement This is not simply the lack or absence of enduringly involvement. Even in products we are not enduringly involved, at the time of purchase, at least, we often become involved (e.g., purchase of a car battery or greeting cards). But for some products we do not even feel this "purchase decision involvement." This comes from low or absent perceived risk, which in turn results from total perceived brand parity and low item cost. If we feel no purchase decision involvement, we are going to choose that product casually based on price or convenience etc., and not exhibit any brand loyalty.

If you now think back to the Miata and its loyal owners, to Macintosh and its loyal users, and to The Body Shop and its frequent patrons, you will find this model at work. What is immediately apparent is that breaking through the brand parity barrier; these iconic brands stand alone and distinguished, carefully garnering the identity and the experience dear to their fans.

BRAND EQUITY

You have understood brand loyalty. Now, meet a closely related concept: *brand equity*. In a sense, it is the mirror image of brand loyalty. Brand loyalty is the consumer's commitment to a brand. Brand equity is the brand's power to attract the patronage and commitment of its customers.

Assume for a moment that one day a three-star hotel property removes all signs that identify it by name. You are given a tour of the hotel and then asked how much you would consider a reasonable price for a night's stay at the hotel. Suppose you said $70. Next, assume that you are also invited by Marriott Hotel Corporation to tour one of their new properties, a three-star hotel almost identical to the first one, and asked how much you would pay for a night's stay there. Would your answer be $60, $70, $90, or what?

It turns out that just such a study was actually done. A few years ago, when Marriott Hotels built a new chain of mid-priced inns, they tested two alternative names for the property: *Fairfield Inn* and *Fairfield Inn by Marriott*. The results: Survey respondents who saw the property under the second name estimated a reasonable price that was 35% more than that estimated by the other group of respondents who were shown the same property but under the first name (i.e., Fairfield Inn). That is the power of the brand name! This is "brand equity." [19]

Brand equity may be defined as "the enhancement in the perceived utility and desirability that a brand name confers on a product." Brand equity comes from the value of that brand to the consumer compared to other brands. It is the overall superiority of a product carrying that brand name over similar products carrying other brand names.

Brand equity reflects the greater confidence that consumers place in the brand than they do in the competing brands. This confidence then translates into consumer preference for the brand, brand loyalty, and even a willingness to pay a premium price for the brand. For example, a study by McKinsey & Company and Intelliquest Inc. found that consumers tend to buy brands with low brand equity like Gateway only at a discounted price compared to those of such brands as Dell or IBM. The resulting market share and profit potential translate into financial gains, so much so that the brand-owning company's net worth is raised. For example, when Cadbury-Schweppes bought the Hires and Crush brands of soft drink from Procter & Gamble, it paid a total price of $220 million; of this amount, 90 percent is said to be associated with the brand equity itself.

What is the difference between brand loyalty and brand equity? As we mentioned earlier, brand loyalty is a characteristic of the consumer—Tom is brand loyal to Coke and Nicole is not; this tells us about the brand loyalty of Tom and Nicole toward Coke. But it does not tell us anything about the brand equity of Coke. There will always be some people who would not like or be loyal even to the best brand. So, what makes a brand powerful is how consumers perceive the brand and how many consumers perceive it that way. Brand equity comes, in other words, from the sum total of the consumption values the brand is perceived to offer, accumulated across all of that product category's target consumers.

Brand Equity as Value Delivered by the Brand

A brand's perceived value is the sum total of physical and psychological benefits the consumer receives from the brand. This perceived value comes from four sources. [21] (See Figure 16.4)

1. **Need Satisfaction** Value comes from the brand's potential to satisfy the consumer's needs—the purpose for which the consumer seeks the brand to begin with. The better the brand satisfies those needs, the greater the perceived brand value and, in turn, the more the consumer will value and desire that brand.

2. **Value for the Money** Value comes from the brand's perceived utility relative to its costs, based on a comparison of what is received with what is given up.

3. **Trustworthiness** Brand value encompasses the consumer's trust—the trust in the brand's commitment to quality and to its customers;

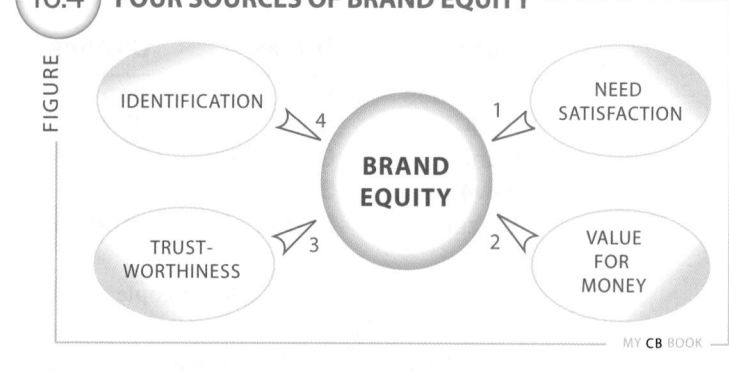

FIGURE **16.4** **FOUR SOURCES OF BRAND EQUITY**

that the brand will maintain its strengths, and that it will not compromise its quality or otherwise take advantage of consumers. An example of a trust-failure is the press story a few years ago about Sears automotive shops doing unneeded repairs on cars; this story diminished consumer trust and, in turn, Sears lost some of its brand equity.

4. **Identification** **Identification** is the degree to which consumers identify themselves with the brand, or feel some attachment to it. In effect, consumers would say that it is their brand; it is the kind of brand they would be happy to be associated with. Often, identification occurs because the brand is associated with things, persons, ideas, or symbols we find engaging. In particular, celebrities and role models are often used to develop identification. But even more potent drivers of identification are the firm's social policies, such as environmentalism, kindness to animals, etc. Benetton has long employed shocking images of social issues (e.g., AIDS research, racial harmony); it hopes to generate bonds of identification among its core consumers for whom such images strike an emotional chord. Identification suffers when the brand marketer adopts some policy that goes against the value system of its consumers.[22]

Your brand's equity will be high when it scores well on all four components. As a manager, you can identify which components are weak, work to improve those aspects of the brand, and thus raise your brand's equity.[23]

BRAND PERSONALITY

I Am Your Brand. I've Got Your Traits.

What do consumer perceptions about brands include? First and foremost, target consumers have to be aware of the brand name. If very few people know a brand's name, then that brand has no equity. On the other hand, a lot of people could be aware of it, but if they don't think much of it, then too it has no equity. Thus, brand name awareness is a necessary condition, but brand equity also includes **brand associations**—what consumers think the brand is, does, or stands for. Brand associations include both tangible and intangible qualities, such as, for example, that Harmon Kardon keeps acoustic fidelity; that W Hotels offer artistic living spaces; that Levi's Manufacturing Co. supports diversity in the workplace; that Tommy Hilfiger clothing is trendy; or that Mercedes is the subtle statement of success. Associations like these are the basis of all value perceptions about the brand.

One important category of these perceptions is brand personality. People have personalities, of course, as we saw in an earlier chapter, but do brands have personalities, too? To answer this question, let us begin with a quiz. Below is a list of qualities, i.e., personality traits, we associate with people. Following this list is a set of brands in a few product categories (cars, soft drinks, clothing, etc.). Can you match individual brands in each product category with the following qualities?[7]

A. Sincere   B. Exciting   C. Competent   D. Sophisticated   E. Rugged

Cars	Drinks	Clothes	Misc.
Mercedes	Root Beer	Gap	WSJ
Audi	Coke	Nike	Kodak
Honda	Gatorade	Club Crown	Wall Street Journal
Rav4	Snapple	Banana Republic	Apple Computer
Blazer	Perrier	Lands' End	Campbell Soup

How did you do? Most people would assign various cars to the "qualities" list as Honda (A), Rav4 (B), Audi (C), Mercedes (D), and Blazer (E). Likewise, soft drinks as: Coke (A), Snapple (B), Gatorade (C), Perrier (D), and Root Beer (E). We'll leave other items for you to explore. As this trivia should convince you, brands do have personalities—that is, as consumers, we do see brands as possessing personalities.

If we describe ourselves and other people as having certain qualities known as personality traits, and as consumers if we use products and brands to convey the types of people we are, it makes sense that we end up describing products and brands also by the same human traits. Thus, just as people are cool, urbane, macho, aggressive, fun, and contemporary, so too are brands. **Brand personality** refers to the set of human qualities by which consumers describe a brand. Obviously, different consumers may see the brand differently, and thus brand personality, as seen by consumers, may vary from consumer to consumer. The question is, just what are the dimensions of brand personality?

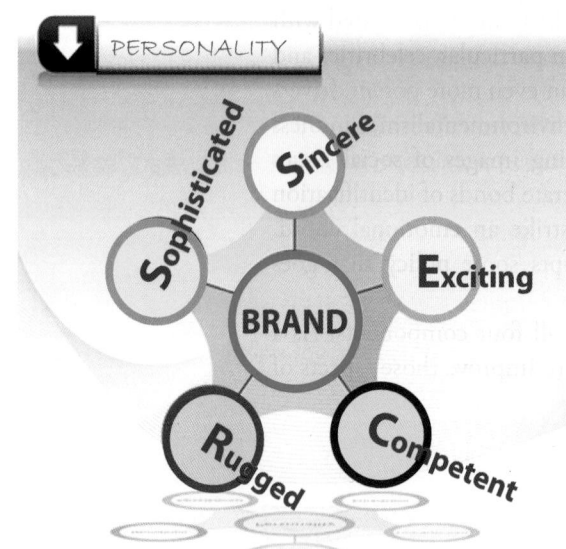

A brand can be described by hundreds of qualities (good or bad). Many of these brand personality descriptors may be synonyms for one another (e.g., cool and trendy), and many others are closely related (e.g., prestigious and classy). Stanford marketing professor Jennifer Aaker analyzed a battery of such descriptors that consumers use for brands and came up with a manageable set of overarching dimensions—called the *Five Brand Personality Dimensions*. You can remember these by using the acronym SECTS (if you paraphrase "rugged" as "tough"). That these dimensions are also five in number, just like *The Big Five* of human personality (see Chapter 5, where they were nick-named OCEAN), is a happy coincidence. And an intuitive reading also shows a broad correspondence of individual dimensions within OCEAN and SECTS:

Conscientiousness is Competence; Agreeableness is Sincerity; Openness and Extraversion crisscross over Excitement and Sophisticated; finally, Neuroticism's opposite, Stability, is like Ruggedness. Remember, the correspondence is intuitive, broad, and suggestive.

SECTS: THE FIVE DIMENSIONS OF BRAND PERSONALITY

Sincere—down-to-earth, family-oriented, genuine, old-fashioned.
Exciting—spirited, young, up-to-date, outgoing.
Competent—accomplished, influential, high-performing.
Rugged—athletic and outdoorsy.
Sophisticated—pretentious, wealthy, condescending

MEASURING BRAND PERSONALITY

Measuring brand personality using SECTS is easy. Each dimension of SECTS is scored by using a set of six adjectives, as shown in Table 16.4. The scores can then be profiled for any brand or a set of brands for comparison.

100% STRENGTH
100% BEAUTY

what are you made of ?

TAGHeuer

SWISS MADE SINCE 1860

Humans have personalities. Brands also have personalities. Brand Tag Heuer "casts" this watch in the likeness of Internationally known Chinese actress Zhang Ziyi.
(Used with the permission of Tag Heuer Watch Company.)

TABLE **16.4** MEASURING BRAND PERSONALITY

Q. How well do the following words describe brand _____ .

Does not describe at all 0 1 2 3 4 5 Describes very well

SINCERE	EXCITING	COMPETENT	RUGGED	SOPHISTICATED
Down-to-earth ____	Trendy ____	Hard-working ____	Outdoorsy ____	Glamorous ____
Honest ____	Spirited ____	Successful ____	Western ____	Good-looking ____
Family-oriented ____	Up-to-date ____	Reliable ____	Masculine ____	Charming ____
Wholesome ____	Contemporary ____	Secure ____	Tough ____	Smooth ____
Cheerful ____	Imaginative ____	Leader ____	Strong ____	Upper class ____

Scoring: To score each personality dimension, simply add the ratings for all the items of a dimension. The scores will range from 0 to 30. While dimension scores summarize the brand personality efficiently, individual item ratings are useful for more diagnostic understanding.

Source: Adapted from Jennifer Aaker, Dimensions of Brand Personality, Journal of Marketing Research, Summer 1997, Vol. 34, 347-57. Reproduced with the permission of The American Marketing Association.

MY CB BOOK

HOW BRANDS ACQUIRE PERSONALITY

How do brands acquire their personality? There are at least three sources:

1. Marketer Communications Intentionally, marketers convey to consumers certain symbolic brand images: they depict their brands in association with certain people (e.g., celebrities like Peyton Williams Manning), person-images (e.g., the cowboy for Marlboro cigarettes), or human-like animated characters (e.g., the Pillsbury Doughboy). One recent trend in brand personality advertising is to display a brand and a human model side by side, striking visual similarity—as was done in recent print ads for Tag Heuer. For want of a term, we would call it **homophyly**, which the dictionary defines as "resemblance arising out of common ancestry,"[8] but which we will define here as "resemblance arising out of identification."

Other marketer-managed signals also promote the intended brand personality. Indeed, all other elements of the marketing mix build a brand's personality. The brand's name, logo, price, packaging, and even the store where the brand is sold contribute to the brand's personality. The brand name Obsession gives the cologne *ruggedness,* whereas Eternity makes it *sincere* even though both colognes are from the same maker, Calvin Klein. Indeed, some of these elements of marketing mix are a way of giving tangible form to the intended brand personality. Visit, for example, a M.A.C store, and see how young store associates are "decorated" M.A.C style; more than anything else, these visual ambassadors personify the trendy, edgy, *exciting* personality of the brand.

2. Consumers' Social Observations In their everyday life, consumers observe who is using which products, and then assign the qualities of those users to the brand. Thus, if consumers see a lot of urban youth wearing Diesel brand jeans and clothing, then Diesel will acquire, in the consumer's eye, the personality of being urban and youthful. If consumers also see these same youths (donning Diesel outfits) with conservatively well-kempt hair, driving nice cars, and patronizing upscale restaurants and clubs, then they would attribute to Diesel the personality of rich, yuppie, fashionable, sophisticated, urbane, and youthful (sort of like Banana Republic or Kenneth Cole brands). On the other hand, if they were to see the Diesel youth donning punk rock hairdos and tattoos, then the personality attributed to Diesel would be rebellious, unorthodox, on-the-edge and youthful (sort of like the brand personality of Hot Topic and Torrid clothing lines).

3. Cultural Gatekeepers In every culture, there are a number of public figures who influence the image of activities, ideas, and products. By adopting a product (without commercial gains from the marketer), by displaying it through personal use, by taking a position on it, by praising it or critiquing it, these cultural gatekeepers inevitably define and influence the brand image for the rest of us.

Two examples will illustrate this: Nike's Air Force One and Menolo Blahnik.

Air Force One No, we are not talking about the presidential plane. We are talking about Nike's basketball shoe designed in 1981. By itself it is so plain (a thick sole, some vent air holes on the top, and a Velcro ankle strap) that unless you knew of it already, you wouldn't give it a second look. And while it endured for two decades—thanks to an occasional lift from hip-hop celebrities—it achieved cult status in November 2001 when rapper Nelly made it the theme of his single, appropriately titled "Air Force One," which became an instant hit. Some lyrics in it include: "You couldn't get this color if you had a personal genie. I am a sneaker pro, I love Pumas and shelltoes. But can't nothin' compare to a fresh crispy white pair..." While the company (Nike) has occasionally brought out limited editions of other colors, the white-on-white, the subject of Nelly's paean, is now the most coveted shoe among hip-hop fans and pretenders alike.[9]

Manolo Blahnik The designer of this high fashion shoe is one of the most revered shoe designers of the century, but that doesn't put it on the consumer's wish list. Rather it is the roster of its famous fans—Madonna, Patti Labelle, and Winona Ryder. Of course, what really expanded its circle of admirers is its frequent appearance on the fashionable TV show *Sex and the City.*

SAVVY MARKETER

How

Marketer Communications

Brands

Consumers' Social Observations

Acquire

Cultural Gatekeepers

Personality

CONSUMER RELATIONSHIPS WITH BRANDS

So, by now, you have gained an intense knowledge of consumer loyalty toward brands. You can separate consumers who would stick with your brand no matter what, from those who would ditch you in a heartbeat just to get a 25-cent promotional deal. As a brand marketer, you also know what factors enhance brand loyalty and what factors diminish it. You have been offering (and will continue to offer) consumers unmatchable performance. And you will manage all elements of your marketing mix to build and project the desired brand personality. You are happy already that your brand commands a good degree of loyalty from a considerable segment of your target consumers. Still, something is bugging you.

What is bugging you is that your brand is no Miata and definitely no iPod. Your brand commands its users' loyalty, but they are not ecstatic about it. There are no fanatics, and there is no public display of love for your brand—like the Miata owners who wed their cars in a public ceremony and the iPod bedecked consumers walking in a trance. Or like the thousands of brainy teens with a hint of nerdy looks and hundreds of funky graphic artists who flock to the nearby Apple showcase stores, to learn one more cool acrobatic move in that amazing digital music and graphics space.

In our quest to understand how consumers relate to their brands so intimately, we want to take you to an even higher plane. We want to talk about consumer-brand relationships, the consumer romance with brands, consumption communities, brand-tribes, and brandfests.

Meet My Brand—My Buddy, My Alter-ego

In a recent ad from Toshiba, the printer is shown brooding, "I do all the work of copying, and all he does [referring to a copying associate] is bring her those copies, and now he is her sushi buddy!"

This is animism at work. **Animism** refers to the belief that objects (products) possess souls; i.e., they have consciousness just like humans do. A Chrysler 300M ad declares: "The technology has changed, but the soul lives on." The fact that advertisers use this technique and that consumers accept it (acceptance here means, simply, not rejecting something as nonsensical or absurd) shows that consumers see it as something that could exist, that could happen, at least on some implicit, latent level of thought and feeling.

While the Toshiba Printer in the ad is a lonely subject of unrequited love, other products and brands are luckier. There are many products and brands that consumers notice, yearn for, adopt and incorporate into their lives, and develop special feelings toward. Consumers develop relationships with these products and brands, just as they have relationships with people. At first, this proposition may seem absurd. You may like, adore, or even love a product or a brand, but to say that you have a relationship with it may seem a stretch to you. But as some consumer psychologists peek deeper into the consumer mind, more and more they are finding manifestations of humanlike relationships between people and their brands.

This is not to say that all people have relationships with all the products they use. Far from it. In fact, there are many products and brands that consumers possess and use without a moment's thought about them. (We call such products "low involvement" products, remember?) At the same time, for each of us, there is at least one product or brand toward which we feel a little personal, a little like it were human. We call this view of how consumers feel toward some products and brands **consumer-brand relationships**.[10]

How is it that consumers can be said to have a relationship with brands? A **relationship** is based upon a sentiment in which one feels a special sense of being connected. In a relationship, one feels that there is interdependence between two entities. Seen in this light, we as consumers do have a relationship with some of the products we consume. We depend on our cars, and our cars depend on us for proper care. If we are enduringly involved with our cars, then we also come to harbor some feeling toward them; we come to see them as having a special place in our lives. The brand becomes something more than a mere instrument for getting the job done. With the brand Jeep, for example, not the destination, but the journey itself is meaningful. This relationship is driven by six factors[11]:

1. Humanistic Qualities in Brands   First, we bestow on some products the same qualities that humans have, and by virtue of those qualities, we then begin to see those products as almost human-like entities.

We think of soup as a nurturer, for example. Jell-O becomes a happy cheery friend. Audi TT is a muscular car that packs 300 horsepower and can be thought of as a muscular, agile, robust, high-speed horse. The point is not simply that we think soup is good nutritional food that nurtures; but rather that we think it is our benefactor and that it nurtures us just as our mothers did. That Jell-O is a cheery friend who would actually lift us, like a friend, out of our blues. And that Audi TT will take us places with gusto, and like the horse of the cowboy era, it will care for its master and owner, never letting us down. Since consumers think of these products as possessing specific human (or animal) qualities, they find them comforting as personal friends and companions, whose company they hope will bring the same satisfaction that other humans (and pets) bring them.

Consumer researchers even have a term for this: **Anthropomorphizing** the brand—giving the brand a humanlike quality. And marketers recognize and promote this by giving brands a human-like character: Mr. Peanut, Mr. Clean, Ronald McDonald, Frisch's Big Boy, the Pillsbury Doughboy, etc.

2. Self-definition by Brand   This is the mirror image of the foregoing. Instead of giving a product or brand certain humanistic qualities, consumers begin to define themselves (and others) by a product category, or by a brand. For example, as in "She is a Real Coke Girl," or "Here comes the Tommy Hilfiger Girl," or even, he is "a meat and

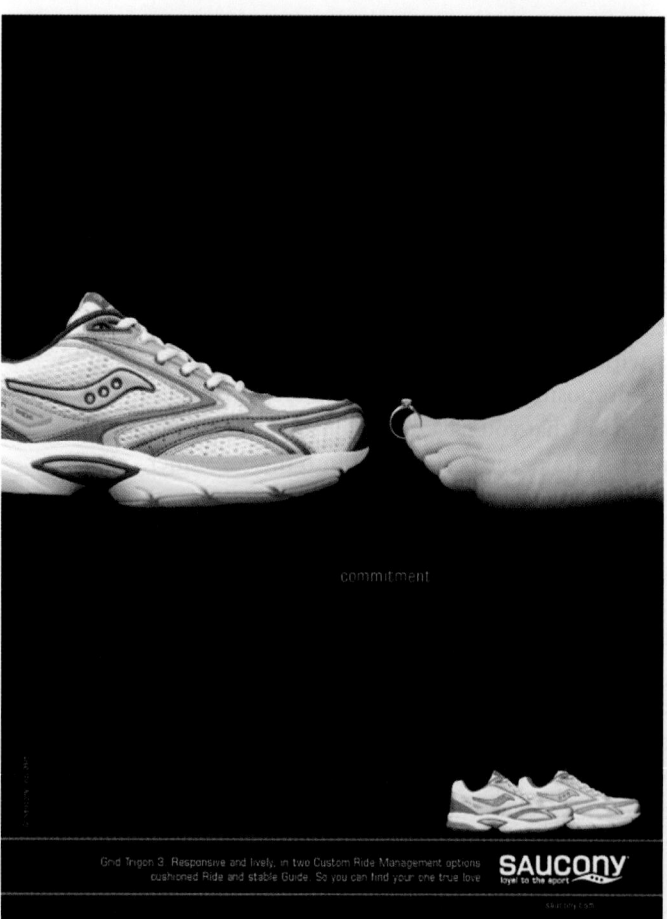

Anthropomorphizing the Brand

Few brands rise to the level where consumers see them as other *beings*, just like themselves. Brand Saucony captures the deep commitment its ardent fans feel to the brand. It's a commitment so deep and an enchantment so intense that the brand and the consumer feel wedded to each other.

(Image: courtesy of Saucony)

potatoes guy." Consumers adopt the brand (product) identity—identifying themselves as possessing the essential quality of the brand (product)—like sophisticated or rugged or simple and competent. Consequently, consumers begin to view the brand as somehow related to them.

3. Surrogate Other If a possession is inherited or received as a gift from a loved one, then the consumer comes to view that object just as he or she views that person. For example, suppose Tim received an antique clock from his grandmother whom he loved dearly; now every time he remembers his grandma, he reaches out to that clock, to connect with it—looking at it, touching it, dusting or polishing it just one more time, even kissing it. Conversely, every time he looks at the clock, it brings back happy memories of grandma and the time spent with her. In a similar vein, we save our loved ones' letters; we also save their favorite perfume or cologne or even favorite flower arrangement. It is almost as if the spirit of the person lives in the brand. Thus, we develop a personal relationship with a product or brand because we see it as a repository of all the memories of the person we loved.[12]

4. Connected With Our Life Projects The fourth source of brand relationships is the role brands and products play in consumers' life projects. **Life projects** are enduring, ongoing, significant endeavors undertaken by consumers to achieve certain life goals. These goals include the social roles consumers take on (ascribed or taken voluntarily) such as father, teacher, mentor, or a committed boy-friend or girl-friend, etc. Life projects also include personal growth and self-actualization goals, such as the desire to become an accomplished musician, a renowned historian, or a crusader against environmental pollution, etc. Products and brands that help consumers fulfill these role responsibilities or accomplish personal-growth goals become the targets of consumer attachment and emotional investment. These products are then viewed as co-strivers in whatever they (the consumers) are trying to achieve in their lives. Consider an example:

> "I use Mary Kay everything. Makeup, lipstick, moisturizer, toner. I think Mary Kay is responsible for how my skin looks now. I do, I really do. ..."[13]

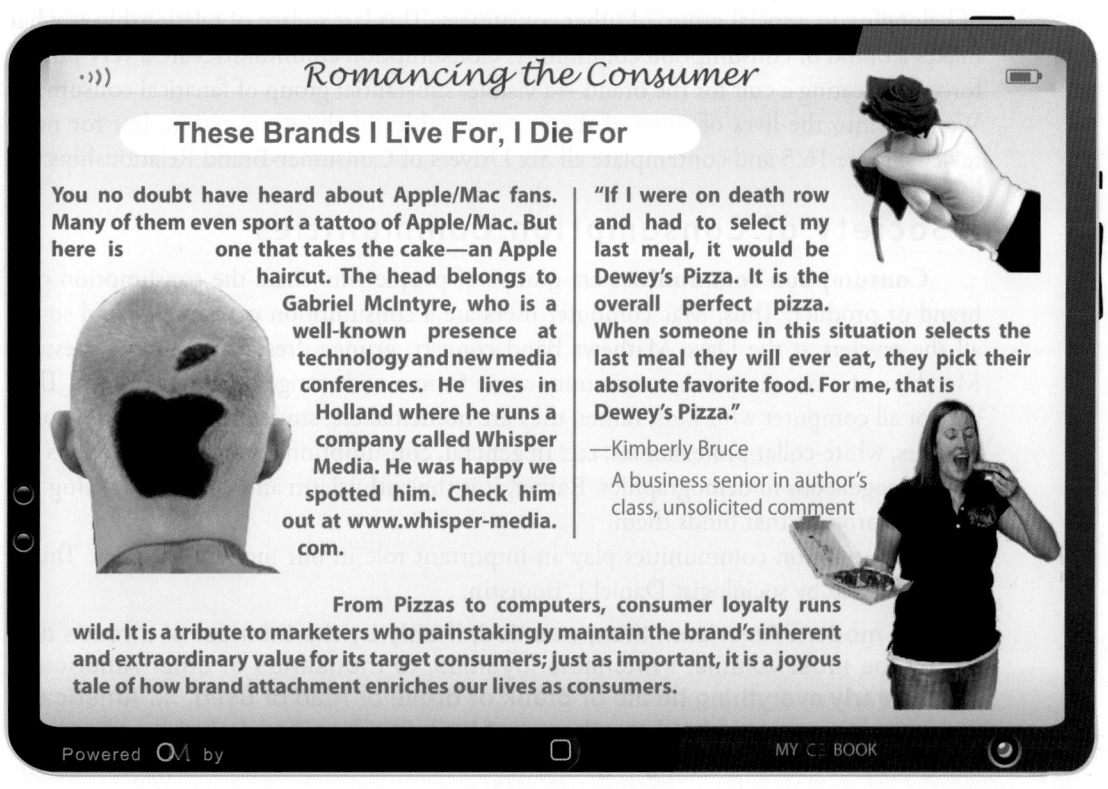

Romancing the Consumer

These Brands I Live For, I Die For

You no doubt have heard about Apple/Mac fans. Many of them even sport a tattoo of Apple/Mac. But here is one that takes the cake—an Apple haircut. The head belongs to Gabriel McIntyre, who is a well-known presence at technology and new media conferences. He lives in Holland where he runs a company called Whisper Media. He was happy we spotted him. Check him out at www.whisper-media.com.

"If I were on death row and had to select my last meal, it would be Dewey's Pizza. It is the overall perfect pizza. When someone in this situation selects the last meal they will ever eat, they pick their absolute favorite food. For me, that is Dewey's Pizza."

—Kimberly Bruce
A business senior in author's class, unsolicited comment

From Pizzas to computers, consumer loyalty runs wild. It is a tribute to marketers who painstakingly maintain the brand's inherent and extraordinary value for its target consumers; just as important, it is a joyous tale of how brand attachment enriches our lives as consumers.

Powered OM by   MY CB BOOK

5. Important Role in Our Everyday Life Come to think of it, everyday life is in itself its own project. We get up, we bathe, and we groom; we have coffee and breakfast; we commute to work; we take a lunch break; we commute back home; we enjoy dinner and conversation; we watch TV; and we go to bed. This daily routine is intertwined with consumption. Some of the consumption we carry on in a taken-for-granted manner, of course, but some of it we conduct with full consciousness, at least some of the time. And consequently, we come to see a relationship between these products and brands and our lives. We speak here not of deep involvement (of the type some Miata owners display toward their cars) but simply of a pleasant feeling, for example, of being served well by our faithful Saturns or Hondas or Lexuses.

Even objects of routine consumption, when strung together with hundreds of repeat performances, come to occupy a relished place in our consciousness. The jasmine fragrance of the bathing soap we use; the M.A.C mascara we apply to adorn our eyelashes; the car that helps us complete our daily commutes; the coffee and bagel or cereal and orange juice or milk and pancakes or tea and sushi we eat as our breakfast. All these so called "mundane consumptions" do come to define for us the "episodes" of everyday life. These episodes are not of mere consumption, abstracted from our subjective lives—the lives we construct and experience in our minds. Rather, their consumption is intertwined with the non-consumption life going on at the same moment. When we are commuting, we are not merely commuting, but we are also making plans for a presentation at work. When we are applying mascara, we are also admiring our physical beauty; when we are drinking beer, we are also enjoying our conversations with our drinking buddies. When we are sipping our coffee and eating our sandwiches, we are also perhaps reminiscing about the events of the previous night; or about the friends we will meet at the networking event later this evening. Invariably then, these products and brands, consumed in lockstep with non-consumption related mental activities, become an important prop in the drama that is everyday life. (In 2005, McDonald's ran an advertising series showing just such vignettes with the theme "McGriddles and Coffee. My Time. My Thoughts.")

6. Membership in a Consumption Community Lastly, we may have a relationship with a brand through a relationship with other consumers. The brand is then seen as a way of belonging to a social group of other consumers. This last source of relationship is what makes a brand or consumption community. Consumption communities are a very potent force for creating a cult for the brand—a visible, substantial group of fanatical consumers. We peek into the lives of some of these communities in the next section, but for now, review Figure 16.5 and contemplate all Six Drivers of Consumer-Brand Relationships.

A Society of Consumption Communities

Consumption communities are groups of people who share the consumption of a brand or product. Thus, Mac computer users are a consumption community, and so are all the revelers at the Dave Mathews Band concert, grunge dressers, and cross-dressers. Members of a consumption community come from a wide range of demographics. They are not all computer whiz kids; rather, they are homemakers, students, retirees, blue-collar workers, white-collar professionals, etc. In general, consumption community members are not homogeneous in demographics. Rather, it is the enthusiasm and emotion of using the brand or product that binds them.

Consumption communities play an important role in our modern societies. This is best explained by sociologist Daniel J. Boorstin:

> **The modern American, then, was tied, if only by the thinnest of threads and by the most volatile, switchable loyalties, to thousands of other Americans in nearly everything he ate or drank or drove or read or used. …. Americans were increasingly held to others not by a few iron bonds but by countless gossamer webs knitting together the trivia of their lives.**[14]

In the Pre-industrial Age, communities were formed on the basis of religious,

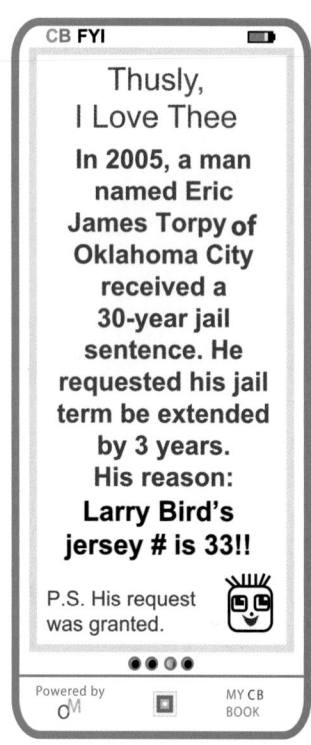

16.5 SIX DRIVERS OF CONSUMER BRAND RELATIONSHIP

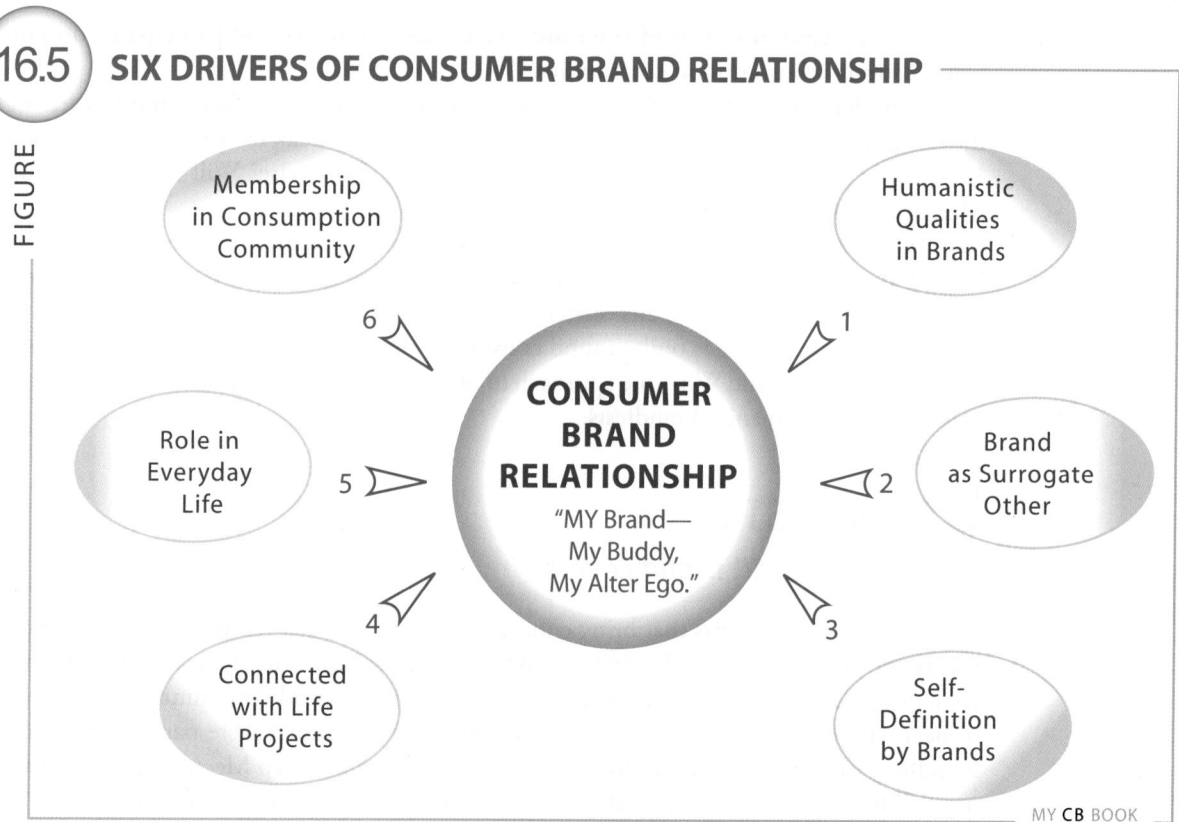

MY **CB** BOOK

political, ethnic, or geographical ties. The bonds between members were strong, members interacted frequently, and they shared many interests. But in the Post-industrial Age, these communities became much weaker, and neighborhoods are now a collection of inhabitants who often remain strangers to one another. Instead, product consumption based communities have burgeoned. There are consumption activities that occur in public spaces or in proprietary market spaces such as bowling alleys, billiard clubs, tennis clubs, health clubs, and nightclubs. Consumers identify themselves as being part of a community merely by virtue of sharing a common consumption product or service.

Consumption communities are everywhere, more than we realize. The most known is, probably, the Harley Owners Group (HOG). But there are also communities of Miata, Citroën, and MINI Cooper owners; participants in yoga classes, marathon runs, Latin dance lessons, etc.; collectors of baseball cards and Renaissance paintings, and, of course, users of iPods, among others.

What Makes Consumption Communities Tick?

Scholars have identified four elements or properties that make a community tick—by that we mean function: (a) consciousness of the kind, (b) geographical proximity, (c) temporal convergence, and (d) high context.[15] .See Figure 16.6.

Some communities score low on these, others score high. The higher the score, the more cohesive that community is and the stronger the member identification with the community. Consider students in an online course. What kind of a community do they form? These students can download lessons posted on the Web, submit assignments, ask questions, send emails, and post messages or topic-specific opinions on message boards. However, this community, if one can call it a community at all, scores low on all four criteria. First, the students taking this course are geographically dispersed. Second, they engage in "product consumption" at different, uncoordinated times, so there is high temporal separation. Third, they don't interact face to face, which makes it a "low context" interaction. Finally, in the online course, there are no group activities, and if there is any collaboration among students, it is in small groups rather than with the class as a whole. Indeed, as a group, these students don't consider themselves as part of any community, and thus lack any **consciousness of the kind**. As a result, online course participants do not make a strong "consumption community."[16]

Now that you understand the four elements, can you assess other communities on these four characteristics and rate them on whether they are weak or strong communities. Most likely HOG will qualify as a strong community. What else? Will Friendster.com? Members of MySpace.com?

There are two kinds of consumption communities: product or activity based and brand based. The first kind is built around consumers sharing a common product category. Examples are bikers, golfers, net surfers, roller-bladers, country music fans, and punk rockers. The second type is built around consumers sharing a specific brand; examples are Harley, Apple, Jeep, and Wii. One approach to building a strong brand-based consumption community is to organize brandfests.

BRANDFESTS
Party Time for All Brand Lovers

Brandfests are events that bring consumers together in geo-temporally concentrated events and entail coordinated activities and brand happenings. Since here all four elements come together, brandfests are an excellent way to build a brand community. The Saturn owners who came to Spring Hill, Tennessee one recent summer were participating in a brandfest. Jeep organizes camps for its owners and fans, called Jeep Meet. Brandfests must meet all four criteria mentioned above for a consumption community to exist.

Consciousness of the Kind The very decision to attend and join a brandfest raises the consciousness of there being a community of brand users. Many do arrive with trepidation, anxious as to whether they will fit in, but—in no small part due to the socialization and nurturing effort of other brand veterans, devotees, advocates, and evangelists, as well as brand hosts (e.g., company personnel)—they slowly ease into a state of psychological comfort, of being seen as belonging to the group.

High Context Members begin as strangers but develop close acquaintances, even lasting friendships that endure and continue beyond the confines of the event. High context interactions are those for which it is necessary to be familiar with the speaker's context (background, culture, and style) to understand what is being communicated. Emotionally charged communications are high context because words go beyond their literal meaning,

Geographically Concentrated Consumers from geographically dispersed areas come together in one location.

Temporality Members (interacting with the brand, with the marketer, and with other consumers) are all brought together within a compact time frame.

Brandfests connect consumers with the rest of the community of consumers, of course, but they also deepen consumers' relationships with the brand and with the company.

BRANDFESTS AND BRAND BONDING

Brandfests are a great way to bond the consumer with your brand. Your customers already like the one specific unit of the brand that they own. Now suddenly, they are face to face with the company behind the brand; they tour the plant, see the product being "born," and they talk to the designers and makers of the brand, who are proud of their creation. The hosting role the company plays inevitably endears the company to them.[17]

You take them behind the scenes and show them the full life of the brand—in flesh and blood, so to speak. Through product demos, product use, and maintenance lectures and seminars, you also teach them the hidden features of the brand. And, you also show them newer brand concepts in the works, thus feeding their brand excitement further.

Equally important, they see an incredibly large group of other brand users—they

SAVVY MARKETER

realize in no uncertain terms (if they didn't already know) that there is really a community out there, totally fanatic and evangelical about the brand. And, most of all, they have fun (music, food, conversations, new friends). Can anything beat this kind of event in building consumer bonds with the brand?

In the context of a Jeep Meet, for example, a relationship with a product means that consumers become more involved in an off-road jeep qua vehicle—e. g., as one brandfest attendee reported, "Earlier I was not into off-road trips; now I will be, using my off-road vehicle." Brand involvement also deepens, as illustrated by a quote from another brandfest attendee: "Toward the brand Jeep, I feel more affectionate, so I'll buy other things that are Jeep related."

16.6 **FOUR ESSENTIAL ELEMENTS OF CONSUMPTION COMMUNITIES**

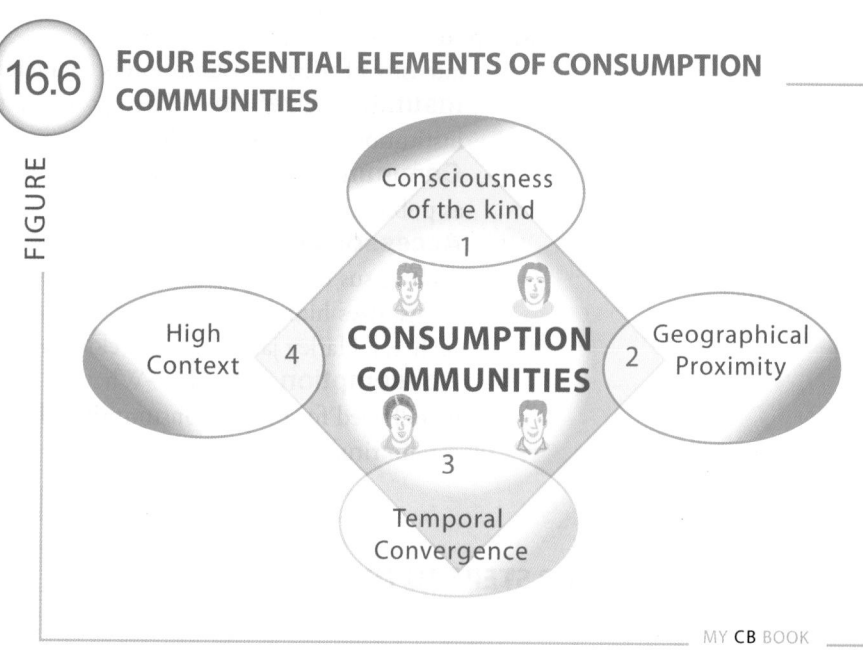

MY **CB** BOOK

CONSUMPTION TRIBES

Because these groups of consumers show tribe-like behavior while consuming specific products, they are also called consumption tribes. **Consumption tribes** are consumption communities that consume a product in a public place, in some ritualistic setting. A tribe differs from an isolated consumer who may be deeply involved in a specific product, such as a consumer who might only wear Nike clothing, or loves her Saab, or has a huge collection of Elvis music and paraphernalia. Conversely, **tribal consumption** is consumption of brands and products that is public and where there is some participation in planned events of the community.

All consumption can be marked along two dimensions: consumption venue (which can be either public/group or private/individual) and consumption event (which can be either everyday or organized). If all of your consumption of a product is at a private place such as your home and/or when you are alone, then your consumption is individual, not tribal, no matter how passionate your consumption of that product. Likewise, if the consumption is an everyday usage event and no more, then also it is individualized consumption. Only when at least some of the consumption occurs through participation in an organized public event does it become a tribal consumption. Products consumed in tribal communities can also be consumed in private and individually, but the more the product is used in public and group consumption events at specially planned gatherings, the more it becomes an object of tribal

Tribe members are happy to spot each other. (Photo courtesy: Nathan Tolbert)

consumption.

The intensity of tribal consumption is characterized by four dimensions:

- **Institutionalization**—Whether or not there is a formal organization or institution consumers can join.
- **Community Events**— Whether or not special large gatherings are organized as public consumption events.
- **Accessorization**—The extent to which the consumer uses the product by itself versus he or she accessorizes the product (e.g., placing decals on the car) or accessorizes himself/herself (i.e., using the product with other related products; such as a Harley jacket, Harley clothing, Harley credit card, key chains, etc).
- **Consumption Rituals**—Whether there are certain consumption rituals to be followed for proper consumption? For example, the game of football follows certain rituals.

Thus, the higher it rates on each of these four dimensions, the more intense is the tribal nature of the consumption. (See Figure 16.7.) To understand these qualities of tribal consumption, let us visit one such tribe—the French Roller Skaters (see box on an adjacent page).

One more point: The consumption community need not be a single entity; often it includes more than one subgroup. For example, among the Harley motorcycle riders, there are the hard core Hell's Angels, with the bad boy/bad girl image, and the adventuresome biker who just likes the identity of being a biker. Among roller skaters, there are fitness skaters, and there are urban youth stunt skaters.

The most important feature of the consumption community is that it gives the consumer a sense of identity and belonging to some larger group. Such community linkage is especially important in modern societies where big cities are dubbed "lonely spaces" for an average consumer, and he or she desperately needs something to hang on to—something with which to identify.

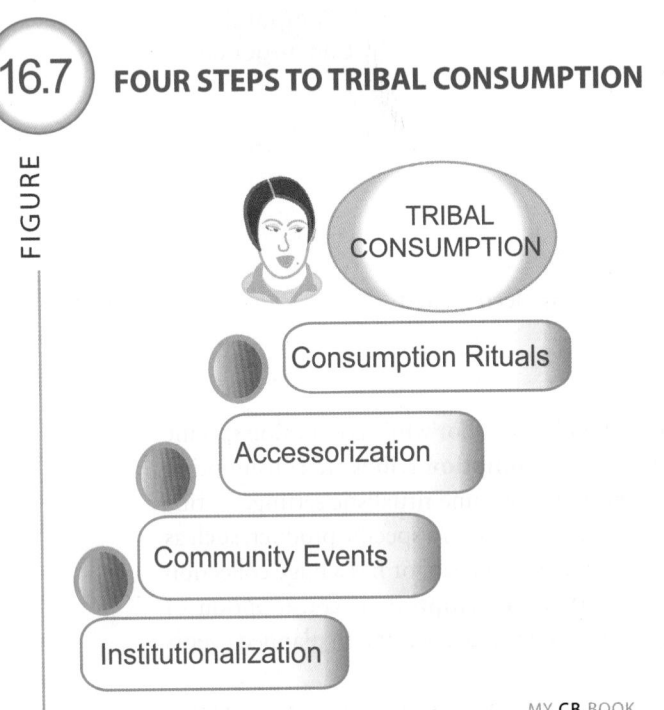

FIGURE **16.7** **FOUR STEPS TO TRIBAL CONSUMPTION**

TRIBAL CONSUMPTION

Consumption Rituals

Accessorization

Community Events

Institutionalization

MY **CB** BOOK

FOUR ROLES IN CONSUMPTION COMMUNITIES

French professors Bernard Cova and Veronique Cova have researched this topic, identifying four roles of individuals with respect to any tribe: Practitioners, participants, devotees, and sympathizers or spectators (see Figure 16.8). *Practitioners* are those who have adopted the use of the product on an everyday basis; *Participants* are those who attend special gatherings; *devotees* join the club or organization; and *sympathizers* or *spectators* do not belong to any formal organization of the consumption community, do not participate in gatherings, and do not use the product on an everyday basis. They could either be curious spectators, or sympathizers of the consumption participants. The next time you run into one such community, interview a few members and try to place them into one of these four groups.

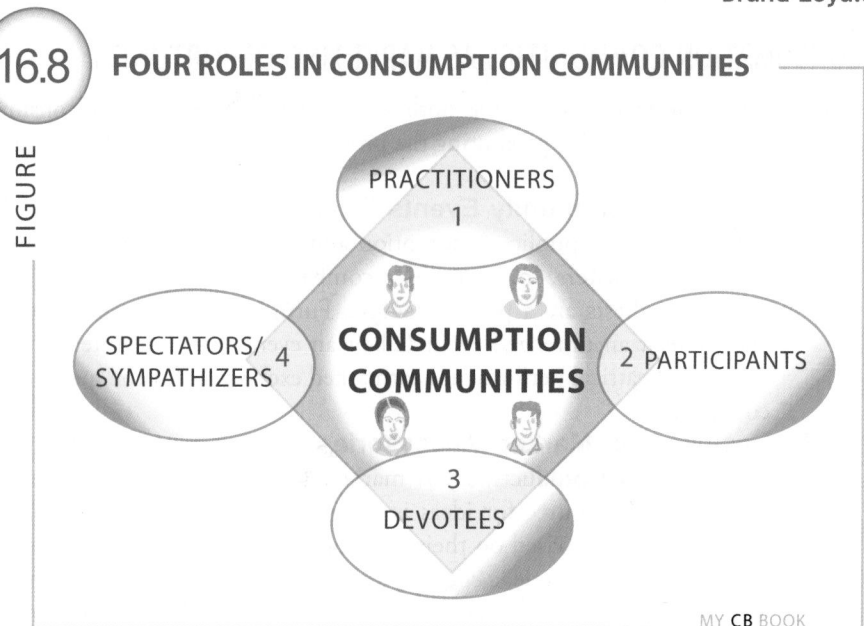

16.8 **FOUR ROLES IN CONSUMPTION COMMUNITIES**

PRACTITIONERS 1

SPECTATORS/ SYMPATHIZERS 4 **CONSUMPTION COMMUNITIES** 2 PARTICIPANTS

3 DEVOTEES

MY **CB** BOOK

How to Research Consumption Tribes

Suppose you, as a marketer, wanted to do some firsthand consumer research on one of these tribes. How would you do it? Here is a quick guide:

S A V V Y MARKETER

1. **Secondary Research** Find and read everything published about a particular consumption community—newspaper and magazine stories; TV and radio news and special reports; books; e-zines; personal Web pages; and discussion groups, forums, and chat rooms.

2. **Observation** Simply observe the users of the product as consumers use it in public places. For example, if we are interested in roller-blades, then we should observe who uses them (young or old, males or females or both, and from what socio-economic classes), where they use them (in skating rinks, on city sidewalks, in the suburban cul-de-sacs, on school grounds, etc.), on what occasions (weekends, nights, days, evenings, summer, all year long, holidays, etc.), for what purpose (fun, commute, competitive games, etc.), with whom (alone, with a pal, with a group of friends, coworkers, etc.), in what mindset (it is fun, "have to do it," efficient means of commuting, it is cool, goes with lifestyle, etc.), and with what other accoutrements (casual clothing, special clothing, accessories, etc.).

3. **Direct Questioning** Directly question a representative group of consumers who are members of the consumption communities. This can take the form of focus group discussions, one-on-one interviews, or more structured surveys. Here, we can ask consumers directly about their purpose and mindset in consumption, what their self-perceptions are as consumers of that product, whether they differentiate themselves from other subgroups of their consumption communities, and how they think outsiders perceive their community.

4. **Participant Observation** The final phase and the ultimate method for learning to understand a consumption tribe deeply is participant observation. Become a member of the tribe by consuming the product yourself, attending consumption community events, and mingling freely with community members. This method offers insight in two ways: (a) by experiencing the consumption firsthand and then reflecting on that experience; and (b) by knowing and analyzing the inner thoughts and subjective experiences of other consumers—as revealed by these other consumers, in their words and in their deeds.

CONSUMPTION COMMUNITIES AS MARKETING OPPORTUNITY

S A V V Y
MARKETER

How

Organize Community Events

to

Create Accessories

Nurture

Extend Products

Communities

Consumption communities provide both a special target segment of consumers and a special avenue or channel for promoting the product. Here is how marketers can utilize this opportunity[18]:

1. **Organize Community Events** Community members are always looking for opportunities for public consumption and for other pretexts of coming together. So for roller skaters, for example, a company could organize a big roller skating event. Brandfests are a prime example. Furthermore, a company could organize and sponsor an unrelated event (albeit an event that is of interest to members), such as a theatrical performance earmarked exclusively for the members of a brand community.

2. **Design and Market Accessories** Since community members like to accessorize their products, smart marketers should create accessories and market them. The best source for ideas is to see what some innovative consumers may have already improvised on their own, or to think of anything else that would be functional. For example, a specially designed, oversized water or drink bottle with a special logo might appeal to roller-bladers, especially if sold along with color coordinated outfits.

    Often community members use special paraphernalia (e.g., outfits) along with the primary products associated with their core consumption. Marketers of these accessories could add branding appeal for these paraphernalia by licensing an apt brand name. For example, they might add a designer name like *Calvin Klein* or a celebrity name like *Tiger Woods*.

3. **Product Extensions** These products expand the market and the communities by creating easier to use products that would appeal to the timid, not so bold, or not so skilled, as opposed to more high performance product versions would appeal to diehards.

Keep one point in mind: If there are sub-communities, as there usually are, then the marketer should conduct the marketing program so as not to annoy one sub-community just to please another.

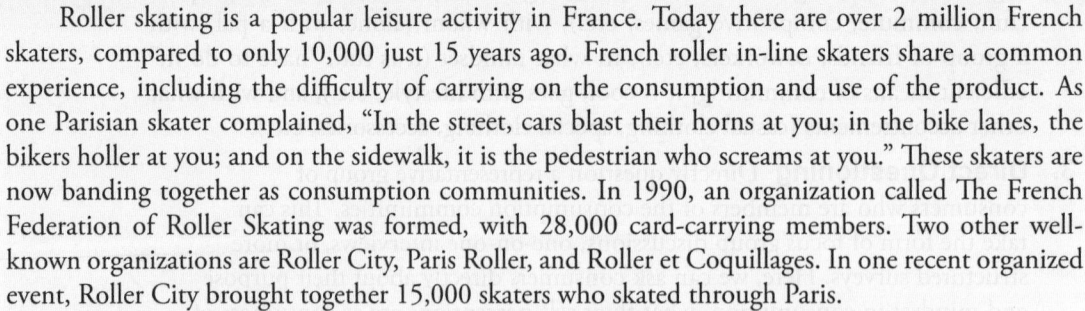

French Roller Skaters as a Consumption Community

Roller skating is a popular leisure activity in France. Today there are over 2 million French skaters, compared to only 10,000 just 15 years ago. French roller in-line skaters share a common experience, including the difficulty of carrying on the consumption and use of the product. As one Parisian skater complained, "In the street, cars blast their horns at you; in the bike lanes, the bikers holler at you; and on the sidewalk, it is the pedestrian who screams at you." These skaters are now banding together as consumption communities. In 1990, an organization called The French Federation of Roller Skating was formed, with 28,000 card-carrying members. Two other well-known organizations are Roller City, Paris Roller, and Roller et Coquillages. In one recent organized event, Roller City brought together 15,000 skaters who skated through Paris.

And of course there are regular unorganized gatherings such as those at Plage du Prado in Marseilles where hundreds of skaters congregate daily. In Paris around 10 pm on Fridays, there are regular local gatherings called Friday Night Fever. At Place d'Itilie, about 3000 to 5000 skaters congregate every week. Similar gatherings also occur on Friday evenings in Bordeaux, Lyon, Marseilles, Rennes, and Strausbourg.

Whereas spectator sports are a popular activity for consumption communities, such as watching the soccer games, and having large private parties on Superbowl evenings (a North American happening), French skaters present a good example of a consumption community centered on participant sports.

Source: Information based on Bernard Cova and Veronique Cova, "Tribal Aspects of Postmodern Consumption Research: The Case of French in-line roller Skaters," *Journal of Consumer Behavior*, 2000(1), 1, 67-76.

DEEP INVOLVEMENT

Extreme Interest in Things

We repeat this subtopic from Chapter 2 because it relates to brand loyalty intimate... is defined as a consumer's *extreme interest* in a product or activity on an ongoing basi... product fanaticism. Devotees like Gabriel McIntyre have a haircut styled like the Appl... fanatic about things they deeply care about. They use them for enjoyment, to derive... even to define their identity for themselves. What are you deeply involved in? Cars?... Cooking? Shoes? If you are, then you know how a significant part of your consumer beha... searching, browsing, buying, collecting, caring, nurturing, and relishing—is dedicate... deep involvement. You also know firsthand, then, how your deep involvement is, for... of motivation—perhaps even a reason to live!

Deep involvement produces deep brand loyalty. And deep personal relationships with the brand and with objects that carry that brand name. The wedding ceremony in Pennsylvania's Pocono Mountains a few years ago where 250 consumers married their Miatas is a rare happening, but it is a telling proof that the idea of "relationships" consumers feel with and for some brands is REAL and ALIVE.

The Cool Factor : Code Mystique for Brands

Coolness is a nebulous concept, hard to define, even harder to dissect. Brands earn this label, sometimes, based on performance excellence or a new feature—e.g., cars equipped with a system that would auto-correct their steering if they stray out of their lane. Sometimes, an innovation that solves a previously unrealized problem, e.g., Post-It Notes. But a new factor is design. The aesthetics and sensory appeal of the product, achieved through artistic design, can instantly make a product look and feel cool. The most well known cases are, of course, the Apple iMac and, more recently, the iPod and the iPhone. But design is taken to new heights when it is deployed to achieve both aesthetic and sensory pleasure as well as functional performance enhancement. Case in point: Bang and Olufsen's line of home electronics products. Its BeoCom2 phone is sculpted from a single piece of aluminum, and its ring tone is scored by a composer, delivering superior clarity and uniqueness.

Ironic that a phone would leave you speechless.

Interesting things happen when a sculptor and composer collaborate over a phone. The BeoCom 2 is formed from a single piece of aluminum with an original ring tone scored to set it apart. The result is a phone that enhances communication, especially nonverbal. Find your nearest Bang & Olufsen store at www.bang-olufsen.com or call 888 625 3421.

Courtesy Bang and Olufsen

Its BeoVision5 TV monitor works in sync with BeoLab5 sound system. Both are cast in aluminum to enhance the look and feel of consumers' living spaces. The design pleases the senses when the product is being used, but also when it is not. Indeed, its ad images are cool too. The BeoCom2 ad proclaims, "Ironic, that a phone would leave you speechless." Its TV ad says, "its beauty almost renders the 'on' button irrelevant." The consumer—albeit a certain kind of consumer—finds these designs cool. You could almost hear him or her echo the brand's message: "Ironic that my phone leaves me speechless," and "I watch TV for hours and then I turn it on." Can you think of a better scenario for consumer-brand connections?

So much pleasure is gained from viewing the aluminum framed plasma screen and matching sound system that its beauty almost renders the 'on' button irrelevant. It makes watching TV as enjoyable as watching what's on it. Find your nearest Bang & Olufsen store at www.bang-olufsen.com or call 888-625-3421.

The all-powerful BeoVision 5 & BeoLab 5

(S)UMMARY

We began this chapter with a description of brand loyalty. We defined behavioral brand loyalty as consistent purchase of the same brand, and attitudinal brand loyalty as high liking for the brand. Combining these two concepts, brand loyalty is the consistent repurchase of the same brand based on favorable attitude toward and preference for it. We then presented a model of brand loyalty, which is based on three factors: performance, self-connection, and consumer involvement.

To take our understanding of *brand loyalty* to a higher level, we presented a comprehensive model of brand loyalty. This model highlights positive and negative forces pertaining to market and consumer factors. We also described four drivers of brand equity. And finally, we discussed the concept of brand personality and outlined its five dimensions, nicknamed *SECTS*.

In the final section, we presented a fascinating topic: consumption and brand communities, and how they get formed. These communities manifest shared public consumption and play an important role in modern-day consumption. Members exhibit, often, tribe-like rituals and norms for product usage, and they accessorize their use of products and even themselves with brand paraphernalia. Companies can foster brand communities by organizing brandfests, which serve to create and foster relationships between consumers and brands and the companies that stand behind those brands.

CB Blog

16

BRANDS—
SHORTHAND FOR QUALITY, PROPS FOR IDENTITY

To consumers, a brand is many things. It is a name to refer to the specific version of a product they want. It is shorthand, also, for all the qualities the physical thing contains, and all the benefits its use will deliver. It is assurance that the brand will do what the brand says it will. It is also a badge for its user, reflecting for the user a certain kind of persona. It is the target of consumption, consumed by the consumer. But it is also the subject of consumption, with the consumer being the target—the brand consumes the consumer!

Consumers are fanatical about some brands. They depend on some brands, and, in turn, the brands depends on them. By constantly thinking about them and by repeatedly consuming them, we become attached to them, yearning for their presence, whenever pertinent. We connect to them as if they were people, like friends, trusting and trustworthy. And through them, we connect to other people. In consumption communities and at consumption events called brandfests—a new form of public discourse built around a brand. We celebrate brands, and in so doing, we celebrate our lives as consumers.

With such a rich potpourri of brand mantras, it is hard to overstate the import of understanding the role brands play in consumer lives. This chapter has been our foray into the world of brand consumption. Explore it as a consumer and relish your current brand relationships even more. Explore it as a marketer and strategize how you can offer greater brand value to your target consumers.

CONSUMER BEHAVIOR

MY CB BOOK .COM

KEY TERMS

Animism
Anthropomorphizing
Attitudinal brand loyalty
Behavioral brand loyalty
Brandfests

Brand loyalty
Brand personality
Brand tribes
Consumer brand
    relationship

Communities
Consumption
Consumption tribes
Homophyly
Latent loyalty

Life projects
Store loyalty
Spurious loyalty
Tribal consumption

YOUR TURN

REVIEW+Rewind

1. How would you define brand loyalty? If a consumer repeatedly buys the same brand, can we call him or her brand loyal? Why or why not?

2. What is *behavior scan*, and what is its utility to marketers? How well does it help marketers in assessing consumer brand loyalty?

3. Explain the three factors in the simple model of brand loyalty. Using this model, how would you build brand loyalty for high and low involvement consumers?

4. Explain the four faces of brand loyalty. Give an example of each.

5. List and explain the dimensions of brand personality. How do marketers create brand personality?

6. Can consumers have relationships with brands? Why do these relationships get formed?

7. What are the four defining characteristics of brand communities? Do brandfests satisfy these conditions? Why or why not?

8. What are consumption tribes? What are the four dimensions that determine the intensity of tribal consumption?

9. How can marketers (a) research and (b) utilize the concept of tribal consumption?

THINK+Apply

1. Identify any five brands to which you are loyal. Discuss why you are loyal to those brands, using the explanation offered in this chapter.

2. Assume you are a marketing manager for (choose one): (a) a music CD store; (b) a book store; (c) a clothing store; (d) a brand of cola; or (e) a brand of hair color. You want to know what proportion of your customers are brand (store-) loyal and why or why not. Prepare a questionnaire for a consumer research project to address this issue.

3. Assume you have completed the above-mentioned survey. Based on the ideas presented in the chapter, what sort of reasons do you expect to find for consumers being loyal or not loyal to the brand or store for the product category you have chosen? Next, as a marketing manager, prepare a plan of action to increase loyalty among the currently non-loyal consumers. Identify separate actions for each of the possible factors.

4. For which of the following products would a marketer be able to create tribe-like brand consumption communities: (a) electric shaver, (b) beer, (c) video games, (d) Yoga, (e) shopping at Target, and (f) shopping at Whole Foods (www.wholefoods.com). Why or why not? Describe how.

PRACTICE+Experience

1. The chapter describes four types of brand loyalty based on consumer attitudes and behaviors. Interview five consumers and identify to which segment each of them belongs, if any.

2. Spend some time as a participant observer in a consumption community. Describe and comment on how those communities compare with the textbook descriptions in the chapter.

3. Put together a survey to measure (a) involvement, (b) brand loyalty, and (c) brand personality. Interview ten consumers, asking them to describe their preferred brands of (a) jeans, (b) cars, (c) laptops, and (d) cell phones. Obtain these descriptions as open-ended answers (take notes). Next, have them fill out the survey for each product category. Analyze your data. For example, are brand loyalty scores higher for high involvement consumers? Are brand personality scores remarkable only for high involvement consumers? Do consumers' open-ended descriptions correlate their scores on the questionnaires?

In the Marketing Manager's Shoes

Most concepts in the chapter have some lessons for the marketing manager, i.e., they suggest what to do differently in practice; indeed, often these applications are implicit in our explanations of the concepts and models in the chapter. Identify at least five specific applications of the chapter's concepts, all of which should be entirely new—different from the examples cited here.

17 Consumer Behavior in e-Marketplace

Searching, Shopping, and Connecting

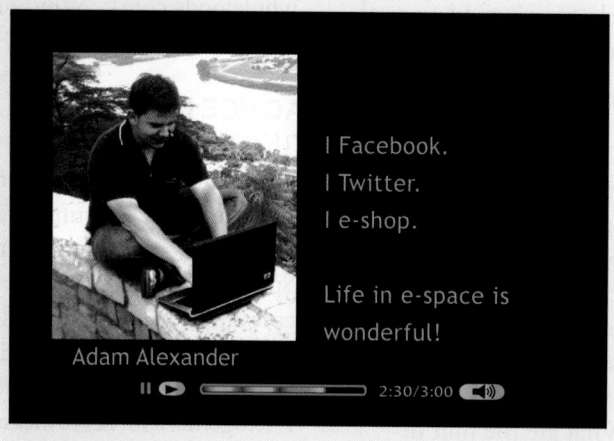

I Facebook.
I Twitter.
I e-shop.

Life in e-space is wonderful!

Adam Alexander

2:30/3:00

LEARN . APPLY . EXPERIENCE

OBJECTIVES

1 The Geography and Demographics of Consumers on the Web

2 Factors for and Barriers to Consumer Internet Use

3 Goals and Motivations of Online Shoppers and Experiential Browsers

4 Pre- and Post-Purchase Factors in Consumer e-Satisfaction

5 Social Network Sites (*SoNets*) and Consumer Gratifications

6 The Role of the Internet Beyond Shopping: Religious and Other Web Connectors

Questions of the Eve: Boxers or Briefs, Pre or iPhone?

• good a.m., Twitter friends! Trying to be cheerful despite gloomy, misty morning in which hair becomes non-sweet cotton candy. 5:30 AM, JUN 12th from mobile web

. Qs. of the eve: boxers or briefs, Pre or iPhone? The women here, like Caterina Fake (former flickr co-founder) are more open to Pre! 5:30 PM JUN 4th from mobile web

• BIG NEWS: just met the guy who knows the guy whose investment co invested in Palm PRE! He confirmed it kicks fricking ... ! 5:37 PM, JUN 4th from mobile web

• as you all know, I've been tortured with desire for this little iPhone killer. 5:01 AM JUN 5th from mobile web

• I heard that that uber-typer @anamariecox uses the iPhone to update us all every 4 min and I challenge her to a Pre/iPhone Duel! 5:17 AM JUN 5th from mobile web

• Here is what my spot poll revealed at the Founder's Club party. MOST of the male CEOs weren't interested in Palm Pre. Women were Pre-curious. 5:17 AM JUN 5th from mobile web

• I predict that women will be the sleeper "early adopter" customers of the Palm Pre. Okay, enough about phones today! 5:19 AM JUN 5th from mobile web

Laurel Touby, in one of her cheery moments

Photo credit: Stacy Kranitz

Tweets: New consumer chatter that builds brands

* Name Laurel Touby
* Location New York, NY
* Web http://www.mediabistro.com
* Bio as the founder of mediabistro.com, my Tweets are highly personal musings about the media industry and the people who make media.

161 Following
4,846 Followers

Source: http://twitter.com/laureltouby. Posts (or *Tweets* as they are known) are displayed on Twitter with the most recent entry at the top; that order is reset here chronologically. (Used with permission)

INTRODUCTION

Twitter is a microblogging *and* social networking site that consumers of all ilk have taken a fancy to. It allows members to post, in less than 140 characters, their answers to a simple question: "What are you doing right now?" Founded in August 2006, it had acquired 2 million users by 2008; by the end of February 2012, it had registered 200 million users worldwide![1]

Consumers like Touby use it to stay connected with friends and business associates as well as to keep up with happenings in whatever sphere of activity interests them. While not everyone is as devoted to the Internet for his or her shopping and social needs as the netizens of Twitter, Facebook, MySpace, Bebo, and other social networking sites are, most of us have had at least some familiarity and experience with the Internet. Of course, around the world, not everyone has access to the Internet, and of those who use the Internet, not everyone uses it for shopping, or even for social networking. While online retail revenues are on a sharp rise to a whopping $348 billion, they still represent only 6% of total retail sales.[2] To tap the full potential of online buying, as marketers, we need to understand why consumers shop or do not shop on the Internet, and, more generally, why they do or do not spend time in e-space. The goal of this chapter is to understand the motivations and experiences of online consumers.

We begin the chapter by describing the Internet Consumer Universe: How many consumers are online worldwide and for what purposes? Next, we recognize a principal distinction between two types of online consumers: goal-oriented shoppers and experiential browsers. We examine the motives of each group, and explore the features of Internet shopping that satisfy these motives. Following this, we present a model of e-satisfaction, highlighting the attributes and behaviors of online vendors that produce it. We then describe segments among online shoppers.

We turn, next, to Social Networking Sites (SNS) to recognize their pervasive presence in the lives of consumers worldwide. We examine the demographic profile of the two major SN sites, namely, Facebook and Twitter. We then explore why marketers too inhabit the SN sites and whether consumers who "friend" or "follow" these brands also throw some dough their way.

In the last section, we return to the use of Internet per se, and describe how the Internet has turned the youth (teens and college students) into market mavens. We conclude with a look (very brief) at how the Internet is enriching the lives of faith seekers. We chose this last domain to drive a point home: The marketers of commercial and noncommercial firms alike can harness the Web to bring consumers value.

THE INTERNET CONSUMER UNIVERSE: GEOGRAPHY AND DEMOGRAPHICS

TABLE 17.1 THE INTERNET UNIVERSE

REGION	INTERNET USERS	
	Within Region %	Within WORLD %
Africa	11.4	5.7
Asia	23.8	44.0
Europe	58.3	22.7
Middle East	31.7	3.3
North America	78.3	13.0
Latin America	36.2	10.1
Australia	60.1	1.0
WORLD	30.2	100

Source: Excerpted from www.internetworldstats.com

MY CB BOOK

The Internet Consumer Around the World

Globally, 2.1 billion people were online in 2011 (up from 361 million in 2000), accounting for 30.2% of the total world population.[3] The penetration of the Internet varies across nations. In North America, 78.3% of the adult population is online. Oceania/Australia is next, with 60.1% of people there online; Europe is 58.3%; the lowest usage of the Internet is in Africa, with only 5.7% of its population using the Internet. See Table 17.1. However, it is in Africa that the Internet usage has grown the highest (1100%) since 2000, compared to the world average growth of 336%.

The top ten countries account for 17% of all Internet

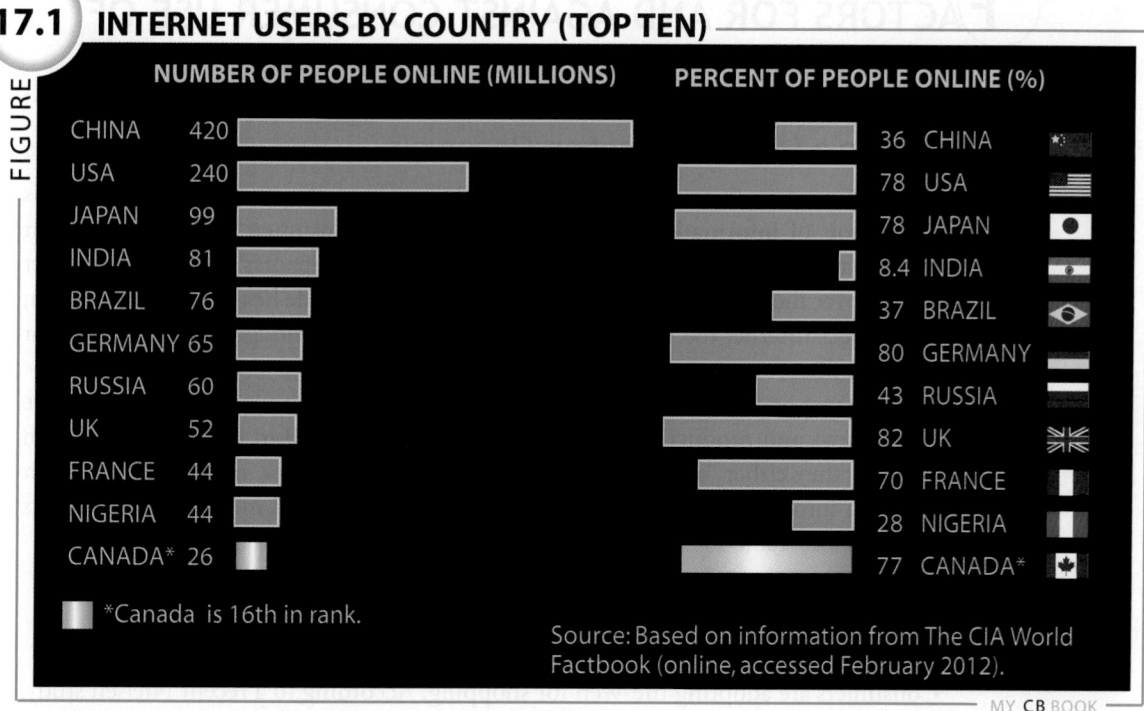

MY **CB** BOOK

17.1 INTERNET USERS BY COUNTRY (TOP TEN)

users. China tops the list with 420 million Internet users, with USA and Japan in the second and third place, with 240 and 99 million, respectively. (See Figure 17.1)

The distinction of having the largest number of Internet users does not imply, of course, the most Web-engaged nation. That distinction belongs to Norway, with 91% of its population using the Internet (not counting the small island nations of Falkland and Iceland, with 100 and 93% reach, respectively). Among the Top Ten nations, UK has that distinction, with 82% reach; Germany, USA, and Japan trail closely with 80, 78, and 78% reach, respectively. China has a modest 36% reach; India is at bottom, with only 8.4% reach. Outside of the Top Ten list, Canada (16th in rank) has a reach of 77%, with 26 million Internet users. See Figure 17.1.

The absolute lowest (counting all countries with 100,000 or more consumers online) is Bangladesh, with only 0.3% of its population online (not shown in figure).[4]

Demographic Profile of Internet Users

The adoption of the Internet has not been even across demographic groups. Among U. S. consumers, women have adopted the Internet slightly more. Younger consumers are more on the Internet than older consumers. Caucasians lead whereas Hispanics lag African-Americans somewhat. And Internet use increases, as expected, with income, education, and suburban and urban (rather than rural) residence. See Table 17.2.

TABLE 17.2 DEMOGRAPHICS OF INTERNET USERS

Total Adults		**74%**
SEX	Women	75
	Men	73
AGE	18-29	87
	30-49	82
	50-64	72
	65+	41
ETHNIC	Whites	77
	African Americans	64
	Hispanics	58
AREA	Urban	71
	Suburban	74
	Rural	63
HH INCOME	Less than $30,000/yr	57
	$30,000- $49,999/yr	77
	$50,000- $74,999/yr	90
	$75,000 or more	94
EDUCATION	Less than high-school	35
	High school	67
	Some college	85
	College+	95

Source: Demographics of Internet Users, Pew Internet and American Life Project, March '02 Survey; updated Jan. 2009. http://www.pewinternet.org/trends.asp

MY **CB** BOOK

FACTORS FOR AND AGAINST CONSUMER USE OF THE INTERNET

Internet as a Huge Information Reservoir

All consumers familiar with the Internet are aware of its principal property: It is a huge reservoir of information. As many as 65% of all consumers expect government agencies to have a Web site; 63% expect all commercial companies to provide product information over the Internet; 67% expect the Internet to provide healthcare information; and 69% expect Internet to contain news. Obviously, this percentage is much higher for Internet users than for nonusers (about 80% versus 40%).[5]

The Internet in fact meets these expectations. Of the consumers who go online looking for news and product and service information, some 70 to 87% (depending on the topic) say they either "always" or "mostly" do find it.[6] However, not everyone finds it easy to search information online. Some factors make it a helpful medium, while others act as barriers. See Table 17.3.

ONLINE SHOPPING BEHAVIOR

Consumers are adopting the Web for shopping. According to a recent Nielsen study, some 875 million consumers had bought a product online within the previous three months. The five top product categories were (with percent of online shoppers in parentheses) books (41%), clothing (36%), videos (24%), airline tickets (24%), electronics (23%), and groceries (14%).[7] Although large and growing, the online revenue ($348 billion) is still a small proportion (6%) of total retail sales, so the potential for online consumer spending is substantial. To understand this potential, let us see what consumers are buying online, and what they are not buying.

PRODUCTS CONSUMERS BUY ONLINE

Would you buy your wedding dress online? What about your engagement ring? A new painting by an unknown artist? A car tire? A designer brand Italian leather sofa from an Italian merchant? Exotic fruit from a merchant in Hawaii? Milk? Bread? Beer? Well, it depends. You could buy your wedding dress online, for example, if you have first searched and identified a similar dress in a bricks-and-mortar (b&m) store. The Italian sofa? Yes, if the vendor can certify their pedigree and authenticity. The same goes for exotic fruit. Tires? Yes, if you don't need them immediately. Here is what consumers buy or do not buy online and under what conditions:

Digital Products Digital products are products that exist in or can be transformed into digital form, such as computer software, music, pictures, video, and information material such as manuals, brochures, books, educational lessons, etc. Since these products can be transported digitally, they are available for downloading immediately.

Branded Products with Established Preferences Lands' End clothing, Calvin Klein Cologne, Oolong tea, and any number of other products, which consumers have already tried and formed preferences for—they are willing to buy them online, especially if they want to avoid physical shopping.

Technical Products from Trusted Vendors Thousands of consumers buy online printers, cables, and computer components (memory, sound cards, etc). These are products that are specified by technical attributes, and, therefore, there is nothing to inspect in person. Consequently, and as long as they can trust the vendor, consumers feel no hesitation buying these products online.

Products Not Needed Immediately If a consumer got a busted tire and if he needed a new one immediately, then he could not afford to wait for it to arrive in the mail. But if the product were not needed immediately, and if it were a branded product

TABLE 17.3 FACTORS FOR AND AGAINST CONSUMER INFORMATION SEARCH ON THE INTERNET

HELPFUL FACTORS	BARRIERS
• **Data Warehouse** The Internet is a vast storage medium. It is a huge warehouse of information where one can access merchants worldwide.	• Lack of Access to Computer and the Internet Not everybody has access to a computer, the Internet, and a high-speed connection.
• **Accessible Anytime, Anywhere** This information is accessible anywhere—anywhere the consumer has access to an Internet device (e.g., a PC, a web-enabled cell phone, etc). Moreover, the Internet information warehouse is always open, 24 hours a day, seven days a week.	• Lack of Internet Literacy Many consumers' use of the Internet is limited to emails; they do not have the necessary Internet literacy to search efficiently.
• **Searchability** The ability for consumers to search for information quickly. Just by typing a keyword, the consumer can get information from multiple vendors all at once (in contrast to the physical world, where the consumer has to contact multiple vendors individually).	• Massive, Undifferentiated Information Many search engines present a huge number of information documents. For example, on google.com (a popular search engine) if you type "online business degree," in .23 seconds, the number of entries that show up is 4,430,000! Now, you have to click on them individually only to find that most of them are poorly selected and have low relevance.
• **Reorganization of Information** The ability to manipulate, organize, and store information easily. The information on the Internet can also be configured and organized easily by the consumer in any format; for example, you can sort a list of brands and vendors by price (ascending or descending order), by make and model, by features, by location, and so on. Moreover, you can also store this re-configured information instantly on a file (by bookmarking the page, for example), for perusing later.	• Information Overload Even when information is selected by using shopbots and the displayed database is all relevant, it is still large in size, totaling to some 20 to 50 brands;
	• Impersonalness The information comes in low-context. By "low-context" we mean that there is no human element in communication, no nonverbal gestures, and no referent opinion. Thus, the Internet is good for objective information, but if you wanted some nonverbal and symbolic information, the Internet is not the place to look.

MY CB BOOK

(e.g., Goodyear tire, Alphanumeric shirts, or Akademik jeans), and came in standard sizes, colors, etc., then consumers would not hesitate to buy them online.

Products Generally Not Bought Online

New Experiential Products   Experiential products are those that consumers need to try or actually use in order to enjoy them and judge their value or utility. New cologne? Consumers have to smell it. A new make or model of car? They have to test drive it. They would not buy it online, at least not before having experienced it at a bricks-and-mortar store.

Small Ticket, Bulky Items If the product's price were, say, three dollars and shipping and handling (S&H) cost were four dollars, then consumers would be unlikely to buy it online. Unless, of course, if multiple items could be combined so that the cumulative value would make total shipping costs a small proportion.

Perishables Milk, bread, and other groceries are not bought online, unless the online vendor has a local distribution center and can deliver frequently.

High Touch Products One characteristic of products is "high touch"—products that require touch and feel, and consequently cannot be judged or bought in virtual space. Dress material, designs for home furnishing, cologne, jewelry, accessories—these are all products that call for "high touch" shopping, possible only in bricks-and-mortar stores.[8]

PSYCHOLOGY OF ONLINE SHOPPERS

When asked why they shop online, the Number 1 reason consumers give is *convenience*. In a recent Pew/Internet survey, 78% of internet users agreed that shopping online is convenient and 68% agreed that it saves them time. The greatest problem was the security of credit card and personal information, with 75% of online consumers expressing such concern. Another negative factor was lack of user-friendliness of information: 32% of online shoppers felt the information was sometimes confusing, and 30% felt overwhelmed.[9]

To describe the psychology of online shoppers more in-depth, we must first briefly review some concepts of shopping in general, recapitulating important ideas from preceding chapters. Shopping does not mean buying; rather it means visiting stores. Consumers visit stores, sometimes for buying, but sometimes just for browsing. Browsing may culminate into a purchase, but, regardless, the process of browsing itself is seen by many consumers as enjoyable. Indeed, consumers browse, and continue to browse, only as long as they are deriving enjoyment. Once, the enjoyment stops, they stop browsing and leave the store. When the principal reason for shopping is enjoyment-seeking, it is called *hedonic shopping*. On the other hand, when shopping (i.e. visiting the store) is driven by intent to buy something, that is called *utilitarian shopping*. In utilitarian shopping, the process of examining and evaluating the merchandise may be tedious, but it continues until the goal is accomplished, i.e., the right product or brand is identified. That is why, utilitarian shopping is also called task-oriented or goal-directed shopping.[10]

These two motives apply equally well to online stores. Consumers could visit online stores either for hedonic experience or for the utilitarian purpose of making a purchase. However, a majority of consumers visit online stores for utilitarian rather than hedonic motives. That is, a majority of them are "buyers" rather than "browsers." In a recent survey, 71% of online consumers reported that their most recent online purchase had been planned, whereas 29% said they had been browsing when they made their most recent online purchase.[11]

What is important to online buyers versus browsers? Let us examine their psychology.

GOAL ORIENTED ONLINE SHOPPERS

Goal oriented online shoppers go on the Internet with a purchase goal in mind—they want to buy something. The question is, instead of going to a mall or a physical store, why do they like to go shopping online? Their reasons (or motivations) are two: (1) efficient and effective shopping; and (2) freedom and control.[12]

Efficient and Effective Shopping

The primary motive of goal-oriented shoppers to go online is to make the required purchase more efficiently as well as more effectively than they consider possible offline. This efficiency and effectiveness comes from certain enabling features of online stores, namely: (a) convenience, (b) access to a wider assortment, (c) comprehensive product information, (d) easy product comparisons, (e) best prices, and (f) memorized shopping history.

Convenience Sure, consumers could go to the mall; but that would mean driving to the mall, finding parking, walking up to the store, finding the merchandise, dealing with the sales clerk, carting the merchandise to the car, loading it, and then driving back home and unloading it. Online stores remove all this hassle. This convenience can be a strong motive, particularly for time-starved consumers. Moreover, consumers can shop online anytime, and from anywhere (wherever they have access to the Internet).

Access to a Wider Assortment However, convenience can only go so far. Beyond convenience, consumers want to find what they want. Can they find it on the Internet? Indeed, much more than do bricks-and-mortar stores, online stores display a much wider assortment. For example, if you are looking for shoes, at Footsmart.com, you can find 19 types of men's shoes; 74 types of women's shoes, 25 varieties of walking shoes, 22 varieties of slippers and 16 types of therapeutic shoes! Not only do online stores carry a wider assortment, but

HOW THE WEB ENABLES EFFICIENT AND EFFECTIVE SHOPPING
- Convenience
- Access to wider assortments
- Comprehensive product information
- Easy product comparisons
- Best prices
- Stored shopping history

MY CB BOOK

you can also find an online store for a rare item of merchandise. Suppose you wanted to buy a pair of retro-western women's boots; where would you go? Whom would you ask? The chances are, you wouldn't know. But on the Internet, type "retro women's boots," and back comes a list of stores; click on the first name on the list (Caboots.Zoovy.com), and the next page will prove a feast for your eyes. See Exhibit 17.1.

Comprehensive Product Information Consumers who shop online also seek and find comprehensive product information. For example, the LG Electronics Web site (www.lge.com) gives detailed information on its new 3D Cinema TV with Smart TV. It is often difficult in b&m stores, to find knowledgeable salespersons who can match this level of product information.

Easy Product Comparisons Moreover, on the Web, it is possible to compare competing products or brands side-by-side. For example, online store www.bizrate.com offers side by side comparison across alternatives. In the physical world, the two product brochures are unlikely to list the features in the same order, thus making comparisons cumbersome.

Best Price The Internet is also a haven for price-based comparison-shoppers. This is not only because it enables access to stores worldwide, but also because there are shopping agents (e.g. mysimon.com, pricescan.com) that search the entire e-space and assemble the requested product in a list with ascending price order. For example, on Pricescan.com, searching for Coby TF-DVD7100 7 inch Portable DVD Player will get you 11 vendors, with prices ranging from $107 to $189. See Exhibit 17.2.

Memorized Shopping History Finally, the best thing about the Web is that an online store can record and save information from your previous visits. Thus, if you register with a site and give it your address and payment information once, you don't have to give that information again. On your next visit, it even brings up the products you might have searched before. At the Lands' End store, for example, you can create your own model (a visual model to your size), and store it. Not only does this tool enable you to check how a particular clothing item will look on you, but you can also retrieve this model every time you visit the store.

Thus, online shopping makes searching, selecting, and acquiring products more efficient (saving time and effort), and also more effective (better product selection).

Greater Freedom & Control

The second motive for goal-driven shoppers to shop online is that they feel more freedom and greater control when they shop online. They feel that they are free to do whatever they like and are in control of their shopping. This sense of freedom and control comes from six features of online shopping:

Shop Anytime, Anywhere On the Internet, the stores are open 24/7. And you can shop from anywhere, as long as you have access to the Web. Furthermore, when shopping online, you, the consumer, do not need to be groomed, dressed, and presentable. You know what that kind of freedom means to you.

EXHIBIT 17.1

The Wide Assortment on the World Wide Web

SHOES GALORE

Shoes from Caboots Co.
(www.caboots.zoovy.com)
(Used with permission)

MY CB BOOK

EXHIBIT

17.2 **HOW THE INTERNET ENABLES EASY PRICE COMPARISONS**

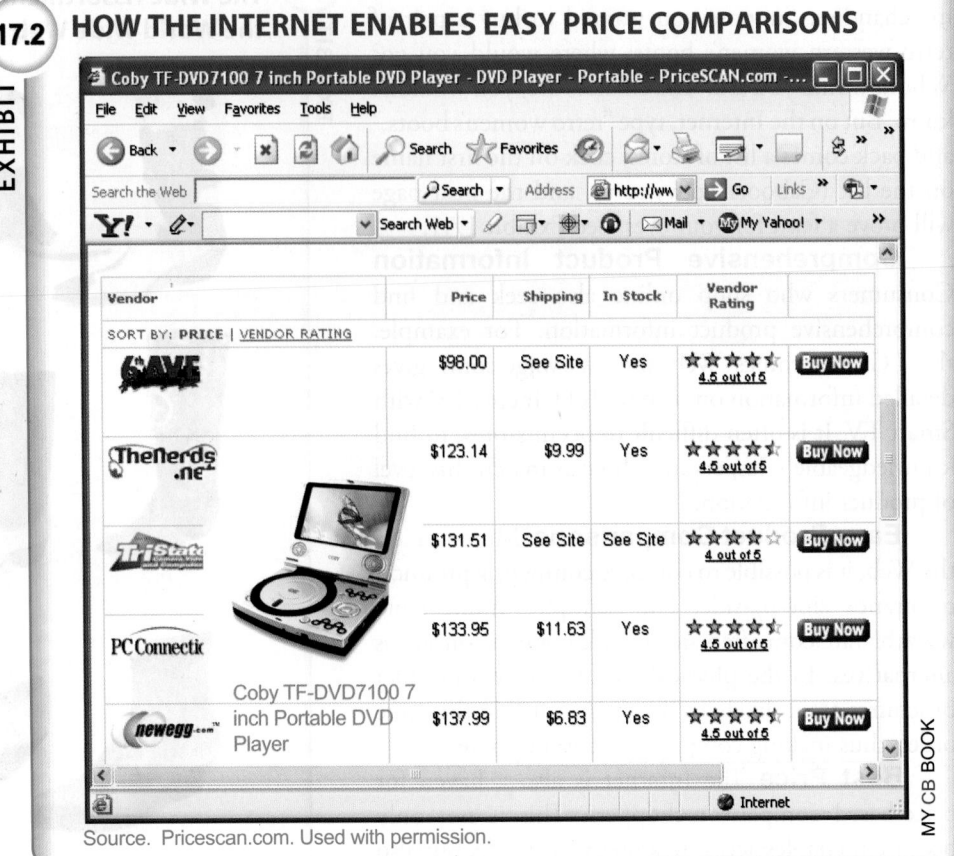

Source. Pricescan.com. Used with permission.

No Pressure from Salespersons On the Internet, there is no salesperson to shadow you, and no salesperson to intimidate you. For example, some men (and women too) might feel awkward entering Victoria's Secret (the physical store). But on the Web, there is no such fear.

No Obligation to Buy In physical stores, if a salesperson spends time with us, we sometimes feel obligated to buy something. Online shoppers feel free from such perceived normative pressures.

Control What Information to See Online store visitors also feel they have control over what information to see. For example, if you go to the Alfa Romeo Web site (www.alfaromeo.com), and if you click on MiTo, you get the option to view the exterior or interior, review "personalization" options, and watch the car being driven on water balloons!

Multi-trip Purchase Because the effort to visit online stores is low, as an online visitor you don't have to conclude your purchase in a single trip. You can leave the store any time, and return to it later, by "bookmarking" the page (i.e., by saving the Web page). Many Web sites "remember" the products you viewed, and they save your shopping carts from previous trips.

Order-tracking Online shoppers also feel that they have greater control over their orders. Once you place an order, you typically receive an e-mail confirmation. Subsequently, you can track the order simply by typing your tracking number into the vendor's web site.

It is important to note that while these features make online shopping desirable, by enabling freedom and control, not every consumer views these as sources of freedom and control. Indeed, for a majority of consumers, when it comes to shopping, there is nothing like the real store.

HOW THE WEB GIVES CONSUMERS GREATER FREEDOM AND CONTROL
> Shop anytime, anywhere
> No pressure from salespersons
> No obligation to buy
> Control what information to see
> Multi-trip purchase
> Order-tracking

MOTIVES OF EXPERIENTIAL BROWSERS

Experiential browsers are consumers whose principal motive for going to the Web is fun and excitement. Just as visitors to an amusement park go there and ride the rides for fun and enjoyment, so do many consumers go online to find enjoyment. Such consumers are called *Web surfers*.

There are four potential sources of fun and enjoyment on the Web. That is, within the overall motive of fun and enjoyment, there are four more specific motives that online surfers seek: (1) explore favorite topics or products; (2) treasure hunt; (3) game-like exchanges; and (4) multi-media sensations.

1. Explore favorite topics or products If you are a sports fan, you watch ESPN on TV and read Sports Illustrated, and you enjoy them. And you enjoy browsing sports paraphernalia in sports stores. Now, the Internet is one more medium for you to extend your love of sports and experience the joy of sports in some new ways. For example, on ESPN.com, not only can you read all the sports stories (which you could also read in a sports magazine), but you also can visit the photo gallery (something you cannot do with a magazine); you can chat with other sports fans; and you can express your opinion on current issues. For example, if you visited ESPN Web site recently, you could have answered this opinion question: How did Michael Jordan's two seasons with the Wizards impact his legacy: (a) Enhanced it; (b) Diminished it; or (c) Nothing changed.

Browsers go on the Internet to explore and gain deeper knowledge about their pet topics. If you are interested in, say, exotic cars, you type in "exotic cars" in the Google search field and, instantly, a list of sites shows up. Click on one (www.fantasycars.com) and you can spend some enjoyable time looking at such exotic cars as Josse, Marcos, Isdera, Vector, and Stola, for example.

Thus, consumers who are enduringly involved in a topic go online to have fun—exploring and learning about their favorite topics. The Internet enables this due to two features it has. First, it has search engines (e.g., Google, Searchme), which cull together a virtual library of hundreds of sites for you to explore. Second, there are topic-specific sites, such as ESPN.com which offer a wealth of information, with easy to search and explore features.

2. Treasure hunt The second motive of browsers is **treasure hunting**—finding something unusual. This something can be a product or a special deal. For example, suppose you were surfing ESPN.go.com, and you clicked on "People and Chat." The Web page that appears next features an ad. For e-kiss. Yes, you can send someone a personalized animated card featuring audio-video of a kiss in motion. Now, you did not know that, did you? And you realize that not only is this an unusual product, but that such a product is, in fact, not even feasible in bricks-and-mortar stores.

Another kind of treasure find is a price deal or a bargain. Bargain hunting is a strong motive for browsers, both online and offline. However, only the Internet brings bargains home to the browsers without the prolonged process of physically roaming from store aisle to store aisle. And consumers just love the "thrill of the bargain."[13]

The Internet has at least four features that enable treasure hunting. First, there are search engines and shopping bots (like mysimon.com), which act as virtual scavengers, scoping out the entire e-space. These shopping bots are primarily useful to the goal-oriented shoppers, but, often, during net-surfing, these sites present whatever they find anyway, and some of these finds can be rare either as a product or in price. Then, there are targeted pop-up ads, which display ads relevant to the topic the consumer is browsing. Third, browsers often register at sites to receive interesting offers, and then receive opt-in-e-mails (e-mails that consumers opt to receive), such as Groupon, LivingSocial, etc. Finally, there are sites such as eBay that are like treasure warehouses both for unusual and usual products, often at bargain basement prices. These four features of the Internet offer ample opportunities for consumers to find some unexpected treasures. Consumers who

TREASURE HUNT

Search engines

Pop-up ads

Opt-in emails

Auction sites

SOURCES OF ENJOYMENT FOR WEB SURFERS
> **Exploring favorite topics or products**
> **Treasure hunt**
> **Game-like exchanges**
> **Multi-media sensation**

MY CB BOOK

know this, therefore, make browsing part of their leisure activity.

3. Game-like Exchange In b&m stores, you like an item, pay a fixed price, and take the item home. This exchange itself is nothing special. Occasionally, when you happen to visit a flee market or a car or estate auction, then you get to bargain and bid, and this, especially the bidding process, can be quite a game. Some consumers go to these auctions regularly, and even become addicted, feeling the adrenalin as they wait to see if someone ups the bid they just made. Now, on the Internet, you can go to an auction every day. eBay.com is the most famous of them, but now there are newer Web sites such as uBid and zolabid.com where you can post your *urgent* need for a product (even pizza) or service (e.g., you need a pet sitter within the next one hour!) and receive immediate bids from neighborhood suppliers (the mobile app automatically knows your location!).

4. Multi-media Sensation The fourth source of enjoyment, and the motive for online browsing, is the multi-media sensation of the Web. If you go to the BMW Web site (www.BMWfilms.com), for example, you can watch four short films (duration: 8 minutes 40 seconds, each). Likewise, if you go to the Levi's Web site (US.Levi.com), the home page opens on a close up shot of the back pocket of Levi's Type I Jeans, a close up shot so close that you can see every stitch and the yarn of the dark blue denim; you can also see an intriguing picture of a denim clad model—the view alters between different shots. Inside ("inside" for a Web site means the deeper layers of the Web site), there is more of a feast, including five games. One of these games features a section of a pair of jeans with rivets; your challenge is to connect, with the clock running, all the rivets by clicking on them in the order in which they appear. There are 21 of them, and they appear at random locations. Such multi-media exposure to a game, where the product itself is a hero, can be fun in itself, but it can also "rivet" you to the product.

HOW THE WEB ENABLES TREASURE HUNTS
> Search engines as virtual scavengers
> Targeted pop up ads
> Opt-in emails
> eBay and other auction sites

Readers must note that the Web content is a moving target, and by the time you maybe reading this, the particular content we mentioned may have already been "retired.")

These four elements, then, are the sources of enjoyment and motivations for online browsers. Table 17.4 summarizes the goals, experiences, and the Internet's enabling features for the two types of online shoppers.

FLOW ONLINE

No matter which particular source of enjoyment is at work on a Web site, the essential source of online browsing enjoyment is what has been termed *flow*. **Flow** refers to a situation where the consumer gets immersed in the site navigation, losing a sense of time. Flow is correlated to the fun that surfers feel in Web site surfing, in the use of Web sites for leisure and recreational purposes, and the amount of time spent surfing. Flow comprises several elements: (1) a challenging task; (2) focused attention; (3) loss of self-consciousness; (4) perceived control over the stimulus; (5) clear task demands; (6) unambiguous feedback; and (7) intrinsic enjoyment.[14]

ELEMENTS OF FLOW
> A challenging task
> Focused attention
> Loss of self-consciousness
> Perceived control over the stimulus
> Clear task demands
> Unambiguous feedback
> Intrinsic enjoyment

Outcomes of flow include: (1) increased sense of control, (2) prolonged participation, (3) liking for the Web site, (4) a fun experience, and (5) purchase and revisit intentions[15]

To help consumers experience a state of flow, Web sites should offer:

. **A balance between the task challenge and consumer skills**
. **Unambiguous demands on the consumer—a sense of knowing what one is supposed to do. This is also called "inherent transparency" of a site navigation path.**[16]
. **A sense of perceived control—minimal pop up ads, no need to register**

TABLE **17.4**	GOALS & EXPERIENCES OF GOAL-ORIENTED VERSUS EXPERIENTIAL ONLINE SHOPPERS: SELECTED EXCERPTS FROM RESEARCH	
GOAL-ORIENTED SHOPPER		**EXPERIENTIAL SHOPPER**

GOALS AND MINDSET

GOAL-ORIENTED SHOPPER	EXPERIENTIAL SHOPPER
• You know exactly what you want [online], you order it and go away. • Show me what I want fast, and get me on my way. • I don't think any body goes online to have an enjoyable experience.	• Online shopping is a fun way to shop. • I constantly browse [online]. That is what I do in my spare time. • I am a software guy, and its always interesting to see what the latest program will do, so I visit all kinds of software companies [online].

WHAT THEY EXPERIENCE

GOAL-ORIENTED SHOPPER	EXPERIENTIAL SHOPPER
• In a store, a salesperson spends time with me and I feel obligated to buy. No such pressure online*. • You can even shop naked. • The single most satisfying aspect of online shopping is] the freedom to shop when and where I want. So easy and convenient.	• It makes me sound like a cheese ball, but I like the chancy-ness of auctions. • Promos seem to beckon me. • Online has made me into a collector. • I have developed friendships with [fellow eBay users] and they all communicate with me. They are all over the U.S. and it's something, and I feel like a family.

HOW THE WEB STORES OFFER THAT EXPERIENCE

GOAL-ORIENTED SHOPPER	EXPERIENTIAL SHOPPER
• The online is the world's store in your face. • I know that I have the full information at hand online. At a store, I only know what the clerk knows, I don't know the Clerk. • If you have a real person involved, the transaction might go wrong.	• I find wonderful deals. Online coupons have made my Christmas Shopping almost a game. What wonderful deals. • I like reviews at Amazon.com, you read about what people like and dislike, and it is kind of like an online community. • A good site will surprise you with stuff you had no idea existed.

Source: Mary Wolfinbarger and Mary C Gilly, " Shopping online for Freedom, Control, and Fun," California Management Review 2001,vol. 43, no-2, 34-55. Copyright ©2001, by the Regents of the University of California. Reprinted from the California Management Review, By permission of The Regents.

MY CB BOOK

before further browsing, not too many links to click or too many screening questions, etc.

MARKETING IMPLICATIONS

Now that you know why online shoppers shop online, what would you do if you are a Web merchant? Clearly, since you know that three out of four online shoppers are goal-oriented, you need to provide, first and foremost, features that are important to them. So, as an online retailer, you must feature the widest assortment of products possible. If you sell Italian sofas, for example, then carry a virtually unlimited collection of sofas; at the same time, organize your inventory in easy-to-scan categories. Make detailed information available, but organize it under sub-headings that consumers may or may not choose to view. Make possible side-by-side comparisons between two or more alternative brands. Give consumers the option to list products in rank order by price, by make, and by other relevant features. Finally, make your company's Web site remember the history of browsing by visitors who have registered, and you should definitely offer them the option to save their shopping carts.

In addition, to cater to experiential browsers, you need to

OUTCOMES OF FLOW
> **Increased sense of control**
> **Prolonged participation**
> **Liking for the Web site**
> **A fun experience**
> **Purchase and revisit intentions**

MY CB BOOK

TO HELP CONSUMERS EXPERIENCE THE FLOW
> **Match task challenge with consumer skills**
> **Make demands on the consumer that are unambiguous**
> **Make navigational paths transparent**
> **Enable a sense of control**

MY CB BOOK

make your Web sites fun to navigate. Again, if you sell Italian leather sofas, you might feature some interesting facts about leather, and, maybe give a behind-the-scenes look at the making of the sofas. If you sell golf clubs, make the site a golfing information site rather than merely a golf-merchandise selling site; however, you must organize the site such that the goal-oriented shoppers can see the "golf-clubs" (or "products") button clearly on the home page, so they are not hindered by information intended for experiential browsers.

SAVVY MARKETER

To satisfy the "treasure hunt" motive of browsers, feature some rare merchandise, and also feature one or two items at a "terrific bargain." You may also feature one or two items available for auction, or at least feature some product/activity related contests of skill or chance, like the game of rivets at the Levi's Web site. Finally, any animation and sensory features will go a long way in fulfilling the sensation-seeking motive of the browsers. The leather sofa retailer could feature an animation where the consumer is able to change colors on any sofa to see how it will look in that color, place the sofa in various style rooms (e.g., contemporary, classic, etc.), or even show some photos of a person sitting on that sofa. In e-space, the possibilities of building audio-visual sensations around your product are virtually limitless. At the very least, the Web pages must be aesthetically pleasant to look at.

E-SATISFACTION

Satisfaction With Online Sellers

We discussed satisfaction with bricks-and-mortar stores in Chapter 13. The factors that lead to customer satisfaction with bricks-and-mortar stores also apply to online stores, but, in addition, a few new factors become relevant.[17] These factors pertain to pre-purchase and post purchase stages. See Figure 17.2.

PRE-PURCHASE FACTORS

Pre-purchase factors are four:

1. Site navigation Site navigation can be confusing (if buttons are not easy to locate) and tedious (requiring too many mouse clicks), or the Web site can be visually clear, well organized, and a breeze to get through (only a few mouse clicks lead to the desired information). To be satisfied, consumers must find site navigation easy.

2. Quality of product information The Web site should provide quality information. Easy navigation means only that it gets you "there" (i.e., to the correct page) efficiently; but once you get there, what do you find on that page? Is the information comprehensive or sketchy, and is it easy to understand and process? For example, is the information about various models and alternatives described in the same format, and is it possible to sort out various alternatives by price, features, makes, etc.? Also, are product reviews by experts and other users available?

3. Shopping cart and order ease The third factor for satisfaction is the ease of item selection and ordering procedures. For example, to enable multi-session shopping, the Web site should have the feature of saving your shopping cart. Also, shipping and handling costs should be reasonable, clear, and available *before* you place the item in the shopping cart. A notable example of shopping ease is Amazon.com's *one-click purchase* feature.

4. Privacy and trust features Finally, since you are going to be giving your credit card information to the online seller, you would want to know that the site offers secure transactions, and that privacy policies are clearly stated and reassuring.

POST-PURCHASE FACTORS

There are four features of online retailers post-order behavior that can cause your customers satisfaction or dissatisfaction. See Figure 17.2.

Keeping the consumer informed First, after you place the order, you like to be kept informed about the status of the order. Good online retailers such as Amazon.com send you an e-mail soon after you place the online order, confirming the details of your order, and a follow up e-mail when the order is shipped. Moreover, many Web sites enable "order-tracking," so that you can go online and track the progress of your order any time.

Order fulfillment After placing the online order, you hope and expect the merchandise to arrive on time and you expect it to be exactly what you ordered. Receiving a Darth Vader costume in the wrong size or receiving it a day after the Halloween is no fun.

Problem resolution A mistake in order fulfillment is bad enough, but if getting that mistake corrected requires you to jump through hoops, then that is only going to aggravate you even more. The Web site should feature clear instructions on what to do if you have any problem with your order. And you should definitely be able to return the wrong merchandise, with ease and cost-free. In a recent survey of online consumers, as many as 67% of online shoppers desired that a retailer's agent pick up the product returns, and nearly 35% considered this a "must have" feature.[18]

Multi-channel customer support As a consumer, sometimes you just want to speak to a live person to explain your need or problem. Good online retailers offer consumers the option of contacting customer service through multiple channels. On the FTD.com Web site (an online flower retailer), for example, if you click on customer service, it offers you four options: a toll free phone number (1-800-send-FTD), an e-mail option, a postal mail address, and chat with a service representative.

A recent research study, focused on pre-purchase factors, confirms that Convenience (i.e., Ease of navigation) is the Number 1 determinant of consumer satisfaction with their online experience; Site design (e.g., uncluttered screen) and Financial security (i.e., privacy and trust features) were close second.[19] See Exhibit 17.3.

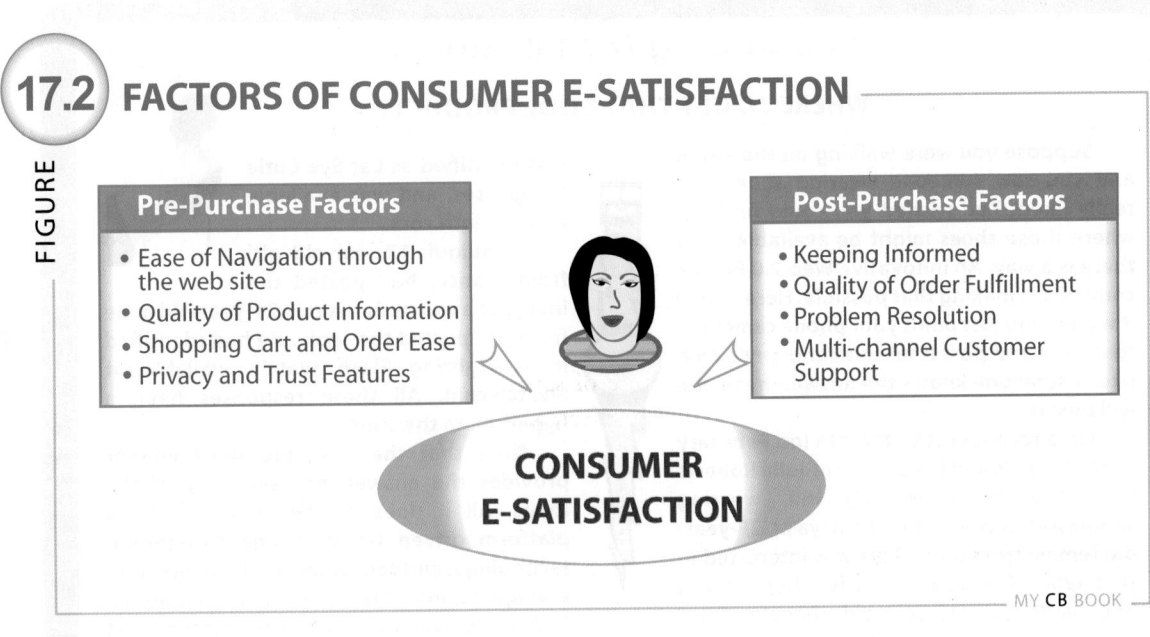

FIGURE 17.2 FACTORS OF CONSUMER E-SATISFACTION

EXHIBIT **17.3**

SATISFYING ONLINE SHOPPERS

What Consumer Research Reveals...

In a recent survey of Internet shoppers, members of an NFO panel were surveyed by sending them an online survey via email. A total of 2108 panel members (prescreened to ensure that they had shopped online) were mailed the survey; 1007 members returned the survey.

The results showed that convenience was the most important driver of satisfaction; closely following it were site design and financial security. Product information (its quality and adequacy) also played some role. However, the product offerings (the variety and number of product offerings) played a less significant role in consumer satisfaction

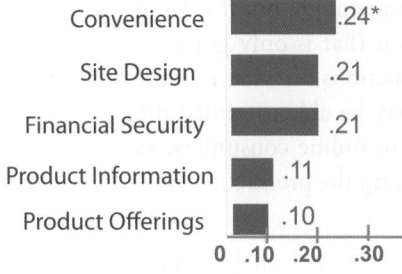

Convenience .24*
Site Design .21
Financial Security .21
Product Information .11
Product Offerings .10

0 .10 .20 .30

*Represents regression coefficients. A higher value implies greater importance of the factor. Thus, convenience, site design, and finacial security are twice as important as product information and product offerings.

Measuring Components of e-Retail Experience

Q1. Compared to bricks & mortar retail stores, how would you rate Internet storefront on the following aspects:
(Much worse than 1 2 3 4 5 6 7 Much better than)

A. Convenience
- Ease of browsing 1 2 3 4 5 6 7
- Total shopping time 1 2 3 4 5 6 7
- Convenience 1 2 3 4 5 6 7

B. Merchandise--Product offerings
- Number of product offerings 1 2 3 4 5 6 7
- Variety of product offerings 1 2 3 4 5 6 7

C. Product Information
- Quality of information 1 2 3 4 5 6 7
- Adequacy of information 1 2 3 4 5 6 7

D. Financial Security
- Financial security of the transaction 1 2 3 4 5 6 7

Q2. Rate the site design for Internet storefronts
(Scale: 1 Poor – 5 Excellent)
Presenting uncluttered screen 1 2 3 4 5
Providing easy to follow search paths 1 2 3 4 5
Presenting information fast 1 2 3 4 5

Q3. Overall, how do you feel about your Internet shopping experience
Very displeased 1 2 3 4 5 6 7 Very pleased
Very dissatisfied 1 2 3 4 5 6 7 Very satisfied

MY CB BOOK

Source: Excerpted from David M. Szymanski and Richard T. Hise, "e-Satisfaction: An Initial Validation," *Journal of Retailing*, Vol. 76(3) 2000, 309-322. © The New York University. Used with permission.

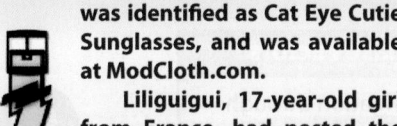

Romancing the Consumer

WHERE TO GET THAT COOL PRODUCT?

Suppose you were walking on the street and you saw someone wearing shoes you really liked. You wished you could find out where those shoes might be available. Now there is a way. An innovative Web 2.0 French company is making that possible. Here is how it works: you just point your phone camera at that shoe and post it on this company's Web site. If someone knows the answer, he or she will post it.

On a recent visit to the site (on February 5, 2012), we found the picture of Julia Roberts from the movie Notting Hill, wearing sunglasses. It was posted by Asya M, 28-year-old female from USA. Asya was interested in that type of sunglasses. A few hours later, Shokoladnaya (18-year-old female from Russian Federation) had posted the answer: It

was identified as Cat Eye Cutie Sunglasses, and was available at ModCloth.com.

Liliguigui, 17-year-old girl from France, had posted the image of a watch. Sanjeet K, 21-year-old male from UK, posted the reply. He had identified it as Lighting Flash Watch available at Swatch.com. All these responses have a hyperlink to the store.

Note that the company itself neither provides the answer, nor sells any of the items. All it does is offer a social media platform driven by an image recognition technology, and consumers find it interesting enough to join what it calls its *mutual aid fashion community*. Find this company at *wheretoget.it*!

MY **CB** BOOK

Powered O by

STICKINESS: CONSUMER LIKING FOR WEB SITES

The foregoing list of factors produces satisfaction among goal-oriented online shoppers. But liking for the Web site requires more. The ability of a Web site to attract and keep visitors returning is referred to as the **stickiness** of the Web site. What factors drive stickiness?

The information content continues to be an important factor, of course, but a few other features become influential. These are: graphics style and multimedia sensory experience, personalization, and communities.

Graphics and multi-sensory features The first factor luring consumers is the graphics and multi-sensory features of a Web site. For many users, well-designed graphics and multi-sensory (i.e., audio visual) features can enhance the experience, particularly for the fun-seeking surfers.

Personalization Personalization on online sites means giving users the information they seek without their asking for it. Web sites track consumers' online click-stream and analyze these data to identify consumer tastes and preferences—what kind of things the consumer searches for. Then the next time you visit that web site, it automatically presents information relevant to your interests. A prime example is Amazon.com's personalization: When you visit that site from your computer, it automatically flags books and titles likely to be of interest to you.

Communities Finally, many consumers like a Web site based on communities it features. Microsoft, for example, has a community site for users to chat. Users post their questions and comments; another consumer answers their question. Many users like to answer other users' questions and they like to read comments others have posted. For a prime non-commerce example that charms as well as glues its visitors to the Web site, visit and "get stuck" to 1000awesomethings.com.

STICKINESS
Multi-sensory experiences
Personalizaton
Communities

How Consumers Perceive Online Shopping

Consumers know that every purchase they make entails some risk. Many consumers perceive these risks to be greater in the online channel. A recent study examined four types of risks consumers perceived in online shopping: financial risk (defined in the study as the risk of credit card information being misused), performance risk (defined as the difficulty of judging quality), psychological risk (defined as one's personal information not being kept private), and time/inconvenience risk (online purchase might turn out to be more time taking or more hasslesome). The study's findings are shown in Figure 17.3.[20]

Consumers' risk perceptions are attenuated by two factors: prior experience and risk-averse personality trait. Consumers who have shopped online before are the ones most likely to shop again. This is because their prior experience turned out to be positive and risk-free. And consumers who are risk-averse perceive greater risk in online shopping.

Of course, this risk is mitigated, even for expensive items, by two factors. First, longevity of online channel for that product category. And second, the reputation of the online retailer. In one study, if the online store was that of an established retailer, consumers expressed greater likelihood of buying a product even if the brand name itself was new.[21]

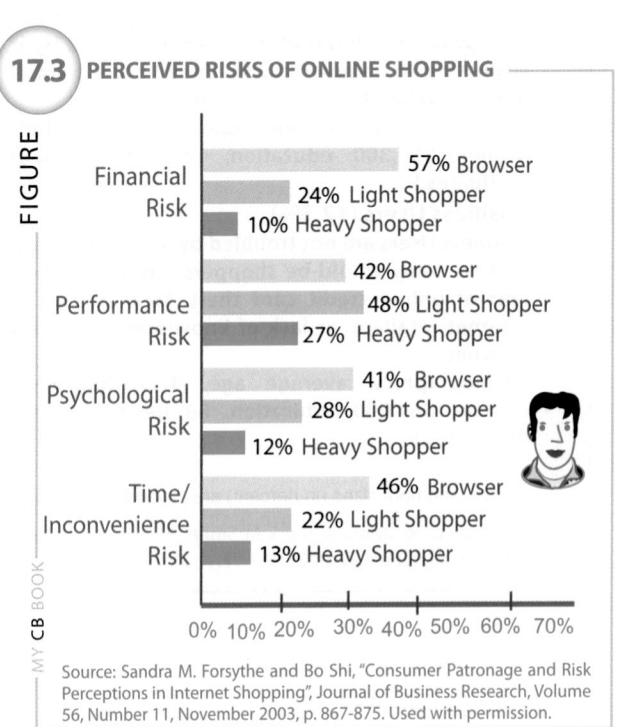

17.3 PERCEIVED RISKS OF ONLINE SHOPPING

Source: Sandra M. Forsythe and Bo Shi, "Consumer Patronage and Risk Perceptions in Internet Shopping", Journal of Business Research, Volume 56, Number 11, November 2003, p. 867-875. Used with permission.

SEGMENTS AMONG ONLINE SHOPPERS

Not all consumers shop online for the same reason. Some prefer to shop online because of convenience. Others go online because they believe they get a better assortment. Those who are price-sensitive and do comparison-shopping even in the bricks-and-mortar stores probably go online in search of better prices. A recent research study identified four segments among online shoppers, and likewise four segments among non-shoppers. Their profiles are presented in Exhibit 17.4.

EXHIBIT 17.4

SEGMENTS AMONG ONLINE SHOPPERS AND NON-SHOPPERS

A. SEGMENTS AMONG ONLINE SHOPPERS

Shopping Lovers (11.1%)
As its name implies, this segment loves to shop online and accounts for the highest level of purchases among online consumers. They find Internet shopping fun and hassle free.
(Demographics: average age, 44; household income, $60,200; education, 36 percent college graduates.)

Adventuresome Explorers (8.9%)
Versatile and prolific in their online use; higher than other segments in the use of their computer for information exploration on diverse topics ranging from news, financial stocks, job opportunities to hobbies, photographs, and online news groups and chats). Online shopping is fun for these people; it is just one more adventure for them to explore.
(Demographics: average age, 45.8; household income, $61,500; education, 35 percent college graduates.)

Suspicious Learners (9.7%)
Their computer literacy is low. They are just learning how to use the Internet. They are frustrated by it, struggling to complete tasks. They find it "hard to judge merchandise quality on Internet."
(Demographics: average age, 49.6; household income, $59,300; education, 42 percent college graduates.)

Business Users (12.5%)
Business Users are not troubled by any of the issues that so many would-be shoppers struggle with- fear of online credit card theft, lack of trust of Internet retailers, or lack of knowledge about the Internet.
(Demographics: average age, 47.5; household income, $64,000; education, 88 percent college graduates.)

B. SEGMENTS AMONG ONLINE NON-SHOPPERS

Fearful Browsers (10.6%)
Even though they do not purchase online, they do like to visit online vendor sites. However, they are onlook- ers, not buyers. Along with other non-shopper segmetns, this segment is fearful of several online risks (e.g., unseen product, shipping charges, credit card information security).
(Demographics: average age, 44; household income, $63,700; education, 43 percent college graduates.)

Shopping Avoiders (15.6%)
People in this segment like to use the Internet to look at financial information (stocks, trends); check or send e-mail messages; read on-line news or magazines; play games; and to conduct business-related work. But they abhor shopping online, holding values which are inconsistent with Internet shopping (e.g.,   to see products in person, hassle-free return, and credit card security).
(Demographics: average age, 56; household income, $61,700; education, 70 percent college graduates.)

Technology Muddlers (19.5%)
People in this segment use the computer the least of any segment, and are the least computer-literate. Just like the preceding segment, they also have strong hesitation to give their credit card number to a Web site, and want to see merchandise in person.
(Demographics: average age, 49.3; household income, $54,400; education, 62 percent college graduates.)

Fun Seekers (12%)
Among the eight segments, this is the highest in computer use. Using the web for entertainment (e.g., games; online chats, hobby topics, et.c). But they do not like using it for shopping, fearing privacy concern and feeling a need to see products in person.
(Demographics: average age, 49.3; household income, $48,100; education, 25 percent college graduates.)

Note: Segment sizes (in percent) are proportion of all online consumers. Of these, online *shoppers* made up 42.2%.

Source: W. R. Swinyard and S. M. Smith, "Why People Shop Online: A Lifestyle Study of the Internet Consumer," *Psychology & Marketing*, June/July 2003, 567-97. © 2003 Wiley Periodicals, Inc. (Used with permission of John Wiley & Sons, Inc.)

MY CB BOOK

INTERNET BEYOND SHOPPING

Welcome to Web 2.0

Web 2.0 refers to the new capabilities of the Web, realized in recent years. Some authors use the term to refer to the comeback of e-retail business after the 1999 dot-com crash. However, the term is best reserved to refer to an expansion of the Web's capabilities that enable consumers a more creative role. This differs from the Web 1.0 era, when consumers could merely access the content placed on it by merchants and organizations who hosted Web portals. But in the Web 2.0 era, consumers are able to create their own content on the Web and post it for all to see. Wikipedia is an early example, but today, it takes the form of online posting by consumers of comments, reviews, photos, video, etc., on such Web sites as YouTube and Flickr. The Web 2.0 has created a new generation of authors, penning their life stories, trivial and grave alike, and posting blogs on everything from local Wal-Mart store to Presidential elections. These are also called Consumer Generated Media (CMG), and businesses are increasingly utilizing them both to reach these Web 2.0 savvy consumers (for example via advertising on these sites) and to listen in to the consumer pulse.

Consumers on Social Networking Web sites

Social Networking sites are a category of consumer generated media (CMG). **Social networking sites** (let us call them *SoNets*) are Web portals that enable consumers to have their own Web pages, invite others to join their personal online group of friends, and share content and messages with one or many among them. Consumers post a profile of themselves, post other contents (text, music, photos, and video), and invite friends to view, tag, and comment. Users can post new entries on a "wall"—a text box that automatically gets tagged with date and time of posting, visible to friends and guests. Users can also post entries on their friends' individual walls, and, of course, they can use e-mail and instant messaging to communicate via these sites.

There are, literally, hundreds of SoNets: MySpace, Facebook, Sodahead, Twitter, etc. Facebook, Twitter, and LinkedIn are the most popular in North America and also widely in use around the world. But each country or region has its own favorite: Nexopia is popular in Canada, Bebo in the U.K., Xing in Germany, Hi5 in parts of Europe, Orkut in Brazil,

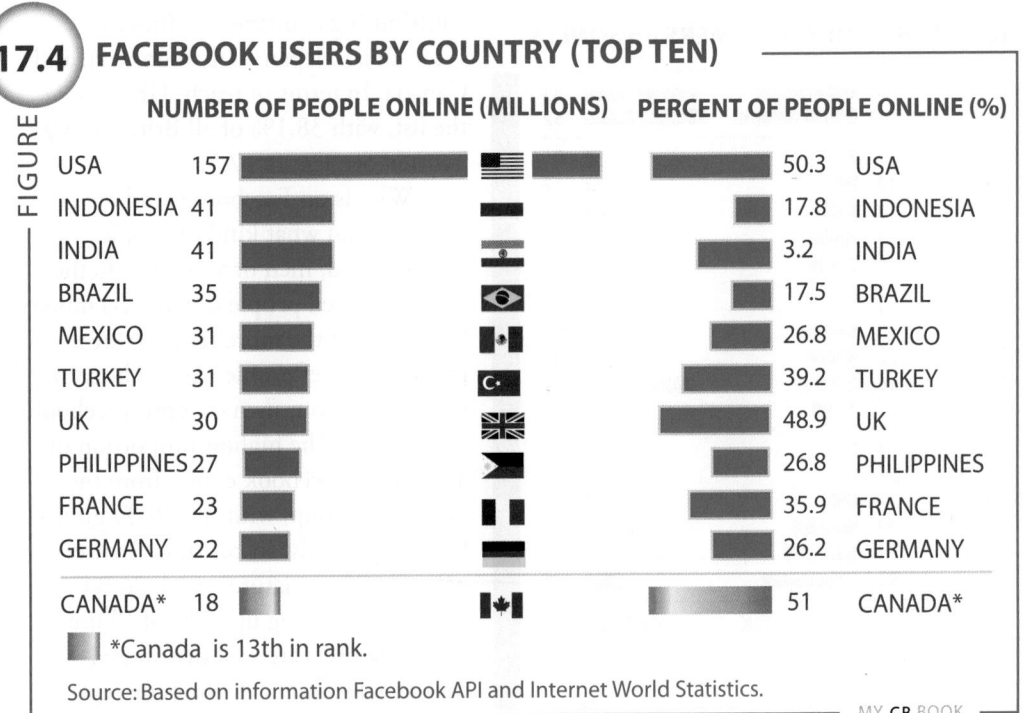

FIGURE 17.4 FACEBOOK USERS BY COUNTRY (TOP TEN)

	NUMBER OF PEOPLE ONLINE (MILLIONS)		PERCENT OF PEOPLE ONLINE (%)	
USA	157		50.3	USA
INDONESIA	41		17.8	INDONESIA
INDIA	41		3.2	INDIA
BRAZIL	35		17.5	BRAZIL
MEXICO	31		26.8	MEXICO
TURKEY	31		39.2	TURKEY
UK	30		48.9	UK
PHILIPPINES	27		26.8	PHILIPPINES
FRANCE	23		35.9	FRANCE
GERMANY	22		26.2	GERMANY
CANADA*	18		51	CANADA*

*Canada is 13th in rank.

Source: Based on information Facebook API and Internet World Statistics.

17.5 TWITTER USERS BY COUNTRY (TOP SIX)

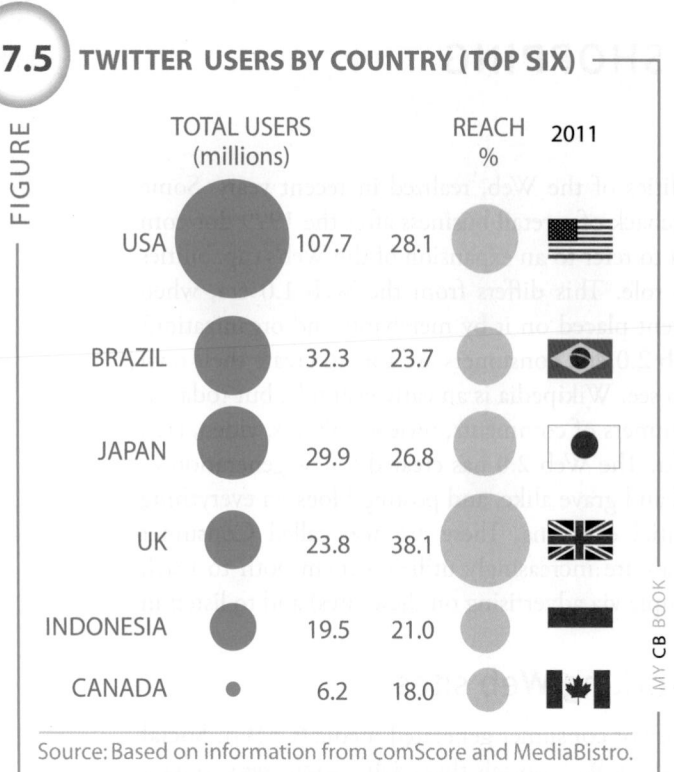

	TOTAL USERS (millions)	REACH %	2011
USA	107.7	28.1	
BRAZIL	32.3	23.7	
JAPAN	29.9	26.8	
UK	23.8	38.1	
INDONESIA	19.5	21.0	
CANADA	6.2	18.0	

Source: Based on information from comScore and MediaBistro.

Orkut and Hi5 in South America and Central America, and Friendster, Orkut, Xiaonei, Cyworld in Asia (Cyworld especially in South Korea) and the Pacific Islands, Renren in China, and ibibo—stands for *I build, I bond*—in India, Tuenti in Spain, and Sonico in Latin America.

The granddaddy of all these is, of course, Facebook. Launched in February 2004, As of December 2011, it reported 845 million average monthly users. Entirely free to consumers, its business potential is evident from its filing of an IPO (Initial Public Offering) application on February 2, 2012—it expected to raise $5billion in market capitalization value. By some estimates, it is expected to reach 1 billion users sometime by August 2012![22]

Twitter is the second most popular SoNet, launched in 2006 and by February 2012 boasting 300 million users worldwide, and growing. Twitter is in a class by itself. It is a microblogging site that allows users to post a short message limited to 140 characters as an answer to the question: What are you doing right now? Called *Tweets*, and *Retweets* when you forward someone else's Tweet, these posts have mushroomed—110 million Tweets are posted everyday!

Given their massive reach, and corresponding gigantic influence on consumers, we profile their reach and audience briefly. For Facebook, USA provides the largest number of users (157 million). However in terms of reach—percentage of population—three countries lead the pack: Canada (51% of the population is on Facebook), USA (50.3%), and UK (48.9%). See the Top Ten list in Figure 17.4.

17.6 DEMOGRAPHICS OF CONSUMERS on *SONETS*

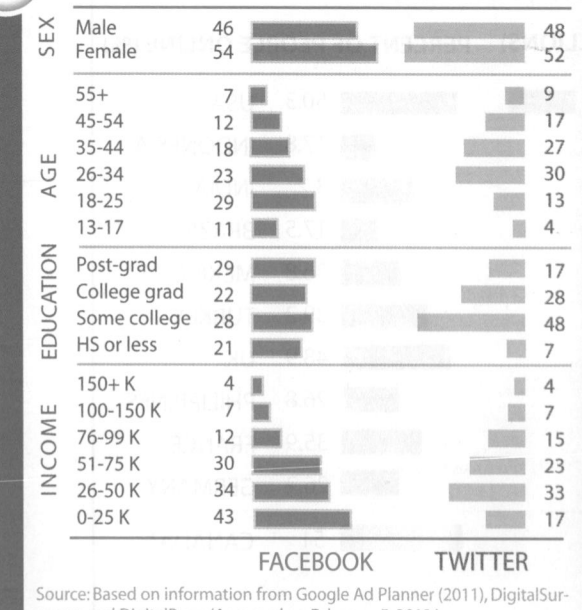

		FACEBOOK	TWITTER
SEX	Male	46	48
	Female	54	52
AGE	55+	7	9
	45-54	12	17
	35-44	18	27
	26-34	23	30
	18-25	29	13
	13-17	11	4
EDUCATION	Post-grad	29	17
	College grad	22	28
	Some college	28	48
	HS or less	21	7
INCOME	150+ K	4	4
	100-150 K	7	7
	76-99 K	12	15
	51-75 K	30	23
	26-50 K	34	33
	0-25 K	43	17

Source: Based on information from Google Ad Planner (2011), DigitalSurgeons, and DigitalBuzz. (Accessed on February 5, 2012.)

For Twitter, the top six contributing countries are (in order) USA, Brazil, Japan, UK, Indonesia, and Canada. In terms of reach, UK tops the list, with 38.1% of all British using Twitter! See Figure 17.5.

Who is on Facebook? And on Twitter? And what kind of people? Young or old; men or women? Do the more educated people use SoNets more? Or less? And the more rich? Figure 17.6 provides a brief profile. As can be seen, women edge out men on both Facebook and Twitter. The highest proportion of all users of Facebook comes from the 18-25 age group, with the 26-34 group following closely; in contrast, Twitter's users are more mature—with 26-34 and 35-44 making up 57% of all users. Facebook users are well distributed over all education categories (except

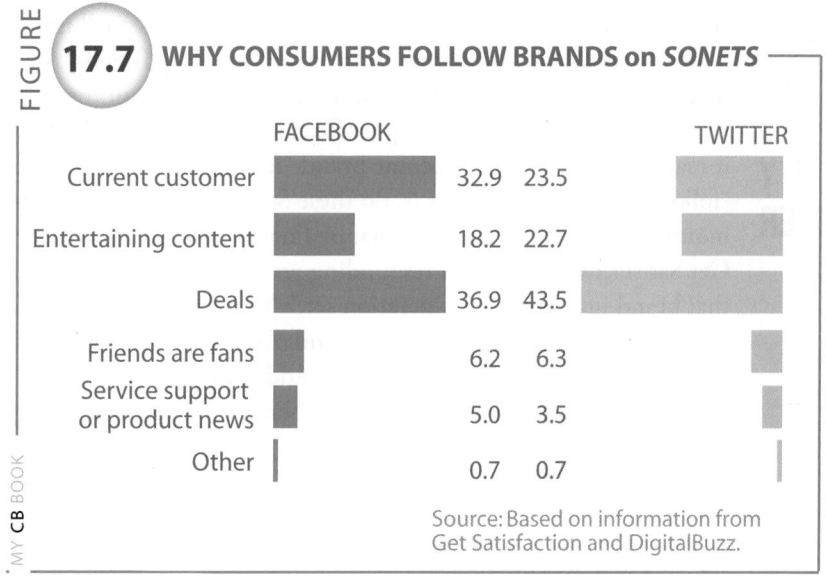

FIGURE **17.7** WHY CONSUMERS FOLLOW BRANDS on *SONETS*

	FACEBOOK		TWITTER
Current customer	32.9	23.5	
Entertaining content	18.2	22.7	
Deals	36.9	43.5	
Friends are fans	6.2	6.3	
Service support or product news	5.0	3.5	
Other	0.7	0.7	

Source: Based on information from Get Satisfaction and DigitalBuzz.

post graduate) including a large proportion (41%) with high school or less education; in contrast, Twitter users are concentrated in some college, college, and even post-graduate degree holders. In income, Facebook and Twitter both have a well distributed profile, with 77 and 73% of users coming from <$75,000 income groups. See Figure 17.6.

BRAND ACTIVITY ON SOCIAL MEDIA

Marketers go, as they should, where the consumers are. So it is natural that marketers too came to inhabit the SoNet world. Some 4 million brands are on Facebook![23] And about 150 of them have over one million fans![24] Facebook member consumers join the brand communities by a simple tool Facebook features: *Like*. If you want to "follow" a brand, simply click on the icon *Like*, and , in an instant, you are connected. By 2011, the three top brands with the largest number of Facebook-based brand "fans" were Coco Cola (with 26.4 million fans), Disney (with 23 million fans) and Starbucks (with 22 million fans).[25]

Why do SoNet members become "fans" of the brands on SoNets? According to a study by a company called Get Satisfaction, a significant number of them do so because they are already the users of the brand; the most cited reason is, however, the deals they get on these sites (36.9% for Facebook and 43.5% for Twitter). See Figure 17.7. A small proportion (about 6%) join a brand's fan community because their friends

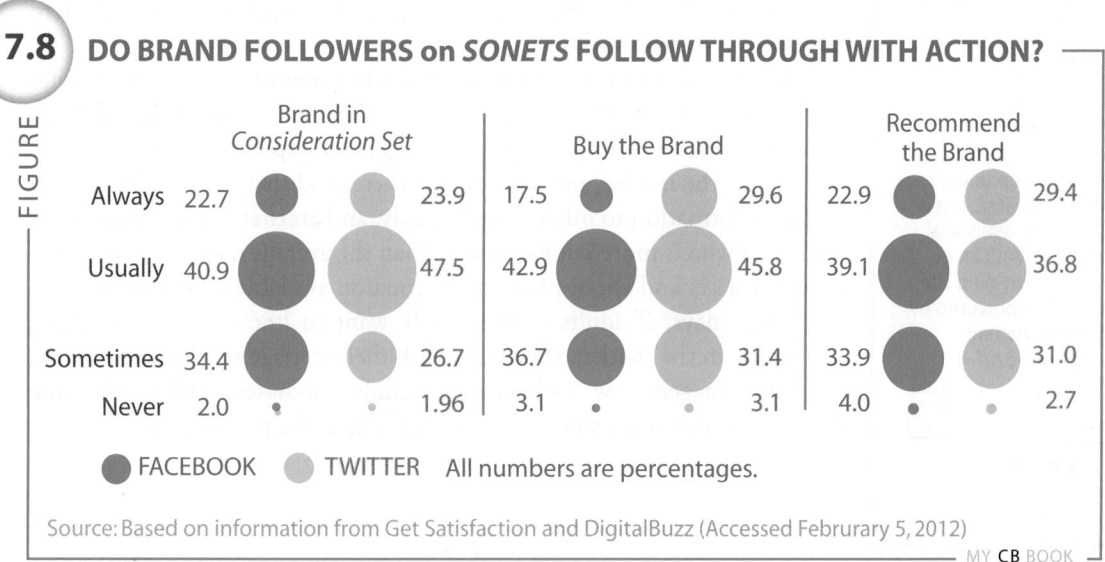

FIGURE **17.8** DO BRAND FOLLOWERS on *SONETS* FOLLOW THROUGH WITH ACTION?

	Brand in *Consideration Set*		Buy the Brand		Recommend the Brand	
Always	22.7	23.9	17.5	29.6	22.9	29.4
Usually	40.9	47.5	42.9	45.8	39.1	36.8
Sometimes	34.4	26.7	36.7	31.4	33.9	31.0
Never	2.0	1.96	3.1	3.1	4.0	2.7

● FACEBOOK   ○ TWITTER   All numbers are percentages.

Source: Based on information from Get Satisfaction and DigitalBuzz (Accessed Februrary 5, 2012)

are on it. Although this number is small, the power of small numbers should not be underestimated when it comes to friends influencing friends. After all, it is this "sharing" that forms the core raison d'être of online brand communities.

SAVVY MARKETER

One other question of import for marketers who inhabit the SoNets is this: Does it matter that consumers become brand "friends" on Facebook, and likewise brand "followers" on Twitter? That is, do these SoNet members put their money where their mouth is—or where their click-happy fingers are. The answer, according to the same Get Satisfaction survey is a resounding *yes*. As many as 70% of brand "fans" always put that brand into their "consideration set," "usually" or "always." See Figure 17.8. A similar proportion actually does buy that brand. And 2 out of 3 "fans" will recommend the brand to others, "usually" or "always." Add "sometimes," and you get almost all of them (96 to 98%) happy to recommend the brand to others! See Figure 17.8.

INTERNET IN THE LIFE OF TEENS
And, Now, of College Students

> I multi-task every single second I am online. At this very moment, I am watching TV, checking my email every two minutes, reading a newsgroup about who shot JFK, burning some music to a CD and writing this message.
>
> — A 17-year-old boy[26]

The Internet is the telephone, television, game console, and radio wrapped up in one for most teenagers. Teens go online to chat with their friends, kill boredom, see the wider world, and follow the latest trends—**sometimes all at once**. Multitasking is their way of life. And the emotional hallmark of that life is enthusiasm for the new ways the Internet lets them connect with friends, expand their social networks, explore their identities, and learn new things.[27]

To enable their instant messaging (IM) to convey emotions, teens have invented a new hieroglyphics of *emoticons* [text-based sequence of characters that depict human emotions, such as a tearful eye] and a growing list of abbreviations to help them speed their way through multiple, simultaneous online conversations."[28]

While social communications (e-mails and IM) and recreational activities (playing online games, downloading music, listening to music online, etc.,) dominate their use of the Internet, teenagers also use it considerably to find out what is "cool" in fashion and music (more than half of them) and to do online product research (65% of them), and actual purchasing (more than 30%).

Internet Mavens

This has brought about a major change in teens: it has turned them into *Internet market mavens*.

In an earlier chapter, we defined **market mavens** as consumers who possess market information about a cross-section of products and are generally more knowledgeable (than the general population) about what is available in the market and what is new there; and they serve as a source of market information to others. Analogously, an **Internet market maven** is a consumer who is more knowledgeable than the average consumer about the e-marketplace, and about product information available on the Internet.

These days, if adults in the family want to know about something happening in the market, they would ask their teenage son or daughter! As a result, teenagers now influence the family purchases significantly more than even much older sons and daughters did in the pre-Web era.

CB FYI

The Pope Embraces *YouTube*

January 23, 2009 was a, well, *holy* day in the life of *YouTube*. The Vatican got its own YouTube channel and started broadcasting news clips of its activities and Pope Benedict's messages. Embracing this latest communication tool of the cyber age, the 81-year old Pope welcomed it as a gift, commenting that such new technologies respond to the "fundamental desire" of people to communicate. But he also cautioned against excessive immersion in online social networking sites, lest it isolate users from real social interactions. The Vatican of course, has, its own Web site, launched in 1995, powered by three computers named *Michael, Gabriel, and Raphael*!

Source: www.vatican.va

Powered by oᴹ   MY CB BOOK

And College Students Are Internet Market Mavens

This trend among teens started some 10 years ago. Those teens are today 20-30 years old; they are in colleges and in their post-college early careers. And with ten+ years of experience under their click-happy fingers (!), they are Internet market mavens par excellence. Thus, just like their teen siblings, or even more so, not only do they search and shop online rather fearlessly, they inform and influence, as well, the purchase decisions of older generations (parents, grandparents, supervisors, and mentors). Now, as a marketer, you know why it pays to have teens and adolescents (20-30 year olds) become the fans of your brands on SoNets!

CYBERSPACE AND THE PURSUIT OF FAITH FINDING RELIGION ONLINE

Beyond commerce, beyond social connections, the Internet has also become a way for many consumers to seek spiritual happiness. According to a recent study (by Pew Internet & American Life Project), about 28 million Americans have surfed a religious Web site. This is more than the number of U.S. consumers who have gambled online, done online banking, traded stocks online, or used online dating services.[29]

A little more than one in three of them have downloaded religious music, e-mailed a request for a prayer, given spiritual guidance to someone, and/or bought a religious item online. About one in ten have participated in religious chat rooms. About 4% have participated in online worship, 3% have taken an online religion course, and 3% have used a faith-oriented match-making service. Perhaps the most noteworthy fact about online religious surfers is that they are very open-minded about other religions, eager to learn about them: 50% of them went online to look for information about another faith. See Table 17.5.

Internet Religion Does Not Make Churches Irrelevant

The Internet brings religion closer to members of congregations as well as non-members. For non-members, the Internet serves as a more convenient and psychologically comforting avenue. Not connected to or socialized into any offline congregation, they find it easier to relate to other "virtual" worshippers. The Pew Internet report summarizes it thus:

TABLE 17.5 WHAT DO ONLINE RELIGION SURFERS DO ONLINE?	%
Looked for information about their faith	67
Looked for information about another faith	50
Downloaded religious music	38
e-mailed a prayer request	38
Given spiritual guidance via e-mail	37
Bought religious items online	34
Downloaded sermons	25
Sought spiritual guidance via e-mail	21
Participated in religious chat rooms	10
Participated in online worship	4
Taken an online religious course	3
Used a faith-oriented matchmaking service	3

Source: Excerpted from Pew Internet & American Life Project Religion Surfer Survey, shown in "Cyber Faith: How American Pursue Religion Online," at www. PewInternet.org

MY CB BOOK

> **By creating better ties within a pre-existing community, by creating a Web presence, and by facilitating discussions that can be difficult to hold in other settings, congregations tightened bonds within their groups, re-established connection with former members, and in some cases, expanded mission on a global scale.[30]**

SUMMARY

We began this chapter by describing the Internet consumer universe—the number of people using the Internet worldwide and in major countries. Worldwide, 2.1 billion (30.2%) consumers were online in 2011. Norway tops the list (91%) and (counting only the countries with population of more than 1 million) Bangladesh bottoms it (0.3%).

The most common use of the Internet is for e-mail. A majority of consumers consider the Internet as a legitimate and expected source of information both for commercial and noncommercial information, and indeed, they find that their expectations are well met.

Next, we discussed the two broad groups of consumers who go online: goal-oriented shoppers and experiential Internet surfers. The goals and motives of each group are different. Goal-oriented shoppers seek efficiency in purchasing and a sense of freedom and control. Certain features of the Web in general, and individual Web sites, in particular, satisfy these goals. On the other hand, experiential browsers go online seeking enjoyment, and here, too, certain other features of the Web become relevant. These features

were discussed. We also discussed a research-based segmentation scheme with four segments each among e-shoppers and e-non-shoppers.

We next discussed consumer life on Social Networking Sites (SoNets). Among more than 300 SoNets in existence, Facebook and Twitter top the list (with more than 850 and 300 million users, respectively). We examined the demographic profile of these users. And we discussed the benefit to marketers who inhabit these SoNets, noting that consumers who become fans of a brand on Facebook take positive action as well, buying and recommending that brand.

Next, we examined the role the Internet plays in the lives of youth (teens and college students). The Internet has transformed them into market mavens, a phenomenon of note for marketers. We concluded the chapter with a brief look at how the Internet also serves consumers to enhance their religious experience. Our coverage serves as illustration of how marketers—of commercial and non-commercial enterprises alike—can harness the Internet to bring more value to consumers.

KEY TERMS

Bookmark
Digital products
Emoticons
Experiential products
Experiential browsers

Flow
Goal-oriented online shoppers
High touch products
Internet maven
Low-context information

Social networking sites
Treasure hunt
Web site stickiness
Web surfers

YOUR TURN

REVIEW+Rewind

1. Which type of products are most and least appropriate for buying online? Why?
2. Describe the major differences between the goals, motivations, and experiences of goal-oriented shoppers versus experiential browsers.
3. Describe factors that determine whether or not an online shopper will be satisfied with the online shopping experience.
4. Name major segments of Internet consumers and briefly describe their Internet surfing behavior.
5. Describe the demographic profile of users of Social Networking Sites (SoNets).

THINK+Apply

1. Reflecting on your own recent online shopping experience, assess the extent to which each of the goals of goal-oriented shoppers described in the chapter were true for you.
2. If you wanted to target each of the four segments described in the chapter for (a) clothing and (b) electronic appliances, discuss for each product line how your Web design and online marketing would be different for each segment.
3. As a marketer of the following products, which SoNet (Facebook or Twitter) will you spend money on (explain why): (a) Men's Warehouse for men's suits; (b) Gap clothing; (c) Kenneth Cole clothing; (c) and travel packages.

PRACTICE+Experience

1. Visit the Web sites of two vendors of the same product and rate each on the attributes that online goal-oriented shoppers seek. Now, repeat this exercise from the perspective of experiential browsers.

2. Interview three consumers about their most recent online shopping experiences. Ask them to describe one instance where they were satisfied, and one instance where they were not. Then ask for reasons for their satisfaction or dissatisfaction. Summarize your findings and comment on the extent to which the reasons discussed in the chapter were or were not verified in these consumer experiences.

3. Interview five consumers to assess their online shopping behavior pattern. Then determine which of the segments described in the chapter best fits them. Then, think about what you would do differently (in respect to Web design and other marketing efforts) to reach and appeal to each type of these consumers.

In the Marketing Manager's Shoes

Put yourself in a marketing manager's shoes. Most concepts in the chapter have some lessons for the marketing manager, i.e., they suggest what to do differently in practice; indeed, often these applications are implicit in our explanations of the concepts and models in the chapter. Identify at least five specific applications of the chapter's concepts, all of which should be entirely new, different from the examples cited here.

CB Blog

17

e-CONSUMPTION: GOOGLE, DEAR READER, GOOGLE!

The Internet. What will life be without it? Its use is growing everyday, both in population penetration and range of online activity.

Since you are reading this book, you are the kind who depends on the Internet for information. For your class projects; or for your work projects. And, of course, you surf the net for entertainment and for product information. You already buy at least a few products on the net. The Internet is transforming the way consumers shop. It has empowered consumers vis-a-vis marketers. And savvy marketers are removing the few barriers that consumers have historically experienced. Such as the difficulty of returning the merchandise—by integrating online and physical stores—thus, you can buy online and return the merchandise in the neighborhood physical store. And new tools to visualize the merchandise, and sometimes, customize it.

Beyond commerce, the more fascinating uses of the net are in our social lives. Using new tools on social networking sites (SoNets), we can find new friends and stay connected with our fans, 24-7. Twitter has uncovered a latent demand of our psyche: To gather "followers" and to "tweet" them with the minutiae of everyday life. As a recent Time magazine (Time, June 05, 2009) article so insightfully observed, getting a glimpse, on a dynamic basis, of the daily routines of our friends and peers is strangely satisfying and brings us "social warmth" we never knew.

Want to experience a state of flow? Transport yourself to the Web site www.flickr.com. You can have hours of entertaining photo journey. And then jump over to pinterest.com, where consumers have posted photos of everyday goods, to spotlight their eye-candy-ish charm. There, in the Facebook manner, you can register your "like," and "request an invite" so that you may then post the photos of your own favorite things, for other "community members" to "like" and savor.

If your goal is more task-oriented information search, then Google or Yahoo or MSN, Bing or Search Me, or any number of other search portals will serve you well. This book has depended a lot on these search engines. For the information we printed; and also for the information we did not—you see, knowing that you could always search the Web for anything, we felt less the need to answer every potential "What is that" question.

Hint, hint: Google (or Bing), dear reader, google (or bing)!

CONSUMER BEHAVIOR

Marketers, Public Policy, and the Slightly Unethical Consumer

Deceived, Intoxicated, and, Finally, Enlightened

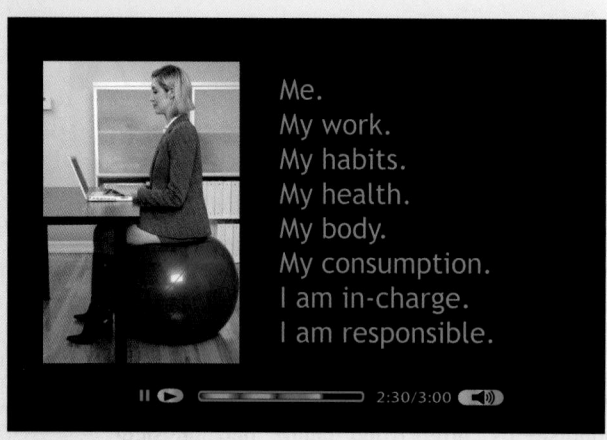

Me.
My work.
My habits.
My health.
My body.
My consumption.
I am in-charge.
I am responsible.

2:30/3:00

LEARN . APPLY . EXPERIENCE

Supersized Fast-Food: I Loved It But Nobody Told Me It Will Supersize Me!

On July 24, 2002, the Supreme Court of the State of New York registered a complaint against the four biggest U.S. based fast-food chains: McDonald's, Burger King, Wendy's, and KFC Corporation. The plaintiff was Caesar Barber, a 57-year-old resident of the Bronx County (New York). At 5'2" height, he weighed 275 lbs. He suffered from diabetes and has had two heart attacks. His complaint: The fast-food chains were responsible for his health condition. How? For fifty years, he had eaten fast food four to five times a week.[a]

On February 17, 2003, Judge Robert Sweet of the State Supreme Court threw out the case. His ruling: The complaint fails to allege that the defendants' products were dangerous in any way other than that which was open and obvious to a reasonable consumer.[b]

On October 29, 2009, a class action suit was filed against big banks, in the district court of Miami, Florida. The suit alleged that the banks charged overdraft fees without notifying the customers that they were protected for overdrafts. When customers signed for checking or debit account with their banks, they were automatically enrolled in overdraft protection. In 2008, consumers spent nearly $24 billion in overdraft fees (Center for Responsible Lending).

I like what marketers offer but I have to be vigilant.

Banks maintain that the overdraft is in consumers' interest as a preferable outcome (versus their payment to merchants being declined). Yes, that is legal, of course. But if banks cared for consumers' interests, they will not also resort to sophisticated accounting techniques: Banks entered the orders not in the order in which they occurred, but, instead, they entered them at the end of the day in the order of their amounts. On a particular day, suppose you had a credit balance of $10; and suppose that at 3 p.m. that day you bought coffee for $4.0, and then at 5 p.m. gas for $20. You should have to pay overdraft fee only once, not twice. But the banks would deduct the larger transaction first ($20 for gas), thus earning themselves two overdraft transactions and a fee of $70.0. What if you deposited $40.0 at 10 am that day? Sorry, that won't help. The banks enter all purchases/withdrawals first and all deposits last!!

On May 24, 2011, Bank of America settled the suit for $410M. Other banks named in the suit were J.P. Morgan Chase, CitiGroup, Wells Fargo, Fifth-Third, and Nations Bank. These banks separately settled the suit with amounts ranging from 9.5 million (Fifth Third Bank) to $203m (Wells Fargo).[c]

---

a. Various sources: Fox News, "Ailing Man Sues Fast-Food Firms," July 24, 2002; Pacific Research Institute, Capital Ideas, Vol. 7, No. 31, Aug 8, 2002; Fat Chance: Caesar Barber Sues Fast Food Restaurants Over His Poor Health (Editorial), Bookrags, Aug 15th, 2002. b. Jonathan Wald. CNN Money, February 17, 2003. c. Daily Finance, Catherine New, 11/08/2011.

INTRODUCTION

In the lawsuits you just read about, who was right?

At the core of the landmark lawsuit is the issue of the division of responsibility for consumption choices between individuals who make them freely and the marketers who make those choices available. "Where should the line be drawn," Judge Sweet had asked, "between individual responsibility and society's responsibility?" By society, Judge Sweet meant the government and the institutions, including the marketers. On the one hand, we would expect individual consumers to know that fast food eaten frequently and predominantly cannot but lead to ill health; on the other, individual consumers cannot be expected to be able to fully evaluate the exact outcomes of consuming products. Furthermore, since marketers have inside knowledge about the products, the onus of sharing full knowledge about the products lies with them—the marketers.

While there may be temptation to discount consumer Barber's action as an attempt to extort money from big corporations and to gain fame, it is worth noting that among the compensation and remedy demanded by the plaintiff were these items: (a) an order mandating the defendants to label their products with ingredients and their harmful effects; and (b) funding of an educational program to inform children and adults of the dangers of eating fast food.

Note also that Judge Sweet dismissed the case on grounds that the effects of eating fast food should be obvious to an average consumer; but he left open the possibility that the plaintiffs had not demonstrated that the fast-food chains knew of certain long term health effects that an average consumer could not be expected to know about. And no matter how self-serving the lawsuit might appear, it did serve to awaken everyone—consumers, governments, and marketers alike, to pay more attention to what is in our food, that which we consume in fast-food chains as well as that which we consume at home. And the fast- food chains have since leapfrogged to a menu that includes more healthy options and also more informative labeling.

> The (ill) effects of eating fast food should be obvious to an average consumer.

At any rate, before rushing to judgment in either direction, readers should read the entire filing, available at Findlaw.com.

In this chapter, we examine marketer practices that deceive and harm the consumer interest. To counteract these, we describe how governments and public policy protect the consumer against marketer malpractices. Herein, we describe Consumer Bill of Rights as well as various government agencies and laws enacted to protect the consumer. Second, we examine consumers' own behaviors that are self-destructive, as if the consumer were intoxicated on consumption. Ranging from addiction to crime to mindless indulgence, these constitute what some call "the dark side" of consumer behavior. Finally, we describe an emerging trend of islands of enlightened behavior, among some marketers and among some consumers, embracing the move toward an ethic of more mindful and sustainable consumption.

DECEPTION: ETHICS IN MARKETING

Marketers give us products, we consume them. They charge us money, and, as consumers, we are happy to pay. We derive the benefits we seek from those products, and marketers get financial rewards in return. This exchange relationship is mutually beneficial. But as is true of all relationships, these marketer-consumer relationships also have to rest on mutual trust. Unfortunately, that trust is sometimes broken—from both sides. Some marketers occasionally engage in opportunistic practices that make them exorbitant sums of money but at the cost of consumer wellbeing. Many of these practices positively harm the consumer; others detract from benefits the consumer was promised. These malpractices can be grouped into four categories:

1. Selling unsafe products
2. Unfair Pricing
3. Misinformation and deception
4. Intrusion and Over-commercialism

1. SELLING UNSAFE PRODUCTS

All products have the potential of being unsafe—even seemingly safe products. The milk we drink could upset our stomachs, the clothes we wear could give us skin irritation, the electric bulb could ignite fire, and our cell phones could, conceivably, permeate our brains with some unfriendly, IQ-depleting electromagnetic waves. We depend on marketers to ensure that the products they put out in the market are safe. Fortunately, most of them are—both because most marketers act responsibly and because our governments are watching them. (More on specific governmental agencies, later.)

Policing by government agencies can, however, never eliminate unsafe products completely. A recent study by Consumer Reports magazine found that dozens of unsafe products do manage to find their way onto retail shelves. And many items banned in U.S.A. end up in foreign markets. In U.S.A., the injuries and property damage caused by unsafe products costs some $700 billion annually.[1] What is required is a commitment on the part of marketers to ensure product safety.

Sometimes, products that are potentially unsafe enter the marketplace without the marketer's awareness of their being unsafe—such as when milk gets contaminated or when third party suppliers accidentally use a restricted ingredient (e.g., peanuts in a product labeled peanut-free). Conscientious marketers cooperate with government in withdrawing such products from the market as soon as they are detected. (See inset.)

Of real concern are instances when a marketer knowingly allows unsafe products to be sold just to make money. Some critics point to the marketing of Vioxx as a case-in-point. Read Vioxx stories (Google it!) and then decide for yourself.

2. UNFAIR PRICING

Nobody wants to pay more. But consumers don't resent a price just because it is high; rather, they resent it when they believe it is unjustified; when they suspect that the marketer is indulging in **price gouging**—a practice wherein the seller hikes up the price just to take advantage of some short-term shortage or emergency circumstances. In the State of Florida, where Hurricane Katrina took a heavy toll on people, during the year 2005, the government received 3464 written price-gouging complaints.[2] According to research,[3] consumers infer price unfairness on the basis of three judgments:

a. **Internal reference price;**
b. **Differential pricing to different customers; and**
c. **Opportunistic price hike by the seller.**

Consumers generally carry in their heads an "internal reference price"—a price they expect the item to cost. Often this is based on their knowledge of the price levels of comparable items. Now, if they find the price being offered to exceed this internal reference price substantially, they suspect unfair pricing. As to differential pricing to different customers, if they judge it to be set arbitrarily or to be discriminatory by customer demographics, they suspect foul play. (However, consumers tend not to resent price concessions offered to less resourced persons, e.g., senior citizens, or persons whose presence in the same servicescape is deemed desirable, e.g., no cover charge for women.) Finally, if they find the price to be opportunistic (e.g., snow shovel prices doubled the day after the day of a snow storm), they judge that price to be unfair. Also a price is judged to be unfair when the cost of an add-on service or the charges for a minor customer noncompliance are disproportionate,

RECENT PRODUCT RECALLS

U.S.

. On January 4, 2006, Trader Joe's Company recalled Gourmet Chocolate Fudge Original Code BB because the product may have contained walnuts, which were not declared on the label (!).

. On June 29, 2011, Toyota Motor Sales, USA, Inc. announced to recall approximately 45,500 Highlander Hybrid and 36,700 Lexus RX 400h vehicles sold in the U.S. due to a potential power supply circuit fuse problem.

USA and CANADA

. The U.S. Consumer Product Safety Commission and Health Canada announced on October 11, 2011 the recall of B.O.B.® single and double strollers (about 411,700 units in the U.S. and 27,000 units in Canada), due to strangulation hazard posed by canopy drawstring.

U.K.

. On October 10, 2011, Morphy Richards issued a recall notice on its Double Over Electric Blanket (model # 75311), due to potential to overheat.

AUSTRALIA

. On August 29, 2011, Haircare Australia recalled 158 bottles of "Brazilian Blowout" after the Australian Competition and Consumer Commission (ACCC) discovered its high formaldehyde content that may cause cancer.

MY CB BOOK

such as fuel surcharge (by rental car companies), address-correction charge (by a mail delivery service), late fee for missing a deadline by a few minutes (for movie returns), or minor error in payments (e.g., you paid your credit card company $35 instead of the required minimum of $35.15, and you got charged $15 fee!).

What can marketers do to combat price unfairness perceptions? First, they have to ask themselves whether their goal and business ethic is to make exorbitant profits and be opportunistic or, instead, to be fair in deed as well as in word. If they choose to be fair, then the following actions can help:

S A V V Y
MARKETER

a. **Educate consumers about the value of the item, and about the item's superiority over its competitors' products or over comparable alternatives;**

b. **Make their costs and effort transparent (e.g., the quality of materials used, the level of skills needed, etc.);**

c. **Explain the extent of control or latitude (or a lack of it) they have at their command in the value-chain;**

d. **Make information about price deals available openly and to everyone;**

e. **Ensure that price differentials offered to different customer groups seem logical to all customers (e.g., dynamic pricing practices by airlines).**

f. **Not be a stickler on business procedural compliance, allowing instead for small human failures.**

g. **Help consumers keep track of deadlines.**

3. MISINFORMATION AND DECEPTION

Marketing's Curse

Selling Unsafe Products

Unfair Pricing

Misinfor- mation

Over-com- mercialism

When consumers buy a product, they buy it believing what the marketers say the product will do. Marketers do not always tell the whole truth about a product, hide the demerits of the product, or make exaggerated claims about product benefits. Such exaggerations are particularly frequent for product categories that promise miracles—rapid weight loss, memory enhancement drugs, hair regrowth formulas, training programs promising jobs and careers, etc. Most established and brand name health insurance companies do business honestly. Many mail order agencies, however, are not as honest, hiding substantive details in complicated policy documents; or they blatantly stretch the truth. A case in point:

> In September 2005, Financial Services Authority (FSA), a U. K. governmental agency, in its review of 25 policies that offer cover for critical insurance, found that some policy documents (a) used scare tactics by citing misleading data—e.g., that there were 100,000 cases of cancer every year, but the policy did not provide insurance for all those types of cancer; (b) hiding exclusions in small print; and (c) deliberately using language likely to mislead—for example, it asked, "What will you do if you are unable to work because of an illness?" This statement gives the impression that it is an income protection policy, which, of course, it is not.[4]

Sometimes, consumer deception occurs inadvertently. Cell phone services represent such a situation. Cell phone service companies refer to their plans as nationwide coverage; it means only that the service areas include locations from all parts of the country, not that service is available in all locations of the country. Consumers assume, of course, that they can call anywhere in the U.S. Furthermore, consumers can't always keep track of when they are entering a roaming area (which costs a higher rate) and sometimes the call switches to "roaming" even in the midst of a conversation.

While most marketers act honestly, a few resort to defrauding the consumer and they devise clever ways to do it. Many State governments publish a list of prevalent consumer frauds. A short excerpt from one such list appears in Exhibit 18.1.

4. INTRUSION AND OVER-COMMERCIALISM

The Ills of Advertising

The fourth, and last in our list, problem with marketing is its attribute of intrusion and over-commercialism. First, consider intrusion. Marketers typically interrupt us when we are not looking to buy anything, and we are either busy with productive work or are enjoying life's everyday pleasures. Telemarketers call us anytime they will, even at our dinner hours. E-mails show up in our email servers from merchants we never sought and whose merchandise has no relevance to us or even is demeaning to our dignity. Commercial messages show up on our PCs in the form of banner ads and pop ups and on our mobile phone screens when we are in the midst of typing in our short-message-text (SMS). And of course, all those commercial breaks on network TV annoyingly interrupt our entertainment.

Advertising is a double-edged sword, actually. On one hand, it provides consumers information about all the products and brand choices available in the marketplace. On the other, by interrupting TV and radio programs, and by constant repetition, it becomes annoying. These are gains and losses for the consumer as an individual. Then there are some societal benefits and harms. The principal societal benefit is that it keeps the economic system moving, particularly the system that depends on the economies of large-scale production and distribution. Its societal harms are three: (i) materialism, (ii) value-corruption, and (iii) falsity/no sense.[5]

Materialism **Materialism** is a set of consumer beliefs that sees the acquisition and consumption of more and more products and services as the route to life's satisfaction and happiness. And advertising spreads materialism, social critics argue, by parading an endless array of goods in an enticing way.

Value-corruption Social critics accuse advertising of corrupting our values. In addition to materialism, it promotes self-centeredness and greed (the slogan, "You can have it all."), insensitive competitiveness (Nike's briefly used slogan, "You don't win a silver; you lose a gold."!), disrespect for tradition, etc. Some would argue, for example, that a 1995 campaign for Calvin Klein brand of clothing depicting scantily clad pictures of

---

EXHIBIT 18.1

A LIST OF SELECTED CONSUMER FRAUDS

There are somewhere between 800 and 1,000 frauds and schemes being practiced at any one time. Every consumer is a potential victim. Below are some more prevalent consumer frauds.

● **BAIT AND SWITCH FRAUDS** A company advertises a product at an exceptionally low price. When you go to buy it, the salesperson tells you that the advertised product is sold out. Or you might be told, "You really don't want the cheap merchandise." The salesperson will then try to sell you a similar but more expensive product.

Bait and switch is illegal. However, there must be sufficient evidence against a business before legal action can be taken.

● **EARN-AT-HOME SCHEMES** A company promises high profits for making products such as costume jewelry, pillows, or toys. The company will promise to buy the finished products but will require some money upfront. But later on, the company would reject the finished product as not up to its standards. Or the company is simply not to be found.

● **MEDICAL MIRACLE CURE FRAUDS** These frauds are prevalent among elderly people, especially those who suffer from arthritis. Remember, there are no miracle patent medicines that can do anything for people that a reputable doctor's care cannot do.

● **LOTTERIES** A person offers to sell a winning lottery ticket or a "law firm" says someone has left you a winning lottery ticket, but you must send money so a computer can verify your identity. The "winning" ticket may be counterfeit or not exist.

● **CONTEST SCAMS** These are fake contest notices stating that one has won a "free" prize, and in order to redeem any prize the victim should send "x" amount of money.

● **DOOR-TO-DOOR HOME REPAIR** These involve someone coming to the door and offering home repair work quickly at what seems like a reasonable cost. But, they suddenly "discover" that it will cost much more than the original estimate.

● **DEATH VULTURE FRAUDS** This category is possibly one of the lowest forms of all con games. They visit close members of a bereaved family and attempt to collect sums of money for items which they maintain were purchased by the deceased before his death.

Source: South Carolina Department of Consumer Affairs http://www.scconsumer.gov/publications/frauds_schemes.htm

MY CB BOOK

---

children promoted sexuality in young children; worse, among adults it promoted, critics argue, pedophilia! Some social critics charge that advertising promotes stereotypes about sexes (genders), race and ethnicity ("Two wongs won't make a white.""[6]), the elderly ("I have fallen and I can't get up."[7]), etc.

Falsity/No Sense Some of the advertising is misleading. But at a more benign level, much of it fills our airwaves with ad-speak that is trite and trivial, confusing, and plain silly. It has the effect of making commonplace the telling of half-truths and other self-serving silliness, and justifying cynicism.[8]

PUBLIC POLICY—ITS ROLE IN CONSUMER PROTECTION

Governments at the federal, state, and local levels enact various laws that influence both business behavior and consumer behavior. These laws establish public policy that influences consumer behavior in four ways: (1) by constraining choices, (2) by mandating certain products and services, (3) by setting up facilitative infrastructure, and (4) by protecting the consumer in his or her purchases.

PUBLIC POLICY WATCH-DOG

Constraining Choices

Mandating Choices

Facilitative Infrastructure

Consumer Protection

1. CONSTRAINING CHOICES

No matter where on earth you live, you can pretty much consume what you wish. Unless it is harmful to you; or to those around you. Thus, you cannot imbibe alcohol unless you are 18 or 21, depending on where you live; you cannot drive without a license; and you may not park your car anywhere you like. You may not smoke in enclosed public facilities, carry firearms in public transportation vehicles, or use cell phones during a flight. And you must wear clothes in public places.

Governments constrain choices in two ways: one by imposing controls directly on the consumer (as in the foregoing examples), and second, by imposing control on businesses who make products available to consumers, e.g., by banning the manufacture and/or distribution of certain products (e.g., marijuana). Government regulations also monitor negligent consumer behavior. **Negligent behavior** puts a person or others at risk and imposes heavy costs on society or otherwise deteriorates its quality of life in the long run.

Many government regulations are intended to protect other consumers from the consumption of individuals. In August 2004, British government imposed, for example, a fireworks restriction—firecrackers were banned between 11 pm and 7 am. The goal: residents can now sleep undisturbed.[9] China already had a similar ban. However, the Chinese government recently lifted the ban for the Lunar New Year's Day and loosened its restrictions, now limiting the ban only to the hours of midnight to 7 am during the 14-day period. The 12-year old ban was lifted because the Chinese tradition required that the Lunar New Year be celebrated with fireworks. This tradition is based on the Chinese belief that the sounds of firecrackers will scare away a monster called "nian" and are, therefore, a symbol of good luck.[10]

Governments also control what products may be consumed in public places, for example, by prohibiting smoking, drinking, and gambling in public buildings. In recent times, smoking was banned on airplanes, even on transcontinental or trans-Atlantic flights. In Hong Kong and Singapore, restrictions are very severe for those who are caught transporting drugs. The Singapore government has also used controls to affect the use of credit by its people. The Monetary Authority of Singapore, Singapore's central bank, has clamped down on consumer credit because it feared that Singaporeans were finding it too easy to borrow money.

2. MANDATING CHOICES

Governments not only forbid some choices, they mandate others. **Compliance** refers to the government mandate for consumers to obey defined rules and regulations with respect to purchase, payment, and, more importantly, product usage, including disposal. To obtain compliance, governments pass laws and issue regulations with penalties. In many countries, governments require the use of certain products, such as motorcycle helmets by riders and seat belts by drivers and passengers of automobiles.[11] All passengers must wear seat belts in Canada, and likewise in the U.K.; and in most states in USA.

Many consumer choices are regulated indirectly and in ways invisible to consumers—by mandating manufacturers to make products with certain construction and/or ingredients. Two examples will suffice. In U.S.A. and Canada, since 1996, if you ate a bowl of cereal, you would also be giving your body a good vitamin—specifically vitamin 'B' in the form of folic acid. Folic acid is a crucial vitamin that your body needs for cell replication and growth. Its deficiency leads to anemia and starves rapidly growing tissue of essential elements. In 1996, FDA began to require that all enriched flour, rice, pasta, and other grain products such as cereals contain 140 mcg of folic acid per 100 grams. Although pregnant women need to take as much as 400 mcg of folic acid a day (since the fetus has special needs for its growing tissues), for most of us, this government mandate quietly takes care of our tissue growth needs.[12] As of 2010, 50 countries have regulations mandating wheat flour fortification with folic acid.[12n]

For our second example, we travel across the globe to the world's largest democracy—India. Consumers in India cannot buy non-iodized salt—its sale was banned by a regulation passed in October 2005 by the Indian Ministry of Health and Family Welfare. Why? Because a World Health Organization (WHO) study has identified Iodine deficiency to be the world's leading cause of preventable mental retardation. The Indian government has determined that no State in the country was free from iodine deficiency. By mandating that all salt sold in India be iodized, the government has taken a crucial step in advancing consumer wellbeing.[13]

3. FACILITATIVE INFRASTRUCTURE

The third mechanism by which government policy shapes consumer behavior is the development of infrastructure. Governments can influence consumer behavior by establishing incentives and infrastructures to encourage certain consumer behaviors. Examples: Public recycling facilities, trash cans located on city streets, express lanes for car poolers, park-and-ride facilities, rapid public transit in metro areas, financial incentives for energy efficient appliance usage, and bike routes for bikers. (The U.S. government's 1990 Clean Air Act gives local communities a mandate to build bicycling into their transit plans).

4. PROTECTING THE CONSUMER FROM MARKETERS

Finally, governments play a very intense role in enacting and enforcing laws to protect consumers from marketers and marketing practices. In effect, all elements of the marketing mix (product, promotion, price, and place) are covered in various laws meant to protect the consumer. In 1914, the U.S. Congress established the Federal Trade Commission (FTC) as a body of specialists with the power to investigate and enforce laws that require businesses to engage in fair business practices. The scope of what is or is not a fair business practice has been constantly evolving. That scope, and consumer protection, received a shot in the arm with the passage of the Consumer Bill of Rights. These rights, set forth by President John F. Kennedy, and then passed into law are:

1. **The right to safety**
2. **The right to be informed**
3. **The right to be heard**
4. **The right to choose**

The U.S. Congress has passed many additional laws designed to protect the consumer from being misled by businesses (see list of selected laws in Exhibit 18.2).

For example, a law termed lemon law protects a car buyer against being sold a

CB Good to Know

Your Blinds Are Safe and Here is Why...

A study by the U.S. Consumer Product Safety Commission had found that the matte-finish models of inexpensive imported mini-blinds were treated with lead stabilizers to make the blinds more durable. However, sunlight and heat can cause the plastic to deteriorate, releasing lead dust, which is harmful to young children if they ingest it by touching or licking the slats. The response from retailers was mixed: Home Depot and Lowe's stores stopped selling the blinds; Hechinger and Wal-Mart posted warnings and announced they would phase out the old blinds as new unleaded versions came in. Most stores offered refunds or exchanges. Ultimately, the Consumer Product Safety Commission banned the blinds from being imported. However, the greater safety comes at a price—an increase of 15 percent for the new unleaded versions.

Why did we choose a dull topic of blinds, you might ask. After all blinds are the last thing on our minds.

Precisely, our point. Thanks to benevolent government regulations. Without them, we will have to keep thousands of similarly "boring" products on our minds. Now you know!

Public policy regulations enable us to enjoy carefree consumption. So get up, get out, and vote, the next time a law-maker is being elected. Thank you.

substandard car. If the car breaks down or fails to perform as expected within 90 days of the purchase, the car dealer is required to make good on the purchase and to pay punitive damages to the customer. Similarly, in many states, there are "cool off" laws that give a customer 72 hours to return a product without penalty. On surface, these laws may appear tedious and uninteresting to you, but dig a bit (Read *CB Good to Know* feature box: "Your Blinds Are Safe and Here Is Why"), and discover how they make our everyday living possible and easy.[14]

Governments around the world make consumer lives worry free by regulating businesses. See Exhibit 18.3.

Most businesses themselves try to reduce a customer's perceived risk by offering warranties and written satisfaction guarantees. But the reason these warranties and guarantees are effective and helpful to consumers is that the government enforces business compliance with them. And in the area of pricing, unit pricing and price disclosure laws reduce opportunities for price gouging and deceptive pricing practices.

Regulation of Advertising

One of the FTC's (Federal Trade Commission) most important duties is to oversee all advertising and ensure that no company engages in deceptive advertising. (See Exhibit 18.4) The FTC defines **deceptive advertising** as that which "has the capacity to deceive a measurable segment of the public." A classic example of the regulation of deceptive advertising is the case of Listerine. Warner-Lambert, the manufacturers of Listerine, claimed in its advertising from 1921 to 1975 that Listerine would prevent or lessen common colds and sore throats. In 1975, the FTC determined that the claim was misleading and ordered **corrective advertising**—advertising whose message includes a correction of a previous

---

EXHIBIT 18.2

SELECTED U.S. CONSUMER PROTECTION LAWS

- NATIONAL TRAFFIC AND SAFETY ACT Established in 1958, this act sets safety standards for automobiles and tires.
- AUTOMOBILE INFORMATION DISCLOSURE ACT Established in 1958, this act prohibits automobile dealers from changing the factory price of new cars.
- FAIR PACKAGING AND LABELING ACT Established in 1966, this act regulates the packaging and labeling of consumer goods by requiring manufacturers to identify the amount and type of contents contained within it.
- FEDERAL CIGARETTE LABELING AND ADVERTISING ACT OF 1965 This act required that every cigarette package state: "Warning: The Surgeon General Has Determined That Cigarette Smoking Is Dangerous to Your Health."
- CONSUMER PRODUCT SAFETY ACT Established in 1972, this act set up safety standards for consumer products and outlined penalties for companies that did not follow them.
- TOY SAFETY ACT ESTABLISHED IN 1984 This act makes it possible for the government to immediately recall dangerous toys.
- THE NUTRITION LABELING AND EDUCATION ACT This was created in 1990 to guide consumers in choosing processed foods and products with dietary supplements. The bill enables the FDA to give approval to those products with beneficial health effects and to stop those that make false claims.

Source: Federal Regulations (usgovinfo.about.com/od/uscongress/a/fedregulations.htm)

MY CB BOOK

deception). Accordingly, the company was required to insert the following disclaimer in its future advertising: "while Listerine will not prevent colds or sore throats or lessen their severity, ..." [this was followed by whatever new selling appeal it wanted to employ, such as countering bad breath.]

The FTC requires that companies substantiate any claims made in an advertisement by documenting all verifiable benefits in company files. A **verifiable benefit** is one that can be verified by independent laboratory tests, such as whether a brand cleans clothes whiter than a competitor's brand, or whether a shampoo will prevent hair thinning. The stipulation is that the company must have clinical tests of the product's performance on file before making such advertising claims.

Advertising to Children

Because younger children (under age seven) in general cannot differentiate between a commercial and a program, and many older children do not comprehend the persuasive intent of commercials, special regulations apply to children's advertising. In addition, Better Business Bureau (BBB), a non-governmental organization, monitors advertising

---

EXHIBIT 18.3

GOVERNMENT REGULATION IN EUROPE AND CANADA

> In the European Union, CE (Conformité Européenne—"European Conformity") is a mandatory conformity mark for products placed on the market in the European Economic Area. It forces manufacturers to ensure that the products conform with the essential requirements of the applicable EC directives. Under this directive, which was passed into law in January 2003, all consumers purchasing goods in any EU Member State are entitled to a basic set of consumer rights.

> The regulating body in the UK is (Health and Safety Executive (HSE.gov.uk). In UK, the law gives consumers this basic right: The product you buy must: (a) be of satisfactory quality, (b) be fit for the purpose, and (c) match its description.

> In Canada, on December 15, 2010 the Canada Consumer Product Safety Act received royal assent and, into force since June 20, 2011, is now Canadian law. The Act prohibits the manufacture, importation, advertisement or sale of any consumer products that pose an unreasonable danger to human health or safety;

Consumer Protection from Unfair Trading Practices Act
- requires industry to report serious incidents or deaths related to a consumer product and to provide the government with information about product safety issues;
- requires manufacturers or importers to provide test/study results on products when asked;
- allows Canada's minister of health to order recalls of consumer products; and
- imposes significant fines and penalties for non-compliance with the Act.

Sources: www.ce-marking.org/what-is-ce-marking.html; http://www.canadianlawsite.ca/consumer-protection.htm; HSE.gov.uk.

MY CB BOOK

EXHIBIT 18.4

FTC REGULATIONS ON ADVERTISING   Protecting by Laws

The Federal Trade Commission Act allows the FTC to act in the interest of all consumers to prevent deceptive and unfair acts or practices. A representation, omission or practice is deceptive if it is likely to:
1. Mislead consumers, and
2. Affect consumers' behavior or decisions about the product or service.

In addition, an act or practice is unfair if the injury it causes, or is likely to cause, is:
a. substantial;
b. not outweighed by other benefits; and
c. not reasonably avoidable.

An ad claim can be misleading if relevant information is left out or if the claim implies something that's not true. For example, a lease advertisement for an automobile that promotes "$0 Down" may be misleading if significant and undisclosed charges are due at lease signing.

In addition, claims must be substantiated by scientific data (on file), especially when they concern health, safety, or performance.

Source: Federal Regulations (usgovinfo.about.com/od/uscongress/a/fedregulations.htm)

No Bull

MY CB BOOK

practices of businesses. To monitor children's advertising, it has a special unit called Children's Advertising Review Unit (CARU). CARU has issued special guidelines for children's advertising (See Exhibit 18.5). It behooves all marketers to understand the spirit and logic of those guidelines and follow them, as many well-intending businesses do.

PROTECTING CONSUMER PRIVACY

Privacy has always been important to consumers; now in the age of transactions at a distance (where you don't know the merchant) it is becoming a major concern. There are three domains of privacy: (a) our purchases; (b) our personal information; and (c) our financial information. We give this information to sellers and we don't want sellers making that information public. Fortunately, laws in many countries protect consumers against such misuse. To protect our privacy on the Web, and especially for the vulnerable group that is children, US Government has enacted a law called Children's Online Privacy Protection Act (COPPA) in effect since 2000. Read about it in Exhibit 18.6. In Canada, the Office of the Privacy Commission protects consumer privacy under the Personal Information Protection and Electronic Documents Act (PIPEDA).

No To Virgin, Yes To Apple

In December 2008, Britain's Advertising Standards Agency (ASA) ordered Virgin Media to stop running its ad campaign titled "Hate To Wait?" The campaign featured various everyday situations where people got impatient and wanted instant gratification. One execution showed a speed-dating scene in which one woman found even the short interlude too long and would ring the bell even before a guy introduced himself. To consumers who hate to wait, Virgin was pitching its high internet download speed broadband connection. Rival British Telecom filed a complaint, charging that its advertised speed was not available at peak times and that the ads therefore misled consumers. The agency upheld the complaint and ordered Virgin to stop the ads.

However, it turned down a complaint against Apple by rival IBM. In one ad, in its now famous "I'm a Mac" campaign, Apple had advertised that PCs running on Windows software were more susceptible to virus infections. The complaint was that it misled consumers into believing that all PCs were susceptible to infection and that Macs were not. Rejecting the complaint, the ASA argued that consumers understood that not all PCs, but only those running on Windows were subject to more infections and that it is not that Macs were not subject to infection but that they were less subject to infections, a claim which the agency judged to be truthful.

Source: Based on information in Rob Beschizza, "UK regulators uphold complaint against Virgin download caps," December 11, 2008: "Advertising regulator agrees with Apple: Windows is virus-stricken and insecure," December 25, 2008 Posted in Gadgets.bpoingboing.net.
(http://gadgets.boingboing.net/2008/12/25/british-ad-regulator.html)

CARU GUIDELINES FOR ADVERTISERS
Self-Regulation at Work

EXHIBIT 18.5

1. Products and content which are inappropriate for children should not be advertised or promoted directly to children.

2. Advertisers should always take into account the level of knowledge, sophistication and maturity of the target audience. Younger children have a limited capacity for evaluating the credibility of information they receive. Advertisers, therefore, have a special responsibility to protect children from their own susceptibilities.

3. Realizing that children are imaginative and that make-believe play constitutes an important part of the growing up process, advertisers should exercise care not to exploit unfairly the imaginative quality of children (e.g., suggesting unreasonable expectations of product quality or performance).

4. Advertisers are urged to capitalize on the potential of advertising to influence behavior by developing advertising that, wherever possible, addresses itself to positive and beneficial social behavior, such as friendship, kindness, honesty, justice, generosity and respect for others.

5. Care should be taken to incorporate minority and other groups in advertisements in order to present positive and pro-social roles and role models wherever possible. Social stereotyping and appeals to prejudice should be avoided.

* CARU stands for Children's Advertising Review Unit, a division of Better Business Bureau. a non-governmental, industry self-regulatory agency.
Source: CARU Web site.

MY CB BOOK

CONSUMER NEGLIGENCE AND CONSCIENCE

Marketers' misdemeanors—Ponzi schemes, deceptive advertising, and price gouging—become widely known because of the publicity they receive. But often consumers too indulge in marketplace behaviors that are unethical. The basic concept of ethic is "don't do unto others what you wouldn't want others do to you." But an even more simple guide rule to remain ethical can be this: Don't do anything you wouldn't want the concerned marketer to know about. Many consumer acts would violate this ethical rule, such as stealing from a store, reporting false information about yourself (e.g., mis-reporting your age to qualify for a transaction, making false claims for loss recovery under warranties and property insurance, etc.).

Table 18.1 presents a list of common unethical practices and the findings of a study in six countries. As this table shows, ethical norms do differ across countries, likely reflecting local cultures.[18]

Beyond general ethics (or the lack of them), some consumer behaviors are criminal, such as shoplifting. Consumers also indulge in negligent consumption—practices that are harmful to them and/or to others in the society. These include excessive gambling, drinking, smoking, or doing anything in excess, in fact—binge eating, watching TV or cyber surfing several hours a day, neglecting sleep, etc. Here we discuss five such negligent consumption behaviors: (1) compulsive consumption, (2) shoplifting, (3) feeding our bodies badly, (4) texting while driving, and (5) eco-unfriendly consumption.

1. THE CURSE OF COMPULSIVE BUYING

Compulsive buying can be defined as a chronic tendency to purchase products far in excess of both a person's needs and resources. We all know people who are compulsive buyers, always shopping, always buying stuff, some of which they may never use, or stuff they already have more of than they can use, and buying it even if they can barely afford it or even when they are short on money. They are compulsive buyers. To score yourself on compulsive buying, take the test in Table 18.2.

According to research, compulsive buyers have a lower self-esteem, are more depressed, show a greater tendency to fantasize, experience greater "emotional lift" at the time of purchase, experience remorse in the post-purchase phase, and accumulate a much higher debt. Moreover, research has found that compulsive buying is motivated less by a desire to possess things,

> Compulsive buyers have a lower self-esteem and have a greater tendency to fantasize.

EXHIBIT 18.6

COPPA—THE CHILDREN'S ONLINE PRIVACY PROTECTION ACT

The primary goal of the Children's Online Privacy Protection Act (COPPA) is to give parents control over what information is collected from their children online and how such information may be used.

The Rule requires operators of commercial Web sites and online services to:

1. Post a privacy policy on the homepage of the Web site and link to the privacy policy on every page where personal information is collected.

2. Provide notice about the site's information collection practices to parents and obtain verifiable parental consent before collecting personal information from children.

3. Give parents a choice as to whether their child's personal information will be disclosed to third parties.

4. Provide parents access to their child's personal information and the opportunity to delete the child's personal information and opt-out of future collection or use of the information.

5. Not condition a child's participation in a game, contest or other activity on the child's disclosing more personal information than is reasonably necessary to participate in that activity.

6. Maintain the confidentiality, security and integrity of personal information collected from children.

Source: http://www.ftc.gov/bcp/conline/pubs/buspubs/coppa.htm and www.coppa.org/comply.htm

MY CB BOOK

and more as a means of maintaining self-esteem.[20]

Compulsive Consumption

A related behavior is compulsive consumption, and it comes in various forms: alcoholism, eating disorders, compulsive gambling, compulsive exercising, compulsive videogaming or Internet surfing, and compulsive sexuality.[21] **Compulsive consumption** can be defined as an uncontrolled and obsessive consumption of a product or service frequently and in excessive amounts, likely to ultimately cause harm to the consumer or others. In the consumer research literature, three characteristics of compulsive consumption have been reported. Compulsive consumers experience a drive or urge to engage in a behavior, deny harmful consequences, and face repeated failure in attempts to control that behavior.[22, 23]

Marketing professors Ron Faber and Tom O'Guinn have advanced a three-factor theory of compulsive buying.[24] Those three factors are biological, psychological, and sociological. See Figure 18.1.

Biological Factors Biologically, two subfactors are responsible: genetics and brain chemical deficiency. Some of the compulsive behavior is hereditary—sons of alcoholics have been found, for example, to be at a higher risk of becoming alcoholics even when separated from the parent. And a neurotransmitter called serotonin (whose deficiency causes depression) has been found to lead to compulsive behaviors.

Psychological Factors Psychologically, childhood experience of inadequacy and rejection, continuing in adult years as chronic self-esteem void, cause compulsive buying and compulsive consumption behaviors. Incidents that produce self-esteem loss (e.g., a rebuke by the boss at work) have been found to lead the consumer to go shopping or engage in yet another episode of binge eating or gambling or whatever.

Sociological Factors Finally, sociologically, our culture and social values and norms determine whether the biological and psychological factors would find their outlet

TABLE 18.1 SELECTED UNETHICAL CONSUMER PRACTICES

Questionable Consumer Behaviors	Overall	Rank	NATIONALITY					
			UK	Brunei	H. K.	France	USA	Austria
Drinking a can of soda in a supermarket without buying it.	1.8	1	2.2	1.2	1.4	1.7	1.3	2.9
Using long distance phone access code that does not belong to you.	1.8	2	2.2	1.5	1.3	1.6	1.2	3.0
Reporting a lost item as stolen to an insurance company to collect money.	2.3	4	2.5	1.7	2.0	2.1	1.3	3.9
Changing price tags on merchandise in a store.	1.9	3	2.1	1.3	1.5	1.8	1.3	3.4
Not saying anything when the waitress miscalculates the bill in your favor.	2.3	6	3.2	1.6	2.4	2.5	1.8	2.2
Getting too much change and not saying anything.	2.7	8	3.2	2.4	3.4	2.5	2.2	2.5
Taking towels from hotels and blankets from aircraft as souvenirs.	3.1	11	3.6	3.2	3.6	3.0	3.0	2.3
Renting one double bedroom hotel room for more than two people.	2.3	6	3.1	2.2	2.5	2.2	2.0	1.8
Taking advantage of free trial periods.	3.0	9	3.6	3.0	3.4	3.6	3.2	1.6
Cutting in when there is a long line.	3.1	10	3.7	3.3	2.8	3.8	3.4	1.5

Note: Overall ranking ascends from less favorable (1) to more favorable (5) responses.

Source: Emin Babakus, T. Bettina Cornwell, Vince Mitchell, and Bodo Schlegelmilch, "Reactions to Unethical Consumer Behavior across Six Countries," Journal of Consumer Marketing, 21(4), 2004, 254-263. Reproduced with Permission. Courtesy Emerald Publishing Group.

MY CB BOOK

in compulsive buying or some other impulse control disorder. Sometimes, cultures dilute the seriousness of a disorder or even suggest shopping as a cure for a 'negative situation'—as in the bumper sticker in USA: "When the going gets tough, the tough go shopping"; such social nod further feeds the compulsive shopping frenzy.

An individual consumer can act on two factors: chemical deficiency and self-esteem. Both medical consultation and psychological counseling can do the suffering consumer some good.

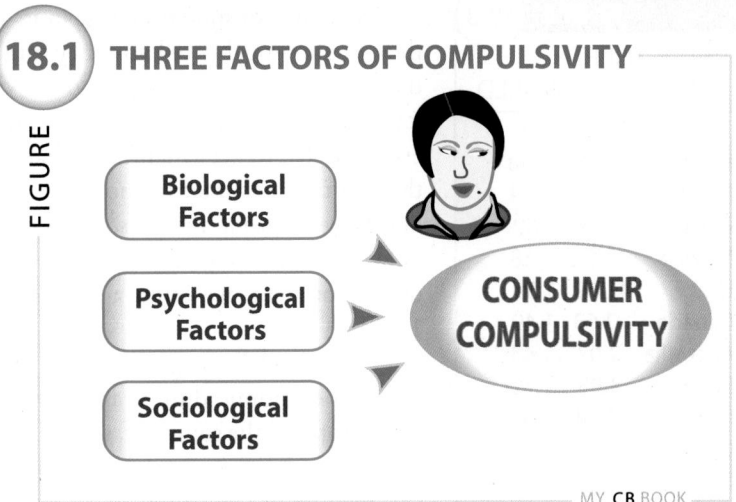

FIGURE 18.1 THREE FACTORS OF COMPULSIVITY

Biological Factors
Psychological Factors
Sociological Factors

CONSUMER COMPULSIVITY

MY CB BOOK

2. THE MENACE OF SHOPLIFTING

Shoplifting is a crime. Yet it happens. Worldwide, retail industry loses more than $100 billion a year ($119 billion in the year ended June 2011, 1.45% of sales, up 6.5% from the preceding year). India tops the list at 2.38% with Taiwan at the bottom .91%. Because the size of the total economy varies across countries, in absolute terms, the largest loss is in the U.S. ($41.69 b); in comparison, India's loss is only $0.78B. The retail theft loss and the theft prevention surveillance costs combine to increase the cost of goods by about $200 per family on an average ($435 in the U.S.).[25]

The shoplifting misadventure is not limited to prankster teenagers, professional thieves, or the starving, destitute, with no option left. It is done by "regular" people and at least occasionally, even by the affluents, as the case of Academy Award-nominated actress, Winona Ryder attests.[26]

Highest

Shop Lifting

Lowest

TABLE 18.2 MEASUREMENT OF COMPULSIVE BUYING

Q1. If I have any money left at the end of the pay period, I just have to spend it.

Strongly Agree 1	Somewhat Agree 2	Neither Agree Nor Disagree 3	Somewhat Disagree 4	Strongly Disagree 5

2. How often have you done each of the following?	Very Often 1	Often 2	Some times 3	Rarely 4	Never 5
a. Felt others would be horrified if they knew of my spending habits.	—	—	—	—	—
b. Bought things even though I couldn't afford them.	—	—	—	—	—
c. Write a check when I knew I didn't have enough money in the bank to cover it.	—	—	—	—	—
d.. Bought myself something in order to make myself feel better.	—	—	—	—	—
e. Felt anxious or nervous on days I didn't go shopping.	—	—	—	—	—
f. Made only the minimum payments on my credit cards.	—	—	—	—	—

To score yourself, enter your responses into the following equation and calculate the total:
Your Score = -9.69 +(Q1 X .33) +(Q2a X .34)+(Q2b X .50)+(Q2c X .42)+(Q2d X .33)+(Q2e X .38)+(Q2f X .31)

If your score is less than or equal to -1.34, you are classified as a compulsive buyer. If you score this low, you may want to reflect on your motivations and resolve to identify strategies to overcome this behavior.

Are You a Compulsive Buyer?

Note. An Excel worksheet is available at www.mycbbook.com/compusive.htm

MY CB BOOK MEASUR

Source: Ronald J. Faber and Thomas C O'Guinn, "A Clinical Screener for Compulsive Buying," *Journal of Consumer Research*, 19, December 1992, pp.459-69. Copyright © 1992 *Journal of Consumer Research*, The University of Chicago Press, Used with permission.

MY CB BOOK

TABLE 18.3		
RETAIL THEFT AROUND THE WORLD		
	$b	%
India	.78	2.38
Russia	4.01	1.74
Brazil	2.38	1.69
Mexico	2.92	1.68
U.S.	41.69	1.59
Canada	3.63	1.49
Australia	2.07	1.43
Spain	3.95	1.40
Italy	4.68	1.37
UK	7.82	1.37
China	1.14	1.11
Japan	9.64	1.04
Taiwan	.59	.91

Source: The Global Retail Theft Barometer 2011, Joshua Bamfield, Centre for Retail Research, UK, October 18, 2011.

MY CB BOOK

Why do consumers engage in it? If you ask someone who has shoplifted, they would probably tell you they forgot to pay for it; or that they didn't have the money but wanted the product. Or even that because the store makes a lot of money. Whatever be their expressed reasons, one thing is sure: no one ever expected to get caught. But that is, at best, the most circumstantial factor that led the consumer to shoplift on that particular occasion; the real reason lies deeper—inside the person. To capture both types of factors—those that lie deep inside the person and those that lie outside—in one's circumstances or environment, we build a three-factor model of shoplifting. (See Figure 18.2.)

This model recognizes three core "internal" factors: personal values, personal economic duress, and perceived unfairness. First, the fundamental reason for, and the source of, shoplifting is consumers' personal value system—their sense of right or wrong. If a person's personal value were that stealing is sin, then he or she would never even harbor the thought, and would abhor the very idea of stealing. Second, a person's economic duress can motivate him/her toward using whatever means to find life's essentials. And third, if a consumer perceived marketers in general and a merchant in particular to be unfair to him or her, he or she would be inclined to abandon any qualms about stealing. These three factors then form the consumer's general attitude toward stealing.

Attitudes lead to behavior, as you read in Chapter 7. Accordingly, consumers' attitude toward stealing should, when it is pro-stealing, lead to stealing behavior. It does—but it requires two situational, "external" factors: opportunity and absence of risk. First, there has to be an opportunity to steal. If items are in locked showcases, no one can steal them. Second, if the apprehension to get caught is high, then people will not steal them. That is why security cameras in stores are the best deterrent. Also if the laws are severe, it exacerbates the risk. In some societies, stealing is punished by

FIGURE 18.2 A MODEL OF CONSUMER SHOPLIFTING BEHAVIOR

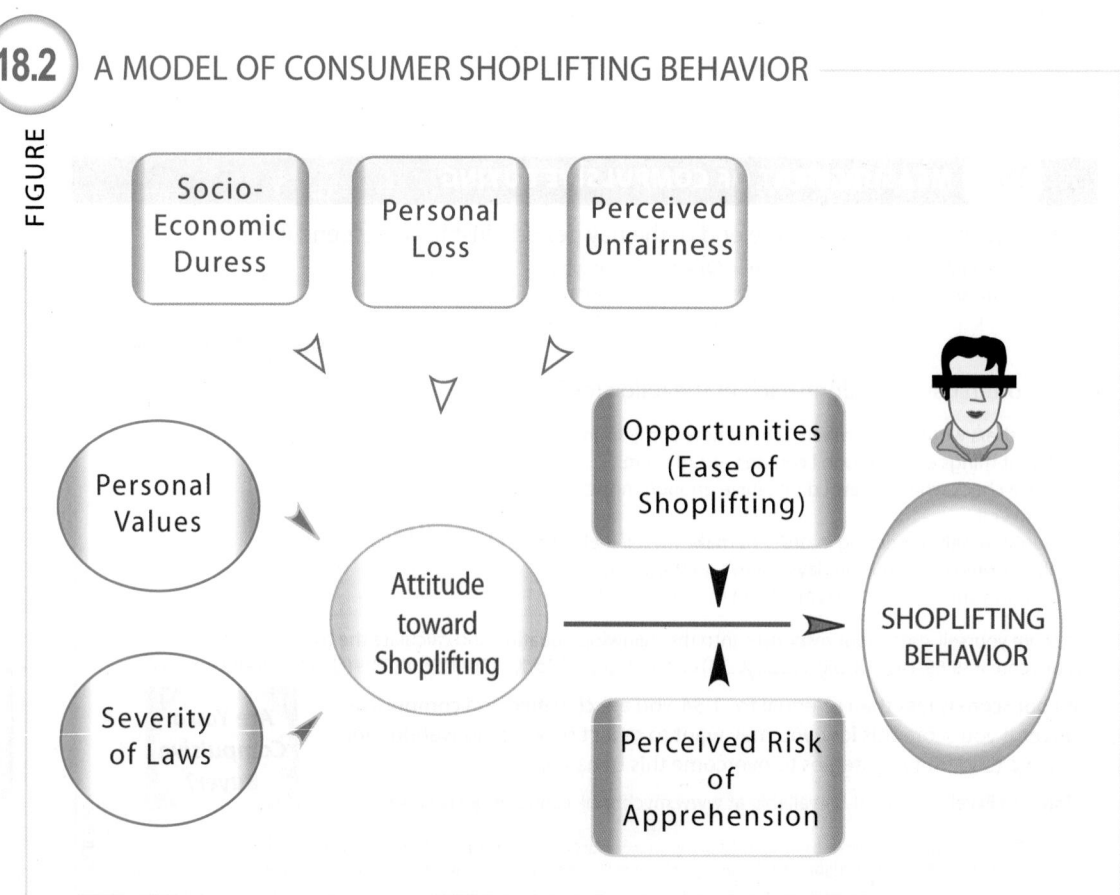

MY CB BOOK

cutting off a thief's limbs, thus purging theft altogether.

To demotivate shoplifting then, society needs both: good personal ethics on the part of consumers and a vigilant watch in the store.

3. FEEDING OUR BODIES BADLY

Food consumption is intended to supply our bodies the calories and the nutrients it needs. Instead, a large number of us end up feeding it with food that supplies a ton-load of calories far in excess of its requirement but starves it of essential nutrients. Plain and simple, it is a gross abuse of our bodies—in effect, we are failing to protect our most valuable asset.

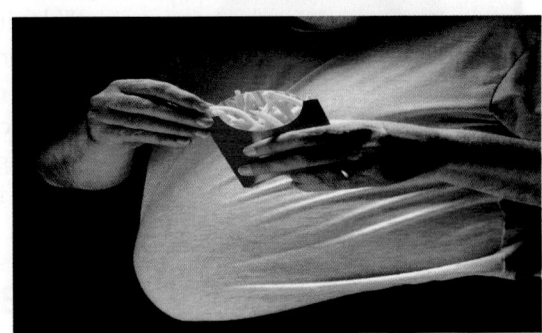

This puts our bodies out of shape—a condition called *overweight* and *obesity*. But obesity is now a culturally loaded term, with some public minders taking the high moral ground that the obese do not have the rectitude to down-size. Although obesity overtly manifests as large body size, the shape or size of the body is not the main issue. The issue is the resulting health problems: high bad cholesterol, triglyceride, sugar, etc., causing diabetic and heart diseases that hamper everyday living and pose serious life threats.

The problem is that these problems arise slowly, festering over several years of bad eating, thus remaining largely invisible in their onslaught. And then, suddenly, it is too late and the bad eating behavior too entrenched to modify.

Just how serious is this problem?

Every fourth person on earth is too fat.

Which country leads on obesity? That dubious distinction belongs to the Western Pacific Islands of Naura and Tonga; according to a recent WHO report, nine out of every 10 adults in those Island nations are overweight.

Around the world, about 300 million people are obese (World Health Organization). Obesity is now classified as a growing epidemic. According to a UK's Department of Health estimate, among children aged 2-15, as many as 25% were overweight (22% among boys and 27% among girls); and 5.5% of boys and 7.2% of girls were found to be obese (up from less than 1% in 1975). Worldwide, the report places about 155 million (one in ten) children to be overweight; about 45 million of them (about 3%) obese.[30]

Obesity is determined by Body Mass Index (BMI). To calculate it, divide your weight in kilograms by the square of your height in meters. If your BMI is <25, congratulations. If, for one of your friends, this number comes to 25 or more but less than 30, then he or she is "overweight." If this number comes to 30 or more, your friend is obese. Furthermore, if the number is over 40, that person is "morbidly obese," at serious health risk.[31]

More than 75% of women over the age of 30 are overweight in countries as diverse as Barbados, Egypt, Mexico, South Africa, Turkey and United States; over 75% men are overweight in such countries as Argentina, Germany, Greece, Kuwait, and New Zealand.

In general, there are three factors responsible for obesity: genetics and ethnicity, sedentary lifestyle, and dietary habits. (See Figure 18.3.)

Genetics and Ethnicity For some consumers, their genetics make their metabolism work in a manner that there is no fat build up; others are not as blessed. Likewise, some ethnic groups are more susceptible to fat build up. But we can control the influence of this factor by monitoring the other two culprits.

Sedentary Lifestyle If our lifestyles are sedentary and we do not exercise enough, then we are bound to gain weight.

300 million

# of people around the world who are classified as **obese**

55 USA
32 Canada
25 UK

Annual per capita consumption of soda in gallons

I sit to work and
I sit to workout.

Dietary Habits   Finally, our diets are perhaps the most to blame—not only does an average person not consume the five foods of the so-called food pyramid, but our diets are positively unhealthy. Americans drink an equivalent of 55 gallons of soda a year—up from 20 gallons in 1970 (Canada 32 and U.K. 25 gallons a year, according to Euromonitor, 2012).[33]

At least two of these factors are entirely within consumers' power to control. Even the much maligned fast-food chains now have a broader menu with many healthy items. McDonald's now offers, on its Web site, opportunity to see exactly what you are getting—how many calories, fat, protein, carbs, sodium, etc. For example, a McMeal consisting of a hamburger, small French fries with ketchup will give you 500 total calories, with 20 grams of fat, 30 milligrams of cholesterol, 1040 milligrams of sodium, 66 grams of carbs, and 15 grams of protein. Substitute it with a bacon ranch salad with grilled chicken for mere 260

FIGURE **18.3** THREE FACTORS CAUSING OBESITY

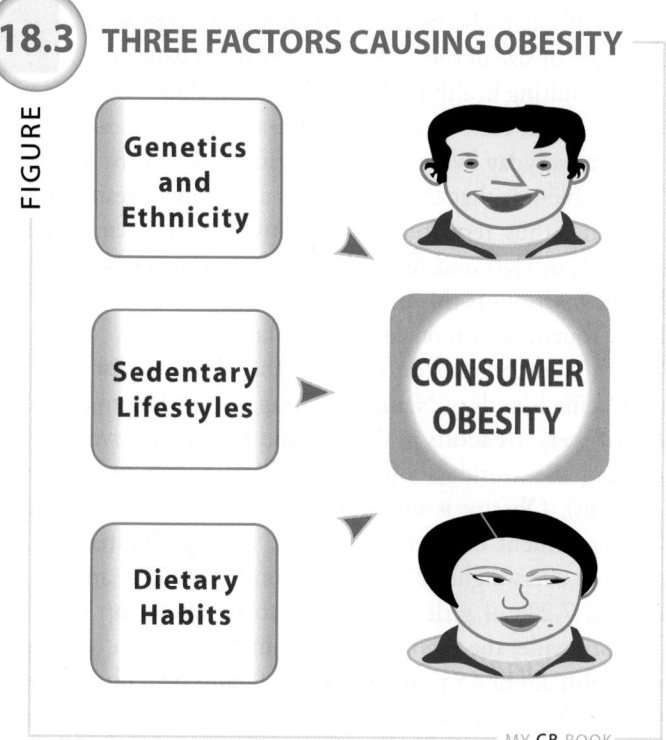

Genetics and Ethnicity

Sedentary Lifestyles

Dietary Habits

CONSUMER OBESITY

MY **CB** BOOK

Great Taste Now Comes in 600 Calories!   *Romancing the Consumer*

ThinDish is a Web-based information service that offers consumers information on restaurants that offer low calories, low fat dishes. This Winnetka, California, headquartered company partners with restaurants that offer dishes with less than 600 calories. Following the US Department of Agriculture (USDA) 2010 Dietary Guidelines for Americans (DGA), the partnering restaurants also make the dishes—not all of their menu but the featured ThinDishes—meet these additional criteria: at least 30% of calories come from protein, sodium less than 700 mg, less than 20 gm fat (i.e., less than 30% of calories), and carbs less than 40% of RDA. Some recent entries gleaned from the site:

• Shah Abbas restaurant, Beverly Hills, two dishes;
• Modo Mio, Pacific Palisades, 5 dishes;
• Delphi Greek, Los Angeles, 10 dishes;
• Taste, Melrose, 4 dishes

thin dish™

calories; add Newman's Own® Low Fat Balsamic Vinaigrette for a mere 40 more calories. You can check out various other health food combinations; the helpful nutrition calculator will tell you—what you choose, of course, is entirely up to you.

A lot of people are motivated to lose weight but face two hurdles: a lack of clear direction on diet and years of conditioning of the body that now craves for certain foods. A new book can help overcome both these barriers: *Why We Get Fat—And What To Do About It*, Gary Taubes, Knopf, 2010.

It is a myth that we have to sacrifice the pleasures of our taste buds to lose those extra pounds. Healthy food can be very tasteful and you can indulge in every imaginable food, albeit with some changes in the frequency of trips to the fast-food places. And it is easy to cultivate some natural exercise habits that can in fact become pleasurable: park your car a little farther and walk and smell the air; shun the elevator and race up the stairs with a colleague; at parties and in clubs, stand and walk rather than sit.

For inspiration, take a tour of the Mayo Clinic in Rochester; there, some doctors have their workstations set up on treadmills set to run at one mile an hour (which helps them burn one hundred calories an hour while working normally). One of them, Dr. James Levine, even has a similar treadmill for his visitors![33]

4. RECKLESS DRIVING: A HUGHLY UNINTELLIGENT CONSUMER BEHAVIOR

Worldwide, about 1.2 million people get killed in road accidents annually. Additionally, around fifty million people get injured or disabled. Also, globally, of the total road accidents (a) more than half involve drivers who are between the age of 15 and 44 years, and (b) 73% involve male drivers.[33] World Health Organization Report calls road fatalities an "epidemic" that by 2030 will become the world's fifth biggest killer.

In USA, automobile accidents cause more than 3 million people to be injured annually, with more than 2 million resulting in permanent disability or more than 40,000 in death. In Canada, a Transport Canada 2002 estimate puts the death number at 2936 and injuries at 227, 768.[34] And in the U.K., in 2007, reckless driving caused 30,720 people to be killed or seriously injured (Department of Transport).[34] One of the most regrettable factors underlying reckless driving is the use of cell phones. Holding the cell phones in one hand impairs quick reaction time, and emotionally tangled cell-talk (e.g., getting angry, immersed, etc.) detracts attention from the road. Reading or writing SMS text messages is worse, as this activity occupies both our eyes and hands. Actually, reading text messages is worse than writing them because some users manage to type in without constantly looking at the phone. A recent study by Car and Drive magazine found that texting impairs reaction times even more than does drunk driving![36] (See inset.)

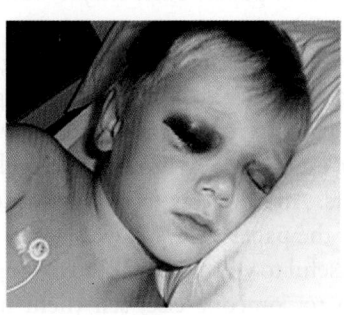

My name is Frank P. Brady of Asheville, NC. On April 28, 2001, I was driving in Coral Springs, Florida, with my family, when a car rear-ended our car. The other driver, a young person, had been distracted by his cell phone. My son, Patrick, then 2 years, got seriously injured, receiving brain injury. It has taken 8 years for my son to re-train his brain. He is a straight "A" student now, but is considered by the state and federal government as still being disabled because he has trouble reading. (Personal communication.)

SHUT UP AND DRIVE!

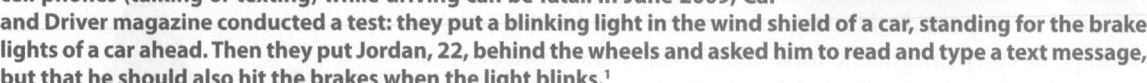

You are driving and a blue light blinks on your cell phone, indicating someone just sent you a text message. You hit the "ok" button to read the message from your pal asking when you would be reaching your rendezvous spot. Quickly you type in the answer: "In 10 minutes if no traffic." Now face the black truth: There is a slight chance you will not reach—at all!

Worried parents have always pleaded with their teenage kids to not use their cell phones while driving. But now there is scientific proof that using cell phones (talking or texting) while driving can be fatal. In June 2009, Car and Driver magazine conducted a test: they put a blinking light in the wind shield of a car, standing for the brake lights of a car ahead. Then they put Jordan, 22, behind the wheels and asked him to read and type a text message, but that he should also hit the brakes when the light blinks.[1]

At a speed of 70 miles an hour, it took Jordan 0.50 second while reading and .48 second while typing in the text message, compared to his baseline reaction time of .39 second (yes, reading is more distracting than typing!). Does a delay of .1 to .2 second matter? Yes, absolutely. At 70 miles an hour, a 0.1 second delay will take you 10.3 feet farther before you stop; a .67 second slower reaction time (Eddie's delay while texting) will take you 68 feet closer to the car ahead; and that will put you, sometimes, in the "belly" of that car!

The researchers also had Jordan get drunk (to the legal limit) and repeat the tests (without using cell phones). All delayed reaction times were shorter than they were with phone use. You read right: Using phones while driving is more dangerous than driving drunk! In July 2007, five teenagers were killed by a driver who was texting.[2] So the problem is not only that you text while driving, but that another driver does. His/her addiction to smartphone could kill YOU!!

In many of us, there is an almost addictive urge to instantly view our phone messages. And there is this misguided belief that "I am cautious" and that, "because it has not happened to me so far, it will never happen to me."

You are right. The probability of a cell-phone-use-caused accident is low, very low, perhaps one in a thousand or even lower. That means, it will happen only once, if you text, say, 1,000 (or 10,000) times while driving. But that one time is more than enough to meet death, worse, be maimed. It boggles all intelligent, thinking people as to why this simple fact of texting-while-driving is not clear to otherwise intelligent drivers: One chance is all fatality needs!

So you see, there is a small chance you will not make it to your rendezvous at all, all because you chose to text while driving. Granted, the chance is teeny-weeny, but, when in your life the best is yet to come, should you be, dear reader, taking that c h a n c e ? ? ?

> **PLEDGE CARD**
> I luv txting. But i don't wanna die young. I pledge 2 ignor sms whl drvin. And limt cell-talk to emrgncy minm. i wanna liv. wfm!
> Signed_____
> Date _____

MY **CB** BOOK

5. ENVIRONMENTAL ABUSE: OUR THROWAWAY SOCIETY

In industrialized countries (aptly called *throwaway societies*), the volume of throwaways can be enormous. The U.S. leads many countries in household solid waste production: about 4.4 pounds per person per day (compared to 2 to 3 pounds per capita in Europe). This comes to 1600 pounds of trash per person per year, making up some 220 tons of waste materials every year. The majority (71%) of it consists of paper; other major waste components are metals, plastics, and glass. (See Exhibit 18.7.)

Now the big question is: What are you going to do about it? There are three things you can do—the "3Rs of waste action": reduce, reuse, and recycle. We discussed recycling in Chapter 12. Here, we discuss 'reduce' and 'reuse'. First, you can reduce the waste. How? By buying items in packages that generate less waste. For example, buy products in bulk sizes (avoid single serving sizes) and in refillable containers. Another way to reduce waste is by using products conservatively (e.g., use both sides of the paper).

Second, reuse or help someone else reuse what is not useful to you. Instead of throwing away old furniture, appliances, and clothing, give them to someone else, sell them in garage sales, or donate them to charities. With a combination of reduce and reuse, you can contribute significantly to the sustainability of our environment.

The third R is recycle. Do not throw away the packages and containers and paper products (e.g., newspaper) as garbage; instead recycle them. Reduce and reuse can make some impact; however, it is unlikely that a substantial number of consumers in modern consumer societies will embrace these courses of action. Recycling is, however, more doable. Want to know what to recycle? Just Google "recycling guide." We did, and the third entry (when accessed on January 18, 2012) was titled "The World's Shortest Comprehensive Recycling Guide," available at

obviously.com/recycle.

Check it out.

(Also read more on this topic in Special Topic #5, p. 514-531.)

EXHIBIT **18.7**

WHAT IS IN AMERICA'S TRASH

Metals 15.3m tons (8.5 %)

Glass 12.5m tons (7.0 %)

Yard Trimmings 31.6m tons (17.6%)

Plastics 14.4m tons (8.0 %)

Paper 71.6m tons (40.4%)

Other (e.g., rubber, leather, textiles, wood, miscellaneous inorganic wastes) 20.8m tons (11.6%)

Food Scraps 13.2m tons (7.4 %)

Source: General Overview of What's in America's Trash, Consumer Handbook for Reducing Solid Waste, U.S. Environmental Protection Agency, Information; posted on its Web site http://www.epa.gov/epaoswer/non-hw/reduce/catbook/what.htm

MY CB BOOK

THE THREE-FACTOR MODEL OF ECOLOGICAL CONSUMPTION

Reduce, reuse, and recycle are three prongs of an overarching consumer behavior, we call *ecological consumption*. **Ecological consumption** refers to a consumer's mindset wherein the consumer highly values and is actively conscious of the sustainability of our planet's natural resources and is committed to channel his/her consumption in a manner that promotes, rather than deteriorates, the ecological balance between our planet's natural resources and living organisms including, of course, humans. We build a three-factor model to understand this mindset, shown in Figure 18.4.

The three principal factors are Environment as value, Perceived personal benefits and costs, and Social norms. Among these three factors, the first is the most fundamental. The consumer must believe that it is utmost important to preserve the health of our environment, and must place it high up on his/her value system. The second factor is

FIGURE **18.4** THREE-FACTOR MODEL OF PRO-ENVIRONMENTAL CONSUMPTION

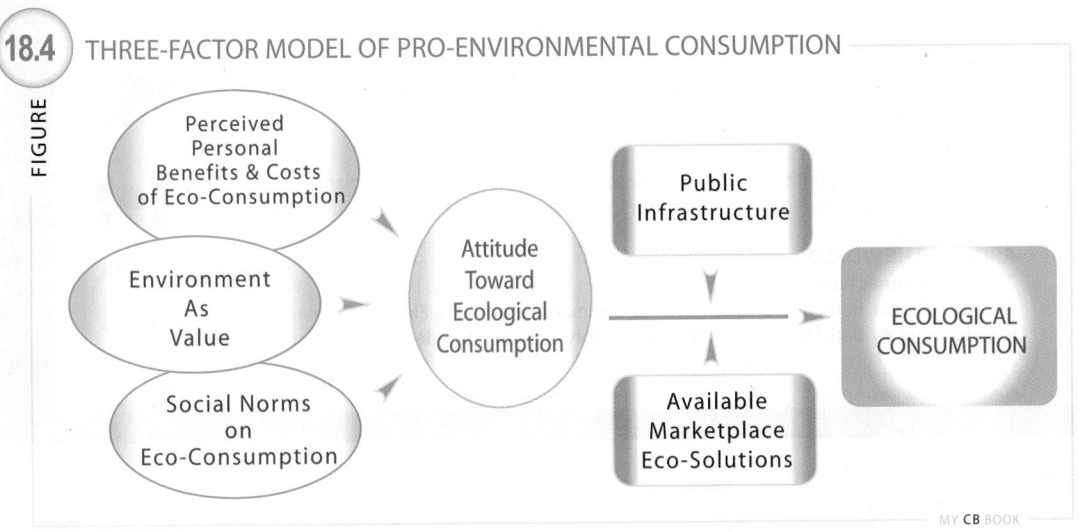

Perceived Personal Benefits & Costs of Eco-Consumption

Environment As Value

Social Norms on Eco-Consumption

Attitude Toward Ecological Consumption

Public Infrastructure

Available Marketplace Eco-Solutions

ECOLOGICAL CONSUMPTION

MY **CB** BOOK

perceived personal benefits and costs of engaging in ecological consumption. Personal benefits include both tangible (e.g., better health from organic eating) and intangible (satisfaction of implementing one's value system and identity) rewards. Third, social norms—what one's referents command or wish—aid this mindset. They reinforce the already motivated consumer and compel an otherwise unwilling individual.

SAVVY MARKETER

These three "internal" factors produce pro-ecology attitudes. To convert this attitude into behavior, two "external" factors are needed: public infrastructure and available marketplace solutions. Public infrastructure includes the availability of recycling facilities, public transportation, alternative energy production and distribution, bike routes, etc. Marketplace solutions include the wide availability of eco-friendly products and reverse channels. A utopian vision of marketplace "eco-readiness" would be the one where ecological products are available in comparable quality, at convenient outlets, and at a price premium (if any) that is affordable for a majority of consumers. Realizing this vision requires a strong ecological ethics both on the marketer's part and on the consumer's part. Let us elaborate on this ethic.

It Takes A Village

Because ecological health requires action by consumers en masse, governments need to play a strong advocacy role, raising citizen awareness by bringing home the importance of a healthy environment and the urgency of preserving it. This can be done through informational and educational campaigns by governmental and social agencies. For instance, Waste Watch is a UK based organization promoting action on waste reduction, reuse, and recycling. In Australia, Resource NSW, an agency of the Government of New South Wales, in partnership with many social and corporate organizations, has developed a program of public education, called the Murfy educational program, with a Murfy character and related icons on recyclable products.

CONTAINER RETURN LAWS   Saving packaging waste

Some governments offer infrasturcutre to facilitate your eco-consumption behavior. If you live in one of these places, hope you are doing your part to save our planet.

> **U.S.A**
  California, Connecticut, Delaware, Hawaii, Iowa, Maine, Massachusetts, Michigan, New York, Oregon, and Vermont.

> **CANADA**
  12 provinces Alberta, British Columbia, Manitoba, New Brunswick, Newfoundland, Northern Territories, Nova Scotia, Ontario, Prince Edward Island, Quebec, Saskatchewan, and Yukon Territory

> **AROUND THE WORLD**
  21 other countries have the law:
  Australia, Austria, Barbados, Belgium, Croatia, Denmark, Estonia, Fiji, Finland, Germany, Guam, Iceland, Israel, Kiribati, Micronesia, Netherlands, Norway, Palau, Sweden, Switzerland, and Turkey

MY CB BOOK

Sources: www.bottlebill.org/

On Marketers' part, *reverse channel* is an important program. You can bring back empty bottles to retailers, for example, if you live in one of the eleven U.S. states, one of the 12 Canadian provinces, and in one of the 21 countries around the world. (See list in inset.) With container laws (California, Connecticut, Delaware, Hawaii, Iowa, Maine, Massachusetts, Michigan, New York, Oregon, and Vermont).[37] Outside the U.S., 22 other countries have container return laws (Austria, Belgium, Denmark, Finland, Germany, Netherlands, Norway, Sweden, and Switzerland).[38] The retailers charge a small deposit (e.g., usually, 5 cents a bottle) when you buy the product, and refund that money when you bring back the empty container. That is incentive enough for many consumers.

If enough consumers don't seek out environment-friendly products, our consumption will continue to put at risk the sustainability of our planet for future generations.

Eco-friendly products mean both recycled and recyclable content and eco-friendly production and distribution processes. For example, Aveda, which makes its cosmetics only from natural ingredients, also ensures that the ingredients themselves were produced without harmful chemicals and with non-polluting processes. Another company is Anakiri.

Now, the question is, will you, as a consumer, seek out products like Aveda and Anakiri cosmetics to make your contribution to the environment? Governments can induce manufacturers, and they can even compel them, but the ultimate success of any such manufacturer initiative depends on consumers—if enough consumers don't seek out environment-friendly products (which may be more expensive), our consumption will continue to put at risk the sustainability of our planet for future generations.

Romancing the Consumer

HELPING US CONSUME ETHICALLY

k, so you are interested in buying products that are produced by companies that follow ethical business practices. The problem is, you don't know which companies and products qualify. Don't you wish there were a source to guide you through all this? Well, now there is.

An organization based in the UK has dedicated itself to this very mission: The Ethical Consumer Research Association (ECRA), a non-profit workers' cooperative founded in 1988 to "provide information on the companies behind the brands and to promote the ethical use of consumer power." Its subsidiary Ethical Consumer Information Systems Ltd. has developed a rating system for companies and products both adaptable to changing ethical norms and wholly transparent to users for critical review. Its database, available at its Web site (www.ethiscore.org) contains ratings of some 30,000 companies, evaluated on five criteria:

- Environment (Nuclear Power, Climate Chnge, Pollution & Toxins, Habitats & Resources)
- People (Human Rights, Workers' Rights, Supply Chain Policy, Irresponsible Marketing, Armaments)
- Animals (Animal Testing, Factory Farming, Animal Rights)
- Politics (Political Activity, Boycott Call, Genetic Engineering, Anti-Social Finance, Company Ethos)
- Product Sustainability (Organic, Fair Trade, Positive Environmental Features, Other Sustainability)

Want to buy an MP3 Player? The highest scoring brands are Archos, mobiBLU, Pure PocketDAB Radio, and Rio (all scoring 12 out of 20); the lowest, Hitachi MP3 player. The iconic iPOd is in the comfortable middle (score 9). Craving for chocolate bars? The highest scoring brand is Plamil chocolate (score 15 out of 20); the lowest, Galaxy Chocolate (score 3.5); Lindt receives a comfortable 10.5. Click on the company name and you will get the detailed breakdown scores on the five evaluation criteria.

visit www.corporatecritic.org for in-depth company research

For consumers eager to consume with a conscience—in terms of our planet's ecology and our collective societal ethos—such wealth of information is invaluable. It is an incentive as well for companies to reassess their business practices and strive forward toward a higher ethical standard in the production of goods.

(Source. www.Ethiscore.org)

Powered by MY BOOK

THE ENLIGHTENED CONSUMER

As we write this, world economy is nose-diving into what some predict to be a recession. (Greece's economy was on "life support system" with a second bailout of $173 billion from the European Union in March 2012.) In the wake of housing bubble bust and banking crises that began in early 2008, millions of consumers around the world have fallen on hard times, financially speaking. To cope, they have curbed their spending. Such deprivation is unfortunate, but there is a silver lining.

According to some observers, the financially strapped consumers have learned a lesson in frugality. Buying thrifty has become new chic. Anthropologist Robbie Blinkoff conducted a study in Fall 2008 in five cities and noted that consumers' outlook on shopping has changed. The old "intoxicated" mindset of "I shop, therefore I am" has given way to a new mantra: "I shop because I need stuff, but it doesn't define me!"[50]

Will this mindset prove enduring? With the return of good economic times again, will consumers maintain their frugal ways? This is hard to predict; in fact our hunch is that consumer shopping habits will, in short order, stretch back to keep pace with the returning prosperity.

But at least compulsive (and impulsive) shopping habits are likely to stay under control. Consumers who have succeeded in breaking free of their addictive shopping/consumption will have no reason to give up that personal victory anytime soon.

In the area of environmental sustainability, too, there is evidence of the rise of consumer awareness. Since 2007, Wal-Mart has been tracking consumers' willingness to buy five key eco-friendly products, and this index has been rising.

A 2008 survey by the market research firm TNS, impressive in scope (interviews with 13,000 consumers in 17 countries), revealed a pleasantly surprising finding: A staggering 94% of Thai respondents and 83% of Brazilians were willing to pay more for environmental friendliness; and even in the Western world, used to years of abundant consumption, as many as 45% of British and 53% of American respondents were willing to dig deeper into their pockets to help the environment. Among U.S. consumers, 26% reported that they actively sought environmentally friendly products.

We haven't *gone* green.
We started that way.

ANAKIRI
BioEnergetic Skin Care

Enabling this consumer desire for sustainable consumption are the sustainability initiatives of some select enlightened business firms. Case in point: in 2007, Proctor & Gamble set itself a 5-year goal of developing and marketing at least $50 billion in cumulative sales of "sustainable innovation products." By the end of 2011, it had reached $40 billion goal post.

Of course, not all businesses are so progressive, and the segments of enlightened consumers are in a minority, and their ranks are unlikely to swell anytime soon. But their very presence gives cause for optimism.

As students of consumer behavior, we should rethink our consumption. We should resist every temptation to indulge in abusive and excessive consumption—compulsive shopping, mindless eating, reckless driving, addiction to our mobile phones, buying or consuming without paying, and ecology-deteriorating consumption. That is the call of our new age. It is an invitation to become:

A World-class Consumer: Educated. Ethical. Enlightened.

...

CB Blog   18

Consumer Wellbeing—It Takes Three To Tango!

Marketers bring us good products, mostly. Or, at least, products consumers desire. Occasionally, they sneak in products they know are harmful to consumers, which consumers wouldn't buy or consume if they knew the truth. Fortunately, such greed-driven, consumer-harming marketing practices are few and far between. Most marketers understand the brand-damaging consequences of deceitful marketing, and some are held in check by our governments.

Either way, our consumer life in most of the civilized world is infinitely worry-free because of a climate of responsible marketing and our public policy watchdogs. We should, as consumers, be thankful to our benevolent laws and our vigilant government agencies on the one hand, and our mostly conscientious, self-enlightened marketers on the other, for creating a climate of consumer trust. Sure, there are some unscrupulous marketers, but they are the proverbial exceptions that prove the rule.

Materialism, vanity, fast food—it is too easy to blame marketers for these consumer traits and gratifications. Yes, marketers advance them, but no more than our culture does in general—and definitely no more than consumers want, desire, and wish. These are not the gifts or curses of modern marketing, and they are not limited to Westernized nations.

Take India, for example. There, fast food is everywhere. Every block has a shop making, on site, high calorie, salty, spice-bomb samosas and kachoris, and sugar-syrup-soaked gulabjamuns. In restaurants and in homes, flat dough breads are deep-fried, and vegetable curries float in a sumptuous quantity of oils. (Ah, to partake of those dishes is heavenly!) "Fast food" is partially a misnomer, as is "junk food." The correct term should be fat, or fatty, food." Some foods that contain a lot of fat are fast, while some are junk; however, not all fast food is fatty. And a lot of "fat" food is, in fact, produced through laborious, creative cuisine. Every nation on earth is a "fat food" nation, and every culture is a "fat food" culture. It has always been this way, and it will always remain so.

Fortunately, in each culture and in every nation, fat food exists side by side the enclaves of bountiful, nutritious, salubrious edibles, both in nature and man-made.

The responsibility is clear: It takes three to t.a.n.g.o.—the conscientious marketer, a vigilant public policy, and a self-monitoring consumer. The world of goods offers a plethora of options, healthy and not so healthy, vane and modest, exorbitant and frugal, lustful and soulful. The choice is, ultimately, the consumers' to make.

Life is wonderful!

CONSUMER BEHAVIOR

SUMMARY

In this chapter, we covered three broad topic areas: questionable marketing practices, government regulation of marketing practices, and consumers' unethical behaviors. Among questionable marketing practices, we discussed (a) selling unsafe products, (b) unfair pricing, (c) misinformation and deception, and (d) intrusion and over-communication.

Product safety is closely monitored by the U.S. government's Consumer Product Safety Commission, in Canada by Health Canada, and in the UK by Health and Safety Executive (HSE), and most marketers ensure that products they sell are safe. Conscientious marketers voluntarily recall products if and when they are discovered to be unsafe. Unfair pricing is a practice where the seller charges a price to take advantage of a situation, a practice also called *price gouging*. Consumers suspect price gouging when the price is too high to be justified by possible costs, when it exceeds their "reference price," and when they see sellers exploiting a temporary situation. They also perceive unfair pricing if the price charged to them is disproportionately higher than the price usually charged to comparable other customers.

Misinformation and deception in advertising and selling takes the form of product benefit claims that are untrue or exaggerated. Deception in advertising and in selling messages is regulated by U.S. Government's Federal Trade Commission, and in the UK by Advertising Standards Agency (ASA).

The fourth practice, and last in our list, is intrusion and over-communication. By nature, advertising intrudes on our activity of the moment, and when repeated frequently (over-communication), it becomes irritating. Commercial messages also are criticized as a cause of materialism and corrupted values (instant gratification, obsession with one's body, etc.), a concern especially for advertising directed at children.

Next, we discussed the role of government in protecting the consumer. By regulation and laws, it mandates many of consumers' choices (e.g., wearing a helmet) and constrains others (can't smoke in public buildings, etc.). It also facilitates desirable consumption by making infrastructure facilities available (e.g., a biker's path on city streets). Finally, and most importantly, through its various agencies and laws, U.S. Federal Government, and then State Governments as well, monitor many marketer practices, guaranteeing four basic rights to consumers: the right to safety, the right to be informed, the right to be heard, and the right to choose. Similar laws exist in most other countries.

Of special concern are children as targets of commercial messages. In addition to government agencies, a self-regulatory organization called Children's Advertising Review Unit (CARU) of the Better Business Bureau (BBB) closely monitors advertising directed at children. Children are also protected online by a law enacted in April 2000, called Children's Online Privacy Protection Act (COPPA).

In the third and last section, we discussed consumers' own behaviors—unethical or self-damaging. We discussed five such practices: compulsive consumption, shop-lifting, feeding our bodies badly, reckless driving, and eco-unfriendly consumption. For the first three of these, we presented three-factor models, comprising consumer values and motivations as well as environmental facilitators/deterrents. For reckless driving, we presented recent scientific proof that the use of cell phones while driving is suicidal and therefore "very unwise." Finally for ecological consumption, we developed a comprehensive model wherein three fundamental factors (environment as a value, personal benefits/costs, and normative pressures) produce pro-ecology attitudes. To implement these attitudes into behavior, public infrastructure and marketplace solutions play a facilitative role.

Thus, for consumer wellbeing, and, in turn, marketers' as well, all three players in the marketplace—marketers, consumers, and public policy—need to have strong ethics.

KEY TERMS

Compliance
Compulsive buying
Compulsive consumption
Consumer Bill of Rights

Corrective advertising
Cyber privacy
Deceptive advertising
Impulse control disorder

Lemon law
Negligent consumer behavior
Price gouging
Verifiable benefit

YOUR TURN

REVIEW+Rewind

1. List the four marketing practices discussed in the chapter that could be harmful to consumers. Explain each briefly.

2. What factors lead consumers to infer the incidence of price gouging? What could marketers do to avoid consumers wrongly suspecting that they (the marketers) are engaging in price gouging?

3. Name the four approaches by which the government influences consumer behavior, and give an example of each.

4. Name some agencies involved in consumer protection. Then name some regulations or laws for the same purpose.

5. What four rights did President Kennedy's Consumer Bill of Rights give consumers?

6. How does FTC define deceptive advertising? And what is meant by "corrective advertising"?

7. List any five guidelines that COPPA has proposed.

8. List any five unethical consumer behaviors.

9. Explain the three factors in the three-factor theory of compulsive buying.

10. Draw the model of consumer shoplifting.

11. What factors lead to consumer obesity? Which of these factors is the consumer (versus the marketer) responsible for?

THINK+Apply

1. Is consumer deception always to be blamed on the marketer? Are consumers also to blame? Why or why not?

2. Why do some thinkers consider advertising a bad thing? Do the issues in those criticisms bother a typical consumer? Why or why not?

3. List any three negligent consumer behaviors. Then propose an action plan to reduce their incidence. Think of actions for each party: public policy, the marketer, and the consumer him/herself.

4. List any five unethical consumer behaviors you are aware of from your everyday life. Next suggest what could be done to motivate the consumer away from these behaviors.

5. Review the model of consumer shoplifting. Then write a memo for the management of a mall on possible actions to reduce shoplifting in their malls.

PRACTICE+Experience

1. Interview a few consumers about their personal experiences with price gouging. Next ask them, for each specific instance, what made them conclude that the vendor (or marketer) was price-gouging.

2. Interview a few consumers to ask what sort of behaviors they would consider unethical on the part of consumers. Ask them if they personally know of any incidents of unethical consumer behaviors. Then ask them why, in their opinion, some consumers engage in these behaviors. Summarize your findings.

3. Interview a few consumers (if possible, overweight consumers) about their concerns about the growing obesity problem? Next obtain their views about the extent to which the consumer versus fast-food chains and food marketers, in general, are responsible. Ask them if they are aware of nutrition information now available on Web sites of individual fast-food chains and in the restaurants, and if they use it and why or why not? Ask them why consumers in general may not use such information? Summarize your findings.

In the Marketing Manager's Shoes

Put yourself in a marketing manager's shoes. Most concepts in the chapter have some lessons for the marketing manager, i.e., they suggest what to do differently in practice; indeed, often these applications are implicit in our explanations of the concepts and models in the chapter. Identify at least five specific applications of the chapter's concepts, all of which should be entirely new, different from the examples cited here.

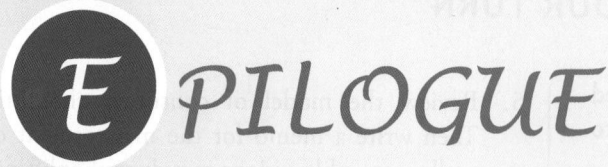

EPILOGUE

Marketing Meets the Consumer

Insight, Foresight, and the Marketer Response

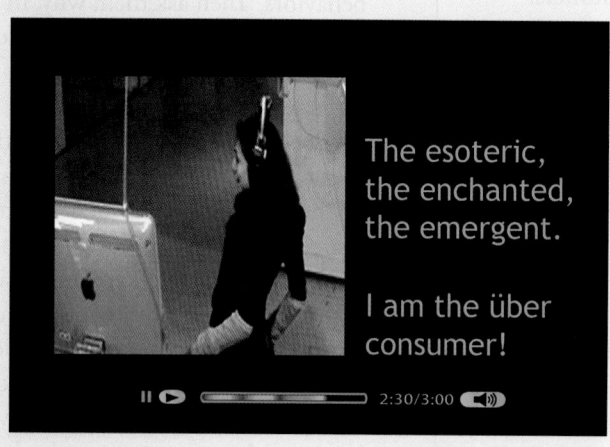

The esoteric,
the enchanted,
the emergent.

I am the über
consumer!

2:30/3:00

LEARN . APPLY . EXPERIENCE

OBJECTIVES

1 Segmentation and Target Identification

2 5Ps of Marketing

3 Deep Consumer Profiling

4 The Concept of Personalization

5 CB-Informed Marketer Response Strategy

6 A Glimpse into the Future World of Consumption

Consumer Insights and The Marketer's Response

Now that we understand consumer behavior, the inevitable question is, how can we put all this knowledge to use to serve the consumer better? As customer-oriented marketers, we already know that we serve our business interests best by satisfying the consumer. Understanding consumer behavior—how consumers seek and obtain happiness in the marketplace—should enable us to fashion a marketing program that accords with our target consumers' modes of thinking, feeling, and acting. To satisfy consumers, marketing programs must respond well to consumers' motivations and needs, their hopes and aspirations, and their identities and life projects. In this section, we develop some key ideas for a consumer-behavior informed, responsive marketing program.

Basically, from a consumer behavior standpoint, there are three parts to a marketing planning project: (a) segmentation and target identification, (b) deep consumer profiling, and (c) responsive offering presentation. (See Figure E1.) First, because no marketer can satisfy and serve all consumers, we must recognize salient differences among consumers and identify the consumer segments we can serve best (through segmentation and targeting). Next, we should research and understand consumer behaviors of the chosen groups (through deep consumer profiling). Finally, we must create offerings (e.g., products or services, pricing, and associated messages) that respond well to our target consumers' world-views (responsive offering presentation). Let us look at each.

FIGURE E1 THREE STEPS TO MARKETING RIGHT

MY **CB** BOOK

SEGMENTATION AND TARGET IDENTIFICATION

Some differences between consumers are obvious; for example, age, sex, race, income, education, social class, and geographic location. Collectively known as demographics (described in Chapters 14 and 15), these form the first bases for segmenting consumers. The next set of characteristics pertains to psychographics, and, in Chapter 6, we have covered some well-known psychographics-based segmentation schemes such as VALS™ and PRIZM. Many research companies offer other, country-specific psychographic segmentation schemes; as a marketer, you should avail yourself of these, and choose the one that seems most appropriate. Beyond these established ways of segmenting the market, virtually any of the other consumer characteristics discussed in this book can be used to segment your market: values, motives, perceptions, attitudes, loyalty, and involvement, among others.

Take values. Values can segment consumers into those who are materialistic versus those who are not; pro-lifers versus pro-choicers; environmentalists; consumers who value animal rights; and nationalists versus globalists. All can be useful in defining segments. In terms of motivation, consumers may differ on where they fall on Maslow's hierarchy. Product-specific motivations could also differ. For example, some consumers might buy a motorcycle as a more economical means of transportation than a car; others might buy one to experience outdoor adventure and the thrill of the ride; and still others might want one as a badge of a particular lifestyle. Consumers may also be classified as those with low involvement versus those with high involvement; those who are brand (or store) loyal versus those who are not; knowledgeable versus novice consumers; those who have "recognized a problem" versus those who have not; avid information seekers versus information minimizers; technophiles versus technophobes; net-surfers versus non-surfers; those who love to shop versus those who dread shopping; and so on.

These and many other concepts covered throughout the book are all useful bases for segmenting your market. Contemplating all of these criteria may appear to be an arduous task, but identifying the right consumer segment to serve is a singularly important responsibility in marketing planning. Admittedly, segmentation is less important if your product is one that can be mass-marketed. On the other hand, if you want to identify a niche market or an emergent market, contemplating and evaluating all of these consumer differences can be a very fruitful exercise. The benefit of reading this book is that you are now aware of a comprehensive list of variables by which to segment your target consumers.

DEEP CONSUMER PROFILING

Once you have identified your target market segment you must now prepare a comprehensive, deep profile of this segment. By *comprehensive deep profile*, we mean a description of as many of the consumer concepts as possible, as covered in this book. For example, suppose that your target segment consists of college seniors from upper middle-class families in metropolitan areas with a cosmopolitan outlook. Now, for this segment, describe everything: their values, motivations (e.g., achievement- or ego-needs), their lifestyles, and their activities and interests. For example, what kinds of music do they like? Are they into fine arts, fine wines, dining, sports, or community volunteering? What is their culture, their ethnic identification, and their self-concept? What are their life themes, and what are some of their current life projects? Also, describe their perceptions about the marketplace, your product category, your brand, and competitor brands. Is this product category one of high or low involvement to them? How knowledgeable are they about this product category and about your brand? In what ways do they see the product as related to their life themes? What are their reference groups? And which reference groups do they consider relevant, and from whom do they seek influence when selecting a brand from your product category? What specific product benefits are they seeking? What are their evaluation criteria? Which brands are in their evoked and consideration sets? What is their attitude toward your brand, on all three of the attitude components (know, feel, do)? Are they comparison shoppers, impulse buyers, coupon clippers? And so on.

To prepare such a profile, you will need to do in-depth consumer research. Initially, qualitative research using focus groups and in-depth interviews may be used. These may be followed by large-scale quantitative studies. If your product typically engages hedonic, social, and identity (rather than exclusively utilitarian) product values, then you may also want to deploy creative research methods such as visual collage construction or ethnographic studies (see Appendix 1). In essence, you are preparing a dossier on your target consumers. Such in-depth profiling might in turn reveal important sub-segments, and you must, naturally, recognize them and profile them individually. You may also revisit your decision to target or not to target a specific segment or sub-segment in the first place.

Actually, *targeting* might be a misguided term, notwithstanding its use in marketing for more than four decades. A better term would be *frame-forming*. "Targeting" implies that consumers are the target (as in a bull's eye). What marketers need to do instead is to adjust their *frame of view*, and to bring the consumer into the frame so they (marketers) can then keep the consumer in focus. Mere semantics? Actually, no. Labels do reflect our implicit view of a phenomenon, and, in turn, they guide (and misguide) our actions themselves.

RESPONSIVE OFFERING PRESENTATION

The third and final step is *responsive offering presentation*. By "offering," we mean the product or service with all its associated entities—its branding, packaging, assortments, warranties, prices, distribution channels, and advertising messages. The so-called "augmented product," that is. This offering must be responsive to all of the elements of the deep profiles you will have prepared—responsive to how consumers think, feel, and act. Essentially, this entails planning the 5Ps of marketing—four of which are classic, and the fifth a recent realization. Let us briefly discuss each.

Fashioning 5Ps of Marketing

Product The principal instrument of creating consumer satisfaction is the product. For established consumer needs, product design should create configurations that best meet the needs of target consumers. In a car, for example, do your target consumers want fuel economy or high performance, style or comfort? What amenities do they want? Many needs are latent, but placing yourself in the consumers' proverbial shoes and making keen observations can suggest products for hitherto unmet needs—this is how teeth whitening strips or Torrid stores for plus-sized teenage girls were conceived. Observing consumers' changing lifestyles can also uncover needs for new services such as speed-dating or SleepStream (an app for iPhone).

Pricing Several characteristics of the psychological makeup of your target consumers should inform your pricing decisions. Price should obviously be set at a level your target consumers can afford, based on their income. Beyond that, a product's desired image (e.g., economy or prestige) affects pricing. Consumers' reference price and price-quality associations also dictate pricing levels. If the target segment is price-sensitive and given to

Three Steps

SEGMENTATION & TARGET IDENTIFICATION

to

DEEP CONSUMER PROFILING

Marketing

RESPONSIVE OFFERING PRESENTATION

RIGHT

comparison-shopping, then the prices would have to be set at competitive levels. The more the product is bought for reasons beyond the utilitarian, the less price-sensitive consumers are. Likewise, the more the product plays a role in consumers' life-themes, the less price-sensitive the consumer is. Less price sensitivity means consumers are willing to pay more for intangible dimensions of the product or service, such as the prestige of the brand.

Place Marketers have a choice of a wide array of retail stores and distribution channels. Through classical conditioning, the image of the store rubs off on the product and brand; and, conversely, the brand's image rubs off on the store. That is why Target (a U.S.-based department store company) has commissioned renowned artist Philippe Starck to create signature merchandise exclusively for itself, and why Sears/K-Mart stores carry the Martha Stewart brand. The reciprocal conditioning between product image and store image occurs primarily for products with social and ego-identity value components (e.g., clothing, accessories), but not noticeably for primarily utilitarian products (e.g., appliances). Stores themselves carve out their personae through atmospherics, making them more or less inviting for browsers. In making place decisions, marketers also need to decide if they should sell their products on the Web—either exclusively, or in addition to bricks-and-mortar stores. Likewise, bricks-and-mortar stores need to decide if they should have a storefront on the Web as well. This depends, in large part, on whether or not the target market is net-savvy.

Promotions Promotions, as you know, consist of personal selling, publicity, sales promotions, and advertising. In personal selling, one of the most significant factors is whether the consumer looks to the salesperson as an informational and expert referent or, alternatively, as an identificational referent. Furthermore, the salesperson's product knowledge should dovetail with customers' own product knowledge levels and should complement their need for more information. Sales promotions are a valuable tool for *attracting* deal-seeking consumers, but their periodicity and predictability should be managed so as not to create an enduring expectation in the consumer's mind. *Publicity* is non-advocate communication (i.e., independent of the marketer), either in the mass media (e.g., a newspaper article on the brand) or through person-to-person word-of-mouth. Because dissatisfied consumers talk (and they talk more than do satisfied consumers), it is imperative for marketers to resolve consumers' dissatisfaction, for example, through effective service recovery. Beyond that, advertising in newsworthy ways itself creates publicity (or *buzz*, if you will); for example, CBS's Egg-writing—a laser-inscribed program promo short text, such as *CSI: Crack the Case on CBS*—or a TV commercial by Honda wherein a very voice-talented choir simulates, using only their mouths, the aural and sensory experience of driving a Honda.

Advertising (or, speaking more broadly, marketing communications) is also the field in which consumer behavior concepts most intimately influence marketing practice. Different media reach different consumers, defined both in terms of demographics and psychographics (e.g., *Self* magazine for image-focused teenage girls, and *Men's Health* magazine for fitness-obsessed adult men). Within the ad itself, the persons shown using the product should be similar to the target consumers in both demographics and lifestyle. Brand advertising should even capture the desired mood and the attitude of the prospective consumer. Celebrities must be carefully chosen to serve as a type of referent (namely, informational or identificational) that your target segment is seeking. The specific appeal itself must be determined through a careful consideration of the total consumer profile. It has to be congruent with the consumer's culture (e.g., individualistic or collective), address the consumer's motives, help bolster his or her self-concept, be an instrument of identity projection, and create the kind of brand relationship the target consumer seeks. If the consumer has misconceptions, then the firm should set out to correct them. If the consumer has no brand knowledge, then the marketer should focus on imparting that knowledge. If consumer cognitions about the brand are already adequately and truthfully formed, then advertising should move toward creating emotions and feelings by attaching some element of feeling to the product (see Chapter 7, *Romancing the Consumer: Rational Brands Go Emo!*).

5Ps of Marketing

- PRODUCT
- PRICE
- PLACE
- PROMO-TION
- PERSONAL-IZATION

Advertising also should be fashioned according to the diverse levels of consumer involvement—more visual, with banner copy for low-involvement consumers, and a detailed product story for high-involvement consumers. Marketers should also harness the enthusiasm and interest of highly involved consumers in order to build brand communities by organizing brandfest events (as does Chrysler for Jeep, among others).

Personalization Personalization refers to how a business organization treats an individual consumer—as a number, or as a person. This is the "how" dimension of business transactions. It is most pertinent to the consumer-marketer interface, the interaction between the consumer and the marketer. Whether that interaction is face-to-face or via telecommunications, consumer-initiated or marketer-initiated, pre-purchase or post-purchase, it should be functional (meets consumers' needs), efficient (minimizes consumer inconvenience and costs), and socially rewarding (addresses the consumer's need to feel respected and valued as a person). Functionality, efficiency, and social reward are judged, of course, from the consumer's point of view, not the marketer's. Interactive Voice Response (IVR) systems might be efficient from the marketer's point-of-view, but if they force the consumer into a mile-long nested menu, then, from the consumers' point-of-view, they constitute a negative value. (See *Valuespace*, McGraw-Hill, 2001; www.myvaluespace.com.)

Once the consumer is connected with a real human (see www.gethuman.com, described in Chapter 12), the challenge is even greater—the live human should be, well, *human*. She/he should have good listening skills, be knowledgeable about the product, and, most importantly, genuinely enjoy people.

Everything in this book about consumers will help a marketer fulfill this role responsibility. Consumers experience approach-avoidance conflicts; they make attributions (e.g., "Why is this salesperson recommending this option?"); they make quick inferences and form distorted perceptions; they need mnemonics to remember market information; they need recognition cues to recall a brand message (aided recall); they sometimes enter the marketplace trying to form evaluation criteria (therefore, don't push them toward a quick decision); they enjoy browsing. To get information, women approach the salesperson quickly, while men like to discover it on their own. And most important, rather than being persuaded, consumers persuade themselves. Review these concepts in the book from time to time, as you plan your marketing programs to connect with your consumers. The utility of re-reading about various consumer behavior concepts in this book can never be overemphasized. After all, the purpose of a marketing program is not merely to go through the routine, or to see that the system runs efficiently, or to play the standard script. Instead, it is to *satisfy* the consumer. The consumer—the curious, engaged, distracted, bored, hassled, anxious, confident, risk-averse, venturesome, task-focused, playful and spontaneous, self-doubting, motivated, unmotivated, minimally involved, enduringly involved, angry, delighted, frugal, indulgent consumer, living out his/her self-concept, and seeking from the marketer products that will advance his or her current life projects.

To understand this consumer deeply, and then to innovate responsive offerings is, dear marketer, your sacred task. And it is also your grand opportunity to do well for yourself by doing well by the consumer. To prepare you for that task, we hope this book has served you well, and that it has given you reasons to revisit the many CB concepts illuminated herein.

KEY TERMS

Frame Forming
Personalization
Deep consumer profiling
Responsive offering
   presentation

CB Blog

DEAR MARKETER: ROMANCE YOUR CONSUMERS ANEW

*A*s a marketing manager, and now armed with all this knowledge about the consumer, how do you feel? Kind of Mel Gibson-esque power (as in WHAT WOMEN WANT) to read the consumer mind and manipulate it to your advantage? Gloating because you now know exactly how to classically condition the consumer mind, to engineer consumer attitudes, to harness consumers' reference groups, and to mastermind their decision processes? That is (recall from Chapter 1) the old-fashioned, selling-oriented view of marketing. The new customer-oriented view is that the purpose of marketing is to create and present an offering that will meet consumer needs and create genuine value for the consumer.

In this view, consumer knowledge empowers the marketer, not to manipulate, but to respond to the consumer's strivings and wishes; to their modes of thinking and feeling, to their common values. In this view, consumers accept classical conditioning when the brand is paired with the symbols they want the brand to have; they embrace the brand's intended social image if it conforms to their idea of what is currently cool. And it is they who choose (beforehand and independent of marketing) what reference groups, what social icons, what cultural divas they will adore. What marketers can do is, simply but importantly, respond.

In this latter perspective, marketers place themselves on the side of consumers. Together, they try to create solutions to consumer problems, offerings that deliver values consumers seek—captured in the acronym USER (Chapter 1). It is this partnership that the study of consumer behavior in this book has, we hope, prepared you for. Both in terms of skills and knowledge as well as in terms of perspective and world-view.

Marketing is not about outsmarting the consumer. It is, rather, about casting your company, your product, your brand in the consumers' image. It is about making your brand offerings (5Ps) more adorable, from the consumer's vantage point. It is about creating products and services, and crafting the symbolic images to accompany them, that bring consumers real value—tangible and intangible, material as well as fantastic, in ways that promote their physical, social, and psychological wellbeing.

The only legitimate mission of marketing is, or should be, to create real value for the consumer. Understanding consumer behavior helps us grasp the quintessential value of consumption and to understand how we should, as marketers, fulfill marketing's ultimate purpose: to become co-creators of the consumption value humans seek.

Let us commence this journey anew, with a new zeal to serve our new consumer-emergent, empowered, enchanted.

MY CB BOOK .COM

REVIEW+Rewind

1. What do the following terms mean:
   (a) Personalization, (b) deep consumer profiling, and (c) frame forming.
2. Describe some bases of segmenting a market.
3. Briefly explain the three-step process described in the chapter for marketers to apply this book's lessons.

Welcome to the World of Future Consumption

Before we conclude the Chapters portion of the book, we bring you some news on future consumption possibilities.

You have already read in this book about several new technologies that are enabling and empowering the consumer in new ways. You have read about augmented reality—point your mobile phone camera toward, say, a pub, and you can view its menu, for example. You have read about Zaarly, which is eBay in reverse, and with bidding windows set in minutes, not days—request anything you need here and now, say within the next 30 minutes and receive real time bids from sellers! Web-based company Zazzle promises to enable you to custom-design anything, literally anything! And using social media, you can connect to anyone in the world, continents away.

Technology is going to change our world of consumption in still other ways. Let us review them briefly.

First, the future consumer is going to be Internet savvy, even in Third World countries. Foretelling this are not just the MySpace and FaceBook generation teens, but also some innovative projects designed to bridge the "big divide" between the "have" and "have not" nations. One example: a project in India by a technology training company named NITT; organized under the aegis of its Cognitive Research Team, the project is called *Hole in The Wall Project*. The company's office complex sits in the middle of a slum near New Delhi, separated by a wall. One day, NITT's chairman, Sugata Mitra, got an idea. He cut a hole in the wall, placed in it a computer screen facing the slum side, turned on the Internet, and watched quietly. Within hours, kids from the slum neighborhood were learning to surf the net on their own. So he formulated a plan to put Internet computer kiosks in poor neighborhoods in Delhi. Now the project has been embraced by the government and is expanding to other states. And children who don't even go to school are learning a wealth of information. Assuming 200 children learn from each Kiosk over, say, the next five years, there will be, among the very poor in India, 100 million otherwise unschooled but computer-literate children!

Second, technology-suffused consumption is going to make waves. The doorways that opened automatically on Star Trek's Enterprise Ship, for example, will someday be abundantly in use. Already Tanaka of Japan is offering a door that opens as you approach it, not only automatically, but also exactly in the size of your silhouette—you see, the slates slide out individually to accommodate your body but nothing more. This technology can help isolate a room from outside elements (hot or cold air, dirt, insects, bacteria, etc.), maximize privacy, and make possible more aesthetically appealing doorways.

Then again, wearable technology is making big strides. This is taking two directions: (a) technological functions woven into clothing, such as cell phones, viewing screens, body condition/health monitors, etc., and (b) experiential clothing—clothing that enables hedonic and sensational wearing experiences. First,

Kinetic dress—the outer skirt develops blue circles as the wearer interacts with other people.
(photo courtesy CuteCircuit)

consider the functions woven into clothing. One such product is the accessory nerve.

Accessory Nerve is a sleeve-like textile device that you wear on your sleeve. Its embedded technology connects to your mobile phones (via Bluetooth). When you receive a phone call, the phone won't ring; instead the sleeve will form a pleat pattern, each pattern distinct for a pre-programmed caller. That way you will know who is calling. If you are in a meeting, you simply flatten the pleats, and the caller will get a text message saying, "I'll call you back later." The accessory nerve allows users to exchange information and greetings in a subtle and intimate way. The device is in prototype development at Cute Circuit. (See picture.)

Among experiential clothing products, you've already read about the Hug Shirt (Chapter 1). The same company (Cute Circuit) is experimenting with other ideas. Among them:

The Kinetic Dress The dress closely follows the body of the wearer. When seated and alone, it is black; then as the wearer moves and interacts with others, blue, luminescent embroidery patterns begin to appear. It even creates a halo around the wearer.

The Mystique Dress This dress follows closely the mood of the wearer, depending on the context. In the beginning, as soon as you wear it, let us say in the morning, it is a short, knee-length, pale gray. Later as the day dawns, it begins to lengthen and show strands of red. By evening, it is a full-length, totally red dress.

Another kind of experiential technology will be embedded in public environments. An intriguing example of this is a product currently in development, called Embedded Theater (ET). ET will allow you to experience your surroundings (say, a street scene) in a new way: the objects and persons in your vicinity will begin to speak to you, or you will hear imaginary conversations as if they are coming from people you are seeing on the street at the moment.

With this technology, you wear a headset with sensors and a belt with embedded wireless network capabilities. Then, as you move through a city, the system receives audio files that are dynamically adjusted in volume to create a "tridimensional audioscape," depending on the direction of your gaze or on the objects you are viewing. The system understands your location in the environment, and the sensor understands the direction in which you are looking. It then creates a fictional audio landscape, in three-dimensions, that corresponds exactly to real-world objects and locations. For example, as you walk to the right of a statue, you might hear the statue whispering in your left ear; turning to look at the statue, the sound would now be in front of you. Or, you could hear a conversation in the street between two people that took place three hundred years ago. The path you take and the places you explore will actively affect the course of the narrative, so that you will experience your environment like never before.

Embedded Theater, ET (photo courtesy CuteCircuit)
(www.cutecircuit.com)

One last thing. Consumers in all countries are going to get more exposure to diverse cultures of the world. Barring some countries, whose politics and policies will keep them isolated, the future consumer is going to become more and more global.

It is in the human psyche that consumers will forever seek novel experiences. Marketers must constantly innovate "offerings" that produce these experiences. This is the marketers' challenge. And their privilege.

Welcome to the fascinating world of future consumption!!

SPECIAL TOPICS

PSYCHOLOGY MEETS ECONOMICS:

Why Consumers Can't Count Their Money Correctly

Priya Raghubir, Stern School of Business, New York University

Consumers feel happier if they discover that the complimentary ticket they received was priced at $200 rather than $100. They see greater value in two 10% discounts than in a single 20% discount. And they buy a $200 appliance placed next to a $220 model but not when it is placed next to a $180 model. Economics calls these consumer behaviors "irrational." Psychology considers them "normal." This paper illuminates why.

The "Irrational" Consumer Goes to Market

Barbara and Jenny, two friends, both traveled on frequent flyer miles from San Francisco to New York over Spring break. During the flight, Barbara found out that the person sitting next to her had paid $475 for his ticket; Jenny found out that the person in the seat next to her had paid $936. Later, when they told each other about this, Barbara felt sad: "I am always unlucky. I saved only a half of what you saved"!

Vicky had always wanted a pashmina scarf. In her local store they sold for US $99.0. When she went to India she found the same scarves selling for 500 Rupees each (approximately US $9.99). She was delighted and bought herself a pale pink scarf. She took pleasure in knowing that she spent only $10. Her friend, Christie, on her trip to India went to an upscale store where the prices were displayed in U.S. dollar currency. There, she found the scarves selling for $19.99 and bought three of them. Back home, Vicky was kicking herself for not having bought more scarves; Christie, on the other hand, could barely contain her joy.

Geeta and Rita, two friends in college, always hung out together. When they went out shopping or clubbing, they would always buy each other coffee, beer, or lunch, in turn—ignoring small price differences between what each bought for the other. Once, they went on a vacation together to Europe. There, suddenly, they started accounting for every penny they paid for each other's meal or drink, ensuring that in the end, they evened out. Back in the USA, they resumed their old pattern![1]

Barbara, Vicky, and Geeta. Three perfectly rational consumers. Just like you and me. Yet, their behavior in the above episodes is, from an economics point-of-view, totally irrational. A free plane seat is a free plane seat, period. So why should it matter (to Barbara) how much a fare paying passenger paid for it? The price of a scarf marked in rupees was, when converted in dollars before buying it, still only $9.99, so why did it not seem (to Vicky) a deal enough to buy more than one unit of the highly desired scarves. And, the fellow vacationer (Rita) is the same friend, so why should the joint consumption, and paying for it in turn, change (for Geeta) from one of mutual friendly favors to bean counting?

It is clear that economic theory fails to explain these everyday behaviors of consumers. In this chapter we draw on current and classical theories of consumer psychology to understand how consumers act in the marketplace when they are deciding whether or not to pay, and how much to pay, for a product or service. Our main point is that both the prices on products and the money that consumer have are valued subjectively.

What is money? Does money in another shape, size, color, or form feel different? Is it spent differently? Saved differently? Recalled differently? Stored differently?

What are prices? Does a price communicated using another set of words or numbers or currency feel more or less expensive? Does the sequence in which a price is seen before or after other prices, or before or after information about the product or service, affect how attractive or unattractive it appears?

The anecdotes above suggest that the answer to all these questions is a resounding, unequivocal "Yes!" We invoke psychological rules to explain how consumers process information when they are making economic transactions. These rules draw on psychological concepts covered earlier in the book, as applied to the domain of money and prices.

PERCEPTION

As you understood from the chapter on perception (Chapter 3), we do not perceive an object or its price, *objectively*. Rather, we perceive it *subjectively*. Therefore, the object or price perceived depends on the context and on us, the perceiver. This subjectivity in perception entails many biases in our perception. To understand these biases, let us review a few additional consumer episodes, in the Box titled PSYCH RULES. Read them now, and pause for a minute to contemplate whether you would have acted differently. Done? Okay, read on.

REFERENCE POINTS

One of the most influential ideas in how people perceive money and prices is the idea that their values are not an absolute, but are based on a "reference point" against which they are evaluated.[2] That is why:

- **A free ticket evaluated against a full price ticket of $936 will seem to be a much greater benefit to the consumer than the same ticket valued against a full price ticket of $475.**

PSYCH RULES !

■ Bob and Jay liked going out Friday night for a beer at the beach. They would happily pay $5 for a pint at the hotel bar which had a balcony facing the ocean, but hated paying the same price for the same beer at the beachside kiosk that was right on the beach!

■ Allan was planning a trip to Vegas. He was going to be staying with friends, and wanted to get the cheapest flight possible. He narrowed his options down to two flights that cost the same: one with a free hotel night stay over but a less convenient departure time; and the other with a slightly better departure time, but no additional free hotel. Despite the less convenient times, and a friend's apartment being available to stay, Allan took the first offer!

■ Lisa's mother used a special "age-defying" cream that Lisa would buy for her for Mother's Day. But she would always wait for the brand to offer a "free gift," which comprised a set of six items like a lipstick, etc. The thing was that Lisa (and her mother) rarely used any of the products they received in the free gift hamper, but Lisa still liked to wait for the sale before making her purchase and always inspected her free gift packet carefully! On one occasion, she had got a free full sized lipstick that was in a color she never wore. While the brand made a number of other lipsticks in her preferred shades, she hesitated buying them at full price after that.

■ Michael and Ben, two students of economics, both liked to shop on price. But while Michael was more satisfied the more he had paid for a pair of shoes, Ben was happier when he had purchased it on sale. Ben was particularly happy when he saw that the "regular price" advertised against the sale price he had paid was higher than what Michael had paid for his shoes!

■ Ed and Tom, dormmates, friends, and competitors in college, both started a similar job after graduating. Ed got the job in his college town. Tom got a job in a big city where, as both Ed and Tom knew, the cost of living was higher by at least 20% than in their college town. When Ed saw his offer of $60,000 p.a., he was delighted about making a "real" salary. However, when his dormmate, Tom, told him he was being paid $65,000, Ed's euphoria evaporated!

These anecdotes are taken from the author's research files.

- An annual salary of $60K seems high when evaluated against a student stipend; but when evaluated against a friend's salary of $65K, it appears to be low. This is despite the fact that in real terms (adjusting for cost of living) the lower salary in a lower-cost city will buy more.
- A sale price evaluated against a regular price will seem a better value than the sale price just on its own.
- A $5 pint of beer will appear to be more affordable when purchased from an expensive hotel than from a cheap beachside kiosk.

So, you see, change the reference points, and perceptions change!

How Reference Points are Formed

You might now ask, where do these reference points come from? Consumers acquire these reference points in many different ways.[3] They can be based on:

- One's past experience (as in the example of Ed assessing his salary against his student stipend, or Sandy not buying the spa treatment at a higher price).
- One's knowledge of what others pay (as in the example of Jenny feeling that her frequent flyer purchase was a better deal).
- One's knowledge of what other vendors or stores offer for the same price (as in the case of Allan being tempted to choose the less convenient flight time to get the offer with a free hotel room that he would not use).
- Consumers' beliefs as to what is fair (as in the case of Bob and Jay feeling ripped off by the beachside kiosk charging the same price for a beer as the adjacent hotel, since they know that the kiosk's costs of operation are much lower than the hotel's operational costs).
- Consumer expectations of what the product would be available for eventually (as in the case of Lisa waiting for the sale to buy her mother's gift).

The useful thing to know for students of consumer psychology is that many of these reference points come from marketers.[4] The manner in which a consumer perceives your price is determined to a large extent by how you communicate the price. See box, "How Marketers Create Reference Points."

The interesting thing is that consumers actually view the same amount spent for the same product as a "gain" when they pay less than their reference point; and they view it as a "loss" when they pay more than their reference point. No matter how natural it seems to you, economics calls this behavior "irrational." Psychology explains why it is but natural for us to perceive and react this way!

How Marketers Create Reference Price Points

■ Manufacturer's suggested retail price: MSRP ....
■ Past or regular price information: Was .... Now ....
■ Competitor's Price .... Our price ....

Why Is My Loss More Than Your Gain?

Here is another interesting phenomenon. To most consumers, the joy of a five dollar "gain" is less than the felt pain of a five dollar "loss!" How come? The law of asymmetry, technically called *prospect theory*, explains it.[5]

Prospect Theory suggests that the perceived disutility (that is, "pain") of a loss is greater than the perceived utility (that is, "joy") of a gain of the same amount. Let's see how it translates into everyday consumer decisions.

MARKETING IMPLICATIONS

Marketers can put Prospect Theory to good use.[6] Here is how:

1. TWO SMALLER GIFTS ARE BETTER THAN ONE LARGE GIFT: That is, rather than offering a single gift, i.e., a single lump sum "gain," offer the same amount in two or more separate rewards. The value the consumer will assign to two separate rewards, A and B, will be higher than the value they will assign to the reward C (where C = A+B). Likewise, two coupons for 10% discount each would be valued more by consumers than a single 20% discount coupon. Even more noteworthy, two sequential half discounts will be valued more than a single discount. Thus, if an item costs, say, $100, then two sequential discounts of 10% will result in a net price of $81, compared to the net price of $80.0 with a single discount of 20%; however, consumers are likely to perceive the former a better value than the latter!

2. BUNDLING THE PRICE: If two items are priced at $50 and $25, then it is better to bundle them and sell them at $75. Why? You see, to a consumer a price is a "loss." And having to incur a loss twice is more painful than incurring a loss once. (This is the mirror opposite of "gaining two rewards is more pleasurable than gaining one of same total value.") By the same logic, if a credit card company has to impose a late fee of, say, $25 and a returned check fee of $29, then it is better to bundle them into a single invoice for $54. The $54 fees can still be itemized, but knowing of them (and paying them) in a single transaction is better than knowing of them at two separate points in time.

3. DEDUCT TAX AT SOURCE: Prospect theory would also imply that if consumers have to pay tax on their income after receiving the income, it will hurt them more than paying tax at the time of receiving the income, i.e., receiving a net income. You now know why it is painful for restaurant waiters who receive a bulk of their income without any tax withheld at source to declare the whole amount of their income in tax filings. Luckily, sales tax is deducted at source, and it is just as well with consumers.

4. CHARGE MORE NOW, REBATE IT LATER (SILVER LINING): A final implication of prospect theory is that when there is a large loss (e.g., as in the case of a high price that a consumer needs to pay) with a small gain (e.g., a discount), then separating the gain (e.g., in the form of a cash back offer or money back) would lead to greater utility than netting the gain out from the cost (as the benefit of receiving the gain is greater than the reduction in the disutility due to a lower price). To illustrate: Suppose an item costs $100, and the seller is prepared to sell it for $80.

Then, rather than giving an instant cash discount of $20, it is better to charge the full price and then let the consumer receive $20 in a cash rebate. This is because the pain of paying $100 is a little more than the pain of paying $80, but the joy of getting $20 back more than makes up for this small increase in initial pain. Yes, for the consumer, the pain of paying $80 now is *higher* than the pain of paying $100 now net of the pleasure of $20 cash rebate received later.

> To consumers, the joy of a five dollar "gain" is less than the pain of a five dollar "loss!"

Option 'A' Buy this item for $100 now, then receive $20 cash back.

Option 'B Buy it now for a discounted price of $80.

"I will take Option 'A'. I want my cash back."

REFERENCE POINTS AS ATTRACTION & COMPROMISE

Two applications of reference points are especially useful to marketers of multiple options in a product line.[7]

The Attraction Effect: Suppose a travel agent offers two packages to Las Vegas: Package 'A': air plus three nights in a four star hotel, priced at $299; Package 'B': air plus two nights in the same four star hotel, priced at $199. Now, suppose, the travel agent adds a third option, Option 'C': air plus two nights in a *three* star hotel, also priced at $199. What do you think would happen? Believe it or not, the sales of Option 'B' will receive a boost. This is because, to consumers, with Option 'C' as a reference, Option 'B' suddenly looks more attractive!

The Compromise Effect: Next, consider an option in a product line that is high quality and high priced (say, business class airfares), and a second option that is relatively lower priced and of relatively lower quality (say, economy class). If the company now introduces a third option that is priced still higher but is also of higher quality (e.g., first class seats), what do you think will happen now? The sales of the middle-priced option (e.g., business class seats) will increase! This is because, to the consumer, the business class fare now seems a good compromise option.

Unintended Reference Points: While attraction and compromise effects of reference points can be used by marketers to manage consumer perceptions of the price of their products, some other reference points created by marketers have unintended effects. Understanding these can help us avoid them.

a. Prevent Sale Price from Becoming a Reference Point A sale price works by inducing a consumer to buy because the consumer uses the regular price as a reference point. But when the item is often on promotion, the reverse happens: the consumer begins to use the sale price as a reference point, and, consequently, never buys on regular price.[8] Remedy: avoid frequent promotions. And offer them at irregular intervals.[9]

b. Make Comparisons Difficult Rather than offering the regular item on sale, create a somewhat different version of the same item for sale. Make a different package—different in color, size, etc. For example, if the regular item is 50 grams of a candy bar for 50 cent, offer a 40 gram bar for 30 cents, only during the promotion period. Or bundle two bars together and offer them for 80 cents. Or a limited time bundle with premium.

Furthermore, make the difference as vivid as possible. If you are a pizzeria for example, you could offer pizzas in three non-comparable forms: single servings as a triangular slice, those in an individual pie as a circle, and those in a large party pack as squares, making it more difficult for consumers to compare the sizes and prices across the three offerings.[10]

Extending this principle further, if you want consumers not to be able to use your competitors' price as a reference point, then differentiate your brand sufficiently from your competitors' brands. If differentiation in the core product itself is infeasible, at least differentiate it on superficial features such as package size and shape. Of course, follow the opposite strategy—make your brand look as similar as possible—when your price is advantageous.

MONEY ILLUSIONS

Reference points are one source of biased perception. The second source is what we will call *money illusions*. This takes three forms: 1. Visual appearance biases, 2. number reading biases, and 3. face value biases.

1. Visual Appearance Bias—Bigger Is Better

In our everyday life, we are exposed to money in certain shapes and sizes, and we get used to those shapes and sizes, valuing them more. And we inherently value larger numbers, larger sizes and larger shapes more. This inherent bias leads us to value money according to its form rather than its actual value. As a consequence:

a. Gift certificates or checks may be viewed as worth less than an equivalent amount in cash.[11]

b. Payments by a credit card may be perceived to be less painful than by cash. Buying food and paying five dollars on your cafeteria debit card is less painful than paying cash, or even than by a credit card.[12]

c. Amounts of a larger denomination are valued more and therefore may be less likely to be spent. That is, if you have a $50 bill, you may be less likely to buy anything than if you have, say, only a $10 bill.[13]

d. Notes (that are representative of higher denominations) are likely to be valued more than coins, leading to consumers spending coins more readily than bills. That is why many restaurants bring back "change" in coins and small notes, as they are more likely to be left as tips.

e. Monetary forms that are more colorful and less serious are likely to be spent more readily.[14]

f. Larger coins may be valued more than smaller coins (even when the latter are of higher value), especially by young children.[15]

2. Number Reading Biases

Left to right processing: Since we read from left to right, we tend to ignore the cents at the right most digits. This leads to the well-known effect of "99 cent pricing." This implies that a price of $3.99 is perceived to be cheaper than a price of $4.00. This also suggests that when discounts are offered they should be across the whole number. For example, if a product priced at $425 is to be discounted, it will be more effective to discount it to $399 than to discount it to $400. By the same token, offering a discount of $10 is more effective than offering a discount of $9.99.

3. Face Value Biases

Face value biases occur in that the face value of a price or currency influences us more immediately than the implicit real value.[16] This effect is most vivid in foreign currencies.[17]

A price of 200 units in a foreign currency feels much more than a price of, say, 120 units in our own currency, even if in monetary value the latter might be of much higher than the former. Now you know why Vicky could not bring herself to buy more than one 500 Rupees pashmina scarf; and why, once back in US, re-connected with the dollar currency, she regretted not having spent Rupees 1000.00 to 1500.00 buying those scarves.

PRICE As A SIGNAL

Why is it that consumers sometimes are happy paying a higher price; and, sometimes, unenthusiastic about buying a product at a reduced price? This is because they use price as a signal, to infer other things. Here is how signaling works:

Price as a Signal for Quality Often consumers don't have the expertise to judge a product's quality. In such cases, they use the product's price as a signal of quality.[18] That is why they are happier buying a more expensive item. Recall that Michael was happy even though he paid a lot for his shoes. From an economics point-of-view, consumers should be less willing to pay a higher price. However, from a psychological point of view, if consumers use high prices as a signal of high quality, then, they should be more willing to buy a high-priced product.

Conversely, consumers may use a lower price as a signal of low quality. If the promotion is steep, this too may backfire. If a product's regular price is, say, $1, and it is promoted at 50 cents, then consumers would infer that the product must cost less than 50 cents to make. At such a low cost, it may not be worth even 50 cents. So they would then never buy the product at its regular price, and may not even buy it at deeply discounted promotional prices.

The Emotional Side of Price

After reading through the rest of this book, it should come as little surprise to you that price also has an emotional side. That is, consumers experience some emotions when they pay a particular price rather than another.

a. Excitement of sweepstakes Consider the excitement of taking part in a sweepstake. Even though the economic value of a sweepstake may be mere pennies, the possibility, however small, that a person could win one big prize, adds feelings of excitement to the purchase. Therefore, promotions that are more exciting are better at generating sales than the regular "percentage off" or "dollar off" promotions that merely represent a reduction in the economic price that a consumer has to pay. Likewise, in an auction, the excitement fueled by winning a bid may lead consumers to over-pay (compared to the economic utility of that deal). The *fact* of winning leads to extra utility.

b. Feelings of self-worth Making an expensive purchase can make consumers freshly aware or cognizant that they can afford it and are therefore worth it. This is another reason why Michael may be happier paying a full price even if he knew that he could probably find a lower price elsewhere.

c. Feelings of smartness On the other hand, finding a deal and paying a lower price may help the consumer feel that he/she is smart.[19] This is the reason why Ben was happy with his purchase of shoes at the discounted price. The different ways in which Michael and Ben relate to prices is based on their individual differences: one appears to be insecure about his self-worth and needs the purchases he makes to reassure himself; the other appears, in contrast, to be less than secure about his smarts or feels guilty about buying himself indulgences, and, consequently, uses his purchases to reassure himself that they are good value.

d. Feelings of guilt In the domain of self-gifts, consumers often feel guilty about rewarding themselves with hedonic pleasures. This is one of the reasons that they would prefer to get something as a gift from another person, rather than buying it for themselves, as in the case of Tully who loved her gift of a spa treatment when she received it as a gift. Even though the funds would come from the same joint account, she would not allow herself to buy it for herself.

e. Feelings of embarrassment Frequently consumers may forego the satisfaction of positive emotions in order to avoid negative emotions, such as embarrassment, anxiety or uncertainty. Despite the fact that coupons are widely used, consumers may still feel embarrassed about using one at a checkout counter when there is a large line behind them; or at a dinner for Valentine's day; or for a gift for a special person. This is because they don't want to look cheap to others, and to the extent that the use of a coupon or promotion suggests that they are money-conscious, they may wish to avoid this impression by not using it.

Memory Games with Price

How much did I pay for that puppy in the window?

One of the reference points for price is the price in one's mind already. Actually, "in memory," we should say, since that is where all prior information is stored. Our memory often plays games when it comes to our recall of price.

One thing about memory is, as you read in Chapter 4, that there is a lot of information in it, and all of it is not equally easy to retrieve. Depending upon the situation, our memory recalls things selectively.

1. Low levels of price recall One of the most amazing findings was based on a field study where researchers asked consumers who had just placed an item in their shopping basket how much they had paid for it.[20] They found that as many as half of the consumers did not recall the price of the item minutes after they had placed it into their basket, even when they had purchased it on the basis of it being on deal or having a low price. Thus, there is evidence that price does not enter into the equation in the traditional manner that economists would argue that it does. Instead, consumers encode a price in broad categories such as a "good" price, or a "low" price, or a "bargain" or a "steal" or a "rip-off." They make their decisions on the information coded this way rather than on the actual price of the product. As a consequence then, what is needed for a promotion to induce

consumer purchase is that the promotional discount be just sufficient so as to be coded as a "good deal," and no more. Keeping this insight in mind, managers should not give away too much money in promotions, but rather should find the level worthy of the "it's a good deal" coding.

2. Biases in the recall of money Recent work in consumer psychology has shown that consumers have strong biases in their recall of how much money they have. The larger the denomination of a monetary instrument, the more accurate they are, but as the number of each note or coin increases, they underestimate the amount that they are carrying.

3. Biases in the recall of spending Can you recall how much you spent last month on your credit card bill? Or on your last vacation? The fact is that these are difficult tasks as they are made up of identifying individual transactions and then aggregating them. People can forget not only the fact of the transaction, but the amount of it. They are more likely to forget transactions that are infrequent, distant in time, small in value, and those associated with a lower pain of paying (e.g. by credit card). This could be one of the reasons why people overspend on their credit cards, as they lose track of their expenses.[21]

4. Biases in the recall of prices Finally, consumers are more likely to recall prices that stood out—these are likely to be the less expensive prices than they had searched for. Thus, prices of products on promotion may be better recalled overall than their regular prices.[22]

To summarize, memory biases in how people recall information can also lead to departures from traditional economic theory.

CONCLUSION:
THE IRRATIONAL CONSUMER—NOT THAT IRRATIONAL AFTER ALL

The way consumers think, act and feel in the marketplace is a function of psychological factors that go beyond our traditional understanding of economics. By accepting that consumer perceptions may be based on reference points and the effort they put into a decision, the fact that consumers use price as a signal of quality, that they use their feelings to make decision, and the fact that they do not use all the information at their disposal (either memory based, or available in their context) but use only a subset of it, which is then integrated in a manner that allows them to make a decision that is "good enough" rather than the best decision that they could make, one can get at a better understanding of why consumers react to prices the way they do. And that understanding can help marketers understand how to set and communicate prices so as to be in sync with the consumer's ways of encoding them.[23, 24]

Endnotes (on p. 531)

CONSUMERS in SEARCH of PROPER PLEASURE
How Brand Stories Help Consumers Enact Dramas in Their Lives

Arch G. Woodside, Boston College, USA

Consumers are hardwired to tell stories of their consumption. Through storytelling, consumers interpret, make sense of, and relive their original consumption experience. Such re-experiencing through storytelling, Aristotle calls "proper pleasure." Residing in our unconscious and behind these stories is an archetype—the hero of the story if you will. While brand communications often tell brand stories of their own, few rise to the level of successfully incorporating the archetypes specific consumers are trying to achieve—archetypes such as the hero, the anti-hero, or the rebel, for example.

We illustrate the role of such archetypes in brand communications though a brand consumption story about Versace and the archetype some consumers might well experience—namely, the siren, the seductress in a Versace coat. This story is vivid proof that archetypes are real, and it is an invitation to brand managers to become familiar with the repertoire of various archetypes, or else miss an opportunity to bring consumers "proper pleasure" they (the consumers) are seeking.

"So Where the Bloody Hell Are You?"

Thus asks the tag line in a new TV commercial campaign for Australian Tourism. The commercial shows vignettes uniquely available for experiencing in Australia. This tag line, and the commercial which employs it, was not invented in thin air. Rather, the Australian Tourism Board had done extensive consumer research. The tagline represents the "gist" of a story that the viewer of the TV commercial is supposed to learn and enjoy about the brand—Australia. In this essay, we will explain:

• How consumers build stories around brands they consume
• How these stories bring them "proper pleasure"
• How the telling and listening of stories helps them become mythical "heroes"
• How brand communications help, or can help, consumers experience their "proper pleasure," achievable through the realization of aspired mythical icons

Jung on Myths and Icons

According to psychologist Carl Jung, each of us has a mythical icon in our unconscious mind that we want to implement.[1] We may be a 16-year old regular teenager or a college student or a 40-year old dad of two, and that is how we think of ourselves most of the time. But existing often unconsciously in our psyche there is another image of ourselves—this image is sometimes an alter ego—different from our regular visible image, such as "accountant by day, cowboy by night"; or alternatively, it may be the extension of our regular self stretched out to its outer limits—e.g., a slightly altruistic person by day, Robinson Crusoe by night; or merely a shopper ostensibly, but a warrior deep within; or a soccer mom in casual appearance but Supermom inwardly. We live and relive these myth icons of self by reflective thoughts and by fantasizing about them, and by constructing these fantasies around our everyday chores and everyday consumptions. We build them also by narrating the stories to ourselves and to others, and in these narrations we sometimes stretch, embellish, dramatize, and give heroic qualities to everyday consumption experiences. Brands help us play out such myths. But by telling them first in drama-based ads, or in vignette-based narratives, brands also help us experience the stories vicariously.

While all archetypes exist in all of our psyches, each of us tends to enact a limited set of them in our lives—we tend to form scripts unconsciously, based in part on early personal experiences and the associations of these experiences with specific archetypes. Put simply, with experiences in our cultures, or from mythical stories prevalent in our cultures including movies, we become familiar with a set of mythical icons (e.g., the Superman) and then adopt one of those as our own alter-ego (our archetype).

How Consumers Experience Brand Stories

Myths have heroes. Likewise, all stories have a protagonist—the main character in the story. Often, they also have an antagonist—the character who blocks the mission of the protagonist. Eventually, the protagonist wins. This is recognized, in popular parlance, as the triumph of the hero over the villain.

Consumers both live the myth stories and then they tell them. They live these stories in that, modeling after the archetype in the myths, they try to enact the product drama, i.e., the drama surrounding the product's use, in a manner that will make them the protagonist in the related myth story. Living the stories enables consumers to achieve archetype outcomes: become Mr. Evil—an anti-hero—by donning a WWII helmet and a black leather jacket, and riding a Harley-Davidson motorcycle on a Saturday afternoon, even though this consumer might be an accountant five-days a week.

Next, after living the story during brand consumption, consumers try to tell the stories of their consumption. Let us closely consider four questions:

1. **Why do consumers tell stories?**
2. **How do the stories consumers tell illustrate the underlying myth icons?**
3. **What are the components of a good story?**
4. **What should brand managers do to help consumers tell stories?**

Q1. Why Do Consumers Tell Stories?

Humans (consumers) tell stories:

- To make sense as to what is happening and what has happened;
- To experience the inherent pleasure in telling and hearing stories; and
- To build in one's mind a repertoire of relevant myth icons—the icons one finds personally meaningful

Q2. How Do the Stories Employ Myth Icons?

Substantial research literature provides justification for storytelling theory in consumer psychology as well as for creating and testing the impact of storytelling in marketing contexts. This literature has confirmed that consumers often include products and brands in reporting their own lived experiences.[2] They frequently assign roles, actions, and relationships to brands in the stories they tell themselves and to others; brands in these stories are depicted as enablers of archetype myths.[3] For example, drinking Mountain Dew enables the slacker myth;[4] a **slacker** is a person rebelling against the dominant life themes of work and family—someone seeking to hang out and experience fun with friends at the expense of productive work.

Q3. What are the components of a good story?

Classical drama is almost always a good story. It includes several incidents increasing in excitement and suspense preceded by conditions/settings that initiate the unconscious/conscious identification of one or more goals. Actions by a protagonist and possibly by additional actors result in an outcome. Along the way, some obstacles prevent progress toward success. These obstacles and the struggle against them serve to increase the emotion and involvement in a story. When the protagonist achieves the final goal, the viewer feels an emotional peak.

Storytelling and listening is a pleasure for both the storyteller (original consumer) and the story listener (who now enjoys the "original" consumption vicariously).[5]

The protagonist experiences the highest emotional state when the protagonist seizes the opportunity, buys the brand, and/or experiences the brand and witnesses the outcome.

Archetypes in Consumer Stories

The brand stories that consumers live and tell are built around archetypes. Recall that archetypes are original pro-

totypes (or "models") based on which subsequent similar "products" are built. Well, then, consumers do not build brand consumption stories in vacuum; rather, they always have some image of an ideal person or an ideal consumption setting they are trying to replicate. These images are stored in their memory from popular culture, or from their own past experiences.

These images are the archetypes. These images are also placed there, sometimes, by brand marketers. A number of brands in our culture have icons. How? By telling good stories—stories that are anchored in archetypes that individual consumers find appealing. Let us take a tour of a selected sample of them. (See Tables 1.)

Q4. What should brand managers do to help consumers tell stories?

If you are a brand manager, you cannot but be eager to apply the concept of archetype in building your brand story. You now want to build an archetype-based brand story. The question is which archetype and how? To address that question, let us understand how the brand stories consumers adopt come to be. Figure 1 depicts the processes surrounding the construction of archetypal brand stories. The 7 substeps in this process are:

1. **Each consumer has certain archetypes he or she aspires to accomplish. For instance, some consumers may wish to enact in their lives the archetype of the Supermom, and others of a siren.**
2. **Only certain archetypes are relevant to a given product category and to a given brand. For example, the archetype of siren is unlikely to be relevant to a brand of washing machine but the archetype of the Supermom might well be.**
3. **The brand stories that brand managers build, which may or may not be based on any archetype.**
4. **The brand stories consumers construct for some brands, basing those stories in aspired archetypes. Consumers may construct stories of their own, or adopt stories told by brand managers.**
5. **Brand managers attempting to build archetype-based brand stories tap into the pool of archetypes. That archetype may or may not be the one the consumer finds relevant or aspires to.**
6. **Brand manager researches the consumer so as to identify proper archetype.**
7. **The consumer accepts and tells the desired brand story and derives *proper pleasure*.**

Note that not all products lend themselves to archetype-based myth consumption for all consumers. And consumers don't construct such stories for all products. But just as likely, they intuitively "sight" opportunities in some brands to play out their aspiring archetypes. And then they play out an archetype, first imagining the archetype as they use the brand, and then later when narrating the brand consumption story. They may not be aware of the archetype or may not know it by that name (of course they don't know the concept of archetype itself, either) and may be living it out at the

TABLE 1	From the Mother of Goodness to the Siren—Archetypal Stories in Brand Communication

The Hero A hero is somebody who commits an act of remarkable bravery or shows great courage, strength of character, or another admirable quality. Michael Jordan, Tiger Woods, Joe DiMaggio, the Power Puff Girls, and Forrest Gump are examples of real-life and fictional heroes (you have to have a sister or daughter who is six years old to know about the Power Puff Girls). The consumer presents her/himself to her/himself as a hero by adopting brands worn/advocated by well-known heroes. Perhaps the most known example of a brand helping consumers enact this archetype is Nike.

The Anti-Hero "Yeah, I'm bad!" captures the essence of the anti-hero. Silver and black clothing personifies the anti-hero stance—witness the bad boys of the NFL, the Oakland Raiders. "Anti-Hero" and "Alien" are brand names of skateboards designed to enable users to enact this archetype. "Anti-Hero Scumbag T-shirts" are also available to wear while riding your Anti-Hero skateboard. Take a look at http://www.skatewarehouse.com/TSANTIHERO.html.

The Mother of Goodness Purity, nourishment, and motherly warmth define the mother-of-goodness archetype. The brand, Just Juice, reflects purity—no water or other filler additives is the promise inherent in the name. "Soup is good food," is the famous Campbell's Soup tag line that personifies the mother-of-goodness.

The Powerbroker Being the supreme authority, possessing dominant influence, represents the powerbroker. The following story illustrates a brand's application of the powerbroker archetype.
There's a famous TV advertisement from about 20 years ago for brokerage firm E.F. Hutton. In the ad, a group of people sit at a crowded, noisy restaurant or something, and one stuffy guy says to another stuffy guy, "My broker is E.F. Hutton, and E.F. Hutton says ... " and the whole crowd of mostly stuffy guys falls silent, listening. The tag line: "When E.F. Hutton talks, people listen." (http://www.thestreet.com/basics/gettingstarted/999737.html)
The fact that many Americans over 50 can fill in the blank when asked ("When ___ talks, people listen") illustrates the power of archetype storytelling applications to building brand awareness and preference.

The Wise Old Man Being experienced and offering reliable, tested, high performance are attributes of the wise old man. Levi's invented jeans during the California gold rush of 1849, and the brand often presents itself as having the attributes of the wise old man.

The Loyalist Trust, loyalty, and reassurance are marks of the loyalist. All sport fan clothing displays of the loyalist archetype. Illustrations of the loyalist include the following behaviors:
· Wearing the apple brand's icon as a tattoo;
· Screaming, "We are Penn State!"
· A NFL football player identifying his alma mater as, "The Ohio State University!"
· Wearing a Wisconsin cheese head hat;
· Displaying the Nike swoosh on hats, jerseys, and jackets.

The Little Trickster Humor, non-conformity, and the element of surprise are attributes central to the little trickster. Being a little trickster offers release, liberation, and fun—overcomes conscience and super ego controls. The little trickster is the child's version of the anti-hero. A child's love of Sponge Bob Square Pants morphs into a teen's love of James Dean's movies with the rebel archetype. Dennis-the-Menace line of clothing and wigs permits the wearer to enact tricks on nearby neighborhood adults unwittingly assigned the role of Mr. Wilson—a child's production of scripts illustrative of the little trickster.
(See http://www.a2zkids.co.uk/products/costumes/books_nursery_rhymes_and_fairytales/dennis_the_menace.html#)

The Siren A brand personifying the attributes of a siren enables its consumer to become irresistibly attractive. The name and commercial displays of Allure by Chanel is an example of one marketer's attempt to tap into this archetype. Sea nymphs luring sailors onto rocks is an early description of a siren—note the inherent danger of doom to the person responding to a siren's call. Successfully adopting a siren stance is, for the consumer, an inherently, unconsciously, dangerous act, and it helps overcome boredom. Thus, wearing Allure—becoming a siren by proxy—adds spice to a relationship or situation.

Prepared by Arch Woodside for **MyCBBook**

FIGURE 1	HOW BRANDS BUILD ARCHETYPAL STORIES

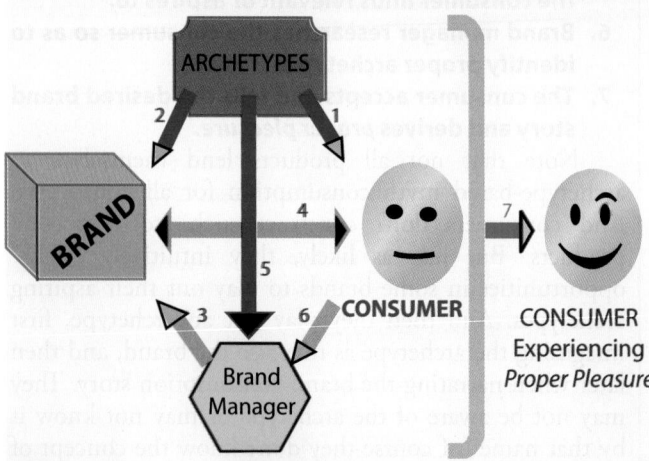

Legand (Figure 1)

1. Core archetypes the consumer aspires to achieve.
2. The archetype most fitting for the brand.
3. The brand stories that brand managers build.
4. The brand stories consumers build, accept, and relish. This link reflects consumer-brand relationship.
5. The archetype the brand manager taps to build stories.
6. Brand manager researches consumer brand stories.
7. Consumer tells (or listens to) the archetype-based story.

level of the subconscious; in that case the story they tell may have the archetype in an implicit (not explicit) form. This is best illustrated in the Versace brand story from a consumer (see below).

A Versace Coat and the Siren:
A Fascinating Brand Story based on Archetype

Now let us tell you one of the most fascinating consumer stories we have heard and read. This one comes from a blog (Web log) and is about a British woman, Pollee, buying and using a Versace coat. In the story, Pollee buys a Versace coat, wears it sans knickers (no underpants), and transforms herself into a *siren*. Read the story in Exhibit 1.

Note in the story that Pollee also buys lingerie at Rigby & Pellar (a retail store) and she decides to pull "into a garage to use the loo [bathroom]." She decides to surprise her "man of the moment" [live-in boyfriend] by removing her dress and knickers in the loo to wear only her coat and lingerie (likely a slip and stockings) home to "my man." She is stopped by two police officers for using a cell phone while driving (illegal in Britain) and the officers ask her why she was wearing a coat on such a warm (August) evening. "Quick as a flash I told them I was going to a fancy dress vicars and tarts party."

This story expresses characteristics of the Versace coat assisting in a courtship (i.e., dating) relationship and participating directly in a secret affair. In Pollee's account, the man of the moment morphs into "my man" with no hindrances apparent to a possible committed relationship. Versace is a co-conspirator with Pollee in a secret affair when she wears the coat without knickers—a highly emotive, private bonding that leads to a risky exposure to police officers. In the story's ending in the blog, Pollee includes a happy face symbol, suggesting that her secret affair drama with Versace leads to her achieving her goal for the evening. The opening segments of the story in the blog (not reproduced in Exhibit 1) include a hint of a brief imbalanced relationship among Pollee, fur coats, and design shops. Pollee twice mentions that she "wouldn't wear fur." But her addition, "I'm inconsistent," indicates both an imbalanced state as well as her achieving balance by having learned to live with a little inconsistency. The imbalance is likely resolved in the subsequent "acts," by her assumption of the siren role, which gives her the pretext to break free from all the norms of her "everyday self."[6]

For You, the Brand Marketer, the Wisdom of Consumer Stories

If you are a brand manager, you have probably already "sighted" the amazing opportunity this storytelling consumer action, and our theoretical analysis, offers. Here let's briefly summarize it for you. Crafting an archetype-based story—wherein a brand is a supporting actor—enables a consumer to achieve conscious and/

EXHIBIT 1 **POLLEE'S STORY**

"I am a Siren and I wear Versace"

Pollee, a British woman, writes a story about her purchase and consumption of a Versace coat

Out on shopping one day, she had just bought new lingerie from a store and then at a second hand ladies wear shop in Beauchamp Place (London) she found her prized purchase: a beautiful cream colored cashmere coat—Versace at a price of £150, of which she writes:

> The feel of the cashmere was sooo soft ....epitomised luxury all the way. The fit of the coat was wonderful and I felt like I was one of those film stars sweeping into the room wearing the most wonderful outfit.

On her way back home she stopped to pick up some food and then while using the restroom, on a whim she thought of surprising her "man of the moment" by showing off her purchases (lingerie and the coat) by donning them. She did, and on a further whim, she decided to not redress her shirt and skirt ("no knickers," so to speak).

As luck would have it, cops pulled her over for using the cell phone while driving. They asked her to get out of the car. "I got out of the car...trying the hardest not to reveal what was (or wasn't) underneath my coat." writes Pollee.

The cops were asking Pollee why she was wearing a coat when it was so hot.

> "Quick as a flash I told them I was going to a fancy dress vicars and tarts party. [Refers to a party where the theme requires guests to arrive dressed up as either a vicar or a prostitute. It is a very English tradition.]

> 'Let's have a look' said the youngest one, who was the one if I had a choice I would have accepted a drink from! I pulled up my coat to show the top of a leg and told them that was all they were getting! They laughed and we all went our separate ways.....thank goodness.

> Five or six minutes later I arrived at my man's house, 'nice coat' he said as I wafted in like a film star…

> As I tried to kiss him he shifted me out of the way as the football was on. I resorted to standing in front of the TV and slowly unbuttoning my two buttons......luckily he ….. ;-)

—Pollee (posted 24 August, 2001)

Source: Pollee's blog can be read in full at http://www.dooyoo.co.uk/fashion/versace/

---

or unconscious goals. Such storytelling helps build very favorable consumer-brand relationships (e.g., committed partnerships, best friendship, flings, or a secret affair, see Fournier 1998).[7] The storytelling analysis in this chapter includes self-oriented thinking by the storyteller with near-conversational interactions with the primary brands appearing in the stories (e.g., Pollee's, "Versace did not let me down"). Consequently, learning—not only thinking about—what buyers and users say to the brand and what the brand says first provides valuable clues for designing highly effective marketing and advertising strategies.

Narrative reports and drama enactments are more likely to encourage vicarious participation while "lecture" forms of advertising tend to evoke argumentative forms of thinking.[8] Given that learning via storytelling is more memorable and retrievable than lecture-based learning,[9] learning the stories consumers tell in natural settings represents a useful grounding for crafting naturalistic stories or fantasies that are acceptable and enjoyable to the intended audience.

Consumer storytelling research provides evidence as to how and why brands become icons in the informants' own words. Informant-reported enactments of the iconic roles played by brands likely include symbols and expressions that match with imprinted unconsciously driving myths that affect the informants' behavior—the originating core myths may be uncovered via word searches using blog search engines (e.g., Technorati, Blogdigger, etc.). Consequently, becoming aware of the consumer enactments of imprinted myths via brand icons provides direction for story genre and consumer-brand relationships (e.g., the Fairy godmother myth is one plotline worthy of producing alternative enactments to encourage one segment of travelers to visit Paris; showing alternative scenes of a protagonist wearing a Versace coat sans knickers is a story gist useful for rejuvenating romance in a tired relationship).

Summary

While commercials in *lecture* formats quickly become irretrievable (to say nothing of irritable), commercials that employ a *drama* format engage the consumer. Consumers are hardwired to attend to, tell, and retrieve *stories*. Consumers are driven to tell stories to others to achieve deeper understanding—bring to consciousness relationships their consumption of brands and products have to archetypes. Archetypes are "prototypes" of characters (e.g., superman, supermom, vixen) and qualities (e.g., altruism, seduction, etc.) consumers dream about and try to implement and achieve.

It is through consumption stories consumers tell others that they understand and validate their consumption experience—"How do I know what I think until I hear what I have to say?" Classical drama storytelling enables consumers to achieve Aristotle's "proper pleasure" (i.e., the pleasure of experiencing the consumption experience by interpreting the original experience) and to experience one or more specific archetype primary forms.

Lecture format in commercials is a good option to communicate a brand's features and benefits. However, in many product categories, consumers buy brands more than for the features and the benefits that these brands offer—they buy and consume them to enact archetype experiences. Classical dramas as formats in advertising include but go beyond showing features and benefits to connect consumers to archetypal outcomes. The brand stories in these dramas should therefore invoke and connect with the archetypes.

Conclusion

A substantial proportion of consumption experiences are "realized" by consumers through the telling of stories to themselves and to others—stories built around the brand's use. Brand communications also sometimes tell such stories, but, in order to be effective, they should resonate with what consumers are trying to achieve through brand consumption. To achieve such resonance, brand managers should listen to stories consumers tell.

This requires ethnographic studies, but weeks and months of ethnographic data entailing consumer stories will be of no avail without knowledge of archetypes. Existing unconsciously behind these stories are archetypes—the heros in the stories if you will. To identify the specific archetype in a story, the manager must become familiar with the repertoire of archetypes and the kinds of myths and stories associated with them. Our description of a sample of these archetypes along with current marketing examples is a demonstration of the living, vivid reality that archetypes are present in current brand dramas. Our essay is thus an invitation to brand managers to study archetypes and harness their potential in their brand communications.

Endnotes

1. Jung, C.G. (1959). The archetypes and the collective unconscious. Princeton, NJ: Princeton University Press.
2. See Arnould, E.J. & Wallendorf M. (1994). Market-orientated ethnography: Interpretation building and marketing strategy formulation. *J. of Marketing Research*, 31, 484 -503. ; Hirschman Hirschman, E. (1986). Humanistic inquiry in marketing research: Philosophy, method, and criteria. J. of Marketing Research, 23, 237-250. Hirschman, E. (2000a). Consumers' use of intertextuality and archetypes. Advances in Consumer Research, 27, 57-63. Hirschman, E. (2000b). Heroes, monsters, and messiahs. New York: Andrews McMeel.; Kozinets, 2002; Moore, 1985; Woodside & Chabet, 2001); also see Stern, B. (1994). Classical and vignette television advertising dramas: Structural models, formal analysis, and consumer effects. Journal of Consumer Research, 20, 601-615.
3. Fournier, S. (1998). Consumers and their brands: Developing relationship theory in consumer research. *J. of Consumer Research*, 24, 343-374.
4. See Holt, D.B. (2003). What becomes an Icon Most? *Harvard Business Review*, 3, 43-49.
5. See Gergen K. J. & Gergen M. M. (1988). Narrative and the self as relationship. *Advances in Experimental Social Psychology*, 21, 17-56; Delgadillo, Y. & Escalas, J.E. (2004). Narrative word of mouth communication: Exploring memory and attitude effects of consumer storytelling. Advances in Consumer Research, 31, 186-92.
6. For additional interpretations of Pollee's story, See Woodside, A.G., Sood, S. (2007), "Advancing consumer storytelling research," *Psychology & Marketing*, forthcoming.
7. Fournier, S. (1998). Consumers and their brands: Developing relationship theory in consumer research. *J. of Consumer Research*, 24, 343-374.
8. See Boller, G.W. (1990). The vicissitudes of product Experience: 'Songs of our consuming selves.' *Advances in Consumer Research*, 17, 621-626; Boller, G.W., Babakus, E., & Olson, J.C. (1989). Viewer empathy in response to drama ads: Development of the VEDA scale. Unpublished working paper number 402-489. Memphis State University: Fogleman College of Business and Economics; Booth, W.C. (1961). The Rhetoric of Fiction. Chicago: University of Chicago Press.
9. See Bruner, J. (1990). Acts of meaning. Cambridge, MA: Harvard Business School Press, 1990; Schank, R.C. (1990). Tell me a story: A new look at real and artificial memory. Cambridge, U.K.: Cambridge University Presss Wertime, K. (2002). Building Brands & Believers. Singapore: Wiley (Asia).

The Online Life of Coffee Aficionados:
A Netnography of An Online Consumption Culture

Robert V. Kozinets, York University, Canada

Coffee is just another product for you too. You could just as well be selling those turnip twaddlers of flame retardant condoms, but as long as you are having fun and paying your bills, that is all that matters to you, right? I am afraid that it is not quite that simple for many of us. We take our coffee very seriously, and to have it demeaned in such a manner is a slap in the face. Coffee is much more than a tool. It is passion, it is intrigue, mystery, seduction, fear, betrayal, love, hate, and any other core human emotion that you can think of, all wrapped into one little bean.

—Peter, posted on <alt.coffee> 08/14/2000

This is one of many posts on online discussion groups that you may encounter and benefit from as a consumer researcher. Capture, read, and delve into enough of them, and you will begin to build some of the deeper insights that mark the best marketers. This work of understanding online communities is part of a new approach to consumer research called *netnography*. Just what is netnography? And what can the passionate online musings of coffee fans such as Peter teach marketers about consumers and their brands—not just brands of coffee but brands of any product category? To find out, read on.

Alt.Coffee: Coffee Wisdom on the Net

Alt.coffee has been serving up coffee wisdom for well over a decade. It attracts the attention of well over one hundred thousand consumers. Online communities like this exist for any number of other products. Consumers, particularly those consumers who are deeply interested in particular products or brands, inhabit such communities, in the physical world and online. In online worlds and social groups, they hang out, chat, educate and entertain themselves and one another. They do it in forums, on blogs, in virtual worlds like Second Life, and on social networking sites like Facebook. And in the process they take their product experience to a new height.

You can join a community, or simply watch it as a lurker. And you can learn a lot from it. About the community, about online worlds, and about consumption in general. A new breed of consumer researchers is doing just that. We call them *netnographer*s. They perform ethnography—a technique from anthropology—on the Internet. The insights they discover can be amazing. Let us study their ways.

Ethnography: Inside A Culture

Let us first meet Netnography's elder sibling, *ethnography*. The word *ethnography* literally means 'writing about a culture.' Anthropologists, who specialize in studies of culture, employ this method and use "participant observation" as their approach. This means that, in order to write about a culture, an ethnographer will live in a community as a member, observing and participating in the life of that community. Ethnographers study the unique meanings, practices and products of particular social groups. Because it is a technique of careful observation and reflection, the most important instrument in conducting an ethnography is not a machine, a recording device, or a piece of software. It is the ethnographer. Professional ethnographers hone their skills with many years of fieldwork. They learn how to observe fine details, to record them unobtrusively, to learn new languages, to use interview techniques, and to carefully analyze meanings.

Unlike other forms of research, ethnography is all about the specific. Ethnographers study the members of a specific group, like the Bora Bora tribe or a football fan club. Within those groups, they seek to learn about specific things that make the group unique—their particular customs, their particular foods, their rituals; their ways of greeting; how they are being affected by the world today. And so on.

One of the greatest things about ethnography is its flexibility. The method is constantly adapted to study new types of cultures as they emerge. And so it is no surprise that it has come to be adapted to study online social worlds.

Now Meet Netnography

Anthropologists already know how to conduct ethnographies in face-to-face situations. However, the online world is different. Communications that take place through a computer are "mediated" communications. Text and pictures are used rather than the spoken word. People may not be who they seem to be. People can take more care and time to represent themselves. The type of information that is collected is different. Conversations are automatically saved, and linger in time. There are many conversations that are public, and anyone in the world can enter it, or listen in. All of these things make ethnography on the Internet very different from face-to-face ethnography.

Like ethnography, netnography is very flexible. It can be adapted to studying many different kinds of online communities. It can study social networking sites like Facebook, blogs or microblogs like Twitter, and virtual worlds like Second Life, Webkinz, or Habbo Hotel. And it can study the many forums, bulletin boards, and newsgroups that pepper the Internet. Like ethnographers, a good netnographer must be a highly skilled data collector and interpreter, using skills that usually require many years of training and practice to develop. Netnography also has certain rules, adapted to the special qualities of the Internet. To learn more about the techniques of netnography, see Exhibit 'A'.

Netnography is faster and less expensive than traditional ethnography. It can allow almost up-to-the-minute assessments of consumers' collective pulse. Because it is unelicited, it is more natural and less disruptive than focus groups, surveys, or interviews. It does not force consumers to choose from predetermined researcher assumptions, like surveys do. Instead, it offers a wealth of grassroots information on the symbolism, meanings, and consumption patterns of online consumer groups. It offers a powerful window into the naturally occurring reality of consumers.

These are potent opportunities. However, there are matching challenges. It is relatively easy to download a few newsgroup postings, summarize them, and call oneself an online anthropologist. But skilled anthropology requires a finely-tuned instrument: the researcher. Raw data (or even medium-rare data) is not information. The form of online data can also be difficult to work with. Anonymity and deception can make conclusions more challenging.

But the opportunities are huge. Netnography offers us an opportunity to gain empathy with consumer groups. To truly understand consumers as full and multifaceted human beings—not a stereotype, not a collection of numbers. To hear their own stories, in their own words. Read their chosen names. Learn to speak in their language. Begin to see through their eyes. Learn their "tribal dance."

Online Communities: What Are They?

Some would say that there are no mass markets anymore. That is because consumers are all not the same. Some would say that there is no mainstream anymore. That is because consumer culture has split into a new world of consumer tribes. The modern marketplace has fragmented into smaller groupings of communities and tribes.

Motorcycle enthusiast gatherings and fan clubs were just the start. Many groups share a connection based upon their enthusiasm and knowledge for a consumer activity, from Harley-Davidson to Star Trek to the Apple iPhone.

EXHIBIT 'A'

How to Research Online Communities

Although netnography is inherently an open-ended form of inquiry, ethnographers choose from related field procedures and often confront similar methodological issues. Common ethnographic procedures that help shape researchers' participant-observation include:

1 **Making cultural entrée.** This includes carefully plotting strategy, surveying the online field, previewing different forums and sites, creating web-pages, contacting culture members

2 **Collecting data.** This includes planning for the collections of: (a) observational, downloaded data, including text, photos, images, and audiovisual productions, (b) elicited data such as interviews, and (c) reflective research field-notes

3 **Analyzing data.** This includes qualitative coding and categorization, and the derivation of more abstract themes and theories from the coded observational data; computer-assisted qualitative data analysis software programs are often helpful to assist with the analysis of large amounts of netnographic data

4 **Striving for trustworthy interpretation.** This encompasses carefully analyzing different types of data, keeping the data in context, analyzing the social act of communication and not the anonymous poster, other pragmatic methods for avoiding overstretching the interpretation

5 **Ensuring ethical standards.** This often follows human subject research laws and includes gaining informed consent where appropriate to do so, appropriately citing online sources, and providing opportunities for culture member feedback.

These consumer gatherings are not limited to fan clubs, conventions, bike rallies, in-store and in-home meetings, by any means. They spill out into virtual space. There,

they gather structure, momentum and followers.

The New Consumer's wiring is tribal. As beings who are increasingly mediated by technology, consumers plug into networks to connect. Their communication runs in feedback loops, expressing information and emotion through pictures and words . And these communications can provide many valuable insights to the marketer/researcher.

Tourists to Insiders:
Types of Community Members

The members of online communities may be categorized in terms of their level of involvement with the online community and also their level of involvement with the consumption activity. "Tourists" lack strong social ties to the community. They also don't have a very deep interest in the activity. "Minglers" have strong social ties to the community but have a low level of interest in the consumption activity. "Devotees" have strong consumption interests, but few attachments to the online group. Finally, "insiders" have strong ties to the online group and to the consumption activity. Insiders tend to be long-standing and frequently referenced members. See Exhibit 'B'.

Marketing research and word-of-mouth marketing tend to be most interested in devotees and insiders. Insiders often speak for other members of the community, and they often speak the most and the loudest. Online communities also inspire loyalty and devotion. The recommendation of members often carries weight with other members. Marketing researchers and marketers interested in online word-of-mouth and influence may find it useful to track and understand the flow of influence in online communities. How do tourists and minglers become insiders and devotees? How are they influenced? How do members of social networks, on social networking sites and in other online venues, teach each other about products, companies, and brands? These are questions that netnography can help answer. We illustrate this with a study of online coffee culture.

Online Coffee Culture:
A Treasure for Netnographers

As a leading cultural anthropologist has noted: "Coffee is among the preeminent vessels of meaning in consumer culture."[2] There are rich layers of meaning that underpin the coffee aficionados' experiences of coffee, both in the physical world and on the net.

As is true of any community, the coffee community has its own language, and on the net this special language becomes even more colorful, peppered liberally with such coffee-lingo as baristas and JavaJocks, cremas and roastmasters, tampers and superautomatics, livias and tiger flecks. Learning this language can be an interesting exercise for any student of coffee culture browsing the online chatter, but it is the subtext of the postings, the banter among the online members, the way that the communications are shared and shaped that is fascinating and draws the reader—and the researcher—in. Consider the post in Exhibit C. What can we learn here? At least four things.

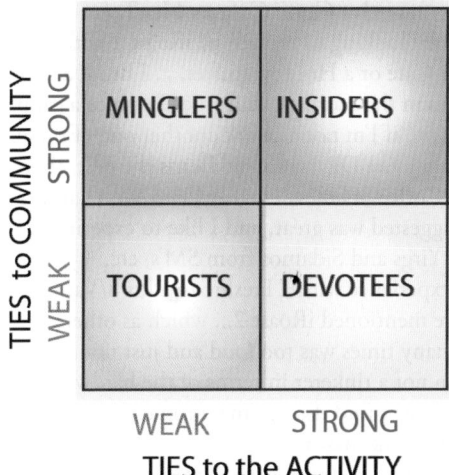

EXHIBIT B
TYPES OF COMMUNITY MEMBERS

	TIES to the ACTIVITY (PRODUCT/BRAND)	
	WEAK	STRONG
TIES to COMMUNITY — STRONG	MINGLERS	INSIDERS
TIES to COMMUNITY — WEAK	TOURISTS	DEVOTEES

1. Communities Are All About Taste

The first thing that we can learn is that community, like coffee, is all about "taste."

The famous French sociologist Pierre Bourdieu said that taste distinguishes, and it distinguishes the distinguisher. One way that we show our taste is to use a special language.

Showing taste is what George is doing in his alt.coffee posting. He is sharing his needs and asking for advice, but he is also making many fine distinctions to show his knowledge and expertise. Note the different terms George uses. Is it "coffee" he drinks? Not really. He drinks "french press," "espresso," and "cappa ." Notice George's use of brand names. He is not just looking for any coffee bean roaster, he is looking for either a "HotTop" or a "Gene Café" to replaces his broken "iRoast 2." What will he put in it? Not just ordinary coffee beans. He will roast "DP [dry-processed] Ethiopian," "DP Yirgs," "Harrar," and Sidamos." Where from? From quality, coffee bean retailers like "CoffeeWholesalers" and SM's [Sweet Maria's].

Then, George gets a little bit technical. He says that he is "not a tinkerer in terms of hardware," but he does talk about finding "the optimal profile for a given bean." As he describes his needs, he talks about roasting beans towards "the second crack" of the bean, and discusses when they "develop a sheen."

What do we learn on <alt.coffee>? Even in this one post, we are repeatedly taught how to be a coffee connoisseur. Why does George drink "french press" and not just coffee? The reason is because "basic coffee," the type that most of us enjoy, is garbage. At least, it is to a coffee connoisseur.

Proper coffee, flavorful coffee, needs to be properly prepared. And, although it is not enjoyed all the time, the most discussed form of coffee on the newsgroup is

EXHIBIT C

alt.coffee   Search this group

"George Anthony"   22 May 2007
Advice requested—Gene Cafe vs HotTop

Hello, I am looking to replace an iRoast 2 with either a Gene Cafe or a HotTop roaster. ... I drink a cup of french press in the morning and an espresso or a cappa in the afternoon, if I'm not at work another one of these during the day. I like DP Ethiopian beans the best, the Harrar from Coffee Wholesalers that [Tim Wolf] and [Barney J] suggested was great, and I like to experiment with the DP Yirgs and Sidamos from SM's, etc.

I have experience with a Freshroast Plus 8/Variac and the above mentioned iRoast 2... which as others have stated many times was too loud and just not a great product. I am not a tinkerer in terms of the hardware, but I do attempt to find the optimal profile for a given bean. I'm not a dark roast fan.

Depending on the bean, I roast to somewhere in the neighborhood of the second crack, sometimes up to it, sometimes into it for a short period... my beans only develop a sheen after a few days.

I want a machine that will deliver the best possible roast, that's priority one. . . . If the Gene Cafe, which appears to offer more input into the roast process, produces inferior results, I'd go with the HotTop. If the results are comparable, I'd lean towards the Gene Cafe. [Any Advice?]

---

espresso. Real coffee, essential coffee, precious coffee is espresso.

Making a great cup of espresso, we learn from George and others on the group, is a complicated affair. George tells us about the preparation of the bean. It needs to be roasted to perfection. And the preparation of the espresso is also complicated. It involves attending carefully to the water, the grind, timing the shot, knowing your machine, keeping its screen and filter clean, tamping it, maintaining the correct temperature, the degree of the roast, the air humidity, the internal boiler temperature, and even such mystical elements as the mood of the coffee-maker.

This is not just a matter of making good espresso. It is a way to show taste. It is a way to show your status. A way to show that you have the time for pleasure, hedonism, and indulgence. A way to show that you have upper class tastes and abilities. There is a type of elitist or "snob appeal" to coffee knowledge. Like all cultures, it has elements that are familiar to insiders, but that confuse and exclude outsiders.

Insiders—They are experts who have taken control. They are using their skills, their intelligence, and their resources to look behind the scenes into the world of coffee production. They want to understand what it is that makes a particular type of coffee superior, and then to capture it. They are "prosumers"—a combination of the consumer and the producer. They are active, involved consumers. This need to show devotion by actively producing is found

in a lot of other consumption groups, such as sports and music fans, and fans of different TV shows like *Lost and Heroes*. It is also becoming a way that more and more people interact with what has been called "Web 2.0."

2. Online Communities Teach Consumers How to Consume

The second thing we learn is about how community members teach one another. Consider the interactive exchange on alt.coffee between several participants, in Exhibit D.

alt.coffee   Search this group

Kafein_stttrykker   April 25, 2:31 p.m.
Subject: Oxygenation While Brewing

I was in NYC last week, and had the opportunity to go to Jack's Stir Brew (rated as the best coffee in the U.S. by various surveys). Jack claims that his brewing method, which stirs the grinds and water during brewing and pipes in oxygen, results in a less acidic coffee. The house coffee is a very dark, very strong brew, and it's true that it's very smooth with little acidity.

The question is how to do stir brewing and oxygenation at home.

Raging Storm   Apr 25, 4:31 pm
Subject: Oxygenation While Brewing

If Jack uses piped oxygen, does this mean pure bottled oxygen. I guess food standards wouldn't allow for pumped ambient air? If oxygen reduces acidity, there won't be much pure oxygen from a vac pot. I would solve the acidity problem by roasting darker.

Indiana Smith   Apr 25, 8:23 pm
Subject: Oxygenation While Brewing

They sell little aerosol cans of oxygen at Target. Google "Oxygen plus". You'd have to rig some sort of valve and tubing, would not be hard. Stirring - a spoon, a stick, etc.

Usually oxidized food is a bad thing, you want to keep oxygen AWAY from food, so I dunno about the whole idea.

"Kafein_stttrykker" is trying to figure out how to duplicate "the best coffee in the U.S." He traveled to New York and spoke to the person who apparently produces the best cup of coffee in the world. Apparently, it involves stirring the grinds and piping in oxygen. He asks other members of the group how to do this at home.

"Raging Storm" doesn't directly answer the question, but discusses "food standards" and the use of an alterative brewing method, the "vac pot." He then offers his own advice about what he sees as an "acidity problem."

Then, "Indiana Smith" directly answers the question, suggesting some creative engineering. But he also questions the entire idea of adding oxygen to coffee.

The key to understanding these postings is their relationship to a question. "Kafein" has traveled to New York and sought out wisdom from Jack, one of the world's anointed masters of coffee brewing. The quest for a perfect cup of coffee is not simply a metaphor. To these people, it is real. And it is a quest that is shared.

Great coffee is rare. And this rarity is communicated in conversations about scarcity, about which machine to use, which coffee bean, what timing, which device. These members are always trying to make their coffee better.

One member cautioned that only one out of every five pulls is worth drinking. Some coffeephiles say that it has taken them months to train their tastebuds. And now that they have trained their tastebuds, they are slave to coffee.

Repeatedly, we see postings talking about how much money this hobby requires. But also how much it is worth it. One coffeephile said that he spent huge amounts of money to keep himself from being subjected to the unbearable taste of ordinary coffee. There was no end to his involvement. First, he learned to enjoy espresso in fine restaurants. Then, he bought a good espresso maker. Then, he needed to buy a quality roaster, then a better one. Now, he needs better coffee beans, and is trying different coffee bean wholesalers (many of them on the Internet).

Where did this need come from? What is the origin of this motivation? He blames his fellow alt.coffee

coffeephiles. So do many of the other posters. They teach, learn, and encourage each other to love coffee and to demand better coffee for themselves.

This is the force of culture, acting through online communities. It is a type of gravitational pull in the world of consumption. It drives increasing investments in a new cultural interest.

3. Passion for Brands

The third thing we learn from these online community postings is that good coffee is about passion, artistry, and authenticity. Good coffee is not just a drink. The experience of making and drinking good coffee shows that you are a fully realized human being.

Coffee makers are artists, they have tastes "like a seasoned sommelier or vintner" ["Angelo," posted on <alt.coffee> 08/09/2000]. Several posters claim that they would not visit a café whose baristas did not love coffee.

Passion matters. The baristas or coffee makers should love their work and this will come through in the coffee: "Coffee is the passion of a barista and a lifelong profession" ["Peter," posted on <alt.coffee> 08/13/2000].

The need for passion clearly comes through in an online debate. In the posting that opens this section, Peter, a more passionate coffee drinker (an ex-employee of Starbucks) was angry at a current Starbucks employee, and insulted him in the strongest terms possible.

Peter's revealing comments were applauded by many different members of the online community. They also revealed some important and shared impressions of Starbucks. The bad feelings towards Starbucks are reflected in two negative newsgroup nicknames for Starbucks. First, Starbucks is an expensive and faceless corporate entity. It is called "*$". Second, it carelessly kills mom-and-pop, more authentic local stores, and the drink it brews is called "corporate coffee."

The need for an authentic coffee is expressed by another online poster, Fred (Exhibit E).

Fred is not talking about coffee flavor, or even about economics. He is talking about passion. He is saying that vendors or manufacturers should have a genuine passion for the product. This is a longing for better days, a longing

EXHIBIT E

alt.coffee	Search this group

Fred   11/19/2000

What I am coming to in my own life and consumer behavior is that I want to support and savor the true specialty items while I can. I'd rather eat Barry's fudge… than Godiva 'faux specialty' chocolates. And I'd rather drink the local café's coffee than Starbucks's because, well, those tiny, passionate companies are more precious than Starbucks… Any corporation with food chemists can make Starbucks' product, IMO [in my opinion]. Only a passionate, driven romantic would keep making top-notch specialty coffee day in and day out. Lose Starbucks and another clone clicks into that economic eco-niche. Lose a lover or a hero and you might wait a long time until another comes along.

that also drives coffee newsgroup members to produce their own quality coffee. To make your own great cup of coffee and to support local cafes is not only a statement about coffee and your taste. It is also a way to express positive human values in the world. As Fred says later in his post, doing this helps to maintain "a world of beauty and passion."

4. Religiously Devoted to Coffee

Fourth and final, we learn that consumers bring religious zeal for consumption of products they love. Consider the quest of coffee consumers. Consider their search. Consider the way they link coffee consumption to human values. To bettering the world. And now, consider this segment from a post by "Jerry" that lovingly details, in several pages of text, his exact experiences with his new coffee maker (Exhibit F).

As with Fred's "passion," his David and Goliath-story "hero," and 'world of beauty,' the language Jerry uses here is romantic and idealistic. It is even prophetic and Biblical. The crema (or oil from the coffee beans) is "beautiful," and

EXHIBIT F

alt.coffee [Search this group]

Jerry   11/02/2000

I hit the brew switch [on his new Livia 90 cappuccino/espresso maker]... at first, nothing. Then... beautiful reddish-brown crema... the "tiger flecks" I had heard so much about but rarely had seen flowed forth and fell just short of two ounces in 25 seconds. I stood just admiring the crema when suddenly a voice called, "The milk! The Milk!"

it "flowed forth" much like a river of milk and honey might do for an Old Testament figure. Jerry did not remember to steam the milk, but he told about how it occurred to him as "a voice" that "called [un]to him." The drama and might be a parody. But it occurs repeatedly in the culture and the community. For example, other postings call the lack of passion by a "Starbucks Jock" "Sacrilege!" and the placing of sugar in espresso the mark of one who "has no soul."

And what is the term that this community of coffeephiles uses for their ultimate cup of espresso? It is elusive. A religious experience. It is the holy grail of the coffee dream quest. They call it a "god shot." (See Exhibit G.)

God shot is a name for the perfect shot of espresso, a moment of glory. It is mysterious, and cannot be captured,

EXHIBIT G

alt.coffee [Search this group]

JebZT38   11/17/2002

Just when you least expect it, the God shot cometh. I expect very little and usually that's the kind of shot I get, average. But today I got TWO God shots, and the only thing I can figure is that maybe the humidity had something to do with it?"

reproduced or summoned at will. It is a moment when human being and nature are reunited.

This interpretation does not suggest that coffee consumption is actually a religion for these coffeephiles. But for them it has religious aspects of search, passion, and transcendence. It is very meaningful to them. They hold it dear. Caring about coffee, caring about these experiences, is a part of their identity. Because these metaphors are highly motivational and persuasive, they should be of great interest to marketing researchers and to marketers.

Lessons for Marketers

This research looks at the interactions of consumers with one another. These interactions occur naturally. They occur in a community. The consumer interaction is not artificial, nor controlled by the marketer or marketing researcher, as in a focus group or an interview.

Netnography reveals interesting consumer insights, language, motivations, consumption patterns and symbols. It provides feedback on brands and products. The method achieves all of this in a manner that is far more unobtrusive, convenient and accessible than traditional ethnography. It is also far more economical.

Think about the marketing of coffee. If you were a coffee marketer, would this sort of information be valuable? Without an ethnographic study, what sort of picture would you have of consumers? You might have interesting figures on how much coffee was bought, where it was bought, at what price it was bought. You might have information about the responses to different promotions, like a sampling campaign at Costco or Tesco, or a coupon. You might even have information about what consumers said as they answered various surveys, things like taste is more important than price, or that they like a "deep, full-bodied flavor." But what does this type of investigation give us? In contrast, what does an ethnography—on the Internet or in person—provide?

Online consumers tend to be knowledgeable and educated, and they provide interesting consumption insights. Online posters appear to spend large amounts of time and money on their focal consumption activity. The data they provide can be extraordinarily rich. By carefully evaluating their ideas, marketing researchers can obtain useful information similar to that obtained from "lead users."[3] This information can be very useful to marketers, as it can:

1. reveal consumers' language and motivations
2. help us understand positioning and choice sets
3. tell us about innovative trends to follow
4. clue us about new product concepts to launch

For example, the posts above talked about oxygenating and stirring coffee to create better flavor. Could a company build a machine to do this? It might require oxygen canisters and an automatic stirring device. If it made a better cup of coffee, do you think these coffeephiles would buy it? Could it lead to a brand new market for "oxygenating" coffee machines?

In research like this, we step into the world of the consumer in a very dramatic way. We are not forcing them to check our boxes, or speak our language. Instead, we are forced to learn their language. We gain not only knowledge, but understanding. We see interactions and learning, taste and conflict in their natural state.

Certainly not all consumers are this passionate, devoted, or articulate. Not everyone who drinks coffee is an espresso aficionado who goes on quests for the perfect cup of coffee and writes long postings to describe their latest coffee brewing adventures. But netnography reveals that at least some coffee consumers are this way. We see the creative, artistic person who is sometimes—perhaps more than we think—behind the mask of the coffee consumer.

Netnography reveals the true face of these consumers. And it is an interesting face. It is an interesting face because it is rich and full of details. It is interesting because it talks about taste. It is interesting because it is artistic, creative, and can serve as a source of new ideas for new products or marketing campaigns. It is interesting because this is not just a closed community, but an open one, that anyone interested in coffee can learn from and join. It is interesting because it has the potential to be very influential. And it is interesting because it reveals the deeply committed members who form the core of the culture. We might call it a picture of the community's soul.

> Netnography reveals the true face of these consumers. And it is an interesting face because it is rich and full of details... because it is artistic, creative, and can serve as a source of new ideas for new products or marketing campaigns.

Beyond Coffee Culture

We used the study of coffee as an example. But there are online communities discussing just about any type of product or service you can imagine, from cars to soap, restaurants to private schools, music to movies, pets to data processing. And they also talk about brands, and not just big brands but little brands, too. This talk goes on in a lot of online community places. In social networking sites like Facebook and MySpace. In virtual worlds like Stagecoach Island and Second Life. On blogs. On Twitter. In company and personal web-sites and forums.

For marketers and marketing researchers, the payoff from exploring these communities and their consumption experiences could be considerable. In these communities, consumers endlessly discuss their taste, as we saw in this example. This information can help to understand preferred attributes and choices. Consumers discuss their preferences, both in terms of products and brands. They complain about functions and forms—and many other things. They discuss new products that they would like to see, identifying areas for new product development.

Consumers also self-select themselves into groups. These naturally occurring groups can guide grassroots segmentation and targeting strategies. Consumers also endlessly discuss the meanings of brands and products. They talk about brand differences with honesty, and passion, setting the stage for examinations of positioning strategy.

Netnography: The Labor and The Reward

However, netnography in any of these communities requires skill and devotion. You need to be able to gather cultural knowledge and analyze it like a detective. You need to be able to follow a cultural investigation through to all of the touchpoints that matter—both online and in the physical world. You must read beyond the postings. You must become fluent in online language. You need to understand the implications and limits of the method. You need to know how hard to push your data, and when you cannot stretch it any longer. You need to follow good ethical research guidelines. You need to take the time to do it right.

My coffee netnography covered 33 months of gradually gaining understanding. See Exhibit 'H' for "How I Did Netnography." A good netnographer will become completely immersed in the phenomenon and the culture.

In a world where the mainstream has gone away, understanding the ways and the language of different electronic tribes is an important way to begin communicating. Used wisely and carefully, netnography can inform marketing, new product development, and advertising on the deep meanings that communities bring to their members' consumption experiences. It reveals motivations, hopes, fears, dreams. It can show us the unexpected and the real. It can offers us a window into the rich and complex world of the consumer.

In the right hands, netnography can reveal the human face of the brand.

EXHIBIT H — How I Did Netnography

1 I began by seeking out all of the groups that contained the term "coffee" in my trusty search engine.

2 After investigating the hits, I examined the potential newsgroups: <alt.coffee>, <alt.food.coffee>, and <rec.food.drink.coffee>, as well as several others.

3 I chose <Alt.coffee> because it had by far the highest traffic—approximately 75 messages per day.

4 I contacted different members of the group, and let them know that I was doing research there.

5 I followed <alt.coffee> and related newsgroups, read the messages, and downloaded a wide variety of messages, for 33 months.

6 I also dove deep into coffee culture, online and off. Online, I read and searched coffee-related web-pages, web-rings, and mailing lists. In my daily life, I began reading books about coffee. I also ramped up my coffee drinking experiences. I conducted a number of informal discussions and meetings with several coffee connoisseurs.

7 From the large pool, I selected (and downloaded and printed) 179 postings, based on their apparent interestingness and usefulness. Qualitative research often focuses on special cases that are of high interest. To learn about the limits of coffee consumption, I studied not the average coffee drinker but the high-performance coffee connoisseur.

8 The postings were pre-classified into different topics. A thread is a set of interrelated bulletin board postings. Threads were chosen for their rich content, descriptive qualities, and relevant topic matter. As well, I favored threads where a lot of different community members were part of the conversation.

9 The coding of the postings involved both analysis and interpretation. Categories and themes were derived from a close examination of their similarities and differences. For this research, the volume of text was 198 double-spaced 12-point font pages, from 65 distinct e-mail addresses and user names.

10 I sought to form conclusions about the meaning of the data. At the same time, I looked for evidence that might contradict these conclusions. As evidence was found, the conclusions changed until they could accommodate all of the findings. This process is called "hermeneutic circling." It resulted in several early themes being rejected. This qualitative data analysis process is disciplined and rigorous, but also creative and playful.

11 In the conduct of research, ensuring ethicality was very important. I identified myself in postings to the community, told members about the observation, and provided my credentials. Because the board is public space, and is searchable, I made sure that nothing was said about the community or its members that could harm them if it was published.

12 After I had written my interpretations, I passed them to nine online informants to ask their opinion. This is called a "member check." I received mostly positive comments from members. Some said that they were "impressed" by the netnographic study. Others thought it was "perceptive" and even "fantastic." Members also had several useful suggestions, which I implemented. Member suggestions added some new facts about the group. They also changed the way that I wrote about basic coffee, brand use, and religious devotion.

> In a world where the mainstream has gone away, understanding the ways and the language of different electronic tribes is an important way to begin communicating. Used wisely and carefully, netnography can inform marketing, new product development, and advertising on the deep meanings that communities bring to their members' consumption experiences. It can offers us a window into the rich and complex world of the consumer.

ENDNOTES

[1] Kozinets, Robert V. (1999), "E-Tribalized Marketing?: The Strategic Implications of Virtual Communities of Consumption," *European Management Journal*, 17 (3), 252-264.

[2] Sherry, John F., Jr. (1995), "Bottomless Cup, Plug-in Drug: A Telethnography of Coffee," *Visual Anthropology*, 7, 351-370.

[3] Von Hippel, Eric (1986), "Lead Users: A Source of Novel Product Concepts," *Management Science*, 32, 791-805.

[4] Spiggle, Susan (1994) "Analysis and Interpretation of Qualitative Data in Consumer Research," *Journal of Consumer Research*, 21 (December), 491-503.

Acknowledgement
All images of coffee in cups are courtesy of Elisabeth85@flickr
The image of "coffee beans heart" on is courtesy of J Gorge@flickr
The image of coffee machines is courtesy of Lotzman Katzman

GENDER BENDER BRAND HIJACKS AND CONSUMER REVOLT
The Porsche Cayenne Story
Jill Avery, Simmons School of Management, USA

Larson tells you that he bought his new Ford Mustang because of its performance characteristics, touting its 4.6 liter V8 engine that generates 315 horsepower and torque power like he's never felt before. He and his dad spent years in their garage rebuilding old Mustangs from the 1960s when he was growing up.

The crowd is thick at the bar and John has to shout so that the bartender can hear. As John yells, "A cosmopolitan with Stolichnaya Razberi," the crowd surrounding him goes quiet and then erupts into laughter. John quickly adds, "...for my girlfriend. And a Jose Cuervo tequila shot for me."

Carlo laughs when you ask him whether he smokes Marlboro cigarettes in order to be a cowboy. He tells you that Marlboros generate the densest smoke, thick and syrupy, just like he likes it. He's always smoked Marlboro because that's what the older boys in his neighbor smoked when he was a teenager.

Walking out of the theater, Dalton just shakes his head when you ask him whether he liked the movie he has just seen, Confessions of a Shopaholic, starring Isla Fisher as a Manhattan writer with a shopping addiction. Smiling, he points to his girlfriend who gushes about the movie. While she is speaking, he rolls his eyes and pretends to slit his own throat.

Brands are Gender Identity Markers

In today's world, the things we buy serve as identity markers, communicating who we are or who we would like to be to others around us. People who know us use our consumption as clues to understand who we are, and they judge us based on what we buy, use, and do. Our consumption communicates a lot of different things about who we are. Think about how the clothes someone wears helps tells us whether they are rich versus poor, conservative versus liberal, old versus young, yuppie versus bohemian, urban versus rural, showy versus modest, hip versus mainstream.

One central part of who we are is our gender identity—our sense of ourselves as women or men. Larson, John, Carlo, and Dalton are typical guys and they choose products, brands and consumption experiences that reflect who they are. What these consumers have realized is that the products and brands they use and the consumption experiences they choose contribute to their identity as men. Their masculinity is judged by the cars they drive, the drinks they order, the cigarettes they smoke, and the movies they like. Buy the wrong thing and one's masculinity is questioned; buy the right thing and one's masculinity is secured. Across many different product

categories, things are gendered. Think about how easy it is for you to match the following products with either men or women:

- Harley-Davidson motorcycle vs. Vespa scooter
- Mountain Dew vs. Diet Coke
- Chevy Corvette vs. Volkswagen Cabriolet
- Jack Daniels whiskey vs. Turning Leaf chardonnay
- Entourage vs. Sex in the City

Marlboro vs. Virginia Slims

Throughout history, marketers have created gendered brands, creating their brands and the stories they crafted about them in their advertising to appeal either to men or to women. One classic example comes from The Altria Group, formerly known as Philip Morris. The Marlboro cigarette brand, known today for its rugged American West imagery, actually began life as a cigarette targeted towards women. Early advertising for Marlboro from the 1920s featured the tagline "Mild as May." It was only in the 1960s that Marlboro created the Marlboro cowboy and the mythical place he inhabits, "Marlboro Country," which has fueled the masculine image the brand enjoys in the marketplace today. Today, the Marlboro brand team hosts smokers at the Marlboro Crazy Mountain Ranch in Montana to let them live out their cowboy fantasies. At the same time that the company was giving the Marlboro brand a masculine make-over, it introduced Virginia Slims, a cigarette targeted to women, that featured taglines like "It's a woman thing" and a more elegant, narrow shape, tapered to mimic a woman's fingers.

Diet Coke vs. Coke Zero

A more contemporary example comes from The Coca-Cola Company. For years, Diet Coke has reigned as the top selling diet soda in the marketplace. However, Diet Coke's sales have been fueled almost entirely by women. Why? Consumer research told marketers at Coca-Cola that men, increasingly conscious about their weight, would like less calories in their soda, but that they were turned off by Diet Coke and other diet sodas because of their ubiquitous appeal among women. It was only when Coca-Cola in 2005 introduced Coke Zero that men flocked to the category. Coke Zero was launched in a black can, which starkly contrasted with Diet Coke's white and silver can, reflecting, as Coca-Cola's marketers claimed, the fuller flavored, bolder drink inside. Coke Zero's irreverent launch advertising was also designed to pull in men, as was its sponsorship of the 2008 "Coke Zero 400" NASCAR race. With the launch of Coke Zero, today's men can finally drink diet soda with impunity!

High Tech Does Gender

Even in product categories normally thought of as gender-neutral, gendered products are emerging. In today's world, it is tough to find a college student without his or her cell phone or laptop computer—these devices have increasingly become extensions of ourselves. These tech gadgets are increasingly becoming gendered, shedding their androgynous designs for masculine or feminine elements. The new HP Mini Vivienne Tam Edition is an example. Touted as "The World's First Digital Clutch," this new, ultrathin and ultralight notebook computer is sleeved in a gorgeous design featuring peony flowers designed by fashion designer, Vivienne Tam. The notebook contains a "tech-chic" virtual experience inside which allows users to walk on a virtual fashion catwalk and customize their computer with Vivienne Tam wallpaper, screensavers, and games. A recent post to an Ask Slashdot web forum illustrates how technology is becoming increasingly gendered and the trouble this presents for men who have bought the wrong product:

Photo: Popazreal

HP Vivienne Tam

"I recently purchased a 10 inch white MSI wind. As you can see it's a small computer and it's good for what I use it for. I get a lot of comments from women saying it is 'cute' or 'adorable.' Not the good kind of cute that will get me the attention I want though, the kind of cute that says they think I have a different presence than I actually want to portray. So how can I make my netbook more manly, or at least have some witty line to respond to the their comments?" (basementman)

Why Do Marketers Create Gendered Brands?

Gendered brands deliver value to consumers, and therefore, deliver value to marketers. A brand has identity value for consumers if it helps them create their identities. Consumers will pay more for and remain loyal to a brand that has symbolic value that they can use to shape who they are. Brands with high levels of identity value derive a great deal of their brand equity from what the brand says about its users rather than what the product itself actually does. Given that our gender identity is so central to who we are, brands that help us be more masculine or feminine are especially prized by us as consumers. That is a reason why marketers are so anxious to create gendered brands.

However, creating a gendered brand also has its downsides. Whenever you have a brand that targets one gender, you are leaving half of your potential audience untapped. Marlboro could potentially double its sales if it could appeal to women as well, couldn't it? Gillette, "The Best a Man Can Get," now tells women to "Reveal the Goddess in You," managing a full line of men's and women's shaving products. This is the trap into which many marketers of gendered brands fall. Once they have become successful in penetrating the market associated with one gender, they look longingly at the large market populated by the other gender and think, "What if…?"

Gender-Bending Brands

Stagnant sales in many mature product categories are causing managers to look for new ways to increase their business. **Gender-bending**—taking a brand that has historically been targeted to one gender and now targeting it to the other gender—is becoming a more common occurrence. Many times, managers who want to gender-bend their brands merely adjust their brand names to include the opposite gender; for example, Procter and Gamble uses "Gillette" for its male products and "Gillette for Women" for its female products to distinguish them from each other. This helps clarify to a woman that the traditionally male brand is now making products for her and also helps protect the products men use from feminine intrusion. Other marketers create separate brand names for men and women; in the deodorant category, for example, Procter and Gamble offers a brand for each gender: Secret targets women while Old Spice targets men. Unilever sells body wash for women under the Dove brand name and body wash for men under the Axe brand name. Consumers don't know both brands are developed in the same laboratories and manufactured on the same lines. But some marketers do not adjust the names of their brands at all; instead, using the original brand names, they just launch new brand extensions targeting the opposite gender.

©istockphoto.com/Don Bayley

Gender-bending of motorcycles

This is when the trouble can start. When a consumer is using a brand to create a certain type of identity (including a gender identity), changing the brand's identity meanings is risky. Consumers rely on these identity meanings to communicate who they are and feel threatened when the brand begins to mean something else. The identity signals the consumers were using to communicate their gender identity to others begin getting all mixed up and the brand becomes less attractive to its consumers because its symbolic value is diluted. Consumers' response to changing identity meanings is particularly negative when the new identity meanings coming in are undesirable. Many luxury brands that have tried to launch lower priced product lines under the same brand have experienced backlash from their existing affluent consumers who do not want to be associated with "the riff-raff." Indie bands are often accused by their fans of selling out to the mainstream. Cool kids stop wearing a certain fashion when the less cool adopt it.

Gender Polarization and Politics

Consumer research has indicated that men may be particularly hostile to the incursion of feminine identity meanings into their brands. Why? Let's begin by looking way back in time. In virtually all cultures throughout history, there have been certain objects that have been kept for the exclusive use of men. Women were forbidden to touch, or sometimes even look at, these objects, which generally included items or spaces deemed sacred for religious or cultural reasons or which gave men power, for fear that they would contaminate them.[1] For example, Tahitian women were forbidden to touch men's fishing or hunting tools.[2] In contemporary times, these traditions still exist. Sociologists have shown that men at The Citadel, a military college for men which recently went co-ed, believed that women could contaminate the ring given to men upon their graduation just by touching it.[3] Consumer researchers have confirmed that men are especially leery of purchasing products and brands traditionally associated with women.[4] It seems that women can contaminate brands just as they contaminated sacred totems and talismans.

Why do men want to protect their consumption items from women? Because "being a man" is commonly defined as "not being a woman." Masculinity is understood as the antithesis of what is feminine. The two genders are polarized, constraining men to act like men, and women to act like women. However, gender is not just polarized, it is also political in many cultures. Androcentrism, where men and masculinity are more highly valued than women and femininity, reigns in many societies, both historical and contemporary. Calling a man effeminate is a severe insult in many cultures and most men try to avoid associating themselves with feminine characteristics, personality traits, behaviors, and possessions. In order to maintain their position at the top of the social hierarchy, men must avoid acting like women, and this constrains male consumers' choices in the marketplace.

©istockphoto.com/
Thomas Perkins

How men react when women start using male-gendered brands

So, what happens when brands traditionally used by men are targeted towards women? Let's take a look at a recent example from an online netnographic study I conducted among Porsche owners during the launch of the first non-sports car in the brand's history.[5]

Gender-Bending Porsche Cayenne SUV

Porsche may well be one of the world's most gendered brands. Treasured for their superior German engineering, award-winning design, and racing victories, Porsche sports cars are also valued by their owners for their masculine identity meanings. Since the brand's inception, Porsche has been linked with masculine imagery. Well known as "chick magnets," Porsches are purchased by men young and old in order to attract the opposite sex. Jokes, movie and book plots, and real life stories abound about men purchasing their first Porsches during their mid-life crises, trying to compensate for their decreasing attractiveness with a car that catches women's eyes. Porsche is such a male brand that in all of the movies featuring Porsche cars over the past forty years, 91% of the Porsche drivers have been male. Much of Porsche's brand equity derives from its identity meanings.

In 2003, in an effort to expand their market share, the parent company of Porsche launched the Porsche Cayenne SUV, the brand's first vehicle that was not a sports car. Although the company claimed it was targeting men who owned Porsche sports cars who also needed an SUV to transport their growing families, Porsche owners believed that the Cayenne was targeted towards women. Their collective howl of disbelief echoed around the

Photo: Christiaan Ploeger

Porsche 997 Carrera (top) and Porsche Cayenne (bottom)

world. *The New York Times* captured the spirit of their response: "There may be no vision more heretical to a testosterone-poisoned 911 owner than that of a suburban mother loading groceries into the back of her Porsche after dropping her children off at soccer practice."[6] In the article, a current Porsche sports car owner laments: "Every SUV I've seen is driven by some soccer mom on her cellphone. I hate these people, and that Porsche would throw me into that category made me speechless." A reporter from *Forbes* magazine concurred, "Porsche goes soccer mom…Has Porsche lost its soul?"[7] Existing Porsche owners felt betrayed and contaminated, as the following posts from the Web forum Rennlist.com illustrate:

"The Cayenne makes me feel like my favorite jazz record shop has decided to carry britteny spears records." (aaronschen)

"My GOD say it ain't so! I keep telling myself that if I wish and hope and pray hard enough… that it won't happen. That this SUV thing is all just a bad dream… I can just see it know… Some rich Soccer Mom driving the damn thing to pick up her kids with a bumper sticker that reads, Proud parent of

an honor student and a Baby on Board sticker next to the Barney stick on sunshade with a baby seat in back... NO! Just shoot me now!" (Doc).

So what happened? Many predicted that existing Porsche owners would abandon the brand now that women were using it, as it no longer represented the masculine identity they needed. But existing Porsche owners had too much at stake to just leave a brand that had become an essential piece of their identity. Instead, they banded together in web forums around the world to fight against the Porsche Cayenne SUV to ensure that the masculine identity meanings they were using stayed safe. They fought by protesting the brand in their online conversations with one another, in interviews they gave to the news media, and at local Porsche events. The ways in which they fought against the SUV turned out to be much more detrimental to the Porsche brand than if they had just abandoned it.

"Not Me": Derogating the SUV

First, existing owners began to label consumers who purchased the SUV with derogatory names, such as "soccer mom," "pretender," and "yuppie," as a way of distancing themselves from the incoming new owners. This name-calling was designed to humiliate consumers who had already bought a Cayenne, to show them their lowly place within the Porsche owner community, and to deter new consumers from buying them by imbuing the brand with derogatory feminine stereotypes. Cayenne owners were denied entry into the community of Porsche users. Here is an example from the Web forum Rennlist.com:

> "It'll be piloted by folks who woulda bought the Mercedes Benz/Range Rover if there weren't five of them in the subdivision already, who wouldn't consider a Lexus because it's 'jap crap' and who think BMW/VW is beneath them. They're not enthusiasts, they're consumers. They won't know or care that old time P-snobs will shun them."

In *the New York Times,* existing owner Robin Sun claims, "People will buy these Porsche SUV's because they're a fad, and they'll embarrass the real Porsche crowd. They're not going to know how to drive and they'll do stupid things."

"Not Real": Denying Legitimacy to the SUV

Second, existing owners began to claim that the Cayenne was not a "real Porsche," citing its feminine design, cupholders, automatic transmission, and shared

Brittany Spears in my favorite jazz record shop!!!

Photo: Christiaan Ploeger

Porsche 997 GT3 (top) and Porsche Cayenne (bottom)

componentry and assembly by Volkswagen as inauthentic elements. These arguments were put forth to deter Cayenne sales and to draw a boundary line between the Porsche SUV and the Porsche sports cars to protect the sports car owners from negative attributions being made about the Cayenne. This was used to exclude the Cayenne and its owners from Porsche race events and on-road greeting rituals practiced by Porsche owners, as seen in the following post from the Web forum Rennlist.com:

> "One thing is for sure: The SUV is NOT my brother! I always accepted the other models in the family—the 928s, 924s, Boxsters, etc. They were all sports cars. But the SUV: never!" (993RS)

"Not Porsche": The Porsche Brand is Contaminated by the SUV

Finally, the existing owners began differentiating between the "new Porsche" and the "old Porsche," claiming that the Porsche brand had been irreversibly harmed by the launch of the SUV. The existing owners switched their loyalties, disentangling themselves from the "new Porsche" and attaching themselves to the "old Porsche". This allowed them to continue owning their cars which represented the "old Porsche," while distancing themselves from the Cayenne and the new identity meanings it brought.

> "For me, it is religion... no sense in arguing about it or trying to convert me. I am not a fan, I am not going to BE a fan, and I am no longer a prospective customer... I like both of the P cars I have, but I have bought my last one. The pepper is a stupid strategic mistake... and stupid is forever." (Gretch)

All of these consumer actions were intended to stop the dilution of the identity meanings associated with the original Porsche brand. The valuable identity meanings previously associated with the parent brand did not transfer to the new Porsche Cayenne SUV brand extension. Existing Porsche owners became gatekeepers of Porsche's identity meanings, allowing some types of Porsche owners (namely sports car owners) access to them, but prohibiting access to Cayenne owners.

A Word to the Marketer: The Wisdom of Gender-Bending

Did Porsche make a mistake by launching the Porsche Cayenne SUV? Short term sales were spectacular. In the first selling year, Porsche sold more SUVs worldwide than sports cars and sales of the SUV have continued to be strong. Women who would never have considered the brand before are now actively purchasing the Porsche SUV and Porsche has added many new users to its consumer base. Hence, there are very tangible short term rewards that accrue to firms who gender-bend their brands. However, the response of Porsche's existing consumers gives us insight into the longer term, more intangible risks that gender-bending has on brands. The Porsche brand's identity meanings, an important contributor to its brand equity, are diluted when women use the brand. Existing owners feel "contaminated" by new owners and either leave the brand or construct barriers between themselves and the SUV drivers, keeping the valuable masculine identity meanings for themselves and taking them away from the brand extension and the contaminated parent brand.

Do the short term rewards outweigh the longer term risks of the loss of identity value and/or the loss of hard-core customers? That depends on the value we place on the brand equity Porsche receives from its identity meanings. For brands with low "gender identity equity," gender-bending is a low risk option, as consumers are using the brand for reasons other than building their identities. For brands with high "gender identity equity," the risk from gender-bending is high, as illustrated in the Porsche example. In this case, managers should evaluate alternative branding strategies, such as developing a new brand for the opposite gender, rather than contaminating the original gendered brand.

GENDER BENDER BRAND STRATEGIES		
Gender Equity Level	Gender-Bending Risk	Branding Strategy
Brand with Low Gender Identity Equity	Low	• Gender-bend the existing brand
Brand with High Gender Identity Equity	High	• Mainly focus on only one gender • Create separate brands for each gender

Boys and Their Toys

Let's return to Larson, John, Carlo, and Dalton, whom we introduced at the beginning of the chapter. These four men rely on the gendered identity meanings of the brands they use to communicate who they are (and who they are not). The brands serve as important props for Larson, John, Carlo, and Dalton to show others who they are as men. The Ford Mustang brings Larson back to his childhood when the Mustang was the muscle car of choice for 1960's greasers and evokes heroic memories of his father. Jose Cuervo's Web site and advertising promises John that he can "live notoriously well," by learning how to properly down a tequila shot without "pussyfooting around," playing up the fact that only real men have the courage to drink tequila straight-up. Carlo becomes a rugged cowboy when he smokes his Marlboro's. And Dalton distances himself from the movies his girlfriend enjoys by labeling them "chick flicks." As long as the Mustang, Jose Cuervo, and Marlboro brands maintain their masculine identity meanings, Larson, John, and Carlo will continue to use them. As long as Stolichnaya Razberi and Confessions of a Shopaholic maintain their feminine identity meanings, John and Dalton will avoid them.

Brand managers fill their brands with imagery, stories, and personality to appeal to either men or women, infusing them with gendered identity meanings. Being a brand manager of a gendered brand requires understanding and respecting the identity meanings that consumers use, and protecting them so that the identity message the brand sends when a consumer uses it supports the identity needs of the brand's consumers.

ENDNOTES

[1] Herdt, G.H., *Guardians of the Flutes: Idioms of Masculinity*. (McGraw-Hill, New York, 1981).

[2] Lombroso, Cesare, Guglielmo Ferrero, Nicole Hahn Rafter, and Mary Gibson, *Criminal Woman, the Prostitute, and the Normal Woman*. (Duke University Press, Durham, NC, 2004).

[3] Addelston, Judi and Michael Stirratt, "The Last Bastion of Masculinity: Gender Politics at The Citadel," in Masculinities in Organizations, edited by Cliff Cheng (Sage, Thousand Oaks, CA, 1996), p. 54.

[4] Alreck, Pamela L., Robert B. Settle, and Michael A. Belch, "Who Responds to 'Gendered' Ads, and How?" *Journal of Advertising Research* 22 (2), 25 (1982).

[5] Avery, Jill, "Saving Face by Making Meaning: The Negative Effects of Consumers' Self-Serving Response to Brand Extension". Doctoral Dissertation, *Harvard Business School* (2007).

[6] Tanz, Jason, "Wounded to a Quick by a Porsche Gone Astray", *New York Times*, New York, (December 13, 2002).

[7] Meredith, Robyn, "Porsche Goes Soccer Mom," *Forbes*, (February 2002), 169(3), 54-56.

THE ENCHANTED CONSUMER
POSTMODERN CONSUMPTION EXPERIENCE AND TRENDS
The Esoteric, the Experiential, and the Emergent

Beatlemania! If you happen to be in London, you may join this tour by an enterprising Beatles fan, Gregory S. He will show you Sir Paul McCartney's workspace, the studio where "Hey Jude" was recorded, and the famous Apple studio where Beatles played their last gig on the rooftop. The tour sells out on most days.[1]

In New York city, at an East Village monastery, you can dine with Rasanath Dasa (cost $20 per person). Rasanath Das is an engineer with an MBA from Cornell University. He has been an investment banker for Bank of America and a strategy consultant for Deloitte. But now he is a monk and a spiritual thinker. "Wow! Fantastic experience!" says Brad Svrluga who dined with the monk recently. "The vegetarian lunch was delicious and conversation vibrant. For the hour and half I was at the monastery I forgot I was in fast paced NYC," opines Kristine Michelsen-Correa.[2]

This is the stuff consumer researchers call *postmodern*. Experiential. Authentic. Global. An increasing number of consumers—certainly only a niche segment by any stretch but substantial and growing nonetheless—are seeking it. They are consuming, not just products, but also the symbols behind them, and their meaning. The "consumption of meaning" comes into full focus when the goods being consumed are intangible—such as art and memories and virtual life. How consumers consume the meaning of these symbolic and experiential goods and what life satisfaction they derive from such consumption is our topic in this note. We also take an inventory of recent and emerging trends in consumer behavior, ranging from the rising power of women to globalism to digital autobiographies.

OBJECTS OF DESIRE
DEEP MEANING IN CONSUMPTION

What does your car mean to you? Do your sunglasses have a special meaning for you? Do you have a special attachment to your pair of jeans? Your CB textbook? And, would you feel sad giving away your old high school football outfit? To explore the symbolic meaning of goods, we have selected eight unique and significant consumption entities, here simply called *consumption potpourri*. This is a rich cornucopia of the culture of consumption itself, so let us immerse ourselves and experience it.

1. APPROPRIATION OF PRODUCTS
"How I Anoint What I Buy"

The clothes you wear, the car you drive, the mobile phones you use—these products are produced by the ton and bought by millions of other consumers. How is it, then, that you come to consider your car as your own, separate from other identical units of the same brand; you come to view your jeans as something special and unlike

any others; and you come to like your own mobile phone so much that if you were to lose it, replacing it by another exactly identical unit wouldn't be the same thing? When you bought it—the car, the pair of jeans, the cell phone—it was one of the countless many; but after you acquired it, something happened to it; you did something to it, so it somehow became different, unique, and special to you. What you did is called **appropriation**—the process of making something one's own.[3] Although consumers never say so, they are always attempting to appropriate their acquisitions—the products they acquire as gifts or as purchases, at least the important ones. When objects are appropriated, they somehow become special, and as such they become sources of extra satisfaction. Let us see how this process of appropriation works.

Basically, appropriation entails investing ourselves in the product and somehow separating and distancing the product from its original existence as a mass produced unit. This process consists of five rituals: selection, acquisition, exchange, possession, and usage.[4]

appro priation

Selection Ritual This is the process the consumer undertakes to identify and select the desired object. The fact that the consumer selected it from so many other products makes that brand or object more salient to the consumer. The more time the consumer spends in selecting the product, the more he/she sees himself/herself invested in it. Somehow the very process of selection puts the self into the product and distinguishes the specific object from others (notwithstanding similarity in a physical sense).

Thus, products whose selection entails much personal investment of time will become more thoroughly appropriated. In particular, when we choose a specific product after rejecting several others, then by contrast with those products we reject, we feel an affinity toward those we select. Moreover, in the process of selection, if we were to judge products also by how well they reflect our personalities, then we would experience that much more affinity and personal feeling toward the chosen product.

Exchange Ritual An exchange ritual is an event surrounding the acquisition of a product as a gift from someone. A product received as a gift becomes unique because it includes the memory of the gift-giver. Occasionally, we also buy products as self-gifts, and in these instances, the memory of the cause for celebration serves to distinguish the product in our minds as something special.

Acquisition Ritual Many consumers follow certain acquisition rituals; for instance, they take along their best friends when they go to take possession of a new car, they wear special clothing to get a diamond or the like, or they consult an astrologer to decide exactly when to buy an engagement ring. In many ethnic cultures, certain days are considered more auspicious for acquiring a significant new product like a car or a house. Many ethnic groups also perform certain religious rituals, such as worshipping in the name of the newer possession or anointing the object itself.

Possession Ritual Often consumers try to modify a product before they take possession of it—for example, by retrofitting or customizing a new car, or by remodeling a house. When we acquire previously owned objects (e.g., a house, car, clothing, etc.), often we attempt to transform or alter them, in part to exorcise the ghost of the previous owner, so to speak. For example, we change the paint or window treatments on a house, or we get new wheel covers on the car. Through these rituals and transformations, we appropriate all objects we consider significant in our lives.

Usage Ritual Finally, we appropriate some objects simply by using them; somehow, they seem to mold themselves to our individual bodies and idiosyncratic behaviors. As I drive my car, I feel it is getting used to the way I drive so it is now mine and special. Likewise, as I break in my shoes, or wear my jeans, I see them progressively fitting better and better over time (in part because they become softer with washing). I also personalize a product through some modifications in its use—for example by selecting the ring tones for my cell phone, I make a mass produced phone unique, special, and *my* own.

Sometimes, we perform these rituals as second nature and sometimes, with great fanfare (e.g., driving out in a new car to show it off). Regardless, such rituals result in products becoming anointed, and such anointment both begins and nurtures our attachment

deep meaning in consumption

virtual living
appropriation
wireless consumer
authenticity
technology consumption
gift exchange
media fiction consumption
body adornment

to the products we acquire and own. That is why our products become very especial to us.

2. CONSUMING AUTHENTICITY
"Bringing the Glorious Past into Present Life"

Authentic *Random House Dictionary* defines *authentic* as "Conforming to fact and therefore worthy of trust, reliance, or belief; Having a claimed and verifiable origin or authorship; not counterfeit or copied." Here, in the context of consumer products, we will define **authenticity** as the genuineness of an object in its likeness as it existed at a time in history or when it first originated.

Authenticity is an important source of value and life satisfaction for consumers. Although consumers differ in the extent to which they seek authentic experience, most consumers do enjoy authentic experience at least occasionally in their lives. Who among us has not paused at Dick Clark's American Band Stand or Planet Hollywood to look at a dress originally owned by Marilyn Monroe? (You can pick up some fascinating memorabilia from one of the five Dick Clark's in the USA: Branson, MO; Molly Pitcher on the New Jersey Turnpike; Chandler, AZ; Phoenix, AZ; and Salt Lake City, UT. And you can find Planet Hollywood in New York City; London, UK; Riyadh, Saudi Arabia; Olympia Mall, Kuwait; Bali, Indonesia; and Dubai, UAR, among other cities.) Original? Well, almost!

Some consumers seek authenticity as an occasional experience. Others want to incorporate it into their everyday lives. Likewise, some are deeply attached to a particular domain of interest; others are curious but not possessed by it. Thus, the Elvis Presley Museum in Memphis attracts thousands of visitors every week; some come for the first and only time, and they enjoy viewing all the Elvis artifacts. Later in their lives, they will occasionally remember this experience with fond memory, but beyond that they will go about their lives without thinking of Elvis. Others will wrap themselves in the Elvis experience—visiting the Memphis museum frequently, having several Elvis items (replicas) in their homes, listening to Elvis music, reading his biographies, and frequently talking about him with friends and even strangers.

Authenticity in objects comes in two forms: original and in replica. In the original form, the object is

authenticity

believed to have actually existed in a specific time period and to have been used in a specific circumstance. Thus, an "original" Marilyn Monroe dress is indeed the one that was actually worn by Ms. Monroe. In contrast, in a replica, authenticity is judged by how similar the object is to the original real object—e.g., the dress on display is not the one actually worn by Ms. Monroe, but the dress she actually wore looked exactly like this one.[5]

Consumer enjoyment and satisfaction gained from the experience of authenticity also comes in two forms: exploration and connection.[6] For consumers who are not enduringly involved in the domain of the authentic experience, viewing an authentic object or witnessing a replica of an authentic historical event is simply an **exploration**, an act of getting to learn and know about that object or event. These consumers feel the joy of simply seeing the object or the place from times past; it satisfies their curiosity and gives them the satisfaction of knowing a slice of the past more directly, more intimately. The second group of consumers—those who are enduringly involved in the specific domain—feel the experience as a much more personal event. Viewing an authentic object or being in an authentic place gives them the sense of **being connected** with the past, somehow being part of that era. It is for them a fantasy world come true.

Exploration-oriented consumers are quite satisfied with the replica form of authenticity. **Connection-seeking consumers** seek out, in contrast, authenticity in its original form; they are unlikely to experience the same joy by viewing or experiencing a replica—they want the "real thing." Moreover, connection-seeking consumers will not stop at simply viewing the authentic exhibit; rather they will want to bring back with them a substantial part of the authentic exhibit (in replica form, of course)—tangible objects with which they can then surround themselves in everyday life.

The foregoing description refers to historical objects and events. But there is, these days, a significant trend of authenticity in everyday commercial products. This sort of authenticity resides in "the genuineness and uniqueness of an object in its first origin." The product was created uniquely from materials and by craftsmanship sourced from places and persons/artisans not already found in other mass produced goods. These products incorporate some unique combination of local ingredients, resources, culture, and the skills of individual artisans, and are thus distinguished from mass produced goods. Starbucks and Anthropologie are good examples. Authentic brands, when they expand in scale, retain their claims to authenticity by maintaining their original "formula" of making and selling goods.

3. GIFT-EXCHANGE AS CONSUMER BEHAVIOR
"I Will Love You if You Love Me"

Gift-exchange—perhaps no other custom among humans is so pregnant simultaneously with economic and social meaning. In every culture and nation, people of virtually all ages and economic means expend considerable time, money, and thought on buying gift items. For several weeks preceding Christmas day, for example, in most of the Western world, consumers are on a mission and adventure, combing stores to find suitable gifts for as many as 20 to 30 persons. For some, it is a period of economic hardship, as they scrape together enough money to buy gifts for everyone on their lists. And this economic burden is joined by considerable social risk as each gift must fit the recipient's expectations and still be within the buyer's budget. One wrong move, and it could jeopardize the relationship with the intended gift recipient. Therefore, let us understand the consumer psychology of gift-exchange.

A **gift** is defined as a tangible or intangible product given voluntarily by one person to another, through some ritual presentation and embodying some symbolic representation of the giver's sentiments for the recipient.[6]

The Cultural Meaning of Gift Exchange

The very idea of gift-exchange (regardless of the specific gift occasion or the gift item) is embedded in culture. Every society imposes certain obligations about gift-giving. In fact, we all have three obligations: an obligation to give, an obligation to receive; and an obligation to reciprocate. All gifts have some symbolic meaning. Basically, a gift-giver expresses empathy—saying in effect that "I share in your life, in your joy, in your celebration; I am happy because you are happy." Not giving a gift when expected communicates that the expected giver does not wish to maintain a relationship with the assumed recipient. Conversely, the recipient has the obligation to receive. Not accepting a gift would imply that the targeted recipient does not accept either the relationship itself or the specific sentiment the gift conveys. Third, reciprocation is a core norm between gift-exchange partners. **Reciprocation** means returning the favor in like manner. Once accepted, the recipient is expected to reciprocate at some future time. Non-reciprocation will convey a desire not to maintain the relationship.[7]

There is one exception to the norm of reciprocity. Generally speaking, reciprocity is expected among status equals (i.e., people of equal status) but not from status subordinates (e.g., personal assistants, valets, servants, mail-persons, etc.); to these recipients, the gift generally conveys appreciation for the services rendered. Occasionally, status superiors may also not reciprocate (or not reciprocate with the same personal touch), signifying that the gift is viewed as a token of gratitude from the gift-giver for their patronage or tutelage. Every gift serves three functions:[8]

1. **Social Integration** The gift integrates the giver into the social group. By giving the gift, the giver in effect says to the recipients, "I want to integrate myself into your group, into your society. I want to be seen as part of it."

2. **Social Distance Reduction** By giving a gift, the gift-giver gets closer to the recipient. It is a means of building a relationship with the desired person or increasing the distance (by not giving the gift) from those who are less desired. We fashion our gifts accordingly, being generous or incorporating a personal touch for the former group or people, and barely meeting the obligatory expectation in the latter case. When properly used, gifts serve as social lubrication.

3. **Tangible Expressions of Relationships** Not only do gifts build relationships (i.e., reduce social distance), but they also specify the nature of the relationship. Gifts exchanged by family members are different from those exchanged by coworkers, which in turn are different from gifts between lovers.

Cultural Meaning

Beyond these general functions, specific gifts are means of conveying one's identity or status.[9] Gift givers consider gifts a reflection of their own identities and status as well as the status of the intended recipient. Certain characteristics of gifts convey status and identity. These characteristics are market price, brand name reputation, and uniqueness. (See Figure 1.) Other characteristics convey expressiveness. **Expressiveness** refers to the extent to which the gift is accompanied by the giver's sentiment. Purely utilitarian gifts (e.g., coffee mugs) are low in expressiveness. Non-utilitarian gifts (e.g. flowers) are high in sentiment. Often, utilitarian gifts possess expressive qualities because of the prestige of the brand name, such as Godiva chocolates.

In purely obligatory gift situations, often the

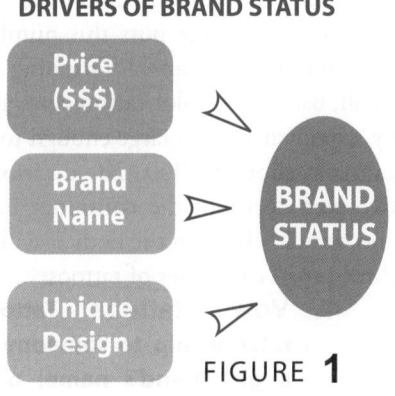

DRIVERS OF BRAND STATUS

Price ($$$)

Brand Name

Unique Design

BRAND STATUS

FIGURE **1**

recipient tries to "signal" what items he or she is expecting or can use. Sometimes this signaling is explicit, as in a bridal registry. Many cultures do not allow such explicit signaling. For example, in Eastern cultures, the concept of a bridal registry does not exist, and it would be considered rude to indicate what one wants as a wedding gift—although, as in everything else, even here, city dwellers are adopting some modified version of the concept.

When the gift recipient is not forthcoming with any such indication, the gift giver may try to "read" the intended recipient's wishes or needs, especially if he or she feels sentimental toward the latter and is consequently motivated to delight the gift recipient. The more correctly the giver is able to read these wishes and fashion the gift accordingly, the more expressive and sentimental the gift becomes. Some gifts are acquired or produced with personal labor and skills; other givers transform the gift item with some personal touch. The more the giver invests personal effort in finding the gift or in producing or modifying the gift, and correspondingly, the farther the giver removes the gift from the realm of a marketable (or market-available), mass-produced commodity, the greater the expressiveness of the gift.

Because gifts have cultural meaning, the selection of a gift is a serious consumer task, filled with great social risks. The social risk stems from the following potential errors:

1. **Status Incongruence** The gift item may be perceived inappropriate to the status of the giver and/or the receiver

2. **Disproportionate** The gift might violate the norm of reciprocity—unequal to the gift previously received by the gift-giver

3. **Impersonal** The gift might be considered less personal or more personal than desired.

When relationships are in the formative stage, the risk is one of over-reaching rather than under-reaching; the exchange parties must start with relatively impersonal gifts and progress in small steps to more personal gifts—constantly reading with each exchange episode the recipient's acknowledgement and acceptance of the giver's sentiments.

Such is the fascinating world of gift exchange and the all too important role gifts play in our lives.

4. CONSUMPTION OF BODY ADORNMENTS
"My Body is a Scrapbook."

All humans are motivated to look good. That goal leads to three forms of consumption: (1) regular grooming rituals, such as applying makeup; (2) permanently altering the body mass, such as by pumping iron or through liposuction; and (3) making relatively permanent marks on the body, such as piercings and tattoos. All three forms of consumption have the same underlying motives, although some motives are more prominent in one form than in

PSYCHOLOGY OF GIFT-GIVING

EXHIBIT 1

Although there are literally hundreds of occasions for gift-exchange, and thousands of possible gift items, they can all be characterized along following dimensions.

- Structured versus Emergent
- Ritualistic versus Expressive
- Utilitarian versus Aesthetic
- Anticipated versus Surprise
- Altruistic versus Agonistic

First, gift occasions can be structured or emergent. Structured occasions are standard occasions that occur repeatedly on the same predetermined days. Christmas and Valentine's Day are examples of structured occasions for an entire population of consumers, and birthdays, and anniversaries are standard for individual consumers. Emergent occasions are those that are not predetermined and do not repeat in a regular pattern. Examples are baby shower, weddings, hospitalization, etc.

Second, gifts are either anticipated or a surprise. Most gifts are expected by their recipients; the occasion demands it; social norms nearly mandate it. Occasionally, however, consumers indulge in gift-giving just to show extra caring for the recipient, as a pleasant surprise.

Third, and related to the above characteristic, is the concept of ritualistic gift. Ritualistic gifts are given simply because it is a ritual, the occasion demands it. There are no personal feelings on the part of gift giver. Weddings, baby showers, birthdays of close relatives, Christmas, promotion of a close colleague, farewell party, etc., are all examples of ritualistic gifts. Positively expressive gifts on the other hand are given to people one has special feelings for. These may be given on ritualistic occasions, but they go beyond mere obligation. Positively expressive gifts, as opposed to merely ritualistic gifts, are chosen with consideration of the recipient's needs (often unexpressed) or preferences and one goes beyond the call of duty, in expense as well as in involvement in finding the gift.[E1]

Fourth, gifts differ in their "self-serving" content. Altruistic gifts are those given largely for the recipient's benefit, with no consideration of immediate personal gain. In contrast, agonistic gifts are intended to gain an immediate personal advantage. Most business gifts tend to be of this type.

Finally, gifts can be utilitarian—products the gift recipient can use for his or her currently felt needs, e.g., a small appliance, kitchen utensils, or an airline ticket. Alternatively, gifts can be aesthetic or symbolic—items whose principal value is not material but sentimental or intangible, e.g., jewelry, pictures, artwork, etc. Of course many products when given as gifts are a mix—utilitarian but at the same time also symbolic, e.g., a monogrammed shirt, a picture frame, or intimate apparel.[E2]

E1 for further reading, see Mary Ann Mcgrath and John Sherry, "giving voice to the gift: the use of projective techniques to recover lost meanings," *j. of consumer psychology*, 2 (2), 1993, 171-191.

E2 this section is based on diverse literature: John Sherry (1983, "Gift giving in anthropological perspective," *J. of Consumer Research*, vol. 10, (sept), 157-167; Mary Wolfinbarger (1990), "Motivations and symbolism in gift-giving behavior," in Advances in Consumer Research volume 17, eds. Marvin E. Goldberg, Gerald Gorn and Richard W. Pollay, pages: 699-706; Cele Otnes, Julie A Ruth, Constance C. Milbourne (1994), "The pleasure and pain of being close: men's mixed feelings about participation in valentine's day gift exchange," in *Advances in Consumer Research*, Vol. 21, eds. Chris t. Allen and Deborah Roedder John, 159-164.

another. We explore these in the context of tattoos.[10]

Tattooing has its roots in ancient history when tribal societies engraved their bodies with symbols of animals, gods, and elements of nature. In modern times, and in the West, the revival or renaissance of tattooing began in the late 1950s with the influence of artists like Lyle Tuttle, who founded the Tattoo Museum and Hall of Fame in San Francisco. The academic and commercial art worlds began taking notice of tattooing as an art form; gallery showings of tattoos as an art form increased, creating general awareness among consumers.

SOCIAL RISKS IN GIFT-GIVING
Beware what you give!

1. **The gift is below status —yours or the recipient's**
2. **The gift does not reciprocate for what you received**
3. **The gift is too impersonal or too personal**

Furthermore, this "art culture" positioning of tattooing attracted both better artists and a better clientele—not merely those who were on the fringe of society. At one time, only rough bikers, rebels, and sailors got tattoos, but now middle class consumers, college students, sports heroes, and media celebrities have all taken to getting tattoos.

Although no current statistics are available, according to a 1990 survey by American Households (unpublished) of 10,000 random households, 3% of the respondents had a tattoo.[10] A source puts this number in 1996 at 12 to 20 million Americans.[11] Tattooing costs money. Even a small, basic, one-color tattoo costs about a $100; a tattoo by a renowned artist large enough to cover the entire back can cost about $5,000. The decision to get a tattoo is a two-part decision: the consumer has to select a symbol and decide where on the body it will be applied. There are three broad categories of tattoos:

1. **"Vow" tattoos** Tattoos that signify a relationship to someone or something (e.g., a girl friend's name) or a commitment to

someone.

2. **Group affiliation tattoos** Tattoos depicting a gang or sports team symbol.
3. **Symbolic tattoos** Tattoos of birth signs, symbols signifying some self-association like occupation, hobbies, etc.

In terms of body site, men generally tend to get them on arms; women choose from a greater range of locations: in addition to arms, they use ankles, thighs, back, lower back, hips, etc.

In general, consumer motivations for getting tattoos can be summed up in five categories, shown in Exhibit 2.

Males tend to view tattoos primarily as symbols of self-concept or self-control. In contrast, women view them primarily as a beauty aid and decoration, although self-identity is as strong a motive for them as for men. When aesthetic beauty is the principal motive, designs are chosen not because they symbolize anything about the consumer but because they are beautiful art works and because consumers think they look good on the body. Many consumers choose astrological or religious symbols both because of their beliefs in the power of supernatural beings and also to show their identities as religious persons. Many consumers choose tattoos depicting their favorite stars, sports team names, significant others, and romantic interests,

and for these consumers the primary motivation is group affiliation. For Latinos, for example, tattoos on the hand often signify ethnic pride and group affiliation—the most common symbols popular among Latinos are Christian religious symbols (e.g., angels, crosses, devils, fairies).[12]

Alienation is perhaps the motive that comes closest to the motives of the earliest adopters of tattoo consumers in modern times—those on the fringe of society. They adopted tattooing simply as a means of rebelling against the mainstream, a sort of "in your face" gesture. Consumers of this ilk are the ones who go heavy—getting multiple tattoos and covering large areas of the body.

EXHIBIT 2

CONSUMER MOTIVES FOR GETTING TATTOOS

Aesthetic beauty Aesthetic value as art and decoration of the body

Magic/Mystery Belief in the power of certain symbols to bring good luck or toprotect oneself from evil

Affiliation Desire to affiliate with certain people, groups, or institutions

Self-esteem Renders tangible the feeling of one's control over one's body

Identity construction Construction, restructuring, and definition of self-identity

Self-esteem comes from feeling a sense of freedom to get whatever tattoo one wants and to put it on one's body. As one tattooee (a 30-something female who recently had been divorced) said, "My body is NOW mine, so I can do whatever I like with it." This ability to alter one's body becomes a powerful symbol of self-definition.

Finally, the most potent motivation is identity construction and identity display. A body is really a surface on which consumers want to write, for the whole world to see, their identities. For many consumers, tattoos become a collection and the body a vehicle for displaying collections. One consumer, who had gotten tattoos from 35 different artists, described his body as a "scrapbook" symbolizing his life history. Consumers who see tattoos as a means of identity construction and identity display have to deliberate a lot in choosing their tattoos—a misstep could permanently engrave the wrong identity on their bodies.

5. CONSUMPTION OF MEDIA FICTION
"Dear Producer: Don't Forget I Am the Armchair Director."

Today television reaches all corners of the world, including the remote villages of third-world countries. Most consumers are exposed to at least some TV on a regular basis. Whereas some of this TV viewing is to get news and information, much of it is for entertainment.

Millions of consumers around the world become regular viewers of specific program series such as *The Apprentice*, *Survivor*, *Friends*, or *The Real World*. Not only do they watch these, but they then spend considerable time discussing the episodes with friends and family and often thinking about them. They become enduringly involved. This enduring consumption of TV episodes becomes a significant source of life satisfaction for many consumers, who manifest a fan-like devotion to the show. What is the nature of this consumption experience? What is the source of satisfaction here?

Consumer researchers have identified three components of this consumption experience: (1) meaning negotiation, (2) belief consumption, and (3) artifact consumption.[13] **Meaning negotiation** refers to seeing meaning in the episode, understanding the episode, and accepting it as logical and plausible. If a show or a movie has events that do not seem logical, then we typically do not like the show; we reject it as silly or implausible. Sometimes we are not sure we have understood the meaning, so to validate our views, we discuss the event or episode with others, and through their agreement or correction, we come to establish the meaning or validate our own opinions.

Belief consumption refers to believing in the core values and concepts underlying the show. The popular TV show *Will and Grace*, for example, is based on the theme of people living an alternative lifestyle; in watching the show regularly, we in effect accept the legitimacy (and normality) of that lifestyle. Finally, by consuming the artifacts—the accoutrements that accompany the show—consumers bring the show more squarely into their lives. We illustrate these three "benefits" with *The X-Files* in Exhibit 3.

6. TECHNOLOGY CONSUMPTION EXPERIENCE

"Gizmos: I Love Them, I Hate Them"

It is difficult these days to get teenagers and young adults (and sometimes even more mature people) to focus on listening to you. Their fingers are busy texting and their eyes are taking in the video on their mobile screens, even as you are speaking to them directly. In college classrooms across the nations, students adroitly "toggle" their eyes, ears, and minds between the professor's words and the more alluring screens on their various media devices. They are constantly multitasking, silently congratulating themselves on mastering this art. In their minds, they are learning and processing at double or triple pace twice or three-times the amount of information. Some elders and professors marvel at this unique skill of youngsters; others are saddened that the learner time that should have been devoted to reflection and thought as the speaker pauses is now "utilized" for thorough devotion to alternative media.

Technology in consumers' lives is a "mixed blessing" —referred to in marketing as a *paradox*. Consumer researchers David Glen Mick and Susan Fournier have identified eight paradoxes of technology:[14]

Control/Chaos Your caller ID service gives you control of whether or not to take the call. But it also gives your friends reason to suspect that you are screening your calls.

Freedom/Enslavement A cell phone gives you freedom not to be tied to a place if you are expecting a call; at the same time, you now have to take it everywhere, and you feel so helpless on days you forget to take it with you.

Also because people can reach you no matter where you are, you feel enslaved.

New/Obsolete You are fascinated by the newness of a model of car or phone, but also saddened at the thought that it too will soon be obsolete.

Competence/Incompetence Technology makes you feel more competent, more able. For example, using publishing software, you can now publish professional quality resumes, invitation cards, and reports, and you can automatically spell-check the document. At the same time, the same software can be daunting to learn or can suddenly produce errors from which you wouldn't know how to recover. And you can suddenly feel technology-illiterate and thus experience a new level of incompetence.

Efficiency/Inefficiency Using the Internet to gather information and even shop can be efficient. At the same time, sometimes you can spend hours surfing the net or getting an online merchant to answer your questions or resolve problems.

Fulfills/Creates Needs Having an e-mail account is great—so you can now send messages to friends and acquaintances. But suddenly, you start receiving junk mail, so now you need software to block unwanted e-mails (although many e-mail services such as AOL now provide this utility to subscribers).

Assimilation/Isolation Big screen TV becomes an excuse for having a Super Bowl party so you can have friends and feel socially connected; at the same time, the TV becomes the focal point of the occasion, replacing social conversations.

Engagement/Disengagement Creating a PowerPoint presentation can be a fascinating, all-absorbing creative task with opportunities for customization. On the other hand, in the presentation, the form takes over the substance, and there is less opportunity to establish an emotional connection with the audience—the kind that an erudite speaker can make speaking directly without any technological aid.

Consumer Experience of Paradoxes

How does a consumer experience these paradoxes? What mental and psychological reactions does the experience of these paradoxes create? And how do consumers manage that experience? CB Researchers David Mick and Susan Fournier have outlined a model, shown in Figure 2.

As shown in the model, consumers experience the paradox as a conflict or with ambivalence; for example, I know that the computer will raise my competence, but also that I will have to understand the manual. Even the anticipation of such a paradox, let alone the actual experience of it, produces conflict or ambivalence among

CONSUMPTION OF MEDIA FICTION: X-FILES CONSUMPTION COMMUNITY EXHIBIT 3

X-Philes are fans of the daring TV show that premiered on September 10, 1993, on the American TV network Fox Channel. Its grand finale was a 2-hour long show that aired on May 19, 2002, ending a 9-year block-buster run. The show featured two FBI agents, Fox Mulder and Dana Scully, with each episode oriented toward solving a crime case. What was unusual about the show is that it juxtaposed truth and fiction drawn from popular conspiracy theories and also belief in supernatural powers. The show's creator, Chris Carter, once stated that the show was based on three maxims: "Trust No One," "I Want to Believe," and "The Truth is Out There." More than 14 million viewers, typically young, urban, educated consumers, tuned in every week. A small but significant proportion of this group are X-Philes, the show's ardent fans who not only watched the show but also spent hours in chat rooms, attended fan conventions, and bought and sported show-related merchandise.

Embracing the show's driving maxims, the fans themselves seemed to be driven by analogous supra-beliefs: "I Want to Believe," "The Meaning is Out There," and "Trust This One." This is how these supra-beliefs translated into consumption behaviors.

Negotiating Aesthetic Consumption Standards

Media events that are consumed are always evaluated against some unwritten aesthetic standards (for example that "the story should be internally consistent"); if the media product (e.g., a TV show or a movie) falls short of this standard, the consumer views the consumption as not enjoyable. This judgment-making is itself a consumption experience. Fans typically communicate about what they found substandard and what was above par in meeting the unwritten aesthetic standard. For example, one chat room participant wrote:

> "What is up with these killer kitties? A cat cannot kill a human! Even if it is possessed by some spiritual dude."

Another fan initially interpreted the feral cats shown in one episode as a nonphysical manifestation. However, after an explanation from another X-phile member, she altered her interpretation:

> "Ok, I have thought better of it. … The feral cats were probably real… I just assumed they were illusions because they vanished at the end of the episode. Could be… doesn't have to be. I'll go with it."

This is what we mean by meaning negotiation being a part of consumption experience —and it is both a challenge and source of consumption satisfaction. This meaning negotiation (not just understanding the logic of a show, but also that the understood meaning meets a shared aesthetic standard) is why most consumers discuss and opine about any media event they consume. Thus, consumption occurs at two times: once when consumers are watching the show, and second when consumers are discussing it (to validate their perception of its meaning).

Consuming Beliefs About Mysterious Experiences

X-Philes also shared their real-world encounters with mysterious things. One fan posted: "A couple of nights ago, I saw these two bright lights just hanging in the sky…" And another one wrote: "People think these UFOs are just Hollywood fantasies. It is not true! Don't be a fool. Be a believer!" X-philes thus consume their beliefs in mysterious objects first while viewing the show and later validate them through assertive sharing with others like them who also want to believe in these mysteries.

Consuming the Artifacts

There is a poster behind Mulder's desk that says "I want to Believe." A fan wanted to know where he could buy one. Possessing this poster and other merchandise is yet another way for fans to connect to the show, to bring the shows' mysterious themes into their own lives. On the X-Net there is considerable buying and selling of such merchandise and exchange among the members. Now, first the possession of artifacts is in itself a way of bringing the show into one's life in a tangible way; but, equally valuable, using exchange as a mechanism to acquire them brings consumers into interaction with other community members, and this in turn is a means of social adhesion and community building.

13. Based on Robert V. Kozinets, "'I Want to Believe': A Netnography of X-Philes' Subculture of Consumption," *Advances in Consumer Research*, eds. M. Brucks and D. MacInnes, Vol. 24, p. 470-475.

A MODEL OF TECHNOLOGY CONSUMPTION EXPERIENCE

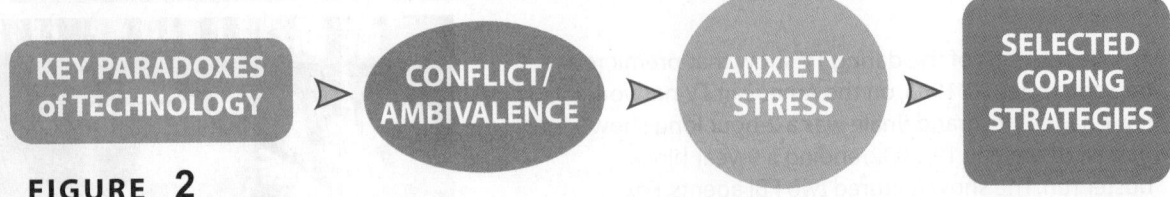

KEY PARADOXES of TECHNOLOGY ▷ CONFLICT/ AMBIVALENCE ▷ ANXIETY STRESS ▷ SELECTED COPING STRATEGIES

FIGURE 2

consumers. Next, this conflict or ambivalence produces anxiety—anxiety about how to avoid the negative side of technology while embracing the positive side. Some consumers cope with such anxiety by delaying the adoption of new technology. Others adopt it but with cautious and limited use (e.g., be very circumspect in posting on Facebook).[15]

7. THE WIRELESS CONSUMER

"I am not really here, but 'here' is nowhere."

Wireless phones. They are everywhere these days. Their availability to the masses was presaged by a TV commercial a few years ago. In that TV ad, a teenager in the backseat of a car taps her window to catch the attention of a tycoon in a stretch limo in the adjacent lane. She asks, "Excuse me, do you have a cell phone?" Annoyed, the wealthy old tycoon answers, "Of course I do," to which the young girl cheerily chirps, "So do I. So do I!"

Today, nearly every consumer in the Western world carries a cell phone, and most in the developing nations have access to one. Whereas men and women are equally represented in the wireless world, men tend to use wireless communication more often than women (8.3 calls per day versus 5.5 by women), in part because men use their phones for work—three times more often than do women.[17] Until only a few years ago, the principal reason and use of cell phones was for work and business. Today, its dominant use is for personal and social communications, especially among the masses. Its principal defining feature—mobility—has given a new sense of freedom and control to consumers. No longer are they tied down to a place. They can connect anytime, anywhere, to anyone whose cell phone number they know. Furthermore, as more consumers avail themselves of Web access service on their cell phones, more and more of them will also access any information, anytime, anywhere.

The latest development in wireless phones is, of course, the incorporation of a digital photography feature. You simply point the "eye" of the combined device toward someone or something, and you capture the image instantly. This digital image can then be downloaded onto your PC. If your cell phone is also equipped with a wireless Internet application, you can then e-mail that picture instantly to a friend.

Ethnographic studies[18] in Europe, the United States, and Latin America have revealed that cell phones have brought several changes to consumers' lives, as described below.

Increased Personalness A cell phone is not shared with others. It is with the consumer always, as a constant personal companion. Consumers give their cell phone numbers only to their selected friends (and coworkers). So, calls received on the cell phone are somehow more important, more personal. Teenagers, who had to put up with parental eavesdropping on their conversations, finally feel a new sense of privacy.

Emotional Security Because consumers can call their friends and family anytime, they believe they have instant access to social support in their hour of need. Many parents buy their teenage children cell phones so they can keep tabs on their whereabouts, and of course, teenagers constantly are able to connect with their friends at will; in fact they are chattering with their friends all the time. Loneliness is now a thing of the past. In surveys, teenagers report that because of cell phones, they have expanded their circle of friends and casual acquaintances.

The Blurring of the Private and the Public Because we are accessible to friends, family, coworkers, and bosses all the time, the distinctions between work time and non-work time, between being at home and being at work, and between private and public have blurred. Increasingly, consumers have lost their hesitation about carrying on personal conversations in public places, and, conversely, business related conversations in social company.

The camera feature now available on many wireless phones has raised fresh concerns about privacy. Anybody can take anyone's picture, and without his or her

wireless consumer

knowledge.

Spontaneity Cell phones have also given consumers a greater degree of spontaneity. When they are late for meetings—social or business—they feel no regret, simply because they can just call the other party to advise of the delay. In turn, there is less pressure to be punctual. Moreover, now there is less planning and more tentativeness in setting up a time and place for a meeting, often leaving these details to the last minute. This tentative scheduling allows consumers to micro-manage their time and squeeze the maximum utility and pleasure, so to speak, out of whatever they are doing at a given moment. This spontaneity is a new source of perceived freedom.

Marketers' Alert: A Mixed Opportunity

For marketers, mobile phones enable anytime, anywhere access to consumers. This phenomenon opens a floodgate of new opportunity. Imagine you are in a supermarket, passing by the cereal aisle, and suddenly your phone rings, announcing a coupon for a brand of cereal available for you to download on the phone. This place-based communication has given rise to a new term in marketing practice—**contextual marketing**—the practice of sending consumers messages pertinent to the purchase and consumption situation of the moment. Obviously, this practice also has the danger of being seen by consumers as a grave intrusion into their privacy, and marketers have to be cautious in using this application. One barrier, of course, is that the consumer has to pay for the received call, but, even more important, such an unsolicited context-based marketing message can create an emotional backlash against the company.

But consumers can use their cell phones to order a product anytime, anywhere, and they can also use them to make payments using their digital wallets. This means that vendors of impulse-purchase products (e.g., street hawkers, event-based vendors, etc.) will have to be Internet ready (including possessing the ability to accept digital payments) if are to avail themselves of this opportunity to do business.

The ideal utilization of this new marketing channel is one that gives consumers what they want, and this would mean piggybacking marketing messages onto services/applications that consumers are already seeking. Two such applications are already on the horizon. First, consumers wish to stay connected to people and events pertaining to their areas of interest. Thus, teenagers want to know, for example, about music events; most consumers want to be in the know, on a real time basis, about sports; and some consumers want to have up-to-date information about financial markets. And they want to communicate such information to their friends. Marketers can build interest-based information Web sites (accessible on wireless phones) and communities for which consumers can voluntarily register.

Second, marketers can integrate their messages with two existing features of cell phones—ring tones and "wallpaper." Marketers can create wallpapers that incorporates their logos or brief text messages, which consumers can then download. Likewise, commercial jingles can be re-formulated as ring tones. Of course, consumers will seek and accept these only if the wallpaper designs and tones are intrinsically "cool." A company named Zingy (Zingy.com) offers precisely this service and represents a creative example of how marketers can exploit this new channel in a way which, rather than intruding on consumers' privacy, offers them something they welcome.

Third, the cameras on wireless phones can also change shopping. A consumer in a store can simply point and shoot a picture of the merchandise and then e-mail it to someone to seek advice. Marketers should be on the lookout for opportunities to observe and understand how this "virtual shopping pal" phenomenon affects consumer behavior in the store.

New marketing applications with mobile phones are emerging even as we write. With augmented reality apps, consumers can point their smart phone cameras at a store and find out merchandise and pricing information without even entering the store.

8. VIRTUAL IDENTITY
"Finally, I am my dream-self."

In the physical world, we have an identity we can't alter. We have to be what we are The virtual world has liberated us. We no longer need to be hampered by our identities in the physical world. Millions of consumers are enjoying this new found freedom.

Increasingly, consumers are living in a virtual world. Consumers, young and old, spend considerable time online. Checking out information, reading stories, playing online games, and chatting with people of similar interests. From MySpace to Facebook, and from YouTube to Flickr and Pinterest, consumers are placing their autobiographies online, for the whole world to see. These autobiographies— called *my profile* in e-space and comprising pictures, films, stories, likes/dislikes, etc.,—are sometimes real and true. Sometimes, they are made up, reflecting the identity consumers wish they had.

Now Second Life takes this feature to a new level. You can construct for yourself a new identity, complete with physical metamorphosis and personality overhaul. We need not elaborate. After all, you will be Googling it soon, won't you?

FORESIGHTS
TEN TRENDS IN CONSUMER SPACE

What will the future of consumer behavior be like, say, over the next decade? What will change and in what manner? Forecasting the future is always risky business, yet not to form an educated expectation could be even riskier as it would leave us unprepared to face the future. In this section, we survey the broad environment of consumption, describe the social and cultural milieu, and project ten upcoming trends in consumer behavior.

TEN TRENDS IN CONSUMER SPACE

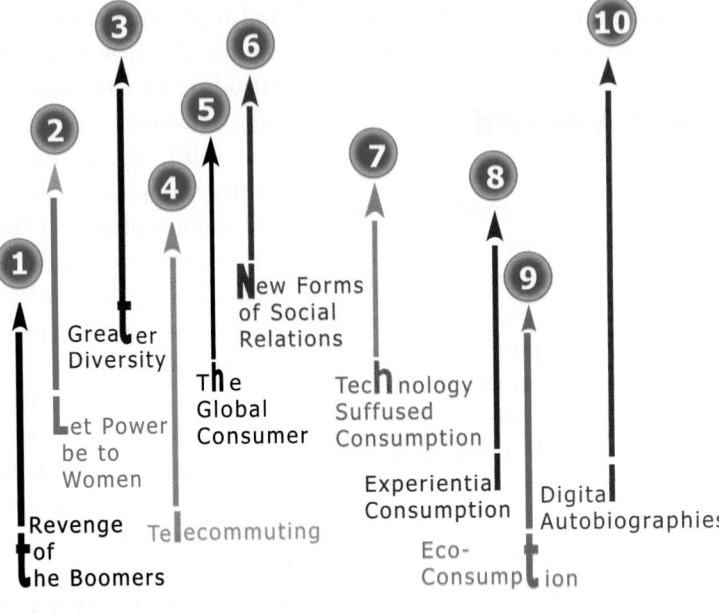

1. Revenge of the Boomers
2. Let Power be to Women
3. Greater Diversity
4. Telecommuting
5. The Global Consumer
6. New Forms of Social Relations
7. Experiential Consumption
8. Technology Suffused Consumption
9. Digital Autobiographies
   Eco-Consumption
10.

1. THE REVENGE OF THE BOOMERS

Baby boomers (those born in America between 1946 and 1964) are up in arms. They are 78 million in number, and 38 million of them will be in the age range of 55-75 over the next decade. Call them self-centered, materialistic, dreamers, anything. Just don't call them old. They don't see themselves that way, and they definitely don't want to look their age. Yes, they are up in arms, fiercely battling their aging looks. Hair coloring, anti-wrinkle creams, Botox, liposuction, they will take them all. Whatever it takes. And they will have the money to afford it all. After all, unlike their predecessor cohorts, they are vibrant and active, and they don't plan to retire anytime soon.

Elsewhere, especially in the cultures of the East, aging and aged looks actually bring more respect, so the pursuit of age-reversal is going to be much more subdued there. But growing ranks of 70, 80, and 90-somethings, especially in Japan, are buoyed by rising longevity and will create unprecedented levels of demand in health and elder care, as well as for innovations in medicine.

2. POWER TO WOMEN

Women are not going to abandon the apron anytime soon (not all of them and not entirely), but the days when a woman's place was, by definition, in the home are long over—at least in much of the Western world. Women now outnumber men among college students (54%),[18] and a recent report shows that academic achievement scores are higher for girls than for boys.[19] In most of the industrialized world,

women aged 25-34 outnumber men in possessing at least a college degree.[20]

With degrees under their belts and an 8-10 year longevity advantage over men, women's life-time earning capacities will be substantially improved. Already, 30% of working-women in the United States earn more than their husbands.[21] A significant number of men, especially those who worked in high tech industries, have been laid off, whereas their spouses took up or continued working in their jobs in the growing service industries (health care, retail, etc.). And men are quickly becoming adept at raising the kids and completing domestic chores, thereby earning the appellation "Mr. Mom."

The contemporary woman, in industrialized and third world countries alike, is surely and rapidly moving toward an egalitarian role in corporate, government, and household affairs. Increasingly, then, marketers will have to treat women as having equal importance in decision-making about all major purchases. Conversely, even to market household consumables, they will also have to include men in their target audiences.

3. GREATER DIVERSITY

As we move toward the middle of the second decade of the new millennium, there will be greater population diversity, certainly in the U.S., but also in Europe, especially in those countries with growing service economies (e.g. Switzerland). In the United State, the largest growth will be in the Hispanic population. Also, the number of immigrants from the newly liberated countries of Eastern Europe (e.g., Poland) will increase, and the current inflow into the nation's universities of international students (who later become permanent U.S. residents and join the work force) will continue. There will also be growing diversity in lifestyles and a public recognition of it.

With all this "mixing" of ethnicities and lifestyles, there will be greater cosmopolitanism (a population open-minded enough to change and to accept differences among people) peacefully co-existing with population enclaves still steeped in ethnocentric conservatism. At any rate, and undeniably, marketing will have to adjust to acknowledge and embrace this diversity. In the language, culture, people, and consumption of products depicted both in the media at large and in advertising in particular, smart marketers will promote their products and services both to the new niches of non-majority groups, as well as through mass-marketing campaigns that embrace people of all sorts. As an example of the former (new niches of the non-majority population), in addition to such channels as BET (Black Entertainment Television) and Telemundo, the International Cable Channel now features programs in Japanese, Chinese, Hindi, French, and German. As an example of the latter (i.e., incorporating diverse consumers into a single general marketing campaign), TCM (Turner Classic Movies) recently experimented with a new programming idea: every Thursday, it showed eight hours of movie entertainment from the famed Bollywood (Bombay's Hollywood).

4. TELECOMMUTING

Telecommuting—the practice of working at a distance from a formal place of employment—will grow. The basic motivation for telecommuting for individuals comes from the need for workers to play multiple roles simultaneously, most notably working as well as raising children. And this latter role is being thrust increasingly onto men (i.e., the "Mr. Mom" phenomenon). Also, if a company moves, the employee with a preference for the current location may not want to. Besides, the desire to be free to be wherever, whenever, is a basic human motivation. For corporations, the motivation for adopting this practice comes from the fact that real estate in business districts, particularly in major metropolitan areas, is very expensive, so it pays to let employees work from home. Corporations also find it cost-effective to outsource many operations to free-lance skilled designers, artists, engineers, consultants, etc., who work from their homes.

Enabling this trend is technology. With network computer technology, it is now possible for any employee to gain access to any of a company's databases and information, so employees can work from home or from the road; millions of salespersons already do. Moreover, a supervisor in a central location can "emulate" the screen on a distant employee's computer both to monitor and to support the employee's work. Also, video conferencing, Web-based broadcasting of audio-visual presentations (dubbed "webinars"), and other related technologies will reduce the need for central location-based corporate meetings. Finally, new advances in wireless communication are giving everyone the capability to communicate with anyone, anytime.

What will be the impact of telecommuting on consumer behavior? Well, employees are consumers too. Telecommuters will dress more casually (so the market for business suits will be down and casual clothing up), will more likely fix lunch at home (increasing the demand for easy-to-fix, supermarket-based "meal solutions" like pre-cut salad in bags), and will order more delivered food. Because of isolation from coworkers, telecommuters will also look increasingly for opportunities to participate in local professional and social organizations. And marketers who organize such networking activities will need to be responsive to this need.

5. THE GLOBAL CONSUMER

The marketplace will increasingly become global. By this we mean that products and styles with origins in diverse regions and cultures of the world, both far and near, will become available in every region and every nation of the world. Historically, and for the most part, culture has migrated from the West to the East; in contrast, the future will see an all-directional cross-pollination. Fashions of the West will be available in the East, and the West in turn will borrow heavily  from the East. These imported products and styles will be available (and desired by consumers) both in original, historical forms as well as in adaptations (e.g., kimonos as loungewear and kimono-style Western dresses in the West; pure McDonald's style burgers and local pita-bread based adaptations in the Middle East). This cross-pollination will be most notable in fashion clothing, furnishings, food, and music; moreover, it will be most apparent in the consumption by youth of all nationalities.

Such globalization will not mean homogenization. Far from it. Indeed, consumers in each country as a whole

An African-American couple enjoys this ethnic wedding ensemble,

will continue to retain their national cultures, both in values and attitudes and in overt consumption styles and substance (e.g., a majority of Indians living abroad, even 100 years from now, will believe in extended family living and will continue to wear *saree* and *kurta* on special occasions and eat *chapaati* as their everyday food). Nor will the population of consumers within any nation look homogeneously globalized. Rather multiple cultures of consumption will be present simultaneously, such that slowly but surely more and more imported cultures of consumption will exist side by side with the indigenous ones.

This cultural diffusion will present a challenge and opportunity to marketers. They will have to be quick-footed, scan the globe for transferable material culture, test-market new ideas and prototypes, and bring cross-cultural potpourri to market at the right time to the right consumers.

6. NEW FORMS OF SOCIAL RELATIONS

There will be a continuing decline in conventional sources of social advice and support—kith and kin, life-long friends, and strong local communities—which will therefore lose their reach and influence over individuals. Not only has there been a trend away from extended families, but also a decisive trend away from the conventional family type. And it is in the nature of modern contemporary living that life-long friendships and integration into a local community are hard to achieve and maintain. This is the result of increased urban mobility; it is also due to a task-oriented, utilitarian mindset about relationships that most people growing up in contemporary modern societies acquire. In such settings, there are voids—and an unfulfilled need for having someone to share one's emotions with, to turn to for advice, and to generally feel connected.

What will fill this void? Look for the emergence of a new industry—let us call it the **Industry of Social Relations**. Increasingly, consumers will turn

to commercialized sources of social support. Already, dating services are burgeoning, one quirk being "speed dating"—in musical-chairs style, eligible singles meet prospective partners for 3 minutes each to identify an initial match. A professional organization is experimenting with a similar practice for speed networking.[22] As another example, a number of parents—frazzled moms and dads—are turning to so called "Parent-Coaches," self styled professionals who advise parents (by phone or via e-mail) what to do to rein-in a cranky child.[23] Marketing opportunities exist for organizing this industry. Opportunities exist for market-based personal conversation partners—and we don't mean 1-900 phone lines. Rather, we mean human-to-human, wholesome, personal conversations, with someone willing to lend an empathetic ear. *Love doctors* in the mall, if you will.

7. TECHNOLOGY SUFFUSED CONSUMPTION

During a recent conference in Chiang Mai, a fellow attendee ("Jane") recorded the entire performance of a local folk dance on her iPad, lifting up her eyes only for a few second if at all. Bereft of an iPad or a video camera, I was blessed to watch it, instead, the only way I could: directly with my eyes in real time in real (physical) space. Of course, Jane had the benefit of being able to watch and re-watch it later and also bring that joy to friends and family.

In other domains, now there are cars in the making that will sense a potential collision with an object or a person in its path and stop automatically. And a breath-analyzer device installed in the car will automatically disable the car if you are intoxicated! In entertainment, with Tivo or Replay, consumers can watch any TV program anytime, untethered to the programming schedule. And now there is computerized clothing. Small computer chips and digital circuits are built into clothing. They will unobtrusively monitor your pulse rate and other biological functions and automatically send information to your doctor. And, of course, the "hug shirt" (see Chapter 1) will let you send a virtual hug to someone far away.

Then, there is the wired household. Imagine this: your refrigerator and your pantry are fitted with small computers. They automatically sense when your milk carton or your box of cereal is about to run out and needs replenishing, and they will reorder the pre-specified quantity from pre-specified vendors (don't worry, you will have control to intervene if necessary). Virtual shopping will be even more advanced, both online and offline. You and your mom (who lives on the other coast or continent) will be able to shop together. Already, you can do it on the Lands' End Web site. In the future, you could be shopping in a physical store and be able to beam to your mom a real size real time view of the clothing you are trying on.

Technology will bring new convenience to physical store shopping. Using their wireless phones, shoppers will be able to make payments (at an increasing number of retail stores) using "digital cash." And consumers will be able to scan the merchandise on a handheld, wireless, mouse-like device anywhere in the mall, then deposit the device (actually called a "frog") at a central Kiosk (called a "pond"), and leave—and someone will assemble all the merchandise from various stores and deliver it to the customers' homes.

A recent gift of digital and wireless technology is *augmented reality*: adding a super-layer of digitized information on a physical scene (a la the "yellow mass of linearly arranged pixels" on top of the image of the line of scrimmage on a football field). And with Buddha—a mobile application for iOS and Android phones, you can find if anyone in the room has the same interests as you, and then make an instant friend.

Thusly, and more and more, our consumption is going to be technology-suffused.

8. EXPERIENTIAL CONSUMPTION

Marketing scholars have always maintained that consumers don't buy products; rather they buy product benefits. And the experience of consuming them. Now smart marketers are taking note. There is a new form of car rental—in metropolitan areas like New York and Washington, D.C., for example. Consumers arrive on the Metro (subway); pick up a car; go around town, do their shopping or whatever; return the car; hop on the metro; and go home. They don't have to hassle with maintaining and owning a car.

Reality shows are on the rise. They are a hit because they are an excellent source of vicariously lived life experiences. Many of course are juvenile in taste, appropriate to the youth they target. An untapped market opportunity exists, however, for a mature audience equivalent. Many video games, like *SimCity*, are hits because they allow consumers to experience life vicariously, with interactivity to boot.

Stores like The Body Shop and restaurants like Rainforest are a hit because of the sensory experiences they offer. Many consumers love electronic pets because they come as close as possible to giving consumers the experience, but without the hassle of taking care of the pet. For example, a robotic pooch called *I-Cybie* not only

barks and wiggles but also walks and does tricks like pushups and headstands. Now, a human robot is also available—called *Robosapien* and made by Wow Wee International. (www.WowWee.com.) The robot can do household chores plus entertain you by dancing and talking back to you. In other domains, consumers are increasingly trying out yoga, adventure camps, and other exotic leisure activities. Marketers who can offer these and other experiential products will have ample opportunities to advance their fortunes.

9. ECO-CONSUMPTION

Another noteworthy trend is **eco-consumption**—consumers engaging in everyday behaviors that keep our environment and natural resources more sustainable. This trend includes:

(1) Buying and using products that are more eco-friendly;

(2) Reducing overall consumption, especially of critical natural resources (e.g., driving less, car pooling, switching off idle devices, etc.); and

(3) Recycling and reusing products (e.g., recycling waste, selling or donating old clothes).

Several recent surveys have revealed that eco-consciousness is on the rise, dramatically in some domains and some populations. *Wal-Mart Sustainability Live Better Index* has been tracking consumers' decisions to purchase five key eco-friendly products since April 2007. This index shows that concern for the environment has a growing presence in the shopping baskets of the retailer's 200 million annual customers. In its April 2008 survey, it found  that the index had gone up by 37% since the previous year. Of course, the adoption of green products is not uniform across the board. Wal-Mart's index revealed that the adoption rate for concentrated liquid detergent was 76.3%, and for paper products it was 67.5%. However, for organic milk, the adoption rate was a mere 1.58%.

A 2008 survey by the market research firm TNS, impressive in scope (interviews with 13,000 consumers in 17 countries), revealed a pleasantly surprising finding: Eco-consciousness (and consumption) is much greater in developing than in developed nations. A staggering 94% of Thai respondents and 83% of Brazilians were willing to pay more for environmental friendliness, whereas only 45% of British and 53% of American respondents were willing to dig deeper to help the environment. Of course, actual practice lags intentions, as it always does, in every culture and every nation. Among U.S. consumers, 26% report that they actively seek environmentally friendly

EXHIBIT 4

HOW GREEN ARE CONSUMERS

EIGHT SEGMENTS

Eco-Centrics
Encourage in a wide variety of green activities
Well-informed and activity involved
Willing to pay more for eco-friendly products
Respectful Stewards
Community and culturally focused
Idealistic
Willing to pay more for eco-friendly products
Proud Traditionalists
Hard-working; focused on family
Run environmentally responsible homes
Experiment with eco-friendly products
Frugal Earth Mothers
Prudent, lower-income women
Save money wherever possible
Focused on "good and wholesome"
Skeptical Individualists
Highly educated, high-income men
Not community- or spiritually- focused
Skeptical about corporate green initiatives
Eco-Chic
Young adults- see green as new hip
Impulse buyers and early adopters
Like "the cause" but haven't considered the
state of the environment in-depth
Green Natives
Young, lower-income shoppers
Have not registered cause/effect of
environmental responsibility
Eco-Villains
Middle income men; small/mid-sized metro
areas
Black-and-white perspective
Have dismissed environmental concerns
outright; do not seek eco-friendly products

Source: TNS Research Group

products. On the flip side, 44% of U.S. respondents are skeptical that global warming exists.

The diversity in eco-consciousness among consumers should be of special interest to the readers of this book. TNS analyzed the U.S. part of its data and found eight segments, ranging from Eco-Centrics at one end (most eco-conscious) to Eco-Villains at the other (those who totally dismiss any environmental concerns). (See Exhibit 4.) The demographic profile of these segments (Table 1) also reveals interesting patterns: Whereas Eco-Centrics are mostly Caucasians (77%, slightly higher than their proportion, 69.7%, in the total U.S. population), among Respectful Stewards, the next most eco-conscious segment, Hispanics are a majority (86%, seven times their population proportion of 12.5%!). This reflects, in part, the high eco-consciousness of people in their (or their parents' and grandparents') countries of heritage.

Thus, although a significant segment of the population in every nation will continue to be skeptical of eco-criticality (the sense that our environment is threatened), the ranks of pro-environmental segments are going to grow. In addition, those already eco-conscious and eco-active are going to expand their eco-friendly consumption practices. This trend will be fueled by several factors:

- **More Information on Eco Issues** As governments, media, celebrities, and opinion leaders speak out on these issues more and more, the resulting public conversations will make an average consumer wake up and take note.
- **More Options for Action** Increasingly, a greater range of products that are eco-friendly will become available. Marketers will innovate new eco-friendly products, sometimes to meet new demand, sometimes to attain their government-imposed carbon emission limits, and not infrequently to distinguish their wares from those of competitors. Examples: Green Depot (a green version of Home Depot) for home remodeling and Green Elegance

TABLE 1   DEMOGRAPHIC PROFILE of EIGHT GREEN CONSUMER SEGMENTS

	Male	Female	Average Age	Ethnicity	Household Income
Eco-Centric	34%	66%	45.9	77% Caucasian	33%>100k
Respectful Stewards	41%	59%	41.7	86% Hispanic	38%<35k
Proud Traditionalists	65%	35%	48.6	94% Caucasian	52%$35k-100k
Frugal Earth Mothers	23%	77%	48.3	85% Caucasian	100%<$100k
Skeptical Individualists	67%	33%	37.7	81% Caucasian (10% Asian)	11%>$100k
Eco-Chic	56%	44%	38.5	75% Caucasian	100%<100k
Green Naives	24%	76%	38.4	56% Caucasion (27% African American)	100%<100k (skews to lower end)
Eco-villains	70%	30%	43.2	87% Caucasian	100%<$100k

Source: TNS Research Group: Shades of Green Segmentation

Weddings for "green weddings" (also check out www.greatgreenweddings.com).

• **More Government Incentives** Many governments, across the world and across the states, have been and will be offering incentives for eco-friendly consumption (e.g., hybrid cars, solar panels, wind turbines, etc.)

• **New Economics of Eco Consumption** Whereas many eco-friendly products do and will continue to cost more (e.g., organic cotton), consumers will discover that many other eco-friendly products actually cost less to use (e.g., CFL bulbs, hybrid cars, local produce, etc.).

• **Being Trendy** In some circles and for some products, eco-conscious consumption is likely to become a source of social value. (Remember four exchange values consumers seek? See Chapter 1.)

For a segment of consumers, it will become fashionable to be seen "consuming green." This trend is going to take hold both in the comfortable middle to upper class segments and among the super rich, luxury segments. For middle and upper class consumers, the trend will be driven by ideology, a true belief in the value of pro-environmental consumption; accordingly, consumers in this segment will buy eco-friendly products, fully aware that, often, they will pay more, but willing to make the sacrifice. In the luxury segment, on the other hand, it will become fashionable to flaunt one's conspicuous eco-consumption (e.g., the 2012 BMW ActiveHybrid 750 Model starts at $100,000!).

This growing trend spells opportunity for marketers. To avail themselves of this opportunity, indeed to stay viable in many product categories and/or consumer segments, marketers will have to study, track, and understand these drivers of consumers' eco-consumption.

10. DIGITAL AUTOBIOGRAPHY

These days, if you are not on Facebook, MySpace, Bebo, or the like, or if you are not "twittering," you are perhaps nobody. This trend of acquiring some real estate in cyber space (e.g., a Web page) and filling it with stuff about oneself and about people and things important to oneself seems to have caught people's fancy. We call this trend *digital autobiography*—the use of the Web to *create* and *share* personal stories and opinions.

According to some Web stat trackers (e.g., Techcrunch.com, web-strategist.com), by February 2012, MySpace had 200 million visitors, and Facebook had close to 1 billion!

There are three types of "online community portals" where consumers can create their digital autobiographies:

(1) Social networking sites (*SoNets*), e.g., Facebook, Bebo, Multiply, etc.

(2) Blogs (e.g., blogspot) and discussion forums (e.g., iPod lounge), etc.

(3) Creative work-sharing sites, such as Flickr, HP Expression Center (http://expressioncenter. wetpoint.com), Pinterest, etc., where members display their creative work (photos, art, craft, etc.), and the most notable of them all, Second Life.

Consumers join these online community portals, create a "My Profile," and post photos. But the adventure goes beyond. Photo sharing site Flickr.com has a project called "What's in my bag," for example, where members post pictures of the contents of their bags (purses, schoolbags, even travel suitcases), sometimes with short "biographies" of the items. Flickr also has a project called *365 days*, which invites members to take one photograph every day for a year. The portal states the project's purpose thus:

> **Your year-long photo album will be an amazing way to document your travels and accomplishments, your haircuts and relationships. Time moves surprisingly fast.**

On blogging sites, members post their profiles and then write blogs regularly. On the blogging site called *blogspot*, one member who goes by the name *Politics After 50* (with a slogan "Its never too late to be pissed off") has this recent entry: "I've mostly been following Twitter on the Iran elections since the American media is so freaking useless …." And a woman with the online identity of *Omyword* introduces herself:

> **I am a writer, comic, voice and film actor. Most of my career I spent having the blood sucked out of me by corporate America…Now I am independently unwealthy and living for a little while in Paris.**

Members also use the *SoNets* to share their interests. On MySpace, a member under the alias "The Professor" describes his interests in music: 60's soul, britpop, Mod, northern soul, some electronica and some hip hop, jazz. He describes his general interests as: clothes, movies, clothes, scooters, clothes, drinking, clothes, etc... On Twitter, a member, Steven Delgado, writes in his *profile*: "I make things run on alternative fuels."

Whereas the trend started with college students captivated by Facebook, no longer is digital autobiography limited to Generation Y members. Today, more than half of Facebook users are outside of college, and the fastest growing demographic is those 25 years old and older (Web-strategiest.com).

Consumer motives for creating content on the community portals can be hypothesized to include:

(1) **Feeling connected.** Phone calls and text-messaging are good for one-to-one communication; *SoNets*

enable one-to-many communication. If you go shopping, why be limited to telling just one or two friends by calling them? Instead, why not post it on Twitter? Another benefit *SoNets* offer is that users can feel connected *constantly;* in cyber space, they are "present" and communicating with friends 24-7. Thus, one-to-many and constant connectivity are two advantages of *SoNets* (over cell phones and emails) that will lure an increasing number of consumers in the years to come.

(2) **Self-validation.** Express opinions, display creative work, post snippets of personal doings, and have your worth affirmed by visitor comments, or sometimes by the sheer count of visitors, the number of Facebook Friends and Twitter Followers you have acquired. Seeking self-validation is an inherently human motive (need), and now community portals enable us to do it on a grander scale!

(3) **Enjoyment.** Some consumers have taken to deriving extreme recreation from browsing and creating content on these sites. "I am addicted to Twitter," says one "tweeter." Twitter in fact brings out the human tendency to be fascinated with the minutiae of life. Before Twitter was launched, many analysts were skeptical, asking, "Who wants to know where you are and what you are doing?" Twitters' sky-rocketing success has shown that it is precisely that sort of stuff—the small things we do every day—that fascinates us and our close friends (i.e., "Followers").

For these and other gratifications that consumers can obtain from such online pursuits and pastimes, expect the Digital Autobiography trend to grow.

CONCLUSION

In this chapter, our goal was to make excursions into some unique domains of consumption—things consumers consume and activities consumers undertake fervently—with a fan-like zeal. From a potentially larger list, we chose eight. One of them comes from the world of entertainment (media fiction); two come from technology (technology per se and wireless communication); two from the domain of niche consumption (body adornment and authenticity); two from the domain of the ubiquitous yet non-mundane consumer behavior (gift exchange and appropriation); and one—the most nascent and most pregnant with

3 Motives

FEELING CONNECTED

for

SELF-VALIDATION

Digital

ENJOYMENT

Autobiography

possibilities—about the über consumption of virtual identities.

In each of these excursions, we learned something that is, well, quite esoteric—gaining insights that are rare. We never would have known, but do now, that in consuming media, for example, we are engaged in the quite complex process of meaning negotiation, and that, in watching media, we are consuming our own beliefs. Reciprocity norms govern gift exchange as a socio-cultural consumer practice. We seek authenticity, sometimes as exploration and sometimes as connectivity. Technology is a mixed blessing, and consumers have to learn both to harness and to cope with it. Wireless communications empower us with anytime anywhere communicability but also enslave us always to be accessible. We also dissected how consumers anoint important things they buy, making them their own and, in their minds, unique, even though the products were mass-produced by a firm.

Next, projecting into the next 10 years or so, we identified ten trends: (1) the revenge of boomers, (2) the growing power of women, (3) greater ethnic diversity, (4) more telecommuting and working from home; (5) globalization of consumption, (6) new forms of social relations, (7) technology suffused consumption, 8) experiential consumption, (9) eco-consumption, and (1) digital autobiographies. Each of these trends offers opportunities and challenges to marketers. It behooves all students of consumer behavior— and marketers are forever *students of consumer behavior—* to keep a keen eye on these and other emerging trends.

CB FYI

Sustainable Dancing

In 2008, a new dance club opened in Netherlands, called WATT. The club uses rain water in toilets and serves "biological" beer. But what makes the club really avant garde in sustainable consumption is how the power for lights and music in the club is generated—from the energy of the dancers, captured by "energy converters" under the floor you are dancing on!

Sustainable Dance Club (SDC), the organization behind WATT, now offers a sustainable dance floor (SDF) for sale, in both fixed and mobile versions. The Club is hoping to take this innovative product, and its message, world-wide. Check it out at sustainabledanceclub.com

Sustainable dance floor at WATT

Powered by dM

MY CB BOOK

A.
Endnotes

1. Service offered through the networking site Vayable.

2. Service offered through the networking site SideTour.

3. For further reading: P. Ostergaard, J. A. Fitchett, and C. Jantzen, "On Appropriation and Singularisation: Two Consumption Processes," Adv. in Cons. Res, 26, 0. 405-8.

4. Ferraro, Rosellina, Jennifer Edson Escalas, and James R. Bettman (2011), "Our Possessions, Our Selves: Domains of Self-Worth and the Possession-Self Link," J. of Consumer Psychology, 21 (2), 169-177.

5. Technically, these two forms of authenticity are called 'indexicality' and 'iconicity'. K. Grayson and R. Martinec, "Fact or Fiction? The "Authentic" Homes of Shakespeare and Sherlock Holmes," Advances in Cons. Res, 2002(29), 44; G. Bamossy and V. Universiteit, "Truth or Myth? Commercializing the "Authentic" Vincent Van Gogh," Advances in Cons. Res., 29, 2002, 44-45.

6. Author.

7. Based on Sherry, John, Jr. (19833, "Gift Giving in Anthropological Perspective," J. of Consumer Research, Vol. 10, (Sept), 157-167.

8. For further reading, see Mary Ann McGrath and John Sherry, "Giving Voice to the Gift: The Use of Projective Techniques to Recover Lost Meanings," J. of Consumer Psychology, 2 (2), 1993, 171-191.

9. M.Wolfinbarger (1990), "Motivations And Symbolism In Gift-Giving Behavior," In Advances in Cons. Res, Vol. 17, P. 699-706; Cele Otnes, Julie A. Ruth, Constance C. Milbourne (1994), The Pleasure And Pain Of Being Close: Men's Mixed Feelings About Participation In Valentine's Day Gift Exchange, In Advances in Cons. Res, Vol. 21, P.: 159-164.

10. A. M. Velliquette, J. B. Murray, and E. H. Creyer, "The Tattoo Renaissance: An Ethnographic Account of Symbolic Consumer Behavior," in Advances in Cons Res, XXV, 1998, 461-467; Joel Watson, "Why Did You Put That There?: Gender, Materialism, and Tattoo Consumption," in J. W. Alba and J. W Hutchinson (eds.), Advances in Cons Re, XXV, 1998, 453-460.

11. W.T. Tope, "State and Territorial Regulation of Tattooing in the United States," J. of the American Academy of Dermatology, 1995, 32, 791-799.

12. Melissa Blouin, "Tattoo You: Health Experts Worry About Artful Trend," Northwest Arkansas Times, Sunday, July 14, 1996, C4.

13. Allan Govenar, "The Variable Context of Chicano Tattooing," in Marks of Civilization, ed., Arnold Rubin, Los Angeles, CA: Museum of Cultural History, 209-218.

14. Quoted in Watson, ibid.

15. Based on Robert V. Kozinets, "'I Want to Believe': A Netnography of the X-Philes' Subculture of Consumption" Advances in Consumer Research, Vol. 24, p. 470-475.

16. This section is based largely on David Glen Mick and Susan Fournier, "Paradoxes of Technology: Consumer Cognizance, Emotions, and Coping Strategies," J. of Cons Res, 1998, 25, Sept. 1998, 123-143.

17. Adapted and paraphrased from consumer interviews reported by researchers Mick and Fournier (1998), Ibid.

18. Adapted from Hassan Fattah, "America Untethered,"American Demographics, March 2003, 35-39.

19. See as an example Risto J. Moisio (2003), "Negative Consequences of Mobile Phone Consumption," in Advances in Cons. Res. Vol. 30, P: 340-345

20. P. Francese, "Top Trends for 2003", Amer. Demographics, Jan 2003, 48-51

21. Michelle Conlin, "The New Gender Gap," Business Week, May 26, 2003, 75-82

22. Ibid, p.77.

23. Newsweek, May 12, 2003, Peg Tyre and Daniel McGinn, "She Works, He Doesn't," 45 –52.

24. Barbara Carton, "Need a Game Plan for a Cranky Kid? Call a 'Parent Coach', The Wall Street Journal, May 22, 2003, pp. A1, A7.

B.
Endnotes for Raghubir paper

1. These anecdotes are based on various papers referenced at the end of this chapter.

2. Kahneman, Daniel and Amos Tversky (1979). Prospect theory: An analysis of decision under risk. Econometrica, 47, 263-291.

3. Raghubir, Priya, J. Jeffrey Inman, and Hans Grande (2004), "The Three Faces of Price Promotions: Economic, Informative and Affective," California Management Review, 46 (4), Summer, 1-19.

4. Winer, Russell S. (1988), "Behavioral Perspectives on Pricing: Buyers' Subjective Perceptions of Price Revisited," in T. M. Devinney, ed., Issues in Pricing: Theory and Research, Lexington, MA: Lexington Books, 35-57

5. Kahneman, Daniel and Amos Tversky (1979). Prospect theory: An analysis of decision under risk. Econometrica, 47, 263-291.

6. Thaler, Richard. H. (1985). "Mental accounting and consumer choice," Marketing Science, 4 (3), 199-214.

7. Simonson, Itamar (1989). Choice based on reasons: The case of attraction and compromise effects. J. of Consumer Research, 16, 158-172.

8. Winer, R.l S. (1986), "A Reference Price Model of Brand Choice for Frequently Purchased Products," J. of Cons. Res., 13 (Sep), 250 - 256.

9. Krishna, Aradhna (1991), "Effect of Dealing Patterns on Consumer Perceptions of Deal Frequency and Willingness to Pay," J. of Marketing Research, 28 (4) (November), pp 441-51

10. Robert E. Krider, Priya Raghubir, and Aradhna Krishna (2001), "Pizzas: π or Square? Psychophysical Biases in Area Comparisons," Marketing Science, 20(4), Fall, 405-425.

11. Raghubir, Priya and Joydeep Srivastava (2008) "Monopoly Money: The Effect of Payment Coupling and Form on Spending Behavior," Journal of Experimental Psychology: Applied, 14(3), September, 213-225.

12. Prelec, Drazen and Duncan Simester (2001), "Always Leave Home Without It: A Further Investigation of the Credit-Card Effect on Willingness to Pay," Marketing Letters, 12 (February), 5-12.

13. Bruce, V., D. Gilmore, L. Mason, and P. Mayhew (1983). "Factors in the Perceived Value of Coins," J. of Econ Psych, 4 (Dec.), 335-347.

14. Raghubir, Priya and Joydeep Srivastava, "The Denomination Effect," J. of Consumer Research, forthcoming.

15. Kirkland, J. and D. Flanagan (1979). "Long-term Memory and the Value-Size Hypothesis," Perceptual & Motor Skills, 48 (June), 1149-1150.

16. Shafir, Eldar, Peter Diamond, P., and Amos Tversky (1997). Money Illusion. Quarterly J. of Economics, 112, 341-374.

17 Raghubir, Priya, and Joydeep Srivastava (2002), "Effect of Face Value on Monetary Valuation in Foreign Currencies," J. of Consumer Research, 29(3), December, 335-347.

18. Desmet, Pierre (2002). A study of the potential effects of the conversion to euro. J. of Product and Brand Management, 11(3), 134-146.

19. Raghubir, Priya, and Kim P. Corfman, (1999), "When do Price Promotions Affect Brand Evaluations?" J. of Marketing Research, Vol. XXXVI (May), 211-222.

20. Chandon, Pierre, Brian Wansink, and Gilles Laurent (2000), "A Benefit Congruency Framework of Sales Promotion Effectiveness," J. of Marketing, 64 (Oct), 65-81

21. Schindler, Robert M. (1992), "A Coupon is More Than a Low Price: Evidence From a Shopping-Simulation Study," Psychology and Marketing, 9 (Nov/Dec), 431-451

22. Dickson, Peter R., and Alan G. Sawyer (1990), "The Price Knowledge and Search of Supermarket Shoppers," J. of Marketing, 54 (July), 42-53.

23. Srivastava, Joydeep, and Priya Raghubir (2002), "Debiasing Using Decomposition: The Case of Memory-Based Credit Card Expense Estimates," J. of Consumer Psychology, 12(3), 253-264.

24. Krishna, Aradhna and Gita V. Johar (1996), "Consumer Perception of Deals: Biasing Effects of Varying Deal Prices," J. of Experimental Psychology: Applied, 2 (3), 187-206.

RESEARCHING THE CONSUMER

Dear Consumer: May We Hang Out With You for a While?

Laskerville—a code-named small town outside Chicago. The town has a population of 8,000 to 10,000, not counting the three or four visitors who slip in and out of town. You can see them in the market square, in local bars, at car dealerships, even at the funerals. It is they who have given the town this code name, and the townspeople don't even know it.

They are researchers from the Chicago-based Foote, Cone & Belding (FCB) advertising agency, whose founder's name was Albert Lasker. Since 1989, the researchers would cast away their business suits and don jeans and boots. To mingle with the villagers. To chat with them casually. About whatever interests them—the villagers. Trying to get a fix on what turns the wheels in small-town U.S.A.

Laskerville, you see, was chosen because it is typical of small towns across the nation. And a lot of advertisers want to sell to very common folks in these very common towns. What better way to find out about their attitudes, lifestyles, concerns, and mores, than to observe them firsthand in their natural habitat.[1]

INTRODUCTION

You don't have to live in Laskerville to know about consumer research. In one form or the other, we have all experienced it first hand. If you visit a restaurant, on the table there, you might find a comment card, requesting your opinion on your experience during the visit. If you are in a mall, someone might approach you with a request to answer a few questions. Sometimes when your phone rings, there is a marketing researcher on the line, wondering what you think of the detergent you are currently using, whether you have an opinion on the upcoming election, what your future computer needs might be, or how you spend a typical weekend.

These are not idle questions someone decided to ask to kill some free time on a Friday afternoon. These are questions, instead, designed to understand you as a consumer—what products you buy, how you buy them, and what your experience is with them. These questions determine whether the consumer type that you represent would be a prospect for a company's product or service, what kind of specific product or service design changes might appeal to you and to the kind of consumers you represent, and how that product or service may be offered to you. Researching consumer behavior is critical for marketing success.

Lest you shudder at the thought of someone watching you in the supermarket, remember a supermarket is a public

space and surveillance cameras are watching you in retail stores all the time anyway. More importantly, all consumer research, if done properly and ethically, aims to bring more value to you, the consumer. As marketers, we can learn a lot by simply observing shoppers quietly; and by hanging out with consumers. Actually, there are a number of other methods of researching the consumer, each with its own charms and challenges. In this chapter, we describe them all—the various methods of researching the consumer.

Two Types of Consumer Information: Qualitative and Quantitative

Consider these two questions:

Q1. Why do you like Rainforest Cafe? Is it because of their:
1. Food quality;   2. Menu variety;   3. Atmosphere;
4. Value price;   5. Other

Q2. How do you feel when you dine at a Rainforest Cafe? Describe your experience and feelings during your first visit there?

These two questions are meant to obtain two different types of information, respectively called *quantitative* and *qualitative*. **Quantitative information** is information collected in a form that can be easily coded into numerical value. **Qualitative information** is information that is collected and presented in the consumer's own words and cannot be easily coded into numerical value. The quantitative questions contain pre-specified responses for consumers to choose and mark; qualitative questions leave the response totally unspecified, thus offering the consumer an opportunity to give the answer in his or her own words.[2]

An important question is, when should we use qualitative versus quantitative research? The answer lies in a simple but unique difference in the way we form the question. In Q1 on Rainforest Cafe, notice that we are providing the list of possible answers; in Q2, in contrast, we are leaving it for consumers to provide the answer. Why? It is because, in Question 1, we assume we already know the range of possible reasons for consumers to like or dislike Rainforest Cafe, and we just want to find out which of the possible reasons are true for how many consumers. In contrast, Q2 implies that we don't know the possible answers, or are not sure what sort of reasons might exist for people to visit Rainforest Cafe. Moreover, quantitative research method lets us know only the cut and dry reasons for consumer behavior; in instances where we believe that the underlying reasons for a specific consumer behavior are, instead, some deep felt human experiences, then we resort to qualitative research.

Thus, the principal reason we choose to employ qualitative research is that we do not want to restrict the consumer to limit his or her answers to pre-assigned response categories; instead the consumer is free to use his or her own words, and describe his or her experience and reasons with all its intricacies and mystique, if you will. As researchers, when we use qualitative research methods, we are looking to "discover" consumers' personal experiences we do not know about, and we are looking to understand their consumption values, motives, attitudes, opinions, perceptions, preferences, experiences, actions, and future intentions. As you can see, this type of research—qualitative research—can be quite rewarding, even fun. Let us see how it is done.

QUALITATIVE RESEARCH

There are six principal methods of qualitative research: focus groups, directed interview, motivation research, observation, participant observation, and interpretive research. Let us describe each below.[3]

Focus Groups

With **focus groups**, a small group of consumers is assembled in a room, and a moderator steers the group discussion along certain questions of interest to the marketer. The group members can range in number from 6 to 15 and are generally chosen by **convenience sampling** (a method in which respondents are recruited based on convenient availability) but are pre-screened to represent the target market. The moderator is a trained marketing research professional, and he or she generally uses a discussion guideline (a list of issues to probe). A good moderator endeavors to avoid biasing the opinions expressed by the group members. He or she also tries to ensure that no one member dominates the discussion, that all group members get a chance to have their say, and that the discussion stays focused on the topic at hand. The discussion room is generally a specially equipped room, with a one-way mirror on one of its walls. Behind the mirror, client companies' executives sit and watch the group session. Also, the focus group is generally audio and/or video recorded for later review and analysis of data. Focus groups are often used in consumer research, principally to explore various facets of consumers' world-view about the topic at hand.

Since focus groups are not a statistical sample of the target population, the findings of focus group research are not projectable to the entire population of target consumers. Rather, focus groups offer a window into the consumer's mind, bringing to surface things the marketer may not have known about the consumer and his or her view of the product. What the marketer discovers through focus group

(and other qualitative research methods) he/she can then use to design specific questions for a subsequent large-scale quantitative research study. Thus, the principal utility of focus group research is to "explore" the consumer behavior about which marketers didn't know much to begin with. In this role, focus groups have several applications:

- **Generating ideas for product improvements or new products. We can learn of the problems consumers currently face in using the product, or of how the product can be made more convenient in use.**
- **Understanding consumer's hopes and fears about a new product; this understanding can then help the marketer in designing a communication campaign that would respond to these hopes and fears.**
- **Understanding consumer perceptions of competing brands. A firm can display its own brand (keeping the sponsor's identity undisclosed) and competing brands and engage the consumer group in comparing these.**
- **Testing new concepts. New product concepts, packaging prototypes, new brand names, and certainly, advertising photo boards or finished commercials can all be presented to focus group members for their feedback.**

Directed Interview

If you can get hold of some old episodes of *Tonight Show with Jay Leno*, you are seeing directed interview in action; except that Leno is interested merely in helping the celebrity guest put on display some aspect of his or her life that would interest the audience, not in learning anything about the guest *as a consumer*. But Leno does have a broad interview guide—a set of topics to broach with his guests. In consumer research, we do the same. We interview a sample of consumers one-on-one on a topic area. This method is called directed interview.

Directed interview (also called in-depth interview or simply depth interview) is a method of learning about consumers' views and activities in a particular topic area by asking mostly pre-conceived questions in a conversational format. By pre-conceived questions, we mean that the main topic areas to cover and the sort of questions to ask have been thought out in advance. These are written down in what is known as an "interview guide." The interview guide is broad in three respects: first, the interviewer does not have to read the questions exactly; rather he or she should phrase the questions conversationally. Second, the guide contains not only the topic areas and loose phrasing of questions, but also directions for probing. Third, the interviewer is expected to exercise discretion both to skip a question (for example, if it has been already covered by the respondent's answer to another question) and to probe whenever necessary (for example when a response is too brief) even if the guide does not specifically ask for it.

Of course, the guide contains no predetermined answers (remember, it is qualitative research). The interviewer (who is generally trained in this free-flowing interview method) uses the 'guide' to ask initial questions and then follows up with new questions formed on the spot based on the consumer's answers. The interviewer records consumers' answers verbatim, either manually by writing them down or by a mechanical recording device such as an audio or video recorder. All survey respondents are asked the same broad set of questions although of course the specific follow up questions differ.

Motivation Research

Motivation research (MR) is research directed at discovering the reasons (i.e., motives) for a person's behavior—reasons the consumer is either unaware of or is unwilling to admit in direct questioning. In consumer behavior, motivation research is conducted to find out the conscious or subconscious reasons that motivate people to buy or not to buy a particular product, or to engage or not engage in other marketplace behaviors (e.g., browsing, shoplifting, fanatic love for a product, etc.). Motivation research uses a number of techniques—all disguised and non-structured—disguised in that the consumer is not able to figure out that the researcher is trying to find out his or her (the consumer's) deep motives; non-structured in that the answers are not pre-structured for the respondent to choose from; rather, the consumer is encouraged to say whatever comes to mind.

Observation

In our everyday life, we learn a lot by observing people. We learn about what people do and how they do what they do. If people learn about people by watching people, why couldn't marketers learn about consumers by watching consumers? This simple art of observing people has been the stock-in-trade for anthropologists who study culture. With varying degrees, it has also been one of the methods in consumer research for as long as consumer research has existed. But now it is being revived with new vigor. One consumer researcher, Paco Underhill, has spent a lifetime on it. His firm, Envirosell, has placed video cameras and human observers in shopping malls and stores around the world, observing some fifty thousand shoppers a year. An excerpt from his research findings, reported in a book titled *Why We Buy*, reveals the power of observation.

> **We did a supermarket study for a dog food manufacturer. We staked out the pet food aisle and observed consumers picking up the food ration of their dogs. We noticed something interesting: dog food ('main course', if you will) was being bought by adults and while adults were placing the dog food in the cart, children were picking dog treats (e.g., flavored biscuits). Seldom did adults themselves picked these treats. However, they readily accommodated their children's pleas for dog treats. Perhaps children loved their dogs more; or perhaps they just found feeding Fido those doggie cookies loads of fun. (p. 18).[4]**

The marketing implications are clear. While dog food should be advertised to adults, dog treats should be advertised to children; and in the store, they should be placed on a lower shelf where children can reach them.

Now, then, some basic principles about observations. **Observation** is a method of discovering some information about consumers by simply recording what they do without intruding. Thus, we do not ask them any questions directly (as we do in directed interviews); in fact, we don't even let them be aware that they are being followed or observed. We do not intrude or bother them or interfere with whatever they are doing; rather we record their activity in as natural a form as it occurs. The consumer activity can be recorded by the human eye (i.e., observed by a person) or it can be recorded by mechanical devices such as a video recorder. We can even time their pace by using a stopwatch.

This method has several features worth noting. First, we observe consumers naturally—"in situ," so to speak; we are thus uncovering what consumers do, not what they say they do. Consequently, the observed behavior is more close to truth. Second, and this is a limitation of observation as a method—we can only observe the behavior, not consumer attitudes and perceptions. Thus, we know how consumers act but not why they act the way they do. We cannot learn, for example, which product features they like and which they dislike, and we certainly cannot learn of their deep seated motives for buying or not buying or using or not using a product. Third, while the method is simple to implement in the data collection phase (all we do is place some recorders and some human observers in strategic locations), it requires both patience and skill in data interpretation. A typical observation study would produce at least a hundred hours of tape (some may produce as many as a thousand hours of tape), and a group of researchers has to view them, some portions more than once, patiently; furthermore, the researcher viewing the video has to have the knack of "seeing" something of insight in a forest of data.

Participant Observation

Suppose you want to understand a French family's food consumption behavior—what kind of food do they eat, when and how, with what kinds of rituals, do they eat certain foods with certain beverages, at certain times? How often do they entertain, and what food do they serve on these occasions? Etc, etc., The best way to find that out is to live with a French family as a house guest for a week or so. This is "participant observation" at work.

Participant observation takes the observation method one step further. We are no longer simply observing quietly, unobtrusively; rather we are observing and living everyday life with our consumers. **Participant observation** is a method of research where the researcher observes consumers in their natural setting, living life in their midst as they do. He or she arranges to spend time with a consumer or consumers in their natural setting and simply goes about doing daily chores, participating in life as it unfolds. Often the consumers being researched do not know that the researcher is an outsider and is observing them. The Laskerville project, described at the beginning of this chapter, is a prime example of this research method.

This method enables a firsthand look at consumers' behaviors and offers a deep understanding, perhaps more than any other method can. It is also extremely time consuming and requires a skilled and trained observer, who must earn the trust of the host family or host community.

Interpretative/Ethnographic Research

Interpretative research is a class of qualitative research methods where a researcher obtains a thick slice of consumer behavior data and interprets them for meaning. The researcher usually has training and special skills in data collection and meaning analysis and bases his or her interpretation based on an extensive understanding of the social and cultural characteristics of that setting. These types of studies are also called **ethnographic studies**. The term *ethnographic* means taking the cultural perspective of the population being studied. Thus, the behavior of specific consumers is interpreted from the vantage point of the consumers themselves. The question the researcher asks is, What meaning does a particular consumer behavior have for the consumer him- or herself? How does it make sense within the context of the culture that the consumer group shares?[5] Interpretive research is also called *post-modern research*. The focus of the post-modern research is on understanding the meaning of a product or consumption experience in a consumer's life. The purpose here is not limited to the buying decision, but rather it covers the consumer's lifestyle, his or her well-being, satisfaction, and so on and the role that material objects and worldly activities play in his or her life.[6] The research methods themselves are not new, but they are being used with new rigor and enthusiasm, and more importantly, the perspective is new. It is called "post-modern" because, after some half a century of widespread use of quantitative survey research and use of sophisticated statistical techniques, the attention is turning back to qualitative data, and to a goal to capture, rather than the black and white, cut and dry quantifiable information, the "touchy feely" stuff. To capture consumers' emotions, raw feelings, intimate experiences, and subjective feelings. To uncover deep seated motives, aspirations, hopes, and emotions. [7, 8]

The methods include extended field research, consumer narratives and creative expressions. The Laskerville project described at the beginning of the chapter, is an example. **Field research** entails spending extended time in the field, observing consumers but not necessarily living there to become one of them. The researcher may retain his or her identity as an outsider. (Thus, participant observation is one type of field research where the researcher camouflages his or her identity and becomes one of the consumers.) For an example, see Odyssey Project (Exhibit). **Consumer narratives** is a method where consumers are encouraged to write long narratives (or maintain a journal) about their experience as a consumer in a particular domain, such as using make up or buying clothes, or getting cosmetic surgery.

Finally, **creative expression** (our name for this group of

EXHIBIT A1	CREATIVE EXPRESSIONS

McCann Ericsson, an advertising agency, asked housewives to draw pictures of how they felt when they saw cockroaches. The study was sponsored by the marketer of Combat roach killer. The product, a poison, was in trays designed to kill cockroaches that fell in it. But women were not buying it. The creative expression drawings revealed the deep-seated reason: some women saw their husbands (who would sneak in at night) as cockroaches and wanted to have the pleasure of spraying the cockroaches and *watch them squirm to death!*

MYCBBOOK

techniques) is a method wherein consumers are encouraged to express their feelings in creative ways such as by drawing, by acting out, or by finding suitable pictures. A noteworthy example is ZMET (see box, next page).[9]

Netnography

A new branch of ethnography is *Netnography*—ethnography on the net. In this method, the researcher studies online consumption communities, enrolling as a member of the group so as to access online postings (data) as well as to actively join the online chat (participant observation). Read more about this method (along with an illustrative application to online coffee culture) in the Special Topics section.

Advantages and Disadvantages of Interpretative Research

The advantages of interpretive research are manifold. First, the researcher is able to encounter consumers and consumption activities in their natural settings, thus eliminating the artificialness of surveys, focus-group rooms, or laboratory settings. Also, a thicker slice of everyday activity is sampled—for example, one observes a consumer for one hour or one day or one week as necessary rather than for a few minutes. The researcher observes firsthand the consumer activity, rather than inquire about it of respondents. Even when the consumer is interviewed, the researcher's own observations supplement the consumer's answers. Besides, the questioning is much more open ended and qualitative rather than close ended and quantified. Because of the extended mutual exposure between the researcher and the consumer, a greater trust is built, which then leads to consumer answers being more sincere. Finally, the consumer activity being analyzed and questioned is much more immediate and physically present. For example, a researcher who observes certain possessions in a consumer's house can actually point to them rather than ask the question in the abstract.

This method also has some shortcomings. It requires highly skilled and well trained researchers who are less preoccupied with recording but more oriented to constantly interpreting what they are observing. It is obviously very time consuming and very expensive. In addition, the interpretation of data is too subjective, despite following certain analytic procedures. Finally, the methods are good

THE CONSUMER BEHAVIOR ODYSSEY PROJECT

EXHIBIT A2

Ethnographic Research

The Consumer Behavior Odyssey was a qualitative research project involving personal visits by an interdisciplinary team of academic consumer researchers to a variety of consumer sites. The project was undertaken in summer 1986 by a group of leading consumer researchers (trained in such disciplines as sociology, psychology, anthropology, consumer behavior, and marketing research) who traveled in a recreational vehicle (RV) from coast-to-coast on a journey of discovery, so to speak. The data collection methods consisted of taped interviews, still photos, on-site recording of diaries, and day-end writing of reflections in a journal. Researchers visited department stores and garage sales, county fairs and tourist resorts, opera performances and rock concerts, and picnics and weddings (i.e., virtually any "consumption site" that came their way). The objective was to observe in a nonintrusive way the acquisition, consumption, and disposition of products and services wherever these occurred.

Motorized versus Nonmotorized Mobile Homes

In one of their projects, The Odyssey researchers visited and observed the owners and renters of motorized and nonmotorized mobile homes. They found notable differences in the "consumption experience" of mobile home living by these two groups. Nonmotorized mobile homeowners seemed to view their mobile units as much more of a "home" than did the owners of motorized mobile homes. The former parked their units more permanently, shared community activities with others in the RV park, and externally personalized (e.g., named their units by their last names) and beautified their mobile units. The latter, in contrast, did not engage in any joint activities with their "neighbors," were preoccupied more with traveling and reaching their destinations than with relaxing in one spot in their units, and did not attempt any personalization in the external appearance of their mobile units.

This consumer perspective could not have been discovered by the more conventional quantitative methods. It can be helpful to marketers of mobile homes, travel accessories, and travel destinations to identify these two different groups of consumers.

Further reading: Russell W. Belk, Melanie Wallendorf, and John F. Sherry, "The Sacred and the Profane in Consumer Behavior, Theodicy on the Odyssey," *J. of Consumer Research*, June 1989, 16, 1-38. Russell W. Belk, "The Role of the Odyssey in Consumer Behavior and in Consumer Research," in *Advances in Consumer Research*, ed. by Paul Anderson & Melanie Wallendorf, 1987, vol. XIV, p. 357-361, Provo, UT: Association for Consumer Research. Russell W. Belk, John F. Sherry, and Melanie Wallendorf, "A Naturalistic Inquiry into Buyer and Seller Behavior at a Swap Meet," *J. of Consumer Research*, March 1988, Vol 14, 449-470. Harold H. Kassarjian, "How We Spent Our Summer Vacation: A Preliminary Report on the 1986 Consumer Behavior Odyssey," *Advances in Consumer Research* 14, pp. 376-77.

MYCBBOOK

at generating hypotheses, but not at confirming hypotheses or suggesting generalizable principles. Overall, they can uncover some rare insights on the consumer, which can then be confirmed by quantitative methods described next.

QUANTITATIVE RESEARCH

Have you read a film review lately? That is qualitative information. Now, have you seen a beauty contest (like Miss America Pageant)? Or, the Olympic games? Remember, how judges give a numerical score to each contestant. That is a quantitative measure. In **quantitative research**, the consumer responses themselves need not be numerical (although we often ask them to circle some numbers); the main characteristic of quantitative research is that we offer the consumer a set of predetermined responses to choose from; we are later able to easily code this information into numbers by simply assigning a different number to each response category. Thus, gender information can be easily coded as male=1 and female=2; or the converse. So can a 'Yes' and 'No' answer, or an 'agree'/'disagree' answer.

Quantitative research can use either of two broad methods: survey and experiment.[7]

SURVEYS

A **Survey** is a method where consumers are asked a question and requested to mark one of the pre-specified response categories. The researcher may read (on the phone or in face-to-face settings) a series of predetermined questions, one at a time, and records the consumer's answers. Alternatively, in a self-administered questionnaire (sent by mail or given in person), respondents can write in the answer themselves. [Often, questionnaires contain a few questions that seek open-ended verbatim responses (i.e., in their own words), so such parts of surveys are *qualitative*.]

Basically, the method is useful to elicit consumers' beliefs, opinions, attitudes, perceptions, and so on. It has several advantages and disadvantages. Advantages are quick data collection in a relatively short time, and ability to reach consumers in widespread geographic locations. The disadvantage is that consumers will give the answers they consider safe to give. Also, consumers do not like to appear ignorant and will therefore make up an answer even if they have never before thought about the topic. When the topic might be one in which consumer motivations might be hidden or where consumers may hesitate to candidly share their opinion, qualitative disguised techniques discussed before are more appropriate.

With the advent of the Internet, online surveys are becoming quite common. You might be surfing the Net and suddenly an ad pops up, inviting you to fill in a survey (usually some incentive is offered such as free coupons or entry into a sweepstake. The big advantage of online surveys is of course the cost savings as the consumer enters the responses directly into the computer thus avoiding the need for someone to later enter the information.

EXPERIMENTS

One limitation of survey methods is that questionnaires are limited to assessing consumer opinions and thoughts that exist in the consumer mind. However, often we are interested in finding out how consumers will respond to some potential market offering or communication. Moreover, surveys measure what respondents say they will do, not what they will actually do. An experiment overcomes this shortcoming. An **experiment** is a method in which the researcher places respondents in a situation that does not normally occur and then observes or records their response.

A prime example of experimental research in marketing is test marketing. **Test marketing** is a method of testing a marketing mix on a limited market as a precursor to deciding whether to implement that mix in the entire market. Suppose, for example, that you wanted to launch a new product. Rather than launch it in the entire nation (and incur huge losses in case the product does not sell), you could launch it in two cities and observe consumer response. Or let us say that you simply wanted to test the relative appeal of two types of packages, or two different price levels, or two different advertisements or any combination of these. You could select two matching cities (i.e., cities similar in their demographic profiles) and place one package, price, or advertisement (called

a stimulus) in one city and the second stimulus in the second city, and observe which elicits a more favorable consumer response. These are called *field experiments*, because they are conducted in natural marketplace settings and often consumers are unaware of their being in an experimental research.

A second variety of experiment is called *laboratory experiment* or *lab experiment* for short. In lab experiment, consumers are invited to the research laboratory and then presented with a stimulus. Consumers are aware that they are participating in some research, but the research purpose is typically camouflaged. For example, suppose you want to find out what consumer perceptions of taste of a new type of candy would be if the candy is presented under one brand name versus another and when it is priced low versus when it is priced high (say, 99 cents versus $1.25 for a bar). To find this out, we invite, say, 500 consumers to our lab and at random assign them to one of the four lab rooms. Consumers in each lab room are offered a candy bar, asked to try it and then rate the candy on a number of features such as quality, taste, price reasonableness, and even such image dimensions such as luxurious, rewarding, sophistication, etc. The candy bar remains the same, only the price and brand names are different. Consumer ratings for each of the four groups reveal which brand name and price combination appeals to consumers the most.

SIMULATION

Simulation is a special form of quantitative, experimental method, in which researchers create real-world conditions in a laboratory to study the behavior of consumers. By observing their behavior in this laboratory setting, marketers are able to forecast how they (the consumers) would behave in the real marketplace. Just as astronauts use a flight simulator to train for the real flight, so too marketers simulate the marketing mix (i.e., create the market mix on a smaller scale in the laboratory) before investing money on the full-fledged marketing program.

Pretest market lab simulation is a specific procedure for testing new-product concepts and prototypes. In a typical procedure, consumers representative of the target market are recruited by mall interception and invited to view a TV program and look at some product samples. They are also shown a 15-minute program segment, a pretaped TV program with one change: One of the commercials has been substituted by the test commercial. After viewing the program, the consumers are surveyed on the perceptions and persuasive impact of the commercial. Next, they are given some shopping money (say, $3.00) and are requested to examine the mock up store display that contains the new test brand as well as other brands. Consumer purchases are recorded and later these consumers are called back to obtain their reactions to the test product. The data can then be analyzed by statistical models to predict the performance of the new product in the real world.

MEASUREMENT SCALES

No matter which quantitative method we use, to measure consumer responses, we must use some numerical scales. We describe a few of these scales below.

Ranking scales ask consumers to simply rank order various items, as shown below.

Please rank the following attributes of wireless phone service in terms of their importance to you, assigning 1 to the most important and five to the least important.

Attribute	Rank
Voice quality	———
Speed of connection	———
Signal clarity	———
Signal availability	———
Reach (area covered)	———

Semantic differential scales ask consumers to rate a product or brand or an ad, etc., on a pair of opposite adjectives, as shown below.

Sprint Wireless phone service is:

Poor	1 2 3 4 5	**Excellent**
Economical	1 2 3 4 5	**Uneconomical**
Low quality	1 2 3 4 5	**High quality**

My opinion of Sprint Wireless phone service is:

Favorable	1 2 3 4 5	**Unfavorable**
Negative	1 2 3 4 5	**Positive**
I dislike	1 2 3 4 5	**Like it very much**

Another scale is *Likert scale* which requests a numerical rating, but asks respondents about the degree to which they agree or disagree with statements:

Please express your opinion on the following questions about seat belts, by circling an appropriate number.

1. Strongly Disagree   2. Disagree   3. Feel Neutral
4. Agree   5. Strongly Agree

Seat belts prevent injuries.	1 2 3 4 5
Seat belts are inconvenient.	1 2 3 4 5
In case of an accident, seat belts can trap you	1 2 3 4 5

Measurement scales can also be pictorial, rather than numerical. Such a scale is particularly useful for less literate respondents, or respondents who speak a different language. When the research purpose is to measure the emotions the respondent experiences, pictures of various facial expressions can be used.[11] Pictorial scales are also especially useful for researching children as consumers.

THE INTERNET AND VIRTUAL REALITY: NEW TOOLS OF CONSUMER RESEARCH

Imagine a focus-group discussion without the discussants really present in the same room. This is focus group online. The discussion groups communicate on the Internet via discussion forums moderated by a host, in real time. The participants are recruited in advance and asked to log on to their PCs at a prespecified time. Everybody, including the moderator, is ready to communicate online. Everything else is the same as in the conventional focus group. The only difference is that the participants can be continents apart.

The advantages of online focus groups compared to its conventional counterpart are time savings, costs savings, and ability to bring together consumers or users from around the world. An added feature of this medium of discussion is that new product concepts can be presented via computer graphics so that they are more realistic than conventional paper-and-pencil concept descriptions. (Of course, this feature of computer graphics can be utilized also in face-to-face discussion groups.) Its disadvantages are lack of face-to-face interpersonal dynamic, and reliance on "verbalizable responses," thus making emotional responses more difficult to surmise.[9]

Online focus groups constitute an interesting use of information technology. However, as is true with any new application of a technology, consumer researchers should be aware of some still-unanswered questions about this method. Is an online focus-group moderator able to establish rapport with and communicate trust to the discussion group members? In comparison to face-to-face focus groups, do online respondents assume that they are being exposed to a large number of online users, or do they assume anonymity because no one can identify them? Finally, does such anonymity bring forth more candid or less candid responses? As experience with the method grows, these questions will get answered.

Virtual Reality Techniques in Consumer Research

An even more advanced use of technology is virtual reality simulations. Virtual reality (VR) refers to interactive, computer-generated 3D immersive displays of images and sound. The VR equipment consists of a stereoscopic head-mounted display, body suit, and glove to provide tactile and sensory input. With virtual reality, test environments can be simulated to be indistinguishable from their real (physical) versions.[10]

To show how this technique is utilized, let us describe two of its typical applications: virtual shopping and virtual test marketing.

VIRTUAL SHOPPING

Using computer technology, a store aisle can be simulated on the computer. Sitting in front of a video game type of screen, consumers can walk through the aisle, look at a shelf display, examine a product, read the label, request additional information, learn if a coupon is available, put the item back on the shelf, or place it in a cart (depicted by a visual icon), and so forth, all with the click of a mouse. The computer displays whatever information the consumer wants, and in turn keeps a record of consumer activity. Thus, it is a useful tool to study consumers' information-seeking behavior, as well as consumer responses to alternative shelf displays. A version of this system, called *Visionary Shopper*, has been tested in the United Kingdom. It will cost a fifth of the conventional simulated test-marketing approaches.

VIRTUAL TEST MARKETING

In an actual VR test marketing project, the goal was to evaluate demand for electric cars.[12] Respondents were placed in front of a multimedia display. The screen flashed newspaper stories from an imagined future time. This was done to move respondents forward in time. Respondents then interacted with the program and a laser disk full of an array of verbal, pictorial, text, and video material. Respondents could look at the car display, walk around it, talk to salesmen, read press reports, ask other consumers, and so on. After this simulation, they were asked to drive a conventional car with the engine replaced by an electric engine. Following the real-world test drive, they returned to their computers to answer questions on their attitudes and preferences. The proprietary name of this technique is *Information Acceleration*, designed by MIT professor Glen Urban and his colleagues.

Advantages of Virtual Reality Techniques

Virtual-shopping research has several advantages over other methods. Compared to conventional focus-group and concept-test research, and also conventional store simulation tests, the virtual-shopping method is able to simulate the real-world shopping environment much more realistically. In the virtual-shopping experiment, the consumer is exposed to very realistic shelf displays, complete with the clutter of competing brands; even the hustle-bustle and the sight and sound of other shoppers can be simulated. Another advantage is that the computer is able to record much more detailed data about the shopper behavior. These data include the amount of time the shopper took to examine the product and make the decision, the content of information he or she sought and examined, the sequence in which the information was examined, the sequence in which brands were examined and products chosen, and so forth.[13]

A Virtual-Reality Consumer Research Project

EXHIBIT A4

VIRTUAL STIMULI, REAL SUBJECTS

A snack manufacturer wanted to find out if its line of snacks included items that consumers perceived as close substitutes. If two or more items were perceived as substitutes, then the firm could trim the line without reducing sales (but reducing the costs). On the flip side, the firm wanted to know what snack products of the competition were perceived to be substitutes of the firm's own products. If there was a competitor's snack product against which the firm's product was briefly compared but then rejected as not being a good substitute, this would suggest a gap in the firm's own product line. The firm could fill this hole by bringing out a new product.

To answer these questions, the firm employed a virtual-shopping experiment. Four hundred consumers were recruited from six shopping malls across the United States. They were invited to the local simulation lab repeatedly to buy snack products from a virtual vending machine—vending machine on the computer screen. Since they were invited for repeated shopping trips, it was possible to first study their preferences and then custom-design the vending machine inventory to force a reconsideration of their choices. For example, in a subsequent shopping trip, the vending machine display was manipulated to show the item of a particular consumer's preference as being "out of stock." The consumer was thus forced to consider substitutes (although he or she was free to buy or not buy a substitute). This enabled the researcher to study consumer perceptions of what was a close substitute of their favorite brand versus what was not.

This method had three advantages: First, it was much less costly to set up vending machine displays on the computer screens than would have been the case with the physically real displays. Second, the "out-of-stock" manipulation could be custom designed for each consumer based on the knowledge of what his or her current preference was. Finally, the consumer perception and preference data could be collected unobtrusively. □

Read more: Raymond R. Burke, "Virtual Shopping," *ORMS Today*, 22, no. 4 (August 1995), pp. 28-34.

CB 2.0

In this section, we discuss two advanced methods of consumer research: information processing research and mechanical measures.[16]

INFORMATION PROCESSING RESEARCH

Information-processing research studies what information consumers are looking for, looking at, paying attention to, considering, and using to make decisions. Ultimately, we hope to discover what information led consumers to choose certain brands or products and services.

A number of procedures are available for conducting such research. We can quietly observe consumers, keeping an eye on the information they are acquiring and evaluating; or we could ask them to share with us their information acquisition and processing behavior. All these procedures have, as a group, certain merits and demerits. The merit is that as consumer researchers, we come closer to understanding what goes on inside the mind of the consumer. It tells us what effect certain information has on the final decision. The disadvantage is that it is very time consuming, but it can offer valuable insight on consumer decisions. Overall, the insights we obtain serve as guidance on how to present product information to consumers. Let us discuss two principal procedures briefly, Information boards and protocols. Note that these methods are really a hybrid of quantitative and qualitative methods—Information boards more quantitative and protocols more qualitative; however in their precision in data recording and/or interpretation, they are akin to quantitative methods.

Information Boards

An **information board** is a table of information with brand names in the rows and attribute names in the columns. Cells contain the information about the extent to which the brand specified in the corresponding row contains the attribute specified in the corresponding column. Initially, all the cell entries are covered; the consumer participating in the research study is asked to make a brand decision by uncovering the cells in whatever order he or she desires, and as many or as few cells as he or she feels necessary to come to a decision. Some brand names may be hypothetical (often designated by letters of the alphabet (e.g., brand K), or one of the brands may be the sponsor's brand. As the consumer uncovers the cells, the sequence of this uncovering is recorded.

Later, the researcher analyzes consumers' sequence of "information acquisition." Based on the sequence, the researcher draws inferences about the evaluative criteria consumers use in appraising alternative brands and the comparison process they employ in making their choice.

This kind of research helps a marketer understand which product features are important to consumers, and which features should be emphasized in marketing communications. It is possible, for example, that the very last attribute uncovered on the information board was the one on which the marketer's brand was edged out by a competitor's brand, even though the former was superior on all the preceding attributes. The marketer now has the choice of either improving this last-considered feature in his or her brand, or educate the consumer about his or her brand's considerable superiority on all the features taken as a group.

An information board can be a simple card or wooden board with pegs on the cells for hanging information cards. More often, it is an electronic information board created and displayed on a computer. The research participant simply clicks on the desired cell to reveal the information. The computer automatically records the sequence of uncovering the information cells.

Protocols

Information boards indicate to the consumer researcher only what information the consumer "acquired," not what information was "processed," much less how it was processed. For example, after uncovering a cell in the information board study, the consumer may simply decide to discard that information from further consideration, but the researcher has no way of knowing this.

SEARCH MONITOR

EXHIBIT A5

One menu-driven microcomputer-based program for information search experiments is called Search Monitor. Devised by consumer researcher Marrie Brucks (marketing professor at University of Arizona), Search Monitor enables the consumer to obtain information on various alternatives by offering a battery of such questions as:

    Q. What type of .. does brand .. have?
    Q. What price is brand .. in store ..?
    Q. Does brand .. have a ..?

The consumer chooses a question from the list and fills in the blanks with the desired brand, store, and feature name. Then the answer appears on the screen. In some applications, the researcher can build in delays in response times in order to make the respondent realize that information search will consume time just as it does in the real world. The program permits the researcher to design the question menu, key in the answers according to the product and brands being studied, and vary the waiting times before the answer will appear on the screen.

Read more: Merrie Brucks, "Search Monitor: An Approach for Computer Controlled Experiments Involving Consumer Information Search," *Journal of Consumer Research,* 15 (June 1988), 117-21.

MYCBBOOK

The "protocol" method, in contrast, allows a peep into the consumer's mental processing. In the **protocol** method, the consumer is asked to speak his or her thoughts out loud. For example, a consumer making a selection in a supermarket aisle would be asked to say what information he or she is looking at, thinking of, deciding about. The researcher who is accompanying the consumer and recording the respondent's spoken thoughts would periodically prompt the respondent with questions like "Now what are you thinking?"; "Why did you just look at that?"; "Why did you put that brand down?"; or "Why did you finally select that?" These consumer thoughts, spoken aloud and recorded, are called protocols. The protocols are later analyzed to gain insight into consumers' decision-making process.

There are two types of protocols: concurrent and retrospective. **Concurrent protocols** are the consumer thoughts recorded at the time of decision making, such as in the supermarket aisle when the consumer is actually making a brand selection. Concurrent protocols can also be combined with data from information boards so that we gain information on both consumers' information acquisition and processing.

Retrospective protocols are consumers' reports on the decision process for a decision they made in the recent past. For example, a researcher might contact recent car buyers and ask them to describe the process of information search and alternative evaluation they went through in making their car purchase. The researcher would begin by asking such questions as "When did you begin thinking of buying a car?"; "What cars did you consider in the very beginning?"; "Then what did you consider about these cars, and how did you narrow down the field?" In effect, the consumer is remembering and "reconstructing" the decision process. Obviously, the less time elapsed since the decision was made, and/or the more significant the decision, the more accurate would be the protocols.

An obvious criticism of concurrent protocols is that they might interfere with the actual information processing task; that is, if the consumer didn't have to verbalize his or her thoughts, his or her information processing may have been different. Researchers have found, however, that after a few initial minutes of performing the required "speak out" task, respondents return to their normal way of making shopping decisions.

MECHANICAL MEASURES

The research methods we have discussed so far all use verbal responses—the answers consumers tell us. And this is true whether they tell us using quantitative scales or free-flowing prose. However, many of the responses actually also occur in the physical body—in the eyes, on the skin, and in the brain—they occur as physical activity (change in temperature, pressure, or electric current, etc.) Mechanical measures are intended to measure these bodily responses to

marketing stimuli. These are briefly discussed below.

One device to capture consumers' information processing is an eye camera. The camera records the pupil movement as the consumer looks through a piece of information. This method can be used to study consumer's information acquisition while reading or viewing an advertisement, looking at aisle displays and examining package information on products in a supermarket, or participating in an experiment such as an information board.

The researcher uses data gathered by the eye camera to identify the information at which the consumer gazed the longest. Such data help the researcher pinpoint the selective appeal and use of information by the consumer.

GSR

Galvanic Skin Response (GSR) measures the amount of skin resistance to electric current between two electrodes. When a consumer reacts to any stimuli, her or his sweat glands are activated; this, in turn, reduces the skin resistance. Thus, GSR activity indicates consumer response to a stimulus, such as an item of information (e.g., price) or an emotional message in an advertisement.

Brain Activity

When consumers process any information or react to any marketing stimulus, electric impulses are generated in the brain. These impulses can be measured by sensors attached to the skull, which generate electroencephalographic (EEG) measures.

One of the brain activities measured in this way is called *alpha activity*. Alpha activity inversely measures the degree of the brain's attentiveness. When we are sleeping, resting, or otherwise inactive, the alpha activity is high; when we are paying attention to a commercial, the alpha activity is low. During the viewing of different ads, viewers' alpha activity levels would vary, and accordingly they will serve as indicators of the ad's ability to attract and hold viewer attention.

SUMMARY

Methods of researching consumer behavior are either qualitative or quantitative. Qualitative methods include focus groups, directed interview, motivation research, observation (Simple and Participant), and interpretative research. Quantitative methods entail surveys or experiments. Surveys find out what consumers think, know, or feel already. Experiments, in contrast, present some new stimuli and seek consumer reactions to these stimuli. Some major topics researched by quantitative methods are consumer attitudes, image or self-concept measurement.

Although these methods differ in their technique as well as goals, the common purpose is to help marketers understand the consumer—to get inside consumers' minds, to know what concerns them, what they like and dislike, how they perceive various marketing stimuli, how they respond to them, and why they respond that way. ■■■

MARKET SEGMENTATION

WHERE MARKETING STRATEGY MEETS CONSUMER INSIGHTS

Market Segmentation Perhaps no other concept in marketing is more potent than the concept of segmentation. The core idea is that all consumers are not alike, and that to satisfy individual consumers, we must bring them market offerings designed to meet their specific needs. Market segmentation is the process of identifying key differences among a population of consumers and clustering them into distinct groups corresponding with their different needs and characteristics. These resulting groups are called market segments.

In an absolute sense, seldom are any two consumers entirely identical. In this sense, then, every consumer is a segment unto himself/herself. But many of the differences are minor, and for practical reasons it is wise to not pay heed to every little difference. We end up grouping consumers, therefore, into *broad* groups, using grouping criteria that imply significant differences. For example, we could group consumers simply by their sex, treating men and women as two distinct segments. Or we could cluster all people into brown-eyed and blue-eyed consumers; however, this grouping would not be very helpful (except to perhaps those marketing colored contact lenses or eye makeup). Thus the core goal of segmentation is to identify consumer groups whose marketplace behaviors will be significantly different.

What are the desirable features of good segmentation schemes? These are:

1. A manageable number

If you divide your customers into too many segments, it would be difficult to attend to their fine-tuned differences and impossible to target them individually. Thus, no marketer can deal with, say, 100 or even 50 segments. Typically, eight to ten should do, preferably fewer. (Note: The PRIZM scheme—see Chapter 6—comprises 66 segments, but that is an omnibus scheme for the *entire* country population; from these, marketers would select, typically, 8 to 10 segments, at most, to target. If you were to identify segments among your existing customers, however, then a smaller number of segments, say a maximum of ten, would be more manageable.)

2. Internally homogeneous, mutually heterogeneous

Consumers within any segment should be as similar as possible while consumers in different segments should be maximally diverse across segments.

3. Segment size

The resulting segments should not be too small. Otherwise it will not be profitable to target each segment separately.

4. Segments should be measurable

The criteria by which different segments are defined should be easy to measure. Broadly speaking, demographics (age, income, etc.) are easiest to measure whereas psychographics entail more complex scales.

5. Segments should be accessible

It should be possible to target different segments by different marketing mixes. In relative terms, geographic segments are the easiest to target (by place-based media and by physical outlets); likewise, income and affluence are easy to target by pricing (e.g., in airlines, coach and business classes). Psychographics are targeted, less easily, by message design contents that depict prototype consumers of the target lifestyles. Human attributes that have no other targetable correlates are difficult to target, such as, say, left-handed versus right-handed persons or blonds versus brunettes. In such instances, segmentation is still useful, leaving accessibility to self-selection (less efficient but the only possible method): Consumers will self-select themselves to those market offerings that fit their needs.

BASES OF SEGMENTATION

A. Demographics

   Sex, age, income, education, social class, family life cycle stage, ethnicity (see Chapters 14 and 15)

B. Psychographics

   Motives, values, personality, lifestyles

C. Benefits

   From utilitarian to hedonic and symbolic; from features to experiences

D. Marketplace Behaviors

   a. Brand loyal/disloyal (see Chapter 16)

   b. Heavy, medium, light user

   c. Shopping style (e.g., economic vs. experiential shopper; see Chapter 13)

   d. Knowledge base (novices vs. experts; see Chapter 11)

   e. Tech savvy (tech clueless to geeks)

   f. Communications role (role in market conversations, e.g., opinion leaders, buzzers, connectors, etc.; see Chapter 10)

A. Demographics.

Demographics are **objective** characteristics of people, both as a group and as individuals. Thus, the academic discipline called *demography* studies the structure of population in a nation or a group—population growth, age distribution, birth rates, mortality rates, income distributions, and so on. For example, Japan now bears the dubious distinction of being the most aged nation in the world (with 23% of people 65+ and only 13% of people 0-14 years of age). In contrast, China's population is much younger, with only 9% in the 65+ age group, and India's population is also much younger, with 30% in the 0-14 age group (read more in Chapter 14). Now, imagine if you were considering exporting a line of adolescent clothing, which country would you target. No wonder, multinational corporations from the West are now keen on investing more in China and India than in Japan.

Demographics also differentiate individuals within any population. And accordingly, they serve as an important set of bases for identifying the segments. Let us consider some key demographics.

SEX Sex is the most obvious differentiator, based in our biology, and giving us two natural segments, males and females. The two segments behave differently in three ways:

1. They need and desire different products;
2. They desire different features in the same products;
3. They connect with marketing communications differently;

Correspondingly, marketers have four avenues of targeting those two segments :

a. Target Male And Female Segments Separately With products dedicated entirely to one segment or the other.

Examples: Men's clothing vs. Women's clothing. Many stores cater only to women; e.g., Chico's, Bebe, Talbots, etc. Others cater only to men: e.g., Men's Warehouse; Man Alive. In Media, Vogue and Cosmopolitan target women, while GQ and Esquire target men.

b. Differentiating A Common Product For The Sexes For the longest time, cars were cars. Especially the sedans. They were, in their core, designed to be gender neutral, which actually assumed that men were the drivers. This mold was broken recently when Volvo designed a concept car called *YCC (Your Concept Car)*, designed by women for women (read more about it in Case 1-1).

c. Crossing Over to Attract the Other Segment Hardware stores historically had assumed men to be the principal customer group. Now they have realized that women—especially single independent women—also need home improvement. So companies like Home Depot are refashioning themselves to be female-friendly (hiring more women as in-store advisors, and organizing classes for women customers).

d. Appealing to a Woman's Mojo Targeting the two sexes with different products in product categories that are inherently gender specific (e.g., clothing, cosmetics) is a no-brainer. The real creativity lies in exploring whether or not the marketing of truly gender-neutral products need to be fashioned differently. A start-up venture in Africa did just that: Fenomenal Woman was set up to sell insurance exclusively to women. The marketing approach differs in that it organizes market conversations and community building, appealing directly to a woman's inner mojo. Read more about this case and the psyche of the two sexes in Chapter 14.

AGE Age is another biological characteristic of humans. Many of our needs differ by age, and so do many of our tastes. These differences therefore call for separating consumers by age. Some companies find it useful to target particular age groups defined in terms of small age-bands: for example: 0-5, 6-12, 13-18 for toys, baby clothing, baby or child food, etc. Some brands segment their consumers by age-defined life stages: youth, adolescents, mature middle age, seniors, etc. Abercrombie & Fitch (a clothing

brand), for example, targets adolescents with its flagship stores A&F; in recent years, it opened a new store brand to appeal to teenagers, called *Halston*. And Abercrombie (with *Fitch* dropped) Kids to catch consumers early in life. A popular age segmentation in US is Boomers, Generation X, Generation Y, and Seniors. These groups differ not only in their chronological marker but, more importantly, in their psyche due to the particular time period they experienced while they were growing up. More about age-related consumer psychology in Chapter 14.

ETHNICITY

Ethnicity is another useful demographic characteristic of consumers. This demographic captures both biological and cultural variables. Some needs of consumers of different ethnic origin differ due to differences in their biological makeup, such as hair care needs. Other preferences differ

due to cultural values and practices. The latter (values and practices) affect consumer preferences for products (e.g., more spicy versus less spicy foods; ethnic clothing, etc.) as well as for market-mix elements (e.g., use of coupons and of credit cards). Most noteworthy is the need to tailor communications to ensure congruence with the values and mores of particular ethnic groups.

INCOME, EDUCATION, AND OCCUPATION

Often these three demographic characteristics go together. Often, but not always. Consider the early history of segmentation: This practice was started by General Motors. Henry Ford is reputed to have once said that customers can have their cars in any color as long as it's black. Rival General Motors broke out of this mold and invented segmentation—creating three separate divisions: Chevrolet for the low income, Oldsmobile for the middle class, and Buick for the high income consumer segments. Later for the super-rich, it added Cadillac.

Education is a good basis of segmenting the consumers for those products and services that correlate with educated tastes. Examples: Barnes & Noble; Classical versus Pop music; public TV vs. commercial TV; patronage of the arts; ethnic foods; etc.

Occupation determines interests (often in combination with income and education). Carpenters and auto mechanics are more likely to go for Jimmy Buffet concerts and outback barbecues than say college professors or doctors—the latter more for, say, philharmonics and ethnic food.

Family Life Cycle is formed by a person's marital status and size of family. We will consider all the stages later (in Chapter 14), but let us consider here four of these stages: young singles, young married, married with children at home, and empty nesters. For young singles, social and leisure activities will be of prime interest (music, fashion clothing, etc.); the young married couples would be most interested in starter homes and the furnishings to go with it. Married with children couples are most preoccupied with their children's education; they need activities that center around children. Empty nesters have a lot of time and take to traveling and exploring.

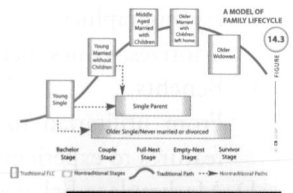

PSYCHOGRAPHICS

Psychographics are people's mental make ups and behavioral patterns. They include motives, values, personalities, lifestyles, etc. Beyond their demographics, consumers differ also on their psychographics: in their motivations (actualizers versus enjoyers), values (which is more important: comfort or environment?), and finally in lifestyles. *Lifestyles* refer to patterns of living. Thus, a farmer's lifestyle will be different than a teacher's; a politician's different from a sportsman's. Las Vegas appeals to "enjoyers," whereas MBA colleges appeal to actualization-seekers. Green energy appeals to ecology-minded consumers. In lifestyle, European budget hotels and Eurail cater to backpacker explorers; cruise lines cater to worry-free, chores-free, indulgent leisure seekers.

INSIGHTS NEEDED FOR SEGMENTATION

The concepts of psychographics are fully discussed in Chapters 5 and 6. We have described the psychographic segmentation only briefly here, because this concept entails multifaceted dynamic consumer psychology, to appreciate which you need to read the rest of the book.

In Chapters 2 through 6, we describe how a consumer's mental makeup is constructed, starting with motivation—the fundamental force driving a consumer's psychographics—in Chapter 2. So read on the rest of the book.

■ ■ ■

C ASES

FROM Air Stocking TO ZIPCARS
From Classic to Romantic

Classic

The quality of being straightforward and unemotional.
Also: Left brain, logical; relates to utilitarian consumption (focused on utility value in the USER framework)

Romantic

The quality of being sensitive to feelings.
Also: Right brain, emotional.
Focused on social, ego/identity, and recreational values in the USER framework).
Post-modern.

CASE STUDY ① A Car for Women, by Women

CB *raison d'être* (Ch 1) (Q1, Q2, Q3); Motives (Ch 2) (Q4); Gender (Ch 14) (Q5)   Classic

Imagine a Car like this one: The front end of the car is very low, lower than most other cars. The rear window is very steep and extends all the way to the edge of the trunk lid. And the fenders are curved convex and (thanks to the extended front and rear wind shields) they are visible from the driver's position. For the first time, you can see all four corners of your car's outside. And see the roads better.

There is no hood. Only a garage mechanic can get to the engine by lifting the front end of the chassis. There is no cap for the gas tank. Rather you just push the nozzle into the pressure-lid covered gas intake. And there is a wind-shield washer fluid filler outside (remember, you can't lift the hood), next to the gas tank intake, and it too is similarly capless. The two doors of the coupe are gull-wing to allow very easy entry and exit. And the car can run on flat tires for a while.

You are puzzled and then it hits you: This car is dedicated to minimizing any demands on the driver. What car is this and how did they ever dream these things? Here is the skinny on it.

The car is a Volvo, not actually available yet, but in the works. A few years ago, Volvo put together a women-only product design team. The teams focus-grouped hundreds of women drivers, and brainstormed among themselves, bringing "gender empathy" to the project. Project name: Your Concept Car (YCC)—a car designed by women for women.

How else is the car different? Let us count the ways.
- **The gear shifter is in the steering wheel, and the brake is invisible—it is electronic.**
- **The space released by the relocated gear box is now expended on an oversized storage center console, with three compartments, of varying sizes: a small one for keys and coins and cell phone; the second, larger one, for purse, umbrella, etc.; and the third holds your laptop.**
- **There is a cooler and also a wastebasket.**
- **Individual chair car seats in the back fold up and slide back (more cargo space!).**
- **The engine cuts off at stoplights and comes**

back to life with a tap at the accelerator.
- **There is parallel parking assist.**
- **It has "ergo vision." When you buy your car, your body is scanned at the dealership and the information is stored in your car's digital key. Insert it in the center console, and, voila, your seat, steering wheel, pedals, head restraint, and seat belts adjust automatically.**
- **And those seats, they come equipped with detachable pads with changeable fabric coverings. So also the carpets.**

In short, this feels more like your living room than a car. And those sleek, feminine contours in the *bodyline*— what woman can resist these? Can you?

DISCUSSION QUESTIONS

1. Does the YCC project illustrate the value of understanding consumers? How?
2. Which of the four values (USER) will this car satisfy for women consumers who may buy it?
3. Does the idea of designing a car especially for women a sound one, especially in this age of equality among the sexes?
4. Will the car appeal to women's motives and emotions? How likely will they want to buy this car compared to other cars they might be considering? Why?
5. Would it not be advisable to position the car simply as an attractively designed car, rather than tying it down to one of the genders? Why or why not?

Source: Volvo Web site (used with permission). Additional sources: Edmunds.com; Howstuff works.com.

CASE STUDY **2** **Don't Wear Your Stockings! Spray Them**

(CB raison d'être (Ch 1) (Q1, Q2, Q3); Motives (Ch 2) (Q2); Values (Ch 5) (Q4))

Classic

Say goodbye to all those runs in your stockings. And in Hot Summer, no more need to suffer the confining fabric garment on your legs. Instead of wearing stockings made of fabric, now all you do is hold a can and spray the stockings directly on your legs. The can sprays silk powder and the powder coating makes it look like you are wearing a panty hose.

This innovative product was introduced in Japan, in February 2003, by C.C. Medico Co. Ltd of Japan. Japanese women had bought about 1 million cans in that year itself. And they continue to buy the product with enthusiasm.

The sprayed-on stockings last a day. Don't worry, they won't wash away in rain—they are waterproof. Of course, you can wash them off with soap and a loofah.

A Southwest flight attendant who tried it on a flight had this to say, " I haven't sweated it off. It hasn't rubbed off on my clothes or on the seat."

Said another: "I would rather wear this than a hose; it makes my skin more smooth."*

You can buy it at beauty.com (search Air stocking). It comes in three colors: Terra-cotta, natural, and bronze. Alas, for the fish-net look, you will have to stay with the real thing. But in Air Stockings, you get to show your pedicured toes.

Check it out at www.airstockings.com

* From the company's web site.

(Source: Based on a report *CBS: On You Side*, April 29, 2004 and information at www.airstockings.com.)

Source: www.airstocking.com

DISCUSSION QUESTIONS

1. If women find this product appealing, does it not show that marketing creates new needs in consumers? Explain.

2. Why will women find this product appealing? Or, why not? Describe the mindset of the prospective consumer.

3. The product has yet to gain popularity in USA and other European and Asian countries. Why might its adoption by consumers be slower outside of Japan?

4. Draw a means-ends chain for this product.

CASE STUDY **3** **Cars By The Hour**

Classic

Suppose you didn't have to own a car. And yet, you could get a car to drive whenever, wherever you wanted it. With all the hassle, not to mention the costs, of maintenance, repair, insurance and parking, that is something you may have occasionally dreamed of. Well, that dream is now a reality.

A company named Zipcar has made it possible. Founded in 2000, the company offers cars for hourly or daily driving in selected locations in cities like San Francisco, Minneapolis, Boston, New York City, Chapel Hill (North Carolina), and Washington, D.C. Here is how it works:

• **Apply online for a membership and you will receive a Zipcard. By using a phone or online, reserve your car.**

• **Walk to the car, and just hold your Zipcard**

to the windshield. The doors will unlock.

• **Drive away.**

• **At the end of your trip, simply bring the car back to the same spot.**

And the cars you will get are new models of cool cars like BMW, Volvo, Mini Cooper, Prius Hybrid, etc. With a fleet of 1500 cars and growing, you are bound to get a car you will like, including a pick up if you need one. In most locations, you will need to walk only a block or two (which may actually do you some good, compared to your current door-to-door driving routine). Check out the locations and rates, for Georgetown, for example. You can find similar maps, for other locations, on its friendly Web site.

The company's Web site also cites these environmental benefits.

ENVIRONMENTAL BENEFITS

- **Fewer Cars:** Forty percent of Zipcar members decide against owning a car. Each Zipcar replaces about 20 privately owned vehicles.

- **Drive Less:** Car usage of individuals is reduced by as much as 50%.

- **Newer Cars:** Older cars are replaced with newer cars that are safer and more environmental friendly.

- **Green Spaces:** Fewer parking spaces are required.

- **Urban Congestion:** Fewer cars on the road means less congestion, saving everyone time and thus improving nation's productivity.

Proudly, it displays a banner that pronounces:

Imagine a nation with a million fewer cars on the road—we do.

The company also offers a program for Universities for on campus access to Zipcars. Some 20 universities have joined the program including Harvard, MIT, American University, Tufts, Princeton, and Columbia.

Look out, one maybe coming soon to your neighborhood.

TOTAL COST OF OWNERSHIP
Your Car

How much do you pay for your car per month:

Car payment (incl. depreciation)	= $287
Finance charge	= $ 62
Insurance	= $ 75
Gas	= $ 23
License, registration, taxes	= $ 46
Maintenance	= $ 71
Parking	= $175

Total $839 per month, $10,068 per year
vs. ZIPCAR

Zipcar cost (based on 10 trips a month of 2 hour average duration) = $2,400 per year ($6,000 for 25 trips a month)*

* Based on $10 per hour rate.

DC--Georgetown Car Name	Where It Lives	Price (/hr)	Price (daily)
S40 Savannah	20th/H St NW	$10.75	$72
xB Benedict	20th/H St NW	$8.75	$62
Element Elsa	33rd/Water St NW--On Street	$10.75	$72
Tacoma Pickup Tonya	Foggy Bottom/GWU Metro	$10.75	$72
Escape Elliott	Foggy Bottom/GWU Metro	$10.75	$72
Matrix Mammoth	Foggy Bottom/GWU Metro	$8.75	$62
V50 Velma	Georgetown Central	$10.75	$72
xA Africa	Georgetown Central	$8.75	$62
3 Menudo	Georgetown Central	$8.75	$62
xA Alexis	Ritz Carlton Hotel at 1155 23rd St. NW	$8.75	$62
Matrix Martian	Ritz Carlton Hotel at 1155 23rd St. NW	$8.75	$62
MINI Megalon	Ritz Carlton Hotel at 1155 23rd St. NW	$10.75	$72
Matrix Mordicai	Wisconsin Av/O St NW (CVS)	$8.75	$62

Note. Prices include gas, insurance, and XM Satellite Radio.

DISCUSSION QUESTIONS

1. As a consumer, would you want Zipcar to come to your neighborhood? What needs, USER exchange values, and motives will it satisfy?

2. As a consumer research specialist, would you recommend to Zipcar they come to your neighborhood? What factors make a region/neighborhood an ideal site for a car share service like Zipcar?

3. Identify the values Zipcar might engage. Then draw a means-ends chain.

4. What demographic and psychographic characteristics make a consumer an ideal candidate for becoming a Zipcar member?

5. Should your University or company sign up with Zipcar? Why or why not?

Applying psychographics (Ch 6) | Classic

CASE STUDY ④ Going to the Ball Game?
Take Your Psychographics With You

A student group was given a project with this objective: To identify the psychographic profile of sporting event season ticket holders.

The student group proceeded as follows. They listed 10 psychographic factors that they believed would differentiate season ticket holders from non-holders. Of these, they chose five they expected to be most differentiating. They also named, as directed to do, two factors that they expected *not* to differentiate the two groups.

Next, they wrote five AIO statements to measure each factor, making sure that the items tapped, separately, an activity, an interest, and an opinion; they tried to include as well some negatively worded items. For each factor, then, they selected the three items they thought best measured the factor.

Next, they removed the factor names and jumbled all 21 statements. And they placed a 5-point scale: 1-Does not describe me at all, 5-Describes me very well. Adding some questions on demographics completed the questionnaire.

Their task was to find a convenient sample of 10 season ticket holders and ten non-season ticket holders. With permission from the manager, they surveyed customers at an Applebee's restaurant. With 20 surveys completed, they entered the data in an Excel sheet and computed the mean score on each statement for each of the two groups separately. Their findings are summarized in Table 1.

Now they were eager to examine the tabulated results and write a verbal profile of the season ticket holders. They were aware that the sample was not representative and their findings could be entirely off base. But they were to assume that the data represented a large random sample. They hoped the findings would at least enable them to answer the central question: Do season ticket holders differ, in their psychographics, from non-holders?

DISCUSSION QUESTION. The student group is keeping its report a secret. Can you piece together your own report? And while you are at it, you can't help critiquing the group's effort. Sure, go ahead; that too will be immensely useful.

TABLE **1**

*In the table, items marked asterisk are reverse-coded so that each score actually shows pro-factor average. To illustrate, "I think going to bars is a waste of money" means the opposite of "social drinkers." To make it a pro-factor item, a rating of '1' was *recoded* as '5', of '2 as '4', '4' as '2', and '5' as '1'. Holders score 4.2, more than the score of non-holders, 3.4, thus implying that holders are more of a social drinker than non-holders.

Source: From author's *Research Files*.

Psychographic Profiles of Sporting Events Season Ticket Holders vs. Non-holders

(Scale: 1-Does not describe me at all, 5-Describes me very well.)

FACTOR	Season Ticket Holders	Non-holders of Season Ticket
SENSATION SEEKING		
I crave excitement.	3.8	3.0
I enjoy the outdoors.	4.4	4.2
It is important to experience life to the fullest by trying new things.	3.6	3.2
COMPETITIVENESS		
I only play to win.	4.2	2.8
I don't think it is important to win a game as long as you are having fun.*	2.8	1.8
I would not enjoy a situation in which there is a winner and a loser.*	4.0	3.0
SOCIAL DRINKER		
I only drink on the weekends.	4.0	2.6
I think going to bars is a waste of money.*	4.2	3.4
I would rather go to a bar than stay at home.	3.4	2.6
EXTROVERTED		
Having a positive attitude is important to me.	3.4	4.8
I would rather spend time with others than by myself.	4.4	3.2
I go out with my family/friends every weekend.	4.6	3.6
NEWS JUNKIE		
I never watch the news.*	2.8	2.0
I would like to know what's going on in the rest of the world.	3.2	4.2
The local news does not provide enough information.	3.2	2.8
SUPERSTITIOUS		
I do not have an umbrella open indoors.	3.2	3.6
I do not believe in lucky numbers.*	2.6	3.4
I would like to visit a psychic.	2.0	2.8
INTERNET SAVVY		
I would feel comfortable buying on the Internet.	4.0	3.4
I believe a computer without the Internet is worthless.	3.4	2.8
I do research on new products online	2.4	2.4

CASE STUDY (5) NASCAR—Balancing Your Attitude

Classic

Attitude Molding (Ch 8); Learning to interpret consumer research data

Two Consumer Researchers (Professors Vassilis Dalakas and Aron Levin) surveyed 220 NASCAR fans attending a race. In the survey, respondents were asked to name their favorite driver and then they rated themselves on how much they identified with the named driver (a questionnaire called Sports Spectator Identification Scale (SSIS) was used for this rating). Survey respondents were also asked to indicate their least favorite driver and to name the companies that sponsored the driver. Next, their attitudes toward 11 NASCAR drivers and attitudes toward brands and companies who sponsor them were measured.

On the ten–point scale that the SSIS uses, respondents scored 7.66 for Dale Earnhardt, Jr., 7.39 for Jeff Gordon, 6.87 for Mark Martin, 8.34 for Tony Stewart, and 7.66 for Dale Jarrett. Note that these are ratings not across all respondents but only across all those who named a specific driver as their favorite.

Was the sponsoring company liked more by the sponsored drivers' fans than by an average race visitor? Their findings are summarized in the table below.

As the marketing manager of one of the companies that participates in NASCAR sponsorship, you wonder what lessons these findings hold for you? Failure to draw those lessons can cost you a big fortune.

TABLE

ATTITUDE TOWARD A COMPANY/BRAND

Company/Brand	Average Attitude Among All Visitors	Average Attitude among Fans of the Sponsored Driver	Average Attitude among Visitors Who Chose This Driver as Their Least Favorite	Correlation (Sponsor versus Driver Atttiude)*
Budweiser (Dale Earnhardt, Jr.)	8.49	9.39 (61**)	5.20 (5)	.370
UPS (Dale Jarett)	7.80	9.50 (10)	6.50 (2)	.412
Home Depot (Tony Stewart)	7.53	9.54 (13)	6.67 (18)	.397
GM Goodwrench (Kevin Harwick)	7.48	9.14 (7)	4.64 (11)	.535
Dupont (Jeff Gordon)	6.50	9.42 (36)	3.87 (52)	.681
Viagra (Mark Martin)	5.97	7.62 (13)	1.0 (2)	.170
Miller Lite (Rust Wallace)	5.96	6.0 (4)	3.60 (14)	.289
Coors Light (Sterling Marlin)	5.82	5.67 (3)	3.08 (12)	.228

Note. Attitudes measured on a 0-10 point scale.

* Correlation between attitude toward the brand/company and attitude toward the sponsoring driver. The scores can range from -1.0 to +1.0, with a larger number signifying a higher correlation.

** Numbers in parentheses are number of respondents.

Source: Excerpted from Vassilis Dalakas and Aron Levin, "The Balance Theory Domino: How Sponsorship May Elicit Negative Attitudes," in press. (Used with permission.)

* In reading the table, small respondent numbers, say, less than five, are not meaningful to draw any inferences from.

MY CB BOOK

DISCUSSION QUESTIONS

1. Are the findings in Table consistent with Heider's Balance Theory (Chapter 8)? Explain your answer.

2. Do all brands benefit from sponsorships? Which companies are benefiting more or less? If you were a marketing manager of a company, and if you decided to stop NASCAR sponsorships, for which company would the loss be the least and for which ones the most?

3. Why are the correlations so different across companies? What do these wide-ranging correlations show for specific companies?

4. Since all drivers will have both their fans as well as *dislikers*, how would you, as a marketer, choose the driver to sponsor?

5. Suppose some drivers became available and if you were (a) Coors Light or (b) the company behind Viagra, would you sign up that driver (dumping your current driver) and which driver will you sign? Why or why not?

Source: Vassilis Dalakas and Aron Levin, "The Balance Theory Domino: How Sponsorships May Elicit Negative Consumer Attitudes," *Advances in Consumer Research*, Volume 32, 2005, p. 91-97. (Reprinted by permission)

CASE STUDY 6 How I Bought My Car

By: Stephanie Riesling

One of my most memorable experiences as a consumer occurred only about three months ago. In January this year, I purchased a brand new Mazda 3. I considered many things when deciding what car to buy, what features to get on it, and what color to get. The first thing that I had to decide was what kind of car I wanted to buy. Many things went along with this, such as price, reliability, and looks. I wanted something that was in my price range, that looked good, and also that had been known to last for a long time.

One afternoon my boyfriend and I drove to different car lots in our area just to glance around. When that day was done I had narrowed my choices down based on looks and price because these were the things I could see from driving around. My choices were the Corolla, Mazda 3, Ion, and Civic. Over the next couple of days I read Consumer Reports on these cars, I talked to people about their experiences, and I surfed the Internet reading a lot about these cars. Finally, I decided that I wanted to go back to the Mazda dealership. Honestly, even though I did extensive research I really just liked the way the Mazda 3 looked the best. And although I was trying to keep my options open I knew in the back of my mind that was the car I wanted.

When it came to features I knew I wanted a five speed and four doors, the rest could be negotiated. I was pleasantly surprised to find out that the Mazda 3 gets 35 miles to the gallon expressway and averages 33 miles per gallon. With gas prices soaring the way they are this was a huge added bonus in my mind. There were certain features that I knew going in that I could live without. When it came to power windows and locks, I could do without. Although I would like to have them on my car, keeping the overall cost down was more important to me.

Finally after looking at about 35 Mazda 3s, going from the cargo net to the interior color, I had narrowed it down to two cars, one was red and one was black. This is the decision that I agonized over. I went home and printed out a picture of each car and carried them with me for two days constantly looking at them. Finally, I went back to the lot and had the salesman pull the cars side by side so I could compare them in person. I think I must have walked circles around the cars at least twenty times comparing every inch. Finally, I decided the black color made the car resemble a Cavalier and the red one just looked sharp and speedy so I went with the velocity red with metallic in it. When actually purchasing my car I had a sense of nervousness and excitement mixed together. I was about to own a beautiful brand new car but I felt like I was signing my life away. It was a lot of money but it was worth it.

I am delighted with it. I would buy the car all over again.

(Stephanie Riesling is a 20-something senior and a resident of Greater Cincinnati and Northern Kentucky area.)

DISCUSSION QUESTIONS

1. Review various concepts in Chapter 11 (Consumer Decision Making) and see which of the methods, procedures, and decision rules did this consumer apply?

2. Is this a typical experience of consumers buying a car? How might this experience differ across consumers?

3. Did this consumer experience any post-choice dissonance? Why or why not?

Consumer Research Findings from Millward Brown

Tweens are a group to be reckoned with. They're complex, demanding, and difficult to understand. They're a challenging group for marketers but vitally important to get to know.

Today's tweens (9-14 year-olds) are more affluent than those of any previous generation, and there are more of them. They're more vocal and powerful. Not only do they have their own pocket money, but they also wield influence beyond their spending power.

Millward Brown's research for the book *BRAND-child* found that in more than half of tweens' households (58%), parents ask their kids' advice when it comes to buying high ticket items like cars, or the tweens actually tell their parents what they should buy (see charts below).

In India, 71% of tweens claim to influence cars bought by their parents. In America the corresponding figure is 63% and over half of 9-14 years-olds in Brazil, China, Japan and Germany also believe that they affect this purchase. Motor manufacturers such as Ford, Honda, VW and Vauxhall have all recently developed marketing activity acknowledging the role of the child in brand choice.

Additionally, today's tweens are tomorrow's adult consumers. On estimate, the average US tween will have an uninflated per capita income of $2m (£1.07m) throughout their life. How they spend this income will partly be driven by the brand associations formed at a young age.

Kids and brands

Mental associations, shortcuts and loyalties to brands begin to form at a very early age. And many habits formed as tweens can persist long into adulthood. As early as six months of age, babies are beginning to form mental images of corporate logos and mascots. At the age of three, before they can read and write, one out of five US children is making specific requests for brand-name products.

The research shows that overall brand loyalty increases sharply from the age of 10, and peaks around the age of 30 (see graph on page 55). There is a pattern of strengthening bonds with brands that starts and grows throughout the tween years.

However, on average tweens are 40% less loyal to brands than adults. Furthermore, among kids, around half of all brands change their 'typology' (a measure of overall brand equity) every two years, highlighting an extremely rapid migration of attitudes.

But why this promiscuity? Children are programmed to want to explore and experience, and this is just as true of brands as it is of other things. Tweens are less brand loyal simply because they have had less experience and involvement with brands. But this is not the only reason.

The news and promotions bombarded at kids in an attempt to drive sales and build loyalty often does little to build strong brand foundations. Most mothers have been browbeaten into buying a particular

Understanding the teen mind (Ch 14); Teen influence in families (Ch 14);
Referent influence type (Ch 10); An example of deep profiles (Epilog)

Classic

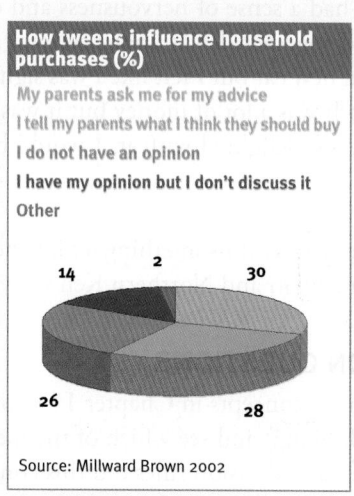

How tweens influence household purchases (%)

- My parents ask me for my advice
- I tell my parents what I think they should buy
- I do not have an opinion
- **I have my opinion but I don't discuss it**
- Other

14   2   30
26   28

Source: Millward Brown 2002

Tweens claiming to influence car buying parents (%)

India	71
America	63
China	59
Brazil	59
Japan	53
Germany	51
Spain	40

Kids bonding to car brands (%)

	Germany	Spain	Brazil
New MINI	13	8	15
Ford Focus/Ka	0	15	3
VW Golf	12	8	6
New Beetle	12	9	7

Source: Millward Brown 2002

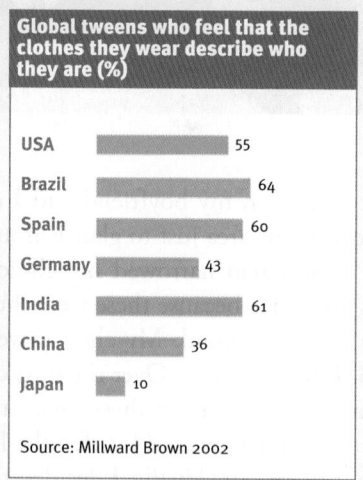

Global tweens who feel that the clothes they wear describe who they are (%)

USA	55
Brazil	64
Spain	60
Germany	43
India	61
China	36
Japan	10

Source: Millward Brown 2002

brand strategy february 2005

DISCUSSION QUESTIONS

1. Tweens influence family purchases of important products such as a car. What is the nature of this influence (normative, informational, identificational)? Why would parents give in to influence from their teen children?

2. Does this finding imply that marketers should direct their brand communications for all family consumption products to tweens as well as adult family members?

3. Consider the finding that brand loyalty among tweens is 40% less than adults. Is this likely to be true for all products? Which of the three reasons cited in the study will become less influential as tweens grow up?

4. What role might the concept of involvement play in (a) tweens' influence on family purchases, and (b) tweens' brand loyalty?

5. Discuss each of the "Tips for Marketers."

Interesting Insights into Tween Psyche

product which comes with a free gift or promotion, only to find the product itself being ignored. Such promotions rarely generate loyalty, although they may drive short-term sales. And with more promotional activity around, it's easy for tweens to jump from one brand to another.

Tween tribes

On average, eight in 10 of today's urban tweens need to feel part of a group, and what the group says, goes. The lowest agreement score on 'It is important to me to feel part of a group' was seen in Germany (71%), and the highest in Brazil (89%). In China 81% agree that it's important to feel part of a group. Half of all girls and around four in 10 boys believe that 'the clothes they wear describe who they are'.

Peer pressure drives how tweens behave and what brands they buy. Tweens want to belong, so it's no surprise that brands play such a big role in helping them do this. And kids beneath the tween threshold feel their own pressure. In a phenomenon known as 'fish streaming', younger children look up to tweens and aspire to use their brands. Brand tracking work showed that children with older siblings were more likely to pick up on PlayStation on its initial release. Those without older siblings took around a year longer to reach the same level of brand exposure.

As kids move from tween to teen, peer pressure diminishes. But tweens have a strong emotional need to fit in and feel secure, and this is one of the major contributors to both strong and weak brand loyalty among this group.

David Chantrey is group account director at Millward Brown. Millward Brown has conducted BRANDZ research for WPP and interviewed over 2,000 urban tweens worldwide for Martin Lindstrom's book BRANDchild.

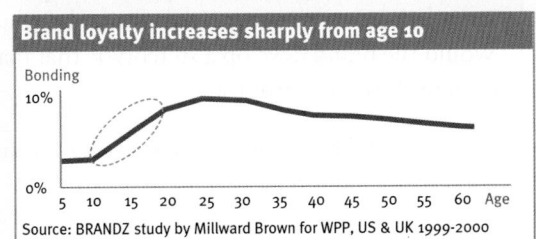

Brand loyalty increases sharply from age 10

Bonding
10%

0%

5 10 15 20 25 30 35 40 45 50 55 60 Age

Source: BRANDZ study by Millward Brown for WPP, US & UK 1999-2000

Children aged 6-8 who favoured Playstation initially

	No older siblings	With older siblings
1999	45%	57%
2000	57%	64%

Source: Millward Brown, 1999/2000

Tweens who feel peer pressure to buy certain products

Age:	12-13	14-15	16-18
Yes:	54%	30%	17%

Source: The Center for a New American Dream, 2002 Youth Survey

55

Tips for marketers

● **Whether you're marketing kids' brands or grown-up brands, consider tweens as a potential target:** Establish how many tweens know your brand and what they think of it. Understand the role tweens play in purchase decisions in your category. If you decide to include tweens as a target, consider how you'll manage the brand relationship from child to adult.

● **Make ethics your number one priority when marketing to tweens:** Never forget that tweens are still children and the ethical responsibility that comes with this. Products need to be safe, and as marketers you need to be honest, keep your word, and earn the trust of both tweens and their parents.

● **Make sure brands work around how tweens live, not around traditional business hours:** Once they reach the age of eight or nine, today's kids are a 24/7 generation and expect 24/7 brands and instant gratification.

● **Make sure your concept has potential to keep evolving over time:** Today's tweens thrive on upgrades – product evolution now needs to happen over weeks and months, not years. However, there must be a sense of consistency that ties subsequent evolutions together – know exactly what your brand stands for and remain true to it.

● **Build peer-to-peer marketing programmes around community leaders and put tweens at the centre:** Belonging to a group is crucial in tween life. Tweens look up to their leaders and inspire each other. Peer-to-peer marketing will play an increasingly important role in creating successful tween brands, and the most successful will use viral marketing tools to enable tweens to market for them.

● **Think and act mobile:** You will increasingly need to be where your target is, which won't be in front of the TV. TV ads may well be used to inspire, but interactive channels will increasingly do the informing.

● **Be flexible and patient with your own lack of understanding of how the tween world operates:** Tweens hate to be sold to but love to be respected. They want to be listened to, heard and understood. Marketers should spend time with them; listen to them; talk to them; discover what they dream about. The future of a brand rests in their hands.

Marketing Advice from a World-Class Brand Communications Expert

CASE STUDY 8 Grandpa, You Are Driving My Car!!

Classic

Brand Positioning (Ch 1, 3) and who drives it (Ch 1, 3); Understanding age segments (Ch 14)

Look at Honda Element. Overall, a boxy rectangle. With an almost vertical hatchback. The Color is vivid maroon with black trim. Inside, the seats come off. The carpets are all rubber. You can hose them out.

Scion is even more boxy (the full height back is entirely vertical). XB comes with customizable entertainment console—you can place Sirius Satellite and XM radio.

The cars were designed to appeal to youth, Gen Y—the group of seven million Americans born between 1977 to 1995.

In concept tests, indeed Gen Y liked them. (Somewhere, when the older ones among us were asleep, the square look seems to have become hip.) What appealed to Gen Y the most in the car is how roomy it was. It was, in fact, a dorm room on wheels. So they could carry half of their belongings if they like. And driving the car was just an extension of lounging in their dorm room. With entertainment and all.

This all seems sensible. There is only one problem. The Gen Y is not driving it. Instead, it is their parents—boomers or even seniors driving them. The targeted age of Element, Scion, Matrix was each between 27 and 20. Actual age: 42 to 45. This is the story for car after car. Dodge Neon is 39 instead of the anticipated 23; Pontiac Vibe 48 compared to targeted 30 years.[1]

The snag; the cars, designed to be inexpensive, still cost a hefty $18 to 22 K. And few Gen Y have that kind of money. What are they buying instead: 4 to 10 years older models of Civics, Corollas, Jeeps, Ford Escorts, etc. Or family hand-downs as their parents replace their own cars with new ones.

One option might be to strip down the model even more to bring down the price to say $12,000. But this strategy has its own risks. For starters, the car may be left bereft of any thing desirable at all. (Remember Echo?). Second, they will embrace the brand only as a stop gap, yearning to graduate to better brands as soon as they can afford. So a scaled down skeleton brand will be a poor strategy to lure youngsters into becoming "customers for life."

That older people like the Hondas and Scions seems a puzzle only at first. Come to think of it: room on wheels, movable seats, easy to hose, aren't all these features inherently appealing to older people as well. And the vertical body structure means easy to get in and out—something even more valuable to seniors. Oh, the square boxy look, didn't someone say, among the new generation, it is hip to be square?!

Incidentally, Toyota name means too mainstream, so just as GM did years ago with Saturn, the company set up Scion as a separate division. Now the company has come up with a more mainstream yet sleek design, in tC (see Chapter 1) which appeals to youth, but for 20-somethings, it is pricey. So the search for a car as sleek as a tC and as "cool" as Element or the vertical back Scion and still within a youth's budget continues.

DISCUSSION QUESTIONS

Q1. Why would a car designed for Gen Y appeal to more mature consumers?

Q2. Are the sources of value from a car like the Element or the Scion identical for the two groups of consumers—20-somethings and forty-somethings? How might they differ? Would each group consider the car "cool" and in the same way?

Q3. If a group other than the originally intended adopts a product/brand, will this then discourage the originally intended group to move away from the product/brand? Would the brand develop a stereotype that may then limit its appeal to some groups?

Q4. Does the Element and Scion story mean age is not a good segmentation basis? Discuss.

[1.] A report by CNW Marketing Research. For a more fact-filled report, see "The Car is for Kids, but Gramps is Driving," NY Times (www.nytimes.com/2005/07/03/automobiles/03Auto.html); also: 50-plus Marketing (www.20plus30.com/50plusmarketing/archive/2005_09_01_archive.html).

Ruehl No. 925
The Abercrombie & Fitch Consumer Grows UP!

Classic

Understanding latent consumer needs/niche lifestyle positioning (Ch 1. 6)
Targeting age segments (Ch 14)

If you walk casually in Greenwich (New York, City), you will pass right by it. It's a clothing store, owned by Abercrombie & Fitch (A&F), with the name of the store so inconspicuous that you won't notice it. The store front, with no display windows, looks more like a house than a store. The name of the store: Ruehl #925!

Once inside, you will find none of the mega size steamy posters of bare-chested, models that decorate the parent company's stores. Instead you will get a wide range of clothes, a bit more fashionable and a bit more expensive.

Abercrombie & Fitch (A&F) is implementing a life-stage need identification concept. It knows that most of its current customers are college students; when they graduate and enter the job market, they take their patronage, at least for part of their casual wardrobe, elsewhere, such as to stores like Banana Republic or Polo. Now to lure them, the company has embarked a new store concept, where it features casual clothing, still bearing the same urban casual look, of course, but somewhat upgraded in quality, and, correspondingly, in price as well. Its media advertising and in-store poster displays are also subdued as far as overt sexiness is concerned. And the new stores are designed more like a vintage apartment with soft lighting that invites lingering and lounging.

In part it resembles Hollister, the A&F's other brand extension a few years ago. Hollister, you might know, similarly has no visible store front or nameplate, but looks and feels more like an apartment than a store. Walk inside and at the entrance you will find chair and cocktail tables, littered with book and magazines. Merchandise aisles are dimly lighted and are set in meandering lanes so the whole walk thru the store feels more like a walk through a *Homerama* house. If you buy something, you will have to find the cash register which is set in the center of the store and looks more like a DJ booth in a clubby lounge—yes, with living-room style sofa seating in the foreground. And as you browse through the merchandise, you can watch on giant screens scenes from the surfing haven beaches of California's, so as to experience the surfer lifestyle.

While Hollister appeals to a high school teenage segment a few years younger than a typical, still-in-college A&F customer, Ruehl is designed to capture a just-gradu-

ated, new career person. And like Hollister, Ruehl also sells items beyond the expected, including: vintage books, art, newspapers, magazines and CDs.

What's with the name of the new store chain, Ruehl No. 925! Nine-to-Five, get it?.

And Ruehl is a created family name of an imaginary German immigrant. The story on company's Web site goes:

> **"A German immigrant moved to the United States circa 1850 and opened a fine leather goods shop that stayed in his family for generations. His great grandson, 100 years later, decided to enter the apparel business, focusing on denim and inspired by screen idol James Dean."**

Ruehl #925 sells, you see, not just merchandise, but, rather, it tells you a story. It wants you to feel as if, in shopping there and while wearing its merchandise, you are living a story. The question is whether that story is the one you want to live.

DISCUSSION QUESTIONS

1. Will the store appeal to recent college graduates who are now seeking a more mature, career centered merchandise, and would otherwise go to stores like Banana Republic and Kenneth Cole?

2. How well does the store meet the challenge of looking more mature than but still connected to the A&F image? Should it?

3. "Consumers seeking career wardrobe just want good, stylish career clothing. They are not there for the dimly lighted store atmosphere. They are in other words, more in a "find-the-merchandise, goal-oriented" mode, not in a leisurely browsing mode." Do you agree or disagree, and do you believe the store ambience will hinder or help attract the target group and sell them the merchandise.

4. Design a research study to identify consumer segments to whom the store will appeal? What mindset will make this segment an ideal prospect for the store?

CASE STUDY (10) A Conservative British Store Turns Emotional

In April 2011, Prince William and Catherine Middleton danced their first dance to the tune of "Your Song," recorded in 1970 by British music icon Elton John. This particular version was rendered by Ellie Goulding. Goulding's rendition had reached #2 in the UK in 2010. Those familiar with the lyrics of the song will know it is a very emotional song ("And you can tell everybody this is your song.... How wonderful life is now you're in the world."), so it was an apt choice for the Royal couple.

The curious fact is, however, that Goulding had first recorded the song for a TV advert for John Lewis, a venerable British retailer! In that now famous advert, it played in the background as various consumers were shown packing their Christmas gifts (presumably bought from John Lewis) and as the camera artfully captured their emotions for the intended recipients. Such emotional advertising is new to retailers in general, much less to a classic, conservative retailer whose main tag line all these years has been a more matter-of-factly "never to be undersold!" What gives?

John Lewis is one of the two largest and iconic stores in the U.K. (the other one being Marks & Spencer). It sells clothing, furniture, electronics, and cosmetics to groceries, hairbrushes and buttons. With the onslaught of credit-crunched and down economy, in 2008, the retailer's sales had plunged (reflecting a general trend in retail sales) by one-third. However, in 2009, the sales were 15% higher than the previous year. Industry observers credit the reversal to an advert it had run in 2009: That advert had followed the life of a woman from cradle to adulthood, passing through the life stages of childhood, school, college, marriage, children, and so on, all squeezed within 90 seconds, interspersed with products from Lewis, and filmed to the musical score of Billy Joel's 1977 "She is Always a Woman," sung here by recording artist Fyfe Dangerfield. The £6 million, 90 second ad had been created by Creative agency Adam & Eve and had been watched on YouTube within one week of posting by 100, 000 viewers. Reporting on its widespread grip on public's hearts, Dailymail of UK

had reported : "… this 'moving' ad has got Britain talking—and sobbing into their breakfast bowls."

The retailer continued with similarly emotional adverts during 2010, and then during the Christmas 2011 season. In the 2011 ad, a boy is shown finishing the chores quickly on the eve of Christmas, so he could go to bed early, so he could get up early the next morning, so he could hand over his gift to his parents early. Such eagerness to give (not receive but gift) on the part of a 10-year-old is inherently heart-warming.

In the first week of December, the sales for this 150-year-old store sales were the largest ever for that week, with a 2% rise from the previous year, at a down-economic time when most retailers reported declining sales. (dailymail.co.uk 12th December 2011). Thus the emotional campaigns the retailer embraced three years ago had at last stopped the bleed!!

Discussion Questions:

1. Emotional advertising works for John Lewis? Why?

2. Was there a risk in adopting such advertising? Specify.

3. What are the prerequisites for a store to adopt this kind of advertising? Did John Lewis have those attributes?

Source: Campaign of the Year: John Lewis, *Brand Republic,* campaignlive.co.uk, 15 December 2011; "John Lewis Builds on Trust to Break out as Advertiser," Emma Hall, *Ad Age,* June 13, 2011; "Ellie Goulding Covers Elton John's 'Your Song' For a Smash Hit," Bill Lamb, About.com Guide

Classic

Consumer Evaluation of Innovation: Application (Ch 4)

CASE STUDY ⑪ "Don't Breathe.... Buy Our Diesels"

Don't Breathe. Don't Think. Share Your Bath Water. But Buy our Diesels.

Is this anyway to sell clothing?
Here is one market research report proclaiming:
- 294 days in planning
- 16, 497 hours of collating
- 348 bits of clip art
- 27 vague conclusions reached.

One of those conclusions is Result #08. It is a psychographic analysis of the ways in which individuals put their hands in their pockets. Put one thumb in your back pocket, and you are a "passive type"; both thumbs in the two back pockets would make you a "shy type"; one thumb in front pocket makes you a "confident type" and put both thumbs in your two front pockets, and you are definitely an "aggressive type."

The truth is that there was no research to uncover this or any of the other 26 results the company has posted on its Web site. These are just tongue-in-cheek spoofs on market research. From a company called DIESEL.

It is not that the company doesn't believe in market research; it just doesn't believe in anything that is conventional, expected, normal. Another of its ad campaigns features scenes of street protests with young 20-somethings carrying posters that read such off-the-wall slogans as "Share your bath water," "Legalize the 4-day Weekend," and "World Needs more love letters."

Finally, its Web site features a guide for being "young forever"—with some 20 illustrated pages showing models born in 1880s but frozen in time with their fresh youthful adolescent looks, and such irreverent tips as "Don't Breathe," "Don't have Sex," and "Don't think." The one with "Don't Breathe" has a quote from Mario Derion, born 1891 (Yes, 1891, and still looking 20) that reads: "I limit my breathing to just a few times a day. It helps me stay as beautiful as a century ago. After living so long, I may smell and what do I care. I look absolutely breathtaking."

Is this anyway to sell clothing?

If the proof of pudding is in eating it, the answer is a resounding "Yes." This Italian maker of blue jeans and related fashion merchandise has seen its sales boom, doubled from some 300 million in 1998 to more than 600 million units in recent years. It has more than 200 stores in major cities spanning the globe from Miami to Berlin, and expanding exponentially. It churns out about 1500 new designs every six months, more than half in denim, made to look soft and worn. Its edgy designs include such items as a man's pants with racing stripes and Hindu lettering. Its appeal is international, but mention that to Diesel owner Renzo Rosso, and he would correct you promptly: "I want to mask that we are multinational. Individuality is the sex appeal of the brand."

Sex appeal? Maybe that is why even Karl Lagerfesld, the famous high fashion designer himself, sports Diesel clothing. And its Research Result #29 shows: 18% of Diesel fans are plain "bored," 14% lazy, and 25% are "horny." While the company shows these psychographic profiles as tongue-in-cheek spoof, they do underscore the point that the brand appeals to persons of certain psychographic profile. What the company won't reveal, of course, is just what the true psychographics of its fans are.

DISCUSSION QUESTIONS

1. Visit the company's web site www.Diesel.com and explore the brand and its communications. Based on this exploration,
(a) Draw a psychographic profile of its target customers.
(b) Describe the brand's image/brand personality.

Source: Based on information on the company's Web site (www. Diesel.com) and Gail Edmondson, "Diesel is Smokin'" *Time*, February 10, 2003, p.64.

CASE STUDY (12) A Festival of Love
Courtesy of Your Government!

Call of a Nation: The Romancing Singapore Campaign

There is a dinner party in progress. Guests are 30 eligible unmarried men and women, strangers to one another. A few months later, there will be a mass wedding, and then a few weeks later, tango parties. The food will include generous portions of ginger and pumpkin broth, oysters, and chocolate torte—items chosen for their reported aphrodisiac value. Who is paying the bill? The Government of Singapore and its partners in the government's *Romancing Singapore* campaign.

Started in February 2003, the campaign is an unprecedented and bold government move to socially engineer, among Singaporeans, well, ROMANCE! Romance within marriage, that is, and expressly designed to make babies. Faced with a declining birth rate and shrinking population, the government considers it a matter of national priority. And it is incentivizing love-making as a patriotic duty.

For marketers, this is a one-of-a-kind business opportunity. Some 80 businesses have partnered with government on its *Romancing Singapore* campaign. Its Web site promotes specially branded Eau de Parfum and Chocolate Truffle cake called Aphrodisiac!

An entertainment entrepreneur, famous in Singapore as Dr. Love, has, in conjunction with the Singapore government, launched a TV show called "Dr. Love's Super Baby-Making Show." Nine couples will participate, and the couple having the baby first will be the winner of the $100,000 (USD).

Dr. Love has started another business, Meggpower. The company calls itself "A bio-communication" company and purports to sell a "wireless hormonal monitoring service." It will text-message or email a subscriber when she is due to ovulate. Based on its monitoring of the members' hormonal cycle, the company will also recommend totally customized diets to enhance conception.

Want some beach reading this Summer? Pick up a copy of "When Boy Meets Girl. The Chemistry Guide." Want to learn some creative tips on dating? Pick up a copy of "Dare to Date." Both are free! They are published by the Singapore government.

Incidentally, the *Romancing Singapore* campaign is not a one shot campaign. Rather, it is an ongoing celebration. The idea is to keep the issue in continuous awareness of people.

Some readers might wonder why love making—a behavior that comes naturally to most humans—needs to be promoted at all? The answer is three fold: first, it is love making within a marriage; second, it is love-making undertaken to procreate. And the third reason has to do with the value system and life themes of Singaporeans.

Singapore is an achievers' society. Everyone, especially the educated Chinese, is driven to work hard and obtain success. These educated Chinese—the native people—just don't have the time for leisure and forming a family. *Romance Singapore* is therefore a lifestyle and value priority altering mission. Its goal is nothing less than to shape your world-view and your life-theme. It is to make you respect and embrace leisure and family life. It is not merely hedonic and personal; it is, rather, a patriotic duty. If you are a citizen of Singapore, your nation is calling you. So get some romance. Make babies. Will You?

DISCUSSION QUESTIONS

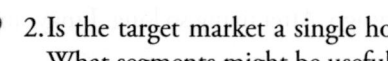 (Sources: RomancingSingapore.com.sg; Wow-her.com.sg; Loveclinic.com.

1. Is the persuasion the Singapore government is attempting a low or a high involvement context for the consumer? Which model of attitude is applicable, and to what extent is the government utilizing the guidelines suggested by various models of attitude? Specifically, which route to attitude change is the government trying to pursue?

2. Is the target market a single homogeneous group? What segments might be useful to recognize?

3. In terms of people's reasons for not getting married and not making babies, what factors might be responsible? How might the campaign work (or fail to work) depending on the specific factor?

4. What other new components to the program would you suggest, speaking from a consumer behavior point-of-view?

5. Does the government's sponsorship of such programs raise any ethical issues? Discuss.

CASE STUDY 13 — Selling Victoria's Secret in Saudi Arabia

When you see women in Saudi Arabia, all in long black wrapper dresses, you would not guess that, underneath, many of them wear fancy, colorful underwear. So these women in Saudi Arabia would seem to be a natural target market for Victoria's Secret. Except one big snag: Saudi culture does not permit open display of lingerie in a store.

Buying underwear is a nightmare for Saudi women. Since women salespersons are not allowed to sell in public places, stores that sell lingerie employ only male salespersons, and women customers must ask male salespersons for help in assessing their bra sizes. Once the bra size is determined, the salesperson would speak it out loud and an assistant would dig out the merchandise from hidden shelves. The whole experience of having to discuss their bodies with male salesmen is so embarrassing, that many women would just guess their bra size; as a result, a majority of Saudi women are reported to be wearing the wrong size bras.

It is against this background, that Lingerie Perdu, a Western style lingerie store opened on the first day of Ramadan in November 2001 on Tahlia Street in Jeddah, Saudi Arabia. How, Al-Mashat, the store's owner did it is a lesson in creative trans-cultural marketing—marketing that respects a host culture's mores and yet creates a trans-cultural experience for the consumer.

The task of designing the store was assigned to Los Angeles based Chase Design. Chase chose the name Perdu, French for lost. Saudi Arabic women are fascinated with France, and France is the country they most associate with lingerie. It also captures the experience of a woman who enters the store and can happily feel lost in the two story store that features translucent glass and has mysterious ambiance.

Lingerie Perdu Store in Saudi Arabia
Design: Chase Design Group, Los Angeles, U.S.A.

Because of the Wahhabi principles of Islam practiced in Saudi Arabia, stores can't show female body parts or pictures of women wearing lingerie. So what Chase Design did was to use language and poetry in a rich sensual way. First, it created a custom alphabet, altering English characters to look more like Arabic letters and vice versa. This bilingual wordmark appeared more sensual; and it bridged the visual gap between the English and Arabic letters. Then, it selected poetry and words that evoke the experience of wearing lingerie.

In the middle of the store, a large banner hangs from the ceiling to the floor, with these poetic words inscribed in English: Wrap this beautiful robe of words around you and dream. Also hanging are many other long banners with words like "passion," "love," "dreams" etc., inscribed both in English and Arabic. These words also appear on signage, display cases, and even shopping bags.

Because of Saudi laws, Perdu does not have any female employees. Lifelike mannequins are not allowed so Perdu features abstract, fabric wrapped shapes.

Banners that hang from high ceilings and create the feminine ambience in the store
Lingerie Perdu Store in Saudi Arabia
Design: Chase Design Group, Los Angeles, U.S.A.

And, stores can't have mirrors in the dressing rooms. So, one day local religious police (called *mutawa*) came in and took down the mirrors in the store's fitting rooms. But mirrors or no mirrors, Saudi women are enjoying this new experience of shopping lingerie—Victoria Secret style. Minus of course the images of Tyra Banks.

Source: Logolounge.com

DISCUSSION QUESTIONS

1. Culture in Saudi Arabia seems to promote among women extreme modesty (where they should not flaunt their bodies); yet, many women there are as ea-ger to acquire and consume the fashionable clothing and luxurious lingerie from western countries. What role does culture play in consumer desires—does it encourage or curb consumption?

2. Is it important for a marketer, especially a designer of physical marketspace (i.e., a store) to be fully aware of the culture of its customers? How did Chase Design Group, a U.S. firm, meet this challenge?

3. What lessons can we learn from this story about culture and marketing?

CASE STUDY 14 GOING MY WAY? LET's GoLoCo

What the Internet enables is access to data, anytime, anyplace, and from anywhere and anybody, instantly. This enables instant connectivity, with an information databank and with people. This in turn has opened up new opportunities for consumers, and consequently, for pioneer marketers. One such pioneering marketer is Robin Chase, who in early 2007 launched a company called GoLoco.

It is a Web site for members to find others in the area who might be interested in sharing a road trip with you. It maybe a daily commute to work, or getting to an event in town, or an out-of-town trip. It will find you

GoLoco - How does it work?
Meeting friends.
0:00 / 0:37

other people who might be planning to make the same trip. They will share expenses with you, and some conversation. Or you can ride with them instead and share expenses and conversation.

Posting your forthcoming trip or daily commute does not obligate you to accept whoever applies. All it does is make the connection. In fact, you can control who sees your profile and your postings. When you post a trip, you invite your friends and any group you like

(e.g., work group). Some groups (e.g., Soccer teams) and some organizations also are members so it is easy to see which groups are available.

When you sign up for the site, you deposit some money. Likewise, every poster does. When the site connects you, and you finalize the agreement, the site transfers a computed amount (50 cents a mile plus parking and toll costs, divided by the number of total passengers) from the rider's funds to the driver's funds, and takes a 10% commission as transaction fee.

According to a recent U.S. Department of Transportation (DOT) estimate, some 88% of Americans commute to work and 75% of them commute alone (86% of all commuters). DOT has also estimated that on average, American households spend $7825 on transportation, annually. Car pooling will at least halve your costs. And if cost savings don't get you, you could do it for our environment: In a recent estimate, our personal cars were the source of 20% of total US energy-related CO_2 emissions.

So if you commute or take many road trips (or even if you take just a few), you could enroll (yourself and your organization) today and start saving—your cash and your environment. Will you?
Check it out at www.GoLoco.org

DISCUSSION QUESTIONS

Q1. Who will be the prime prospect for this service? Describe this consumer in terms of (a) driving needs and habits, (b) demographics, and (c) psychographics.

Q2. What factors will encourage a consumer to participate in this program, and what factors will hinder? What will be the nature and sources of satisfaction for consumers who participate? Will these motivations and satisfactions be different for drivers versus riders?

(See next page.)

CASE STUDY (15) "So I Got a New Face"

(A Personal Narrative by Shay Sayre)

Attitude formation on significant matters (ch 7); consumers' identity projects (Ch 5,16, Special Topic 5).

Romantic

California Girl

I am 49 and a single mother of two. My employment takes me to Southern California. Southern California—where appearance is the established medium of exchange. I live near the beach so I am constantly exposed to youth, fitness and beauty. Weather encourages abbreviated dresses, necessitates fitness, and requires youthfulness. … A 1996 national survey by American Society for Plastic and Reconstructive Surgery showed that of the 87,000 breast augmentations reported nationally, 25% were in California. You see celebrities all the time. In this capital of "hedonic consumption," who can be oblivious to appearance?

Media—the Hyperreal Persuaders

My cohorts in the media were film stars Marilyn Jones and Liz who all were preoccupied with snagging men, and television's Jeanie and Samantha (*Bewitched*) whose sole preoccupations were looking good for the men they loved. During this age of "commercialized feminism," women were encouraged to emulate fabricated perfection depicted by advertising's Ivory complexions, Breck-girl hair, and Coke bottle figures.

Likewise, today's media continue to provide a visual plethora of visual justifications for the good looks. Television commercials imply that everyone colors gray hair. Magazine ads depict men conquering baldness with hair transplants, and women enjoying new popularity with silicon implants; Cosmetic advertisements boast complexions instantly transformed by tanning creams. Video and film personalities are ageless reminders of the power of surgical restoration. All around, I see synchronized endorsements of manufactured body images.

Friends are Having a Ball

Daily activity furnishes the creative moments in which the matrices of my identity are transformed to a new actuality. There are friends who drop names of surgeons, suggest anti-aging treatments, and recall their own transformative experiences. Among friends, silver-haired Irene hosts a tea party in a white, low cut cotton frock that proudly reveals her implant acquisitions; Elisabeth hugs her beau-de-jour, a man twenty years younger who is obviously infatuated by her purchased-youth-enhancements; Bali Bill is surrounded by saronged female companions who are probably unaware of his hair transplant; Linda sports tight pants proudly purchased to fit her newly liposucked thighs; and Grecian Formula improved Ray kisses a twenty-something fiancée at his retirement celebration.

Mirror Tells Me the Truth

Once my mirror reveals signs of the aging process, I began to consider dealing with the sun-baked skin that could push me way out of the socially acceptable envelope. Group snapshots [of friends at parties] are cruel reminders that I lack the cosmetic advancements implemented by most of my friends.

Blood is Thickest

My family members pull in different directions. Mother doesn't count because she loves me whatever. But my sister, a surgical nurse herself, is a devout advocate of surgical solutions to nature's mistakes. Beverly has subjected many parts of her body to the knives of various care givers: Navy surgeons for breast implants during a husband's military career; a surgeon-employer for a face and brow lift; a physician friend for liposuction. All procedures are free of charge, but none are free from payment—implants break; nerve damage inhibits facial movement; cellulite comes back in a less desirable location than the one from which it is removed. Photographs are the only remaining evidence of a pre-surgery sister.

Daughter Aubyn believes that nature should be allowed to take its course, and son Ryan contends that "outward is as inward does." Purists be damned, I think. If they are against it, then it must be a good idea. After all, what do offspring understand about the ageing process.

Money and Affordability

Even in the capital of hedonism, the cost of cosmetic surgery is substantial. One can expect to pay in the neighborhood of $10,000 for a basic face lift. I am faced with a pending costly repair to my residence devastated by termites, and then there is the uncertainty of potential unemployment. But considering the alternative—aging and reclusion—I rationalize the expense as an investment in myself. A gift to me.

When the physician is chosen, the date is set and the cash paid, my surgery is a *fait accompli*. I write a poem to commemorate the occasion: *Changing Faces*. (See next page.)

Shay Sayre is a professor of consumer behavior at California State University at Fullerton.

Source: Excerpted from Shay Sayre, "Facelift Forensics: A Personal Narrative of Cosmetic Surgery," *Advances in Consumer Research*, 1999, Vol. 26, 178-83. (Used by permission of the Assoc. for Consumer Research)

DISCUSSION QUESTIONS

1. Identify various influences (both in terms of sources and nature of influence) on this consumer's decision to get a face lift surgery.

2. Does this narrative illustrate the role of bodies in consumers' identities? Explain.

3. What decision rule did Ms. Sayre most likely use?

4. What model of attitude would likely explain Ms. Sayre's pro-surgery attitude?

CASE STUDY (16) Consuming Brands, Experiencing Selves: A Tale of Two Consumer Life Projects

Jean's Life Story

Jean is 59 years old and lives with Henry, her husband of 40 years, in a middle-class suburb of a northeastern city not farther than 10 miles from the town in which both she and he were born. While Henry will soon retire, Jean still works—60 hours and six days a week-- tending a small neighborhood bar in her blue-collar hometown.

Jean grew up in the house her Italian grandfather built. It is the house her brother, his wife, and two of their three grown children now occupy. The house is a symbol of all Jean believes in: it is at once family, independence, and hard work.

Jean "didn't grow up with very much," both in the way of money or family support. The illegitimate child of a father she would never know, Jean was somewhat an outsider in her own home. Many aunts and uncles were against her remaining in the family at all. Jean soon discovered that superior performance of household tasks offered a surefire mechanism through which she could fit in with her family and garner their support. To this day, Jean wants desperately to be affirmed by society in the roles she values most: mother and wife. Accomplishment as a cook and housekeeper remain a major source of happiness, pride, and satisfaction in Jean's life.

What do I do everyday? I cook. I clean. My white clothes are white. You can pick up a sheet of mine that is 10 years old and people think they are brand new. I iron them…… Everybody always says what a beautiful house I have. That makes me feel good.

With no more than a high school education, Jean discovered the value of diligence and hard work. She lives by one of her mother's credos: "You want, you work, you get." As Italian wife and mother, she loves to make Spaghetti sauce:

My mother always used to make the sauce too. All

Italians do. When you make sauce, it's like your trademark. (My youngest brother) Johnny always says that he can tell people by the sauce that they make. Everybody loves my sauce. My brother Frankie says I make the best sauce he ever had, and he is a gourmet.

When I make the sauce, it takes all day. I let it cook on the stove for 8 hours. I have a really big pot. Stainless steel from Revere Ware. 12 quarts. I blend the Pastene tomatoes in the blender. Whole tomatoes. And I add a little can of the Hunts special sauce. Then I fry up the sausage in a frying pan with the Bertolli olive oil and a little bit of onion, pepper. Pastene tomatoes, I always buy those, they are the best. They make the best sauce. You can tell the difference… I buy the best vinegar. Progresso.. Bounty paper towels, they are the best…Maytag, they say that is the best…Frigidaire makes the best fridge…Krups makes the best coffee….Electrolux is the best vacuum. It's expensive, yeah, but…

I always used the Bon Ami but then I noticed that it started scratching the sink…. I tried the Comet and that really is better.

After 40 years of shopping, cooking, and cleaning, Jean has become somewhat of an expert consumer (" You ask me how I know it is good tomatoes? I've been making the sauce for 40 years and you ask me how I know?")

Karen's Life Story

Karen is a recently divorced 39-year-old single Mom, raising two girls aged 8 and 12 while working full-time as an office manager. Karen's demographics in large part speak to her current life situation: money is tight and Karen is busy. Her day starts at 5:00 A.M. to give her time for exercise while still getting the kids off to school and herself to work before the 8:00 A.M. check-in. Afternoons

---

Contd. from previous page

—A poem by Shay Sayre (See story on facing page)

CHANGING FACES

Cosmetic surgery is a notion I entertain regularly amid the voices of caution that punctuate my peace.

"Why not grow old like everyone else," snarls my son.
"If it will make you happy, dear" smirks mom.

What do they know?
Do they have the skin of Cochise?
Do they view the world beneath billowing lids?
Do they dread passing reflective surfaces?

The knife is my magic wand,
a Maginot Line keeping time on the other side.
I'll have no second thoughts,
I'll have no second thoughts

are crazy, with Karen running the kids back and forth to dance classes, music lessons, and Girl Scouts. In her "spare time," Karen is trying to fix up the new apartment she just rented, meet new friends, and decide on a car to replace her broken-down Ford.

> What's my life like? A blur. A rush. A rush from the minute I get up in the morning. I go from one thing to another all day long….. I have clothes over there to fold and put away, and the food shopping is still out. The kids have homework to do. You wanna help?

Karen has the added project of negotiating a prominent midlife crisis. She experiences a sense of disparity between what she has attained and what she "really wants." A powerful sense tells her that the 40-year mark is a last chance opportunity for pursuing significant paths of change. Another strong voice tells her to focus, instead, on raising her children in this new single-parent world.

> Should I go back to school and get the degree I never finished? Should I move out of this town and go somewhere else? I dunno. The kids…
>
> Wherever am I going to find a man, where? I never thought that I would be the one left alone after the divorce. Never, I am turning 40, and there aren't that many available men that age in general left anymore, let alone good ones, and God forbid they live in this small town. Wherever am I going to find a man?

One of the few areas of life satisfaction for Karen is that she has managed to maintain a youthful appearance. She adheres closely to a regular exercise routine ("I run three miles every day at 5:30, no matter what) and a highly scripted personal care regimen.

> People always tell me that I do not look my age. I mean, I work hard not to, so that's good.

Speaking of the products and brands she buys, Karen says:

> I don't really know what all I buy. I am thinking about it, and it seems I don't buy many brands…. I don't spend a lot of time at the store. I don't really remember when all I started using that (brand). I guess it just really didn't, it just really does not matter to me that much. A lot of things are just here because I never tried anything else and I just use that brand out of habit. It works. It gets me through.
>
> I always buy Comet… I hate Ajax… At work I use Gateway [Computer]. I don't really care that it is a Gateway, but we only had the choice between an Apple and the Gateway and I am definitely not an Apple person….. I buy Success Rice. Success Rice is the only one in the kind of rice that I want. Ready in five minutes. The others take twenty-five.
>
> Mop and Glo? That was my ex-husband Jim. I never

really did like that… Palmolive? That was Jim… The Dove started with him… Mayonnaise? I just bought the brand Jim told me… Cereals? I just buy what is demanded of me.

But when it came to cosmetics, Karen spoke excitedly:

> I use Mary Kay everything. Makeup, lipstick, moisturizer, toner. I think Mary Kay is responsible for how my skin looks now. I do, I really do. I do not think that my skin would be this, so young today if I had used any other brand. I mean, I do see it. I really can tell the difference. I can't live without it now…

Karen also embraces Reebok, the brand of running shoe she dons each morning at 5:30 A.M.

> I started running again when umm, right after I decided to leave Jim. I used to run in college when I was training for tennis tournaments. I was quite good at distance running. So, I picked it back up. I wear Reebok running shoes. Me and my Reeboks. They are beat up by now. Want to see them? Like a favorite pair of jeans, you know? You go through so much together.

And Karen drinks Coke Classic, not a diet soft drink:

> I think I am one of the last people that still drinks Coke. Everyone I know wants a Diet Coke all the time. It's always diet something. Everyone knows I drink regular Coke. Because I sort of make a statement when I don't drink Diet that I don't do what everybody else does, that I don't really care about the extra calories that much, that I can afford it. Sorta like, "so there!"

DISCUSSION QUESTIONS

1. Describe the main life themes of Jean and Karen and how products play a role in these life projects.
2. Who is more involved in consumption (across the board) and why?
3. Is either of them using products to construct self-identity? Who? Which products? How?
4. Jean has strong opinions on a range of products (whereas Karen has opinions only on a few products). How would you explain the role having an opinion plays in consumer's life theme and/or self-identity?

(Source: Excerpted from Susan Fournier, "Consumers and their Brands: Developing Relationship Theory in Consumer Research," *Journal of Consumer Research*, Vol. 24, March 1998, 343-373. ©Journal of Consumer Research, University of Chicago Press.)

CASE STUDY (17) Money for Nothing and Hits for Free

The artists are rich, the record labels are filthy rich, and copyright laws have not been extended to the Internet and I am on a college budget.

Thus wrote a college student who had frequently downloaded many songs from the Internet. The student was one of 22 participants in a study by marketing professors Aron M. Levine, Mary Conway Dato-on, and Kenneth Rhee. The three professors were interested in uncovering consumers' reasons, or rather justifications, for engaging in free and unauthorized music downloading from Web sites such as Napster. This was not a vain question, mind you, since consumers could download music, for example, because they were unaware that such a practice could be illegal or unethical, or alternatively, because they saw little chance of being caught. The range of responses they obtained revealed both the reasons and then more; their responses can be organized in following categories (categories are ours, not respondents'):

1. **No real harm to companies or artists**
2. **No norms are violated**
3. **CDs are too expensive**
4. **Napster is actually doing them good**
5. **Companies and artists are too rich already**

There were, of course, a few respondents who did recognize harm to companies and artists.

The three marketing professors followed up their qualitative study with a quantitative study, surveying 210 student respondents by a questionnaire. Included in the questionnaire was a scale to measure respondents' attitude toward unethical behavior in general (designed by two other marketing professors, Scott Vitell and Jim Muncy, see Table 1). Respondents answer on a five-point Likert scale: 1—"strongly believe it is wrong" to 5—"strongly believe it is not wrong." Also included in the survey were, of course, measures of the extent to which respondents engaged in music-downloading and the degree of their agreement with some statements about music downloading—statements derived from the earlier qualitative study.

The Ethical attitude scale had four factors:
1. **Willful Wrongdoing:** such as drinking soda in the store without paying for it, and changing price tags.
2. **No Harm, No Foul:** such as taping a movie, returning merchandise bought elsewhere, etc.
3. **Deceptive Practices:** such as lying about a child's age, using expired coupon, stretching truth on taxes, etc.
4. **Passive Benefiting:** Server miscalculates, cashier returns too much change, etc.

Summarized in Table 2 are findings on how the downloaders (63% of all respondents) and non-downloaders (37%) scored on these ethical attitude dimensions and on beliefs about downloading practices.

One noteworthy finding was that music downloaders actually purchased more CDs on an average! Now explain that!

TABLE 2

ATTITUDES AND BEHAVIORS OF MUSIC DOWNLOADERS	Downloaders	Non-Downloaders
ETHICAL ATTTITUDE		
1. Willful Wrongdoing	1.52	1.22
2. No Harm, No Foul	4.12	3.47
3. Deceptive Practices	2.63	2.14
4. Passive Benefiting	2.57	2.02
BELIEFS about DOWNLOADING		
1. Harms companies	2.87	3.41
2. Harms artists	2.83	3.39
3. Companies make excess profits	4.16	3.89
4. CDs contain few good songs	4.06	3.57
Does Downloading Affect CD Buying		
No. of CDs in Collection	3.33	2.64
No. of CDs Purchased during Past 6 Months	2.41	2.11

Levin, Aron, Mary Conway Dato-on, and Ken Rhee. (2004) "Money For Nothing and Hits For Free: The Ethics of Downloading Music from Peer-to-Peer Web Sites." *Journal of Marketing Theory & Practice* 12 (1): 48-60. Used with permission.

DISCUSSION QUESTIONS

1. Which of the practices in the Ethical Attitude Scale do you yourself consider unethical? Discuss why.

2. Does the practice of free music downloading influence consumer's CD purchasing? Does this practice harm the artists or recording companies?

3. The availability of music online (whether free or at a fee) is here to stay; it is a sign of the times, i.e., The Internet Age. How should recording companies and artists adapt to this new reality?

TABLE 1

STATEMENTS USED TO MEASURE ETHICAL STANDARDS

- Changing price tags on merchandise in a retail store.
- Drinking soda in a supermarket without paying for it.
- Giving misleading price information to a clerk for an un-priced item.
- Using a long distance access code you didn't buy.
- Reporting a lost item as "stolen" to an insurance company in order to collect the money.
- Returning damaged merchandise when the damage is your own fault.
- Not saying anything when the server miscalculates the bill in your favor.

- Getting too much change and not saying anything.
- Taping or burning a CD instead of buying it.
- Moving into a new residence, finding that the cable TV is still hooked up, and using it rather than signing up and paying for it.
- Using an expired coupon for merchandise.
- Lying about a child's age in order to get a lower price.
- Stretching the truth on an income tax return.
- Using a coupon for merchandise you did not buy.
- Taping a movie off the TV.
- Returning merchandise after trying it and not liking it.
- Using computer software games that you did not buy.

CASE STUDY (18) Villains in TV Shows

We Say We Hate Them, But We Yearn to Watch Them

"I sure hope Lex is gone tonight."
"Hopefully Lex will be out tonight."
"I hope Lex goes home tonight!"
"I want Lex out tonight."
"I would like to see Lex go."

The cyber chat was abuzz with hopes as the hour for the TV broadcast later that evening for Episode 12 of *Survivor* was approaching.

The Plot Participants are organized into two teams and the teams are taken to some remote locations away from civilization. Each team is responsible for finding food, shelter, water, etc. The teams also contest in some survival games. The losing team is required to vote one of their members out. As the teams dwindle, they are combined into one and further trimming continues till only two players remain. The winner is then chosen by a vote from the rest of the players (who were eliminated in the previous episodes).

This CBS show was watched every week by some 28 million consumers. And many viewers did more than watch. During the week, they brooded over the events of the past episodes and forecasted what the next episode will, or rather should, bring. Many of them shared their thoughts, fears, and hopes in chat rooms, which were hosted by CBS. Two marketing professors decided to study this chatter. Professors Vassilis Dalakas and Jeff Langenderfer collected the postings, sampling various chat rooms during the period of one hour before and one hour after each episode of *Survivor III*, and analyzed the text of the postings. What they found is an eye-opener:

1. Viewers formed strong liking and disliking for characters:
Some postings after Episode #5:
"I detest Lindsey."
"I hate Brandon!"
"Silas, u suck….all muscles and no brain"
"Don't get me started on Lindsey, that horrible witch!"

2. So much so that they created user names indicating love or hate feelings:
Lindseysucks, Loser_Linda, Ethan2win, Ethansucks, Ethan_Lover, Lexsucks, Lexisthebest

3. Viewers Rooted for their heroes, of course:
"Ethan has been a good guy; he should win."
"I wanted Kim to win. She was working so hard."

4. But they rooted against those they disliked even more passionately:
" I sure hope Lex is gone tonight."
" I'd rather see Tom win than Lex and I don't like Tom …

but I despise Lex even more."
"If 'big Tom' doesn't win, I'll boycott the next show."

5. Viewers felt satisfaction when their heroes won but they felt delight when their "villains" suffered:
"The right person won… Finally a survivor who deserved it."
"Tell him [Silas] I did a happy dance when he got the boot."
"Almost cried with joy when Brandon was voted out!"

That viewers come to love some characters and hate others is expected. That they would want their heroes to win and villains to lose is also expected. Finally, we would expect viewers to be happy when their heroes win, but that they would also be joyed when their villains lose is interesting even if not surprising. This much the postings revealed.

But the real intrigue is in an insight Professors Dalakas and Langenderfer offer: When a player whom the viewer hated and expected to be eliminated in a particular episode was not eliminated, the viewer interest and anticipation for the next episode increased!

But then (and this is our quandary, not researchers'):

FYI In the first season of Big Brother, another reality TV series, viewers were able to vote off the "house guests" at the show. As a result, all of the "villains" were eliminated by the fans right away. The contestants who were left were all liked by the audience, and the audience interest in the show nose-dived. In subsequent seasons, the elimination procedure was changed, and dislikable characters were retained longer. Audience interest remained strong till the end.

Do consumers themselves have this self-realization that while they are wishing for their villains to be ousted or suffer in the next episode, they should really be wishing for them to survive the next episode?

[Source: Excerpted from Vassilis Dalakas and Jeff Langenderfer, "Consumer Satisfaction with Television Viewing: Insight for the Entertainment Industry," unpublished manuscript.]

DISCUSSION QUESTIONS

1. Do you agree or disagree that this is how it really happens: that most consumers really experience greater emotional pleasure if their villains are not voted out.

Contd. on next page

CASE STUDY ⑲ How Green Is Your School?

Colleges are at the forefront of becoming environment-friendly. Recently, The Daily Green (an online magazine by Hearst Magazine Group) highlighted what it called the "The Ten Greenest Colleges in America." At the top of that list is a small college in Bal Harbor, Maine, the College of the Atlantic. It was the first college to go carbon neutral, a benchmark it reached in 2007. It is also perhaps the only college in the world that serves, in its student cafeteria, only organic foods, for breakfast, lunch, and dinner alike. Actually, this is not surprising: the college only has one major, human ecology—the study of humans' relationship with our planet.

Among the Big Schools, at the top of the list were University of California, Harvard, and Duke (in that order). Harvard runs its fleet of school trucks on vegetable oil from its dining facilities. Duke only buys green energy. And the University of California leads in encouraging biking, and UC Berkeley has established the first certified organic kitchen in a college setting.

Becoming green is a multi-pronged program. It entails such wide ranging actions as making buildings green, reducing waste, recycling more, consuming less paper, and buying green energy.

One notable winner is Berea College, located 45 miles northwest of Lexington, Kentucky. It is notable for its integration of living, ecology, and learning. That learning occurs in a five acre area called *Ecovillage*, which houses a student residential hall and a child-development laboratory. Each year, resident students select a project from a menu: composting, carpooling, gardening, making green cleaning supplies, and the like.

Apartments are constructed to minimize energy use and to incorporate many "passive solar design elements" such as a southern orientation, concrete floors for thermal mass, pop-out windows for stack ventilation (passive cooling), window overhangs for seasonal shading, additional day-lighting through tube skylights, low-emissivity window glazing, and light colored roof and wall surfaces. The installed appliances

Ecologically designed residential apartment building (with garden in the foreground) at Berea College's *Ecovillage*

are all energy-efficient, and fixtures made from recycled materials; there is even a waste water heat recovery system, and an outdoor clothesline.

DISCUSSION QUESTIONS

1. Will you enjoy living in such an eco-village? Why or why not?
2. Will your college be one to install an eco-village like this? What can you yourself do to spur this transformation at your institution?
3. How will you make this a "high involvement" issue among the student body at your college? What attitude formation strategies will you adopt?

Based on reports in Brian Clark Howard, "10 of the Greenest Colleges in America," thedailygreen online magazine and http://www.berea.edu/sens/ecovillage/

Contd. from the previous page

2. Why do viewers come to like some characters and hate others? Shouldn't they like those who provide them greater emotional experience? Does it have to do with their self-concepts? How so?

3. From this it would follow that program directors should keep the intensely disliked characters "alive" until the last moment!! They should, it follows, even "manage" the outcome—i.e., rather than let the team players eliminate a player

people hate, they should maneuver to keep that player until the last episode. Should they do it and what are the ethics of this, if any?

4. As a show's consumer researcher, how would you assess when the optimal point of hatred is reached so that program directors don't "engineer" the villains' retention beyond that point?

THE REAL TRUTH ABOUT BEAUTY

Brand Dove Asks Women When They Feel Beautiful

Marketers spend millions of dollars (or Euros or yens) every year, helping women achieve beauty. They assume that women are chasing beauty and they believe their brands help them achieve it. But just what is beauty and what do women feel about it? This question has never been researched. Until now. In 2004, UK based Unilever's Dove brand commissioned a study, pioneering in conception and vision, vast in scope, and an eye-opener in its findings. According to the company:

> The Dove campaign for real beauty (CFRB) was inspired by the global study "the real truth about beauty: a global report." Launched in 2004, the CFRB aims to serve as a starting point for societal change and act as a catalyst for widening the definition and discussion of beauty. The campaign supports the Dove mission to make more women feel beautiful every day by widening stereotypical views of beauty. For more information, visit campaignforrealbeauty.Com

Below are some key findings:

Feeling Positive
90% of American women consider their looks average or above average.
Claiming "Looks," Not Beauty
36% say their looks are above average; in contrast, only 18% say their "beauty" is above average.
Redefining Beauty
75% of women agree that beauty does not come from a woman's looks, but from her spirit and life.
Owning Beauty
79% of women wish a woman could be considered beautiful even if she is not "physically perfect."

Relationship Over Beauty
Women consistently rated relationship as most important and beauty as least important.
Feel beautiful when:
- they feel loved (70%)
- husband/significant other:
  » Looks at them admiringly (68%)
  » Does something special for them (65%)
  » Goes out with them for a special occasion (64%)

The study produced a wealth of information, covering such issues as women's self-perceptions of their looks, their opinions on media's depiction of beauty, and how they experience their self-esteem. Study these findings in the charts that follow.

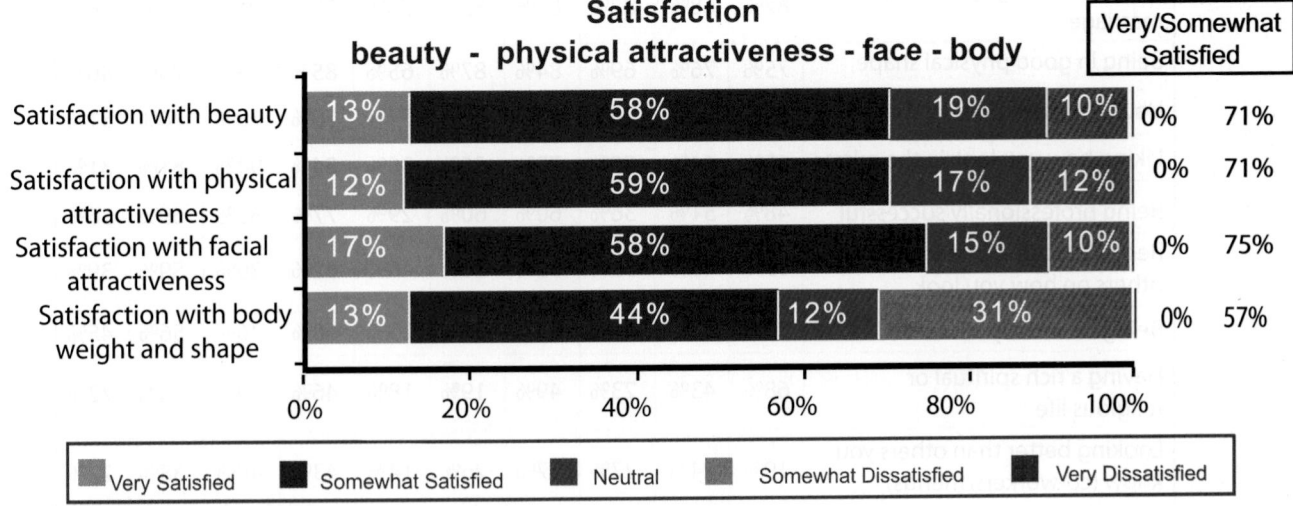

Satisfaction
beauty - physical attractiveness - face - body

					Very/Somewhat Satisfied
Satisfaction with beauty	13%	58%	19%	10%	0% 71%
Satisfaction with physical attractiveness	12%	59%	17%	12%	0% 71%
Satisfaction with facial attractiveness	17%	58%	15%	10%	0% 75%
Satisfaction with body weight and shape	13%	44%	12%	31%	0% 57%

0% 20% 40% 60% 80% 100%

■ Very Satisfied ■ Somewhat Satisfied ■ Neutral ■ Somewhat Dissatisfied ■ Very Dissatisfied

C2 - How satisfied would you say you are with your own beauty?
C3 - How satisfied would you say you are with your own physical attractiveness?
C41 - Now thinking about your face, how satisfied would you say you are with your facial attractiveness?
E1 - How satisfied would you say you are with your current body weight and shape?

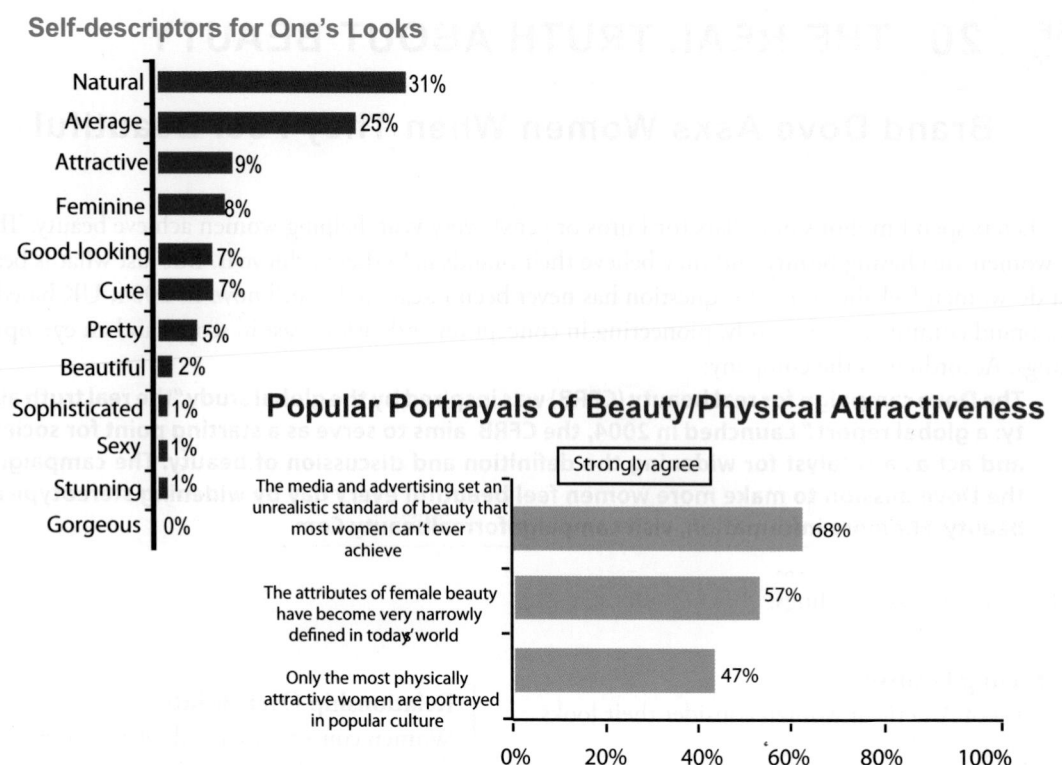

Self-descriptors for One's Looks

- Natural — 31%
- Average — 25%
- Attractive — 9%
- Feminine — 8%
- Good-looking — 7%
- Cute — 7%
- Pretty — 5%
- Beautiful — 2%
- Sophisticated — 1%
- Sexy — 1%
- Stunning — 1%
- Gorgeous — 0%

Popular Portrayals of Beauty/Physical Attractiveness

Strongly agree

- The media and advertising set an unrealistic standard of beauty that most women can't ever achieve — 68%
- The attributes of female beauty have become very narrowly defined in today's world — 57%
- Only the most physically attractive women are portrayed in popular culture — 47%

(0% 20% 40% 60% 80% 100%)

D6, D2, D1 - Now I am going to read you a list of statements, and I'd like you to tell me to what extent you agree or disagree with each. Please use a 10-point scale where 1 means you "Completely disagree" and 10 means you "Completely agree."

Top 3 boxes of 10 pt. scale Strongly agree

Importance in Making "You" Feel Beautiful

	USA	CAN	GRN	ITA	FRA	NLD	PRT	BRA	ARG	JPN
Being loved	91%	89%	91%	91%	82%	84%	92%	94%	93%	70%
Doing something you really love to do	88%	84%	83%	88%	80%	91%	91%	96%	96%	68%
Taking good care of yourself	86%	86%	77%	79%	72%	80%	84%	97%	84%	78%
Having a strong relationship or marriage	82%	68%	82%	86%	82%	78%	90%	91%	89%	56%
Being in good physical shape	75%	76%	69%	84%	87%	65%	85%	85%	79%	46%
Having a close circle of friends	65%	78%	76%	68%	64%	74%	78%	78%	76%	51%
Liking how you look in the mirror	65%	64%	70%	79%	56%	36%	84%	94%	81%	31%
Being professionally successful	48%	51%	36%	60%	60%	29%	77%	83%	69%	36%
Receiving compliments from others on how you look	35%	43%	55%	52%	50%	46%	62%	80%	59%	39%
Being financially succesful	50%	57%	41%	53%	37%	23%	68%	76%	56%	45%
Having a rich spiritual or religious life	68%	43%	23%	49%	19%	18%	46%	79%	56%	72%
Looking better than others you know (co-workers/friends)	19%	24%	27%	37%	26%	14%	43%	48%	38%	22%

*Cell entries are percent of total respondents who checked the top 3 boxes on the 10-point scale.

Q. Now thinking about yourself, how important is each of the following in making you feel beautiful? Please use a 10-point scale where 1 means "Not at all important" and 10 means it is "Extremely important."

Perceptions about Beauty

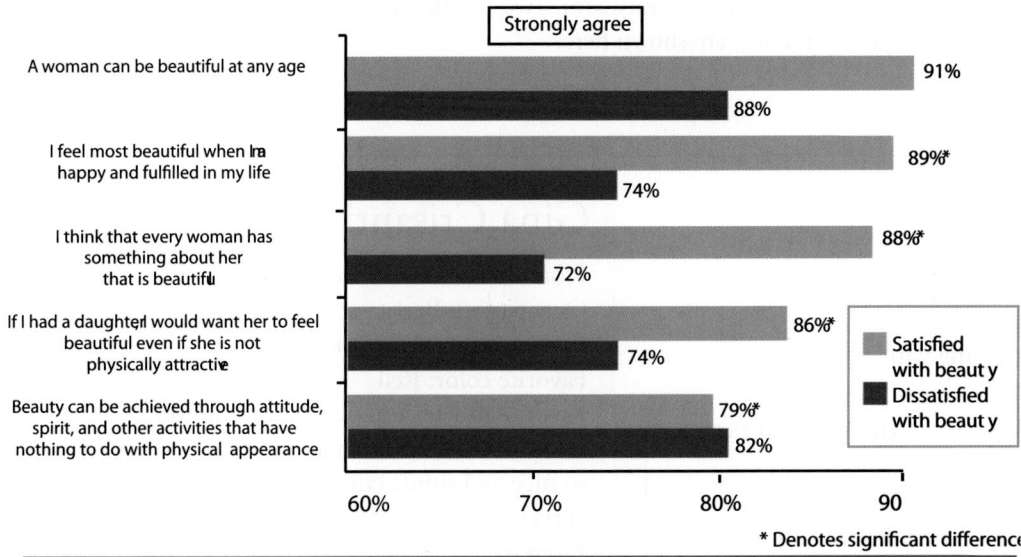

Strongly agree

A woman can be beautiful at any age — 91% / 88%

I feel most beautiful when I am happy and fulfilled in my life — 89%* / 74%

I think that every woman has something about her that is beautiful — 88%* / 72%

If I had a daughter I would want her to feel beautiful even if she is not physically attractive — 86%* / 74%

Beauty can be achieved through attitude, spirit, and other activities that have nothing to do with physical appearance — 79%* / 82%

Legend:
- Satisfied with beauty
- Dissatisfied with beauty

* Denotes significant difference

C2-C42, C61-C63, C56 - How satisfied would you say you are with your own beauty? Now I am going to read you a list of statements, and I'd like you to tell me to what extent you agree or disagree with each. Please use a 10-point scale where 1 means you "Completely disagree" and 10 means you "Completely agree".

Top 3 box of 10 pt. scale
Satisfaction top 2 box
Dissatisfaction bottom 2 box
Ranked on total respondents

The Media and Beauty

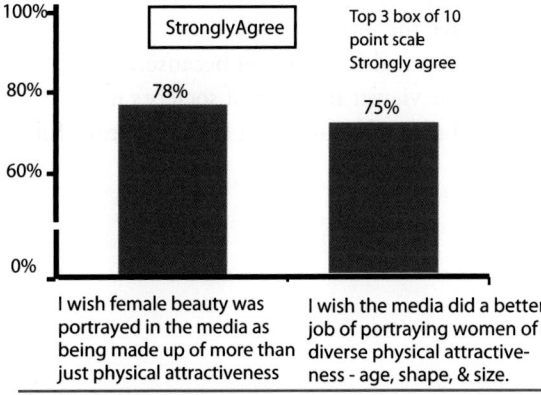

Strongly Agree

Top 3 box of 10 point scale Strongly agree

78% — I wish female beauty was portrayed in the media as being made up of more than just physical attractiveness

75% — I wish the media did a better job of portraying women of diverse physical attractiveness - age, shape, & size.

Q. Now I am going to read you a list of statements and I'd like you to tell me to what extent you agree or disagree with each. Please use a 10-point scale where 1 means you "completely disagree" and 10 means you "completely agree."

Better Ways to Depict Women in the Media
Total Respondents - Top Two Choices

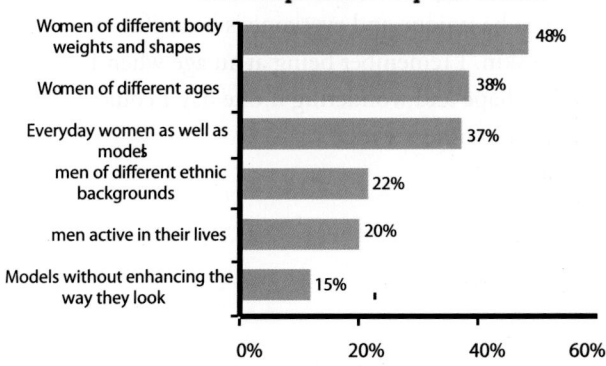

Women of different body weights and shapes — 48%

Women of different ages — 38%

Everyday women as well as models — 37%

men of different ethnic backgrounds — 22%

men active in their lives — 20%

Models without enhancing the way they look — 15%

D8 - I am going to read you a list of things regarding the media. Please tell me in which two of the following ways, if any you must think the media could be doing a better job of depicting women in the media and advertising

Commenting on this trail-blazing study, Naomi Wolf, well-known author, feminist and social critic, wrote:

> It appears that American women have deconstructed the beauty myth.
> When I first wrote about the oppressive power of prevailing norms of "the physical ideal" in 1991, very few women felt comfortable challenging them. It was taken for granted... that the ideal was tall, young, thin, blond, Caucasian, and large-breasted...
> [Now, this report shows] a majority of women have worked out a beauty philosophy that is inclusive, not exclusive, related to their inner lives, not their weight on a scale or the number of lines in their faces, and, most importantly, psychologically empowers them as attractive women on their own terms.

Based on the study, Unilever's Dove brand designed and implemented a communication campaign titled Campaign for Real Beauty. See it at www.campaignforrealbeauty.com. Two profiles from that campaign (Shanel Lu and Gina Crisanti), which also appeared in print ads, are shown here.

Shanel Lu

Hometown: Landover, Maryland
Occupation: Manicurist
Favorite food: Anything with curry
Favorite color: Red
Favorite movie: Old classic sappy love stories
Beautiful time:
I felt absolutely beautiful on my wedding day. That was one moment in my life when I was the queen of the night. It was a special day when everything was about me. I felt like I was floating on a cloud. Throughout the day, everyone was surrounding me with loving comments and reminding me of how beautiful I looked.
You're excited about this campaign because…

I absolutely love what it represents. I love the thought of being a part of an ad that would potentially touch many young girls to tell them that it is alright to be unique and everyone is beautiful in their own skin. I remember being at an age when I felt out of shape and wondering if one day I could be beautiful in others' eyes.

Gina Crisanti

Hometown: Fort Worth, Texas
Occupation: Barista at Argo Tea Café
Favorite food: Artichokes
Favorite color: Red
Favorite movie: You Can Count on Me
Favorite curves: The small of my back, because it's so nice and subtle compared to some of my other curves.
Interests:
I love being out in the sun, exploring the city, playing catch, rollerblading, jogging, yoga, shopping, hanging out at the lake, and, of course, spending time with friends and family.
Surprising fact:
I've never seen Star Wars or The Matrix.
Beautiful time:
In general, I feel beautiful when I keep a positive attitude, take responsibility for what is within my control and leave the rest up to life.
You're excited about this campaign because…
It encourages the viewer to let go of society's narrow, fantastical idea of beauty, and embrace beautiful reality.

DISCUSSION QUESTIONS

1. What does the Dove Report show about women's self-concept and the role beauty plays in it?

2. Would the Dove campaign appeal to women? More than an ad that, say, presents beautiful models of the type the media has been criticized for depicting as "the beauty ideal"? Support your answer with findings from the study (or despite the findings).

3. The import and significance of the study, and of the Dove campaign based on it, reaches far beyond—by presenting a new vision about beauty, the campaign is an invitation to society at large to break free of the false beauty ideal. Comment on this statement and also outline some ideas as to how a marketer or a social agency might bring this message to societies at large.

FURTHER READING

ACTION (INTENT, BEHAVIOR SHAPING)

1. We Are What We Consume: the Influence of Food Consumption on Impulsive Choice. Arul Mishra and Himanshu Mishra (2010), *Journal of Marketing* Research (December). Published, 2010.

2. *Mindless Eating – Why We Eat More Than We Think.* Wansink, Brian. New York: Bantam-Dell. (2006).

3. Mindless Eating and Healthy Heuristics for the Irrational. Wansink, Brian; Just, David R; Payne, Collin R. American Economic Review, May2009, Vol. 99 Issue 2, p165-169.

4. Spending on the Fly: Mental Budgets, Promotions, and Spending Behavior. Stilley, Karen M.; Inman, J. Jeffrey; Wakefield, Kirk L. *Journal of Marketing*, May2010, Vol. 74 Issue 3, p34-47.

5. Breaking the Impulse Buying Cycle: Post-Impulse Purchase Affect and Its Impact on the Propensity for Future Impulse Buying. Spiteri-Cornish, Lara.; Chattopadhyay, A. and Wang, Q. (2009).

6. Consumer Responses to the Depth and Minimum Claimed Savings of "Scratch and Save (SAS)" Promotions. Choi, Sungchul; Stanyer, Mike; Kim, Moontae. *Psychology & Marketing*, Aug2010, Vol. 27 Issue 8, p766-779.

7. Stealth Marketing: How to Reach Consumers Surreptitiously. Kaikati,Andrew M.; Kaikati, Jack G. *California Management Review, 2004.*

8. The Influence of Bite Size on Quantity of Food Consumed: A Field Study. Mishra, Arul; Mishra, Himanshu; Masters, Tamara M. *Journal of Consumer Research*, Feb2012, Vol. 38 Issue 5, p791-795

9. Exploring Impulse Buying and Variety Seeking By Retail Shoppers: Towards a Common Conceptual Framework. Sharma, Piyush; Sivakumaran, Bharadhwaj Marshall; Roger. *Journal of Marketing Management*, May2010, Vol. 26 Issue 5/6, p473-494,

10. The Effect of Partitions on Controlling Consumption. Cheema, Amar; Soman, Dilip. *Journal of Marketing Research* (JMR), Dec2008, Vol. 45 Issue 6, p665-675.

11. The Effects of Reduced Food Size and Package Size on the Consumption Behavior of Restrained and Unrestrained Eaters. Scott, Maura L.; Nowlis, Stephen M.; Mandel, Naomi; Morales, Andrea C. *Journal of Consumer Research*, Oct2008, Vol. 35 Issue 3, p391-405.

12. Building Trust to Increase Purchase Intentions: the Signaling Impact of Low Pricing Policies, Tiffany Barnett White; Hong Yuan. *Journal of Consumer Psychology*, Oct 2011.

13. From Point of Purchase to Path to Purchase: How Preshopping Factors Drive Unplanned Buying. Bell, David R; Corsten, Daniel; Knox, George. *Journal of Marketing*, Jan2011, Vol. 75 Issue 1, p31-45.

14. Price, Scarcity, and Consumer Willingness to Purchase Pirated Media Products. Anthony Miyazaki; Alexandra Aguirre Rodriguez; Jeffrey Langenderfer. *Journal of Public Policy and Marketing*, 28. 1 (Spring, 2009): 71-84.

15. Encouraging Individuals to Save For their Future: Augmenting Current Efforts With Positive Visions of the Future. Ellen, Pam Scholder; Joshua L. Wiener; and M. Paula Fitzgerald. *Journal of Public Policy & Marketing* (forthcoming).

16. Walking In Memphis: Testing One DMO's Marketing Strategy to Millennials. Loda, Marsha D.; Coleman, Barbara C.; Backman, Kenneth F. *Journal of Travel Research*, Feb2010, Vol. 49 Issue 1, p46-55.

17. Watching Food-Related Television Increases Caloric Intake in Restrained Eaters. Shimizu, Mitsuru and Brian Wansink. *Appetite*, 2011, 57:661-664.

18. Finns and Functional Foods: Socio-Demographics, Health Efforts, Notions of Technology and the Acceptability of Health-Promoting Foods. Niva, Mari; Mäkel, Johanna. *International Journal of Consumer Studies*, Jan2007, Vol. 31 Issue 1, p34-45

19. Just Thinking About Exercise Makes Me Serve More Food: Physical Activity and Calorie Compensation. Werle, Carolina O. C.; Brian Wansink and Collin R. Payne. (2011), *Appetite*, 56:2 (April), 332-335.

20. Healthy Convenience: Nudging Students toward Healthier Choices in the Lunchroom. Hanks, Andrew S.; David R. Just; Laura E. Smith and Brian Wansink (2012), *Journal of Public Health*, forthcoming.

21. What Would Batman Eat? Priming Children to Make Healthier Fast Food Choices. Wansink, Brian; Mitsuru Shimizu and Guido Camps (2012), *International Journal of Pediatric Obesity*, forthcoming.

22. The 100-Calorie Semi-Solution: Sub-Packaging Most Reduces Intake Among the Heaviest. Wansink, Brian; Collin R. Payne and Mitsuru Shimizu (2011), Obesity, 19:5 (Spring), 1098-1100.

23. Linking Trust to Use Intention for Technology-Enabled Bank Channels: the Role of Trusting Intentions. Dimitriadis, Sergios; Kyrezis, Nikolaos. *Psychology & Marketing*, Aug 2010, Vol. 27 Issue 8, p799-820.

24. Third-Person Perception and Purchase Behavior in Response to Various Selling Methods. Tal-Or, Nurit; Shilo, Shiri; Meister, Talia. *Psychology & Marketing*, Dec 2009, Vol. 26 Issue 12, p. 1091-1107.

25. Effectiveness of Promotional Premiums: the Moderating Role of Affective State in Different Contexts. Chang, Chingching. *Psychology & Marketing*, Feb2009, Vol. 26 Issue 2, p175-194.

26. Effectiveness of Price Discounts and Premium Promotions. Palazon, Mariola; Delgado-Ballester, Elena. *Psychology & Marketing*, Dec2009, Vol. 26 Issue 12, p1108-1129.

ADVERTISING (EFFECTS)

27. Sequence Matters: A More Effective Way to Use Advertising and Publicity. Loda, Marsha D.; Coleman, Barbara Carrick. *Journal of Advertising Research*, Dec2005, Vol. 45 Issue 4, p362-372.

28. An Examination of Consumer Responses toward Attribute- and Goal-Framed Messages. Putrevu, Sanjay.

Journal of Advertising, Fall2010, Vol. 39 Issue 3, p. 5-24.

29. Movie theatre Commercials: the Impact of Scent and Pictures on Brand Evaluations and Ad Recall. Lewin, May O. and Maureen Morrin, (forthcoming) *Journal of Consumer Behaviour*.

30. Advertising's New Audiences. Millan, Elena S.; Mittal, Banwari. *Journal of Advertising*, Fall2010, Vol. 39 Issue 3, p81-98.

31. Beauty as a Tool: the Effect of Model Attractiveness, Product Relevance and Elaboration Likelihood on Advertising Effectiveness. Trampe, Debra; Stapel, Diederik A.; Siero, Frans W.; Mulder, Henriëtte. *Psychology & Marketing*, Dec2010, Vol. 27 Issue 12, p1101-1121.

32. Explaining the Joint Effect of Source Credibility and Negativity of Information in Two-Sided Messages. Eisend, Martin. *Psychology & Marketing*, Nov2010, Vol. 27 Issue 11, p1032-1049.

33. Making Unique Choices or Being Like Others: How Priming Self-Concepts Influences Advertising Effectiveness. Chang, Chingching. *Psychology & Marketing*, Apr2010, Vol. 27 Issue 4, p399-415.

34. The New Science of Viral Ads. Teixeira, Thales. *Harvard Business Review*, Mar2012, Vol. 90(3), p25-27.

35. Effects of Model Body Size and Product Price on Advertising Effectiveness, Purchase Intention and Body-Related Behaviors. Polonsky, Maxim; Kareklas, Ioannis. *Advances in Consumer Research*, 2010, Vol. 37, p880-882.

36. Humor and Ad Liking: Evidence That Sensation Seeking Moderates the Effects of Incongruity-Resolution Humor. Galloway, Graeme. *Psychology & Marketing*, Sep2009, Vol. 26 Issue 9, p779-792.

37. Informational and Transformational Responses to Celebrity Endorsements. Lord, Kenneth R.; Putrevu, Sanjay. *Journal of Current Issues & Research in Advertising*, Spring2009, Vol. 31 Issue 1, p1-13.

38. Beliefs of and Attitudes Toward Political Advertising: An Exploratory Investigation. Jin, Hyun Seung; An, Soontae; Simon, Todd. *Psychology & Marketing*, Jun2009, Vol. 26 Issue 6, p551-568.

39. Effects of Age, Need For Cognition and Affective Intensity on Advertising Effectiveness. McKay-Nesbitt, Jane; Manchanda, Rajesh V.; Smith, Malcolm C; Huhmann, Bruce A. *Journal of Business Research*, Jan2011, Vol. 64 Issue 1, p12-17.

ADVERTISING APPEALS

40. A Content Analysis of Guilt Appeals in Popular Magazine Advertisements. Huhmann, Bruce A.; Brotherton, Timothy P. *Journal of Advertising*, Summer97, Vol. 26 Issue 2, p35-45.

41. Guilt Appeal: Persuasion Knowledge and Charitable Giving. Hibbert, S.; Smith, A.; Davies, A and Ireland, F. (2007) *Psychology and Marketing*, Vol 24, Issue 8, 723-742.

42. Consumer Responses toward Sexual and Nonsexual Appeals. Putrevu, Sanjay. *Journal of Advertising*, Summer2008, Vol. 37 Issue 2, p57-69.

43. Comparative and non comparative Advertising:

Attitudinal Effects Under Cognitive and Affective Involvement Conditions. Putrevu, Sanjay; Lord, Kenneth R. *Journal of Advertising*, Jun94, Vol. 23 Issue 2, p77-91.

44. Go Green!! Should Environmental Messages Be So Assertive?? Kronrod, Ann; Grinstein, Amir; Wathieu, Luc. *Journal of Marketing*, Jan2012, Vol. 76, 1, p95-102

45. Sex in Advertising … Only on Mars and Not on Venus? Dahl, Darren W.; Jaideep Sengupta and Kathleen D. Vohs (2011), *Marketing Intelligence Review-GFK*, 3(1), 54-57.

AUTHENTICITY

46. Authenticity: What Consumers Really Want (Hardcover) Pine, II, B. Joseph; Gilmore, James. Harvard Business School Press Books, Oct. 01, 2007.

47. A Journey to the Authentic: Museum Visitors and their Negotiation of the Inauthentic. Hede, Anne-Marie; Thyne, Maree. *Journal of Marketing Management*, Jul2010, Vol. 26 Issue 7/8, p686-705.

48. Brand Authentication: Creating and Maintaining Brand Auras. Alexander, Nicholas. European *Journal of Marketing*, 2009, Vol. 43 Issue 3/4, p. 551-562.

49. Authenticity: Further theoretical and Practical Development. Gundlach, Hugh; Neville, Benjamin. *Journal of Brand Management*, Apr2012, Vol. 19 Issue 6, p484-499.

50. Authentic Subcultural Membership: Antecedents and Consequences of Authenticating Acts and Authoritative Performances. Beverland, Michael B.; Farrelly, Francis; Quester, Pascale G. *Psychology & Marketing*, Jul2010, Vol. 27 Issue 7, p698-716.

51. Projecting Authenticity Through Advertising. Beverland, Michael B.; Lindgreen, Adam; Vink, Michiel W. *Journal of Advertising*, Spring2008, Vol. 37 Issue 1, p5-15.

BRAND ATTITUDE

52. The Consumer Psychology of Brands. Schmitt, Bernd. *Journal of Consumer Psychology*, Jan2012, Vol. 22 (1), p7-17.

53. Brands On The Brain: Do Consumers Use Declarative Information Or Experienced Emotions To Evaluate Brands? Esch, Franz-Rudolf; Möll, Thorsten; Schmitt, Bernd; Elger, Christian E.; Neuhaus, Carolin; Weber, Bernd. *Journal of Consumer Psychology*, Jan2012, Vol. 22 Issue 1, p. 75-85.

54. Changing Your Mind About Seeing a Brand That You Never Saw: Implications for Brand Attitudes. Howard, Daniel J.; Kerin, Roger A. *Psychology & Marketing*, Feb2011, Vol. 28 Issue 2, p168-187.

55. the Relevance of Irrelevance in Brand Communication. Albrecht, Carmen-Maria; Neumann, Marcus M.; Haber, Tobias E.; Bauer, Hans H. *Psychology & Marketing*, Jan2011, Vol. 28 Issue 1, p. 1-28.

56. Measurement of Implicit and Explicit Attitudes Toward Barack Obama. Nevid, Jeffrey S.; McClelland, Nate. *Psychology & Marketing*, Oct2010, Vol. 27 Issue 10, p989-1000.

57. How to Repair Customer Trust After Negative Publicity: the Roles of Competence, Integrity, Benevolence and Forgiveness. Xie, Yi; Peng, Siqing. *Psychology & Marketing*,

Jul2009, Vol. 26 Issue 7, p572-589.

58. Brand Positivity and Competitive Effects on the Evaluation of Brand Extensions. Kapoor, Harish; Heslop, Louise A. *International Journal of Research in Marketing*, Sep2009, Vol. 26 Issue 3, p228-237.

BRAND PERSONALITY

59. Effects of Brand Personality on Brand Trust and Brand Affect. Sung, Yongjun; Kim, Jooyoung. *Psychology & Marketing*, Jul2010, Vol. 27 Issue 7, p639-661.

60. The Differential Roles of Brand Credibility and Brand Prestige in Consumer Brand Choice. Baek, Tae Hyun,;Kim, Jooyoung; Yu, Jay Hyunjae. *Psychology & Marketing*, Jul2010, Vol. 27 Issue 7, p662-678.

61. Consumers' Implicit Theories About How Personality Influences Their Brand Personality Judgments. Pragya Mathur ; Shailendra P. Jain; Durairaj Maheswaran. *Journal of Consumer Psychology*, **February2012.**

62. gender Dimensions of Brand Personality. Bianca Grohmann. *Journal of Marketing Research*, 2009, 46 (1), p. 105-119.

63. Does Brand Social Power Mean Market Might? Exploring the Influence of Brand Social Power on Brand Evaluations. Crosno, Jody L.; Freling, Traci H.; Skinner, Steven J. *Psychology & Marketing*, Feb2009, Vol. 26 Issue 2, p91-121.

64. Competing for Consumer Identity: Limits to Self-Expression and the Perils of Lifestyle Branding. Chernev, Alexander; Hamilton, Ryan; Gal, David. *Journal of Marketing*, May2011, Vol. 75 Issue 3, p66-82,

BRAND RELATIONSHIP (COMMUNITY)

65. Brand Community: Drivers and Outcomes. Stokburger-Sauer; Nicola. *Psychology & Marketing*, Apr2010, Vol. 27 Issue 4, p347-368.

66. How We Relate To Brands: Psychological And Neurophysiological Insights Into Consumer–Brand Relationships. Reimann, Martin; Castaño, Raquel; Zaichkowsky, Judith; Bechara, Antoine. *Journal of Consumer Psychology*, Jan2012, Vol. 22 Issue 1, p128-142.

67. The Coherence of Inconsistencies: Attitude–Behaviour Gaps and New Consumption Communities. Moraes, Caroline; Carrigan, Marylyn; Szmigin, Isabelle. *Journal of Marketing Management*, Feb2012, Vol. 28 Issue 1/2, p103-128.

68. I Won't Leave You Although You Disappoint Me: the Interplay Between Satisfaction, Investment and Alternatives in Determining Consumer-Brand Relationship Commitment. Sung, Yongjun; Choi, Sejung Marina. *Psychology & Marketing*, Nov2010, Vol. 27 Issue 11, p1050-1073.

69. How Global Brands Travel With Consumers: An Examination of the Relationship Between Brand Consistency and Meaning. Bengtsson, A.; Bardhi, F.; Venkatraman, M. *International Marketing Review Journal*, 2010, 27(5), 519-540.

70. Brands as Relationship Partners: Warmth, Competence, and In-Between. Susan Fournier; Claudio Alvarez. *Journal of Consumer Psychology*, March 2012.

71. Anti-brand Communities, Negotiation of Brand Meaning, and the Learning Process: the Case of Wal-Mart. Hollenbeck, Candice R. and George M. Zinkhan. *Consumption, Markets & Culture*, 2010 (13), 325-345.

72. Betrayed By the Buzz? Covert Content and Consumer-Brand Relationships. Ashley, Christy; Leonard, Hillary A. *Journal of Public Policy & Marketing*, Fall2009, Vol. 28 Issue 2, p212-220.

CHILDREN AS CONSUMERS

73. Children's Understanding of Television Advertising: A Grounded Theory Approach. Andronikidis, Andreas I.; Lambrianidou, Maria. *Psychology & Marketing*, Apr2010, Vol. 27 Issue 4, p299-322.

74. Wishful Identification with Fictional Characters: An Assessment of the Implications of Gender in Message Dissemination to Children. Lonial, Subhash C.; Van Auken, Stuart. *Journal of* Advertising, 1986, Vol. 15 Issue 4, p4-42.

75. Children's Perceptions of Characters: Human Versus Animate Assessing Implications For Children's Advertising. Van Auken, Stuart; Lonial, Subhash C. *Journal of Advertising*, 1985, Vol. 14 Issue 2, p13-61.

76. The Active Role of Children as Consumers. Ironico, Simona. *Young Consumers*, 2012, Vol. 13, 1, p30-44.

CONSUMER INTEREST

77. Consumerism: Search for the Consumer Interest. David A. Aaker; George S. Day. Simon and Schuster, 1982.

78. Countering Consumption in a Culture of Intoxication. Fry, Marie-Louise. *Journal of Marketing Management*, Dec2010, Vol. 26 Issue 13/14, p1279-1294

79. From Nutrients to Nurturance: A Conceptual Introduction to Food Well-Being. Block, Lauren G.; Grier, Sonya A.; Childers, Terry L.; Davis, Brennan.; Ebert, Jane E. J.; Kumanyika, Shiriki; Laczniak, Russell N.; Machin, Jane E.; Motley, Carol M.; Peracchio, Laura; Pettigrew, Simone; Scott, Maura; Van Ginkel Bieshaar, Mirjam N. G. *Journal of Public Policy & Marketing*, Spring2011, Vol. 30 Issue 1, p5-13

80. Toward a General Model of Consumer Empowerment and Welfare in Financial Markets with an Application to Mortgage Servicers. Bone, Paula Fitzgerald. *Journal of Consumer Affairs*, Summer2008, Vol. 42 Issue 2, p165-188.

81. Evolution of the Empowered Consumer. Davies, Andrea and R. Elliott. (2006) European *Journal of Marketing*, Vol 40, Issue 9/10 pp. 1106-1121.

82. Towards Dimensionalizing Warranty Information: The Role of Consumer Costs of Warranty Redemption. Jain, Shailendra Pratap, Rebecca Slotegraaf, and Charles Lindsey. *Journal of Consumer Psychology (2007)*.

CULTURE

83. Consumer Expectations and Culture: The Effect of Belief in Karma in India. Kopalle, Praveen K.; Lehmann, Donald R.; Farley, John U. *Journal of Consumer Research*, Aug2010, Vol. 37 Issue 2, p251-263.

84. Consumer Myths and the Gay Men and Women Who Believe them: A Qualitative Look at Movements and Markets. Gudelunas, David. *Psychology & Marketing*,

Jan2011, Vol. 28 Issue 1, p53-68.

85. Face As a Mediator of the Relationship Between Material Value and Brand Consciousness. Liao, Jiangqun; Wang, Lei. *Psychology & Marketing*, Nov2009, Vol. 26 Issue 11, p987-1001.

86. Dilemmas of Culture and Marketing Strategy. Asser, Maarten Nijhoff; Hodges, Silvia. *CPA Practice Management Forum*, 2010, Vol. 6 Issue 2, p5-10.

87. Looks Good Enough to Eat: How Food Plating Preferences Differ Across Cultures and Continents. Zampollo, Francesa, Brian Wansink, Kevin M. Kniffin, Mitsuru Shimizu, and Aki Omori. (2012), *Cross-Cultural Research*, 46, forthcoming.

88. Cross-Cultural Influences on Cross-Border Vacationing, Lord, Kenneth R.; Sanjay Putrevu, and Shi Yi Zheng (2008), *Journal of Business Research*, Volume 61, No. 3, 183-190.

89. Cultural Value, Consumption Value and Global Brand Image: A Cross-National Study. Park, Hye-Jung; Rabolt, Nancy J. *Psychology & Marketing*, Aug2009, Vol. 26 Issue 8, p714-735.

90. Driving and Surviving: A Cross-Cultural Investigation of Truck Drivers' Consumption-Related Experiences in the United States and Vietnam. C. Scott Rader, Society for Marketing Advances Annual Conference, 2008.

DECISION MAKING (PREFERENCE)

91. Consumer Uncertainty, Revisited. Shiu, Edward M.K.; Walsh, Gianfranco; Hassan, Louise M.; Shaw, Deirdre. *Psychology & Marketing*, Jun2011, Vol. 28 Issue 6, p584-607.

92. Consumer Evaluations of Hybrid Products. Rajagopal, Priyali; Robert E. Burnkrant. *Journal of Consumer Research*, Aug2009, Vol. 36 Issue 2, p232-241.

93. How and When Alphanumeric Brand Names Affect Consumer Preferences. Gunasti, Kunter and William T. Ross. *Journal of Marketing Research*, 2010, 47(December),1177-1192.

94. The Influence of Implicit Attitudes on Choice When Consumers Are Confronted with Conflicting Attribute Information. Dempsey, Melanie A.; Mitchell, Andrew A. *Journal of Consumer Research*, Dec2010, Vol. 37(4), p614-625.

95. Consumer Decision Making and Variety of offerings: the Effect of Attribute Alignability. Herrmann, andreas; Heitmann, Mark; Morgan, Robert; Henneberg, Stephan C.; Landwehr, Jan. *Psychology & Marketing*, Apr2009, Vol. 26 Issue 4, p333-358.

96. Leaving the Store Empty-Handed: Testing Explanations for the Too-Much-Choice Effect Using Decision Field theory. Jessup, Ryan K.; Veinott, Elizabeth S.; Todd, Peter M.; Busemeyer, Jerome R. *Psychology & Marketing*, Mar2009, Vol. 26 Issue 3, p299-320.

97. The Interplay among Category Characteristics, Customer Characteristics, and Customer Activities on In-Store Decision Making. Inman, J. Jeffrey, Russell S. Winer, and Rosellina Ferraro. *Journal of Marketing*, 2009, 73 (September), 19-29.

98. The Discriminating Consumer: Product Proliferation and Willingness to Pay for Quality. Bertini, Marco; Wathieu, Luc; Iyengar, Sheena S. *Journal of Marketing Research (JMR)*, Feb2012, Vol. 49 Issue 1, p39-49.

99. The Brand Anchoring Effect: A Judgment Bias Resulting From Brand Awareness and Temporary Accessibility. Esch, Franz-Rudolf; Schmitt, Bernd H.; Redler, Joern; Langner, Tobias. *Psychology & Marketing*, Apr2009, Vol. 26 Issue 4, p383-395.

100. Assimilation and Contrast in Price Evaluations. CUNHA Jr., Marcus; Shulman, Jeffrey D. *Journal of Consumer Research*, Feb2011, Vol. 37 Issue 5, p822-835.

101. What Moderates the Too-Much-Choice Effect? Scheibehenne, Benjamin; Greifeneder, Rainer; Todd, Peter M. *Psychology & Marketing*, Mar2009, Vol. 26 Issue 3, p229-253.

102. Shall I Tell You Now or Later? Assimilation and Contrast in the Evaluation of Experiential Products Wilcox, Keith; Roggeveen, Anne L.; Grewal, Dhruv. *Journal of Consumer Research*, Dec2011, Vol. 38 Issue 4, p763-773.

103. Testing the Tyranny of Too Much Choice Against the Allure of More Choice. White, Chris M.; Hoffrage, Ulrich. *Psychology & Marketing*, Mar2009, Vol. 26 Issue 3, p280-298.

DEMOGRAPHICS (ETHNICITY)

104. Ethnicity and Brand Connections. Schumann, David W. and Edith Davidson in J. Priester, D. MacInnis, C.W. Park (eds.) Handbook of Brand Relationships, M.E. Sharpe Publishers (forthcoming).

105. Whitewashing America: Material Culture and Race in the Antebellum Imagination. Bridget T. Heneghan. Univ. Press of Mississippi, 2007.

106. How Social Insecurity and the Social Meaning of Advertising Reinforce Minority Consumers' Preference For National Brands. Wyatt, Rosalind J.; Gelb, Betsy D.; Geiger-Oneto, Stephanie. *Journal of Current Issues & Research in Advertising*, Spring2008, Vol. 30 Issue 1, p61-70.

107. Marketing to American Latinos (Part 1): A Guide to the in-Culture Approach (Book). Sharp, Charles L. *Journal of Consumer Marketing*, 2002, Vol. 19 Issue 2/3, p168-171.

108. White Response to Potentially Discriminatory Actions in a Services Setting. Baker, Thomas L.; Meyer, Tracy. *Psychology & Marketing*, Feb2011, Vol. 28 Issue 2, p188-204.

109. Why Do I Identify With thee? Let Me Count Three Ways: How Ad Context Influences Race-Based Character Identification. Brumbaugh, Anne M. *Psychology & Marketing*, Nov2009, Vol. 26 Issue 11, p970-986.

110. Is the Customer Always Right? the Potential for Racial Bias in Customer Evaluations of Employee Performance. Lynn, Michael; Sturman, Michael. *Journal of Applied Social Psychology*, Sep2011, Vol. 41 Issue 9, p2312-2324.

111. Learned Helplessness as an Explanation of Elderly Consumer Complaint Behavior. LaForge, Mary C. *Journal of Business Ethics*, May89, Vol. 8 Issue 5, p359-36.

DEMOGRAPHICS (GENDER)

112. A Proposed Model of Online Consumer Behavior: Assessing the Role of Gender. Richard, Marie-Odile; Chebat, Jean-Charles; Yang, Zhiyong; Putrevu, Sanjay. *Journal of Business Research*, Sep2010, Vol. 63 Issue 9/10, p926-934.

113. Exploring the Origins and Information Processing Differences Between Men and Women: Implications for Advertisers, Putrevu, Sanjay (2001), *Academy of Marketing Science Review* [Online], 2001 (10).

114. Salesperson Race and Gender and the Access and Legitimacy Paradigm: Does Difference Make a Difference? Jones, Eli; Moore, Jesse N.; Stanaland, andrea J. S.; Wyatt, Rosalind A. J. *Journal of Personal Selling & Sales Management*, Fall98, Vol. 18 Issue 4, p71-88.

DEMOGRAPHICS (SENIORS)

115. Older Consumers' Tv Home Shopping: Loneliness, Parasocial Interaction and Perceived Convenience. Lim, Chae Mi; Kim, Youn-Kyung. *Psychology & Marketing*, Aug2011, Vol. 28 Issue 8, p763-780.

116. Older Consumer Responses to Marketing Stimuli: the Power of Subjective Age. Moschis, George P.; Mathur, Anil. *Journal of Advertising Research*, Sep2006, Vol. 46 Issue 3, p339-346.

117. Understanding Older Consumers Through Cognitive Age and the List of Values: A U.K.-Based Perspective. Sudbury, Lynn; Simcock, Peter. *Psychology & Marketing*, Jan2009, Vol. 26 Issue 1, p22-38.

118. The Relationships Among Family and Social Interaction, Loneliness, Mall Shopping Motivation and Mall Spending of Older Consumers. Youn-Kyung Kim; Jikyeong Kang; Minsung Kim. *Psychology & Marketing*, Dec2005, Vol. 22 Issue 12, p995-1015.

Demographics (Youth)

119. Gen Buy: How Tweens, Teens, and Twenty-Somethings Are Revolutionizing Retail. Keel, Astrid L. *Psychology & Marketing*, Oct2011, Vol. 28 Issue 10, p1087-1088.

120. So, you're a Millennial—Create us a Facebook Presence. Looney, B., Ryerson, A. T. *Journal of American Academy of Business*, Cambridge, volume 17, No. 1, Summer, 2011.

121. Tuning In and Tuning Out: Media Multitasking Practices and Experiences Among Generation Y Consumers. Fleura Bardhi, andrew Rohm, and Fareena Sultan, (2010) *Journal of Consumer Behaviour*, 9 (4), 316-332.

122. The Perfect Gift Card: An Exploration of Teenagers' Gift Card Associations. Tuten, Tracy L.; Kiecker, Pamela. *Psychology & Marketing*, Jan2009, Vol. 26 Issue 1, p67-90.

123. Pester Power—A Battle of Wills Between Children and their Parents. Lawlor, Margaret-Anne; Prothero, andrea. *Journal of Marketing Management*, May2011, Vol. 27 Issue 5/6, p561-58

124. Millennials and Whole Person Marketing: How the Shift From a Protected and Confident Generation to Cynical Philosophers Is Changing How Brands Are Perceived. Donohue, Mary, E.; Vincent, Carter; Scott, Comber and Molly R. Jensen (2011), *Proceedings of the 2011 Marketing Educators' Association Conference*, San Diego, CA.

e-CONSUMER

125. Does Involvement Matter in Online Shopping Satisfaction and Trust? Martín, Sonia San; Camarero, Carmen; José, Rebeca San. *Psychology & Marketing*, Feb2011, Vol. 28 Issue 2, p145-167.

126. How to Foster and Sustain Engagement in Virtual Communities. Porter, Constance Elise; Donthu, Naveen; MacElroy, William H.; Wydra, Donna. *California Management Review*, Summer2011, Vol. 53 Issue 4, p80-110.

127. Exploration and Its Manifestations in the Context of Online Shopping. Demangeot, Catherine; Broderick, Amanda J. *Journal of Marketing Management*, Dec2010, Vol. 26 Issue 13/14, p1256-1278

128. Online Communities and the Sharing of Extraordinary Restaurant Experiences. Watson, Pamela; Morgan, Michael; Hemmington, Nigel. *Journal of Foodservice*, Dec2008, Vol. 19 Issue 6, p289-302.

129. Perceived Ease of Use in Prior E-Commerce Experiences: A Hierarchical Model for Its Motivational Antecedents. Sun, Tao; Tai, Zixue; Tsai, Ke-Chuan. *Psychology & Marketing*, Sep2010, Vol. 27 Issue 9, p874-886.

130. Cybermarketscapes: Consumer Behavior in Virtual Retail Environment. Lukošius, Vaidotas and Elise Truly Sautter. *Networked Minds Conference*, East Lansing, Michigan State University, MI, September 27-29, 2001.

131. Believe It or Not: the Perceived Credibility of Blogs in Tourism. Mack, Rhonda W., Blose, Julia E. and Bing Pan. (2008). *Journal of Vacation Marketing*, (14)2.

132. Modeling Consumer Adoption of Mobile Shopping For Fashion Products in Korea. Ko, Eunju; Kim, Eun Young; Lee, Eun Kyung. *Psychology & Marketing*, Jul2009, Vol. 26 Issue 7, p669-687.

133. Consumers' Rules of Engagement in Online Information Exchanges. Poddar, Amit; Jill R. Mosteller; and Pam Scholder Ellen. *Journal of* Consumer Affairs, 2009, 43(3), 419-448.

134. Consumers' Intentions to Remain Loyal to Online Reputation Systems. Wang, Hui-Chih; Doong, Her-Sen; Foxall, Gordon R. *Psychology & Marketing*, Sep2010, Vol. 27 Issue 9, p887-897.

135. Designing the E-Servicescape: Implications for Online Retailers. Hopkins, Christopher D.; Grove, Stephen J.; Raymond, Mary Anne; LaForge, Mary C. *Journal of Internet Commerce*, 2009, Vol. 8 Issue 1/2, p23-43.

136. Avatars as Information: Perception of Consumers Based on their Avatars in Virtual Worlds. Bélisle, Jean-François; Bodur, H. Onur. *Psychology & Marketing*, Aug2010, Vol. 27 Issue 8, p741-765.

137. Value-Driven Internet Shopping: the Mental Accounting theory Perspective. Gupta, Sumeet; Kim, Hee-Woong. *Psychology & Marketing*, Jan2010, Vol. 27 Issue 1, p13-35.

138. Toward an Integrated Framework for Online Consumer Behavior and Decision Making Process: A Review. Darley,

William K.; Blankson, Charles; Luethge, Denise. *Psychology & Marketing*, Feb2010, Vol. 27 Issue 2, p94-116.

139. The Potential Implications of Web-Based Marketing Communications for Consumers' Implicit and Explicit Brand Attitudes: A Call for Research. Madhavaram, Sreedhar; Appan, Radha. *Psychology & Marketing*, Feb2010, Vol. 27 Issue 2, p186-202.

140. Consumer Trust in the Online Retail Context: Exploring the Antecedents and Consequences. Chen, Jun; Dibb, Sally. *Psychology & Marketing*, Apr2010, Vol. 27 Issue 4, p323-346.

141. The Relationship Between Trusting Beliefs and Web Site Loyalty: the Moderating Role of Consumer Motives and Flow. Gupta, Reetika; Kabadayi, Sertan. *Psychology & Marketing*, Feb2010, Vol. 27 Issue 2, p166-185.

Ecological Consumption

142. Further Insights into Perceived Value and Consumer Loyalty: A 'Green' Perspective. Koller, Monika; Floh, Arne; Zauner, Alexander. *Psychology & Marketing*, Dec2011, Vol. 28 Issue 12, p1154-1176.

143. Generativity and Self-Enhancement Values in Eco-Friendly Behavioral Intentions and Environmentally Responsible Consumption Behavior. Urien, Bertrand; Kilbourne, William. *Psychology & Marketing*, Jan2011, Vol. 28 Issue 1, p69-90.

EMOTIONS (MOOD)

144. Affect and Its Effects on Compensatory Consumption. Garg, Nitika. *Advances in Consumer Research*, 2006, Vol. 33 Issue 1, p248-249.

145. Psychological Ownership And Affective Reaction: Emotional Attachment Process Variables And The Endowment Effect. Shu, Suzanne B.; Peck, Joann. *Journal of Consumer Psychology*, Oct2011, Vol. 21 Issue 4, p439-45.

146. The Many Shades of Rose-Colored Glasses: An Evolutionary Approach To The Influence Of Different Positive Emotions. Griskevicius, Vladas; Shiota, Michelle N.; Nowlis, Stephen M. *Journal of Consumer Research*, Aug2010, Vol. 37(2), p238-250.

147. I Was Pleased a Moment Ago: How Pleasure Varies with Background and Foreground Reference Points. Heyman, J.; A. Schwartz, B. Mellers; and S. Tishcenko. *Motivation and Emotion* 28:1 (2004): 65-83.

148. If You Feel it Now You Will Think it Later: the Interactive Effects of Mood Over Time on Brand Extension Evaluations. Sar, Sela; Duff, Brittany R.L.; Anghelcev, George. *Psychology & Marketing*, Jun2011, Vol. 28 Issue 6, p561-583.

149. International Consumer Admiration and the Persistence of Animosity. Maher, Amro, Paul Clark and Ahmed Maher. (2010) *Journal of Consumer Marketing*, 27(5), 414-424.

150. Retail therapy: A Strategic Effort to Improve Mood. Atalay, A. Selin; Meloy, Margaret G. *Psychology & Marketing*, Jun2011, Vol. 28 Issue 6, p638-659.

151. Integrating Emotions in the Analysis of Retail Price Images. Zielke, Stephan. *Psychology & Marketing*, Apr2011, Vol. 28 Issue 4, P330-359.

152. Consumer Response to Online Apparel Stockouts. Kim, Minjeong; Lennon, Sharron J. *Psychology & Marketing*, Feb2011, Vol. 28 Issue 2, p115-144.

153. Using Emotional Benefits as a Differentiation Strategy in Saturated Markets. Barrena, Ramo; Sánchez, Mercedes. *Psychology & Marketing*, Nov2009, Vol. 26 Issue 11, p1002-1030.

154. Mood Self Verification Explains the Selection and Intake Frequency of Comfort Foods. Wansink, Brian; Payne, Collin. *Advances in Consumer Research*, 2007, Vol. 34, p189-190.

155. Negative Emotions as Motivators of Consumption. Kapoor, Harish. *Advances in Consumer Research*, 2008, Vol. 35, p949-950

ETHICS (CONSUMER)

156. Aggressive Driving: A Consumption Experience. Ruvio, Ayalla A.; Shoham, Aviv. *Psychology & Marketing*, Nov2011, Vol. 28 Issue 11, p1087-1112.

157. Globesity: A Planet Out of Control? Francis Delpeuch, Bernard Maire, Emmanuel Monnier and Michelle, Holdsworth, 2009.

158. How Ethical Is Ethical? An Analysis of the Perception of Ethical Consumerism by British Consumers. Spiteri-Cornish, L. (2010). Coventry University, UK.

159. Understanding Unethical Retail Disposition Practice and Restraint from the Consumer Perspective. Rosenbaum, Mark S.; Kuntze, Ronald; Wooldridge, Barbara Ross. *Psychology & Marketing*, Jan2011, Vol. 28 Issue 1, p29-52.

ETHICS (MARKETER)

160. the Ethical Aspects of Direct to Consumer Advertising of Prescription Drugs in the United Kingdom: Physician Versus Consumer Views. Reast, Jon; Palihawadana, Dayananda; Shabbir, Haseeb. *Journal of Advertising Research*, Sep2008, Vol. 48 Issue 3, p450-464.

161. The Use of Humor to Mask Deceptive Advertising. Shabbir, Haseeb; Thwaites, Des. *Journal of Advertising*, Summer2007, Vol. 36 Issue 2, p75-85.

162. Is Food Marketing Making Us Fat? A Multi-Disciplinary Review. Chandon, Pierre and Brian Wansink (2011), *Foundations and Trends in Marketing*, 5:3, 113-196.

FAMILY (AS A CONSUMING UNIT)

163. Using Vignettes to Study Family Consumption Processes. Grønhøj, Alice; Bech-Larsen, Tino. *Psychology & Marketing*, May2010, Vol. 27 Issue 5, p445-464.

164. Adolescents' Perceptions of Family Communication Patterns and Some Aspects of their Consumer Socialization. Kim, Chankon; Lee, Hanjoon; Tomiuk, Marc A. *Psychology & Marketing*, Oct2009, Vol. 26 Issue 10, p888-907.

165. Dual Spousal Work Involvement: An Alternative Method to Classify Households/Families, Schaninger, Charles M. and Sanjay Putrevu (2006), *Academy of Marketing Science Review* [Online] 2006 (8).

GENDER (IDENTITY)

166. The Effect and Moderation of Gender Identity Congruity: Utilizing "Real Women" Advertising Images. Feiereisen, Stéphanie; Broderick, Amanda J.; Douglas, Susan P. *Psychology & Marketing*, Sep2009, Vol. 26 Issue 9, p813-843.

167. Sex-Typing of Leisure Activities: A Test of Two theories. Zinkhan, George M.; Prenshaw, Penelope J.; Close, Angeline Grace. *Advances in Consumer Research*, 2004, Vol. 31 Issue 1, p412-419.

168. Gender Effects in Advertising. Cramphorn, Michael F. *International Journal of Market Research*, 2011, Vol. 53 Issue 2, p147-170

169. Gender Roles in Advertising. Knoll, Silke; Eisend, Martin; Steinhagen, Josefine. *International Journal of Advertising*, 2011, Vol. 30 Issue 5, p867-888.

INFORMATION PROCESSING

170. Sophisticated But Confused: the Impact of Brand Extension and Motivation on Source Confusion. DeRosia, Eric D.; Lee, Thomas R.; Christensen, Glenn L. *Psychology & Marketing*, May2011, Vol. 28 Issue 5, p457-478.

171. The Power of Strangers: the Effect of Incidental Consumer Brand Encounters on Brand Choice. Ferraro, Rosellina; Bettman, James R.; Chartrand, Tanya L. *Journal of Consumer Research*, Feb2009, Vol. 35 Issue 5, p729-741

172. I Imagine, I Experience, I Like: the False Experience Effect. Rajagopal, Priyali; Montgomery, Nicole Votolato. *Journal of Consumer Research*, Oct2011, Vol. 38 Issue 3, p578-59

173. Lack of Attribute Searchability: Some Thoughts. Mittal, Banwari. *Psychology & Marketing*, Jun2004, Vol. 21 Issue 6, p443-462.

174. The Effects of Cognitive Thinking Style and Ambient Scent on Online Consumer Approach Behavior, Experience Approach Behavior, and Search Motivation. Vinitzky, Gideon; Mazursky, David. *Psychology & Marketing*, May2011, Vol. 28 Issue 5, p496-519.

175. the Effects of Counterfeiting on Consumer Search, Gentry, James W.; Sanjay Putrevu and Clifford J. Shultz II (2006), *Journal of Consumer Behavior*, Volume 5, Number 3, 245-256.
Affective Influences on Evaluative Processing, Herr, Paul M.; Christine M. Page; Bruce E. Pfeiffer and Derick Davis (2012), *Journal of Consumer Research, 38, 833-845.*

176. The Impact of Product Knowledge on Consumer Product Memory and Evaluation in the Competitive Ad Context: the Item-Specific-Relational Perspective. Lee, Byung-Kwan; Lee, Wei-Na. *Psychology & Marketing*, Apr2011, Vol. 28 Issue 4, p360-387.

177. Anarchy of Effects? Exploring Attention to Online Advertising and Multiple Outcomes. Goodrich, Kendall. *Psychology & Marketing*, Apr2011, Vol. 28 Issue 4, p417-440.

178. The Spacing Effect in Marketing: A Review of Extant Findings and Directions for Future Research. Noel, Hayden; Vallen, Beth. *Psychology & Marketing*, Nov2009, Vol. 26 Issue 11, p951-969.

179. Consumer Evaluations of Brand Extension: the Roles of Case-Based Reminding on Brand-to-Brand Similarity. Shen, Yung-Cheng; Bei, Lien-ti; Chu, Chia-Hsien. *Psychology & Marketing*, Jan2011, Vol. 28 Issue 1, p91-113.

180. Feeling Happier When Paying More: Dysfunctional Counterfactual Thinking in Consumer Affect. Yoon, Sukki; Vargas, Patrick T. *Psychology & Marketing*, Dec2010, Vol. 27 Issue 12, p1075-1100.

181. The Role of Consideration Sets in Brand Choice: the Moderating Role of Product Characteristics. Suh, Jung-Chae. *Psychology & Marketing*, Jun2009, Vol. 26 Issue 6, p534-550,

182. Consumers' Inferences about Quality Across Diverse Service Providers. Reimer, Anja; Folkes, Valerie. *Psychology & Marketing*, Dec2009, Vol. 26 Issue 12, p1066-1078.

183. Do Experts and Novices Evaluate Movies the Same Way? Plucker, Jonathan A.; Kaufman, James C.; Temple, Jason S.; Qian, Meihua. *Psychology & Marketing*, May2009, Vol. 26 Issue 5, p470-478.

184. The Influence of Source Credibility on Attitude Certainty: Exploring the Moderating Effects of Timing of Source Identification and Individual Need For Cognition. Nan, Xiaoli. *Psychology & Marketing*, Apr2009, Vol. 26 Issue 4, p321-332.

INFLUENCE (SOCIAL)

185. Same Destination, Different Paths: When and How Does Observing Others' Choices and Reasoning Alter Confidence in Our Own Choices? Cait Poynor Lamberton; Rebecca Walker Naylor; Kelly L. Haws. *Journal of Consumer Psychology*, 2012 (forthcoming).

186. Social Information in the Retail Environment: The Importance of Consumption Alignment, Referent Identity, and Self-Esteem. Dahl, Darren W.; Argo, Jennifer J.; Morales, Andrea C. *Journal of Consumer Research*, Feb2012, Vol. 38 Issue 5, p860-871.

187. What Drives Immediate and Ongoing Word of Mouth? Berger, Jonah; Schwartz, Eric M. *Journal of Marketing Research (JMR)*, Oct2011, Vol. 48 Issue 5, p869-880.

188. Determining Influential Users in Internet Social Networks. Trusov, Michael; Bodapati, Anand V; Bucklin, Randolph E. *Journal of Marketing Research (JMR)*, Aug2010, Vol. 47 Issue 4, p643-658.

INVOLVEMENT

189. Segmenting the Market Through the Determinants of Involvement: the Case of Fair Trade. Bezençon, Valéry; Blili, Sam. *Psychology & Marketing*, Jul2011, Vol. 28 Issue 7, p682-708.

190. Combined Influence of Selective Focus and Decision Involvement on Attitude-Behavior Consistency in a Context of Memory-Based Decision Making. Van Kerckhove, Anneleen; Vermeir, Iris; Geuens, Maggie. *Psychology & Marketing*, Jun2011, Vol. 28 Issue 6, p539-560.

191. Product Involvement in Organic Food Consumption: Does Ideology Meet Practice? Tarkiainen, Anssi;

Sundqvist, Sanna. *Psychology & Marketing*, Sep2009, Vol. 26 Issue 9, p844-863.

192. The Impact of Involvement on Satisfaction for New, Nontraditional, Credence-Based Service offerings. Prenshaw, Penelope J.; Kovar, Stacy E.; Burke, Kimberly Gladden. *Journal of Services Marketing*, 2006, Vol. 20 Issue 6/7, p439-452

LEARNING (KNOWLEDGE)

193. Does Cue Competition Reduce Conditioned Liking of Brands and Products? Walther, Eva; Ebert, Irena; Meinerling, Katrin. *Psychology & Marketing*, May2011, Vol. 28 Issue 5, p520-538.

194. Consumer Response to Complex Advertisements: the Moderating Role of Need For Cognition, Knowledge and Gender, Putrevu, Sanjay, Joni Tan and Kenneth R. Lord (2004), *Journal of Current Issues and Research in Advertising*, Volume 26, Number 1, 9-24.

195. When Consumers Cope with Price-Persuasion Knowledge: the Role of Topic Knowledge. Kachersky, Luke; (Christian) Kim, Hyeong-Min. *Journal of Marketing Management*, Feb2011, Vol. 27 Issue 1/2, p28-40.

196. Does Brand Spelling Influence Memory? The Case of Auditorily Presented Brand Names. David Luna; Marina Carnevale; Dawn Lerman. *Journal of* Consumer Psychology, March 2012.

197. A Model of Consumer Financial Numeracy. Huhmann, Bruce A.; McQuitty, Shaun. *International Journal of Bank Marketing*, 2009, Vol. 27 Issue 4, p270-293.

198. Knowing Too Much: Expertise-Induced False Recall Effects in Product Comparison. Mehta, Ravi; Hoegg, Joandrea; Chakravarti, Amitav. Journal of Consumer Research, Oct2011, Vol. 38 Issue 3, p535-554.

199. Differential Effects of Subjective Knowledge, Objective Knowledge, and Usage-Experience on Decision Making: An Exploratory Investigation. Raju, P.S.; Lonial, Subhash C. and Mangold, W. Glynn, *Journal of Consumer Psychology*, Vol. 4, No. 2, 1995, 153-180.

200. Practice Makes Perfect? When Does Massed Learning Improve Product Usage Proficiency? Lakshmanan, Arun, Charles D. Lindsey, and H. Shanker Krishnan. *Journal of Consumer Research*. 2010.

MEANS-END CHAIN

201. Consumer (Goal) Satisfaction: A Means-Ends Chain Approach. Orsingher, Chiara; Marzocchi, Gian Luca; Valentini, Sara. *Psychology & Marketing*, Jul2011, Vol. 28 Issue 7, p730-748.

202. Choice as an End Versus a Means. Choi, Jinhee; Fishbach, Ayelet. *Journal of Marketing Research* (JMR), Jun2011, Vol. 48 Issue 3, p544-554

MOTIVATION

203. The Course of Motivation. Touré-Tillery, Maferima; Fishbach, Ayelet. *Journal of Consumer Psychology*, Oct2011, Vol. 21 Issue 4, p414-423.

204. Public Commitment as a Motivator for Weight Loss. Nyer, Prashanth U.; Dellande, Stephanie. *Psychology &*

Marketing, Jan2010, Vol. 27 Issue 1, p1-12.

205. Value-Based Segmentation of Luxury Consumption Behavior. Wiedmann, Klaus-Peter; Hennigs, Nadine; Siebels, Astrid. *Psychology & Marketing*, Jul2009, Vol. 26 Issue 7, p625-651.

206. You Like What I Like, but I Don't Like What You Like: Uniqueness Motivations in Product Preferences. Irmak, Caglar; Vallen, Beth; Sen, Sankar. Journal of Consumer Research, Oct2010, Vol. 37 Issue 3, p443-45.

207. Autotelic Need for Touch, Haptics and Persuasion: the Role of Involvement. Peck, Joann; Johnson, Jennifer Wiggins. *Psychology & Marketing*, Mar2011, Vol. 28 Issue 3, p222-239.

208. Motivational Consequences of Perceived Velocity in Consumer Goal Pursuit. Huang, Szu-chi; Zhang, Ying. *Journal of Marketing Research (JMR)*, Dec2011, Vol. 48 Issue 6, p1045-1056.

PERCEPTION (Sensory Marketing)

209. The Impact of 3d Virtual Haptics in Marketing. Jin, Seung-A Annie. *Psychology & Marketing*, Mar2011, Vol. 28 Issue 3, p240-255.

210. To Touch or Not to Touch; That Is the Question. Should Consumers Always Be Encouraged to Touch Products, and Does It Always Alter Product Perception? Marlow, Nigel; Jansson-Boyd, Cathrine V. *Psychology & Marketing*, Mar2011, Vol. 28 Issue 3, p256-266.

211. Multisensory Design: Reaching Out to Touch the Consumer. Spence, Charles; Gallace, Alberto. *Psychology & Marketing*, Mar2011, Vol. 28 Issue 3, p267-308.

212. Money: A Bias for the Whole, By Himanshu Mishra; Arul Mishra and Dhananjay Nayakankuppam (2006), *Journal of Consumer Research*, 32 (March), 03/2006.

213. Product Scent and Memory. Krishna, Aradhna; Lwin, May O.; Morrin, Maureen. *Journal of Consumer Research*, Jun2010, Vol. 37 Issue 1, p57-67.

214. Consumer World-Mindedness and Attitudes Toward Product Positioning in Advertising: An Examination of Global Versus Foreign Versus Local Positioning. Nijssen, Edwin J; Douglas,Susan P. *Journal of International Marketing*, Sep2011, Vol. 19 Issue 3, p113-133.

215. Do Payment Mechanisms Change the Way Consumers Perceive Products? *Chatterjee, Promothesh; Rose, Randall L. Journal of Consumer Research, Apr2012, Vol. 38 Issue 6, p1129-1139.*

216. Consumer Perceptions of Online Shopping Environments: A Gestalt Approach. Demangeot, Catherine; Broderick, Amanda J. *Psychology & Marketing*, Feb2010, Vol. 27 Issue 2, p117-140.

217. Online Visual Merchandising (VMD) Cues and Consumer Pleasure and Arousal: Purchasing Versus Browsing Situation. Ha, Young; Lennon, Sharron J. *Psychology & Marketing*, Feb2010, Vol. 27 Issue 2, p141-165.

218. Translating Country-of-Origin Effects into Prices. Drozdenko, R. & Jensen, M. (2009). *Journal of Product & Brand Management, 18*(5), 371-378.

PERCEPTION (of PRICE)

219. Perceptions of Fair Pricing. Heyman, J. and B. Mellers. *Handbook of Consumer Psychology*, C. Haugtvedt, F. Kardes, & P Herr (Eds.) (2008).

220. Design for Synergy with Brand or Price Information. Chitturi, Ravindra; Chitturi, Pallavi; Raghavarao, Damaraju. *Psychology & Marketing*, Jul2010, Vol. 27 Issue 7, p679-697.

221. Judging Fairness of Price Increases Following a Disaster. Ferguson, Jodie L., Pam Scholder Ellen and Maria Gabriela Piscopo (2011), *Journal of* Business Ethics, 98(2), 331-349.

222. How Price Increases Affect Future Purchases: the Role of Mental Budgeting, Income, and Framing. Homburg, Christian; Koschate, Nicole; totzek, Dirk. *Psychology & Marketing*, Jan2010, Vol. 27 Issue 1, p36-53.

223. Pricing Strategy and the Formation and Evolution of Reference Price Perceptions in New Product Categories. Lowe, Ben; Alpert, Frank. *Psychology & Marketing*, Sep2010, Vol. 27 Issue 9, p846-873.

224. Getting a Feel for Price Affect: A Conceptual Framework and Empirical Investigation of Consumers' Emotional Responses to Price Information. Peine, Klaus; Heitmann, Mark; Herrmann, andreas. *Psychology & Marketing*, Jan2009, Vol. 26 Issue 1, p39-66.

225. The Effect of Stress on Price Sensitivity and Comparison Shopping. Anglin, Linda K.; Stuenkel, J. Kathleen. Advances in Consumer Research, 1994, Vol. 21 Issue 1, p126-131.

226. Small Sounds, Big Deals: Phonetic Symbolism Effects in Pricing. Coulter, Keith S.; Coulter, Robin A.. *Journal of Consumer Research*, Aug2010, Vol. 37 Issue 2, p315-328.

PERSONALITY

227. The Influence of Personality on Active and Passive Use of Social Networking Sites. Pagani, Margherita; Hofacker, Charles F.; Goldsmith, Ronald E. *Psychology & Marketing*, May2011, Vol. 28 Issue 5, p441-456.

228. Personality, Person-Brand Fit, and Brand Community: An Investigation of Individuals, Brands, and Brand Communities. Matzler, Kurt; Pichler, Elisabeth; Fuller, Johann; Mooradian, Todd A. *Journal of Marketing Management*, Aug2011, Vol. 27 Issue 9/10, p874-890.

229. Trait Superstition and Consumer Behavior: Re-Conceptualization, Measurement, and Initial Investigations. Carlson, Brad D.; Mowen, John C.; Fang, Xiang. *Psychology & Marketing*, Aug2009, Vol. 26 Issue 8, p689-713.

230. The Relationship between Packaging Uniformity and Variety Seeking. Roehm, Michelle L.; Roehm, Harper A. *Psychology & Marketing*, Dec2010, Vol. 27 Issue 12, p1122-1133.

231. A Taste of "Nextopia". Dahlén, Micael; Thorbjørnsen, Helge; Sjödin, Henrik. *Journal of Advertising*, Winter2011, Vol. 40 Issue 4, p33-44.

PERSONALIZATION

232. What Is Personalization? A Conceptual Framework. Vesanen, Jari. European *Journal of* Marketing, 2007, Vol.

41 Issue 5/6, p409-418.

233. Buyer Monitoring: A Means to Insure Personalized Service. Kwortnik, Robert J; Lynn, W. Michael; Ross, William T. *Journal of Marketing Research (JMR)*, Oct2009, Vol. 46 Issue 5, p573-583.

234. Identifying Customer Need Patterns For Customization and Personalization. Xuehong Du; Jianxin Jiao; Mitchell M Tseng. Integrated Manufacturing Systems, 2003, Vol. 14 Issue 5, p387-396.

235. Service Personalization and Loyalty. Dwayne Ball; Coelho, Pedro S.; VÜares, Manuel J. *Journal of Services Marketing*, 2006, Vol. 20 Issue 6/7, p391-403.

236. Leveraging Customer Knowledge -- Profiling and Personalisation in E-Business. Rowley, Jennifer; Slack, Frances. *International Journal of Retail & Distribution Management*, 2001, Vol. 29 Issue 9, p409-41.

PERSUASTION

237. How Potential Tourists React to Mass Media Marketing: Advertising Versus Publicity. Loda, Marsha D.; Norman, William; Backman, Kenneth. *Journal of Travel & Tourism Marketing*, 2005, Vol. 18 Issue 3, p63-70.

238. Autotelic Need for Touch, Haptics, and Persuasion: the Role of Involvement. Peck, Joann; Johnson, Jennifer Wiggins. *Psychology & Marketing*, Mar2011, Vol. 28 Issue 3, p222-239.

POST-MODERN CONSUMPTION

239. Glocal Yoga: Re-Appropriation in the Indian Consumptionscape. Askegaard, Søren; Eckhardt, Giana M. *Marketing Theory*, Mar2012, Vol. 12 Issue 1, p45-60.

240. Performing the High-School Prom in the UK: Locating Authenticity Through Practice. Tinson, Julie; Nuttall, Peter. *Journal of Marketing Management*, Aug2011, Vol. 27 Issue 9/10, p1007-1026.

241. Symbolic Interactionism And The Internet: The Communication Of Identity In Virtual Communities of Consumption And Real Life. Presi, Caterina. 16th EIASM/EMAC Doctoral colloquium in Marketing, Glasgow, Scotland May 18-20, 2003.

242. Happiness For Sale: Do Experiential Purchases Make Consumers Happier Than Material Purchases? *Journal of Consumer Research*, Issue 36, 188 - 198, with J. Irwin, and L. Nicolao, August 2009.

243. Consuming Postcolonial Shopping Malls. Varman, Rohit; Belk, Russell W. *Journal of Marketing Management*, Feb2012, Vol. 28 Issue 1/2, p62-84.

244. The Posthuman: The End and the Beginning of the Human. Campbell, Norah, Aidan O'Driscoll and Michael Saren. *Journal of Consumer Behaviour*, 9, (2), 2010, p86–101.

245. Social Behavior and Brand Devotion Among Iphone Innovators. Arruda-Filho, Emílio J.M.; Cabusas, Julianne A.; Dholakia, Nikhilesh. *International Journal of Information Management*, Dec2010, Vol. 30 Issue 6, p475-480.

246. How Iphone Innovators Changed their Consumption in Iday2: Hedonic Post or Brand Devotion. Arruda-Filho, Emílio J.M.; Lennon, Mark M. *International Journal of*

Information Management, Dec2011, Vol. 31 Issue 6, p524-532.

247. Nationalism and Ideology in an Anticonsumption Movement. Varman, Rohit; Belk, Russell W. *Journal of Consumer Research*, Dec2009, Vol. 36 Issue 4, p686-700.

248. Anti-Consumption and Brand Avoidance. Lee, Michael S.W.; Motion, Judith; Conroy, Denise. *Journal of Business Research*, Feb2009, Vol. 62 Issue 2, p169-180.

249. Retail Spectacles and Brand Meaning: Insights from a Brand Museum Case Study. Hollenbeck, Candice R.; Cara Peters; and George M. Zinkhan. 2008. *Journal of Retailing*, (84 (3)): 334-353.

250. Gift Giving: A Community Paradigm. Candice R. Hollenbeck . *Psychology & Marketing*, 2006(23): 573-595.

251. How to Facilitate Immersion in a Consumption Experience: Appropriation Operations and Service Elements. Carù, Antonella; Cova, Bernard. *Journal of Consumer Behaviour*, Jan/Feb2006, Vol. 5 Issue 1, p4-14.

252. Bridging Aficionados' Perceptual and Conceptual Knowledge to Enhance How they Learn from Experience. Latour, Kathryn A.; Latour, Michael S. *Journal of Consumer Research,* Dec2010, Vol. 37 Issue 4, p688-697.

253. Possession and Access: Consumer Desires and Value Perceptions Regarding Contemporary Art Collection and Exhibit Visits. YU CHEN. *Journal of Consumer Research*, Apr2009, Vol. 35 Issue 6, p925-940.

254. Liquid Relationship to Possessions. Bardhi, F.; Eckhardt, G.; Arnould, E. J. in *Journal of Consumer Research*, 2012, 39.

255. Consuming the Authentic Gettysburg: How a Tourist Landscape Becomes an Authentic Experience. Chronist, Athinodoros; Hampton, Ronald D. *Journal of Consumer Behaviour*, Mar/Apr2008, Vol. 7 Issue 2, p111-126.

256. The Quest for Authenticity in Consumption: Consumers' Purposive Choice of Authentic Cues to Shape Experienced Outcomes. Beverland, Michael B.; Farrelly, Francis J. *Journal of Consumer Research*, Feb2010, Vol. 36 Issue 5, p838-856.

257. A Journey to the Authentic: Museum Visitors and their Negotiation of the Inauthentic. Hede, Anne-Marie; Thyne, Maree. *Journal of Marketing Management*, Jul2010, Vol. 26 Issue 7/8, p686-705.

258. Brand Authentication: Creating and Maintaining Brand Auras. Alexander, Nicholas. European *Journal of Marketing Managment*..

259. Using Semiotics in Consumer Research to Understand Everyday Phenomena. Ogilvie, Madeleine; Mizerski, Katherine. *International Journal of Market Research*, 2011, Vol. 53 Issue 5, p651-668.

260. Adults' Consumption of Videogames as Imaginative Escape from Routine. Molesworth, Mike. Advances in Consumer Research - North American Conference Proceedings, 2009, Vol. 36, p378-383.

261. The Experiential Aspects of Consumption: Consumer Fantasies, Feelings, and Fun. Holbrook, Morris B.; Hirschman, Elizabeth C. *Journal of Consumer Research*, Sep82, Vol. 9 Issue 2, p132-140.

262. Trying to be Cosmopolitan. Thompson, Craig J.; Tambyah, Siok Kuan. *Journal of Consumer Research*, Dec99, Vol. 26 Issue 3, p214-241.

263. For Those About to Rock: A New Understanding of Adolescent Music Consumption. Nuttall, Peter. Advances in Consumer Research - North American Conference Proceedings, 2008, Vol. 35, p624-629

264. Material Man is Not an Island: Coping with Cultural Fracture. Davies, A. Fitchett J.A. (2010), *Journal of Marketing Management*, Vol. 26 (Issue 11-12), p 1145-1160. ISSN: 0267-257X.

265. Buying a Book as a Christmas Gift: Two Routes to Customer Immersion. Addis, Michela; Sala, Giulia. Service Industries Journal, Dec2007, Vol. 27 Issue 8, p991-1006.

266. Collins's Interaction Ritual theory: Using Interaction Rituals to Conceptualize How Objects Become Sacred Symbols. Huggins, Kyle A.; Murray, Jeff B.; Kees, Jeremy; Creyer, Elizabeth H. *Advances in Consumer Research - North American Conference Proceedings*, 2007, Vol. 34, p335-336.

267. Truly, Madly, Deeply: Consumers in the Throes of Material Possession Love. Sirianni, Nancy J.; Lastovicka, John L. *Journal of Consumer Research*, Aug2011, Vol. 38 Issue 2, p323-342.

268. Measures of Expressions of Love. Goff, Brent G.; Pointer, Lucille; Jackson, Gary Brian; Goddard, H. Wallace. Psychological Reports, Oct2007, Vol. 101 Issue 2, p357-360.

269. Consumption Fantasies: A Phenomenological View. Leonard, Hillary A., *Advances in Consumer Research*, 2005, Vol. 32 Issue 1, p229-230.

270. Our Possessions, Our Selves: Domains of Self-Worth and the Possession-Self Link. Ferraro, Rosellina; Jennifer Edson Escalas and James R. Bettman (2011), *Journal of Consumer Psychology*, 21 (2), 169-177.

271. Peacocks, Porsches, and Thorstein Veblen: Conspicuous Consumption As A Sexual Signaling System. Sundie, Jill M.; Douglas T. Kenrick; Vladas Griskevicius; Joshua M. Tybur, Kathleen D. Vohs, and Daniel J. Beal. *Journal of Personality and Social Psychology*, 2011, 100 (4), 664-680.

SATISFACTION

272. Do Satisfied Customers Bad-Mouth Innovative Products? Parthasarathy, Madhavan; Forlani, David. *Psychology & Marketing*, Dec2010, Vol. 27 Issue 12, p1134-1153.

273. Can You Trust a Customer's Expression? Insights into Nonverbal Communication in the Retail Context. Puccinelli, Nancy M.; Motyka, Scott; Grewal, Dhruv. *Psychology & Marketing*, Oct2010, Vol. 27 Issue 10, p964-988.

274. Consumer Discontent Revisited. Lundstrom, W. J.; White, D. S. (2006). *Journal of Academy of Business and Economics*, 6(2).

275. Perceived Justice of Service Recovery Strategies: Impact on Customer Satisfaction and Quality Relationship. Vázquez-Casielles, Rodolfo; Suárez Álvarez, Leticia; Díaz Martín,

Ana Maria. *Psychology & Marketing*, May2010, Vol. 27 Issue 5, p487-509.

276. Complaining: A Function of Attitude, Personality and Situation. Thøgersen, John; Juhl, Hans Jørn; Poulsen, Carsten Stig. *Psychology & Marketing*, Aug2009, Vol. 26 Issue 8, p760-777.

277. Satisfaction in Choice as A Function of the Number of Alternatives: When "Goods Satiate". Reutskaja, Elena; Hogarth, Robin M. *Psychology & Marketing*, Mar2009, Vol. 26 Issue 3, p197-203.

278. Attaining Satisfaction. Cho, Cecile K.; Johar, Gita Venkataramani. *Journal of Consumer Research*, Dec2011, Vol. 38 Issue 4, p622-631.

279. Consumer Loyalty in Sport Spectatorship Services: the Relationships with Consumer Satisfaction and Team Identification. Bodet, Guillaume; Bernache-Assollant, Iouri. *Psychology & Marketing*, Aug2011, Vol. 28 Issue 8, p781-802.

SELF-IDENTITY (AND BRAND SYMBOLISM)

280. Adolescent Girls from a Modern Conservative Culture: the Impact of their Social Identity on their Perception of Brand Symbolism. Souiden, Nizar; M'saad, Bouthaina. *Psychology & Marketing*, Dec2011, Vol. 28 Issue 12, p1133-1153.

281. Sticky Priors: the Perseverance of Identity Effects on Judgment. Bolton, Lisa E.; Reed II, Americus. *Journal of Marketing Research (JMR)*, Nov2004, Vol. 41 Issue 4, p397-410.

282. Matching a Cause with Self-Schema: the Moderating Effect on Brand Preferences. Chowdhury, Tilottama G.; Khare, Adwait. *Psychology & Marketing*, Aug2011, Vol. 28 Issue 8, p825-842.

283. Arts Patronage: A Social Identity theory Perspective. Swanson, S.; Davis, J. C. (2006). *Journal of Marketing theory & Practice*, 14(2), 125-138.

284. The Impact of Collective Guilt on the Preference for Japanese Products. Maher, Amro and Anusorn Singhapakdi (2010) *Journal of the Global Academy of Marketing Science*, 20(2)

285. Consumers' Identification and Beyond: Attraction, Reverence and Escapism in the Evaluation of Films. Addis, Michela; Holbrook, Morris B. *Psychology & Marketing*, Sep2010, Vol. 27 Issue 9, p821-845.

286. Brand-Self Identity Narratives in the James Bond Movies. Cooper, Holly; Schembri, Sharon; Miller, Dale. *Psychology & Marketing*, Jun2010, Vol. 27 Issue 6, p557-567.

287. Creating Visual Narrative Art for Decoding Stories That Consumers and Brands Tell. Megehee, Carol M.; Woodside, Arch G. *Psychology & Marketing*, Jun2010, Vol. 27 Issue 6, p603-622.

288. Brand Consumption and Narrative of the Self. Schembri, Sharon; Merrilees, Bill; Kristiansen, Stine. *Psychology & Marketing*, Jun2010, Vol. 27 Issue 6, p623-637.

289. A Phenomenological Inquiry into the Essence of the Technologically Extended Self, C. Scott Rader, Academy of Marketing Science World Congress, 2007.

290. Real or Relevant Beauty? Body Shape and Endorser Effects on Brand Attitude and Body Image. D'Alessandro, Steven; Chitty, Bill. *Psychology & Marketing*, Aug2011, Vol. 28 Issue 8, p843-878.

291. Gay Men's Identity Attempt Pathway and Its Implication on Consumption. Hsieh, Ming Huei; Wu, Shu Ling. *Psychology & Marketing*, Apr2011, Vol. 28 Issue 4, p388-416.

VALUE (HEDONIC)

292. Hedonic Evaluations of Cars: Effects of Payment Mode on Prediction and Experience. Hoelzl, Erik; Pollai, Maria; Kastner, Herbert. *Psychology & Marketing*, Nov2011, Vol. 28 Issue 11, p1113-1127.

VALUES AND CONSUMPTION

293. Materialism and Its Relationship to Individual Values. Kilbourne, William E.; LaForge, Mary C. *Psychology & Marketing*, Aug2010, Vol. 27 Issue 8, p780-798.

294. The Investigation of Chinese Consumer Values, Consumption Values, Life Satisfaction, and Consumption Behaviors. Xiao, Ge; Kim, Jai-Ok. *Psychology & Marketing*, Jul2009, Vol. 26 Issue 7, p610-624.

295. Developing Practical Procedures for the Measurement of Personal Values in Cross-Cultural Marketing. Munson, J. Michael; McIntyre, Shelby H. *Journal of Marketing Research (JMR)*, Feb1979, Vol. 16(1), p48-52.

296. An Investigation of Old School Values in the Arena Football League. Aiken, K. Damon; Campbell Jr., Richard M.; Sukhdial, Ajay. Sport Marketing Quarterly, Sep2010, Vol. 19 Issue 3, p125-131.

297. Measuring Childhood Materialism: Refining and Validating Schor's Consumer Involvement Scale. Bottomley, Paul A.; Nairn, Agnes; Kasser, Tim; Ferguson, Yuna L.; Ormrod, Johanne. *Psychology & Marketing*, Jul2010, Vol. 27 Issue 7, p717-739.

298. Cross-cultural Consumer Values, Needs And Purchase Behavior. Kim, Jai-Ok; Sandra Forsythe; Qingliang Gu; Sook Jae Moon. *Journal of Consumer Marketing*, 1984, 19(6), 481-502.

299. Of Wealth and Death: Materialism, Mortality Salience, and Consumption Behavior. Kasser, Tim; Kennon M. Sheldon. *Psychological Science*. July 2000, Vol. 11 (4), 348-351.

300. Bringing A Perspective of Transformative Learning to Globalized Consumption. Edmund O' Sullivan. *International Journal of Consumer Studies*, 2003, 27(4), 326-330.

ENDNOTES

CHAPTER 1

1. This and all similar quotes are, unless otherwise specified, from author's research files. Some consumer statements are slightly modified for economy of space, but the original sentiment is preserved. Where only first names are given, names are disguised.

2. Our definition departs from but is compatible with those in the classical marketing literature; for a review, see Janice Hanna, "A Typology of Consumer Needs," *Research in Marketing* 3, J. N. Sheth, ed. (Greenwich, CT: JAI Press, 1980), 83-104.

3. Bagozzi, Richard P., M"arketing as an Organized Behavioral System of Exchange," *Journal of Marketing*, Vol. 38, No. 4 (Oct., 1974), pp. 77-81.

4. See, Pierre Bourdieu, *Distinction: A Social Critique of the Judgment of Taste*, Cambridge, UK: Cambridge University Press, 1984.

5. Banwari Mittal and Jagdish N. Sheth, ValueSpace: Winning the Battle for Market Leadership," NY: McGraw-Hill, 2001.

6. Barry J. Babin, William R. Darden, and Mitch Griffin, "Work and/or Fun: Measuring Hedonic and Utilitarian Shopping Value," *Journal of Consumer Research*, 1994, 20 (March), 644-656; Rajeev Batra and Olli T. Ahtola, "Measuring the Hedonic and Utilitarian Sources of Consumer Attitude," *Marketing Letters*, 2(2), 159-170.

7. Quoted in Anne M. Velliquette, Jeff B. Murray, And Elizabeth H. Creyer, "The Tattoo Renaissance: An Ethnographic Account of Symbolic Consumer Behavior," in Joseph W. Alba and J. Wesley Hutchinson (eds.), *Advances in Consumer Research*, XXV, 1998, 461-467;

8. Source: http://inventors.about.com/library/inventors/blansweringmachines.htm;

9. Source: www.testmark.com/develop/tml_callerid_cnt.html

10. Information about these products was compiled from company Web sites and various news sources.

11. Theodore Levitt, Marketing Myopia, *Harvard Business Review*, July-August 1960.

12. Peter F. Drucker, *Management: Tasks, Responsibilities Practices* (New York: Harper & Row, 1973).

13. Bartels, Bartels, The History of Marketing Thought (3rd Ed.), Columbus: Publishing Horizons, 1988.

14. Information about these products was compiled from company Web sites, press releases, and various news sources.

15. These definitions are adapted from various sources: http://www.asanet.org/public/what.html http://encarta.msn.com/encnet/features/dictionary/DictionaryResults.aspx?search=anthropology; Encarta® World English Dictionary [North American Edition] © & (P)2003 Microsoft Corporation. All rights reserved. Developed for Microsoft by Bloomsbury Publishing PLC.

16. See, story on the Website of Advertising Educational Foundation, posted March 29, 2004: http://www.aef.com/06/news/data/2004/2539.

CHAPTER 2

1. For a foundational discussion of motivation, see John W. Atkinson, *An Introduction to Motivation* (New York, NY: D. Van Nostrand Company, 1964); Edward J. Murray, *Motivation and Emotion* (Englewood Cliffs, NJ: Prentice Hall, 1964).

2. Ibid

3. For an illuminating review of various needs, see Janice Hanna, "A Typology of Consumer Needs," *Research in Marketing* 3, J. N. Sheth, ed. (Greenwich, CT: JAI Press, 1980), 83-104.

4. Abraham H. Maslow, "A Theory of Human Motivation," *Psychological Review* 50 (July 1943), 370-96; also, Abraham H. Maslow, *Motivation and Personality* (New York: Harper & Row, 1970).

5. Maslow, *Motivation and Personality*, 1987, Harper Collins, p. 22.

6. I owe this example to Jagdish N. Sheth, personal communication.

7. Haire, M. (1950). Projective techniques in marketing research. Journal of Marketing, 14, 649¬-656.

8. For an application to consumer Internet Behavior, see Zheng Zhou, Yeqing Bao, "Users' Attitude toward Web Advertising: Effects of Internet Motivation and Internet Ability," *Advances in Cons. Res.*, 29, (2002), 71- 78.

9. For one recent academic study, see J. A. Ruth, "Promoting a Brand's Emotional Benefits," *J. of Cons. Psych.*, 11, 2, 2001, 99-113.

10. As for motivation, so too for emotions; our treatment is necessarily oversimplified due to space limitations. For fuller discussion, see P. T. Young, *Motivation and Emotion* (New York: John Wiley and Sons, 1961); E. J. Murray, *Motivation and Emotion* (Englewood Cliffs, NJ: Prentice Hall, 1964); and George Mandler, *Mind and Body* (New York: Norton, 1984); C. E. Izard, *Human Emotions* (New York: Platinum, 1977), and for a marketing application, see R.R. Bagozzi, M. Gopinath, P. U. Nyer, "The role of emotions in marketing," *J. of the Acad. of Marketing Science*, 1999, 27(2), 184-206.

11. See Robert Plutchik, "A Language for the Emotions," *Psychology Today*, 1980, 13(9), 68-78; R. Plutchik, "Emotions: A General Psychoevolutionary Theory," in K.R. Scherer & P. Ekman (Eds.), *Approaches to Emotion*, Hillsdale, NJ: Erlbaum.

12. See Marsha L. Richins "Measuring Emotions in the Consumption Experience," *J. of Cons. Res.*, 1997, 24 (Sept.),127-146.

13. Based on Morris B Holbrook and Maryl P. Gardner, "Illustrating a Dynamic Model of the Mood-Updating Process in Consumer Behavior," *Psychology & Marketing*, Mar2000, 17(3), 165-194; also see, Gordon C. Bruner, "Music, mood and marketing," *J. of Marketing*, 1990, 54(4), 94-104.

14. For further reading, see J. Russell, "A Circumplex Model of Affect," J. of Personality and Social Psychology, 1980, 39, 1161-1178; and Morris B. Holbrook and Meryl P. Gardner, "Illustrating a Dynamic Model of Mood Updating Process in Consumer Behavior," *Psychology and Marketing*, March 2000, 17(3), 165-194. Also see, Rajeev Batra and Douglas M. Stayman, "The Role of Mood in Advertising Effectiveness," *J. of Cons. Res.* 17,2 (Sept. 1990), 203-14.

15. For a classic review of Mood effects in marketing, see Merryl P. Gardner, "Mood State and Consumer Behavior: A Critical Review," J. of Cons. Res., 1985, 12, 281-300; Harri T.Luomala and Martti Laaksonen, "Contributions from mood research," *Psychology and Marketing*, 2000, 17 (3), 195-233; J. B. Cohen and C. S. Areni "Affect and consumer behavior," *Handbook of consumer behavior,* 1991, 188-240; R. A. Westbrook and R. L. Oliver, "The dimensionality of consumption emotion patterns and consumer satisfaction," *J. of Cons. Res.*, 1997, 18, June, 84-91.

16. For some research on the effects of negative moods, see Sarah Maxwell and Arthur Kover, "Negative Affect: The Dark Side of Retailing," *J. of Bus. Res.*, 56(7), 2003, 553-559; Barry J. Babin and William R. Darden, "Good and Bad Shopping Vibes: Spending and Patronage Satisfaction," *J. of Bus. Res.*, 1996, 35, 201-6.

17. See, Morris Holbrook and Elizabeth Hirschman, "The Experiential Aspects of Consumption: Consumer Fantasies, Feelings, and Fun," *J. of Cons. Res.* 9 (Sept. 1982), 132-40; Elizabeth Hirschman and Morris Holbrook, "Hedonic Consumption: Emerging Concepts, Methods, and Prepositions," *J. of Marketing* 46 (Summer 1982), 92-101.

18. For academic research on hedonic motives, see Meera P. Venkatraman and Deborah J. MacInnis, "The Epistemic and Sensory Exploratory Behaviors of Hedonic and Cognitive Consumers," in *Advances in Cons. Res.* 12, E. C. Hirschman and M. B. Holbrook, eds. 1988,102-7.

19. Russell Belk, Güliz Ger, and Søren Askegaard, "The Fire of Desire:

A Multisited Inquiry into Consumer Passion," *J. of Cons. Res.*, 2003, December, 30, 328-51; also, Russell Belk, Güliz Ger, and Søren Askegaard, "Consumer Desire in Three Cultures: Results from Projective Research," *Advances in Cons. Res.*, 24, 1997, 24-28.

20. Quote borrowed from Belk, Ger, and Askegaard, 1997 (Ibid), p. 26.

21. There is a rich body of academic research literature on the topic of involvement, including: Peter Bloch, "Involvement beyond the purchase process: conceptual issues and empirical investigation," *Advances in Cons. Research*, 1982 Vol. 9, 413-417; Marsha L. Richins, Peter H. Bloch, Edward F. McQuarrie, "How Enduring and Situational Involvement Combine to Create Involvement Response," *J. of Cons. Psych.*, 1992, 1,143-153; Y. Evrard and P. Aurier, "Identification and validation of the components of the person-object relationship," *J. of Bus. Res.*, 1996, 37, 127-134; J.L. Zaichkowsky, "Measuring the Involvement Construct," *J. of Cons. Res.*, 1985, 12, 341-352; J.N. Kapferer and G. Laurent, "Consumer Involvement Profile: A New Practical Approach to Consumer Involvement," J. of Advertising Research; 1986, 25(5), 48-59. Mark B. Traylor, "Product Involvement and Brand Commitment," *J. of Advertising Research*; 1981, 21, 51-56; B. Mittal and M.S. Lee, "A causal model of consumer involvement," *J. of Economic Psychology*, 1989, 10, 363-389; J. C. Andrews, S.S. Durvasula, and S. H. Akhter, "A framework for conceptualizing and measuring the involvement construct in advertising research," *J. of Advertising*, 1990, 19, 27-31.

22. Maslow, *Motivation and Personality*, 1987, 3rd ed., Harper Collins, p. 22.

23. Wayne Weiten, *Psychology: Themes and Variations* (Belmont, CA: Wadsworth, 1989), 596.

24. See, Harold H. Kelley, "Attribution Theory in Social Psychology," *Nebraska Symposium on Motivation*, 15 (1967), 191-241; Harold H. Kelley, "The Process of Causal Attribution," *American Psychologist* 28 (1973), 107-128, and for Cons. Res. on attribution, see Valarie S. Folks, "Recent Attribution Research in Consumer Behavior: A Review and New Directions," *J. of Consumer Research.*, 1988, 14,548-565; W. Sue and M.J. Tippins, "Consumer Attributions of Product Failure to Channel Members and Self: The Impact of Situational Cues," in T.K. Srull (ed.), Advances in Cons. Res., 25, 139-145, Provo, UT: Association for Cons. Res.; B. Weiner, "Attributional Thoughts about Consumer Behavior," *J. of Cons. Res.*, 2000, 27, 382-387. Also see, D. Forlani and Orville C. Walker, Jr., "Valenced Attributions and Risk in New Product Decisions: How Why Indicates What's Next," Psychology & Marketing, 2003, 20(5), 395-432. R. D. Mizerski, L.L. Golden, and J.B. Kernan, "The Attribution Process in Consumer Decision Making," *J. of Cons. Res.*, 1979, 6, 123-140.

CHAPTER 3

1. Read some basic literature on *perception* in Pomerantz, James R. (2003): "Perception: Overview," in Lynn Nadel (Ed.), *Encyclopedia of Cognitive Science*, Vol. 3, London: Nature Publishing Group, pp. 527–537; Gregory, Richard. "Perception" in Gregory, Richard L.; Zangwill, O. L. (1987). The Oxford companion to the mind. Oxford University Press. (pp. 598–601); Bernstein, Douglas A. (5 March 2010). *Essentials of Psychology*, Cengage Learning. pp. 123–124.

2. Bond traders: Ross Diamond on how product placement thrives in the world of 007. (Advertising). New Statesman, Nov 25, 2002,

3. See White, Roderick, "Ambient Media - Best Practice. Admap #454, October 2004.

4. Assembled from various news sources and company Web sites.

5. Paul D. Bolls, Darrel D. Muehling and Kak Yoon, "The effects of television commercial pacing on viewers' attention and memory," *J. of Marketing Communications*, Mar2003, 9(1),17-28.

6. See Rik Pieters and Michel Wedel, "AttentionCapture and Transfer in Advertising : Brand, Pictorial, and Text size effects," *J. of Marketing*, 2004, 68, 36-50.

7. See Stuart Henderson Britt, "How Weber's Law Can Be Allied to Marketing," Business Horizons, February 1975, 21-29.

8. Stuart Rogers, "How a Publicity Blitz Created The Myth of Subliminal Advertising," Public Relations Quarterly, Winter92/93, 37(4), 12-17.

9. See J. A. Bargh, M. Chen, and L. Burrows, "Automaticity and Social Behavior: Direct Effects of Trait Construct and Stereotype Activation," *J. of Personality & Social Psychology*, 1996, 71, 230-44.

1010. For further reading, see Timothy E. Moore, "Subliminal Advertising: What You See IS What You Get," *J. of Marketing*, 46, 1982, 38-47.

11. For academic research on 'mere exposure', see William E. Baker "When Can Affective Conditioning and Mere Exposure Directly Influence Brand Choice," *J. of Advertising*, 1999, 28, 21-46; and Chris Janiszewski, "Preattentive Mere Exposure Effects," *J. of Consumer Research*, 1993, 20, 376-393.

12. Koffka, K. (1935). Principles of Gestalt Psychology. New York: Harcourt, Brace & World.

13. For a recent consumer research study on closure, see David C. Houghton and Rajdeep Grewal, "Please, Let's Get An Answer – Any Answer: Need for Consumer Cognitive Closure," Psychology & Marketing, Nov. 2000, 17, 11, 911-934.

14. See Abhijit Biswas and Edward A. Blair, "Contextual Effects of Reference Prices in Retail Advertising," *J. of Marketing*, 55 (July 1991), 1-12; Robert Jacobson and Carl Obermiller, "The Formation of Reference Price," Advances in Cons. Res.16 (1989), 234-40; Joel E. Urbany, William O. Bearden, and Dan C. Weilbaker, "The Effects of Plausible and Exaggerated Reference prices on Consumer Perceptions and Price Search," *J. of Cons. Res.*, 1988, 15, 95-110; "Consumers' perceptions of promotional framing of price," Indrajit Sinha and Michael F. Smith, *Psych and Mktg*, 2000, 17(3), 257–275.

15. For studies on how consumers use price itself as a surrogate indicator of product quality, see, See Valarie A. Zeithaml, "Consumer Perceptions of Price, Quality, and Value: A Means-End Model and Synthesis of Evidence," *J. of Marketing* 52 (July 1988): 2-22. Also see Steven M. Shugan, "Price Quality Relationships," in Thomas C. Kinnear, ed., Advances in Consumer Research 11 (Association for Consumer Research, 1983), 627-32; and Carl Obermiller and John J. Wheatley, "Price Effects on Choice and Perceptions under Varying Conditions of Experience, Information, and Beliefs in Quality Differences," in Thomas C. Kinnear, ed., Advances in Consumer Research 11 (Association for Consumer Research 1983), 453-58.

16. For a recent summary of research findings on this topic, see, Narasimhan Srinivasan and Subhash C. Jain, (2003) "Country of Origin Effect: Synthesis and Future Direction," (book chapter), Handbook of Research in International Marketing, (ed.) Subhash C. Jain , Edward Elgar, MA, 458-476. Some of the notable research studies on this topic are Jyh-shen Chiou, "The Impact of Country of Origin on Pretrial and Posttrial Product Evaluations: The Moderating Effect of Consumer Expertise," Psychology & Marketing, 2003, 20, 10, 935-954; W. Li and R. S. Wyer, Jr. "The Role of Country of Origin in Product Evaluations: Informational and Standard-of-Comparison Effects," *J. of Consumer Psychology* 3, no. 2 (1994), 187-212; Sung-Tai Hong and R. S. Wyer, Jr., "Effects of Country of Origin and Product-Attribute Information on Product Evaluation: An Information Processing Perspective," *J. of Cons. Research*, 16, 2 (September 1989), 175-87; E. Kaynak and T. Cavusgil, "Consumer Attitudes Towards Products of Foreign Origin: Do They Vary across Product Classes," International *J. of Advertising* 2 (1983), 147-57; M. Wall and L. A. Heslop, "Consumer Attitudes toward Canadian-made versus Imported Products," *J. of the Academy of Marketing Science* 14 (Summer 1986), 27-36; M. Wall, J. Liefeld, and L. A. Heslop, "Impact of Country-of-Origin Cues on Consumer Judgments in Multi-Cue Situations: A Covariance Analysis," *J. of the Academy of Marketing*

Science 19, no. 2 (Spring-Summer 1991), 105-14; Chih-Kang Wang and Charles W. Lamb, Jr., "Foreign Environmental Factors Influencing American Consumers' Predispositions Toward European Products," *J. of the Academy of Marketing Science* 8 (Fall 1980), 345-56; D. Tse and G. J. Gorn, "An Experiment on the Salience of Country-of-Origin in the Era of Global Brands," International Marketing Review 9 (1992), . 57-76. W. K. Li, K. B. Monroe, and D. Chan, "The Effects of Country of Origin, Brand, and Price Information: A Cognitive-Affective Model of Buying Intentions," Advances in Consumer Research 21 (1994), 449-57. J. K. Johansson, "Determinants and Effects of the Use of "Made in Labels," International Marketing Review 6 (1989), 47-58. Murray A. Young, Paul L. Sauer, and H. Rap Unnava, "Country-of-Origin Issues," in Salah H. Hassan and Roger D. Blackwell, Global Marketing: Perspectives and Cases (Fort Worth, TX: Dryden Press, 1994), 196-210; Sevgin A. Eroglu and Karen A. Machleit, "Effects of Individual and Product-Specific Variables on Utilizing Country-of-Origin as a Product Quality Cue," International Marketing Review, 6 (November), 1998, 27-41; G. Erickson, J. K. Johansson, and P. Chao, "Image Variables in Multiattribute Product Evaluations: Country-of-Origin Effects," *J. of Consumer Research* 11 (September 1984), . 694-99. C. M. Han, "Country Image: Halo or Summary Construct," *J. of Marketing Research* 16 (May 1989), 222-29; S. Lohr, "Made in Japan or Not: That Is the Question," New York Times 3, no. 1 (April, 1988), cited in L. D. Dahringer and H. Muhlbacher, International Marketing: A Global Perspective (Reading, MA: Addison-Wesley, 1991), p. 354; Giana M. Eckhardt, "Local Branding in a Foreign Product Category in an Emerging Market," *J. of International Marketing*, 2005,13(4), 57-79.

17. See, Lindstrom, Martin, Brand Sense, New York, Free Press, 2010; and Schmitt, Bernd H., *Experiential Marketing: How to Get Customers to Sense, Feel, Think, Act, Relate,* New York: Free Press, 1999.

18. For research on the role of odors in retailing, see Jean-Charles Chebat and Richard Michon, "Impact of Ambient Odors on Mall Shoppers' Emotions Cognitions, and Spending: A Test of Competitive Causal Theories," *J. of Business Research*, July 2003, 56(7), 529-540.

19. see, Peck, Joann & Terry L. Childers, "To Have and To Hold:The Influence of Haptic Information on Product Judgments," Journal of marketing, 2003, Vol. 67, 35-48.

20. For a more indepth description of Perception in marketing, see, Raab, Gerhard, G. Jason Goddard, Riad A Ajami, and Alexander Unger, *The Psychology of Marketing: Cross-Cultural Perspectives*, Surrey, England: Gower Publishing Limited, 2010.

CHAPTER 4

1. For a fuller description of the Pavlov experiments, see Leland C. Swenson, Theories of Learning: Traditional Perspectives/ Contemporary Developments (Belmont, CA: Wadsworth Publishing Company, 1980), pp. 13-30.

2. For academic research on classical conditioning, see, See Gerald Gorn, "The Effects of Music in Advertising on Choice Behavior: A Classical Conditioning Approach," Journal of Marketing (Winter 1982), pp. 94-101; Ronald E. Milliman, "Using Background Music to Affect Behavior of Supermarket Shoppers," *Journal of Marketing* (Summer 1982), pp. 86-91; Richard A. Feinberg, "Credit Cards as Spending Facilitating Stimuli: A Conditioning Interpretation," *Journal of Consumer Research* (December 1986), pp. 348-56.

3. A foundational discussion of modeling can be found in Neal E. Miller and John Dollard, Social Learning and Imitation (New Haven, CT: Yale University Press, 1941).

4. For recent research on this topic see, S.A. Hawkins, S. Hoch, and Myers-Levy, "Low Involvement Learning," *Journal of Consumer Psychology*, 11, 31, 2001, 1-11.

5. George A. Miller, "The Magic Number Seven, Plus or Minus Two: Some Limits on Our Capacity for Processing Information,"

Psychological review 63 (March 1956), pp. 81-97.

6. For research on effects of repetition on memory, see Douglas M. Stayman and Rajeev Batra, "Encoding and Retrieval of Ad Affect in Memory," Journal of Marketing Research, 1991, 28, 232-240; H. R. Unnava and Robert E. Burnkrant, "Effects of Repeating Varied Ad Executions on Brand Name Memory," *Journal of Marketing Research*, 1991, 28, 406-417.

7. For consumer research based on this concept, see William E. Baker , Does Brand Name Imprinting in Memory Increase Brand Information Retention?, *Psychology & Marketing*, Dec2003, 20 (12), 1119-1135.

8. One of the recall cues can be brand names suggestiveness; see, Kevin L. Keller, Susan E. Heckler,and Michale Houston, "The effects of Brand Name Suggestiveness on Advertising Recall," *Journal of Marketing*, 1998, 62, 48-57; and S. Holden and M. Vanheule, "Know the Name, Forget the Exposure: Brand Familiarity versus Memory of Exposure Context," *Psychology & Marketing*, 1999, 16, 479-496.

9. For original exposition of this theory, see, R. Anderson, "A Spreading Activation Theory of Memory," *Journal of Verbal Learning and Verbal Behavior*, 1983, 22, 261-295.

10. For foundational treatment of this topic, see Everett M. Rogers, "New Product Adoption and Diffusion," in R. Ferber, ed., Selected Aspects of Consumer Behavior, Washington, D.C.: NSF Government Printing Office, 1977, pp. 223-38, Everett M. Rogers, *Diffusion of Innovations*, 3rd ed. (New York: Free Press, 1983), p. 281-84. Also see Pam Schroder Ellen, William O. Bearden, and Subhash Sharma, "Resistance to Technological Innovations: An Examination of the Role of Self-Efficacy and performance Satisfaction," *J. of the Academy of Marketing Science* 19, no. 4, (Fall 1991), pp. 297-307; S. Ram and Jagdish N. Sheth, "Hurdling the Barriers to Technological Innovation," *R&D Strategist* (Fall 1990), pp. 4-14.

11. Ibid

12. For a classic treatment of nostalgia, see F. Davis, Yearning for Yesterday: A Sociology of Nostalgia, New York, The Free Press.

13. Based on author's reflections.

14. For recent studies on consumer nostalgia, see Robert M. Schindler and Morris H. Holbrook, "Nostalgia for Early Experiences as a Determinant of Consumer Preferences," *Psychology & Marketing*, 2003, 20, 4, 275-302.

15. Stauth, Georg, and Bryan S. Turner. "Nostalgia, Postmodernism and the Critique of Mass Culture." Theory, Culture and Society 5.2-3 (1988): 509-26.

16. For a scholarly study, see S. Brown, R.V. Kozinets, and J.F. Sherry, Jr. "Teaching Old Brands New Tricks: Retro Branding And The Revival Of Brand Meaning," *J. of Marketing*, 2003, 67, 19-33.

17. Lesley Speed, Together in Electric Dreams: Films Revisiting 1980s Youth. *Journal of Popular Film and Television*, Spring, 2000.

CHAPTER 5

1. See Milton Rokeach, *The Nature of Human Values* (New York: Free Press, 1973); David E. Vinson, Jerome E. Scott, and Lawrence Lamont, "The Role of Personal Values in Marketing and Consumer Behavior," *J. of Marketing* 41 (April 1977), 44–50.

2. The list is protected as intellectual property by Consulting Psychology Press. The examples given here are based on intuition and are merely to serve as illustrations that logically exemplify the two types of values, without implying whether these items in fact belong in the Rokeach list. Interested readers can find a list in Rokeach, ibid; moreover, a simple Google search will bring up hundreds of Web pages listing the values in their entirety, as it did at least as of May 1, 2006.

3. The nine LOV values were developed by the Survey Research Center at the University of Michigan, as reported in Lynn Kahle R. (ed.), *Social Values and Social Change: Adaptation to Life in America*, New

York, Praeger, 1983. An exposition of these values for marketing can be found in subsequent research studies:
Lynn R. Kahle, Sharon E. Beatty, and Pamela Homer, "Alternative Measurement Approaches to Consumer Values: The List of Values (LOV) and Values and Life Style (VALS)," *J. of Consumer Research* 13 (December 1986), pp. 405–409; Sharon Beatty, Lynn R. Kahle, Pamela Homer, and Shekhar Misra, "Alternative Measurement Approaches to Consumer Values: The List of Values and the Rokeach Value Survey," *Psychology & Marketing* 2 (Fall 1985), 181–200.

4. Kahle, Beatty, and Homer, 1986, Ibid.

5. For further reading, see "Value-System Segmentation: Exploring the Meaning of LOV," *Kamakura*, Wagner A. and *Novak*, Thomas P.. *J. of Consumer Research*, Jun 92, 19(1), 119-132.

6. Rajeev Batra, Pamela M. Homer, and Lynn R. Kahle, "Values, Susceptibility to Normative Influence, and Attribute Importance Weights," *J. of Consumer Psychology*, 2001, 11(2), 115-128.

7. Irene Tilikidou and Antonia Delistavrou,, "Utilisation of Selected Demographics and Psychographics in Understanding Recycling Behaviour," Greener Management International, Summer2001, 34, 75-94.

8. Thomas J Reynolds and Jonathan Gardner, Laddering Theory, Method, Analysis, and Interpretation," *J. of Advertising Research*, 28 (January–February 1988), pp. 11–31; also see Thomas J. Reynolds and Alyce Byrd Craddock, "The Application of the MECCAs Model to the Development and Assessment of Advertising Strategy: A Case Study," *J. of Advertising Research* (April/May 1988), pp. 43–54. And for some recent suggestions in research method, see Arch G. Woodside, "Advancing Means-End Chains by Incorporating Heider's Balance Theory and Fournier's Consumer Brand Relationship Typology," *Psychology & Marketing*, Vol. 21, #4, April 2004, 279-294. Also see Gillian Sullivan Mort and Trista Rose, "The effect of product type on value linkages in the means-end chain: Implications for theory and method," *J. of Consumer Behaviour*, Mar2004, Vol. 3 Issue 3, 221-35; and Simon Manyiwa and Ian Crawford, "Determining linkages between consumer choices in a social context and the consumer's values: A means--end approach, " *J. of Consumer Behaviour*, Sep2002, 2(1), 54-71.

9. For research on compulsivity as a personality influence, see George Balabanis , "The relationship between lottery ticket and scratch-card buying behaviour, personality and other compulsive behaviours," *J. of Consumer Behaviour*, Sep2002, 2(1), 7-23.

10. Actually, there are other important theories: among them Humanistic Theories – which view a person's development as a function of his or her view of the world learning from environment as well as pursuit of self-actualization goals, and Social Cognition Theories which see a person's personality as a result of a person's cognition of our own beliefs, values, abilities and of environmental constraints and factors (such as oppression and our value system that makes us view that oppression as unjust can develop us into a rebel and freedom fighter personality.). These theories are not covered here, although many ideas related to them would be covered elsewhere— for example, Maslow's hierarchy of motives which has its roots in Humanistic theory, and many personal ability factors such as locus of control, self-efficacy and self-monitoring which have their basis in Social Cognition Theories.

11. See Freud, S. (1923). *The Ego and the Id*. New York: W.W. Norton & Company

12. For a more formal definition and treatment of personality and trait theory, see Ernest Hilgard, Richard Atkinson, and Rita Atkinson, *Introduction to Psychology*, 6th ed. (New York: Harcourt Brace Jovanovich, Inc., 1975); and Walter Mischel, "On the Future of Personality Measurement," *American Psychologist*, 32 (1977), p. 2.

13. For other views and further reading on personality, see Paul J. Albanese *The Personality Continuum and Consumer Behavior* (Quorum Books, 2002) and Albanese, "The Personality, Consumer Behavior, and Marketing Research: A New Theoretical and Empirical Approach," *Research in Consumer Behavior*, vol. 4, (1990), pp. 1-50. Add Albanese (1990) on p. 18. Also see, Morris B. Holbrook, "The

Psychoanalytic Interpretation of the Consumer Behavior: I Am an Animal," (1988), *Research in Consumer Behavior*, vol. 3, 149-178, and Morris B. Holbrook, Consumer Research: Introspective Essays on the Study of Consumption (Sage, 1995).

14. R.B. Cattell, H.W. Eber, and M.M. Tatsuoka, Handbook for the Sixteen Personality Factor Questionnaire (Champaign, IL: Institute for Personality and Ability Testing, 1970).

15. For a different, equally rigorous view, see John C. Mowen, *The 3-M Model of Motivation and Personality* (Kluwer, 2000). For further reading, see John, O. P. (1990). The "Big Five" factor taxonomy: Dimensions of personality in the natural language and in questionnaires. In L. A. Pervin (Ed.), *Handbook of personality: Theory and research* (pp. 66-100). New York: Guilford; McAdams, D. P. (1992), "The five-factor model in personality: A critical appraisal," *Journal of Personality*, 60, 329-361.

16. This Acronym appears in Rod Plotnik, *Introduction to Psychology*, Sixth edition, Wadsworth, 2002. p.463.

17. Elizabeth C. Hirschman and Barbara B. Stern, "Do Consumer's Genes Influence Their Behavior: Findings on Novelty Seeking and Compulsive Consumption," ACR, XXVIII, Mary C. Gilly and Joan Myers-Levy (eds), 2001, 28, 403-410.

18. J.C. Loehlin, *Genes and Environment in Personality Development*, Newbury Park, CA, Sage, 1992.

19. *Cambridge Advanced Learner's Dictionary* © Cambridge University Press 2003.

20. For a closely related definition, see http://en.wikipedia.org/wiki/Vanity.

21. Richard G. Netemeyer, Scot Burton, and Donald R. Lichtenstein. "Trait Aspects Of Vanity: Measurement and Relevance to Consumer Behavior," *J. of Consumer Research*, 21, March 1995, 612-625.

22. Robert H. Frank, Luxury Fever: Why Money Fails to Satisfy in an Era of Excess, Princeton University Press, 2000.

23. Harold H. Kassarjian, "Personality and Consumer Behavior: A Review," *J. of Marketing Research*, Vol. 8 (November 1971), pp. 409–418. Also see Paul J. Albanese, "The Personality, Consumer Behavior, an Marketing Research: A New Theoretical and Empirical Approach," *Research in Consumer Behavior*, vol. 4, (1990), pp. 1-50.

24. For a state-of-the-art review of self-theory in the context of people's work life, see Robert A. Snyder and Ronald R. Williams, "Self-Theory: An Integrative Theory of Work Motivation," *J. of Occupational Psychology* 55 (1982), p. 257–67. For more current treatment, see Paul J. Albanese *The Personality Continuum and Consumer Behavior* (Quorum Books, 2002), 113-114.

25. For discussions of self-concept, see M. Joseph Sirgy, "Self-Concept in Consumer Behavior: A Critical Review," *J. of Consumer Research* (December 1982), pp. 287–300; also, Harold H. Kassarjian, "Personality and Consumer Behavior: A Review," J. of Marketing Research, Vol. 8 (November 1971), pp. 409–418. M. Joseph Sirgy, "Using Self-congruity and Ideal Congruity to Predict Purchase Motivation," *J. of Business Research*, Vol. 13 (June 1985), pp. 195–206. Warren S. Martin and Joseph Bellizzi, "An Analysis of Congruence Relationship between Self Images and Product Images," *J. of the Academy of Marketing Science*, December 1982, 473–488.

26. Beyond brand choice, many of our leisure activities also are influenced by self-concept; for recent research, see Peggy Sue Loroz, "Golden Age Gambling: Psychological Benefits and Self-Concept Dynamics in Aging Consumers' Consumption Experiences," Psychology & Marketing, Vol. 21(5), May 2004, 323-349.

27. Adapted from Author's working paper of the same title, 2004.

28. Yi-Fu Tuan, Space and Place: The Perspective of Experience, Minneapolis, MN: University of Minnesota Press (1978)

29. William James, The Principles of Psychology 1, 1890, New York, Henry Holt, Quoted in Russell W. Belk, "Possessions and the Extended Self", J. of Consumer Research 15, (1988), pp. 139

30. Russell W. Belk, (1988), ibid pp. 151.

CHAPTER 6

1. Adapted from William D. Wells and Douglas J. Tigert," Activities, Interests, and Opinions," *Journal of Advertising Research* 11 (August 1971), p. 35.

2. Adapted from The Clustered World: How We Live, What We Buy, And What It All Means About Who We Are (Little, Brown And Company) by Michael J. Weiss

3. Adapted from Author's working paper, 2004.

4. "Focus Sponsors Area: One Festival," Ford Motor Company Press Release, April 23, 2001.

5. Hilary Cassidy, "Saucony Laces Up for Lifestyle Effort," *Brandweek*, Feb 5, 2001.

6. Elizabeth Goodgold, **"Talking shop: wonder what makes shoppers tick? 5 retail superstars reveal how to please customers and, more important, how to keep them coming back for more."** *Entrepreneur*, Sept, 2003.

7. Rebecca Piirto, "Global Psychographics," American Demographics 12, no. 12 (December 1990) p. 8.

8. Russell W. Belk, "Materialism: Trait Aspects of Living in the Material World," *J. of Consumer Research* 12 (December 1985), pp. 265—80.

9. Marsha L. Richins and Scott Dawson, "A Consumer Values Orientation and Its Measurement: Scale Development and Validation," *J. of Consumer Research*, 19, 3 (December 1992), p. 385.

10. For academic research on this topic, see Margaret Craig-Lees and Constance Hill, "Understanding Voluntary Simplifiers," *Psychology & Marketing*, 2002(Feb), 19(2), 187-210; Diedre Shaw and Terry Newholm, "Voluntary Simplicity and the Ethics of Consumption," Psychology & Marketing, 2002(Feb), 19(2), 167-186; and Steven Zavestoski, "The Social-Psychological Bases of Anticonsumption Attitudes," *Psychology & Marketing*, 2002(Feb), 19(2), 149-165.

11. Stephen Zavestoski, "The Social-Psychological Bases of Anti-consumption Attitudes." *Psychology & Marketing*, 2002, 19(2), Feb, 149-169.

12. Veblen, Thorstein, *The Theory of the Leisure Class* (Oxford World's Classics), Oxford University Press, USA (January 11, 2008)

13. Clark, Ronald, A., Zboja, James, J., and Goldsmith, Ronald E., "Status Consumption and Role-relaxed Consumption: A tale of two retail consumers," *Journal of Retailing and Consumer Service*s, Vol. 14, Issue 1, January 2007, Pages 45–59.

14. Brooks, John, "Showing Off in America: From Conspicuous consumption to Parody Display," Book Sales; 1st edition, 1984.

15. "A ZIP+4 code uses the basic 5-digit ZIP plus an additional 4-digits to identify a geographic segment within the 5-digit delivery area, such as a city block, a group of apartments, an individual high-volume receiver of mail, or any other unit that could use an extra identifier to aid in efficient mail sorting and delivery." Wikipedia. org (DoA: January 5, 2006).

16. Michael J. Weiss, *The Clustered World*, 2000, New York, Little Brown and Company.

CHAPTER 7

1. Gordon W. Allport, "Attitudes," in C.A. Murchinson, ed., *A Handbook of Social Psychology* (Worcester, MA: Clark University Press, 1935), pp. 798-844.

2. See story in Julia Boorstin, "For God's Sake," *Fortune*, November 24, 2003, p. 62.

3. See, Revole: The Complete New Testament, Nelson Bibles, 2003.

4. For recent research, see Sharon E. Beatty and Lynn R. Kahle, "Alternative Hierarchies of the Attitude-Behavior Relationships: The Impact of Brand Commitment and Habit," *J. of the Academy of Marketing Science*, 1988, 16, 1-10. "The Integrated Information Response Model," Finn, David W.. *J. of Advertising*, 1984, 13(1),

24-33. "Web Commercials and Advertising Hierarchy-of-Effects," Bruner II, Gordon C.; Kumar, Anand. *J. of Advertising Research*, Jan-Apr2000, 40 (1 & 2), 35-43; "Point of View: Does Advertising Cause a "Hierarchy of Effects"?" Weilbacher, William M.. *J. of Advertising Research*, Nov/Dec2001, Vol. 41 Issue 6, p19-26,

5. For research on how the hierarchy works for Web sites, see Gordon Bruner, and Anand Kumar, "Web Commercials and Advertising Hierarchy of Effects," *J. of Adv. Res.*, Jan. 2000, 35-43; and J.S. Stevenson, Gordon Bruner, and Anand Kumar, "Web page Background and Viewer Attitudes," *J. of Adv. Res.*, Jan. 2000, 29-34.

6. Daniel Katz, "The Functional Approach to the Study of Attitudes," *Public Opinion Quarterly*, 1960, Summer, 24, 163-204. Also see, Sharon Shavitt, "The Role of Attitude Objects in Attitude Functions," *J. of Experimental Social Psychology*, 1990, 26, 124-48. Also see R. Grewal, R. Mehta, and F.R. Kardes, "The Role of Social Identity Function of Attitudes in Consumer Innovativeness and Opinion Leadership, *J. of Economic Psychology*, 21, 2000, 233-52.

7. For further reading, see "Why We Evaluate: Functions of Attitudes," Gregory R. Maio and James M. Olson (eds.), Lawrence Erlbaum Associates (November, 1999).

8. For research studies, see "Attitude functions in consumer research: comparing value-attitude relations individualist and collectivist cultures," Gregory, Gary D.; Munch, James M.; Peterson, Mark. *J. of Bus. Research*, Nov2002, 55(11), 933-942. "Attitude Functions in Advertising: The Interactive Role of Products and Self-Monitoring," Shavitt, Sharon; Lowrey, Tina M.; Han, Sang-Pil. *J. of Consumer Psychology*, 1992, 1(4), 337-65. "A reconceptualization of the functional approach to attitudes." Lutz, Richard J., Research in Marketing, 1981, 5, 165-70.

9. The acronym TORA existed in prior writings; TOVA and TOTA are proposed by author to help reader "encoding."

10. Martin Fishbein, "An Investigation of the Relationships between Beliefs about an Object and the Attitude toward that Object," *Human Relations*, 1983, 16, 233-40. For some applied research using this theory, see Richard P. Bagozzi, Hans Baumgartner, and Youjae Yu, "Coupon Usage and the Theory of Reasoned Action," in Rebecca Holman and Michael R. Solomon, eds. Advances in Consumer Research, 1991, 18, 24-27; and Terence A. Shimp and Alican Cavas, "The Theory of Reasoned Action Applied to Coupon Usage," *J. of Consumer Research*, 1984, 11, 795-809.

11. For recent research studies using the Fishbein model, see "Consumer attitude toward US versus domestic apparel in Taiwan,"Wang, Yun; Heitmeyer, Jeanne. *International J. of Cons. Studies*, Jan2006, 30(1), 64-74; "Investigating Consumer Responsiveness to Service Contract Attributes: A Choice Experimental Approach," Oppewal, Harmen; Grant, David J.I.. *Advances in Cons. Res.* 2002, 29(1), 133-138. "Modeling Personal and Normative Influences on Behavior," Miniard, Paul W.; Cohen, Joel B., *J. of Consumer Research*, Sep83, 10(2), 169-71. "An Experimental Investigation of Causal Relations Among Cognitions, Affect, and Behavioral Intention," Lutz, Richard J., *J. of Cons. Res.*, Mar77, 3(4), 197-209; Kulwant Singh, Siew Meng Leong, Chin Tiong Tan, and Kwei Cheong Wong, "A Theory of reasoned Action Perspective of Voting Behavior: Model and Empirical test," *Psychology & Marketing*, 12, No. 1, January 1995, 37-51.

12. For an application of this idea to personal selling, see Arun Sharma, and Michael Levy, "Salespeople's Affect Toward Customers: Why Should It Be Important for Retailers," *J. of Business Research*, July 2003, 56(7), 523-528.

13. See, D.S. Kempf, "Attitude Formation from Product Trial," *Psychology & Marketing*, January 1999, 35-50; and also Michel Laroche, Frank Pons, Nadia Zgolli, Marie-Cecile Cervellon, and Chankon Kim, "A Model of Consumer response to Two Retail Sales Promotion Techniques," *J. of Bus. Res.*, July 2003, 56(7), 513-522.

14. The theory, more properly called a Theory of Trying is owed to marketing professors Richard P. Bagozzi and Paul R. Warshaw: "Trying to Consume," *J. of Cons. Res.*, 17 (September 1990), 127-40.

15. For recent studies, see "The Theory of Trying and Goal-Directed Behavior: The Effect of Moving Up the Hierarchy of Goals," Bay, Darlene; Daniel, Harold. *Psych. & Marketing*, 2003,20(8), 669-684.

CHAPTER 8

1. Source: http://www.spain-info.com/Culture/bullrunning.htm (DoA: December 11, 2005.)

2. Source: http://www.runningofthenudes.com/index.asp (DoA: December 11, 2005.)

3. Source: http://furisdead.com/feat-jcrewvictory.asp (DoA: December 12, 2005).

4. For a State-of-the-art review, see Meyers-Levy, Joan and Prashant Malaviya, "Consumers' Processing of Persuasive Advertisements: An Integrative Framework of Persuasion Theories," *J. of Marketing,* 1999, 63, Special Issue, 45-60.

5. Richard Vaughn, "How Advertising Works: A Planning Model," *J. of Advertising Research,* 1980, 20(5), 27-33; Brian T. *Ratchford,* "New Insights About The FCB Grid," *J. of Advertising Research,* Aug/Sep1987, 27(4), 24-38.

6. This theory was proposed by Richard E. Petty, John T. Cacioppo, and David Schumann, "Central and Peripheral Routes to Advertising Effectiveness: The Moderating Role of Involvement," *J. of Cons. Res.,* 1983, 10, 135-46. Recent research on this topic includes, J. Craig Andrews and Terence A Shimp, "Effects of Involvement, Argument Strength, and Source Characteristics on Central and Peripheral Processing in Advertising," *Psychology and Marketing,* 1990, Fall, 7, 195-214.

7. Also see Peter W. Reed and Michael T. Ewing. "How Advertising Works: Alternative Situational and Attitudinal Explanations," *Marketing Theory,* Mar 2004, 4(1/2), 91-112.

8. Petty, R.E., and Cacioppo, John T. (1986), "The Elaboration Likelihood Model of Persuasion", *Advances in Experimental Social Psych.,* ed. L. Berkowitz, 19, Orlando, FL: Academic Press, 123-205.

9. For recent research, see "Self-Schema Matching and Attitude Change: Situational and Dispositional Determinants of Message Elaboration," Wheeler, S. Christian; Petty, Richard E., Bizer, George Y., *J. of Consumer Res.,* Mar2005, 31(4), 787-797.

10. For a scholarly treatment, see Joel B. Cohen, Joel B. and Americus Reed II (2004), "Multiple Attitudes as Guides to Behavior," Working Paper, Marketing Department, Warrington College of Business, University of Florida, Gainesville, FL.

11. For research on this topic, see Richard J Lutz, "Changing Brand Attitude through Modification of Cognitive Structure," *J. of Consumer Research,* 1975, 1, 49-59.

12. Fritz Heider, "Attitudes and Cognitive Organization," *J. of Psychology,* 21, 1946, 107-12; also, Robert Zajonc "The Concepts of Balance, Congruity, and Dissonance," in *Attitude Change,* P. Suedfeld, ed. Chicago, Ill: Aldine, Atherton, Inc. 1971.

13. See Kelly, H. H. (1973), "The Process of Causal Attribution," *American Psychologist,* 28 (February), 107-28.

14. Settle, Robert B., and Golden, Linda L. (1974), "Attribution Theory and Advertiser Credibility," *J. of Marketing Research,* 11, 181-185; Richard W. Mizerski, Linda L Golden, and *Jerome* B. *Kernan,* "The Attribution Process in Consumer Decision Making," *J. of Consumer Research,* Sep1979, 6(2), 23-40.

15. Bem, D. J. (1972) Self-perception theory, In L. Berkowitz (ed), *Advances in Experimental Social Psychology,* (Vol. 6. pp. 1-62), New York: Academic Press.

16. For various academic studies, see Alice M. Tybout, "The Relative Effectiveness of Three Behavioral Influence Strategies as Supplements to Persuasion in a Marketing Context," *J. of Marketing Res.,* 1978, 15 (May), 229-42. Freedman, J. L. and S. Frazer (1966), "Compliance Without Pressure: The Foot-in-the-Door Technique," *J. of Personality and Social Psychology,* 4 (October), 195-202. Cialdini, R. B. J. E. Vincent, S. K. Lewis, J. Catalan, D. Wheeler, and B. L. Darby (1975), "Reciprocal Concessions Procedure for Inducing Compliance: The Door-in-the-Face *Technique," J. of Personality and Social Psychology,* 31 (February), 206-15. P. H. Reingen, "On Inducing Compliance With Requests," *J. of Cons. Res.,* 1978, 5 (Sept.), 96-102.

17. See Francis Buttle, "What Do People Do With Advertising?" *International J. of Advertising,* 1991, 10(2), 95-110.

18. See "Effects of Absurdity In Advertising: The Moderating Role of Product Category Attitude and the Mediating Role of Cognitive Responses," Leopoldo Arias-Bolzmann, Goutam Chakraborty, and John C. Mowen, *J. of Advertising,* Spring 2000, 29(1), 35-50; "A cross-cultural comparison of cognitive responses, beliefs, and attitudes toward advertising in general in two Asian countries," Durvasula, Srinivas; Lysonski, Steven, Subhash C. Mehta, *J. of Marketing Management,* Winter 1999, 9(3), 48-59; Amitava Chattopadhyay, Darren W. Dahl, Robin J.B. Ritchie, Kimary N. Shahin, "Hearing Voices: The Impact of Announcer Speech Characteristics on Consumer Response to Broadcast Advertising," *J. of Consumer Psychology,* 2003, 13(3), 198-204; Alice M. Tybout, Brian Sternthal, and Bobby J. Calder, "A two-stage theory of information processing in persuasion: an integrative view of cognitive response and self-perception theory," *Advances in Cons. Res.,* 1978, 5(1), 721-723; Self-Validation of Cognitive Responses to Advertisements, Briñol, Pablo; Petty, Richard E.; Tormala, Zakary L., *J. of Consumer Research.,* 2004, 30(4), 559-573.

19. This insight is owed to a classic paper, Herbert E. Krugman, "The Impact of Television Advertising: Learning without Involvement," *Public Opinion Quarterly,* 1965 Fall, 349-356.

20. For research literature on this topic, see Scott B. Mackenzie and Richard J Lutz, and George E. Belch, "The Role of Attitude toward the Ad as a Mediator of Advertising Effectiveness: A Test of Competing Explanations," *J. of Marketing Res.,* 1986, 23, 130-43; Scot Burton and Donald R. Lichtenstein, "The Effect of Ad Claims and Ad Context on Attitude toward the Advertisement," *J. of Advertising,* 1988, 17, 1, 3-11; and Meryl P. Gardner, "Does Attitude toward the Ad Affect Brand Attitude Under A Brand Evaluation Set?" *J. of Marketing Research.,* 1985, 22, 192-98.

21. Also see Jennifer L. Aaker and P. Williams, "Empathy versus pride: The influence of emotional appeals across cultures," *J. of Cons. Res.,* 1998, 25, 241-261; Karen A. Machleit and R. D. Wilson, "Emotional Feelings And Attitude Toward The Advertisement: The Roles Of Brand Familiarity And Repetition," *J. of Advertising,* 1988, 17(3), 27-35.

22. On public attitudes toward advertising, see Sharon Shavitt, Pamela Lowrey, and James Haefner, "Public Attitudes Toward Advertising: More Favorable Than You Might Think," *J. of Advertising. Research.,* 1998 Issue July, 7-22.

23. For comprehensive understanding, see James Price Dillard and Jason W. Anderson, "The Role of Fear in Persuasion," *Psych. & Marketing,* 2004, 21(11), 909-926; Tony L. Henthorne, Michael S. LaTour, and Rajan Nataraajan, "Fear Appeals in Print Advertising: An Analysis of Arousal, and Ad Response," *J. of Advertising,* 1993 (Summer), 59-69; Omar Shehryar and Hunt, David M Hunt, "A Terror Management Perspective on the Persuasiveness of Fear Appeals," *J. of Consumer Psychology,* 2005, 15(4), 275-287; Damien Arthur and Pascale Quester, "Who's Afraid of That Ad? Applying Segmentation to the Protection Motivation Model," *Psych. & Marketing,* 2004, 21(9), 671-696; Lucy Cochrane and P. Quester, "Fear in Advertising: The Influence of Consumers' Product Involvement and Culture," *J. of International Consumer Marketing,* 2005, Vol. 17 Issue 2/3, p7-32; John C. Mowen and Eric G. Harris and Sterling A. Bone, "Personality Traits and Fear Response to Print Advertisements: Theory and an Empirical Study," *Psychology & Marketing,* 2004, 21 (11) 927-943.

24. For research studies, see Stephen M. Smith and Curtis P Haugtvedt, "Understanding Responses to Sex Appeals in Advertising: An Individual Difference Approach," *Advances in Cons. Res.,* 1995, 22 (1), 735-739; Michael S. LaTour and Tony L. Henthorne, "Ethical Judgments of Sexual Appeals in Print Advertising," *J. of Advertising,* 1994 (Fall) 81-90; Stephen J. Gould, "Sexuality and Ethics in Advertising: A Research Agenda and Policy Guideline Perspective," *J. of Advertising,* 1994, 23(1), 73-80; Ming-

Hui Huang, "Romantic Love and Sex: Their Relationship and Impacts on Ad Attitudes," *Psych. & Marketing*, 2004, 21(1), 53-73.

25. See Michael S. LaTour, "Female nudity in print advertising: An analysis of gender differences in arousal and ad response," *Psych. & Marketing*, 1990, 7)1), 65-81.

26. See Golden, Linda L., and Alpert, Mark I. (1987), "Comparative Analysis of the Relative Effectiveness of One-and Two-Sided Communication for Contrasting Products," *J. of Advertising*, 16,18-25; Hastak, Manoj, and Park, Jong-Won (1990), "Mediators of Message Sidedness Effects on Cognitive Structure for Involved and Uninvolved Audience," *Advances in Consumer Research*, 17, 329-336; Crowley, Ayn E., and Wayne D. Hoyer, (1994), "An Integrative Framework for Understanding Two-sided Persuasion," *J. of Consumer Research*, 20, 561-574. Etgar, Michael, and Goodwin, Stephen A (1982), "One-Sided versus Two-Sided Comparative Message Appeals for New Brand Introduction," *J. of Consumer Research*, 8, 460-465; Hastak, Manoj, and Park, Jong-Won (1990), "Mediators of Message Sidedness Effects on Cognitive Structure for Involved and Uninvolved Audience," *Advances in Cons. Res.*, 17, 329-336; Michael A. Kamins, and Henry Assael, "Two-sided versus One-sided Appeals: A Cognitive Perspective on Argumentation, Source Derogation, and the Effect of Disconfirming Trial on Belief Change," *J. of Marketing Research*, 1987, 24, 29-39; Kamins, Michael A., Brand, Meribeth J., Hoeke, Stuart A., and Moe, John C. (1998), "Two-Sided Versus One-Sided Celebrity Endorsements: The Impact on Advertising Effectiveness and Credibility," *J. of Advertising*, 18, 4-10; Belch, George E. (1981), "An Examination of Comparative and Non comparative Television Commercials: The Effect of Claim Variation and Repetition on Cognitive Response and Message Acceptance," *J. of Mark Res.*, 18, 222-249.

27. See Sawyer, Alan G. (1973), "The effects of Repetition of Reputational and Supportive Advertising Appeals," *J. of Mark Res.*, 10, 22-23.

28. See McGuire, William J. (1961), "The Effectiveness of Supportive and Reputational Defenses in Immunizing and Restoring Beliefs Against Persuasion," *Sociometry*, 24, 184-197; "The Application of Attitude Immunization Techniques in Marketing," Stewart W. Either, *J. of Marketing Research*, 1971, 8(February), 56-61.

29. For academic research, see S. Putrevu and Kenneth R. Lord, "Comparative and noncomparative advertising: attitudinal effects under cognitive and affective involvement conditions," *J. of Advertising*, 1994, 23 (June), 77-91; Kawpong Polyorat and Dana L. Alden, "Self-construal and need-for-cognition effects on brand attitudes and purchase intentions in response to comparative advertising in Thailand and the United States," *J. of Advertising*, 2005, 34 (1), 37-48; "Attitude toward a Comparative Advertisement: The Role of an Endorser." Raju, Sekar, Rajagopal, Priyali, Unnava, H. Rao. *Advances in Cons. Res.*, 2002, 29(1), 480-481.

30. William R. Swinyard (1981), "The Interaction between Comparative Advertising and Copy Variation," *J. of Mark Res.*, 18,175-186.

31. For further academic studies on this topic, see G. Belch, "An examination of comparative and noncomparative television commercials: The effects of claim variation and repetition on cognitive response and message acceptance," *J. of Marketing Research*, 1981,18, 333-349; "A cross-country investigation of recall and attitude toward comparative advertising," Donthu, N., J. of Advertising; 1998, 27(2), 111-122; M. Etgar "One-sided versus two-sided comparative message appeals for new brand introductions," *J. of Consumer Research*, 1982, 8, 460-465; "Comparative Advertising Effectiveness: The Role of Involvement and Source Credibility," Gotlieb, Jerry B. and Sarel, Dan *J. of Advertising*, 1991, 20(1), 38-45; "Comparative versus Noncomparative Advertising: A Meta-Analysis," Grewal, Dhruv; Kavanoor, Sukumar; Fern, Edward F.; Costley, Carolyn; Barnes, James, *J. of Marketing*, 1997, 61(4), 1-15; "The Effects of Information Processing Modes on Consumers' Reactions to Comparative Advertising," Thompson, Debora Viana and Hamitton, Rebecca W., Advances in Consumer Research, 2005, 32, 560-560; "Comparative Advertising Effectiveness: A Cross-Cultural Study," Shao, Alan T., Bao, Yeqing Gray, Elizabeth. *J. of Current Issues & Research in Advertising*, Fall 2004, 26(2), 67-80; Modelling consumer response to differing levels of comparative advertising, Del Barrio-García, Salvador; Luque-Martínez, Teodoro. *European J. of Marketing*, 2003, 37 (1/2), 256-274.

32. For research study, see "Source Credibility and Attitude Certainty: A Metacognitive Analysis of Resistance to Persuasion," Tormala, Zakary L., Petty, Richard E.. *J. of Cons. Psychology*, 2004,14(4), 427-442. "Prepurchase Attribute Verifiability, Source Credibility, and Persuasion," Jain, Shailendra Pratap; Posavac, Steven S., *J. of Cons. Psychology*, 2001, 11(3), 169-180; Grewal, Dhruv, Gotlieb, Jerry, and Marmorstein, Howard, "The moderating effects of message framing and source credibility on the price-perceived risk," J. of Consumer Research, June 94, 21(1), 145-54.

33. See Michael A. Kamins, "An investigation into the `match-up' hypothesis in celebrity advertising: When beauty may be only skin deep," *J. of Advertising*, 1990, 19(1) 4-13. Stephen K. Koernig and Albert L. Page, "What If Your Dentist Looked Like Tom Cruise? Applying the Match-Up Hypothesis to a Service Encounter," *Psychology & Marketing*, 2002, 19(1), 91-110. Brian D Till and Michael Busler, "The Match-Up Hypothesis: Physical Attractiveness, Expertise, and the Role of Fit on Brand Attitude, Purchase Intent and Brand Beliefs," *J. of Advertising*, 2000, 29(3), 1-13.

34. For an academic framework, see Robert Cialdini and Noah Goldstein, "Social Influence: Compliance and Conformity," *J. Annual Review of Psychology*, 2004, 55(Feb.), 591-621.

35. For a State-of-the-Art scholarly work on this topic, see Robert B. Cialdini, "The Science of Persuasion," *Scientific American*, Jan 2004 Special Edition, 14(1), 70-77.

CHAPTER 9

1. For a classical description, see Robin M. Williams , 1970, *American Society: A Sociological Perspective*, 3rd ed. New York, Knopf. But note, that treatment is quite dated; the present author has culled only those values that are deemed relevant today and re-profiled them to reflect current embodiment of those values.

2. Paraphrased by author based on such source literatures as Robin M. Williams, *American Society: A Sociological Interpretation*, NY, Knopf, 1960; C.M. Seah, *Asian Values and Modernization*, 1997, Singapore, Singapore University Press; William Theodore de Bary, *Asian Values and Human Rights: A Confucian Communitarian Perspective*, Harvard University Press, 2000; William K. Cummings, "Asian values, education and development," *Compare: A Journal of Comparative Education*, 1996, Vol. 26, Issue 3, 287-95.

3. Geert Hofstede, *Cultural Consequences: International Differences in Work-Related Value* (Beverly Hills, CA: Sage,1980); Geert Hofstede and Michael H. Bond, "Hofstede's Culture Dimensions: An Independent Validation Using Rokeach's Value Survey," *Journal of Cross-Cultural Psychology*, 15 (December 1984), pp. 417-33. Hofstede G. *Culture and Organizations: Software of the Mind*, London: Mc Graw-Hill, 1991.

4. Also see, Fons Trompenaars & Charles M. Hampden-Turner, *Building Cross-cultural Competence: How to Create Wealth from Conflicting Values*. Yale University Press, November 2000; also see, Trompennars F. *Riding the Waves of Culture. Understanding Diversity in Global Business*, New York: Professional Publishing, 1994.

5. See for example, Han Sang-Pil, Shavitt S. Persuasion and Culture: Advertising Appeals in Individualistic and Collectivistic Societies. *Journal of Experimental Social Psychology 1994;* 30 (July): 8-18; Tse DK., Belk RW, Zhou N. "Becoming a Consumer Society: A Longitudinal and Cross-cultural Content Analysis of Print Ads from Hong Kong, The People's republic of China, and Taiwan," *Journal of Consumer Research* 1989; Vol. 15, (March): 457-472; Pollay RW. Measuring the Cultural Values Manifest in Advertising. In *Current Issues and Research in Advertising*, James H. Leigh and Claude R.

Martin (eds), Ann Arbor: MI: University of Michigan Press, 1983. pp 72-92.

6. Although it is not a value but a behavioral characteristic (the way people communicate – explicitly or not), for tactical efficiency, we incorporate it under universal "value" dimensions.

7. Adapted from http://www.japanesekimono.com/kimono_patterns.htm

8. Compiled by author from various sources including: *Signature Bride Magazine*, Spring 1998 issue as cited in **http://www.africanweddingguide.com/history/lobola.html**; and **Sudheer Birodkar,** "Dowry, Sati and Child Marriage"sudheerbirodkar@yahoo.com sudheerbirodkar@yahoo.com

9. For further reading, see Don Slater, *Consumer Culture and Modernity*, Polity Press, 1997; D.A. Briley, M.W. Morris, and I. Simpson, "Reasons as Carriers of Culture," *J. of Consumer Research*, Sept. 2000, 157-77.

10. Further reading: D.A. Ricks, *Big Business Blunders*, Homewood, Illinois, Dow Jones-Irwin, 1983.

11. Several academic studies of cultural themes in advertising across different countries are worth reading; these include Caillat, Zahna., and Barbara Mueller. (1996), "The Influence of Culture on American and British Advertising: An Exploratory Comparison of Beer Advertising," *Journal of advertising Research*, 36 (3), 79 – 87; Cho B, Kwon U, Gentry JW, Jun S, Kropp F. Cultural Values Reflected in Theme and Execution: A Comparative Study of U.S. and Korean Television Commercials. *Journal of Advertising* 1999; 28 (4), 59-73; Cutler, Bob. D., and Raj Shekhar G. Javalgi. (1992), "A Cross-Cultural Analysis of Visual Components of Print Advertising: The United States and European Community, *Journal of Advertising Research*, 32 (Jan/Feb), 71- 80; Mueller, B. (1987), "Reflections of Culture: An Analysis of Japanese and American Advertising Appeals," *Journal of Advertising Research*, (June/July), 51-59; Mueller, B. (1992) 'Standardization vs. Specialization: An Examination of Westernization in Japanese Advertising', *Journal of Advertising Research*, 32 (1), 15-24; Cheng H, Schweitzer JC. Cultural Values Reflected in Chinese and U.S Television Commercials. *Journal of Advertising Research* 1996; May/June: 27-45; Albers-Miller ND, Gelb BD. Business Advertising Appeals as Mirror of Cultural Dimensions: A Study of Eleven Countries. *Journal of Advertising* 1996; 25 (Winter): 57-70.

12. For recent research on ethnocentrism, see Magne Supphelen and Terri L. Rittenburg, "Consumer Ethnocentrism When Foreign Products Are Better," *Psychology & Marketing*, 2001(September), 18(9), 907-28. de Ruyter, K. van Birgelen, and M. Wetzels, "Consumer ethnocentrism in International Services Marketing," *International Business Review*, 1998, 7, 185-202.

13. Edward T. Hall, *Beyond Culture*, Garden City, NJ: Doubleday, 1976.

14. Fuat Firat and Alladi Venkatesh, "Postmodernity: The Age of Marketing" *International Journal of Research in Marketing*, Vol. 10, 1993, pp. 227-249 (Quotation on p. 245).

15. Russell W. Belk, "Hyperreality and Globalization: Culture in the Age of Ronald McDonald," *Journal of International Consumer Marketing* 8 (March/April 1995), pp. 23-37.

16. Also see, Mooij, De M. (1998) *Global Marketing and Advertising. Understanding Cultural Paradox.* Sage Publications: California; and Gannon MJ Associates (1994). *Understanding Global Cultures.* Sage Publications.

CHAPTER 10

1. The term was coined by sociologist Herbert H. Hyman in "The Psychology of Status," *Archives of Psychology*, 38, 1942, No. 269.

2. Francis S. Bourne, "Group Influence in Marketing and Public Relations," in *Some Applications of Behavioral Research,* eds. R. Likert and S.P. Hayes (Basil, Switzerland: UNESCO, 1957).

3. William O. Bearden and Michael J. Etzel, "Reference Group Influence on Product and Brand Purchase Decisions," *J. of Consumer Research* 9, (1982), pp. 183-94.

4. See C. Whan Park and V. Parker Lessig, "Students and Housewives: Differences in Susceptibility to Reference Group Influence,ö *J. of Consumer Research* 4, no. 2 (1977), pp. 102-110. and Robert E. Burnkrant and Alain Cousineau, "Informational and Normative Social Influence in Buyer Behavior," *J. of Consumer Research* 2 (December 1975), pp. 206-215.

5. William O. Bearden, Richard G. Netemeyer, and Jesse E. Teel, "Measurement of Consumer Susceptibility to Interpersonal Influence," *J. of Consumer Research*, March 1989, Vol. 15 Issue 4, 473-81.

6. For a non-U.S. study using this concept, see Byoungho Jin and Byungsook Hong , "Consumer Susceptibility to Salesperson Influence in Korean Department Stores," *J. of International Consumer Marketing*, 2004, 17(1), 33-53.

7. Banwari Mittal, Personal Research Files, 2005, 2006, 2009.

8. Leon Festinger. (1954). "A Theory Of Social Comparison Processes," *Human Relations*, 7 (May), 117–140; *William O. Bearden and Randall L. Rose* "Attention to Social Comparison Information: An Individual Difference Factor Affecting Consumer Conformity," *J. of Consumer Research*, March 1990, Vol. 16 Issue 4, p. 461-71.

9. Tamara F. Mangleburg, Patricia M. Doney, and Terry Bristol, "Shopping With Friends And Teens' Susceptibility To Peer Influence," *Journal of Retailing*, 2004 (80), 101-116.

10. Paul Lazarsfeld, B. Berelson, and H. Gaudet (1948). *The People's Choice.* New York: Columbia University Press.

11. For further reading, see, Everett M. Rogers, "New Product Adoption and Diffusion," in R. Ferber, ed., Selected Aspects of Consumer Behavior, Washington, D.C.: NSF Government Printing Office, 1977, pp. 223-38.

12. Ed Keller and Jon Berry, *The Influentials*, Free Press, 2003.

13. Ed Keller and Jon Berry, Ibid.

14. Ed Keller and Jon Berry, Ibid.

15. Everett M. Rogers, *Diffusion of Innovations*, 3rd ed. (New York: Free Press, 1983), p. 281-84; Frank M. Bass, "A New Product Growth Model for Consumer Durables," Management Science, 15 (January 1969), 215-27.

16. Also see, Katz, Elihu (1973), "The Two-step Flow Of Communication: An Up-to-date Report Of An Hypothesis," in Enis and Cox(eds.), *Marketing Classics*, p175-193.

17. Reported in Deidre Breakenridge, *Cyberbranding: Brand Building in the Digital Economy*, Prentice Hall, 2001, p. 140.

CHAPTER 11

1. M. Joseph Sirgy, "A Social Cognition Model of Consumer Problem Recognition," *J. of the Academy of Marketing Science*, Vol. 15, Winter 1987, p. 53-61.

2. Cheryl Burke Jarvis, "An Exploratory Investigation of Consumers' Evaluations of External Information Sources," in Joseph W. Alba and J. Wesley Hutchinson (eds.), *Advances in Consumer Research*, Vol. XXV, p. 446-452, Provo, Utah: Association for Consumer Research, 1998.

3. See Shelley Chaiken, (1980) for a technical discussion of the terms heuristic versus systematic; and Furse, Punj, and Stewart (1984) for discussion of their use by consumers in one study; Shelly Chaiken, "Heuristic versus Systematic Information Processing and the Use of Source versus Message Cues in Persuasion," *J. of Personality and Social Psychology* 39 (November 1980), pp. 752-66; David H. Furse, Girish N. Punj, and David W. Stewart, "A Typology of Individual Search Strategies among Purchasers of New Automobiles," *J. of Consumer Research* 10, no. 4 (March 1984), pp. 417-31.

4. C. Whan Park and V. Parker Lessig, "Familiarity and Its Impact on Consumer Decision Biases and Heuristics," *J. of Consumer Research* 8 (September 1981), pp. 223-30; James R. Bettman and C. W. Park, "Effects of Prior Knowledge and Experience and Phase of Choice Process on Consumer Decision Processes: A Protocol Analysis," *J. of Consumer Research* 7 (December 1980), pp. 234-48.

5. Narasimhan Srinivasan and Brian T. Ratchford, "An Empirical Test of a Model of External Search for Automobiles," *J. of Consumer Research* 18 (September 1991), pp. 233-42; also see Rajan Sambandam and Kenneth R. Lord, "Switching Behavior in Automobile Markets: A Consideration-Sets Model," *J. of the Academy of Marketing Science* 23, no. 1 (1995), pp. 57-65.

6. B. Mittal, "An Integrated Framework for Relating Diverse Consumer Characteristics to Supermarket Coupon Redemption," *J. of Marketing Res.*, 1996. Also see, Aviv Shoham and Maja Makovec Brencic, "Value, Price Consciousness, and Consumption Frugality: An Empirical Study, *Journal of International Consumer Marketing*, Vol. 17, Issue 1, 2004.

7. Peter L. Wright, "The Harassed Decision Maker: Time Pressure, Distractions, and the Use of Evidence," *J. of Applied Psych* 59 (October), pp. 555-61; C. Whan Park, Easwar Iyer, and Daniel C. Smith, "The Effects of Situational Factors on In-Store Grocery Shopping Behavior: The Role of Store Environment and Time Available for Shopping," *J. of Consumer Research* 15 (March 1989), pp. 4222-33.

8. For a fuller discussion of these and other models, see James R. Bettman, An Information Processing Theory of Consumer Choice (Reading, MA: Addison-Wesley, 1979), pp. 173-228.

9. See Hillel J. Einhorn (1970), "Use of Nonlinear, Noncompensatory Models in Decision Making," Psychological Bulletin 73, pp. 221-30.

10. Amos Tversky, "Elimination by Aspects: A Theory of Choice," Psychological Review 79 (July 1972), pp. 281-99; Kahneman, D. and Tversky, A. (1973) "On the psychology of Prediction," *Psychology Review*, 80, 237-251; — and — (1982). The Simulation Heuristic, In D. Kahneman, P. Slovic and A. Tversky (eds.) Judgement under uncertainty: Heuristics and Biases (pp. 201-208). New York: Cambridge University Press; — and — (1982), "Subjective Probability: A Judgment of Representativeness," *Cognitive Psychology*, July 1972, pp 430-454.

11. C. Whan Park and Daniel C. Smith, "Product-Level Choice: A Top-Down or Bottom-Up process?" *Journal of Consumer Research* (December 1989), pp. 289-299.

12. "Mental Budgeting and Consumer Decisions," Chip Heath and Jack B. Soll, *J. of Consumer Research*, 23,(1) (Jun., 1996), pp. 40-52.

13. For further understanding, see Susan M. Broniarczyk and Joseph W. Alba, "The Role of Consumer Intuitions in Inference Making," *J. of Consumer Research*, 21 (December), 1994, pp. 393-407.

14. Herbert A. Simon, Models of Man (New York: John Wiley & Sons, 1957); also see, Peter L. Wright, "Consumer Choice Strategies: Simplifying versus Optimizing," *J. of Marketing Research* 11 (1975), pp. 60-67.

15. Banwari Mittal, "The Role of Affective Choice Mode in the Consumer Purchase of Expressive Products," *J. of Economic Psychology* 9 (1988), pp. 499-524.

16. See, James R. Bettman and Michael A. Zins, "Constructive Processes in Consumer Choice," *J. of Consumer Research* 4 (September 1977), pp. 75-85; James R. Bettman and C. Whan Park, "Effects of Prior Knowledge and Experience and Phase of Choice Process on Consumer Decision Processes: A Protocol Analysis," *J. of Consumer Research* 7 (December 1980), pp. 234-48; Denis A. Lussier and Richard W. Olshavsky, "Task Complexity and Contingent Processing in Brand Choice," *J. of Consumer Research* 6 (1979), pp. 154-65; also see Peter L. Wright, "Consumer Judgment Strategies: Beyond the Compensatory Assumption," in M. Venkatesan, ed., Proceedings of the Third Annual Conference (Chicago: Association for Consumer Research, (1972), pp. 316-24.

Appendix 11A

1. The present model is author's adaptation and modification. For a review of models in prior literature, see Jagdish N. Sheth, "Models of Buyer Behavior: Conceptual, Quantitative, and Empirical," in A Theory of Family Buying Decisions, (New York: Harper & Row), pp. 17 -33.

2. Ibid.; Harry L. Davis, "Decision Making within the Household," Journal of Consumer Research 2 (March 1976), pp. 241 -60.

3. C. Whan Park, "Joint Decisions in Home Purchasing: A Muddling-Through Process," *J. of Consumer Research* 9 (September 1982), pp. 151 -61.

4. Dennis L. Rosen and Donald H. Granbois, "Determinants of Role Structure in Family Financial Management," *J. of Consumer Research* 10 (September 1983), pp. 253 -58; Charles Schaninger and Chris T. Allen, "Wife's Occupational Status as a Consumer Behavior Construct," *Journal of Consumer Research* 8 (September 1981), pp. 189 -96; Mary Lou Roberts and Lawrence H. Wortzel, "Role Transferral in the Household: A Conceptual Model and Partial Test," *Advances in Consumer Research* 9, (1982), pp. 261 -66.

5. See, Kim P. Corfman and Donald R. Lehmann, "Models of Cooperative Group Decision-Making and Relative Influence: An Experimental Investigation of Family Purchase Decisions." *J. of Consumer Research* 14 (June 1987), pp. 1 -13, also see Rosann L. Spiro, "Persuasion in Family Decision making," *J. of Consumer Research* 10 (March 1983), pp. 393 -402; and Daniel Seymour and Greg Lessne, "Spousal Conflict Arousal: Scale Development," *J. of Consumer Research* 11 (December 1984), pp. 810 -21.

6. James G. March and Herbert A. Simon, Organizations (New York: Wiley, 1958).

7. We borrow the concept of buyer, payer, and user roles from Jagdish Sheth (personal discussion) and as reported in Jagdish Sheth and Banwari Mittal, Customer Behavior: A Managerial Perspective, Thomson, 2004.

Appendix 11B

1. Philip Kotler, Marketing Management: Analysis, Planning, Implementation, and Control (Englewood Cliffs, NJ: Prentice-Hall, 1991), p. 247.

2. Based on research by Erin Anderson, Wujin Chu, and Barton Weitz, "Industrial Purchasing: An Empirical Exploration of the Buyclass Framework," Journal of Marketing 51 (July 1987), pp. 71-86.

3. Wesley J. Johnston and Jeffrey E. Lewin, "Organizational Buying Behavior: Toward an Integrative Framework," *J. of Business Research*, 1996, 35 (January), pp. 1-15.

4. See, Niren Vyas and Arch G. Woodside, "An Inductive Model of Industrial Supplier Choice Process," *J. of Marketing* 48 (Winter 1984), pp. 30-45.

5. For a fuller discussion, see Jagdish N. Sheth, "A Model of Industrial Buyer Behavior," *J. of Marketing*, 37 (October 1973), pp. 50-56.

6. For further reading on relationship buying, see; Jagdish N. Sheth and Atul Parvatiyar, "Relationship Marketing in Consumer Markets: Antecedents and Consequences," *J. of the Academy of Marketing Science* 23, no.4 (1995), pp. 25-71; James C. Anderson, Hakan Hakansson, and Lars Johanson, "Dyadic Business Relationships within a Business Network Context," *J. of Marketing* 58 (October 1994), pp 1-15; I. Bjorkman and S. Kock, "Social Relationships and Business Networks: The Case of Western Companies in China," International Business Review 4, no. 4 (1995), pp. 519-35; Neeli Bendapudi and L. Berry, "Customers' Motivations for Relationships with Service Providers," *J. of Retailing* 73, no. 1 (1997), pp. 15-37; Michael R. Leenders and David L. Blenkhorn, Reverse Marketing: The New Buyer-Supplier Relationship (Free Press, 1996), pp. 164-170.

CHAPTER 12

1. Festinger, L. (1957). A theory of cognitive dissonance. Stanford, CA: Stanford University Press.

2. For a comprehensive treatment and definitive research-based work on Consumer Satisfaction, see Richard L. Oliver, Satisfaction: A Behavioral Perspective on the Consumer, 1997, New York: McGraw Hill.

3. Jagdish N. Sheth and Banwari Mittal, "A Framework for Managing Consumer Expectations," *J. of Market-Focused Management,* (1996), 1, 137-158.

4. For academic studies on consumer satisfaction, see Sivadas, E. and Famie, L. Baker-Prewitt (2000), "An examination of the relationship between service quality, customer satisfaction, and store loyalty", International J. of Retail& Distribution Management, 28, 2, 73-82. Barnes, J. G. (1997), "Closeness, strength, and satisfaction examining the nature of relationships between providers of financial services and their retail customers", *Psychology and Marketing*, Vol. 14 (8), pp. 765-90; Jones, T. O. and Sasser, W. E. (1995), " Why satisfied customers defect", *Harvard Business Review*, November- December, pp. 88-99.

5. In academic literature, these are called technical and functional quality, respectively. See, Christian Gronroos "A Service-Oriented Approach to the Marketing of Services," European *J. of Marketing;* 1978, 8 (12), 588-602. Also, S. A. Taylor and T. L. Baker, "An assessment of the relationship between service quality and customer satisfaction in the formation of consumers' purchase intentions,: *J. of Retailing*, 1994, 70(2), 163-78.

6. SERVQUAL's architects are renowned Services Marketign scholars Professors Zeithaml, Berry, and Parasuraman; see SERVQUAL: A Multiple-Item Scale for Measuring Consumer Perceptions of Service Quality, By: A. *Parasuraman,* Valarie A. *Zeithaml,* Leonard L. *Berry, J. of Retailing,* Spring 1988, 64 (1), 12-40; also see R. Johnson, M. Tsiros, and R.A. Lancioni, "Measuring service quality: a systems approach," *J. of Services Marketing,* 1999, 9 (5), 6-19. F

7. A seminal treatise on consumer satisfaction can be found in Richard L. Oliver, Satisfaction: A Behavioral Perspective on the Consumer, New York, NY: McGraw Hill, 1997. Our discussion here borrows and adapts from this work.

8. Banwari Mittal, Walfried M. Lassar, (1998) "Why do customers switch? The dynamics of satisfaction versus loyalty," *Journal of Services Marketing*, Vol. 12(3), p. 177-194.

9. Reported in William H. Davidow and Bro Uttal, Total Customer Service: The Ultimate Weapon, Perennial (HarperCollins), 1990.

10. MacInnis, Deborah J. and Christine Moorman, "Enhancing Consumers' Motivation, Ability and Opportunity to Process Brand Information from Ads," *Journal of Marketing*, Vol. 55, pp. 32-53, October 1991.

11. Davidow, ibid.

12. Based on literature on customer complaining and post complaining experience; see Jeffery G. Blodgett, Donna J. Hill, S. Tax, Stephen, "The Effects of Distributive, Procedural, and Interactional Justice on Postcomplaint Behavior," *J. of Retailing*, 1997, 73(Summer), 185-210; M.C. Gilly and B.D. Gelb, Post-purchase consumer processes and the complaining consumer,'' *J. of Consumer Research*; 1982, 9(4), 323-28; R.S. Spreng, G. Harrell, and R.D. Mackoy, Service Recovery: Impact on Satisfaction and Intentions, *J. of Services Marketing*, 1995, 9(1), 15-21.

13. See Bradley T. Gale, Managing Customer Value, Free Press, 1994.

14. See, Carmen Tanner and Sybille Wölfing Kast (2003), "Promoting sustainable consumption: Determinants of green purchases by Swiss consumers," Psychology and Marketing, 20(10), 883 – 902; McCarty, J.A., and L.J. Shrum, 'The Recycling of Solid Wastes: Personal Values, Value Orientations and Attitudes about Recycling as Antecedents of Recycling Behaviour', *J. of Business Research*, 1994, 30, 53-62.; Anita L. Jackson and Janeen E. Olsen "An Investigation of Determinants of Recycling Consumer Behavior," *Advances in Consumer Research*, 1993,

20(1), 481-487; Seema Bhate, "An examination of the relative roles played by consumer behaviour settings and levels of involvement in determining environmental behaviour," *J. of Retailing & Consumer Services*, Nov 2005, 12(6), 419-429; Cleveland, Mark; Kalamas, Maria; Laroche, Michel, "Shades of green: linking environmental locus of control and pro-environmental behaviors," *J. of Consumer Marketing*, 2005, 22(4), 198-212; "Beyond the intention-behaviour mythology: An integrated model of recycling," Janette Davies and Gordon R Foxall. Marketing Theory, Mar 2002, 2(1), 29-113; and "The Recycling Cycle: An Empirical Examination of Consumer Waste Recycling and Recycling Shopping Behaviors," Biswas, Abhijit; Licata, Jane W.; McKee, Daryl; Pullig, Chris; Daughtridge, Christopher. *J. of Public Policy & Marketing*, Spring 2000, 19(1), 93-105.

15. Services Marketing, Valarie Zeithaml, Mary Jo Bitner, and Dwayne D. Gremler, McGraw-Hill?Irwin, NY: New York, 2002; and Principles of Service Marketing and Management (2nd Edition) (Paperback), Christopher H Lovelock, and Lauren Wright, Prentice Hall, 2001.

16. For further academic research on the role of consumers' environmental value, see Linda R. Stanley, Karen M. Lasonde. And John Weiss, "The Relationship Between Environmental Issue Involvement And Environmentally-Conscious Behavior: An Exploratory Study," *Advances in Consumer Research*, Volume 23, 1996, 183-188.

CHAPTER 13

1. Penned by author based on several reports: "Bridal Wave Sweeps Store," Chicago Tribune, November 8, 1994. Patrick Collins, "Charge of the White Brigade," Sunday Standard Times, January 15, 1995, 87, 4, E1-E2, New Bedford, Massachusetts. Susan Davis, "No Blushing Brides in Filene's Frenzied Mob," Westwood Suburban World, May 25, 1995, n.p. Although dated, the image of shoppers seen here rings as true today as ever.

2. Paco Underhill, Why We Buy, Simon and Schuster, New York, NY, 1999, p. 98

3. For some research literature on this topic, see Edward M. Tauber, "Why Do People Shop?" J. of Marketing, 36 (october), 1972, 47-8. Danny Bellenger and Pradeep K. Korgaonkar, "Profiling the Recreational Shopper," J. of Retailing, 56, 3, 1980, 77-92; and Barry J. Babin, William R. Darden, and Mitch Griffin, "Work and/or Fun: Measuring Hedonic and Utilitarian Shopping Value," *J. of Consumer. Research.*, 20 (March 1994), 644-56; Robert A. Westbrook and William C. Black, "A Motivation-Based Shopper Typology," *J. of Retailing*, 61, 1985, Spring, 78-103

4. See Peter N. Bloch, Nancy M. Ridgway, and Scott A. Dawson, "Shopping Mall as a Consumer Habitat," *J. of Retailing* 70, no. 1 (1994), 23-42.

5. See "Work and/or Fun: Measuring Hedonic and Utilitarian Shopping Value, Babin, B. J.; Darden, W. R.; Griffin, M. J. of Cons. Res., 1994, 20, 644-656; "Profiling the recreational shopper," D. Bellenger and Pradeep Korgaonkar, J. of Retailing; 1980, 53, 29-38.

6. Kirk L. Wakefield and Julie Baker, "Excitement at the Mall: Determinants and Effects on Shopping Response," *J. of Retailing*, 74(4), 1998, 515-539.

7. Mica Nava (Editor) and Alan O'Shea (Editor), <u>Modern Times: Reflections on a Century of English Modernity</u>, Routledge,1996.

8. Based on prior studies including Edward M. Taylor, "Why do people shop," *J. of Marketing*, 36 (October 1972), 46-59; Robert A. Westbrook and William C. Blake, "A Motivation-based Shopper Typology," *J. of Retailing*, Vol. 61, 1985, 78-103; and Joseph P. Guiltinan and Kent B. Monroe, "Identifying and Analyzing Consumer Shopping Strategies," Advances in Cons. Res., Vol. 7, ed., Jerry Olsen, 1980, 745-748.

9. Rook, "The Buying Impulse," *J. of Consumer Research* (September 1987), 189-99.

10. Thomas and Gardland, "Supermarket Shopping Lists," International *J. of Retail and Distribution Management* 21, no. 2 (1993), 8-14.

11. See, C. Whan Park, Easwer S. Iyer, and Daniel C. Smith, "The

Effects of Situational Factors on In-Store Grocery Behavior: The Role of Store Environment and Time Available for Shopping," *J. of Consumer Research*. 15 (March 1989), 422-33.

12. Quoted in Kahn and McAlister, p.123.

13. Ronald E. Milliman, "Using Background Music to Affect the Behavior of Supermarket Shoppers," *J. of Marketing* 46, no. 3 (1982), 86-91.

14. For further reading on the effect of store atmospherics on consumer shopping behavior, see Robert J. Donovan, John R. Rossiter, Gilian Marcoolyn, and Andrew Nesdale, "Store Atmosphere and Purchasing Behavior," *J. of Retailing*, 70 (3), 283-94, 1994; E. Sherman and A. Mathur, "Store environment and consumer purchase behaviour: mediating role of consumer emotions," *Psych. & Marketing*, 1997, 14(4), 361-378

15. Adapted from Dennis W. Rook, and R.J. Fisher "Normative Influences on Impulsive Buying, *J. of Consumer. Research.*, 1995, 22, 296-304. And Dennis Rook, The Buying Impulse, *J. of Consumer Research.*, 1987, 14(Sept), 189-199.

16. Barbara E. Kahn and Leigh McAlister, Grocery Revolution: The New Focus on the Consumer (Reading, MA: Addison-Wesley, 1996). Also see, Fiona M. Davies, Mark M.H. Goode, Luiz A. Moutinho, and Emmanuel Ogbonna, "Critical Factors in Consumer Supermarket Shopping Behaviour: A Neural Network Approach," *J. of Consumer Behaviour*, 1, 1, 35-49.

17. Ibid., p. 96.

18. For academic research on store patronage, see Mark D. Uncles and Kathy A. Hammond, "Grocery Store Patronage", *International Review of Retail, Distribution and Consumer. Research.*, 5, 3, (July), 1995, 287-302.

19. For further reading, see Dennis W. Rook, "The Buying Impulse," *J. of Consumer. Research.* (September 1987), 189-99; Easwer S. Iyer, "Unplanned Purchasing: Knowledge of Shopping Environment and Time Pressure," *J. of Retailing* 65 (Spring 1989), 40-57.

20. Art Thomas and Ron Gardland, "Supermarket Shopping Lists," International J. of Retail and Distrib. Management 21, 2 (1993), 8-14; Also see Susan Spiggle, "Grocery Shopping Lists: What Do Consumers Write?" in Melanie Wallendorf and Paul F. Anderson eds., Advances in Cons. Res. 14, (Provo, UT: Association for Consumer Research., 1987), 241-45.

21. See Jay D. Lindquist, "Meaning of Image," *J. of Retailing*, Vol. 50 (Winter 1974-75), 31.

22. For academic studies on store loyalty, see Joseph D. Brown, "Determinants of Loyalty to Grocery Store Type," *J. of Food Products Marketing*, 2004, Vol. 10, 3, 1-11; Sawmong, Sudaporn; Omar, Ogenyi. "The Store Loyalty of the UK's Retail Consumers," *J. of American Academy of Business*, Cambridge, Sep2004, Vol. 5, 1/2, p503-509; Michel Laroche, Frank Pons, Nadia Zgolli, Marie-Cécile Cervellon and Chankon Kim, **"A model of consumer response to two retail sales promotion techniques,"** *J. of Business Resesrch.*, 56,, 7, July 2003, 513-522; Francis Piron, "Effects of Service and Communication Initiatives on Retail Grocery Consumers' Loyalty," Singapore Management Review, 2001 2nd Half, 23, 2, 45-61; Laura A. Williams and Alvin C. Burns, "Factors Affecting Children's Store Loyalty: An Empirical Examination Of Two Store Types," *J. of Applied Bussiness. Research.*, Winter2001, 17, 1, 61-82. Cristy E. Reynolds and Arnold, Mark J. Arnold "Customer Loyalty to the Salesperson and the Store: Examining Relationship Customers in an Upscale Retail Context," *J. of Personal Selling & Sales Management*, Spring2000, 20, 2, 89-98. Alan S. Dick and Kenneth R. Lord, "The Impact of Membership Fees on Consumer Attitude and Choice," *Psychology & Marketing*, Jan98, 15, 1, 41-58; Niren Sirohi, Edward W. McLaughlin, and Dick R. Wittink, "A Model of Consumer Perceptions and Store Loyalty Intentions for a Supermarket Retailer," *J. of Retailing*, Summer 1998, 74, 2, 223-45; Bloemer, Josee; de Ruyter, Ko "On the relationship between store image, store satisfaction and store loyalty," Euro *J. of Marketing*, 1998, 32, 5/6, 397-413.

23. For academic studies, see Sudhir Kale and Debabrata Talukdar, "Does Store Brand Patronage Improve Store Patronage?" Review of Industrial Organization, Mar2004, 24, 2, 143-160; André Bonfrer and Pradeep K. Chintagunta, "Store Brands: Who Buys Them and What Happens to Retail Prices When They Are Introduced," Review of Industrial Organization, Mar 2004, 24, 2, 195-218; De Wuif, Kristof; Odekerken-Schröder, Gaby; Goedertier, Frank; Van Ossel, Gino, "Consumer perceptions of store brands versus national brands," *J. of Consumer Marketing.*, 2005, 22, 4, 223-232.

24. For a comprehensive essay on the role of convenience, see Leonard Berry, Kathleen Seiders, and Dhruv Grewal, "Understanding Service Convenience," *J. of Marketing*, July 2002, 1-17.

25. Paul S. Richardson, Arun K. Jain, and Alan Dick, "Household Store Brand Proneness: A Framework," *J. of Retailing* 72, 2, 1996, 159-85; Ogenyi Ejye Omar, "Grocery Purchase Behavior for National and Own-Label-Brands," Service Indus. J. (January 1996), 16, 1, 58-66.

26. Julie Baker, A Parasuraman, Dhruv Grewal, and Glenn B. Voss, "The Influence of Multiple Store Environment Cues on Perceived Merchandise Value and Patronage Intentions," *J. of Marketing*, 2002, April, 66(2), 120-41. Kirk L. Wakefield and Julie Baker, "Excitement at the Mall: Determinants and Effects on Shopping Response," *J. of Retailing*, 1998, 74(4), 515-539.

27. Motives act as goals whose achievement is scripted—by which we mean there is an automatic action code built into our minds, built through repeated action, so that anytime we see an opportunity for gratification, we impulsively reach for it, for example.

28. Suresh Ramanathan and Baba Shiv, "Getting to the Heart of the Consumer: The Role of Emotions and Cognitions (or lack thereof) in Consumer Decision Making," *Advances in Consumer Research*, eds. Mary Gilly and Joan Myers-Levy, 2001, 28, 49-50.

29. Jacqueline J. Kacen and Julie Anne Lee, "The Influence of Culture on Consumer Impulsive Buying Behavior," *J. of Consumer Psychology.*, 2002, 12(2). 163-176.

30. For further reading, see Sharon E. Beatty and M. Elizabeth Ferrell, "Impulse Buying: Modeling Its Precursors," *J. of Retailing*, 1998, 74(2), 169-191. Also see Peter Weinberg and Gottwald Wolfgang, "Impulsive Consumer Buying as a Result of Emotions," *J. of Bussiness Research.*, 10, 1982, Mar, 43-57.

CHAPTER 14

1. John Archer and Barbara Bloom Lloyd, *Sex and Gender*, Cambridge University Press, 2002.

2. Populaiton Referenc Bureau and CIA World Facts. https://www.cia.gov/library/publications/the-world-factbook/geos/xx.html#People

3. Sandra Gill, Jean Stockard, Miriam Johnson, and Suzanne Williams, "Measuring Gender Differences: The Expressive Dimension and Critique of Androgyny Scales," Sex Roles 17, (1987), pp. 375-400 p.380; Sandra L. Bem, "Gender Schema Theory: A Cognitive Account of Sex Typing," Psychological Review 88, (1981), pp. 354-364; Cathy Goodwin, Kelly L. Smith and Susan Spiggle, "Gift Giving: Consumer Motivation and the Gift Purchase Process," *Advances in Consumer Research.* 17, eds. R. Holman and M.R.Solomon, Provo, UT: Asso. for Consumer Research, (1990), pp.690-698; Cele Otnes, Tina M. Lowrey and Young Chan Kim, "Gift Selection for Easy and Difficult Recipients: Social Roles Interpretation," *J. of Consumer Research* 20, (1993), pp. 229-244; Cele Otnes and Mary Ann McGrath, "Ritual Socialization and the Children's Birthday Party: The Early Emergence of Gender Difference," *Journal of Ritual Studies* 8, (1994), pp. 73-93; Cele Otnes, J.A. Ruth and C.C.Milbourne, "The Pleasure and Pain of Being Close: Men's Mixed Feelings About Participating in Valentine's Day Gift Exchange," *Advances in Consumer Research.* 21, eds. Chris T. Allen and Deborah Roedder John, Provo, UT: Assoc. for Consumer Research, (1994), pp. 159-164; Mary Ann McGrath, "Gender Differences in Gift Exchanges: New Directions From Projections,"

Psychology and Marketing 12, (1995), pp. 371-393; Eileen Fischer and Stephen J. Arnold, " Sex, Gender Identity, Gender Role Attitudes, and Consumer Behavior," *Psychology & Marketing* 11, (1994), pp. 163-182.

4. Bureau of Labor Statistics, U.S. Department of Labor Report, 2010. Report by Statistics Canada, 2010; The National Equity Panel Report, UK, 2010.

5. A pioneer in Gender role identity research is noted psychologist and Sandra L. Bem; her theory is documented in her 1993 book, The lenses of gender: Transforming the debate on sexual inequality. New Haven, CT: Yale University Press. Further suggested readings on the topic include Sandra L. Bem, "The Measurement of Psychological Androgyny," *Journal of Consulting and Clinical Psychology*, 42, (1974), pp. 155-162; Sandra L. Bem, "Theory and Measurement of androgyny: A Reply to the Pedhazur-Tetenbaum and Locksley-Colten Critiques," *Journal of Personality and Social Psychology*, 37, (1979), pp/ 1047-1054; Barbara B. Stern, Benny Berek and Stephan J. Gould, "Sexual Identity Scale: A New Self-Assessment Measure," Sex Roles, 17, (1987), pp. 503-519.

6. See Stern et al, ibid.

7. Paco Underhill, Why We Buy, Simon and Schuster, 1999, 102

8. Paco Underhill, Why We Buy, Simon and Schuster, 1999.

9. One domain not covered here is gift-giving; interested readers are directed to: "Gender Differences in Gift Exchanges: New Directions from Projections," *McGrath*, Mary Ann. *Psychology & Marketing*, Aug 95, 12 (5), 371-393; "The Pleasure and Pain of Being Close: Men's Mixed Feelings About Participation in Valentine's Day Gift Exchange," Cele Otnes, Julie A. Ruth, and Constance C. Milbourne, Advances in Cons. Res. , 21, 1994, 159-164; Kay M. Palan, Charles S. Areni, Pamela Kiecker (2001), Gender Role Incongruency And Memorable Gift Exchange Experiences, in *Advances in Consumer Research* Volume 28, eds. Mary C. Gilly and Joan Meyers-Levy, Valdosta, GA: *Association for Consumer Research*, Pages: 51-57. Cele Otnes, Julie A. Ruth, Constance C. Milbourne (1994), The Pleasure And Pain Of Being Close: Men's Mixed Feelings About Participation In Valentine's Day Gift Exchange, in *Advances in Consumer Research* Volume 21, eds. Chris T. Allen and Deborah Roedder John, Provo, UT : *Association for Consumer Research*, Pages: 159-164; Sherry, John, Jr. (19833, "Gift Giving in Anthropological Perspective," *J. of Consumer Research*, Vol. 10, (Sept), 157-167. Mary Finley Wolfinbarger (1990), Motivations And Symbolism In Gift-Giving Behavior, in *Advances in Consumer Research* Volume 17, eds. Marvin E. Goldberg and Gerald Gorn and Richard W. Pollay, Provo, UT : *Association for Consumer Research*, Pages: 699-706.

10. Tina M. Lowrey and Cele Otnes, "Construction of a Meaningful Wedding: Differences in the Priorities of Brides and Grooms," in Gender Issues and Consumer Behavior, Janeen Arnold Costa, ed., (Thousand Oaks: CA: Sage, 1994), pp. 164-83.

11. Darren W. Dahl, Jaideep Sengupta, and Kathleen D. Vohs, "Sex in Advertising: Gender Differences and the Role of Relationship Commitment," Journal of Consumer Research, forthcoming.

12. For further reading, see Bernd H. Schmitt, France Leclerc, and Laurette Dub-Rioux, "Sex Typing and Consumer Behavior: A Test of Gender Schema Theory," *J. of Consumer Research*. 15 (June 1988), 122-28; Barbara B. Stern, "Sex Role, Self-Concept Measures and Marketing: A Research Note," *Psychology & Marketing* 5 (Spring 1988), 85; Janeen Arnold Costa, ed., Gender Issues and Consumer Behavior (Thousand Oaks: Sage, 1994).

13. Adapted from Frieda Curtindale, "Car Dealers Give the Lady Some Respect," American Demographics 14 no. 9 (September 1992), p. 25.

14. Underhill, Ibid

15. Consumers Opt for Quality Time with Loved Ones Over Traditional Gifts This Valentine's Day, Valentine's day 2009 Report, National Retail Federation.

16. See *Metrosexual*, Frederic P. Miller, Agnes F. Vandome, McBrewster John, VDM Verlag Dr. Mueller e. K. Sept 16, 2010.

17. *Branded Male: Marketing To Men*, Mark Tungate, Kogan Page, 2008.

18. This leaves a gap of 2 years (1985-1987) between Gen 'Y' and Teen groups; for all practical purposes, their traits might be deemed to be similar to Gen 'Y'.

19. Based on U.S. Census 2000.

20. Cherryl Russell, "On the Baby-Boom Bandwagon," *American Demographics* 13, no. 5 (May 1991), pp. 24-31.

21. Laura Koss-Feder, "Providing For Parents"--The "sandwich generation" looks for new solutions, *Time*, March 17, 2003.

22. Ibid.

23. Children as Consumers," *American Demographics*, Sept. 1990, pp. 36-39, p. 10.

24. "Older Consumers Follow Different Rules," *American Demographics*, February 1993, pp. 21-22.

25. U.S. Census 2000.

26. For literature on this topic, see Mary C. Gilly and Ben M. Ennis, "Recycling the Family Lifecycle," in *Advances in Consumer Research*, vol. 9, Andrew M. Mitchell (eds.) 1982 (Association for Consumer Research).

27. William H Frey, "Married with Children," *American Demographics*, March 2003, p. 17-21. Also, U.S. Census 2000.

28. U.S. Census 2000.

29. George P. Moschis, "The Role of Family Communication in Consumer Socialization of Children and Adolescence," *J. of Consumer Research*, 11, (1985), pp. 898-913.

30. Pierre Filiatrault and J. R. Ritchie, Ibid.

31. George P. Moschis, "The Role of Family Communication in Consumer Socialization of Children and Adolescence," *J. of Consumer Research*, 11, (1985), pp. 898-913.

32. Adapted from Conway Lackman and John M. Lanasa, "Family Decision Making: An Overview and Assessment," *Psychology and Marketing* 12 no 2 (March -April 1993), pp. 81 -93; and from Les Carlson and Sanford Grossbart, "Parental Style and Consumer Socialization of Children," *J. of Consumer Research* 15, no. 1 (June 1988), pp. 77 -94.

33. Moschis and Moore 1982, Bahn 1986, and James U. McNeal, "The Littlest Shoppers," *American Demographics*, Vol. 14, No. 2 (February 1992), pp. 48 -53.

34. Moschis and Churchill, 1978, Ibid.

35. Carole M. Macklin, "Do Children Understand TV Ads?" *J. of Advertising Research*, 23, (1983), no. 1 pp. 63 -70.

36. See Jean Piaget, The Child's Conception of the World (New York: Harcourt Brace, 1928).

37. Moschis and Moore; Scott Ward and Daniel Wackman, "Children's Purchase Influence Attempts and Parental Yielding," *J. of Marketing Research* 9 (August 1972), pp. 316 -19; G. W. Peterson and B. C. Rollins, "Parent Child Socialization," in M. B. Sussman and S. K. Steinmetz, eds. Handbook of Marriage and Family (New York: Plenum Press), pp. 471 -507; Jan M°ller Jensen, "Children's Purchase Requests and Parental Responses: Results from an Exploratory Study in Denmark," in Flemming Hansen, European Advances in Consumer Behavior, Vol. 2 (Provo, UT: Association for Consumer Research, 1995), pp. 61 -68. Sanford Grossbart, Les Carlson, and Ann Walsh, "Consumer Socialization Motive for Shopping with Children," AMA Educator's Proceedings (1988); Bonnie B. Reece, Sevgin Eroglu, and Nora J. Rifon, "Parents Teaching Children to Shop: How, What, and Who?" AMA Educators' Proceedings (1988) pp. 274 -78; Les Carlson and Sanford Grossbart, "Parental Style and Consumer Socialization of Children," *J. of Consumer Research* 15 (1988), pp. 77 -94.

38. For an exhaustive annotated review of the literature in this area, see Reshma H. Shah, "Toward a Theory of Intergenerational Influence: A Framework for Assessing the Differential Impact of Varying Sources

of Influence on the Preferences and Consumption Values of Adult Children," Unpublished working paper, University of Pittsburgh, 1992. Also see Reshma H. Shah and Banwari Mittal, "The Role of Intergenerational Influence in Consumer Choice: Toward an Exploratory Theory," eds. Merrie Brucks and Debbie MacInnis, *Advances in Consumer Research* (Provo, UT: Association for Consumer Research, 1997), pp. 55-60; Ruby Roy Dholkia, "Intergenerational Differences in Consumer Behavior: Some Evidence from a Developing Country," *J. of Business Research* 12, no. 1 (1984), pp. 19-34; Patricia Sorce, Philip R. Tyler, and Lynette Loomis, "Inter-generational Influence on Consumer Decision Making," *Advances in Consumer Research* 16 (1989), pp. 271-75.

39. Collectively from these sources: Elizabeth S. Moore-Shay and R. J. Lutz, "Intergenerational Influences in the Formation of Consumer Attitudes and Beliefs about the Marketplace: Mothers and Daughters," *Advances in Cons. Res.*, M. Houston, ed., 15 (Ann Arbor, MI: Association for Consumer Research 1988), pp. 461 -67; J. Fry, D. C. Shaw, C. H. von Lanzenauer, and C. R. Dipchard, "Consumer Loyalty to Banks: A Longitudinal Study," *J. of Business* 46, pp. 517 -25; Hill, 1970; L. G. Woodson, T. L. Childers and P. R. Winn, "Intergenerational Influences in the Purchase of Auto Insurance," in W. Locander, ed., Marketing Looking Outward: Business Proceedings, (Chicago: American Marketing Association, 1976, pp. 43 -49.

40. Elizabeth S. Moore, William L. Wilkie, and Richard J. Lutz, "Passing the Torch: Intergenerational Influence as a Source of Brand Equity," *J. of Marketing*, Vol. 56, April 2002, p.28.

41. Elizabeth S. Moore, et al. ibid.

42. Banwari Mittal and Marla R. Stafford, "Consuming As A Family: Modes of Intergenerational Influence On Young Adults," *Journal of Consumer Behavior*, 2010, 9 (4, July-Aug) 239-257.

CHAPTER 15

1. Author's estimate based on an (assumed) the individual average ranging from 10 minutes a day to 6 hours a week.

2. *The Early Sociology Of Race And Ethnicity: Race And Culture,* Kenneth Thompson, Taylor & Francis, 2005.

3. There is no consensus on this issue and opinions among scholars differ vastly.

4. See, Marlene L. Rossman, Multicultural Marketing: Selling to a Diverse America (New York: AMACOM, 1994).

5. Source: Census of Canada, 2006.

6. "London: Resident Population Estimates By Ethnic Group," Office for National Statistics, Neighbourhood Statistics. Retrieved 2009-08-09.

7. Census of Canada, 2006.

8. Office for National Statistics. (UK) ibid.

9. US Census, 2010.

10. Based on U.S. Census 2010 Data.

11. Based on U.S. Census 2010 Data.

12. Based on U.S. Census 2010 Data.

13. Based on U.S. Census 2010 Data.

14. Based on U.S. Census 2010 Data.

15. See, Shelly Reese, "When Whites Aren't a Mass Market," *American Demographics*, March 1997, p. 51-54.

16. See "How to Sell across Cultures," *American Demographics*, March 1994, p. 56-57.

17. Reported in *Business Wire*, July 7, 2005, "Market Research Study Finds Race Matters When African Americans Shop."

18. *Communicating With The Multicultural Consumer: Theoretical And Practical Perspectives*, Barbara Mueller. Peter Lang, 2007.

19. *Adweek.com*, June 13, 2005, "Study: Gaps in Hispanic Consumer Behavior," reporting on a study by Havas' Euro RSCG.

20. Study done by ADVO, Inc. reported in Hispanicad.com, dated October 31, 2005.

21. Rohit Deshpande and Douglas M. Stayman, "A tale of two cities: Distinctiveness theory and advertising effectiveness," *J. of Marketing Research*, February 1994, Vol. 31 Issue 1, 57-64.

22. Patricia Braus, "What Does Hispanic Mean," American Demographics 15, no. 6 (June 1993), pp. 46-51.

23. Computed by author based on U.S. Census data.

24. Quoted in Marlene Rossman, ibid.

25. Barbara Mueller, ibid.

26. See Matthew Heller, "A big slice of home: Mexican retailer Gigante bets on large stores to attract higher-spending U.S. Hispanics," *Latin Trade*, April, 2004.

27. Based on Phinney, J.C., "The Multigroup *Ethnic Identity* Measure: A New Scale for Use with Diverse Groups." *J. of Adolescent Research,* 7, 2 (1992) 156-76.

28. Naveen Donthu, and J. Cherian, "Hispanic Coupon Usage: The Impact of Strong and Weak *Ethnic* Identification," *Psychology and Marketing* 9, 6, 1992. 501-10.

29. Further readings: Rohit Deshpande, Wayne Hoyer, and Navin Donthu. "The intensity of *ethnic* affiliation: a study of the sociology of hispanic consumption," *Journal of Consumer Research* 13, 2, 1986, 214-20. Eun-Ju Lee; Ann Fairhurst, Susan Dillard, "Usefulness of Ethnicity in International Consumer Marketing," *Journal of International Consumer Marketing*, 2002, Vol. 14 Issue 4, 25-49; Osei Appiah, *Ethnic identification on adolescents' evaluations of advertisements, J. of Advertising Research*, Sep/Oct, 2001, Vol. 41, Issue 5, 184-99. Rohit Deshpande and Douglas Stayman. "A tale of two cities: distinctiveness theory and advertising effectiveness," *J. of Marketing Research* 31, 4 (1994): 57–64; Eithel M. Simpson, Thelma Snuggs, Tim Christiansen, and Kelli E. Simples, "Race, homophily, and purchase intentions and the black consumer," *Psychology & Marketing*, October, 2000, vol. 17 issue 10, 877-889; Jerome D. Williams, and Kimberly Dillon Grantham, "Racial and ethnic identity in the marketplace: an examination of nonverbal and peripheral cues," *Advances in Consumer Research*, 1999, vol. 26 issue 1, p451-454; Michel Laroche, Chung Koo Kim; Madeleine Clarke, "The effects of ethnicity factors on consumer deal interests: an empirical study of French- and English-Canadians," *J. of Marketing Theory & Practice*, Winter 1997, vol. 5 issue 1, 100-113.

30. Priscilla Barbara, "Consumer Behavior and Born Again Christianity," *Research in Consumer Behavior*, 2, 1987, 193-222.

31. See, Metin M. Cosgel and Lanse Minkler, "Religious Identity and Consumption," Review of Social Economy, September 2004, Vol. 62 Issue 3, 339-350;

32. Andrew Lindridge, "Religiosity and the Construction of a Cultural-Consumption Identity," *J. of Consumer Marketing*, 2005, Vol. 22 Issue 3, 142-151.

33. Harry Leon Hornbeck, *Engel's Law*, Washington University, 1934.

34. Richard T. Curtin, "Indicators of Consumer Behavior: The University of Michigan Survey of Consumers," Public Opinion Quarterly 46 (1982), 340–52. Also see, E. James Jennings and Paul McGrath, "The Influence of Consumer Sentiment on the Sales of Durables," *J. of Business Forecasting*, 13 (Fall 1994) 17–20.

35. See, James A. Roberts And Eli Jones, " Money Attitudes, Credit Card Use, and Compulsive Buying among American College students," *J. of Consumer Affairs,* Winter 2001, 35(2), 213-241; Alice Hanley, Mari S. Wilhelm, "Compulsive buying: An exploration into self-esteem and money attitudes," *J. of Economic Psychology*, Mar 1992, 13(1), 5-19. Melvin Prince, "Self-concept, money beliefs and values," *J. of Economic Psychology*, 1993, 14, 1,161-173; Mark Oleson, "Exploring the relationship between money attitudes and Maslow's hierarchy of needs," International *J. of Consumer Studies*, 2004, Vol. 28 Issue 1, 83-92; James A. Roberts and Cesar J. Sepulveda, "Money Attitudes and Compulsive Buying: An Exploratory Investigation of the Emerging Consumer," *J. of International*

Consumer Marketing, 1999, 11, 4, 53-74; Diane M. Masuo and Mahendra Reddy, "Comparison of students 'money attitudes': a cross-cultural sampling of selected U.S. and Japan universities," *European Advances in Consumer Research*, Volume 3, 1998, 185-191. For as study on how money attitudes affect consumers' investing behavior, see Steven Michael Burgess, Nick Battersby, Leonard Gephardt, and AntonySteven, "Money Attitudes and Innovative Consumer Behavior: Hedge Funds in South Africa," Advances in Consumer Research, 32, 2005, 315-323.

36. Current Population Survey (CPS), 2011 Annual Social and Economic Supplement (ASEC), U.S. Census, 2011.

37. Further readings: Kath Hamilton and Miriam Catterall, "Toward a Better Understanding of the Low Income Consumer," *Advances in Consumer. Reseqrch.*, 2005, 32, 627-632; Ronald Paul Hill, "Stalking the Poverty Consumer: A Retrospective Examination of Modern Ethical Dilemmas," *J. of Business Ethics*, 2002 Part 1, 37(2), 209-219.

38. For seminal work on this topic , see Alan R. Andreasen, The Disadvantaged Consumer (New York: Free Press, 1975).

39. This is based on a 1963 study by Sociologist David Caplovitz, The Poor Pay More (New York: Free Press, 1967).

40. See Alan R. Andreasen, The Disadvantaged Consumer (New York: Free Press, 1975); David Caplovitz, Ibid; David Hamilton, The Consumer in Our Economy (New York: Free Press, 1962); and Judith Bell and Bonnie Maria Burlin, "In Urban Areas: Many of the Poor Still Pay More for Food," *J. of Public Policy & Marketing*, 1993, 12, Fall, 260-270.

41. Insightful essays on the psychology of the poor include: Ronald Paul Hill and Debra Lynn Stephens, "Impoverished Consumers and Consumer Behavior: The Case of AFDC Mothers," *J. of Macromarketing*, 1997 17, Fall, 32-48; Ronald Paul Hill, "Stalking the Poverty Consumer: A Retrospective Examination of Modern Ethical Dilemmas," *J. of Business Ethics*, May2002 Part 1, 37, 2, 209-219; Hill, "Surviving in a Material World: Evidence from Ethnographic Consumer Research on People in Poverty;" *J. of Contemporary Ethnography*, 2001 Vol. 30 Issue 4, p364-391; Kath Hamilton and Miriam Catterall, "Toward a Better Understanding of the Low Income Consumer," *Advances in Consumer Research*, Volume 32, 2005, 627-632.

42. Linda F. Alwitt and Thomas D. Donley, "The Low-Income Consumer: Adjusting the Balance of Exchange," (Thousand Oaks, CA: Sage Publications, 1996).

43. Brendan Coffey, "Every Penny Counts," Forbes, 09.30.02.

44. Noted in "The State of the Banking Industry," *SOBI*, KPMG Report, April 1 through June 30, 2004.

45. See Warner, W. Lloyd (1949) *Social Class in America*, Science Research Associates, Inc.

46. Del Jones, "Are you proud of your job?" USA TODAY, May 24, 2005.

47. Social capital is one of the three resources (along with cultural and economic) Sociologist Pierre Bourdieu, Pierre Bourdieu, *Distinction: A Social Critique of the Judgment of Taste*, Cambridge, UK: Cambridge University Press, 1984.

48. Among Hindus, social classes, from the highest to the lowest, are the Brahmin (the priest and learned), the Kshatriya (the ruler, prince, and warrior class), the Vaishyas (or the trader class), and the Shudras, the untouchable class--although these caste barriers are weakening (even breaking down) in modern India.

49. Paul Henry, "Modes of Thought that Vary Systematically with Both Social Class and Age," *Psychology & Marketing*, 2000, 17(5), 421-440.

50. Jo Blanden; Paul Gregg and Stephen Machin (April 2005). "Intergenerational Mobility in Europe and North America," The SuttonTrust.

51. According to a survey by *Business week*, reported in Businessweek Online issue of October 2, 2005.

52. Michael J Silverstein and Neil Fiske, "Luxury for the Masses," Harvard Business Review, April 2003, 48-59.

53. *Trading Up: The New American Luxury*, Michael Silverstein and Neil Fiske, John Butman, Penguin Group (USA) Inc.. Edition: 2008.

54. Rource: Richard P. Coleman, "The Continuing Significance of Social Class to Marketing," *J. of Consumer Research*, December 1983, p.277.

55. See Martineau, Pierre (1958), "Social Classes and Spending Behavior," *J. of Marketing*, 23, 121-30. Rainwater, Lee (1960) *And the Poor Get Children*, 1960, Quadrangle Books. Also see, Levy, Sidney J. (1966), "Social Class and Consumer Behavior," in *On Knowing the Consumer*, ed. Joseph W. Newman, New York: John Wiley & Sons.

56. For academic research on social class, see Rajesh Kanwar and Notis Pagiavlas, "When Are Higher Social Class Consumers More And Less Brand Loyal Than Lower Social Class Consumers? The Role Of Mediating Variables," *Advances in Consumer Research*, Volume 19, 1992, 589-595; Scott Dawson, Bruce Stern and Tom Gillpatrick, "An Empirical Update And Extension Of Patronage Behaviors Across The Social Class Hierarchy," *Advances in Consumer.Research*, Volume 17, 1990, 833-838; James E. Fisher, "Social Class And Consumer Behavior: The Relevance Of Class And Status," *Advances in Consumer Research*, Volume 14, 1987, 492-496; Scott Dawson and Melanie Wallendorf, "Associational Involvement: An Intervening Concept Between Social Class And Patronage Behavior," *Advances in Consumer Research*, 12, 1985, 586-591; Terence A. Shimp and J. Thomas Yokum, "Extensions Of The Basic Social Class Model Employed In Consumer Research," *Advances in Consumer Research*, Volume 8, 1981, 702-707; Robert B. Settle, Pamela L. Alreck, Michael Belch, "Social Class Determinants of Leisure Activity," *Advances in Consumer Research*, 6, 1979, 139-145; Rich, Stuart U., and Jain, Subhash C., "Social Class as Predictor of Shopping Behavior," *J. of Marketing Research*, 1968, 5, 41-49; Myers, James H., and Mount, John F. (1973), "More on Social Classes Vs. Income As Correlates of Buying Behavior," *J. of Marketing*, 37, 71-73; Jain, Arun K. (1975), "A Method for Investigating and Representing an Implicit Theory of Social Class," *J. of Consumer Research*, 2, 53-59; and Kernan, Jerome B. (1977), "Retrospective Comment on Martineau's "Social Classes and Spending Behavior," in *Classics in Consumer Behavior*, ed. Louis E. Boone, Tulsa, OK: The Petroleum Publishing Co.

CHAPTER 16

1. Elanie Wells, "Cult Brands," 04.16.01, Forbes.com.

2. Reported in John A. Quelch and David Harding, "Brand versus Private Labels: Fighting to Win," Harvard Business Review, January-February 1996, 99-109. For classical literature on brand loyalty, where these measures are developed, see R. M. Cunningham, "Measurement of Brand Loyalty," The Marketing Revolution, Proceedings of the Thirty-Seventh Conference of the American Marketing Association, Chicago: American Marketing Association, 1956, 39-45. 3 Louise Witt, "Inside Intent," American Demographics, March 1, 2004., 26(2), 34-39.

3. Jacob Jacoby and Robert W. Chestnut, Brand Loyalty Measurement and Management (New York: John Wiley & Sons, 1978), p. 2.

4. See Alan S. Dick and Kunal Basu, "Consumer Loyalty: Toward an Integrated Conceptual Framework," *J. of the Academy of Marketing Science* 22, no. 2 (1994), p. 101.

5. For additional reading, see C.B. Bhattacharya and S. Sen, "Consumer-Company Identification: A Framework For Understanding Consumers' Relationships With Companies," *J. of Marketing*, 2003, 67(2), 76-88, and Understanding the Bond of Identification: An Investigation of its Correlates Among Art Museum Members," Bhattacharya, C.B., Hayagreeva Rao, and Mary Ann Glynn, *J. of Marketing*, 1995, 59(Oct.), 46-57.

6. Adapted from Building Strong Brands, David Aaker, Free Press, 1995.

7. www.dictionary.com (DoA: November 28, 2005)

8. Adapted from Maureen Tracik, "Why This Season's Hot Sneaker Is Nowhere to Be Found," Wall Street J., December 10, 2002, B1.

9. See, Susan Fournier, "Consumers and Their Brands: Developing Relationship Theory in Consumer Research," *J. of Consumer Research,* 24, March 1998, 343-373. Also see, Jagdish N. Sheth and Atul Parvatiyar, "Relationship Marketing in Consumer Markets: Antecedents and Consequences," *J. of Academy of Marketing Sciences* 23, No. 4 (Fall 1995), 255-71.

10. See, Susan Fournier, "Consumers and their Brands: Developing Relationship Theory in Consumer Research," *J. of Consumer Research,* 24, 1998, 343-373; Terrence Shimp and Thomas Madden, "Consumer-Object Relations: A Conceptual Framework Based Analogously on Sternberg's Triangular Theory of Love," *Advances in Cons. Research,* 15, ed. M. Houston, Provo, UT: *Assoc. for Consumer Research,* (1988), pp. 163-168; Craig Thomson, "Caring Customers: Gendered Consumption Meanings and the Juggling Lifestyle," *J. of Consumer Research,* 22, 1996, 388-407; William B. Locander and Howard R. Pollio, "Putting Consumer Experience Back into Consumer Research" *J. of Consumer Research,* 1989 (16) 133-146.

11. Mary Ann McGrath and John Sherry, "Giving Voice to the Gift: The Use of Projective Techniques to Recover Lost Meanings," *J. of Consumer Psychology,* 2 (2), 1993, 171-191.

12. A consumer interviewed by Harvard Researcher Susan Fournier, reported in Susan Fournier, "Consumers and their Brands: Developing Relationship Theory in Consumer Research," *J. of Consumer Research,* 24, March 1998, 343-373.

13. Daniel J. Boorstin, 1974, The Americans: The Democratic Experience, New York, Vintage, 148.

14. Albert M. Muniz and Thomas C. O'Guinn, "Brand Community," *J. of Consumer Research,* 2001, 27(March), 412-32. Also see, John W. Schouten and James H. McAlexander, "Subcultures of Consumption: An Ethnography of the New Bikers," *J. of Consumer Research,* 1995, 22(June), 43-61; and also Muniz, Albert M., Jr.; Schau, Hope Jensen, "Religiosity in the Abandoned Apple Newton Brand Community," *J. of Consumer Research,* 2005 , 31(4), 737-747.

15. Further reading: Rene Algesheimer, Utpal M. Dholkia, and Andreas Herrman, "The Social Influence of Brand Community: Evidence from European Car Clubs, " *J. of Marketing,* 2005, 69 (July), 19-34.

16. For a role of brandfest in building brand equity, see "Brand-fests: Servicescapes for the Cultivation of Brand Equity," McAlexander, James H.; Schouten, John W., Servicescapes: The Concept of Place in Contemporary Markets, 1998, 377-401..

17. This formulation is intuitive, independent of a more scholarly view that interested readers would find rewarding in "Building Brand Community," McAlexander, James H., Schouten, John W., and Koening, Harold F. *J. of Marketing,* 2002, 66(1), 38-54.

18. David A. Aaker, Managing Brand Equity (New York: The Free Press, 1991).

19. See Kevin L. Keller, "Conceptualizing, Measuring, and Managing Consumer-Based Brand Equity," *J. of Marketing* 57 (January 1993), 1-22.

20. See, Walfried Lassar, Banwari Mittal, and Arun Sharma, "Measuring Consumer-Based Brand Equity," *J. of Consumer Marketing* 12, no. 4, (1995), 11-19. Also, Charles Bonghee Yoo and Neveen Donthu, "Developing and Validating a Multidimensional Consumer-based Brand Equity Scale," *J. of Business Research,* April 2001, 52, 1, 1-14.

21. For further reading on 'bonds of identification,' see C.B. Bhattacharya, Hayagreeva Rao, and Mary Ann Glynn, "Understanding the Bond of Identification: An Investigation of Its Correlates Among Art Museum Members," *J. of Marketing,* Oct. 1995, 59(4), 46-57.

22. See, Pierre Francois and Douglas MacLachlan, "Ecological Validation of Alternative Consumer-Based Brand Strength Measures," *International J. of Research in Marketing* 12 (1995) p. 322; R. Kenneth Teas and Terry H. Grapentine, "Demystifying Brand Equity," *Marketing Research* 8, no. 2, (Summer 1996), 25-29.

23. Also, Utpal M. Dholkia, "An Investigation of Some Determinants of Brand Commitment," Advances in Consumer Research, Vol. 24,

eds., Marrie Brucks and Deborah J. MacInnis, 1997, 381-386.

24. See B. Mittal, "An Integrated Framework for Relating Diverse Consumer Characteristics to Supermarket Coupon Redemption," *J. of Marketing Research,* 31, 1994, 533-544; David R. Fortin, "Clipping Coupons in Cyberspace: A Proposed Model of Behavior for Deal-Prone Consumers," *Psychology & Marketing,* June 2000, 17(6), 515-534.

25. A recent study showed that luring banking consumers by incentives takes away from consumer loyalty to banks; see Paul M. Dholakia, "The Hazards of Hounding," Harvard Business Review, 2005, 83(10), 20-24.

CHAPTER 17

1. Twitter CEO Dick Costolo's statement to press on Septemebr 8, 2011, reported in News media.

2. Based on Pew Internet Reports.

3. John B. Horrigan and Lee Rainie, Pew Internet and American Life Project, "Counting on the Internet," December 29, 2002, Found at http://www.pewinternet.org/reports/toc.asp?Report=80 (as of June 7, 2003).

4. InternetWorldStats.com.

5. Based on Pew Internet Reports.

6. Based on Pew Internet Reports.

7. "Trends In Online Shopping: A Global Nielsen Consumer Report," Global Online Shoping Report, Nielsen Company, 2008.

8. See Peterson, R. A., Balasubramanian, S., & Bronnenberg, B. J. (1997). Exploring the implications of the Internet for consumer marketing. *J. of the Academy of Marketing Science,* 25 (Fall), 329-48; Phau, I., & Poon, S. (2000). Factors influencing the types of products and services purchased over the Internet. Internet Research: Electronic Networking Applications and Policy, 10 (2), 102-113; and

9. Tulay Girard, Ronnie Silverblatt, and Pradeep Korgaonkar, "Influence of Product Class on Preference for Shopping on the Internet," JCMC 8(1) October 2002.

10. Sung-Joon Yoon, "The Antecedents and Consequences of Trust in Online Purchase Decision," *J. of Interactive Marketing,* 16, 2, (2002), 2-17.

11. Srini S. Srinivasan, Rolph Anderson, Kishore Ponnavolu, "Customer Loyalty in e-commerce: An Exploration of its Antecedents and Consequences," *J. of Retailing,* 78, (2002), 41-50.

12. Mary Wolfinbarger and Mary C. Gilly, ".comQ: Dimensionalizing, Measuring, and Predicting Quality of the E-tail Experience," Marketing Science Institute Report No. 02-100, (2002). Mary Wolfinbarger and Mary C. Gilly, "Shopping Online for Freedom, Control, and Fun," *California Management Review,* Vol. 43, no. 2, (Winter 2001). Mary Wolfinbarger and Mary C. Gilly, "A Comparision of Consumer Experiences with Online and Offline Shopping," *Consumption, Markets and Culture,* Vol. 4(2), (2000), pp. 187-205.

13. Mary Wolfinbarger and Mary C. Gilly, "Shopping Online for Freedom, Control, and Fun," California Management Review, 43, 2 Winter 2001, 34-55

14. Mihalyi Csikszentmihalyi, Beyond Boredom and Anxiety: Experiencing Flow in Work and Play, San Francisco: Jossey-Bass, 2000.

15. Gautam Chakraborthy, Vishal Lala, David Warren, "An Empirical Investigation of Antecedents of B2B Web sites' Effectiveness," *J. of Interactive Marketing,* Vol. 16, No. 4, (Autumn 2002), pp. 51-72.

16. Thoams Novak, Donna Hoffman, and Yiu-Fai Yung, "Measuring the Customer Experience in Online Environments: A Structural Modeling Approach, " *Marketing Science,* 2000, 19 (1) 22-42.

17. David M. Szymanski, Richard T. Hise, "e-Satisfaction: An Initial Examination," *J. of Retailing,* Vol 76 (3), (2000), pp. 309-322. Chung-Hoon Park and Young-Gul Kim, "Identifying Key Factors

Affecting Consumer Purchase Behavior in an Online Shopping Context," International *J. of Retail & Distribution Management*, 31, (2003(1), pp. 16-29. Andrew G. Parsons, "Non-functional Motives for Online Shoppers: Why We Click," J. of Consumer Marketing, Vol. 19, No. 5, (2002), pp. 380-392. also Evanschitzkya, Heiner; Iyer, Gopalkrishnan R.; Hessea, Josef; Ahlerta, Dieter , E-satisfaction: a re-examination," *J. of Retailing*, Fall2004, 80, 3, 239-247,

18. Raymond Burke, "Technology and the Customer Interface: What Consumers Want in the Physical and Virual Store," *Journal of the Academy of Marketing Science*, Fall 2002, 30(4), 411-432.

19. David Luna, Laura A. Peracchio, and Maria D. de Juan, "Cross-Cultural and Cognitive Aspects of Web Site Navigation," *J. of the Acad. of Marketing Science*, 2002, 30(4), 397-410.

20. Sandra M. Forsythe and Bo Shi, "Consumer Patronage and Risk Perceptions in Internet Shopping," *J. of Business Research*, 56, 11, November 2003, 867-875. Mary Wolfinbarger and Mary C. Gilly, "Shopping Online for Freedom, Control, and Fun," California Management Review, 43, 2 Winter 2001, 34-55

21. Ruby Roy Dholakia and Outi Uusitalo, " Switching to Electronic Stores: Consumer Characteristics and the Perception of Shopping Benefits," *International J. of Retail & Distribution Management*, 30, 10, (2002), 459-469.; also see Klassen, Michael, Pola. B. Gupta and Matthew P. Bunker, "Comparison Shopping on the Internet, *International Journal of Business Information Systems*. (in press)

22. Facebook IPO, Mashable, accessed on January 25, 2012.

23. Facebook Web site.

24. Facebook Web site.

25. Facebook website.

26. Amanda Lenhart, Lee Rainie, Oliver Lewis, "Teenage life online: The rise of the instant-message generation and the Internet's impact on friendships and family relationships," http://www. pewinternet.org, (2001), pp. 10.

27. Elisheva Gross, Jaana juvonen, Shelly L-Gable, "Internet Use and well being in adolescence," UCLA 2001

28. Michael Belch, Kathleen A Krentler, and Laura A. Flurry, "Teen Internet Mavens: Influence in Family Decision Making," *J. of Business Research.*, Forthcoming.

29. Information excerpted from Elena Larsen, "Cyber Faith: How American Pursue Religion Online," Dec. 23, 2001, Pew Internet & American Life Project, available at www. PewInternet.org

30. Elena Larsen, Ibid, p.20.

Chapter 18

1. A source of succinct information on consumer protection under law is provided at http://www.recalledproduct.com/ with many useful links.

2. Caroline E. Mayer "Unsafe Products Reaching Retail Shelves, Consumer Reports Says," *Washington Post*, Tuesday, October 5, 2004; Page E01.

3. Florida State Government Press Release, dated 12-30-2005, "Bronson Announces Price Gouging Included in Top Ten List of Complaints in 2005."

4. See Lan Zia and Kent B. Monroe, and Jennifer L. Cox, "The Price is Unfair! A Conceptual Framework of Price Fairness Perceptions" *J. of Marketing*, 2004, 68 (October), 1-15; and Margaret C. Campbell, "Perceptions of Price Unfairness: Antecedents and Consequences," *J. of Marketing Research*, 1999, 36 (May), 187-99.

5. www.quackwatch.org/01QuackeryRelatedTopics/algae.html

6. Nicky Burridge, "Consumers 'Misled' Over Critical Illness Cover," The Press Association Limited, September 2, 2005.

7. See Rick Pollay and B. Mittal, "Here's the Beef: Factors, Determinants, and Segments in Consumer Criticism of Advertising," *J. of Marketing*, 1993, 57(3), 99-114.

8. A slogan Abercrombie and Fitch used once on its tee-shirts.

9. A tagline in a TV Commercial for Life Alert, a medical service, in 1980s.

10. In Pollay and Mittal, ibid.

11 See report http://news.bbc.co.uk/cbbcnews/hi/uk/newsid_3540000/3540914.stm (DoA: 1/12/2006)

12. For further reading, see http://www.chinadaily.com.cn/english/doc/2005-09/10/content_476636.htm

13. Ward's Auto World, "NTSB: Enforce Seatbelt Laws, Airbag Injuries Will Decline" 32, no. 10 (October 1996), p. 10.

14. For further information, see http://www.newstarget.com/000976. html Based on a report by RxPGnews, see http://www.rxpgnews. com/medicalnews/healthcare/india/article_2694.shtml (DoA 12/15/2005)

15. Anna Mulringe, et al., "Window Blinds That Can Poison Kids," *U.S. News & World Report* 121, no. 2 (July 8, 1996), p. 76.

16. www.ftc.gov/privacy/ privacyinitiatives/financial_rule.html

17. Also see Van Kenhove P., De Wulf K., and Steenhaut S. 2003. The relationship between consumers' unethical behavior and customer loyalty in a retail environment. *J. of Business Ethics*. 44 (4): 261 -278; James R. Coyle, James R., Stephen J. Gould, Pola B. Gupta, and Reetika Gupta (2009), "To Buy or To Pirate": The Ethical Matrix of Music Consumers' Acquisition-Mode Decision-Making," *J. of Business Research*, Vol. 62(10), pp. 1031-1037.

18. Thomas C. O'Guinn and Ronald J. Faber, "Compulsive Buying: A Phenomenological Exploration," *J. of Consumer Research* 16 (September 1989), pp. 147–57.

19. Ibid.

20. For a fascinating theoretical understanding of compulsive consumption, see Elizabeth C. Hirschman, "The Consciousness of Addiction: Toward a General Theory of Compulsive Consumption," *J. of Consumer Research* 19 (September 1992), pp. 155–79

21. Hirschman, Ibid.

22. See Faber and O'Guinn; also Dennis W. Rook, "The Buying Impulse," *J. of Consumer Research* (September, 14, 1987) pp. 189–199; and Dennis W. Rook and Steven J. Hoch, "Consuming Impulses," Advances in Consumer Research 12, E.C. Hirschman and M.B. Holbrook, eds. (Provo, UT: Association for Consumer Research), pp. 23–27

23. Based in part on Ron Faber and O'Guinn "Money Changes Everything – Compulsive Buying from a Biopsychosocial Perspective," *American Behavioral Scientist*, 1992, 35(6), 809-819.

24. Chris E. McGoey, "Shoplifting Facts: Retail Theft of Merchandise," www.crimedoctors.com/shoplifting.html (DoA: 1/16/2006)

25. On December 12, 2001, Winona Ryder, was caught by security surveillance cameras, shoplifting in a Saks Fifth Avenue store in Beverly Hills some 5000 dollars worth of merchandise—as reported in www.courttv.com, "Winona Scissorhands? Actress goes on trial for shoplifting designer duds," updated on October 31, 2002 (DOA: 1/14/2006)

26. Source: National health Interview Surveys 1997-2005.

27. Reported in BBC News, Matthew Davis, "US Slowly Wakes Up to Obesity Crisis," 19 December 2005; www.news.bbc.co.uk

28. Based on a WHO report, see http://www.who.int/nut/documents/obesity_executive_summary.pdf

29. International Obesity Taskforce Report (www.iotf.org/childhoodobesity.asp)

30. A Tuft University Report; see http://president.tufts.edu/ontherecord/issue.php?num=31

31. News "Mayo Clinic Creates 'Office of the Future'" Wednesday, May 25, 2005. Mayoclinic.org (http://www.mayoclinic.org/news2005-rst/2836.html); "Mayo Clinic Developing a Treadmill Workstation," June 13, 2005, Consumeraffairs.com (http://www.consumeraffairs.com/news04/2005/mayo_treadmill.html)

GLOSSARY

A

Acculturation	Learning a new culture.
Achieved social system	When one can change social class through effort and accomplishments.
Active audience theory	Holds that consumers are actively processing the information in the ad, and that it is they who are persuading themselves.
Actual self	Who a person currently is.
Adoption of an innovation	Consumer acceptance of an innovation for continued use.
Advocate sources	Sources that have a vested point-of-view to advocate or promote.
Affective choice mode (ACM)	A choice decision making mode wherein *affect* or liking for the brand ensues based not on attribute information, but based on judgments about how the product will reflect the person.
Agonistic gifts	Gifts are intended to gain an immediate personal advantage.
Agreeableness	Being friendly, sympathetic, warm, kind, and good-natured.
AIDA	Sequence of four stages, or four mental states, that an adopter goes through: awareness, interest, desire, and action.
AIO inventory	AIO stands for "activities, interests, and opinion," and it comprises a set of statements to which respondents indicate their agreement or disagreement on a numerical scale.
Altruistic	Gifts are those given largely for the recipient's benefit, with no consideration of immediate personal gain.
Animism	The belief that objects (products) possess souls, i.e., they have consciousness just like humans do.
Anthropology	The study of humankind in its habitat.
Anthropomorphizing	Giving the brand a humanlike quality
Approach motivation	The desire to attain a goal object.
Approach-approach conflict	Choosing between two desirable options
Approach-avoid conflict	When we find an object desirable as well as undesirable.
Appropriation	The process of making something one's own.
Arousal seeking	the drive to maintain our stimulation at an optimal level.
Arts	Represent a society's appreciation of the aesthetic experience as well as the society's values, obsessions, and life-conditions.
Asceticism	The tenet of Buddhism which teaches rigorous self-denial and active self-restraint in consumption.
Ascribed or assigned group	Is one in which membership is automatic—you don't have a choice.
Ascribed social system	When one's social class is determined by birth.
Aspirational group	When a person is not already a member of the group (real or symbolic) but desires and expects to become a member.
Assimilation	Occurs when a stimulus is perceived to belong to a category.
Associated network	A network of various concepts organized and stored in memory.
Assortment	A store's assortment is the number of different items the store carries.
Atmospherics	The physical setting of the store (includes lighting, colors, cleanliness and organization, scents, and background music).
Attention	Allocation of mental processing capacity.
Attitude hierarchy	Refers to the sequence in which the three attitude components occur.

Attitudes	Learned predispositions to respond to an object in a consistently favorable or unfavorable way.
Attitudinal brand loyalty	Consistent brand preferences reflected in favorable liking for the brand
Attraction of the alternatives	How attractive a consumer finds alternative brands to be
Attribution	The process of assigning causes—i.e., figuring out why something happened.
Attribution motivation	The motivation to assign causes
Attribution Theory	Theory that consumers always assign causes to events.
Authentication	Realizing that one is what one truly is.
Authenticity	The genuineness of an object in its likeness as it existed at a time in history.
Authoritarian families	Families where the head of the household (mother in matriarchal and father in patriarchal family societies) exercises strict authority on children, and children learn to obey their elders in all matters.
Autonomous decisions	Are decisions made independently by the decision maker.
Autonomy	The desire to feel free to do whatever one wants.
Avoidance motivation	the desire to protect oneself from an negative object, such as a bee sting or a stale or unhygienic burger.
Avoid-avoid conflict	Choosing between two options that are equally undesirable.
Awareness set	Comprises all the brands you are aware of as a consumer.

B

Baby Boomers	Americans born between 1946 and 1964.
Baby Busters	Americans who were born between 1965 and 1975
Behavioral brand loyalty	Consistent repurchase of the same brand
Behavioral compatibility	Means consumers won't need to alter their behavioral routines.
Belief consumption in media	Believing in the core values and concepts underlying the show.
Beliefs	Expectations about what something is or is not or what something will or will not do.
Big-spenders	Consumers who like to spend without necessarily being rich.
Biogenic needs	Are conditions of discomfort stemming from our biology as humans.
Bottom-up customization	A process wherein consumers build a product starting from the basic version.
Brand associations	What consumers think the brand is, does, or stands for.
Brand belief	A thought about a specific property or quality of the brand.
Brand equity	The enhancement in the perceived utility and desirability that a brand name confers on a product
Brand image	Consists of all the associations or qualities associated with a brand, including physical, functional, and human.
Brand loyalty	Consumer commitment to a brand based on favorable attitude and preference, manifested by the consistent repurchase of the brand
Brand personality	The set of human qualities by which consumers describe a brand.
Brandfests	Events that bring consumers together in geo-temporally concentrated events and entail coordinated activities and brand happenings.
Browsing	Looking at merchandise without a purchase-intent.
Buddhism	A religion found in such countries as China, Tibet, Sri Lanka, Japan, and Korea, with its principal teaching being that material things cannot bring happiness.

Buzz marketing	The rapid-spreading of product news through word-of-mouth.

C

Cause marketing	Companies sponsor and support some social causes
Central route	When a consumer processes the message with attention.
Character	The behavior of a person, at test particularly in the face of tempting opportunities for opposite behaviors.
Choice group	A group that a person voluntarily decides to join.
Christianity	A system of religion centered around the church and its religious order.
Chunking	The combination of bits into a new unit.
Classical conditioning	A process of learning by an extension of a pre-existing response from one stimulus onto another stimulus through exposure to the two stimuli simultaneously.
Closure principle	Suggests that consumers have a natural tendency to complete a partial stimulus, supplying the missing information from memory (assuming of course that they are already familiar with the complete stimulus).
Cognitive Age	Also known as subjective age, is defined as an individual's perception of how old he or she feels.
Cognitive factors	Refers to a person's mental abilities.
Cognitive learning	Refers to learning by acquiring new information from written or oral communication.
Cognitive responses	The thoughts generated in the mind upon exposure to a message.
Cognitive style	Consumer mindset about the task of processing information.
Collectivism	Individuals are expected to show consideration for the well-being of their family, group, or organization.
Communicability	Refers to the extent to which an innovation is socially visible or is otherwise easy to communicate about in social groups.
Community support	Companies sponsor certain community events, such as an ethnic food festival, Black History Month, or even local high school football teams.
Comparative advertising	The advertised brand compares itself to competing products or brands.
Compensatory model	The consumer arrives at a choice by considering all of the attributes of a product or service and mentally trading off the alternative's perceived weakness on one or more attributes for its perceived strength on other attributes.
Competitive promotional activity	The special price deals available on competing brands
Compliance	Government mandate for consumers to obey defined rules and regulations with respect to purchase, payment, and, more importantly, product usage, including disposal.
Compulsive buying	A chronic tendency to purchase products far in excess of both a person's needs and resources.
Compulsive consumption	An uncontrolled and obsessive consumption of a product or service frequently and in excessive amounts, likely to ultimately cause harm to the consumer or others.
Concept	A name or label given to any object or quality of an object, person, situation, or an idea.
Concept-oriented families	Are those that are concerned with the growth of independent thinking and individuality in children.
Conditional stimulus	A stimulus to which the consumer either does not have a response or has a pre-existing response that needs modification, so a new response needs to be conditioned.

Confucianism	Confucianism is a philosophy, rather than a religion, that guides almost every aspect of Chinese life.
Conjunctive model	The consumer uses certain minimum cutoffs on all salient attributes.
Conscientiousness	Being organized, determined, responsible, and dependable.
Consideration set	Brands which a consumer will consider buying.
Consumer	Anyone engaged in the acquisition and use of products and services available in the marketplace.
Consumer behavior	The mental and physical activities undertaken by consumers to acquire and consume products so as to fulfill their needs and wants.
Consumer Bill of Rights	Rights granted by U.S. Congress to every consumer: 1. The right to safety 2. The right to be informed. 3. The right to be heard. 4. The right to choose.
Consumer impulsivity	A consumer's tendency to buy and/or consume spontaneously, whenever exposed to the stimulus product.
Consumer loyalty	A consumer's commitment to a brand or a store or a supplier, based on a strong favorable attitude and preference, and manifested in consistent repatronage
Consumer problem	Any state of felt deprivation
Consumer sentiment	Refers to a consumer's expectation about his or her financial well-being in the near future
Consumer socialization	Refers to the acquisition of knowledge, preferences, and skills to function in the marketplace.
Consumer-brand relationships	How consumers feel toward some products and brands
Consuming the artifacts	The accoutrements that accompany the show—consumers bring the show more squarely into their lives.
Consumption	Any and all usage of products whether or not the products are actually "consumed" away, i.e., depleted.
Consumption communities	Groups of people who share the consumption of a brand or product.
Consumption constellation	A group of products that are consumed together in a typical consumption setting.
Consumption enmeshed self-identity	The extent to which a person defines his or her identity by consumption.
Consumption tribes	Consumption communities that consume a product in a public place, in some ritualistic setting.
Context	The setting or surrounding in which a stimulus is situated.
Contextual marketing	The practice of sending consumers messages pertinent to the purchase and consumption situation of the moment.
Contrast	A stimulus' distinct difference from its environment or background.
Corrective advertising	Advertising whose message includes a correction of a previous deception
Cultural categories	The division of the world's objects and qualities into groups with given names, e.g., masculine or feminine, upper class or lower class, intellectual or peasant, nerd or jock, modern or traditional, sophisticated or simpleton.
Cultural congruency	Refers to how similar the culture depicted in the Web site is to the audience's culture.
Cultural Gatekeepers	People who, through their position and reputation, exercise influence and promote certain cultural meanings.
Cultural Practices	Supra-logical behaviors that are rooted in the traditions and history of a cultural group.

Cultural symbolism	The meaning that any characteristic or entity comes to have in particular cultures.
Cultural Values	The values a society as a whole embraces.
Culture	Everything humans learn from and share with members of a society
Customer recovery	The actions the company undertakes to remove the cause of dissatisfaction and to convert the dissatisfied and unhappy consumer into a satisfied and happy consumer.
Customs	Ways of doing something.
Cyber-buzz	Buzz through the Internet channel.

D

Deceptive advertising	Advertising that has the capacity to deceive a measurable segment of the public.
Deep involvement	A consumer's extreme interest in a product or activity on an ongoing basis.
Defense mechanisms	Psychological processes we employ to protect our ego.
Deficit hypothesis	The idea that consumers with low prior expertise would seek more information to overcome their knowledge deficit.
Democratic families	Every member is given equal voice. Most family matters are discussed among family members, especially those who would be affected by the decisions.
Democratic justice	Refers to a family norm in which each family member is given a voice in family decisions.
Diffusion process	The spreading of an innovation's acceptance and use through a population.
Digital Products	Are products that exist in or can be transformed into digital form, such as computer software, music, pictures, video, and information material such as manuals, brochures, books, educational lessons, etc
Discretionary income	Personal income left after taxes and after purchase of necessities.
Disjunctive model	A judgment model in which the consumer is willing to make trade-offs between aspects of choice alternatives.
Divestment rituals	Activities we perform before discarding or parting with a product.
Door in the face	The marketer makes a large request that is sure to be refused; subsequently, after the consumer declines the first request, the marketer then makes a much smaller request, which is what s/he wanted of the consumer in the first place.
Downward mobility	Movement into a lower class.
Drive	A force or energy that impels us to act.

E

Early adopters	The first group of consumers who deliberate rather than rush, but are independent in their thinking and are quick to evaluate and reach a decision on an innovation.
Early majority	A large group of consumers who are very deliberate, and adopt an innovation if they do not see much risk in it.
Economics	The study of goods—how they are produced, distributed, and consumed.
E-fluentials	A subgroup of Influentials—the persons who are net-savvy and influence other people both offline and online.
Egalitarian sex role attitudes	The view that men and women are both equal and must share equally in all tasks. In this view, women are as entitled to and capable of pursuing a career as men are.
Ego needs	The need to feel good about ourselves and to have self-esteem.

Ego/identity value	Comes from our need to construct and nurture our identity or self-concept, our sense of ego, our idea of who we are.
Ego-defense	Defending our ego against others' attacks on it.
Elaboration	The active processing of information in conjunction with other information already in the memory so as to identify meaning in the new information.
Elaboration likelihood model	The higher the consumer involvement, the higher the likelihood that the consumer would elaborate on the message.
Elements of Culture	Values; Norms; Rituals; Customs; Myths; Knowledge, Science and Technology; Laws; Arts; and Material Culture
Elimination by aspects	A decision-making model similar to the lexicographic model, but with one important difference. The consumer rates the attributes in the order of importance; and, in addition, s/he defines minimum required values
Elimination stage	Consumers narrow down the set of alternatives for closer comparisons, eliminating those not judged suitable.
Emergent occasions	Those that are not predetermined and do not repeat in a regular pattern.
Emoticons	Text-based sequence of characters that depict human emotions, such as a tearful eye
Emotional hierarchy	The sequence in which we feel first, then act, and think last
Emotions	A sudden surge of feelings.
Enculturation	Learning one's culture.
Enduring involvement	The degree of interest a consumer feels in a product or service on an ongoing basis.
Engel's law	According to Engel's law, the lower the per capita income of a nation or people, the more they tend to spend on basic necessities such as food, housing, and clothing.
Environmental factors	Refers to sources of information and influences surrounding the growing child.
Episodic knowledge	Knowledge that consists of description of events.
Ethnic Identity	Refers to a person's knowledge of his or her membership in a social group and the value and emotional significance attached to that membership.
Ethnicity	Refers to the distinctions among people based on their national or cultural heritage.
Ethnocentrism	The belief in the superiority of one's own culture over all others.
Evaluation criteria	Standards against which consumers evaluate a product.
Evaluative mode	Consuming with the intention of evaluating the product performance.
Evoked set	Subset of the brands in the awareness set
Exchange	An interchange between two parties where each receives from the other something of more value and gives up something of less value.
Experiential browsers/ web surfer	Are consumers whose principal and overall motive for going to the Web sites of online stores is fun and excitement.
Experiential products	Products that we need to try or actually use in order to enjoy them and judge their value or utility to you.
Expertise	Possession of knowledge about a topic, or product—especially knowledge that is not yet common knowledge.
Exploratory shopping	Refers to browsing around after collecting the planned items.
Expressive gift	The extent to which the gift is accompanied by the giver's sentiment.
Extended problem solving	Where search is extensive and deliberation prolonged.

Extended problems	Purchase tasks for products never purchased before, or made long ago, or where risks of wrong choice are high.
Extended self	Comprises all the external entities and objects that we consider, with pride, part of ourselves.
External reference price	the price the marketer uses to anchor a price advantage (e.g., "compare at___").
External stimuli	Sources of information you see outside—in the marketplace and on the street.
Extraversion	Being outgoing, persuasive, and displaying leadership roles
Extrinsic reward	External to the product, e.g., coupons, sweepstakes, rebates,

F

Families	Are two or more persons related by blood, marriage, or adoption.
Family life cycle	How a person advances from one stage to another is called a family life cycle.
Fantasy consumption	Vicarious consumption, consumption by imagining things and situations.
Fashion System	A society's collective ideas (or conventional wisdom) about what is in fashion and what is out of it.
Femininity	Refers to the personality traits of compassion, sensitivity, and politeness. Persons with these traits tend to value interpersonal relations over self-centered gains.
Flaunters	These are consumers who have money and want to show it. They derive pleasure in displaying their wealth, hoping to impress or arouse envy in others. They buy conspicuous items (expensive cars, luxurious clothes, diamonds, etc.) and enjoy their possessions and acquisitions more for their exhibition value than their utilitarian value.
Flow	Refers to a situation where the consumer gets immersed in the site navigation, losing a sense of time.
Foot in the door	A marketer makes a small request to which the consumer cannot (or usually won't) refuse; subsequently, the marketer makes a larger request.
Formal group	Membership is granted by a formal admission into the group.
Forward buy	Buying an item for future consumption.
Framing	The context in which information is presented.
Framing-effect	The bias in the interpretation of the information due to its framing or context.
Functional theory of attitude	Katz's theory that people hold certain attitudes (or come to acquire those attitudes) because these attitudes serve one or more of the following four functions: utilitarian, value expressive, ego-defense, and knowledge.

G

Gender role orientation	Refers to our concepts of the specific behaviors expected of a person by virtue of that person's gender.
Generation X	Are those that are born between 1965 to 1976.
Generation Y	Are those that are born between 1997 to 1984.
Geodemographics	Is the study of relationships between demographics on the one hand and geographic location on the other.
GI Generation	Are those that are born between 1901 to 1924.
Gift	A tangible or intangible product voluntarily given by one person to another, through some ritual presentation and embodying some symbolic representation of the giver's sentiments for the recipient

Goal object	Something in the world the acquisition or attainment of which will bring us happiness—by reducing our current discomfort or tension.
Goal oriented online shoppers	Shoppers who go on the Internet with a purchase goal in mind.
Group	Two or more persons sharing a common purpose.

H

Health Condition	Refers to one's physical health, including ailments, physical strength, and energy levels that one feels for everyday activities.
Hedonic consumption	The use of products/services for the sake of intrinsic enjoyment.
Hedonic motives	Consumer need and desire to obtain pleasure.
Heider's balance theory	Maintains that in any relationship between three entities, a state of unbalance cannot be sustained, and it will be resolved by altering one of the relationships.
Heuristic search	Ad hoc acquisition of information to reach intuitive judgments.
Heuristics	Quick rules of thumb and shortcuts used to make decisions.
High involvement learning	A mode of learning when the product is very important to us as consumers and a lot is at stake.
High touch	Products that require touch and feel, and consequently cannot be judged or bought in virtual space.
High-Context Culture	Culture where to understand something, you need to know the context. Behind everything, there are layers of meaning not immediately apparent.
Hinduism	A system of religious beliefs founded in India
Homophyly	Resemblance arising out of love and identification
Household	A household is one or more persons living in the same quarters.

I

Ideal self	The person we would like to become
Identificational influence	Occurs when a consumer emulates the behavior of another person.
Image congruity theory	We like to associate ourselves with objects (things, activities, and people) that have an image that is congruent with our own image of ourselves.
Immediacy bias	Desire for immediate outcome
Impulse control disorder	Failure to control our impulse to do something.
Impulsive consumer behavior	Refers to a specific purchase and/or consumption activity undertaken on the spur of the moment.
Income	The amount of monetary earnings that person receives periodically on a more or less regular basis.
Independent sources	Those not controlled by marketers and also not known to us personally.
Individualism	The idea that individuals are responsible for their own success, which is achieved through individual ability.
Inept set	Brands in the evoked set that are considered unfit for your needs.
Inference making	The consumer act of assuming the missing information to make a judgment about a product.
Informal group	A group that has few explicit rules about member behavior, e.g. family
Information processing mode (IPM).	In this mode, "the consumer is thought to acquire information about brand attributes, form evaluative criteria, judge the levels of these attributes in various brands, and combine these attribute-levels for overall brand evaluation."

Informational influence	Occurs when a consumer is influenced by the product information someone provides.
Information overload	A condition in which the information being presented is too much to process for you as a consumer.
Innate needs	Needs we are born with.
Innovation	A product or an idea that is new to the consumer.
Innovativeness	Being predisposed to embrace new products, ideas, and behaviors.
Insight	The ability to see the hidden nature of a solution.
Institutions	Permanent groups or entities with a pervasive and universal presence in a society, such as schools, religions, and family.
In-store factors	Characteristics that surround the consumer's decision process inside the store.
Instrumental learning	A process where one learns to act in a certain way that is rewarding.
Instrumental values	The means, paths, or behavioral standards by which we pursue those goals (e.g., honesty, altruism, etc.)
Instrumentality	Refers to valuing things and people merely for their utility.
Interaction quality	The pleasantness of social experience in the acquisition and use of the service.
Intergenerational Influence	Refers to the transmission of values, attitudes, and behaviors from one generation to the other.
Internal reference price	Price we believe to be the right price.
Internal stimuli	Perceived states of discomfort arising from something inside you.
Internet Maven	A consumer who is more knowledgeable than the average consumer about the e-marketplace, and about product information available on the Internet.
Intrinsic reward	The reward built into the product itself
Involuntary attention	Attention that is forced on the consumer.
Involvement	the degree of interest a consumer finds in a product or service or object or activity.
Islam	The religion of the followers of the Prophet Mohammed.

J

Joint decisions	Are those in which more than one decision participant made the decision.
Judgment models	Also called "decision models" and "choice rules," are procedures and rules consumers use to consider various product attributes to arrive at their product choice.
Just noticeable difference (j.n.d.)	The magnitude of change necessary for the change to be noticed.

K

Key informant method	Ask prominent people in a community to name a few persons they consider able to influence others' opinion on a given topic.
Knowledge	The basis of beliefs on which we base actions.
Knowledge function	The ability of an object to serve our need for knowledge and certainty.

L

Laddering	A procedure to map a consumer's view of how a product's use ultimately fulfills his or her higher level values.

Laggards	Consumers who are most hesitant to adopt anything new and who try to resist or postpone adopting the new product or new behavior.
Late majority	Consumers who are very skeptical of anything new, are extremely risk-averse, and resist adopting unless an innovation has been proven useful and safe.
Latent loyalty	When the consumer likes the brand but has been unable to buy it.
Laws	Norms with legal consequences.
Learned needs	Needs that are acquired in the process of growing up and living.
Learning	Acquiring a response to a stimulus.
Learning hierarchy	A sequence of learning wherein cognitions come first, affect next, and action last.
Lemon law	Protects a car buyer against being sold a substandard car.
Lexicographic model	A choice making rule wherein the consumer rank orders product attributes in terms of importance.
Life projects	Enduring, ongoing, significant endeavors undertaken by consumers to achieve certain life goals.
Lifestyle	Our pattern of living
Limited problem solving	The consumer invests some limited amount of time and energy in searching and evaluating alternative solutions.
Limited problems	Nontrivial, but risks are moderate, and the product or service is not overly complex or technical in terms of its features.
Long-term memory	The part of the brain where information we do not currently need is stored away.
Low involvement learning	The learning method when product is relevant but not much is at stake, such as a low priced item of routine use.
Low-context	Meaning that there is no human element in communication, no nonverbal gestures, and no referent opinion.
Low-Context Culture	Culture where to understand the meaning of something, you don't have to look at the context; the thing in itself is self-explanatory; also people are explicit in their communication.

M

Make-goods	recovery offerings or concessions to dissatisfied consumers
Manscaping	Was a term introduced in 2004 by the American TV show Queer Eye for the Straight Guy, and is shorthand for "landscaping" the male body by shaving, trimming, waxing, or brushing the body hair.
Market mavens	Individuals who are generally knowledgeable about the marketplace happenings and possess information about a range of products, prices, distribution outlets, and even special promotions in effect at the time.
Marketer	An individual or an organization with an organizational goal that offers products and services in exchange for the consumer's money or (occasionally) other resources.
Marketer sources	Those that come from the marketer of the product or service.
Marketer System	All the agents involved in bringing the product to the market.
Masculinity	Personality traits of independence, competitiveness, assertiveness.
Maslow's hierarchy of needs	Psychologist Maslow's theory about the order in which humans experience needs.
Match-up hypothesis	The celebrity chosen for promoting a brand should have an image similar to the brand's image (or desired image).
Material Culture	All man-made objects in a society that represent the degree of affluence and progress of a society in contrast to the life lived entirely in and with nature.

Materialism	The extent to which one considers possessing and consuming more and more products as a sign of success and a means of happiness.
Meaning negotiation in media shows	Seeing meaning in the episode, understanding the episode and accepting it as logical and plausible.
Means-end chains	Pathways connecting product attributes to ultimate consumer goals or values.
Membership groups	Those in which an individual claiming to be a member is so recognized by the head or leader and/or key group members, even when the membership is informal.
Memorabilia	Products designed to capture the authenticity of a person, place, or event from a historic period.
Memory	Information storage area of the mind and its stored contents.
Mental activities	Acts of the mind, and they relate to what we think, feel, and know about products.
Metrosexuals	Urban males who have a strong aesthetic sense and spend a great deal of time and money on their appearances and lifestyles.
Modeling	A process whereby learning occurs by observing others
Money attitude	Consumer's view of and orientation toward money—what it means to them and how they want to utilize it.
Moods	Emotions felts less intensely.
Motivation	The human drive to attain a goal object.
Motivation research	A method directed at discovering the reasons (i.e., motives) for a person's behavior–reasons the consumer is either unaware of or is unwilling to admit in direct questioning.
Multiattribute models of attitude	Suggests that overall attitude is based on the component beliefs about the object, weighted by the evaluation of those beliefs.
Myths	Tales and stories handed down from history without known origins and with no test of truth.

N

Need	A discomforting human condition.
Need for cognition	Our discomfort with ignorance, our need for information, our need for understanding the world around us, and our need for knowledge.
Neglectful families	Parents are distant from their children, who are neglected in these families because the parent(s) place more priority on their individual affairs.
Negligent consumer behavior	Consumption that puts a person or others at risk and imposes heavy costs on society or otherwise deteriorates its quality of life in the long run.
Neuroticism	Being emotionally unstable, nervous, and anxious.
Non-marketer sources	Sources of information that are independent of the marketer's control.
Non-profit organization	A firm that offers products and services either free of cost or at a nominal charge insufficient to cover costs or make any profit.
Normative influence	Occurs when a consumer's decision or action is based on his or her desire to conform to the expectations of someone else.
Norms	Unwritten rules of behavior
Nostalgia	A longing for the things and lifestyles of the past.

O

| OCEAN | Openness; Conscientiousness; Extraversion; Agreeableness; Neuroticism |
| Odd pricing | A practice wherein prices are set just below the next round number. |

One-stop shopping	Finding all of the consumer's requirements of related products in one place or from one source.
Openness	Being curious, insightful, imaginative, original, and open to new experiences and diversity.
Opinion leadership	The giving of information and advice, leading to the acceptance of the advocated position by the recipient of the opinion.
Opportunity recognition	Problem recognition aroused by an external, solution stimulus.
Optimism	Is a personality factor that concerns the degree to which a person is hopeful about the future and expects life opportunities for continual personal progress.
Outcome quality	The consequences experienced from the use of the service.
Overprivileged	Those earning substantially above the median income of their group.

P

Paradox	When reality is contrary to the intuitive expectation.
Particularism	Valuing the individuality of each situation
Passive audience theory	The view of the consumer processing the message that consumers' minds sit there, like couch potatoes, passively, and absorb whatever is thrown at them.
Peer-to-peer marketing	A special case of buzz marketing where the goal is not just to spread the word but to get the target audiences to act on the word which comes from their peers.
Perceived justice	The consumer's perception that he or she was treated fairly during the complaint resolution process.
Perceived risk	The degree of loss (i.e., amount at stake) in the event that a wrong choice is made.
Perception	The process by which the human mind becomes aware of and interprets a stimulus.
Perceptual distortion	Information being encoded non-objectively, resulting in the consumer seeing it as being different from reality.
Perceptual maps	Visual depictions of consumer perceptions of alternative brands of a product category in multi-dimensional grids.
Perceptual or Differential threshold	The minimum level or magnitude at which a stimulus begins to be sensed.
Peripheral route	The processing of a message superficially.
Permissive families	Children are given relative independence in conducting their own affairs, especially in their adolescent years.
Personal sources	Family members, friends, and other acquaintances with past experience with and/or greater knowledge of the product category.
Personality	A person's psychological makeup that engenders characteristic responses to the environment in which he or she lives.
Personalization	Refers to a business organization treating a consumer as a person rather than a number.
Pessimism	Tendency to see the future as bleak.
Physical activities	Acts of the human body, and they relate to what we physically do to acquire and consume products.
Picture matching method	Consumers who have just been shown a test advertisement are shown a set of faces with differing expressions and are asked to mark the face that comes closest to how they themselves felt when they viewed the ad.
Planned purchases	Purchases that the consumer planned to buy before entering the store.

Pomosexual	Is a term that stands for *post-modern sexual*, and describes persons who do not identify with any specific classification of sexuality.
Population Pyramid	A bar graph which displays the age and sex distribution of a population.
Possession Rituals	Set of activities we perform to transform or modify products obtained from the marketplace.
Positively expressive gifts	Gifts are given to people for whom one has special feelings
Post-purchase cognitive dissonance	Also known as "buyer's remorse"—post-purchase doubt about the wisdom of one's choice.
Poverty	The level of personal wealth at which a household cannot even pay for all of its basic needs, such as food, clothing, and shelter.
Power Distance	The extent to which the less powerful members of the society accept the authority of those with greater power.
Price gouging	A practice wherein the seller hikes up the price just to take advantage of some short-term shortage or emergency circumstances.
Primary group	Groups with whom a person interacts frequently (not necessarily face-to-face) and considers their opinion or norms important to follow.
Problem recognition	The consumer's realization of the gap between his/her current state and the desired state.
Problem solving	Actively processing information to reach certain judgments that will conclude the issue.
Problem stimulus	One in which the problem itself is the source of information, such as the sight of dirty laundry or the printer's empty ink cartridge.
Product	Any physical or nonphysical product or service that offers some benefit to the consumer, including a place, a person, or an idea offered for exchange.
Product disposal	Dispossessing product remnants after use.
Product placement	Strategy of embedding a product within the media program content
Psychogenic needs	Needs that stem not from our bodies, but from our mental makeup—the way we think about ourselves and about the world.
Psychographics	The sum total of values, self-concepts, personality and lifestyles.
Psychological bonding	The connection consumers feel toward the brand.
Psychology	The study of the human mind and mental processes that influence a person's behavior.
Psychology of price perception	How consumers psychologically perceive prices.
Purchase decision involvement	The degree of concern you experience about making the right choice.
Purposive behavior	When energy is expended to attain some goal object.

Q

Quality cue	Any information used for making inferences about the quality of the product or service.

R

Race	Refers to the distinction among humans based on their genes, from which stem basic differences in the subspecies of humans.
Recall	Becoming conscious of some information residing in LTM without current encounter with it externally.
Reciprocation	Returning the favor in like manner.
Recognition	Refers to identifying a stimulus as having been encountered before.
Recognition set	Brand names the consumer recognizes as being familiar.

Recreation/Hedonic value	Comes from objects and activities when they recreate our moods and regenerate our mental ability—removing our fatigue and boredom, stimulating the senses, and rejuvenating our minds.
Reference groups	Persons, groups, and institutions one uses as points of reference.
Reference price	The price consumers expect to pay.
Referent	Any person, group, or institution that serves as a point of reference
Relationship	A sentiment where one feels a special sense of being connected.
Relative advantage	How much better the innovation is compared to the current product that it would substitute.
Religion	A system of beliefs about the supernatural, spiritual world, about God, and about how humans, as God's creatures, are supposed to behave on this earth.
Religious Affiliation	Membership, in objective terms, in a religion.
Religious Identity	The degree of involvement and commitment in that religion as a system of belief and practice.
Repetition	The incidence of an occurrence more than once.
Resource	Something we own or possess that people value.
Retro products	Products that are designed to capture significant stylistic aspects of some old, once popular but since retired product.
Retrosexual	A man with a generally poor sense of style.
Reverse channel	When the manufacturers and retailers take back old products and empty containers.
Risk Averseness	Preference for avoiding risks.
Ritualistic gifts	Gifts are given simply because it is a ritual, the occasion demands it
Rituals	A set of activities done in a fixed sequence and repeated periodically.
Rote memorization	Rehearsing the information until it gets firmly lodged in our long-term memory.
Routine problem solving	Generally, no new information is considered and consumers usually solve these problems by simply repeating their previous choices.
Routine problems	Are those that, as a consumer, you have solved many times in the past.

S

Sacred	An intangible entity that is other-worldly.
Safety and security need	The need to be protected from danger.
Satisfaction/ dissatisfaction	The positive or negative feeling consumers get with the outcome of product or service consumption.
Satisficing	A consumer's (or a decision maker's) acceptance of an alternative that he or she finds satisfying, acknowledging that there might be a better alternative.
Search strategy	The pattern of information acquisition that consumers utilize to solve their decision problems.
Secondary group	Groups marked by infrequent contacts, and norms of the group are considered less binding or obligatory.
Selection stage	The decision making stage in which an alternative is selected out of several.
Self-actualization	The need to realize one's true potential.
Self-concept	A person's conception of himself or herself.
Self-designation method of identifying opinion leaders	A survey method where the respondents rate or designate themselves on opinion-leadership activities or behaviors.
Self-efficacy	Viewing oneself as effective, in control.
Self-esteem	Holding oneself as valued.

Self-Perception Theory	Bem's theory that we infer our attitude from our own behavior.
Self-selection	Consumers self-select themselves to be customers of the store or consumers of the product or brand that offers the advantage they seek.
Semantic knowledge	Consists of information about objects and their properties.
Semantic memories	Memories for objects and their properties.
Sensation	An event wherein a stimulus comes within the reach of one or more of our five senses: seeing, hearing, smelling, touching, and tasting.
Sensory memory	The ability of our senses to keep information alive briefly.
Shopping	All activities the consumer undertakes while in the store, physical or virtual. This set of activities includes "walking through the stores at a relaxed pace, examining merchandise, comparing products, interacting with sale staff, asking questions, trying things on, and ultimately, though not always making purchases.
Shopping orientation	A consumer's predominant motive for shopping activity.
Short-term memory	The part of the brain where information is being held and being processed currently.
Signaling	Implicitly communicating one's attitudes and desires.
Silent Generation	Those born between 1925 to 1945.
Situational involvement	The degree of interest a consumer takes in a specific situation or on a specific occasion.
Social archetype groups	Categories of persons sharing a lifestyle, such as bohemians, literati, jocks, bookworms, cowboys, etc.
Social capital	The network of friends and professional connections that can be of help in our hour of need.
Social capital	Your social connections, the network of people you know.
Social Class	The relative standing of a person in society in terms of status; a prestige hierarchy in a society
Social self-concept	The way others see us.
Social value	A products ability to enable us to manage our social worlds (as opposed to the physical world).
Socially conscious businesses	Companies that espouse desirable societal values.
Social-oriented families	Families that are more concerned with maintaining discipline and harmony among family members.
Sociology	The study of social systems—groups, organizations, and societies.
Solution stimulus	The information emanating from a solution itself.
Source	Any person or organization that is conveying the message or stands behind the message.
Source attractiveness	The quality of making an emotional connection with the viewer.
Source credibility	Refers to how credible (believable or trustable) the source is judged to be by the target audience.
Source independence	Separation of the source from the company that would benefit from the message.
Source similarity	How similar to themselves consumers see the spokesperson to be.
Spurious loyalty	Loyalty that is incidental, not well-founded
Status consumption	Acquiring and consuming products that signify a status in society.
Status crystallization	A condition when all components of one's social class become consistent.
Stereotype	A perception we come to form about a whole category of things or people.
Stimulus	Any object or event in the external environment.

Stimulus discrimination	A process wherein a consumer perceives two stimuli as different so that the response learned for one stimulus is not repeated for the other.
Stimulus generalization	A process wherein a consumer extends a learned response for one stimulus to other similar stimuli.
Store environment	Refers both to the physical setting and the social stimuli within the store.
Store image	The sum total of perceptions that consumers have about a store.
Store loyalty	A consumer's predominant patronage of a store, based on a favorable attitude and preference
Store personality	Characterization of a store on personality-like qualities such as sophisticated, modern, traditional, tacky, etc.
Structured occasions	Standard occasions that occur repeatedly on the same predetermined times or days.
Subjective norm	What others expect us to do (i.e., normative expectations).
Subliminal perception	the perception of a stimulus without being aware of it.
Subliminal stimuli	Stimuli of which one is not conscious.
Susceptibility to Interpersonal Influence (SIPI)	Consumer motivation to follow other people's expectations and advice.
Symbolic	Items whose principal value is not material but sentimental or intangible
Symbolic groups	Groups Have no provision or procedure for granting membership.
Syncratic decisions	Are decisions in which all parties play an equal role in decision making.
Systematic information search	An organized pattern of seeking information, directed at answering specific questions.

T

Task-oriented shoppers	Shoppers who focus on finding what they came to seek and want to finish the shopping task efficiently.
Telecommuting	The practice of working at a distance from a formal place of employment.
Terminal values	The goals we seek in life (e.g., freedom, wealth, salvation, etc.)
The theory of reasoned action	Attitude toward an object is based on the consequences the object has, weighed by the desirability or undesirability of these consequences.
Thematic apperception test	A form of story completion task based on a series of ambiguous pictures shown to the consumer.
Three-factor theory of compulsive buying	Biological, psychological, and sociological determinants.
Tightwads	People who are obsessive about saving as much money as possible.
Top-down customization	A process wherein consumers build a product starting from the loaded version.
Traditional sex role attitude	The view that a woman's place is in the home and man's place is out of the home, working and earning a living.
Treasure hunting	Finding something unusual and unexpected.
Trialability	The extent to which it is possible to try out the innovation on a smaller scale.
Tribal consumption	Consumption of brands and products that is public and there is some participation in planned events of the community.
Trustworthiness	Perceived benevolence and dependability of the opinion giver.
Two-sided messages	Present both the merits and demerits of a product, brand, or issue.
Two-step flow of communication theory	suggests that communication from mass media reaches the masses in two-steps—first from mass media to opinion leaders and then from opinion leaders to the masses.

U

Übersexual	The word "über" has German roots and means above or superior. Thus, an ubersexual is a variant of metrosexual, a more "refined" male, who is more confident and more focused on his mind than body.
Uncertainty Avoidance	The extent to which people in a society feel threatened by ambiguous situations and want to avoid them.
Unconditioned stimulus	A stimulus to which the consumer already has a pre-existing response.
Underprivileged	Those earning substantially below the median income of their own income group.
Uniqueness seeking	A personality trait wherein a person seeks to be unique, different from others.
Universalism	Belief in the universal application of the same rule
Unplanned purchases	Purchases the consumer did not intend to buy before entering the store.
Upward mobility	When a person moves to a higher social class
Utilitarian	The concrete (not symbolic) outcomes of a product or activity,
Utilitarian value	The set of tangible outcomes of a product usage (or an activity).

V

Value	The sum total of net benefits we receive from an activity or an exchange.
	The ratio of benefits from the product versus the costs the consumer incurs in time, effort, and money.
Value compatibility	Consistency with consumers' deeply held values.
Value-based business practice	The adoption of some socially desirable value as a corporate value, which then guides everything the company does.
Values	Desired end-states of life and preferred paths to achieving them.
Values	A society's ideas as to what in life is worthy of pursuit and how those pursuits should be conducted.
Vanity	Excessive pride in one's appearance and accomplishments.
Verifiable benefit	Benefits that can be verified by independent laboratory tests.
Viral marketing	Seeking the spread of product acceptance from one consumer to another in an exponential fashion.
Vividness	A stimulus' brightness and distinctness.
Voice	Complaining or praising someone or something—the act of expressing one's dissatisfaction or satisfaction
Voluntary attention	Attention given by choice—the consumer chooses to pay attention.
Voluntary simplicity	Acquiring a belief system that too much consumption is undesirable, and, accordingly, living life with fewer products and services.

W

Want	A desire for a specific object or product.
Wayfinding	The ease of finding your way around the store.
Wealth	A consumer's total financial resources.
Weber's law	The larger the base quantity, the larger the magnitude of change needed for the change to be noticed.
Weblogs	Journals or logs people keep on their personal Web sites.
Word-of-Mouth	The consumers' conversations with other consumers about a product or service.

Z

Zapping	Consumers avoiding commercials by switching channels.
Zipping	Consumers avoiding the commercial by fast-forwarding while watching a prerecorded program

INDEX—SUBJECT

Howard, Daniel J. A2n54
Houghton, David C. E3C3n13
Houston, Michale, E4C4n8, E14C14n39
Hoyer, Wayne D. E14C15n29
Hsieh, Ming Huei A11n291
Huang, Ming-Hui E7C8n24
Huang, Szu-chi A8n208
Huggins, Kyle A. A10n266
Huhmann, Bruce A. A2n39, 40, A8n197
Hunt, David M. E7C8n23
Hunter, Gary L. 120
Hutchinson, J. Wesley E2C1n7, E10C11n2
Hyman, Herbert H. E9C10n1

I

Inman, Jeffrey J. 531Bn3, A1n4, A4n97
Irmak, Caglar A8n206
Ironico, Simona A3n76
Irwin J. A9n242
Iyer, Easwar E10C11n7, E11C13n11
Iyer, Gopalkrishnan R. E17C17n17
Iyengar, Sheena S. A4n98
Izard, C.E. E2C2n10

J

Jackson, Anita L. E11C12n14
Jackson, Gary Brian A10n268
Jacobson, Robert E3C3n14
Jacoby, Jacob E15C16n3
Jain, Shailendre Pratap A3n61, 82, E8C8n31
Jain, Subhash C. E3C3n16, E15C15n56
Jain, Arun K. E12C13n25, E15C15n56
James, William E5C5n29
Jansson-Boyd, Cathrine V. A8n210
Jantzen, Christian 531An3
Jarvis, Cheryl B. E10C11n2
Javalgi, Raj S. G. E9C9n11
Janiszewski, Chris, E3C3n11
Jennings, E. J. E14C15n34
Jensen, Hope E16C16n14
Jensen, Jan M. E13C14n37
Jensen, M. A8n218
Jensen, Molly R. A5n124
Jerry, E8C8n32
Jessup, Ryan K. A4n96
Jiao, Jianxin A9n234
Jin, Byoungho E9C10n6
Jin, Hyun Seung A2n38
Jin, Seung-A Annie A8n209
Joann P. E4C3n19
Johar, Gita Venkataramani A11n278
John, Deborah R. E12C14n3, E13C14n9
John, McBrewster E13C14n16
John, O.P. E5C5n15
Johnson, Jennifer Wiggins A8n207, A9n238
Johansson, J. K. E4C3n16
Johanson, Lars E10C11Bn6
Johnson, Miriam E12C14n3
Johnson, R. E11C12n6
Johnston, Wesley J. E10C11Bn3
Jones, Del E15C15n46
Jones, Eli A5n114, E14C15n35
Jones-Irwin, Dow E9C9n10
Jones, T. O. E11C12n4
Johar, Gita V. 531Bn 24
José, Rebeca San A5n125
Juhl, Hans Jørn A11n276
Jun S, Kropp F. E9C9n11
Jung, C.G. 500n1
Just, David R. A1n3, 20

K

Kabadayi, Sertan A6n141
Kacen, Jacqueline J. E12C13n29
Kachersky, Luke A8n195
Kahle, Lynn R. 111, E4C5n3, 4, 6, E6C7n4
Kahn, Barbara E. E12C13n12, 16
Kahneman, Daniel 531Bn2, E10C11n11, 5
Kaikati, Andrew M. A1n7
Kaikati, Jack G. A1n7
Kalamas, Maria E11C12n14
Kale, Sudhir E12C13n23
Kamins, Michael A. E8C8n26, 33
Kang, Jikyeong A5n118
Kanwar, Rajesh E15C15n56
Kapferer, J.N. E3C2n21
Kapoor, Harish A3n58, A6n155
Kareklas, Ioannis A2n35
Kardes, F.R. E6C7n6, E9n219
Kassarjian, Harold H. E5C5n22, 25
Kasser, Tim A11n297, 299
Kast, Sybille W. E11C12n14
Kastner, Herbert A11n292
Katz, Elihu E9C10n16
Katz, Daniel E6C7n6
Kauchak, T. 308
Kaufman, James C. A7n183
Kaynak, E. E3C3n16
Keel, Astrid L. A5n119
Kees, Jeremy A10n266
Keller, Ed E9C10n12, 13, 14
Kelley, Harold H. E3C2n24, E7C8n13
Keller, Kevin L. E4C4n8, E16C16n19
Kempf, D.S. E6C7n13
Kenrick, Douglas T. A10n271
Kent, Robert 329
Kerin, Roger A. A2n54
Kernan, Jerome B. E3C2n24, E7C8n14
Khare, Adwait A11n282
Kiecker, Pamela A5n122, E13C14n9
Kilbourne, William E. A6n143, A11n293
Kim, Chankon A6n164, E6C7n13
Kim, Chung Koo E14C15n29
Kim, Eun Young A5n132
Kim, Hee-Woong A5n137
Kim, Hyeong-Min A8n195
Kim, Jai-Ok A11n294, 298
Kim, Jooyoung A3n59, 60
Kim, Minjeong A6n152
Kim, Minsung A5n118
Kim, Moontae A1n6
Kim, Young Chan E12C14n3
Kim, Young-Gul E16C17n17
Kim, Youn-Kyung A5n115, 118
Kinnear, Thomas C. E3C3n15
Kirkland, J. 531Bn15
Kiyosaki, Robert 196
Kleine, Robert E. E5C5n29
Kleine, Susan S. E5C5n29
Khermouch, Gerry 251
Kniffin, Kevin M. A4n87
Knoll, Silke A7n169
Knox, George A1n13
Ko, Eunju A5n132
Kock, Soren E10C11Bn6
Koening, Harold F. E16C16n17
Koernig, Stephen K. E8C8n33
Koffka, K. E3C3n12
Koller, Monika A6n142

K (continued)

Kopalle, Praveen K. A3n83
Koschate, Nicole A8n222
Koss-Feder, Laura E13C14n21
Kotler, Philip E10C11Bn1
Kozinets, Robert V. E4C4n16, 531An15
Korgaonkar, Pradeep K. E11C13n3, 5
Kovar, Stacy E. A8n192
Kover, Arthur E2C2n16
Krentler, Kathleen A. E17C17n28
Krider, Robert E. 531Bn 10
Krishna, Aradhna 531Bn9, 10, 24, A8n213
Krishnan, Shanker H. A8n200
Kristiansen, Stine A11n288
Kronrod, Ann A2n44
Krugman, Herbert E. E7C8n19
Kumanyika, Shiriki A3n79
Kumar, Anand E6C7n4, 5
Kuntze, Ronald A6n159
Kwon, Cho B. E9C9n11
Kwortnik, Robert J. A9n233
Kyrezis, Nikolaos A1n23

L

Laaksonen, Martti E2C2n15
Lackman, Conway E13C14n32
Laczniak, Russell N. A3n79
LaForge, Mary C. A4n111, A5n135, A11n293
L-Gable, Shelly E17C17n27
Lakshmanan, Arun A8n200
Lala, Vishal E16C17n15
Lamb, Charles W. E3C3n16
Lamberton, Cait Poynor A7n185
Lambrianidou, Maria A3n73
Lamont, Lawrence E4C5n1
Lanasa, John M. E13C14n32
Lancioni, R.A. E11C12n6
Landis, Benson Y. 387
Landwehr, Jan A4n95
Lang, Peter E14C15n18
Langenderfer, Jeffrey A1n14
Langner, Tobias A4n99
Lanzenauer, C. H. E14C14n39
Larsen, Elena E17C17n29
Lassar, Walfried M. E11C12n7, E16C16n20
Laroche, Michel E6C7n13, E11C12n14
Lasonde, Karen M. E11C12n16
Lastovicka, John L. A10n267
Latour, Kathryn A. A10n252
LaTour, Michael S. A10n252, E7C8n23, 24
Lazarsfeld, Paul E9C10n10
Laurent, Gilles E3C2n21, 531Bn20
Lawlor, Margaret-Anne A5n123
Leavitt, Clark 246
Leavitt, Theodore 18
Leclerc, France E13C14n12
Lee, Byung-Kwan A7n176
Lee, Eun-Ju E14C15n29
Lee, Eun Kyung A5n132
Lee, Hanjoon A6n164
Lee, Julie Anne E12C13n29
Lee, M.S. E3C2n21
Lee, Michael S.W. A10n248
Lee, Thomas R. A7n170
Leenders, Michael R. E10C11Bn6
Lehmann, Donald R. A3n83, E10C11An5
Leigh, James H. E8C9n5
Leonard, Hillary A3n72, A10n269
Lenhart, Amanda E17C17n26
Lennon, Mark M. A9n246

PHOTO CREDITS

Cover
Face: Makeup © Olga Melnikova (modified); car: BMW electric concept car i8 ©Philip Lange (Modified); shoe ©tombaky; purse ©Elnur Amikishiyev; Watch ©Olga Sapegina; Tablet PC ©stanca sanda/ smartphone©stanca sanda;All images from Depositphotos.com

CHAPTER 1
p.4 Globe with internet address ©Liubomyr Feshchyn/Depositphotos
p.9 Globe ©istockphoto.com/Kasia Biel (repeated throughout the book);
p.6 Businessman doing yoga ©Katarina Pantelic/Depositphotos
p. 12 Couple doing yoga ©Wavebreak Media Ltd/123RF
p. 14 Miguel Young and Sean Foley: Author
p.15 Man with Tattoo: Author (BM)
p. 21 Piccadilly Circus , London ©Stephen Bures/123RF; coffee cup ©Subbotina/123RF
p. 28 Customer with shopping cart ©LoopAll/ Depositphotos; Manager with a magnifying glass©Danila Bolshakov/Depositphotos
p. 29 Set of apples ©Andrey Khritin/123RF; Apples ©Kurhan/123RF

CHAPTER 2
p. 30 Love this coffee so much, courtesy Kimberly Rose
p. 31 Face marked for plastic surgery ©Doruk Sikman; Face in bandage ©Graca Victoria/ Depositphotos
p. 32 Sms message on mobile phone close-up ©chaoss/Depositphotos (Modified)
P. 46 Young Man Collection of Expressions ©William Perugini/Depositphotos
P. 49 French football fans watching TV © photography33/Depositphotos

CHAPTER 3
p. 54 Wink, courtesy Mischief. The U.K.
p. 60 Fluevog shoe, courtesy Fluevog Co.
P. 60 Houses of Parliament in London UK ©ildar akhmerov/Depositphotos, (superimposed nail polish: in-house)
p. 61 Paint on back and head of woman ©Дмитрий Байрачный/Depositphotos
p. 62 Flower Necktie ©Christian De Araujo/ Depositphotos
p. 63 Wink, Mischief, The U.K.
p. 68 Candy ©Dmitriy Sechin/Depositphotos
P. 69 Invisible Gift Box ©Andrzej Tokarski/ Depositphotos
p. 76 Music of taste ©Denys Fonchykov/ Depositphotos; Tea cup with mint leaves ©Dmitry Pistrov/Depositphotos; Soap with rosemary ©Anton Ignatenco/Depositphotos;
p. 77 Traditional greek jug ©Anton Cheremukhin/ Depositphotos.
p. 78 cup of yogurt (Yagöot) courtesy Yagöot, Ltd., Cincinnati, USA
p. 79 Yagöot store interior, (Photo by Author) used by permission of Yagöot, Ltd., Cincinnati, USA

CHAPTER 4
p. 88 p. 361 father son shaving, Depositphotos/ ©Yuri Arcurs
p. 96 Duracell: courtesy P&G
p 97 Segway: Segway Co.

CHAPTER 5
p 108 Man with blond hair, courtesy Howard French
p. 110 Save the world. ©grapix; Help Haiti Text ©Basheera Hassanali' Charity. Concept of a person helping poor people. ©David Castillo Dominici/Depositphotos
p. 111 Award—Excited young business woman winning a trophy ©Yuri Arcurs; Couple playing video game ©Suprijono Suharjoto; Hug me ©Bruce Shippee/ Depositphotos
p. 112 Car from leaf ©Андрей Музыка/ Depositphotos
p. 114 Cheering Person with Success Words Proud of Accomplishment ©iqoncept; Happy Person Emtions Showing Joy Good Feelings ©iqoncept Lonely Person ©iqoncept/ Depositphotos;
p.118 Psychological Personality Traits Chart Diagram ©John Takai/Depositphotos (Modified).
p. 121 Punk hair child boy ©Ilya Andriyanov/Depositphotos; Identity ©Umberto Leporini/Depositphotos
p. 126 Woman with her shoes ©marcel braendli/Depositphotos

CHAPTER 6
p. 132 Cross country skiing ©scusi0-9/Depositphotos; Sports lifestyle concept ©Tetiana Vychegzhanina/Depositphotos
p. 133 Family at a house ©Elena Elisseeva/ Depositphotos
p. 139 Ceramic pottery at Horezu, Romania ©Xalanx/Depositphotos; Colorful pottery ©Nikolina Petolas/Depositphotos
p. 140 Cyclists biking outdoors ©Алина Исакович/Depositphotos
p. 141 Couple on a deck chair relaxing on the beach ©Yuri Arcurs/Depositphotos
p. 142 Ceramics cup in shape of happy snowman i ©Svyatoslav Lypynskyy/ Depositphotos
p. 148 New York map ©Ingvar Bjork/ Depositphotos
p. 149 Bohemian on bicycle, Randy Pea, Cincinnati, photo courtesy Author; Urban achiever ©Suprijono Suharjoto/ Depositphotos

CHAPTER 7
p. 158 Emotion Gauge Mood Changing from Sad to Happy Moods ©iqoncept/ Depositphotos
p. 167 Thumbs up-thumbs dow... Babii/123rf
p. 169 Tofu and Sov...

Depositphotos
p. 177 Man on treadmill ©Алексей Буравцов/Depositphotos

CHAPTER 8
p.180 Pregnant woman smoking, courtesy NHS, U.K.
p 187 3d small people - megaphone ©Anatoly Maslennikov/Depositphotos; Watch TV ©Vlastimil Šesták/Depositphotos
p. 188 Man passively watching TV ©Dmitro Panchenko/Depositphotos
p 189 Football fan watching TV ©Kirill Kedrinskiy/Depositphotos
p 192. Man on a hook, courtesy NHS, U.K.
p 193 Broccoli ©Stephanie Frey/ Depositphotos

CHAPTER 9
p 200 Blue Witch: Jessica Flint (Charlottesville, VA), as Lavinia from Chrimson Cult (courtesy Jessica Flint)
p. 202 Men traveling on camels in egypt ©Liliya Drifan/Depositphotos; Pilates Silhouettes Set ©Alexander Kaludov/ Depositphotos
p. 203 Natural light ©Leonid Anfimov/ Depositphotos; New light bulb reflet ©arnauld Ehret/Depositphotos
p. 204 sport shoe ©Elnur Amikishiyev/ Depositphotos; Gamepad ©Viachaslau Bondarau/Depositphotos
p. 208 Power distance ©Patrick/CSP
p. 209 Blindfolded ©pressmaster/CSP
p. 210 Makeup kit ©Jakub Pavlinec/ Depositphotos
p. 211 Kimono ©Maslov Dmitry; Flying Lord Hanuman ©Abhishek Poddar/Depositphotos
p. 216 Mexican ©Vinicius Tupinamba/ Depositphotos; A Middle Eastern businessman using a laptop ©Monkey Business/Depositphotos
p. 217 Two scottish men ©Dmytro Konstantynov/Depositphotos
p. 218 Chinese business man ©Peng-Guang Chen/Depositphotos
p. 219 Shhhhh... ©istockphoto.com/Artsem Martysiuk
p. 226 Chinese lantern ©ptahii; tour eiffel by night ©Willy Deganello/Depositphotos
p. 227 German Man ©PILart/Depositphotos; Store-front in India, courtesy author
p. 228 Japan Geisha doll ©Yuriy Chertok/ Depositphotos
p 229 Houses of Parliament in London UK ©ildar ak... ...Football Netherland ©HII CHA...

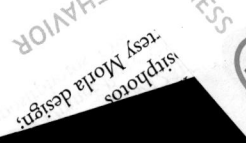

of raviolis ©photography33/Depositphotos

p. 236: Two sailors: ©istockphoto.com/Arthur Kwiatkowski; Elvis Wonders: ©istockphoto.com/Joshua Blake;

p. 237 Three gangsters. ©Artsiom Kireyau/Depositphotos; Group of successful business people ©Vitaly Valua/Depositphotos; Friends gossiping ©Andres Rodriguez/Depositphotos

p. 241 Doctor advises woman patient ©Iurii Sokolov/Depositphotos

p. 248 Beautiful news tv redhead woman on 3d display ©TONO BALAGUER SL/Depositphotos

p. 247 Friends gossiping ©Andres Rodriguez/Depositphotos

p. 249 Persons with Talk Bubbles 3D ©Alexander Limbach/Depositphotos

p. 250 Fasten your seat belt ©Gunnar Pippel/Depositphotos

p 252 Romancing: Beautiful woman applying makeup ©Xalanx; Makeup collection ©Jakub Pavlinec/Depositphotos

CHAPTER 11

p. 256 Fabio, courtesy nationwide;

p. 257 Black smartphone ©Oleksiy Mark/Depositphotos; Touchscreen smart phone. ©Pavel Karnaushenko/Depositphotos; Man ©Alena Root/Depositphotos

p. 277 Road Arrow Signs ©iqoncept/Depositphotos

p. 280 Man holding apple and hamburger ©Marin Conic/Depositphotos

CHAPTER 12

p. 245 Bride (left)©Viktoriia Lesnichenko/Depositphotos; bride (right) ©Ирина Кононова/Depositphotos

p. 307 Ladybug : ©istockphoto.com/arlindo71

p. 309 **Taking orders ©Corepics VOF/**Depositphotos

p. 31 LIKE word and hand cursor. ©kovaleff/Depositphotos

CHAPTER 13

Shopping paper bags ©jrp_studio/Despostphotos

CHAPTER 14

p. 336 Tug of war©Stefano Valle/Depositphotos

p. 341 Latin mexican hispanic sombrero poncho woman ©TONO BALAGUER SL/Depositphotos; Arabic businesswoman with a cell phone ©Kamil Macniak/Depositphotos; Japanese girl with notebook ©pz.axe/Depositphotos; Indian woman ©Hongqi Zhang/123RF;

African American ©woman Iofoto/123RF;

Beauty mask ©Lucian Milasan/
woman in a mirror

p. 346 Boomer man ©Andres Rodriguez/Depositphotos; Boomer woman doctor ©benis arapovic/Depositphotos;

p. 348 Woman before plastic surgery ©Mauricio Jordan de Souza Coelho/Depositphotos

p. 349 Gen X, ©Yuri Arcurs/Depositphotos Gen Y, ©Tyler Olson/Depositphotos

p. 351 Teenager listening music with headphones ©Pere Sanz/Depositphotos

p. 352 Musical Senior Couple ©Lisa F. Young /Depositphotos

p. 353 Ladies in red hats, courtesy Jesse Morgan; Japanese teen ©Vadim Zholobov/Depositphotos(MODIFIED)

p. 359 Parents with child in supermarket ©Monkey Business/Depositphotos

p. 360 Mother and daughter ©Svetlana Khvorostova/Depositphotos

p. 361 father son shaving ©Yuri Arcurs/Depositphotos

CHAPTER 15

p. 366 Monks, courtesy Nathan and Sara Tolbert

p. 367 Young woman in a green shirt ©felix mizioznikov/Depositphotos; African American Man ©Tyler Olson/Depositphotos

p.369 Chinatown Los Angeles at Night ©Chad Anderson/Depositphotos; CN Tower Downtown Toronto © Theresa Scarbrough/Depositphotos; City of westminster london street lights at dawn ©Darrin Henry/Depositphotos

P. 374 Caucasian man © Xalanx/Depositphotos

P. 377 Hispanic man © Mehmet Dilsiz/Depositphotos

p. 379 Hispanic Family ©Andy Dean/Depositphotos

p. 382 Chinese man © Eskay Lim/Depositphotos

p. 383 Woman Applying Makeup ©Robert Byron/Depositphotos; Makeup and cosmetics ©Alisa Foytik/Depositphotos

p. 384 Flag of the UAE©Philip Lange/Depositphotos; Holly mosque of muslims ©alliesinteract/Depositphotos

p. 387 Buddha ©Валерий Шанин/Depositphotos; Virgin Mary with Jesus icon ©Desislava Vasileva/Depositphotos; Statue of Confucius at Confucian Temple in Shanghai, China ©Philip Lange/Depositphotos; Statue of Ganesha, the God of education, knowledge and wisdom in the Hindu ©Rohit Seth/Depositphotos; Abstract background with mosque ©alliesinteract/Depositphotos; Jewish religious holiday Hannukkah. ©Rimma Zubkin/Depositphotos

p. 394 Changing wheels in car workshop ©Markus W. Lambrecht/Depositphotos

p. 395 Doctor with stethoscope ©haveseen/Depositphotos

CHAPTER 16

p. 403 Groom and car, in-house.

Chapter 17

p. 451 praying to Jesus ©alliesinteract/Depositphotos

CHAPTER 18

p. 454 Fitness ball at work: ©istockphoto.com/Michael DeLeon;

p. 455 Mna with unhealthy ©Tatjana Strelkova/Depositphotos; Woman with credit card © Artur Marciniec/Depositphotos; Trick ©inxti74/Depositphotos

p. 470 Fitness ball at work: ©istockphoto.com/Michael DeLeon;

p. 471 Male businessman climbing stairs ©Алексей Зайцев/Depositphotos

p. 472 Teen driving: ©istockphoto.com/Pamela Moore;

EPILOG

p. 481 Businessman with binoculars searching ©Arsenii Gerasymenko/Depositphotos

p. 482 Business target ©Abhishek Poddar/Depositphotos

p. 483 Focussing ©Ala Charnyshova/Depositphotos

Special Topics

p. 519 woman with tattoo ©Miao Long/Depositphotos

p. 521 Couple Watching TV ©Stefano Lunardi/Depositphotos

p. 522 Man using PDA ©Natalia Ulrikh/Depositphotos

p. 524 Power to women©Leon belomlinsky /Depositphotos

p. 526 Ethnic bridal suit, courtesy TK Designs;

p. 527 Save the world. ©grapix/Depositphotos

Researching the Consumer

Running man with shopping cart ©LoopAll #5785027;

3d manager with magnifying glass© Danila Bolshakov #6251486

Market Segmentation

3D man©Ribkov Dagim/ 3D woman © Ribkov Dagim/ Depositphotos

Caucasian man © Xalanx/ Depositphotos

African American Man © Tyler Olson/Depositphotos

Chinese man © Eskay Li/ Depositphotos

Hispanic man © Mehmet Dilsiz/Depositphotos

Musical Senior Couple © Lisa F. Young/Depositphotos

Teenager listening music with headphones © Pere Sanz/ Depositphotos

Doctor with stethoscope © haveseen/Depositphotos

Cyclists biking outdoors © Алина Исакович/Depositphotos

Couple relaxing on the beach © Yuri Arcurs/Depositphotos

About the Authors

Jill Avery is Assistant Professor of Marketing at the Simmons School of Management in Boston. She received a DBA from the Harvard Business School, an MBA from the Wharton School, and a BA from the University of Pennsylvania. She teaches marketing management, brand management, integrated marketing communications, and consumer behavior in the MBA and undergraduate programs and was recognized for distinction in teaching at Harvard College.

Jill's research focuses on brand management and CRM. Her dissertation research on brand communities won the Harvard Business School Wyss award for excellence in doctoral research. Her branding insights have been widely cited in the business press, including *Advertising Age*, *The New York Times*, and *The Economist*.

Prior to her academic career, Jill spent a decade as a brand manager for Gillette, Braun, Samuel Adams and AT&T; and on the agency side managing the Pepsi, General Foods, Bristol-Myers, and Citibank accounts.

Active in pro-bono consulting for entrepreneurial [st]art-ups and non-profit organizations, she serves on [the] Board of Overseers, the Museum of Fine Arts, Boston. [(]@mycbbook.com)

[Rob]ert V. Kozinets is Associate Professor of Marketing [at York] University's Schulich School of Business. [Previously], he was a faculty member at Northwestern's [Ke]llogg School of Management in Chicago and the University of Wisconsin-Madison's School of Business. An anthropologist by training, Rob is a global expert [on online] communities and online research methods. In [netnogr]aphy—online ethnography, [his] understanding of blogs, [a]nd social networking sites. [... "...n]d" by *Canadian Business* [...] appeared in press (e.g., *the* [... Disc]*overy Channel*.

[...]d management and online [... publis]hed in leading marketing [...] *Consumer Tribes* (Elsevier [... Netnogra]*phy: Doing Ethnographic* [... 20]09) and writes a blog, [... w]ww.kozinets.net). (rob@[mycbbook.com])

[... h]olds an MBA from IIMA and [...] University of Pittsburgh. A [...] has taught at SUNY, Buffalo, [... Nor]thern Kentucky University [...] University of New South [...]

[...] published in such journals [... Psyc]*hology & Marketing*, *Journal* [... Journa]*l of Retailing*, and *Marketing*

Theory. He has coauthored three books: *ValueSpace* (McGraw-Hill 2001, www.myvaluespace.com), *Customer Behavior* (Dryden Press, 1998, and Thomson Learning, 2002), and "MYCBBook" (www.mycbbook.com, 2008, 2010, 2013). The present book, arguably his most-labored, is a digest of his understanding of Consumer Behavior, sixth-sensed through a decade of research, teaching, and contemplating consumer behavior. (Ban@mycbbook.com)

Priya Raghubir is Professor of Marketing and the Mary C. Jacoby Faculty Fellow at the Stern School of Business, New York University. Prior to joining NYU, Priya was at the University of California at Berkeley and the Hong Kong University of Science and Technology.

Priya's research interests are in the area of consumer psychology, including psychological aspects of prices and money, risk perceptions, visual information processing, and survey methods. She has published over 50 articles in journals and books, including the *Journal of Consumer Research*, *Journal of Marketing Research*, *Journal of Consumer Psychology*, *Journal of Marketing*, and *Marketing Science*. She is on the editorial boards of *JCR*, *JMR*, *JCP*, *JR* and *Marketing Letters*, and has presented her work over a 100 times at universities, symposia and conferences worldwide.

Priya received her undergraduate degree in Economics from St. Stephen's College, Delhi University, her MBA from the Indian Institute of Management, Ahmedabad, and her Ph.D. in Marketing from New York University. (Priya@mycbbook.com)

Arch Woodside is Professor of Marketing, Boston College. He is a Member and Fellow of the Royal Society of Canada, American Psychological Association, Association of Psychological Sciences, Institute for the Academy for the Study of Tourism, and the Society of Marketing Advances. He is the Founder of the International Academy of Culture, Tourism, and Hospitality Research. He is the Editor-in-Chief of the *Journal of Business Research* and the *International Journal of Culture, Tourism, & Hospitality Research*. He is the author of management, marketing, and consumer research articles appearing in the *Journal of Marketing*, *Journal of Marketing Research*, *Journal of Consumer Psychology*, *Journal of Applied Psychology*, *International Journal of Research in Marketing*, *Annals of Tourism Research*, *Psychology & Marketing*, *Industrial Marketing Management*, *Journal of Retailing*, *Journal of the Academy of Marketing Science*, and 27 additional scholarly journals. His research focuses on business-to-business marketing, consumer research, advertising, tourism research, and case study research. (Arch@mycbbook.com)

[... Av]ery: p. 509-513; Kozinets: [...] [...]0, Raghubir: 491-495; and